CASES, MATERIALS AND NOTES ON PARTNERSHIPS AND CANADIAN BUSINESS CORPORATIONS

Fourth Edition

D1559473

CASES, MATERIALS AND NOTES ON PARTNERSHIPS AND CANADIAN BUSINESS CORPORATIONS

Fourth Edition

by

A. Douglas Harris
Assistant Professor
Faculty of Law
University of Toronto

Ian B. Lee
Assistant Professor
Faculty of Law
University of Toronto

Ronald J. Daniels
Dean
Faculty of Law
University of Toronto

Jeffrey G. MacIntosh
Toronto Stock Exchange
Professor of Capital Markets
Faculty of Law
University of Toronto

Edward M. Iacobucci
Associate Professor
Faculty of Law
University of Toronto

Poonam Puri
Associate Professor
Osgoode Hall Law School
York University

Jacob S. Ziegel
Professor of Law Emeritus
Faculty of Law
University of Toronto

THOMSON

CARSWELL

Doug Harris, Edward Iacobucci, Jeff MacIntosh and Jacob Ziegel acknowledge financial support from the University of Toronto Faculty of Law. Ian Lee acknowledges financial support from the Foundation for Legal Research. Poonam Puri acknowledges financial support from Osgoode Hall Law School.

Library and Archives Canada Cataloguing in Publication

   Cases, materials and notes on partnerships and Canadian business corporations / A. Douglas Harris ... [et al.]. — 4th ed.

ISBN 0-459-24147-8   1. Corporation Law — Canada — Cases. I. Harris, A. Douglas   II. Title: Partnerships and Canadian business corporations.

KE1345.A7C38 2004   346.71′066   C2004-904912-7
KF1415.ZA2C38 2004

The paper used in this publication meets the minimum requirements of the American National Standard for Information Sciences — Permanence of Paper for Printed Library Materials, ANSI X39.48-1984.

Composition: Computer Composition of Canada Inc.

One Corporate Plaza   **Customer Service:**
2075 Kennedy Road,   Toronto 1-416-609-3800
Toronto, Ontario M1T 3V4   Elsewhere in Canada/U.S. 1-800-387-5164
                                                         Fax: 1-416-298-5094
Internet: www.carswell.com   E-mail: carswell.orders@thomson.com

PREFACE TO FOURTH EDITION

As was the case with the third edition, our primary goal in preparing this edition has been to update the materials so that they reflect the important case law and statutory and doctrinal developments that have occurred over the past ten years.

As was also the case with the third edition, it is difficult to reduce the developments over this period to a short list. However, we would highlight the following themes that have been carried forward from the third edition: the continued incursion of securities regulation into areas traditionally thought of as corporate law, the continued expansion of liability of corporate officers and directors under corporate and non-corporate legislation for non-performance and misfeasance by their corporation, and the continued expansion of the scope and use of the oppression remedy. Themes that have been given new life by recent developments include the extent to which directors' fiduciary duties extend to stakeholders in the corporation other than shareholders and the use of poison pills in the Canadian context.

Of course, no one can ignore the plague of alleged and admitted misdeeds that emerged in the early part of the twenty-first century involving US companies like Enron Corp., WorldCom Inc., and Tyco International Ltd., and Canadian companies including Bre-X Minerals Ltd., Livent Inc., and YBM Magnex International, Inc. The legislative and regulatory response to these and other corporate scandals continues to develop even as we finalize this new edition, again primarily in the domain of securities regulation as reflected in US legislation like the *Sarbanes-Oxley Act of 2002*, and in Canada by newly introduced regulatory instruments relating to board composition, certification of financial statements, and audit committees. The academic and popular debate surrounding these scandals has focussed attention on the extent to which regulation, whether under corporate law or otherwise, is a sufficient or appropriate tool to constrain human duplicity.

All of the contributors to this edition owe a significant debt to the contributors to the third edition: Jacob Ziegel, Ron Daniels and Jeff MacIntosh. We also are grateful to John Lundell Q.C., Partner at Lawson Lundell, for his generous assistance with the new British Columbia *Business Corporations Act*. Finally, we wish to extend our sincere appreciation to law students Andrew Gordon, Donald Grant, Adam Lewinberg, Juhee Makkar, James McClary, Carlin McGoogin, Robert Morin, Angela Pomerleau, and James Rempel for their valuable research assistance in the preparation of this edition.

Doug Harris
Ron Daniels
Edward Iacobucci
Ian Lee

Jeffrey MacIntosh
Poonam Puri
Jacob Ziegel

March 31, 2004

ACKNOWLEDGMENTS

We thank the authors, publishers and organizations listed below for their permission to reproduce excerpts from the following materials.

Every effort was made on behalf of the authors to obtain permissions. Should any errors or omissions be brought to the attention of the publishers, appropriate steps will be taken to give proper credit.

Canadian Business Corporations
F. Iacobucci
M.L. Pilkington
J.R.S. Prichard
Canada Law Book Limited

Canadian Corporation Law
F. Iacobucci
Butterworth & Co. (Canada) Ltd.

A Comment on the Social Responsibilities of Life Insurance Companies as Investors
R.H. Mundheim
Fred B. Rothman & Co.
The Virginia Law Review Association

Corporate Control Transactions
F. Easterbrook
D. Fischel
Yale Law Journal

Directors: Myth and Reality
M.L. Mace
President and Fellows of Harvard College

Economic Analysis of Law (3rd ed.)
R.A. Posner
Little Brown and Company

An Economic Analysis of Limited Liability in Company Law
P. Halpern
M. Trebilcock
S. Turnbull
University of Toronto Law Journal

The Independent Director — Heavenly City or Potemkin Village?
V. Brudney
The Harvard Law Review Association

For Whom are Corporate Managers Trustees?
E.M. Dodd
The Harvard Law Review Association

The Four Stages of Capitalism:
Reflections on Investment Management Treatises
R.C. Clark
The Harvard Law Review Association

Mergers and Acquisitions:
Developments in Takeover Techniques and Defense
A. Brownstein
J. Fogelson
M. Lipton
C. Wasserman

Model Business Corporations Act
American Bar Association

A New Look at Corporate Opportunities
V. Brudney
R. Clark
The Harvard Law Review Association

Ontario Corporate Manual
R.A. Kingston
Richard De Boo Ltd.

Principles of Corporate Governance
American Law Institute

The Proper Role of a Target's Management in Responding to a Tender Offer
F. Easterbrook
D. Fischel
The Harvard Law Review Association

Regulating the Market for Corporate Control: A Critical Assessment of the Tender Offer's Role in Corporate Governance
J. Coffee
Columbia Law Review

Report of the Ontario Select Committee on Company Law (1967)
Queen's Printer (Ontario)

Report of the Royal Commission on Corporate Concentration
Supply and Services Canada

A Restatement of Corporate Freezeouts
V. Brudney
M. Chirelstein
Yale Law Journal

The Shareholders' Derivative Action
S.M. Beck
Canadian Bar Review

Share Transfer and Transmission Restrictions in the Close Corporation
D.P. Coates
University of British Columbia Law Review

Shareholders' Voting Rights and Company Control
M.A. Pickering
Stevens and Sons Limited

A Structural Approach to the Corporation
R. Gilson
Stanford Law Review

The Structure of the Corporation
M.A. Eisenberg
Little, Brown and Company

Studies in Canadian Company Law Vol. II (1973)
D. Huberman
J.S. Ziegel
Butterworth & Co. (Canada) Ltd.

Ultra Vires and Some Related Problems
L. Getz
University of British Columbia Law Review

Vicarious Liability in the Law of Torts
P.S. Atiyah
Butterworth's (London)

SUMMARY OF CONTENTS

TABLE OF CONTENTS

**Chapter 7 – Regulating the Exercise of Power by Controlling
Shareholders** 547

TABLE OF ABBREVIATIONS

Frequently Cited Statutes and other Legislative Sources

ABCA	Business Corporations Act, R.S.A. 2000, c. B-9
ALI SECURITIES CODE	American Law Institute, *Federal Securities Code*, May 19, 1978
BCBCA	Business Corporations Act, S.B.C. 2002, c. 57
BCCA	Company Act [Repealed], R.S.B.C. 1996, c. 62
BCSA	Securities Act, S.B.C. 2004, c. 43
BNA	Business Names Act, R.S.O. 1990, c. B.17
CBCA	Canada Business Corporations Act, R.S.C. 1985, c. C-44
CIA	Corporations Information Act, R.S.O. 1990, c. C.39
LPA	Limited Partnerships Act, R.S.O. 1990, c. L.16
MBCA	American Bar Association, Committee on Corporate Laws, *Model Business Corporations Act*, 1984
MCA	The Corporations Act, R.S.M. 1987, c. C225
OBCA	Business Corporations Act, R.S.O. 1990, c. B.16
PA	Partnerships Act, R.S.O. 1990, c. P.5
PRA	Partnerships Registration Act, R.S.O. 1980, c. 371, [repealed 1990, c. 5, s. 12; proclaimed in force May 1, 1991]
QCA	Companies Act, R.S.Q., c. C-38
QSA	Securities Act, R.S.Q., c. V-1.1
SA (or OSA)	Securities Act, R.S.O. 1990, c. S.5
SEA	Securities Exchange Act of 1934, 15 USC §78, U.S. Laws 1934, c. 404

A Note Regarding Case Citations

As part of Carswell's commitment to provide you with convenient and current legal information, case references added to this service also include Westlaw*e*CARSWELL citations.

The following is an example of the Westlaw*e*CARSWELL citation format used on Westlaw*e*CARSWELL and in this service:

2004 CarswellOnt 1234

- "**2004**" is the year of the decision.
- "**CarswellOnt**" indicates that this is a decision from the Province of Ontario added to Westlaw*e*CARSWELL. Similarly, "**CarswellBC**" indicates a decision from the Province of British Columbia added to Westlaw*e*CARSWELL, and so on. Cases originating in Federal Courts have "**CarswellNat**" citations, while a decision from the Supreme Court of Canada will have a cite based on the jurisdiction in which it originated. Thousands of judicial decisions from every jurisdiction across Canada are available on Westlaw*e*CARSWELL.
- "**1234**" indicates that this was the 1, 234th decision added to Westlaw*e*CARSWELL in 2001.

The addition of Westlaw*e*CARSWELL cites will provide a convenient point of reference for those who use Westlaw*e*CARSWELL. Please note, however, that case citations previously added to this service may not necessarily contain Westlaw*e*CARSWELL cases.

Westlaw*e*CARSWELL is a leading, Internet-based legal research service which combines the Internet's simplicity with state-of-the-art searching capabilities. If you would like to learn more about Westlaw*e*CARSWELL or are interested in seeing this valuable product, we invite you to call Customer Relations at 416-298-5140 (Toronto) or 1-800-387-5164 (North America) or visit our website at http://www.carswell.com/.

TABLE OF CASES

Part A

Partnership Law

Chapter 1

Partnership Law Principles

1. VARIETIES OF BUSINESS ORGANIZATION

A question all persons intending to launch a new business must ask themselves is the legal form in which the enterprise is to be conducted. Canadian provincial law recognizes three principal types of organization for conducting a business. These are (1) a sole proprietorship, (2) a partnership and (3) a business corporation. Partnerships are further subdivided into three categories: (a) General Partnerships, (b) Limited Partnerships (LPs) and (c) Limited Liability Partnerships (LLPs).

(a) Sole Proprietorships

The sole proprietorship is both the oldest and simplest form of business organization. As its name indicates, the sole proprietorship has but one owner who has both the prerogative and responsibility of making all ultimate decisions concerning the business. There is nothing in law to prevent a sole proprietorship from becoming a large and powerful enterprise, though most sole proprietorships tend to be small and localized. Quantitatively, sole proprietorships still play an important role in the economy. In the third quarter of fiscal year 2003-2004, for example, 98,400 new sole proprietorships and general partnerships were registered under the Ontario *Business Names Act*, R.S.O. 1990, c. B.17 as am., s. 12(1) ("BNA"), as well as 75 limited partnership business names and 230 Ontario Limited Liability Partnerships and Extra-Provincial LLPs. The number of corporation business names registrations during the same period was 22,100. (Since only sole proprietorships not carrying on business under the owner's true name are required to be registered under the BNA, the recorded figure probably underestimates the total number of new proprietorships by a substantial margin.[1])

---

[1] Written partnership agreements don't come cheap either, and in downtown Toronto the cost apparently runs to between $1,500 and $2,000. They are expensive because they have to be tailored to meet the parties' particular requirements. However, many small partnerships

The attractions of a sole proprietorship are the ease with which such a business may be commenced and dissolved (assuming it is not subject to special municipal, provincial or federal licensing requirements) and the modest expenses involved in starting it up. The disadvantages are that the sole proprietor enjoys none of the advantages that accrue to a business corporation, including the one-person corporation, considered below. In particular, the unincorporated owner is fully liable for all the debts and other obligations incurred by his business regardless of how carefully he segregates it from all his other activities. In law the unincorporated business has no separate personality, no matter how carefully the proprietor segregates his business activities from his personal activities.

(b) Partnerships

The provincial partnerships Acts all define a partnership as the relationship subsisting between two or more persons carrying on business with a view to profit. A general partnership therefore differs from a sole proprietorship in that the former has several owners instead of one and, in most cases, also a more complex organization. Ease of formation and dissolution, general lack of formalities with respect to both (other than compliance with the registration requirements under the BNA and the obligation to give notice to creditors under the *Partnerships Act* if a partner retires) and great flexibility in designing the internal managerial structure of the business are also hallmarks of the partnership. Equally, the general partnership suffers from the same weaknesses as a sole proprietorship and, as compared with the business corporation, including the unlimited liability of each partner, jointly or jointly and severally, for all the debts and other obligations of the partnership. A partner can limit her liability by becoming a limited partner pursuant to the provisions of one of the provincial limited partnerships Acts (or the corresponding provisions in the *Partnerships Act* of those jurisdictions where both types of partnership are treated in the same Act) but this involves her scrupulous abstention from playing any part in the direction of the business. Partners in qualifying professional firms can exclude their liability for the negligent or other described wrongful acts of a partner by registering as a Limited Liability Partnership (LLP), and meeting other statutory requirements, without losing their right to remain active partners as is true in a limited partnership. See further, *infra*, Section 6(b), (c). The disadvantages of unlimited liability for general partnerships can also be circumvented by forming a partnership between incorporated companies, and such partnerships are quite common. Technically speaking, an incorporated general partner is liable for all the debts of the partnership, but if the corporation has few assets the practical effect is the same as if the partner

---

operate without a written agreement, and in such cases the default rules under the *Partnership Act* and general common rules will come into play.

had limited liability for the partnership debts. *Cf. Haughton Graphic Ltd. v. Zivot, infra*, Section 6(b).

(c) Business Corporations[2]

The history of business corporations law and the distinctive attributes of a business corporation are dealt with in Chapter 2. Here it must suffice to summarize the principal features that distinguish the corporation from the unincorporated form of business enterprise. First, the corporation has its own legal personality which is separate from that of its shareholders, directors and officers. This is true even in the case of one-person corporations. The corporation can therefore sue and be sued in its own name, and equally it can enter into contracts even with its own shareholders. Second, the corporation has perpetual succession and is not affected by any changes in, or the deaths or retirements of its members. Third, shareholders are not liable for the debts or other obligations of the corporation. This last advantage alone is sufficient in many instances to make the corporation the preferred business vehicle for investors and entrepreneurs alike.

Incorporation also has some disadvantages, though none of them is serious. Incorporation must be sought from a government agency or official and requires the filing of documents and the adoption of a corporate constitution. Annual returns containing prescribed information must also be filed in many of the provinces. Further, a corporation wishing to do business in more than one province will either have to incorporate federally or obtain an extra-provincial licence to carry on business in the host province. Legal costs are involved ($800 to $1200 for a simple incorporation, and filing fees are usually substantially higher than those payable by sole proprietorships and partnerships. In Ontario, the incorporation fee is $300 and another $60-$80 for a business name registration under the BNA if the corporation carries on business under an assumed name; the CBCA incorporation fee is $200, and in British Columbia it is $350.) Finally, corporations are required to hold meetings, to elect directors and to provide shareholders with information. In the case of one-person and closely held corporations modern legislation has greatly simplified these requirements and they can usually be satisfied easily.

Overall then, the advantages of incorporation greatly outweigh its disadvantages and a corporation is generally a superior business vehicle,

---

[2] "Corporation" and "Company" will be used interchangeably throughout this book to indicate an incorporated business entity unless the context indicates otherwise. "Company" or "limited company" is the term commonly used in the United Kingdom and those parts of the Commonwealth that have adopted the British-type companies legislation. "Corporation" is invariably used in the US, and is the expression now adopted in most of the provincial Acts in Canada and in the federal legislation. British Columbia, Nova Scotia and Newfoundland appear to be exceptions to the rule. US usage is to restrict "company" to partnerships. Thus a newly fashioned business vehicle in US state law, the "limited liability company", involves a form of incorporated partnership.

from a legal perspective, than either the sole proprietorship or the general or limited partnership. Why then would a person or persons choose not to incorporate his or their business? We have no complete set of answers, but the following may provide a partial explanation. First, various types of professionals (*e.g.*, lawyers) are not allowed in many provinces to conduct their business in incorporated form. See further, *infra,* Chapter 3. Second, the promoters may only envisage a short term business relationship (*e.g.*, a joint venture) and may not think it worthwhile to incorporate. Third, partnerships, particularly those of short duration, are often formed between corporations. They may feel their corporate status already protects them adequately from unlimited liability. Fourth, the unincorporated form of business may offer tax advantages. This appears to be the dominant reason for the resurgence of interest in limited liability partnerships. See *infra,* Section 6(b). Having offered these explanations we are bound to add a further one, and this is that many small-business persons may not realize how easy and relatively inexpensive incorporation is and the many advantages it can offer.

2. THE HISTORY OF PARTNERSHIP LAW

Partnership was a well known institution in Roman law (where it was known as a *societas*) and in other ancient legal systems, but partnership law itself developed only slowly in the common law. Initially, the courts of the law merchants were primarily seized of disputes between partners, and equity and the common law apparently did not play a large role until the seventeenth and eighteenth centuries. The industrial revolution and Britain's pre-eminent position as a mercantile nation gave further impetus in the nineteenth century to the development and refinement of partnership principles. The accumulation of case law made the law both uncertain and complex. In 1879 Sir Frederick Pollock, the distinguished British jurist, prepared a Bill for the consolidation and amendment of the law of partnership. In a substantially altered form, it became the foundation of the Act subsequently adopted by the British Parliament and known as the *Partnership Act* 1890, 53 & 54 Vict. c. 39. In 1907, the British Parliament also adopted the *Limited Partnerships Act* of that year, 7 Edw. 7, c. 24. However, its practical impact was negligible because the easy availability of incorporation for small businesses following the House of Lords' seminal decision in *Salomon v. Salomon & Co.* (1896), [1897] A.C. 22 (U.K. H.L.), *infra*, Ch. 2, made this a far superior business vehicle for investors concerned to exclude their liability for the enterprise's debts. In 2000, the British Parliament enacted the *Limited Liability Partnerships Act 2000*. However, unlike its Canadian counterparts, the English LLP has corporate personality and does not constitute a partnership under the *Partnership Act* 1890. See further *Lindley & Banks on Partnerships*, 18th ed. (2002) 2–37 *et seq.* In a very comprehensive report, the English and Scottish Law Commissions have recently recommended substantial changes to the 1897 Act, but these recommendations have not so far been implemented. See The Law Commission and the Scottish Law Commission, *Partnership Law*, Cm 6015, Law Com Report 283, Nov. 2003.

All the Canadian common law provinces have copied the 1890 Act. All of them have also adopted a limited partnerships Act or provisions dealing with limited partnerships, though not necessarily of the British variety. All of them also have requirements with respect to the registration of partnerships which may be contained in the *Partnerships Act* or in a separate Act. See further, *infra*, Section 6(b). The American Uniform State Commissioners approved a *Uniform Partnership Act* (UPA) in 1914, which has been adopted by most of the states, and a *Uniform Limited Partnership Act* (ULPA), subsequently revised in 1984, which has been very influential in Canada as well as the US. Though influenced by the British Act, the UPA is far from being a carbon copy of it; the ULPA is entirely different from the *British Limited Partnerships Act* 1907. See further, *infra*, Section 6(b).

The *British Partnership Act* and its Canadian counterparts are divided into the following principal parts (all the section references below and in the balance of the chapter are to the *Ontario Partnerships Act*, R.S.O. 1990, c. P.5, (unless otherwise indicated):

1. Nature of Partnership (ss. 2–5),
2. Relation of Partners to Persons dealing with them (ss. 6–19);
3. Relation of Partners to One Another (ss. 20–31);
4. Dissolution of Partnership (ss. 32–44);
5. Miscellaneous (ss. 45–46).

The Act is not a complete code and s. 45 (Ont.) provides that the rules of equity and common law applicable to partnerships continue in force except so far as they are inconsistent with the express provisions of the Act.

The materials that follow are designed to expose the student to the principal characteristics of the partnership concept at common law and the modifications introduced by the LP and LLP legislation, and to enable her to obtain a better appreciation of the nature of corporate personality dealt with below in Chapter 2. The materials are not intended to offer anything remotely resembling a compendious treatment of the law of partnership. Three recommended texts for this purpose are *Lindley and Banks on Partnership*, 18th ed. (2002) (the leading British text), *Crane & Bromberg on Partnerships* (1968), a very readable American text in the Hornbook Series (also available in a 1995 practitioners' edition), and Alison R. Manzer, *A Practical Guide to Canadian Partnership Law* (1994, loose leaf).

3. DEFINITION OF PARTNERSHIP

Section 2 of the *Partnerships Act* defines a partnership. Section 3 provides some important guidelines in determining whether or not a partnership exists in the prescribed situations. These rules are themselves of late origin and evolved principally from 1860 onwards.

Prior to that year, the unresolved and much litigated issue was whether a person's entitlement to a share of the profits of another's business was sufficient to make him a partner. The affirmative proposition was laid down in 1775 by De Grey C.J. in a much quoted dictum in *Grace v. Smith* (1775), 2 Wm. Bl. 997, 96 E.R. 587 at 588, that "every man who has the share of the profits of a trade, ought also to bear his share of the loss." This doctrine was approved 18 years later in the leading case of *Waugh v. Carver* (1793), 126 E.R. 525, 2 Hy. Bl. 235:

> and ever since that time until 1860 it was considered as clearly established that, by the law of England, all persons who shared the profits of a business incurred the liabilities of partners therein, although no partnership between themselves might have been contemplated. Subtle distinctions were drawn between sharing net profits and payments varying with them; but it was taken for granted, both by judges and text-writers, that where there was no statutory enactment to the contrary, if net profits were shared, it necessarily followed that liabilities were incurred. (*Lindley on Partnership*, 15th ed., p. 98)

1860 marks the year when the House of Lords, in *Cox and Wheatcroft v. Hickman* (1860), 8 H.L.Cas. 268, 11 E.R. 431, finally repudiated Chief Justice Grey's doctrine. It was not an easy victory because the judges who came to advise the House of Lords were almost evenly divided in their views. The judgments in *Cox and Wheatcroft v. Hickman* do not make easy reading (few judgments in this branch of partnership law do); nevertheless, the extracts that follow will enable the student to obtain a better understanding of the basis for the statutory definition.

Cox and Wheatcroft v. Hickman
(1860), 11 E.R. 431, 8 H.L. Cas. 268

Benjamin Smith and Josiah Timmis Smith carried on business at the Stanton Iron Works in Derbyshire under the name of B. Smith & Son. They fell into financial difficulties and entered into a deed of arrangement with their creditors whereby their business, including the partnership property, was assigned to trustees, who were authorized to carry on business under a new name. The income of the business was to be divided rateably among the creditors, who were given the right to make rules for the conduct of the business, and to wind it up. If the creditors were paid in full, the business was to revert to S and S.

Two of the creditors, Cox and Wheatcroft, were among those appointed trustees. Cox, however, never acted in that capacity, and Wheatcroft resigned after six weeks. Some time later, the other trustees incurred trade debts to Hickman, and gave him bills of exchange which they purported to accept on behalf of the firm. Hickman, who was unaware of the existence of Cox and Wheatcroft, and was ignorant of the existence of the deed, sued them on the bills. The trial judge (Lord Chief Justice Jervis) held them liable. On appeal, the Exchequer Chamber was evenly divided. The verdict was therefore affirmed in the plaintiff's favour. On further appeal to the House of Lords, the judges were summoned to give their opinions. Once again the judges were divided, with Blackburn, Crompton and Williams JJ. affirming the judgment in favour of Hickman and Baron Channell, Lord Chief Baron Pollock, and Wightman J. voting to reverse. The members of the House of Lords (Lords Campbell, L.C., Brougham, Cranworth, Wensleydale and Chelmsford) also voted unanimously in favour of reversal.

The following extracts from counsel's argument and from the judgments of Blackburn J. and Lord Cranworth highlight the legal issues and the contrasting approaches of the judges:

THE ATTORNEY-GENERAL (for Wheatcroft): The claim against the Appellants proceeds on the ground of a supposed partnership among the creditors of the Smiths in the Stanton Iron Works. There was none. The measure of the interest of each creditor who signed the deed is the amount of his debt. That interest is limited and defined. Yet the Court below has held that each creditor, although having only this defined interest, becomes a partner in the company and incurs an indefinite liability. That doctrine cannot be supported. It is contrary to all the principles of partnership.

The facts here do not give any right to Hickman to maintain this action, for if he had heard that Cox and Wheatcroft had been named in the deed as trustees, he must have heard at the same time that Cox never acted in that character, and that Wheatcroft resigned the trust. The trustees who acted in the business are the only persons liable on these bills. The ownership of the property here never was changed at all. The trustees were by the deed to have possession of it for a certain time, but the property itself remained that of the Smiths, the debts should be paid. The joint creditors, who are in fact incumbrancers, have the power to say whether the arrangement shall continue; but that amounts to no more than saying that the security given for their debts be put an end to. It is said that the man who participates in carrying on a trade is a partner in it; that is so under ordinary circumstances, but not under such circumstances as exist here. If these trustees had found, upon the estate leased to the Smiths, and of which they were in possession for a time, a lode of mineral producing £100,000 in a year, the creditors would not have participated therein as partners; they would have got their debts paid a little earlier. The property would still have been that of the Smiths. If they had been partners, the creditors might put the whole into their own pockets; as persons to be satisfied under that deed they had no power to do so. There was no profit here, nor anything in the nature of profit, till the creditors were paid.

A qualified benefit derived from a trade does not make a man a partner in it, *Grace v. Smith* (2 Sir W. Bl. 998), *Mair v. Glennie* (4 Mau. and Selw. 240). It is only when men share profits generally and indefinitely that they become partners: *Waugh v. Carver* (2 H. Bl. 235), where the two persons were to share in agreed proportions all the profits of their respective trades. *Cheap v. Cramond* (4 Barn. and Ald. 663), proceeded on that principle. Neither of these cases resembles the present . . .

BLACKBURN J.: The Defendants in this case are liable as acceptors of the bills of exchange declared upon. The question entirely depends on the effect of the deed of arrangement. If the effect of that deed is such that creditors executing thereby give authority to those managing the Stanton Iron Company, to bind them to third persons in the usual course of business by accepting bills, the Defendants have given such authority. If the effect of the deed is not such that creditors executing that deed give authority to bind them as to third persons, the Defendants are not shown to have given any such authority, for they have never acted as trustees; nor does it appear that they have done any act beyond what was proper to carry out the arrangement contained in that deed.

The principal object of the deed of arrangement is to divide the property of the Smiths amongst the creditors according to the rules observed in bankruptcy; and for this purpose their property is assigned to trustees. The goodwill of the business which had been carried on by the Smiths, was part of their joint estate, and those who had the making of the arrangement appear to have thought it a valuable part of the joint estate. Instead of disposing of it to third persons, or suffering it to be lost, the arrangement made was, that the business should in future be carried on under a new style, that of "the Stanton Iron Company," by the trustees, in the manner stipulated for in the deed to which the creditors are parties. The question is, whether the stipulations are such as to render those creditors who are parties to the deed partners in the Stanton Iron Company, so far, at least, as regards liability to third persons.

Some of the Judges in the Court below have expressed an opinion that there is a distinction between the present question and that which would have arisen if the question had been whether the Defendants were liable for the consideration of these bills. I am, however, of opinion that no such distinction exists. I apprehend that all cases as to liability of partners to contracts are branches of the law of agency, and that the question always is, whether the contract entered into is within the scope of the authority conferred by those, who are sought to be charged, upon the person actually making the contract. But I take it that, as a matter of law, those who are partners in a trading firm, do confer upon those who are permitted to manage the concern, authority to make all contracts which in the exigency of the business are necessary and proper and customary. This *prima facie* authority may be restricted by express agreement, but unless those who deal with the firm have notice of this restriction, they are entitled to hold all who are partners bound by the *prima facie* authority conferred on the manager, and that equally whether the persons sought to be charged were persons to whom the creditors gave credit, or dormant partners, of whose existence they were unaware. I think the justice of this rule, as applicable to dormant partners, very questionable, but I do not think it open to question that it is the rule of law. I think that where, as in the present case, the accepting of bills is a necessary and customary part of the business, the authority to accept them is conferred as much as the authority to contract the debts for which they are given. It is true the authority is limited to accepting bills in the name of the firm, and binds only those included in that firm, but all who are partners are included in the firm . . .

The deed does not provide what is to be done in the case which has actually happened, *viz.*, that of the concern proving insolvent; but the law declares that those who take the profits of a trading concern as such, are liable to the losses, even if they have stipulated to the contrary, *Waugh v. Carver* (Smith's Leading Cases, 786) and the notes thereto.

The phrase, taking the profits as such, is not a happy one, and there is some difficulty at times in defining what it means, but I think it at all events means this: it is not possible, according to the common law, to cause a trading concern to be carried on, on the terms that the advantages of a partnership, including the participation in profits, and the partnership lien and security over the assets of the firm, shall belong to those who have but a limited liability. I am aware of no case or authority inconsistent with the proposition thus guarded. Now, it seems to me, that the present defendants have, by the deed to which they are parties, stipulated that the business shall be carried on for their benefit, and under their control; that they shall be interested in all the property of the firm to such an extent as to have a partnership lien upon it. This shows that they are not merely persons permitting the Smiths or the trustees to carry on the business, and relying on it as a fund for payment, but that they take the profits as such, and having done so, they are partners as regards third persons. I agree that the question is one of agency, *viz.*, whether the defendants authorized the managers of this firm to bind them, but I think it is an incident attached by law to a participation in the profits to the above extent, that such authority is given to those managing the concern. I think, for the reasons I have given, that this arrangement deed does amount to a stipulation for a participation in the profits as such by the creditors.

For these reasons, I am of opinion that the Defendants are liable as acceptors of the bills of exchange declared upon.

LORD CRANWORTH: The liability of one partner for the acts of his co-partner is in truth the liability of a principal for the acts of his agent. Where two or more persons are engaged as partners in an ordinary trade, each of them has an implied authority from the others to bind all by contracts entered into according to the usual course of business in that trade. Every partner in trade is, for the ordinary purposes of the trade, the agent of his co-partners, and all are therefore liable for the ordinary trade contracts of the others. Partners may stipulate among themselves that some one of them only shall enter into particular contracts, or into any contracts, or that as to certain of their contracts none shall be liable except those by whom they are actually made, but with such private arrangements third persons, dealing with the firm without notice, have no concern. The public have a right to assume that every partner has authority from his co-partner to bind the whole firm in contracts made according to the ordinary usages of trade.

This principle applies not only to persons acting openly and avowedly as partners, but to others who, though not so acting are, by secret or private agreement, partners with those who appear ostensibly to the world as the persons carrying on the business . . .

It is often said that the test, or one of the tests, whether a person not ostensibly a partner, is nevertheless, in contemplation of law, a partner, is, whether he is entitled to participate in the profits. This, no doubt, is, in general, a sufficiently accurate test; for a right to participate in profits affords cogent, often conclusive evidence, that the trade in which the profits have been made, was carried on in part for or on behalf of the person setting up such a claim. But the real ground of the liability is that the trade has been carried on by persons acting on his behalf. When that is the case, he is liable to the trade obligations, and entitled to its profits, or to a share of them. It is not strictly correct to say that his right to share in the profits makes him liable to the debts of the trade. The correct mode of stating the proposition is to say that the same thing which entitles him to the one makes him liable to the other, namely, the fact that the trade has been carried on on his behalf, i.e., that he stood in the relation of principal towards the persons acting ostensibly as the traders, by whom the liabilities have been incurred, and under whose management the profits have been made.

Trial Judgement Reversed.

Notes

1 In 1865, in *Bovill's Act*, 28 & 29 Vic. c. 86, the British Parliament sought to clarify the common law position by providing that a receipt of the share of the profits of a business by a creditor in the described circumstances was not sufficient to make him a partner of the business. These provisions were subsequently incorporated in what are now ss. 3.3(a) and (d) and 4 of the Ontario *Partnerships Act*. Sections 1 and 5 of *Bovill's Act* read as follows:

1. The Advance of Money by way of Loan to a Person engaged or about to engage in any Trade or Undertaking upon a Contract in Writing with such Person that the Lender shall receive a Rate of Interest varying with the Profits, or shall receive a Share of the Profits arising from carrying on such Trade or Undertaking, shall not, of itself, constitute the Lender Partner with the Person or the Persons carrying on such Trade or Undertaking, or render him responsible as such . . .

5. In the event of any such Trader as aforesaid being adjudged a Bankrupt, or taking the Benefit of any Act for the Relief of Insolvent

Debtors, or entering into an Arrangement to pay his Creditors less than Twenty Shillings in the Pound, or dying in insolvent Circumstances, the Lender of any such Loan as aforesaid shall not be entitled to recover any Portion of his Principal, or of the Profits or Interest payable in respect of such Loan, nor shall any such Vendor of a Goodwill as aforesaid be entitled to recover any such Profits as aforesaid until the Claims of the other Creditors of the said Trader for valuable Consideration in Money or Money's Worth have been satisfied.

These provisions were critically examined by Sir George Jessel M.R. in *Pooley v. Driver* (1876), 5 Ch. D. 458 (Eng. M.R.), another leading nineteenth-century case. He held that the purported lenders to the partnership had overstepped the dividing line between lenders and partner and had, given the powers vested in them under the loan instruments, become partners in the business. Another aspect of the partnership definition of great practical importance involves the question of when joint ownership of property is deemed to make the owners partners and is discussed in the case that follows.

A.E. LePage Ltd. v. Kamex Developments Ltd.
(1977), 78 D.L.R. (3d) 223, 1977 CarswellOnt 414 (C.A.), affirmed [1979] 2 S.C.R. 155, 1979 CarswellOnt 706, 1979 CarswellOnt 706F.

BLAIR J.A.: This is an appeal from a judgment of Madam Justice Van Camp in which she allowed the claim of the respondent, a real estate agent, for commission under an exclusive listing agreement. During the term of the exclusive listing agreement the property, a large apartment building, was sold through another agent and the amount of the commission claimed was $45,000. Judgment was given against the appellants but not against the corporate defendant, Kamex Developments Limited. The question in this case is whether the appellants constituted a partnership and, if so, whether the defendant March signed the listing agreement as a partner binding the partnership.

The appellants purchased the property in question in 1970, under the name of one of them, "M. Kalmykow in trust". The defendant corporation was then incorporated to hold the property in trust for the appellants. It executed a declaration of trust and concurrently entered into a written agreement with them.

The agreement specified that the property was to be held by the defendant corporation in trust for the appellants in proportion to their interests as set forth therein. It provided that revenues and profits from the property should be paid to them in proportion to their interests and that they should be liable to pay any deficiency to the corporation in the same proportions. It provided for the sale or transfer of the interests of the appellants in the property to third parties after the other appellants named in the agreement had been given a first opportunity of refusal. The agreement also provided that any decision "regarding the sale or other dealings with the said apartment building" was to be made by a majority vote defined as the majority of the interests in the property of the appellants. The evidence disclosed that the appellants met monthly in order to discuss the operation of the property and also the possibility of its sale.

At some stage the property was listed for sale by what is called an open listing. A decision was taken by the appellants as a group that there should be no exclusive listing. Employees of the respondent approached March, one of the appellants, and as a result he executed the exclusive listing agreement. The learned trial Judge found that he signed this agreement on behalf of all the other appellants, and that he was understood to have done so by the employees of the respondent. She also found that he was not authorized by the appellants to sign the exclusive listing agreement and his act had not been approved by them.

Many issues were raised in the course of this argument but because of the nature of the pleadings, it is unnecessary to refer to all of them. The respondent's statement of claim alleged:

> On October 6, 1972, the Plaintiff entered into a written agreement (hereinafter referred to as "The Listing Agreement") with the Defendant, March. At the time of execution of the Listing Agreement, the Plaintiff was advised by March that he was a member of the partnership and had authority to enter into the Listing Agreement on behalf of the partnership. It was a term of the Listing Agreement that such Exclusive Authority was to be irrevocable until one minute before midnight on November 30, 1972.

This pleading confines the respondent to an assertion that it dealt with the appellant March as a representative of a partnership. Hence, the prime issue in this appeal is whether or not the appellants were a partnership. This involves an answer to the elementary question of whether the appellants as co-owners of the property thereby became partners.

A partnership is defined in the *Partnerships Act,* R.S.O. 1970, c. 339, s. 2, as follows:

* * *

The key words of the definition refer to "persons carrying on a business in common with a view to profit". The mere fact that property is owned in common and that profits are derived therefrom does not of itself constitute the co-owners as partners. Section 3, para. I of the *Partnerships Act* reads as follows:

> 3. In determining whether a partnership does or does not exist, regard shall be had to the following rules:
>
> 1. Joint tenancy, tenancy in common, joint property, common property, or part ownership does not of itself create a partnership as to anything so held or owned, whether the tenants or owners do or do not share any profits made by the use thereof.

Whether or not the position of co-owners becomes that of partners depends on their intention as disclosed by all the facts of the case. It is necessary to determine whether the intention of the co-owners was to "carry on a business" or simply to provide by an agreement for the regulation of their rights and obligations as co-owners of a property. The test was stated by Roach, J.A. in *Thrush v. Read*,[[1950] 2 D.L.R. 392, 1950 CarswellOnt 42 (C.A.) at p. 396, as whether:

> on a true construction of the agreement, and having regard to all the circumstances, it should be held that the parties to that agreement intended to become, and thereby became, partners in a joint venture and that therefore they were not merely co-owners of the common property.

At p. 396 [D.L.R.], he said:

> In addition to the joint ownership created by the agreement, it becomes necessary therefore to find within that agreement an intention on the part of the parties thereto to carry on a business in common with a view of profit.

In that case it was clear that the purpose of a mining syndicate was not simply to hold claims as co-owners, but to carry on the business of dealing in mining claims, rights and privileges and turn the same to account. There is no such intention to carry on a business in this case.

This case is comparable to *Robert Porter & Sons Ltd. v. Armstrong*, [1926] S.C.R. 328, 1926 CarswellBC 105 where, on facts not too dissimilar from the present case, it was held that the co-owners of property were not partners. There Duff, J., dealt with the fundamental distinction between partnership and co-ownership at p. 330 [S.C.R.]:

> The real question is whether, from the evidence before us, one ought to infer an agreement in the juridical sense that the property these two persons intended dealing with was to be held jointly as partnership property, and sold as such. Is this what they contemplated? Had they in their minds a binding agreement which would disable either of them from dealing with his share — that is to say, with his share in the land itself — as his own separate property? A common intention that each should be at liberty to deal with his undivided interest in the land as his own would obviously be incompatible with an intention that both should be bound to treat the *corpus* as the joint property, the property of a partnership. English law does not regard a partnership as a *persona* in the legal sense. Nevertheless, the property of the partnership is not divisible among the partners *in specie*. The partner's right is a right to a division of profits according to the special arrangement, and as regards the *corpus* to a sale and division of the proceeds on dissolution after the discharge of liabilities. This right, a

partner may assign, but he cannot transfer to another an undivided interest in the partnership property *in specie*.

The learned trial Judge considered that the intention of the co-owners to purchase the building, hold it as an investment and sell it for profit constituted them as partners in a business carried on for profit. With respect, I am of the opinion that the mere fact that co-owners intend to acquire, hold and sell a building for profit does not make them partners. As Duff, J., said in Robert *Porter & Sons Ltd. v. Armstrong*, at p. 329 [S.C.R.], p. 341 [D.L.R.]:

> Foster and Miller unquestionably intended to buy the property, to sell it again at an enhanced price, and thereby to make profit. Indeed, the sole object of purchasing the land was to dispose of it profitably. No doubt they intended to share the outlay equally between them. As regards the purchase money, the law would, of course, give to either of them a right of contribution against the other for any payment on the joint debt in excess of his own proper share, and on a sale, each would be entitled to share in the price according to his interest. The inevitable result, if the property was held in common and sold, would be that, as between Foster and Miller themselves, the right to share in the profits and the legal responsibility for losses would be equally distributed. But these consequences all flow from the fact that these two persons were jointly responsible for the purchase money, and that each was entitled to an undivided moiety in the equitable estate vested in them, as the result of the contract of purchase.

In this case, the intention of the parties to maintain their rights as co-owners of the property is clear beyond doubt from the documents. In addition, it should be noted that the appellants wished to identify and keep separate their respective beneficial interests in the property for income tax purposes. Their intention would have been defeated if they were regarded as a partnership and the apartment building had become the property of the partnership. The fact that they are obliged by their agreement to offer a right of first refusal to the other co-owners in the event of sale is not inconsistent with their basic right to deal with their respective interests in the property . . .

* * *

Appeal allowed.

Notes

1 *Kamex* was distinguished by Murphy D.C.J. in *Lansing Building Supply (Ontario) Ltd. v. Ierullo* (1989), 71 O.R. (2d) 173, 1989 CarswellOnt

2316 (Dist. Ct.). The three individual defendants and three corporations controlled by them carried on business under a collective name. Through the corporation they held title in real property in common with a view to developing the property and selling it as condominiums. The agreement signed by the individual defendants and the corporations purported to be a co-ownership agreement and disclaimed any intention to enter into a partnership between them. One of the individual defendants ordered building materials from the plaintiff and held himself out as a partner with the other individual defendants. The plaintiff sued the individual defendants for the balance owing on the building supplies on the premise that they were in fact partners.

Murphy D.C.J. upheld the claim and distinguished *Kamex* on two grounds. The first was that the terms of the co-ownership agreement had many of the attributes associated with a partnership (*e.g.*, the provisions that the property was to be held by the defendants as tenants in common, that profits from the venture were to be distributed among the co-owners, and the fact that the right of the co-owners to deal with their interests in the land was severely restricted). The second ground was that that the conduct of the parties was consistent with the existence of a partnership. For a similar case involving the finding of a partnership among co-owners of real property, see *Volzke Construction Ltd. v. Westlock Foods Ltd.* (1986), 45 Alta. L.R. (2d) 97, 1986 CarswellAlta 94 (C.A.).

2 From a practical perspective, how is a third party supposed to tell the difference between a "simple" co-ownership and a partnership when the third party receives an order from one of the co-owners? To be on the safe side, must the third party obtain the signatures of all the co-owners authorizing each of them to contract on behalf of the others? Would it be better for the law to invest the co-owners of commercial property with the same type of usual authority as would be conferred on a co-owner if she were a partner? For the power of a partner to bind the partnership with respect to obligations incurred by the partner while acting within the usual scope of the partner's authority, see PA, s. 6.

3 Where a person purports to act as agent for another, he is deemed to warrant his authority to do so. If he has never been appointed an agent (as apparently was true of March in *A.E. LePage Ltd. v. Kamex Developments, supra*), or has exceeded his authority as agent, the person so holding himself out is guilty of breach of warranty of authority. For the measurement of damages in such a case, see *Wickberg v. Shatsky, infra,* ch. 3(9).

4. LEGAL PERSONALITY OF PARTNERSHIP

Thorne v. New Brunswick (Workmen's Compensation Board)
(1962), 33 D.L.R. (2d) 167, 48 M.P.R. 56, 1962 CarswellNB 8 (C.A.)

McNAIR C.J.N.B. (for the Court): This is a special case stated by the Workmen's Compensation Board under s. 34(8) of the *Workmen's Compensation Act*, R.S.N.B. 1952, c. 255, in which our opinion is sought on a question of law which arose on an application for compensation made to the Board by one Osborne Thorne.

The Act provides for an Accident Fund established and maintained by assessments made against employers in the industries within its scope out of which compensation may be paid by the Board to a workman and his dependents when personal injury or death is caused to him by accident arising out of and in the course of his employment in any such industry.

The facts as stated by the Board may be summarized as follows: In February 1961 Thorne and one Jules Robichaud, both residents of New Brunswick, entered into an oral agreement to carry on in partnership within the Province a combined lumbering and sawmill business. It was agreed Robichaud would have charge of the woods operations, Thorne of the milling operations, and that each partner would personally work in his branch of the undertaking at a remuneration, termed wages, of $75 per week. They commenced business in early February 1961 and, in accordance with the requirements of the Act, duly notified the Board of the new undertaking, filed with it an estimate of wages for the current year, and paid to the Board the provisional assessment applicable to the estimated payroll.

On April 3, 1961 Thorne suffered personal injuries by accident arising out of and in the course of the duties performed by him pursuant to the partnership agreement. He applied to the Board for payment of compensation, alleging he was a workman within the meaning of the Act and entitled thereunder to benefits. Clearly the business carried on by the partners constituted an industry within the scope of the Act and workmen in their employ would be eligible for compensation thereunder.

The question submitted for the opinion of the Court reads:

Based on the foregoing facts was Osborne Thorne, on April 13, 1961, a workman employed by the said partnership within the meaning of the *Workmen's Compensation Act* so as to entitle him to compensation thereunder?

Partnerships are an emanation of the common law, the term "firm" to describe the relationship having been borrowed from mercantile law. The *Partnership Act*, 1890 (U.K.), c. 39, is essentially a codification of the rules of common law and equity. Admittedly under such pre-existing rules no person could enter into a contract with himself or be his own employer and, as a partnership was regarded as having no legal existence distinct from the individuals composing it, no person could be an employee of a firm of which he was a member. We were informed by counsel that from its inception the Workmen's Compensation Board has followed that principle.

It is now, however, contended by the claimant that by virtue of statute law in force in the United Kingdom and in New Brunswick partnerships should be regarded as legal entities or persons distinct from their component members and that, in consequence, the firm of which he is a member was capable of entering into a contract of employment with him. Reliance is placed on principles enunciated in relation to trade unions in *Taff Vale Railway v. Amalgamated Society of Railway Servants*, [1901] A.C. 426 (U.K. H.L.), which were adopted and applied in *I.B.T., Local 213 v. Therien*, 22 D.L.R. (2d) 1, [1960] S.C.R. 265, 1960 CarswellBC 141.

The *Taff Vale* case decided a trade union registered under the *Trade Union Acts* 1871 and 1876 of the United Kingdom, being a legal entity, can be sued in its registered name. In the *Therien* case it was held a trade union certified as a bargaining agent under the *Labour Relations Act* of British Columbia is likewise a legal entity suable in tort. The ratio of the decisions is that the granting by the Legislature of rights, powers, and immunities to such bodies is quite inconsistent with the notion it was not intended they should be constituted legal entities or persons exercising such powers and enjoying such immunities . . .

There is a fundamental distinction between the legislation involved in the *Taff Vale* and *Therien* cases and the *Partnership Act* of New Brunswick, as the latter does not purport to legalize or validate partnership firms, a status or condition already enjoyed by them under the common law. It is contended, however, that by its enactments relating to partnerships the Legislature has given them rights, powers, and attributes not previously possessed and imposed on them duties and liabilities not previously existing, which has resulted in their establishment under the law as legal entities. Support for the new concept is sought not only in the *Partnership Act* but also in O. 48a of our Rules of Court and certain dicta of Farwell J., in the passages from his judgement in the *Taff Vale* case above quoted.

O. 48a was in 1891 incorporated as such into the existing English Rules of Court made under the authority of the *Supreme Court of Judicature Acts* 1873 and 1875. Counsel's suggestion is the provisions of O. 48a were necessitated to meet procedural problems resulting from its members, allegedly resulting from the enactment of the *Partnership Act*, 1890 (U.K.), c. 39.

O. 48a is for the most part a compilation of earlier English Rules. In notes thereto in *Annual Practice 1961* at p. 1151 it is stated:

> This Order repeals 0. 7, r. 2; 0. 9, rr. 6, 7; 0. 12, rr. 15, 16; 0. 16, rr. 14, 15; 0. 42, r. 10; and 0. 45, r. 10 of the R.S.C., 1883, and stands in lieu thereof. Rules 1–10 of the order form a code relating to partnership firms and must be construed together.

An examination of the former Rules reveals that prior to the enactment in 1890 of the *Partnership Act* of the United Kingdom a partnership firm was in English jurisprudence recognized as an entity in the sense partners could sue or be sued in the firm name and execution issue against property of the partnership on a judgment against the firm. The earlier procedural provisions can have no greater significance or effect than they possessed before the *Partnership Act* of 1890 was enacted and, in our view, their incorporation into O. 48a in 1891 lends no support to the contention that Act created for partnership firms a new status.

The nature and purpose of such provisions of O. 48a as were new were discussed in *Worcester City & County Banking Co. v. Firbank, Pauling & Co.*, [1894] 1 Q.B. 784 (Eng. C.A.) at pp. 787-8. Lord Esher M.R., says:

> The first question in this case is whether the writ was properly issued. The writ, which is in form for service within the jurisdiction, was issued against a firm in the firm name. The foundation of the decisions on this subject which have been cited to us is, that, although under the rules a writ may be issued against a firm in the firm name, it is really in effect a writ against all and each of the members of the firm, just as if the writ had been issued against them in their individual names; and it was therefore held under the former rules that, where a writ against partners in their individual names could not be served without leave, they or some of them being resident out of the jurisdiction, neither could a writ be issued without leave against them under the firm name. In the present case the facts are these. I think that it has been made out that this is a Natal firm, i.e., a colonial firm . . . For the present purpose I think that a colonial firm is in the same position as a foreign firm . . . The rules as they existed prior to the making of Order XLVIII.A have been construed to the effect that a writ such as this could not be issued without leave against a foreign firm, the members, or some of the members, of which were resident abroad. That has appeared to those conversant with the matter to involve a hardship, and it was for the purpose of getting rid of that hardship I believe that Order XLVIII.A was framed. In rule 1 of that order the words "and carrying on business within the jurisdiction" are used in addition to those which had been used in the former rules. In conjunction with that rule we have rules 3 and 8 of the same order . . . Reading rule 1 of Order XLVIII.A with rules 3 and 8, it seems to me that it is now immaterial whether the writ is against an English firm or against a foreign or colonial firm . . . If the firm carries on business within the jurisdiction, then whether it is an English or a foreign firm, and whether it also carries on business in a colony or abroad or not, a writ may be issued against the partners in the firm name without leave under Order XLVIII.A r. 1.

See also by Lopes L.J., at p. 789 and Davey L.J., at pp. 790-1.

The reasons so given for the adoption in 1891 of the new provisions contained in O. 48a lend no countenance to the submission the Order constitutes a recognition of a new concept, resulting from the *Partnership Act* of 1890, of a partnership firm as a legal entity distinct from the individuals composing it. As respects New Brunswick law the proposition appears entirely fanciful in light of the fact our first *Partnership Act*, passed in 1921, post-dated by twelve years our adoption of the English O. 48a being found *in toto* in our original Rules of Court of 1909.

Support for the theory advanced by the claimant is also sought in the language of Farwell J., in his judgment in the *Taff Vale* case particularly where he says: "Now it is undoubtedly true that a trade union is neither a corporation, nor an individual, nor a partnership between a number of individuals" (p. 427), and again, "it is competent to the Legislature to give to an association of individuals which is neither a corporation nor a partnership . . . a capacity . . ." (p. 429). From such collocation of words and phrases we are asked to infer judicial recognition by this learned jurist of the new concept.

That such language was never intended by its author to denote such recognition is made clear by his later observations in *Sadler v. Whiteman*, [1910] 1 K.B. 868 (Eng. K.B.).

Our *Partnership Act*, now R.S.N.B. 1952, c. 167, is modelled on the Act of the United Kingdom. Its s. 5 reads:

> 5. Persons who have entered into partnership with one another are for the purposes of this Act called collectively a firm, and the name under which their business is carried on is called the firm name.

Such enactment is identical with ss. (1) of s. 4 of the Act of the United Kingdom. Its s. 4 contains however, as ss. (2), this further enactment:

> (2) In Scotland a firm is a legal person distinct from the partners of whom it is composed . . .

The inclusion of those provisions in the parent Act deprives of all force the suggestion that by other provisions in the Act the Legislature intended to make of partnership firms generally legal entities or persons.

The true principles are, we feel, correctly formulated in *Pollock on Partnerships*, 15th ed., p. 24, where it is said:

> The law of England knows nothing of the firm . . . as an artificial person distinct from the members composing it, though the firm is so treated by the universal practice of merchants and by the law of Scotland. In England the firm-name may be used in legal instruments both by the partners themselves and by other persons as a collective description of the persons who are partners in the firm at the time to which the description refers: and under the Rules of the Supreme Court actions

may now be brought by and against partners in the firm name. An action between a partner and the firm, or between two firms having a common partner, was impossible at common law, and until 1891 it remained open to doubt whether such actions were possible since the *Judicature Acts*; but they are now expressly authorised by the Rules of Court. (Note 80 here follows reading: "Order XLVIII.A, r. 10. But not so as to enable a partner to be in substance both plaintiff and defendant: *Meyer & Co. v. Faber*, [1923] 2 Ch. 421, C.A.) . . .

Ellis v. Joseph Ellis & Co., [1905] 1 K.B. 324 (Eng. C.A.), lends support to the views we entertain. The action, brought under the *Workmen's Compensation Act* 1897 of the United Kingdom which contains a definition of "workman" corresponding closely to that found in the New Brunswick Act, was against the surviving members of a firm by the dependents of a deceased partner who under a mutual agreement worked in the colliery for wages and had, up to the time of his injury, been paid at the stipulated rate out of the proceeds of the business. It was held the Act contemplated the case of a workman employed by some other person or persons and that the deceased, having been himself one of the partners in the firm for which he was working, could not be said to have been employed by them. At p. 329 Collins M.R., says:

It seems to me obvious . . . that a person cannot for the purposes of the Act occupy the position of being both employer and employee.

And Matthew L.J., says, *ibid.*:

The argument on behalf of the applicant . . . appears to involve a legal impossibility, namely, that the same person can occupy the position of being both master and servant, employer and employed. The deceased man in this case was a partner; and the arrangement made between him and his co-partners as to the payment of wages to him was really an agreement with regard to the mode in which accounts were to be taken between the partners, and to the share of profits to be received by him in excess of that received by the other partners in consideration of the work done by him.

Since the argument in the case at bar our attention has been drawn to two recent decisions of the English Court of Appeal in which the word "entity" was used as descriptive of a partnership firm. They are *Davies v. Elsby Brothers Ltd.*, [1960] 3 All E.R. 672 (C.A.) and *Whittam v. W.J. Daniel & Co.*, [1961] 3 All E.R. 796 (Q.B.). In our view their language falls far short of a recognition in English jurisprudence of the doctrine that as a matter of substantive law a partnership is a legal entity or *persona juridica* separate and distinct from the individuals composing it.

Question answered in the negative.

Notes

1 The decision in *Thorne* should be contrasted with the Privy Council's decision in *Lee v. Lee's Air Farming Ltd. (1960)*, [1961] A.C. 12 (New Zealand P.C.), *infra*, Ch. 2, recognizing the legitimacy of an employer-employee relationship between a corporation and its dominant shareholder.

2 Next to the absence of limited liability, the refusal of the common law to recognize its separate legal personality constitutes the weakest link in the choice of the partnership as a form of business organization as compared with the corporation. *Lindley on Partnership*, 16th ed., p. 325, summarizes the consequences as follows:

> The law, ignoring the firm, looks to the partners composing it; any change amongst them destroys the identity of the firm; what is called the property of the firm is their property, and what are called the debts and liabilities of the firm are their debts and their liabilities. In point of law, a partner may be the debtor or the creditor of his co-partners, but he cannot be either debtor or creditor of the firm of which he is himself a member, nor can he be employed by his firm, for a man cannot be his own employer.

With minor exceptions, the provisions of the Act fully support this aggregate view of the partnership. See *e.g.*, ss. 10-11, 19 and 33.

3 Lindley, *op. cit.*, pp. 35 *et seq.* examines the current position under several heads, *viz.* (i) the partnership name; (ii) legal proceedings by and against the firm; (iii) contractual rights and liabilities; (iv) partnership disabilities; and (v) sureties and securities. In all these cases the partnership's lack of legal personality creates serious problems. To some extent, some of the difficulties can be overcome by proper drafting of the partnership agreement and by agreement between the partnership and its employees or creditors. For example, the partnership agreement may provide that the death or retirement of a partner shall not dissolve the partnership or, in the case of an employment contract, that the contract shall not come to an end. Nevertheless, even where such difficulties have been anticipated by the drafter, there may be difficulties in interpretation. See *e.g.*, *Bank of Montreal v. Kiwi Polish Co. (Can.) Ltd.* (1969), 9 D.L.R. (3d) 579, 1969 CarswellBC 7 (B.C. C.A.) reversed [1971] S.C.R. 991, 1971 CarswellBC 91, 1971 CarswellBC 275, and *cf. Zamikoff v. Lundy*, 9 D.L.R. (3d) 637, [1970] 2 O.R. 8, 1970

CarswellOnt 256 (C.A.). The retention of the partnership name, despite changes in the composition of the partnership, also contributes to the appearance of continuity. However, the appearance yields to reality if the partnership becomes insolvent and creditors are obliged to sue individual partners. See *infra*, s. 5(b).

4 Some real or apparent exceptions to the non-entity rule appear in the Act and in other legislation, *viz.*:

(a) PA, s. 5, recognizes the "firm" designation. See also s. 7 with respect to acts or instruments in the firm's name. However, as the judgment in *Thorne* points out, the use of the collective name is only a matter of convenience and has no substantive consequences;

(b) Section 31 limits the effect of the assignment of a partner's share, but this provision can be explained without resort to entity theories of the partnership.

(c) Section 39 of the Act deals with the application of partnership property on dissolution of the partnership and gives priority to the partnership debts. A similar provision appears, in the case of a bankrupt partnership, in the *Bankruptcy and Insolvency Act* ("BIA"), R.S.C. 1985, c. B-3 as am., s. 142(1). See Houlden & Morawetz, *Bankrupty and Insolvency Law of Canada*, 3rd rev. ed. (1992), G§112.

(d) Under the *Income Tax Act*, R.S.C. 1985, c.1 (5th Suppl.) as am., s. 96, a partnership is treated as a separate person resident in Canada for the purpose of computing the partner's share of the partnership's income for the taxation year. The partnership itself, however, is not separately taxed on its notional income. It is only regarded as a conduit for the partners. See further Richard S. Carson, Carl F. Steiss and Kanshall Tikku, *Taxation of Partnerships in Canada*, Ch. 2 and 3 (Butterworths, 1983) and Norman C. Tobias, *Taxation of Corporations, Partnerships and Trusts* (Carswell, 2001).

(e) Rules of Civil Procedure. Ontario's counterpart to O. 48a of the English Rules of Court is now found in Rule 8 of the Rules of Civil Procedure. Rules 8.01, 8.02 and 8.06 read as follows:

Rule 8.01

8.01(1) A proceeding by or against two or more persons as partners may be commenced using the firm name of the partnership.

(2) Subrule (1) extends to a proceeding between partnerships having one or more partners in common.

Rule 8.02

8.02 Where a proceeding is commenced against a partnership using the firm name, the partnership's defence shall be delivered in the firm name and no person who admits he or she was a partner at any material time may defend the proceeding separately, except with leave of the court.

Rule 8.06

8.06(1) An order against a partnership using the firm name may be enforced against the property of the partnership.

(2) An order against a partnership using the firm name may also be enforced, where the order or a subsequent order so provides, against any person who was served as provided in rule 8.03 and who,

(a) under that rule, is deemed to have been a partner;

(b) has admitted having been a partner; or

(c) has been adjudged to have been a partner,

at the material time.

(3) [OMITTED].

As noted by Chief Justice McNair in *Thorne, supra*, the English rules of practice were not intended to change the substantive law but only to remove some awkward procedural hurdles thrown up by the common law. *Quaere*, whether this limited view of their effect is entirely correct of the Ontario rules and their counterparts in the other provinces? Is it true of Rule 8.01(2)? Of Rule 8.06(1)? If a new partner joins a partnership after the partnership has incurred a particular obligation, what is the effect of the creditor securing a judgment in respect of the obligation against the partnership after the new partner has joined the firm? Is the new partner liable for the partnership's old debts? (See PA, ss. 10, 18.) If he is not, why does Ontario Rule 8.06(1) permit execution against the "partnership property" without distinguishing between those who were partners at the time when the obligation was incurred and those who only subsequently became partners?

General Conclusion.

The aggregate view of the common law partnership remains substantially intact and has been only modestly affected by statutory provisions and rules of practice. The American position is more unsettled. There was a lively debate among US scholars about the aggregate and entity theories of partnership at the time of the adoption of the UPA in 1914, although the UPA itself never adopted a formal position. See *Crane & Bromberg on Partnership* (1968), pp. 16 *et seq.* A 1980s report of a subcommittee of the American Bar Association recommended a revision of the UPA and an expanded adoption of the entity approach but fell short of seeking to resolve the old controversy. See UPA Revision Subcommittee, "Should the Uniform Partnership Act be Revised?" (1987), 43 Bus. Law. 121 esp. at 124-25. As previously noted, *supra*, s. 2, the English and Scottish Law Commissions have recommended conferring legal personality on partnerships governed by English and Scottish law.

5. CONDUCT OF THE BUSINESS OF THE PARTNERSHIP

(a) Relationship of the Partners *Inter Se*

Sections 20 to 31 of the *Partnerships Act* contain the statutory presumptive rules governing the partners' relationship towards one another. Read collectively the rules lead to the conclusion that the partners' relationship is based on principles of equality, consensualism, utmost good faith and the personal character of the partnership contract.

(i) Equality

The principle of equality is reflected in the partners' right and obligation to share equally in the profits and losses of the partnership business (s. 24.1), in the right to participate in the management of the business (s. 24.5), to have access to the partnership books (s. 24.9) and in the duty to render to each other true accounts and full information of all things affecting the partnership (s. 28). All these aspects provide important contrasts with the distribution of power within a corporate structure. Particularly instructive is the right to participate in management. Modern business corporations Acts confer no inherent right in a shareholder, even a majority shareholder in a closely held corporation, to participate in the management of the corporation. If the shareholder wants to play such a role he must have himself elected as a director or enter into a "unanimous shareholder agreement." See CBCA s. 146 and, *infra*, Ch. 4.

The fact that, in the absence of a contrary agreement, every partner is entitled to participate in the management of the partnership's affairs explains the reciprocal agency basis of partnership. It also explains the fundamental rule, enshrined in s. 6 of the Act, that "the acts of every partner who does any act for carrying on in the usual way business of the kind carried on by the firm of which he is a member" bind the firm and the partners unless the third party allows that the partner is in fact without authority to act in the matter. The implications of these agency rules are examined more fully in ss. (ii) below.

Although every partner is entitled to play a managerial role, it is not clear whether he is bound to do so. The *Partnership Act* itself is silent on the point. See *Crane & Bromberg, op. cit.*, p. 380, and *cf.* PA, s. 35(b), which entitles the other partner to seek judicial dissolution of the partnership where the respondent partner is permanently incapable of performing his part of the partnership contract.

(ii) Consensualism

The principle of consensualism in the conduct of partnership affairs is clearly evinced in several provisions. Section 20 provides that the mutual rights and duties of partners, whether ascertained by agreement or determined by the Act, may be varied by the consent of all the partners. The rule of unanimity also governs the admission of new partners (s. 24.7) and any changes in the fundamental character of the partnership business (s. 24.8). The consensual character of the partnership relation manifests itself in the rule that, unless otherwise agreed, any partner may determine the partnership at any time by giving notice of his intention to do so to the other partners (s. 26(1)). It is also reflected in the rule in s. 25 that no majority of partners can expel a partner unless the power to do so has been expressly conferred in the partnership agreement. (This does not mean that in the absence of such agreement partners are bound to each other for life even though they are very unhappy together. It means that the parties will have to seek judicial relief under PA, s. 35. They may also be entitled to terminate the partnership under one of the provisions in s. 32.)

One deviation from the unanimity rule appears in s. 24.8, which allows majority opinion to prevail in "ordinary matters" connected with the partnership business. How would you explain this exception?

(iii) Fiduciary Character

The fiduciary obligations of partners to each other is not peculiar to partnership law but applies to all persons occupying positions of trust and exercising powers for the benefit of others. As will be seen (*infra*, Ch. 6), the fiduciary obligations of directors and officers of corporations have been a fertile source of litigation.

In the partnership context, Cardozo C.J. expressed the relevant principles with particular felicity in an oft-cited passage in his judgment in *Meinhard v. Salmon*, 164 N.E. 545 (N.Y. Ct. App., 1928):

> Joint adventurers, like co-partners, owe to one another, while the enterprise continues, the duty of the finest loyalty. Many forms of conduct permissible in a workaday world for those acting at arm's length, are forbidden to those bound by fiduciary ties. A trustee is held to something stricter than the morals of the market place. Not honesty alone, but the punctilio of an honour the most sensitive, is then the standard of behaviour. As to this, there has developed a tradition that is unbending and inveterate. Uncompromising rigidity has been the attitude of courts of equity when petitioned to undermine the rule of undivided

loyalty by the "disintegrating erosion" of particular exceptions. [Citations omitted.] Only thus has the level of conduct for fiduciaries been kept at a level higher than that trodden by the crowd. It will not consciously be lowered by any judgment of this court.

The fiduciary principle is given statutory expression in ss. 28, 29 and 30 of the *Partnerships Act*. Note also the provision in s. 22(1) of the B.C. *Partnership Act*, and peculiar to that Act, that "a partner must act with the utmost fairness and good faith towards the other members of the firm in the business of the firm."

(iv) Personal Character

Finally, the personal character of the partnership relation is evinced in s. 31 of the Act (which deals with the effect of the assignment of a partner's interest in the partnership) and in the rule adopted in s. 33 that the partnership is automatically dissolved on the death or insolvency of a partner. These features should be contrasted with the perpetual succession enjoyed by the modern corporation (see Ch. 2, s. 1) and the presumption of free transferability of its shares.

In the light of some of the aforementioned provisions, the observation has been made that a partnership is an "unstable relationship." In the statutory sense this is undoubtedly true, but it need not be true in a practical sense if the partnership agreement varies or excludes (as it usually will to some extent) the de-stabilizing provisions in the *Partnerships Act*. In particular, a well-drafted agreement will contain, *inter alia*, provisions with respect to the admission of new partners and the retirement of old ones, the effect of death or bankruptcy, the distribution of responsibilities, the provision of capital and the division of losses and profits.

(b) Liability Towards Third Parties

From a practical point of view, a person's liability for the debts or other obligations of a firm is one of the most litigated aspects of partnership law. This is not surprising, since the problem usually arises when the partnership (assuming there was a partnership to begin with) is insolvent and a creditor is trying to secure payment of its debt.

Five types of situation must be distinguished:

  (i) liabilities incurred by the partnership before the defendant became a member of it;

 (ii) liabilities incurred by the partnership while the defendant was a member of it;

(iii) liabilities incurred by the business while the defendant held himself out, or allowed himself to be held out, as a partner in the business;

(iv) liabilities incurred by the business after the defendant had retired as a partner but before the creditor became aware of the change; and

(v) liability attaching to a person by virtue of the provisions of the *Partnerships Registration Act*, R.S.O. 1980, c. 371 (now repealed), the equivalent provisions in the other provinces, and, less clearly, under the *Business Names Act*, R.S.O. 1990, c.B-17, as am.

Each of these situations will be briefly considered in turn. In addition, something must be said about an important procedural aspect about suing partners in respect of joint obligations.

(i) Pre-partnership Liabilities

Since partnership is a consensual relationship, it is easy to understand why PA, s. 18(1), provides that a person who is admitted as a partner into an existing firm does not thereby become liable to the creditors of the firm for anything done before he became a partner. The converse side of the coin is that retirement does not exonerate a partner from debts and other obligations incurred by the firm before his retirement, and s. 18(2) so provides. (In the first type of situation, would the creditors have an enforceable claim against the new partner if she had agreed as part of her admission to the firm to assume joint liability with the other partners for the existing debts of the firm?)

(ii) Liability as Partner

The elementary proposition that a partner is liable jointly with the other partners for all debts and obligations of the firm incurred while he is a partner is codified in s. 10 of the Act. This liability is inherent in the partnership relationship and is independent of any rights of contribution and indemnity which a partner may have against another partner under ss. 24.1 and 24.2. Another equally basic proposition, again derived from general principles of agency law, is that it is not necessary that the partner whom it is sought to hold liable actually approved or authorized the contract giving rise to the indebtedness. The firm will be liable, and therefore the partner will be liable, if his co-partner "does any act for carrying on in the usual way business of the kind carried on by the firm of which he is a member." See s. 6 of the Act. The same principles govern a partner's liability for acts performed by other agents of the firm. He will only have a valid defence if he can show that the third party knew that the person with whom he was dealing had no authority to bind the firm in the particular matter or did not know or believe him to be a partner. *Id.*

Liability of the firm, and therefore of its partners, for wrongful acts and omissions of a partner is dealt with in ss. 11–13 of the Act. Note carefully that while a partner only incurs joint liability with his fellow partners under s. 10, her liability under s. 13 is joint and several. The distinction between the two types of liability is anomalous and used to cause substantial procedural difficulties. These have largely been overcome by the means explained, *infra*, s. 6(b).

(iii) "Holding out" Liability

A person may be held liable as a partner, even if she never was a partner, if the "holding out" principle of s. 15 applies to her. Section 15(1) provides:

> Every person, who by words spoken or written or by conduct represents himself or who knowingly suffers himself to be represented as a partner in a particular firm, is liable as a partner to any person who has on the faith of any such representation given credit to the firm, whether the representation has or has not been made or communicated to the persons so giving credit by or with the knowledge of the apparent partner making the representation or suffering it to be made.

The meaning of "knowingly suffers himself to be represented as a partner" was examined in *Tower Cabinet Co. v. Ingram*, [1949] 1 All E.R. 1033 (D.C.), reproduced later in this section.

(iv) Liability of Apparent Partner

Another aspect of the holding out principle determines the extent to which a person may continue to remain liable as a partner even after he has retired from the partnership. The relevant rules are set forth in PA, s. 36, and are discussed, *inter alia*, in *Ingram, supra*, and in *Dominion Sugar Co. v. Warrell*, [1927] 2 D.L.R. 198, 60 O.L.R. 169 (C.A.).

(v) Registration Requirements

The *Partnerships Registration Act* (PRA) was first adopted in Ontario in 1869 (33 Vic. c. 20) and, therefore, long before the *Partnerships Act* itself was adopted. The other common law provinces have adopted substantially similar provisions. In 1938 the Canadian Uniformity Commissioners also adopted a *Uniform Partnerships Registration Act*, which has been enacted in part or with amendments in New Brunswick, Prince Edward Island and Saskatchewan. For the current version of the *Uniform Act*, see Uniform Law Conference of Canada, *Uniform Statutes*, p. 227, www.ulcc.ca. Ontario repealed the PRA in 1990 and replaced it with the *Business Names Act*. See now the *Business Names Act*, R.S.O. 1990, c. B.17, as am.

The BNA and PRAs have, or had, a common purpose, *viz.*, to enable third parties to ascertain the membership of a partnership and to learn of any changes in the composition of the firm by requiring the filing of these particulars in a public registry office: BNA, ss. 2(3), 4-5 and O.Reg. 121/91. However, there are important differences between the BNA and the old Ontario PRA, of which the following are the most relevant for partnership liability purposes:

(a) The BNA applies to single proprietorships and to corporations carrying on business under an assumed name as well as to partnerships

(s. 2). Business is broadly defined as including every trade, occupation, profession, service or venture carried on with a view to profit (s. 1). The PRA was restricted to trading, manufacturing and mining partnerships.

(b) The BNA does not apply to limited partnerships[3] or to partners carrying on business or identifying themselves to the public "under a name that is composed of the names of the partners" [s. 2(4)].[4]

(c) The civil sanctions were different:

(i) Under the BNA, s. 7(1), a partnership "is not capable of maintaining a proceeding in Ontario" except with leave of the court. The partnership is entitled to leave as of right if it can satisfy the court that the three conditions in s. 7(2) are met. (Presumably, the court may grant permission, on terms or otherwise, even if the conditions are not met.) Under the PRA, an action was also not maintainable as long as the partnership was in breach but the breach could be cured at any time without leave of the court. (Why should the court's leave be necessary under the BNA?)

(ii) The BNA contains no provisions estopping a person whose name appears as a partner in a BNA registration from denying that he is a partner until his name is removed. The PRA contained the following provisions in ss. 5, 6 and 8(1):

5. Whenever any change takes place in the membership of a partnership, in the residence address or address for service of any partner or in the name of a partnership, the partners shall cause to be filed within sixty days after the change takes place a new declaration setting out the information required by section 3.

6. The statements made in any declaration are not controvertible by any person who has signed it nor as against any person not being a member of the partnership by any person who has signed it, or who was actually a member of the partnership therein mentioned at the time the declaration was made . . .

8.(1) No person who signed the declaration under section 1 or a subsequent declaration under section 5 or 17 shall be deemed as against creditors to have ceased to be a partner until a declaration

---

[3] This is because the LPA has its own registration provisions, but how will an outsider know whether she is dealing with an LP or other type of business without searching both registries? The LPA provisions are discussed later in this chapter.

[4] The Ministry brochure issued at the time of the BNA's adoption stated that to satisfy s. 2(4) it was not sufficient for the partnership name to comprise all the partners' surnames; the partners' first names also had to be included. Thus "Smith and Brown" did not satisfy the statutory requirement unless it was changed to read, "John Smith and Jane Brown". Is this interpretation supported by the language of s. 2(4)?

or dissolution under section 7 is made and filed or a declaration is filed under section 5 omitting his name.

The effect of the PRA provisions, coupled with s. 36 of the PA, were discussed in the leading case of *Dominion Sugar Co. v. Warrell*, [1927] 2 D.L.R. 198 (Ont. C.A.). The absence of estoppel provisions in the BNA does not mean that they may not be implied. This is because, given the common law rules on holding out and the provisions in ss. 15 and 36(1) of the PA, it seems safe to conclude that a person who allows herself to be held out as a partner in a BNA registration when she is not, or fails to have her name removed when she ceases to be a partner (if she was a partner), will be estopped from denying her partnership status to a person *who has relied* on the registration. What is the position if the third party has not searched the register? Will/should the courts impute constructive notice of the registration? In other areas of commercial law, courts have generally been reluctant to apply doctrines of constructive notice to the contents of registered documents unless the Act so provided or unless the courts felt it should be inferred from the purpose of the registration requirements. Will the BNA objectives be defeated if constructive notice of a registration is not imputed, or does it depend on the circumstances of the particular case?

(vi) Procedural Aspects of Joint Liability

The rule at common law, confirmed by the House of Lords in *Kendall v. Hamilton* (1879), 4 App. Cas. 504 (U.K. H.L.), was that "if a joint creditor of a firm obtains judgment in an action brought against one partner only, he loses his remedy against the other partners, although he did not know of the other partners when he recovered judgment and the judgment remains unsatisfied". *Lindley on Partnerships*, 15th ed., p. 364. In England, the rule was abolished by s. 3 of the *Civil Liability (Contribution) Act* 1978. In Ontario the rule still appears to be in force, but its practical effect is substantially mitigated by the Rules of Practice. RP 8.01 provides that a proceeding by or against two or more persons as partners may be commenced using the firm name of the partnership. Pursuant to RP 8.06(2), a party who has obtained an order against a partnership using the firm name may apply for leave to enforce it against a person alleged to be a partner if the person has not previously been served with notice of the proceedings. Section 8(2) of the PRA may also have some bearing on the rule in *Kendall v. Hamilton*, though the precise impact of this provision remains uncertain. In addition, s. 139(1) of the *Courts of Justice Act*, R.S.O. 1990, c. C.43, provides:

> 139.(1) Where two or more persons are jointly liable in respect of the same cause of action, a judgment against or release of one of them does not preclude judgment against any other in the same or a separate proceeding.

The commentary prepared by the Ministry of the Attorney General when the legislation was in draft form explained that, "this provision abolishes the rule that judgment against, or a release of, a person who is jointly liable prevents judgment from being obtained against any other joint wrongdoer".

Tower Cabinet Co. v. Ingram
[1949] 2 K.B. 397, [1949] 1 All E.R. 1033 (K.B.)

Tower Cabinet claimed from Merry's the sum of 323l. 17s. od., the price of goods sold and delivered in January and February, 1948. Judgment was obtained and subsequently Tower Cabinet sought to render the appellant, Ingram, liable for the debts of Merry's, alleging that he was so liable under the provisions of ss. 14 and 36 of the *Partnership Act*, 1890.

In January, 1946, Ingram and one Christmas began to carry on business in partnership under the name of Merry's. The partnership was registered under the *Registration of Business Names Act*, 1916, as being carried on by the appellant and Christmas. On April 22, 1947, the parties agreed to dissolve the partnership and the appellant gave notice to the firm's bankers that he had ceased to be a partner in Merry's. He arranged with Christmas that Christmas should notify those dealing with the firm that the appellant had ceased to be connected with it, but no advertisement appeared in the *London Gazette*. During the subsistence of the partnership the firm's notepaper had been headed "Merry's" under which the names A. H. Christmas and S. G. Ingram (the appellant) appeared, indicating that they were both partners. After the dissolution new notepaper was printed on which the name Merry's appeared and "A.H. Christmas, director." In January, 1948, "Merry's" sent, on the old notepaper used by the firm when the appellant was a member, an order to the respondents for six bedroom suites. This order was signed by Christmas as "manager". Christmas had no authority from the appellant to use the paper and its use was in direct conflict with the arrangements made on the dissolution of the partnership.

The master held that the appellant was liable as a partner, not (under s. 14) for holding himself out as a partner, but under s. 36 of the *Partnership Act*, 1890.

LYNSKEY J.: The question is whether the company is (sic) able to make Ingram liable as a partner by reason of the provisions of the *Partnership Act*, 1890, concerned with holding out or with failure to give notice when a man has ceased to be a partner, and credit has been given to the firm as if he were still a partner.

The first section on which the company rely is s. 14. Before the company can succeed in making Ingram liable under this section, they (sic) have to satisfy the court that Ingram by words spoken or written, or by conduct represented himself as a partner. There is no evidence of such representation. The section says "or who knowingly suffers himself to be so represented." The only evidence relating to this is the fact that the order in this case was given by Christmas on notepaper which contained Ingram's name. That would amount to a representation by Christmas that Ingram was still a partner in the firm. But on the evidence and on the Master's finding, that representation was made by Christmas without Ingram's knowledge and without his authority. Such being the finding of fact, which is not challenged, it is impossible to say that Ingram knowingly suffered himself to be represented. The words are "knowingly suffers," not being negligent or careless in not seeing that all the notepaper had been destroyed when he left.

The company also rely on s. 36 of the Act, concerned with the rights of persons dealing with the firm. It is on the construction of the three subsections of that section that this case turns. That section has not been the subject of construction, as far as we have been informed, by any court since this Act was passed. It is said by counsel for the company that the true meaning of that section is that ss. 1 is concerned with the case where it is apparent to the world that a man is a partner in a firm. If it is apparent to the world, and if persons have dealt with the firm, then under ss. 1 notice must be given to those individuals before the liability of a resigned or retired partner can cease. Secondly, he says that ss. 2 equally applies to the position of partners when it is apparent to the world that they were partners, and those two sections are concerned with that particular case. Referring to the old authority, *Farrar v. Delfinne*, counsel for the company says that a distinction must be drawn between what are described by Cresswell J. as partners who are notorious partners and partners who are profoundly secret members of the partnership, and that this section being in the codifying Act, is really reenacting in the form of that statute, the law as it existed in the year 1845 and later. Even in that case, Cresswell J. laid considerable stress on the question of actual notice. He said:

> Todd and the defendant were once in partnership, but they had not been so since the year 1837. The plaintiff dealt with the firm during the partnership, and he continued to do so afterwards; and the question is, whether the defendant is liable in respect of such subsequent dealings now that the partnership is dissolved. The law stands thus: if there had been a notorious partnership, but no notice had been given of the dissolution thereof, the defendant would have been liable. If there had been a general notice, that would have been sufficient for all but actual customers; these, however, must have had some kind of actual notice. If the partnership had remained profoundly secret, the defendant could not have been affected by transactions which took place after he had retired; but if the partnership had become known to any person or persons, he would be in the same situation as to all such persons, as if the existence of the partnership had been notorious. The question for you, therefore, is, was this partnership actually known to the plaintiffs, either by the general report, or by direct communication? Because, if it were, and he did not know, either from notice of the fact, or from surmise, that the dissolution had taken place, you must infer that he

still dealt on the faith of the partnership, and the defendant will therefore be liable.

It is said by counsel for the company who seeks to adopt this judgment in his favour, that s. 36, ss. 1 and 2 are concerned with what are described in that judgment as notorious partnerships, and ss. 3 is concerned with cases of profoundly secret partners. I find difficulty, when looking at the Act itself, in adopting that suggested construction. The form of the section is:

> Where a person deals with a firm after a change in its constitution he is entitled to treat all apparent members of the old firm as still being members of the firm until he has notice of the change.

The whole point depends, in my view, upon what is the meaning in s. 36, ss. 1, of "apparent members" — Apparent to whom? Does it mean apparent to the whole world, or notorious, or does it mean apparent to the particular person with which the section is concerned? The section says:

> Where a person deals with a firm . . . he is entitled to treat all apparent members . . .

In my reading of that sub-section, "apparent members" means members who are apparently members to the person who is dealing with the firm, and they may be apparent either by the fact that the customer has had dealings with them before, or because of the use of their names on the notepaper, or from some sign outside the door, or because the customer has had some indirect information about them. Both ss. 1 and 2 in my view are concerned with cases where they are apparent members.

Sub-section 3 again deals with the particular individual. It does not deal with the public at large. Its words are simple and obvious. It is not concerned merely with questions of apparent members or non-apparent members, but applies the test indicated by the words:

> A partner who, not having been known to the person dealing with the firm to be a partner.

Those words are equally applicable whether he was an apparent partner or a dormant partner. If the person dealing with the firm did not know that the particular partner was a partner, and that partner retired, then as from the date of his retirement, he ceases to be liable for further debts contracted by the firm to such person. The fact that later the person dealing with the firm may discover that the former partner was a partner seems to me to be irrelevant, because the date from which the sub-section operates is from the date of the dissolution. If at the date of the dissolution the person who subsequently deals with the firm had no knowledge at or before that time that the retiring partner was a partner, then ss. 3 comes into operation, and relieves the person retiring from liability.

It has been argued for the company that they knew Ingram was a partner because the order for the goods contained a statement to that effect. In my view, that document, which only came into existence in January, 1948, was a representation by Christmas that Ingram was a partner at that particular date, but that representation was untrue. Ingram was not a partner at that date and it cannot be inferred that that representation gave the company knowledge that Ingram had in fact been a partner before the date of the dissolution of the partnership in April, 1947. Even if the representation did give such knowledge, in my view, the section had already commenced to operate, and it would not avail (subject to s. 14, which was concerned with holding out) to render Ingram liable. The result is that in this case the master was not correct in his view of the effect of the sub-section or of the decision which he cited. It is established here that the company had no knowledge that Ingram was a partner before the date of the dissolution. That being so, Ingram is brought directly within the words of ss. 3, and is therefore under no liability to the company in respect of the debts subsequently incurred by Christmas after Ingram had ceased to be a partner. In my view, this appeal ought to be allowed.

Appeal allowed.

6. SPECIAL FORMS OF PARTNERSHIP

(a) Joint Ventures

Central Mortgage & Housing Corp. v. Graham
(1973), 43 D.L.R. (3d) 686, 1973 CarswellNS 192 (T.D.)

Central Mortgage and Housing Corporation (CMHC) proposed the establishment of a shell housing project in Sydney, N.S., and enlisted the assistance of Bras D'Or, a construction company, to carry out the project. Bras D'Or agreed to erect 21 houses on lands which it provided according to plans and specifications provided by CMHC. CMHC agreed to provide that financing for the houses and all purchasers were to be approved by CMHC. Upon the execution of an assumption agreement by a purchaser satisfactory to both parties, CMHC released Bras D'Or from any further liability for the funds advanced.

The defendants purchased one of the 21 homes. Several defects appeared in the house and the defendants stopped making payments on the mortgage. CMHC commenced an action for foreclosure and sale. The defendants argued that their house had been defectively built and filed a counterclaim for damages against CMHC and Bras D'Or. They alleged that the two were engaged in a joint venture and therefore jointly liable for the damages sustained by the defendants.

JONES J. (after setting out the facts in detail, continued): In the first instance it is necessary to determine the relationships between the parties. The Grahams contend that Central Mortgage and Bras D'Or were jointly involved in the erection of these homes and must answer for any deficiencies. In their submission, Central Mortgage was a builder, partner, joint venturer or principal in this scheme. Central Mortgage, on the other hand, maintains that it acted throughout merely as the lending agency which provided the financial backing for the project. In the result, the only relationship to Bras D'Or or the Grahams was that of mortgagee. There is no great variance in the evidence as to the arrangements made for the erection of these houses. Having regard to that evidence, it is my view that central Mortgage and Bras D'Or were engaged in a joint venture. A joint venture is defined in vol. 1 of Barrett and Seago, *Partners and Partnerships, Law, and Taxation* (1956), at p. 65 as follows:

> Joint adventures may be defined as an association of two or more individuals, corporations or partnerships or some combination of these, for the purpose of carrying on a business venture. Of more recent years, this rather peculiar type of business organization has had increased use and attention. Joint adventures are quite common in building and construction work. A useful and practical result can thus be obtained in that the task might well prove too large for a single firm, corporation or group of individuals. Moreover, a combination of equipment is required together with a pooling of skilled and experienced personnel [to] make this form of organisation an attractive one. Speaking in broad general terms, much of the law of partnership is applicable to joint adventures.
>
> Another definition stresses the fact that the joint adventure is almost invariably concerned with a single undertaking that does not continuously require the attention of every participant.

The authors also stated at p. 67: "It is well settled that a corporation may engage in and be a party to a joint adventure."

Volume 2 of *Williston on Contracts*, 3rd ed. (1959), states at pp. 544-5:

> A form of organization long known to commerce but only recently endowed with a distinctive recognition in law, the joint venture is a convenient means for providing the great concentration of economic resources, knowledge and skill requisite to the accomplishment of large scale construction projects such as public buildings, national monuments and similar structures, bridges, tunnels, super highways and tool roads, power dams, canals and seaways, electric energy projects, atomic reactors and other power sources, to mention but a few of the typical results of joint ventures.

And at pp. 547-8:

> As a means for conducting trade or commerce, the joint venture is rooted deep in the past; but as a legal concept, it has been slow of growth. The early common law did not recognize any relationship between persons as joint venturers apart from that of partners, and required proof of the existence of the requisite elements of such a status.
>
> The courts, however, responding to the urgent problems arising from the need of applying fundamental principles of the common law to new developments in the world of business and commerce, had gradually evolved what may become a distinctive legal relationship: The joint venture. Here, parties combine their resources, usually consisting of capital, knowledge, skill and services, in the conduct of a business venture without organizing a partnership in the legal sense of the word.

And at pp. 549-50:

> Unaided by established precedents of *stare decisis* and faced with the exigencies of rapidly developing and expanding business methods and requirements, the courts have, quite naturally, shown a wide divergence of views in their characterization of the joint venture, and an understandable reluctance to formulate a precise definition of "this case law hybrid of recent origin and undetermined connotation."
>
> The cases show that there has been a complete lack of terminological uniformity or exactitude in the judicial expressions attempting to formulate a definition of joint ventures; and many courts have declared that the particular circumstances and agreement as well as the object of the undertaking must determine the legal nature of the association.
>
> Succinctly expressive of this attitude and of the difficulties confronting the courts in defining the nature of a joint venture is the language in a leading and representative case:
>
> "Precise definition of a joint venture is difficult. The cases are of little help since they are generally restricted to their own peculiar facts. 'Each case in which a coadventure is claimed . . . depends of course for its results on its own facts, and owing to the multifariousness of facts, no case of coadventure rises higher than a persuasive precedent for another.' "

As the author points out at p. 553, a joint adventure is founded entirely on an agreement between the parties. At p. 554, the author refers to the following definitions:

The joint venture is an association of two or more persons based on contract who combine their money, property, knowledge, skills, experience, time or other resources in the furtherance of a particular project or undertaking, usually agreeing to share the profits and the losses and each having some degree of control over the venture. Stated in somewhat greater detail:

It can be said that a joint adventure contemplates an enterprise jointly undertaken, that it is an association of such joint undertakers to carry out a single project for profit; that the profits are to be shared, as well as the losses, though the liability of a joint adventurer for a proportionate part of the losses or expenditures of the joint enterprise may be affected by the terms of the contract. There must be a contribution by the parties to a common undertaking to constitute a joint adventure; and a community of interest as well as some control over the subject matter or property right of the contract.

Whether the parties to a particular contract have thereby created as between themselves, the relation of joint adventurers or some other relation depends upon their actual intention, and such relationship arises only when they intend to associate themselves as such. This intention is to be determined in accordance with the ordinary rules governing the interpretation and construction of contracts.

* * *

The English Courts have tended to look for a partnership agreement before attaching any legal significance to an association between parties. In *Ross v. Canadian Bank of Commerce*, [1923] 3 D.L.R. 339, 54 O.L.R. 59 (P.C.), a much wider view was expressed. The action was brought by a third party against two persons involved in a mining operation. Viscount Cave, L.C., stated at p. 342:

What, then, was the effect of these agreements? It appears to their Lordships to be this: that both before and after the agreements these two persons joined together to form the Patricia Syndicate; that the purpose of the Patricia Syndicate was to carry on the business of developing the mines; and that both parties agreed when the process of development had been completed to transfer the property to a company and to take their profit in the form of shares in that company. That was a combination for the purpose of making profits, even although the receipt of the profits might be deferred until the company had been formed. It appears to their Lordships to be immaterial whether the combination is called a partnership or a joint adventure. Probably it was a partnership. But, in any case, it was a combination, and if it was part of the terms on which the combination was made that a business should be carried on and liabilities should be incurred, and if in the course of carrying on that business liabilities were incurred, either by the combination or the partnership or the syndicate (whichever it is called) or by a member on its behalf, within the limits of the adventure, then those liabilities bound both members of the syndicate and not only the one by whom the liability was actually incurred.

There is little doubt the Privy Council was of the opinion that the defendants were in fact partners.

A number of recent Canadian cases have dealt with the relationship between finance companies and dealers. While the factual situation is different from the present case, the Courts have shown a tendency to examine the arrangements between the financier and dealer in determining their legal relationship to third parties. The leading decision is *Federal Discount Corp. v. St. Pierre*, 32 D.L.R. (2d) 86, [1962] O.R. 310 (C.A.) . . .

I am satisfied on the evidence that Central Mortgage was involved in this project from the very start. Central Mortgage proposed the establishment of a shell housing project in Sydney. Agents of the corporation sought civic approval and directly enlisted Bras D'Or to carry out the project. The project was approved upon the submission of a proposal by Bras D'Or. Central Mortgage provided financing to cover the full cost of the project. The houses were sold to specified individuals only upon approval by Central Mortgage. Central Mortgage provided the plans and specifications and all necessary documentation.

In terms of an agreement between Central Mortgage and Bras D'Or, the construction company agreed to erect 21 houses on lands which it provided according to plans and specifications provided by Central Mortgage at a fixed price. Central Mortgage agreed to provide total financing for the houses. Bras D'Or agreed to the sale of the houses to purchasers approved by Central Mortgage. Upon the execution of an assumption agreement by a purchaser satisfactory to both parties, Central Mortgage released Bras D'Or from any further liability for the funds advanced.

In my view, there was a contribution by both parties of money, property, skill, and knowledge to a common undertaking. There was a joint property interest in the subject-matter even though evidenced only in the mortgages. The parties had a mutual control and management of the enterprise during the construction of the houses and in the sales. The arrangement was limited to this project. There is no doubt that Bras D'Or intended a profit from the project. While there was [not] a mutual sharing of the profits, Central Mortgage clearly had a financial interest at stake and was vitally concerned with the successful completion of the venture. The project was within the operations of Central Mortgage under the *National Housing Act*, R.S.C. 1970, c. N-10. This was made clear by the evidence of the officials of the corporation. Based on the evidence, the arrangement between Central Mortgage and Bras D'Or can be characterized as a joint venture. To the extent that Bras D'Or in carrying on the venture incurred liabilities then both parties were bound.

Judgment for the defendants.

Notes

1 Since the *Graham* case, several attempts have been made to characterize the relationship between a mortgagor and mortgagee as amounting to a joint venture, but none of them has succeeded. See *e.g., Mar-Sand Properties Ltd. v. Central Mortgage & Housing Corp.* (1975), 12 N.B.R. (2d) 597, 1975 CarswellNB 225 (Q.B.); *390346 Ontario Ltd. v. Malidav Holdings Ltd.* (1980), 31 N.B.R. (2d) 72, 75 A.P.R. 72, 1980 CarswellNB 157 (Q.B.); *Fraser-Brace Maritimes Ltd. v. Central Mortgage & Housing Corp.* (1980), 42 N.S.R. (2d) 1, 117 D.L.R. (3d) 312, 1980 CarswellNS 70 (C.A.); and *Central Mortgage & Housing Corp. v. Omega Investments Ltd.* (1981), 34 N.B.R. (2d) 291, 1981 CarswellNB 149 (C.A.). Mr. Justice Jones himself, in a subsequent case, treated his decision in *Graham* as turning on its special facts. Writing in an appellate capacity in *Fraser-Brace Maritimes Ltd. v. Central Mortgage & Housing Corp., supra,* he said (at p. 17):

> The analogy in this case is to *Northern Electric Co. Ltd. v. Frank Warkentin* (1972), 27 D.L.R. (3d) 519, and *Northern Electric Co. Ltd. v. Manufacturers Life Insurance Co. and Metropolitan Projects Ltd.* (1975), 10 N.S.R. (2d) 97; 2 A.P.R. 97. In the latter case this court held the relationship then in issue was basically that of lender and borrower and not one of partnership or joint venture. The *Graham* case, on the other hand, is clearly distinguishable. While on the record Central Mortgage in the *Graham* case appeared as the mortgagee in fact the corporation's involvement was complete. The entire scheme was to place on the market for sale to third parties shell housing. The proposal was being promoted by Central Mortgage and not the contractor. Central Mortgage and the builder were dealing in such manner as to create the appearance of joint participation to the injury of innocent third parties. The question of whether there was a joint venture in the instant case was a matter for the trial judge and I see no basis for disturbing his finding in that regard.

2 The question remains, however, whether, apart from *Graham*, there is any Canadian authority to justify treating a joint venture as a special kind of partnership or as a business association *sui generis*. Mr. Justice Jones relied almost exclusively on American sources. Even in that context we have the weighty opinion of *Crane & Bromberg on Partnership* (1968), p. 189, that:

> A joint venture is an association created by co-owners of a business undertaking, differing from partnership (if at all) in having a more limited scope. In all important respects, the joint venture is treated as a partnership.

They also express the view that "[w]hether a JV is considered a partnership or merely analogized to one, the venturers are governed by the

rules applicable to partners" (p. 192). The viability of the distinction
between a JV and a partnership was seemingly accepted by Mr. Justice
Wachowich in *Canada Deposit Insurance Corp. v. Canadian Commercial Bank* (1986), 46 Alta. L.R. (2d) 111, 1986 CarswellAlta 442
(Q.B.) at 116–118 [Alta. L.R.]. This case involved the characterization
of several loan participation agreements between the Bank and investors. It was argued that one of the participation agreements (the "Cadillac Participation Agreement") amounted to a partnership. Mr. Justice
Wachowich responded (at 118):

> As to the partnership classification, it seems to me that the
> requisite continuity for partnership, which distinguishes a partner-
> ship from a joint venture, is lacking. A partnership is concerned with
> carrying on business whereas a joint venture is usually restricted to
> a specific project. It seems to me that having regard to the fact that
> this relationship arose for the sole purpose of effecting a loan to the
> borrower, the relationship more appropriately reflects a joint venture
> or a syndication as distinct from a partnership.

If the more limited scope of the association is all that separates the
JV from the traditional partnership, there should be little difficulty in
fitting the JV within the framework of the *Partnerships Act*. In fact, s.
32(b) of the Act itself recognizes short term ventures as a partnership
in dealing with the termination of the partnership. Again, in *Mann v.
D'Arcy*, [1968] 2 All E.R. 172 (Megarry J.), a contract between the
plaintiff and the first defendant for the purchase and resale of 350 tons
of potatoes on board the *Anna Schaar*, the parties to share profits and
losses, was treated as a partnership. See the judgment at p. 174. Does
it follow that the BNA (Ontario) and PRA (other provinces) registration
requirements also apply to such short term ventures, and would it be
practical given the short term character of many JVs?

3 One of the cases referred to in *Graham* is Mr. Justice Kelly's seminal
judgment in *Federal Discount Corp. v. St. Pierre*, 32 D.L.R. (2d) 86,
[1962] O.R. 310, 1962 CarswellOnt 146 (C.A.). In this much-cited case
the court denied holder in due course status to the plaintiff, a sales
finance company, which held a promissory note given by the defendants
to a dealer on the ground, *inter alia*, that the plaintiff company and the
dealer were "more nearly engaged in one business, each one in the
conduct of its particular phase being useless without the association of
the other." Mr. Justice Kelly did not suggest that the dealer and the
company constituted a partnership or that they had agreed to share
profits and losses arising from the discounting of consumer paper.
Nevertheless, it could be argued that he was invoking the concept of a
joint venture for the purpose of restricting the normal scope of the
holder in due course doctrine and, no doubt, very properly so. For further
discussion of the *Federal Discount* doctrine, see Ziegel, Geva & Cum-
ing, *Commercial and Consumer Transactions*, rev. 2nd ed. (Emond
Montgomery Ltd., 1990), pp. 743 *et seq.*

(b) Limited Partnerships

(i) Introduction

The concept of a limited partnership is an old one to civilians and was already well established in the Middle Ages where it is said to have originated in Italy. Today such civilian limited partnerships are frequently identified by their French name, *sociétiés en commandites*. The concept, however, is foreign to the common law, under which one is either a partner or one is not.

New York adopted a *Limited Partnerships Act* as early as 1822, and Ontario followed suit with its own LPA in 1849. See 12 Vic., c 45. The United Kingdom introduced an LPA in 1907. However, it never made much of an impact because, after the seminal decision of the House of Lords in *Salomon v. Salomon*, [1897] A.C. 22, 66 L.J. Ch. 35 (H.L.), there were no barriers to using the *British Companies Act* for the incorporation of small businesses, and no significant advantages to using the limited partnership over the incorporation vehicle for such businesses. (*Lindley on Partnership*, 15th ed., p. 928, for example, writes that the number of registered limited partnerships in the years preceding 1983 has been "around the 750 mark.") This was equally true of the Ontario position, but there was an additional reason to discourage use of the limited partnership form of organization. This was the poor drafting of the 1849 Act and the difficulty of complying with its technical and demanding requirements. Although Ontario adopted an entirely new Act in 1980 (see below), the ratio of limited partnerships to general partnerships is still very low. In the third quarter of fiscal year 2003-04 for example, there were only 75 LP business names registrations compared to 98,400 new sole proprietorship and general partnerships registrations.

The Americans adopted a *Uniform Limited Partnership Act* in 1916, and this was revised in 1976. Alberta, Saskatchewan, British Columbia, the Yukon and the Northwest Territories adopted legislation modelled on the original ULPA in the post-World War II period. Ontario adopted a new LPA in 1980 (see now R.S.O. 1990, c. L-16), which is substantially based on the Alberta Act. For further descriptions of the current Canadian and American positions, see L.R. Hepburn & W.J. Strain, *Limited Partnerships* (Richard DeBoo, looseleaf, 1983); Alison Manzer, *A Practical Guide to Canadian Partnership Law*, Ch. 10, (Canada Law, looseleaf, 2002); Clement Bates, *The Law of Limited Partnership* (Rothman & Co., 1997); R.A. Kessler, "The New Uniform Limited Partnership Act: A Critique" (1979), 48 Fordham L. Rev. 159.

(ii) Important Features of the *Ontario Limited Partnerships Act*

General Features. A limited partnership is a partnership consisting of at least one general partner and one limited partner (s. 2(2)), and it is formed simply by filing a declaration under s. 3 of the LPA. As specified in s. 3(2), the declaration need only set out the name and address of the firm and the names of the general and limited partners, the general nature of the business and the contributions made by each partner. This declaration expires after five years, but the limited partnership is not dissolved by such expiry; it only has to pay an extra fee (s. 3(4)).

A limited partner is only liable to the extent of his contribution to the firm (s. 9), but this protection is lost if "he takes part in the control of the business" (s. 13(1)). Exactly what is meant by "control" is not clear, although some help is offered in s. 12(2)(a) which explicitly permits a limited partner to "advise as to [the firm's] management." Do you think an easy line can be drawn between advising and controlling? If a firm consistently follows the advice of a limited partner, could this be construed as amounting to control? Why should participation by a limited partner in the control of the partnership deprive him of his sheltered status? Is it because third parties are misled, or is it because he cannot both have his cake and eat it too? *Cf.* the status of a shareholder-director in an incorporated company; and see the decision in *Haughton Graphic Ltd. v. Zivot* (1986), 33 B.L.R. 125 (Ont. H.C.), reproduced at the end of these notes, *infra*.

Transferability. Section 18 gives a limited partner the right to assign his interest, but the assignee only has limited rights unless either all of the other partners consent in writing to the assignment or the partnership agreement gives the assignor that power. The situation is similar to selling shares in a closely held company, where the by-laws usually require the consent of the other shareholders or give them a pre-emptive right to purchase the shares before they can be sold to a third party.

Withdrawal. Aside from selling his interest, a limited partner has the right to receive the return of his contribution from the firm in four situations, as set out in s. 15: (1) on dissolution; (2) if the partnership agreement provides for it; (3) if no other procedure is specified in the partnership agreement, then after he has given six months notice to all other partners; or, (4) if all the partners consent to the return. However, a limited partner is not entitled to withdraw his contribution unless there are sufficient partnership assets to cover all of the partnership liabilities. Compare these provisions with the right of an Ontario corporation to purchase its shares under OBCA, ss. 30–36.

Dissolution. A limited partnership is dissolved upon the death, retirement or mental incompetence of a general partner or dissolution of a corporate general partner. However, by ss. 21(a) and (b), the remaining general partners can continue the business. Pursuant to s. 23(1)(b), dissolution also occurs when all of the limited partners have withdrawn from the partnership. Furthermore, under s. 15(4), a limited partner can have the partnership dissolved if, although he is entitled to the return of his contribution, it is not forthcoming on his demand, or if the partnership assets are insufficient under s. 14(2)(a) and he would otherwise be entitled to be repaid his contribution.

Legal Personality. Americans have long debated the question of whether a limited partnership has a separate legal personality. The conflict arises because of what observers perceive to be the ambivalent provisions in the ULPA, although there is no explicit section anywhere in that Act (just as there is none in the new Ontario LPA) conferring legal personality on the limited partnership. Is there any reason why a limited partnership cannot have its own personality?

Conclusion. We see that the limited partnership is a very specialized investment vehicle, lying somewhere in its attributes between a corporation and a regular partnership.

(iii) Limited Partnerships and Taxation

One of the reasons for the recent popularity of limited partnerships is the fact that they combine the advantage of limited liability with the benefits of partnership tax treatment.

Avoidance of Double Taxation. Under the *Income Tax Act,* individual partners take their share of partnership income or loss into account when computing their personal income for tax purposes. This is a direct "flow through" of income as opposed to the situation where a corporate investment vehicle is used. In the latter case, the corporation pays tax on its actual or imputed profit and shareholders pay taxes on dividends received by them from the corporation, thus often resulting in "double taxation." Double taxation is said to occur whenever the same income is taxed twice. A discussion of the complexities of the corporate tax system, with its attempts to achieve varying degrees of integration for certain types and amounts of income for certain sorts of corporations is far beyond the scope of this note.

This flow-through feature has made the limited partnership particularly attractive to investors, for example, foreigners investing in Canadian real estate. The individual foreign investor has the cash generated from his project reduced by such deductions as CCA (capital cost allowance). Then, because income flows directly through to him, income for tax purposes can be reduced still further by claiming personal deductions. This contrasts with the alternative of investing through a corporation, which must pay tax based on income before the personal deductions, and at the high flat corporate rate. After that, any distribution to the foreign shareholder would be subject to withholding tax, with the rate ultimately determined by any applicable tax treaty.

Special Incentives. In its efforts to implement specific economic policies through the taxation system, the federal government has intermittently introduced special tax incentives (some of which have since been repealed or are in the course of being phased out) designed to encourage, for example, exploration for oil and gas, Canadian feature films, construction of multi-unit residential buildings (MURB's) and scientific and technologically oriented research and development. The basic incentive in these schemes is the allowance of a rapid expensing for tax purposes of the cost of items which would otherwise be capitalized and offset against income over a much longer period of time, and by allowing any resulting tax losses to offset income of the taxpayer from other sources. While a corporation can store such deductions if it does not have current income to offset the special writeoffs, a partnership will normally flow them through directly to the partners. This treatment avoids any loss because of the time value of money, and ensures that the losses are actually used up rather than being eventually lost because of limitations on their storage time.

(iv) The Proper Law of Limited Partnerships

An LP formed under the laws of another jurisdiction will be recognized in Ontario subject to compliance with the statutory provisions. Section 25(1–4) of the LPA says that no extra-provincial limited partnership shall "carry on business" in Ontario (the expression is defined in s. 25(2)) unless it has filed an appropriate declaration, *etc.*, which must be kept up-to-date (see ss. 25(5–7)). Note the penalties for noncompliance with the Act in s. 35. However, s. 27(l) says:

> A limited partner of an extra-provincial limited partnership is not liable in Ontario as a general partner of the extra-provincial limited partnership by reason only that it carries on business in Ontario without filing the declaration and power of attorney required by this Act.

Furthermore, s. 27(2) provides that the laws of the jurisdiction in which the particular extra-provincial partnership was organized governs the liability of its limited partners.

The common law rule is that the characterization of a partnership and the liability of its partners are determined by the proper law of the limited partnership (i.e. the law of the jurisdiction under which the limited partnership was formed). See *King v. Sarria* (1877), 69 N.Y 24, 25 Am. Rep. 128, Restatement, *Conflict of Laws Second*, ss. 294-295, and J.H.W. Rathwell (1972), 10 Alta. L. Rev. 477, esp. at 478–82.

Apparently, there is nothing to prevent a limited partner from going "forum" shopping and forming a limited partnership in a jurisdiction with the most favourable limited partnership laws, just as there is no common law doctrine precluding the promoters of a company from incorporating in a jurisdiction, Canada, US or elsewhere, with the most favourable business corporations legislation, even though the corporation conducts no active business in the state of incorporation. There was some forum shopping in Canada in the 1970s for provinces with the most favourable LP laws but the trend seems to have been arrested with the introduction of modern LP Acts in most, if not all, of the common law jurisdictions.

(v) Investor Protection

Sections 9-10 of the LPA purport to provide some basic protection for limited partners. What is the nature of this protection? Is the LPA the exclusive source of the limited partner's rights and obligations? *Cf.* PA, s. 46. As is true of the OBCA and CBCA in the corporate area, the LPA has not been considered to provide sufficient protection to investors in publicly traded limited partnership interests. As a result, the provincial securities commissions have imposed additional requirements. The Ontario Securities Commission, for example, considers a limited partnership unit to be a "security" (see definition in s. l(l) of the *Securities Act*, R.S.O. 1990 c. S.5, as am. (S.A.). Thus, if there is a "distribution" (see S.A. 1(1)) and there is no exemption under the Act, compliance with the rigorous prospectus disclosure requirements will be necessary.

Questions

1 Can a person be a general partner and a limited partner at the same time? See LPA s. 5(l). Why would a person wish to be both?

2 Every limited partnership is required by LPA s. 2(2) to have at least one general partner. Are there any legal or policy objections to a general partner being a corporation with few assets? Would this undermine the structure of the LPA and its division between general and limited partners? Would it make a difference if the directors of the general partner corporation were elected by the limited partners? *Cf. Haughton Graphic Ltd. v. Zivot, infra.*

3 Is a limited partnership subject to the registration requirements of the BNA? Compare s. 2(3) of the BNA with s. 28 of the LPA. What incentive is there for a foreign limited partnership operating in Ontario to comply with the registration provisions of the LPA?

4 Suppose a limited partnership is formed in a jurisdiction which permits a greater amount of management participation by the limited partners than is allowed under Ontario law and that the LP conducts all or most of its business in Ontario. Would an Ontario court nevertheless hold that, because of s. 27(2), limited partner is still protected from personal liability? If the court so holds, does this mean that the policy of the Act can be defeated by the simple expedient of registering a limited partnership in the extra-provincial jurisdiction with the more favourable rules? For a discussion of this issue from an American point of view, see Note, "Regulation of Foreign Limited Partnerships" (1972), 52 Boston Univ. Law Rev. 64.

Haughton Graphic Ltd. v. Zivot
(1986), 33 B.L.R. 125 (Ont. H.C.)

EBERLE J.: In this case, the plaintiff claims for payment of a debt for printing services supplied by it to a limited partnership called Printcast

Publishing Network (hereafter called "Printcast"). The existence of the debt and the amount claimed of $128,251.79 are not in dispute. The plaintiff earlier obtained a default judgment against Printcast but that judgment has remained unsatisfied.

The plaintiff sues the two named defendants as limited partners of Printcast on the ground that, in addition to exercising their rights and powers as limited partners, each took part in the control of the business of the limited partnership, within the meaning of s. 63 in Part 2 of the *Partnership Act*, R.S.A. 1980, c. P-2, as amended by R.S.A. 1980 (Supp.), c. 2; S.A. 1981, c. 28 ["the Alberta Act"]. It is common ground that the Alberta law relating to limited partnerships applies in this case.

Facts

In 1980 the defendant Gary S. Zivot (hereafter called "Zivot") promoted Printcast as a limited partnership under Alberta law, for the purpose of launching a magazine called "Goodlife" to be published in the United States. Zivot's Concept was for a structure similar to a radio or television network. The limited partnership was to be the promoter of the concept. It would sign up local affiliates and supply them with common editorial material. Each affiliate would obtain local advertising and would be responsible for addition of local material to fill out the magazine.

At the same time, Zivot incorporated Lifestyle Magazine Inc. (hereafter called "Lifestyle") to be the sole general partner in Printcast. Lifestyle was controlled by Zivot, who was the sole limited partner in the company. During subsequent financing stages, other limited partners were added, including the defendant Herbert Marshall (hereafter called "Marshall").

Lifestyle obtained the concept and the necessary development expertise for Printcast from Century Media Incorporated. That too was a company controlled by Zivot, and used by him as a vehicle for his "media development business". Century Media in turn employed Zivot, its president, as the live body to perform these services. Century Media's role in the matter is not of particular importance, the principal players being: Printcast (the limited partnership); Lifestyle (the general partner); and Zivot and Marshall (two of the limited partners).

Through Zivot's efforts, about $250,000 of seed money was obtained from investors in the latter part of 1981. At the beginning of January 1982, Printcast went into business. The first Step was to sign up affiliates in various cities. In addition, the details of the magazine and its contents had to be worked out and arrangements made with suppliers, including printing.

It is clear on the evidence and admitted by Zivot that commencing in January 1982 Zivot was known to suppliers as the "president" of Printcast. He used this title to introduce himself; he used business cards showing his relationship to Printcast; and when the magazine was published, its masthead showed Zivot as president and Marshall as executive vice-president of Printcast. Although the specific date on which Marshall joined the enterprise is unclear, there is no doubt that he played the role of executive vice-

president of, and was also a limited partner in, Printcast throughout all the
relevant time period.

There is no dispute about any of the above matters and I accept them
as facts.

The arrangements for printing the magazine in Toronto were made
between Nash, the president of the plaintiff, and Zivot, Marshall and two
other employees of Printcast. I accept Nash's evidence that Zivot was
introduced to him as president of Printcast and Marshall as vice-president,
Nash gained the impression that Zivot was the man at the top with complete
and ultimate responsibility for putting the magazine together and getting it
on the market. He also gained the impression that Marshall was in charge
of the administrative side of the business, including the sales and production
aspects of the magazine. A deal was struck for the plaintiff to print the
Toronto magazine and in late 1982, it printed the first five issues. Then
Printcast went into bankruptcy, leaving the plaintiff unpaid for the printing
of three issues.

Before the plaintiff did any printing, it is clear that Nash knew that he
was dealing with a limited partnership. This was part of the information
obtained for him about the credit worthiness of Printcast, and is recorded in
Ex. 3. This information verified that the publishing venture had a capital of
somewhere between $2,000,000 and $3,000,000 of which a substantial
portion was held in certificates of deposit due to mature on July 1 and
November 1, 1982.

Beyond this information, I am satisfied that Nash was neither given
nor obtained further details about the commercial nor the legal nature of
Printcast. Nash admitted that he was not familiar with the structure of a
limited partnership. He was not told of the existence or identity of the general
partner, Lifestyle, nor of Zivot's ownership and control of it. He was not
told that both Zivot and Marshall were limited partners in Lifestyle. Thus,
the contract for printing services could have been made by the plaintiff only
with Printcast itself, and not with the general partner Lifestyle.

Take Part in Control

It was faintly pressed that the defendants could not be personally liable
for the debt because they did not take part in the control of the limited
partnership Printcast within the meaning of s. 63 of the *Partnership Act.*

The evidence, however, is all to the contrary. Zivot admitted that he
was the directing mind of Printcast, that he was responsible for it, and that
he managed it. Whether or not he made all of the managerial decisions, he
said that he was responsible for all of them. Marshall was one of those
directly under Zivot who made many of the managerial decisions in the
areas of sales and administration. Zivot signed cheques on behalf of Printcast; Marshall also had the authority to do so. In fact, Zivot and Marshall
were in complete control of Printcast.

In my opinion, the fact that both defendants were or may have also
been acting as employees or officer of Lifestyle, all unknown to Nash, does

not take the defendants outside the ambit of s. 63. The defendants' submission to the contrary must be rejected on the basis of the evidence which I
accept.

* * *

Section 63 *Alberta Partnership Act*[5]

On that state of facts, and in view of the overwhelming evidence that
both defendants took part in the control of the limited partnership, I come
back to s. 63 of the *Alberta Partnership Act*. It reads as follows:

Liability to creditors.

63. A Limited partner does not become liable as a general partner
unless, in addition to exercising his rights and powers as a limited
partner, he takes part in the control of the business.

Although elaborate arguments were made as to the meaning of the section,
I take a simpler view of it. If a limited partner takes part in the control of
the business, he becomes liable under the statute as a general partner, i.e.
unlimited liability to the extent of his assets. That is what happened in this
case, and it is, effectively speaking, the end of the matter.

The elaborate arguments made only come into play if it should be
found that the plaintiff somehow disclaimed reliance on that section. The
arguments demonstrate that in the United States, where the limited partnership is also recognized, there are two lines of authority. One line of authority
recognizes that in a statutory provision such as s. 63 of the Alberta Act,
there is no room for consideration of whether or not the plaintiff relied upon
the personal liability of the limited partner. It is simply a question of whether
or not the limited partner took part in the control of the business and this
question becomes largely a quantitative matter. An example of this line of
authority is commonly taken to be *Delaney v. Fidelity Lease Ltd.*, 526 S.W.
2d 543 (Tex., 1975) in the Supreme Court of Texas.

On the other hand, there is a line of cases which espouses what is called
the "specific reliance" test. An example commonly referred to is *Frigidaire
Sales Corp. v. Union Properties Inc.*, 14 Wash. App. 634, 544 P. 2d 781
(Wash., 1975) in the Court of Appeals of Washington State. This view may
be more fully explained by stating that "liability for a partnership's obligation to a creditor should not be imposed upon a limited partner who takes
part in the control of the business unless, as a result of the limited partner's
conduct, the creditor believed that the limited partner was a general partner".
See Basile, "Limited Liability for Limited Partners: An Argument for the
Abolition of the Control Rule" (1985), 38 Vanderbilt L. Rev. 1199, p. 1208.

---

[5] For the corresponding section under Ontario law see s. 12(1) of the *Limited Partnership
Act*, R.S.O. 1990, c. L-16 [Eds.].

After explaining the "specific reliance" test as above, Basile asserts that the Delaney decision, *supra*, correctly points out that the American statutory provision under discussion, which is indistinguishable from s. 63 of the Alberta Act, does not by its terms require creditor reliance as a predicate for holding a limited partner liable.

This comment identifies the problem in this case. Section 63 does not contain any requirement of reliance. If reliance was a necessary precondition to unlimited liability for a limited partner, appropriate words should be in the statute. To conclude that the words in the section require such a condition would not, in my view, be an interpretation of the words used in the section, but would be a clear addition of a second, distinct requirement to the only one currently found in the language of s. 63.

In any event, mere knowledge by the plaintiff that a magazine was being promoted and published by a limited partnership does not assist the defendants at all. What engages the liability of the limited partner is his taking part in the control of the business.

Accordingly in my view the defences must fail.

I do not think the outcome would be any different if, contrary to my findings, Zivot had explained fully to Garwood the legal particulars of the limited partnership, the legal relationship of the persons and entities concerned, the precise nature of the liability of each of them, and to whom the liabilities were owed. I say this because under s. 63 of the Alberta Act it is clear that the legal relationships can be altered by activity on the part of the limited partner. Absent some unusual situation where it might be argued that the creditor had in some way estopped himself from relying on s. 63, the result in this case would have been the same even if Mr. Zivot's evidence were to have been accepted.

In addition to the American sources cited, I was referred also to a Canadian article, "The Control Test of Investor Liability in Limited Partnerships" by R.D. Flannigan contained in (1983), 21 Alta. L. Rev. 303. This article recognizes that the reliance test is not part of the definition of taking part in the control of the business but rather that reliance is an element that is added to the control test in order to reduce the number of instances where general liability will be imposed upon limited partners. The author offers the additional test in order to allow that which is patently prohibited by the legislation, i.e., participation in control by a limited partner: see pp. 317 and 318.

There is a surprising absence of authority in Canada on the issues raised in this case. The only recent case to which I was referred is *Elevated Construction Ltd. v. Nixon* (1969), 9 D.L.R. (3d) 232 (Ont. H.C.). In his decision, Osler J. really dealt with different aspects of the *Limited Partnerships Act*, R.S.O. 1980, c. 241, but . . . in *obiter* he touched upon the question of the degree of control of the business that must be exercised by a limited partner in order to make him liable as a general partner. He pointed out that the cases are far from exhaustive, referring only to three cases from 1857 and one from 1877, all of which refer to the same limited partnership. He concluded by saying at 655 [O.R.]:

> The cases are of little assistance in determining where the line is to be drawn beyond which a limited partner is deemed to be taking part in the control of the business and each case will presumably have to be decided upon its own facts.

In opposition, the defendants relied upon s. 59 of the Alberta Act under the heading *Business dealings by partner with partnership* which commences "A Limited partner may loan money to and transact other business with the Limited partnership . . ." Emphasis was placed upon the permission to "transact other business with the limited partnership". The short answer to this submission was, I think, correctly put by counsel for the plaintiff, i.e., that, while s. 59 permits the transaction of business with the limited partnership, it does not permit the transaction of business by a limited partner on behalf of the limited partnership.

Finally it was submitted on behalf of the defendants that to hold them liable in this case means that a person who is an officer or director (or I suppose a senior employee) of the corporate general partner in a limited partnership would always be fixed with unlimited liability for the debts of the limited partnership by virtue of s. 63 of the Alberta Act on the ground that he is the person who has control of the corporate general partner. This conclusion does not logically follow. The section only applies to a person who, in addition to being an officer, director, senior employee, or other directing mind of the corporate general partner, seeks also to take advantage of personal limited liability as a limited partner in the limited partnership. In other words, s. 63 applies only if two conditions are met. One is that the person be a limited partner and the second is that he take part in the control of the business of the limited partnership. The section does not apply to someone whose sole role in, and connection with, the limited partnership is that of an officer, director or other controlling mind of the general partner . . .

Action allowed.

Question and Notes

1 Do you agree with Eberle J.'s decision in this case? With his reasoning? Could the decision have been justified on other grounds, *viz.*, that Zivot held himself out as "president" of Printcast? Is it proper for the court to lift the corporate veil of an incorporated general partner to show that a limited partner is the directing mind of the general partner? Is this approach warranted by the language or underlying policy of s. 12(1) of the LPA?

2 *Haughton Graphic* was considered by the B.C. courts in *Nordile Hold-*

ings Ltd. v. Breckenridge (1992), 66 B.C.L.R. (2d) 183 (C.A.), aff'g [1990] B.C.W.L.D. 860 (S.C.). This was a case where, as in *Haughton*, the general partner of the limited partnership was incorporated and the defendants occupied dual positions as limited partners and as shareholders and officers of the general partner. At trial, Esson C.J. concluded that the defendants "clearly took part in the management" of the limited partnership business within the meaning of s. 64 of the B.C. *Partnership Act.* He also followed Eberle J. in rejecting the "specific reliance" analysis adopted in some American cases. Nevertheless, he exonerated the defendants because of an exclusionary provision in a statutory disclosure statement supplied to the plaintiff before the transaction, which was incorporated in the purchase agreement.

This ground for the decision was also adopted in the Court of Appeal, which affirmed the trial judgment. The appellate judges, however, gave a narrow reading to s. 64 of the B.C. Act. Relying on the plaintiff's concession that the defendants had acted in the management of the limited partnership "solely" in their capacities as directors and officers of the general partner, Gibbs J.A. reasoned that "[a]cting solely in one capacity necessarily negates acting in another capacity." McEachern CJBC was worried that imposing personal liability on persons in the defendants' position would "destroy the *Salomon* principle." For a searching critique of the judgments see Lisa Philipps, "The Amazing Three-Headed Limited Partner: Reflections on Old Loopholes and New Jurisprudence" (1993) 21 C.B.L.J. 410.

(c) Limited Liability Partnerships (LLPs)

LLPs are an American innovation. The legislation was inspired by the loan and savings crisis in the US in the 1980s when law firms, especially in Texas and California, were being sued for their partners' alleged involvements in the mismanagement and wrongful diversion of loan and savings associations' funds. Partners in other law firms also came to appreciate their vulnerability to liability suits based on partnership principles of joint and several liability even though negligence was only proven against one of the partners. Partners in accounting firms quickly came to share the same concerns, since they too were exposed to similar and even greater risks because the large accounting firms are multinational in character and act for enterprises around the globe.

Texas was the first US state to adopt remedial legislation, and it did so in 1991. Similar legislation has now been adopted in many other states, but the legislation differs considerably in scope and detail. See R.W. Hamilton, "Registered Limited Liability Partnerships: Present at Birth (Nearly)" (1995), 66 Col. L. Rev. 1065. However, all the acts had a common objective, which was to restrict liability to the partner(s) directly at fault or vicariously liable for the acts of persons under his or their supervision.

In Canada, LLP legislation was first enacted in Ontario in 1998 in the form of amendments to the Ontario PA. See SO 1998, c.2, ss. 1-8. Alberta followed a year later. However, the scope of the Alberta provisions is significantly broader than the Ontario provisions. Since then the other common law provinces have followed suit with the exception of Newfoundland, Prince Edward Island and British Columbia. For a close analysis and critical evaluation of the Canadian legislation see Richard Bowes, "Limited Liability Professional Partnerships" (2000) 34 C.B.L.J. 3. For a practitioner's perspective, see Alison Manzer, *op. cit.*, Ch. 10. Note carefully that the Ontario provisions only benefit the members of qualifying professions. So far only accountants and lawyers meet these requirements. See further, below, "Preconditions to Acquiring LLP Status".

The United Kingdom adopted the *Limited Liability Partnership Act* in 2000. The Act has the same objectives as the North American legislation but accomplishes them by different means. See *Lindley and Banks on Partnership*, 18th ed., (2002), paras. 2–37 *et seq.* Under the British legislation the LLP is a body corporate with separate legal personality and unlimited capacity. The LLP is governed not by the *Partnership Act* 1890 but by its own provisions. Most importantly, the members of the LLP are agents of the LLP and not of each other (s.6(1)) and are in general not liable for the LLP's debts and obligations. The members may also be employees of the LLP. In sum, the British LLP is a hybrid form of corporation and partnership.

Scope of Protection under the Ontario provisions. Section 10 of the OPA reads, in part, as follows:

> 10.(1) Except as provided in subsection (2) every partner in a firm is liable jointly with the other partners for all debts and obligations of the firm incurred while the person is a partner, and after the partner's death the partner's estate is also severally liable in a due course of administration for such debts and obligations so far as they remain unsatisfied, but subject to the prior payment of his or her separate debts.
>
> (2) Subject to subsection (3), a partner in a limited liability partnership is not liable, by means of indemnification, contribution, assessment or otherwise, for debts, obligations and liabilities of the partnership or any partner arising from negligent acts or omissions that another partner or an employee, agent or representative of the partnership commits in the course of the partnership business while the partnership is a limited liability partnership.
>
> (3) Subsection (2) does not affect the liability of a partner in a limited liability partnership for the partner's own negligence or the negligence of a person under the partner's direct supervision or control.
> [Subs. (4) and (5) are omitted.]

As will be seen, the operative provisions are those in s. (2) excluding a partner's direct or indirect liability arising from "negligent acts or omissions" of another partner or an employee, agent or representative of the partnership. Sub-section (3) affirms a partner's liability for the partner's own negligence or the negligence of a person under the partner's direct supervision or control. It seems, therefore, that members of an Ontario LLP continue to have joint and several liability for the partnership's contractual debts, for liability arising out of a partner's fraudulent conduct or breach of trust or fiduciary obligations, and for strict liabilities arising by operation of law, *e.g.*, under employment standards legislation. Many large accounting and law firms across Canada have availed themselves of the new legislation, but none of the provincial LLP provisions appears so far to have been tested in actual litigation. This suggests either that the new provisions have been completely successful in their objectives or that the LLP firms have been able to settle any claims against them without explicit resort to the legislation. Ontario s. 10(2) above should be compared with the exculpatory language in s. 11.1 of the Alberta Act. This protects the non-culpable partners from debts, obligations or liabilities of the partnership or another partner arising from "negligence, wrongful acts or omissions, malpractice or misconduct" of another partner, employee or representative of the partnership. Alberta borrowed this formulation from the Texas model. Bowes, *supra*, at 34.

The expansive Alberta provisions, and those of other provincial and US states of comparable width, are important because of the Ontario provisions in s. 44.4 of the Ontario Act providing for the recognition of extra-provincial LLPs. Section 44.4(4) provides that an EPLLP will be recognized in Ontario and will be governed by the partnership law under which it was formed but must register its name under the *Ontario Business Names Act* (s.44.4(1)). Consider whether s. 44.4 would oblige an Ontario court to recognize an Alberta LLP even though most of the partnership's contacts are with Ontario.

Preconditions to acquiring the status of an Ontario LLP (ss. 44.1–44.3). There are four such requirements, *viz.*: (a) there must be a written agreement between two or more persons designating their partnership as an LLP to be governed by the OPA; (b) the partnership is formed to carry on a profession governed by an act that permits practice of the profession by an LLP, and the governing body of which profession requires its members to maintain a minimum amount of liability insurance; (c) the LLP's name is registered under the OBNA; and (d) the LLP's name must include the words "LLP", "L.L.P." or "s.r.l." as a suffix to the partnership's name. The other provincial acts have comparable provisions.

Part B

Business Corporations Law

Chapter 2

Evolution of Business Corporations Law and the Nature of Corporate Personality

1. THE HISTORY OF CANADIAN BUSINESS CORPORATIONS LAW

The evolution of Canadian corporations law has been much influenced by British and American law. The British influence is the older of the two. Since a knowledge of the history of British company law is also important for an understanding of the early Canadian developments, it will be appropriate to start with it here.

British Origins. The common law recognizes two principal forms of incorporation, *viz.* (a) incorporation by exercise of the royal prerogative (usually referred to as incorporation by letters patent or, more colloquially, royal charter), and (b) incorporation by a private or general act of the legislature. Until well into the eighteenth century incorporation by royal charter was by far the most common method. Even it was used very sparingly until the sixteenth and seventeenth centuries to incorporate companies with commercial purposes such as the Hudson Bay Company, the London East India Company and the Levant Company for overseas trade and colonization of territories. These early charters were usually accompanied by monopolies of one description or another. Limited liability was not expressly conferred by these charters and limited liability for investors did not become a controversial issue until the early part of the nineteenth century.

By the turn of the eighteenth century there was a lively trade in royal charters of companies, and this was accompanied by frenetic speculation in the shares of these companies. The South Sea Company was the most notorious of them. It nearly collapsed in 1720 amidst much scandal and allegations of corruption in high places. That same year Parliament adopted the "*Bubble Act*" (6 Geo. 1, c. 18), an obscure piece of legislation, the only sure feature of which was that it substantially froze the development of British company law for over a century and generally cast commercial companies under a pall.

The beginning of the industrial revolution in the United Kingdom was accompanied by growing pressure for the repeal of the *Bubble Act* and a more accessible form of incorporation. The *Bubble Act* was repealed in 1825, but the first general Act for the incorporation of companies, the *Joint*

Stock Companies Act (7 & 8 Vic. cc. 110 & 111), was not adopted until 1844. This Act introduced incorporation by registration, the method that has remained in dominant use in the U.K. since then and subsequently became the standard model of incorporation in most of the Commonwealth. However, the Act of 1844 still withheld the privilege of limited liability. The difficulties were compounded because the courts held that the joint stock companies were merely large partnerships and that each shareholder was a partner, even though the management of the companies was usually vested in directors or trustees.

The battle for limited liability was finally won in 1855 with the adoption of the *Limited Liability Act* (18 & 19 Vic., c. 133). This Act also introduced the requirement that incorporated companies with limited liability include the term "Limited" or "Ltd." as part of the company's name so as to warn the public of this "dangerous" new entity! The 1855 Act and earlier legislation was replaced in 1862 by the *Companies Act* (25 & 26 Vic., c. 89). This is the title by which all subsequent general companies legislation in the U.K. has come to be identified. The 1862 Act also became the model for several of the later Canadian provincial Acts.

Nineteenth Century Canadian Developments. None of the Canadian provinces and territories adopted general incorporation legislation before the middle of the nineteenth century. Prior to this period, incorporation by private Act was the common procedure and was used substantially for the same purposes as in the U.K.

The first general legislation consisted of two Acts, both passed in 1849, one for Upper Canada and the other for Lower Canada. These authorized the incorporation of joint stock companies for the construction of roads and bridges. Both provided for incorporation by registration of appropriate documents with the registrar of the counties through which the road was to pass or in which the work was to be situated. The 1849 Acts were followed by a more broadly aimed Act of 1850 which permitted the incorporation of companies for "manufacturing, mining, mechanical and chemical purposes." This too was a registration Act and was modelled on a New York statute of 1848.

In 1860 another general Act was adopted for the incorporation of commercial companies and this provided for incorporation by judicial decree. In 1864, a third general Act, *viz.* by Letters Patent issued under the seal of the Governor in Council. According to Wegenast (*The Law of Canadian Companies* (1931)), the idea of incorporation by letters patent pursuant to a general Act may have been suggested by an English Act of 1844 for the incorporation of joint stock banks. The letters patent method of incorporation exerted great influence on the general incorporation Acts of other provinces and on federal corporate legislation. It was not abolished in Ontario until 1970, and not by the federal government until the adoption of the *Canada Business Corporations Act* (CBCA) in 1975.

The first general incorporation Act was adopted by the federal Parliament in 1869. This repealed the pre-Confederation legislation providing for incorporation by registration and judicial decree and re-enacted the Act of 1864. The 1864 Act also served as a model for the subsequent incorporation legislation of New Brunswick, Manitoba and Prince Edward Island. The other provinces (British Columbia, Alberta, Saskatchewan and Nova Scotia) adopted at different times the British method of incorporation by registration and also adopted many of the other provisions in the British Act of 1862. One of the unfortunate consequences of this schism was that at a crucial conceptual level Canada was divided into two camps, since the method of incorporation also brought in its train important substantive differences. A further difficulty arose because it was not always easy to determine how much of the English jurisprudence, built as it was around companies incorporated by registration, was relevant to companies incorporated by letters patent. That rift has only been healed (and only partly at that) over the past 30 years with the re-introduction of incorporation by registration.

Twentieth Century Developments. Until the 1960s, Canadian corporation law developments largely consisted of fleshing out and amending the nineteenth century legislation, and there were few basic conceptual changes. A new era in corporate legislation was introduced in 1970 with the adoption of an entirely new Act, the Ontario *Business Corporations Act* (OBCA) (R.S.O. 1970, c. 53). The Act largely implemented the recommendations of the Interim Report of the Select Committee on Company Law ("Report of the Lawrence Committee") which was published in 1967. The new Ontario Act replaced incorporation by letters patent with incorporation by registration, permitted the incorporation of one-person corporations, largely immunized third parties from the effects of the *ultra vires* doctrine, regularized pre-incorporation contracts, introduced a new regulatory framework for the issuance and transfer of investment securities, partially codified the duties of directors and officers, regulated insider trading in the corporation's securities, permitted derivative actions and improved minority shareholder protection in other important respects.

In 1971, a federal task force led by Robert Dickerson, John Howard and Leon Getz submitted to the federal government its Proposals for a New Business Corporations Law for Canada. The draft Act largely mirrored changes and concepts that had already been adopted in the Ontario Act. One major difference was that the draft Act went further than the Ontario Act in its protection of minority shareholder rights. The federal government enacted the draft Act in 1975 with only minor changes. Since then, the CBCA has become the template for many of the subsequent provincial business corporations Acts. The Act has been adopted, more or less verbatim, in Alberta, Saskatchewan and Manitoba, and has been substantially followed in New Brunswick. The Act's influence was also pronounced in important amendments adopted in Nova Scotia in 1982 and in the Quebec Act of 1980. In 1982, Ontario repealed its own Act of 1970 and replaced it with a new Act, the *Business Corporations Act,* 1982 (S.O. 1982, c. 4). With modest exceptions, the Act closely tracked the federal Act. In 1978, the Newfoundland government published the Barry Report. This likewise

recommended adoption of the federal model. In 2001 the federal government adopted substantial amendments to the CBCA. See S.C. 2001, c.14,
and W.D. Gray and C.W. Halladay, *Guide to the CBCA Reform: Analysis
and Precedents* (Carswell 2002), and the Symposium on the amendments
in (2003-4) 39 C.B.L.J. 4-137. The changes largely benefited publicly held
corporations, but protection of minority shareholder interests was also enhanced in important respects.

British Columbia's position is *sui generis*. The province adopted a new
Companies Act in 1973 which incorporated (or anticipated?) many of the
features of the federal Act of 1974 but was not a carbon copy of it. B.C.
adopted an entirely new Act in 2002, the *Business Corporations Act*, SBC
2002, c.57 (BCBCA), which received royal assent on October 31, 2002,
and will come into force by regulation. When proclaimed, the new Act will
repeal the *Company Act*, RSBC 1996, c.62. The new Act will

> remedy many of the shortcomings and ambiguities in the *Company
> Act* and will introduce more modern provisions in many areas. It will
> however retain the contract model of incorporation and its concomitant
> flexibility (which will be enhanced), a decision having been made not
> to adopt the *Canada Business Corporations Act* model, which will
> continue to be available for anyone wanting to use the alternative
> model.

See John O.E. Lundell, "Introduction to the British Columbia Business
Corporations Act", *Continuing Legal Education*, Vancouver, May 2003,
§1.1.

Development of Securities Legislation. Even a skeletal history of modern Canadian business corporation law would be seriously incomplete without some mention of securities legislation, an area in which until recently
Canada has generally led the Commonwealth. The aim of securities regulation is to provide an informed, transparent and honest market in the
publicly issued and traded securities of corporations. The Canadian legislation accomplishes this by a policy of full and continuous disclosure of all
relevant information and by imposing a comprehensive regime of supervision and registration of securities and members of the securities industry.
The difference between corporate legislation and securities legislation is
that corporate legislation is generally only concerned with corporations
incorporated under the laws of the enacting province whereas securities
legislation applies to corporations (and other issuers) regardless of where
the issuer was incorporated.[1] As a result, a corporation with publicly held

---

[1] Another distinction that is sometimes drawn is that corporation law is concerned with the
organization and constitution of corporations and their internal government, whereas securities law focuses on the protection of investors in the marketplace. However, the securities
legislation does not follow such neat distinctions, and there is, in fact, a good deal of overlap,
as was freely admitted in several of the judgments in *Multiple Access Ltd. v. McCutcheon*
(1982), 138 D.L.R. (3d) 1 (S.C.C.). In the ultimate analysis, securities law covers whatever

securities often finds itself subject to the concurrent and, not infrequently, overlapping laws of several jurisdictions. Another important difference between corporation and securities legislation is that while rights and duties under the former are usually privately enforced (or not enforced at all), in the case of securities legislation, the investor has the assistance of a powerful watchdog with a wide range of administrative and quasi-judicial powers and, in the case of Ontario at least, with the human and financial resources to use them.

A new era in securities regulation began with the 1965 report of the Kimber Committee in Ontario. In addition to strengthening disclosure and reporting requirements, the Report recommended legislation with respect to proxies and proxy solicitations, insider trading and takeover bids. The Kimber Committee recommendations were quickly implemented in the *Securities Act*, 1966. In 1978, Ontario adopted a revised *Securities Act, 1978*, which introduced the principle of continuous disclosure and conferred new (and controversial) protection for minority shareholders in private control transactions. This is the Act which is in force at the present time (see R.S.O. 1990, c. S-5), though it was amended in important respects in 1987. British Columbia and Quebec have also adopted new securities Acts, the former in 1985 and the latter in 1982. As noted below, the fallout from the Enron and other very recent corporate and securities market scandals in the US, leading to the Congressional adoption of the *Sarbanes-Oxley Act* and much tighter enforcement of state and federal securities regulation, has also reverberated in Canada.

Federal involvement in securities regulation has been discussed inter- mittently in the post-war period. In 1979, the federal government published a three-volume report on Proposals for a Securities Market Law for Canada prepared by a task force led by Philip Anisman. The Proposals were never implemented, partly because of provincial opposition (particularly from Quebec) and more particularly because of lack of political will in Ottawa. However, the rapid globalization of securities markets, the US scandals noted above and their Canadian counterparts, and serious weaknesses in the provincial regulatory structure, have again focussed attention on the need for a national securities regime in Canada. In spring 2003 the federal gov- ernment established a Wise Persons' Committee (*sic*) to review the Cana- dian position. The Committee's report, published in December 2003, unan- imously supported the establishment of a national securities commission, albeit one in which the provinces would have a strong voice in the structure of the commission and the administration of the federal securities legisla- tion. See *WPC Committee to Review the Structure of Securities Regulation in Canada* (Dept. of Finance, Ottawa, Dec. 2003). Nevertheless, as of this

---

the regulators deem necessary for the protection of investors in publicly traded issues in their jurisdictions, a position that is strongly criticized by law and economics scholars. They believe that shareholder rights should be determined by the incorporating jurisdiction and that maintenance of this distinction is essential to encourage provinces to compete for the adoption of investor-friendly corporate legislation.

writing (March 2004), Quebec, Alberta and British Columbia continue to oppose the establishment of an overarching national securities regime and the future of the Committee's recommendations remains seriously unsettled.

Distinction Between Canadian and US Corporate and Securities Law. The growing influence of American corporate and securities law on Canadian corporate and securities law should not mislead the reader into assuming that the two national regimes are interchangeable and that both operate in substantially identical political, economic and legal environments. There are many important differences between the Canadian and American positions, as is shown by the following illustrations:

1. The number of publicly traded companies in the US is far larger, proportionate to population as well as in absolute terms, than the number of Canadian companies;
2. Even more important, the US market for publicly traded shares is much more liquid and deeper than the Canadian market. One Canadian study (Fowler & Rorke, 1988) found that only 5.3% of the securities listed on the Toronto Stock Exchange (TSX) were widely traded, that 35.3% were moderately traded, and that 59.4% were infrequently or thinly traded. These figures have important implications for the type of securities regime appropriate in the Canadian context and the need for regulatory oversight;
3. The concentration of share ownership is much higher in Canada than it is in the US. As of 1990, only 14% of the companies in the TSX 300 Composite Index were widely held among investors. 60.3% of the shares were owned by a single shareholder exercising legal control, and 25.4% were owned by one shareholder with effective control or by two or three shareholders each of whom owned 10–20% of the outstanding shares. In contrast, in the US 63% of the Fortune 500 companies were widely held, and only 18% of the companies were controlled by a single shareholder or group of shareholders with effective control. The higher concentration of Canadian share ownership leads to fewer investor-manager conflicts but increases the potential for inter-investor friction as well as triggering other consequences; and
4. The Canadian market is characterized by highly interconnected corporate relationships. Of the 100 most profitable Canadian companies in 1987, close to 45% held 10% or more of the voting shares of another company on the TSX Composite List. This familial relationship is also reflected among the directors of Canada's largest companies, many of whom hold two or more appointments.

There are also important differences at the legal level. While all the provinces and the Territories have their own business corporation legislation, with modest exceptions, Canada has not experienced the "Delaware" phenomenon.[2] Again, unlike the US, Canada still has no national securities commission but, given the importance of the Ontario securities market, the Ontario Securities Commission often acts as a surrogate federal securities commission. Further, the *Ontario Securities Act* confers substantially broader powers and greater discretion on the OSC than are enjoyed by the SEC under US legislation.

See further Daniels and MacIntosh, "Toward A Distinctive Canadian Corporate Law Regime" (1991) 29 O.H.L.J. 863.

Influence of Law and Economics Movement. Corporations law lends itself particularly well to economic analysis. However, until comparatively recently, the relevance of economic theory in testing the efficiency and impact of legal doctrines was substantially ignored in the corporate law courses of even leading North American law schools. What was true of law schools was even more true of textbooks and of statutes and judicial decisions. The position has changed dramatically over the past 30 years. There are now dozens, perhaps hundreds, of first rate articles, Canadian as well as American, many symposia exploring the interface between economic learning and corporate law rules and a large number of books and "readers" whose dominant theme is the economic approach to corporate and securities law. In this genre, particularly influential have been the writings of (Judge) Frank Easterbrook and Daniel R. Fischel, subsequently published by them in book form in *The Economic Structure of Corporate Law* (Harvard UP, 1991). An excellent analysis from an Anglo-Canadian perspective is Brian R. Cheffins, *Company Law: Theory, Structure and Operation* (Clarendon Press, 1997).

SELECTED ANGLO-CANADIAN BIBLIOGRAPHY

P. Anisman, "The Proposals for a Securities Market Law for Canada: Purpose and Process" (1982), 19 O.H.L.J. 329; *Gower & Davies' Principles of Modern Company Law*, 7th ed. (2003); R. Daniels and J. MacIntosh, "Toward a Distinctive Canadian Corporate Law Regime" (1991), 29 Osgoode Hall L.J. 863; R. Daniels and B. Langille, Eds., "Symposium on the Corporate Stakeholder Debate: The Classical Theory and Its Critics" (1993) 43 U.T.L.J. 297-796; T. Hadden, R.E. Forbes, and R.A. Simmonds, *Canadian Business Organization Law* (Butterworths, 1984); A. Douglas Harris (Ed.), *WPC — Committee to Review the Structure of Securities Regulation in Canada — Research Studies* (Department of Finance, Ottawa, 2003); D.L. Johnston, *Canadian Securities Regulation*, 3rd ed., (Butterworths, 2002); E.E. LaBrie and E.E. Palmer, "The Pre-Confederation History of Corporations in Canada" in Ziegel (Ed.), *Studies in Canadian Company Law*, (1967), vol. 1, Ch. 2; "Special Lectures of the Law Society of Upper Canada," *Corporate Law in the 80's* (De Boo, 1982); K.P. McGuiness, *The*

---

[2] See further Wayne D. Gray, "Corporations as Winners under the CBCA Reform" (2003), 39 C.B.L.J. 4, especially Part IV and the appendix.

Law and Practice of Canadian Business Corporations (Butterworths, 1999); Ontario Legislative Assembly, *Interim Report of the Select Committee on Company Law* ("Lawrence Report") (1967); F.W. Wegenast, *The Law of Canadian Companies*, Ch. 2 (1931); Bruce Welling, *Corporate Law in Canada*, 2nd ed. (Carswell, 1991); J.S. Ziegel, "The New Look in Canadian Corporation Laws" in *Studies in Canadian Company Law*, vol. 2, Ch. 1 (1973).

2. NOTE ON THE CONSTITUTIONAL POSITION

As described in the preceding section, both the federal and provincial governments have enacted general business corporation legislation and, in the case of the provinces, securities legislation as well. This short note is intended to explain the constitutional basis of their jurisdiction and to deal with some related constitutional problems.

There is no specific provision in the *Constitution Act* 1867–2002 generally enabling the federal government to incorporate companies. However, in the leading case of *Citizens Insce. Co. of Canada v. Parsons* (1881-2) 7 A.C. 96, the Privy Council found the jurisdiction in the "Peace, Order and Good Government" clause of s. 91 of the *Constitution Act*. Sir Montague Smith reasoned that since the provinces were restricted in their jurisdiction to the "incorporation of companies with provincial objects" [*Constitution Act*, s. 92(11)] "it follows that the incorporation of companies for objects other than provincial falls within the general powers of the parliament of Canada" (*ibid.*, at p. 116). Apart from its residuary power the federal government also has ancillary incorporation powers under several of the specific heads of s. 91 (*e.g.*, s. 91(15) relating to banks and banking) and has exercised them.

The provinces enjoy express incorporation powers by virtue of s. 92(11) of the *Constitution Act*. What remained unclear, however, until the long-standing doubt was resolved by the Privy Council in *Bonanza Creek Gold Mining Co. v. R.*, [1916] 1 A.C. 566 (P.C.), was the meaning of the power to incorporate companies "with provincial objects." The Privy Council held that the words merely meant that a province could not endow a provincial corporation with the *right* to carry on its activities in another jurisdiction but that it did not preclude a province from conferring on a corporation the *capacity or power* to carry on business elsewhere if the extra-provincial jurisdiction was willing to allow it to do so. In practice, the provinces readily grant the permission subject to some modest filing or registration requirements and the payment of a fee. See further *infra*, Ch. 3, s. 2. To all intents and purposes therefore, a provincially incorporated company, *qua* company, enjoys almost as much mobility as a federally incorporated company. However, federally incorporated companies appear to enjoy greater prestige and, for reasons stated below, they cannot be prevented from commencing business in a province before they have complied with provincial registration or filing requirements and paid a fee.

A recurring issue has been the extent to which federal corporations are subject to provincial regulation. The answer is that it depends on the characterization of the provincial legislation. If it is solely of a corporate character it will be ineffectual, but if it has a double character — if it can be justified, that is, as legislation affecting property or civil rights — it will be valid so long as it does not conflict with the federal legislation. This proposition was reaffirmed by the Supreme Court of Canada in *Multiple Access Ltd. v. McCutcheon* (1982), 138 D.L.R. (3d) 1. The Supreme Court also held that mere duplication or overlap between federal and provincial provisions is not sufficient; there must be actual conflict between them to trigger the paramountcy doctrine. In two earlier decisions, *John Deere Plow Co. v. Wharton*, [1915] A.C. 330, and *Great West Saddle v. R.*, [1921] 2 A.C. 91, the Privy Council applied a different test, *viz.* whether the provincial requirements "impair" or "sterilize" the status and essential capacities of the federal corporation. However, it seems unlikely that this was intended to be the exclusive test of the validity of provincial legislation. The Privy Council itself, in applying the sterilization test to provincial securities legislation, drew some very refined distinctions. *Cf. A.G. Man. v. A.G. Can.*, [1929] A.C. 260, with *Lymburn v. Mayland*, [1932] A.C. 318.

The main controversy has been with respect to the validity of provincial legislation which sterilizes the business activity of a federal corporation, assuming the legislation is otherwise a legitimate exercise of provincial power under s. 92(13) of the *Constitution Act*. The judgments of the Privy Council in *John Deere Plow* and *Great West Saddlery* make it clear that the business activities of federal corporations enjoy no immunity from provincial control and restrictions. Nevertheless, the impression has continued to linger on, based as it is on the actual decisions in these two cases, that the provincial legislation will be invalid if it amounts to a total or substantial prohibition of the federal corporation's prospective or subsisting charter activities. The contrary position was clearly upheld by the Supreme Court of Canada in *Can. Indemnity Co. v. A.G. B.C.*, [1977] 2 S.C.R. 504, 73 D.L.R. (3d) 111, in affirming the validity of B.C. legislation establishing a government controlled monopoly in automobile insurance. In the latter case a unanimous court approved the following statement by McGillivray J.A. in *R. v. Arcadia Coal Co. Ltd.*, [1932] 2 D.L.R. 475, at 487-8:

A provincial Legislature may enact laws, province wide, of general application (i.e., including the public generally) in respect of any of the subjects enumerated in s. 92 and in so doing may completely paralyze all activities of a Dominion trading company provided that in the enactment of such laws it does not enter the field of company law and in that field encroach upon the status and powers of a Dominion company as such.

For further discussion of the constitutional position, see P.W. Hogg, *Constitutional Law of Canada*, 4th ed. (1997), Ch. 23, and J.S. Ziegel, *Studies in Canadian Company Law* (1967), vol. 1, Ch. 5.

Impact of the Canadian Charter of Rights and Freedoms.
Corporations also benefit from the protective provisions of the *Charter*, though not to the same extent as individuals. See further, *infra*, Section 5(b).

3. INCORPORATION AND ITS CONSEQUENCES

(a) Statutory Provisions

B.C. BUSINESS CORPORATIONS ACT
S.B.C. 2002, c. 57 as am.

3 (1) When a company is recognized — A company is recognized under this Act

   (a) when it is incorporated under this Act,
   (b) if the company results from the conversion, under this or any other Act, of a corporation into a company after the coming into force of this Act, when the conversion occurs,
   (c) if the company results from an amalgamation of corporations under this Act, when the amalgamation occurs, or
   (d) if the company results from the continuation into British Columbia of a foreign corporation under this Act, when the continuation occurs.

(2) A company was recognized under a former *Companies Act*

   (a) when it was incorporated under that Act,
   (b) if the company resulted from the conversion, under the former *Companies Act* or under any other Act, of a corporation into a company before the coming into force of this Act, when the conversion occurred,
   (c) if the company resulted from the amalgamation of companies under the former *Companies Act*, when the amalgamation occurred, or
   (d) if the company resulted from the continuation into British Columbia of a foreign corporation under the former *Companies Act*, when the continuation occurred.

* * *

10 (1) Formation of company — One or more persons may form a company by

(a) entering into an incorporation agreement,

(b) filing with the registrar an incorporation application, and

(c) complying with this Part.

(2) An incorporation agreement must

(a) contain the agreement of each incorporator to take, in that incorporator's name, one or more shares of the company,

(b) for each incorporator,

(i)   have a signature line with the full name of that incorporator set out legibly under the signature line, and

(ii) set out legibly opposite the signature line of that incorporator,

(A) the date of signing by that incorporator, and

(B) the number of shares of each class and series of shares being taken by that incorporator, and

(c) be signed on the applicable signature line by each incorporator.

(3) An incorporation application referred to in ss. (1)(b) must

(a) be in the form established by the registrar,

(b) contain a completing party statement referred to in s. 15,

(c) set out the full names and mailing addresses of the incorporators,

(d) set out

(i)   the name reserved for the company under s. 22, and the reservation number given for it, or

(ii) if a name is not reserved, a statement that the name by which the company is to be incorporated is the name created by adding "B.C. Ltd." after the incorporation number of the company, and

(e) contain a notice of articles that reflects the information that will apply to the company on its incorporation.

* * *

13 (1) Incorporation — A company is incorporated

(a) on the date and time that the incorporation application applicable to it is filed with the registrar, or

(b) subject to ss. 14 and 410, if the incorporation application specifies a date, or a date and time, on which the company is to be incorporated that is later than the date and time on which the incorporation application is filed with the registrar,

(i)   on the specified date and time, or

(ii) if no time is specified, at the beginning of the specified date.

(2) After a company is incorporated under this Part, the registrar must issue a certificate of incorporation for the company and must record in that certificate the name and incorporation number of the company and the date and time of its incorporation.

(3) After a company is incorporated under this Part, the registrar must

    (a) furnish to the company
        (i) the certificate of incorporation, and
        (ii) a certified copy of the incorporation application and a certified copy of the notice of articles,
    (b) furnish a copy of the incorporation application to the completing party, and
    (c) publish in the prescribed manner a notice of the incorporation of the company.

* * *

17 Effect of incorporation — On and after the incorporation of a company, the shareholders of the company are, for so long as they remain shareholders of the company, a company with the name set out in the notice of articles, capable of exercising the functions of an incorporated company with the powers and with the liability on the part of the shareholders provided in this Act.

18 Evidence of incorporation — Whether or not the requirements precedent and incidental to incorporation have been complied with, a notation in the corporate register that a company has been incorporated is conclusive evidence for the purposes of this Act and for all other purposes that the company has been duly incorporated on the date and time shown in the corporate register.

* * *

30 Capacity and powers of company — A company has the capacity and the rights, powers and privileges of an individual of full capacity.

* * *

87 (1) Liability of shareholders — No shareholder of a company is personally liable for the debts, obligations, defaults or acts of the company.

(2) A shareholder is not, in respect of the shares held by that shareholder, personally liable for more than the lesser of

(a) the unpaid portion of the issue price for which those shares were issued by the company, and

(b) the unpaid portion of the amount actually agreed to be paid for those shares.

(3) Money payable by a shareholder to the company under the memorandum or articles is a debt due from the shareholder to the company as if it were a debt due or acknowledged to be due by instrument under seal.

CANADA BUSINESS CORPORATIONS ACT
R.S.C. 1985, c. C-44, as am.

5 (1) Incorporators — One or more individuals not one of whom

(a) is less than eighteen years of age,

(b) is of unsound mind and has been so found by a court in Canada or elsewhere, or

(c) has the status of bankrupt,

may incorporate a corporation by signing articles of incorporation and complying with s. 7.

(2) Bodies corporate — One or more bodies corporate may incorporate a corporation by signing articles of incorporation and complying with s. 7

* * *

8. (1) Certificate of incorporation — Subject to subsection (2), on receipt of articles with incorporation, the Director shall issue a certificate of incorporation in accordance with section 262.

(2) Exception — failure to comply with Act — The Director may refuse to issue the certificate if a notice that is required to be sent under subsection 19(2) or 106(1) indicates that the corporation, if it came into existence, would not be in compliance with this Act.

9. Effect of certificate — A corporation comes into existence on the date shown in the certificate of incorporation . . .

15. (1) Capacity of a corporation — A corporation has the capacity and, subject to this Act, the rights, powers and privileges of a natural person.

(2) *Idem* — A corporation may carry on business throughout Canada.

(3) Extra-territorial capacity — A corporation has the capacity to carry on its business, conduct its affairs and exercise its powers in any jurisdiction outside Canada to the extent that the laws of such jurisdiction permit . . .

45. (1) Shareholder immunity — The shareholders of a corporation are not, as shareholders, liable for any liability, act or default of the corporation except under ss. 38(4), 146(5) or 226(5).

Note

Section 38(4) of the CBCA deals with reduction of capital, s. 146(5) with shareholder agreements, and s. 226(5) with actions against shareholders after dissolution of the corporation. For the OBCA sections corresponding to the CBCA provisions reproduced above, see ss. 4–7, 15-16, and 92(l).

INTERPRETATION ACT
R.S.C. 1985, c. I-21 as am.

21. (1) Words establishing a corporation shall be construed

  (a) as vesting in the corporation power to sue and be sued, to contract and be contracted with by its corporate name, to have a common seal and to alter or change it at pleasure, to have perpetual succession, to acquire and hold personal property for the purposes for which the corporation is established and to alienate that property at pleasure;

  (b) in the case of a corporation having a name consisting of an English and a French form or a combined English and French form, as vesting in the corporation power to use either the English or the French form of its name or both forms and to show on its seal both the English and French forms of its name or have two seals, one showing the English and the other showing the French form of its name;

  (c) as vesting in a majority of the members of the corporation the power to bind the others by their acts; and

  (d) as exempting from personal liability for its debts, obligations or acts individual members of the corporation who do not contravene the provisions of the enactment establishing the corporation.

(b) The Nature of Corporate Legal Personality and its Consequences

Salomon v. Salomon & Co.
[1897] A.C. 22 (H.L.)

Aron Salomon sold his business as a leather merchant and wholesale boot manufacturer to a limited company with an authorized capital of 40,000 shares with a par value of £1 each. The only shareholders in the company were Salomon, his wife, four sons and a daughter, each of whom subscribed for one share. The sale price of the business was approximately £38,800, which was to be satisfied by the issuance to Salomon of 20,000 shares (i.e., representing a consideration of £20,000), and the payment to him either in cash or debentures, of some £16,000. In fact, at the first meeting of the directors of the company, it was decided that Salomon should be paid £6,000 in cash, and should be issued debentures amounting to £10,000, and secured upon the assets of the company.

When the company was wound up a year later it was found that if the amount realised from the assets of the company were to be first to be applied in payment of the debentures, there would be no funds left for payment of the ordinary creditors.

The liquidator claimed that the company was a mere alias or agent of Salomon, that Salomon was liable to indemnify the company against the claims of the ordinary creditors and that no payment should be made on the debentures held by Salomon until the ordinary creditors had been paid in full.

The trial judge, Vaughan Williams J., gave judgment against Salomon, and this was confirmed by the Court of Appeal. A further appeal was taken to the House of Lords:

LORD MACNAGHTEN: My Lords, I cannot help thinking that the appellant, Aron Salomon, has been dealt with somewhat hardly in this case.

Mr. Salomon, who is now suing as a pauper, was a wealthy man in July, 1892. He was a boot and shoe manufacturer trading on his own sole account under the firm of "A. Salomon & Co." in High Street, Whitechapel, where he had extensive warehouses and a large establishment. He had been in the trade over thirty years. He had lived in the same neighbourhood all along, and for many years past he had occupied the same premises. So far things had gone very well with him. Beginning with little or no capital, he had gradually built up a thriving business, and he was undoubtedly in good credit and repute.

It is impossible to say exactly what the value of the business was. But there was a substantial surplus of assets over liabilities. And it seems to me to be pretty clear that if Mr. Salomon had been minded to dispose of his business in the market as a going concern he might fairly have counted upon retiring with at least 10,000*l.* in his pocket.

Mr. Salomon, however, did not want to part with the business. He had a wife and a family consisting of five sons and a daughter. Four of the sons were working with their father. The eldest, who was about thirty years of age, was practically the manager. But the sons were not partners: they were only servants. Not unnaturally, perhaps, they were dissatisfied with their position. They kept pressing their father to give them a share in the concern. "They troubled me," says Mr. Salomon, "all the while." So at length Mr. Salomon did what hundreds of others have done under similar circumstances. He turned his business into a limited company. He wanted, he says, to extend the business and make provision for his family. In those words, I think, he fairly describes the principal motives which influenced his action.

All the usual formalities were gone through; all the requirements of the *Companies Act*, 1862, were duly observed. There was a contract with a trustee in the usual form for the sale of the business to a company about to be formed. There was a memorandum of association duly signed and registered, stating that the company was formed to carry that contract into effect, and fixing the capital at 40,000*l*. in 40,000 shares of 1*l*. each. There were articles of association providing the usual machinery for conducting the business. The first directors were to be nominated by the majority of the subscribers to the memorandum of association. The directors, when appointed, were authorized to exercise all such powers of the company as were not by statute or by the articles required to be exercised in general meeting; and there was express power to borrow on debentures, with the limitation that the borrowing was not to exceed 10,000*l*. without the sanction of a general meeting.

The company was intended from the first to be a private company; it remained a private company to the end. No prospectus was issued; no invitation to take shares was ever addressed to the public.

The subscribers to the memorandum were Mr. Salomon, his wife, and five of his children who were grown up. The subscribers met and appointed Mr. Salomon and his two elder sons directors. The directors then proceeded to carry out the proposed transfer. By an agreement dated August 2, 1892, the company adopted the preliminary contract, and in accordance with it the business was taken over by the company as from June 1, 1892. The price fixed by the contract was duly paid. The price on paper was extravagant. It amounted to over 39,000*l*. — a sum which represented the sanguine expectations of a fond owner rather than anything that can be called a businesslike or reasonable estimate of value. That, no doubt, is a circumstance which at first sight calls for observation; but when the facts of the case and the position of the parties are considered, it is difficult to see what bearing it has on the question before your Lordships. The purchase-money was paid in this way: as money came in, sums amounting in all to 20,000*l*, were paid to Mr. Salomon, and then immediately returned to the company in exchange for fully paid shares. The sum of 10,000*l*. was paid in debentures for the like amount. The balance, with the exception of about 1000*l*. which Mr. Salomon seems to have received and retained, went in discharge of the debts and liabilities of the business at the time of the transfer, which were thus entirely wiped off. In the result, therefore, Mr. Salomon received for his business about 1000*l*. in cash, 10,000*l*. in debentures, and half the nominal capital of the company in fully paid shares for what they were worth. No other shares were issued except the seven shares taken by the subscribers to the memorandum, who, of course, knew all the circumstances, and had therefore no ground for complaint on the score of overvaluation.

The company had a brief career: it fell upon evil days. Shortly after it was started there seems to have come a period of great depression in the boot and shoe trade. There were strikes of workmen too; and in view of that danger contracts with public bodies, which were the principal source of Mr. Salomon's profit, were split up and divided between different firms. The attempts made to push the business on behalf of the new company crammed its warehouses with unsaleable stock. Mr. Salomon seems to have done what he could: both he and his wife lent the company money; and then he got his debentures cancelled and reissued to a Mr. Broderip, who advanced him 5000*l*., which he immediately handed over to the company on loan. The temporary relief only hastened ruin. Mr. Broderip's interest was not paid when it became due. He took proceedings at once and got a receiver appointed. Then, of course, came liquidation and a forced sale of the company's assets. They realized enough to pay Mr. Broderip, but not enough to pay the debentures in full; and the unsecured creditors were consequently left out in the cold.

In this state of things the liquidator met Mr. Broderip's claim by a counterclaim, to which he made Mr. Salomon a defendant. He disputed the validity of the debentures on the ground of fraud. On the same ground he claimed rescission of the agreement for the transfer of the business, cancellation of the debentures, and repayment by Mr. Salomon of the balance of the purchase money. In the alternative, he claimed payment of 20,000*l*. on Mr. Salomon's shares, alleging that nothing had been paid on them.

When the trial came on before Vaughan Williams J., the validity of Mr. Broderip's claim was admitted, and it was not disputed that the 20,000 shares were fully paid up. The case presented by the liquidator broke down completely; but the learned judge suggested that the company had a right of indemnity against Mr. Salomon. The signatories of the memorandum of association were, he said, mere nominees of Mr. Salomon — mere dummies. The company was Mr. Salomon in another form. He used the name of the company as an alias. He employed the company as his agent; so the company, he thought, was entitled to indemnity against its principal. The counter-claim was accordingly amended to raise this point; and on the amendment being made the learned judge pronounced an order in accordance with the view he had expressed.

The order of the learned judge appears to me to be founded on a misconception of the scope and effect of the *Companies Act*, 1862. In order to form a company limited by shares, the Act requires that a memorandum of association should be signed by seven persons, who are each to take one share at least. If those conditions are complied with, what can it matter whether the signatories are relations or strangers? There is nothing in the Act requiring that the subscribers to the memorandum should be independent or unconnected, or that they or any one of them should take a substantial interest in the undertaking, or that they should have a mind and will of their own, as one of the learned Lords Justices seems to think, or that there should be anything like a balance of power in the constitution of the company. In almost every company that is formed the statutory number is eked out by clerks or friends, who sign their names at the request of the promoter or promoters without intending to take any further part or interest in the matter.

When the memorandum is duly signed and registered, though there be only seven shares taken, the subscribers are a body corporate "capable forthwith," to use the words of the enactment, "of exercising all the functions of an incorporated company." Those are strong words. The company attains maturity on its birth. There is no period of minority — no interval of incapacity. I cannot understand how a body corporate thus made "capable" by statute can lose its individuality by issuing the bulk of its capital to one person, whether he be a subscriber to the memorandum or not. The company is at law a different person altogether from the subscribers to the memorandum; and, though it may be that after incorporation the business is precisely the same as it was before, and the same persons are managers, and the same hands receive the profits, the company is not in law the agent of the subscribers or trustee for them. Nor are the subscribers as members liable, in any shape or form, except to the extent and in the manner provided by the Act. That is, I think, the declared intention of the enactment. If the view of the learned judge were sound, it would follow that no common law partnership could register as a company limited by shares without remaining subject to unlimited liability.

Mr. Salomon appealed; but his appeal was dismissed with costs, though the Appellate Court did not entirely accept the view of the Court below. The decision of the Court of Appeal proceeds on a declaration of opinion embodied in the order which has been already read.

I must say that I, too, have great difficulty in understanding this declaration. If it only means that Mr. Salomon availed himself to the full of the advantages offered by the Act of 1862, what is there wrong in that? Leave out the words "contrary to the true intent and meaning of the *Companies Act*, 1862," and bear in mind that "the creditors of the company" are not the creditors of Mr. Salomon, and the declaration is perfectly innocent: it has no sting in it.

* * *

Among the principal reasons which induce persons to form private companies, as is stated very clearly by Mr. Palmer in his treatise on the subject, are the desire to avoid the risk of bankruptcy, and the increased facility afforded for borrowing money. By means of a private company, as Mr. Palmer observes, a trade can be carried on with limited liability, and without exposing the persons interested in it in the event of failure to the harsh provisions of the bankruptcy law. A company, too, can raise money on debentures, which an ordinary trader cannot do. Any member of a company, acting in good faith, is as much entitled to take and hold the company's debentures as any outside creditor. Every creditor is entitled to get and hold the best security the law allows him to take.

If, however, the declaration of the Court of Appeal means that Mr. Salomon acted fraudulently or dishonestly, I must say I can find nothing in the evidence to support such an imputation. The purpose for which Mr. Salomon and the other subscribers to the memorandum were associated was "lawful." The fact that Mr. Salomon raised 5000*l.* for the company on debentures that belonged to him seems to me strong evidence of his good faith and of his confidence in the company. The unsecured creditors of A. Salomon and Company, Limited, may be entitled to sympathy, but they have only themselves to blame for their misfortunes. They trusted the company, I suppose, because they had long dealt with Mr. Salomon, and he had always paid his way; but they had full notice that they were no longer dealing with an individual, and they must be taken to have been cognisant of the memorandum and of the articles of association. For such a catastrophe as has occurred in this case some would blame the law that allows the creation of a floating charge. But a floating charge is too convenient a form of security to be lightly abolished. I have long thought, and I believe some of your Lordships also think, that the ordinary trade creditors of a trading company ought to have a preferential claim on the assets in liquidation in respect of debts incurred within a certain limited time before the winding-up. But that is not the law at present. Everybody knows that when there is a winding-up debenture-holders generally step in and sweep off everything; and a great scandal it is.

It has become the fashion to call companies of this class "one man companies." That is a taking nickname, but it does not help one much in the way of argument. If it is intended to convey the meaning that a company which is under the absolute control of one person is not a company legally incorporated, although the requirements of the Act of 1862 may have been complied with, it is inaccurate and misleading: if it merely means that there is a predominant partner possessing an overwhelming influence and entitled practically to the whole of the profits, there is nothing in that that I can see contrary to the true intention of the Act of 1862, or against public policy, or detrimental to the interests of creditors. If the shares are fully paid up, it cannot matter whether they are in the hands of one or many. If the shares are not fully paid, it is as easy to gauge the solvency of an individual as to estimate the financial ability of a crowd.

* * *

Appeal allowed.

Notes

1 Nowadays *Salomon v. Salomon* is usually cited for the proposition that the corporation's legal personality is separate and independent from its members' personalities. Contemporary observers however saw the decision in a different light. To them it validated the use of the *Companies Act* 1862 (a consolidating measure) and its predecessor, the *Companies Act* of 1856, for the incorporation of private or closely held companies even if the prescribed minimum of seven shareholders were related to one another and all but one of the shareholders, as in *Salomon's* case, only held one qualifying share.

This result was by no means a foregone conclusion. As an English scholar has shown (Paddy Ireland, "The Triumph of the Company Legal Form, 1856-1914" in John Adams (Ed.), *Essays for Clive Schmitthoff*, p. 29, Professional Books Limited, 1983), in introducing the 1856 Act; the British government did not contemplate, and certainly did not intend, that it could be used to incorporate economic partnerships and sole proprietorships although there was nothing in the Act itself that precluded it being used for these purposes. The government's assumption was widely shared. Between 1856 and 1862 only 4,859 new companies were incorporated altogether and even later, according to one estimate, only 5–10% of all important business organizations were incorporated. Influential judges and members of the Bar (including Vaughan Williams J., the trial judge in *Salomon*, and Lindley L.J. in the Court of Appeal) continued to be strongly opposed to making incorporation available to economic partnerships. This explains the striking differences in approach in *Salomon* between the lower courts and the House of Lords.

2 Several factors appear to have brought about the changes in attitude. First, as already mentioned, there was no requirement in the 1862 Act for seven unconnected incorporators or a requirement that shares of the company must be offered for sale to the public. English courts have traditionally been less instrumentally oriented than their American peers in construing legislation and therefore much less reluctant to give words their ordinary meaning even if this leads to anomalous results. Second, there were prominent barristers such as Francis B. Palmer, the author of a leading company law text that is still widely used in England, who thought British partnership law constituted a trap for the unwary investor and who welcomed the 1856 Act as a solution to these difficulties. Palmer published in 1877 an influential text, *Private Companies: Their Formation and Advantages*, which did much to encourage the incorporation of private companies. Third, the "Great Depression," which hit Victorian England and lasted from 1873-1896, reminded the business community of the vulnerability of unincorporated partnerships and made incorporation and the limited liability it conferred very attractive.

These cumulative factors presumably influenced the law lords in *Salomon* in deciding to reverse the Court of Appeal's decision. The House of Lords' decision also appears to have won widespread approval. The report of the Loreburn Committee in 1906 on company law amendments recommended the formal recognition of private companies and their being relieved from several onerous requirements incumbent on public companies. These recommendations were implemented in the *Companies Act* of 1907.

3 As will have been noted, in *Salomon*, Aron Salomon not only claimed not to be responsible for the company's debts; he also claimed to be a secured creditor of the company in respect of the amount owing under the debenture originally issued in his favour and subsequently mortgaged by him to Broderip. The House of Lords also upheld this claim although (in Lord Macnaghten's case) not without some misgivings. Salomon was much criticized in the trade press of 1893 for putting

forward his preferred status (see G.R. Rubin, "Aron Salomon and his Circle" in John Adams (Ed.), *supra*, at 108-109), but it followed logically from the asserted separate personality of the company and its shareholders.

In Canada, there are still no serious restrictions on a shareholder being able to become a secured creditor of his own company. Those that exist will be found under provincial fraudulent conveyances and preferences legislation and the comparable provisions in the federal *Bankruptcy Act*. In the U.K., the *Insolvency Act* 1986, s. 245(3)(a), invalidates a floating charge given to a person "connected" with the company if given within two years preceding the "onset" of insolvency, whether or not the company was able to pay its debts at the time the floating charge was given. There is an exception if fresh cash, goods or services have been provided to the company as consideration for the floating charge or if any debt of the company is reduced or discharged: s. 245(2). See further, Farrar, Furey and Hannigan, *Farrar's Company Law*, 3rd ed., p. 712 (Butterworths, 1991). In the US, federal courts fashioned a judicially constructed remedy, under the so-called *Deep Rock* doctrine, by treating a non-arm's length shareholder's claim in bankruptcy as inequitable and subordinating it to the claims of other creditors. (Recall the similar provision in s. 4 of the *Ontario Partnership Act*). See further, *infra*, this chapter, Section 4.

Lee v. Lee's Air Farming Ltd.
[1961] A.C. 12 (P.C.)

The appellants husband formed the respondent company for the purpose of carrying on the business of aerial top dressing. He held all the issued shares of the company with the exception of one. He was appointed governing director of the company for life and, pursuant to the company's articles of association, was appointed chief pilot of the company at a salary arranged by him. Article 33 also provided that in respect of such employment the relationship of master and servant should exist between him and the company.

The husband was killed while piloting the company's aircraft in the course of aerial top dressing. His widow, the appellant, claimed compensation under the New Zealand *Workmen's Compensation Act*, 1922. On a case stated for its opinion on a question of law, the New Zealand Court of Appeal held that since the deceased was the governing director in whom was vested the full government and control of the company, he could not also be a servant of the company. The widow appealed.

LORD MORRIS: . . . The substantial question which arises is, as their Lordships think, whether the deceased was a "worker" within the meaning of the *Workers' Compensation Act*, 1922, and its amendments. Was he a person who had entered into or worked under a contract of service with an employer? The Court of Appeal thought that his special position as govern-ing director precluded him from being a servant of the company. On this view it is difficult to know what his status and position was when he was performing the arduous and skilful duties of piloting an aeroplane which belonged to the company and when he was carrying out the operation of top-dressing farm lands from the air. He was paid wages for so doing. The company kept a wages book in which these were recorded. The work that was being done was being done at the request of farmers whose contractual rights and obligations were with the company alone. It cannot be suggested that when engaged in the activities above referred to the deceased was discharging his duties as governing director. Their Lordships find it impos-sible to resist the conclusion that the active aerial operations were performed because the deceased was in some contractual relationship with the com-pany. That relationship came about because the deceased as one legal person was willing to work for and to make a contract with the company which was another legal entity. A contractual relationship could only exist on the basis that there was consensus between two contracting parties. It was never suggested (nor in their Lordships' view could it reasonably have been suggested) that the company was a sham or a mere simulacrum. It is well established that the mere fact that someone is a director of a company is no impediment to his entering into a contract to serve the company. If, then, it be accepted that the respondent company was a legal entity their Lordships see no reason to challenge the validity of any contractual obligations which were created between the company and the deceased . . .

Nor in their Lordships' view were any contractual obligations invali-dated by the circumstance that the deceased was sole governing director in whom was vested the full government and control of the company. Always assuming that the company was not a sham then the capacity of the company to make a contract with the deceased could not be impugned merely because the deceased was the agent of the company in its negotiation. The deceased might have made a firm contract to serve the company for a fixed period of years. If within such period he had retired from the office of governing director and other directors had been appointed his contract would not have been affected. The circumstance that in his capacity as a shareholder he could control the course of events would not in itself affect the validity of his contractual relationship with the company. When, therefore, it is said that "one of his first acts was to appoint himself the only pilot of the company," it must be recognised that the appointment was made by the company, and that it was none the less a valid appointment because it was the deceased himself who acted as the agent of the company in arranging it. In their Lordships' view it is a logical consequence of the decision in *Salomon's* case that one person may function in dual capacities. There is no reason, therefore, to deny the possibility of a contractual relationship being created as between the deceased and the company. If this stage is reached then their Lordships see no reason why the range of possible contractual relationships should not include a contract for services, and if the deceased as agent for the company could negotiate a contract for services as between the company and himself there is no reason why a contract of service could not also be negotiated. It is said that therein lies the difficulty, because it is said that the deceased could not both be under the duty of giving orders and also be under the duty of obeying them. But this approach does not give effect to the circumstance that it would be the company and not the deceased that would be giving the orders. Control would remain with the company whoever might be the agent of the company to exercise it. The fact that so long as the deceased continued to be governing director, with amplitude of powers, it would be for him to act as the agent of the company to give the orders does not alter the fact that the company and the deceased were two separate and distinct legal persons. If the deceased had a contract of service with the company then the company had a right of control. The manner of its exercise would not affect or diminish the right to its exercise. But the existence of a right to control cannot be denied if once the reality of the legal existence of the company is recognised. Just as the company and the deceased were separate legal entities so as to permit of contractual relations being established between them, so also were they separate legal entities so as to enable the company to give an order to the deceased . . .

Appeal allowed

Question

Suppose, in *Lee's* case, the company had violated a statutory duty to supply its employees with an airworthy aircraft. Could the widow have sued the company (in tort or contract) for breach even though the evidence showed that her husband was primarily at fault for failing to ensure the aircraft's air worthiness? What public policies are served in permitting a sole incorporator to wear several hats? Is there a point beyond which the law should refuse to accept the consequences of corporate legal personality? See, *infra*, this chapter the Notes on Corporate Personality, One-Person Corporations and Limited Liability and the extensive materials following the Notes on Lifting the Corporate Veil.

Kosmopoulos v. Constitution Insurance Co.
(1983), 149 D.L.R. (3d) 77 (Ont. C.A.)

ZUBER J.A.: This is an appeal by the defendant insurers from a judgment of Mr. Justice Richard Hollard awarding the plaintiff Andreas Kosmopoulos $89,852.37. Although a number of issues were raised at trial the single argument now advanced by the appellants is that the plaintiff Andreas Kosmopoulos, as a shareholder of a corporation, has no insurable interest in the assets of that corporation and his claim must fail. The plaintiff resists this argument but also cross-appeals asking judgment against the defendant insurance agency if the main appeal should succeed.

The facts are set out by the trial judge as follows:

> The plaintiff, Andreas Kosmopoulos, is forty-one years old and came to Canada from Greece some sixteen years ago with his wife. With her assistance he opened a leather goods store at 652 Yonge Street, Toronto. He, his wife, and some occasional help, manufactured a substantial percentage of the goods sold in a separate small room at the back of the retail area.

> Mr. Kosmopoulos and his wife were not fluent in English and, according to his evidence, which I accept, he relied on the assistance of his solicitor, Mr. Amourgis, in connection with the documents involved in starting up the business. Mr. Amourgis advised the incorporation of Kosmopoulos Leather Goods Limited. This was done, according to Mr. Kosmopoulos, in order to protect his personal assets. He was the sole shareholder and director. The lease of the business premises was also in his name, was renewed in his name and was never assigned to the limited company. Mr. Kosmopoulos considered that he owned the business and that the incorporation was for his protection only. The business was carried on under the name of Spring Leather Goods and the sign "Spring Leather Goods" appeared in a prominent position above the doorway to the store and the word "Spring" also appeared in a vertical position immediately to the left of the entrance. The bank account for the business was in the name of Spring Leather Goods but the bank was aware that the business was carried on by a limited company and the account was personally guaranteed by Mr. Kosmopoulos.

> The late Aristides Roussakis, an employee of the defendant Roussakis Insurance Agency Limited, was Mr. Kosmopoulos's insurance agent. The store was opened about March 10th, 1972, and about this time Mr. Roussakis attended at the store to arrange for insurance coverage. Mr. Roussakis was also of Greek extraction and the conversation between him and Mr. Kosmopoulos was conducted in Greek. Mr. Roussakis inspected the premises. As a result of this visit, a policy of insurance was issued by the General Accident Group covering from March 14th, 1972 to March 14th, 1975. The insured was shown as Andreas Kosmopoulos O/A Spring Leather Goods. This policy was subsequently renewed but was not in force on the date of the loss, May 24th, 1977. By the date of the loss, this policy had been replaced by subscription policies with Simcoe-Bay Group and Commercial Insurance Company. The defendant insurers are subscribing companies to the two replacement policies. Both replacement policies showed the insured as Andreas Kosmopoulos O/A Spring Leather Goods. The business premises were inspected on behalf of the replacement underwriters.

* * *

A fire started next door to the leather goods store on May 24th, 1977, and the premises and contents sustained damage from fire, smoke and water.

* * *

The risk was known to the agent and had been inspected by employees of the insurers. No evidence was adduced that it made the slightest difference to the risk that the business was carried on in the name of Spring Leather Goods by a limited company rather than by Mr. Kosmopoulos personally. In these circumstances can it be said that Mr. Kosmopoulos had no insurable interest and that his action against the insurers must fail?

The concept of "insurable interests" is described in Brown and Menezes, *Insurance Law in Canada* (1982), at p. 67 as follows:

* * *

The insurable interest finds its most celebrated definition in a judgment of Lawrence J. in *Lucena v. Craufurd et al.* (1806), 2 Bos. & Pul. (N.R.) 269 at pp. 302-3, 127 E.R. 630 at p. 643 (H.L.):

A man is interested in a thing to whom advantage may arise or prejudice happen from the circumstances which may attend it . . . And whom it importeth, that its condition as to safety or other quality should continue: interest does not necessarily imply a right to the whole, or a part of a thing, nor necessarily and exclusively that which may be the subject of privation, but the having some relation to, or concern in the subject of the insurance, which relation or concern by the happening of the perils insured against may be so affected as to produce a damage, detriment, or prejudice to the person insuring: and where a man is so circumstanced with respect to matters exposed to certain risks or dangers, as to have a moral certainty of advantage or benefit, but for those risks or dangers he may be said to be interested in the safety of the thing. To be interested in the preservation of a thing, is to be so circumstanced with respect to it as to have benefit from its existence, prejudice from its destruction. The property of a thing and the interest devisable from it may be very different; of the first the price is generally the measure, but by interest in a thing every benefit or advantage arising out of or depending on such thing may be considered as being comprehended.

If the law had nothing more to say with respect to insurable interest, this case would be easily resolved. It is obvious that the plaintiff Andreas Kosmopoulos was "so circumstanced" with respect to the assets of his limited company that he had "benefit from its existence, prejudice from its destruction".

In 1925, the House of Lords again dealt with the concept of insurable interest in *Macaura v. Northern Ass'ce Co., Ltd.*, [1925] A.C. 619. In that case Macaura sold lumber, both felled and standing, to a limited company in exchange for shares in the company. As the company continued to operate Macaura also became a substantial creditor of the company. The timber was destroyed by fire. The fire insurance policies were in the name of the plaintiff Macaura and a bank. In dealing with the plaintiff's claim, Lord Buckmaster said . . .:

> Turning now to his position as shareholder, this must be independent of the extent of his share interest. If he were entitled to insure holding all the shares in the company, each shareholder would be equally entitled, if the shares were all in separate hands. Now, no shareholder has any right to any item of property owned by the company, for he has no legal or equitable interest therein. He is entitled to a share in the profits while the company continues to carry on business and a share in the distribution of the surplus assets whenthe company is wound up. If he were at liberty to effect an insurance against loss by fire of any item of the company's property, the extent of his insurable interestcould only be measured by determining the extent to which his share in the ultimate distribution would be diminished by the loss of the asset — a calculation almost impossible to make. There is no means by which such an interest can definitely be measured and no standard which can be fixed of the loos against which the contract of insurance could be regarded as an indemnity. This difficulty was realized by counsel for the appellant, who really based his case upon the contention that such a claim was recognized by authority and depended upon the proper application of the determination of insurable interest given by Lawrence J. in *Lucena v. Craufurd*. I agree with the comment of Andrews L.J. upon this case. I find equally with him a difficulty in understanding how a moral certainty can be so defined as to render it an essential part of a definite legal proposition. In the present case, though it might be regarded as a moral certainty that the appellant would suffer loss if the timber which constituted the sole asset of the company were destroyed by fire, this moral certainty becomes dissipated and lost if the asset be regarded as only one in an innumerable number of items in a company's assets and the shareholding interest be spread over a large number of individual shareholders . . .

In *Macaura* the plaintiff was not the sole owner of the company; he owned "practically the whole interest" or "almost all the shares". In the case at hand, Mr. Kosmopoulos was the sole owner and the problems of calculating the interest of an insured shareholder envisaged by Lord Buckmaster would be greatly simplified. However, it must be conceded that the reasoning in *Macaura* is not dependent on the extent of the plaintiff's shareholding. The rationale of the case is summed up by Lord Wrenbury who said at p. 633:

> My Lords, this appeal may be disposed of by saying that the corporator even if he holds all the shares is not the corporation, and that neither he nor any creditor of the company has any property legal or equitable in the assets of the corporation.

It will be seen that the House of Lords narrowed the definition of insurable interest from the benefit/detriment concept expressed in *Lucena v. Craufurd*, to a direct property interest: see Brown and Menezes, *Insurance Law in Canada* (1982), at p. 82 *et seq.*

The question then is whether this court is obliged to accept *Macaura* as the law in Ontario. *Macaura* has been twice referred to in the Supreme Court of Canada.

* * *

[Zuber J.A. proceeded to discuss the two SCC cases *Guarantee Co. of North America v. Aqua-Land Exploration Ltd.* (1965), [1966] S.C.R. 133, 1965 CarswellOnt 77, and *Wandlyn Motels Ltd. v. Commerce General Insurance Co.*, [1970] S.C.R. 992, 1970 CarswellNB 13, 1970 CarswellNB 13F, and continued as follows:]

I conclude therefore that the Supreme Court of Canada has accepted the rule in *Macaura* only to the extent that it needed to decide the *Aqua-Land* case, i.e., that one shareholder of three had no insurable interest in the assets of the corporation. Therefore, the issue of whether a sole shareholder has an insurable interest in the assets of the corporation, in my view, remains open in this province.

Previously this conclusion would have had very little practical importance because both Ontario and federal legislation required that a corporation have a plurality of shareholders. Now, however, both the Ontario *Business Corporations Act*, R.S.O. 1980, c. 54, and the *Canada Business Corporations Act*, 1974-75-76 (S.C.), c. 33, provide for corporations with a single director and a single shareholder. The question, then, is whether the *Macaura* rule should be accepted in its entirety in Ontario to compel a court to hold that the sole owner of a single-shareholder, single-director company can have no insurable interest in the assets of that company. In my view the rule should not be accepted to this extent as part of the Ontario law. As mentioned earlier, the sole owner of a limited company fits well within the definition of those who might have an insurable interest as defined in *Lucena v. Craufurd, supra*. I can see no reason for imposing the rigidity of the *Macaura* rule on this recent development in company law.

In coming to this conclusion I derive some comfort from the judgment of the Supreme Court of Tennessee in *American Indemnity Co. v. Southern Missionary College* (1953), 260 S.W. 2d 269. In that case, Southern Missionary College was insured against burglary by the American Indemnity Company. A burglary loss was suffered by a college store which was separately incorporated but which was wholly owned and controlled by the college. The insurers resisted the loss on the grounds that the college had no insurable interest in the assets of the college store. The definition of insurable interest applied by the Supreme Court of Tennessee appears to be almost identical to the definition in *Lucena v. Craufurd* . . .

In concluding that the college had an insurable interest in the assets of the college store, Chief Justice Neil said at p. 272:

> We think the two corporations are separate entities, but their existence as such is a mere fiction of the law. The subordinate corporation does the bidding of its parent down to the minutest detail. The domination of the parent over its offspring was so complete as to make them practically indistinguishable except in name. There can be no other reasonable conclusion from the admitted facts but that Mercantile Enterprises was an agency or instrumentality of the complainant, and all property including the money burglarized was in reality the property of the latter, subject of course to the claims of creditors of the former.

And, at p. 273:

> It cannot be questioned that the Southern Missionary College would, upon the dissolution of Collegedale Mercantile Enterprises, Inc., be entitled to all the assets of the latter subject to the claims of creditors. Its insurable interest is comparable to the interest which a stockholder has in specific corporate property, i.e., dividends and assets upon liquidation.

I find the foregoing reasoning persuasive and applicable to this case.

In some future case where the sole owner of a corporation takes out insurance in his own name to cover the assets of his corporate alter ego, an insurer may be able to show that this amounted to a misstatement material to the risk and thereby avoid liability. Such a case is not easy to imagine and, in any event, is not this case . . .

Appeal dismissed.

On appeal ([1987] 1 S.C.R. 2), the Supreme Court affirmed the Court of Appeal's decision but on different grounds. Justice Wilson (writing for herself and Beetz, Lamer, LeDain and LaForest JJ.) did not agree that this was an appropriate case for lifting the corporate veil. However, she held that a shareholder does have an insurable interest in the corporation's property and she declined to follow *Macaura* and the Supreme Court of Canada precedents holding the contrary.

Justice McIntyre was not willing to go quite so far in adopting an expansive definition of insurable interest. He thought it was sufficient to hold that the shareholder in a one-person corporation has a sufficient interest in the corporation's property to take him/her out of the *Macaura* rule.

In the passages that follow, the extract from Justice Wilson's judgment is limited to the issue of lifting the corporate veil; Justice McIntyre's judgment is substantially reproduced in full.

WILSON J. . . .

(a) *"Lifting the Corporate Veil"*

As a general rule a corporation is a legal entity distinct from its shareholders: *Salomon v. Salomon & Co.*, [1897] A.C. 22 (H.L.). The law on when a court may disregard this principle by "lifting the corporate veil" and regarding the company as a mere "agent" or "puppet" of its controlling shareholder or parent corporation follows no consistent principle. The best that can be said is that the "separate entities" principle is not enforced when it would yield a result "too flagrantly opposed to justice, convenience or the interests of the Revenue": L.C.B. Gower, *Modern Company Law* (4th ed. 1979), at p. 112. I have no doubt that theoretically the veil could be lifted in this case to do justice, as was done in *American Indemnity Co. v. Southern Missionary College, supra*, cited by the Court of Appeal of Ontario. But a number of factors lead me to think it would be unwise to do so.

There is a persuasive argument that "those who have chosen the benefits of incorporation must bear the corresponding burdens, so that if the veil is to be lifted at all that should only be done in the interests of third parties who would otherwise suffer as a result of that choice": Gower, *supra*, at p. 138. Mr. Kosmopoulos was advised by a competent solicitor to incorporate his business in order to protect his personal assets and there is nothing in the evidence to indicate that his decision to secure the benefits of incorporation was not a genuine one. Having chosen to receive the benefits of incorporation, he should not be allowed to escape its burdens. He should not be permitted to "blow hot and cold" at the same time.

I am mindful too of this Court's decision in the *Aqua-Land Exploration Ltd.* case, *supra*, in which the Court did not "lift the veil" in order to find that one of three shareholders in a corporation had an insurable interest in its asset. So also in the *Wandlyn Motels Ltd.* case, *supra*, the Court refused to regard a motel owned by a man who held all but two of the shares of the insured, Wandlyn Motels Ltd., as the property of that corporation. If the corporate veil were to be lifted in this case, then a very arbitrary and, in my view, indefensible distinction might emerge between companies with more than one shareholder and companies with only one shareholder: for a recent comment on the arbitrary and technical distinctions that would be created by lifting the corporate veil in this case, see Jacob S. Ziegel, "Shareholder's Insurable Interest — Another Attempt to Scuttle the *Macaura v. Northern Assurance Co.* Doctrine: *Kosmopoulous v. Constitution Insurance Co.*" (1984), 62 Can. Bar Rev. 95, at pp. 102-03. In addition, it is my view that if the application of a rule leads to harsh justice, the proper course to follow is to examine the rule itself rather than affirm it and attempt to ameliorate its ill effects on a case-by-case basis.

McINTYRE J.: . . . I would dismiss the appeal. In doing so, however, I would not go as far as my colleague [Wilson J.] has gone in rejecting totally the limited definition of an insurable interest in *Macaura v. Northern Assurance Co.*, . . . , and adopting the expansive definition of Lawrence J. in *Lucena v. Craufurd* . . . I would prefer to adopt the approach of Zuber J.A. in the Court of Appeal. He was of the view that the *Macaura* rule should not be accepted to compel a holding that a sole shareholder and sole director of a company could not have an insurable interest in the assets of the Company. Modern company law now permits the creation of companies with one shareholder. The identity then between the Company and that sole shareholder and director is such that an insurable interest in the Company's assets may be found in the sole shareholder. This approach fits well with *Lucena v. Craufurd* without opening the concept of insurable interest to indefinable limits.

Note

For comments on *Kosmopoulos*, see Ziegel (1984), 62 Can. Bar Rev. 95, and Stuesser (1987), 13 C.B.L.J. 226. Is there a meaningful distinction between lifting the corporate veil in the case of one-person corporations to allow recovery under an insurance policy and deeming the sole shareholder to hold an insurable interest in the corporation's assets? Would the Supreme Court have reached the same conclusion if (a) the insurance policy had been held in the names of *several* owners of the unincorporated business, or (b) new shareholders had joined the corporation after its incorporation by the pre-incorporation owner?

The question of whether, and when, the corporate veil should be lifted *in favour of* the corporation's shareholders and officers continues to be troublesome. (Cases of lifting the corporate veil against its shareholders are considered in detail later in this chapter.) In *Rogers, Rogers and Cornwall v. Bank of Montreal*, [1985] 5 W.W.R. 193, aff'd [1987] 2 W.W.R. 364 (B.C. C.A.) Mackenzie J. refused to lift the veil in favour of the officers of a public corporation who claimed personal damages against the bank and receivers appointed by the bank under a secured debenture for trespass and conversion of the corporation's property and for conspiracy to injure the plaintiffs. Mackenzie J. followed such earlier precedents as *Hunt v. T.W. Johnstone Co. Ltd.* (1976), 69 D.L.R. (3d) 639 (Sask.); *Tunstall v. Steigman*, [1962] 2 Q.B. 593 (C.A.), and *Re TIW Industries Ltd; TIW Industries Ltd. v. Clarkson Co. Ltd.* (1984), 48 C.B.R. (N.S.) 66 (Ont.). Similarly, in *Meditrust Healthcare Inc. v. Shoppers Drug Mart* (2002), 220 D.L.R. (4th) 611, 2002 CarswellOnt 3380 (C.A.), the Ontario Court of Appeal refused to lift the corporate veil to allow a parent corporation to sue the defendant for conspiring to injure the business activities of the plaintiff's subsidiary.

On the other hand, in *Houle v. Canadian National Bank*, [1990] 3 S.C.R. 122, the Supreme Court affirmed a decision of the Quebec Court of Appeal allowing the former shareholders of a corporation damages against the bank for the premature calling in of a loan to a closely held corporation. The plaintiffs alleged that as a result of the bank's action, a prospective purchaser of the company's shares substantially reduced its offer, causing them to suffer substantial damages.

There is also a line of cases, of which *Kummen v. Alfonso & Wagner*, [1953] 1 D.L.R. 637 (Man. C.A.) and *Ashcroft v. Curtin*, [1971] 3 All E.R. 1208 (C.A.) are examples, in which Canadian and British courts have allowed an employee-shareholder to include a claim for lost profits by his company, or a claim based on the reduced value of his shares, as part of a claim for special damages against a tortfeasor. (See further B.G. Hansen and D.J. Mullan, "Private Corporations in Canada: Principles of Recovery for the Tortious Disablement of Shareholder-Employees", in Lewis Sklar (Ed.), *Studies in Canadian Tort Law*, ch. 8, pp. 247-253). These cases can probably be distinguished on the ground that the defendant had clearly breached a duty of care to the plaintiff and that the corporate veil was only being lifted for the purpose of showing the full extent of the plaintiff's loss.

NOTES ON CORPORATE PERSONALITY, ONE-PERSON CORPORATIONS, AND LIMITED LIABILITY

Since it was decided, *Salomon v. Salomon* has stood for two basic propositions in modern corporations law, *viz.* (a) that a corporation has a legal existence separate and apart from the personalities of its shareholders, and (b) that there is no requirement that shareholders must hold their shares beneficially and therefore no objection to a *de facto* one-person corporation. It will be convenient to deal with these propositions separately.

The Nature of Corporate Personality. Some of the consequences of the separate legal personality of the modern business corporation are spelled out in the statutory provisions reproduced at the beginning of this section; many more will be encountered in later chapters of this Casebook. The law reports are replete with cases in which the courts have loyally applied the House of Lords' prescription in *Salomon v. Salomon*. But what is the nature of the personality that *Salomon v. Salomon* tells us is brought into being on incorporation?

Legal scholars, philosophers and political scientists have long debated the nature of corporate and group personality. There are two principal schools of thought, though each in turn has spawned a host of offspring of its own. The subscribers to the fiction theory argue that corporate personality is a legal creation and that, as Chief Justice Marshall of the US Supreme Court observed in *Dartmouth College v. Woodward*, (1819) 4 Wheat. 518, at 636, a corporation is "an artificial being, invisible, intangible, and existing only in contemplation of law." A similar sentiment is reflected in Coke's report of the *Sutton Hospital Case* (1613), 10 Co. Rep. 23a, where it was said that "a corporation aggregate of many is invisible, immortal and rests only in intendment and consideration of the law." The supporters of the *realist* school, on the other hand, assert that "when a group reaches a sufficient level of organization, when it can make decisions and when it has a continuity of experience, then a new personality has actually come into existence, regardless of whether the state accords it legal recognition." Bonham & Soberman, "The Nature of Corporate Personality" in *Studies in Canadian Company Law* (Ziegel ed.), vol. 1, at p. 6. For further discussion of the various theories see G.W. Paton & David P. Derham, *Jurisprudence* (1972), 4th ed., pp. 407 *et seq.*; Radin, "The Endless Problem of Corporate Personality" (1932), 32 Col. L. Rev. 643; and Pollock, "Has the Common Law Received the Fiction Theory of Corporations?" (1911), 27 Law Quar. Rev. 219.

Yet another approach is adopted by members of the contractarian law and economics school, of which Judge Easterbrook and Daniel Fischel are leading exponents. See *The Economic Structure of Corporate Law*, ch. 1(1991). The contractarians argue that the corporation is only a nexus of intersecting contracts between shareholders, creditors of the corporation, employees, management and the board of directors and that to understand how the corporation works one must study the contracts, explicit or implicit, between the relevant parties. ("Contract", in this context, is used in a non-technical sense to describe the terms binding the various constituencies and the stimuli to which they respond.) This theory, in other words, is market driven, and for good reason. Its proponents believe that, given an efficient market, the players are better able to determine what is in their best interests than are paternalistic courts or legislators and that the principal role of corporation statutes is to provide default rules to fill the gaps where the parties have failed to write an explicit contract or its terms are otherwise incomplete.

Given this consensual view of the corporate universe, it is not clear what importance its subscribers attach to the legal personality of the corporation and whether they would ally themselves with the realist or fiction theory of incorporation, or with neither. They would probably treat it as an instrumentalist question — i.e., to view incorporation as a vehicle for facilitating the efficient operation of the firm and its constituencies — and therefore apply the personality theory that will best promote the contractual interests in a given case. Whatever the merits of the various theories, it seems fairly clear that modern Canadian business corporations legislation has embraced the fiction theory. This is evident not only from the fact that the Acts uniformly recognize one-person corporations (see the statutory extracts, *supra*) but also from the CBCA provision (s. 5(2)) allowing an existing corporation to incorporate another.

Equally striking is the fact that the CBCA corporation comes into existence without apparently having any shareholders (*cf.* ss. 6, 8, and Forms 1 and 2). And of course there is no requirement that only an existing business can be incorporated — or for that matter that the corporation must maintain

an active existence (*cf. Camp bell v. Taxicabs Verrals Ltd.* (1912), 27 O.L.R.
147); though the latter rule has now been modified by CBCA, s. 212. Further
support for the fiction theory can be found in the Director's powers under
the CBCA to revive a dissolved corporation (s. 209) and the various provisions for lifting the corporate veil. See, *infra*, s. 4. These provisions would
not be necessary if every corporation had an "authentic" existence separate
and apart from its shareholders. CBCA s. 15, conferring on a corporation
the capacity and powers of a natural person, may appear to contradict the
fiction theory of the CBCA, but the exception is more apparent than real:
the provision was inserted for reasons of expediency and not because the
drafters were inspired by natural law or realist theories of corporate personality. See further the discussion of the *ultra vires* doctrine, *infra*, ch. 4(3).

These remarks are not intended to dismiss out of hand the relevance
of the realist theory with respect to business corporations, and there are at
least two areas in which it can make important contributions to contemporary problems. The first is in determining to what extent a corporation is a
citizen of the community in which it operates, with the obligations and
opportunities that this implies, and not merely a profit centre. See further,
infra, ch. 4. The second question involves corporate criminal liability. Can
a corporation meaningfully commit a crime, how does one establish the
necessary *mens rea*, and what purpose is served by holding a corporation
criminally liable? See, *infra*, this chapter, s. 5(b).

One-Person Corporations. As Prof. Gower observed (*Principles of
Modern Company Law*, 6th ed., p. 99), *Salomon v. Salomon*:

> [O]pened up new vistas to company lawyers and the world of com-
> merce. Not only did it finally establish the legality of the one-man
> company and showed that incorporation was as readily available to the
> small private partnership and sole trader as to the large public company,
> but it also revealed that it was possible for a trader not merely to limit
> his liability to the money which he put into the enterprise but even to
> avoid any serious risk to the major part of that by subscribing for
> debentures rather than shares.

Not all commentators were enamoured of this result and some thought
it was "calamitous". However, some of the critics appear to confuse the
question of whether the law should permit one-person corporations with the
issue of limited liability. Clearly, they are separate issues. The Lawrence
Committee thought the law should recognize what had become an established business fact, and it disagreed with the objections raised by the
Jenkins Committee in the U.K. in a 1962 report to the legalization of one-
man companies.

The Lawrence Committee's endorsement for simplifying the legal
requirements for incorporation were accompanied in Ontario (and later in
other provinces) by corresponding expedition in the administrative handling

of incorporation applications. This development is graphically described in the following extract from a news item in *The Globe and Mail* of 10 May 1983:

> "15-MINUTE CORPORATIONS IN SIX CITIES GET COMPANY". Aspiring tycoons with $200 and a free quarter-hour can now get quickie incorporations from the provincial Government in seven Ontario cities.
> The latest while-you-wait incorporation outlet for time-pressed capitalists opened in Kingston yesterday, complementing service already provided in Toronto, London, Thunder Bay, Sudbury, Ottawa and Windsor.

Limited Liability. Even more striking than the easy availability of incorporation is the easy availability of limited liability for owner-managed as well as investor-owned corporations. Limited liability was not an issue before the 19th century and, as has been seen, it was only secured in the U.K. in 1855 after a prolonged struggle. Even then it was only seen as a victory for modern capitalism; it was not appreciated (and perhaps not intended?) that the privilege also extended to owner-managed corporations until the House of Lords so decided in *Salomon v. Salomon*. The fact that the common law legislatures have done nothing to reverse the decision suggests that public opinion accepts the results with equanimity. Before jumping to the conclusion that this is correct and in determining whether the present law strikes a reasonable balance between the interests of shareholders, directors and creditors of limited liability corporations, we need to see what protection existing legislation affords a corporation's creditors.

The principal provisions are the following:

1. *A cautionary suffix.* The Canadian Acts invariably require the addition to the corporation's name of one of the words "Corporation," "Limited," "Incorporated" or the abbreviations "Inc.," "Ltd." and "Corp.," (or their equivalents in French) to warn creditors that they are dealing with a limited liability entity. See *e.g.*, CBCA s. 10(1), BCBCA, s. 23, OBCA, s. 10(1). How does this assist involuntary creditors? Legislation also frequently requires a corporation to set out its name in legible characters "in all contracts, invoices, negotiable instruments and orders for goods or services". See *e.g.*, CBCA, s. 10(5), *Business Names Act*, R.S.O. 1990, c. B.17, s. 2(6), and BCBCA s. 26(1). Note also that a corporation is not precluded from adopting a trade name so long as it continues to comply with s. 10(5): CBCA s. 10(6), OBCA, ss. 10(6), and registers the assumed name under the *Business Names Act*, R.S.O. 1990, c. B.17 as am., s.2(1). It has been held in Ontario that failure to comply with the OBCA disclosure requirements imposes no personal civil liability on the corporation's officers or directors since the OBCA (and the same is true in the CBCA) only treats non-disclosure as an offence under s. 252: *Watfield Inter-*

national Enterprises Inc. v. 655293 Ontario Ltd. (1995), 21 B.L.R. (2d) 158, 1995 CarswellOnt 540 (Gen. Div.). Failure to comply with the OBN requirements gives rise to a criminal penalty under s. 10 and the corporation's inability to maintain proceedings in Ontario without the court's leave: s. 7(1) and (2).

Nevertheless, there are many reported cases where the officer or director of a corporation has been held personally liable for non-disclosure of the fact that he was contracting on behalf of a corporation, especially where he had previously dealt with the other party in an individual capacity before the incorporation of the company. In *Turi v. Swanick* (2002), 61 O.R. (3d) 368, 2002 CarswellOnt 3041 (S.C.J.), Spiegel J. also held that a lawyer who incorporates a company for a small business person is under a contractual and common law duty to inform his client, first, that the client must be careful to use the company's legal name in entering into contracts on behalf of the company and, second, of the legal consequences of the client failing to follow this procedure.

In a still more telling case, *Wolfe v. Moir* (1969), 69 W.W.R. 70, 1969 CarswellAlta 36 (T.D.), the defendant Gordon L. Moir was held personally liable for injuries suffered by the plaintiff while skating on a roller skating rink in Lethbridge ("Fort Whoop-Up") owned by Chinook Sport Shop Ltd. Gordon L. Moir and his wife were the company's shareholders and officers and Gordon Moir apparently also acted as manager of the skating rink. The skating rink was advertised in the *Lethbridge Herald* in the following fashion:

> Roller Skating
> Tonight
> 8:00 to 10:30 p.m.
> Moir's Sportland
> (Fort Whoop-Up)
> Special Group Rates.

Moir had previously served as recreation director for the city of Lethbridge and his name was well known in the community. Sinclair J. also found that the names "Fort Whoop-Up" or "Moir's Sportland" had not been registered by Moir or his company under s. 72 of the Alberta *Partnership Act*, R.S.A. 1955, c. 230, s. 21(1) requiring a company or partnership carrying on business under an assumed name to file a declaration disclosing the assumed name. Similarly, Moir's company had failed to comply with s. 82(1)(c) of the *Companies Act*, R.S.A. 1955, ch. 53, Alberta's then-counterpart to OBCA s. 15(1).

On the strength of these facts, Sinclair J. held Moir personally liable for the plaintiff's injuries. He reasoned, *inter alia*, as follows:

> In the present case, as I have already pointed out, other than for the evidence of Mr. and Mrs. Moir that the business was operated by Chinook Sport Shop Ltd. of which they were, re-

spectively, secretary and president, there was nothing to indicate that the usual corporate formalities were gone through. It seems to me that for a person to successfully rely upon what is, after all, the extraordinary protection from personal liability granted to an individual by *The Companies Act*, it is incumbent upon him to establish that at least the formalities prescribed by the statute have been complied with. This he has failed completely to do.

Further, in my view, the effect of sec. 82 (1) (*b*) of *The Companies Act* is that if a person chooses to advertise and to hold himself out to the public without identifying the name of a company with which he is associated, he runs the risk of being held personally liable. There are many cases in which an individual has been held personally responsible for an obligation because he did not make it clear when the obligation was incurred that he was acting on behalf of a company.

Sinclair J. did not examine the Partnership and Companies Acts provisions to determine what sanctions they imposed for non-compliance with the registration and disclosure provisions and, of course, *Wolfe v. Moir* was decided before Watfield, *supra*. Nor apparently did the plaintiff give evidence that he thought his admission contract to the skating rink was with Moir personally. Nevertheless, it seems clear that Sinclair J.'s decision was based, in part at least, on liability by estoppel.

2. *Rules Concerning the Raising and Maintenance of Share Capital*. The rules are quite technical and are discussed in detail, *infra*, Ch. 11. Briefly, they are designed to ensure that the corporation receives cash or its true equivalent for its issued shares, and that management does not declare dividends or redeem or purchase the corporation's shares when the corporation is insolvent or if this would make it insolvent. See CBCA ss. 35-36, 42. Note carefully however that there is no obligation under the CBCA, the OBCA, or (it seems) the BCBCA for a corporation to have a minimum paid up capital, This apparent laxity is in striking contrast with the requirements for both public and closely held corporations obtaining in many Western European countries. How useful are such capital requirements and how does one determine what is an adequate minimum amount of capital?

3. *Publicity*. All the Acts require the filing of information in a public office stating the location of the corporation's head office or registered office and giving the names of its current directors. See *e.g.*, BCBCA, ss. 10-11, 407 and Form 1; CBCA s. 19 and Forms 3 and 6, s. 263 and Form 22; and the *Corporations Information Act*, R.S.O. 1990, c. C.39. Prescribed records must also be maintained at the corporation's head office and made accessible there to shareholders and creditors or (in B.C.'s case) to any person. See BCBCA, s. 42 ; CBCA, s. 21; OBCA, ss. 140, 145. Note again however that, with the exception of the CBCA, the Canadian Acts do not generally impose a requirement

for the public filing of the corporation's balance sheets or other financial information. (Such filing requirements apply however to public corporations under the various Securities Acts.) For the CBCA provisions, see s. 160(1). The contrary position obtains under the British *Companies Act* where such requirements apply to private as well as public companies. For the particulars see Gower & Davies' *Principles of Modern Company Law*, 7th ed., pp..558-61. U.K. companies are exempt from the requirements if they opt to incorporate with unlimited liability for their members. Few have done so. In 1979, out of 65,727 newly registered companies with share capital, only 297 were incorporated without limited liability. See *A New Form of Incorporation for Small Firms: A Consultative Document* (London: Cmnd 8171, Feb. 1981), para. 4.2. This is a striking commentary on the importance which shareholders attach to limited liability and the price they are willing to pay to get it.

4. *Directors' Liability.*

(a) Directors and officers of a corporation are generally liable for failing to exercise reasonable care, diligence and skill in the discharge of their obligations and for breach of their fiduciary duties. See BCBCA, s. 142, CBCA, s. 122, OBCA, s. 134 and, *infra*, chs. 5-6. These duties are owed to the corporation and ordinarily only the corporation can enforce them.

(b) Directors are also liable for breach of specific prohibitions. See BCBCA s. 154(1), CBCA, ss. 118, 123(4) and OBCA ss. 130, 135(4).

(c) Exceptionally, directors are liable for unpaid wages owing to the corporation's employees whether or not the directors have been negligent. See CBCA, s. 119 and OBCA, s. 131, and *Mesheau v. Campbell* (1983), 141 D.L.R. (3d) 155 (Ont. C.A.), *infra*, this Section. These provisions are of American origin. Another even more important provision, but of Canadian origin, is found in s. 227.1 of the *Income Tax Act*, which was introduced in 1981. This holds directors jointly and severally liable with the corporation for failure to deduct or withhold required taxes or to remit such taxes to Revenue Canada. A due diligence defence is available to directors under s. 227.1(3) and, predictably, it has attracted much litigation. See Lynn Campbell, "Directors' Diligence under the Income Tax Act" (1990) 16 C.B.L.J. 480.

(d) Directors' Liability in Tort. Faced with the prospect of an insolvent company and an unenforceable judgment, plaintiffs increasingly seek to overcome the hurdle of limited liability by suing one or more of the directors/officers or lower level employees of the company in tort alleging that they were personally implicated in the wrongdoing. For recent examples of such actions, see *ADGA Systems International Ltd. v. Valcom Ltd.* (1999), 43 O.R. (3d) 101, 1999 CarswellOnt 29 (C.A.) (reproduced below), *C. Evans & Sons Ltd. v. Spritebrand*, [1985] 2 All E.R. 415 (C.A.), *London Drugs Ltd. v. Kuehne & Nagel*

International Ltd., [1992] 3 S.C.R. 299 (in the latter case the tortious approach was adopted to overcome a disclaimer of liability clause in the contract between the plaintiff and the defendant corporation), and *Williams v. Natural Life Health Foods Ltd.* [1998] 1 W.L.R. 830 (H.L.). Other examples are *Henry Electric Ltd. v. Union Electric Supply Co. Ltd.* (1986), 6 W.W.R. 78 (B.C. C.A.) and *James V. Barnett v. M.N.R.* (1985), 85 D.T.C. 619.

It was already settled by the early 1920s that the representative character of the defendant as an officer, director, or employee of a company did not shield him from personal liability for such traditional torts as trespass, assault, libel, and at least some types of negligence even if the officer or director was acting in the normal course of his duties. See Atkin L.J.'s judgment in *Performing Rights Society Ltd. v. Ciryl Theatrical Syndicate Ltd.*, [1924] 1 K.B. 1 at 14-15. In *London Drugs Ltd.*, *supra*, Trainor J., at first instance, went so far as to assert that the B.C. courts now recognize that "there is no general rule that an employee cannot be sued for tort committed in the course of carrying out the very services for which the plaintiff had contracted with his employer", but he cast the net too widely. One important exception was carved out in McCardie J.'s well known judgment in *Said v. Butt*, [1920] 3 K.B. 497 (Eng. K.B.), which continues to be treated as good authority in Canada, as well as in England. This case held that an officer of a company could not be sued for procuring breach of contract between the company and the other contracting party. Subsequent Ontario courts interpreted the judgment to mean that officers and directors could not be sued generally for committing economic torts if they were acting within the normal scope of their office. However, this notion was firmly scotched by Carthy J.A. in *ADGA Systems*, *supra*, in delivering the unanimous judgment of the Ontario Court of Appeal. In his opinion, the principle in *Said v. Butt* only applies to subsisting contracts between the company and the plaintiff; it does not apply where, as in *ADGA Systems*, the officer is accused of procuring breach of contract between the plaintiff company and its own employees. The last word has not been said on the subject and the important issues of policy await further clarification by the Supreme Court of Canada. See also the notes following the reproduction of Carthy J.A.'s judgment, *infra*.

Statutory liability for a company's tort is also frequently imposed on directors and officers under environmental protection legislation but subject to a due diligence defence. A *cause célèbre* in this area which provoked consternation among directors was the conviction of two directors of Bata Industries Ltd. in *R. v. Bata Industries Ltd.* (1992), 9 O.R. (3d) 329 (Prov. Div.) for failure to ensure compliance with Ontario's anti-pollution legislation.

(e) Under former BCCA, s. 14, a company could not carry on business without at least one shareholder. If it did, the directors and officers were personally liable for debts contracted by the company if the company carried on business without a member for more than 6 months. This provision was of British origin but was rarely invoked in practice. *Cf. Jarvis Motors (Harrow) Ltd. v. Carabott*, [1964] 3 All E.R. 89. What purpose did it serve, and how could it be applied to one-member companies? See further Gower & Davies, op. *cit.*, pp. 191-92.

5. *Relief under the Oppression Remedy.* The statutory oppression remedy, which is also of British origin, was historically designed to overcome restrictive common law rules making it very difficult for minority shareholders to sue management. See now BCBCA, s. 227, CBCA, s. 241 and OBCA, s. 247. However, the definition of "complainant" in CBCA s. 238(c) and (d) includes the Director of the CBCA* and "any other person who, in the discretion of a court, is a proper person to make an application under this Part." When these provisions were first adopted it was not envisaged that they would apply to general creditors and that creditors could seek relief from allegedly oppressive or unfairly prejudicial conduct by a corporation and its management. However, the contrary has been held in a series of cases beginning with *First Edmonton Place Ltd. v. 315888 Alberta Ltd.* (1988), 40 B.L.R. 28 (Alta. Q.B.), stayed on appeal (1989), 45 B.L.R. 110 (Alta. C.A.), and allowing relief directly against the offending officers or directors. See further Ziegel (1993), 43 U.T.L.J. 511, 526-29 and *Downtown Eatery (1993) Ltd. v. Ontario* (2001), 54 O.R. (3d) 161, 2001 CarswellOnt 1680 (C.A.). From a creditor's point of view, these precedents provide a promising avenue to piercing the corporate veil and by-passing the restrictive impact of shareholders' limited liability.

6. *Directors' Duties to Creditors where the Corporation is insolvent or in the vicinity of Insolvency.* It is basic common law doctrine, now codified in the Canadian business corporations Acts, that directors must act in the best interests of the corporation and, in the discharge of their duties, must act in good faith and exercise such skill and care as a reasonably prudent person would exercise in comparable circumstances. *Cf.* CBCA s. 122(1). Until the mid-1970s "best interests of the corporation" was always understood to mean best interests of the corporation's shareholders; creditors were expected to fend for themselves. However, starting in 1976, an important line of Australian and New Zealand *dicta* and decisions embraced the concept that directors' allegiance shifted to protection of creditor interests when the corporation was insolvent or near insolvency. Ziegel, *supra*, at 517–21. The courts reasoned that when a corporation becomes insolvent the shareholders no longer have an equity in it requiring protection and that the corporation's assets notionally become the creditors' assets, since the

---

* The Director of the CBCA is a federally appointed official responsible for the administration of the CBCA and is not an officer or agent of any corporation.

assets would be liquidated and the proceeds distributed among the creditors if the corporation became bankrupt. *Cf. Bankruptcy and Insolvency Act*, R.S.C. 1985, c.B-3 as am., s.136 with respect to the ranking of creditors' claims in bankruptcy. The Commonwealth jurisprudence was subsequently confirmed in s. 214 of the English *Insolvency Act* ("wrongful trading provision") holding directors personally liable if the company continues to trade at a time when the directors ought to realize that it is unlikely that the company will be able to meet its new obligations. Similar legislation has been adopted in Australia and New Zealand.

The shift in Commonwealth doctrine was not felt in Canada until December 15, 1998, when it was adopted in the *Peoples* case[3] by Justice Greenberg of the Montreal Bankruptcy Court. He held Peoples' directors liable in negligence for failing to protect Peoples' creditors' interests after it should have been obvious to them that Peoples could not avoid bankruptcy. Greenberg J.'s decision was reversed on appeal by the Quebec Court of Appeal.[4] The Supreme Court of Canada granted leave to appeal on August 28, 2003 and the appeal is expected to be argued in late spring 2004. The *Peoples* case has attracted much attention and Greenberg J.'s reasoning has been followed in several lower court Ontario judgments. See further Symposium (2004) 39 C.B.L.J. 336–411, Wayne Gray, (2003) 39 C.B.L.J. 4, and Ziegel, *Annual Review of Insolvency Law* (Carswell 2004), p.134, and *infra* Ch. 5.

7. *Group Enterprise Theories*. Even a mediumsized modern corporation is likely to have one or more affiliates. Large corporations, and especially multinational corporations, will often have dozens of affiliates located in many countries. The creation of affiliates is designed to serve a variety of functions to take advantage of tax provisions, to comply with national ownership and other requirements and, not least, in the case of hazardous activities, to limit the parent corporation's exposure for liabilities incurred by an affiliate. Frequently, control of the group will be exercised from head office and an affiliate may have only negligible assets to meet large tort claims. In this circumstance, courts have often been called upon to lift the corporate veil and to treat the group of corporations as a single entity for tax, tort and other purposes. The results have been very mixed. See further, *infra*, Section 4, *De Salaberry Realties Ltd. v. Minister of National Revenue et seq.*

Conclusion. In light of the above analysis it will be seen that the existing Acts offer creditors little assurance that a corporation will be able to, and will in fact, meet its obligations to them. They do not even ensure that the

---

[3] *People's* [sic] *Department Stores Ltd. (1992) Inc. (Re)* (2001), 23 C.B.R. (4th) 200.
[4] *People's Department Stores Inc. (trustee of) v. Wise* (2003), 224 D.L.R. (4th) 509 (Que. C.A.).

corporation will commence life with a reasonable amount of capital nor do they encourage public appreciation of the corporation's financial position by requiring the filing of financial returns for closely held corporations. Though the prospects have recently improved, the possibility of suing the directors and officers for negligence in the conduct of the corporation's affairs as an indirect means of recovering what is owing to creditors is at best a long shot and few such attempts have succeeded in the past absent self-dealing and other forms of opportunistic conduct. See further, *infra*, Ch. 5.

Given creditors' vulnerability under the existing statutory regimes, how do we explain their apparent acquiescence? There are no sure answers but the following are some possible explanations: (a) in the case of closely held corporations, lenders, landlords, and other large creditors frequently require personal guarantees from directors and shareholders; (b) knowledgeable creditors can also protect themselves by requiring the corporation to put up security or by retaining a security interest in inventory and equipment being supplied to the corporation; (c) banks and other financial institutions accepting deposits from the public are closely supervised by provincial and federal authorities, and depositors are protected by depositors' insurance; (d) in other sensitive industries (*e.g.*, those involving motor vehicle dealers, real estate agents and travel agents) licensing and bonding requirements are quite common; (e) insurance is also mandatory for the most common and important source of tort claims, i.e., those arising out of automobile accidents; (f) creditors, being themselves often incorporated, have nothing to gain by knocking a system from which they too derive so many benefits; (g) in the case of closely held corporations, and absent calculated fraud, it is unlikely the directors/shareholders would be worth suing even if the law were to hold them personally liable. If they were sued they would probably seek relief in personal bankruptcy.

There appears to be surprisingly little hard data about many of the proffered hypotheses and, until the 1980s, there was surprisingly little discussion about the economic rationales of limited liability and when it was appropriate to hold shareholders and/or management personally liable for externalities created by a company's activities, particularly in the non-contractual area. The dike was breached with a seminal article by Halpern, Trebilcock and Turnbull, "An Economic Analysis of Limited Liability in Corporation Law" (1980), 30 U.T.L.J. 117, an extract from which is reproduced at the end of this section. Since then many more articles have appeared extending and deepening the economic and legal analyses.

We continue first with a selection of cases and other materials illustrating the exceptions to the rule of limited liability discussed in the preceding notes.

Mesheau v. Campbell
(1983), 39 O.R. (2d) 702, 141 D.L.R. (3d) 155 (C.A.)

WEATHERSTON J.A. (for the court): Section 114 of the *Canada Business Corporations Act*, S.C. 1975, c. 33 provides in part as follows:

114(1) Directors of a corporation are jointly and severally liable to employees of the corporation for all debts not exceeding six months wages payable to each such employee for services performed for the corporation while they are such directors respectively.

(2) A director is not liable under subsection (1) unless

    (a) the corporation has been sued for the debt within six months after it has become due and execution has been returned unsatisfied in whole or in part;

    (b) the corporation has commenced liquidation and dissolution proceedings or has been dissolved and a claim for the debt has been proved within six months after the earlier of the date of commencement of the liquidation and dissolution proceedings and the date of dissolution; or

    (c) the corporation has made an assignment or a receiving order has been made against it under the *Bankruptcy Act* and a claim for the debt has been proved within six months after the date of the assignment or receiving order.

The issue in this appeal is whether the directors are liable to an employee for an unsatisfied judgment debt against a corporation on a claim for wrongful dismissal. In my opinion, they are not.

The plaintiff says he has complied with all the conditions of the section. He sued his employer, Emblem Mat Corporation, for damages within six months after his wrongful dismissal. The action was not defended. The plaintiff proved his claim and obtained a judgment, execution of which has been returned unsatisfied in whole. The defendants are, and were at all material times directors of the employer.

A cause of action similar to that created by s. 114 of the *Canada Business Corporations Act* was created by s. 52 of the *Ontario Joint Stock Companies Letters Patent Act*, S.O. 1874, c. 35 whereby it was enacted:

52. The Directors of the Company shall be jointly and severally liable to the labourers, servants and apprentices thereof, for all debts not exceeding one year's wages, due for services performed for the Company whilst they are such Directors respectively; but no Director shall be liable to an action therefor, unless the Company has been sued therefor within one year after the debt became due, nor yet unless such Director is sued therefor within one year from the time when he ceased

to be such Director, nor yet before an execution against the Company has been returned unsatisfied in whole or in part; and the amount due on such execution shall be the amount recoverable with costs against the Directors.

As to that section, Osler J.A. said in *Welch v. Ellis* (1895), 22 O.A.R. 255 at 258 that:

Our enactment would appear to have been borrowed from some of the laws of the State of New York, which provide that the stockholders of the company in the events contemplated, shall be liable for all debts that may be due and owing to their "labourers, servants and apprentices" for services performed for the corporation . . .

The Ontario section limits the liability of directors to one year's wages, but otherwise follows the form of the New York statute. The liability is for services performed for the corporation. Section 114 follows precisely the same form, except that the benefit of the section has been extended to all employees, not merely to "labourers, servants and apprentices", and the temporal limit is six months.

In *Zavitz v. Brock et al.* (1974), 3 O.R. (2d) 583, 46 D.L.R. (3d) 203, the question was whether the plaintiff came within the class of persons entitled to the benefit of the section of the Ontario *Corporations Act*, R.S.O. 1960, c. 71 [now R.S.O. 1990, c. C.38] then in force, namely, clerks, labourers, servants, apprentices and other wage earners. Arnup J.A. said at p. 590 [O.R.]:

Some further limited assistance is gained from the fact that the right of a person in the prescribed class to sue is a right to claim "for all debts due . . . for services performed for the company, not exceeding six months wages, and for the vacation pay . . .".

Mr. Brown argued for the plaintiff that the arrangement of phrases in the Ontario statute made it significantly different from s. 114 of the *Canada Business Corporations Act*, and that under the latter act the directors are liable for all debts, however created, subject to a quantitative limit equal to six months' wages. I do not agree. The history of the section and its manifest purpose make it perfectly clear that the words "all debts" are modified by the phrase "for services performed for the corporation" and are subject to the quantitative limit of six months' wages payable to each such employee.

A claim for damages for wrongful dismissal is a claim for unliquidated damages. It is not a debt, nor is it "for services performed for the corporation". In *Mullen v. Millar* (1924), 55 O.L.R. 563 [affirmed 56 O.L.R. 345, [1925] 2 D.L.R. 321], it was held that the plaintiffs could not succeed under the Ontario statute then in force because they had not yet entered the employ of the company. In the present case, the plaintiff's cause of action arose after his employment was terminated. In neither case was the debt "for services performed for the corporation".

Appeal allowed; cross-appeal dismissed.

Notes

Section 114(1) of CBCA 1975 is s. 119(1) in the current Act. The corresponding provision in the OBCA is s. 131(1). *Mesheau v. Campbell* is only one of a larger number of divided cases dealing with the issue whether a claim for termination pay can be characterized as a "debt". The conflict was resolved by the Supreme Court of Canada in *Crabtree (Succession de) c. Barrette*, [1993] 1 S.C.R. 1027, 1993 CarswellQue 25, 1993 CarswellQue 155, discussed by Bryan C.G. Haynes in (1994) 23 C.B.L.J. 283. The Court supported the *Mesheau* line of cases.

Canadian directors have reacted with increasing alarm to the proliferating number of federal and provincial statutes (said now to exceed more than a hundred) imposing personal liability on directors for the company's debts, and are agitating for relief. In a number of high profile cases directors have resigned en masse on the eve of a company's bankruptcy because of the spectre of personal liability (it is probably too late at that stage); lawyers are also cautioning clients about the downside of becoming directors. Indemnity insurance ("D & O insurance") is available to protect officers and directors against personal liability, but it is expensive and there is a substantial deductible. See further Ron Daniels, "Must Boards Go Overboard? An Economic Analysis of the Effect of Burgeoning Statutory Liability on the Role of Directors in Corporate Governance" (1995), 24 C.B.L.J. 229.

Employees' pursuit of directors for unpaid wages is in part a reflection of the low preference which unpaid wages enjoy in bankruptcy. See *Bankruptcy and Insolvency Act*, s. 136(1). In particular, wages claims are subordinated to security interests in favour of lenders and others granted by a company prior to its bankruptcy. To remedy the position two solutions have been canvassed since 1970. One is to give wage claims superpriority status in bankruptcy. The other is to create a federally operated wage earner protection fund similar to the fund existing in many Western European countries. See Donald J.M. Brown, *Final Report of the Commission of Inquiry into Wage Protection in Insolvency Situations* (Ontario, Min. of Labour, Oct. 1985). Bill C-22 of 1991, which enacted important amendments to the *Bankruptcy and Insolvency Act*, provided for such a fund but, because of widespread opposition, it was dropped in the enacted version of the bill. See Ziegel, "How Can We Throw in the Towel Over a Measly 10 cents a Week?", *The Globe & Mail*, 26 Dec. 1991. In the most recent discussion of the issue, a Senate of Canada Committee has recommended that unpaid wages and vacation pay should have superpriority over secured claims against an employer's inventory and accounts up to a maximum of

$2,000 or one pay period per employee claim. See Standing Senate Committee on Banking and Commerce, 15th Report, *Debtors and Creditors Sharing the Burden: A review of the Bankruptcy and Insolvency Act and the Companies' Creditors Arrangement Act,* Nov. 3, 2003, pp. 87–96.

ADGA Systems International Ltd. v. Valcom Ltd.
(1999), 43 O.R. (3d) 101, 1999 CarswellOnt 29 (C.A.)

CARTHY J.A. (for the Court): This appeal presents for consideration once again the troublesome issue of the liability of officers and directors of a corporation for acts done in pursuance of a corporate purpose.

The plaintiff, ADGA Systems International Ltd., has claimed that a competitor, the defendant Valcom Ltd., raided its employees and caused the plaintiff economic damage. The plaintiff also claims against three of its own employees for breach of fiduciary duty in acceding to the importunes of Valcom Ltd. The issue in controversy on this particular appeal is the claim by the plaintiff against the director and two employees of Valcom Ltd. for their personal involvement in this recruitment program. Those three defendants brought a motion for summary judgment seeking to dismiss the claim against them. The motion was dismissed by Mercier J. The Divisional Court then heard an appeal from that order, allowed the appeal, and dismissed the claim against those three defendants. The plaintiff now appeals to this court and seeks to justify proceeding to trial against MacPherson, the Director of Valcom Ltd. and Ewing and McKenzie, senior employees of Valcom Ltd. The question is whether the respondents can be sued for their actions as individuals, assuming those actions were genuinely directed to the best interests of their corporate employer. In my view a cause of action does exist against the respondents and a trial is required to determine the merits of that action

* * *

Analysis

* * *

My first observation is that I recognize the policy concern expressed by the Divisional Court, and other General Division judges, over the proliferation of claims against officers and directors of corporations in circumstances which give the appearance of the desire for discovery or leverage in the litigation process. This is a proper concern because business cannot function efficiently if corporate officers and directors are inhibited in carrying on a corporate business because of a fear of being inappropriately swept into lawsuits, or, worse, are driven away from involvement in any respect in corporate business by the potential exposure to ill-founded litigation. That being said, it is not appropriate to extend the reasoning of

ScotiaMcLeod[5] beyond its intended application by reading it as protecting all conduct by officers and employees in pursuit of corporate purposes. The common law should not develop on an ad hoc basis to put out fires. When a policy issue arises, here from modern business realities, the courts must proceed on a principled basis to establish a framework for further development which recognizes the new realities but preserves the fundamental purpose served by that area of law. For this reason I intend to analyze the development of law in this field from its beginnings.

That beginning is found in the House of Lords' decision in *Salomon v. Salomon & Co. Ltd.*, [1895-9] All E.R. 33 (H.L.), which established that a company, once legally incorporated, must be treated like any other independent person, with rights and liabilities appropriate to itself. From time to time, litigants have sought to lift this "corporate veil", by seeking to make principals of the corporation liable for the obligations of the corporation. However, where, as here, the plaintiff relies upon establishing an independent cause of action against the principals of the company, the corporate veil is not threatened and the *Salomon* principle remains intact.

The distinction between an independent cause of action and looking through the corporation was confirmed by the subsequent case of *Said v. Butt*, [1920] 3 K.B. 497. This is a King's Bench decision but has been adopted in Canada and throughout the United States. (See, for instance, *Kepic v. Tecumseh Road Builders* (1987), 18 C.C.E.L. 218 at p. 222, 23 O.A.C. 72; and *Golden v. Anderson*, 64 Cal.Rptr. 404 (1967) at p. 408.)

In *Said v. Butt*, the plaintiff was engaged in a dispute with an opera company which refused to sell him tickets to a performance. The plaintiff purchased a ticket through an agent and when he appeared at the opera the defendant, an employee of the opera company recognized him and ejected him. The plaintiff sued the employee for wrongfully procuring the company to break a contract made by the company to sell the plaintiff a ticket.

The court held that there was no contract because the company would not knowingly have sold a ticket to the plaintiff. Nevertheless, on the assumption that there was a contract, the court considered the implications to the defendant employee. McCardie J. stated at p. 504:

> It is well to point out that Sir Alfred Butt possessed the widest powers as the chairman and sole managing director of the Palace Theatre, Ld. He clearly acted within those powers when he directed that the plaintiff should be refused admission on December 23. I am satisfied, also, that he meant to act and did act *bona fide* for the protection of the interests of his company. If, therefore, the plaintiff, assuming that a contract existed between the company and himself, can sue the defendant for wrongfully procuring a breach of that contract, the gravest and widest consequences must ensue.

---

[5] *Montreal Trust Co. of Canada v. ScotiaMcLeod Inc.* (1995), 26 O.R. (3d) 481 (C.A.).

After detailing the mischief that would flow from permitting such claims to be made McCardie J. concluded at p. 506:

> I hold that if a servant acting *bona fide* within the scope of his authority procures or causes the breach of a contract between his employer and a third person, he does not thereby become liable to an action of tort at the suit of the person whose contract has thereby been broken . . . Nothing that I have said to-day is, I hope, inconsistent with the rule that a director or a servant who actually takes part in or actually authorizes such torts as assault, trespass to property, nuisance, or the like may be liable in damages as a joint participant in one of such recognized heads of tortious wrong.

For present purposes, I extract the following from McCardie J.'s reasons. First, this is not an application of Salomon. That case is not mentioned anywhere in the reasons. Second, it provides an exception to the general rule that persons are responsible for their own conduct. That exception has since gained acceptance because it assures that persons who deal with a limited company and accept the imposition of limited liability will not have available to them both a claim for breach of contract against a company and a claim for tortious conduct against the director with damages assessed on a different basis. The exception also assures that officers and directors, in the process of carrying on business, are capable of directing that a contract of employment be terminated or that a business contract not be performed on the assumed basis that the company's best interest is to pay the damages for failure to perform. By carving out the exception for these policy reasons, the court has emphasized and left intact the general liability of any individual for personal conduct.

The third point of interest arises from this excerpt from the reasons at p. 505:

> The explanation of the breadth of the language used in the decisions probably lies in the fact that in every one of the sets of circumstances before the Court the person who procured the breach of contract was in fact a stranger, that is a third person, who stood wholly outside the area of the bargain made between the two contracting parties. If he is in the position of a stranger, he will be prima facie liable, even though he may act honestly, or without malice, or in the best interests of himself; or even if he acts as an altruist, seeking only the good of another . . .

The court was there referring to the stranger as the wrongdoer but the same principle might be applied in the converse situation where the stranger is the victim. This suggestion, was picked up later in the dissenting reasons of La Forest J. in *London Drugs Ltd. v. Kuehne & Nagel International Ltd.*, *infra*, to the effect that a jurisprudential division line might be drawn between those who contract with the company, or voluntarily deal with it, and can be taken to have accepted limited liability, and strangers to the company whose only concern is not to be harmed by the conduct of others. On that theory, those harmed as strangers to the corporate body naturally look for liability to the persons who caused the harm and those who have in some manner accepted limited liability in their dealings with the company would be limited in recourse to the company. As evidenced by the decision in *London Drugs v. Kuehne* that theory of demarcation of liability has not been adopted in Canada.

The consistent line of authority in Canada holds simply that, in all events, officers, directors and employees of corporations are responsible for their tortious conduct even though that conduct was directed in a *bona fide* manner to the best interests of the company, always subject to the *Said v. Butt* exception.

In *Lewis v. Boutilier* (1919), 52 D.L.R. 383 at p. 389 (S.C.C.), the president of a company was held personally liable for negligently putting a boy to work in a dangerous area of a sawmill where he was killed. It was held to be no defence to the president that the corporation that owned the sawmill might also be liable.

In *Berger v. Willowdale A.M.C.* (1983), 41 O.R. (2d) 89 at p. 98, 145 D.L.R. (3d) 247 (C.A.) . . . this court dealt with a claim by an employee against the president of her employer corporation for damages arising from slipping on an icy sidewalk. Under the *Workmen's Compensation Act*, employees could not be sued for such workplace accidents. However, executives were excluded from the definition of employees under the *Workmen's Compensation Act*. The court held that, given the existence of a duty of care owed by the president to this employee, and a failure to respond appropriately to that duty, damages against the president were recoverable even though the action against the company was barred by the provisions of the *Workmen's Compensation Act*. The fact that the duty of care co-existed in the employer and president did not constitute a bar to a claim against the executive officer.

In *Sullivan v. Desrosiers* (1986), 76 N.B.R. (2d) 271 (C.A.) . . . the plaintiffs were surrounding landowners of a hog farm who claimed that their lands had been polluted by a manure lagoon on the site of the farm. The issue before the Court of Appeal was whether the owner of the company could be held personally liable.

At p. 277 Hoyt J.A. stated:

The question here is whether Mr. Sullivan, who was the manager and principal employee of the company that committed the nuisance, may be responsible along with the company. I see no reason why, because of his involvement in creating and maintaining the nuisance, Mr. Sullivan should not also be responsible.

And at p. 278:

Nor am I attracted to the submission that Mr. Sullivan is protected by reason of the rule in *Salomon v. Salomon & Co.*, [1897] A.C. 22. The question here, as I have pointed out, is not whether Mr. Sullivan was acting on behalf of or even if he "was" the company, but whether a legal barrier, here a company, can be erected between a person found to be a wrongdoer and an injured party thereby relieving the wrongdoer of his liability. In my opinion, once it is determined that a person breaches a duty owed to neighbouring landowners not to interfere with their reasonable enjoyment of their property, liability may be imposed on him and he may not escape by saying that as well as being a wrongdoer he is also a company manager or employee.

The Supreme Court of Canada again considered the issue of an employee's liability for acts done in the course of his duties on behalf of the employer in *London Drugs Ltd. v. Kuehne & Nagel International Ltd.*, [1992] 3 S.C.R. 299, 97 D.L.R. (4th) 261. The plaintiff delivered a transformer to a warehouse company for storage. An employee of the warehouse company negligently permitted the transformer to topple over, causing extensive damage. Even though there was a contractual relationship between the company and the customer, the majority held in favour of the claim against the employee.

Iacobucci J. stated at pp. 407-08:

There is no general rule in Canada to the effect that an employee acting in the course of his or her employment and performing the "very essence" of his or her employer's contractual obligations with a customer does not owe a duty of care, whether one labels it "independent" or otherwise, to the employer's customer . . .

The mere fact that the employee is performing the "very essence" of a contract between the plaintiff and his or her employer does not, in itself, necessarily preclude a conclusion that a duty of care was present.

La Forest J. dissented on this issue and was prepared to relieve the employee from personal liability in tort where the tort occurred in the context of a breach of contract between the employer and the customer, and so long as the employee's tort was in the course of duties. His analysis of the distinction between the voluntary and involuntary creditor is, and will continue to be, of interest as policy questions impact upon the evolving jurisprudence in this area. At p. 349 he stated:

The distinction between voluntary and involuntary creditors is also useful in this area. As commentators have pointed out (Halpern, Trebilcock and Turnbull, "An Economic Analysis of Limited Liability in Corporation Law" (1980), 30 U.T.L.J. 117), different types of claimants against the corporation have differing abilities to benefit from being put on notice with respect to the impact of the limited liability regime. At one end, creditors like bond holders and banks are generally well situated to evaluate the risks of default and to contract accordingly. These "voluntary" creditors can be considered to be capable of protecting themselves from the consequences of a limited liability regime and the practically systematic recourse by banks to personal guarantees by the principals of small companies attests to that fact.

At the other end of the spectrum are classic involuntary tort creditors exemplified by a plaintiff who is injured when run down by an employee driving a motorcar. These involuntary creditors are those who never chose to enter into a course of dealing with the company and correspond to what I have termed as the classic vicarious liability claimant.

These Canadian authorities at the appellate level confirm clearly that employees, officers and directors will be held personally liable for tortious conduct causing physical injury, property damage, or a nuisance even when their actions are pursuant to their duties to the corporation.

* * *

Although the jurisprudence on this subject has followed a very straight path since the decisions in *Salomon v. Salomon* and *Said v. Butt*, in recent years in this jurisdiction judges hearing motions to dismiss claims have tended to smudge these principles, inspired, in my view, and as expressed by them, by the legitimate concern as to the number of cases in which employees, officers, and directors are joined for questionable purposes. The assumption has filtered into reasons for judgment that the employee is absolved if acting in the interests of the corporation, the employer, even in cases that do not raise the *Said v. Butt* defence.

An immediate example is found in the reasons of the Divisional Court in this case where at p. 214 of the reasons it is stated:

There was no evidence to show that what these appellants did was to further their own interests in any respect. All evidence points to the fact that their actions were done as part of their duties of employment and to further the interests of Valcom.

The judgment then proceeds to analyze the jurisprudence in support of the above conclusion. Dealing with the appellate authorities referred to by the Divisional Court, the first is *Craik v. Aetna Life Insurance Co. of Canada*, [1995] O.J. No. 3286 (Gen. Div.), Court File No. 95-CQ-64403, affirmed by the Court of Appeal [1996] O.J. No. 2377. The facts are somewhat similar to those before this court, but the decision of Cumming J. and the oral endorsement of this court appear to pivot on the fact that the pleadings asserted that the corporation acted tortiously but did not assert that the employees acted in any personal capacity. The claim against the employees was struck out.

* * *

The Divisional Court placed its prime reliance on the judgment in *ScotiaMcLeod Inc.* and in doing so created a much broader canvass for the reasoning of this court than it was, by its language, intended to fill. That case concerned whether a reasonable cause of action was pleaded against certain individual directors of the defendant company. The plaintiff's complaint was that, as a result of certain filing statements, it had been misled into making investments in the defendant corporation's debentures.

The dismissal of the claim against what I will call a group of non-active directors was upheld because the pleading did not allege any negligence against them. The plaintiff sought to hold those directors vicariously liable for the negligence of the corporation, and no attempt was made in the pleading to single out their activities as individuals. This is similar to the situation in *Craik v. Aetna, supra.* On the other hand, two of the directors who had attended and made representations at a due diligence meeting were alleged to have been directly and personally involved in the marketing of the debentures and to have made representations which were relied upon by the plaintiffs. The action against those active directors was permitted to go to trial.

An excerpt from the reasoning of Finlayson J.A. in *ScotiaMcLeod Inc.*, at pp. 490-91 O.R., pp. 720-21 D.L.R., has been quoted from time to time by General Division judges and, here, by the Divisional Court, as suggesting some limitation on the liability of directors and officers who are acting in the course of their duties:

> The decided cases in which employees and officers of companies have been found personally liable for actions ostensibly carried out under a corporate name are fact-specific. In the absence of findings of fraud, deceit, dishonesty or want of authority on the part of employees or officers, they are also rare. Those cases in which the corporate veil has been pierced usually involve transactions where the use of the corporate structure was a sham from the outset or was an afterthought to a deal which had gone sour. There is also a considerable body of case-law wherein injured parties to actions for breach of contract have attempted to extend liability to the principals of the company by pleading that the principals were privy to the tort of inducing breach of contract between the company and the plaintiff: see *Ontario Store Fixtures Inc. v. Mmmuffins Inc.* (1989), 70 O.R. (2d) 42 (H.J.C.), and the cases referred to therein. Additionally there have been attempts by injured parties to attach liability to the principals of failed businesses through insolvency litigation. In every case, however, the facts giving rise to personal liability were specifically pleaded. Absent allegations which fit within the categories described above, officers or employees

of limited companies are protected from personal liability unless it can be shown that their actions are themselves tortious or exhibit a separate identity or interest from that of the company so as to make the act or conduct complained of their own.

The operative portion of this paragraph is the final sentence which confirms that, where properly pleaded, officers or employees can be liable for tortious conduct even when acting in the course of duty. That this is clearly the intent of what was being stated is evidenced by the conclusion that the action should proceed against two defendants; against whom negligent conduct had been properly pleaded. The reasoning of *ScotiaMcLeod* has been recently applied by this court in decisions which confirm my interpretation.

* * *

Conclusion

It is my conclusion that there is no principled basis for protecting the director and employees of Valcom from liability for their alleged conduct on the basis that such conduct was in pursuance of the interests of the corporation. It may be that for policy reasons the law as to the allocation of responsibility for tortious conduct should be adjusted to provide some protection to employees, officers or directors, or all of them, in limited circumstances where, for instance, they are acting in the best interests of the corporation with parties who have voluntarily chosen to accept the ambit of risk of a limited liability company. However, the creation of such a policy should not evolve from the facts of this case where the alleged conduct was intentional and the only relationship between the corporate parties was as competitors. Any such evolution should await facts which are apposite to the policy concerns and should probably be articulated as a definitive extension of the defence in *Said v. Butt*. Such a development would be in the direction indicated by La Forest J. in his dissenting reasons in London Drugs and thus may have to await further consideration by the Supreme Court. In the meantime the courts can only be scrupulous in weeding out claims that are improperly pleaded or where the evidence does not justify an allegation of a personal tort. A principled development of jurisprudence is the tradition and the strength of the common law and must take precedence over incidental attempts to abuse the law as it develops.

* * *

Appeal allowed.

Notes and Questions

1 For a searching examination of the reasoning in *ADGA Systems* see "Workshop Presentations: Directors' and Officers' Liability" (2001) 35 C.B.L.J. 1-71. Given Carthy J.A.'s explanation of the basis of

McCardie J.'s decision in *Said v. Butt*, why was the same reasoning not also applied by the Supreme Court in *London Drugs* to exempt the negligent employee from personal liability? From a policy perspective, is there a difference between protecting a director against liability for causing the company to breach its contract and protecting an employee who accidentally drops goods in a warehouse belonging to a customer of his employer? If the underlying concern is that the employer may be judgment-proof and that holding the employee liable will encourage an employer to carry insurance, why does the same reasoning not apply to the director in *Said v. Butt*?

2 In *Williams v. Natural Life Health Foods Ltd.*, [1998] 1 W.L.R. 830 (H.L.), the plaintiff acquired a franchise from the defendant company for the operation of a health food shop. Prior to signing the contract, the company sent the plaintiffs detailed financial projections in the preparation of which the second defendant had played a prominent part. The plaintiffs did not know the second defendant and had little contact with him before the contract was signed. The turnover from the plaintiffs' franchise was much less than predicted by the company and the plaintiffs sued both the company and the second defendant for negligent representation relying on the rule in *Hedley Byrne*. The action against the second defendant failed. The House of Lords held, reversing the Court of Appeal, that to establish the liability of a director or employee for negligent representation a plaintiff had to show an assumption of personal responsibility by the director or employee. That burden had not been discharged in the present case. Does the judgment have wider implications or is it only further evidence of the House of Lords' reluctance to expand the scope of liability for economic torts?

HALPERN, TREBILCOCK AND TURNBULL,
An Economic Analysis of Limited Liability in Corporation Law
(1980), 30 U.T.L.J. 117, 147–150 (footnotes omitted)

We now attempt to derive some implications from the foregoing analysis for the form of an efficient liability regime for corporations.

First, in the case of large, widely held companies, a limited liability regime, as a general rule, is the most efficient regime. By skewing the distribution of business risks amongst different shareholders, an unlimited liability regime would create a significant measure of uncertainty in the valuation of securities and threaten the existence of organized securities markets, thus inducing costly attempts by creditors and owners to transact around the regime. The case for a limited liability regime for this class of company is very compelling. The attenuated nature of the moral hazard factor in widely held companies does not create a strong countervailing consideration.

Second, in the case of small, tightly held companies, a limited liability regime will, in many cases, create incentives for owners to exploit a moral hazard and transfer uncompensated business risks to creditors, thus inducing costly attempts by creditors to reduce these risks. An unlimited liability regime for this class of enterprise (perhaps the 'private company', recognized by mainly corporation statutes with respect to financial disclosure and securities regulation exemptions, having fewer than, say, fifty shareholders, restrictions on share transfers, and no right to make public offering) would seem to be the most efficient regime. The availability of an organized securities market is not, of course, a major countervailing factor with this class of company.

A major effect of adopting an unlimited liability regime in this context would be to shift to the corporation and its owners the onus of proposing contractual arrangements to creditors which limit the liability of the owners — (where these are desired). Requiring explicit negotiation of such arrangements is likely to improve flows to creditors about allocation of risks and sharpen the focus of creditors' incentives to monitor a corporation's activities. We acknowledge that the case for an unlimited liability regime for this class of company is not as compelling as the case for limited liability for large, widely held companies, given that in the former case, with fewer parties involved, most creditors and owners can contract around either regime at low cost, thus making the choice of liability regime relatively inconsequential. We also recognize that difficulties may be associated with attempting to distinguish by law small from large corporations for the purpose of applying different liability regimes, and that the distinction may induct some perverse and wasteful incentive effects as firms seek to manipulate internal structures to ensure compliance with the requirements of the preferred regime. However, our empirical intuition remains that, on balance, an unlimited liability regime is the most efficient regime for small, closely held companies.

Third, in cases where, as a general rule, a limited liability regime is the most efficient regime (large, widely held corporations, in our analysis), there is a case for a limited number of exceptions to the regime where some form of unlimited liability seems desirable. These exceptions might embrace the following classes of case:

A. MISREPRESENTATION

An exception is called for in the case of misrepresentations to creditors as to the legal status of a firm or its financial affairs, as in *Royal Stores v. Brown* and *Pacific Rim Installations Ltd. v. Tilt-Up Construction Ltd.* Here the party responsible for the misrepresentation should be personally liable for corporate debts induced by the misrepresentation, but, in addition, as we elaborate below, the directors of the corporation might be made personally liable (subject to offsetting insurance of compensation arrangements) to strengthen management incentives to have this form of behaviour monitored by corporate officers and employees.

B. THE INVOLUNTARY CREDITOR

In cases such as *Walkovsky v. Carlton*, transaction costs are such that a firm can transfer uncompensated business risks to this class of creditor. *Rockwell Developments Ltd. v. Newtonbrook Plaza Ltd.*, where a firm unilaterally imposed costs on another party through unmeritorious legal proceedings, involved similar considerations. Again, it can be argued that the directors of the company should be personally liable to this class of creditor. In the large, widely held corporation where this exception would apply, such a rule would minimize the information costs that owners would face in monitoring each other's wealth, would reduce creditors' transaction costs in enforcing claims, and would focus incentives to adopt cost-justified avoidance precautions on that body of persons (the directors) in such a class of corporation best able to respond to those incentives.

C. THE EMPLOYEE

Amongst corporate creditors, employees, as a class, probably face the most severe informational disabilities, have the least ability to diversify risk of business failure, and may have the strongest equity argument (in terms of relative capacity to absorb losses). This proposition is not universally true, as some employees will possess both superior information on corporate finances and high job mobility (*e.g.*, corporate executives and professional employees), while some trade creditors may be afflicted with similar disabilities to those of the less informed, less mobile corporate employees. However, fashioning a rule that clearly differentiates these situations is likely to be difficult, and present rules governing the liability of directors for limited amounts of unpaid wages of "employees" in the *Canada Business Corporation Act* may represent defensible approximations of optimal rules.

The net effect of these proposals would seem to be to obviate the need for the elaborate veil-piercing, subrogation, and consolidation rules in corporate bankruptcies advocated by Landers. In the case of small, tightly held corporations, the unlimited liability regime which we have proposed would seem responsive to many of the parent-subsidiary and affiliated company problems with which he is concerned. In the case of large, widely held companies, involuntary creditors and employees, under our proposals, receive special protection. Other creditors, prejudiced by intra-group transactions induced by moral hazard considerations, would have to rely on the misrepresentation exception. This exception is necessarily a much more limited response to creditor problems than the unlimited liability regime proposed for small, closely held corporations because any substantial move in the direction of unlimited liability in the case of large, widely held companies will engender the kind of costs that have led us generally to reject such a regime in this case. Our proposals would also contemplate as unnecessary and undesirable many of the provisions in the federal *Bankruptcy Act* and the new Bankruptcy Bill with respect to "reviewable transactions" and the liability of corporate Agents. The operational uncertainty (and consequent costs) associated with these provisions would be reduced under the relatively straightforward rules that we have proposed.

Note

The authors refer to several well known Canadian and American authorities on lifting the corporate veil. Some of these are reproduced in the section that follows. The Halpern article and the phenomenon of mass torts have provoked a strong revival of interest in the rationales of limited liability in close and publicly held corporations and in the question of when it is appropriate to deny the benefits of limited liability, particularly in the context of claims by involuntary creditors. See, *inter alia*, Easterbrook & Fischel, "Limited Liability and the Corporation" (1985), 52 U. Chi. L. Rev. 89; Hansmann & Kraakman, "Toward Unlimited Shareholder Liability for Corporate Torts" (1991) 100 Yale L.J. 1879; and Grundfest, "The Limited Future of Unlimited Liability: A Capital Markets Perspective" (1992), 102 Yale L.J. 387. On the Hansmann-Kraakman proposal, see the notes following *Walkovsky v. Carlton* in the next section of this chapter.

4. LIFTING THE CORPORATE VEIL

It will be obvious from the ease with which legislators allow corporations to be created that the doctrine of *Salomon* can be easily abused and corporate personality can be used as a veil behind which to shield conduct prejudicial to the corporation's creditors and others. This section explores the extent to which the courts have been willing to pierce the corporate veil even without the aid of specific statutory authority to do so. Commentators have long despaired of finding a single or coherent principle to explain the judicial response. Nevertheless, in studying the cases that follow, students will find it helpful to distinguish between the following types of case:

(i)   those involving allegations of fraudulent conduct on the part of the company's principals;

(ii)   those where the company was clearly undercapitalized to meet its foreseeable financial needs;

(iii)   those involving tort claims against the company;

(iv)   cases where the company was not incorporated for *bona fide* business reasons but for other reasons, typically to take advantage of tax loopholes; and

(v)   non-arm's length transactions between parent and subsidiary companies.

The student is of course welcome to construct his/her own taxonomy!

Clarkson Co. Ltd. v. Zhelka
64 D.L.R. (2d) 457, [1967] 2 O.R. 565 (H.C.)

Selkirk promoted, incorporated and controlled several companies, including St. George Developments Ltd., Langstaff Land Developments Ltd., Fidelity Real Estate Ltd., and Industrial Sites and Locations Ltd. In 1959, Industrial bought some land, and being without money or other assets at that time, paid for it in part with cash advanced by Langstaff and St. George. In 1960, Industrial conveyed the land to Zhelka, the sister of Selkirk, in return for a $120,000 promissory note. In 1961 Zhelka mortgaged the land to Gelberg, and when Gelberg began foreclosure action, part of the land was sold, and the cash applied to pay off the mortgage and a Province of Ontario tax lien. Interest adjustments paid to Zhelka somehow found their way into the bank account of Fidelity Real Estate.

Selkirk was adjudged a bankrupt in 1960, and the Clarkson Co. Ltd. was appointed as trustee in bankruptcy. Clarkson sought a declaration that the land, registered in the name of Zhelka, was held by Zhelka or by Industrial as trustee for Selkirk, alleging that Industrial was a mere agent and the alter ego of Selkirk, directed by Selkirk to the prejudice and confusion of his personal creditors.

THOMPSON J. (after stating the facts, continued): I unhesitatingly conclude that the conveyance to Miss Zhelka and the entire transaction with her was without consideration and voluntary and entered into with the intention of protecting the lands against resort thereto by the creditors and others having claims against Industrial. Undoubtedly, Selkirk was the moving factor behind the whole plan.

* * *

It is my view that there is a resulting trust in Industrial and that it never was intended that Miss Zhelka should take any beneficial interest in the property conveyed; and that despite the fact that she subsequently mortgaged the lands to Gelberg for the convenience of one of the associated companies.

I have no doubt that the conveyance is open to attack by the creditors of Industrial under the Statute of Elizabeth, 13 Eliz., c. 5, now the *Fraudulent Conveyances Act*, R.S.O. 1960, c. 154. The Court would not lend its assistance, however, to the grantor in the recovery of the property, were it sought by Industrial upon the principle of the maxim *in pari delicto, potior est conditio possidentis* . . .

Even if the plaintiff were successful in its contention that Industrial is merely the agent or the *alter ego* of Selkirk, it is doubtful whether the plaintiff claiming through Selkirk, the bankrupt, could acquire any greater rights than he could in the face of the maxim quoted. It is also questionable as to whether, in that event, it could avoid the transaction under the general policy of the bankruptcy law or as a "settlement" within the meaning of s. 60 of the *Bankruptcy Act*, R.S.C. 1952, c. 14. It would, however in such event, be open to attack by the trustee as a conveyance fraudulent as against creditors of the debtor.

These considerations, however, become academic by reason of the fact that the plaintiff does not attack the transaction as a settlement or otherwise under the *Bankruptcy Act*, nor as a conveyance fraudulent against the debtor's creditors. The case is framed upon the premise that the property is held by the defendants or one of them as agent or trustee for the debtor and that it constitutes part of his estate or property passing to the plaintiff upon bankruptcy.

Such considerations become still more academic in the light of the view I ultimately adopt as to the relationship between the debtor Selkirk and Industrial.

There can be little doubt that the companies forming Selkirk's corporate structure were interrelated in the sense that there were transfers of assets from one to another or advances of money as between them, although none of them was a subsidiary of another in the true sense of the word.

It equally appears from the evidence that the only person to benefit financially from or to receive moneys arising from their operation was Selkirk himself.

The picture as to their procedures, however, is not altogether clear. The absence of records leaves substantial gaps in the evidence. Selkirk, himself, the one who, if he would, could have thrown much light upon the scene, was not called as a witness. Too much has been left to unsafe conjecture and frequently that which might have developed into proof has become arrested on the border of suspicion.

* * *

The evidence clearly demonstrates that George A. Selkirk always had and retained in fact complete control over all these companies upon which the evidence touches. He dictated the corporate policy in each case and was the moving and directing force in all of their business operations. The directors and officers, and particularly in the case of Industrial, were his nominees, including members of his immediate household and family, and were subject to his influence and I have no doubt to his domination. To all intents and purposes Industrial and its associated companies were one-man companies.

In reaching such conclusions, I am, I may say, quite uninfluenced by any alleged admissions or statements said to have been made by Selkirk. There are instances throughout the evidence of statements alleged to have been made to others by him. He is not a party to the action and such could not form admissible evidence for the plaintiff. Either one must consider them as entirely hearsay or as self-serving statements.

We are here, of course, primarily concerned only with Selkirk's relationship to Industrial. His connection with the other companies and their interconnection with Industrial is only of importance in so far as it may tend to establish a pattern of conduct. Industrial, despite its default in Government returns and irregularity in its proceedings, was regularly incorporated and has been kept alive as a corporate entity. Its charter has not been revoked under s. 326 [am. 1964, c. 10, s. 8] of the *Corporations Act*, R.S.O. 1960, c. 71, although, apparently, it has been under departmental investigation. In 1963, it was still being taxed and some $14,000 levied against it under the *Corporations Tax Act* (ex. 21).

There is no evidence to indicate that when Industrial was incorporated in 1958, that Selkirk was insolvent; and nowhere is evidence to be found tracing any of Selkirk's personal assets into the hands of Industrial. The only indication that any of his personal assets passed into any of his companies is in the dictum in *Selkirk v. M.N.R.* earlier referred to. There is no intimation that at that time Selkirk was insolvent or that the transfer was in any way irregular or questionable. It does appear that later the Langstaff company advanced moneys to Industrial, but by the same token, it appears that Industrial still later advanced or repaid to Langstaff an approximately equal sum. I can see nothing unlawful or illegal per se, as against the personal creditors of Selkirk, in these interchanges of funds between companies. Even if there were an unlawful element, the only persons who were injured or damnified would be the shareholders or creditors of the companies involved. It is true that Selkirk has benefited personally from activities of his companies in dealings or transactions of questionable validity.

Industrial seldom had a bank account. Rental from the buildings upon the lands in question was received by his nominee or nominees rather than by Industrial. None of it, however, has been traced into his own hands, although one might suspect that some of it at least did reach him. In any event, only a small portion of it accrued due and was paid before his bankruptcy.

Fidelity Real Estate Ltd. appears recently to be the only one of the companies operating with a bank account and Industrial was indirectly the recipient of some of its funds.

The moneys paid to Miss Zhelka upon the settlement of the Gelberg action, some $9,249, went into the Fidelity bank account. These were really the funds of Industrial. Out of that account were paid some of Selkirk's personal bills for clothing, a retaining fee to a solicitor acting for him upon a criminal charge or charges of fraud pending against him and a sum offered by him by way of restitution in connection with such charge.

Whether Selkirk was entitled to moneys by way of salary or otherwise from Fidelity does not appear. If he was, at the time of such payments, a director of Fidelity as he once was, and the moneys were merely a loan or an advance to him, the transaction of course would fall within the prohibition of the *Corporations Act* respecting loans to shareholders.

The sum and substance of all this is that Selkirk has received some comparatively minor benefits from the operation of his companies and at times in a manner which, so far as regularity is concerned, is questionable. An aura of suspicion has been cast about him. I have no doubt that where his personal advantage is concerned he would go a long way.

But the question remains, in what way has his association with his corporate offspring injured, defeated or prejudiced his personal creditors? Apart from a small portion of the rents which he may have received, if any, from the buildings on the Steeles Ave. lands, it would appear that all benefits have accrued since his bankruptcy and really fall into the category of after-acquired property, to which recourse by the trustee is under the provisions of the *Bankruptcy Act.*

This is not a case where a debtor or a prospective debtor has transferred his own assets to a corporation of his making for the purpose of avoiding existing personal liabilities or obligations; nor is it a case where he has personally made a secret or clandestine profit by such a transfer.

There is here no claim of complaint by any creditor, if such there now be, of Industrial or its associated companies, nor by any director or shareholder.

In a critical analysis of the situation, one asks oneself just where is any fraud upon Selkirk's personal creditors being perpetrated by the operation of his companies and his conduct with relation thereto? To me the evidence falls short of establishing that.

No doubt his creditors are disappointed at their inability to have access to his corporate assets and particularly where he himself is reaping some financial benefit therefrom. But that must of necessity be, so long as the Legislature provides for and encourages the formation of private corporations. Without such, of course, enterprise and business adventure would be stifled. Limited liability is one of the landmarks of incorporation.

The plaintiff as trustee in bankruptcy for some reason apparently has not seen fit to follow any funds reaching the hands of his debtor as after-acquired property nor to intervene with respect thereto.

The cases in which the Courts, both in this Province and in England, have seen fit to disregard the corporate entity or personality, and instead to consider the economic realities behind the legal facade, fall within a narrow compass. The Legislature, in the fields of revenue and taxation, and particularly with respect to true subsidiaries, has made much greater departure in this respect. Such cases as there are, illustrate no consistent principle. The only principle laid down is that in the leading case of *Salomon v. Salomon & Co., Ltd.,* [1897] A.C. 22; and in general such principle has been rigidly applied. Briefly stated, it is that the legal persona created by incorporation is an entity distinct from its shareholders and directors and that even in the case of a one man company, the company is not an alias for the owner.

The exceptions would appear to represent refusals to apply the logic of the *Salomon* case where it would be flagrantly opposed to justice.

Counsel have presented me with an exhaustive review of these authorities. I can see no useful purpose in here reiterating it. The conclusions to be drawn from the cases as a whole were well stated by Mr. Justice Masten in his article on "'One Man Companies' and their Controlling Shareholders" at 14 Can. Bar Rev. 663 (1936), where he discusses the authorities.

In questions of property and capacity, of acts done and rights acquired or liabilities assumed, the company is always an entity distinct from its corporators. It is not an alias or a sham and the principle of the *Salomon* case stands unimpaired.

If a company is formed for the express purpose of doing a wrongful or unlawful act, or, if when formed, those in control expressly direct a wrongful thing to be done, the individuals as well as the company are responsible to those to whom liability is legally owed.

In such cases, or where the company is the mere agent of a controlling corporator, it may be said that the company is a sham, cloak or *alter ego*, but otherwise it should not be so termed.

Whether an individual has constituted the company his agent is a question of fact in each case. A controlling or total share interest does not in itself establish such agency. Due regard must be had to law of principal and agent relating to the formation of the relationship.

Although the instant case may be close to the line, the plaintiff has failed to satisfy me that I should declare Industrial to be his *alter ego* or his mere agent for the conduct of his personal business or for the purposes of the conveyance in question to the defendant Zhelka. In the result, the action must be dismissed.

As I have previously intimated, I think the defendant Zhelka has invited these proceedings. I fail to see how the plaintiff, as trustee for the creditors of Selkirk, could afford to stand idly by in the face of her earlier statement in the Gotfried action that she was holding the lands in question for her brother. It was, as events have proven, a false statement, or at least a totally irresponsible one; but the plaintiff in my view on the strength of it was justified in seeking judicial investigation of the whole matter.

In view of the relationship between the defendants and of the fact that the alternative plea by the corporate defendant that Miss Zhelka holds the lands in trust for it is virtually a plea asserting its own fraud against its creditors, I do not feel that it should have costs.

Judgment for defendant.

Notes and Questions

1   In the light of the exceptions to the *Salomon* principle referred to in his judgment and illustrated by the later materials in this section, was Thomson J. correct in claiming that "[i]n questions of property and capacity . . . the company is always an entity distinct from its corpora-tors", and that it is only if a company is formed "*for the express purpose*" of doing a wrongful or unlawful act that the corporate veil will be lifted (italics added)? *Cf.* Thomson J.'s cautious attitude with Lord Denning's much more robust approach in *Littlewoods Mail Order Stores Ltd. v. Inland Revenue Commissioners*, [1969] 3 All E.R. 855. Lord Denning said:

> The doctrine laid down in *Salomon v. Salomon & Co. Ltd.* has to be watched very carefully. It has often been supposed to cast a veil over the personality of a limited company through which the courts cannot see. But that is not true. The courts can and often do draw aside the veil. They can, and often do, pull off the mask. They look to see what really lies behind. The legislature has shown the way with group accounts and the rest. And the courts should follow suit.

2 Given Selkirk's disregard of the separateness of his various corporations, should the court have treated them as one entity in claims by creditors of one of the associated corporations? Would this be unfair to the creditors of the other corporations, or would it depend on whether they thought they were dealing with that particular corporation, a group of corporations, or Selkirk personally? See the notes following *De Salaberry Realties Ltd. v. M.N.R.*, *infra* this section, and in particular the decision in *Stone v. Eacho*, 127 F. 2d 284 (4th Cir. 1942).

3 There have been a substantial number of cases over the past 25 years in which Canadian courts have lifted the corporate veil in order to reach a wrongdoer. See *e.g. Oasis Hotel Ltd. & Surowiec v. Zurich Ins. Co.* (1981), 28 B.C.L.R. 230 (C.A.); *Sask. Economic Dev. Corp. v. Patterson-Boyd Mfg. Corp.*, [1981] 2 W.W.R. 40 (C.A.); and *Manley Inc. v. Fallis* (1977), 2 B.L.R. 277 (Ont. C.A.), In *Big Bend Hotel Ltd. v. Security Mut. Casualty Co.*, [19 B.C.L.R. 102 (S.C.), a fire damaged a hotel and its contents and a claim for compensation was brought against the hotel's insurance company. The hotel company had failed to disclose in its application for insurance that its principal shareholder had previously suffered a fire loss and that a fire insurance policy issued to him had been cancelled. In denying the plaintiff's claim, Callaghan J. reasoned as follows:

> Applying the test set out in *Gore Mutual, supra,* to the evidence led in this case, I have concluded that the insurers, if they had known of the prior fire loss, would have declined to accept the risk.
>
> But the plaintiff submitted that the application was made on behalf of Big Bend Hotel Ltd. and that company had not previously sustained a fire loss and thus, even if there was "wickedness of mind" on the part of Vincent Kumar, that should make little difference as K & S Enterprises Limited, the owner of the Fort Hotel, was a separate legal entity. It was then submitted that the corporate veil should not be lifted and reliance was placed on the reasoning enunciated in *Salomon v. Salomon*, [1897] A.C. 22.
>
> On the whole, Canadian and English Courts rigidly adhere to the concept set out in *Salomon, supra,* that a corporation is an independent legal entity not to be identified with its shareholders.
>
> However, there are exceptions to the general rule and courts have lifted the corporate veil to take into account the actions of the

individual members, particularly in cases of improper conduct or fraud. In *Gilford Motor Company v. Holmes*, [1933] Ch. 935, the defendant had contracted with the plaintiff company, his former employer, not to solicit that company's customers. In order to avoid this undertaking the defendant formed a company and the company solicited the customers. The English Court of Appeal held that the plaintiff was entitled to an injunction against both the defendant and his company, notwithstanding that the company was not a party to the covenant, as the defendant company was a "mere cloak or sham".

In *Jones and another v. Lipman and another* (1962), 1 W.L.R. 832, the defendant tried to avoid completing an agreement to sell his house by conveying it to a company formed solely for that purpose. Russell J. stated at p. 836:

> The defendant company is the creature of the first defendant, a device and a sham, a mask which he holds before his face in an attempt to avoid recognition by the eye of equity.

* * *

Here, Vincent Kumar clearly omitted to disclose a fact which he knew was material to the insurers, and such failure to disclose is fraudulent. In these circumstances, it is appropriate to lift the corporate veil; equity will not allow an individual to use a company as a shield for improper conduct or fraud.

Rockwell Developments Ltd. v. Newtonbrook Plaza Ltd.

[1972] 3 O.R. 199, 27 D.L.R. (3d) 651, 1972 CarswellOnt 902 (C.A.)

ARNUP J.A. (for the Court): Samuel Kelner, a solicitor in Toronto, appeals from the order of Parker J., dated November 5, 1971, whereby Kelner was ordered to pay personally the defendant's costs of the action brought against it by Rockwell Developments Ltd. (hereafter "Rockwell"), which action, by a judgment of Parker J., dated March 19, 1970, was dismissed with costs payable by Rockwell to the defendant. The defendant moves to quash Kelner's appeal on the ground that no appeal lies to this Court from an order of Parker J., as to costs only, save by his leave, and an application made to Parker J., for leave to appeal was dismissed.

The appeal and the motion to quash do not fall into neat separate compartments. The power of Parker J., to make the order as to costs against Kelner is involved also in the question of whether there is a right to appeal from that order. I therefore state the facts which are involved in the consideration of both the motion to quash and the appeal itself.

For a number of years prior to 1967 Kelner, while practicing law with Mr. Irwin Cooper, had been interested in the purchase and development of real estate in Metropolitan Toronto. It was his practice to incorporate separate limited companies for each separate real estate development in which he became interested. Rockwell was a private Ontario company incorporated "in the 1950s" and "did a variety of business transactions from that time, from time to time". In 1967 it had outstanding 26 common shares, one held by Kelner, one by Cooper, one by a girl in their law office, and 23 by Planet Development Corporation Limited. It is Kelner's evidence that the shares held by the three individuals, who were also the directors, were held in trust for Planet Development Corporation Ltd., and that he in turn was the beneficial owner of all of the shares of Planet.

In 1967 Kelner became interested in lands in the Town of Markham, owned by Newtonbrook Plaza Ltd. a company which (in the language of Parker J., in his judgment after the trial) was "owned by" one Abraham Parsham. An offer to purchase was made by Rockwell, signed by Kelner as its secretary, to Newtonbrook Plaza Ltd., accepted by the latter, the acceptance being signed on its behalf by Parsham as president. Because of a difficulty respecting the zoning of the land, Rockwell asserted a right to close the transaction with an abatement in the purchase price, while Newtonbrook asserted that Rockwell could either close the transaction in accordance with its terms, or call it off.

Rockwell executed and registered some form of document described as an "assignment". Following tenders by each side upon the other, Rockwell sued Newtonbrook for specific performance with an abatement in price, and Newtonbrook in a separate action sued Rockwell for a declaration that the original agreement of purchase and sale was null and void, claimed an order expunging the registration of the assignment, and further claimed damages for slander of title. These two actions were tried together, over a period of five days. In a reserved judgment dated March 19, 1970, Parker J., dismissed the action of Rockwell with costs, directed in the second action that the Rockwell assignment be expunged from the Registry Office, and since it was admitted by counsel for Newtonbrook that the property had greatly increased in value since July, 1967, Parker J., granted that company no other relief and directed that there be no costs in the action it had brought.

The costs of Newtonbrook in Rockwell's action were taxed at $4,800 and were not paid by Rockwell. Kelner was examined as an officer of the judgment debtor corporation, following which a substantive motion was made to Parker J., by Newtonbrook for an order directing that Kelner pay personally the costs directed by the original judgment to be paid by Rockwell to Newtonbrook. Kelner made an affidavit on that motion and was cross-examined thereon.

From the material filed on such motion a number of additional facts emerged. There was no resolution of the directors of Rockwell authorizing Kelner to enter into the offer to purchase on its behalf; the deposit of $10,000 was advanced by Kelner and his partner Cooper from their own funds, direct to Newtonbrook or its agent, and did not go through the bank account of Rockwell nor was there any entry in Rockwell's books of account respecting it. The tendered sum of $28,000 which preceded the action was also advanced by Kelner and Cooper, and did not go through the bank account or books of Rockwell. In due course both the deposit of $10,000 and the tendered amount of $28,000 found its way back to Kelner and Cooper. There was no resolution of the directors authorizing the institution of Rockwell's action against Newtonbrook, nor the defence of the action of Newtonbrook against Rockwell. There was no resolution respecting the retainer of solicitors, although solicitors were retained to prosecute Rockwell's action and to defend Newtonbrook's action against it.

Both in 1967 and subsequently, Rockwell had literally no assets except a small bank account, which had dwindled from about $400 in 1964 to $31.85 in October, 1970, when Kelner was examined as an officer of Rockwell in aid of the judgment. On the last-mentioned date Rockwell's solicitors had not been paid; by the time the motion was heard they had been paid, by Kelner and Cooper, against the moneys going direct from Kelner and Cooper to the solicitors, with no entry in the books of account of the company.

Kelner described the putting up of the deposit, the tender money, and the amount required to pay Rockwell's solicitors as being "shareholders' loans", and stated that "our accountant would pick this up in due course". There is no reference anywhere in the books or records of Rockwell to any shareholders' loans. . . .

* * *

Turning to the merits of the appeal, it would appear that while he did not discuss the cases apart from the *Sturmer* and *Curry* decisions, Parker J., was addressing his mind to the issues as I have expressed them herein. As already indicated he found that "Kelner was the actual contracting party and the person who set this process in action . . . he was the actual litigant and Rockwell was only a nominee to hold title".

With great respect, I am unable to agree with these conclusions. The use of a "one man company" for the carrying on of business transactions, authoritatively recognized and expressed in *Salomon v. Salomon & Co.*, [1897] A.C. 22, and the correlative propositions that the property of the company is distinct from that of its members, and its transactions create legal rights and obligations vested in the company itself as opposed to its members, continue today. The subject is discussed in Gower, *Modern Company Law*, 2nd ed. (1957), at pp. 62-6.

I can find no basis for the finding that Mr. Kelner was the "actual contracting party". He was undoubtedly the individual who would ultimately benefit, in whole or in part, from the contract, but the contract was made with the company alone. Mr. Kelner could not have sued upon it, nor could he himself have been sued. Both he and Mr. Parsham were pursuing the same course of action; they were quite content to enter into contracts made by the companies which they respectively controlled.

It was undoubtedly the fact that Kelner was "the person who set this process in action", in the sense that he was the individual who, on behalf of the company, gave instructions to its solicitors, but this does not, in my view, justify a finding that he was "the actual litigant". Nor can I find justification for the finding that "Rockwell was only a nominee to hold title". This seems to imply that Rockwell was a trustee for Kelner, but it is contrary to all established principles of company law to suggest that a corporation is a trustee for its shareholders, or even for its single shareholder. On the evidence, there were to be other shareholders — certainly Mr. Cooper, according to Kelner's evidence — and there is a reference in the judgment of Parker J., at trial to the real estate agent who negotiated the transaction, and who was known to Kelner, and to the evidence that "at the time the deposit was paid there was an agreement between (the agent) and Mr. Kelner that (the agent) could have up to fifty per cent of the deal".

In argument Mr. Rolls conceded that "if this was a true corporate transaction, my case would be difficult or impossible". He sought to avoid the *Salomon* principle by reference to the fact that there was nothing in the minute book or the books of account of the company concerning the transaction and indeed, apart from the fact that the company had made the offer to purchase, there was nothing in the corporate records as such, respecting the purchase.

Unquestionably, the handling of the corporate records, both as to the minute book and as to the books of account, was slipshod, but no one connected with Rockwell was in a position to complain except Kelner himself. There was no allegation of fraud on the part of Kelner except one suggestion, not seriously pressed, that Kelner had "facilitated a fraudulent preference" by seeing to the payment of the account of the company's solicitors, after the motion herein had been launched, so that those solicitors were paid in preference to "other creditors". As already indicated, these fees were paid by Kelner and Cooper from their own funds, allegedly as an advance on behalf of the corporation. If this was a fraudulent preference, it is still open to Newtonbrook to attack it if so advised.

* * *

Motion to quash dismissed; appeal allowed.

Notes

1 In *Iron City Sand & Gravel Div. v. West Fork Towing Corp.*, 298 F. Supp. 1091 (N.D. W. Va., 1969), the plaintiff brought an action against the defendant corporation and its principal shareholder, Paul Pitrolo, for the value of two of the plaintiff's barges that sank allegedly due to the defendant corporation's negligence while bailee of the barges. The court found no negligence and dismissed the claim. Had it been necessary to do so, the court indicated that it would have accepted the plaintiff's contention that West Fork was merely Paul Pitrolo's alter ego. Christie J. reasoned as follows (at p. 1098):

The Court recognizes the principle that ownership of all or almost all of the shares of a corporation by one individual does not afford sufficient ground for disregarding the corporate entity, nevertheless, where such ownership is combined with the other factors involved in this case, particularly the inadequate capitalization, see 63 A.L.R. 2d 1951, we find little difficulty in holding that West Fork Towing Corporation was the "alter ego" of Paul Pitrolo. . . . If this court were to treat West Fork Towing Corporation as a separate legal entity it would be attributing to it a status which, according to the evidence, was never attributed to it by Paul Pitrolo. That this is the case is demonstrated by the fact that, insofar as the evidence shows, Paul Pitrolo made all the corporate decisions required of West Fork Towing Corporation, he loaned the corporation the money with which it purchased its operating equipment and he leased the corporation the land upon which it was operated. The offices of West Fork Towing Corporation were located in a building owned by a corporation controlled by Paul Pitrolo, in which another corporation owned by Pitrolo — Pitrolo Pontiac Company — was also located. While separate accounts were maintained for West Fork Towing Corporation, it appears that these accounts were prepared, at least part of the time, by employees of Pitrolo Pontiac Company in offices which West Fork Towing Corporation shared with Pitrolo Pontiac. Thus, in denying an independent status to West Fork Towing Corporation, the Court would only be recognizing the rule of law that when the corporate fiction is a mere simulacrum, an alter ego or business conduit of an individual, it may be disregarded in the interest of securing a just determination of an action.

2 The cost decision in *Rockwell Developments* has not sat well with legislators or with other courts. See now Ontario Rules of Civil Procedure, Rule 56, Security for Costs (Rule 56.01(d), below), and the decision in *269335 Alberta Ltd. v. Starlite Investments Ltd.* (1987), 18 C.P.C. (2d) 161, 1987 CarswellAlta 148 (Q.B.).

Rules of Civil Procedure

56.01 (1) The court, on motion by the defendant or respondent in a proceeding, may make such order for security for costs as is just where it appears that,

(a) the plaintiff or applicant is ordinarily resident outside Ontario;
(b) the plaintiff or applicant has another proceeding for the same relief pending in Ontario or elsewhere;
(c) the defendant or respondent has an order against the plaintiff or applicant for costs in the same or another proceeding that remain unpaid in whole or in part,
(d) the plaintiff or applicant is a corporation or a nominal plaintiff or applicant, and there is good reason to believe that the plaintiff or applicant has insufficient assets in Ontario to pay the costs of the defendant or respondent;

(e) there is good reason to believe that the action or application is frivolous and vexatious and that the plaintiff or applicant has insufficient assets in Ontario to pay the costs of the defendant or respondent; or

(f) a statute entitles the defendant or respondent to security for costs.

The courts have taken a firm approach to the interpretation of rule 56.01(d). While it is a generally accepted principle in the application of rule 56.01 that an impecunious plaintiff should not be ordered to give security for costs (because this would lead to poor plaintiffs being stopped in their tracks by orders for security for costs), the courts have exercised caution in applying this principle to rule 56.01(*d*). In *Smith Bus Lines Ltd. v. Bank of Montreal* (1987), 20 C.P.C. (2d) 38, 1987 CarswellOnt 457 (H.C.) the court held that "impecuniosity" is different from having "insufficient assets in Ontario to pay the costs of the defendant", and that in order to establish impecuniosity a corporate plaintiff must prove that monies are not available from its shareholders or other sources to deposit as security.

The Court of Appeal's judgment in *Newtonbrook Plaza* should be compared with the more recent judgment of the Court in *642947 Ontario Ltd. v. Fleischer* (2001), 56 O.R. (3d) 417, 2001 CarswellOnt 4296 (C.A.). Sweet Dreams Corporation was involved in litigation with the other party to the appeal. Halasi and Krauss controlled Sweet Dreams. As a condition to obtaining an interim injunction from the trial judge, Sweet Dreams gave an undertaking with respect to costs if the injunction was discharged and its case was unsuccessful. The injunction was discharged and the trial judge held Halasi and Krauss personally liable on Sweet Dreams' undertaking. Halasi and Krauss appealed. Speaking for the Court, Laskin J.A. reversed the trial judge on Sweet Dreams' liability on the undertaking. However, he also made it clear that had Sweet Dreams been liable on its undertaking the trial judge would have been justified in lifting the corporate veil to hold H and K personally liable. Laskin J.A. reasoned, in part, as follows:

[68] Typically, the corporate veil is pierced when the company is incorporated for an illegal, fraudulent or improper purpose. But it can also be pierced if when incorporated "those in control expressly direct a wrongful thing to be done": *Clarkson Co. v. Zhelka* at p. 578. Sharpe J. set out a useful statement of the guiding principle in *Transamerica Life Insurance Co. of Canada v. Canada Life Assurance Co.* (1996), 28 O.R. (3d) 423 at pp. 433-34 (Gen. Div.), affd [1997] O.J. No. 3754 (C.A.): "the courts will disregard the separate legal personality of a corporate entity where it is completely dominated and controlled and being used as a shield for fraudulent or improper conduct."

[69] These authorities indicate that the decision to pierce the corporate veil will depend on the context. They also indicate that the separate legal personality of the corporation cannot be lightly set aside. Yet,

however restrictive corporate law principles for piercing the corporate veil may be, in the context of an undertaking to the court, the trial judge's findings support going behind Sweet Dreams and imposing personal liability.

[70] She found that Sweet Dreams had no assets to honour its under-taking, that Halasi and Krauss controlled Sweet Dreams and that when Halasi and Krauss tendered the undertaking for Sweet Dreams they knew it had no assets. All of these findings are reasonably supported by the evidence. Moreover, Halasi was a sophisticated developer and Krauss was a lawyer. They tendered an undertaking to the court, which they knew was worthless, to gain an advantage. When called on to honour the undertaking, they tried to hide behind a shell company, which they controlled, to escape liability. In the words of Sharpe J. in Transamerica Life, Sweet Dreams was "completely dominated and controlled" by Halasi and Krauss, and used by them "as a shield for . . . improper conduct".

Question: Why should an undertaking to a court be treated more seriously than a contractual undertaking by a corporation when its directors know the corporation has no assets with which to honour its obligations?

De Salaberry Realties Ltd. v. Minister of National Revenue
(1974), 46 D.L.R. (3d) 100, 74 D.T.C. 6235, 1974 CarswellNat 166 (Fed. T.D.)

DECARY J.: The appeal is from income tax assessments for the years 1963, 1964, and 1965, confirmed by a judgment of the Tax Appeal Board on September 3, 1970, and pertaining to the profit realized by the appellant in selling land alleged to be purchased only for shopping center purposes.

At the opening of the hearing the Court refused to permit that the transcript of evidence before the Tax Appeal Board be put as exhibit on the ground that the appeal is a trial *de novo* and that such a way of proceeding would prevent the Court from questioning the witnesses and judging their credibility. The Court requested counsel to establish the chain of authority for the final policy and decision-making for the two ultimate beneficial owners, the Bronfman and the Steinberg families . . .

The evidence discloses that, during the pertinent years, the way of proceeding for each group, was to cause to have a company incorporated per one or few purchases. It would be naive to believe that the multiplicity of companies ensuing was wanted for business reasons and not for tax reasons. Indeed each company sells one or a few parcels of land whereas the group sells many.

The Court cannot confine itself, for passing judgment on the course of conduct, to the one of the appellant but must resort to the one of the groups. I do not conceive a medical doctor having to make a diagnosis on the general state of health of a patient that would examine only his right arm. Complete examination is required for the medical doctor and so is it needed in the present instance: the appellant is a member of the body of the Bronfmans and of the Steinbergs.

Considering that finding, the rule of *Salomon v. A. Salomon & Co. Ltd.*, [1897] A.C. 22 (H.L.), cannot be invoked for refraining the Court from passing judgment on the course of conduct of the groups of the sister companies and of the parent companies of the appellant.

The Steinberg group had a case in this Court that was decided by my learned brother Heald J., where the facts were, in substance, similar to those of the present case inasmuch as the finding of law was concerned. That case is the one of *Wilderton Shopping Centre Inc. v. M.N.R.*, [1972] C.T.C. 319, [1972] D.T.C. 6277, which is on appeal to the Appeal Division of this Court. In view of the fact that I consider the course of conduct of the group rather than the one of the appellant I do not consider that I should wait for the judgment of the Appellate Division. I agree with the result of the judgment of my learned brother Heald.

It is in evidence that Cemps Investments Ltd. is owned and controlled by trusts settled by the Bronfman family and that Steinberg's Ltd. is owned and controlled by the Steinberg family.

As to the Bronfman family, the Cemps Investments Ltd. owns all the shares of Cemps Holdings Ltd., now the Fairview Corporation of Canada Limited. The business of Cemps Holdings Ltd. is, *inter alia*, to manage the dealing in land of its wholly owned or partly owned subsidiaries which are subsidiaries or grandchildren corporations of Cemps Investments Ltd. The sub-subsidiaries are the legal owners of land at the times relevant to this appeal.

As to the Steinberg family, Steinberg's Limited owns all the shares of Ivanhoe Corporation. The business of Ivanhoe Corporation is the same as the one of Cemps Holdings Ltd., it owns shares of subsidiaries that are legal owners of land at the times relevant to this appeal.

After a careful study of the market possibility and the population growth, Cemps Holdings Ltd. or Ivanhoe Corporation causes a company to be incorporated to purchase a parcel of land. No attention is given to the matter of zoning before purchasing because it is assumed that any difficulty in that respect can be overcome.

Plans are prepared that are in fact pre-plans, costing $3,000 to $5,000, whereas definite plans, blues, would cost close to $50,000. These facts are in evidence. The officers and directors of each of these sub-subsidiaries, sister companies, are the same persons; the objects of the companies are similar; they are managed by their parent company which in turn, on a general policy level, is governed by their grandparent company. The structure is the same in the Bronfman and in the Steinberg group.

Though there may be only one or two purchases, the area being large, too big for the needs, there are many sales made by the sub-subsidiaries, sister companies of the appellant; in fact, it is in evidence that the two parent companies, Cemps Holdings Ltd. and Ivanhoe Corporation are often approached by people wanting to buy land though no advertisement is made by them. I deduce that it has to be known that their subsidiaries have excess land and that they are willing to sell. Notice should be taken that it is not the sub-subsidiaries that are approached but the subsidiaries, Cemps Holdings Ltd. and Ivanhoe Corporation. That indicates that the centre of policy and decision-making is not at the level of the sub-subsidiaries but closer to the grandparent companies, Cemps Investments Ltd. and Steinberg's Ltd. The directors of Cemps Holdings Ltd. and Ivanhoe Corporation are nominees of their parent company and therefore under their influence.

By purchasing, even if forced to, more land than reasonably required, it is evident that the appellant, like the group, has the intention to sell the excess which is of no other use. It is inventory for the appellant. The appellant is an instrument of his parent company and its grandparent company in purchasing and selling land.

I do regard the appellant as a legal entity distinct from the other companies of each group but I look at each group to find out the course of conduct which stamps the one of the appellant, an instrument of the group.

That the appellant is an instrument of the group is revealed by its thin capitalization: $1,000 divided in 100 shares of a par value of $10 each. With such a thin capitalization the appellant made two purchases amounting to nearly two millions. Funds had to be obtained from the two groups. That is a strong clue that the appellant is nothing but an instrument of its grandparent companies of the two families, but a liability of such an amount warrants a certainty of available funds from the groups.

The little, if any, attention paid to zoning and the assumption that any difficulty in that regard could be overcome, have been proven wrong in the present case for the two purchases of the appellant. In my opinion, such carelessness about zoning indicates strongly that the main objective is to acquire land that can always be disposed of if the plans are frustrated. To me, that and the thin capitalization are the birth of a sham or of a docile instrument. Primarily there is a slight desire of building a shopping centre and secondarily there is an intention to sell land. Such a way of doing, in my opinion, is not serious and is prompted only for possible tax advantages. To grasp the magnitude of the Bronfman and the Steinberg groups, I think it is required to know of the corporations of each group.

In the Bronfman group, there are the trusts owning all the shares of Cemps Investments Limited and that company owns all the shares of Cemps Holding Limited at times relevant to this appeal, now the Fairview Corporation of Canada Limited, and Cemps Holdings Limited owned 50% of the shares of the appellant at the time of purchase and sale of land by the appellant.

The Fairview Corporation of Canada Limited owns all the shares of the Fairview Corporation Limited which, in turn owns all the shares in two other companies; 51% of the shares of one company; 50% of the shares of five companies; 33-$\frac{1}{3}$% to 30.1% of the shares of three companies. There were 13 companies in the Bronfman group in 1972 after many subsidiaries were amalgamated during the years 1967 to 1969. There were about 10 companies so amalgamated. At the times relevant to this case the total of the companies in the Bronfman group was over 10 companies.

In the Steinberg group, the family owns all the shares of Steinberg's Limited which in turn owns all the shares of Ivanhoe Corporation. The latter company in turn owned all or a substantial part of the shares of 18 companies in the Montreal district.

In the Bronfman group, we have a great-grandparent corporation, a grandparent corporation, a parent corporation and two wholly owned sub-subsidiary corporations and eight companies where the interest of the parent corporation, Ivanhoe, is 50% or more. In the Steinberg group, there are the grandparent corporation, the parent corporation and 18 companies wholly or partially owned by the parent company.

It is my opinion that such pyramiding of corporations, in each group, demonstrates the extent of the need not to restrict the scrutiny of the course of conduct to the one of the appellant which is only an instrument in the hands of the groups.

In each group the directors of the subsidiaries, of the sub-subsidiaries and of the sub-sub-subsidiaries are nominees of the great-grandparent or grandparent corporation from where emanates the general policy-making and decision-taking of the group.

The Court takes note that the sister companies, those in each group of the same level as the appellant, do not deal with each other but deal only with their respective parent company, that is, Cemps Holdings Ltd. for those of the Bronfman group and Ivanhoe Corporation for those of the Steinberg group. Each of these sister companies has the same general objects and their business is essentially similar. Each one buys and sells land. If one is isolated from its sister companies there are only one or two purchases and a few more sales. When they are reunited, then their dealings are impressive and indicate that their business includes buying and selling in the ordinary course of events.

Furthermore, these sister companies are all instruments of their parent companies, Cemps Holdings Ltd. and Ivanhoe Corporation, which have caused them to be incorporated; have determined their thin capitalization; have made the market and population growth surveys; have seen that pre-plans of architects be drafted that could be used for any supermarket: the said pre-plans cost at most $5,000 whereas blues would cost $50,000; have been approached by people wanting to buy land owned by the appellant and its sister companies; have authorized the sale of land of the appellant and its sister companies; have dictated the course of conduct of the sister companies; have received and have obeyed the policy-making and the decision-taking of Cemps Investments Ltd. or Steinberg's Limited, their parent company, and grandparent or great-grandparent of the sister companies.

In such a pattern there is no room for any free will on the part of the appellant and its sister companies; they are, directly, instruments of their parent corporation and, indirectly, of their grandparent or great-grandparent corporation.

In view of these facts the course of conduct of the appellant must not be viewed in an isolated way but in taking into account the activities of its group. In such a light there is no doubt that the course of conduct of the appellant is the one of trader in land, and even in isolating the appellant, which should not be done, the course of conduct, then, is also that of a trader in land.

I have perused the activities of both groups to ascertain their course of conduct and also to ascertain the course of conduct of one of their instruments, the appellant.

I have disregarded the entity of the appellant in having recourse to the activities of both groups in order to judge the course of conduct of the appellant. There are precedents and authors that justify my collecting of the evidence.

In Palmer and Prentice, *Cases and Materials on Company Law (1969)*, we find these remarks at p. 49:

> An attempt was made to specify the criteria which, if satisfied, would indicate that a subsidiary company was carrying on the business of the parent company by Avory J. [sic] in *Smith, Stone and Knight Ltd. v. Birmingham Corporation*, [1939] 4 All E.R. 116, noted (1939), 3 Mod. L. Rev. 226:
>
> > Were the profits treated as profits of the company? — When I say "the company" I mean the parent company — secondly, were the persons conducting the business appointed by the parent company? Thirdly, was the company the head and brain of the trading venture? Fourthly, did the company govern the adventure, decide what should be done and what capital should be embarked on the venture? Fifthly, did the company make the profits by its skill and direction? Sixthly, was the company in effectual and constant control?

Applying these criteria it can be said that the profits were treated as profits of the parent company: a prospectus for the issue of shares in the Ivanhoe company reveals that fact; the appointments of the persons conducting the business of the appellant were made by the two parent companies and are the same people and they also act in the parent company; the parent company is the head and brain of the trading venture; the policy is established by the parent company; the capital to be brought in the venture was decided by the parent company, whether or not, once and for all, or in each instance, and that makes no difference; it is by the skilled direction of the parent company that the profit was made; the parent company is in effectual and constant control of the appellant or the said officers of both companies are the same people paid by the parent.

Ibid., on the same page, we read:

In a similar vein the decision *City of Toronto v. Famous Players Canadian Corporation Ltd.*, [1935] 3 D.L.R. 685, [1935] 3 D.L.R. 327 (C.A.), established that the business of one company can embrace the apparent or normal business of another where it can be said "that the second company is in fact the puppet of the first; when the directing mind and will of the former reaches into and through the corporate facade of the latter and becomes, itself, the manifesting agency. In such a case it is not accurate to describe the business as being carried on by the puppet for the benefit of the dominant company. The business is in fact that of the latter.

In the present instance, the appellant is the puppet of the two parent companies, it being owned 50-50; the mind and will of the parent companies reach through the facade of the appellant. The parent companies carry [on], in fact, the business of the appellant.

* * *

The business of the appellant is not apparent unless recourse is to be had to the group to ascertain the overall course of conduct, otherwise only a part of the course of conduct is apparent, the appellant being a shield; the appellant, being a subsidiary, has to be reckoned with as to the ownership of the land but its conduct must be ascertained by the course of conduct of the whole group; the appellant's parent companies are in fact in an intimate and immediate domination of the appellant which has no independent functioning of its own.

* * *

In Gower, *Principles of Modern Company Law*, 3rd ed. (1969), we read at pp. 194-5 as to holding and subsidiary companies:

The most striking limitation imposed by the Companies Acts on the recognition of the separate personality of each individual company is, however, in connection with associated companies within the same group enterprise. As we have seen, it has become a habit to create a pyramid of inter-related companies, each of which is theoretically a separate entity but in reality part of one concern represented by the group as a whole.

In the present case we have a pyramid of corporations and the appellant is part of the group of companies.

Ibid., at p. 200, we read:

It may therefore be said that not only has the veil been lifted in the interests of the Revenue but further steps have been taken in the interests of members towards recognizing "enterprise entity" rather than corporate entity.

As to group enterprises, which is the case we are concerned with we read, *ibid.*, at p. 213:

> Consideration of the cases in which the courts have treated a company as the agent of its controlling shareholder suggests that they are more ready to do so where the shares are held by another company. In other words, they are coming to recognize the essential unity of a group enterprise rather than the separate legal entity of each company within the group.

There is, in the present case, an essential unity of group enterprise which, for purposes of evidence of course of conduct, I recognize rather than the course of conduct of the separate legal entity of the appellant.

[Decary J. proceeded to consider American doctrine, and concluded]:

> Upon the evidence adduced, I find that the appellant, being a member of a horizontal group of sister companies incorporated for the same object and a member of a vertical group, there being a parent and a grandparent company for the Bronfman family and for the Steinberg family, must have its course of conduct determined by the one of its sister companies, its parent companies and its grandparent company because the appellant is only an instrument in the carrying on of the business of its parent companies and of its grandparent company, whose business of the parent and grandparent companies include, *inter alia*, directly or indirectly, the real estate one, under many forms and shapes, and the course of conduct of the appellant is hereby determined to be the one of a trader in land as a member of the horizontal business group and of the vertical business group of the member-companies, and the membership not being, in fact, for business reason as shown, *inter alia*, by the thin capitalization of the appellant and its dominance by its parent companies, consequently the profit realized in 1963, 1964 and 1965 on the sale of parcels of land is one made in the turning into account of inventory and is income of the appellant under the provisions of ss. 3 and 4 of the *Income Tax Act*.

Appeal dismissed.

[Decary J.'s judgment was affirmed on appeal to the Federal Court of Appeal (1976), 70 D.L.R. (3d) 706.]

Notes

1 In *Jodery Estate v. Nova Scotia (Minister of Finance)*, [1980] 2 S.C.R. 774, 1980 CarswellNS 78, 1980 CarswellNS 82, the issue was whether 12 grandchildren, the beneficiaries under the will of Roy A. Jodrey, were liable to pay succession duties under the Nova Scotia *Succession Duties Act*. The deceased who, prior to his death, was resident and domiciled in Nova Scotia, had sought to avoid the impact of the Act by

incorporating three companies under Alberta law. (1) The JBH company was the parent company and issued each of the grandchildren 100 shares at $1 per share paid by the grandchildren; (2) JCG was a subsidiary company and issued 100 common shares, all of which were beneficially owned by the parent company; (3) WRI was the third company but was not related to the first two companies. It issued two common shares, both of which were owned by the deceased. The deceased transferred to WRI his shares in a Nova Scotia investment company in exchange for a promissory note for $3,735,200. He also added a codicil to his will revoking an earlier bequest to his grandchildren and substituting a bequest to the subsidiary company including the note of WRI.

A majority of the Supreme Court of Canada (Martland, Pigeon, Beetz, and Chouinard JJ.), affirming the decision of the Nova Scotia Court of Appeal, held that the grandchildren were "beneficially entitled" to the deceased's estate and therefore subject to succession duties. Martland J., referring to the relationship between the parent company and its subsidiary, said:

> Both companies were incorporated on the same day in the same office by the same lawyers. Neither the parent company nor the subsidiary company engaged in any business activity between their dates of incorporation and the date of Mr. Jodrey's death. Neither of them had any creditors. Both of them had the same directors. Both had the same officers.
>
> This is eminently a case in which the court should examine the realities of the situation and conclude that the subsidiary company was bound hand and foot to the parent company and had to do whatever its parent said. It was a mere conduit pipe linking the parent company to the estate.

Dickson J., supported by Ritchie and McIntyre JJ., dissented vigorously and reaffirmed his confidence in the fundamental soundness of the *Salomon* principle:

> There is a tendency to think loosely in terms of a parent owning the assets of its wholly owned subsidiary but that is not so in law. No one would suggest that a person owning 100 shares of Canadian Pacific is the owner of, or has a beneficial interest in, the assets of Canadian Pacific. No distinction can be made in principle between ownership of 100 shares in a major corporation and ownership of all of the issued shares in a small company. In neither case does the shareholder own any asset other than shares. And the situation is unaffected by the fact that one or more shareholders may have voting control and thereby be in a position to acquire the assets or a portion thereof on wind-up, or upon a distribution of assets other than on wind-up. If shareholders are beneficially entitled to the property of a corporation in which they hold shares, then s. 2(5) would not have been necessary.

It is fundamental that a company as a body corporate is in contemplation of law an entity separate and distinct from shareholders who compose it. The principal of *Salomon v. Salomon & Co. Ltd.*, *supra*, is still very much part of our law and in general the courts have rigidly applied it.

Prof. Durnford, in "The Corporate Veil in Tax Law" (1979), 27 Can Tax J. 282, takes a dim view of the Canadian courts' willingness to pierce the corporate veil in favour of the tax collector. In his view, "in the Canadian law of taxation, the corporate veil is in tatters." How does one reconcile the courts' willingness to lift the veil in parent-subsidiary relationships with their reluctance to do so in actions against natural shareholders?

The Supreme Court's decision in *Covert* should be contrasted with its later decision in *Stubart Investments Ltd. v. R.*, [1984] 1 S.C.R. 536, 1984 CarswellNat 222, 1984 CarswellNat 690. The question before the Court was whether a corporate affiliate, established solely for tax planning purposes, should be ignored on the ground that the new corporate structure served no *bona fide* business purpose. The business purpose test was adopted in the US as far back as 1934 (see *Gregory v. Helvering*, 293 U.S. 465 (S.C., 1935)) and is an established doctrine of US tax law. It was belatedly embraced by the House of Lords in *W.T. Ramsay Ltd. v. Inland Revenue Commissioners*, [1981] 2 W.L.R. 449 (U.K. H.L.). In *Stubart*, the Supreme Court was urged to follow suit. The Supreme Court refused to do so on the grounds that a taxpayer's right to organize its affairs was deeply entrenched in Canadian law and implicitly recognized in the *Income Tax Act*, and that adoption of the business purpose test would create too much uncertainty.

Is the Supreme Court's position in *Stubart* consistent with the majority decision in *Covert*? Does *Stubart* involve a repudiation of the earlier Canadian case law canvassed in Decary J.'s judgment in *De Salaberry Realties*?

For many years, s. 245 of the Canadian *Income Tax Act* contained a general anti-tax evasion provision. The federal tax officials regarded the provisions as ineffectual and, following a White Paper on Tax Reform issued on June 18, 1987, the federal government enacted a new s. 245. Subsection 245(2) provides that if a transaction is an "avoidance transaction", the "tax consequences" will be determined as is reasonable in the circumstances to deny the tax benefit that would otherwise result from the transaction.

An avoidance transaction is defined in ss. 245(3) as any transaction that, in the absence of the general anti-avoidance rule, would result directly or indirectly in a tax benefit. However, a transaction is not considered to be an avoidance transaction if the transaction "may reasonably be considered to have been undertaken or arranged primarily *for bona fide purposes other than to obtain the tax benefit*." (italics added.)

For further details of these changes, see David Duff, *Canadian Income Tax Law* (Emond Montgomery, 2003), p. 169–183.

2 *The Deep Rock Doctrine.* In many cases the creditors or other security holders of an insolvent corporation, which is being liquidated or reorganized in receivership or bankruptcy proceedings, instead of attempting to hold the sole or controlling shareholder personally liable for the subsidiary's debts, seek merely to have the court deny such shareholder the right to enforce a claim as a creditor or secured creditor of the insolvent corporation. Most of the cases arise under the *Bankruptcy Act* and the Supreme Court of the United States, in administering that Act, has evolved the so-called Deep Rock doctrine (so named from Deep Rock Oil Corporation, the subsidiary in *Taylor v. Standard Gas & Electric Co.*, 306 U.S. 307, 59 S.Ct. 543 (1939)), under which the claim of the controlling shareholder (usually but not always a holding company) may be subordinated to other claims, including the claims of preferred shareholders, on various grounds.

Mr. Justice Douglas explained the rationale of the doctrine as follows:

> Though disallowance of such claims will be ordered where they are fictitious or a sham, these cases do not turn on the existence or non-existence of the debt. Rather they involve simply the question of order of payment. At times equity has ordered disallowance or subordination by disregarding the corporate entity. That is to say, it has treated the debtor-corporation simply as part of the stockholder's own enterprise, consistently with the course of conduct of the stockholder. But in that situation as well as in the others to which we have referred, a sufficient consideration may be simply the violation of rules of fair play and good conscience by the claimant; a breach of the fiduciary standards of conduct which he owes the corporation, its stockholders and creditors. [*Pepper v. Litton*, 308 US 295, 310].

The doctrine was originally applied in *Taylor v. Standard Gas & Electric Co.* (in reorganization of subsidiary corporation, holding company's claim as creditor subordinated to creditors and preferred shareholders of subsidiary because of a series of acts of improper management of subsidiary for the benefit of the parent and because of the inadequate capitalization of the subsidiary). See Cary and Eisenberg, *Cases and Materials on Corporations* 136-138 (Concise 6th ed., 1988). Compare the provisions of the *Partnerships Act* (Ont.), s. 4, the *Partnership Act* (B.C.), s. 5, and see also *Sukloff v. A.H. Rushforth & Co.*, [1964] S.C.R. 459, 1964 CarswellOnt 39.

According to a West Coast author, there is evidence of judicial willingness to import principles of equitable subordination into Canadian law although without specific reliance on American precedents. See J. Thomas English, "Salomon v. Salomon Revisited" (1989), 47 Advocate 261, discussing *Laronge Realty Ltd. v. Golconda Investments*

Ltd. (1986), 7 B.C.L.R. (2d) 90, 1986 CarswellBC 496 (C.A.) and *Canada Deposit Insurance Corp. v. Canadian Commercial Bank* (1987), 67 C.B.R. (N.S.) 136, 1987 CarswellAlta 329 (Q.B.). Compare Prof Telfer's treatment of the topic in "Transplanting Equitable Subordination: The New Free-Wheeling Equitable Discretion in Canadian Insolvency Law?" (2002) 36 CBLJ 36. Prof Telfer is critical of the importation of the US doctrine into Canada and believes the same results could be arrived at by invoking the oppression remedy in the federal and provincial business corporations Acts.

For a stimulating and much-cited exchange on piercing the corporate veil in parent-subsidiary cases, with special reference to bankruptcy situations, see Landers, "A Unified Approach to Parent, Subsidiary, and Affiliate Questions in Bankruptcy" (1975), 42 U. Chic. L.R. 562; Posner, "The Rights of Creditors of Affiliated Corporations" (1976), 43 U. Chic. L.R. 499; Landers, "Another Word on Parents, Subsidiaries and Affiliates in Bankruptcy", id. at 527.

3 A still more radical approach to the problems of parent-subsidiary relationship in bankruptcy was adopted by the US federal court in *Stone v. Eacho*, 127 F.2d 284 (4th Cir., 1942). Tip Top Tailors was incorporated under Delaware law. Its principal place of business was in Newark, N.J. It operated nine retail stores in various cities of the US, one of them being in Richmond, Va. Tip Top Tailors caused a separate corporation to be incorporated under the same name under Virginia law but the court found it conducted no business of its own and was merely the alter ego of the parent company. The Delaware corporation dealt with its Richmond store precisely in the same way as it dealt with its other (unincorporated) stores.

The Delaware corporation was adjudged bankrupt and the appellant Stone was appointed its receiver. Two days later, two creditors attached the property in the Richmond store as property of the Virginia corporation. On the following day a successful bankruptcy petition was filed against the Virginia corporation by Stone as receiver of the Delaware corporation. He subsequently also filed a claim for $39,069.67 as the amount owing by the Virginia corporation to the Delaware corporation. The trustee in bankruptcy of the Virginia corporation resisted the claim and argued that, at all events, it be postponed to the claims of other creditors on the ground that the Virginia corporation was a mere instrumentality or department of the Delaware corporation.

There was no evidence that the alleged creditors of the Virginia corporation were aware of its existence or had intended to extend credit to it as distinct from extending credit to the parent corporation. The Fourth Circuit Court of Appeals accordingly concluded, distinguishing the *Deep Rock* doctrine, that the fairest solution would be to ignore the Virginia corporation entirely and to treat all creditors as creditors of the parent corporation. The court stated (at p. 288):

But in a case such as this, where both corporations are insolvent, where the business has been transacted by and the credit extended to the parent corporation, and where the subsidiary has no real existence whatever, there is no reason why the courts should not face the realities of the situation and ignore the subsidiary for all purposes, allowing the creditors of both corporations to share equally in the pooled assets. As said in Latty, *supra*: "Perhaps the fairest way of dealing with the situation when both the parent and the subsidiary corporations are insolvent is to let all the creditors of each share pro rata in the pooled assets of both. Such procedure would be especially equitable where the claimants are creditors of both the parent and the subsidiary."

4 *Employee problems*. In *Minister of National Revenue v. Blackburn* (1976), 66 D.L.R. (3d) 191, 1976 CarswellNat 7, 1976 CarswellNat 7F (Fed. C.A.), the question was whether certain employees who prior to a certain date were employed by one corporation and who thereafter were employed by another corporation, were "employed by the same employer" within the meaning of ss. 149(2) of the *Unemployment Insurance Act*, 1971. The Federal Court of Appeal said:

> While, from many points of view, as far as the employees were concerned, there was no change in their position after the corporate reorganization — they were still employed doing the same things in the same business, which had been purchased from the old corporation by the new corporation — nevertheless, their employer after the time in question, was the new corporation and not the old corporation. In such circumstances we are forced to the conclusion that they were not "employed by the same employer" within the ordinary meaning of those words and we have not been able to find anything in the context to justify giving those words any meaning other than the ordinary meaning. The result seems hard in the circumstances of this case but the condition imposed by Parliament cannot, for that reason, be ignored in some cases and applied only in cases where it is more obvious why Parliament would have imposed it.

In the field of labour relations the legislatures have intervened by providing that collective bargaining agreements are binding on the transferee of a business regardless, it would seem, of the nature of the prior relationship between the transferor and the transferee. See *e.g.*, the *Labour Relations Act*, 1995, S.O. 1995, c. 1, Sch. A, s. 69, and the Labour Relations Code, R.S.B.C. 1996, c. 244. Apart from statutory prescriptions, the courts have also shown themselves quite ready to lift the corporate veil in parent-subsidiary relationships for the purpose of respecting collective bargaining and picketing rights. See *e.g.*, *Nedco Ltd. v. Clark* (1973), 43 D.L.R. (3d) 714, 1973 CarswellSask 99 (C.A.), followed in *Sask. Joint Board v. Can. Pioneer Management Ltd.* (1978), 78 C.C.L.C. 552 (Sask. L.R.B.).

The Ontario *Employment Standards Act*, 2000, S.O. 2000, c. 41, offers another striking example of the legislature lifting the corporate veil in intercorporate relations to discourage employers from evading the social purposes of the Act by transferring some or all of the employer's assets to an associated corporation, thus leaving the employer, in the event of bankruptcy, unable to satisfy employee claims for unpaid wages or vacation pay and other entitlements established under the Act. The relevant current provisions read as follows:

1. (1) In this Act,

* * *

"employer" includes,

      (a) an owner, proprietor, manager, superintendent, overseer, receiver or trustee of an activity, business, work, trade, occupation, profession, project or undertaking who has control or direction of, or is directly or indirectly responsible for, the employment of a person in it, and

      (b) any persons treated as one employer under s. 4, and includes a person who was an employer; ("employeur")

* * *

4. (1) Subsection (2) applies if,

      (a) associated or related activities or businesses are or were carried on by or through an employer and one or more other persons; and

      (b) the intent or effect of their doing so is or has been to directly or indirectly defeat the intent and purpose of this Act.

(2) The employer and the other person or persons described in ss. (1) shall all be treated as one employer for the purposes of this Act.

(3) Subsection (2) applies even if the activities or businesses are not carried on at the same time.

(4) Subsection (2) does not apply with respect to a corporation and an individual who is a shareholder of the corporation unless the individual is a member of a partnership and the shares are held for the purposes of the partnership.

(5) Persons who are treated as one employer under this section are jointly and severally liable for any contravention of this Act and the regulations under it and for any wages owing to an employee of any of them.

5 The common employer doctrine was recently applied by the Ontario Court of Appeal in an arresting set of facts in *Downtown Eatery (1993)*

Ltd. v. R. (2001), 54 O.R. (3d) 161 2001 CarswellOnt 1680. A was employed as manager of a night club "For Your Eyes Only". FYEO was not incorporated and A was in fact paid by Best Beaver, one of a number of associated companies owned by HG and BB. A was wrongfully dismissed and recovered substantial damages in an action against Best Beaver. The judgment was not satisfied and the sheriff went out and seized $1,855 in cash on the premises of FYEO. Downtown Eatery claimed that the money belonged to it and brought action against A. A in turn counterclaimed against all of the companies owned by HG and BB and against HG and BB personally. The Court of Appeal held that A was entitled to recover on the basis that the group of companies constituted his common employer and because HG and BG were guilty of oppressive conduct under the OBCA. This was because, by reorganizing the group of companies and causing Best Beaver to go out of business (although for otherwise legitimate reasons) and transferring BB's assets to the other companies while A's claim was awaiting trial, they effected a result that was unfairly prejudicial to A.

The judgment of Borins and McPherson JJ.A. addressed the common employer claim in the following passage:

[34] In our view, in June 1993, when Alouche was dismissed, there was a highly integrated or seamless group of companies which together operated all aspects of the For Your Eyes Only nightclub. Twin Peaks owned the nightclub premises and leased them to The Landing Strip which owned the trademark for For Your Eyes Only and, significantly for a nightclub, held the liquor and entertainment licences. Downtown Eatery operated the nightclub under a licence from The Landing Strip and owned the chattels and equipment at the nightclub. Best Beaver served as paymaster for the nightclub employees. Controlling all of these corporations were Grad and Grosman and their family holding companies, Harrad Corp. and Bengro Corp.

[35] Grad and Grosman could easily have operated the nightclub through a single company. They chose not to. There is nothing unlawful or suspicious about their choice. As Wood J. said in Sinclair, "it is a perfectly normal arrangement frequently encountered in the business world."

[36] However, although an employer is entitled to establish complex corporate structures and relationships, the law should be vigilant to ensure that permissible complexity in corporate arrangements does not work an injustice in the realm of employment law. At the end of the day, Alouche's situation is a simple, common and important one — he is a man who had a job, with a salary, benefits and duties. He was fired — wrongfully. His employer must meet its legal responsibility to compensate him for its unlawful conduct. The definition

of "employer" in this simple and common scenario should be one that recognizes the complexity of modern corporate structures, but does not permit that complexity to defeat the legitimate entitlements of wrongfully dismissed employees.

6 *Group Entities and Tortious Liability.* The leading case in England now as to the circumstances in which English courts are willing to ignore the corporate veils separating the members of a corporate group is *Adams v. Cape Industries Plc* (1989), [1990] 1 Ch. 433 (Eng. C.A.). In this case, the Court of Appeal unambiguously reaffirmed the legitimacy of a parent company establishing subsidiaries even if its purpose in doing so is to shield the parent company from liability in tort in the event of claims being brought involving the allegedly defective character of the products distributed by the subsidiaries. The defendant Cape Industries, an English company, presided over a group of subsidary companies that mined asbestos in South Africa and marketed it in various countries and subdivisions thereof, including Texas in the US. Employees of a Texas company using the asbestos products claimed to have been injured by them and brought a class action against the subsidiaries and Cape Industries. Cape did not defend the action and default judgment was entered against it in Texas. Cape did not carry on business and had no office in Texas when the action was instituted against it.

The plaintiffs sought to enforce the Texas judgment in England. Under English conflict of laws rule, a foreign judgment is only enforceable in England if the defendant has either submitted to the jurisdiction of the foreign court or was present in the foreign jurisdiction when the action was instituted. Since Cape had not submitted to the Texas jurisdiction and had no office in Texas at any material time, the plaintiffs had to persuade the Court of Appeal either that the subsidiaries were only a façade or that it was appropriate to lift the corporate veil between Cape and its subsidiaries in order to do justice between the parties. Scott J., at trial, and the Court of Appeal on appeal were satisfied that the subsidiary involved in the distribution of the asbestos in Texas (and inferentially elsewhere in the US) had a genuine existence and emphatically rejected the notion that English law permits the corporate veil to be lifted among members of a group of companies even where the plaintiff is an involuntary creditor. The Court of Appeal said:

> We do not accept as a matter of law that the court is entitled to lift the corporate veil as against a defendant company which is the member of a corporate group merely because the corporate structure has been used so as to ensure that the legal liability (if any) in respect of particular future activities of the group (and correspondingly the risk of enforcement of that liability) will fall on another member of the group rather than the defendant company. Whether or not this is desirable, the right to use a corporate structure in this manner is inherent in our corporate law. Mr. Morison urged on us that the

purpose of the operation was in substance that Cape would have the practical benefit of the group's asbestos trade in the United States of America without the risks of tortious liability. This may be so. However, in our judgment, Cape was in law entitled to organise the group's affairs in that manner and (save in the case of A.M.C. to which special considerations apply) to expect that the court would apply the principle of *Salomon v. A. Salomon & Co. Ltd.* [1897] A.C. 22 in the ordinary way.

Question: Would *Cape Industries* be decided the same way in Canada? Is there a persuasive reason for Canadian courts to adopt a common employer doctrine for the protection of employees and to refuse to extend a similar level of protection for involuntary creditors of a member of a group of companies?

Walkovsky v. Carlton
223 N.E.2d 6 (N.Y.C.A., 1966)

FULD J.: This case involves what appears to be a rather common practice in the taxicab industry of vesting the ownership of a taxi fleet in many corporations, each owning only one or two cabs.

The complaint alleges that the plaintiff was severely injured four years ago in New York City when he was run down by a taxicab owned by the defendant Seon Cab Corporation and negligently operated at the time by the defendant Marchese. The individual defendant, Carlton, is claimed to be a stockholder of 10 corporations, including Seon, each of which has but two cabs registered in its name, and it is implied that only the minimum automobile liability insurance required by law (in the amount of $10,000) is carried on any one cab. Although seemingly independent of one another, these corporations are alleged to be "operated . . . as a single entity, unit and enterprise" with regard to financing, supplies, repairs, employees and garaging, and all are named as defendants. The plaintiff asserts that he is also entitled to hold their stockholders personally liable for the damages sought because the multiple corporate structure constitutes an unlawful attempt "to defraud members of the general public" who might be injured by the cabs.

The defendant Carlton has moved, pursuant to CPLR 3211(a)7, to dismiss the complaint on the ground that as to him it "fails to state a cause of action". The court at Special Term granted the motion but the Appellate Division, by a divided vote, reversed, holding that a valid cause of action was sufficiently stated. The defendant Carlton appeals to us, from the non-final order, by leave of the Appellate Division on a certified question.

The law permits the incorporation of a business for the very purpose of enabling its proprietors to escape personal liability . . . but, manifestly, the privilege is not without its limits. Broadly speaking, the courts will disregard the corporate form, or, to use accepted terminology, "pierce the corporate veil", whenever necessary "to prevent fraud or to achieve equity" . . . In determining whether liability should be extended to reach assets beyond those belonging to the corporation, we are guided, as Judge Cardozo noted, by "general rules of agency". (*Berkey v. Third Ave. Ry. Co.*) In other words, whenever anyone uses control of the corporation to further his own rather than the corporation's business, he will be liable for the corporation's acts "upon the principle of *respondeat superior* applicable even where the agent is a natural person". . . Such liability, moreover, extends not only to the corporation's commercial dealings . . .

In the Mangan case . . . (*supra*), the plaintiff was injured as a result of the negligent operation of a cab owned and operated by one of four corporations affiliated with the defendant Terminal. Although the defendant was not a stockholder of any of the operating companies, both the defendant and the operating companies were owned, for the most part, by the same parties. The defendant's name (Terminal) was conspicuously displayed on the sides of all of the taxis used in the enterprise and, in point of fact, the defendant actually serviced, inspected, repaired and dispatched them. These facts were deemed to provide sufficient cause for piercing the corporate veil of the operating company — the nominal owner of the cab which injured the plaintiff — and holding the defendant liable. The operating companies were simply instrumentalities for carrying on the business of the defendant without imposing upon it financial and other liabilities incident to the actual ownership and operation of the cabs . . .

In the case before us, the plaintiff has explicitly alleged that none of the corporations "had a separate existence of their own" and, as indicated above, all are named as defendants. However, it is one thing to assert that a corporation is a fragment of a larger corporate combine which actually conducts the business. (See Berle, The Theory of Enterprise Entity, 47 Col.L.Rev. 343, 348–350.) It is quite another to claim that the corporation is a "dummy" for its individual stockholders who are in reality carrying on the business in their personal capacities for purely personal rather than corporate ends. . .Either circumstance would justify treating the corporation as an agent and piercing the corporate veil to reach the principal but a different result would follow in each case. In the first, only a larger *corporate* entity would be held financially responsible . . . while in the other the stockholder would be personally liable . . . Either the stockholder is conducting the business in his individual capacity or he is not. If he is, he will be liable; if he is not, then, it does not matter — insofar as his personal liability is concerned — that the enterprise is actually being carried on by a larger "enterprise entity". (See Berle, "The Theory of Enterprise Entity", 47 Col.L.Rev. 343.)

* * *

The individual defendant is charged with having "organized, managed, dominated and controlled" a fragmented corporate entity but there are no allegations that he was conducting business in his individual capacity. Had the taxicab fleet been owned by a single corporation, it would be readily apparent that the plaintiff would face formidable barriers in attempting to establish personal liability on the part of the corporation's stockholders. The fact that the fleet ownership has been deliberately split up among many corporations does not case the plaintiff's burden in that respect. The corporate form may not be disregarded merely because the assets of the corporation, together with the mandatory insurance coverage of the vehicle which struck the plaintiff, are insufficient to assure him the recovery sought. If Carlton were to be held individually liable on those facts alone, the decision would apply equally to the thousands of cabs which are owned by their individual drivers who conduct their businesses through corporations organized pursuant to s. 401 of the Business Corporation Law, Consol. Laws, c. 4 and carry the minimum insurance required by subdivision 1 (par. [a]) of s. 370 of the Vehicle and Traffic law, Consol. Laws, c. 71. These taxi owner-operators are entitled to form such corporations . . . and we agree with the court at Special Term that, if the insurance coverage required by statute "is inadequate for the protection of the public, the remedy lies not with the courts but with the Legislature." It may very well be sound policy to require that certain corporations must take out liability insurance which will afford adequate compensation to their potential tort victims. However, the responsibility for imposing conditions on the privilege of incorporation has been committed by the Constitution to the Legislature (N.Y. Const. art. X, §1) and it may not be fairly implied, from any statute, that the Legislature intended, without the slightest discussion or debate, to require of taxi corporations that they carry automobile liability insurance over and above that mandated by the Vehicle and Traffic Law.

This is not to say that it is impossible for the plaintiff to state a valid cause of action against the defendant Carlton. However, the simple fact is that the plaintiff has just not done so here. While the complaint alleges that the separate corporations were undercapitalized and that their assets have been intermingled, it is barren of any "sufficiently particularized statements". . . that the defendant Carlton and his associates are actually doing business in their individual capacities, shuttling their personal funds in and out of the corporations "without regard to formality and to suit their immediate convenience" . . . Such a "perversion of the privilege to do business in a corporate form" . . . would justify imposing personal liability on the individual stock-holders . . . Nothing of the sort has in fact been charged, and it cannot reasonably or logically be inferred from the happenstance that the business of Seon Cab Corporation may actually be carried on by a larger corporate entity composed of many corporations which, under general principles of agency, would be liable to each other's creditors in contract and in tort.

In point of fact, the principle relied upon in the complaint to sustain the imposition of personal liability is not agency but fraud. Such a cause of action cannot withstand analysis. If it is not fraudulent for the owner-operator of a single cab corporation to take out only the minimum required liability insurance, the enterprise does not become either illicit or fraudulent merely because it consists of many such corporations. The plaintiff's injuries are the same regardless of whether the cab which strikes him is owned by a single corporation or part of a fleet with ownership fragmented among many corporations. Whatever rights he may be able to assert against parties other than the registered owner of the vehicle come into being not because he has been defrauded but because, under the principle of *respondeat superior*, he is entitled to hold the whole enterprise responsible for the acts of its agents.

In sum, then, the complaint falls short of adequately stating a cause of action against the defendant Carlton in his individual capacity . . .

* * *

KEATING J. (dissenting): The defendant Carlton, the shareholder here sought to be held for the negligence of the driver of a taxicab, was a principal shareholder and organizer of the defendant corporation which owned the taxicab. The corporation was one of 10 organized by the defendant, each containing two cabs and each cab having the "minimum liability" insurance coverage mandated by s. 370 of the Vehicle and Traffic Law. The sole assets of these operating corporations are vehicles themselves and they are apparently subject to mortgages.

From their inception these corporations were intentionally undercapitalized for the purpose of avoiding responsibility for acts which were bound to arise as a result of the operation of a large taxi fleet having cars out on the street 24 hours a day and engaged in public transportation. And during the course of the corporations' existence all income was continually drained out of the corporations for the same purpose.

The issue preceded by this action is whether the policy of this State, which affords those desiring to engage in a business enterprise the privilege of limited liability through the use of the corporate device, is so strong that it will permit that privilege to continue no matter how much it is abused, no matter how irresponsibly the corporation is operated, no matter what the cost to the public. I do not believe that it is.

Under the circumstances of this case the shareholders should all be held individually liable to this plaintiff for the injuries he suffered . . . At least the matter should not be disposed of on the pleadings by a dismissal of the complaint. "If a corporation is organized and carries on business without substantial capital in such a way that the corporation is likely to have no sufficient assets available to meet its debts, it is inequitable that shareholders should set up such a flimsy organization to escape personal liability. The attempt to do corporate business without providing any sufficient basis of financial responsibility to creditors is an abuse of the separate entity and will be ineffectual to exempt the shareholders from corporate debts. It is coming to be recognized as the policy of law that shareholders should in good faith put at the risk of the business unencumbered capital reasonably adequate for its prospective liabilities. If capital is illusory or trifling compared with the business to be done and risks of loss, this is a ground for denying the separate entity privilege." (Ballantine, *Corporations* [rev. ed., 1946] §129, pp. 302-303.)

In *Minton v. Cavaney* . . . the Supreme Court of California had occasion to discuss this problem in a negligence case. The corporation of which the defendant was an organizer, director and officer operated a public swimming pool. One afternoon the plaintiffs' daughter drowned in the pool as a result of the alleged negligence of the corporation.

Justice Roger Traynor, speaking for the court, outlined the applicable law in this area. "The figurative terminology 'alter ego' and 'disregard of the corporate entity,'" he wrote, "is generally used to refer to the various situations that are an abuse of the corporate privilege . . . The equitable owners of a corporation, for example, are personally liable when they treat the assets of the corporation as their own and add or withdraw capital from the corporation at will . . . when they hold themselves out as being personally liable for the debts of the corporation . . . or *when they provide inadequate capitalization and actively participate in the conduct of corporate affairs"*. . . (italics supplied).

Examining the facts of the case in light of the legal principles just enumerated, he found that "[it was] undisputed that there was no attempt to provide adequate capitalization. [The corporation] never had any substantial assets. It leased the pool that it operated, and the lease was forfeited for failure to pay the rent. Its capital was 'trifling compared with the business to be done and the risks of loss'" . . .

It seems obvious that one of "the risks of loss" referred to was the possibility of drownings due to the negligence of the corporation. And the defendant's failure to provide such assets or any fund for recovery resulted in his being held personally liable.

In *Anderson v. Abbott*, the defendant shareholders had organized a holding company and transferred to that company shares which they held in various national banks in return for shares in the holding company. The holding company did not have sufficient assets to meet the double liability requirements of the governing Federal statutes which provided that the owners of shares in national banks were personally liable for corporate obligations "to the extent of the amount of their stock therein, at the par value thereof, in addition to the amount invested in such shares" (U.S. Code, tit. 12, former §63).

The court had found that these transfers were made in good faith, that other defendant shareholders who had purchased shares in the holding company had done so in good faith and that the organization of such a holding company was entirely legal. Despite this finding, the Supreme Court, speaking through Mr. Justice Douglas, pierced the corporate veil of the holding company and held all the shareholders, even those who had no part in the organization of the corporation, individually responsible for the corporate obligations as mandated by the statute . . . ".

The policy of this State has always been to provide and facilitate recovery for those injured through the negligence of others. The automobile, by its very nature, is capable of causing severe and costly injuries when not operated in a proper manner. The great increase in the number of automobile accidents combined with the frequent financial irresponsibility of the individual driving the car led to the adoption of s. 388 of the Vehicle and Traffic Law which had the effect of imposing upon the owner of the vehicle the responsibility for its negligent operation. It is upon this very statute that the cause of action against both the corporation and the individual defendants is predicated.

In addition the Legislature, still concerned with the financial irresponsibility of those who owned and operated motor vehicles, enacted a statute requiring minimum liability coverage for all owners of automobiles. The important public policy represented by both these statutes is outlined in s. 310 of the Vehicle and Traffic Law. That section provides that:

> The legislature is concerned over the rising toll of motor vehicle accidents and the suffering and loss thereby inflicted. The legislature determines that it is a matter of grave concern that motorists shall be financially able to respond in damages for their negligent acts, so that innocent victims of motor vehicle accidents may be recompensed for the injury and financial loss inflicted upon them.

The defendant Carlton claims that, because the minimum amount of insurance required by the statute was obtained, the corporate veil cannot and should not be pierced despite the fact that the assets of the corporation which owned the cab were "trifling compared with the business to be done and the risks of loss" which were certain to be encountered. I do not agree.

The Legislature in requiring minimum liability insurance of $10,000, no doubt, intended to provide at least some small fund for recovery against those individuals and corporations who just did not have and were not able to raise or accumulate assets sufficient to satisfy the claims of those who were injured as a result of their negligence. It certainly could not have intended to shield those individuals who organized corporations, with the specific intent of avoiding responsibility to the public, where the operation of the corporate enterprise yielded profits sufficient to purchase additional insurance. Moreover, it is reasonable to assume that the Legislature believed that those individuals and corporations having substantial assets would take out insurance far in excess of the minimum in order to protect those assets from depletion. Given the costs of hospital care and treatment and the nature of injuries sustained in auto collisions, it would be unreasonable to assume that the Legislature believed that the minimum provided in the statute would in and of itself be sufficient to recompense "innocent victims of motor vehicle accidents . . . for the injury and financial loss inflicted upon them".

* * *

The defendant contends that a decision holding him personally liable would discourage people from engaging in corporate enterprise.

What I would merely hold is that a participating shareholder of a corporation vested with a public interest, organized with capital insufficient to meet liabilities which are certain to arise in the ordinary course of the corporation's business, may be held personally responsible for such liabilities. Where corporate income is not sufficient to cover the cost of insurance premiums above the statutory minimum or where initially adequate finances dwindle under the pressure of competition, bad times or extraordinary and unexpected liability, obviously the shareholder will not be held liable (Henn, *Corporations*, p. 208, n. 7).

The only types of corporate enterprises that will be discouraged as a result of a decision allowing the individual shareholder to be sued will be those such as the one in question, designed solely to abuse the corporate privilege at the expense of the public interest . . .

[Desmond C.J. and Van Voorhis, Burke and Scileppi JJ. concurred with Fuld J. Bergan J. concurred with Keating J.]

Questions

1   What was the ratio of Fuld J.'s judgment? Would plaintiff's pleadings have been upheld as stating a cause of action if plaintiff had limited his claim against the group of companies?

2   In what sense was it true to say, as Judge Keating claimed it was, that Seon Cab Corporation was a corporation "vested with a public interest"? Did the Seon Cab Corporation differ, in this respect, from any other corporation?

3   Could a supplier of gas to the Seon Cab Corporation have relied on the theory of Judge Keating's dissent as a basis for action against the corporation? Is that theory persuasive in connection with a claim in contract?

4   Shareholder liability for corporate torts: the Hansmann-Kraakman proposal. Dissatisfaction with the limited liability shield and its impact on tort victims has encouraged commentators to search for solutions. We saw earlier (*supra*, this chapter) the solution offered by Halpern *et al.* A more recent proposal, which has provoked much discussion, is one by Professors Hansmann and Kraakman ("Toward unlimited shareholder liability for corporate tort" (1991), 100 Yale L.J. 1879) involving the imposition of *pro rata* liability on shareholders rather than full individual liability for the torts of their corporation. The authors reason that the threat of even *pro rata* liability will give the market an incentive to monitor a corporation's risky activities and impound the risk in the reduced price of the shares without significantly impairing the availa-

bility of equity capital. Do you share the authors' optimism, and would it matter if a corporation did find it difficult to sell shares under such a regime? Would mandatory insurance for hazardous activities not be a better alternative? Would management of a publicly held corporation in any event not have sufficient incentives to carry adequate insurance? How would the authors' proposal affect shareholders in closely held corporations or concentrated shareholdings in public corporations? What procedural problems would *pro rata* liability give rise to? In the context of the Canadian constitution, could a non-incorporating province impose a personal liability regime on shareholders? On these and other questions raised by the Hansmann-Kraakman proposal, see Susan Woodward, "Limited Liability in the Theory of the Firm" (1985), 141 J. Institutional & Theoretical Econ. 601; David W. Leebron, "Limited Liability, Tort Victims, and Creditors" (1991), 91 Col. L. Rev. 1565; and Jos. A. Grundfest, "The Limited Liability of Unlimited Liability: A Capital Markets Perspective" (1992), 102 Yale L.J. 387.

5. LIABILITY OF CORPORATION IN TORT AND CRIMINAL LAW

(a) Liability in Tort

ATIYAH, Vicarious Liability in the Law of Torts
(1967) 381–3 (footnotes omitted)

The growth of corporations coincided largely with the development and extension of vicarious liability in English law; and, indeed, it may well be that the coming of large and powerful corporations such as the railway companies was itself a powerful factor which encouraged the courts to extend the doctrine of vicarious liability. Throughout the whole of the nineteenth century there was a gradual extension of the liability of corporations in tort. In 1818 it was held that trover lay against a corporation; in 1842 a corporation was held liable in trespass for the act of its servant in seizing some property of the plaintiff; in 1846 it was held that a corporation was liable for misfeasance as well as for nonfeasance; and in 1851 a corporation was held liable for an assault by its servants. Doubts were expressed in 1854 as to whether a corporation could be held guilty of a tort involving malice, but in 1858 it was held that corporation could be liable in defamation despite the need to show "presumed malice" or "malice in law", and it was also intimated that even actual malice could be established against a corporation. In the following year the argument that a corporation, "having no soul cannot be actuated by malice" was dismissed as "more quaint than substantial", and despite protests by Lord Bramwell as late as 1886, liability even for malicious torts was firmly established by the end of the century.

Similarly, early doubts as to whether corporations could be held liable for fraud, were in due course brushed aside.

Throughout the nineteenth century little attempt was made to analyze the nature of the liability thus imposed on corporations or to decide whether it was vicarious liability or personal liability. From the practical point of view it was generally quite immaterial whether a corporation was to be treated as liable because it had itself committed a tort, or whether it was liable because its servants acting in the course of their employment had done so. Even where the tort was committed on the actual instructions of the corporations' directors or managers it was just as easy to hold the corporation vicariously liable for acts of the directors or managers, as to charge the corporation with personal liability.

Nevertheless, it has become clear in the course of the present century that, in legal theory at any rate, a distinction can, and sometimes must, be drawn between the vicarious and personal liability of a corporation in much that same way as is done with the liability of individuals. That a corporation could be treated as personally guilty of a tort was implicit in the line of decisions holding that the doctrine of common employment did not apply to a personal breach of duty by an employer. The whole essence of these cases was that the liability, not being vicarious, was not defeated by the doctrine of common employment, and it was never suggested that there was any distinction in this respect between a corporation and an individual. These cases could generally be explained as cases of nonfeasance or omissions, for plainly there is less difficulty in holding a corporation personally liable for an omission than for an act, but even this last step was finally taken. In *Asiatic Petroleum Co. v. Lennard's Carrying Co.*, [1915] A.C. 705 (U.K. H.L.), the question was whether the appellant shipping company was entitled to limit its liability under the provisions of the *Merchant Shipping Acts* which withhold this privilege where a shipowner has been guilty of "actual fault or privity". It was held by the House of Lords that a corporation can be guilty of "actual fault or privity" if such fault or privity can be established against "somebody who is not merely a servant or agent for whom the company is liable on the footing *respondeat superior*, but somebody for whom the company is liable because his action is the very action of the company itself."

This decision thus recognizes that there are some servants or agents of a corporation who can be treated as the "directing mind and will of the corporation, the very ego and centre of the personality of the corporation", whose acts will be attributed to the corporation, not by way of vicarious liability, but on the footing that their acts are those of the company itself. The subsequent development of this form of liability belongs largely to the criminal law for it is only in that branch of the law that the distinction between personal and vicarious liability generally has any practical significance. The cases on criminal liability show that there is often serious difficulty in deciding whether the acts of a particular servant of the company are to be treated as the acts of the company itself, but the most recent cases show a tendency to restrict this concept to those servants who may be said to be "the brains" of the company, such as directors, managers and other "responsible officers". Although there may still be some circumstances in which the distinction between personal and vicarious liability of corporations may be relevant in the law of tort it is true to say that in general little practical importance attaches to it in this branch of the law.

(b) Corporate Criminal Liability

Introductory Note. Given the predominance of business corporations as the preferred form of business organization, it is not surprising that much attention has focussed on the problems that arise in seeking to apply traditional criminal law concepts and penological theories to offences committed by corporations. Two major issues have dominated the debate. The first is, why should corporations be held criminally responsible at all? The second is, under what circumstances should criminal responsibility be ascribed to corporations, particularly in the case of *mens rea* offences?

So far as the first issue is concerned, scholars, law reform committees and judges have long debated the rationale of imposing criminal sanctions on an artificial body existing only in contemplation of law and that, to quote Lord Chancellor Thurlow's oft-quoted epigram, has "no soul to damn: no body to kick". Starting from these premises, it was long supposed that *mens rea* could not be attributed to a corporation and, equally, that of the traditional aims of criminal punishment — deterrence, incapacitation, rehabilitation and retribution — only deterrence made any sense in the case of corporations. Even that has been questioned on the ground that deterrence can be accomplished just as effectively by civil and administrative law remedies. Another complaint is that a meaningful fine usually hits the pockets of those who are least to blame, the shareholders of the convicted corporation or the corporation's employees if the sanction is severe enough to force the closing down of a plant.

There is of course another side to the coin. Large corporations are real persons, not legal fictions, as any one of the many thousands of employees of such mega-companies as IBM, General Motors or Bell Canada will attest, and they exert enormous influence over the economic, and frequently social, welfare of the communities in which they are located. Corporations also commit real crimes, including such latter day varieties as anti-trust violations, racketeering, drug money laundering, financial frauds, and industrial pollution. Civil sanctions in such cases, it is argued, are not sufficient and the stigma of a criminal conviction is as telling for a corporation as it is for an individual accused.

For comprehensive discussions of these themes, see *inter alia*, "Developments in the Law — Corporate Crime: Regulating Corporate Behavior through Criminal Sanctions" (1979), 92 Harv. L. Rev. 1227; Brent Fisse, "Reconstructing Corporate Law: Deterrence, Retribution, Fault and Sanctions" (1982), 56 So. Cal. L. Rev. 1141; John Coffee Jr., "'No Soul to

Damn: No Body to Kick': An Unscandalized Inquiry into the Problem of Corporate Punishment" (1981), 79 Mich. L. Rev. 386; and Jennifer A. Quaid, "The Assessment of Corporate Criminal Liability on the Basis of Identity" (1998) 43 McGill L.J. 67.

So far as the second issue is concerned (on what basis criminal liability should attach to corporations), different common law jurisdictions have adopted different theories. For offences requiring proof of a *mens rea*, the established Anglo-Canadian doctrine is that only the mental state of those directing the corporation's affairs will be ascribed to the corporation (the so-called "identification" or "organic" theory of corporate criminal liability). In the US, on the other hand, the federal courts have frequently applied a simpler doctrine of *respondeat superior*. Between these two extremes there are many variations, as will be seen from the materials reproduced in this section. In Canada, a new set of complications has been introduced with the adoption of the *Charter of Rights and Freedoms*.

We begin our overview with the Supreme Court of Canada's decision in the *Canadian Dredge & Dock Co.* case.

Canadian Dredge & Dock Co. Ltd. v. The Queen
(1985), 19 D.L.R. (4th) 314, 1985 CarswellOnt 939, 1985 CarswellOnt 96
(S.C.C.), affirming (1981), 56 C.C.C. (2d) 193, 1981 CarswellOnt 1243
(C.A.)

Introduction

A number of corporations were charged with conspiracy to defraud contrary to ss. 338(1) and 423(1)(d) [now ss. 380(1) and 465(1)(c) respectively] of the *Criminal Code*. The allegations arose out of the rigging of bids for dredging contracts in Hamilton harbour. Senior officers of the corporate accused (in each case, a general manager, vice-president or president) agreed in advance which company would submit the low (and hence winning) bid, in every case at an inflated price. The losing bidders (and co-conspirators) received payments from the winning bidder and/or occasionally a profitable subcontract. In some cases, the senior officers who orchestrated the fraudulent scheme kept for themselves the side payments which, under the agreement, were to have been paid to their corporation.

Four corporate defendants appealed their convictions on these charges and the dismissal of their appeals by the Ontario Court of Appeal. The grounds of appeal were as follows:

(i) One corporate defendant challenged the doctrine that a corporation could be convicted for a *mens rea* offence under the "identification" theory of corporate criminal liability;

(ii) Two of the defendants argued that a corporation is not criminally liable where the directing mind of the corporation "is, at the material time:

(a) acting in fraud of the corporation;

(b) acting wholly or partly for his or her own benefit, or

(c) acting contrary to instructions that he not engage in illegal actions in the course of his duties." (*Ibid.*, DLR, at 319).

(1) *The Identification Theory of Corporate Criminal Liability.*

Speaking for a unanimous Supreme Court, Estey J. affirmed the correctness of the "identification" theory of corporate criminal liability. The following lengthy extract from his judgment (*ibid.*, at 322-332) relates both the history of corporate criminal liability in Anglo-Canadian law and the policy choices that faced the common law courts:

ESTEY J. The position of the corporation in criminal law must first be examined. Inasmuch as all criminal and quasi-criminal offences are creatures of statute the amenability of the corporation to prosecution necessarily depends in part upon the terminology employed in the statute. In recent years there has developed a system of classification which segregates the offences according to the degree of intent, if any, required to create culpability.

(a) Absolute liability offences

Where the Legislature by the clearest intendment establishes an offence where liability arises instantly upon the breach of the statutory prohibition, no particular state of mind is a prerequisite to guilt. Corporations and individual persons stand on the same footing in the face of such a statutory offence. It is a case of automatic primary responsibility. Accordingly, there is no need to establish a rule for corporate liability nor a rationale therefor. The corporation is treated as a natural person.

(b) Offences of strict liability

Where the terminology employed by the Legislature is such as to reveal an intent that guilt shall not be predicated upon the automatic breach of the statute but rather upon the establishment of the *actus reus*, subject to the defence of due diligence, an offence of strict liability arises: see *R. v. City of Sault Ste. Marie* [1978] 2 S.C.R. 1299. As in the case of an absolute liability offence, it matters not whether the accused is corporate or unincorporate, because the liability is primary and arises in the accused according to the terms of the statute in the same way as in the case of absolute offences. It is not dependent upon the attribution to the accused of the misconduct of others. This is so when the statute, properly construed, shows a clear contemplation by the Legislature that a breach of the statute itself leads to guilt, subject to the limited defence above noted. In this category, the corporation and the natural defendant are in the same position. In both cases liability is not vicarious but primary.

(c) Offences requiring mens rea

These are the traditional criminal offences for which an accused may be convicted only if the requisite *mens rea* is demonstrated by the prosecution. At common law a corporate entity could not generally be convicted of a criminal offence. Corporate criminal immunity stemmed from the abhorrence of the common law for vicarious liability in criminal law, and from the doctrine of *ultra vires*, which regarded criminal activities by corporate agents as beyond their authority and beyond corporate capacity. At the other extreme in the spectrum of criminal offences there are certain crimes which cannot in any real sense be committed by a corporate as a principal, such as, perjury and bigamy, whatever the doctrine of corporate criminal liability may be. As a corporation may only act through agents, there are basically only three approaches whereby criminal intent could be said to reside or not reside in the corporate entity:

   (i) a total vicarious liability for the conduct of any of its agents whatever their level of employment or responsibility so long as they are acting within the scope of their employment;

  (ii) no criminal liability unless the criminal acts in question have been committed on the direction or at the request, express or clearly implied, of the corporation as expressed through its board of directors;

(iii) a median rule whereby the criminal conduct, including the state of mind, of employees and agents of the corporation is attributed to the corporation so as to render the corporation criminally liable so long as the employee or agent in question is of such a position in the organization and activity of the corporation that he or she represents its *de facto* directing mind, will, centre, brain area or ego so that the corporation is identified with the act of that individual. There is said to be on this theory no responsibility through vicarious liability or any other form of agency, but rather a liability arising in criminal law by reason of the single identity wherein is combined the legal entity and the natural person; in short, a primary liability. This rule stands in the middle of the range or spectrum. It is but a legal fiction invented for pragmatic reasons.

* * *

At common law there was no difficulty in finding liability in a corporation in the law of torts, even though the state of mind of the corporation was established by imputing to that corporation the intentions and the conduct of its servants and agents. Thus, in the law of torts, the courts from the earliest times found vicarious liability in the corporation on the principles of agency. On the other hand, the common law of England has shrunk back from the application of the doctrine of vicarious liability for the determination of corporate liability in criminal law for the acts of its agents (with the four exceptions already noted). This led to an irrational result, namely: general corporate immunity from liability under the criminal law at a time when the corporation, for a variety of reasons, had become the principal vehicle of commerce in the community. The State itself, through corporate and taxation legislation particularly, had actually promoted or at least facilitated this result. Early in the century the courts began to dismantle the principle of corporate immunity in the criminal law. Procedural and other obstacles to the imposition of corporation criminal liability were overcome: see Leigh, "Criminal Liability of Corporations and Other Groups", 9 Ott. L.R. (No. 2) 247 at pp. 248-9 (1977). Perhaps the last major procedural impediment, the impossibility, as seen by some courts, of punishing a corporation when the only statutory sanction imposed was imprisonment . . . was removed in 1909 by the *Criminal Code Amendment Act*, 1909 (Can.), c. 9, s. 2 (the predecessor to the present s. 647 of the *Criminal Code*) which allowed the substitution of a fine in lieu of any punishment where a corporation is convicted. Ironically, the destruction of the most difficult barrier, the attribution of *mens rea* to a corporation, began in earnest in a case in civil law: *Lennard's Carrying Co., Ltd. v. Asiatic Petroleum Co., Ltd.*, [1915] A.C. 705. The House of Lords was concerned with a corporation's civil liability for damages under a statute which afforded a defence where such loss occurred without its "fault or privity". At issue was whether the "fault" of a director, who was active in the operations of the corporation, was in law the fault of the corporation itself. The Lord Chancellor, Viscount Haldane, laid down the general principle of corporate liability which is still the guiding principle in United Kingdom law (at pp. 713-4):

> a corporation is an abstraction. It has no mind of its own any more than it has a body of its own; its active and directing will must consequently be sought in the person of somebody who for some purposes may be called an agent, but who is really the directing mind and will of the corporation, the very ego and centre of the personality of the corporation. That person may be under the direction of the shareholders in general meeting; that person may be the board of directors itself, or it may be, and in some companies it is so, that that person has an authority co-ordinate with the board of directors given to him under the articles of association, and is appointed by the general meeting of the company, and can only be removed by the general meeting of the company . . .

Convictions were thereafter sustained under a variety of statutes including those establishing offences requiring proof of the element of *mens rea*, the courts applying the words of the House of Lords in *Lennard's* case, *supra*, in attributing to the accused corporation the actions of the "directing mind". See *Director of Public Prosecutions v. Kent and Sussex Contrac tors, Ltd.*, [1944] K.B. 146 at pp. 155-6, where Viscount Caldecote L.C.J. said:

The offences created by the regulation are those of doing something with intent to deceive or of making a statement known to be false in a material particular. There was ample evidence, on the facts as stated in the special case, that the company, by the only people who could act or speak or think for it had done both these things . . .

These general principles found application in the courts of this country in a series of cases. In *R. v. Fane Robinson Ltd.*, [1941] 3 D.L.R. 409, the Court of Appeal of Alberta set aside an acquittal of two companies where two of its directors and officers conspired with another to defraud an insurance company by inflating the charges made by the defendant company to the insurance company for automobile repairs. Ford J.A., for the court, found . . . that the two officers were the:

acting and directing will of [the accused corporation] generally and in particular in respect of the subject-matter of the offenses with which it is charged, that their culpable intention (*mens rea*) and their illegal act (*actus reus*) were the intention and the act of the company and that conspiracy to defraud and obtaining money by false pretenses are offenses which a corporation is capable of containing.

In so doing the court followed the United Kingdom authorities, including *Lennard's*, *supra*, and found the company criminally liable stating . . . :

if the act complained of can be treated as that of the company, the corporation is criminally responsible for all such acts as it is capable of committing and for which the prescribed punishment is one which it can be made to endure.

The court expressly avoided finding criminal liability through the doctrine of *respondeat superior*.

* * *

The transition from virtual corporate immunity from criminal liability to virtual equality with humans in like circumstances under the criminal law is traced in greater detail by Jessup J., as he then was, in *R. v. J.J. Beamish Construction Co. Ltd.*, *supra*. Three years later, Schroeder J.A., of the Court of Appeal of Ontario, in *R. v. St. Lawrence Corp. Ltd.*, *supra*, . . . again reviewed this transition. In the end, Schroeder J.A. adopted the same statement of the governing principle as Jessup J. had in *Beamish*, *supra*, although the earlier case is not cited . . .

This rule of law was seen as a result of the removal of the officer or managerial-level employee from the general class of "inferior servants or agents" for whose acts the corporate employer continued (as in the case of the human employer) to be immune from vicarious liability in criminal law. This result is generally referred to as the "identification" theory. It produces the element of *mens rea* in the corporate entity, otherwise absent from the legal entity but present in the natural person, the directing mind. This establishes the "identity" between the directing mind and the corporation which results in the corporation being found guilty for the act of the natural person, the employee. Such is the power of legal reasoning. It is the direct descendant of Blackstone's famous theorem: "The husband and the wife in law are one and that one is the husband." It is a full brother of the *dictum* in corporate law that merging corporations cease to exist but find a continuance in the amalgamated company. In order to trigger its operation and through it corporate criminal liability for the actions of the employee (who must generally be liable himself), the actor-employee who physically committed the offence must be the ego, the "centre" of the corporate personality, the "vital organ" of the body corporate, the *alter ego* of the employer corporation or its "directing mind". Schroeder J.A. in *St. Lawrence, supra*, for example, refers to the officer or senior management employee as the corporation's "primary representative . . . through whom the company acts, speaks, and thinks" . . . The terminology "primary representative" comes from, or is coincidentally used in, C.R.N. Winn., "Criminal Responsibility of Corporations", 3 Camb. L.J. 398 (1929), where it is stated, at p. 404:

> the conspiring minds are in fact the minds of the directors, or other primary representatives. It is submitted that no mere conspiracy of inferior agents could affect the corporation with criminal guilt. If the guilty intention in the minds of the primary representatives is attributed to the corporation in this case where, more than anywhere, it is the vital element of the offence, it seems that it will always be proper to attribute to a corporation the guilty state of its primary representatives when they do criminal acts on its behalf in the exercise of its powers.

At p. 407 the learned author continues:

> It is clear, on the one hand, that to seek to hold a corporation criminally liable for the acts of all its servants within the scope of their employment would be an innovation. The criminal law has never applied the maxim "*respondeat superior*," and to seek to ingraft from without what has not taken spontaneous growth might prove an experiment foredoomed to failure.

* * *

The principle of attribution of criminal actions of agents to the employing corporate principal in order to find criminal liability in the corporation only operates where the directing mind is acting within the scope of his authority (*Beamish, supra*, . . . and *St. Lawrence, supra*, in the sense of acting in the course of the corporations' business . . . Scattered throughout the submissions on behalf of the four appellants, was a translation of the directing-mind rule to a requirement that for its application the directing mind must, at all times, be acting in the scope of his employment. Conversely, the argument went, if the directing mind was acting totally outside the "scope of the employment", the attribution of the acts of the directing mind to the corporate employer would not occur. The terminological problems arise from the fact that the concept of vicarious liability in the law of torts has been traditionally fenced in by the concept of the employee acting within "the scope of his employment" and not, in the classic words, "on a frolic of his own". The identification theory, however, is not concerned with the scope of employment in the tortious sense. "Scope of employment" in the *St. Lawrence* judgment, *supra*, and the other discussions of that term in Canadian law have reference to the field of operations delegated to the directing mind.

* * *

(2) *Scope of the Identification Doctrine.*

So far as the scope of the identification doctrine was concerned, Estey J. gave it considerable elasticity (*ibid.*, at 336-337):

> The identity doctrine merges the board of directors, the managing director, the superintendent, the manager or anyone else delegated by the board of directors to whom is delegated the governing executive authority of the corporation, and the conduct of any of the merged entities is thereby attributed to the corporation. In *R. v. St. Lawrence Corp. Ltd.* and nineteen other corporations, [1969] 3 C.C.C. 263, 5 D.L.R. (3d) 263, [1969] 2 O.R. 305 (Ont. C.A.), and other authorities, a corporation may, by this means, have more than one directing mind. This must be particularly so in a country such as Canada where corporate operations are frequently geographically widespread. The transportation companies, for example, must of necessity operate by the delegation and subdelegation of authority from the corporate centre; by the division and subdivision of the corporate brain, and by decentralizing by delegation the guiding forces in the corporate undertaking. The application of the identification rule in *Tesco, supra,* may not accord with the realities of life in our country, however appropriate we may find to be the enunciation of the abstract principles of law there made.

(3) *Acting in Fraud of the Corporation.*

Once it was established that the corporations constituted part of the corporate mind and will, the defendant corporations were obliged to raise this defence because the Ontario Court of Appeal, reaffirming earlier Anglo-Canadian precedents, had held that it made no difference that the delinquent corporate executive was using his office to defraud the corporation. This curious doctrine, apparently based on the analogy of a corporation's tortious liability for the acts of its agents committed in the course of their ostensible employment, had been strongly criticized by commentators and Estey J.

had no difficulty in exposing its weaknesses. However, in delineating what he described as "the outer limit of the delegation doctrine" (sic), he added some new wrinkles which are bound to create difficulties in future cases. He said (*ibid.*, at 351):

> In my view, the outer limit of the delegation doctrine is reached and exceeded when the directing mind ceases completely to act, in fact or in substance, in the interests of the corporation. Where this entails fraudulent action, nothing is gained from speaking of fraud in whole or in part because fraud is fraud. What I take to be the distinction raised by the question is where all of the activities of the directing mind are directed against the interests of the corporation with a view to damaging that corporation, whether or not the result is beneficial economically to the directing mind, that may be said to be fraud on the corporation. Similarly, but not so importantly, a benefit to the directing mind in single transactions or in a minor part of the activities of the directing mind is in reality quite different from benefit in the sense that the directing mind intended that the corporation should not benefit from any of its activities in its undertaking. A benefit of course can, unlike fraud, be in whole or in part, but the better standard, in my view, is established when benefit is associated with fraud. The same test then applies. Where the directing mind conceives and designs a plan and then executes it whereby the corporation is intentionally defrauded, and when this is the substantial part of the regular activities of the directing mind in his office, then it is unrealistic in the extreme to consider that the manager is the directing mind of the corporation. His entire energies are, in such a case, directed to the destruction of the undertaking of the corporation. When he crosses that line he ceases to be the directing mind and the doctrine of identification ceases to operate. The same reasoning and terminology can be applied to the concept of benefits.

> Where the criminal act is totally in fraud of the corporate employer and where the act is intended to and does result in benefit exclusively to the employee-manager, the employee-directing mind, from the outset of the design and execution of the criminal plan, ceases to be a directing mind of the corporation and consequently his acts could not be attributed to the corporation under the identification doctrine. This might be true as well on the American approach through *respondeat superior*. Whether this is so or not, in my view, the identification doctrine only operates where the Crown demonstrates that the action taken by the directing mind (a) was within the field of operation assigned to him; (b) was not totally in fraud of the corporation, and (c) was by design or result partly for the benefit of the company.

On the facts, the defence did not prevail because "the appellants received benefits in the form of contracts and subcontracts, direct payouts and other benefits." Further, "the directing minds were acting partly for the benefit of the employing appellant and partly for their own benefit." (*Ibid.*, at 352-353.) It could not be said that any of the corporations had been defrauded in the narrow sense used above, even though some of the benefits of the illicit scheme were diverted to individuals who were the directing mind and will.

* * *

(4) *Effect of Corporate Officer Acting in Violation of Express Orders.*

Estey J. was much less sympathetic to this defence and rejected it summarily on the ground that (p. 341): "If the law recognized such a defence, a corporation might absolve itself from criminal consequence by the simple device of adopting and communicating to its staff a general instruction prohibiting illegal conduct and directing conformity at all times with the law." (*Ibid.*, at 341). However, cognizant of the distinction between offences of "strict liability" (i.e. offering a due diligence defence: see *R. v. Sault Ste. Marie (City)* (1978), 40 C.C.C. (2d) 353, 85 D.L.R. (3d) 161, 1978 CarswellOnt 24, 1978 CarswellOnt 594 (S.C.C.), and those requiring *mens rea* (as at bar), he noted that such a communication would be relevant with reference to offences of strict liability. In respect of offences of *mens rea*, it was irrelevant.

(5) *Notes and Questions on Estey J.'s Judgment.*

(a) As Estey J. himself concedes, Canadian law invests considerable elasticity in the doctrine of identification. Estey himself speaks of "more than one directing mind", of "delegation and subdelegation of authority" from the corporate centre, and of "division and subdivision of the corporate brain". The Canadian case law supports this relaxed approach. Thus in *R. v. Marketplace* (1979), 51 C.C.C. (2d) 185, 1979 CarswellBC 806 (C.A.), the corporate employer was held criminally liable for the fraudulent representations of a used car salesperson, and in *R. c. Spot Supermarket Inc.* (1979), 50 C.C.C. (2d) 239, 1979 CarswellQue 248 (C.A.), the corporation was held liable for the theft of retail sales taxes by a supervisor in charge "of the office and accounting". (Both these cases are referred to approvingly in the judgment of the Ontario Court of Appeal in the present case and should be contrasted with the much narrower view of the scope of the delegation doctrine adopted by the House of Lords in *Tesco Supermarkets Ltd. v. Nattrass* (1971), [1972] A.C. 153 (U.K. H.L.).)

What then is the distinction in Canada between the identification doctrine and liability based on a straight theory of delegation? If high hierarchical status is not an essential prerequisite (is such a test meaningful anyway in close corporations?), is it the vesting of discretionary powers in the delegate? If yes, how much, and what kind of discretion?

Commonwealth v. Beneficial Finance Co., 275 N.E.2d 33 (1972). The weaknesses of the identification test were persuasively exposed in this case by the Massachusetts Supreme Judicial Court. The defendant corporations were charged with having bribed and conspiring to bribe various public officials. The actual offences were committed by lower echelon officials in the employ of the corporations, none of whom was a "high managerial agent" as defined in the ALI Model Penal Code, s. 2:07 (1962). The trial judge had charged the jury that the state must prove the guilty official had been placed in a position by the corporation "Where he had enough power, duty, responsibility and authority to act for and on behalf of the corporation to handle the particular business . . . in which he was engaged at the time that he committed the criminal act, with power of decision as to what he would or would not do while acting for the corporation, and that he was acting for and in behalf of the corporation in the accomplishment of that particular business or operation or project, and that he committed a criminal act while so acting."

In an exhaustive judgment, the Supreme Judicial Court approved the direction and rejected the ALI test as too narrow and unresponsive to the realities of modern corporate structures. The court also gave the following policy reasons (at pp. 83-84):

> To permit corporations to conceal the nefarious acts of their underlings by using the shield of corporate armor to deflect corporate responsibility, and to separate the subordinate from the executive, would be to permit "endocratic" corporations to inflict widespread public harm without hope of redress. It would merely serve to ignore the scramble and realities of the market place. This we decline to do. We believe that stringent standards must be adopted to discourage any attempt by "endocratic" corporations' executives to place the sole responsibility for criminal acts on the shoulders of their subordinates.
>
> We believe that our decision is supported by basic considerations of public policy. The President's Commission on Law Enforcement and Administration of Justice, Task Force Report — Crime and Its Impact — An Assessment (1967) provides a sound rationale for imputing criminal responsibility to the corporation for the acts of lower echelon corporate officials who have the authority to act on behalf of the corporation. The report states at p. 104 that "[w]hite collar crime does serious damage to social and economic institutions . . . Thus, crimes such as bribery and violation of conflict of interest statutes strike deeply at responsible, impartial government." The report further points out at p. 108 that: "A pervasive problem affecting enforcement is the fact that white collar crime is often business crime and business crime is often corporate crime. Where corporate defendants are involved, the only criminal sanction available is the line. As noted previously, fines may be inadequate as deterrents for a variety of reasons. There are also serious practical problems in imposing sanctions upon corporate employees. It is very difficult to obtain the conviction of the true policy formulators in large, complex corporations. The top exec-

utives do not ordinarily carry out the overt criminal acts — it is the lower or middle management officials who, for example, attend price-fixing meetings." The President's Commission concluded, at p. 108, that: "where corporate misconduct is involved, the offenders — and particularly the offenders against whom evidence of guilt can be obtained — act as part of a corporate hierarchy and, ordinarily, follow a pattern of corporate behavior. Individual responsibility is therefore reduced — the offenders are often following orders from above, either explicit or implicit. Moreover, the fact that acts are performed to further the interests of the corporation, and not merely the offenders' personal interests, helps to rationalize misconduct. Thus in the *Electrical Equipment* cases, personal explanations for the acts were, for the most part, sought in the structure of corporate pressures. The defendants almost invariably testified that they came new to a job, found price-fixing an established way of life, and simply entered into it as they did into other aspects of their job."

(b) Although Estey J. refers to the fraud and lack of benefit exceptions to the identification theory as "defences", he also suggests that a burden falls upon the Crown to prove that the conduct was not totally in fraud of the corporation and, by design or result, partly for the benefit of the company. Are these really "defences" or are they part of the substantive case which must be proved by the prosecution and if so, why? What is the difference in practice?

(c) Estey J. suggests that to be "totally in fraud" of the employed, the acts of the directing minds would have to be directed towards "executing a scheme to deprive their respective employer corporations of any and all dredging business or benefit therefrom" (*ibid.*, at 351) and "aimed at the destruction of the respective corporate employers . . . (*ibid*). How frequently do you think these restrictive requirements will be made out; i.e., how often will the directing mind be directing his (or her) "entire energies" to the *total destruction* of the corporate undertaking?

(d) If, as Estey J. held, the enjoinder by top management to lower echelon executives not to break the law is not a defence when a charge is brought against the corporation involving a *mens rea* offence, why should it be a defence to a strict liability offence? Does the distinction lie in the fact that in a strict liability offence the corporation is held vicariously liable for the acts of all its employees whereas in *mens rea* offences its liability is restricted to members of its directing mind? Do you find this a plausible distinction?

(e) *Conclusion.* Estey J.'s judgment for the Supreme Court in *Canadian Dredge* leaves many loose ends that will require clarification in future cases.

(f) *Important Amendments to Criminal Code, Bill C-45, Stat. Can. 2003, c.21.*[6] One of the last acts of the Chrétien Parliament in 2003 was to enact fundamental changes to the *Criminal Code* involving the criminal liability of corporations, and indeed the criminal liability of many other organizations as well, whether incorporated or not. Bill C-45 was partially enacted in response to the 1992 Westray mining disaster in Nova Scotia in which 26 miners lost their lives. The tragedy was said to have been caused by the mining company's non-compliance with health and safety requirements. The Crown never initiated criminal proceedings against the company or its directors — presumably because of the difficulty of proving their culpability under the existing tests of liability — and proceedings against two of the mine's managers were eventually dropped.

The key features of Bill C-45 are summarized in the following passage in a leading article on Bill C-45:[7]

> Bill C-45 constitutes a fundamental change, if not a revolution, in corporate criminal liability. It creates a new regime of criminal liability that applies not only to corporations, but unions, municipalities, partnerships and other associations of persons. It replaces the traditional legal concept of corporate liability based on the fault of the corporation's "directing mind(s)", the board of directors and those with the power to set corporate policy, with liability tied to the fault of all of the corporation's "senior officers". That definition includes all those employees, agents or contractors who play "an important role in the establishment of an organization's policies" or who have responsibility "for managing an important aspect of the organization's activities".[8] It will no longer be necessary for prosecutors to prove fault in the boardrooms or at the highest levels of corporation: the fault of even middle managers may suffice. It also provides that the conduct of the organization's "representatives" will be attributed to the organization and defines a representative to include not only directors, employees and partners, but also agents and contractors. In a word, Bill C-45 significantly expands the net of corporate and organizational liability.

---

[6] For an excellent exposition of the changes see Todd Archibald, Kenneth Jull and Kent Roach, "The Changed Face of Corporate Criminal Liaibility" (2004) 48 C.L.Q. 367. See also Department of Justice, *A Plain Language Guide. Bill C-45 — Amendments to the Criminal Code Affecting the Criminal Liability of Organizations*, www.canada.justice.gc.ca/en/dept/pub/c45/index.html.

[7] Archibald *et al., supra*, note 1 at 368. The editors are indebted to Prof. Kent Roach for permission to reproduce this passage.

[8] *Criminal Code* s. 2 as amended by Bill C-45 s. 1.

The Impact of the *Charter of Rights and Freedoms* on Corporations*

The *Charter of Rights and Freedoms* (*Constitution Act*, 1982) raises important problems of its application to corporations and its interaction with corporation law. There are two related questions: can corporations invoke the protections of the *Charter* and, if so, to what extent? Since 1982, courts have approached these questions on a right-by-right basis, taking into account both the wording of the *Charter* provision and the nature of the right.

Application. The *Charter* employs various terms in referring to those protected by its provisions. Among these are "everyone" (ss. 2, 7, 8, 9, 10, 12, 17), "every citizen" (ss. 3 and 6), "every person who has the status of a permanent resident" (s. 6(2)), "any person" (ss. 11 and 19), "individual" (s. 15) and "anyone" (s. 24). The words "everyone", "any person" and "anyone" seem synonymous, whereas "citizen" and "permanent resident" have more particular meaning. The fact that the CBCA, the OBCA, and other provincial corporations Acts confer on corporations "the capacity and . . . the rights, powers and privileges of a natural person" (CBCA, s. 15, OBCA s. 15), suggests that corporations should be able to invoke the protection of the *Charter*. However, in *Skapinker v. Law Society of Upper Canada*, [1984] 1 S.C.R. 357, 1984 CarswellOnt 796, 1984 CarswellOnt 800 the Supreme Court of Canada held that the federal and provincial interpretation Acts do not apply to the *Charter*. A more persuasive argument is advanced by Hogg in *Constitutional Law of Canada*, (Carswell 1997, looseleaf) at 34-2, where he notes that many rights contained in the *Charter* "would be seriously attenuated if they did not apply to corporations." The right to "freedom of the press and other media" (s. 2(b)) seems particularly applicable to corporations, given the paucity of media businesses operating as sole proprietorships and partnerships. It would also seem irrational to restrict to natural persons the right to a fair trial (s. 11) or the right against unreasonable search and seizure (s. 8).

Some rights, on the other hand, seem by their nature inapplicable to corporations, even where the right applies to "everyone". The right to "freedom of conscience and religion" (s. 2(a)) has been held not to apply to corporations. *R. v. Big M Drug Mart Ltd.*, [1985] 1 S.C.R. 295, 1985 CarswellAlta 316, 1985 CarswellAlta 609 at 314. Conscience and religion both reflect a particularly human quality, the ability to "believe"; a corporation cannot "believe" in religion in that sense. Another example is the s. 7 right of "everyone" not to be deprived of "life, liberty and security of the person" contrary to the tenets of fundamental justice, which relates to the interests of individual human beings and does not in itself reflect "corporate" interests. See *Irwin Toy Ltd. c. Québec (Procureur general)*, [1989] 1 S.C.R. 927, 1989 CarswellQue 115F, 1989 CarswellQue 115 at 1004 [S.C.R.].

---

* This note is largely the work of James T. McClary, J.D. II student, Univ. of Toronto, 2003-4, for whose assistance the editors express their grateful appreciation.

Many procedural rights in the *Charter* relate to arrest or detention and the conduct of the trial. Because corporations cannot be arrested, detained or asked to testify, they cannot claim (a) protection against arbitrary imprisonment (s. 9), (b) various arrest-related rights under s. 10, (c) the right to reasonable bail (s. 11(e)) and (d) rights relating to testifying at trial (ss. 11(c), 13 and 14). See, for example, *R. v. Amway of Canada Ltd./Amway du Canada Ltée*, [1989] 1 S.C.R. 21, 1989 CarswellNat 690, 1989 CarswellNat 204 at 37–40 [S.C.R.].

The equality right (s. 15) confers its protections on "every individual" and these words have been understood (Hogg, *op. cit.*, p. 34-4) to be restricted to natural persons. Certainly, the reference to discrimination based on "race, national or ethnic origin, colour, religion, sex, age or mental or physical disability" points toward solely human concerns. However, the Supreme Court of Canada has consistently avoided deciding whether corporations are entitled to invoke equality rights and has usually decided such cases on other grounds. See Dale Gibson, *The Law of the Charter: Equality Rights* (Carswell 1990) and Gerald Chipeur, "Section 15 of the Charter protects People and Corporations — Equally" (1985-86), 11 C.B.L.J. 304.

Standing. A corporation will have standing to invoke the *Charter* if its rights have been infringed by legislation or actions of the Crown. A more controversial question is whether, and to what extent, a corporation may challenge legislation on the grounds that it infringes a right held only by natural persons. In *Big M Drug Mart, supra,* the defendant corporation successfully challenged a law prohibiting the selling of goods on a Sunday by invoking the right to freedom of religion. The law was held to be an infringement of s. 2(a) because it compelled the observance of the Christian sabbath. Justice Dickson held that although s. 2(a) of the *Charter* did not apply to corporations, Big M Drug Mart could invoke the right as a defence to a criminal charge because "no one can be convicted of an offence under an unconstitutional law" (*ibid.* at 313).

However, the Court reached a different conclusion in *Irwin Toy, supra.* Irwin Toy Ltd. sought a declaration that a law prohibiting advertising to children was unconstitutional on various grounds, including the s. 7 right to "life, liberty and security of the person". (The s. 7 argument was that penal sanctions under the act were impermissibly vague.) The court refused to consider the s. 7 argument. It distinguished *Big M Drug Mart* by noting that this was a civil suit and no criminal charge was pending against Irwin Toy.

The question whether a corporation has standing to defend a civil suit by invoking the rights of natural persons was discussed in *Canadian Egg Marketing Agency v. Richardson*, [1998] 3 S.C.R. 157, 1998 CarswellNWT 118, 1998 CarswellNWT 119. CEMA, which is a federal agency created under federal law, brought a civil suit requesting an injunction against two corporations that were violating federal law by selling eggs outside the territory of production. The Supreme Court held that the defendant corporations had standing to invoke mobility rights (s. 6) (*viz.* the "right to pursue gaining of livelihood in any province") and freedom of association (s. 2(d)) in defending the suit, although such rights are not enjoyed by corporations. Drawing a parallel with *Big M* (and distinguishing *Irwin Toy*), the Court reasoned that even though the corporations did not face criminal charges, they were brought to court involuntarily and were faced with the coercive power of the state, and therefore should be permitted to make the constitutional arguments. See further Andrew Bernstein, "The Yoke of *Canadian Egg*: Corporate Standing under the Charter" (2000), 33 C.B.L.J. 247.

Chapter 3

The Process of Incorporation

In this chapter we consider a number of issues associated with the incorporation and classification of corporations and the conceptual difficulties presented by pre-incorporation contracts.

1. PLACE OF INCORPORATION

As we have seen, the federal government, the provinces and the territories have concurrent jurisdiction to incorporate corporations. Incorporators therefore can elect to incorporate under federal, provincial or territorial law and, what is more, they generally have a choice of thirteen laws since none of the corporations Acts require the incorporators to be resident in the province or territory of incorporation. (Some of the Acts impose Canadian nationality and/or residency requirements for directors, however. See e.g., CBCA s. 105(3) and OBCA s. 118(3).) If the incorporators see an advantage in doing so, they may even incorporate offshore (a choice usually dictated by tax reasons) since the normal conflict of laws rule is that the validity of the incorporation, the status of the corporation and its general personal law will be governed by the law of its incorporation. See J.G. Castel, *Canadian Conflict of Laws*, 5th ed. (2002) 30.1. However, the conflict of laws rule must be applied with caution. Section 302(2) of the US *Restatement (Second) of Conflict of Laws* indicates that the local law of the state of incorporation will not be applied "in the unusual case where, with respect to the particular issue, some other state has a more significant relationship to the occurrence and the parties." Some American courts have refused to apply the law of incorporation to closely held corporations in determining management-shareholder relationships where there was no significant link between the jurisdiction of incorporation, the corporation's place of business and the shareholders' places of residence. Furthermore, certain provisions of California and New York corporations statutes apply to corporations with a close connection to the state, even if they are incorporated elsewhere.

The Competition for State and Provincial Charters: the Delaware Phenomenon

In the US, the "full faith and credit" clause in the US Constitution requires states to recognize extra-state corporations and, starting at the turn of the century, this led to keen competition among several states to attract new incorporations (and subsequent reincorporations of existing corporations) by offering incorporators flexible corporations Acts favourable to management. The race was won by Delaware. The Delaware government claims that more than one-half of all publicly traded corporations in the US are incorporated in the state, including 58% of Fortune 500 companies, more than any other state, figures that are consistent with earlier data compiled by Roberta Romano in *The Genius of American Corporate Law* (1993).

Early commentators generally interpreted the Delaware phenomenon as a competition in laxity (a "race to the bottom") and urged federal intervention. The seminal exposition of this thesis was published in 1974 by Professor William Cary, a Columbia University law professor and former SEC commissioner. See "Federalism and Corporate Law: Reflections upon Delaware" (1974), 83 Yale L.J. 663, and Nader, Green & Seligman, *Constitutionalizing the Corporation: The Case for the Federal Chartering of Giant Corporations* (1976).

Cary's thesis was strongly attacked by "law and economics" practitioners, of whom Professor Ralph K. Winter Jr., formerly of the Yale Law School and now a federal Senior Circuit Judge on the Second Circuit Court of Appeals, was one of the first ("State Law, Shareholder Protection, and the Theory of the Corporation" (1977), 6 J. Legal Stud. 251). Professor Winter argued that the market for state charters is no different than the market for any other competitive product and that a corporation's managers would not choose a "laxer" jurisdiction unless it was in the shareholders' interest to do so. In his view, management would be restrained from sacrificing shareholder interests by the same competitive forces — in capital markets, product markets, employment markets and the market for corporate control — that deter managerial rent seeking and abuses in general.

Subsequent investigators sought to verify empirically Professor Winter's *a priori* theorizing. They agreed that the data supported him, although there were significant differences in their actual findings. Richard Dodd and Peter Leftwich ("The Market for Corporate Charters: Unhealthy Competition versus Federal Regulation" (1980), 53 J. Bus. 259) examined the share performance on the New York Stock Exchange of 140 firms that changed domicile jurisdictions between 1927 and 1977. They found that shareholders of reincorporating corporations earned persistently abnormal returns averaging 30.25% in the 25 months prior to, and including, the month of the switch. Professor Romano's findings were much more modest. Her data, based on the performance of share prices 99 days before and after the reincorporating event, showed cumulative average residuals ranging from 0.65% for tax-motivated reincorporations to 8.6% for firms reincorporating in anticipation of merger and amalgamation activity. The overall average for all firms was 4.1%. ("Law as Product: Some Pieces of the Incorporation Puzzle" (1985), 1 J.L. Econ. & Org. 225. See also by the same author, "The State Competition Debate" (1987), 8 Cardozo L. Rev. 709 and "Competition for Corporate Charters and the Lessons of Takeover Statutes" (1993), 61 Fordham L. Rev. 843.)

More recent work attempts to quantify the claimed benefits of Delaware incorporation: Robert Daines' analysis ("Does Delaware Law Improve Firm Value?" (2001), 62 J. Fin. Econ. 559) suggests that Delaware firms were, all else equal, worth more than non-Delaware firms in the majority of years during his sample period of 1981 to 1996, although others dispute the significance and persistence of this effect. (See Lucian Bebchuk, Alma Cohen and Allen Ferrell, "Does the Evidence Favour State Competition in Corporate Law" (2002), 90 Cal. L. Rev. 1775, and Guhan Subramanian, "The Disappearing Delaware Effect" (2002) Harvard Law and Economics Discussion Paper No. 391.)

Current contributions to the US debate question the extent to which Delaware is subject to actual competition for incorporations: if Delaware faces no real threat from any single other state (the competition appearing to be between Delaware and a corporation's home state only), should we question the extent to which competitive forces in fact discipline the production of state corporate law? (See Lucian Bebchuk and Assaf Hamdani, "Vigorous Race or Leisurely Walk: Reconsidering the Debate on State Competition Over Corporate Charters" (2002), 112 Yale L.J. 553, Robert Daines, "The Incorporation Choices of IPO Firms" (2002), 77 N.Y.U.L. Rev. 1559, and Marcel Kahan and Ehud Kamar "The Myth of State Competition in Corporate Law" (2002), 55 Stanford L. Rev. 679.)

Shopping for favourable corporation laws has never been a prominent feature in Canada nor have the provinces and the federal government actively competed for incorporations. The Canadian tradition, in fact, has been in the opposite direction, and many have argued that provincial and federal administrators are more interested in promoting greater uniformity among provincial and federal corporation laws than in widening the gap between them. See Ziegel, *Studies in Canadian Company Law*, vol. 2 (1973), 62–67. There are probably many reasons for the absence of a Canadian Delaware. One of them undoubtedly is that, until the early 1970s, the differences among the provincial Acts and between the provincial and federal Acts were not as pronounced as were those among the various state laws in the US (although this does not explain why one of the provinces or the federal government did not strike out on its own with a view to capturing a larger share of the corporations market). Another reason may be the greater conservatism of Canadian corporation lawyers and their unwillingness to expose their clients to an unfamiliar corporate law regime. Whatever the true explanation, the general practice is to incorporate provincially in the province where the corporation expects to carry on its business if no significant extra-provincial operations are envisaged, and to incorporate federally if the corporation expects to conduct business in several provinces.

Ron Daniels examined the Canadian position in a pioneering study published in 1991 ("Should Provinces Compete? The Case for a Competitive Corporate Law Market" (1991), 36 McGill L.J. 130). He saw no intrinsic reasons why the market for provincial and federal charters should not be as competitive as it is in the US, and claimed that the Canadian market was more dynamic than was generally assumed. He found, for example, that the federal government's share of incorporations dropped from 17.8% in 1980 to 9.1% in 1986 while Quebec's share increased from 6.3% in 1979 to approximately 17% in 1986. (He admitted, however, that the changing Quebec political environment probably had more to do with these fluctuating figures than the relative attractiveness of the federal and Quebec corporate regimes.) He also found discernible changes in the rates of incorporation and the market share of incorporations of British Columbia, Alberta and Ontario, though again these differences may have been based on macroeconomic rather than corporate factors. His overall conclusion was that the trend suggested by the data for a more competitive Canadian charter market should be encouraged and not deplored.

Douglas Cumming and Jeffrey MacIntosh re-examined the Canadian market nine years later and concluded that theory and empirical evidence indicated that institutional barriers had limited the extent of competitive corporate law production and also argued that Canadian legislators sought to maximize uniformity, as opposed to revenues derived from a competitive incorporation business ("The Role of Interjurisdictional Competition in Shaping Canadian Corporate Law" (2000), 20 Int'l. Rev. L. & Econ. 141). In a subsequent study ("The Rationales Underlying Reincorporation and Implications for Canadian Corporations" (2001), 22 Int'l. Rev. L. & Econ. 277), the same authors found evidence that interprovincial reincorporations tended to be prompted by the transaction costs of carrying on business, while federal reincorporations had a more substantive law-shopping component, and that reincorporation did not consistently enhance or diminish firm value.

2. EXTRA-PROVINCIAL LICENSING AND FILING REQUIREMENTS

Under the Ontario *Extra-Provincial Corporations Act*, R.S.O. 1990, c. E.27, corporations incorporated in a Canadian province other than Ontario ("Class 1 Corporations") or in a territory of Canada or under the CBCA ("Class 2 Corporations") are not required to obtain a licence under the act to carry on business in Ontario. Corporations incorporated under the laws of a jurisdiction outside Canada are subject to the full force of the provincial requirements applicable to extra-provincial corporations. The requirements for corporations required to be licenced as extra-provincial corporations differ considerably in detail among provinces but share several basic features. First, it is an offence for such corporations to carry on business in the province without a licence, although prosecutions for non-compliance are rare. Second, an unlicenced extra-provincial corporation is usually not capable of maintaining an action or other proceeding before a provincial court or tribunal "in respect of a contract made by it." Ont. EPCA s. 21 (1). However, the defect can usually be cured retroactively by obtaining the licence. Third, the granting of the licence is usually discretionary with the designated official (although refusals apparently are rare), and the official is authorized to attach conditions. Ont. EPCA s. 5(5). Fourth, in common with domestic corporations, extra-provincial corporations are usually required to make annual filings of pertinent information. See *e.g.*, the *Ontario Corporations Information Act*, R.S.O. 1990, c. C.39, s. 4.

A critical feature of the licensing requirements is that they are triggered only if the extra-provincial corporation is "carrying on business" in the province. The definition of "carrying on business" has provoked a considerable volume of litigation. See *e.g.*, *Weight Watchers International Inc. v. Weight Watchers of Ontario Ltd.* (1972), [1973] 1 O.R. 549, 31 D.L.R. (3d) 645, 1972 CarswellOnt 295 (H.C.). Section 1(2) of Ont. EPCA makes it clear that an extra-provincial corporation will be deemed to carry on its business in Ontario if, *inter alia*, it has a "resident agent, representative, warehouse, office or place where it carries on its business in Ontario," but Ont. EPCA s. 1(3) is also a common provision, providing that an extra-provincial corporation does not carry on its business in Ontario by reason only that, "(a) it takes orders for or buys or sells goods, wares or merchandise; or (b) offers or sells services of any type, by use of travellers or through advertising or correspondence."

3. CONTINUANCE UNDER THE LAW OF ANOTHER JURISDICTION

An important feature of the CBCA and its provincial counterparts is the ability of a corporation "to "continue" its corporate existence under the law of another jurisdiction (referred to in the US as "reincorporation"). See CBCA ss. 187-188 and OBCA ss. 180-81. A corporation may wish to do so for one of a number of reasons: because of tax advantages, because it has shifted its business operations to the new jurisdiction, because of a desire to amalgamate with a corporation in the other jurisdiction or simply because the corporate climate is more hospitable in the second jurisdiction.

Whatever the reason, every continuance involves a two-step procedure. First, the emigrating corporation must obtain the consent of the authorities in the jurisdiction of its incorporation (the "export" step). Second, it must meet the requirements of the federal or provincial Act under which it seeks to be continued (the "import" step). Not surprisingly, it is easier to meet the requirements of the immigrating jurisdiction (can you see why, perhaps based on the discussion of regulatory competition earlier in this chapter?)

than it is to meet the requirements of the emigrating jurisdiction — an interesting reversal of the hurdles normally confronting immigrating individuals. Note carefully that, as in the case of mergers and amalgamations within the same jurisdiction, continuance under the law of another jurisdiction does not affect the migrating corporation's prior obligations, property rights and involvement in all prior civil, criminal and administrative proceedings pending before continuance. See CBCA s. 187(7) and OBCA s. 181(9). Does this mean that continuance involves no change in the status of the corporation?

In *Canada (Director appointed under s. 260 of the Business Corporations Act), Re* (1991), 80 D.L.R. (4th) 619, 1991 CarswellOnt 128 (C.A.), the substantive issue was whether the CBCA "export" provisions can be successfully evaded by a "three-cornered amalgamation" which, in the case, involved the Varity Corporation amalgamating with a newly incorporated CBCA corporation and the publicly held shares of Varity being exchanged for shares in a Delaware corporation. The Ontario Court of Appeal held that s. 185 of the CBCA could not be interpreted to confer on the Director under the Act wide discretionary power to veto amalgamations on the ground of inadequate protection of shareholders.

4. CLASSIFICATION OF CORPORATIONS

Many different types of classification exist for corporations. The following notes are limited to those types that are relevant for the purposes of modern business corporations Acts.

(a) Shares of "Widely Held" and "Closely Held" Corporations

It will readily be appreciated that corporations vary widely in the number of shareholders, value of assets and involvement in the securities market and that a statutory framework that may be appropriate for a corporation with widely dispersed shareholders may be quite inappropriate for a closely held corporation ("CHC") with few shareholders. Chapter 10 provides an historical overview of the comparatively recent process by which Canadian corporations law has addressed itself seriously to the distinction, although the process of adaptation is still incomplete. The CBCA and the OBCA differ in their definitional approach, as well in the substantive consequences, of the definitional criteria.

Following the distinction first drawn in the *British Companies Act 1907* between a "private company" and a "public company", the present OBCA distinguishes between a "non-offering corporation" and an "offering corporation". OBCA s. 1(1) defines an "offering corporation" as a corporation that is offering its securities to the public within the meaning of subsection (6) and that is not the subject of an order of the Ontario Securities Commission deeming it to have ceased to be offering its securities to the public. Section 1(6) deems a corporation to be offering its securities to the public only where,

(a) in respect of any of its securities a prospectus or statement of material facts has been filed under the *Securities Act* or any predecessor thereof, or in respect of which a prospectus has been filed under *The Corporations Information Act* . . . or any predecessor thereof, so long as any of such securities are outstanding or any securities into which such securities are converted are outstanding; or

(b) any of its securities have been at any time since the 1st day of May, 1967, listed and posted for trading on any stock exchange in Ontario recognized by the Commission regardless of when such listing and posting for trading commenced.

The distinction between offering and non-offering corporations is material under the OBCA for the purposes of: ss. 20 (financial assistance by corporation), 111 (mandatory solicitation of proxies), 112 (information circulars), 115(2) and (3) (minimum number of directors and outside directors), 138(1) (insider liability), 148 (exemption from audit requirements), 158(1) (audit committee) and Part XV (compulsory acquisitions).

The CBCA does not provide a single distinction for all purposes under the Act (as does the OBCA with the definition of "offering corporation"), but rather relies on different distinctions in different contexts. For example, the CBCA defines a "distributing corporation" as a corporation that is a "reporting issuer" under provincial securities legislation that provides that definition (B.C., Alberta, Saskatchewan, Manitoba, Ontario, Quebec, Nova Scotia and Newfoundland), and, in the case of a corporation that is not a "reporting issuer", a corporation

(i) that has filed a prospectus or registration statement under provincial legislation or under the laws of a jurisdiction outside Canada,

(ii) any of the securities of which are listed and posted for trading on a stock exchange in or outside Canada, or

(iii) that is involved in, formed for, resulting from or continued after an amalgamation, a reorganization, an arrangement or a statutory procedure, if one of the participating bodies corporate is a corporation to which subparagraph (i) or (ii) applies.

The following are the material provisions of the CBCA that rely on the definition of "distributing corporation": ss. 2(1) (definition of "squeeze-out transaction"), 21 (access to corporate records), 49(9) (limits on restriction on transfer of shares), 102 (minimum number of directors and outside directors), 135(1.1) (notice of shareholder meetings), 149 (mandatory solicitation of proxies), 160 (filing of financial statements), 163 (dispensing with auditor), 171 (audit committee), 174 (constrained shares), Part XI (insider trading) and Part XVII (compulsory and compelled acquisitions).

In other contexts, the CBCA refers to a corporation engaged in a "distribution to the public", as in s. 82(2) (applicability of trust indenture provisions). Finally, in still other contexts, the CBCA relies on other *indicia* of closely-held corporations, as in ss. 149(2)(b) (number of shareholders required for mandatory solicitation of proxies) and 160(1) (filing of financial statements).

(b) One-person Corporations

The only significant substantive issue associated with the legal validity of one-person corporations concerns the holding of meetings. Etymologically, a meeting requires two or more persons and that is also the general corporate law rule: *Cowichan Leader Ltd., Re* (1963), 42 D.L.R. (2d) 111, 45 W.W.R. 57, 1963 CarswellBC 149 (S.C.). Most Acts accordingly provide that where a corporation only has one shareholder he or she alone may constitute a meeting. The same rule applies to a corporation that has only one director. See CBCA s. 139(4), OBCA s. 101(4), CBCA s. 114(8) and OBCA s. 126(12). These provisions should be read in conjunction with the equally common provisions recognizing the validity of unanimous resolutions in writing. See CBCA s. 142(1) and OBCA s. 104(1).

(c) Constrained Share Corporations

Federal and provincial legislation permit corporations with publicly issued shares to restrict their transfer to comply with Canadian ownership and control requirements. See CBCA s. 174, Regs., Pt. 9 and OBCA s. 42(2).

(d) Professional Corporations

The 1967 Lawrence Report favoured permitting members of professions to incorporate themselves, subject to safeguards for the protection of the public, reasoning that

> carrying on a professional practice in corporate form permits classification of the legal relationships between shareholders of the company and third parties; simplifies or eliminates difficulties arising by virtue of the withdrawal, retirement or death of members of a professional partnership; expedites transfer of interests in the practice from one person to another or to incoming members of the practice; and permits the accumulation of partnership profits for the purpose of re-investing in fixed assets or for other purposes. In addition, there are, under existing law, very real income tax advantages which would accrue to

the professional person or partnership on incorporation of the practice. There seems to be no reason why all these advantages should not be available to those who are active in professional life. (*Ontario Select Committee on Company Law, Interim Report* (1967), para. 2.2.4.)

OBCA s. 3.1(2) permits a professional corporation to practise a profession governed by an act if that act expressly permits the practise of that profession by a corporation or if the act is one of those listed in s. 3.1(2)(b) (which includes legislation relating to accountants and lawyers). Ontario amended the *Law Society Act*, R.S.O. 1990, c. L.8, in 1991 to permit lawyers to practice through corporations. The OBCA makes it clear that the liability of a member of a profession for a professional liability claim is not affected by the fact that he or she is practising through a professional corporation and that shareholders of professional corporations remain liable under their governing legislation for acts of employees and agents of the corporation. Section 61.05(1) of the *Law Society Act* further provides that the professional, fiduciary and ethical obligations of persons practising law are not diminished by the fact that they are practising law through a professional corporation and apply equally to the corporation and its directors, officers, shareholders, agents and employees. For applications of similar provisions, see *Corkery v. Foster Wedekind* (1987), 45 D.L.R. (4th) 159, 1987 CarswellAlta 262 (Q.B.) and *Bancorp Financial Ltd. v. Thomas N. Mather Professional Corp.*, [1985] 3 W.W.R. 190, 1985 CarswellAlta 10 (Q.B.).

It appears that interest in professional corporations in Canada is (or was) largely motivated by tax considerations. Assuming the enabling legislation retains the element of personal liability for the members of the corporation, "[t]he striking feature of the non-tax advantages and disadvantages of professional incorporation is how relatively inconsequential they appear to be." (J.R.S. Prichard, "Incorporation by Lawyers" in Evans & Trebilcock (Eds.), *Lawyers and the Consumer Interest* (1982), Ch. 10, p. 303.) Until 1978 there were clear tax advantages in incorporation by professionals because of the availability of the small business deduction and the opportunities for income splitting. Amendments to the *Income Tax Act* since then have returned professionals to the commonalty of other taxpayers, subject to limited remaining opportunities for income splitting with a spouse and, for the most sophisticated taxpayers, deferral, supporting Prof. Prichard's conclusion that "the current situation results in close to tax neutrality for small firms and a modest tax disincentive to incorporation for large firms in most circumstances" (*ibid.*, p. 313).

(e) Unlimited Liability Companies

Alone among Canadian jurisdictions, Nova Scotia permits the incorporation of "unlimited liability companies" ("ULCs"), which are corporations without limits on the liability of their members (see *Companies Act*, R.S.N.S. 1989, c. 81, s. 9(c)). A ULC's name may not include the words "limited" or "incorporated", although it can use the words "company" or "Co." and identify itself as a ULC. The liability of members of a ULC is unlimited, but, unlike partners who bear direct liability to creditors on an ongoing basis, the liability of ULC members arises only on the winding up of the ULC in the event its assets are insufficient to meet its obligations. Members can limit their personal liability to third parties by contract, and there are numerous limitations on the liability of former members (*Companies Act*, s. 135). In addition, investors in a ULC typically insulate themselves from unlimited personal liability by interposing a limited liability corporation or limited partnership between themselves and the ULC.

The principal reason for using a ULC is the fact that US tax rules permit the ULC to elect to be taxed as a partnership in the US, even though it is a corporation for all purposes (including tax) in Canada.

5. INCORPORATION TECHNIQUES

Historically there were major differences in the methods of incorporation employed in various jurisdictions. Generally speaking, in the Western provinces (excluding Manitoba), Nova Scotia and Newfoundland, incorporation was effected by delivery to the incorporating official, commonly known as the Registrar of Companies, of two documents entitled, respectively, the memorandum of association and the articles of association. The former constituted the basic constitutional document of the company, containing its name, capital structure and a statement of its proposed business.

In the remaining provinces, and federally, incorporation was effected by making an application to a public official for a grant of Letters Patent of Incorporation. The letters patent granted contained information approximately equivalent to the contents of the memorandum, but there was no requirement to file, in support of it, the by-laws which corresponded to the articles of association and contained the internal regulations of the corporation.

Those jurisdictions employing the memorandum and articles of association are generally referred to as "registration" or "memorandum" jurisdictions, and it has been held that the duty of the incorporating officer is to ensure that the documents filed comply with the provisions of the statute, and in particular, that the proposed company has no objects which are illegal, and that there is no objection to the use of the proposed name. Upon being satisfied as to this, he is bound to accept the documents and issue a certificate of incorporation. He cannot decline to register the documents if the Act has been complied with and, at common law, *mandamus* would lie to compel him to do so: *R. v. Companies Registrar, ex parte Bowen*, [1914] 3 K.B. 1161; and *cf. Re Crown Lumber*, [1943] 4 D.L.R. 415.

In the letters-patent jurisdictions, conversely, a grant of letters patent creating a corporation was an act of the executive, and the Minister involved could, in his absolute and uncontrolled discretion, refuse to grant letters patent or impose arbitrary terms for their issue.

The Lawrence Report concluded that the letters patent system was "an historical anachronism which ought not to be preserved; and that modern public policy no longer requires that a corporation can come into being only by Ministerial Act" (*Ontario Select Committee on Company Law, Interim Report* (1967) para. 1.1.6).

Ontario and the other former letters-patent jurisdictions, other than PEI, have all now moved towards a system involving a minimum of administrative discretion with respect to the grant of corporate status. Under this regime, incorporation is effected by delivering to the incorporating officer a document called "articles of incorporation". See *e.g.*, CBCA ss. 6-8 and OBCA ss. 4-6. The articles of incorporation in these jurisdictions correspond to the memorandum of association in memorandum jurisdictions. There is no requirement in the non-memorandum jurisdictions to file the by-laws which correspond to the articles of association of a memorandum company. However, it is possible to entrench in the articles of incorporation provisions which would otherwise be proper subject matter for by-laws. See CBCA s. 6(2) and OBCA s. 5(3). As is true in the memorandum jurisdictions, if the documents are in order the incorporating officer is required to issue a certificate of incorporation. An appeal lies from the officer's refusal to do so. See CBCA s. 246 and OBCA ss. 251-252.

Three of the former memorandum jurisdictions — Alberta, Saskatchewan and Newfoundland — have also adopted the terminology and incorporation techniques of the federal Act, consistent with their general adoption of that Act, but the other memorandum jurisdictions (B.C. and Nova Scotia) have so far retained the British legacy, although with some modifications in the case of the new British Columbia *Business Corporations Act*, S.B.C. 2002, c. 57 ("BCBCA"). Under the BCBCA the memorandum is replaced by a document called the "notice of articles", the articles will no longer be publicly filed, and the incorporators will enter into a brief "incorporation agreement" intended to preserve the contractual basis of the memorandum corporation (described in Section 7 below).

6. CORPORATE NAMES

One of the more important matters that must be decided upon in the incorporation process is the selection of a corporate name. The legislation in all jurisdictions seeks to regulate the use of corporate names, primarily with a view to ensuring that the public will not be misled by confusingly similar corporate names. The statutory provisions vary from province to province, both in the degree of their complexity and in the detail of their requirements, and the relevant statute must be consulted in each case to determine the appropriate requirements. See, for example, CBCA ss. 10–13 and OBCA ss. 8-9. CBCA s. 11(2) and OBCA s. 8 also allow the use of assigned unique number names.

Whether by detailed statutory provision, regulation or administrative practice, a common theme in the regulation of corporate names is the protection of the public against deception. See, for example, OBCA ss. 9(l)(b) and CBCA s. 12(1) and Regulations, Part 2. The statutes and regulations generally speak of a likelihood of deception, confusion, *etc.*, regardless of any intention to deceive: *cf. Re F.P. Chapple Co. Ltd.* (1960), 25 D.L.R. (2d) 706 (Ont. C.A.).

The following passage, from Iacobucci, Pilkington and Prichard, *Canadian Business Corporations* (1977), p. 34, conveys the flavour of the sort of protection sought to be conferred by corporate name legislation:

> In deciding whether a name will probably lead to confusion with an existing business name, consideration is given to such factors as the nature of the business and the class of persons likely to be affected, the visual and auditory impact of the two names, the use of descriptive and generic terms, and the time and mode of use of a name which may have stamped it with a particular identity (*Re C.C. Chemicals Ltd.* (1967), 63 D.L.R. (2d) 203 (Ont. C. A.); *Re Office Overload and Driver Overload Ltd.*, [1968] 1 O.R. 292 (H.C.J.); *Re Compro Ltd. and Combined Engineered Products Ltd.* (1974), 44 D.L.R. (3d) 21 (Ont. Div. Ct.); *Canadian Motorways Ltd. v. Laidlaw Motorways Ltd.* (1973), 40 D.L.R. (3d) 52 (S.C.C.) per Laskin, J. (as he then was) at p. 64). Even where companies are engaged in different lines of business, they will not be allowed to use similar names which might lead the public to believe they are associated with each other (*Re Ebsco Investments Ltd. and Ebsco Subscription Services Ltd.* (1975), 56 D.L.R. (3d) 501 (Ont. Div. Ct.)). The phrase "likely to deceive" is thus interpreted to mean "probably will mislead or confuse in the circumstances". See also, *Action Plumbing Ltd. v. Registrar of Companies*, [1977] 1 W.W.R. 123 (Alta. C.A.).

Apart from the protection accorded to corporate names (and any goodwill associated with them) under corporate legislation, there is also the protection accorded by the common law concerning passing off and federal trademark legislation. For a discussion of the relationship between these forms of protection, see *Fastening House Ltd. v. Fastway Supply House Ltd.* (1974), 45 D.L.R. (3d) 505, 3 O.R. (2d) 385 (H.C.).

A name conflict that attracted media attention involved Brick's Fine Furniture Ltd. in Winnipeg and Brick Warehouse Corporation, which started its corporate career in Alberta but later established outlets across the Prairies and in Ontario. Brick's Fine Furniture was incorporated under Manitoba law and allegedly established its business in Winnipeg long before Brick Warehouse opened a branch there. Brick Warehouse was incorporated under the CBCA and also registered its name under the federal *Trade Marks Act*. The Manitoba courts apparently took the position that they had no jurisdiction to restrain a federally incorporated company from using its name even if it was confusing and that only the federal authorities could make such an order. Proceedings were subsequently initiated in the Federal Court of Canada, which resolved the issue by requiring both parties to post signs in their stores indicating that they were not associated with one another (an arrangement that remains in place fifteen years later, at least on Brick Fine Furniture Ltd.'s Internet site). See *Brick's Fine Furniture Ltd. v. Brick Warehouse Corp.* (1989), 25 C.P.R. (3d) 89 (Man. C.A.) and *Brick Warehouse Corp. v. Brick's Fine Furniture Ltd.* (1992), 42 C.P.R. (3d) 158 (Fed. T.D.).

7. THE NATURE OF THE CORPORATE CONSTITUTION

The differences between the memorandum and letters patent, and now CBCA type, jurisdictions go well beyond the methods of incorporation to some important conceptual distinctions. Although their significance has been reduced by legislation, an understanding of the distinctions remains important in studying the British jurisprudence and in considering the residual differences not resolved by the modern Canadian Acts.

(a) Pre-CBCA Distinctions

Before the adoption of the CBCA and its provincial counterparts, the most relevant distinctions relating to the nature of the corporate constitution were the following:

(1) In the absence of statutory restrictions, a letters patent corporation was deemed to have the capacity and powers of a natural person; a memorandum company, on the other hand, was subject to the doctrine of *ultra vires* as a result of the decision in *Riche v. Ashbury Ry. Carriage & Iron Ore Co.* (1875), L.R. 7 H.L. 653 (H.L.).

(2) In the memorandum jurisdictions the articles of association constituted a public document and outsiders were deemed to have constructive notice of its contents. The by-laws were never required to be filed under the letters patent Acts and accordingly this doctrine of constructive notice did not apply to them.

(3) In the memorandum jurisdictions the memorandum and articles of association constitute a contract between the shareholders and, as construed by the courts, a mutually enforceable contract between the shareholders and the company. See BCBCA s. 19(3), and s. 14 of the U.K. *Companies Act,* 1985. According to Prof. Gower (*Principles of Modern Company Law,* 6th ed. (1997), p. 115-6), the wording of s. 14 "can be traced back with variations to the original Act of 1844 which adopted the existing method of forming an unincorporated joint stock company by deed of settlement (which did of course constitute a contract between the members who sealed it) and merely superimposed incorporation on registration." There was no corresponding

provision in the letters patent Acts. This did not of course mean that the letters patent and by-laws were not binding on the corporation and its members, but it meant that the source of their binding character, and its extent, depended on the express or implied terms of the statute. Curiously, Canadian case law never clearly resolved the conceptual issue. In a sparsely reasoned judgment, the court in *Rands v. Hiram Walker, Gooderham and Worts Ltd.*, [1936] O.R. 488, [1936] 4 D.L.R. 186 held that the by-laws had contractual effect between shareholders and their company, but it is not clear how much, if anything, turned on this characterization. In *In re Good & Jacob Y. Shantz Son & Co.* (1910), 21 O.L.R. 153, 158, MacLaren, J.A. clearly was of the view that the by-laws were not contractual in nature. See also Wegenast, *Law of Canadian Companies*, (1931) p. 244.

(4) The deemed consensual character of the constitution of a memorandum company also brought in its train other important consequences which have survived to some extent to the present day. First, the allocation of powers between the directors and shareholders was regarded as an internal question to be resolved by the company's constitution. Accordingly, BCBCA s. 136(1) provides "The directors of a company must, subject to this Act, the regulations and the memorandum and articles of the company, manage or supervise the management of the business and affairs of the company". The British Act does not contain even this presumption in favour of the directors' managerial authority. Second, although its scope remains unclear, there is ample authority for the proposition that residual authority remains with the shareholders in general meeting to break a deadlock among directors (*Barron v. Potter*, [1914] 1 Ch. 895, 83 L.J. Ch. 646), to ratify *ultra vires* acts of the directors (*Irvine v. Union Bank of Australia* (1877), 2 A.C. 366; *Bamford v. Bamford*, [1970] Ch. 212, [1969] 1 All E.R (1969)), and to commence action in the company's name (*Marshall's Valve Gear Co. v. Manning, Wardle & Co.*, [1970] 1 Ch. 267, 78 L.J. Ch. 46). This conception of the shareholders in general meeting as possessing residual authority in company affairs also underlies the rule in *Foss v. Harbottle* (1843), 2 Hare 461, 67 E.R. 189.

The position for the most part was very different in the letters-patent jurisdictions. To begin with, it is clear that the directors derive their managerial authority from the Act and not from the corporation's constitution. See Wegenast, *supra*, pp. 353-4, *Kelly v. Electrical Construction Co.* (1907), 16 O.L.R. 232, and *infra*, Ch. 4. Typically, the letters-patent Acts provide or provided (as the CBCA s. 102(1) and OBCA s. 115(1) now provide) that "Subject to any unanimous shareholder agreement, the directors shall manage, or supervise the management of, the business and affairs of a corporation." The shareholders were not given the option of modifying the statutory prescription other than by way of a unanimous shareholder agreement.

The directors' exclusive managerial authority was also emphasized in letters-patent jurisdictions in the usual statutory provision giving directors the exclusive power to adopt bylaws, albeit subject to a requirement for shareholder approval at the next annual meeting of the corporation. On the other hand, in interpreting the statutory by-law making powers, the Canadian courts were not willing to construe them as broadly as the British courts were in reviewing the validity of amendments to articles of association. *Cf. Hutchings v. Can. National Fire Ins. Co.* (1917), 27 Man. R. 496, 33 D.L.R. 752 (C.A.), affirmed [1918] A.C. 451, 39 D.L.R. 401 (P.C.) with *Sidebottom v. Kershaw, Leese & Co. Ltd.*, [1920] 1 Ch. 154, 89 L.J. Ch. 113 (C.A.). The Canadian courts apparently also reserved the general common law right, applied originally to municipal institutions, to test the reasonableness of the by-laws of letters patent corporations. This supervisory jurisdiction was never extended to memorandum companies, although the position has now been changed by statute. See *Edmonton Country Club Ltd. v. Case*, [1975] 1 S.C.R. 534, and the discussion of the "oppression remedy," *infra*, Ch. 11.

Finally, the residual authority of the shareholders in a letters patent jurisdiction has never been clearly defined or put on a sound conceptual footing. Many cases established that the rule in *Foss v. Harbottle* (with its implication of shareholders' power of ratification) applied to letters patent as well as memorandum companies, but beyond this one cannot speak with any assurance. See Wegenast, *supra*, pp. 267, 352, and S.M. Beck, "An Analysis of Foss v. Harbottle" in Ziegel (Ed.), *Studies in Canadian Company Law* (1967), vol. 1, Ch. 18 at pp. 552–556.

For further discussions of the above issues, see M. Neuman, "Letters Patent and Memorandum of Association Companies" in *Studies*, *supra*, vol. 1, Ch. 3, and B. Slutsky, "The Division of Power between the Board of Directors and the General Meeting," *ibid.*, vol. 2, Ch. 4 (1973).

(b) Current Position

The significant changes in the differences between memorandum and letters-patent jurisdictions introduced in the 1970s federal and provincial legislation are the following:

(1) The doctrine of *ultra vires*, so far as it affects the position of third parties, and the doctrine of constructive notice with respect to the contents of public corporate documents, has been abolished in the CBCA, the OBCA and the BCBCA. See, *infra*, Ch. 4.

(2) The entrenched nature of the directors' power is confirmed in CBCA s. 102(1), OBCA s. 115(1) but subject to important qualifications involving unanimous shareholder agreements (CBCA s. 146, OBCA s. 108), shareholder proposals (CBCA s. 137, OBCA s. 99) and shareholders' concurrent powers to initiate by-law changes (CBCA ss. 103, 137, OBCA ss. 99, 116).

(3) Both the CBCA s. 120(7.1), and OBCA s. 132(8), confirm the shareholders' power to ratify a voidable contract in which an officer or director has a material interest.

(4) The courts are given an explicit power in favour of shareholders and other "complainants" to enjoin the corporation and its officers from violating the Act, its regulations or the corporation's constitution and to

require compliance with their provisions. See CBCA s. 247, OBCA s. 253(1) and, *infra*, Ch. 11(5).

It will be seen therefore that the important constitutional differences that remain between the memorandum and CBCA type jurisdictions are those involving (a) the allocation of powers between management and shareholders; (b) the scope of the shareholders' general residual powers; and (c) the permissible scope of by-laws and articles of association. As has been seen, the latter two differences were of uncertain scope before and remain so under the new legislation. The student should also appreciate that differences that may appear important in law often are much less so in practice, particularly according to accounts of the corporation asserting that shareholders have ceased to exercise a meaningful managerial or supervisory role in the affairs of the corporation.

(c) Note on the Scope of the Contract Created by the Memorandum and Articles of Association in Memorandum Jurisdictions

(1) It is clearly established that the memorandum and articles do not constitute a contract between the company and a non-member. In *Eley v. Positive Government Security Live Assce. Co.* (1876), 1 Ex. D. 88, 45 L.J.Q. B. 451 (C.A.), the articles, which were prepared by Eley, provided that he should be the company solicitor. He subsequently became a member, but his employment was later terminated, and he sued for breach of contract. It was held that the articles could not be relied upon to support his claims, since at the critical time of incorporation, he was not a party to them.

(2) BCBCA s. 19(3), does not expressly provide that each member is deemed to contract with the company, though this has been held to be its effect: *Hickman v. Kent or Romney Marsh Sheepbreeders' Association*, [1915] Ch. 881, 84 L.J. Ch. 688.

It follows, in principle, that not only are the members bound to the company but that the company is also bound to the members: *Wood v. Odessa Waterworks Co.* (1889), 42 Ch. D. 636, 58 L.J. Ch. 628 (Ch. Div.).

It is also clear that a contract exists between the members *inter se*. Finally, there is abundant authority for the view that the contractual force of the memorandum and articles is, so far as members are concerned, limited to contractual rights or imposing burdens upon them in their capacity as members.

(3) In *Hickman v. Kent or Romney Marsh Sheepbreeders' Association* [1915] 1 Ch. 881, 84 L.J. Ch. 688, it was suggested that for a right to be conferred upon a member *qua* member, it must be part of the provisions applicable to all members. In *Rattfield v. Haity*, [1960] Ch. 1, the articles required every member who intended to transfer his shares to notify the directors who were then required to take the shares at a fair value. The plaintiffs duly gave notice, but the defendant denied liability to take up and pay for the shares, and plaintiff sought to compel them to do so, and succeeded. It was held that the obligation to acquire the shares was imposed

upon the directors as members. Would the result have been different if the directors had not been required by the articles to be members?

(4) It is generally considered that the remedy available to a member who complains of a breach of the articles is a declaration or injunction, but not damages. There is authority for the proposition that a shareholder cannot sue a company for damages in respect of his position as shareholder unless he is also in a position to rescind his membership contract, and does so: *Houldsworth v. City of Glasgow Bank* (1880), 5 App. Cas. 317, and *Phili pzyk v. Edmonton Real Estate Board* (1975), 55 D.L.R. (3d) 424 (Alta. A.D.). Do BCBCA s. 228, OBCA s. 253, and CBCA s. 247, permit damages to be awarded? *Cf. Goldhar v. Quebec Manitou Mines Ltd.* (1976), 9 O.R. (2d) 740, *infra*, Ch. 11.

(5) There is an ongoing debate with respect to the relationship between s. 14 of the English Act and the rule in *Foss v. Harbottle*. The traditional reconciliation between the two rules is that under s. 14 a member is only entitled to enforce individual rights and that the rule in *Foss v. Harbottle* precludes a shareholder from suing for breach of a duty only owed to the company. It is often said that directors' and officers' duties lie only to the company. Nevertheless, it is now recognized, both in the memorandum and letters patent type jurisdictions, that there may be a concurrent breach of duty to the shareholders and to the company. However, the principle is somewhat differently formulated in the two systems. *Cf.* Gower, *op. cit.,* pp. 120, with *Goldex Mines Ltd. v. Revill* (1975), 7 O.R. (2d) 216, 54 D.L.R. (3d) 672 (C.A.), *infra*, Ch. 11.

(6) In view of the heavy judicial gloss on s. 14 and the conflicting interpretations placed on the section, Prof. Gower concludes (*op. cit.,* p. 122) that "What is clearly needed is either a review of all the relevant authorities by the House of Lords or a revised version of section 14." Given the unsatisfactory British position, the Alberta Law Reform Institute felt that "There is no need to resort to the artificial implication of a contract, and indeed, the notion that there is a contract is likely to interfere with the proper working out of rights and obligations which arise because of relationships the nature of which is determined by law." (*Proposals for a New Alberta Business Corporations Act* (1980), vol. 1, p. 21.)

Does CBCA s. 239 make it any easier to distinguish between individual and derivative rights of a shareholder, and to determine the circumstances when an action can only be brought by, or on behalf of, the corporation? See *Re Goldhar & Quebec Manitou Mines Ltd.* (1977), 9 O.R. (2d) 740, 61 D.L.R. (3d) 612 (Div. Ct.), *infra*, Ch. 11.

8. ALTERATION OF THE CORPORATE CONSTITUTION

All corporate legislation includes provisions of varying degrees of comprehensiveness and complexity governing the method by which the constitution of the corporation may be altered. See, *e.g.*, CBCA ss. 173–180 and OBCA ss. 168–170. It is impossible here to summarize in any useful way the details of the mechanisms prescribed by the various statutes for effecting an alteration, or the extent to which the corporate constitution is, in each jurisdiction, subject to alteration.

Three general characteristics of the statutory requirements are common, however. First, to effect an alteration of the constitution requires, in each case, a special procedure, generally in the form of a shareholders' resolution that must be agreed to by more than a mere majority of the shareholders. Second, if rights are attached to the shares of a particular group or class of shareholders (*e.g.*, preferred shares) that are, in some sense, unique, provision is generally made for the shareholders holding those shares to give their consent separately to any alteration of those rights. Third, modern corporate legislation commonly provides that shareholders who disagree with, and vote against certain proposed alterations, are entitled to have their shares bought from them at a valuation. This so-called "appraisal remedy" is examined in Ch. 12.

The limitations imposed by these provisions are principally procedural in character and must, of course, be observed if the alteration is to be effective. In addition, however, there are substantive limitations.

First, a shareholder cannot, without his consent, be required to take or subscribe for more shares or have his liability to contribute to the assets of the company increased:

> The doctrine of limited liability operates to protect the holders of fully-paid shares not only from the claims of creditors of the company, but also from obligations, financial or other, sought to be imposed by other shareholders of the company. It would be a strange thing and contrary to all jurisprudence, if the purchaser of shares in a public company could be required all of a sudden and against his will, at the instance of the company or a majority of its shareholders, to contribute to the operating expenses, or capital requirement needs of the company.

Per Dickson, J. in *Edmonton Country Club Ltd. v. Case*, [1975] 1 S.C.R. 534, 44 D.L.R. (3d) 554, 565.

Second, the principle that a majority may not exercise its powers in fraud of, or so as to oppress, a minority also operates as a limitation upon the power to alter the constitution.

9. PRE-INCORPORATION CONTRACTS

The fact that Anglo-Canadian law does not recognize the existence of a corporation until a certificate of incorporation has been issued or other prescribed conditions have been met, creates significant legal and practical difficulties where a promoter purports to conclude a contract on behalf of a proposed corporation. This may happen in a variety of circumstances: the promoter may feel it important to get the commitment of the other party to the contract before he has an opportunity to change his mind; the other party may insist on the contract being concluded by a given date; the existence of the contract may be a pre-condition of the promoter being able to attract other investors to the corporation, and so forth. The promoter often wants to avoid personal liability on the contract and, since most promoters are not lawyers, she probably believes she can secure this immunity by signing the contract in a representative capacity. Frequently the promoter is also under the mistaken impression that the corporation has already been incorporated or that compliance with the statutory incorporation requirements is only a minor inconsequential formality.

Part (a) of the following materials explores the common law status of pre-incorporation contracts, while Part (b) deals with the important statutory reforms introduced in the business corporations acts. In considering the legal position, students will find it helpful to distinguish between the following situations:

1. Both parties to the contract (the promoter and the contracting party) know that the company has not yet been incorporated.
2. The promoter knows that the company has not yet been incorporated but the contracting party does not.
3. Neither party to the contract knows that the company has not yet been incorporated; the promoter mistakenly believes that the company has been incorporated and the contracting party relies on the promoter's representations.

Where the company is eventually incorporated, consider also the differences between the situations where the corporation purports to ratify or adopt the pre-incorporation contract, and where it does not ratify or adopt the contract.

Finally, as you read these materials and the claims that each contracting party (i.e., the party that is not the promoter) is making, consider whether or not it should matter if the contracting party made any inquiry, prior to concluding the contract, into the assets or solvency of the corporation purporting to enter into the contract. Is there an element of a windfall if the promoter is held personally liable on the contract where the contracting party made no such inquiries?

(a) Common Law Position

Kelner v. Baxter
(1866), L.R. 2 C.P 174 (Common Pleas)

The plaintiff was a wine merchant and the proprietor of the Assembly Rooms at Gravesend. In August, 1865, it was proposed that a company should be formed for establishing a joint-stock hotel company at Gravesend to be called The Gravesend Royal Alexandra Hotel Company, Limited, of which the following persons were to be the directors, *viz.* L. Calisher, T.H. Edmands, M. Davis, Macdonald, Hulse, N.J. Calisher (one of the defendants), and the plaintiff. The plaintiff was to be the manager of the proposed company; Mr. Dales (another of the defendants) was to be the permanent architect. One part of the scheme was that the company should purchase the premises of the plaintiff for the sum of £5,000, of which £3,000 was to be paid in cash, and £2,000 in paid up shares. The stock *etc.* was to be taken at a valuation. This agreement was carried into effect and completed, the other defendant (Baxter) being the nominal purchaser on behalf of the company. In December a prospectus was settled. On the 9th of January, 1866, a memorandum of association was executed by the plaintiff and the defendants and others.

Pending the completion of the sale, the plaintiff continued to carry on the business and for that purpose purchased additional stock. On the 27th of January, 1866, an agreement was entered into for the transfer of this additional stock to the company on the following terms:

"January 27th, 1866.

"To John Dacier Baxter, Nathan Jacob Calisher, and John Dales, on behalf of the proposed Gravesend Royal Alexandra Hotel Company, Limited.

"Gentlemen, — I hereby propose to sell the extra stock now at the Assembly Rooms, Gravesend, as per schedule hereto, for the sum of £900, payable on the 28th of February, 1866.

(Signed) "John Kelner."

Then followed a schedule of the stock of wines, etc., to be purchased, and at the end was written as follows:

To Mr. John Kelner.

"Sir, — We have received your offer to sell the extra stock as above, and hereby agree to and accept the terms proposed.

(Signed)   "J.D. Baxter,
                            "N.J. Calisher,
                            "J. Dales,

"On behalf of the Gravesend Royal Alexandra
Hotel Company, Limited."

Pursuant to this agreement the goods in question were handed over to the company and consumed by it in the business of the hotel. On the 1st of February a meeting of the directors took place which the following resolution was passed: "That the arrangement entered into by Messrs. Calisher, Dales, and Baxter, on behalf of the company, for the purchase of the additional stock on the premises, as per list taken by Mr. Bright, the secretary, and pointed out by Mr. Kelner, amounting to £900, be, and the same is hereby ratified." There was also a subsequent ratification by the company, *viz.* on the 11th of April, but this was after the commencement of the action.

The articles of association of the company were duly stamped on the 13th of February and on the 20th the company obtained a certificate of incorporation under the *Companies Act* 1862.

The company having collapsed, the present action was brought against the defendants upon the agreement of January 27th.

Erle C.J. rendered judgment for the plaintiff for £900. He refused the defendants leave to introduce oral evidence to show that it was not the parties' intention that they should be held personally liable on the contract. He did however give them leave to move to enter a nonsuit on the ground that the agreement of January 27th did not make them personally liable.

ERLE, C.J.: I am of opinion that this rule should be discharged. The action is for the price of goods sold and delivered: and the question is whether the goods were delivered to the defendants under a contract of sale. The alleged contract is in writing, and commences with a proposal addressed to the defendants, in these words: — "I hereby propose to sell the extra stock now at the Assembly Rooms, Gravesend, as per schedule hereto, for the sum of £900, payable on the 28th of February, 1866." Nothing can be more distinct than this as a vendor proposing to sell. It is signed by the plaintiff, and is followed by a schedule of the stock to be purchased. Then comes the other part of the agreement, signed by the defendants, in these words, — "Sir, We have received your offer to sell the extra stock as above, and hereby agree to and accept the terms proposed." If it had rested there, no one could doubt that there was a distinct proposal by the vendor to sell, accepted by the purchasers. A difficulty has arisen because the plaintiff has at the head of the paper addressed it to the plaintiffs [*sic*: read defendants?] on behalf of the proposed Gravesend Royal Alexandra Hotel Company, Limited," and the defendants have repeated those words after their signatures to the document; and the question is, whether this constitutes any ambiguity on the fact of the agreement, or prevents the defendants from being bound by it. I agree that if the Gravesend Royal Alexandra Hotel Company had been an existing company at this time, the persons who signed the agreement would have signed as agents of the company. But, as there was no company in existence at the time, the agreement would be wholly inoperative unless it were held to be binding on the defendants personally. The cases referred to in the course of the argument fully bear out the proposition that, where a contract is signed by one who professes to be signing "as agent," but who has no principal existing at the time, and the contract would be altogether inoperative unless binding upon the person who signed it, he is bound thereby: and a stranger cannot by a subsequent ratification relieve him from that responsibility. When the company came afterwards into existence it was a totally new creature, having rights and obligations from that time, but no rights or obligations by reason of anything which might have been done before. It was once, indeed, thought that an inchoate liability might be incurred on behalf of a proposed company, which would become binding on it when subsequently formed: but that notion was manifestly contrary to the principles upon which the law of contract is founded. There must be two parties to a contract; and the rights and obligations which it creates cannot be transferred by one of them to a third person who was not in a condition to be bound by it at the time it was made. The history of this company makes this construction to my mind perfectly clear. It was no doubt the notion of all the parties that success was certain: but the plaintiff parted with his stock upon the faith of the defendants' engagement that the price agreed on should be paid on the day named. It cannot be supposed that he for a moment contemplated that the payment was to be contingent on the formation of the company by the 28th of February. The paper expresses in terms a contract to buy. And it is a cardinal rule that no oral evidence shall be admitted to shew an intention different from that which appears on the face of the writing. I come, therefore, to the conclusion that the defendants, having no principal who was bound originally, or who could become so by a subsequent ratification, were themselves bound, and that the oral evidence offered is not admissible to contradict the written contract.

WILLES J.: I am of the same opinion. Evidence was clearly inadmissible to shew that the parties contemplated that the liability on this contract should rest upon the company and not upon the persons contracting on behalf of the proposed company. The utmost it could amount to is, that both parties were satisfied at the time that all would go smoothly, and consequently that no liability would ensue to the defendants. The contract is, in substance, this, — "I, the plaintiff, agree to sell to you, the defendants, on behalf of the Gravesend Royal Alexandra Hotel Company, my stock of wines;" and, "We, the defendants, have received your offer, and agree to and accept the terms proposed; and you shall be paid on the 28th of February next." Who is to pay? The company, if it should be formed. But, if the company should not be formed, who is to pay? That is tested by the fact of the immediate delivery of the subject of sale. If payment was not made by the company, it must, if by anybody, be by the defendants. That brings one to consider whether the company could be legally liable. I apprehend the company could only become liable upon a new contract. It would require the assent of the plaintiff to discharge the defendants. Could the company become liable by a mere ratification? Clearly not. Ratification can only be by a person ascertained at the time of the act done, — by a person in existence either actually or in contemplation of law; as in the case of assignees of bankrupts and administrators, whose title, for the protection of the estate, vests by relation . . .

Both upon principle and upon authority, therefore, it seems to me that the company never could be liable upon this contract: and, as was put by my Lord, construing this document *ut res magis valeat quam pereat*, we must assume that the parties contemplated that the persons signing it would be personally liable. Putting in the words "on behalf of the Gravesend Royal

Alexandra Hotel Company," would operate no more than if a person should contract for a quantity of corn "on behalf of my horses." As to the suggestion that there should have been a special count, that is quite a mistake. There need not be a special count unless there was a person existing at the time the contract was made who might have been principal. The common count perfectly well represents the character of the liability which these defendants incurred. It is quite out of the question to suppose that there was any mistake. The document represents the real transaction between the parties. I think that the course taken at the trial was perfectly correct, and that the rule should be discharged.

Rule Discharged

[The concurring judgments of Byles and Keating JJ. are omitted.]

Notes

1 Do you agree with Willes J.'s reasoning that "we must assume that the parties contemplated that the persons signing [the contract] would be personally liable"? If the defendants anticipated this result, why did they sign the contract "on behalf of" the proposed company? The evidence at trial was that the plaintiff was to be the manager of the proposed company and that the company was in fact incorporated on February 20, 1866, i.e., before the agreed date for the payment of the stock. Do these facts cast a better light on the parties' probable intentions, assuming they thought about the legal position at all?

2 Can you suggest how, in the realm of pre-incorporation contracts, the court could have overcome or distinguished the common law rule that a contract cannot be made with a non-existent principal? In view of the fact that the court treated the purported ratification of the contract by the Hotel Company as a total nullity, what obligations, if any, did the company assume with respect to the stock received by it, and to whom?

3 It was established at common law that the "non-ratification" rule cannot be avoided by recourse to such devices as "adopting" the contract (*Relpetti Ltd. v. Oliver-Lee Ltd.*, 52 O.L.R. 315, [1923] 3 D.L.R. 1400 (C.A.)) or resort to a "provisional contract" (*Hudson- Mattagami Exploration Mining Co. v. Wettlatufer Bros. Ltd.*, 62 O.L.R. 387, [1928] 3 D.L.R. 661 (C.A.)). What is required at common law is a fresh contract, a requirement which, in the absence of a new written document, presents considerable difficulties. See generally, Getz, "Pre-incorporation Contracts: Some Proposals" (1967), U.B.C. L. Rev. 381, 382–387. For examples of cases in which the requirement has been satisfied, see *Howard v. Patent Ivory Mnfg. Co.* (1888), 38 Ch. D. 156; *Heinhuis v. Blacksheep Charters Ltd.* (1988), 46 D.L.R. (4th) 67 (B.C.C.A.); and *Brown Brothers Motor Lease Canada Ltd. v. Kirkpatrick* (1992), 67 B.C.L.R. (2d) 141, 1992 CarswellBC 127 (C.A.). The

latter cases indicate contemporary Canadian courts' willingness to relax the strict common law requirements.

4 Since the decision in *Kelner v. Baxter* was based on the assumed intention of the parties, it is of course open to the promoter in other cases to show that he had expressly excluded his personal liability. A Canadian common law decision where this defence succeeded is *Dairy Supplies v. Fuchs* (1959), 18 D.L.R. (2d) 408, 28 W.W.R. 1 (Sask.). Two men proposed to form a company to run a dairy business. They bought equipment from the plaintiff company and made it clear that the plaintiff was to look to the dairy company, and not them, for payment, and the evidence established that this was the agreement. The dairy company did not pay, and a claim against the promoters personally was unsuccessful.

Black v. Smallwood
[1966] A.L.R. 744 (High Court of Australia)

BARWICK C.J., KITTO, TAYLOR AND OWEN JJ.: On 22nd December, 1959, the appellants purported to enter into a contract for the sale of certain land at Ingleburn to Western Suburbs Holdings Pty. Ltd. The contract incorporated the conditions of sale approved by the Real Estate Institute of New South Wales and was executed by the appellants as vendors and it bore the following subscription as the signature of the purchaser:

Western Suburbs Holdings Pty. Ltd.

Robert Smallwood

J. Cooper   } Directors.

It was subsequently found that Western Suburbs Holdings Pty. Ltd. had not at that time been incorporated but it is common ground that both the appellants and the respondents, Smallwood and Cooper, who subscribed the name Western Suburbs Holdings Pty. Ltd. to the form of contract and added their own signatures as directors, believed that it had been and that the latter were directors of the company. Thereafter the appellants instituted a suit for specific performance against the respondents alleging that by a written contract between the appellants as vendors and the respondents who described themselves therein as "Western Suburbs Holdings Pty. Ltd." agreed to purchase the subject land from the appellants. No attempt was made at the trial to make this allegation good but, without amendment, the case proceeded as one in which the appellants sought to impose a liability in accordance with the terms of the contract upon the respondents as agents contracting on behalf of a principal not yet in existence.

Upon the trial the appellants were successful in obtaining a decree for specific performance but on appeal to the Full Court the decree was set aside and the suit dismissed. All members of the Full Court thought the case was covered precisely by the decision of the Court of Appeal in *Newborne v. Sensolid (Great Britain) Ltd.*, [1954] 1 Q.B. 45, and although one of their number was, perhaps, more than disposed to doubt the correctness of that decision, the Court as a whole decided that it should be followed. It is from this decision that this appeal is brought. At the outset of the case we should say that the decision in *Newborne's Case* is directly in point but we propose to deal briefly with the arguments that were presented to us and which, if they were accepted, would establish that decision to be wrong . . .

Kelner v. Baxter was cited as an authority for the proposition that there is a rule of law to the effect that where a person contracts on behalf of a nonexistent principal he is himself liable on the contract. But we find it impossible to extract any such proposition from the decision. In that case it appears from the contract itself that the defendants had no principal; they had purported to enter into a contract, on behalf of the "proposed Gravesend Royal Alexandra Hotel Company," and the fact that they had no principal was obvious to both parties. But it was not by reason of this fact alone that the defendants were held to be liable; the court proceeded to examine the written instrument in order to see if, in these circumstances, an intention should be imputed to the defendants to bind themselves personally, or perhaps, to put it another way, whether, the intention being sufficiently clear that a binding contract was intended, there was anything in the writing inconsistent with the conclusion that the defendants should be bound personally. The decision was that, in the circumstances, the writing disclosed an intention that the defendants should be bound . . . We should add that we fully agree with the observations of Fullagard in *Summergreene v. Parker* [(1950) 80 C.L.R. 304 at 23, 324] concerning the basis of the decision in *Kelner v. Baxter*. He said: "I do not myself think that *Kelner v. Baxter* or any of the cases cited affords any assistance in the present case. Where A, purporting to act as agent for a nonexistent principal, purports to make a binding contract with B, and the circumstances are such that B would suppose that a binding contract had been made, there must be a strong presumption that A has meant to bind himself personally. Where, as in *Kelner v. Baxter*, the consideration of B's part has been fully executed in reliance on the existence of a contract binding on somebody, the presumption could, I should imagine, only be rebutted in very exceptional circumstances. But the fundamental question in every case must be what the parties intended or must be fairly understood to have intended . . . "

* * *

WINDEYER J.: . . . In many cases courts have had to decide whether an agent had, in the particular case, incurred a personal liability on a contract in writing made by him on behalf of a principal. And these decisions have sometimes turned upon narrow differences in wording, which seem to be the progeny by miscegenation of early technical rules relating to the form of the execution of deeds . . . But here that question does not really arise, for the document which the respondents signed does not purport to be a contract made by them as agents for the supposed company. They thought that the company existed and that they were in fact directors. It is therefore impossible to regard them as having used the name of the company as a mere pseudonym or firm name or as having intended to incur a personal liability. The reason for the formation of the company may have been to ensure that they would not be personally liable. It is however suggested that, notwithstanding the form of the document, a personal obligation to perform the contract has been imposed upon them by law, because at the time they inserted the name of the company as purchaser there was no such company in existence.

So far as this proposition is based upon *Kelner v. Baxter* it must fail. The facts of this case differ essentially from the facts of that. Some statements in textbooks and in judgments that abbreviate the effect of that decision can be at least misleading, unless they be read with the facts well in mind. For example, Latham C.J. said that there "the intention was . . . evident that the proposed company and not the persons purporting to act as agents should be the contracting parties, and yet the court found no difficulty in substituting the agents for the supposed principal as the contracting party": *Summergreene v. Parker* [(1950) 80 C.L.R. 304 at 314]. But it is wrong to read this as meaning that whenever a person contracts professedly on behalf of a principal not yet in existence or already gone out of existence, the so-called agent is "substituted" as the contracting party and becomes personally liable to perform the contract or pay damages for non-performance. Doubtless in *Kelner v. Baxter* both the plaintiff and the defendants expected that payment for the goods would be made from the funds of the company that was in process of being formed. That, however, was not a term of the contract. And when the goods were bought it was well-known to all concerned that the company had not yet been formed. The plaintiff, in his letter to the defendants offering to supply the goods, had referred to it as the "proposed" company; and, as Asprey J. has pointed out, the more ample report of the case in the Law Journal [36 L.J.C.P 94] shows that the plaintiff was himself a participant in the project. The defendants were in fact the buyers of the goods. Their statement that they were buying on behalf of the proposed company was taken to mean, and could in the circumstances only mean, that they contracted to buy the goods with the intent and to the end that the company when formed might have the benefit of them. The words "on behalf of" do not necessarily imply agency in the relevant legal sense, any more than does the word "for" when a man says "I am buying this for" someone whom he names. The words cannot be regarded as indicative of agency for a principal when it is known to the user of the words that there is no principal in existence. The defendants in *Kelner v. Baxter* therefore contracted as principals. They were not substituted as principals. They were the principals. The contrast with this case is obvious. Here, instead of both parties knowing that the company was not in existence, they both, appellants and respondents, thought that it was.

However, counsel for the appellants contended that the respondents could nevertheless be liable to perform the contract as purchasers on the basis of a supposed rule that a person who contracts, professedly as agent, for a nonexistent principal is always personally liable on the contract: and he contended that the respondents signed the contract as agents, and therefore they could be compelled to perform it, being a type of contract specifically enforceable in equity. In my view neither the major nor the minor premise of the argument can be accepted. The minor premise, that the respondents contracted as agents, I have dealt with above and rejected.

The major premise, the supposed general rule, cannot I consider be supported. Counsel sought to extract it from statements in judgments in cases decided before *Collen v. Wright* [(1857) 7 E. & B. 301; 8 E. & B. 647]. That decision, he argued, only displaced earlier doctrine to a limited extent and left intact a general proposition that an agent for a non-existent principal is personally liable on the contract . . . But we have no such rule . . . It would, I think, be contrary to now-established principle to hold a man personally liable on a contract when he did not intend personally to contract and when, the transaction being in writing, the writing could not upon its true construction, when read in the light of what both parties took to be the facts, mean that he had done so. The purported contract in this case was a nullity, for the supposed purchaser did not exist when it was made. The suit for specific performance therefore must fail.

We do not have to consider whether the respondents might have been held liable to the appellants in proceedings of a different kind. I would merely say on the facts appearing from the transcript, the appellants might it would seem have a cause of action in the nature of an action for breach of warranty of authority — that is on an implied warranty that they were directors of an existing company which had power to make a contract to purchase land . . . However, the question does not arise for us in these proceedings and I do not express any concluded opinion on it . . .

Appeal dismissed.

Note

In *Newborne v. Sensolid (Great Britain) Ltd.*, [1953] 1 All E.R. 708, [1954] 1 Q.B. 45, a contract was concluded between Leopold Newborne (London) Ltd. and the defendant for the supply of goods to the defendant. The contract was signed "Leopold Newborne (London) Ltd." and underneath appeared the plaintiff's name "Leopold Newborne." The defendant repudiated the contract and an action was commenced in the name of Leopold Newborne (London) Ltd. It was then discovered that the company had not been incorporated at the time of the making of the contract. Newborne then sought to enforce the contract personally, relying on the decision in *Kelner v. Baxter*. He failed both before Parker J. and the Court of Appeal on the ground that the contract was made, not with the plaintiff, whether as agent or as principal, but with a limited company which at the date of the contract was non-existent and that therefore the contract was a total nullity.

Lord Goddard C.J. said (at p. 710):

> Those cases are well established and we are not departing in any way from the principle they lay down, but we cannot find that the plaintiff purported to contract as agent or as principal. He was making the contract for the company, and, although counsel has argued that, in signing as he did, he must have signed as agent, for a company can only contract through an agent, that is not the true position. A company makes a contract. No doubt, it must do its physical acts through the directors, but their relationship is not the ordinary one of principal and agent. The company contracts and its contract is authenticated by the signature of one or more of the directors. This contract purports to be made by the company, not by Mr. Newborne. He purports to be selling, not his goods, but the company's goods. The only person who has any contract here is the company, and Mr. Newborne's signature is merely confirming the company's signature. The document is signed: "Yours faithfully, Leopold Newborne (London) Ltd.", and the signature underneath is that of the person authorised to sign on behalf of the company.

In *Phonogram Ltd. v. Lane* [1981] 3 All E.R. 182 (C.A.), a case which was concerned with the construction of s. 9(2) of the U.K. *European Communities Act*, 1972, Lord Denning M. R., deprecated the fine common law distinction between a contract signed "for" and a contract signed "as agent." Oliver J. thought the real question in every case was the true intention of the parties and that the liability of a signor did not turn on the distinction drawn in *Newborne's* case.

Wickberg v. Shatsky & Shatsky
(1969), 4 D.L.R. (3d) 540 (B.C. S.C.)

DRYER J.: In 1965 a corporation by the name of Rapid Addressing Systems Ltd. was carrying on business in Vancouver selling and servicing certain business machines and supplies. Three men named Kane, Grant and Weston were shareholders in this company and active in its management. Late in 1965 or early in 1966, the two defendants came into the picture along with a Mr. Spaner and purchased an interest in and became directors of Rapid Addressing Systems Ltd. It was then intended that with the new capital so brought into the company the business would be expanded to handle a wider range of machines and new premises were obtained and a wider franchise secured, though there is some question as to whether or not a written franchise agreement was executed on both sides. The directors decided to incorporate a new company under the name of Rapid Data (Western) Ltd. which would take over the assets and the disclosed liabilities of Rapid Addressing Systems Ltd. This proposed new company was not, in fact, incorporated but the business was carried on (quite improperly) under the name of Rapid Data (Western) Ltd., *e.g.*, stationery was prepared and used with that name, the sign over the new premises bore that name, *etc.*

In the spring of 1966, it was decided not to go ahead with the incorporation of Rapid Data (Western) Ltd. and a little later it was decided to incorporate a company known as Celer Data Ltd. which, again, would take over the assets and the disclosed liabilities of Rapid Addressing Systems Ltd. The incorporation papers regarding this company were sent to the Registrar of Companies on May 9, 1966, and the company's certificate of incorporation is dated May 11, 1966.

In the meantime the directors of Rapid Addressing Systems Ltd. decided they needed a new manager for their business and the plaintiff was approached through a hiring agency. The plaintiff had been engaged in sales or managerial activities for some years and at this time was so engaged by another firm. On May 6th, the plaintiff attended at the new premises of the business and met the two defendants and some of their associates and was offered employment as manager. On Monday, May 9, 1966, the terms were agreed upon and the plaintiff was hired as manager. He asked for a written contract and he was given a letter on the letterhead of Rapid Data (Western) Ltd. signed by the defendant L. Shatsky as president, saying that he was hired as general manager of the company at a salary of $15,000 *per annum*, "to be reviewed six months from this date". This was filed as ex. 1. A few days later the defendant Lawrence Shatsky told the plaintiff that the business was to stop using the name Rapid Data (Western) Ltd. and to carry on under the name Rapid Data (Western), i.e., the word "Ltd." was to be dropped. From then on, though the company still used some stationery bearing the name "Rapid Data (Western) Ltd.", the business was, to all intents and purposes, carried on under the name "Rapid Data (Western)".

The business was not successful and on August the 26, 1966, the plaintiff, after refusing to work on straight commission, was given a notice terminating his services . . .

The plaintiff now brings this action against the two defendants. Counsel for the plaintiff contends (1) that the defendant Lawrence Shatsky is liable as a party to the contract, ex. 1, since it was signed by him as agent for a nonexistent principal; and (2) that Lawrence Shatsky and Harold Shatsky are each liable for breach of warranty of authority in that they warranted the existence of Rapid Data (Western) Ltd. and warranted Lawrence Shatsky's authority to sign the contract on behalf of Rapid Data (Western) Ltd.; and (3) that the business by which the plaintiff was employed was a firm in which Lawrence Shatsky and Harold Shatsky were partners and that consequently each of them is liable for the losses suffered by the plaintiff arising from the nonperformance of the contract, ex. 1.

The first contention, *viz.*, that Lawrence Shatsky is liable since he signed ex. 1 on behalf of Rapid Data (Western) Ltd., a non-existent corporation, is based upon the principle said to be established by *Kelner v. Baxter*

(1866), L.R. 2 C.P 174. In my opinion the plaintiff's claim under this heading cannot succeed by reason of the principle laid down in *Black et al. v. Smallwood* (1966), 39 A.L.J.R. 405. In *Kelner v. Baxter* both parties knew that the company was not in existence. In *Black v. Smallwood* both parties thought that the company in question was in existence. In the case at bar the plaintiff thought that Rapid Data (Western) Ltd. was in existence and the defendants knew that it was not. Counsel for the plaintiff contends that that distinction makes the rule laid down in *Black et al. v. Smallwood* inapplicable. No authority is cited in support of this distinction. In my opinion, the distinction between *Kelner v. Baxter* and *Black et al. v. Small wood* is that in *Kelner v. Baxter* the decision was that in the circumstances the writing disclosed an intention that the defendant should be bound whereas that was not the case in *Black et al. v. Smallwood*. (See *Black et al. v. Smallwood* at p. 406.) It follows that, in my opinion, the reasoning in *Black et al. v. Smallwood* is not inapplicable to the case at bar. Here the parties did not have the same view as to the facts at the time the contract was entered into. Nevertheless it was not the intention of the parties or either of them when the contract was made that Lawrence Shatsky who signed as a director should be personally liable on the contract and therefore, on the principle laid down in *Black et al. v. Smallwood*, he cannot be held liable on the contract. That does not mean, of course, that he could not be liable for breach of warranty of authority or for fraud if they were pleaded and proven. Breach of warranty of authority is pleaded and I will deal with it now.

In my opinion, the defendants undoubtedly so acted as to warrant to the plaintiff that Rapid Data (Western) Ltd. was a legal entity and that they had the power to represent it and to speak for it when entering into ex. 1 with the plaintiff. At the same time I feel that the plaintiff knew very shortly after the date of ex. 1 that the business was not being carried on by an incorporated company known as Rapid Data (Western) Ltd. I cannot and do not accept the evidence of the plaintiff that he did not attach any significance to the dropping of the term "Ltd." from the name of the business nor can I accept his evidence that he did not know of the existence of Rapid Addressing Systems Ltd. until that firm went into bankruptcy. On the other hand I feel I should say that in my opinion the conduct of the defendants in using the name Rapid Data (Western) Ltd. when they not only knew there was no corporation so named but had abandoned any intention of forming a corporation with that name, is reprehensible. I find it difficult to understand how any adult, even with less experience in the business world than the parties to this action, could be as ignorant of the significance of corporate names and their right to use such names and the effect of such user on other persons as has been alleged here.

However, at the time of entering into ex. 1, the plaintiff did not know that Rapid Data (Western) Ltd. was not incorporated and the defendants did, but, I can see no causal connection between the damage suffered by the plaintiff and the breach of the warranty as to its existence. The fact that

Rapid Data (Western) Ltd. was not incorporated and the fact that Rapid Data (Western) Ltd. was not the operator of the business did not cause the plaintiff's loss. Moreover, as pointed out above, shortly after he commenced working and shortly after the date of Ex. 1 the plaintiff knew that the business was being carried on under the name Rapid Data (Western) which should have alerted any normal businessman to the fact that it was a firm rather than a corporation. If, as he says, he attached little significance to the omission of the word "Ltd.", he would surely have attached little significance to the presence of that word in the name of the operator of the business originally presented to him. His loss, as I see it, resulted from the fact that the business was not a success, not from the breach of warranty. It may be that the plaintiff would be able to recover judgment for damages for wrongful dismissal against Rapid Data (Western) Ltd. if it existed, but, in the facts here, such a judgment would be no less an empty one than one recovered against Rapid Data (Western) since, although neither that firm nor its owner, Rapid Addressing Systems Ltd. (see below) has assets to pay it, the non-existent Rapid Data (Western) Ltd. is no less judgment proof. The plaintiff would be entitled to recover against the defendants under this head only that which he had lost by reason of the breach of warranty. See *Mayne & McGregor on Damages* 12th ed., para. 635, and *Bowstead on Agency,* 13th ed., arts. 125, 127 and 128 at pp. 392, 397 and 404. At p. 392 Bowstead says:

> Where the agent is not personally liable on the contract, an action for breach of warranty of authority would only produce nominal damages, because since the company or association has no existence and so no funds, it would hardly be possible to prove a loss arising from the lack of authority: the case would be like that of an insolvent principal. Any effective liability would have to be in deceit, or possibly in negligence.

The plaintiff is therefore, as I see it, entitled only to nominal damages for this breach of warranty. He is entitled to such nominal damages against both defendants . . .

Judgment for plaintiff.

Notes

1 What was the effect of the plaintiff being told by the defendant Shatsky, a few days after he had received the written contract of employment, "to stop using the name Rapid Data (Western) Ltd. and to carry on under the name Rapid Data (Western)", i.e., that the word "Ltd." was to be dropped? Did it mean that as from that date onwards there was a new implied contract of employment between the plaintiff and the principals of Rapid Data (Western) unincorporated? Who were the principals, and would it have been in the plaintiff's interest to have relied on the second contract rather than the first?

2 A judgment similar to *Shatsky* was rendered in another pre-incorporation case, *Delta Construction Co. Ltd. v. Lidstone* (1979), 96 D.L.R. (3d) 457, 29 Nfld. & P.E.I.R. 70 (Nfld., S.C. T.D.). The defendants, wishing to form Algo Enterprises Limited, instructed a solicitor and, on April 2, 1975, signed the memorandum and articles of association. The documents were left with the solicitor in the belief that he was to be the third subscriber and that he would complete the incorporation. About a month later, needing the company's seal, Lidstone went to the solicitor's office and received a seal from a clerk. The seal was used in connection with banking documents, a bank account was opened, and, later, the seal was passed to a solicitor for Central Mortgage and Housing Corporation to be used in connection with a real estate transaction. In August, 1975, the defendants became aware, through the solicitor for CMHC, that the company had not been incorporated. Their solicitor was contacted and he advised that the company would be incorporated without delay. It was not incorporated until October 22, 1975.

In the meantime, in May, 1975, Lidstone requested the plaintiff to do work for Algo Enterprises Limited. He was well known to the plaintiff's manager as the plaintiff had done work for companies in which Lidstone had an interest. The work to be done consisted mainly of the rental and use of earth-moving equipment, at various times, between May 26, 1975, and September 26, 1975. The value of the work done was $17,845. Approximately $3,200 was paid, before the company was incorporated, by cheques drawn on a bank account in the name of Algo Enterprises Limited. The project foundered and the balance, approximately $14,645, was not paid. Noel J. said (at p. 463):

> Did the plaintiff suffer damages as a result of Lidstone's breach of warranty?
>
> At most Lidstone represented that an existing company, Algo Enterprises Limited, required work to be done by the plaintiff. The plaintiff was, clearly, expected to extend credit to the company but Lidstone did not warrant that the company had any assets, that it was solvent, or that the plaintiff's account would be paid. The decision to extend credit was made by the plaintiff. Since the project foundered, it is reasonable to suppose that if the plaintiff is successful in this suit for the balance of its account, assuming the defendants to be solvent, it would be in a better position than it would have been in had the company been in existence as the parties believed. In short, the non-existence of the company would be a windfall to the plaintiff. If the defendants are obliged to pay the plaintiff's account, in effect, they would be guarantors of the account which neither they nor the plaintiff intended should be the case.

3 What should be the measure of damages for false warranty of authority where the company has never been incorporated and, unlike in *Wickberg v. Shatsky*, has never done any business? How can one tell whether or not the incorporated company would have been successful? In the interests of contract performance and greater care in the use of the corporate form, should a court make every presumption against the defendant and assume that the corporation would have been properly financed and properly managed?

4 Apart from the liability of the purported agent for false warranty of authority, what liability is incurred by the person who has actually received the benefit of the plaintiff's work? What is the common law position where the party contracting with the assumed corporation refuses to pay for benefits conferred by the corporation?

(b) Statutory Reforms

Ontario Select Committee
on Company Law, Interim Report (1967)

1.5.5. The law in Ontario and, it would appear, in all the common law Provinces of Canada, is to the effect that no pre-incorporation contract is binding upon a company, no matter how or by whom the contract is made. For the company to be bound by such a contract or, alternatively, to obtain the benefit of it, a new contract must be made between the newly-incorporated company and the contracting party. Whether or not the contracting party has a remedy against the promoter (to whom he may or may not have intended to look for liability) depends, in the present state of the law, in large part upon caprice: the manner of execution of the particular contract. The multifarious judicial decisions seeking to apply the rule of *Kelner v. Baxter* have not consistently protected the separate interests of the parties to the preincorporation contract.

1.5.6. The various States of the United States have, in large part, rejected the rule of law embodied in *Kelner v. Baxter* by determining, through judicial decisions, that a corporation may, either expressly or even by the slightest implication, "adopt" or "ratify" a promoter's contract made on its behalf prior to incorporation. The American courts have also held the promoters liable on pre-incorporation contracts in certain circumstances, even in cases where the corporation has adopted or ratified the contract and thus become liable under it. By this artificiality the plaintiff has acquired two defendants, one of which we can surmise he never intended to have.

1.5.7. To the Committee it appeared that two basic questions of policy were involved in this topic: Should companies be bound by pre-incorporation contracts made on their behalf, perforce, and without power to reject them? And, secondly, if a company is to be bound by a contract made before the company comes into existence, what class of persons should have that authority? Argued from the company's standpoint, it should not be possible for the traditional management functions of the directors and officers to be abrogated by permitting promoters to bind companies in contract prior to incorporation. On the other hand, the contracting party, presumably a member of the public acting in good faith, should not be left without redress if the company is not bound by the contract, whether by election or otherwise. Again from the company's standpoint, the two questions posed above are really one: Is there any class of persons who should have the authority to bind a company in contract prior to its incorporation? In the opinion of the Committee, the answer to this latter question should be in the negative. The Committee recommends, however, that the so-called rule in *Kelner v. Baxter* should be repealed in that the Ontario Act should provide that a company may by its unilateral act, whether express or implied, be permitted to adopt and therefore take the benefit and assume the liabilities of a contract made in its name or on its behalf prior to incorporation. The promoters should cease to be liable under any contract so adopted by a company. Pursuant to these rules it would follow that promoters would bear the risk of non-adoption of pre-incorporation contracts — a risk which is properly inherent in the role of promoter. Companies, on their part, would be free to assume the benefits of pre-incorporation contracts made on their behalf. The Act should provide that in cases where the contract is not adopted by the company, the company should be required to restore to the promoters, in specie or otherwise, any benefit acquired by the company under the pre-incorporation contract not adopted after incorporation.

1.5.8. These recommendations, however, do not fully resolve the difficulties arising in pre-incorporation contract situations. Circumstances could exist, it seemed to the Committee, in which a company should not be permitted, by non-adoption, to avoid obligations under pre-incorporation contracts made on its behalf and, conversely, the promoters should not, in some circumstances, be freed from liability because the company adopts the contract. For example, if the promoters in fact become the sole or dominant shareholders and directors of the company on whose behalf a pre-incorporation contract as entered into, should the contracting party not have the right to enforce contractual liability against either the company or the promoters as the contracting party may elect? We therefore recommend that the Act be amended to include a provision to the effect that a contracting party may make an application to a judge of the High Court of Ontario designated by the Chief Justice of the High Court for an order that the promoters and the company will be jointly and severally liable under a pre-incorporation contract if, under the circumstances, it is just and equitable in the interests of the contracting party for such liability to be imposed.

* * *

The Select Committee's recommendations were implemented in s. 20 of the 1970 Ontario Act as reproduced below. (For the current provisions, which follow those in the CBCA set out below, see OBCA s. 21).

20. (1) In this section,

(a)   "contractor" means a person who enters into a pre-incorporation contract in the name of or on behalf of a corporation before its incorporation;

(b)   "other party" means a person with whom a contractor enters into a pre-incorporation contract;

(c)   "pre-incorporation contract" means a contract entered into by a contractor in the name of or on behalf of a corporation before its incorporation.

(2) A corporation may adopt a pre-incorporation contract entered into in its name or on its behalf, and thereupon the corporation is entitled to the benefits and is subject to the liabilities that were contracted in its name or on its behalf and the contractor ceases to be entitled to such benefits or to be subject to such liabilities.

(3) Where a pre-incorporation contract is not adopted by a corporation, the contractor is entitled to the benefits and subject to the liabilities under the contract and is entitled to recover from the corporation the value of any benefit received by the corporation under the contract.

(4) Whether or not a pre-incorporation contract is adopted by the corporation, the other party may apply to the court which may, notwithstanding subsections (2) and (3), make an order fixing or apportioning liability as between the contractor and the corporation in any manner the court considers just and equitable under the circumstances.

* * *

The federal provisions appear in CBCA s. 14.

14. (1) Subject to this section, a person who enters into, or purports to enter into, a written contract in the name of or on behalf of a corporation before it comes into existence is personally bound by the contract and is entitled to its benefits.

(2) A corporation may, within a reasonable time after it comes into existence, by any action or conduct signifying its intention to be bound thereby, adopt a written contract made before it came into existence in its name or on its behalf, and on such adoption

(a)   the corporation is bound by the contract and is entitled to the benefits thereof as if the corporation had been in existence at the date of the contract and had been a party thereto; and

(b)   a person who purported to act in the name of or on behalf of the corporation ceases, except as provided in subsection (3), to be bound by or entitled to the benefits of the contract.

(3) Subject to subsection (4), whether or not a written contract made before the coming into existence of a corporation is adopted by the corpo-

ration, a party to the contract may apply to a court for an order respecting the nature and extent of the obligations and liability under the contract of the corporation and the person who entered into, or purported to enter into, the contract in the name of or on behalf of the corporation. On the application, the court may make any order it thinks fit.

(4) If expressly so provided in the written contract, a person who purported to act in the name of or on behalf of the corporation before it came into existence is not in any event bound by the contract or entitled to the benefits thereof.

Questions and Notes

1   Borins J.A. provided an extensive review of the legislative history and evolution of OBCA s. 21 in *Sherwood Design Services Ltd. v. 872935 Ontario Ltd.* (1998), 39 O.R. (3d) 576, 1998 CarswellOnt 1739 (C.A.) at pp. 593–600 [O.R.].

2   What significant differences do you see between the above statutory provisions? For a critical analysis of them, see Iacobucci, Pilkington and Prichard, *Canadian Business Corporations* (1977), 53–59, and Maureen A. Malone, "Pre-incorporation Transactions: A Statutory Solution?" (1985), 10 Can. Bus. L.J. 409.

3   Another approach is represented by the Alberta statute, which uses the concept of a "deemed warranty" from the promoter to the other party that (i) the corporation will come into existence within a reasonable time and (ii) that the corporation will adopt the contract within a reasonable time after the corporation is incorporated. The promoter is liable to the other party for damages for a breach of this warranty, and the measure of damages for a breach of the warranty is the same as if the corporation existed when the contract was made, the promoter had no authority to make the contract on the corporation's behalf, and the corporation refused to ratify the contract. See the Alberta *Business Corporations Act*, RSA 2000, c. B-9, s.15 and BCBCA s. 20, which follows this deemed warranty approach.

4   Why should a promoter be held personally liable if the contract is not adopted by the corporation and the other party to the contract was not aware at the time of its conclusion that the corporation did not yet exist? The Federal Proposals (paras. 69-70) rationalized the new rule on the ground that the common law distinctions between the personal liability of a promoter and his liability on other grounds (principally for breach of warranty of authority) are difficult to apply and that the latter are not always adequate substitutes for contractual remedies. A further reason given by the Proposals is that "as a matter of business reality, the promoter is usually in control of the pre-incorporation and immediate post-incorporation process and is able to protect himself." Do you find these reasons convincing?

5 Why does CBCA s. 14(2) only enable a corporation to adopt a *written* pre-incorporation contract? (Note carefully that the OBCA s. 21(2) does not adopt this restriction). The Federal Proposals justified the requirement of a written contract on the ground that "this seems the only way of ensuring full disclosure of the terms of the contract, which is an essential protection for the corporation" (para. 71). Do you agree? What is the promoter's position when there is no written contract?

6 Does CBCA s. 14(2) prevent the promoter from assigning the contract to the corporation? Would such an assignment relieve him from personal liability?

7 Why should the court be empowered under the above provisions to impose personal liability on the promoter even though the pre-incorporation contract has been adopted by the corporation? The Federal Proposals thought the power was necessary to prevent a promoter evading liability "by procuring the adoption of a contract by a shell corporation with insufficient assets to meet its obligations under the contract" (para. 72). Do you find this explanation convincing? For a reported case in which the court was invited to exercise its discretion under the Ontario Act to impose liability on the promoter, but declined to do so, see *Bank of N.S. v. Williams* (1976), 12 O.R. (2d) 709, 70 D.L.R. (3d) 108. Van Camp J. said (at p. 112):

> This section was introduced into the Act in 1970 and I have been referred to no authority as to the exercise of the discretion thereunder. My understanding is that section was introduced to clarify the doubt that existed as to whether a company could adopt a contract made on its behalf before incorporation and release the person who signed on its behalf from liability. I can understand that there may be times when the company and the one who contracted on its behalf should not be able to agree as to the assumption of liability to the detriment of the person with whom the contract was made. However, in the situation before me, Mrs. Aikins was not misled as to which party she was advancing the moneys to, nor did any action of Mr. Williams or the company mislead her as to who would be assuming responsibility for repayment. Consequently, I am not exercising any discretion under that section to apportion the liability of the company between it and Mr. Williams.

8 Under what circumstances is a court likely to hold a corporation liable for a pre-incorporation contract not adopted by it? Do you agree with the Federal Proposals (para. 72) that the appropriate conditions may exist if a fraudulent promoter seeks to evade his obligations "by hiding behind a corporation that he in fact dominates." What "obligations" has he in fact assumed? Are the Federal Proposals consistent in holding the promoter personally liable where the corporation is not incorporated, on the ground that he has it in his power to make sure that it is incorporated, and to continue to hold him liable even if the corporation is incorporated?

9 What is the effect of contractual exclusion of the promoter's personal liability on the promoter's ability to enforce the contract personally where the company is never incorporated? In *Guido v. Swail* (1982), 3 ACWS (3d) 52 (Ont.), the defendants orally agreed to sell plaintiff certain shares. A draft purchase agreement in writing evidenced plaintiffs' intention to contract on behalf of a corporation to be incorporated and without incurring personal liability. The defendants subsequently repudiated the agreement and the plaintiffs brought an action for specific performance. Smith J. dismissed the action on the ground that, having excluded their personal liability, the plaintiffs could not now rely on OBCA ss. 21(1) and (2) to make the contract binding where no incorporation had occurred. Do you agree with this reasoning and, if you do, does this mean that there is no binding agreement where the promoter has excluded his personal liability unless and until a corporation is formed and ratified the agreement?

10 What significance attaches to the fact that CBCA s. 14(1) speaks of a person entering into a "contract" on behalf of a corporation not yet in existence? In *Westcom Radio Group Ltd. v. MacIsaac* (1989), 70 O.R. (2d) 591 (Div. Ct.), the defendant was sued on an advertising contract that she had signed on behalf of her employer. Unknown to the defendant, however (as well as the plaintiff), the business had never been incorporated.

In the Divisional Court, Austin J. upheld the lower court's ruling that the defendant was not liable on the contract. Notwithstanding that OBCA s. 21(1) was invoked in the appeal, Austin J. was troubled by the following difficulty (at 439):

> In coming to any conclusion about the case at bar, the starting point must be to determine whether the plaintiff intended to contract with the non-existent company exclusively. If so, then the purported "contract" is a nullity. Whether the defendant will be personally liable under the OBCA will depend upon the interpretation of the word "contract" in s. 21(1). It is probable that the intention of the legislators was to remedy the perceived unfairness of the *Black* principle, but it is questionable whether the current wording of the Act includes purported agreements which are in law nullities. While there is no explicit statement in any of the Canadian cases to the effect that the OBCA or the CBCA has "obliterated" the *Kelner, Black* distinction, such reasoning seems implicit.

Professor Ziegel argued ((1990) 16 Can. Bus. L.J. 341, at p. 345) that "It is abundantly clear that the drafters were only using the word [contract] in a colloquial sense and that they fully appreciated that there was no binding contract with the corporation . . . The result of [Westcom's] reading of s. 21(1) of the OBCA . . . is to make nonsense of the whole subsection and to deprive it of all meaning."

In *Szecket v. Huang* (1998), 42 O.R. (3d) 400, 1998 CarswellOnt 4783 (C.A.), the Ontario Court of Appeal apparently sided with Professor Ziegel. Although the Court declined to overrule *Westcom*, it characterized the *Westcom* two-step inquiry as "unnecessarily complex" and stated that the lower court judge's analysis based on *Westcom* "represented one of the problems arising from the common law of pre-incorporation contracts, which the legislature intended to remedy by the enactment of s. 21." *Szecket v. Huang* was a case where both parties knew that the company purporting to contract had yet to be incorporated.

Finally, an Ontario court considered the application of OBCA s. 21 in the situation where the promoter knew that the company had not been incorporated but the other party did not. In *1080409 Ontario Ltd. v. Hunter* (2000), 50 O.R. (3d) 145, 2000 CarswellOnt 2399 (S.C.J.), Pepall J. resolved the dilemma of the apparent conflict between *Westcom* and *Szecket v. Huang* by distinguishing both prior cases based on the state of knowledge of the parties as to the incorporated status of the company. On the facts before him, however, he reached a result consistent with the analysis in *Szecket v. Huang* following what he described as "the undeniable legislative intent" of OBCA s. 21.

See also Poonam Puri, "The Promise of Certainty in the Law of Pre-Incorporation Contracts" (2001), 80 Can. Bar Rev. 1051.

Landmark Inns of Canada Ltd. v. Horeak
[1982] 2 W.W.R. 377, 18 Sask. R. 30 (Q.B.)

MAURICE J.: This is an action for damages arising out of the alleged breach by the defendant of a contract to lease certain premises in the plaintiff's Gordon Place Shopping Centre in the city of Regina.

The action involves the interpretation of s. 14 of the Business Corporations Act of the province of Saskatchewan, R.S.S. 1978, c. B-10.

The facts are as follows: the defendant and three partners agreed to set up an optical and contact lens business in the city of Regina. The partners intended to form a limited company to operate the business. One of the partners, Dennis Cantin, noticed that the plaintiff had space to lease in its Gordon Place Shopping Centre. The defendant contacted Harvey Komberg, president of the plaintiff company, by telephone on 18th October 1979, and followed up by letter of 19th October 1979. As a result, through the plaintiff's leasing agent for the property, Frances Olson Realty Limited, the defendant received in October 1979 an offer to lease. The defendant signed the offer to lease on 25th October 1979. The tenant in the offer to lease was shown as South Albert Optical and Contact Lenses Ltd. At the time the defendant signed the offer he designated himself as chairman and affixed thereto a seal purporting to be the corporate seal of South Albert Optical and Contact Lenses Ltd. The plaintiff accepted the offer to lease on 31st October 1979. In early November 1979, the defendant met with Kornberg in Winnipeg. He presented Kornberg with some drawings prepared by the defendant's architects, which involved some renovations to the demised premises. The drawings called for a demising wall, a washroom and a rear door to be installed in the premises. The plaintiff had the work done by a construction firm, which completed the work by 3rd December 1979. The defendant and his partners met in November 1979, and decided not to lease plaintiff's premises, but rather to lease premises in Regina's Southland Mall instead. By letter of 22nd November 1979, sent by the defendant's solicitor to the plaintiff, the plaintiff was advised that the leasing of premises at Gordon Place Shopping Centre would not proceed. This letter was received by the plaintiff on 3rd December 1979.

After reviewing the letter, Kornberg telephoned the defendant, and the defendant confirmed that the lease would not be proceeded with. The plaintiff immediately advised its leasing agent to obtain a new lease for the premises. The agent was successful in obtaining a new tenant for the premises, who leased the premises from the plaintiff as of 1st June 1980. A company by the name of South Albert Optical and Contact Lenses Ltd. was incorporated on 25th February 1980 by the defendant and his partners. On 19th March 1980 the directors and shareholders of his (sic) company held a meeting and adopted the lease entered into by the defendant in its name. South Albert Optical and Contact Lenses Ltd. was not actively carrying on business at the time of the hearing of this matter. The plaintiff commenced action against the defendant for damages resulting from the refusal to proceed with the lease. The plaintiff claims for six months' lost rental from 1st December 1979 to 1st June 1980, at a monthly rental of $1,494.16 per month. The lease was to be a net lease, meaning that the tenant was to be responsible for taxes and common expenses of the premises. I find that the monthly taxes would have been $217.33 and the monthly common expenses would have been $81.50, for a total loss of rent per month of $1,792.99. The plaintiff also claims for the amount it paid to the construction firm to have the premises prepared in accordance with the drawing submitted to it by the defendant, which the defendant expected the plaintiff to act upon. The expenditure was as follows:

amount paid to put in dividing wall	$2,300.00
amount paid to put in washroom	$1,500.00
amount paid to put in rear door	$ 350.00
Total	$4,150.00

The plaintiff also claims the sum of $500, which it paid to its lawyers for services rendered in reviewing the offer to lease. At the time the defendant submitted the offer to lease to the plaintiff, a deposit of $2,988.33 was made to apply on the first and last months' rent.

Section 14 of the Business Corporations Act read as follows [see OBCA s. 21 (Eds.)] Subsection (1) codifies the law on pre-incorporation contracts, as stated in the leading case of *Kelner (Kelmer) v. Baxter* (1866), L.R. 2 C.P 174; also see *Dairy Supplies Ltd. v. Fuchs* (1959), 28 W.W.R. 1, 18 D.L.R. (2d) 408 (Sask. C.A.).

The defendant, having entered into a written contract in the name of South Albert Optical and Contact Lenses Ltd. before it came into existence, is personally bound by the contract unless the provisions of s. 14(2) or (4) of the Act apply to the transaction.

The defendant says that the purported adoption of the lease by South Albert Optical and Contact Lenses Ltd. on 19th March 1980 has the effect of ceasing to make him bound by the lease in accordance with s. 14(2). I cannot agree with this contention. The lease was repudiated when the defendant's solicitor wrote to the plaintiff on 22nd November 1979 advising that the lease would not be proceeded with. The defendant confirmed this in a telephone conversation with Kornberg.

Martin C.J.S., in the case of *Can. Doughnut Co. Ltd. v. Can. Egg Products Ltd.*, 11 W.W.R. 193, [1954] 2 D.L.R. 77, affirmed [1955] S.C.R. 398, [1955] 3 D.L.R. 1, stated at p. 86:

> The authorities are to the effect that an express declaration by one party made either before or at the date fixed for performance that he refuses to recognize the contract as binding discharges the other party from further liability: the latter is freed from further performance and may sue for damages.

The plaintiff accepted the repudiation and obtained a new lease for the premises. The contract having been repudiated, which repudiation was accepted, the contract was at an end. It could not therefore be adopted by the company at a later date.

The defendant says that, as the lease shows the name of the tenant to be South Albert Optical and Contact Lenses Ltd. and it was signed by the defendant as chairman under the seal of the company, the contract expressly provides that the defendant was not to be bound by the contract in accordance with s. 14(4) of the Act.

I cannot agree with this contention either. The section clearly contemplates that the contract will be entered into by a person in the name of or on behalf of a corporation. In this case the lease was entered into in the name of South Albert Optical and Contact Lenses Ltd. To relieve a person of personal responsibility, the contract must contain something more. As the section says, it must contain an express provision that a person who enters into a written contract in the name of a company before it comes into existence is not personally bound by the contract. The lease contains no such provision . . .

Judgment for plaintiff.

Questions and Notes

1 Does Saskatchewan's section 14(1) (which is substantially the same as CBCA s. 14) distinguish between the situations where the other party to the contract knows the corporation is not yet in existence at the time of the making of the contract and those where he does not know? Ought it to?

2 Was Maurice J. correct in stating that s. 14(1) "codifies the law on pre-incorporation contracts" in *Kelner v. Baxter*?

3 Can a promoter effectively repudiate a pre-incorporation contract before the company is incorporated? If he can, was there an effective repudiation by the defendant in the present case? Is the company bound by such a repudiation?

4 In *Okinczyc v. Tessier* (1979), 8 R.P.R. 249 (Ont. H.C.), a contract for the purchase of a parcel of land was signed between the plaintiff (vendor) and the defendant Tessier. The agreement included the following provision:

> It is understood between the parties that the purchaser is buying above described property in trust for a limited company which is to be incorporated.

The corporation, the Niagara Montrose Apartment Corporation, was incorporated on December 30, 1978, its first directors being Tessier and Blenkarn. Blenkarn was Tessier's solicitor. The corporation was the vehicle through which the development was to take place if the project went ahead. The project was abandoned and Tessier failed to close on the agreed date.

The plaintiff sought to hold Tessier personally liable on the contract. Steele J. found (at p. 256) that "there were no organizational resolutions or minutes of any meetings [of the corporation] and that there was never a shareholders' or directors' meeting of the company and the company has no assets."

What result? Is the absence of a formal resolution adopting a pre-incorporation contract fatal in the case of a one-person corporation? See OBCA ss. 104 and 129, and *cf. Eisenberg v. BNS*, [1965] S.C.R. 681, *infra*, Ch. 10. Do the CBCA and OBCA pre-incorporation provisions apply to a contract signed "in trust" for a corporation still to be incorporated? What would be sufficient evidence of the adoption of a contract by a one person corporation whose sole beneficial shareholder is the person who signed the pre-incorporation contract?

In *Solomon v. Cedar Acres East, Inc.*, 317 A.2d 283 (Pa. 1974), the plaintiff, an architect, sued the promoter and the defendant corporation for specific performance of a pre-incorporation agreement or for damages for breach of contract. The facts were as follows. On November 13, 1966, the promoter entered into an agreement with four other men for the creation of the defendant corporation. Two days later, on November 15, 1966, the plaintiff and the promoter entered into a contract requiring the plaintiff to perform architectural services for the development of a 52-acre tract of land on which the promoter held an option. The plaintiff was to become a 5 per cent owner of any corporation formed for the development of the tract and was to receive 5 per cent of the profits of such corporation as well as other compensation for his services. The agreement made no reference to the defendant corporation. The plaintiff had performed some preliminary architectural work for the promoter prior to the agreement of November 15 and performed additional services after this date but did no further work after December 8, 1966.

The defendant corporation was apparently incorporated at the beginning of December. On December 21 the promoter assigned to the corporation the option to buy the 52-acre tract. The corporation refused to honour the agreement of November 15 or to pay the plaintiff anything for the pre-incorporation services rendered by him.

In dismissing the plaintiff's (appellant's) claim against the corporation, the Pennsylvania Supreme Court reasoned as follows (284-285):

> The appellant admits that no express ratification ever occurred. He argues, however, that ratification can be inferred because the corporate defendant benefited from the use of architectural plans knowing that such plans were prepared by the appellant. Knowledge that the plans were prepared by the appellant, however, is not knowledge of all of the material facts contained in the agreement of November 15, 1966. The corporated defendant had no knowledge of that agreement or that it provided for the issuance of stock to the appellant and for profit sharing by the appellant. These material facts were unknown to anyone except the promoter and the appellant. Ratification of a contract by one not a party to the contract requires that the ratifying party be in possession of all the material facts and act with such knowledge. *McRoberts v. Phelps*, 391 Pa. 591, 138 A.2d 439 (1958); *Schwartz v. Mahoning Valley Country Club*, 382 Pa. 138, 114 A. 2d 78 (1955). The only shareholder of the corporate defendant who had knowledge of all of the material facts concerning the November 15, 1966 agreement was the promoter. His knowledge, however, cannot be imputed to the corporate defendant. Knowledge possessed by a single promoter having only a minority interest cannot bind the corporate defendant.

5 In *G.M.A.C. of Can. Ltd. v. Weisman* (1979), 23 O.R. (2d) 479, 6 B.L.R. 213 (Co. Ct.) the defendant concluded a contract with a dealer in Windsor for the purchase of a Chevrolet van. The purchaser's signature appeared on the contract as "Universal Sports (Newfoundland) Ltd., per S. J. Weisman". The evidence was that a company under this name was to be incorporated under Newfoundland law; in fact none ever was. What was the result? Should Ontario or Newfoundland law be applied to determine Weisman's liability? (Assume Newfoundland has no CBCA-type pre-incorporation provisions.) For further discussions of the choice of law rules governing corporate affairs see *American Restatement, Conflict of Laws* 2d s. 301 (1971), and J.G. Castel, *Canadian Conflict of Laws*, 5th ed. (2002) Ch. 31. In determining which law governs the parties' rights and obligations, should a distinction be drawn between those cases where a company is incorporated and those where it is not? Is it constitutionally competent for the CBCA to regulate pre-incorporation contracts or is it a question of "property and civil rights" beyond the federal domain? Professor Malone, *supra*, this section, questions the federal competence but she appears to overlook the ancillary powers doctrine.

6 Defendants, real estate developers in Oregon, applied for a loan through the plaintiff for the purpose of developing a parcel of land. The plaintiff was in the business of lending money and securing loans from other sources. The plaintiff informed the defendants that any loan would have to be made to a corporation so as to overcome the usury restrictions under the then Oregon law on loans to individuals. As a prerequisite to seeking a loan commitment for defendants, the plaintiff required a "good faith" deposit from the defendants. The deposit took the form of a note made payable to the plaintiff. When plaintiff was preparing the note he asked the defendants what corporation would borrow the money and execute the good faith deposit note. Defendants did not have any corporation but told plaintiff the corporation's name would be "Iron Mountain Investment Co., Inc." The note was so prepared and signed by the personal defendant for the corporation. Plaintiff knew at this time there was no corporate entity. The corporation was never incorporated and the defendant defaulted on the note. Assuming the relevant facts had occurred in Canada, would the defendant be held liable under the CBCA or the OBCA? *Cf. Sherwood and Roberts- Oregon, Inc. v. Alexander* (1974), 525 P 2d 135 (Ore.).

Chapter 4

Management and Control of the Corporation

1. CORPORATE GOVERNANCE: THE ROLE OF LEGAL AND MARKET INSTRUMENTS

(a) Introduction

This chapter (and following chapters) of the casebook explore the governance structure of the corporation. In particular, the mechanisms by which managerial action is facilitated, monitored and controlled are discussed. At the core of these chapters is the problem of ensuring the accountability of managers to the goals of the corporation. That is, irrespective of the particular goals to which the corporation is devoted, there is a natural propensity for corporate actors to deviate from these goals in an effort to maximize their own welfare. Corporate law, in conjunction with a variety of other instruments, can serve to limit the scope for such opportunism.

(b) The Challenge of Berle and Means

The concern over opportunism by corporate managers has been a central theme of corporate law scholarship ever since the publication of Berle and Means' seminal treatise on the subject of corporate governance in 1932. (Adolf A. Berle and Gardiner C. Means, *The Modern Corporation and Private Property*, rev. ed. 1967.) The central subject of their work was the considerable scope for unfettered discretion that managers of the largest corporations in America enjoyed because of the separation of ownership and control in these corporations. The high degree of separation of ownership and control in American corporations during the 1920s and 1930s was marked by the growing level of dispersion of share ownership of the largest industrial corporations. For instance, in 1929, 88 of the 200 largest corporations in the United States were found not to have a controlling shareholder, and only 22 were corporations privately owned or controlled. By the time a second edition of their study was prepared in 1967, Berle and Means could report that, as of 1963, 169 of the 200 largest US corporations had dispersed ownership, while only 5 were privately owned or controlled. According to Berle and Means, the effect of this growing dispersion of share ownership was to dull the incentive for any particular shareholder to assume the responsibility for controlling the affairs of the corporation. In essence, the growing dispersion of share ownership transformed shareholders into passive principals of the corporations they owned.

If shareholders were unable to exercise control over the modern corporation, where did control over these large enterprises reside? Berle and Means asserted that the members of a new managerial elite filled the vacuum left by the failure of scattered shareholders to exercise control. But, in contrast to the shareholders of the corporation, the members of this elite held only minor ownership interests in the capital of the corporation. The obvious implication of the separation of ownership and control was that management, because it lacked a direct stake in the corporation, would not be motivated to advance the welfare of the corporation and its owners. The legacy, therefore, of the separation of ownership and control was to submerge the profit motive as the primary force motivating corporate action. The conception of corporate America that Berle and Means held was of large aggregations of capital being directed by managers who were virtually unaccountable to any constituency but themselves.

(c) Enter the Contractarians

(i) Introduction to the Corporate Contract

The analysis fashioned by Berle and Means has had a profound effect on the way in which subsequent scholars, judges and policy-makers have viewed the corporation. But while their prognosis of corporate governance remained virtually unchallenged for almost four decades after the original publication of *The Modern Corporation and Private Property*, by the 1970s their analysis received close scrutiny by scholars belonging to the law and economics movement. At one level, the work of the new scholars built on the original work by Berle and Means. At another level, it deepened and, sometimes, contradicted it. Essentially, by expanding the analysis of Berle and Means, these scholars have been able to evaluate a broad range of conflicts that beset the modern corporation. Among the most notable works in this genre is a book by Frank Easterbrook and Daniel Fischel, *The Economic Structure of Corporate Law* (1991), and the following articles: Michael Jensen and William H. Meckling, "Theory of the Firm: Managerial Behaviour, Agency Costs and Ownership Structure" (1976), 3 J. Fin. Econ. 305; Eugene Fama, "Agency Problems and the Theory of the Firm" (1980), 88 J. Pol. Econ. 288; Eugene Fama and Michael Jensen, "Separation of Ownership and Control" (1983), 26 J. Law and Econ. 301 and "Agency Problems and Residual Claims" (1983), 26 J. Law and Econ. 327; Frank Easterbrook and Daniel Fischel, "Corporate Control Transactions" (1982), 91 Yale L.J. 698; and Ronald Gilson, "A Structural Approach to Corporations: The Case Against Defensive Tactics in Takeovers" (1981), 33 Stan. L.R. 819.

At the core of the law and economics analysis of the corporation is the conception of the corporation as a nexus of contractual relationships among the corporation's shareholders, creditors, managers, employees and suppliers. Implicit in these contractual relationships is the delegation from principal to agent of functional authority over corporate affairs. Although this delegation allows for specialization of tasks, it entails the danger that the delegates (the agents) will use their delegated authority to pursue their own goals at the expense of those goals favoured by the delegators (the principals). The conflicts ("agency conflicts") that arise naturally from the delegation of authority are the principal unit of analysis of these theorists. More specifically, from the law and economics perspective, the purpose of corporate law is to achieve the cost-effective reduction of agency costs.

The agency conflict of greatest relevance to Berle and Means' concern is, of course, that occasioned by the delegation of authority from shareholders to managers in the corporation. Jensen and Meckling, *supra*, modelled the problems that inhere in this relationship by first examining the case where ownership and control are concentrated in a single person — the owner-manager. Obviously, when corporations are controlled by owner-managers, there is no scope for agency conflict. If the owner-manager engages in "diversion", by diverting corporate assets to her personal use, or in "shirking", by failing to render her maximum effort in the performance of her duties *qua* manager (by slacking on the job or by opting for a quieter life by pursuing relatively safe investment projects that do not maximize profits), then she will bear the full costs of such behaviour in the form of reductions in the amount of profit she realizes *qua* shareholder. As a general matter, therefore, when ownership and control are fused, the prospect of debilitating agency conflicts is minimized because the costs of opportunistic behaviour are reflected back onto the party engaging in such behaviour.

When, however, the connection between ownership and management is severed, or, at least, attenuated, the prospect for agency conflict and its accompanying costs is enhanced. Take, for example, the case of a small family-run firm that has as its sole asset a local corner variety store. Assume that the only shareholders of the company are a husband and wife. The couple provide the initial capital that facilitates the acquisition of the store, the purchase of its opening inventory, and the payment of sundry operational expenses. The couple are also the only managers of the store, and, in conjunction with their role in providing capital, are owner-managers. Also, the store lacks any significant creditors.

Now assume that the couple decide that they want to establish a chain of variety stores and require sources of outside capital to facilitate this growth. If the couple sell 40% of the firm to raise the necessary capital for expansion, it can be seen that the calculus governing the decision whether or not to engage in opportunistic behaviour is altered by their diminished ownership interest. Prior to the sale, a dollar of income expended on generating some level of personal benefit, in the form of lavish office facilities, exotic "business" travel, expensive cars, corporate jets, *etc.*, cost the couple a full dollar in terms of the final profit they will realize from the store's operation. After the sale, however, a dollar of firm revenue used to pay expenses incurred by the couple only costs the couple 60 cents. If the amount of personal benefit received exceeds 60 cents per dollar of expenditure, the couple will have benefited from this outlay. As a consequence, they will increase the amount of expenses they incur in the execution of their managerial duties because they bear only a portion of the costs entailed by that expenditure. Similarly, the sale of the ownership interest will also increase the propensity of the couple to shirk more than they would have if they were the exclusive owner-managers. Simply put, the greater the ownership stake sold by the couple to outside investors, the greater the incentive facing the couple to engage in opportunistic behaviour.

It can be seen that the analysis invoked by Jensen and Meckling is simply a formal way of modelling the problem of the separation of ownership and control originally described by Berle and Means. That is, the problem of separation of ownership and control gives rise to the agency conflict. It is important to note, however, that in contrast to Berle and Means' dim prognosis on the capacity of shareholders to control endemic agency conflicts, several economic theorists share confidence in the capacity of shareholders, even those in widely held corporations, to anticipate and control agency conflicts. This optimism flows to some extent from the contractual conception of the corporation: it does not make sense for a party to enter into a disadvantageous contract; hence, the fact that outsiders are willing to enter into the corporate contract suggests that there is some assurance of agency fidelity. Contractarians would predict that agency conflicts are controlled to the point where an additional dollar spent in inducing a certain kind of managerial behaviour is exactly equivalent to the benefit thereby generated.

There are two foundations for the conclusion that corporations will be structured so as to minimize agency costs. First, there are important incentives for private actors to choose a corporate framework that provides investors with assurance that managerial agency problems will be cost-effectively minimized. Second, there exist several legal and market mechanisms that corporate actors can rely on to discipline managers.

On the question of incentives, return to the example of the family-owned corner store. The family, who initially own the entire firm, decide to sell 40% of the firm to outside investors. They have the choice between two corporate law rules. One, the "permissive" rule, would allow them discretion to use corporate funds to buy themselves a house. The other, the "restrictive" rule, would prevent them from making such a purchase. Prior to selling a share of the firm, the family chooses the relevant corporate law rule. If the family chooses the permissive rule, investors will anticipate that the family are likely to divert corporate funds to buy themselves a house, even if they would not otherwise have done so, since this, in effect, gives the family a 40% discount on the purchase (paid for by outside investors). Investors confronted with the permissive rule therefore will lower their estimate of the value of a 40% share of the firm. The family, by choosing the permissive rule, realizes a smaller amount in the sale of an ownership stake in the firm; they are punished for choosing the permissive rule. In contrast, if the family chooses the restrictive rule, investors would be willing to pay more for the stake; the family would be rewarded for their decision.

Incentives thus exist for corporations to choose sensible governance structures. But this is not to say that very strict legal rules are always optimal. If, for example, the restrictive rule in the example not only prevented the acquisition of the house, but it also prevented the family from earning a salary, which would in turn induce the family not to work for the store, the costs of the rule may exceed its benefits — if so, the family would have an incentive not to choose such a regime. In addition, the wisdom of a strict legal rule must be weighed against alternative market mechanisms that may create a better combination of strictness on certain dimensions and laxity on others.

What are the mechanisms identified by contractarian theorists to control agency conflicts in corporations? Theorists point to a number of market and legal instruments. Legal instruments typically restrain managerial opportunism by imposing *ex post* costs on managers engaging in such activities. The statutory and common law duties enumerated in the following chapters set out standards against which managerial conduct will be evaluated. If detected, departures from these duties impose significant *ex post* penalties. (However, for a critical analysis of the capacity of legal instruments to discipline managerial behaviour, see: Roberta Romano, "The Shareholder Suit: Litigation Without Foundation?" (1991), 7 Journal of Law, Economics, and Organization 55 (shareholder litigation is a weak, if not ineffective, instrument of corporate governance).)

Market instruments operate at two levels. Like legal rules, market mechanisms can, by direct intervention, impose significant costs on self-serving management. But markets play a second role in furnishing information to the corporation's principals, which enhances the quality of supervision by corporate owners. If market signals furnish owners with information of managerial shirking or diversion, then owners can discipline managers in a variety of ways.

(ii) Voting — Independent and Instrumental Value

A. OVERVIEW

At the core of many of the legal and market control mechanisms used by owners to constrain managerial self-interest is the institution of shareholder voting. Voting is a powerful control mechanism that may be useful in itself or it may, in an instrumental fashion, be used to facilitate the operation of other mechanisms. On its own, the institution of shareholder voting vests owners with the ability to determine the membership of the board of directors of the corporation. Although some corporate constitutions articulate rules for determining the composition of corporate boards that depart from simple majority rule, for the most part, majority rule is the dominant decision rule for board elections. As numerous commentators have observed, corporate boards often do not manage the corporation, they are vested with the responsibility of appointing and supervising the managers of the corporation. If management fails to perform as expected, then it is the responsibility of the board to instigate changes to management. Thus, if shareholders, as owners of the corporation, are dissatisfied with the board's vigilance in ensuring optimal managerial performance, it is within the power of shareholders to voice their discontent by altering the composition of the board.

In addition to voting for positions on corporate boards, most corporate statutes provide that shareholders are entitled to vote on the occurrence of enumerated events. Generally speaking, these events involve substantial changes to the structure of the corporation. Amalgamations, change of incorporating jurisdiction, sale of substantially all of the company's assets and various changes to the rights and obligations of investor constituencies are events that trigger the voting mechanism. In contrast to the simple majority voting rules that govern election of board members, voting on fundamental corporate changes is typically subject to supra-majority (greater than 50%) voting rules. It is useful to note that the initial position of the supra-majority voting rules triggered by the initiation of substantial corporate changes fetters not only management's ability to generate agency costs for the owners of the firm, but also limits the capacity of various investor constituencies to impose agency costs on each other. For instance, supra-majority rules constrain the ability of majority shareholders to adopt changes that augment their own wealth at the expense of minority shareholders.

B.   INFORMATION PROVISION AND COLLECTIVE ACTION PROBLEMS

The independent capacity of shareholder voting to constrain agency costs is a function of the magnitude and quality of information that is available to shareholders. The greater the information available to shareholders concerning the performance of corporate agents, the more rational and effective their voting. But while information is of unequivocal value to shareholders, it cannot be produced, assimilated and disseminated without cost. As a result, the optimal level of information investment by a firm's principals is a function of the costs and benefits of information generation. Rationally, shareholders should, on an aggregate basis, invest in information activities to the point where the benefits that are received from such expenditure are equal to the costs.

Unfortunately, the likelihood of generating an optimal level of information provision by corporate shareholders is undermined by the presence of various coordination problems. These problems arise because, in economic jargon, shareholder information possesses "public good" attributes

— the good must be produced jointly, and once supplied, it is difficult, if not impossible, to exclude others from consuming it. (The theory of public goods is developed by Samuelson, "The Pure Theory of Public Expenditure" (1954), 36 Rev. of Econ. Statistics 386.) Because an investment in the provision of a public good cannot be recouped, these goods will normally be undersupplied by the private market. In the case of corporate information, its public goods character means that shareholders must overcome endemic collective action problems in order to produce collectively an amount of information commensurate with the importance of the issue subject to the vote. Shareholders will reason that, since the benefits from an investment in information activities will accrue to all shareholders irrespective of their individual contribution, it is better to "free ride" on the investment of other shareholders than to contribute oneself. Of course, if this is a rational strategy for one shareholder, it is equally rational for all similarly situated shareholders, and, predictably, investment in information-related activities will be sub-optimal. (Collective action problems are discussed at length in Robert Clark, *Corporate Law* (1986), pp. 389–400 and Easterbrook and Fischel, "Voting in Corporate Law" (1983), 26 Journal of Law and Economics 395.)

The problem of generating optimal information investment by widely dispersed corporate shareholders bears strong resemblance to the familiar "prisoner's dilemma" problem. (For a full exposition of the prisoner's dilemma, see: D. Mueller, *Public Choice*, (1979) Ch. 2; Coleman, *Markets, Morals and the Law*, (1988) Ch. 10.) This problem arises when there exist strong incentives for rational, self-interested actors to pursue non-cooperative outcomes, even though a mutually advantageous and superior outcome is realizable through cooperation. There are two reasons why corporations may not be vulnerable to the most pessimistic collective actions scenario described above. First, an individual shareholder may own a sufficiently large percentage of shares that the collective action problem is not insuperable. Collective action problems arise if each shareholder anticipates that her behaviour has only a trivial impact on corporate activities. But large shareholders will anticipate that their actions, including gathering information and voting sensibly, could affect outcomes. At the extreme, a "controlling shareholder", that is, a shareholder that can elect a majority of the board of directors by virtue of votes from her shares alone, anticipates that her decisions will with certainty affect a vote. Controlling shareholders therefore have incentives to monitor managers closely and govern behaviour accordingly. Canada, in contrast to the United States and the United Kingdom, has a significant number of large corporations with controlling shareholders, which diminishes concern about collective action problems: see R. Daniels and J. MacIntosh, "Towards a Distinctive Canadian Corporate Law Regime" (1991) 29 Osgoode Hall L.J. 863; R. Daniels and E. Iacobucci, "Some of the Causes and Consequences of Corporate Ownership Concentration in Canada" in R. Morck, Ed., *Concentrated Corporate Ownership* (2000). Note, however, that controlling shareholders, while overcoming collective action problems, do not eliminate concerns about self-interested, sub-optimal governance. Controlling shareholders may take advantage of minority shareholders by causing the corporation to take actions that benefit the controller while harming minority shareholders. Later chapters discuss these problems.

Aside from controlling shareholders, large but non-controlling shareholders may also be able to overcome collective action problems. Shares in Canada and other market economies are increasingly owned not by individuals, but rather by various kinds of large aggregations of capital (for discussion, see R. Daniels and E. Waitzer, "Challenges to the Citadel: A Brief Overview of Recent Trends in Corporate Governance" (1994) 23 Canadian Business Law Journal 23). These "institutional investors" include private and public pension funds, mutual funds, insurance companies and banks. Such shareholders do not fit the Berle and Means model of atomistic shareholders each with trivial share ownership, but rather may own a significant number of shares. Institutional shareholders may have shareholdings large enough to induce them to invest in information.

Second, aside from the role of large shareholders in overcoming collective action problems, markets themselves can address such problems by providing information to shareholder-voters. If, for example, markets, through their natural operation, are able to furnish shareholders with reliable information concerning agency cost levels, then it is possible that pervasive collective action problems can be overcome. (For a further discussion of the operation of equity markets with particular attention to the control of managerial agency costs, see: Ronald Gilson and Reinier Kraakman, "The Mechanisms of Market Efficiency" (1984) 70 Va. L. Rev. 549.)

C. MARKETS AND INFORMATION PROVISION

I. The Capital Market. Of the various markets whose operation furnishes shareholders with valuable information, the most important is the capital market. The capital market comprises numerous bond and equity markets that are located in countries throughout the world. Although these markets are located within distinct domestic boundaries, the rapid advances in technology, combined with diminished barriers to capital mobility, permit commentators to speak realistically of one global capital market. Although less than one per cent of the securities of all companies incorporated in Canada are traded on a Canadian stock market, these companies are the largest and most profitable in the country.

Capital markets play a central role in controlling agency costs. At the time that a shareholder makes her initial investment, capital markets, if perfectly efficient, will ensure that the price that is paid for securities of a corporation fully reflects the magnitude of expected costs generated by agency conflicts. This means that shareholders will not suffer reductions in their wealth by managerial shirking or diversion because these costs were anticipated at the time of initial investment and were impounded into the price paid for their shares.

Of course, there are limits to the extent to which managerial opportunism can be accurately anticipated at the time of initial investment. Foresight is not perfect, and management may embark on a course of action that was not foreseeable when the shareholder made her initial investment. By incorporating the consequences of management misconduct into share prices, capital markets furnish shareholders with a signal of corporate performance. Accordingly, if the price of a corporation's securities increases at a rate that compares favourably with the securities of corporations having similar characteristics, the investor can be reasonably confident that the corporation in which she has invested is being well managed. Conversely, if the share price of the corporation underperforms industry competitors, the spectre of managerial incompetence is raised.

How efficient are capital markets in pricing agency conflicts? At the outset it is important to note that efficient pricing is not predicated on every investor being fully informed of the magnitude of these costs; efficient pricing only requires (i) that some subset of fully-informed investors, i.e., "marginal investors", be able to accurately price the magnitude of expected agency costs, and (ii) that the price paid by marginal investors not diverge significantly from the price paid by less informed investors for shares purchased within the same time frame on the market.

The accuracy of capital market pricing is a subject that has attracted considerable and sustained scholarly attention in the corporate finance literature. Essentially, the efficiency of capital markets is determined in relation to different types of data. The conclusion that the market is "efficient" with respect to a certain data set is just a shorthand way of saying that there are no opportunities for dedicated stock analysts and traders to realize long term abnormal positive returns from devising and executing trading strategies based on a given data set. (The focus is on "*abnormal* positive returns" because all investors expect positive returns in the normal course of events — this is why they invest.) Empirical tests of market efficiency have found that capital markets are generally "efficient" with respect to publicly available information, i.e., information that is disclosed in the financial press and in various publicly available offering documents. Not surprisingly, the empirical evidence also demonstrates that markets are not efficient with respect to "insider information", i.e., information respecting the performance of the company that is not publicly available. (For a full discussion of capital market efficiency, see: E. Fama, "Efficient Capital Markets II" (1991) 46 J. Finance 1575; Gordon and Kornhauser, "Efficient Markets, Costly Information, and Securities Research" (1985), 60 New York Univ,. L.R. 76 1; Note, "The Efficient Capital Markets Hypothesis, Economic Theory and the Regulation of the Securities Industry" (1976-77), 29 Stan. L.R. 1031; Shiller, "Fashions, Fads and Bubbles in Financial Markets", in John C. Coffee, Jr., Louis Lowenstein, Susan Rose-Ackerman, Eds., *Knights, Raiders and Targets: The Impact of Hostile Takeover* (1988), pp. 56 *et seq.*)

II. The Product Market. Another market that provides useful information to shareholders is the product market. This market is simply the market in which the corporation's goods are bought and sold. The success or failure of a company's goods on the product market is governed by the price, quality, and service characteristics of the corporation's products. If a company supplies a product that is superior to competing products, then the company's profits should increase. Conversely, if a company's product fails to earn the patronage of a sufficient range of consumers, then a powerful, but crude, information signal will be made to the principals of the corporation. Dismal product market performance sends a signal to investors about managerial performance, particularly if a corporation is performing poorly while its industry peers are thriving. Shareholders can threaten to alter the composition of the board through their voting power if the board refuses to discipline senior management. Increasingly in the last several years, the threat of shareholder discipline has provoked a number of boards in leading North American corporations to initiate the ouster of reigning senior managers.

D. DIRECT CONTROL OF AGENCY COSTS THROUGH MARKETS

So far, we have only considered shareholder voting as an independent agency cost control mechanism. In this vein, the operation of various markets works to enhance the quality of shareholder voting by increasing the amount of information available to shareholders. Other markets exert a powerful impact on managerial behaviour by imposing direct penalties on opportunistic managerial behaviour. The effectiveness of these markets is not contingent upon the ability of shareholders to overcome collective action problems.

I. The Managerial Market. The managerial market is the market where the services of corporate managers are traded. The threat of having to compete in the managerial market encourages managers to act in their principals' best interests. A manager who shirks or diverts will, if the managerial market is efficient, suffer reductions in the salary she may have otherwise received corresponding to the magnitude of the agency costs she is expected to generate for present or future employers. Clearly, if these costs are fully impounded into an opportunistic manager's expected pay, then the manager derives no net benefit from engaging in opportunistic behaviour. Any immediate gain from opportunism is offset by reductions in the value of the manager's human capital. Of course, the effectiveness of this mechanism turns on the ability of the market to evaluate the performance of the manager under consideration in isolation from her team. But linking even crude measures of managerial performance, like share price, to managerial pay can offer valuable incentives to managers to perform their duties diligently.

The managerial market also serves another important role in the control of agency costs. To the extent that individuals within the firm aspire to replace managers above them, they may be motivated to scrutinize closely the performance of senior management in an effort to detect conduct that will invite discipline and removal by the principals of the corporation.

Obviously, the removal of opportunistic managers presents opportunities for the employees formerly below them. The more generous the promotion or bonus that is correlated with successful "whistle-blowing", the more powerful the incentive to search for managerial opportunism.

II. The Product Market. As discussed, the product market can discipline managers indirectly, by providing information to shareholders about performance. The product market can also sanction managers directly for inferior performance. *In extremis*, an egregious failure of the company to compete successfully in the product market will result in the bankruptcy of the firm. Even if the corporation successfully reorganizes and continues to operate after bankruptcy, management is replaced following most bankruptcies. Thus, managers have an incentive to avoid failure in the product market.

III. The Market for Corporate Control. The final, and, perhaps, the most powerful market safeguard against the generation of agency costs, is the "market for corporate control". Essentially, this mechanism, which was first identified by Henry Manne (Manne, "Mergers and the Market for Corporate Control" (1965), 73 J. Pol. Econ. 110), operates by transferring control of mismanaged corporations (i.e., corporations beset by high levels of agency costs) to owners more willing or able to discipline self-serving managers. The transfer of control is effected by the use of the hostile takeover bid. The principal attraction of the hostile bid is that it can operate independently of the consent of target management. Once control is amassed by an acquirer (51% of voting stock is necessary for legal control but a smaller percentage is often sufficient for *de facto* control), she can exercise the voting rights conferred by control and oust existing management by electing new directors. The acquirer of control profits by purchasing shares at a price that reflects significant agency problems, reducing those problems once in control, and then realizing the greater value of the shares.

There is considerable empirical evidence that supports this rather crude description of the market for corporate control. Scholars have found strong evidence that many corporations that are the subject of hostile takeovers are poorly managed companies, and that successful takeovers increase the aggregate value of target corporations (see discussion, *infra*, in Chapter 6).

Significantly, like legal rules and the managerial market, the market for corporate control is effective in both discouraging deviations from shareholder wealth maximization before they occur, and penalizing such behaviour if it does indeed occur. The fear of a possible takeover, and consequent threat of job loss, serves as a powerful countervailing force on management shirking and diversion. The more credible the threat from the control market, the more willing incumbent managers will be to adopt strategies that reduce the risk of a takeover. Perhaps the most potent defensive tactic is self-imposed restraint on shirking and diversion; by diminishing opportunistic behaviour, the share price of the corporation will rise and attenuate the gains accruing to an acquiror from a control shift.

(d) The Role of Corporate Law in the Contractarian Model of the Corporation

In any contract, parties have an economic incentive to adopt value-maximizing rules. For example, if a warranty is worth $10 to a customer, but would only cost a seller $5, then the parties can *both* be made better off by including a warranty in a contract. They will each try to capture a larger share of the value by haggling over a price, but including a warranty at any price greater than $5 and less than $10 makes both better off. Similarly, if corporations are simply a nexus of contracts, it makes sense to conclude that investors and entrepreneurs (managers) would agree on a set of corporate law rules that maximize value and minimize agency costs. This analysis then invites the question: if a corporation is simply a nexus of contracts, what role is there for corporate law as a body of law distinct from contract law? That is, does acceptance of the contractarian view of the corporation abolish the need for corporate law?

There is further reason to question the justification for corporate law. We have reviewed how markets discipline managers in a variety of ways. If these markets work to align the interests of managers and shareholders, is corporate law redundant?

Lest the reader fear that this casebook was written (and purchased) in vain, let us quickly reassure you that corporate law can serve a vital role despite these important considerations. First, many of the markets we describe only work successfully *because* of the law. For example, the market for corporate control depends on the ability of an acquirer of shares to vote to oust directors; voting rules are a matter of corporate law. Capital markets depend on the rules that corporate law establishes for determining how investors realize returns. For example, it takes corporate law to establish many of the rights associated with share ownership that in turn make shares valuable.

Second, there are important advantages from having the rules operate as a matter of corporate law rather than simple contract. Whenever parties enter into a contract, there are costs associated with reaching agreement; economists refer to these as "transaction costs." Under the contractarian model, corporate law reduces transaction costs by providing a "standard form contract" that offers private actors an off-the-rack set of corporate rules that represent what most parties would want. Entrepreneurs can offer investors this "contract" simply by incorporating. This saves parties (and society) considerable transaction costs given the large number of incorporations that occur in any given period of time. Moreover, many rules that corporate law establishes are complicated, and it would be very difficult (costly) for parties themselves to specify their content in a contract. For example, incorporation gives rise to fiduciary duties that have been refined over 150 years of company law. Incorporation also gives rise to a corporation with a separate legal personality, as we have seen in Chapter 2, which in turn means that a debt obligation of the corporation is not (generally) a debt of the shareholder, and equally, a debt of a shareholder is not that of the corporation. Replicating such rules through private contract would be complicated and costly: see H. Hansmann and R. Kraakman, "The Essential Role of Organizational Law" (2000) 110 Yale L. J. 439.

The contractarian view does not, therefore, lead to a conclusion that corporate law serves no meaningful purpose, rather it suggests that corporate law can facilitate the contracting process by providing a standard form contract. This in turn has implications for the kind of corporate law we should observe. In particular, corporate law under the contractarian view should strive to offer parties terms that they would want, but should give private parties the option to contract around a particular term if they prefer to do so. Corporate law under this view ought to play an "enabling" role that facilitates contracting by offering a set of default rules, and should generally avoid a "mandatory" role that requires parties to adopt particular rules. Unless there is some kind of market failure that engenders mistrust of private contracting, corporate law should seek to give parties what they want and allow them something different if they so choose.

(e) Critique of the Contractarian Model of the Corporation

Criticism of the agency theorists' model of corporate governance can be pitched at two distinct levels. The first and most obvious criticism is to express skepticism with the capacity of markets to effectively control agency costs. In this respect, the criticism against the model reflects not different underlying values or ideologies, but only different perceptions regarding empirically testable hypotheses. Critics of the idea of leaving corporate law to private parties would, for example, emphasize the string of recent, spectacular failures of large, public corporations, like Enron and WorldCom, and contend that regulators must step in to fill the corporate governance void. Contractarians are likely to respond that these failures, spectacular though they may have been, pale beside the successes resulting from the private choice of corporate governance regimes.

Criticisms of contractarianism seem most potent in relation to the claims made by the most strident proponents of the model, who assert that the cost of all agency conflicts is anticipated and reflected back onto managers by the mechanisms enumerated above (see, for instance, Jensen and Meckling, *supra*, p. 328). But in order for this extreme claim to be valid, the various instruments set out above must operate with a high degree of efficiency. We know, however, that this is unlikely: product and managerial markets often suffer from various structural imperfections, capital markets are not efficient in relation to certain sets of information, the corporate control market only operates above certain threshold levels of agency cost and, finally, legal rules may be incorrectly articulated and applied.

It is also common for critics of the enabling, rather than the mandatory or regulatory, model of corporate law to provide evidence of the apparent dysfunction of institutions on which the contractual model of corporations appears to place considerable reliance. Consider the following two excerpts about the role of the board of directors.

MACE, Directors: Myth and Reality
(1971), 184–194, 205-206

The business literature describing the classical functions of boards of directors typically includes three important roles: (1) establishing basic objectives, corporate strategies, and broad policies; (2) asking discerning questions; and (3) selecting the president

. . .

In a final summary of my study of directors, I found that in large and medium-sized companies where the president and board members own only a few shares of stock:

1. Presidents with *de facto* powers of control select the members of the boards.

2. Presidents determine what boards do and do not do.

3. Directors selected are usually heads of equally prestigious organizations with primary responsibilities of their own.

4. Heads of businesses and financial, legal, and educational organizations are extremely busy men with limited motivation and time to serve as directors of other organizations.

5. Most boards of directors serve as advisors and counselors to the presidents.

6. Most boards of directors serve as some sort of discipline for the organization — as a corporate conscience.

7. Most boards of directors are available to and do make decisions in the event of a crisis.

8. A few boards of directors establish company objectives, strategies, and broad policies. Most do not.

9. A few boards of directors ask discerning questions. Most do not.

10. A few boards evaluate and measure the performance of the president and select and de-select the president. Most do not.

Mace surveyed the scene again some ten years later and found "little evidence to suggest that business leaders are responding affirmatively and constructively to rectify the shortcomings of board practices." Mace, "Directors: Myth and Reality — Ten Years Later", (1979), 32 Rutgers Law Review, 293, 297. McDougall and Fogelberg conducted a similar study in Canada: see *Corporate Boards in Canada: How Sixty-Four Boards Function* (1968). More recently, the Toronto Stock Exchange launched a study, under the leadership of Peter Dey, of how boards operate and recommended several "best practices", like having a majority of directors that are otherwise unrelated to the corporation: see Toronto Stock Exchange, *Where Were the Directors?* (1994) (the "Dey Report"). Even more recently, the report of the Joint Committee on Corporate Governance (involving representatives from the accountancy profession and stock exchanges, including the Toronto Stock Exchange), entitled *Beyond Compliance: Building a Governance Culture* (2001) (the "Saucier Report") concluded that while corporate governance had improved since the Dey Report, there remains room for improvement. For example, corporate reporting on compliance with stock exchange best practices is frequently unsatisfactory.

EISENBERG, The Structure of the Corporation
(1976), p. 148

Because it is inherently undesirable for law and practice to be in a state of visible opposition, the drastic skew between the legal and working models of the board would be of serious concern even if no specific dysfunctional consequences could be perceived. In fact, however, a number of such dysfunctions can be identified. On a relatively particularistic level, many legal rules have been shaped on the premise that the board manages the corporation's business in fact as well as in the law. For example, by proceeding from the assumption that officers play a subordinate role to the board, the rules governing the authority of officers frequently embody an unrealistically restrictive view of an officer's power of position. Standards of care, by the same token, often seem to be pitched to the outside director rather than the executive, as if the former were really running the business. In duty-of-loyalty cases, the courts have often given disproportionate weight to the fact that outside directors have approved a transaction in which executives are interested, while the legislatures have sometimes gone so far as to provide that approval by outside directors is sufficient to sterilize an otherwise infected transaction. In a wider context, the skew between belief and reality has led to what might be called the quack-cure problem — the danger that belief in the validity of the received legal model will forestall meaningful regulation by lulling shareholders, legislators, and the public into the illusion (which often seems deliberately conjured up) that a dis-interested board is supervising the corporation's affairs.

Given that market imperfections clearly exist, and given the criticisms of boards offered by Mace and Eisenberg, is the managerial model of corporate governance propounded by Berle and Means validated? To concede some scope for uncontrolled agency costs is not to accept Berle and Means' strong claim that management is unfettered by any external constraint. Clearly, the various mechanisms enumerated above serve to impose some limitations on managerial discretion, although the precise contours of the domain accorded managerial discretion by these limitations is far from settled. Furthermore, to the extent that agency costs are left uncontrolled by the corporate governance regime, it is important to compare these costs with the benefits that are achieved from the separation of ownership and control, and with the existing regulatory alternatives. In terms of the former, the benefits from disentangling ownership and control are substantial and are related to specialization; owners are freed from selecting managers on the basis of factors unrelated to managerial skill, i.e., wealth and risk preferences. It can be surmised that the benefits of specialization outweigh whatever residual costs remain. In terms of the latter, the recognition that agency costs are not fully addressed by the current corporate governance regime does not support its rejection. To do so would require the critic to propose some alternative set of institutional arrangements that permit the same benefits as the current regime but at lower cost. As always, the question is not "Is this system flawless?" but rather, "How does this system compare to others?" Are government officials drafting mandatory rules likely to choose better rules than entrepreneurs and investors, who, after all, invest their own money and time in the corporation?

In contrast to the empirical nature of the criticisms canvassed above, the second major set of criticisms levelled against the contractarian model is normative in character. For instance, Victor Brudney's reservations regarding the model relate to the implications of the contractual metaphor for corporate law reform ("Corporate Governance, Agency Costs, and the Rhetoric of Contract" (1985), 85 Col. L. Rev. 1403). According to Brudney (at p. 1404):

> the rhetoric of contract proceeds on doubtful assumptions about the circumstances of the parties, imports inappropriate normative consequences to govern the relationships thus assumed, and serves the ideological function of legitimating substantially unaccountable managerial discretion to determine corporate activities and to serve itself at the expense of investors.

Brudney is concerned, in particular, with the hostility of the model to regulatory intervention. If parties have, through their autonomous and fully informed conduct, created a mutually acceptable bargain, then the scope for state intervention is greatly confined.

A similar line of argument is developed by Robert Clark. He finds the contractual metaphor "troublesome" because it fails to accurately depict reality, engenders facile optimism about the optimality of existing rules and institutions, deflects attention from underlying value judgments, and is highly indeterminate in application. Clark also criticizes the advisability of viewing shareholders as principals of the corporation. Clark compares the power of principals in "pure" agency relationship with shareholders in the modern corporation and finds that shareholders lack many of the rights routinely accorded legal principals. (Robert Clark, "Agency Costs Versus Fiduciary Duties," in *Principals and Agents: The Structure of Business*, Pratt and Zeckhauser, Eds. (1985), Ch. 3.)

Finally, Bruce Chapman argues that the contractual theory of the corporation is impoverished for its failure to take into account other values unrelated to contract ("Trust, Economic Rationality, and the Corporate Fiduciary Obligation", (1993) 43 University of Toronto Law Journal 547). He notes that adepts of the law and economics approach construe the corporate fiduciary obligation as being properly owed to shareholders "only because all efficient corporate contractors would recognize that shareholders, as residual claimants, put the highest value on control of the corporation" (at 548). He then proceeds to challenge this view on the basis that:

> competitive corporate contracting cannot achieve all that this view promises unless it is aided by the very value that a contractual understanding of the fiduciary obligation denies, namely, the duty of loyalty and trust. Trust plays an essential role in modern economics, and without it, or without the coordination that is provided by institutional loyalty, even efficient wealth-maximizing corporate contracting can make us all worse off. That too, unfortunately, is the stuff of competition. Nor can the concept of trust be very easily accommodated into the contractual model of the corporation. Properly interpreted, the concepts of trust and loyalty present a deep challenge not only to the contractual model, but also to the very conventions of instrumental rationality upon which the model is based. (At 549.)

2. AN INTRODUCTION TO THE LEGAL MODEL OF THE CORPORATION

(a) Introduction

The remainder of this chapter examines the basic structure of corporate governance that is set out in the CBCA and its cognate legislation. First, we consider the effect of an apparent tension, if not conflict, between a corporation's internal choice of rules and an apparently mandatory provision in the relevant corporate statute. How does one's view of the appropriate role of corporate law affect the outcome in *Bushell v. Faith*? Second, we turn to questions of how to interpret potentially ambiguous corporate rules. Are the interpretations of the courts consistent with the contractarian perspective, or do they instead suggest the Berle and Means description of the clear primacy of corporate managers over investors? Third, we review how a regime of privately chosen corporate rules interacts with those who were not party to those choices. In particular, we examine how third parties entering into contracts with the corporation are affected by the failure of a corporation to live up to its internal code of conduct. We also examine the significance of the private choice of corporate objectives. This raises important questions of corporate social responsibility: is there a duty, or even a capacity, of corporate actors to account for constituencies seemingly outside at least a narrow view of the "corporate contract"? Again, in all these cases, ask how the alternative conceptions of corporate law as either facilitating contracting or regulating behaviour affect legal outcomes.

(b) Mandatory Versus Enabling Interpretations of Corporate Statutes

Absent a statutory right or a power in the corporate constitution, shareholders have no right to remove a director prior to the expiration of his term of office (*Imperial Hydropathic Hotel Co., Blackpool v. Hampson* (1882), 23 Ch. D. 1 (C.A.)). The power to remove directors can be an important exercise of ultimate control by the shareholders, and the CBCA and OBCA now make provision for removal in s. 109 and s. 122, respectively, by ordinary resolution at a special meeting. The British Columbia *Business Corporations Act* allows shareholders to remove directors, but, unless otherwise specified in the articles or memoranda, only by special resolution. For firms incorporated prior to the passage of the BCBCA, a special resolution requires a three-quarters majority, as was the case under predecessor acts; for other firms, it requires a two-thirds majority.

The OBCA stipulates that the articles cannot provide for removal of a director by a greater number of votes than provided in s. 122 — an ordinary resolution. See: OBCA 5(5).

A way around a similar, though not identical, U.K. statute was sanctioned by the House of Lords in the following case. How does one's conception of the role of corporate law affect one's evaluation of the outcome in this case?

Bushell v. Faith
[1970] A.C. 1099, [1970] 1 All E.R. 53 (H.L.)

The articles of association of Bush Court (Southgate) Ltd provided that "in the event of a Resolution being proposed at any General Meeting of the Company for removal from office of any Director, any shares held by that Director shall on a poll in respect of such Resolution carry the right to three votes per share . . ." The company had an issued capital of 300 shares, held as to 100 by the appellant Bushell, and as to 100 each by the respondent Faith and his sister Bayne. Bushell & Bayne proposed an ordinary resolution at a general meeting of the Company to remove Faith as a director. On a show of hands the resolution was passed 2-1; Faith demanded a poll and the resolution was defeated 300-200. At trial an injunction was issued restraining Faith from acting as a director. The Court of Appeal reversed ([1969] 1 All E.R. 1002) and Bushell appealed to the House of Lords.

LORD UPJOHN: My Lords, this appeal raises a question of some importance to those concerned with the niceties of company law, and the relevant facts, which are not in dispute, can be very shortly stated. The respondent company Bush Court (Southgate) Ltd (a formal party to the proceedings) was incorporated on 19th September 1960, and at all material times had an issued capital of 300 fully paid-up shares of £1 each held as to 100 shares each by a brother and his two sisters namely the appellant Mrs. Bushell, the respondent Mr. Faith and their sister Dr. Kathleen Bayne.

The respondent was a director but his conduct as such displeased his sisters who requisitioned a general meeting of the company which was held on 22nd November 1968, when a resolution was proposed as an ordinary resolution to remove him from his office as director. On a show of hands the resolution was passed, as the sisters voted for the resolution; so the brother demanded a poll and the whole issue is how votes should be counted on the poll having regard to special art. 9 of the company's articles of association.

The company adopted Table A in Sch I to the *Companies Act 1948*, with variations which are immaterial for present purposes. The relevant articles of Table A are:

> 2. Without prejudice to any special rights previously conferred on the holders of any existing shares or class of shares, any share in the company may be issued with such preferred, deferred or other special rights or such restrictions, whether in regard to dividend, voting, return of capital or otherwise as the company may from time to time by ordinary resolution determine.

> 62. Subject to any rights or restrictions for the time being attached to any class or classes of shares, on a show of hands every member present in person shall have one vote, and on a poll every member shall have one vote for each share of which he is the holder.

Special art. 9 is as follows:

> In the event of a Resolution being proposed at any General Meeting of the Company for the removal from office of any Director, any shares held by that Director shall on a poll in respect of such Resolution carry the right to three votes per share and regulation 62 of Part I of Table A shall be construed accordingly.

Article 96 of Table A, which empowers a company to remove a director by ordinary resolution, is excluded by the articles of the company so that the appellant relies on the mandatory terms of s. 184(1) of the *Companies Act 1948*, which so far as relevant is in these terms:

> A company may by ordinary resolution remove a director before the expiration of his period of office, notwithstanding anything in its articles or in any agreement between it and him . . .

It is not in doubt that the requirements of sub-s. (2) have been satisfied. So the whole question is whether special art 9 is valid and applicable, in which case the resolution was rejected by 300 votes to 200, or whether that article must be treated as overridden by s. 184 and therefore void, in which case the resolution was passed by 200 votes to 100. So to test this matter the appellant began an action for a declaration that the respondent was removed from office as a director by the resolution of 22nd November 1968, and moved the court for an interlocutory injunction restraining him from acting as a director. This motion comes by way of appeal before your Lordships.

The appellant argues that special art 9 is directed to frustrating the whole object and purpose of s. 184 so that it can never operate where there is such a special article and the director in fact becomes irremovable. So she argues that, having regard to the clear words "notwithstanding anything in its articles" in s. 194, special art 9 must be rejected and treated as void. The learned judge, Ungoed Thomas J, so held. He said: "It would make a mockery of the law if the courts were to hold that in such a case a director was to be irremovable", and later he concluded his judgment by saying: "A resolution under art 9 is therefore not in my view an ordinary resolution within s. 184. The [appellant] succeeds in the application."

The respondent appealed, and the Court of Appeal (Harman, Russell and Karminski L.JJ.) allowed the appeal. Harman LJ did so on the simple ground that the 1948 Act did not prevent certain shares or classes of shares having special voting rights attached to them and on certain occasions. He could find nothing in the 1948 Act which prohibited the giving of special voting rights to the shares of a director who finds his position attacked. Russell L.J. in his judgment gave substantially the same reasons for allowing the appeal and he supported his judgment by reference to a number of recent precedents particularly those to be found in Palmer's Company Precedents [17th ed., 1956] but, with all respect to the learned Lord Justice, I do not think these precedents which, so far as relevant, are comparatively new can be said to have the settled assent and approbation of the profession, so as to render them any real guide for the purposes of a judgment; especially when I note the much more cautious approach by the learned editors of 5 Ency Forms & Precedents (4th ed.) 1966, p. 428, where in reference to a form somewhat similar to special art 9 they state in footnote 14:

> The validity of such a provision as this in relation to a resolution to remove a director from office remains to be tested in the courts.

My Lords, when construing an Act of Parliament it is a canon of construction that its provisions must be construed in the light of the mischief which the Act was designed to meet. In this case the mischief was well known; it was a common practice, especially in the case of private companies, to provide in the articles that a director should be irremovable or only removable by an extraordinary resolution; in the former case the articles would have to be altered by special resolution before the director could be removed and of course in either case a three-quarters majority would be required. In many cases this would be impossible, so the Act provided that notwithstanding anything in the articles an ordinary resolution would suffice to remove a director. That was the mischief which the section set out to remedy; to make a director removable by virtue of an ordinary resolution instead of an extraordinary resolution or making it necessary to alter the articles.

An ordinary resolution is not defined nor used in the body of the 1948 Act although the phrase occurs in some of the articles of Table A in Sch I to the Act. But its meaning is, in my opinion, clear. An ordinary resolution is in the first place passed by a bare majority on a show of hands by the members entitled to vote who are present personally or by proxy and on such a vote each member has one vote regardless of his shareholding. If a poll is demanded then for an ordinary resolution still only a bare majority of votes is required. But whether a share or class of shares has any vote on the matter and, if so, what is its voting power on the resolution in question depends entirely on the voting rights attached to that share or class of shares by the articles of association.

I venture to think that Ungoed Thomas J. overlooked the importance of art 2 of Table A which gives to the company a completely unfettered right to attach to any share or class of shares special voting rights on a poll or to restrict those rights as the company may think fit. Thus, it is commonplace that a company may and frequently does preclude preference shareholders from voting unless their dividends are in arrear or their class rights are directly affected. It is equally commonplace that particular shares may be issued with specially loaded voting rights which ensure that in all resolutions put before the shareholders in general meeting the holder of those particular shares can always be sure of carrying the day, aye or no, as the holder pleases.

Counsel for the appellant felt, quite rightly, constrained to admit that if an article provided that the respondent's shares should, on every occasion when a resolution was for consideration by a general meeting of the company, carry three votes such a provision would be valid on all such occasions including any occasion when the general meeting was considering a resolution for his removal under s. 184.

My Lords, I cannot see any difference between that case and the present case where special voting rights are conferred only when there is a resolution for the removal of a director under s. 184. Each case is an exercise of the unfettered right of the company under art 2 whereby:

> any share in the company may be issued with such . . . special rights
> . . . in regard to . . . voting . . . as the company may from time to time
> by ordinary resolution determine.

Parliament has never sought to fetter the right of the company to issue a share with such rights or restrictions as it may think fit. There is no fetter which compels the company to make the voting rights or restrictions of general application and it seems to me clear that such rights or restrictions can be attached to special circumstances and to particular types of resolution. This makes no mockery of s. 184; all that Parliament was seeking to do thereby was to make an ordinary resolution sufficient to remove a director. Had Parliament desired to go further and enact that every share entitled to vote should be deprived of its special rights under the articles it should have said so in plain terms by making the vote on a poll one vote one share. Then, what about shares which had no voting rights under the articles? Should not Parliament give them a vote when considering this completely artificial form of ordinary resolution? Suppose there had here been some preference shares in the name of the respondent's wife, which under the articles had in the circumstances no vote; why in justice should her voice be excluded from consideration in this artificial vote? I only raise this purely hypothetical case to show the great difficulty of trying to do justice by legislation in a matter which has always been left to the corporators themselves to decide.

I agree entirely with the judgment of the Court of Appeal, and would dismiss this appeal.

LORD DONOVAN: My Lords, the issue here is the true construction of s. 184 of the *Companies Act 1948*; and I approach it with no conception of what the legislature wanted to achieve by the section other than such as can reasonably be deduced from its language.

Clearly it was intended to alter the method by which a director of a company could be removed while still in office. It enacts that this can be done by the company by ordinary resolution. Furthermore, it may be achieved notwithstanding anything in the company's articles, or in any agreement between the company and the director.

Accordingly any case (and one knows there were many) where the articles prescribed that a director should be removable during his period of office only by a special resolution or an extraordinary resolution, each of which necessitated, *inter alia*, a three to one majority of those present and voting at the meeting, is overridden by s. 184. A simple majority of the votes will now suffice; an ordinary resolution being, in my opinion, a resolution capable of being carried by such a majority. Similarly any agreement, whether evidenced by the articles or otherwise, that a director shall be a director for life or for some fixed period is now also overreached.

The field over which s. 184 operates is thus extensive for it includes, admittedly, all companies with a quotation on the Stock Exchange. It is now contended, however, that it does something more; namely, that it provides in effect that when the ordinary resolution proposing the removal of the director is put to the meeting each shareholder present shall have one vote per share and no more; and that any provision in the articles providing that any shareholder shall, in relation to this resolution, have "weighted" votes attached to his shares, is also nullified by s. 184. A provision for such "weighting" of votes which applies generally, i.e. as part of the normal pattern of voting, is accepted by the appellant is unobjectionable; but an article such as the one here under consideration which is special to a resolution seeking the removal of a director falls foul of s. 184 and is overridden by it.

Why should this be? The section does not say so, as it easily could. And those who drafted it and enacted it certainly would have included among their numbers many who were familiar with the phenomenon of articles of association carrying "weighted votes". It must therefore have been plain at the outset that unless some special provision were made, the mere direction that an ordinary resolution would do in order to remove a director would leave the section at risk of being made inoperative in the way that has been done here. Yet no such provision was made, and in this Parliament followed its practice of leaving to companies and their shareholders liberty to allocate voting rights as they pleased.

When therefore it is said that a decision in favour of the respondent in this case would defeat the purpose of the section and make a mockery of it, it is being assumed that Parliament intended to cover every possible case and block up every loophole. I see no warrant for any such assumption. A very large part of the relevant field is in fact covered and covered effectively. And there may be good reasons why Parliament should leave some companies with freedom of manoeuvre in this particular matter. There are many small companies which are conducted in practice as though they were little more than partnerships, particularly family companies running a family business; and it is, unfortunately, sometimes necessary to provide some safeguard against family quarrels having their repercussions in the boardroom. I am not, of course, saying that this is such a case; I merely seek to repeal the argument that unless the section is construed in the way the appellant wants, it has become "inept" and "frustrated".

I would dismiss the appeal.

LORD MORRIS OF BORTH-Y-GEST. My Lords, it is provided by s. 184(1) of the *Companies Act 1948* that a company may by ordinary resolution remove a director before the expiration of his period of office. The company may do so notwithstanding anything to the contrary in its articles. So if an article provided that a director was irremovable he could nevertheless be removed if any ordinary resolution to that effect was passed. So also if an article provided that a director could only be removed by a resolution carried by a majority greater than a simple majority he would nevertheless be removed if a resolution was passed by a simple majority.

Some shares may, however, carry greater voting power than others. On a resolution to remove a director shares will therefore carry the voting power that they possess. But this does not, in my view, warrant a device such as special art 9 introduces. Its unconcealed effect is to make a director irremovable. If the question is posed whether the shares of the respondent possess any added voting weight the answer must be that they possess none whatsoever beyond, if valid, an *ad hoc* weight for the special purpose of circumventing s. 184. If special art 9 were writ large it would set out that a director is not to be removed against his will and that in order to achieve this and to thwart the express provision of s. 184 the voting power of any director threatened with removal is to be deemed to be greater than it actually is. The learned judge thought that to sanction this would be to make a mockery of the law. I think so also.

I would allow the appeal.

[Lord Reid and Lord Guest where also of the opinion that the appeal should be dismissed.]

Question

Is the decision in *Bushell* explicable on the basis that it involved a small, private company? Is this a case where the statute should differentiate between the private and public company in terms of what is permissible? For a comment on *Bushell*, see Prentice, (1969), 32 Mod. L. Rev. 693.

(c) Directorial Power and Interpreting the Corporate "Contract"

In the following cases there is a dispute over the interpretation of legal rules concerning directors. Are the results consistent with a contractarian view that sees shareholders as principals and directors as their agents, or do they confirm the Berle and Means view that directors can exercise virtually unfettered discretion? Where the cases limit director power, is this the result of a concern that the law should impose regulatory restrictions on the scope of director power, or simply the result of the court's attempt to interpret the corporate contract implicitly adopted by the parties?

Kelly v. Electrical Construction Co.
(1907), 16 O.L.R. 232 (Ex. D.)

Action to set aside the election of the board of directors of the defendant company which was an Ontario corporation. At the annual meeting, four absent shareholders, who were represented by proxy, were not allowed to vote. The evidence showed that the directors had adopted a by-law in 1897 stating that "all instruments appointing proxies shall be deposited at the head office of the company at least one day before the date at which they are to be used". This by-law was not confirmed at the next annual meeting of shareholders but was confirmed at a shareholders' meeting in 1905.

MULOCK C.J.: The first question to determine is whether the by-law respecting proxies passed by the board of directors on May 13th, 1897, or any by-law, was in force at the election of directors held on February 5th, 1907.

Section 47 of the *Companies Act* declares that the directors may from time to time make by-laws . . . to regulate "(e) the requirements as to proxies . . . but every such by-law . . . unless in the meantime confirmed at a general meeting of the company duly called for that purpose, shall only have force until the next annual meeting of the company, and in default of confirmation thereat shall at, and from that time only, cease to have force, and in that case no new by-law to the same or the like effect shall have any force until confirmed at a general meeting of the company."

The directors' by-law of May 13th, 1897, was not confirmed at the next annual meeting after its passage, and thus it ceased "to have force." The only kind of by-law capable of confirmation by the shareholders under the provisions of sec. 47 is one in force at the time of such annual meeting. Thus the by-law in question not being in force at the time of the annual meeting of May 16th, 1905, was not capable of confirmation, but the shareholders at their annual meeting of May 16th, 1905, purported to pass a by-law in the exact language of that of May 13th, 1897, respecting proxies, and it was contended that if the shareholders' by-law did not operate as a confirmation of the directors' by-law it could be supported as a by-law originating in the first instance at a shareholders' meeting, and that, irrespective of the statute, the shareholders had inherent power to pass it as a piece of domestic legislation necessary for the proper carrying on of the affairs of the company.

This contention, I think, cannot prevail. The presumption that a corporation has implied power to pass by-laws necessary for the proper management of its affairs arises only in the absence of express power. Here the *Companies Act* declares what powers, in respect of proxies, shall be enjoyed by a corporation subject to its provisions, and therefore the question here is not what powers arise by implication, but what are the powers of the corporation having regard to its express statutory powers.

Section 63 of the *Companies Act* enacts that "at all general meetings of the company every shareholder shall be entitled to as many votes as he holds shares in the company, and may vote by proxy," and sec. 47 declares that the board of directors may pass by-laws regulating the requirements as to proxies. These two sections must be read together, their effect being that each shareholder is entitled to the right to vote by proxy subject to the one qualification, namely, compliance with the requirements of a directors' by-law, which, if not confirmed within the time limited for that purpose, ceases to exist.

Section 47, empowering directors to pass by-laws respecting proxies, impliedly withholds such power from the general body of shareholders. As stated by Vaughan, B., in *Rex v. Westwood* (1830), 7 Bing. 1, at p. 29:

> Wherever a charter confers an express power of making by-laws, as to a particular subject, on a certain part of the corporation (more especially

where, as in this case, those terms are very general and comprehensive), there is no ground on which a presumption can be raised of an implied power existing in the body at large; but that such power is expressly taken from that body according to the rule, *Expressum facit cessare tacitum.*

Were the rule otherwise there might in the present case be in existence at the same time previous to the election two inconsistent by-laws, one passed by the board of directors, the other by the shareholders, prescribing conflicting regulations respecting proxies. It cannot, I think, be seriously argued that the statute contemplated such a possibility. I am therefore of opinion that the express power conferred by sec. 47 upon the board of directors to pass by-laws respecting proxies deprives the body at large of any inherent power to deal with that subject, and therefore the shareholders' by-law of May 16th, 1905, if regarded as originating with that body, is null and void. Then the directors' by-law of May 13th, 1897, not having been confirmed by the shareholders within the time fixed by sec. 47, also became null and void. The plaintiffs did not, by their statement of claim, attack the by-law on the ground that it was merely a shareholders' by-law. Nevertheless this point came up for consideration at the trial, and the defendants unsuccessfully endeavored to discover a directors' by-law to serve as foundation for the shareholders' by-law.

Note

The by-laws, like articles of association, are the rules for the internal governance of the corporation. Control over their initiation is an important allocation of power. Section 103 of the CBCA and s. 116 of the OBCA vest the power to make by-laws in the directors subject to the articles, by-laws or a unanimous shareholder agreement providing otherwise. Thus, the corporate constitution may provide for a sharing of power, may give the power exclusively to one group, or may simply leave the statutory allocation in place. In one sense the power is always shared, for s. 103(2) of the CBCA and s. 116(2) of the OBCA require shareholder approval of all by-laws, and any amendment or repeal. Section 103(5) (s. 116(5) of the OBCA) is an alternate route, through a shareholder proposal in s. 137 (s. 99), for initiation of a by-law. This will be discussed further in Chapter 9.

Automatic Self-Cleansing Filter Syndicate Co. Ltd. v. Cuninghame
[1906] 2 Ch. 34, 7 5 L.J. Ch. 437 (C.A.)

The articles of association of the Automatic Self-Cleansing Co., provided that "the management of the business and the control of the company shall be vested in the directors, subject nevertheless . . . to such regulations . . . as may from time to time be made by extraordinary resolution" (a vote of three quarters of the shareholders). At a general meeting called by the directors at the request of a major shareholder who had arranged for the sale of the company's assets, a resolution approving the sale was passed by a simple majority and the directors were instructed to carry the transaction into effect. The directors were of the opinion that the sale on the terms set out was not for the benefit of the company and refused to do so.

COLLINS M.R.: This is an appeal from a decision of Warrington J., who has been asked by the plaintiffs, Mr. McDiarmid and the company, for a declaration that the defendants, as directors of the company, are bound to carry into effect a resolution passed at a meeting of the shareholders in the company on January 16 . . .

[At the trial] Arington J. held that the majority could not impose that obligation upon the directors, and that on the true construction of the articles the directors were the persons authorized by the articles to effect this sale, and that unless the other powers given by the memorandum were invoked by a special resolution, it was impossible for a mere majority at a meeting to override the views of the directors. That depends, as Warrington J. put it, upon the construction of the articles. First of all there is no doubt that the company under its memorandum has the power in clause 3(k) to sell the undertaking of the company or any part thereof. In this case there is some small exception, I believe, to that which is to be sold, but I do not think that that becomes material. We now come to clause 81 of the articles, which I think it is important to refer to in this connection. [His Lordship read the clause.] Then come the two clauses which are most material, 96 and 97, whereby the powers of the directors are defined. [His Lordship read clause 96 and clause 97(1).] Therefore in the matters referred to in article 97(1) the view of the directors as to the fitness of the matter is made the standard; and furthermore, by article 96 they are given in express terms the full powers which the company has, except so far as they "are not hereby or by statute expressly directed or required to be exercised or done by the company", so that the directors have absolute power to do all things other than those that are expressly required to be done by the company; and then comes the limitation on their general authority — "subject to such regulations as may from time to time be made by extraordinary resolution". Therefore, if it is desired to alter the powers of the directors that must be done, not by a resolution carried by a majority at an ordinary meeting of the company, but by an extraordinary resolution. In these circumstances it seems to me that it is not competent for the majority of the shareholders at an ordinary meeting to affect or alter the mandate originally given to the directors, by the articles of association. It has been suggested that this is a mere question of principal and agent, and that it would be an absurd thing if a principal in appointing an agent should in effect appoint a dictator who is to manage him instead of his managing the agent. I think that the analogy does not strictly apply to this case. No doubt for some purposes directors are agents. For whom are they agents? You have, no doubt, in theory and law one entity, the company, which might be a principal, but you have to go behind that when you look to the particular position of directors. It is by the consensus of all the individuals in the company that these directors become agents and hold their rights as agents. It is not fair to say that a majority at a meeting is for the purposes of this case the principal so as to alter the mandate of the agent. The minority also must be taken into account. There are provisions by which the minority may be over-borne, but that can only be done by special machinery in the shape of special resolutions. Short of that the mandate which must be obeyed is not that of the majority — it is that of the whole entity made up of all the shareholders. If the mandate of the directors is to be altered, it can only be under the machinery of the memorandum and articles themselves. I do not think I need say more . . .

[The judgment of Cozens-Hardy L.J. has been omitted.]

Notes and Questions

1 In *Scott v. Scott*, [1943] 1 All E.R. 582 (Ch.D.), a resolution authorizing a dividend to be paid to each preference shareholder was passed at the general meeting. The company's articles provided that: "The directors may from time to time pay to the members such interim dividends as appear to the directors to be justified by the profits of the company." In an action brought by the defendants challenging the validity of the resolution, Lord Clauson speaking for the court stated:

> I do not think it is suggested that if this resolution is a resolution for the payment of an interim dividend that it could possibly be held to be valid, it having been passed by the company in general meeting. If it was, then the annual general meeting impugned upon the sphere of activity which, in the most express terms, is confined to the directors . . . How the directors can manage the business if they are to be interfered with in such an ordinary financial matter . . . I cannot conceive. It seems to me it is quite clear that this resolution, if it is not aimed at declaring an interim dividend, is aimed at interfering with the management of the business by the directors and, as such, it is in my view wholly inoperative, and the general meeting had no power to pass it.

In *Macson Dev. Co. Ltd. v. Gordon* (1959), 19 D.L.R. (2d) 465 (N.S. S.C.), the president of the plaintiff company, having obtained the resignation of his fellow directors in order, as he told them, to facilitate the company's liquidation, held a meeting at which he appointed a second director and shortly thereafter convened a meeting of directors which passed a resolution authorizing a law suit. Subsequently, at a special general meeting of the shareholders who were the "resigned" directors, a resolution was passed disapproving of the action and authorizing its discontinuance. A notice of motion was brought to strike out the name of the company as plaintiff on the ground that the institution of the action was unauthorized.

McDonald J. held that, as sole remaining director, the president had the power under the Articles to fill up a vacancy, as he and the newly appointed director constituted a quorum. By virtue of another Article which delegated the entire management of the company into the hands of the directors, the shareholders' resolution was invalid and could not overrule the decision of the directors. Accordingly, the action was properly brought.

As Gower points out in *Modern Company Law* (4th ed.), p. 146:

> the result of the cases appears to be that the directors have ceased to be mere agents of the company . . . Both they and the members in general meeting are primary organs of the company between whom the company's powers are divided. The general meeting retains ultimate control, but only through its powers to amend the articles (so as to take away, for the future, certain powers from the directors) and to remove the directors and to substitute others more to its taste. Until it takes one or other of these steps the directors can, if they are so advised, disregard the wishes and instructions of the members in all matters not specifically reserved (either by the Act or the articles) to a general meeting. And, as we shall later see, the practical difficulties in the way of effectively exercising even this measure of supervision are very great owing to the directors' control over the proxy-voting machinery. The old idea that the general meeting alone is the company's primary organ and the directors merely the company's agents or servants, at all times subservient to the general meeting, seems no longer to be the law as it is certainly not the fact.

Hayes v. Canada-Atlantic & Plant S.S. Co.
181 F. 289 (1st Cir. 1910)

At common law, the directors had no authority to delegate their powers without special authority from either the relevant companies Act or the by-laws. This rule was said to arise from the principle of *delegatus non potest delegare*. Whether the board should be considered a delegate, particularly when its powers derive from the statute and not by grant from the shareholders, is problematic. The maxim has been altered both in corporate statutes and in most corporate constitutions. The reality in the public company is that directors can only operate by delegating discretionary authority to committees, officers and agents.

Section 115 of the CBCA (s. 127 of the OBCA) authorizes the directors, subject to the articles or by-laws, to appoint one of their number as managing director, or to appoint a committee of directors and delegate to it "any" of the powers of the directors. The open-ended power of delegation is cut down extensively by s. 115(3) of the CBCA (s. 127(3) of the OBCA), which withholds powers of particular importance, such as issuing securities, declaring dividends, adopting by-laws and approving a take-over bid circular.

In those instances, and the others listed, only the board can act. In sum, the delegation is limited to the ordinary course of business. In most public companies, delegation to an executive committee is the rule.

There is no restriction on delegation in the BCBCA. Section 136 vests management power in the directors, but s. 137 permits the articles to transfer all or part of these powers to one or more other persons. The attitude of the courts to such delegation is illustrated by the decision in *Hayes v. Canada-Atlantic & Plant S.S. Co.*, a case which may well have influenced the drafting of s. 115(3) of the CBCA.

PUTNAM, CIRCUIT JUDGE: [W]e might leave the case here, but it is perhaps better to open the record in some respects quite fully. The charter provides as follows:

(2) The directors may annually appoint from among themselves an executive committee for such purposes and with such powers and duties as the directors or by-laws determine; and the president shall be *ex officio* a member of such executive committee.

The formal by-laws of the corporation provide as follows:

Sec. 8. The directors shall annually appoint from among themselves two directors, who, with the president, shall form an executive committee, and said committee shall have full powers of the board of directors when said board is not in session.

Section 8 is expressed literally in very broad terms, in that it purports to vest the committee with the "full powers" of the board of directors. Hayes maintains that this expression, "full powers" has no limitation whatever, while a true construction limits it to the ordinary business operations of the corporation. It must be so limited, as we will see on further examination of the charter and by-laws. Also, although Perry had a majority interest, absolute or contingent, and was the treasurer of the corporation, and although it appears that the proceedings attempted at the alleged meetings of the executive committee and of the directors were hostile to his interests in a fundamental way and to such an extent as to deprive him of the treasurership, and although also it is said that all this does not bear directly on the case; nevertheless, we should exhibit what was attempted to be done by Hayes and Gale for the purpose of showing in a concrete way that it is not tolerable that the by-law in question should have the construction which Hayes claims for it.

The Canadian joint-stock companies act (32-33 Victoria, Chapter 15) directs that the affairs of a corporation shall be managed by a board of directors, and that, in the absence of other provisions in a special way or in the by-laws of the company, the directors shall elect the president and shall regulate the allotment of stock, and the forfeiture of stock for nonpayment, and the transfer of stock. It also provides among other things, for by-laws regulating the number of the directors, their term of service, the amount of their stock qualification, and their remuneration, if any, and "the appointment, functions, duties and removal of all agents, officers and servants of the company, the security to be given by them to the company and their remuneration." In addition to the above, we have already quoted the by-law under which the executive committee was constituted, in effect that the directors should annually appoint from among themselves two directors who with the president should constitute such committee.

Hayes and Gale, at the alleged meeting held on June 6, 1904, undertook to transact the following matters: They removed Perry from his office of treasurer and appointed Gale in his place. They directed payment to Hayes of the salary, and of the $506.33 in dispute, although his salary had never before been fixed or authorized. They fixed an annual salary for Gale as managing director at $1,854.20. They amended the by-laws so that special meetings of the shareholders could be called only by the president. They amended, as we have said, the by-law establishing the executive committee so that the committee should consist of only one director besides the president; and they amended the by-law providing for meetings of the directors so that they could be called only by the president.

It is not worthwhile to follow all through the meeting of the executive committee held June 24, 1904. A crucial matter which we need in this connection is that all the proceedings were in the pecuniary interests of Hayes and Gale, and they were the only persons who were voting in relation thereto. These two persons, when they undertook to amend the by-law by virtue of which they were constituted a committee, so tied up the corporation that no special meeting of the stockholders or directors could be called except by one of themselves; that is, the president. In other words, they proceeded in such a way that, if their action had been effectual, the two men, acting in their own pecuniary interests, would have absorbed the entire powers of the corporation for an indefinite period. The two also assumed, by implication, the power of issuing stock, thus shutting out, if they saw fit, the possibility of the existing shareholders obtaining control of the stock at any meeting thereof which any of them might find some legal method of calling. It is certainly intolerable to maintain that the words "full powers", in the provision for the appointment of the executive committee, practically divested the directors of all their functions, and built up a new foundation for it in lieu of that formally established. Such an assumed absorption of the powers of the creator by the created is too absurd to receive the approbation of any court of law. We recite these facts because they exhibit in a concrete way, by illustration, the impossibility of giving force to the words "full powers" in the by-law referred to except with limitations restricting them to the ordinary business transactions of the corporation. Having in mind that neither the president nor any director of a corporation is entitled to compensation for his services without some special provision of statute or some action of the stockholders or other directors, and having in view the limitations necessarily implied for the reasons we have stated, we must hold that the matter of such compensation was specifically retained for the personal action of the directors by the particular enumeration thereof, notwithstanding that there were other powers, of a general nature, which might well have vested in the executive committee, which would fully satisfy the call of the words "full powers" . . .

Sherman & Ellis v. Indiana Mutual Casualty
41 F.2d 588 (7th Cir. 1930)

A prudent management decision in some cases may be to contract for the management services of third parties who possess particular expertise. This is often the case in the realm of services such as hotel management, entertainment, and restaurants. The important legal question is the extent to which management may be vested in third parties. The matter has been left to the courts to sort out, with the line between permissible and impermissible delegation often being a very fine one. In *Sherman & Ellis*, the defendant insurance company granted its management to the plaintiff insurance company for a period of twenty years. The contract contained the following term:

> That for and during a period of twenty years from the date hereof, it will supply without compensation other than the payment specified in article II, paragraph First, hereof, the underwriting and executive management for the Mutual Company in the person of its President, Frank H. Ellis, or such other of its officers as it may from time to time designate, who shall be competent to perform the services of chief executive head and underwriting manager of the Mutual Company, to the end that the same competent management which the Indiana Manufacturers Reciprocal Association has enjoyed in the past may continue uninterrupted for the benefit of the Mutual Company policy holders . . .

EVANS CIRCUIT JUDGE: The line of demarcation between cases which recognize the right of officers of a corporation to delegate certain managerial duties to a stranger and cases which deny such authority is not entirely clear or easy to follow. That corporations may, at least for a limited period, delegate to a stranger certain duties usually performed by the officers, is clear.

On the other hand, it is equally well settled that there are duties, the performance of which may not be indefinitely delegated to outsiders . . .

The case of *Jones v. Williams*, 40 S.W. 353, is as strong as any that appellant has cited, and illustrates, perhaps as well as any, the extent to which the courts have gone in upholding such delegations of authority. There the Board of Directors gave an outsider the position of editor and manager of a large daily paper for a period of five years, during which time said outsider was to determine the editorial policy of the paper. But the facts in that case fall short of those presented in the instant suit. The period of control there fixed was five years. Here it is twenty years. There a larger part of the board's official duties was undelegated. Here nothing of importance was left for the board of directors, but the unimportant, the ministerial duties.

It is true the statutes of most of the states authorizing the organization of corporations are of general application and are easily complied with. Yet we cannot believe that the requirements therein found or the official duties therein prescribed are mere formalities or only directory in character. This is particularly true of insurance companies upon whose conservative management and financial responsibility a multitude of policyholders are dependent. The grant of corporate power by a state is upon the hypothesis that these powers shall be exercised by the corporation's officers, annually elected by the stockholders and not by the officers of another corporation.

Reverting to the language of this agreement for a moment, it appears "that for and during the period of twenty years from the date hereof it [appellant] will supply . . . the underwriting and executive management . . . in the person of its president, Frank H. Ellis, or such other officer as it may from time to time designate," and that "during said twenty-years period" the casualty company shall elect the officer furnished by appellant for its underwriting manager who "shall have general supervision and charge of the underwriting affairs of the corporation."

Such an agreement negatives the thought that appellant was merely the soliciting agent of the casualty company. It contemplated the substitution of appellant for the officers of the casualty company. What was the casualty company's business? To write casualty insurance and adjust the losses growing out of such insurance. If there existed a conflict of opinion between the board and appellant, whose voice under this contract would control? Obviously, appellant's. The length of time during which the agreement was to operate likewise indicated that not only managerial powers were delegated, but the entire policy of the casualty company business was to be fixed and determined by appellant. No other conclusion can be drawn from this agreement and the evidence than that the casualty company was to be merely an instrumentality through which appellant was to conduct a casualty insurance business in the state of Indiana. The agreement which accomplished this result transcends the spirit and theory upon which corporate franchises are based, and is void.

Kennerson v. Burbank Amusement Co.
260 P. 2d 823 (Calif. C.A. 1953)

PETERS J.: Inasmuch as the directors must exercise and maintain control over corporate affairs in good faith, they are prohibited from delegating such control and management to others and any contract so providing is void. By this contract with Kennerson the Board has attempted to confer upon him the practical control and management of substantially all corporate powers. The sole asset of this corporation was the management of, and the fixtures in, the Manor Theatre building. By the contract the Board has attempted to transfer all control over bookings, personnel, admission prices, salaries, contracts, expenses and even fiscal policies to Kennerson. While the contract provides that moneys are to be banked in the name of Burbank, Kennerson is authorised to book "other forms of entertainment" so that he could, without restraint, change the very nature of the enterprise, and could even assign his powers to others. The fact that Kennerson is under a duty to make periodic reports to the Board does not constitute a sufficient retention of control over discretionary corporate policy to comply with the rule.

Kennerson admits that it is the law that a board cannot divest itself of its fundamental powers by contract, but contends that the requirements that Kennerson must report and account saves this contract from violating this rule . . . as long as the corporation exists, its affairs must be managed by the duly elected Board. The Board may grant authority to act, but it cannot delegate its function to govern. If it does so, the contract so provided is void . . .

A case quite similar to the instant one is *Long Park v. Trenton-New Brunswick Theatres Co.* 77 N.E. 2d 633. There the New York Court of Appeals held invalid, as at matter of law, a contract to manage a theatre business, which contract was somewhat similar to the one here involved. There the board delegated to another corporation the right to manage all the theatres leased or to be leased by the granting corporation. As in the instant case, full and uncontrolled authority over books, policies, admission prices and personnel was granted. The court held that by such a contract "the powers of the directors over the management of its theatres, the principal business of the corporation, were completely sterilized". Such restrictions and limitations upon the powers of the directors are clearly in violation of s. 27 of the General Corporation Law ("The business of a corporation shall be managed by its board of directors.").

The court in *Long Park* was also influenced by the fact that the management contract could not be changed by the directors but could only be changed pursuant to a decision of an arbitrator. As Peters J. noted in *Kennerson*, the problem is one of degree. If substantially all corporate powers are delegated, the contract will be held void and unenforceable. An example of a valid management contract is contained in *Cullen v. Governor Clinton Co.*, 110 N.Y.S. 2d 614 (1952). A management contract was entered into by the owners of the Governor Clinton Hotel. When the contract was challenged, the court ruled as follows:

> Whether the hotel could better be operated through the medium of a management company presented a question of business judgment. If the decision had been arrived at as the result of an honest, prudent and careful belief of the directors that it was for the best interest of the hotel company, then that determination would not be subject to inter-

ference by the courts, even though an error in judgment may have been committed.

Question

The result of the cases seems to be that the directors may make a valid decision to enter into a management contract to have the business operated by a third party as long as in so doing they still continue to function as a board of directors with ultimate control over the business.

What if, in *Kennerson*, the board had decided to lease the theatres in return for a percentage of the profits? Is there any difference between that undoubtedly valid act and what took place in *Kennerson* or in *Long Park?*

Realty Acceptance Corp. v. Montgomery
51 F.2d 636 (3rd Cir. 1930)

An important question in the context of the employment of a senior officer or a service director is the relationship between the individual's contractual rights and the company's rights to amend or repeal its by-laws or articles of association. American and Commonwealth courts have upheld the validity of individual contracts in the face of the corporation's undoubted power to amend its by-laws or articles of association or to not re-elect or to remove a director.

JUDGE MORRIS: By this action of covenant tried to the court without the intervention of a jury under R.S. §649 (28 USCA §773), Henry G. Montgomery, the plaintiff, seeks to recover from Realty Acceptance Corporation, the defendant, damages for the breach of its contract under seal, of September 23, 1924, employing plaintiff as its president and as the president of the Stuyvesant Corporation, all of whose capital stock was owned by the defendant, from the date of the contract to December 31, 1929, at a salary, from October 1, 1924, to December 31, 1929, at the rate of $25,000 a year, payable in equal monthly installments. The main breaches alleged are the removal of the plaintiff from the presidency of each corporation by the respective boards of directors in December 1926, and the nonpayment of any salary for the years 1927 to 1929, inclusive.

Defendant, a Delaware corporation, admits the contract and that, prior to its execution, it was authorized by its board of directors. It likewise admits the ouster and the nonpayment of salary for the three years. It makes no claim that plaintiff was incompetent. It asserts, however, in avoidance of liability, that its by-laws and those of the Stuyvesant Corporation, chartered under the laws of New York, both provided, at the time the contract was made, that the president:

shall be chosen annually by the Board of Directors and shall hold his office until his successor shall have been duly chosen and qualified or

> . . . he . . . shall have been removed in the manner hereinafter provided, and . . . may be removed, either with or without cause, by the vote of a majority of the whole Board of Directors . . .

that plaintiff's removal by both companies was carried out in strict conformity with the by-laws; that the by-laws were valid and nullified or became by implication a part or condition of the contract; and that the contract was void for the further reason that it was against public policy.

Plaintiff does not deny that the by-laws were in existence at the time the contract was entered into; that they were valid; that he had knowledge thereof; or that the removal proceedings were had in strict conformity therewith. He takes the position, however, that, as there was no statutory inhibition against the employment of officers of Delaware or New York corporations for a fixed term, as the by-laws were amendable, article X, "by the affirmative vote of a majority of the whole Board of Directors . . ." and as the making of the contract employing plaintiff for a fixed term was expressly authorized by more than a majority of defendant's board of directors, the contract was a *pro tanto* supersession of the by-laws, and must prevail over them.

Many cases deal with the relation of by-laws and contracts under varying circumstances. The Superior Court of New York ruled, in *Martino v. Commerce Fire Ins. Co.*, 47 N.Y. Super. Ct. 520, that a contract of employment for a definite time prevailed over a by-law declaring that certain employees of the class to which plaintiff belonged should hold office during the pleasure of the board. The Appellate Division of the Supreme Court of that state decided in *Reiss v. Usona Shirt Co.*, 159 N.Y.S. 1031, 1033, that:

> the fact that the by-laws of the defendant, as known to the plaintiff, provided that the treasurer should be elected each year, and that he could be removed with or without cause by the directors, did not necessarily render such an agreement as was asserted by the plaintiff *ultra vires* the corporation.

Cuppy v. Stollwerck Bros., 216 N.Y. 591, III N.E. 249, 251, was an action to recover salary due, under a contract of employment, for one year, from which plaintiff was discharged at the end of four months under the authority of a by-law providing "the Board of Directors by a majority vote may . . . remove a director or officer and by like vote fill the vacancy . . ." The court held that, "while the by-law empowered the board of directors to remove a director or officer, it did not authorize them to terminate a contract with one whom they had employed for a definite term. The fact that the plaintiff had been elected a director in no way alters the situation. His election as director was in pursuance of his contract of employment. It did not supersede the contract and render his contract which was for a definite term terminable at will . . ."

In *Nelson v. James Nelson & Sons, Limited*, [1913] 2 K.B. 471, the facts were that plaintiff was elected managing director of the defendant for the term of four years. Before the expiration of that term, the directors revoked the appointment. The defendant contended that the article of association providing that the directors might revoke the appointment of any managing director appointed by them became by implication a part of the contract and authorized plaintiff's removal. The court denied this contention, saying:

> Is there any prohibition in the articles against the directors appointing a managing director for a fixed term, provided he remains a director and performs his duty satisfactorily? If there is one it is to be extracted from the words "and may revoke such appointment". But I think sufficient meaning is given to these words if they are read "and may exercise the power of revoking the appointment when the company or directors may legally do so" . . . Article 85(b) is, I believe, a very ordinary one in articles, and it would seem greatly to the prejudice of the company if, while they could employ a clerk for a fixed term, they could not offer so important an official as a managing director any security of tenure, but only an appointment at will or pleasure.

If the by-law may not be read into the contract of employment, it would seem to be of no importance that the by-law of the defendant provides for removal "either with or without cause" . . .

To read into a contract of employment for a definite period, expressly authorized by the board of directors, a by-law amendable by a majority of the board, and thus nullify the contract, would sacrifice substance and straightforwardness for form and procedure. Defendant's further contention that, if the contract be upheld at the expense of the by-law, boards of directors may by contract of employment for terms of years perpetuate their business policy and deprive succeeding boards of the power to afford relief, is not convincing. It sticks in the bark, for the evil possibilities suggested have their true foundation, not in the supremacy of contract over by-law, but in the futility of a limitation which rests solely upon a by-law amendable by a majority of the board. Were there doubt of the board's power to amend by necessary implication through solemnly authorized, inconsistent acts, the limitation would constitute no barrier to the commission of the suggested acts by a board so disposed, for the board could formally and expressly repeal the by-law containing the limitation and thereupon with all regularity authorize the contracts for terms of years.

I am of the opinion and find that the contract made by the defendant pursuant to the express authority of its board of directors, which had express power to amend at will the by-laws of the defendant, modified, in its legal effect, all inconsistent by-laws and prevails over them.

Nor was the contract one against public policy. It was not tainted with fraud. The restraint thereby placed upon the future freedom of action of defendant's board of directors cannot be said to have been in fact or principle injurious to the public interest. The term of office therein fixed was neither permanent, unlimited nor for life, but, in view of plaintiff's relation to defendant and his familiarity and grasp of its business, was for a reasonable period only. The contract was in conflict with no statute . . .

The defendant takes the position, however, that the contract, even if valid, was subject to the implied condition that the plaintiff should remain a duly qualified director, and shows that, pursuant to the authority of the by-laws of the two companies, he was removed as a director of each by their respective boards on December 31, 1926. His salary was paid to the end of 1926. But these facts are of no avail to the defendant. The contract was breached by the defendant while plaintiff was still a director of each company. Upon defendant's breach, plaintiff's cause of action was complete, and he was under no obligation longer to keep himself qualified for the presidency. Moreover, the contract contained an implied condition that the defendant would do nothing to defeat the rights of plaintiff under the contract, would do nothing to render his performance thereunder impossible. Yet defendant, the sole stockholder of the Stuyvesant Corporation, through its representatives, the directors of Stuyvesant, removed plaintiff's qualification for the presidency of that corporation by removing him from its board. That act constituted neither a defense to the prior breach nor a termination of defendant's liability under the contract. If of any legal effect, it was a further breach of the contract by the defendant.

The contract was not only valid, it was breached by the defendant.

Southern Foundries (1926) Ltd. v. Shirlaw
[1940] 2 All E.R. 445, [1940] A.C. 701 (H.L.)

Shirlaw was appointed managing director of Southern Foundries Ltd. for a period of ten years. The articles of the Company provided for the appointment of a managing director and also provided that he be subject to the same provisions as to removal as the other directors but "subject to the provisions of any contract between him and the company." The article also provided that if the managing director ceased to be a director "he shall *ipso facto* and immediately cease to be a managing director." When Federated Foundries acquired control of Southern it adopted a new set of articles. Pursuant to the new articles, it removed Shirlaw as a director who then ceased to be managing director.

LORD PORTER: It is common ground, and, indeed, long-established law, that a company cannot forgo its right to alter its articles, but it does not follow that the alteration may not be, or result in, a breach of contract. The principle is perhaps most clearly enunciated first in *Allen v. Gold Reefs of West Africa Ltd.* [1900] 1 Ch. 656, a case in which a company was held entitled to alter its articles so as to obtain a lien on fully paid shares, though before the alteration it had a lien only upon partially-paid shares. Lindley M.R. states the position thus:

> A company cannot break its contracts by altering its articles, but, when dealing with contracts referring to revocable articles, and especially with contracts between a member of the company and the company respecting his shares, care must be taken not to assume that the contract involves as one of its terms an article which is not to be altered. ... It is easy to imagine cases in which even a member of a company may acquire by contract or otherwise special rights against the company, which exclude him from the operation of a subsequently altered article: [1900] 1 Ch. at 673-4.

The principle was also clearly enunciated in *Bailey v. British Equitable Assurance Co.* [1904] in 1 Ch. 374, in which a participating policyholder had taken out a policy which the Court of Appeal thought entitled him to have the whole of the profits distributed, and he was held entitled to a declaration that the assurance company ought to distribute the whole of such profits. The action was necessitated because the company, which, when the policy was taken out, had been formed, and was operating under a deed of settlement providing for the distribution of the whole of the profits, at a later date proposed to register itself with limited liability, to substantiate a memorandum and articles for the deed of settlement, and, under the terms of the articles, to carry part of the profits to a reserve fund. The Court of Appeal affirmed a declaration by Kekewich J. that the company ought to continue to distribute the entire profits arising from the participating branch of its business, and Cozens Hardy M.R. said:

> But the case of a contract between an outsider and the company is entirely different, and even a shareholder must be regarded as an outsider in so far as he contracts with the company otherwise than in respect of his shares. It would be dangerous to hold that in a contract of ... service ... validly entered into by a company there is any greater power of variation of the rights and liabilities of the parties than would exist if, instead of the company, the contracting party had been an individual: [1904] 1 Ch. at 385.

The general principle, therefore, may, I think, be stated thus. (i) A company cannot be precluded from altering its articles thereby giving itself power to act upon the provisions of the altered articles, but so to act may nevertheless be a breach of contract if it is contrary to a stipulation in a contract validly made before the alteration. (ii) Nor can an injunction be granted to prevent the adoption of the new articles. In that sense, they are binding on all and sundry, but for the company to act upon them all none the less render it liable in damages if such action is contrary to the previous engagements of the company. If, therefore, the altered articles had provided for the dismissal without notice of a managing director previously appointed, the dismissal would be *ultra vires* the company, but would nevertheless expose the company to an action for damages if the appointment had been for a term of (say) 10 years and he were dismissed in less. Once it is established that the appointment is for a time certain and the dismissal before its termination, the result follows, and I do not understand the appellants to contend to the contrary. The complication lies in the facts (i) that the respondent has been dismissed, not from his office of managing director, but has been removed from his position of director, and (ii) that the removal has been effected, not by the Southern company, but by the Federated Company. So far as the first matter is concerned, the decision must, I think, be reached by applying the well-known principle laid down by Cockburn C.J. in *Stirling v. Maitland* (1864) 5 B & S 841 at 852:

> I look on the law to be that, if a party enters into an arrangement which can only take effect by the continuance of a certain existing state of circumstances, there is an implied engagement on his part that he shall do nothing of his own motion to put an end to that state of circumstances under which alone the arrangement can be operative. I agree that if the company had come to an end by some independent circumstance, not created by the defendants themselves, it might very well be that the covenant would not have the effect contended for; but if it is put an end to by their own voluntary act, that is a breach of covenant for which the plaintiff may sue. The transfer of business and the dissolution of the company was certainly the act of the company itself, so that they have by their act put an end to the state of things under which alone this covenant would operate.

If, therefore, the Southern company had altered their articles in such a way as to enable them to remove the respondent from his directorship at will, and had so removed him, I, in common, I believe, with all your Lordships, would regard their action as coming under the dictum of Cockburn C.J. as an actionable breach of contract.

In reaching this conclusion I find myself unable to accept the dissenting judgment of Sir Wilfrid Greene M.R., who took the view that under the contract the plaintiff was expressly appointed managing director, not for 10 years, but only for such a period not exceeding 10 years as he remained a director, and that no term could be implied which would prevent the company from terminating the respondent's directorship, with the result that he ceased to be capable of retaining his position as managing director.

However, no such alteration was made. The new articles did away with all former grounds of removal and termination of the director's office, and left it to the Federated company at their absolute discretion to keep or remove a director of the Southern company. That change, it is said, is no breach, or, at any rate, is not contended to be a breach, of the respondent's contract, and his later removal is the act of Federated, and not of the Southern company, and one, therefore, for which the latter company is not responsible. This contention was negatived by Sir Wilfrid Greene M.R., as well as the other two members of the Court of Appeal. As, however, the main argument appears to have been grounded upon the question of the true construction of the contract the matter now under consideration was treated as subsidiary, with the consequence that it was dealt with very shortly in the Court of Appeal.

I cannot say that I have found the solution an easy one, and obviously, having regard to the divergence of view in your Lordship's House, the matter is one which tends itself to a conflict of opinion. Some support for the appellants' contention was sought in *Bluett v. Stutchbury's Ltd.* (1908) 24 T.L.R. 469. The case is very shortly reported, and the exact grounds of the decision are not easy to ascertain, but they lend some countenance to the appellants' argument, inasmuch as in that case, as in this, the articles had been altered so that the retention or dismissal of the director from his directorship was left to the determination of a third party. Cozens Hardy MR is reported to have said that, in such circumstances, if the third party deprived the managing director of his directorship, and, he necessarily ceased to be managing director, the company could not prevent that action, and were in no sense the authors of the dismissal.

If the true view be that the only action taken by the company was the alteration of the articles, and if, indeed, thereafter they were in no way implicated in the act of the Federated company in removing the respondent, and could not help themselves, then the appeal must succeed. However, though it is true that ultimately the Southern company could not prevent the Federated company from removing the respondent from his directorship, the act of removal is not, I think, solely the act of the Federated company. Rather it is the combined act of both, an act impossible to the latter but for the act of the former, and not resulting in a breach of contract until the power of dismissal given by the former was acted upon by the latter. To say that the Southern company could have helped themselves if they removed the respondent from his directorship, but could not do so where they authorized the removal by another, would seem to me to treat what is at best a technicality as if it were the substance of the case. It is the Southern company's act which has resulted in the respondent's removal, and none the less so though his dismissal required two acts, and not one, for its accomplishment. I would affirm the judgment of the Court of Appeal.

Shindler v. Northern Raincoat Co.,
[1960] 2 All E.R. 239, [1960] 1 W.L.R. 1038

Shindler sold the defendant company to Loyds Ltd. who, pursuant to a power in the defendant's articles, appointed him managing director for ten years. Loyds later sold the company to Maudlebery Ltd., who did not wish to employ Shindler. Accordingly, it removed him as director by vote at a general meeting and he thus ceased to be managing director.

DIPLOCK J.: [It] was contended on behalf of the defendant company that, as a matter of law, he was not wrongfully dismissed. In support of that contention, counsel for the defendant company relied on a number of cases, of which the most important are *Bluett v. Stutchbury's Ltd.* (1908) 24 TLR 469 and the decision of Harman J. in *Read v. Astoria Garage (Streatham) Ltd.* [1952] 1 All E.R. 922.

The argument for the defendant company on this matter derives some support from the cases referred to and from another case, *Nelson v. James Nelson & Sons Ltd.* [1914] 2 K.B. 770. The argument is put thus — where a company's articles of association include art. 68, the directors have no power to appoint a managing director on terms which purport to exclude the company's right to terminate his appointment *ipso facto* on either his ceasing to be a director or if the company shall by resolution in general meeting resolve that his tenure of office as managing director be determined. That argument can be put in alternative ways, either that the agreement for a fixed term which does not incorporate the right of the company as set out in art. 68 is *ultra vires*, or else that the agreement for a fixed period of employment must be subject to the implied term that it is determinable in either of the circumstances set out at the end of art. 68.

It seems to me that this point is concluded against the defendant company by the decision of the House of Lords in *Southern Foundries (1926) Ltd. v. Shirlaw* [1940] 2 All E.R. 445; [1940] A.C. 701. That case was somewhat complicated and gave rise to a division of opinion in the House of Lords. Two of their Lordships (Viscount Maugham and Lord Romer) who were the most familiar with the Chancery side came to one conclusion and three of their Lordships (Lord Atkin, Lord Wright and Lord Porter) who were perhaps more familiar with the common law side, came to another. There are some references in subsequent cases in the Chancery Division which suggest that it is difficult to ascertain what *Southern Foundries (1926) Ltd. v. Shirlaw* determined. It does, however, seem to me that all five of their Lordships in the *Southern Foundries* case were agreed on one principle of law which is vital to the defendant company's contention in the present case. That principle of law is laid down in *Stirling v. Maitland* (1864) 5 B & S at p. 852, where Cockburn C.J. said:

> if a party enters into an arrangement which can only take effect by the continuance of a certain existing state of circumstances, there is an implied engagement on his part that he shall do nothing of his own motion to put an end to that state of circumstances, under which alone the arrangement can be operative.

Applying that respectable principle to the present case, there is an implied engagement on the part of the defendant company that it will do nothing of its own motion to put an end to the state of circumstances which enables the plaintiff to continue as managing director. That is to say, there is an implied undertaking that it will not revoke his appointment as a director, and will not resolve that his tenure of office be determined . . .

3. THE SCOPE OF THE "CORPORATE CONTRACT"

This section asks what parties are properly the subject of concern under corporate law, as opposed to other areas of law. In particular, in the following cases there arises the question of how constituencies other than managers and investors interact with the corporation. Should private choices by managers and investors on how initially to structure the corporation prevail over the interests of other parties that come into important contact with the corporation? In reading the cases, again consider how one's view of corporate law might affect outcomes. Are the cases explained by a regulatory view of corporation law that mistrusts private choices of objectives? Or are the cases better explained by a contractual view of corporations? We examine agency doctrines and how parties entering into explicit contracts with the corporation are affected by internal corporate rules, and then examine important questions of corporate goals and social responsibilities. We begin with a brief description of the *ultra vires* doctrine.

(a) Note on the *Ultra Vires* Doctrine

The "*ultra vires* doctrine" is referred to at various points in this chapter. This was a rule that held that a corporation, particularly one in a memorandum jurisdiction, had no legal capacity to act in any way that was not specifically authorized by its incorporating documents. Only if an act was *intra vires*, or within the powers of the corporation, did the corporation have the capacity to pursue it. The doctrine has been dramatically limited, indeed virtually eliminated, by modern corporate law statutes: unless corporate powers are explicitly restricted, it is assumed that the corporation has the powers of a natural person. Consider the following provisions of the CBCA:

15. (1) A corporation has the capacity and, subject to this Act, the rights, powers and privileges of a natural person.

    (2) A corporation may carry on business throughout Canada.

    (3) A corporation has the capacity to carry on its business, conduct its affairs and exercise its powers in any jurisdiction outside Canada to the extent that the laws of such jurisdiction permit.

16. (1) It is not necessary for a by-law to be passed in order to confer any particular power on the corporation or its directors.

    (2) A corporation shall not carry on any business or exercise any power that it is restricted by its articles from carrying on or exercising, nor shall the corporation exercise any of its powers in a manner contrary to its articles.

    (3) No act of a corporation, including any transfer of property to or by a corporation, is invalid by reason only that the act or transfer is contrary to its articles or this Act.

Question

Why would a corporation, or its promoters, ever seek to limit corporate powers?

(b) Agency Doctrines and the Corporation

Since a corporation is only an artificial entity in the contemplation of law, it must act through natural persons to conclude contracts and enter into transactions generally. This section deals with the rules governing a corporation's liability for the acts of its agents.

A natural principal is liable for the acts of an agent if the agent had actual, usual or apparent or ostensible authority to commit the acts from the principal. "Usual" authority means authority ascribed to the agent by common or trade understanding by virtue of the particular office held by him. "Apparent" or "ostensible" authority means the authority with which the agent has been clothed as a result of the principal's express or implied representations. Such representations may be implied from the principal's conduct or acquiescence as well as from his spoken or written words. See further F.M.B. Reynolds, *Bowstead on Agency*, 15th ed., (1985) Ch. 3 and *Freeman and Lockyer v. Buckhurst Park Properties (Manager) Ltd.*, [1964] 2 Q.B. 480, per Diplock L.J., *infra*, this section.

These basic agency rules also apply to corporations, but they are greatly complicated here by a number of factors. The first is that many corporations have complex organizations — there are many "agents" and many "principals" — and it may not be easy to determine which superior manager or officer in the chain of command is entitled to make representations with respect to the apparent authority of an inferior agent. Again, at the same level of authority, the "principal" may in fact comprise a group of individuals of greater or smaller size. This will be true, for example, where the question is whether the board of directors have held out one of their number as president or managing director although he was never formally appointed to this position. Or again the question may arise whether the corporation is bound by the acts of *de facto* directors because the shareholders knew of, and acquiesced, in their assumption of office.

A second complication is that the courts superimposed special corporate rules on the normal agency rules. The most important of these was the constructive notice rule, usually associated with *Ernest v. Nicholls* (1857), 6 H.L. Cas. 401, 10 E.R. 1351, that outsiders are deemed to be familiar with the contents of those of the corporation's constitutional and related documents that are filed in a public office. Consequently, if these documents impose restrictions on an agent's authority (by which is included the authority of organs such as the board of directors or a committee of directors) the outsider will be bound even though the agent was acting within his usual authority or was clothed with apparent authority. The outsider will not be allowed to plead his ignorance of the restrictions.

Almost simultaneously with the constructive notice rule, the English courts also introduced an important qualification to it, generally referred to as the "indoor management" rule or the rule in *Royal British Bank v. Turquand* (1856), 6 E. & B. 327, 119 E. R. 886, after the case which gave it birth. In the latter case, Jervis C.J. explained the qualification as follows:

> We may now take for granted that the dealings with these companies are not like dealings with other partnerships and that the parties dealing with them are bound to read the statute and the deed of settlement. But they are not bound to do more. And the party, here, on reading the deed of settlement, would find not a prohibition from borrowing, but a permission to do so on certain conditions. Finding that the authority might be made complete by a resolution, he would have a right to infer the fact of a resolution authorising that which on the face of the document appeared to be legitimately done.

In other words, the constructive notice doctrine was confined to actual restrictions on a corporate agent's authority; it did not require an outsider to satisfy himself that the internal regulations of the corporation had actually been complied with. In this way, as Prof. Prentice has pointed out, the courts sought to balance the corporation's interest not to have its assets dissipated by unauthorized acts of its agents with the interests of outsiders to be able to conduct business with the corporation's agents without undue restrictions. Prentice, "The Indoor Management Rule" in Ziegel (Ed.), *Studies in Canadian Company Law*, vol. 1, p. 309 (1967).

(c) The Indoor Management Rule

While the indoor management rule has now been codified in Canada, as discussed below, the following case serves as useful background to an understanding of the modern statutes.

Freeman & Lockyer v. Buckhurst Park Properties (Mangal) Ltd.
[1964] 2 Q.B. 480, [1964] 1 All E.R. 630 (C.A.)

Kapoor, a property developer, and Hoon formed the defendant company to purchase and resell a large estate. K personally agreed to pay the running expenses and to be reimbursed out of the proceeds of the resale. K. and H. and a nominee of each were appointed directors of the company. The articles of association contained power to appoint a managing director but none was appointed. K. instructed the plaintiffs, a firm of architects, to apply for planning permission to develop the estate and do certain other work in that connection. The plaintiffs executed the work. The plaintiffs claimed their fees, the amount of which was not in dispute, from the defendant company. The county court judge held that, although K. was never appointed managing director, he had acted as such to the knowledge of the board of directors of the defendant company and he gave judgment for the plaintiffs. The defendant company appealed. The Court of Appeal found as a fact that K. had no actual authority, but that he had ostensible authority as he had acted throughout as managing director to the knowledge of the board of directors.

DIPLOCK L.J. (after stating the facts continued as follows): We are concerned in the present case with the authority of an agent to create contractual rights and liabilities between his principal and a third party whom I will call the "contractor." This branch of the law has developed pragmatically rather than logically owing to the early history of the action of *assumpsit* and the consequent absence of a general *jus quaesitum tertii* in English law. But it is possible (and for the determination of this appeal I think it is desirable) to restate it upon a rational basis.

It is necessary at the outset to distinguish between an "actual" authority of an agent on the one hand, and an "apparent" or "ostensible" authority on the other. Actual authority and apparent authority are quite independent of one another. Generally they co-exist and coincide, but either may exist without the other and their respective scopes may be different. As I shall endeavor to show, it is upon the apparent authority of the agent that the contractor normally relies in the ordinary course of business when entering into contracts.

An "actual" authority is a legal relationship between principal and agent created by a consensual agreement to which they alone are parties. Its scope is to be ascertained by applying ordinary principles of construction of contracts, including any proper implications from the express words used, the usages of the trade, or the course of business between the parties. To this agreement the contractor is a stranger; he may be totally ignorant of the existence of any authority on the part of the agent. Nevertheless, if the agent does enter into a contract pursuant to the "actual" authority, it does create contractual rights and liabilities between the principal and the contractor. It may be that this rule relating to "undisclosed principals," which is peculiar to English law, can be rationalised as avoiding circuity of action, for the principal could in equity compel the agent to lend his name in an action to enforce the contract against the contractor, and would at common law be liable to identify the agent in respect of the performance of the obligations assumed by the agent under the contract.

An "apparent" or "ostensible" authority, on the other hand, is a legal relationship between the principal and the contractor created by a representation, made by the principal to the contractor, intended to be and in fact acted upon by the contractor, that the agent has authority to enter on behalf of the principal into a contract of a kind within the scope of the "apparent" authority, so as to render the principal liable to perform any obligations imposed upon him by such contract. To the relationship so created the agent is a stranger. He need not be (although he generally is) aware of the existence of the representation but he must not purport to make the agreement as principal himself. The representation, when acted upon by the contractor by entering into a contract with the agent, operates as an estoppel, preventing the principal from asserting that he is not bound by the contract. It is irrelevant whether the agent had actual authority to enter into the contract.

In ordinary business dealings the contractor at the time of entering into the contract can in the nature of things hardly ever rely on the "actual" authority of the agent. His information as to the authority must be derived either from the principal or from the agent or from both, for they alone know what the agent's actual authority is. All that the contractor can know is what they tell him, which may or may not be true. In the ultimate analysis he relies either upon the representation of the principal, that is, apparent authority, or upon the representation of the agent, that is, warranty of authority.

The representation which creates "apparent" authority may take a variety of forms of which the commonest is representation by conduct, that is, by permitting the agent to act in some way in the conduct of the principal's business with other persons. By so doing the principal represents to anyone who becomes aware that the agent is so acting that the agent has authority to enter on behalf of the principal into contracts with other persons of the kind which an agent so acting in the conduct of his principal's business has usually "actual" authority to enter into.

In applying the law as I have endeavored to summarise it to the case where the principal is not a natural person, but a fictitious person, namely, a corporation, two further factors arising from the legal characteristics of a corporation have to be borne in mind. The first is that the capacity of a corporation is limited by its constitution, that is, in the case of a company incorporated under the *Companies Act*, by its memorandum and articles of association; the second is that a corporation cannot do any act, and that includes making a representation, except through its agent.

Under the doctrine of *ultra vires* the limitation of the capacity of a corporation by its constitution to do any acts is absolute. This affects the rules as to the "apparent" authority of an agent of a corporation in two ways. First, no representation can operate to estop the corporation from denying the authority of the agent to do on behalf of the corporation an act which the corporation is not permitted by its constitution to do itself. Secondly, since the conferring of actual authority upon an agent is itself an act of the corporation, the capacity to do which is regulated by its constitution, the corporation cannot be estopped from denying that it has conferred upon a particular agent authority to do acts which by its constitution, it is incapable of delegating to that particular agent.

To recognise that these are direct consequences of the doctrine of *ultra vires* is, I think, preferable to saying that a contractor who enters into a contract with a corporation has constructive notice of its constitution, for the expression "constructive notice" tends to disguise that constructive notice is not a positive, but a negative doctrine, like that of estoppel of which it forms a part. It operates to prevent the contractor from saying that he did not know that the constitution of the corporation rendered a particular act or a particular delegation of authority *ultra vires* the corporation. It does not entitle him to say that he relied upon some unusual provision in the constitution of the corporation if he did not in fact so rely.

The second characteristic of a corporation, namely, that unlike a natural person it can only make a representation through an agent, has the consequence that in order to create an estoppel between the corporation and the contractor, the representation as to the authority of the agent which creates his "apparent" authority must be made by some person or persons who have "actual" authority from the corporation to make the representation. Such "actual" authority may be conferred by the constitution of the corporation itself, as, for example, in the case of a company, upon the board of directors, or it may be conferred by those who under its constitution have the powers of management upon some other person to whom the constitution permits them to delegate authority to make representations of this kind. It follows that where the agent upon whose "apparent" authority the contractor relies has no "actual" authority from the corporation to enter into a particular kind of contract with the contractor on behalf of the corporation, the contractor cannot rely upon the agent's own representation as to his actual authority. He can rely only upon a representation by a person or persons who have actual authority to manage or conduct that part of the business of the corporation to which the contract relates.

The commonest form of representation by a principal creating an "apparent" authority of an agent is by conduct, namely, by permitting the agent to act in the management or conduct of the principal's business. Thus, if in the case of a company the board of directors who have "actual" authority under the memorandum and articles of association to manage the company's business permit the agent to act in the management or conduct of the company's business, they thereby represent to all persons dealing with such agent that he has authority to enter on behalf of the corporation into contracts of a kind which an agent authorised to do acts of the kind which he is in fact permitted to do usually enters into in the ordinary course of such business. The making of such a representation is itself an act of management of the company's business. *Prima facie* it falls within the "actual" authority of the board of directors, and unless the memorandum or articles of the company either make such a contract *ultra vires* the company or prohibit the delegation of such authority to the agent, the company is estopped from denying to anyone who has entered into a contract with the agent in reliance upon such "apparent" authority that the agent had authority to contract on behalf of the company.

If the foregoing analysis of the relevant law is correct, it can be summarised by stating four conditions which must be fulfilled to entitle a contractor to enforce against a company a contract entering into on behalf of the company by an agent who had no actual authority to do so. It must be shown:

(1) that a representation that the agent had authority to enter on behalf of the company into a contract of the kind sought to be enforced was made to the contractor;

(2) that such representation was made by a person or persons who had "actual" authority to manage the business of the company either generally or in respect of those matters to which the contract relates;

(3) that he (the contractor) was induced by such representation to enter into the contract, that is, that he in fact relied upon it; and

(4) that under its memorandum or articles of association the company was not deprived of the capacity either to enter into a contract of the kind sought to be enforced or to delegate authority to enter into a contract of that kind to the agent.

The confusion which, I venture to think, has sometimes crept into the cases is in my view due to a failure to distinguish between these four separate conditions, and in particular to keep steadfastly in mind (a) that the only "actual" authority which is relevant is that of the persons making the representation relied upon, and (b) that the memorandum and articles of association of the company are always relevant (whether they are in fact known to the contractor or not) to the questions (i) whether condition (2) is fulfilled, and (ii) whether condition (4) is fulfilled, and (but only if they are in fact known to the contractor) may be relevant (iii) as part of the representation on which the contractor relied.

In each of the relevant cases the representation relied upon as creating the "apparent" authority of the agent was by conduct in permitting the agent to act in the management and conduct of part of the business of the company. Except in *Mahony v. East Holyford Mining Co. Ltd.*, it was the conduct of the board of directors in so permitting the agent to act that was relied upon. As they had, in each case, by the articles of association of the company full "actual" authority to manage its business, they had "actual" authority to make representations in connection with the management of its business, including representations as to who were agents authorised to enter into contracts on the company's behalf. The agent himself had no "actual" authority to enter into the contract because the formalities prescribed by the articles for conferring it upon him had not been complied with. In *British Thomson-Houston Co. v. Federated European Bank Ltd.*, where a guarantee was executed by a single director, it was contended that a provision in the articles, requiring a guarantee to be executed by two directors, deprived the company of capacity to delegate to a single director authority to execute a guarantee on behalf of the company, that is, that condition (4) above was not fulfilled; but it was held that other provisions in the articles empowered the board to delegate the power of executing guarantees to one of their number, and this defence accordingly failed. In *Mahony's* case no board of directors or secretary had in fact been appointed, and it was the conduct of those who, under the constitution of the company, were entitled to appoint them which was relied upon as a representation that certain persons were directors and secretary. Since they had "actual" authority to appoint these officers they had "actual" authority to make representations as to who the officers were. In both these cases the constitution of the company, whether it had been seen by the contractor or not, was relevant in order to determine whether the persons whose representations by conduct were relied upon as creating the "apparent" authority of the agent had "actual" authority to make the representations on behalf of the company. In *Mahony's* case, if the persons in question were not persons who would normally be supposed to have such authority by someone who did not in fact know the constitution of the company, it may well be that the contractor would not succeed in proving condition (3), namely, that he relied upon the representations made by those persons, unless he proved that he did in fact know the constitution of the company. This, I think, accounts for the passages in the speeches of Lord Chelmsford and Lord Hatherley which are cited by Slade J. in *Rama Corporation Ltd. v. Proved Tin & General Investments Ltd.*

The cases where the contractor's claim failed, namely *Houghton & Co. v. Nothard, Lowe & Wills*; *Kredilbank Cassel G.m.b.H. v. Schenkers Ltd.*; and the *Rama Corporation* case, were all cases where the contract sought to be enforced was not one which a person occupying the position in relation to the company's business which the contractor knew that the agent occupied would normally be authorised to enter into on behalf of the company. The conduct of the board of directors in permitting the agent to occupy that position, upon which the contractor relied, thus did not of itself amount to a representation that the agent had authority to enter into the contract sought to be enforced, that is, condition (1) was not fulfilled. The contractor, however, in each of these three cases sought to rely upon a provision of the articles giving to the board power to delegate wide authority to the agent as entitling him to treat the conduct of the board as a representation that the agent had had delegated to him wider powers than those usually exercised by persons occupying the position in relation to the company's business which the agent was in fact permitted by the board to occupy. Since this would involve proving that the representation on which he in fact relied as inducing him to enter into the contract comprised the articles of association of the company as well as the conduct of the board, it would be necessary for him to establish first that he knew the contents of the articles (that is, that condition (3) was fulfilled in respect of any representation contained in the articles) and secondly that the conduct of the board in the light of that knowledge would be understood by a reasonable man as a representation that the agent had authority to enter into the contract sought to be enforced, that is that condition (1) was fulfilled. The need to establish both these things was pointed out by Sargant L.J. in *Houghton's* case in a judgment which was concurred in by Atkin L.J.; but his observations, as I read them, are directed only to a case where the contract sought to be enforced is not a contract of a kind which a person occupying the position which the agent was permitted by the board to occupy would normally be authorised to enter into on behalf of the company.

I find some confirmation for this view of Sargant L.J.'s judgment in the dictum of Atkin L.J. in the *Kreditbank Cassel* case, another case of an "abnormal" contract. He says:

> If you are dealing with a director in a matter in which normally a director would have power to act for the company you are not obliged to inquire whether or not the formalities required by the articles have been complied with before he exercises that power.

I therefore disagree with the conclusion which Slade J. draws in the *Rama Corporation* case as to the law laid down in *Houghton's* case and the *Kreditbank Cassel* case; but if I am wrong as to this, I think that *Houghton's* case, as construed by Slade J., is contrary to the decisions of the Court of Appeal in *Biggerstaff v. Rowatt's Wharf Ltd.* and the *British Thomson-Houston* case, and I prefer and would follow the latter.

In the *Biggerstaff* case the agent (who had never been appointed managing director) had been permitted by the board to manage the affairs of the company, that is, to perform the functions of a managing director, although it does not appear whether the board knew that he described himself to the contractor as such. In the *British Thomson-Houston* case the agent was the chairman of the board who was permitted by them to manage the affairs of the company. In each case the contract was a normal contract, that is of a kind which a director managing the affairs of the company (whether described as a "managing director" or not) would be authorized to enter into on behalf of the company. In each case it was held that by permitting a person holding the office of director to manage the affairs of the company, the board had represented that he had authority to enter into the "normal" contract sought to be enforced. The only relevance of the articles, in my view, was to show that the delegation of powers of management to the agent which the board had by their conduct represented that they had made was not one which was prohibited by the articles, that is, that condition (4) was fulfilled.

In the present case the findings of fact by the county court judge are sufficient to satisfy the four conditions, and thus to establish that Kapoor had "apparent" authority to enter into contracts on behalf of the company for their services in connection with the sale of the company's property, including the obtaining of development permission with respect to its use. The judge found that the board knew that Kapoor had throughout been acting as managing director in employing agents and taking other steps to find a purchaser. They permitted him to do so, and by such conduct represented that he had authority to enter into contracts of a kind which a managing director or an executive director responsible for finding a purchaser would in the normal course be authorized to enter into on behalf of the company. Condition (1) was thus fulfilled. The articles of association conferred full powers of management on the board. Condition (2) was thus fulfilled. The plaintiffs, finding Kapoor acting in relation to the company's property as he was authorized by the board to act, were induced to believe that he was authorized by the company to enter into contracts on behalf of the company for their services in connection with the sale of the company's property, including the obtaining of development permission with respect to its use. Condition (3) was thus fulfilled. The articles of association, which contained powers for the board to delegate any of the functions of management to a managing director or to a single director, did not deprive the company of capacity to delegate authority to Kapoor, a director, to enter into contracts of that kind on behalf of the company. Condition (4) was thus fulfilled.

I think the judgment was right, and would dismiss the appeal.

Appeal dismissed.

[Concurring judgments were delivered by Wilimer and Pearson L.JJ.]

Statutory Reform

The indoor management rule is now largely found in corporate statutes. The following provisions of the CBCA are representative:

17. No person is affected by or is deemed to have notice or knowledge of the contents of a document concerning a corporation by reason only that the document has been filed by the Director or is available for inspection at an office of the corporation.

18. (1) No corporation and no guarantor of an obligation of a corporation may assert against a person dealing with the corporation or against a person who acquired rights from the corporation that

(a) the articles, by-laws and any unanimous shareholder agreement have not been complied with;

(b) the persons named in the most recent notice sent to the Director under section 106 or 113 are not the directors of the corporation;

(c) the place named in the most recent notice sent to the Director under section 19 is not the registered office of the corporation;

(d) a person held out by a corporation as a director, an officer or an agent of the corporation has not been duly appointed or has no authority to exercise the powers and perform the duties that are customary in the business of the corporation or usual for a director, officer or agent;

(e) a document issued by any director, officer or agent of a corporation with actual or usual authority to issue the document is not valid or not genuine; or

(f)   a sale, lease or exchange of property referred to in subsection
189(3) was not authorized.

(2) Subsection (1) does not apply in respect of a person who has, or
ought to have, knowledge of a situation described in that subsection by
virtue of their relationship to the corporation.

Sherwood Design Services Inc. v. 872935 Ontario Ltd.
(1998), 39 O.R. (3d) 576, 1998 CarswellOnt 1739 (Ont. C.A.)

The following case deals with the purpose and meaning of the statutory
indoor management rule. Two of the judges discuss s. 19 of the OBCA,
which is analogous to s. 18 of the CBCA reproduced above.

ABELLA J.A.: An agreement to buy the assets of Sherwood Design
Services Inc. was signed by [K, M and P] "in trust for a corporation to be
incorporated". The purchase price was $300,000. In addition, [K, M and P]
signed a promissory note in the amount of $45,000. This amount was
payable on demand in the event that the transaction did not close. There
was no reference to a company to be incorporated in the promissory note.
At the request of the purchasers, Sherwood informed its major clients that
the business was being sold, causing Sherwood to lose its contracts with
them.
   A numbered company, 872935 Ontario Limited, was incorporated on
December 15, 1989. A partner in the law firm retained by the purchasers,
gave evidence that it was his responsibility to incorporate shell companies
for use by the firm's clients as the need arose. 872935 Ontario Limited was
to be used for the benefit of [K, M and P] in connection with their purchase
of Sherwood's assets.
   Several days before the scheduled closing, on January 11, 1990, the
solicitor for the purchasers sent a letter to the vendor's lawyer stating:

> I wish to advise that 872935 Ontario Limited which was incorporated
> on December 15, 1989 has been assigned by [our law firm] as the
> corporation that will complete the asset purchase from Sherwood De-
> sign Services Inc.

Accompanying this letter were unsigned copies of a certified copy of the
directors' resolution adopting the asset purchase agreement, a certificate of
incumbency, and an undertaking to re-adjust "for your review and consideration".
   The transaction was not completed. On the closing date, January 22,
1990, no one attended on behalf of the purchasers. Sherwood eventually
sold the business for $125,000. The numbered company was assigned by
the purchasers' law firm to other clients in April 1990 for the purpose of

completing a different commercial real estate transaction, purchasing a commercial building. The numbered company thus became a company with assets able to answer any liability the earlier transaction may have attracted.

* * *

[Abella J.A. relied on the rules governing pre-incorporation contracts in s. 21 of the OBCA to decide the case. She held in favour of the appellants (i.e., the original plaintiffs who had sued the numbered company).]

[CARTHY J.A., concurring, agreed with Abella J.A. on s. 21, but offered the following observations about the importance of the indoor management rule found in s. 19 of the OBCA:]

The core of the trial judge's findings and of the reasons of Borins J.A. is that the January 11, 1990 letter written by Mr. Nichols did not represent the act of the corporation. I disagree with this basic premise. Nichols had the authority of the law firm and the sole director, Fuller, and his individual clients, to utilize the corporation in the transaction. His letter speaks both as an agent for the corporation and as reflecting instructions from the individual clients. However, none of this has any significance in light of the indoor management rule which prevents the corporation from disputing the ostensible authority held out by the letter of January 11. The recipients of that letter were entitled to adopt its terms at face value and, in this case, to approach the closing of the transaction expecting to deal with the corporation.

Section 19 of the Ontario *Business Corporations Act, 1982*, S.O. 1982, c. 4, reads in part:

> a corporation . . . may not assert against a person dealing with the corporation, or with any person who has acquired rights from the corporation that . . . a person held out as . . . agent of the corporation . . . does not have authority to exercise the powers . . . that are usual for such . . . agent.

The vendor was a person dealing with the corporation when it received the letter from Nichols, and it now purports to have acquired rights from the corporation. The solicitor certainly held out the authority to speak on behalf of the corporation when he referred to it as the creature of his legal firm, with the clear inference that a member of the firm is the nominal director. The solicitor also had ostensible authority to speak for his individual clients.

The company cannot, therefore, dispute the authority of the solicitor to write the letter of January 11 and is bound by whatever legal implication arises from the words "has been assigned by Miller Thompson as the Corporation that will complete the asset purchase from Sherwood Design Services Inc."

* * *

[BORINS J.A. dissented, holding that the corporation was not bound by the contract under s. 21, nor was the indoor management rule relevant. His comments on the latter issue are as follows:]

> I have also had the opportunity to read the concurring reasons of Carthy J.A. I am respectfully unable to agree with his conclusion that the appellant, Sherwood, is entitled to the protection afforded by s. 19 of the O.B.C.A.

The relevant language of s. 19 reads as follows:

> 19. A corporation or a guarantor of an obligation of a corporation may not assert against a person dealing with the corporation or with any person who has acquired rights from the corporation that . . .
>
> (d) a person held out by a corporation as a director, an officer or an agent of the corporation has not been duly appointed or does not have authority to exercise the powers and perform the duties that are customary in the business of the corporation or usual for such director, officer or agent . . .
>
>> except where the person has or ought to have, by virtue of the person's position with or relationship to the corporation, knowledge to that effect.

Section 19 is the codification of the indoor management rule. It is derived from *Royal British Bank v. Turquand* (1856), 119 E.R. 886, 6 E. & B. 327 (Ex. Ch.), which stands for the proposition that a person contracting with a corporation, and dealing in good faith, may assume that acts within its constitution and powers have been properly and duly performed and is not bound to inquire into whether acts of internal management have been regular.

For the purpose of this appeal, the "person" referred to in s. 19(d) is Sherwood. In my view, s. 19(d) does not apply for the reason that, when Mr. Nichols wrote to Sherwood's solicitors on January 11, 1990, Sherwood had not had any contractual dealings with the respondent corporation. Its contract was with the individual respondents "in trust for a corporation to be incorporated". This is not a case where a party is seeking to enforce against a corporation a contract entered into on its behalf by an agent who the corporation alleges had no authority to contract on its behalf, where the corporation would be foreclosed by s. 19(d) from asserting the agent's lack of authority. Rather, it is a case where a party is seeking to enforce against a corporation a contract entered into on behalf of a non-existent corporation which it is alleged was adopted by the corporation, subsequent to its incorporation, within the meaning of s. 21(2). Section 21, directed as it is to pre-incorporation contracts, is premised on the circumstance that the contracting party did not deal with the corporation against whom it seeks to enforce the contract, but dealt with a person who contracted on behalf of a corporation to be incorporated. On the other hand, s. 19 is premised on the circumstance that the "person" seeking to enforce rights against a corporation had direct dealings with the corporation through "a director, an officer or an agent of the corporation".

The application of s. 19(d) was not before the trial judge for consideration. Consequently, he made no express finding of fact relative to the applicability of the indoor management rule. The findings of fact of the trial judge are reviewed in paras. 45–49 [pp. 591-92 *ante*]. He found that Mr. Nichols' letter of January 11, 1990, did not constitute an act of the corporation, and that Mr. Nichols was not acting on behalf of the corporation when he wrote the letter. In my respectful view, the trial judge's findings of fact do not support the conclusion that, in writing the letter, Mr. Nichols was an agent of the corporation, or had been held out by it as its agent.

If I am wrong in my opinion that s. 19(d) does not apply to the circumstances of this case and that the findings of fact of the trial judge do not support its application, there is a further reason why Sherwood is not entitled to the protection of s. 19(d). At common law, a person contracting with a corporation was precluded from relying on the indoor management rule if the circumstances were such as to put him or her on inquiry which they failed to make: see *Morris v. Kanssen*, [1946] A.C. 459 at p. 475, [1946] 1 All E.R. 586 (H.L.); *Rolled Steel Products (Holdings) Ltd. v. British Steel Corp.*, [1986] Ch. 246 at pp. 284-85. In my view, the closing language of s. 19 reflects this principle.

Sherwood cannot presume in its own favour that the letter of January 11, 1990, was an act of the corporation signifying its intention to be bound by the pre-incorporation contract, if an inquiry that it ought to have made would have disclosed that the corporation was unaware of the contract at that time. As I have pointed out, the unsigned draft resolution of the directors adopting the contract was sufficient to place Sherwood's solicitors on notice that the corporation had not adopted the contract. This document, together with the other unsigned documents sent with the letter, made it obvious that the corporation had not been formed, and, thus, had not had the opportunity to direct its mind to whether it would adopt, or reject, the pre-incorporation contract . . .

Appeal allowed.

(d) Corporate Goals and Social Responsibilities

Since at least the 1930s there has been a growing debate about the role of the business corporation in modern society. There are many approaches to the question, but two principal schools of thought. The contractarian view is neutral about the *content* of the goals that a corporation, or any other organization, might choose to pursue. However, this view further holds that once the choice has been made and the metaphorical contract entered into, a single party should not be granted the power to modify unilaterally the corporate contract. Given that the goal of investors in for-profit corporations (as opposed to non-profit corporations or charities) is to realize a positive return on their investment, it is a reasonable assumption under the contractarian view that the goal of a corporation is to make profit. If a person saves for retirement by investing in a share rather than gives to charity, it is presumably because she hopes to realize gains that will help support her in retirement. Once such an objective is chosen, a contractarian would view it as opportunistic for any given agent to choose to pursue a different goal. On the other hand, if a goal other than profit were explicitly adopted from the start, any investor or contributor to the enterprise would have no grounds for complaint.

The other school of thought rejects the contractarian model, particularly given its focus on profit maximization, as much too narrow and as divorced from the realities of modern society. Its adherents contend that business corporations, both individually and collectively, have an enormous influence on the welfare of employees, consumers and the communities in which they operate and that responsible corporate managers have long recognized this fact in seeking to strike a reasonable balance between the interests of shareholders and the other constituencies affected by corporate behaviour. These debates are not simply academic. They have a direct bearing on the outcome of litigation, as will be seen both from the cases reproduced in this section and in later chapters. Acceptance of one or other of these contending philosophies also affects such seemingly unrelated questions as whether employees and other non-shareholder constituencies should be represented on the board of directors, whether directors may use their legal powers to frustrate takeover bids on the ground that a new management would be unsettling to the corporation's employees, and whether corporations should desist from investing in countries with oppressive regimes. The present section begins with some case law which places these conflicts in context, and concludes with extracts from the writings of scholars and others discussing the role of the modern corporation in a broader context. Again, ask yourself how one's view of the appropriate role of corporate law affects one's view of the outcomes in this case.

Dodge v. Ford Motor Company
204 Mich. 459, 170 N.W. 668, 3 A.L.R. 413 (1919)

The Ford Motor Company was incorporated in 1903 under the laws of Michigan with authorized capital stock of $150,000 of which $100,000 was then issued, $49,000 for cash, $40,000 for patents and $11,000 for other property. In 1908, the authorized and issued capital was increased to $2,000,000 by the declaration of a stock dividend out of accumulated profits. Thereafter its directors regularly declared cash dividends at the rate of 60 per cent per year on the increased capital of $2,000,000 and between December, 1911, and October, 1915, also declared additional special cash dividends from time to time amounting in all to $41,000,000. Thereafter no special dividends were declared except one of $2,000,000 declared on November 8, 1916, before the answers in the present case were filed, and Henry Ford, who controlled the board of directors, had stated that no more special dividends would be declared at present and that the greater portion of the profits should be put back into the business in order to expand it, thereby increasing employment and selling a larger number of cars at a lower price per car. The surplus of the corporation at July 31, 1916, was $112,000,000 and it had cash and municipal bonds amounting of nearly $54,000,000. On November 2, 1916, the directors voted to expend $11,325,000 to erect blast furnaces and other plant in which to manufacture iron and other products for use in the manufacture of cars, and also $5,150,000, out of a program calling for $9,895,000 for a substantial duplication of existing plant. Thereupon, two minority stockholders, owning one tenth of the company's stock, brought suit to compel the declaration of an additional dividend of not less than 75 per cent of the accumulated cash surplus. The court ordered the declaration of a dividend of $19,275,385.96. Defendants appealed.

OSTRANDER J.: When plaintiffs made their complaint and demand for further dividends the Ford Motor Company had just concluded its most prosperous year of business. The demand for its cars at the price of the preceding year continued. It could make and could market in the year beginning August 1, 1916, more than 500,000 cars. Sales of parts and repairs would necessarily increase. The cost of materials was likely to advance, and perhaps the price of labour, but it reasonably might have expected a profit for the year of upwards of $60,000,000 . . .

In justification, the defendants have offered testimony tending to prove, and which does prove, the following facts. It had been the policy of the corporation for a considerable time to annually reduce the selling price of cars, while keeping up, or improving, their quality. As early as in June, 1915, a general plan for the expansion of the productive capacity of the concern by a practical duplication of its plant had been talked over by the executive officers and directors and agreed upon, not all of the details having been settled and no formal action of directors having been taken. The erection of a smelter was considered, and engineering and other data in connection therewith secured . . .

The plan, as affecting the profits of the business for the year beginning August 1, 1916, and thereafter, calls for a reduction in the selling price of the cars . . . In short, the plan does not call for and is not intended to produce immediately a more profitable business but a less profitable one; not only less profitable than formerly but less profitable than it is admitted it might be made. The apparent immediate effect will be to diminish the value of shares and the returns to shareholders.

It is the contention of plaintiffs that the apparent effect of the plan is intended . . . to continue the corporation henceforth as a semi-eleemosynary institution and not as a business institution. In support of this contention they point to the attitude and to the expressions of Mr. Henry Ford . . .

"My ambition," said Mr. Ford, "is to employ still more men to spread the benefits of this industrial system to the greatest possible number, to help them build up their lives and their homes. To do this we are putting the greatest share of our profits back in the business."

With regards to dividends, the company paid sixty per cent on its capitalization of two million dollars, or $1,200,000, leaving $58,000,000 to reinvest for the growth of the company. This is Mr. Ford's policy at present, and it is understood that the other stockholders cheerfully accede to this plan . . .

He had made up his mind in the summer of 1916 that no dividends other than the regular dividends should be paid, "for the present".

The record, and especially the testimony of Mr. Ford, convinces that he has to some extent the attitude towards shareholders of one who had dispensed and distributed to them large gains and that they should be content to take what he chooses to give. His testimony creates the impression, also, that he thinks the Ford Motor Company has made too much money, has had too large profits, and that although large profits might be still earned, a sharing of them with the public, by reducing the price of the output of the company, ought to be undertaken. We have no doubt that certain sentiments, philanthropic and altruistic, creditable to Mr. Ford, had large influence in determining the policy to be pursued by the Ford Motor Company — the policy which has been herein referred to.

It is said by his counsel that:

> Although a manufacturing corporation cannot engage in human-
> itarian works as its principal business, the fact that it is organized for
> profit does not prevent the existence of implied powers to carry on
> with humanitarian motives such charitable works as are incidental to
> the main business of the corporation . . .

In discussing this proposition, counsel have referred to decisions [citations omitted]. These cases, after all, like all others in which the subject is treated, turn finally upon the point, the question, whether it appears that the directors were not acting for the best interests of the corporation . . . There should be no confusion (of which there is evidence) of the duties which Mr. Ford conceives that he and the stockholders owe to the general public and the duties which in law he and his co-directors owe to protesting, minority shareholders. A business corporation is organized and carried on primarily for the profit of the stockholders. The powers of the directors are to be employed for that end. The discretion of directors is to be exercised in the choice of means to attain that end and does not extend to a change in the end itself, to the reduction of profits or to the non-distribution of profits among stockholders in order to devote them to other purposes . . .

As we have pointed out, and the proposition does not require argument to sustain it, it is not within the lawful powers of a board of directors to shape and conduct the affairs of a corporation for the merely incidental benefit of shareholders and for the primary purpose of benefiting others, and no one will contend that if the avowed purpose of the defendant directors was to sacrifice the interests of shareholders it would not be the duty of the courts to interfere.

We are not, however, persuaded that we should interfere with the proposed expansion of the business of the Ford Motor Company. In view of the fact that the selling price of products may be increased at any time, the ultimate results of the larger business cannot be certainly estimated. The judges are not business experts . . . We are not satisfied that the alleged motives of the directors, in so far as they are reflected in the conduct of the business, menace the interests of shareholders. It is enough to say, perhaps, that the court of equity is at all times open to complaining shareholders having a just grievance . . .

The large sum appropriated for the smelter plant was payable over a considerable period of time. So that, without going further, it would appear that, accepting and approving the plan of the directors, it was their duty to distribute on or near the first of August, 1916, a very large sum of money to stockholders . . .

It is obvious that an annual dividend of sixty per cent upon $2,000,000 or $1,200,000 is the equivalent of a very small dividend upon $100,000,000, or more.

The decree of the court below fixing and determining the specific amount to be distributed to stockholders is affirmed . . .

[Steere, Fellows, Brooke and Stone JJ. concurred with Ostrander J.]

Notes

1 The reasoning in *Dodge v. Ford Motor Co.* should be compared with Plowman J.'s reasoning in *Parke v. Daily News, Ltd., infra,* this chapter. Does the court in *Dodge* exclude the possibility of a Michigan corporation engaging in any type of public welfare activity not linked to profit maximization, or is it only the directors' conscious decision to limit a corporation's profits that attracted the court's censure? Would a Canadian court applying the CBCA or OBCA provisions have reached a different conclusion on the principal issue from that reached by the Michigan court?

2 As will be noted, it was part of the plaintiff's complaint in *Dodge* that the directors were under a duty to distribute so much of a company's profits as were not required for legitimate business purposes. The general Anglo-Canadian rule is that directors are not obliged to declare

dividends unless the corporation's constitution so provides or the corporation has lawfully bound itself to do by the terms of issue of a particular security. Typically the by-laws leave the declaration of dividends to the directors' discretion. The modern American view appears to be that "the mere existence of an adequate corporation surplus is not sufficient to invoke court action to compel . . . a dividend. There must also be bad faith on the part of the directors." Stewart, "Judicial Review of Dividend Policy in Suits by Minority Shareholders" (1974), 12 Am. Bus. L. J. 43, 45, cited in Frey, Choper *et al.*, *Cases and Materials on Corporations*, 2nd ed., p. 1067.

Miles v. Sydney Meat-Preserving Co. Ltd.
(1913), 16 C.L.R. 50 (H.C.A.), affirmed (1914) 17 C.L.R. 639 (P.C.)

A company had originally been established by deed of settlement for the purpose of carrying on the business of meat preserving, and as an exporter of processed meat. It was subsequently incorporated by special Act, with the same purposes. The Act provided that the regulations might be altered, but not in opposition to the general scope or true intent and meaning of the deed of settlement, and that no dividends should be paid except out of profits. By the deed of settlement it was provided that the clear *bona fide* net profits arising from the operations of the company should be applied in payment to the shareholders of a dividend in proportion to the number of shares held by them, and that the directors should every half year determine upon such dividend or dividends or bonus out of such clear profits (if any) as they in their judgment, conforming to the provisions of the deed, should see fit; and that the directors might in their discretion out of the profits of each half year set apart and appropriate such sum as they might think advisable for increasing the works or plant or to a reserve fund, and that after such appropriation the balance (if any) should be available for payment of dividends. A majority of the shareholders were graziers.

No dividends were ever paid by the company, but it was the settled policy of the company, which was approved by a majority of the shareholders and was publicly announced, to carry on their operations, not with a view to paying dividends to the members, but with a view to benefiting the pastoral industry generally, although such a policy involved the benefiting of such of the members as were interested in that industry, and the affairs of the company were conducted in accordance with that policy. The plaintiff, a shareholder and director of the company, sought: a declaration that the defendant company and its directors were not entitled to carry on the business of the company in the interest only of those members concerned to maintain the price of cattle, or in the interest of squatters and graziers generally; and an injunction restraining that carrying on of the business of the company otherwise than with a view to earning profits for distribution among all members, regardless of whether they were graziers or squatters.

A majority of the High Court of Australia dismissed the claim, Griffiths C.J. saying, in the course of his judgment (p. 64):

> [The plaintiff's] whole case is based upon the conduct of the directors in not trying to earn a profit for the purpose of immediate distribution. He contends that in the case of every company which is established for gain, in the sense that dividends may be declared out of profits, an implied contractual duty is imposed upon the directors of endeavouring to earn profits so as to be able to distribute them. If this is so, the duty must surely extend to making the largest possible profits, and to distributing the profits when earned. This last obligation is expressly negatived by *Burland v. Earle* In my opinion, no such contractual duty is known to the law. In the case of a great many companies the practical question arises whether they shall be carried on for the purpose of earning immediate profits or with the motive of indirectly achieving some ulterior object which the members may consider beneficial. Take, for instance, the case of a company formed to establish communication by water or land with a new suburb or newly settled locality. If the contention of the appellant is sound, the company would be bound to charge such tolls and dues as would produce the largest immediate profit, without regard to the encouragement of settlement in the new locality. Again, a trading company which thought fit to expend part of its income upon providing good and wholesome residences for its employees instead of distributing it in dividends could be enjoined from doing so. In my judgment, such matters are entirely matters of internal management with which the Court has no authority to interfere.

Isaacs J., dissenting, observed (p. 68):

> It was urged that the decision in this point would have an important bearing on ordinary trading corporations under the Companies Acts. To this I assent, but I think it would be regarded as a new idea if shareholders were told that companies formed to carry on business operations, were never bound to try and make a profit, in other words, that such a company is not intended to make its trading operations a commercial success. If the respondents are right, a bank would be justified in devoting its capital to bolstering up the outside business concerns of such of its shareholders as could control the management, and, as fast as profits came in, appropriate them to extending its facilities for further assistance to those enterprises, telling the rest of the shareholders that dividends were expressly provided for in the articles yet that paying dividends was no part of its scheme, and would never be countenanced.

Questions

Is the majority's reasoning in *Miles* consistent with the court's reasoning in *Dodge v. Ford Motor Co.* and the English case law reviewed in Plowman J.'s judgment in *Parke v. Daily News Ltd., infra*? What is the significance of majority shareholder approval of directors' non-dividend policy? Can it legitimate conduct that is *ultra vires* the company, and not merely beyond the powers of the directors?

Parke v. Daily News Ltd.
[1962] 1 Ch. 927, [1962] 2 All E.R. 929 (Ch. D.)

Daily News Ltd. (D.N.), as a major part of its business, owned two well-known London newspapers. The newspapers employed about 2,800 persons. Two wholly owned subsidiaries owned the copyrights to the newspapers. The newspapers were not profitable and, in order to salvage their value before it was too late, the directors of D.N. decided to look for a purchaser for the newspapers, including their plant, premises and copyrights.

Associated Newspapers Ltd. (A.N.) eventually agreed to purchase the newspapers for £1,925,000 together with a small additional sum to be determined subsequently. The sale was completed on October 17, 1960. Prior to the sale the board of directors of D.N. had decided that, after meeting all the necessary expenses arising from the cessation of the newspaper, the balance of the sale price should be used exclusively for the benefit of the staff and pensioners of the newspapers, and more particularly for (1) payments in lieu of notice, (2) payment of a third week's holiday to each employee entitled to it, (3) provision for pensioners of the newspapers, and (4) compensation for those employees who would lose their jobs based on their length of service with the company. The agreement between D.N. and A.N. expressly provided that A.N. was not to be responsible for any liabilities incurred or other obligations owing by D.N. to its former employees.

The agreement between D.N. and A.N. was not made contingent on its approval by the shareholders of A.N. D.N. first advised its shareholders of the agreement on October 17, 1960. On January 20, 1961, D.N. sent the shareholders notice of a meeting at which the shareholders were to be asked, *inter alia*, to approve disbursement of the balance of the sale price of the newspaper assets as described above. Shortly afterwards the plaintiff, who held a substantial number of shares in D.N., commenced a representative action against D.N. and its directors seeking a declaration that the proposed resolution was *ultra vires* the defendant company and illegal, and enjoining D.N. from disposing of the assets as proposed.

Plowman J. stated the facts and, after finding that D.N. was not contractually bound to its former employees to pay them compensation for the loss of their jobs and had not obligated itself to do so in its agreement with A.N., continued as follows:

PLOWMAN J.: It is the plaintiff's submission that in these circumstances the proposed payment of compensation is gratuitous and *ultra vires* the defendant company. Mr. Finer, on behalf of the plaintiff, referred me to a large number of authorities, but it will be sufficient for me to refer to two or three of them. The first is the well-known case of *Hutton v. West Cork Railway Co.* [(1883) 23 Ch. D. 654 C.A.)]. That was a case where a company had transferred its undertaking to another company and was going to be wound up. After completion of the transfer, a general meeting of the transferor company was held at which a resolution was passed to apply (among other sums) a sum of 1,000 guineas in compensating certain paid officials of the company for their loss of employment, although they had no legal claim for compensation. It was held by the Court of Appeal (Baggallay L.J. dissenting) that the resolution was invalid, as the company was no longer a going concern and only existed for the purpose of winding up. On the facts, of course, it differs from the present case in that (among other things) here the defendant company has transferred only part (albeit the main part) of its undertaking and is proposing, not to wind up, but to continue trading. In an oft-cited judgment, Bowen L.J. said:

> Now the directors in this case have done, it seems to me, nothing at all wrong. Let us clear the ground, because my sympathies are rather with the judgment of Fry L.J., if one could really exercise sympathy in a case where questions of law have to be decided. Not only have they done nothing wrong, but I confess I think the company have done what nine companies out of ten would do, and do without the least objection being made. They have paid, perhaps liberally, perhaps not at all too liberally, persons who have served them faithfully. But that, of course, does not get rid of the difficulty. As soon as a question is raised by a dissentient shareholder, . . . sympathy must be cut adrift, and we have simply to consider what the law is. In this particular instance the plaintiff is a person who stands *prima facie* in the condition of those who are bound by the vote of a general meeting acting within the powers of a general meeting, but he complains that the majority propose to expend certain purchase money which the company are receiving from the Bandon company in two ways which he thinks are beyond their powers. In the first place he says that the majority are going to spend money in compensating the managing director and other officials, who are being extinguished by this transfer to the Bandon company, for the loss of their places. Now the compensation which is to be awarded is not compensation for any legal loss they have sustained: because I understand that these gentlemen could always have been discharged, and have received notice amply sufficient to prevent them from having any cause of legal grievance, and they simply have been asked in the usual way to cease to serve the masters who have no further cause for their services. In the second place, the

plaintiff complains that money is sought to be paid for remuneration of the directors.

After dealing at that point with the question of remuneration of directors, with which I am not concerned, Bowen L.J. went on to say:

> Now can a majority compel a dissentient unit in the company to give way and to submit to these payments? We must go back to the root of things. The money which is going to be spent is not the money of the majority. That is clear. It is the money of the company, and the majority want to spend it. What would be the natural unit of their power to do so? They can only spend money which is not theirs but the company's, if they are spending it for the purposes which are reasonably incidental to the carrying on of the business of the company. That is the general doctrine. *Bona fides* cannot be the sole test, otherwise you might have a lunatic conducting the affairs of the company, and paying away its money with both hands in a manner perfectly *bona fide* yet perfectly irrational. The test must be what is reasonably incidental to, and within the reasonable scope of carrying on, the business of the company. Applying that kind of view, what is the character of these payments? First of all, I ask myself what is the kind of touchstone or test to apply if the company was an ordinary going concern; and, secondly, whether this company is still in the same position as an ordinary railway, or whether it has not become a railway company of a very limited kind, a business adventure of a very exceptional sort, and its business contracted accordingly within very narrow and easily defined units.

After dealing further with the question of directors' remuneration, Bowen L.J. goes on to say:

> Directors, under those circumstances, often do get money. But whenever they get it it is in the nature of a gratuity voted. That does not get rid of the difficulty, because one must still ask oneself what is the general law about gratuitous payments which are made by the directors or by a company so as to bind dissentients. It seems to me you cannot say the company has only got power to spend the money which it is bound to pay according to law, otherwise the wheels of business would stop, now can you say that directors who have got all the powers of the company given to them by section 90 of the *Companies Clauses Consolidation Act*, are always to be limited to the strictest possible view of what the obligations of the company are. They are not to keep their pockets buttoned up and defy the world unless they are liable in a way which could be enforced at law or in equity. Most businesses require liberal dealings. The test there again is not whether it is *bona fide*, but whether, as well as being done *bona*

fide, it is done within the ordinary scope of the company's business, and whether it is reasonably incidental to the carrying on of the company's business for the company's benefit. Take this sort of instance. A railway company, or the directors of the company, might send down all the porters at a railway station to have tea in the country at the expense of the company. Why should they not? It is for the directors to judge, provided it is a matter which is reasonably incidental to the carrying on of the business of the company, and a company which always treated its employees with Draconian severity, and never allowed them a single inch more than the strict letter of the bond, would soon find itself deserted — at all events, unless labour was very much more easy to obtain in the market than it often is. The law does not say that there are to be no cakes and ale, but there are to be no cakes and ale except such as are required for the benefit of the company. Now that I think is the principle to be found in the case of *Hampson v. Price's Patent Candle Co.* The Master of the Rolls there held that the company might lawfully expend a week's wages as gratuities for their servants; because that sort of liberal dealing with servants eases the friction between masters and servants, and is in the end, a benefit to the company. It is not charity sitting at the board of directors, because as it seems to me charity has no business to sit at boards of directors *qua* charity. There is, however, a kind of charitable dealing which is for the interest of those who practise it, and to that extent and in that garb (I admit not a very philanthropic garb) charity may sit at the board, but for no other purpose.

Then a little later Bowen L.J. repeats:

[T]he ultimate test is not *bona fides*, but what is necessary for carrying on business. That is the test which Fry L.J. has not applied to this case. Such is the general view of the law I should take about a company which was a going concern. Now let us see whether this company is a going concern in the same sense, and whether we have the same limit with regard to the payment of money.

After considering that matter Bowen L.J. said:

Compensation, and a gratuity for past services generally, without reference to such services as were rendered during the winding up, can no longer be charges or expenditure reasonably incident to the carrying on — not the business of the old company — but what the business of the company would be for the purposes of its continued existence. It was moribund, and would only want to die in peace and distribute its assets, and it would not, as it seems to me, be proper to carry to the revenue account of such a company the money it voted to directors in a liberal spirit for what they had done in past years, or to a managing director for the disappointment and vexation of being deprived of an office for which he had been amply paid. The revenue debts and charges of the company must be viewed with reference to the qualified nature of its existence still left. That being so, I think the resolution as to compensation is clearly wrong. The directors have no right to give it. It might in some instances be worth the while of a company to compensate a meritorious, but dismissed officer, but that kind of justification cannot exist in the case of a dying company. I think that makes the resolution bad, and I think it also renders it necessary to pass some fresh resolution, because I agree with Cotton L.J. that if the meeting has given over to the directors generally a surplus on the assumption that £1,050 can be expended upon officials (which is not a correct assumption), and that the surplus would accordingly have to be increased by the £1,050, it does not at all follow that it meant the directors to have that £1,050. It seems to me, however, that the meeting has not considered it in the right view, and not measured it in the right measure. I do not understand Cotton L.J. to say that no remuneration can be granted to the directors out of the purchase money which is reasonably measured by the services they have rendered in winding up this company and in connection with the completion of the dissolution and transfer; but this resolution is couched in much wider terms and is evidently based upon the idea that they might be charitable with reference to past services done for the company at the time it was a going company, and I think a willing majority has no right to bind a dissentient minority by any resolution so conceived.

The second authority to which I wish to refer is the equally well-known case of *In re Lee, Behrens & Co. Ltd.* That case was concerned with the legality of a deed of covenant entered into by a company at a time when it was a going concern by which it granted a pension of £500 per annum to the widow of a former managing director. Eve J. said:

But whether they be made under an express or implied power, all such grants involve an expenditure of the company's money, and that money can only be spent for purposes reasonably incidental to the carrying on of the company's business, and the validity of such grants is to be tested, as is shown in all the authorities, by the answers to three pertinent questions; (i) Is the transaction reasonably incidental to the carrying on of the company's business? (ii) Is it a *bona fide* transaction? and (iii) Is it done for the benefit and to promote the prosperity of the company?

In the event, the conclusion (or one of the conclusions) which Eve J. reached is:

The conclusion to which in my opinion such evidence as is available irresistibly points is that the predominant, if not the only, considerations operating in the minds of the directors, was a desire to provide for the applicant, and that the question, what, if any, benefit would accrue to the company never presented itself to their minds. If there were nothing more in the case than what I have just indicated, I should feel myself bound in the circumstances to support the liquidator's rejection of this lady's proof,

and the primary ground on which the liquidator had rejected the proof was that the payment was *ultra vires* the company.

The conclusions which, I think, follow from these cases are; first, that a company's funds cannot be applied in making *ex gratia* payments as such; secondly, that the court will inquire into the motives actuating any gratuitous payment, and the objectives which it is intended to achieve; thirdly, that the court will uphold the validity of gratuitous payments if, but only if, after such inquiry, it appears that the tests enumerated by Eve J. are satisfied; fourthly, that the onus of upholding the validity of such payments lies on those who assert it.

Mr. Finer submits that the proposal to pay compensation in the present case was actuated by motives of generosity towards employees, by philanthropy, by a wish to undermine the financial sacrifice being made by the Cadbury family as shareholders, by a desire to ward off criticism and to avoid political repercussions, and that the rights of the shareholders were entirely overlooked. He therefore submits that the payment will not pass the tests laid down by Eve J. [Plowman J. discussed at length *Kaye v. Croydon Tramways Co.*, [1898] 1 Ch. 358, distinguished it, and then continued:]

It is, of course, conceded that if a transaction is *ultra vires*, the mere fact that the failure to carry it out would involve a breach of faith cannot make it *ultra vires*. But it is said that the test of *ultra vires* is not whether the obligation entered into is legally binding (and I accept that) and that by reason of the matters set out in paragraph 19 it was in the company's interest to give the undertaking at the time it was given, or believed by the directors to be so.

The defendants have failed to satisfy me that there is any substance in this. Paragraph 19 is, I think, merely an attempt to justify *ex post facto* a transaction actuated by motives which, and the propriety of which, I must now consider. At this point I want to make it quite clear that the integrity of the defendants is unchallenged, and I am satisfied that their motives have been honourable throughout. But at the end of the day I am not satisfied that the decision to distribute this enormous sum of money was taken simply in the interests of the company as it would remain after the transfer of the newspaper enterprise.

That the decision to dispose of the newspaper business before it became insolvent, so as to leave the other assets intact, was a decision taken in the interests of the shareholders I have no doubt. But the decision embodied in the formula, and I quote it again:

> Subject to the inevitable costs arising to devote the whole of the pur-
> chase price to our staff and pensioners by giving compensation or
> pension benefits as well as the notice money that every employee will
> receive

was a different decision which was, in my judgment, motivated by other
considerations. Predominant among such other considerations was, I think,
the desire to treat the employees generously, beyond all entitlement, and to
appear to have done so.

    I reach this conclusion not only from a perusal of the correspondence
and other documents that I have already read, but also from the evidence
given in the witness-box, limited as it was, and it is right that I should give
one or two instances which I have not hitherto mentioned of the sort of
evidence I have in mind. [His Lordship examined the evidence and continued:] These and other passages appear to me to show that the view was
taken that in respect of the proceeds of an enterprise which they had helped
to build, the employees had claims to consideration to which it was proper
for the defendant company to pay regard, and that the interests of the
shareholders would be satisfied by ensuring that the other assets of the
company remained intact for their benefit. The view that directors, in having
regard to the question what is in the best interests of their company, are
entitled to take into account the interests of the employees, irrespective of
any consequential benefit to the company, is one which may be widely held.
Traces of it appeared in Mr. Redhead's evidence, and Mr. Leach, an accountant of great experience, said in examination-in-chief:

> I think that although obviously the prime duty of directors is to their
> shareholders to conserve the assets, they also have these days a very
> practical obligation to their employees.

Mr. Leach was cross-examined about that statement:

> (Q) One of the matters which affected the conclusion, at least in your
> mind, as I understand it, was that a company's duty these days must
> be regarded as one not only to the shareholders, but also to the em-
> ployees?
>
> (A) Yes. I think I said that the prime duty must be to the shareholders;
> but boards of directors must take into consideration their duties to
> employees in these days.

But no authority to support that proposition as a proposition of law was
cited to me; I know of none, and in my judgment such is not the law.

    In *Greenhalgh v. Arderne Cinemas Ltd.* Lord Evershed M.R. said, in
a different context, that the benefit of the company meant the benefit of the
shareholders as a general body, and in my opinion that is equally true in a
case such as the present.

In my judgment, therefore, the defendants were prompted by motives which, however laudable, and however enlightened from the point of view of industrial relations, were such as the law does not recognise as a sufficient justification. Stripped of all its side issues, the essence of the matter is this, that the directors of the defendant company are proposing that a very large part of its funds should be given to its former employees in order to benefit those employees rather than the company, and that is an application of the company's funds which the law, as I understand it, will not allow.

If this is right, then it appears to me to follow from the *Hutton* case that the proposal to pay compensation is one which a majority of shareholders is not entitled to ratify. The *Hutton* case was followed on this point in *Stroud v. Royal Aquarium and Summer and Winter Garden Society Ltd.*

Declaration accordingly.

Notes

1 Many of the pre-CBCA Canadian corporation statutes conferred explicit powers on corporations to establish funds or trusts for present or former employees and to make philanthropic contributions generally. For example, OBCA 1970, s. 15(2), provided that "A corporation has power as incidental and ancillary to the objects set out in its articles:

> 8. to establish and support or aid in the establishment and support of associations, institutions, funds or trusts for the benefit of employees or former employees of the corporation or its predecessors, or the dependents or connections of such employees or former employees, and grant pensions and allowances, and make payments towards insurance or for any object similar to those set forth in this paragraph, and to subscribe or guarantee money for charitable, benevolent, educational or religious objects or for any exhibition or for any public, general or useful objects . . .

How would *Parke v. Daily News* have been decided under such a provision? How would the case be decided under CBCA, s. 15, in the absence of express restrictions on the corporation's business pursuant to s. 6(1)(f)? Does s. 15(1) entitle the corporation to disburse its funds as it sees fit? CBCA, s. 122(1) requires every director and officer of a corporation in exercising his powers and discharging his duties to "(a) act honestly and in good faith with a view to the best interests of the corporation." How can the best interests of the corporation be determined if the corporation has no objects clauses? Assuming an *ex gratia* payment to former employees is *intra vires* a CBCA corporation, could it be attacked by a shareholder on the grounds of its oppressive or unfairly prejudicial character? See CBCA, s. 241 and OBCA s. 248.

2 Section 719 of the U.K. *Companies Act 1985* provides as follows:

(1) The powers of a company include (if they would not otherwise do so apart from this section) power to make the following provision for the benefit of persons employed or formerly employed by the company or any of its subsidiaries, that is to say, provision in connection with the cessation or the transfer to any person of the whole or part of the undertaking of the company or that subsidiary.

(2) The power conferred by subsection (1) is exercisable notwithstanding that its exercise is not in the best interests of the company.

(3) The power which a company may exercise by virtue only of subsection (1) shall only be exercised by the company if sanctioned

(a) in a case not failing within paragraph (b) or (c) below, by an ordinary resolution of the company, or

(b) if so authorised by the memorandua or articles, a resolution of the directors, or

(c) if the memorandum or articles require the exercise of the power to be sanctioned by a resolution of the company of some other description for which more than a simple majority of the members voting is necessary, with the sanction of a resolution of that description;

and in any case after compliance with any other requirements of the memorandum or articles applicable to its exercise.

(4) Any payment which may be made by a company under this section may, if made before the commencement of any winding up of the company, be made out of profits of the company which are available for dividend.

Does this provision go far enough? Does it go too far?

3 In *Teck Corporation Limited v. Millar*, [1973] 2 W.W.R. 385, 33 D.L.R. (3d) 288 (B.C. S.C.), Berger J. said (at p. 314):

A classical theory that once was unchallengeable must yield to the facts of modern life. In fact, of course, it has. If today the directors of a company were to consider the interests of its employees no one would argue that in doing so they were not acting *bona fide* in the interests of the company itself. Similarly, if the directors were to consider the consequences to the community of any policy that the company intended to pursue, and were deflected in their commitment to that policy as a result, it could not be said that they had not considered *bona fide* the interests of the shareholders.

Is he suggesting that *Parke v. Daily News* would have been decided differently in Canada? And if he is, would you agree with him? Berger

J.'s views should be compared with those expressed by Mr. Justice Freedman in the CNR "Run-Throughs" Report, *infra*.

4 Both OBCA, s. 99 and CBCA, s. 137 contain provisions entitling shareholders entitled to vote at a meeting of shareholders (a) to submit to the corporation notice of a proposal; and (b) to discuss at the meeting any matter in respect of which he would have been entitled to submit a proposal. ("Proposal" is defined in OBCA, s. 99(11) as "a matter that a shareholder entitled to vote proposes to raise at a meeting of shareholders.")

These provisions and their US counterparts (*Securities Exchange Act 1934*, s. 14, and Rule 14a) have been the subject of considerable litigation in the US and much more modest litigation in Canada because of the exemptions contained in the Canadian and US legislation. OBCA s. 99(5)(b) relieves a corporation from having to include notice of a shareholder proposal in the management information circular relating to the meeting where the proposal is "for a purpose that is not related in any significant way to the business or affairs of the corporation." See also CBCA s. 137(5)(b) and s. 137(5)(b.1). For examples of interpretative cases, see *Medical Committee for Human Rights v. SEC*, 432 F.2d 659 (D.C. Cir 1970) and *Variety Corp. v. Jesuit Fathers of Upper Canada* (1987), 38 D.L.R. (4th) 157 (Ont. H.C.). The case law is relevant in the present context because of the light it casts on the legitimacy of corporate concerns with broad social and ethical issues.

Theodora Holding Corp. v. Henderson
257 A. 2d 398 (Del. Ch. 1969)

The plaintiff shareholder brought an action against the defendants alleging various improprieties, one of which involved a gift of the defendant corporation's stock worth about $528,000 to a charitable foundation. The defendant corporation was a personal holding corporation and the charitable foundation was organized by the individual defendant, who exercised *de facto* control over the corporation. The following extract deals with the court's judgment on the validity of the gift.

MARVEL VICE-CHANCELLOR: The next matter to be considered is the propriety of the December 1967 gift made by Alexander Dawson, Inc. to the Alexander Dawson Foundation of shares of stock of the corporate defendant having a value in excess of $525,000, an amount within the limits of the provisions of the federal tax law having to do with deductible corporate gifts, Internal Revenue Code of 1954 §§170(b) (2), 545(b) (2).

Title 8 Del.C. § 122 provides as follows:

Every corporation created under this chapter shall have power to
. . .

(9) Make donations for the public welfare or for charitable, scientific or educational purposes, and in time of war or other national emergency in aid thereof.

There is no doubt but that the Alexander Dawson Foundation is recognized as a legitimate charitable trust by the Department of Internal Revenue. It is also clear that it is authorized to operate exclusively in the fields of "religious, charitable, scientific, literary, or educational purposes, or for the prevention of cruelty to children or animals . . .". Furthermore, contemporary courts recognize that unless corporations carry an increasing share of the burden of supporting charitable and educational causes that the business advantages now reposed in corporations by law may well prove to be unacceptable to the representatives of an aroused public. The recognized obligation of corporations towards philanthropic, educational and artistic causes is reflected in the statutory law of all of the states, other than the states of Arizona and Idaho.

In *A. P. Smith Mfg. Co. v. Barlow*, 13 N.J. 146, 98 A.2d 681, 39 A.L.R. 2d 1179, appeal dismissed, 346 U.S. 861, 74 S.Ct. 107, 98 L.Ed. 373, a case in which the corporate donor had been organized long before the adoption of a statute authorizing corporate gifts to charitable or educational institutions, the Supreme Court of New Jersey upheld a gift of $1500 by the plaintiff corporation to Princeton University, being of the opinion that the trend towards the transfer of wealth from private industrial entrepreneurs to corporate institutions, the increase of taxes on individual income, coupled with steadily increasing philanthropic needs, necessitate corporate giving for educational needs even were there no statute permitting such gifts, and this was held to be the case apart from the question of the reserved power of the state to amend corporate charters. The court also noted that the gift tended to bolster the free enterprise system and the general social climate in which plaintiff was nurtured. And while the court pointed out that there was no showing that the gift in question was made indiscriminately or to a pet charity in furtherance of personal rather than corporate ends, the actual holding of the opinion appears to be that a corporate charitable or educational gift to be valid must merely be within reasonable limits both as to amount and purpose. Compare *Union Pacific R.R. v. Trustees, Inc.*, 8 Utah 2d 101, 329 P.2d 398.

The New Jersey statute in force and effect at the time of the Smith case gift provided that directors might cause their corporation to contribute for charitable and educational purposes and the like "such reasonable sum or sums as they may determine . . ." provided, however, that such contributions might not be made in situations where the proposed donee owned more than 10% of the voting stock of the donor and provided further that such gifts be limited to 51%, of capital and surplus unless "authorized by the stockholders."

Whether or not these statutory limitations on corporate giving were the source of the limiting language of the New Jersey Supreme Court is not clear, the point being that the Delaware statute contains no such limiting language and therefore must, in my opinion, be construed to authorize any reasonable corporate gift of a charitable or educational nature. Significantly, Alexander Dawson, Inc. was incorporated in Delaware in 1958 after 8 Del.C. § 122(9) was cast in its present form, therefore no constitutional problem arising out of the effect on a stockholder's property rights of the State's reserved power to amend corporate charters is presented.

I conclude that the test to be applied in passing on the validity of a gift such as the one here in issue is that of reasonableness, a test in which the provisions of the Internal Revenue Code pertaining to charitable gifts by corporations furnish a helpful guide. The gift here under attack was made from gross income and had a value as of the time of giving of $528,000 in a year in which Alexander Dawson, Inc.'s total income was $19,144,229.06, or well within the federal tax deduction limitation of 5% of such income. The contribution under attack can be said to have "cost" all of the stockholders of Alexander Dawson, Inc. including plaintiff, less than $80,000, or some 15 cents per dollar of contribution, taking into consideration the federal tax provisions applicable to holding companies as well as the provisions for compulsory distribution of dividends received by such a corporation. In addition, the gift, by reducing Alexander Dawson, Inc.'s reserve for unrealized capital gains taxes by some $130,000, increased the balance sheet net worth of stockholders of the corporate defendant by such amount. It is accordingly obvious, in my opinion, that the relatively small loss of immediate income otherwise payable to plaintiff and the corporate defendant's other stockholders, had it not been for the gift in question, is far outweighed by the overall benefits flowing from the placing of such gift in channels where it serves to benefit those in need of philanthropic or educational support, thus providing justification for large private holdings, thereby benefiting plaintiff in the long run. Finally, the fact that interests of the Alexander Dawson Foundation appear to be increasingly directed towards the rehabilitation and education of deprived but deserving young people is peculiarly appropriate in an age when a large segment of youth is alienated even from parents who are not entirely satisfied with our present social and economic system.

Notes

1 The above case should be compared with Eve J.'s approach in *Evans v. Brunner, Mond & Co. Ltd.*, [1972] 1 Ch. 359, L.J. Ch. 294, in which he upheld the resolution of the shareholders of a company of chemical manufacturers authorizing the directors "to distribute to such universities, or other scientific institutions in the United Kingdom as they may select for the furtherance of scientific education and research the sum of £100,000 out of invested surplus reserve account." A shareholder

sought to restrain the corporation from acting on the resolution on the ground that it was *ultra vires* the corporation. There was uncontradicted evidence by the chairman and directors of the company that they desired to encourage a class of men who would cultivate the scientific attitude of mind and be prepared to devote their abilities to scientific education and research, and that from this reservoir of trained experts the company could select the right men to instruct in the scientific investigation necessary for its purposes; and that this was probably the most advantageous and profitable way in which this sum could be expended.

Eve J. disposed of the plaintiff's contention that the proposed expenditure would not benefit the company in the following passage (p. 368):

> For the present purposes I think I must rest on the evidence of those responsible for the conduct of the company's affairs and accept as conclusive their unanimous opinion that this is probably the most advantageous and profitable way to the company in which this sum of money could be expended. They are as I say unanimous on this point; they have not been cross-examined, and there is no evidence given to the contrary. In those circumstances I do not think I should be justified in not accepting that evidence and acting upon it, and so doing I am forced to the conclusion that the advantages to accrue to the company are direct and substantial and not too speculative or too remote.

He also made it clear however that he was not departing from the traditional British test of the validity of such expenditures and that "what the company has to establish to the satisfaction of the Court, is that the proposals embodied in this resolution are incidental or conducive to the attainment of the main object of the company." (p. 369).

2 Should offering corporations be obliged to include in their financial reports to shareholders details of their contributions to charities? What function would such disclosures serve? There is no such requirement in the existing business corporations Acts. See generally, "Corporate Charitable Donations: Shareholders Protection and Public Disclosure" (1969), 5 Col. J. Law and Soc. Prob. 99.

3 A good deal of attention focused in the 1970s upon the subject of political and other contributions by corporations, and upon various forms of payments, broadly described as "bribery", designed to secure competitive advantages for those making them. In some situations such payments, if made to public officials, may constitute criminal offences. In the present context, a question of greater interest is how they will be treated in corporate law. The affair of Polysar Ltd., a Canadian Crown corporation, and its wholly owned marketing subsidiary, Polysar International S.A. (PISA), is a case in point. In 1976, the Honourable J.B.

Aylesworth, Q.C., and Mr. David Stanley were requested by the direc-
tors of Polysar to investigate the payment practices of PISA. Their
Report is included as an appendix to the Proceedings of the House of
Commons Standing Committee on Public Accounts (1977).

The Report found a number of practices engaged in by PISA
which, though perhaps not illegal by Canadian law, were nonetheless
questionable. For example, in one case PISA gave quantity discounts,
in themselves perfectly proper, to one customer, but instead of paying
the discount directly to the customer, the payment was credited to a
numbered account in a Swiss bank, the beneficial owner of which was
unknown to PISA. The authors of the Report concluded that the customer was almost certainly engaged in tax evasion, and may have been
defrauding a minority shareholder. In another case, unusually large,
and probably unjustified, volume rebates were granted, which were
paid to foreign subsidiaries of the customer. The Report concluded that
the rebates were in fact "add-ons", "the real sale price being artificially
inflated and the difference between real price and invoice price being
credited, on the customer's instructions, to a foreign affiliate". The
authors of the Report were of the opinion that the purpose of the
customer was to evade foreign exchange regulations. The Report also
observed (p. 19A: 14):

> It was drawn repeatedly to our attention that the sole criterion applied
> by PISA management to the acceptability of any given manner of
> doing business was whether or not it was consistent with Swiss Law.
> We cannot report to you that we approve of a criterion that what is
> acceptable is what one can get away with. In our experience, any
> business corporations must set certain standards as to what classes
> of business it is prepared to transact. Again in our experience, we
> believe that the corporations with the highest standards in this regard
> are normally those which are most successful. We are not able to
> commend to you the business standards with which PISA has been
> content.

If PISA had been incorporated under the Ontario, British Columbia, or federal legislation as an ordinary commercial corporation, what
remedies would a minority shareholder have in respect of the sort of
payment described in the Report? Cf. generally, "From the Boardroom,"
Harvard Bus. Rev., July-August 1976; Lowenfels, "Questionable Cor-
porate Payments and the Federal Securities Law" (1976), 51 N.Y.U.L.
Rev. 1; Solomon, "Trans-national Conduct of American Multinational
Corporations: Questionable Payments Abroad" (1976), 17 B.C. Ind. &
Com. L. Rev. 303; Freidman & Leonard, "Integrity and Management
Disclosures" (1976), 7 Inst. Sec. Reg. 1; Kane & Butler, "Improper
Corporate Payments: The Second Half of Watergate" (1976), 8 Loyola
L.J. 1; Herlihy & Levine, "Corporate Crisis: The Overseas Payment
Problem" (1976), 8 Law & Policy in International Business 547.

Political contributions by corporations in Canada are subject to a variety of federal, provincial and municipal electoral laws as well as general prohibitions in the *Criminal Code* directed against corrupt practices. See Boyer, "Legal Aspects of the Corporate Political Contribution in Canada" (1978-79), 3 C.B.L.J. 161.

CNR "Run-Throughs" Report

In 1964, Mr. Justice Freedman, then of the Manitoba Court of Queen's Bench, was appointed a Commissioner under section 56 of the *Industrial Relations and Disputes Investigation Act* to inquire into the industrial situation arising from the running of certain trains of the Canadian National Railways through the terminals of Nakina, Ontario and Wainwright, Alberta. In his *Report of the Industrial Inquiry Commission on Canadian National Railways "Run-Through"* (Ottawa: Queen's Printer, 1965) he discussed the company's responsibility towards communities in the run-through situation based on its being a publicly-owned corporation:

THE COMMISSIONER: One ground on which Canadian National was alleged to have a responsibility towards communities in the run-through situation was that it was a publicly owned corporation. More than once the Commission heard the statement that because Canadian National was a government enterprise owned by the people of Canada it owed a special duty to communities. The Commission feels bound to say that this argument has little merit. In the first place, Canadian National, within the framework of statutory controls and public policy applicable to railways in general, was always expected to be operated as an ordinary commercial concern. It is proper that it should today be operated in the same way. In the second place, it would be entirely unfair to impose on Canadian National a burden towards communities from which its competitors, chief among them the Canadian Pacific Railway, would be free. It might perhaps be argued that the company's competitors should also be subject to the same burden. But to say that is to acknowledge the barrenness of the claim that a special responsibility rests on the C.N. by virtue of its being publicly owned.

Another source from which responsibility was said to derive was parentage. Canadian National, it was argued, owed a special duty to a community which it had fathered. This approach, it may incidentally be noted, would exclude from the range of the company's responsibility all communities other than those which it had created. But with regard to this latter group it was submitted that the company's parental status fixed it with a continuing obligation which it was bound to honour. There is a certain plausibility to this argument. At first blush it seems to have considerable value. A moral quality is imparted to it from the concept of the parent-child relationship and the natural duty linked with that relationship. But closer examination reveals that this contention has its limitations. Does the fact of creation impose on the company an obligation from which it can never be freed? At what stage does community infancy come to an end? The Commission was told that Melville was a creation of the company or of one of its predecessors. But this happens to have occurred several decades ago. Must the company still bear a responsibility for the perpetuation of that community, even if sound economic considerations dictated policies for the company in another direction? Then too one company may create a town and be relatively inactive in it, while a second company may later enter upon the scene and be responsible for its real development. Would it be fair to say that the first company, as its creator, owed a special duty to the town which the second did not? Clearly parentage of itself is an unsafe ground upon which to fix liability. It may play some role, but a limited one, and one which should be applied with caution.

A third ground urged upon the Commission was that railroading was traditionally an instrument of national policy, that it was characterized by much regulation and control on the one hand and by government subsidies on the other, and that a railway company would therefore be under a greater duty to a community than would an ordinary commercial enterprise. At least this submission has the merit of putting the railway companies on the same footing and not exposing Canadian National to a liability not shared by Canadian Pacific. It is true that historically railroads have been assigned a role somewhat different from the ordinary mercantile concern. It is also true that over the years this difference in function and treatment has in varying degrees been maintained. But that condition of affairs is the result of public policy. Its source is government action, not company duty. If in an industry already subject to much regulation it should be deemed in the public interest to add a new regulation on the matter of run-throughs, well and good; but that would primarily be a matter for the concern and determination of government. The Commission is therefore of the view that this alleged ground of duty on the part of the company is better dealt with as an aspect of government responsibility — a subject which is considered below — and it will be reserved for such treatment accordingly.

Perhaps the true ground of company responsibility to communities was indicated by the company itself. It is the ground of good corporate citizenship. It has no basis in law, it is unenforceable, and it has very distinct limits. But in the context of a good society it does exist, and it can function as an operating principle. What it consists of and how far it extends were set forth in a brief submitted in the testimony of Mr. W.T. Wilson, the company's Vice-president of Personnel and Labour Relations. In that brief the following preliminary statement was contained:

> It should be emphasized at the outset that Canadian National has no legal obligation to provide assistance to a community adversely affected by its action, far less to perpetuate the existence of that community. Company policy on this matter reflects a desire to be a good corporate citizen by recognizing the interests of communities in the manner of introducing changes which affect them.

The Commission would say at once that it knows no basis in law, in the absence of express contract or government regulation, for imposing responsibility on a company towards a community. A company is not obliged to remain in a town or to continue an uneconomic operation there. It has the right to leave, or to alter or reduce the nature of its activity there. The result of its action may be to prejudice the interests of a community or even to imperil its future, but the company would in no way be answerable.

Not only is that the legal position but it is the economic one as well, except to the extent that a company is prepared to accept a self-imposed duty to act otherwise. It may be that with regard to communities which it created a company would be more readily disposed to accept such a duty. But if this should be so it would still be no more than the expression of good corporate citizenship. Parentage may strengthen a company's sense of obligation. But of itself it does not constitute a separate or independent ground of duty. What force it possesses is merged in the larger ground of good corporate citizenship. Unless that larger ground is actively present, other considerations will be of little avail.

Report of the Royal Commission on Corporate Concentration (1978)

In 1975, the federal government appointed a Royal Commission to inquire into and report upon "(a) the nature and role of major concentrations of corporate power in Canada; (b) the economic and social implications for the public interest of such concentrations; and (c) whether safeguards exist or may be required to protect the public interest in the presence of such concentrations." The Report of the Royal Commission on Corporate Concentration (the "Bryce Commission") was published in 1978. In chapter 16, entitled "Business and Society", the Report deals with the social responsibilities of large corporations and expresses the following cautionary views:

THE COMMISSION: We move now to a discussion, in slightly more specific terms, of what society may legitimately expect from corporations in terms of social responsibility, and how we think corporations should respond. Society's values are continuously changing, and thus the burden of relieving (or of not relieving) various harmful or otherwise undesirable effects for which corporations may in part be responsible will be in constant flux among corporations and the society in which they operate. It is not that long ago that a vista of smoking factory chimneys signalled prosperity: "Where there's muck there's money." The same scene today attracts condemnation. Other examples of this kind of change in public attitude are given by R.W. Ackerman and R.A. Bauer in *Corporate Social Responsiveness: The Modern Dilemna* [sic] (1976):

Well within the memory of the older of the two authors, women were criticized for "taking a job that a man needs." Disposable containers were desirable until quite recently. Cheap and profligate (we can afford it) use of energy was eulogized. Plastics were a triumph of our civilization rather than non-biodegradable solid waste. In the market place, the doctrine of let the buyer beware has been replaced by the doctrine of let the seller beware. Employers were only recently forbidden by law to keep records of the race of their employees. Now it is required in order to develop affirmative action plans. One could go on, but we believe the point is made.

This phenomenon suggests to us first, that, whatever obligations business managers may have to respond to social change, they should not be expected always to be at the forefront of change. Although a business corporation may innovate in economic matters, in the social field it is probably better suited to meet challenges than to foresee and lead social change. Our conclusion in this respect is also, in part, a recognition of the force behind one of the critical arguments we summarized earlier in this chapter.

Second, society should be careful about the *kinds* of social obligations it asks business to assume, and business should be equally cautious in accepting them. In particular, we suggest that social problems within the third category we described earlier, that is those that lie essentially outside business activity, should normally not be treated as things to which corporations can respond (except perhaps through traditional philanthropy). Put another way, business should properly be concerned only with things that are direct consequences of economic activity; it should not undertake external "good works". The line between the two will not be easy to draw, but a recognition that there is a line should help to develop attainable objectives.

That the warning is apposite is shown by the experience of corporations in the United States. According to what we have read, many of the more innovative and ambitious social action programs, such as the establishment of businesses in the ghettos and other schemes of urban redevelopment, were generally unsuccessful. Of course, we do not know all the details of those programs, and the reasons for their apparent failure are no doubt many and varied. Nevertheless, it would be folly to ignore the findings of those who have studied and commented upon them.

Most of these attempts originated in the late 1960s, at a time when social criticism of all kinds was at a peak. There was a popular argument that the skills of business people could be deployed in almost any field of activity and to the solution of almost any problem. Not a few business leaders joined the chorus. While to some the projects were probably little more than public relations exercises with nothing substantive behind them, many no doubt believed sincerely that they could supply the talent and energy that was lacking in government and elsewhere.

At all events, disillusion resulted when business so often failed to solve problems outside its experience and ability. In addition, the widespread assumption that the problems of economic growth and universal affluence had been mastered was shattered in the 1970s, and with it many of the ambitious programs of social reform to which business was expected to commit itself.

E.M. DODD, "For Whom are Corporate Managers Trustees?"
(1932) 45 Harv. L. Rev. 1145, 1160-61

The traditional view of our law is that a corporation is a distinct legal entity. Unfortunately, its entity character has been thought of as something conferred upon it by the state which, by a mysterious rite called incorporation, magically produces "*e pluribus unum*". The present vogue of legal realism breeds dissatisfaction with such legal mysteries and leads to insistence on viewing the corporation as it really is. So viewing it we may, as many do, insist that it is a mere aggregate of stockholders; but there is another way of regarding it which has distinguished adherents. According to this concept any organized group, particularly if its organization is of a permanent character, is a factual unit, "a body which from no fiction of law but from the very nature of things differs from the individuals of whom it is constituted."

If the unity of the corporate body is real, then there is reality and not simply legal fiction in the proposition that the managers of the unit are fiduciaries for it and not merely for its individual members, that they are, in Mr. Young's phrase, trustees for an institution rather than attorneys for the stockholders. As previously stated, this entity approach will not substantially affect our results if we insist that the sole function for the entity is to seek maximum stockholder profit. But need we so assume?

We have seen that the law has already reached the point, particularly in the public utility field, where it compels business enterprises to recognize to some extent the interests of other persons besides their owners. We have seen further that the same trend of public opinion which may in some cases compel such recognition may in other cases encourage and approve it without compelling it. A sense of social responsibility toward employees, consumers, and the general public may thus come to be regarded as the appropriate attitude to be adopted by those who are engaged in business, with the result that those who own their own businesses and are free to do what they like may increasingly adopt such an attitude. Business ethics may thus tend to become in some degree those of a profession rather than of a trade.

Such a development of business ethics which goes beyond the requirements of law and beyond the dictates of enlightened self-interest is impossible in these days when most business is incorporated unless it can touch incorporated business enterprises as well as those conducted by individual owners. As a practical matter, this can happen only if the managers of such corporations have some degree of legal freedom to act upon such an attitude without waiting for the unanimous consent of the stockholders. That the duty of the managers is to employ the funds of the corporate institution which they manage solely for the purposes of their institution is indisputable. That that purpose, both factually and legally, is maximum stockholder profit has commonly been assumed by lawyers. That such is factually the purpose of the stockholders in creating the association may be granted. Nevertheless, the association, once it becomes a going concern, takes its place in a business world with certain ethical standards which appear to be developing in the direction of increased social responsibility. If we think of it as an institution which differs in the nature of things from the individuals who compose it, we may then readily conceive of it as a person, which, like other persons engaged in business, is affected not only by the laws which regulate business but by the attitude of public and business opinion as to the social obligations of business. If business is tending to become a profession, then a corporate person engaged in business is a professional even though its stockholders, who take no active part in the conduct of the business, may not be. Those through whom it acts may therefore employ its funds in a manner appropriate to a person practising a profession and imbued with a sense of social responsibility without thereby being guilty of a breach of trust.

———————

Professor Dodd's article elicited a spirited response from Professor Berle in (1932), 45 Harv. L. Rev. 1365. He maintained that:

> you cannot abandon emphasis on the view that business corporations exist for the sole purpose of making profits until such time as you are prepared to offer a concrete and reasonably enforceable scheme of responsibilities to someone else.

However, Professor Berle later recognized that public opinion had swung in favour of Professor Dodd's thesis.

AMERICAN LAW INSTITUTE, Principles of Corporate Governance: Analysis and Recommendations (1994)

§ 2.01. The Objective and Conduct of the Corporation

    (a) Subject to the provisions of Subsection (b) and § 6.02 (Action of Directors That Has the Foreseeable Effect of Blocking Unsolicited Tender Offers), a corporation [§ 1.12] should have as its objective the conduct of business activities with a view to enhancing corporate profit and shareholder gain.

    (b) Even if corporate profit and shareholder gain are not thereby enhanced, the corporation, in the conduct of its business:

        (1) Is obliged, to the same extent as a natural person, to act within the boundaries set by law;

(2) May take into account ethical considerations that are reasonably regarded as appropriate to the responsible conduct of business; and

(3) May devote a reasonable amount of resources to public welfare, humanitarian, educational, and philanthropic purposes.

Comment:

i. *Public welfare, humanitarian, educational, and philanthropic purposes.* Section 2.01(b)(3) permits the corporation to devote a reasonable amount of resources to public welfare, humanitarian, educational, and philanthropic purposes, even if corporate profit and shareholder gain are not thereby enhanced. As in the case of ethical considerations, conduct that appears to be based on public welfare, humanitarian, educational, or philanthropic considerations may be intended to enhance corporate profit and shareholder gain. For example, a donation to public television may be made for reasons comparable to those for sponsoring a commercial, and a contribution to local Red Cross or Community Chest activities may be made for reasons of employee well-being and morale. Furthermore, when considerations of the type described in § 2.01(b)(3) enter into corporate decisions, they are usually mixed with, rather than separable from, considerations of profitability and ethics. In such cases the activity may be justified under § 2.01(a) or § 2.01(b)(2).

Section 2.01(b)(3) goes beyond these justifications and allows corporate resources to be devoted to public welfare, humanitarian, educational, and philanthropic purposes even without a showing of expected profits or ethical norms. It is now widely accepted that the corporation should at least consider the social impact of its activities, so as to be aware of the social costs those activities entail. By implication, the corporation should be permitted to take such costs into account, within reason. For example, the corporation may take into account, within reason, public-welfare concerns relevant to groups with whom the corporation has a legitimate concern, such as employees, customers, suppliers, and members of the communities within which the corporation operates. Furthermore, because of the central position of corporations in the economic structure, the cooperation of corporations in furthering established governmental policies is often critical to the success of such policies. Social policy also favors humane behavior by major social institutions. Finally, social policy favors the maintenance of diversity in educational and philanthropic activity, and this objective would be more difficult to achieve if corporations, which control a great share of national resources, were not allowed to devote a portion of those resources to those ends. However, corporate activity that is justified solely by social considerations should be subject to a limit of reasonableness, because the activity is by hypothesis not solely in furtherance of the corporate business, the relevant considerations do not necessarily bear on the manner in which business should be conducted, and (partly for those reasons) there is no limit inherent in the considerations themselves on the extent to which corporate resources may be devoted to such purposes.

The determination whether the amount of resources used for purposes stated in § 2.01(b)(3) is reasonable in any given case, like the other questions of reasonableness in the law, depends on all the circumstances of the case. Among the principal factors to be considered in the context of § 2.01(b)(3) are the customary level at which resources are devoted to such purposes among comparable corporations in proportion to earnings and assets, and the strength of the nexus between the use of corporate resources and the corporation's business. In general, the greater the amount of corporate resources that are expended, the stronger should be the nexus. Extreme conditions, such as a national emergency, may justify activity beyond that which would be reasonable under normal conditions.

The term "resources," as used in § 2.01(b)(3), refers not only to money contributions, but also to the provision of skills, manpower, physical facilities, and the like.

Determining whether activity is humanitarian, educational, or philanthropic is normally not difficult. The same sometimes cannot be said of determining whether activity is for the public welfare. The type of conduct that most readily falls within this description is activity in aid of a clearly defined governmental policy. One major category of such conduct is activity that, although technically not required by statute, is designed to further the policy underlying a statute, such as activity designed to further policies concerning preservation of the environment or avoidance of discrimination in employment. A second major category is the provision of resources to federal, state, or local governments (*e.g.*, making property available for public use without compensation).

RICHARD A. POSNER, Economic Analysis of Law
3rd ed. (1986), pp. 394–97

While some people criticize the modern corporation for not trying assiduously enough to maximize profits, others criticize it for making profit maximization its only goal. Corporations have long made charitable donations. Why, then, should they not devote a portion of their revenues to other social needs such as controlling pollution or training members of disadvantaged minorities? But charitable donations are not a strong precedent; especially when they are made in the places where the corporation's plants or headquarters are located, they can usually be justified to shareholders as efficient advertising or public relations expenses.

There are economic reasons for questioning both the feasibility and appropriateness of major corporate commitments to social goals other than profit maximization. In competitive markets, a sustained commitment to any goal other than profitability will result in the firm's shrinking, quite possibly to nothing. The firm that channels profits into pollution control will not be able to recoup its losses by charging higher prices to its customers.

The customers do not benefit as customers from such expenditures; more precisely, they benefit just as much from those expenditures if they purchase the lower-priced product of a competing firm that does not incur them. Thus the firm will have to defray the expenses of pollution control entirely out of its profits. But in a competitive market there are no corporate profits, in an economic sense, other than as a short-run consequence of uncertainty (the shareholders being the residual claimants of any excess of corporate revenues over costs). Accounting profits in a competitive market will, in the long run, tend to equality with the cost of attracting and retaining capital in the business. If these profits decline, the firm will, in all likelihood, eventually be forced out of business. True, if it has the usual upward-sloping marginal cost curve at its current output, it may be able to continue in business for a time by reducing its output — but not forever. At its lower output, it will not be able to pay the owners of whatever resources it uses in the production of its output as much as those owners could obtain elsewhere: monopsony is rarely a long-run game (see § 10.9, *supra*). The only exception would be if the owners of these resources (who might be the firm's shareholders) were altruists who received utility from the firm's practice of social responsibility. How likely is that? [Judge Posner considers the position in monopolistic markets and concludes:]

Thus in neither a competitive nor a monopolistic market is it realistic to expect much voluntary effort to subordinate profit maximization to social responsibility. Is this regrettable? Maybe not. There are problems of:

(1) Suboptimization: The manager who tries both to produce for the market at lowest cost and to improve society is likely to do neither very well.

(2) Standard: How are managers to decide what is a politically or ethically correct stance?

(3) Distributive justice: Is it proper that the costs of social responsibility be borne (mainly) by consumers in the form of higher product prices, a form of taxation that is usually regressive? And

(4) Substitution: The exercise of social responsibility by the corporation reduces the ability of the shareholders to exercise social responsibility themselves, while profit maximization increases their wealth and with it the resources they can devote to political contributions, charitable gifts, and the like.

HENRY HANSMANN AND RANIER KRAAKMAN, "The End of History for Corporate Law"
(2001) 89 Georgetown L. J. 439

Much recent scholarship has emphasized institutional differences in corporate governance, capital markets, and law among European, American, and Japanese companies. Despite very real differences in the corporate systems, the deeper tendency is toward convergence, as it has been since the nineteenth century. The basic law of corporate governance — indeed, most of corporate law — has achieved a high degree of uniformity across developed market jurisdictions, and continuing convergence toward a single, standard model is likely . . .

[T]here is today a broad normative consensus that shareholders alone are the parties to whom corporate managers should be accountable, resulting from widespread disenchantment with a privileged role for managers, employees, or the state in corporate affairs. This is not to say that there is agreement that corporations should be run in the interests of shareholders alone — much less that the law should sanction that result. All thoughtful people believe that corporate enterprise should be organized and operated to serve the interests of society as a whole, and that the interests of shareholders deserve no greater weight in this social calculus than do the interests of any other members of society. The point is simply that now, as a consequence of both logic and experience, there is convergence on a consensus that the best means to this end (that is, the pursuit of aggregate social welfare) is to make corporate managers strongly accountable to shareholder interests and, at least in direct terms, only to those interests. It follows that even the extreme proponents of the so-called "concession theory" of the corporation can embrace the primacy of shareholder interests in good conscience. Of course, asserting the primacy of shareholder interests in corporate law does not imply that the interests of corporate stakeholders must or should go unprotected. It merely indicates that the most efficacious legal mechanisms for protecting the interests of nonshareholder constituencies — or at least all constituencies other than creditors — lie outside of corporate law. For workers, this includes the law of labor contracting, pension law, health and safety law, and antidiscrimination law. For consumers, it includes product safety regulation, warranty law, tort law governing product liability, antitrust law, and mandatory disclosure of product contents and characteristics. For the public at large, it includes environmental law and the law of nuisance and mass torts.

Creditors, to be sure, are to some degree an exception. There remains general agreement that corporate law should directly regulate some aspects of the relationship between a business corporation and its creditors. Conspicuous examples include rules governing veil-piercing and limits on the distribution of dividends in the presence of inadequate capital. The reason for these rules, however, is that there are unique problems of creditor contracting that are integral to the corporate form, owing principally to the presence of limited liability as a structural characteristic of that form. These types of rules, however, are modest in scope. Outside of bankruptcy, they do not involve creditors in corporate governance, but rather are confined to limiting shareholders' ability to use the characteristics of the corporate form opportunistically to exploit creditors . . .

An important source of the success of the standard model is that, in recent years, scholars and other commentators in law, economics, and business have developed persuasive reasons . . . to believe that this model offers greater efficiencies than the principal alternatives. One of these reasons is that, in most circumstances, the interests of equity investors in the firm —

the firm's residual claimants — cannot adequately be protected by contract. Rather, to protect their interests, they must be given the right to control the firm. A second reason is that, if the control rights granted to the firm's equity-holders are exclusive and strong, they will have powerful incentives to maximize the value of the firm. A third reason is that the interests of participants in the firm other than shareholders can generally be given substantial protection by contract and regulation, so that maximization of the firm's value by its shareholders complements the interests of those other participants rather than competing with them. A fourth reason is that, even where contractual and regulatory devices offer only imperfect protection for nonshareholder interests, adapting the firm's governance structure to make it directly responsible to those interests creates more difficulties than it solves . . .

(e) Creditors and Corporate Obligations

The following cases discuss the extent to which corporate directors and officers owe duties to creditors in some circumstances.

Canbook Distribution Corp. v. Borins
(1999), 45 O.R. (3d) 565, 1999 CarswellOnt 2016 (S.C.J. [Commercial List])

Edwards Books and Art Limited ("EBAL") was adjudged bankrupt on January 28, 1997. EBAL was a wholly-owned subsidiary of Edsed Investments Limited. Edsed was owned by two holding corporations, each with a 50% share of Edsed. One of the holding corporations was owned by Edward Borins; the other was owned by Eva Borins. Some creditors of EBAL claimed that certain transactions between Edsed and EBAL were improper and harmed EBAL's creditors. One of the questions that arose in this case was whether EBAL's directors' duties to the corporation encompassed a duty to creditors. Ground J. had the following to say after one of the defendants in this case, EBAL's law firm, brought a motion for summary judgment in part on the basis that directors do not owe duties to creditors:

GROUND J.: In this action Canbook also seeks relief in its status as an ordinary creditor of EBAL presumably on the theory that Edward Borins and Eva Borins, as directors of EBAL, owed a fiduciary duty to the creditors of EBAL which duty was breached by EBAL entering into the transaction granting security to Edsed. Canadian law appears to be moving in the direction of recognizing such fiduciary duty, particularly in situations where the corporation was insolvent when it entered into the challenged transaction or the challenged transaction rendered the corporation insolvent. In *Peoples Department Stores Inc. v. Wise*, [1998] Q.J. No. 3571, Greenberg J. considered at some length British, Australian, and New Zealand authorities rec-

ognizing such fiduciary duty and stated as follows commencing at para.
189:

> [para 189] We were invited by counsel for the Trustee-Petitioner to
> consider the notion of creditors as "stakeholders" in a corporation.

> [para 190] Over the past 20 years or so . . .

British, Australian and New Zealand courts have repeatedly held, at
least where a company is insolvent or near to insolvency, that the
directors' duties lies not only towards the company's shareholders, but
that they are also bound to act in the best interests of the company's
creditors . . . The aggregate effect of these developments is to change
radically the traditional corporate law doctrine that the directors' duty
is to promote the welfare of the company's shareholders and that
creditors must be expected to look after themselves. ("Creditors as
corporate stakeholders: The Quiet Revolution — an Anglo-Canadian
Perspective" (1993), 43 University of Toronto Law Journal 511; Jacob
G. Ziegel, Faculty of Law, University of Toronto.)

[para 191] In *Nicholson v. Parmakraft (N.Z.) Ltd.*, [1985] 1 N.Z.L.R.
242, Cooke J. wrote a landmark opinion where he declared at p. 249:

> The duties of directors are owed to the company. On the facts of
> particular cases this may require the directors to consider *inter
> alia* the interests of creditors. For instance creditors are entitled
> to consideration, in my opinion, if the company is insolvent, or
> near-insolvent or of doubtful solvency, or if a contemplated pay-
> ment or other course of action would jeopardise its solvency.

[para 192] This would appear to closely describe the status of Peoples
as it was plunged headlong into the new domestic inventory procurement policy.
and page 250;

I would respectfully adopt the approach of Cumming-Bruce and Templeman L.J. in *Re Horsley & Weight Ltd.* [1982] Ch. 442, 454-456.
Both Lord Justices favoured an objective test: whether at the time of
the payment in question the directors "should have appreciated" or
"ought to have known" that it was likely to cause loss to creditors or
threatened the continued existence of the company . . .

[para 194] The Courts of Australia echoed that holding in Nicholson
and also recorded judgments to the same effect even prior to Nicholson.

[para 195] In *Kinsela v. Russel Kinsela PTY Ltd.*, [1986] 4 N.S.W.L.R.
722, Street C.J. wrote at p. 732:

> The obligation by directors to consider, in appropriate cases, the
> interests of creditors has been recognized also in the High Court
> of Australia. In *Walker v. Wimborne* (1976) 137 CLR 1 Mason J.

said (at 6-7): . . . it should be emphasized that the directors of a company in discharging their duty to the company must take account of the interest of its shareholders and its creditors. Any failure by the directors to take into account the interests of the creditors will have adverse consequences for the company as well as for them.

[para 196] Barwick C.J. concurred in the judgment of Mason J.:

It is, to my mind, legally and logically acceptable to recognise that, where directors are involved in a breach of their duty to the company affecting the interests of the shareholder, then share-holders can either authorise that breach in prospect or ratify it in retrospect. Where, however, the interests at risk are those of cred-itors I see no reason in law or in logic to recognise that the shareholders can authorise the breach. Once it is accepted, as in my view it must be, that the directors' duty to a company as a whole extends in an insolvency context to not prejudicing the interest of creditors (*Nicholson v. Permakreft (NZ) Ltd.* and *Wal-ker v. Wimborne*) the shareholders do not have the power or authority to absolve the directors from that breach.

[para 197] In England, the House of Lords put its stamp of approval on this concept in *Winkworth v. Edward Baron Development Co., Limited et al.*, [1987] 1 All E.R. 114, by Lord Templeman, at p. 118.

But a company owes a duty to its creditors, present and future. The Company is not bound to pay off every debt as soon as it is incurred and the company is not obliged to avoid all ventures which involve an element of risk, but the company owes a duty to its creditors to keep its property inviolate and available for the repayment of its debts. The conscience of the company, as well as its management, is confided to its directors. A duty is owed by the directors to the company and to the creditors of the company to ensure that the affairs of the company are properly administered and that its property is not dissipated or exploited for the benefit of the directors themselves to the prejudice of the creditors.

[para 198] Even though in Winkworth the directors' actions were motivated by the wish to benefit themselves, and that was not the case with the Wise Brothers here, the general rationale of that judgment applies in the present case.

[para 200] We agree with the thrust of those judgments and find that Canadian Corporate Law should evolve in that direction.

[17] It is of course a question of fact to be determined at trial in this action as to whether EBAL was insolvent at the date of granting of security to

Edsed or whether the granting of said security jeopardized the solvency of EBAL or the continued existence of EBAL.

[18] Accordingly I find that Canbook has the status to commence the within action . . . as a creditor of EBAL to whom the directors of EBAL owed a fiduciary duty in the circumstances of the transactions as alleged by Canbook in its claim . . .

Order accordingly.

People's Department Stores Ltd. (1992) Inc., Re
(2003), [2003] Q.J. No. 505, 2003 CarswellQue 145 (C.A.)

The Court in *Canbook* relied heavily on the decision of the trial judge in *Wise*. The trial judgment in *Wise* was overturned on appeal:

PELLETIER J.A.: In late January 1995, retroactively to December 9, 1994, Wise Stores Inc. [Wise] and Peoples Department Stores Inc. [Peoples Inc.] were forced into bankruptcy by Marks & Spencer Canada Inc. [M & S], the Canadian subsidiary of the British retail sales giant. At the time of the bankruptcies, Lionel, Ralph and Harold Wise [the brothers] were the directors of the two bankrupt legal persons, i.e. Wise, the holding body corporate; and Peoples Inc., the subsidiary. They were also majority shareholders of Wise, which held all the issued and outstanding shares of Peoples Inc.

The dispute that must now be resolved pits the brothers against Peoples Inc.'s trustee in bankruptcy. The trustee in bankruptcy reproaches the brothers for unduly favouring Wise to the detriment of Peoples Inc. It is therefore claiming from them nearly $28 million, an amount that, according to the trustee, corresponds to the undue benefit that Wise allegedly derived.

At the end of an extensive and well-crafted judgment, the Superior Court allowed the claim for $4,437,115. In the opinion of the trial judge, the brothers failed to meet their obligations under subsection 122(1) of the Canada *Business Corporations Act* [CBCA].

* * *

[The trustee's] argument could be worded as follows: Compelled to assume the duties imposed on them under paragraph 122(1) CBCA, the brothers did not act in the best interests of the creditors of Peoples Inc., which is tantamount to not acting in the best interests of Peoples Inc.

According to the judge, Canadian corporate law should evolve in that direction, which, he maintained, has in fact been endorsed in a number of countries, as the following opinion expressed by Cooke J. of the Court of Appeal of New Zealand demonstrates [*Nicholson v. Permakraft (NZ) Ltd.*, [1985] 1 N.Z.L.R. 242 at 249 (C.A.)]:

The duties of directors are owed to the company. On the facts of particular cases this may require the directors to consider inter alia the interests of creditors. For instance creditors are entitled to consideration, in my opinion, if the company is insolvent, or near-insolvent, or of doubtful solvency, or if a contemplated payment or other course of action would jeopardise its solvency.

It should first be pointed out that that opinion was obiter, which the two other colleagues of the court did not endorse.

Secondly, and with respect, I believe that, in advocating the extension of that theory to Canadian law, the trial judge encroached on the legislator's field of intervention in that the legislator establishes a general regime of director liability of benefit to third parties aggrieved by the management acts of directors. I am not disposed to follow that approach.

In 1978, the Canadian law was completely revised without the legislators explicit acceptance of the principle of the general liability of directors to third parties. I said apparently because such a shift away from traditional thought would, in my opinion, require an explicit, clear provision. Nothing of the kind is found in that Act of Parliament.

It is true that the role of the courts has evolved over the last few decades and that that of judges is sometimes akin to the role that our democratic system has traditionally given elected officials. This is so in the area of the fundamental rights enshrined in the Canadian *Charter of Human Rights and Freedoms*. Bear in mind, however, that it is exceptional for the courts to be asked to reshape the rules of law, not to mention create them, since the fundamental role of the courts consists in applying and legitimizing the will to which the law gives expression.

In the case at bar, I therefore believe that it is not within the purview of the courts to decide that corporate law should evolve in a manner that the legislator did not provide for in his reform.

The trustee supported a somewhat more restrictive argument before our Court in invoking the context of imminent bankruptcy in order to justify the birth of an interest on the part of the creditors in the management of the corporation. At this stage, I believe it is worthwhile to reproduce an excerpt from a judgment in the United Kingdom that the trial judge cited as a basis for that thesis [*Liquidator of West Mercia Safetywear Ltd. v. Dodd & Anor*, (1988) 4 B.C.C. 30 at 33 (C.A.)]:

But where a company is insolvent the interests of the creditors intrude. They become prospectively entitled, through the mechanism of liquidation, to displace the power of the shareholders and directors to deal with the company's assets. It is in a practical sense their assets and not the shareholders' assets that, through the medium of the company, are under the management of the directors pending either liquidation, return to solvency, or the imposition of some alternative administration.

I am very reluctant to link the rights of creditors with those of share-holders, even when bankruptcy is imminent. I note in passing that the property of the corporation is not that of the shareholders, even from a practical standpoint, and I have difficulty seeing why it would be more likely to become the property of the creditors solely because bankruptcy is imminent. Hence, at first glance, the affirmation in that excerpt seems to me to have excessive scope in Canadian law, although I can understand that the interests of creditors in the way directors manage a corporation may grow with imminent bankruptcy. Major J., writing on behalf of a unanimous Supreme Court in *373409 Alberta Ltd. (Receiver of) v. Bank of Montreal* (2002), [2002] S.C.J. No. 82, 2002 CarswellAlta 1573, 2002 CarswellAlta 1574 does not seem to leave much room for the establishment in Canadian law of the thesis of the interests of creditors in the management acts of a corporation. In that case, the sole shareholder and sole director of a corpo-ration, a Mr. Lakusta, had diverted money intended for his corporation for the benefit of another corporation called Legacy. It was a question of whether his action was legitimate in regard to the bank's participation in what, in the opinion of the receiver, constituted fraud. Major J. said the following:

> In this appeal, Lakusta's diversion of money from 373409 to Legacy may very well have been wrongful *vis-à-vis* the corporation's creditors. However, Lakusta's action was not in fraud of the corporation itself. Since Lakusta directed the funds into Legacy's account with the full authorization of 373409's sole shareholder and director, being himself, that action was not fraud in respect of 373409.

As is the case here in regard to the trustee, the receiver intended to defend the rights of the corporation. The Supreme Court concluded that, even if an apparently fraudulent act was committed in regard to the creditors, the corporation could not reproach its director in any way, because fraud was not committed in regard to the sole shareholder. The receiver's claims were therefore dismissed.

I believe that an identical solution is required in the case at bar.

* * *

Appeal allowed, Robert C.J.Q. and Nuss J.C.A. concurring.

[This case was heard by the Supreme Court of Canada in the Spring of 2004. The SCC has yet to decide the case (as of June, 2004).]

Questions

1 In *373409 Alberta, supra,* a bank was sued for the tort of conversion after it accepted for deposit on behalf of Legacy Holdings Ltd. a cheque initially made out to a different corporation, 373409 Alberta. The sole

shareholder, director and employee of 373409, Lakusta, had altered the cheque to add Legacy as a payee. For the tort of conversion against the bank to be successful, the plaintiff had to show that the bank had not been authorized by 373409 to deposit the cheque to the benefit of Legacy. The Supreme Court of Canada held that Lakusta, the sole shareholder, director and employee of 373409, authorized the payment to Legacy, hence the tort of conversion was unsuccessful. Does this holding imply, as the Quebec Court of Appeal suggests, that there is never a directorial duty to creditors? Is there a difference between a finding that a director had the authority on behalf of the corporation to cause funds to be paid to another corporation, and a finding that a director breached a duty to the corporation (or its creditors) by causing funds to be paid to another corporation?

2 As a general proposition, directors do not owe duties to creditors. Why not?

3 Is it appropriate for directors to owe duties to creditors when the corporation is insolvent (that is, the corporation is unable to pay its debts as they become due), or is close to insolvency? What would a contractual analysis suggest? Delaware law has established that there is such a duty to creditors in the vicinity of insolvency: see discussion in *Geyer v. Ingersoll Publications Co.*, 621 A.2d (Del. Ch. 1992).

Chapter 5

The Duty of Care Owed by Managers and Directors to the Corporation

1. COMMON LAW

City Equitable Fire Insurance Co. Ltd.
[1925] 1 Ch. 407

An order was made for the winding-up of an insurance company that was at one time very profitable. An investigation showed a deficit of some £1,200,000 at the time there were large trading profits. The losses were the result of investments in securities which had depreciated and of diversion of funds by the managing director into another company in which he was interested. The managing director was jailed for fraud. The liquidator brought action against the directors and auditors [pursuant to a power equivalent to s. 215(1)(b) of the CBCA] alleging negligence and breach of duty.

ROMER J.: It has sometimes been said that directors are trustees. If this means no more than that directors in the performance of their duties stand in a fiduciary relationship to the company, the statement is true enough. But if the statement is meant to be an indication by way of analogy of what those duties are, it appears to me to be wholly misleading. I can see but little resemblance between the duties of a director and the duties of a trustee of a will or of a marriage settlement. It is indeed impossible to describe the duty of directors in general terms, whether by way of analogy or otherwise. The position of a director of a company carrying on a small retail business is very different from that of a director of a railway company. The duties of a bank director may differ widely from those of an insurance director, and the duties of a director of one insurance company may differ from those of a director of another. In one company, for instance, matters may normally be attended to by the manager or other members of the staff that in another company are attended to by the directors themselves. The larger the business carried on by the company the more numerous, and the more important, the matters that must of necessity be left to the managers, the accountants and the rest of the staff. The manner in which the work of the company is to be distributed between the board of directors and the staff is in truth a business matter to be decided on business lines. To use the words of Lord Macnaghten in *Dovey v. Cory*:

I do not think it desirable for any tribunal to do that which Parliament has abstained from doing — that is, to formulate precise rules for the guidance or embarrassment of business men in the conduct of business affairs. There never has been, and I think there never will be, much difficulty in dealing with any particular case on its own facts and circumstances; and, speaking for myself, I rather doubt the wisdom of attempting to do more.

In order, therefore, to ascertain the duties that a person appointed to the board of an established company undertakes to perform, it is necessary to consider not only the nature of the company's business, but also the manner in which the work of the company is in fact distributed between the directors and the other officials of the company, provided always that this distribution is a reasonable one in the circumstances, and is not inconsistent with any express provisions of the articles of association. In discharging the duties of his position thus ascertained a director must, of course, act honestly; but he must also exercise some degree of both skill and diligence. To the question of what is the particular degree of skill and diligence required of him, the authorities do not, I think, give any very clear answer. It has been laid down that so long as a director acts honestly he cannot be made responsible in damages unless guilty of gross or culpable negligence in a business sense. But as pointed out by Neville J. in *In re Brazilian Rubber Plantations and Estates, Ltd.*, one cannot say whether a man has been guilty of negligence, gross or otherwise, unless one can determine what is the extent of the duty which he is alleged to have neglected. For myself, I confess to feeling some difficulty in understanding the difference between negligence and gross negligence, except in so far as the expressions are used for the purpose of drawing a distinction between the duty that is owed in one case and the duty that is owed in another. If two men owe the same duty to a third person, and neglect to perform that duty, they are both guilty of negligence, and it is not altogether easy to understand how one can be guilty of gross negligence and the other of negligence only. But if it be said that of two men one is only liable to a third person for gross negligence, and the other is liable for mere negligence, this, I think, means no more than that the duties of the two men are different. The one owes a duty to take a greater degree of care than does the other: see the observations of Willes J. in *Grill v. General Iron Screw Collier Co.* If, therefore, a director is only liable for gross or culpable negligence, this means that he does not owe a duty to his company, to take all possible care. It is some degree of care less than that. The care that he is bound to take has been described by Neville J. in the case referred to above as "reasonable care" to be measured by the care an ordinary man might be expected to take in the circumstances on his own behalf. In saying this Neville J. was only following what was laid down in *Overend & Gurney Co. v. Gibb* as being the proper test to apply, namely:

Whether or not the directors exceeded the powers entrusted to them, or whether if they did not so exceed their powers they were cognisant of circumstances of such a character, so plain, so manifest, and so simple of appreciation, that no men with any ordinary degree of prudence, acting on their own behalf, would have entered into such a transaction as they entered into?

There are, in addition, one or two other general propositions that seem to be warranted by the reported cases: (1.) A director need not exhibit in the performance of his duties a greater degree of skill than may reasonably be expected from a person of his knowledge and experience. A director of a life insurance company, for instance, does not guarantee that he has the skill of an actuary or of a physician. In the words of Lindley M.R.:

If directors act within their powers, if they act with such care as is reasonably to be expected from them, having regard to their knowledge and experience, and if they act honestly for the benefit of the company they represent, they discharge both their equitable as well as their legal duty to the company: [See *Lagunas Co. v. Lagunas Syndicate*].

It is perhaps only another way of stating the same proposition to say that directors are not liable for mere errors of judgment. (2.) A director is not bound to give continuous attention to the affairs of his company. His duties are of an intermittent nature to be performed at periodical board meetings, and at meetings of any committee of the board upon which he happens to be placed. He is not, however, bound to attend all such meetings, though he ought to attend whenever, in the circumstances, he is reasonably able to do so. (3.) In respect of all duties that, having regard to the exigencies of business, and the articles of association, may properly be left to some other official, a director is, in the absence of grounds for suspicion, justified in trusting that official to perform such duties honestly. In the judgment of the Court of Appeal in *In re National Bank of Wales, Ltd.*, the following passage occurs in relation to a director who had been deceived by the manager, and managing director, as to matters within their own particular sphere of activity:

Was it his duty to test the accuracy or completeness of what he was told by the general manager and the managing director? This is a question on which opinions may differ, but we are not prepared to say that he failed in his legal duty. Business cannot be carried on upon principals of distrust. Men in responsible positions must be trusted by those above them, as well as by those below them, until there is reason to distrust them. We agree that care and prudence do not involve distrust; but for a director acting honestly himself to be held legally liable for negligence, in trusting the officers under him not to conceal from him what they ought to report to him, appears to us to be laying too heavy a burden on honest business men.

That case went to the House of Lords, and is reported there under the name of *Dovey v. Cory*. Lord Davey, in the course of his speech to the House, made the following observations:

> I think the respondent was bound to give his attention to and exercise his judgment as a man of business on the matters which were brought before the board at the meetings which he attended, and it is not proved that he did not do so. But I think he was entitled to rely upon the judgment, information and advice, of chairman and general manager, as to whose integrity, skill and competence he had no reason for suspicion. I agree with what was said by Sir George Jessel in *Hallmark's Case*, and by Chitty J. in *In re Denham & Co.*, that directors are not bound to examine entries in the company's books. It was the duty of the general manager and (possibly) of the chairman to go carefully through the returns from the branches, and to bring before the board any matter requiring their consideration; but the respondent was not, in my opinion guilty of negligence in not examining them for himself, notwithstanding that they were laid on the table of the board for reference.

These are the general principles that I shall endeavour to apply in considering the question whether the directors of this company have been guilty of negligence. But in order to determine whether any such negligence, if established, renders the directors liable in damages, it is necessary to consider the provisions of art. 150 of the company's articles of association . . .

The importance of the article for the present purpose is to be found in the later part, which provides that the directors are not to be answerable for insufficiency or deficiency of any security or for any other loss, misfortune, or damage which may happen in the execution of their respective offices or trusts or in relation thereto "unless the same shall happen by or through their own wilful neglect or default respectively." . . . [His Lordship discussed the meaning of wilful default in the above context and then entered into an extensive review of the evidence, finding that some of the directors and the auditor had been guilty of negligence but were protected by Article 150, which required wilful misconduct. The case was appealed to the Court of Appeal so far as the decision absolved the auditors, where the decision of Romer J. was affirmed ([1925] 1 Ch. 500). Article 150 would now be invalidated by s. 205 of the *Companies Act* (1948). Section 122(3) of the CBCA is to the same effect.]

Note

Romer J.'s judgment is considered the *locus classicus* on directors' duty of care. In failing to establish a professional standard for a director, his judgment ensured that an action for breach of duty would rarely succeed. The standard was that of the reasonable person given the individual director's expertise. Moreover, a director was not bound to give his full time to the job and was entitled to rely on the company's officers. A further description of the office of director and the standard the law requires is contained in the judgment of Neville J. in *Re Brazilian Rubber Plantations & Estates Ltd.*, below. The directors were described as follows:

> The directors of the company, Sir Arthur Aylmer Bart., Henry William Tugwell, Edward Barber and Edward Henry Hancock were all induced to become directors by Harboard or persons acting with him in the promotion of the company. Sir Arthur Aylmer was absolutely ignorant of business. He only consented to act because he was told the office would give him a little pleasant employment without his incurring any responsibility. H.W. Tugwell was partner in a firm of bankers in a good position in Bath; he was seventy-five years of age and very deaf; he was induced to join the board by representations made to him in January, 1906. Barber was a rubber broker and was told that all he would have to do would be to give an opinion as to the value of rubber when it arrived in England. Hancock was a man of business who said he was induced to join by seeing the names of Tugwell and Barber, whom he considered good men.

Neville J., in his judgment below, held them not liable for losses sustained in an investment in a rubber plantation, which investment was based on grossly inaccurate reports:

Re Brazilian Rubber Plantations and Estates, Ltd.
[1911] 1 Ch. 425 (C.A.)

NEVILLE J.: The evidence in this case has been brought before the Court in a somewhat inconvenient manner, the public examination having been followed by affidavits upon which no cross-examination has taken place. Inasmuch, however, as the liquidator does not charge the respondents with dishonesty, but with negligence based in the main upon undisputed facts, this state of the evidence is of the less consequence. In my opinion it would have been impossible to sustain a charge of dishonesty against any of the respondents. They were, in my opinion, honest men, who performed what they supposed to be their duty as directors, whether or not they fell short in fact of the obligations imposed upon them by their office. Unfortunately for themselves, they fell into the toils of dishonest men. I have not the promoters of the company before me, and I am unable, therefore, to separate the knaves from their dupes; but it appears clear from the evidence that the report upon which the directors were asked to, and did, act was concocted in London, from the particulars furnished by the original vendors, who appear to have been straightforward men.

In dealing with these particulars, however, the authors of the report allowed their imagination free play. It was upon this report that the prospectus was founded, and it incorporated the misrepresentations contained in its source; notably an exaggeration with regard to the acreage, which was stated as approximately 12,500 acres, while it was reported by the company's agent to contain no more than 2000 acres at the outside, and a misstatement as to the number of trees fit for tapping, which was stated at 400,000 and which the agent of the company upon inspection declared to be 50,000. The contracts mentioned in the prospectus disclosed the fact that the original price paid to the vendors in Brazil, Holderness & Salgado, was 15,000*l.*, while the price to be paid by the company to the promoting syndicate was 150,000*l.*, payable as to 30,000*l.* in cash and as to 120,000*l.* in shares. It appeared that the syndicate had to find 20,000*l.* in cash for prior vendors; the preliminary expenses were put at 5500*l.*, while 3750*l.* was payable by the vendors for obtaining the underwriting of 50,000 shares at $7\frac{1}{2}$ per cent; so that the cash on the sale by the syndicate, which the company was bound to provide, shewed but a small profit . . .

It is upon this question of price that the principal question in this case turns. The particulars of the property given in the report clearly justified the price to be given. But the argument on behalf of the liquidator is that the increase in price was of such a startling character that it ought to have caused the directors to suspect the accuracy of the report and prospectus, especially as it appeared that the report was made by Meiter, whose name appeared as a vendor in one of the contracts disclosed, and that they were bound to make further inquiries which it is suggested would have led to the exposure of the fraud. The matters complained of took place in 1906, the public examination was in 1908, and the matter comes before me in 1910.

I have to consider what is the extent of the duty and obligation of directors towards their company. It has been laid down that so long as they act honestly they cannot be made responsible in damages unless guilty of gross negligence. There is admittedly a want of precision in this statement of a director's liability. In truth, one cannot say whether a man has been guilty of negligence, gross or otherwise, unless one can determine what is the extent of the duty which he is alleged to have neglected. A director's duty has been laid down as requiring him to act with such care as is reasonably to be expected from him, having regard to his knowledge and experience. He is, I think, not bound to bring any special qualifications to his office. He may undertake the management of a rubber company in complete ignorance of everything connected with rubber, without incurring responsibility for the mistakes which may result from such ignorance; while if he is acquainted with the rubber business he must give the company the advantage of his knowledge when transacting the company's business. He is not, I think, bound to take any definite part in the conduct of the company's business, but so far as he does undertake it he must use reasonable care in its despatch.

Such reasonable care must, I think, be measured by the care an ordinary man might be expected to take in the same circumstances on his own behalf. He is clearly, I think, not responsible for damages occasioned by errors of judgment. . . .

In this case, therefore, I must consider whether the directors acted without reasonable prudence in adopting the contract on the information which they possessed. I entirely concur in the view that this must not be tested by considering what the Court itself would think reasonable. The gravamen of the charge of negligence is based upon the absence of an independent report or opinion. Now, in my opinion, men in general take a very different view of the importance of independent testimony from that obtaining in the Courts. Business men have very frequently to act on information derived from interested persons. In so doing the wise men amongst them no doubt make an allowance for exaggeration, but exaggeration and fraud are not the same thing. If the report had been merely exaggerated, there was no fear of the company making a bad bargain; there was ample margin to allow for exaggeration. The directors did make inquiries, but they were from persons whom, it is said, they ought to have known to be interested. One of them, Webb, was a person in a position entitling his opinion and word to great weight, and though reflection would have shewn the directors that he could not have been instructed to act on behalf of the company by persons independent of the promoters, I think the directors were not to be blamed for placing considerable reliance upon his assurances. A certain Lord B., who was at first proposed as a director, was by arrangement to consult his solicitors and to communicate the result to the others — Barber said only in case the report was unfavorable. He did not make any communication, but though he did not join the board himself, he put, as the directors supposed, his cousin upon it. Upon the whole I come to the conclusion that the directors believed that the contract was a beneficial one for the company, and that, notwithstanding the discrepancy in prices and the absence of an independent report, this conclusion was not arrived at by negligence on their part as directors. . . .

Notes

1 In the *Re City Equitable* case, the Court stated that the responsibility of the directors varied with the nature of the company on whose board they served. In which ways should a director's role vary across corporation types? Do different sized corporations implicate fundamentally different roles in the nature of director supervision or only in the intensity of supervision?

2 *Re Brazilian* clearly sets the bar at a low level for directors. However, it at least seems clear that directors who blindly do all that they are asked to do will be held to account. In *Selangor United Rubber Estates Ltd. v. Craddock*, [1968] 2 All E.R. 1073 (Ch. Div.), Ungoed-Thomas J. held that two nominee directors of a company who blindly sanctioned the conveyance of all of the assets of the plaintiff company to another company, thereby enabling one of the principals of the latter company to gain control of the plaintiff company with the plaintiff company's own assets, were liable in equity for the wrongful conversion of the plaintiff company's funds. This arrangement also had the effect of looting minority shareholders of their proportionate interest in the assets of the corporation.

During the trial, one of the directors, Mr. Barlow-Lawson, stated that once he became the nominee director of Cradock, the person who would ultimately gain control of the plaintiff company, "he gave no service to any [other] in the company". The second director, Mr. Jacob, who was an employee of Cradock, stated that he never made any enquiries about the resolutions he voted for (facilitating the arrange- ment) nor did he consider the interests of shareholders other than Cra- dock. Instead, he simply did what Cradock requested of him. In the course of the Court's judgment, Ungoed-Thomas J. stated that:

> It seems to me, however, that both Mr. Barlow-Lawson and Mr. Jacob were nominated as directors of the plaintiff company to do exactly as they were told by Mr. Cradock, and that is in fact what they did. They exercised no discretion or volition of their own and they behaved in utter disregard of their duties as directors in the general body of stockholders or creditors or anyone but Mr. Cradock. They put themselves in his hands, not as their agent or adviser, but as their controller. They were puppets which had no movement apart from the strings and those strings were manipulated by Mr. Cradock. They were voices without any mind but that of Mr. Cradock; and with that mind they are fixed in accordance with the view which I have already expressed on the law. They doubtless hoped for the best but risked the worst; and that worst has now befallen them. ([1968] 2 All E.R. 1073 (Ch. Div.), at 1123.)

3 Director liability for breach of the duty of care is predicated on personal negligence. Gower suggests (*Company Law*, 4th ed., 606 fn. 31) that a valuable reform would be to make all directors jointly and severally responsible for board decisions, leaving it to the courts to provide individual relief where it is justified. Do you agree?

4 Under s. 130 of the Ontario *Securities Act*, the directors' failure in *Brazilian Rubber* to identify the misstatements in the prospectus would have rendered them, *prima facie*, liable to buyers of the securities for damages. Section 130(3) does, however, provide a number of so-called "due diligence" defences for liability. The due diligence defences give the impugned directors the ability to demonstrate that they were not negligent in the preparation of the prospectus. In respect of portions of the prospectus that were prepared by an "expert" (or that summarize an expert report) the standard that the directors must meet to escape liability is that they "had no reasonable grounds to believe and did not believe that there had been a misrepresentation" in the prospectus (s. 130(3)(c)). In the case of other parts of the prospectus (the so-called "non-expertised" parts) the directors are not liable unless they "failed to conduct such reasonable investigation as to provide reasonable grounds for a belief that there had been no misrepresentation." (s. 130(5)). On the facts of *Re Brazilian*, the prior owner's report on the property would *not* be considered to be an expert's report. Thus, the higher standard would apply, and the directors would be required to make a reasonable investigation to confirm the facts in the report or face liability.

2. NOTE ON STATUTORY REFORM AND JUDICIAL INTERPRETATION OF THE STATUTORY DUTIES OF CARE

Much criticism was heaped on the lax standard prescribed in the common law explored above. In the previous edition of this casebook, we stated that: "One of the objectives of corporate law reform in Canada has been to upgrade the standard of care imposed on directors. The result is s. 122(1)(b) of the CBCA, s. 134(1)(b) of the OBCA, and s. 142(1)(b) of the BCCA." The history of the legislative changes in Ontario is reviewed in the excerpt below from *Soper v. R.* (1997), [1998] 1 F.C. 124, 1997 CarswellNat 853, 1997 CarswellNat 2675 (C.A.), while the history of the federal reforms is reviewed in the excerpt from *People's Department Stores Ltd. (1992) Inc., Re* (2003), [2003] Q.J. No. 505, 2003 CarswellQue 145 (C.A.). Interestingly enough, however, in both cases, the court uses this legislative history to support the view that the Ontario and federal statutory provisions essentially *adopt* the common law standard of care. Do you agree with the courts' interpretation of the statutory standard? Was the phrase "in comparable circumstances" really meant to embrace the skill and knowledge of the individual director? Are there other aspects of these provisions that would allow the importation of subjective factors?

You should note that these statutory provisions cover more than just Romer J.'s first proposition from *Re City Equitable* (and ancillary statements regarding the standard of care). Romer J.'s second proposition states, *inter alia*, that a director "is not ... bound to attend all [directors'] meetings, though he ought to attend whenever, in the circumstances, he is reasonably able to do so." None of the Canadian statutory provisions *require* that directors attend meetings. However, the CBCA, the OBCA, and the BCCA all draw a distinction between the director who attends a meeting and one who does not. Section 123 of the CBCA is typical of what the statutes require. It provides that "[a] director who is present at a meeting of directors or committee of directors is deemed to have consented to any resolution passed or action taken at the meeting" unless his dissent is entered in the minutes of the meeting or immediately after the meeting he sends his written dissent to the secretary of the company. The statute provides that if the director votes in favour of (or consents to) a resolution, then the dissent option is foreclosed. By contrast, a director who is not present at a meeting is deemed to have consented to any resolution or action taken unless within seven days after she becomes aware of the resolution she informs the company in the indicated manner of her dissent. This suggests that, in this respect, the statute is somewhat more demanding than *Re City Equitable*. However, suppose that a director who fails to attend a meeting and does not subsequently become aware of a resolution (either by accident or design) learns of the resolution only upon receiving a statement of claim suing her *qua* director for a corporate resolution taken in her absence. Can that director, within seven days of receiving the statement of claim, still send a written notice to the company dissenting from the resolution? For similar provisions, see the OBCA, s. 135 and the BCCA, s. 151.

Romer J.,'s third proposition states that "a director is, in the absence of grounds for suspicion, justified in trusting [an] official [with delegated authority] to perform such duties honestly." The CBCA, by contrast, states:

123.(5) A director has complied with his or her duties under subsection 122(1) [the duty of loyalty and the duty of care] if the director relied in good faith on

(a) financial statements of the corporation represented to the director by an officer of the corporation or in a written report of the auditor of the corporation fairly to reflect the financial condition of the corporation; or

(b) a report of a person whose profession lends credibility to a statement made by the professional person.

The statutory provision is notably different from Justice Romer's proposition. In one respect, it is broader. The CBCA requires only *good faith* reliance; it does not, as Justice Romer's proposition does, require that the reliance be in any way *reasonable* or *non-negligent*. However, in another respect the CBCA is narrower. It does *not* allow for reliance on "officials" (which appears to mean internal managers), but only in respect of financial statements and reports of professionals or "a person whose profession lends credibility to a statement made by that professional person". It is possible that a court might interpret the scope of that provision to include an officer or other employee of the corporation, although that interpretation is by no means obvious. As a matter of statutory interpretation, can the common law rule stand side-by-side the statutory rule? The cases that follow explore the meaning of the statutory duty of care provisions. We turn first to the *Soper* case, which involves the interpretation of a provision in the federal *Income Tax Act* ("ITA") that is virtually identical to that found in the CBCA and OBCA. As the *Wise* case (which follows *Soper*) makes clear, the standard enunciated in *Soper* now appears to represent the *corporate* standard as well.

3. STATUTORY REFORM: DUE DILIGENCE IN THE INCOME TAX CONTEXT

Section 227.1 of the (federal) *Income Tax Act* provides that:

> (1) Where a corporation has failed to deduct or withhold an amount as required by subsection 135(3) or section 153 or 215, has failed to remit such an amount or has failed to pay an amount of tax for a taxation year as required under Part VII or VIII, the directors of the corporation at the time the corporation was required to deduct, withhold, remit or pay the amount are jointly and severally liable, together with the corporation, to pay that amount and any interest or penalties relating thereto . . .

> (3) A director is not liable for a failure under subsection 227.1(1) where the director exercised the degree of care, diligence, and skill to prevent the failure that a reasonably prudent person would have exercised in comparable circumstances.

This provision was introduced in 1981 by Parliament in an effort to ameliorate problems in tax collection and to enhance the degree of care exercised by directors in managing corporate affairs. (For a discussion of the legislative background of the section, see: Edwin Kroft, "The Liability of Directors for Unpaid Taxes," in *Report of Proceedings of the Thirty-Seventh Tax Conference, 1985 Conference Report*, Canadian Tax Foundation, 1986, 30:1-90.). Early case law under the provision (in tandem with the initiation of legal action against the directors of the failed Canadian Commercial Bank) appears to have had a sobering effect on directors' attitudes. For example, *The Globe and Mail* (Marina Strauss, "Directors take stock of changing times," *The Globe and Mail*, October 26, 1987, B1) reported that:

> There was a time when a directorship offered the well-connected businessman a chance to sit back and enjoy a good cigar at a meeting once or twice a year. Today, board members sit up more erectly, and have a keener eye on company business.

The following case is now the leading case interpreting the scope of the section.

Soper v. R.
(1997), [1998] 1 F.C. 124, 1997 CarswellNat 853, 1997 CarswellNat 2675
(C.A.)

ROBERTSON J.A.: In October of 1987 the appellant taxpayer, an experienced businessman, became a director of Ramona Beauchamp International (1976) Inc. (hereinafter RBI) at the instigation of Ramona Beauchamp for two purposes: first, to promote RBI's interests in the marketplace and, second, to lend his name and reputation in conjunction with a proposed listing of RBI on the Vancouver Stock Exchange. At the relevant time the taxpayer was the chief operating officer of Canada-Wide Magazines. RBI operated a talent agency and a modelling school.

At the time the taxpayer joined the Board of Directors of RBI, he knew that it was experiencing financial difficulties. At the November 1987 meeting of the Board he was given a copy of the balance sheet of RBI which, as of 30 September 1987, showed a net loss of $132,000. At no time did any employee or Board member of RBI discuss with the taxpayer the failure of RBI to make certain tax remittances as required under the Act. Ramona Beauchamp, a co-director, had instructed the other directors of RBI not to discuss with the taxpayer anything other than that which was dealt with at directors' meetings attended by the taxpayer. RBI's failure to remit source deductions to the Department of National Revenue was never raised at any Board meeting. At no time did the taxpayer inquire as to whether RBI was complying with its remittance obligations under the Act. The taxpayer remained a director of RBI from October 1987 until his resignation became effective on 10 February 1988 . . .

* * *

IV. THE STANDARD OF CARE

The starting point for an analysis of the common law duty of care is the seminal judgment of Romer J. in *City Equitable Fire Insurance Co., In re*, [1925] Ch. 407 (C.A.).

* * *

The question I must address is whether the standard of care formulated in *City Equitable* has been upgraded pursuant to subsection 227.1(3) of the Act. For purposes of deciding this appeal, that question may be recast more precisely as follows: has the subjective element of the common law standard been eliminated or reduced by statute? In other words, has the largely subjective standard been "objectified "?

* * *

[Robertson J.A. noted the similarity in the duty of care provisions of the ITA and the CBCA.]

Thus, in order to determine whether the common law standard of care was modified by statute, it is both appropriate and instructive to consider not only the due diligence provision set out at subsection 227.1(3) of the *Income Tax Act* but also the analogous, and virtually identical, standard of care provisions found in the *Canada Business Corporations Act*.

* * *

Federal company law dictates that a director must "exercise the . . . skill that a reasonably prudent person would exercise in comparable circumstances." By comparison, at common law a director was required to exercise only that degree of skill which could reasonably be expected from a person of his or her knowledge and experience. It has been suggested that the statutory skill criterion is essentially the same as the common law requirement: see Welling, *supra*, at page 333; see also Kroft, *supra*, at pages 30:42-30:43. In reaching that conclusion, those commentators point to the use of the phrase "in comparable circumstances" and, in conjunction therewith, note that a reasonably prudent person might not be at all skilled in the field of corporate management. Put differently, a reasonably prudent person in comparable circumstances may be, for example, an unskilled person. In my view, it is correct to distinguish in this way between a reasonably prudent person and a reasonably skilled person so as to conclude that the subjective element of the common law standard of skill has not been altered by federal statute.

With respect to the duty of care, the *Canada Business Corporations Act* calls upon a director to "exercise the care . . . that a reasonably prudent person would exercise in comparable circumstances." Once again, however, the statutory enactment of a care requirement does not appear to have altered the common law position that a director be expected to fulfill his or her duties with care by acting reasonably according to the knowledge and experience that he or she actually possessed: see Welling, *supra*, at page 333. Put differently, the relevant legislation does not refer to "a reasonably skilled person" who, presumably, would be deemed to possess a certain level of skill in relation to corporate management. Rather, the statute speaks of a reasonably prudent person and the care that that person would exercise in comparable circumstances. Hence, in the event that the reasonably prudent person is unskilled (which possibility is discussed above), the statute requires only the exercise of a degree of care which is commensurate with that person's level of skill. It is in this manner that skill and care are clearly interconnected. That being said, it is worth emphasizing that it is insufficient for a director to assert simply that he or she did his or her best if, having regard to that individual's level of skill and business experience, he or she failed to act reasonably prudently. I turn now to the third and final element of the standard-diligence.

Upon reflection, it seems arguable to me that the term "diligence" is synonymous with the term "care". That is, diligence is simply the degree of attention or care expected of a person in a given situation. At least, that is the way the term is employed in *City Equitable*. If attention to one's obligations is the essence of diligence, then that aspect of the standard neither adds to nor detracts from the statutory statement in subsection 227.1(3) of the *Income Tax Act*. Others, however, have taken a different approach by contending not only that diligence is an independent element of the statutory standard but also that that requirement, unlike the statutory requirements for skill and care, is more onerous than at common law: see Welling, *supra*, at pages 333-334; see also the Ontario case of *Kerr v. Law Profession Indemnity Co.* (1994), 22 C.C.L.I. (2d) 28 (Ont. Gen. Div.), which deals with the Ontario *Business Corporations Act* [R.S.O. 1990, c. B.16].

Professor Welling posits that the reasonably prudent person serving as a director would surely exercise diligence in attending to his or her duties; a skilled individual should use his or her skills to perform said duties while an unskilled individual should obtain "competent outside advice" in respect of same (*supra*, at page 334). I am reluctant to embrace that analysis unreservedly. Even if a director is unskilled, I fail to see why he or she should not be entitled to rely, as contemplated in *City Equitable*, on advice provided by officials inside the corporation — unless the circumstances are such that the reasonably prudent but unskilled person acting as a director would seek outside advice. If Professor Welling intended his comments on outside advice to apply only to the latter set of circumstances, then there is no disagreement between us. In any event, for purposes of deciding this appeal, I need not attempt to delimit the precise boundaries of the diligence requirement.

In my opinion, it is not surprising that federal legislation has retained the subjective element of the common law standard of care for directors. Even the law of tort adjusts its objective standard of the reasonable person downward so as to account, for example, for the age, experience and intelligence of children. The standard may also be adjusted upward, as it is for professionals: see generally A. M. Linden, *Canadian Tort Law*, 5th ed. (Toronto: Butterworths, 1993), at Chapter 5, section B, beginning at page 117. The reasonable person standard is thus hardly inflexible. It adjusts to the circumstances and to the individual qualities of the actor. This is all the more true in the context of federal company or taxation law where that standard, at least as it applies to directors' duties, is explicitly modified by the phrase "in comparable circumstances".

The legislative history of the *Ontario Business Corporations Act*, whose standard of care provisions are virtually identical to those found in the CBCA, supports my conclusion that the common law standard of care, while altered slightly, has not been significantly upgraded by statute. Notably, the Interim Report of the Select Committee on Company Law (1967) (the Lawrence Report) recommended a legal standard of conduct for Ontario directors that was framed in the following terms (at paragraph 7.2.3):

> Every director of a company shall exercise the powers and discharge the duties of his office honestly, in good faith and in the best interests of the company, and in connection therewith shall exercise that degree of care, diligence and skill *which a reasonably prudent director would exercise in comparable circumstances*. [Emphasis added.]

The intent of the Committee, in suggesting the words that it did, was clearly to upgrade to a professional level the legal standards for directors imposed at common law: see the Lawrence Report, *supra*, at paragraphs 7.2.2 and 7.2.3. However, the original draft provision met with opposition and the Ontario legislature ultimately adopted a different standard, that of the reasonably prudent person. The standard set out in the enacted provision also contained the phrase "in comparable circumstances".

It was in the wake of a concerted lobbying effort by the corporate bar that the word "person" was ultimately inserted in place of the term "director" in the *Ontario Business Corporations Act*. The essence of the corporate bar's position is captured neatly by J. S. Ziegel et al., Vol. 1, *Cases and Materials on Partnerships and Canadian Business Corporations*, 3rd ed. (Toronto: Carswell, 1994), at pages 474-475:

> The concern expressed was that a professional standard could result in liability for a wide group of individuals who serve as directors, ranging from the wife of the majority shareholder in a small company to a prominent chief executive officer of a public company who, because of his prominence, serves on the board to five other public companies.

By abandoning a professional standard for directors, the legislature presumably was signalling to that "wide group of individuals who serve as directors" that they could rest easy since the statutory standard in Ontario was not intended to seriously alter the common law. The reality is that courts have to contend with a wide variety of corporate forms. Bluntly stated, the vast majority of Canadian corporations do not issue shares which trade on the various stock exchanges. The "ma and pa" operation is as much a part of the business fabric of the country as are the enterprises controlled from Bay Street.

Since the language of the *Canada Business Corporations Act* mirrors that of the OBCA, it seems logical to infer that the federal Parliament intended to send out the very same message to existing and potential directors. In any event, had Parliament wished to strengthen the standard of care imposed at common law, it could have easily done so by adopting appropriate language.

[Robertson J.A. contrasted the provision in the British Columbia *Company Act*, R.S.B.C. 1979, c. 59, s. 142(1)(b), which does not contain the phrase "in comparable circumstances".]

This is a convenient place to summarize my findings in respect of subsection 227.1(3) of the *Income Tax Act*. The standard of care laid down in subsection 227.1(3) of the Act is inherently flexible. Rather than treating directors as a homogeneous group of professionals whose conduct is governed by a single, unchanging standard, that provision embraces a subjective element which takes into account the personal knowledge and background of the director, as well as his or her corporate circumstances in the form of, *inter alia*, the company's organization, resources, customs and conduct. Thus, for example, more is expected of individuals with superior qualifications (*e.g.* experienced business-persons).

The standard of care set out in subsection 227.1(3) of the Act is, therefore, not purely objective. Nor is it purely subjective. It is not enough for a director to say he or she did his or her best, for that is an invocation of the purely subjective standard. Equally clear is that honesty is not enough. However, the standard is not a professional one. Nor is it the negligence law standard that governs these cases. Rather, the Act contains both objective elements-embodied in the reasonable person language-and subjective elements-inherent in individual considerations like "skill" and the idea of "comparable circumstances". Accordingly, the standard can be properly described as "objective subjective".

[The court then raised the issue of whether the standard is different as between inside and outside directors.]

At the outset, I wish to emphasize that in adopting this analytical approach I am not suggesting that liability is dependent simply upon whether a person is classified as an inside as opposed to an outside director. Rather, that characterization is simply the starting point of my analysis. At the same time, however, it is difficult to deny that inside directors, meaning those involved in the day-to-day management of the company and who influence the conduct of its business affairs, will have the most difficulty in establishing the due diligence defence. For such individuals, it will be a challenge to argue convincingly that, despite their daily role in corporate management, they lacked business acumen to the extent that that factor should overtake the assumption that they did know, or ought to have known, of both remittance requirements and any problem in this regard. In short, inside directors will face a significant hurdle when arguing that the subjective element of the standard of care should predominate over its objective aspect.

* * *

The final case I wish to discuss in this section dealing with inside directors is *Stevenson Estate v. Canada*, [1996] T.C.J. No. 1599 (T.C.C.). That case provides a quintessential illustration of the difference between the nature of liability for inside as opposed to outside directors and the effect of the subjective element of the standard of care. The company at issue was a family run enterprise whose principal activity was the sale of earthworms. At the relevant time, the directors of that business included "an elderly man of minimal education who had virtually no idea what was going on" and who was a director in name only, as well as "an intelligent woman with considerable business experience" who held the position of Chief Financial Officer of the company (at paras. 11 and 13, per Bowman T.C.J.). The Tax Court Judge held the inside director liable for failure to meet the standard of care set out in subsection 227.1(3) of the Act and, in doing so, noted that that director "was involved in the company's affairs to a degree that she could not have been oblivious to its financial difficulties"; in contrast, the outside director was exonerated on the basis that he "took no part in the financial affairs of the company and could not have influenced the course of events" (*ibid.* at paras. 11 and 13). I turn now specifically to a consideration of outside directors and, in particular, how the standard of care set out in the Act is to be met by them.

In order to satisfy the due diligence requirement laid down in subsection 227.1(3) a director may, as the Department of National Revenue has noted, take "positive action" by setting up controls to account for remittances, by asking for regular reports from the company's financial officers on the ongoing use of such controls, and by obtaining confirmation at regular intervals that withholding and remittance has taken place as required by the Act: see Information Circular, No. 89-2, *supra*, at para. 7.

* * *

While such precautionary measures may be regarded as persuasive evidence of due diligence on the part of a director, in my view, those steps are not necessary conditions precedent to the establishment of that defence . . . As an illustration, I would not expect an outside director, upon appointment to the board of one of Canada's leading companies, to go directly to the comptroller's office to inquire about withholdings and remittances. Obviously, if I would not expect such steps to be taken by the most sophisticated of business-persons, then I would certainly not expect such measures to be adopted by those with limited business acumen. This is not to suggest that a director can adopt an entirely passive approach but only that, unless there is reason for suspicion, it is permissible to rely on the day-to-day corporate managers to be responsible for the payment of debt obligations such as those owing to Her Majesty. This falls within the fourth proposition in the *City Equitable* case: see discussion, *supra*, at page 146-147. The question remains, however, as to when a positive duty to act arises.

In my view, the positive duty to act arises where a director obtains information, or becomes aware of facts, which might lead one to conclude that there is, or could reasonably be, a potential problem with remittances. Put differently, it is indeed incumbent upon an outside director to take positive steps if he or she knew, or ought to have known, that the corporation could be experiencing a remittance problem. The typical situation in which a director is, or ought to have been, apprised of the possibility of such a problem is where the company is having financial difficulties.

* * *

It is important to note that whether a company is in serious financial difficulty, such as to suggest a problem with remittances, cannot be determined
simply by the fact that the monthly balance sheet bears a negative figure.
For example, many firms operate on a line of credit to deal with fiscal
fluctuations. In each case it will be for the Tax Court Judge to determine
whether, based on the financial information or documentation available to
the director, the latter ought to have known that there was a problem or
potential problem with remittances. Whether the standard of care has been
met, now that it has been defined, is thus predominantly a question of fact
to be resolved in light of the personal knowledge and experience of the
director at issue.

Applying the foregoing analysis of the law to the facts of this case, I find
that the taxpayer was under a positive duty to act which arose, at the latest,
in November of 1987 when he received the balance sheet of RBI revealing
that the company was experiencing what the Tax Court Judge found, as a
matter of fact, to be "extremely serious" financial problems (Appeal Book,
at page 43). In light of that finding by the Tax Court Judge, and given the
taxpayer's ample experience in the field of business, the balance sheet of
November 1987 should have alerted the taxpayer to the existence of a
possible problem with remittances. This is all the more true since there was
no indication or evidence that RBI's financial troubles were merely temporary in nature. In the circumstances, however, the taxpayer made no
inquiries in respect of remittance of employee withholdings.

[Robertson J.A. noted that the taxpayer had argued that there was a "conspiracy of silence" to keep information regarding unpaid remittances out of
his purview, in light of the fact that the other directors had been asked not
to discuss with him any matter about the company other than those matters
specifically raised at directors' meeting.]

However, there is no indication that the taxpayer was misled or frustrated
by other company officials during a quest for knowledge about the state of
remittances. In any event, it is unnecessary to decide precisely what steps
the taxpayer in this case should have taken after having learned of RBI's
grave financial situation and, correlatively, the potential for a remittance
problem. Suffice it to say that what the taxpayer did, that is nothing, was
inadequate for the purpose of discharging the burden imposed on him by
subsection 227.1(3) of the Act, given the precarious financial position of
the company.

The difference in outcomes between this case and *Sanford* can be rationalized on the basis of the subjective element of the standard of care. The
Sanford case involved an individual with no management experience who
took active steps and performed her directorial duties reasonably, having
regard to her level of skill and experience, and the corporate circumstances
in which she found herself. Accordingly, she was able to avoid personal

liability for the unremitted amounts. On the contrary, this case concerns an experienced businessman who took no positive steps to ensure remittance of employee withholdings despite the fact that he should have been alerted to a potential problem in that regard. He did absolutely nothing but close his eyes. As a consequence, it can hardly be said that the taxpayer in this case exercised, in his capacity as director of RBI, the degree of care, skill and diligence required by the Act.

For all of these reasons, the appeal must be dismissed. This is one instance in which it is simply not appropriate to visit the taxpayer with costs of the appeal. The issues pursued before this Court transcend his personal interests. Accordingly, no costs should be awarded.

4. STATUTORY REFORM: CORPORATE LAW

People's Department Stores Ltd. (1992) Inc., Re
(2003), [2003] Q.J. No. 505, 2003 CarswellQue 145 (C.A.)

The Wise brothers (Lionel, Ralph, and Harold) were the sole shareholders of Wise Inc. ("Wise"), which owned a chain of department stores in Quebec. Marks and Spencer ran another chain of department stores, owned and operated by Peoples Department Stores Inc. ("Peoples"). Both companies were incorporated under the CBCA. Marks and Spencer sold the Peoples chain to Wise. However, the contract between the two companies forbade Wise from merging its operations with those of Peoples until the purchase price was paid, presumably in order that Marks and Spencer could more easily resume control of Peoples should there be a default in the payment of the purchase price. Thus, while Wise ended up owning all of the shares in Peoples, it had to continue to run Peoples as a subsidiary corporation.

This contractual stipulation caused enormous grief to Wise. Both Wise and Peoples were in parlous financial condition, and the Wise brothers sought ways to cut costs. One of the biggest headaches they had was in relation to the purchase of goods for resale; each company had its own administrative purchasing and inventory apparatus and this was causing major mix-ups in ordering, excess inventory at some stores, and deficient inventory at others. What the Wise brothers did to attempt to cure this problem is described in the judgment of the court.

PELLETIER J.A.: To deal with the growing problems, Lionel Wise, the principal director of the Wise and Peoples Inc. group, approached David Clément, Wise's vice-president for administration and finance. Clément, who had a B.A. in commerce, had been working for Wise since 1980. He developed a solution that was relatively simple, at least in theory. He proposed the integration of the management of the inventories of Wise and Peoples Inc. into a single computer file, as if the two entities constituted only one company that operated some 125 stores. Peoples Inc. would be entrusted with all the purchases required to run the two chains, at least so-called local purchases, i.e. those made in North America. Wise would pay Peoples Inc. upon receipt of the merchandise in its stores. Wise would be given responsibility for purchases made abroad for the two chains, since, before the acquisition, Peoples Inc. did not purchase supplies outside North America and did not have the financial tools required for that type of operation.

Around December 1993, the brothers submitted Clément's proposal to the buyers. They saw it as the solution to their problem. Given how the proposal was received, the brothers accepted it without studying the indirect impact it could have. In short, they relied on Clément's skills and decided that the proposal would be implemented as of February 1994.

On April 27, 1994, at a meeting of Wise's audit committee, attended by Kenneth Stevenson, vice-president of Coopers & Lybrand, Lionel Wise explained the new joint inventory procurement policy. Stevenson, who was mandated by M. & S., did not oppose it. After examining it, the auditors of the company expressed no reservations.

The first real criticism came from certain suppliers who said they were concerned. They saw the new policy as an attempt to put Peoples Inc. in debt for the benefit of Wise. Everyone continued, however, to do business with the group and several people decided to make their bills out in the name of the two companies.

[NOTE: Pelletier J.A. then described how the implementation of this policy, described below as the "inventory procurement policy", resulted in Wise running up large debts to Peoples. This was because Peoples paid for all the inventory that was put on the shelves in *both* stores, and billed Wise for its share. This resulted in Wise constantly owing money to Peoples, however, since it had trouble paying its debts. Ultimately, both Wise and Peoples failed and went into bankruptcy proceedings, with Wise owing Peoples a sum of money that the trial judge fixed at something in excess of $4 million. This inter-corporate debt resulted in prejudice to the creditors of Peoples, since the creditors of Peoples, in effect, had to stand in line with all of the creditors of Wise for this $4 million, rather than having exclusive access to the $4 million (which it would have done had the money been in the till at Peoples). A trustee in bankruptcy was appointed for Peoples, and the trustee commenced action against the Wise brothers *qua* directors of Peoples. Note that in bankruptcy proceedings, the trustee in bankruptcy replaces the board of directors. Thus, the trustee's action is the formal equivalent of an action taken by Peoples Inc. against its own directors. While this action is not formally a *derivative* action (because it was not undertaken by a shareholder in the name of the corporation, but rather by the corporation directly), everything that the court says below regarding the duties of directors is equally applicable to derivative actions. Substantively, the trustee alleged that in adopting the new inventory procurement policy, the Wise brothers had breached both their duty of loyalty to Peoples under CBCA s.122(1)(a) and their duty of care under CBCA s.122(1)(b). In respect of the former, the court noted that the trial judge had found that the directors had acted in good faith, and that there was no fraud or dishonesty in their adoption of the inventory procurement policy. Hence, there could be no breach of the duty of loyalty. The following excerpts deal solely with the issue of the duty of care.]

The general duties provided for in subsection 122(1) are of two types: fiduciary duty (paragraph (a)) and duty of care (paragraph (b)).

First of all, like the appellants, I believe that the judgment impugned confused the two duties enshrined in paragraphs 122(1)(a) and (b). That confusion is not of real importance in this case, since it has no consequence for the conclusions I reach.

"Fiduciary duty" does not refer to the quality of directors' management, but to their personal conduct. The law imposes on directors a duty toward those who entrust them with the mission of managing the pooled assets. This type of duty is related more to the motivation of directors than to the consequences of their actions. In other words, integrity and good faith are gauged according to the reasons that motivate directors to act, not in light of the concrete results of their actions.

Paragraph 122(1)(b) defines the liability of directors in light of the quality of their decisions. Doctrine and jurisprudence often call the obligation that the legislator enshrined therein as the "duty of care".

In applying the resulting rules, the courts have traditionally recognized the problems posed by the *a posteriori* analysis of the decisions made by directors in the heat of action. Thus, it was recognized that they have the right to be mistaken. Gonthier J., then of the Superior Court, summarized the state of the jurisprudence elaborated under the *Canada Corporations Act*,[1] the predecessor of the CBCA:[2]

> [TRANSLATION]
> There is no need to point out the rather limited liability of directors recognized by the courts. They are personally responsible for the action of the company only if they commit a gross fault. It is accepted that directors must show fair and reasonable diligence in managing the company and act honestly, but no more than that, and it has been decided that they need not have special knowledge.

In the wake of the recommendations made by a task force led by Mtre. Robert W.V. Dickerson, the federal legislator adopted the *Canadian Com-*

---

[1] R.S. 1970, c. C-32.
[2] *Crevier v. Paquin*, [1975] S.C. 260 at 265.

mercial Corporation Act,[3] which would shortly become the CBCA In its report, the task force advocated greater liability for directors in order to prevent them from easily evading any liability in the application of a purely subjective criterion in the nature of that established in the British ruling in *In re: City Equitable Fire Insurance Company Ltd.*[4] In regard to the duty of care, the Commission recommended the adoption of legislation drafted as follows:[5]

> Art. 9.19(1) Every director and officer of a corporation in exercising his powers and discharging his duties shall
>
> (b) exercise the care, diligence and skill of a reasonably prudent person.

The legislator did not wholly accept the recommendation in the Dickerson Report, showing somewhat greater timidity in adopting the following text:

> 117.1(1) [now 122(1)] Every director and officer of a corporation in exercising his powers and discharging his duties shall
>
> (b) exercise the care, diligence and skill that reasonably prudent person would exercise in comparable circumstances.

Commenting on the legislation adopted, one of the commissioners, John L. Howard, wrote in 1975:[6]

> The Courts have therefore been understandably reluctant to adjudge in retrospect that a policy error, even if it turned out to be an egregious blunder, entitled the affected corporation or its shareholders to seek compensation for the resulting financial loss. By indirection the CBCA continues this policy, expressly declaring duty of care standards but at the same time preserving the common law defences and setting out a number of provisions that go far to relieve directors and officers of the intolerable burden of being accountable for honest errors of business judgment.

In his opinion, the new law ultimately did not really change the scope of a directors duty of care. That was also the opinion of Robertson J.A. of the Federal Court of Appeal.[7] I believe that the following excerpt from *Soper v. Canada* his reasons, concerning the scope of a provision of the *Income*

---

[3] S.C. 1974-75-76, c. 33.
[4] [1925] 1 Ch. 407.
[5] R. W. V. Dickerson J. L. Howard and L. Getz, *Proposals for a New Business Corporations Law for Canada,* Vol. 11 (Ottawa: Information Canada, 1971) at 74.
[6] John L. Howard, "Directors and Officers in the Context of the Canada Business Corporations Act", Meredith Memorial Lectures, *Canadian Commercial Corporations Act* (Toronto: Richard De Boo, 1975) at 282 to 303.
[7] 149 D.L.R. (4th) 297 (F.C.A.).

Tax Act, subsection 227.1(3), that is almost identical to paragraph 122(1)(b) CBCA, perfectly delineates the duty of care:[8]

> The standard of care set out in subsection 227.1(3) of the Act is, therefore, not purely objective. Nor is it purely subjective. It is not enough for a director to say he or she did his or her best, for that is an invocation of the purely subjective standard. Equally clear is that honesty is not enough. However, the standard is not a professional one. Nor is it the negligence law standard that governs these cases. Rather, the Act contains both objective elements — embodied in the reasonable person language — and subjective elements — inherent in individual considerations like "skill" and the idea of "comparable circumstances". Accordingly, the standard can be properly described as "objective subjective".

That is all I have to say about the general liability that the CBCA imposes on directors personally.

[NOTE: The following excerpt deals with the application of this standard to the facts of the case.]

With regard to the duty of care — and I say this with great respect — the *a posteriori* analysis giving rise to the criticism that the trial judge and the trustee direct at the brothers does not take into consideration the factual context of the adoption of the new policy. In particular, that analysis disregards the real problems that the two corporations had to deal with, the relatively pressing need to find a solution, the apparent logic of the solution found, the fact that it was proposed by a person of proven qualifications and skills, and the fact that its implementation was positively received by the buyers, i.e. the staff members most affected by the problem to be resolved.

In my opinion, assuming for the purpose of the discussion that an a posteriori examination demonstrated that the new policy was not a valid solution to the problems encountered, I believe that its adoption at the time met both the objective and subjective standards of the duty of care as defined in *Soper*.[9]

In my opinion, the brothers acted according to what they, in good faith, considered to be the pursuit of the objects of the corporation, and they showed no reckless disregard for the duty of care.

What is more, I believe that they could rightfully use the defence provided for under paragraph 123(4)(b) CBCA:

123 . . .

---

[8] *Ibid.*, at 317 and 318.
[9] *Soper v. Canada*, 149 D.L.R. (4th) 297 (F.C.A.).

(4) A director is not liable under section 118 or 119, and has complied with his or her duties under subsection 122(2), if the director exercised the care, diligence and skill that a reasonably prudent person would have exercised in comparable circumstances, including reliance in good faith on . . .

(b) a report of a person whose profession lends credibility to a statement made by the professional person.

The brothers sought advice from Clément, their right-hand man. Clément designed the policy and recommended its adoption. In my opinion, the evidence unequivocally bolsters the conclusion that the brothers relied in good faith on the report prepared by Clément, whose B.A. in commerce and professional experience in administration and finance for nearly 15 years inspired confidence in his statements.

[NOTE: The last excerpt deals with the contrast between the fiduciary duty (and duty of care) and the oppression remedy.]

In the same vein, I note, lastly, that the judgment in first instance tends to equate the recourse under subsection 122(1) CBCA with that provided for under section 241 CBCA, better known as an "application re oppression". The trial judge does this, particularly in his comments on *Westfair Foods Ltd. v. Watt*. With respect, I believe that the comparison is inappropriate, since an application re oppression appeals to the notion of fairness, which covers a much broader range of situations than the notion of fiduciary duty and duty of care, dealt with in subsection 122(1) CBCA.

Note

1 For a thoughtful critique of the lower court judgment in *Peoples* (which confused the duty of care and the duty of loyalty), see Edward M. Iacobucci, "A *Wise* Decision? An Analysis of the Relationship Between Share Ownership Structure and Directors' and Officers' Duties" (2002) 36 Can. Bus. L.J. 337.

5. STATUTORY REFORM: ENVIRONMENTAL OBLIGATIONS

R. v. Bata Industries Ltd.
(1992), 9 O.R. (3d) 329, 1992 CarswellOnt 211 (Prov. Div.)

In the yard of the defendant Bata Ltd.'s shoe factory, there was a large chemical waste storage site that stored several decaying, rusting and uncovered containers. Several of the containers held chemicals which were known carcinogens. The Court found that the storage of the containers and the disposal of their contents had been a matter of concern for interested persons for several years prior to 1989, when charges were brought against the company and three of its directors.

In 1983, a union safety officer had raised concern with the storage of the containers with Bata officials. In 1986, the company had met with a representative of a waste disposal company, Tricel, to consider the transport and disposal of the containers. At that time, the Tricel representative expressed concern about the integrity of the receptacles containing the chemicals. Nevertheless, by 1986, the containers still had not been removed, and the company secured quotes from Tricel detailing the costs of disposing 112 barrels of waste. Despite the deteriorating condition of the drums containing the chemicals, they were not removed until 1989.

The directors were charged with failing to take all reasonable care to prevent a discharge contrary to s.75(1) of the *Ontario Water Resources Act* and s.147(a) of the *Environmental Protection Act*. Among other things, the directors argued that they could not be convicted under these sections, as they had met the prescribed due diligence standard. The Court exculpated one of the three directors, and held the other two liable under the *Ontario Water Resources Act*.

ORMSTON PROV. DIV. J.: William Weston accepted . . . employment as general manager of Bata, footwear division, and in 1985 became a director of the board of Bata Industries Limited and vice-president of that company. He was the directing mind and will of the corporation. His mandate was to stop the losses and get the company into a position where it was viable. In addition, he was aware that Mr. T.J. Bata, the founder of the company, had a great personal and sentimental attachment to the Batawa area. Mr. Weston therefore had a secondary objective to keep the company in place: to keep manufacturing shoes in Canada and to keep employing people in the Batawa area.

When he arrived in 1984, there were 700 jobs in jeopardy. In his first year, he reduced the losses from 6.3 million to 4.3 million dollars and increased employment to 1,000.

He did this by familiarizing himself with the production operation and the internal operation of the plant in order to build a product line to market. He then spent 90 per cent of his time marketing, i.e., developing product, following through sampling, seeing customers, going to shoe shows, developing advertising policies. The other 10 per cent of his time, was devoted to the cost-cutting side of the business. He spent 30 per cent of his time "on the road". He reduced middle management, and did everything possible to eliminate and question every expense.

When he left his position in November, 1988, the division had come from a $6.3 million loss position to a $900,000 profit position. Forty per cent of his remunerative package was based on incentive. It was a reducing percentage, decreasing as losses were cut and designed to have a stable company in the long run.

He acknowledges that the environmental concerns were not his first priority: "It was passed on to the department responsible for the particular task". The evidence reveals, however, that as middle management positions were eliminated, the "department responsible for the particular task" became Mr. De Bruyn. A review of the evidence reveals that Mr. De Bruyn's responsibilities eventually included (1) personnel and property management; (2) public relations; (3) the environmental concerns; (4) purchasing officer; (5) health and safety committee; (6) the fiftieth anniversary festivities; and (7) the water treatment plant.

Mr. Weston's successor, Mr. Richler, discovered "Mr. Weston had really cut right to the bone, we didn't have a security guard, or a nurse, I was responsible for the assets of the company and I re-instituted the guard and the nurse".

The evidence reveals that on July 4, 1986, the Bata Shoe Organization issued Technical Advisory Circular (TAC) 298 to its interests around the world. TAC 298 updated previous industrial safety measures with particular attention to environmental concerns. It exhorted all companies to work in co-operation with local authorities to identify problems and carry out precautionary measures. The first area that it recommended addressing was an assessment of environmental exposure and reduction of potential risks. It is a very comprehensive document. Its titles include the following:

1.0 Environment Alert
1.1 Environmental Exposure
1.2 Chemical Manufacturers Action Program
1.3 Health and Safety Standards
1.4 B.S.O. Safety Recommendations
2.0 Safety Control Program
2.1 Methods and Procedures for Stock control of all Chemicals Received in the Factory
2.2 Establishing a file on Material Safety Data Sheets
2.3 Proper Labelling of all Chemical Containers
2.4 Employee Training Programs covering all aspects of safety related chemicals
2.5 Disposal Procedures for Waste Materials

Mr. De Bruyn discussed the chemical waste drum storage problem with Mr. Weston after TAC 298 arrived. Mr. De Bruyn was instructed to get a quote for the cost of removing the waste. In late 1986 or early 1987, Mr. Weston was advised the quote was $56,000. His reaction was: "I was extremely surprised. I felt it was a large sum of money. It's an area of business that I know absolutely nothing about so I had no way of knowing if it was high or considerably too high. So I instructed Mr. De Bruyn to get me an alternative quote." On cross-examination:

Q: Did you ever speak to anyone personally at Tricel?

A: No.

Q. And you felt the quote was too high?

A: I felt that I needed an alternative, I didn't have sufficient information to accept that quote *per se*, I needed an alternative quote to assess its value.

Q: Surely you must have looked at some writings, some memos or letters from Tricel, didn't you?

A: No, I was informed by Mr. De Bruyn that was the quotation that had been given.

Q: And you felt that was too high?

A: I felt it would be irresponsible to spend money without getting an alternative quote.

Q: Between late 1986 and late 1987 . . . did you ever think of phoning up the Ministry of Environment and asking them what should be done with the waste?

A: Personally, I did not, no.

Q: Did you ever contract anyone who might have knowledge about environmental matters to give you some advice? By that, I mean a consultant?

A: No . . . I passed the, the problem was in the hands of the safety and environmental officer and he was dealing with it.

Q: And the safety and environmental officer was Mr. De Bruyn.

A: Yes.

Q: And wasn't it your understanding he certainly didn't have any environmental training, did he?

A: Specific training for environmental control — no.

In late 1987, an alternative quote for $28,000 was obtained. Mr. De Bruyn was instructed to go ahead and accept the quotation and remove the waste. In early autumn of 1988, Mr. Weston was advised that the contractor couldn't honour his agreement to clear the waste.

* * *

I ask myself the following questions in assessing the defence of due diligence:

(a) Did the board of directors establish a pollution prevention "system" as indicated in *R. v. Sault Ste. Marie*? (i.e., was there supervision or inspection? Was there improvement in business methods? Did he exhort those he controlled or influenced?

(b) Did each director ensure that the corporate officers have been instructed to set up a system sufficient within the terms and practices of its industry of ensuring compliance with environmental laws, to ensure that the officers report back periodically to the board on the operation of the system, and to ensure that the officers are instructed to report any substantial non-compliance to the board in a timely manner?

I reminded myself that:

(c) The directors are responsible for reviewing the environmental compliance reports provided by the officers of the corporation, but are justified in placing reasonable reliance on reports provided to them by corporate officers, consultants, counsel or other informed parties.

(d) The directors should substantiate that the officers are promptly addressing environmental concerns brought to their attention by government agencies or other concerned parties including shareholders.

(e) The directors should be aware of the standards of their industry and other industries which deal with similar environmental pollutants or risks.

(f) The directors should immediately and personally react when they have notice the system has failed.

Within this general profile and dependent upon the nature and structure of the corporate activity, one would hope to find remedial and contingency plans for spills, a system of ongoing environmental audit, training programs, sufficient authority to act and other indices of a pro-active environmental policy.

* * *

The prosecution involves only three directors of Bata Industries Limited, namely, Thomas G. Bata, the chief executive officer; Douglas Marchant, the president; and Keith Weston, vice-president of Bata Manufacturing, a division of Bata Industries Limited, located in Batawa, Ontario.

In my opinion, the principle of delegation in environmental matters is aptly summarized as follows [McLeod, "Environmental Protection Legislation", *supra*]:

> Delegation is a fact of life. The *Environmental Enforcement Amendment Act* is not intended to prevent a reasonable degree of delegation. However, the Legislature has clearly declared that environmental protection is too important to delegate entirely to the lower levels of a corporation. Although the Legislature does not expect the Board of Directors or the officers of the Corporations to make all environmental decisions, it is not acceptable for them to insulate themselves from all responsibility for environmental violations by delegating all aspects of compliance to subordinates.

Re Thomas G. Bata

Thomas G. Bata was the director with least personal contact with the plant at Batawa. His responsibilities were primarily directed at the global level of the Bata Shoe Organization. It was established in the evidence that TAC 298, the environmental alert, had been distributed to his companies throughout the world.

He attended on site in Batawa once or twice a year to review the operation and performance goals of the facility. He was a walk-around director while on the site. The evidence of Mr. Riden establishes that the plant managers could not orchestrate a visit for Mr. Bata: "You never knew where Mr. Bata was going to go, believe me. He had a habit of trying to outguess where you wanted him to go". There is no evidence that he was aware of an environmental problem.

Mr. Riden also established that when the Bata Engineering chemical storage problem was brought to Mr. Bata's attention, he immediately directed the appropriate resources ($20,000) to minimize the effect on the environment. The evidence also establishes that when a water problem was identified and funds were required to construct the water treatment plant for the town of Batawa, he (the family) authorized the expenditure of $250,000.

In short, he was aware of his environmental responsibilities and had written directions to that effect in TAC 298. He did personally review the operation when he was on site and did not allow himself to be wilfully blind or orchestrated in his movements. He responded to the matters that were brought to his attention promptly and appropriately. He had placed an experienced director on site and was entitled in the circumstances to assume that Mr. Weston was addressing the environmental concerns. He was entitled to assume that his on-site manager/director would bring to his attention any problem as Mr. Riden had done. He was entitled to rely upon his system as evidenced by TAC 298 unless he became aware the system was defective.

* * *

Although the burden of establishing due diligence was onerous in the absence of more recorded corporate documentation, he has done so in my opinion and is not guilty of the offences charged.

Re Douglas Marchant

Mr. Marchant presents another variation in directors' liability. His responsibility is more than Mr. Bata, but less than Mr. Weston's. This "doctrine of responsible share" is well accepted in American jurisprudence (*United States v. Park*, *supra*) and is applicable in this case.

He was appointed to the Board as president on January 26, 1988. Mr. Richer testified that Mr. Marchant was "down in Batawa once a month" and these visits included a tour of the plant. Mr. Richer brought the storage problem to his personal attention around February 15, 1989.

The evidence, therefore, establishes that for at least the last six months of the time alleged in the charges (February 15, 1989 to August 31, 1989), he had personal knowledge. There is no evidence that he took any steps after having knowledge to view the site and assess the problem. There is no evidence that the system of storage was made safer or temporary steps were taken for containment until such time as removal could be affected.

* * *

In the circumstances, it is my opinion that due diligence requires him to exercise a degree of supervision and control that "demonstrate that he was exhorting those whom he may be normally expected to influence or control to an accepted standard of behaviour": *R. v. Sault Ste. Marie, supra,* and *R. v. Southdown Builders Ltd.* (1981), 57 C.P.R. (2d) (Ont. G.S.P.), p. 59.

He had a responsibility not only to give instruction but also to see to it that those instructions were carried out in order to minimize the damage. The delay in clean-up showed a lack of due diligence: *R. v. Canadian Cellulose Co.* (1979), 2 F.P.R. 256 (B.C. Co. Ct.) and *R. v. Genge* (1983), 44 Nfld. & P.E.I.R. 109 (Nfld. T.D.). There is no corporate documentation between February 15, 1989 and August 31, 1989 to assist him in his defence of due diligence. In my opinion, he has not established the defence of due diligence on the balance of probabilities and is therefore guilty as charged.

* * *

Re Keith Weston

Keith Weston's responsibilities as an "on-site" director make him much more vulnerable to prosecution. He demanded the authority to control his work environment before he took the job. He had experience in the production side and was aware toxic chemicals were used in the process. He was reminded of his environmental responsibilities by TAC 298. In my opinion, Keith Weston has failed to establish that he took all reasonable care to prevent unlawful discharge.

In addition to the evidence previously related in respect to the due diligence of Bata Industries, it is my opinion, red flags should have been raised in his environmental consciousness when the first quote of $58,000 was obtained. Instead of simply dismissing it out of hand, he should have inquired why it was so high and investigated the problem. I find that he had no qualms about accepting the second quote of $28,000 and he had further information other than it was cheaper. This was not an informed business judgment, and he cannot rely upon the business judgment rule, which at its core recognized that a business corporation is profit-oriented and that an honest error of judgment should not impose liability provided the requisite standard of care is met:

* * *

As the "on-site" director Mr. Weston had a responsibility in this type of industry to personally inspect on a regular basis, i.e., "walk-about". To simply look at the site "not too closely" 20 times over his four-year tenure does not meet the mark. He had an obligation if he decided to delegate responsibility to ensure that the delegate received the training necessary for the job and to receive detailed reports from that delegate.

6. THE SECURITIES REGULATORS' PUBLIC INTEREST DUTY OF CARE

One of the most important developments in the corporate law field in the past 30 years is the steadily increasing intrusion of the securities regulators into the corporate law domain. Thus, for example, takeover bids are regulated partly as a matter of corporate law, and partly as a matter of securities law — although increasingly it is the activities of the securities regulators that are pivotal in contested takeover bids, rather than the courts. Similarly, Ontario regulators have promulgated detailed rules governing both "going private" and "related party" transactions — matters that traditionally fell within the corporate law domain. Perhaps most importantly, securities regulators have taken jurisdiction over a wide variety of corporate matters under the "public interest" powers. These powers are so-named because the securities regulators may exercise them when, in their opinion, they believe it is in the public interest to do so. Section 127 of the Ontario *Securities Act* (R.S.O. 1990, c. S.5) is typical and provides:

> 127. (1) The Commission may make one or more of the following orders if in its opinion it is in the public interest to make the order or orders:
>
> 1. An order that the registration or recognition granted to a person or company under Ontario securities law be suspended or restricted for such period as is specified in the order or be terminated, or that terms and conditions be imposed on the registration or recognition.
>
> 2. An order that trading in any securities by or of a person or company cease permanently or for such period as is specified in the order.
>
> 3. An order that any exemptions contained in Ontario securities law do not apply to a person or company permanently or for such period as is specified in the order.
>
> 4. An order that a market participant submit to a review of his, her or its practices and procedures and institute such changes as may be ordered by the Commission.
>
> 5. If the Commission is satisfied that Ontario securities law has not been complied with, an order that a release, report, preliminary prospectus, prospectus, return, financial statement, information circular, take-over bid circular, issuer bid circular, offering memorandum, proxy solicitation or any other document described in the order,
>   i. be provided by a market participant to a person or company,

      ii. not be provided by a market participant to a person or com-
pany, or

     iii. be amended by a market participant to the extent that amend-
ment is practicable.

6.   An order that a person or company be reprimanded.

7.   An order that a person resign one or more positions that the person
holds as a director or officer of an issuer.

8.   An order that a person is prohibited from becoming or acting as a
director or officer of any issuer.

9.   If a person or company has not complied with Ontario securities
law, an order requiring the person or company to pay an administrative penalty of not more than $1 million for each failure to
comply.

10. If a person or company has not complied with Ontario securities
law, an order requiring the person or company to disgorge to the
Commission any amounts obtained as a result of the non-compliance.

If staff believes that the public interest has been violated, then it may
refer the matter to "the Commission" (a defined term that formally excludes
the staff, and includes only the appointed Commissioners), who typically
sit in panels of three. One of the most common sanctions meted out under
the public interest powers is a "cease trade" order (s. 127(1)2), pursuant to
which the Commission may effectively stop any transaction that involves
trading of securities in its tracks. Another common sanction is a "denial of
trading exemptions" (s. 127(1)3), which, when applied to individuals,
means that those individuals cannot trade in their personal securities portfolios for the duration of the order. In the following case, a hearing was
commenced to determine whether a denial of exemptions order should be
made against the directors and officers of Standard Trustco for failing to
disclose vital information to the public. Although the Commission might
have framed the issue solely as one of a failure to carry out statutory
disclosure obligations, it chose quite a different path, enunciating for the
first time a "duty of care" that springs entirely from the regulators' public
interest jurisdiction. As you read the case, compare this duty of care with
that which you have encountered in the previous cases.

Standard Trustco Ltd., Re
(1992), 6 B.L.R. (2d) 241, 1992 CarswellOnt 140 (Securities Comm.)

Standard Trustco was a holding company that held substantially all of
the shares of Standard Trust ("Standard"), a trust company. Representatives
of the Office of the Superintendent of Financial Institutions ("OSFI", the
trust company federal regulator) had expressed extreme concerns to the

board of Standard about its financial condition. Despite this, on July 24, 1990, the board summarily approved the release of a press release to the public (drafted by management) that completely glossed over the company's difficulties and failed to mention most of OSFI's serious concerns about the company's condition. The board also approved payment of the company's periodic dividend to shareholders. OSFI informed the Ontario Securities Commission (OSC) of what had taken place, and the OSC informed Standard that unless appropriate disclosure was forthcoming, it would issue a cease trade order barring all trading in Standard shares. OSFI also threatened to seize control of the company. A press release with appropriate disclosure was put out on July 27, indicating (*inter alia*) that the interim financial statements would be audited. This audit showed an enormous ($50 million) loss, as opposed to a $5 million profit as previously reported. Standard subsequently went into bankruptcy and was liquidated.

While the OSC did not, in 1992, have court-like powers (its powers have since been increased substantially), it did (and still does) have the power to make various orders "in the public interest" against participants in securities markets. One of these is a "denial of exemptions" order, pursuant to which individuals or companies are forbidden from trading any securities that they might own for a stated period of time. In this case, an OSC hearing was commenced to determine whether a denial of exemptions order should be made in respect of any of the directors and/or managers of Standard Trustco and Standard Trust. Note that a denial of exemptions order is a relatively trivial sanction — it merely prevents named persons from trading their personal portfolios of securities. However, at the time, it was the only sanction available to the OSC.

The decision in *Standard Trustco* marks a watershed in the application of the public interest powers. The usual threshold for the issuance of a public interest order is a finding that there has been some "abuse of the capital markets". In *Standard Trustco,* for the very first time, securities regulators suggested that in determining whether there had been such abuse, they would apply their very own "standard of care". As will be seen from the excerpts below, this standard of care may go beyond the standard of care that the courts have enunciated.

ONTARIO SECURITIES COMMISSION:

Under the OBCA, directors and officers in exercising their powers and discharging their duties must act honestly and in good faith with a view to the best interests of the corporation and must exercise the care, diligence and skill that a reasonably prudent person would exercise in comparable circumstances. The standard set out in the LTCA [the *Ontario Loan and Trust Corporations Act,* to which Standard was also subject] is similar except that it substitutes "a reasonably prudent director or officer" for "a reasonably prudent person". In the commentary which accompanied the draft LTCA when it was released for consultation in 1985, it was noted that the "prudent director" test was intended to reflect a greater standard necessary for deposit-taking institutions.

In making our decision in this matter we had to go beyond considering whether the Respondents complied with the OBCA and the LTCA. We had to determine whether the conduct of the Respondents was contrary to the public interest.

Responsibility of Directors

(i) General

As against the Respondent directors it was alleged that they acted contrary to the public interest on July 24, 1990 by voting to approve the Standard Trust unaudited interims and the issuance of the Standard Trustco unaudited interims without making appropriate inquiries in relation to the concerns of OSFI and its requirement for an audit. We believe that this, together with the allegation relating to the misleading press release, was the most serious allegation in this hearing.

Counsel for the Respondent directors submitted that it was appropriate for the directors to approve the financial statements of Standard Trustco and Standard Trust prepared by management as they did and to then have members of management, two of whom were also directors, seek the advice of the company's lawyer and auditor on whether disclosure should be made of OSFI's concerns and whether a note should be added to the financial statements. Counsel for the Respondent directors took the position that there was a basis for the directors to have confidence in management. We are of the opinion that, in relying on management to the extent they did and only taking the steps they did, the Respondent directors failed to exercise the kind of prudence and due diligence that they ought to have exercised, given the information they had about the financial condition of Standard Trust and Standard Trustco on July 24, 1990, and the seriousness of the concerns expressed by OSFI which were shared by CDIC. In reaching this conclusion, we have taken into account the fact that almost all of the directors, if not all, had backgrounds which suggested that they were a relatively sophisticated group. It was not appropriate in the circumstances for the Respondent directors to have placed as much reliance on management as they did, both in terms of relying on management's financial statements and relying on management to consult with the outside lawyer and auditor. Directors should not rely on management unquestioningly where they have reason to be concerned about the integrity or ability of management or where they have notice of a particular problem relating to management's activities. As of July 24, 1990, there was reason for the Respondent directors to question management. First, the Superintendent of Financial Institutions, Standard Trust's senior financial institution regulator, had taken the unusual step of attending a Standard Trust Board meeting together with the Chairman of CDIC and raised very serious concerns calling into serious question management's financial statements involving management's accounting policy and appraisals for which management was responsible.

Second, the Respondent directors were in possession of information on July 24, 1990, which, particularly when considered together with the concerns expressed by Mr. Mackenzie, should have caused them not to rely on management to the extent they did and to make further inquiries . . .

In our view, in the circumstances, it was incumbent upon all of the Respondent directors to make a number of inquiries directly of various people to obtain the necessary information and advice in order to satisfy themselves about the integrity of the interim financial statements before they made the decision to approve and issue the financial statements. We agree that the directors ought to have consulted the auditor and counsel. At the very least, the directors ought to have given management specific direction on the inquiries that were to be made of the outside lawyer and the auditor and insisted that management report back to the Boards with the results of the inquiries so that the Boards could then consider the advice and exercise their judgement on whether to issue the financial statements or make additional disclosure or make further inquiries. Given the seriousness of the issue at hand, the directors should not have felt that they could rely on advice provided by the outside lawyer and auditor to management, when the directors did not even hear or consider the advice prior to exercising their judgement with respect to the financial statements. In addition, the Boards ought to have made a number of other inquiries. Some such inquiries which occurred to us included making inquiries of OSFI and CDIC at the Standard Trust Board meeting; asking the Audit Committees what inquiries they made and discussions they had, particularly in light of their qualified recommendation to the Boards; asking Mr. Hammond about the problems in the mortgage portfolio, such as questions relating to the level of arrears, the loan loss calculation, the loans to Owl Developments, the property appraisals and Standard Trust's experience in collecting on arrears; asking Mr. Howe about the appropriateness of the accrual policy and the reserves, particularly when at least some of the directors knew he had recently expressed some concern about those matters, and perhaps asking Mr. Howe about the accounting practices of other financial institutions; consulting with another accounting firm, for example about the accrual policy, in light of the fact that a longstanding policy which had been followed by the company and accepted by Peat Marwick was put in serious question; providing Mr. Smith or another outside corporate securities lawyer with complete background information and asking for advice relating to the materiality of OSFI's concerns and the course of action they should follow in respect of the financial statements from a legal perspective; asking Mr. Gray, the company's in-house lawyer, for his advice on the same legal matters; asking Mr. Seago whether he had reviewed OSFI's concerns and calculations and had an opinion on them in relation to management's calculations; and perhaps seeking advice from independent property appraisers, particularly in respect of the properties involving Owl Developments.

The Boards should have considered having such people attend meetings of the Boards at which time the directors could have made the inquiries. In the circumstances, the directors should have also asked to see the press release which was to accompany the release of the financial highlights of Standard Trustco and should have reviewed it carefully to ensure that it was not misleading.

[NOTE: The respondents also argued that they could shelter behind OSFI, in two ways. First, OSFI did not specifically object to the release of the interim financial statements. Second, OSFI recommended that the board seek outside legal advice about their disclosure obligations, which they did. The OSC decided that a board is responsible for making its own decisions, and may not rely on those of the regulator.]

Counsel for the non-management directors argued that we should not make any finding against his clients because the Notice of Hearing does not specifically allege that they "authorized or permitted the issuance by Trustco of a press release which was materially misleading." He submitted that there was no nexus between the behaviour of his clients and the capital markets. We are of the view that the non-management directors knew or ought to have known that once they approved the subject financial statements a press release would be issued releasing the financial information. To put it another way, if the directors had not approved the financial statements on July 24, 1990, the misleading press release would not have been issued. We are therefore of the view that by approving the financial statements without making the appropriate inquiries they should bear some of the responsibility for the subsequent release of the misleading information to the public, which provided the nexus to the capital market. In addition, as we discussed, we believe that one of the inquiries they should have made was in relation to the contents of the press release.

As a result, we have found that the Respondent directors failed to exercise the care, diligence and skill that reasonably prudent persons would have exercised in comparable circumstances and that they acted contrary to the public interest on July 24, 1990, by voting to approve the Standard Trust and Standard Trustco unaudited interim financial statements without making appropriate inquiries in relation to the concerns of OSFI. We are of the view that their conduct was abusive of the capital markets.

(ii) Responsibility of Audit Committee Members

* * *

[I]n our opinion the members of the Audit Committees should bear somewhat more responsibility than the other directors for what occurred at the Board meetings on July 24, 1990, not because there was a greater standard of care imposed on them, but rather because their circumstances were different. As members of the Audit Committees, they had a greater opportunity to obtain knowledge about and to examine the affairs of the company than non-members had. As a result, more was expected of them in respect of overseeing the financial reporting process and warning other directors about problems.

* * *

(iii) Responsibility of Mrs. Roman-Barber [the Chairman of the Board of Directors of both Standard Trustco and Standard Trust] and Mr. O'Malley [the President, Chief Executive Officer and a director of Standard Trustco and Standard Trust]

Mrs. Roman-Barber and Mr. O'Malley should bear the greatest responsibility among the directors for what transpired on July 24, 1990 because, similar to the case of the members of the Audit Committees, their circumstances were different. First, they came to the meeting with more information than some of the other directors. For example, Mr. O'Malley was aware that MFI had been sufficiently concerned about the condition of Standard Trust that MFI had conducted an examination of Standard Trust in May, 1990. Mr. O'Malley and Mrs. Roman-Barber were both aware of the problems that Standard Trust and Standard Trustco were experiencing with their mortgage loans to Owl Developments. They had both also heard the concerns expressed by Mr. Di Giacomo after Manulife personnel had conducted a brief due diligence on Standard Trustco. Notwithstanding that Mr. O'Malley and Mrs. Roman-Barber had such additional information, they do not appear to have passed it on to the other directors.

Second, the evidence suggested that Mrs. Roman-Barber and Mr. O'Malley were largely in control of the Board meetings on July 24, 1990. They both had responsibility for setting the order in which matters would be dealt with. Mr. O'Malley told the directors in essence that they should not question Mr. Mackenzie about his comments. Mrs. Roman-Barber terminated the meeting before there appeared to be a decision about what ought to be done in respect of an audit or releasing the financial statements. Also, Mrs. Roman-Barber did not propose that the Board reconvene after the lawyer and auditor were consulted or that the Board reconvene to make appropriate inquiries of others about the financial statements.

Third, Mr. O'Malley and Mrs. Roman-Barber appeared to be the ones who determined that the financial statements should be released on July 24, 1990.

(iv) Responsibility of Outside Directors

Outside directors should play an important and effective role on a Board because of their separation and independence from management. They should ask questions of management and others in order to properly oversee the company's operations and disclosure, particularly where they have notice that the company may have serious financial problems. In some cases it is appropriate for outside directors to make inquiries and have discussions in the absence of management where they have a concern about something which management has done. In this case, the outside directors failed to fulfil their role.

Responsibility of Officers

* * *

We are of the view that the officers did not do all that they ought to have done in the circumstances. Notwithstanding that, with the exception of the conduct of Mr. O'Malley in issuing the press release, we were not satisfied that the evidence presented at the hearing was sufficient for us to find that the conduct of the officers in respect of the allegations against them was abusive of the capital markets such as to warrant our intervention.

Notes

1 Note that the Commission did not feel bound to cite any corporate law precedent at all in enunciating its public interest duty of care. Rather, it simply stated that the securities regulatory duty of care sprang from its jurisdiction to protect the public interest. In short, there are now *two* duties of care that practitioners must worry about — the corporate duty and the securities regulatory duty, which may or may not be the same. This is likely to create uncertainty for corporate legal advisors. This uncertainty is only exacerbated by the fact that, unlike a court, a securities regulatory tribunal is not subject to the doctrine of precedent. Thus, even if the Commission had cited and followed applicable judicial authorities, it could subsequently depart from those standards.

2 The Commission's decision in *Standard Trustco* has been harshly criticized by Jeffrey MacIntosh ("Standard Trustco Case Signals Expansion of the 'Public Interest' Powers of Securities Regulators" (1993), 1 Corporate Financing 38). His concerns focus not only on the uncertainty that the case creates for corporate managers and their legal advisors, but on the manner in which *Standard Trustco* constitutes an unwarranted expansion of the Commission's public interest powers.

7. THE EXPLOSIVE EXPANSION OF STATUTORY DUTIES FOR DIRECTORS

In addition to some of the liabilities sketched out above, there are literally scores (if not hundreds) of Canadian statutes that impose liabilities of one kind or another on directors. This proliferation of liabilities has been harshly criticized for the deleterious impact that they have on board decision-making, particularly when companies are in the vicinity of insolvency. In 1992, in two notorious cases, the directors of two financially distressed companies, Westar Mining Ltd. and Canadian Airlines International Ltd., resigned *en masse* in order to avoid exposure to employee related financial liabilities (see the following section). In the following article, Daniels and Morgan voiced concern with the proliferation of legislated liability on the operation of the Canadian system of corporate governance.

RON DANIELS AND ED MORGAN
"Directors Face Grab-Bag of Liabilities"
(Financial Post, August 12, 1992, at 40)

In the past decade, directors have been made personally liable for corporate misdeeds under a wide range of legislation. By one lawyer's count, more than 106 different federal and provincial statutes, covering subjects as diverse as environmental protection and funeral services, impose civil and criminal liability on the boards of companies operating within Ontario. Significantly, these liabilities seldom work to ensure director fidelity to shareholder interest, but focus on aligning the efforts of directors with other, broader societal goals.

The sheer volume of law undermines the traditional legal assumption that individuals appointed to corporate boards "know the law" prior to or even after their election. The orgy of legislative activity also does violence to the standard model of corporate governance. Because these statutes foist liability on directors for not preventing certain types of corporate action for instance, failure to remit various corporate taxes, or the discharge of environmental waste), directors are forced to abandon their traditional advisory role in favour of another, more alien role that insinuates them deeply into day-to-day corporate operations.

For instance, under the *British Columbia Employment Standards Act*, directors are responsible not only for wages owing to employees, but for severance benefits as well. It is one thing to make directors oversee the prompt payment of wages for services currently provided to the corporation; it is quite another to insist that directors be able to predict the likelihood of massive future terminations, and then to secure the creation of a treasure trove to meet these obligations.

Another difficulty with the grab-bag of liabilities imposed on directors is the tension which all of this creates with the liberal notion that individuals be held accountable only for their own wrongs. The erosion of any causal relationship between liability and individual responsibility is found in the courts' evisceration of the statutory due-diligence defence.

A final problem is the difficulties directors face in securing insurance. Like other specialized lines of insurance, directors and officers liability insurance is subject to fluctuations in capacity that make it hard for companies to assure directors they will be protected for as long as they serve.

Even if a policy can be obtained, D&O insurers frequently exclude coverage for these non-corporate law risks. For instance, the Wyatt Company's 1987 survey on Canadian D&O insurance reported that 91% of the policies excluded coverage for pollution and environmental damage, while 17% excluded coverage for actions taken by regulatory agencies.

Given these insurance, limits, liability-shy individuals invited to serve on corporate boards are left with two basic options: Either decline the invitation or insist as a precondition of appointment that the company agree to refrain from any activity — no matter how productive or worthwhile — that risks inviting some liability.

What accounts for the continued allegiance of legislatures to the statutory liability device? One argument is that conventional forms of liability that are imposed directly on the corporation itself and the actual wrongdoers just don't do the trick. Consequently, innocent bystanders must be enlisted in the crusade against corporate wrongs.

If so, the legislature must show there is a lot of undeterred corporate wrongdoing going on in society, and this wrongdoing derives from defects in quaint systems of fault-based liability.

Legislatures would no doubt be hard-pressed to do so. Indeed, this proliferation of liability likely is an attempt to off-load many of the core responsibilities of the modern welfare system onto the backs and into the pockets of directors.

If a legislature decides that corporations should have greater responsibility for the impact of their activities on the environment, shouldn't it be the legislature that establishes and pays for the monitoring necessary to enforce these goals? Similarly, if the legislature determines that workers dislocated by industrial decline should receive compensation or retraining assistance, then shouldn't the funds for such programs be paid from the consolidated revenue fund, not from the consolidated personal assets of directors and their families?

Ultimately, if the limited liability corporation is to continue to serve as our primary engine of wealth creation, making possible the rich range of social welfare programs to which we are accustomed, legislatures are going to have to signal a retreat from their addiction to unconstrained directorial liability. Otherwise, in our zeal to expand the social welfare agenda and clean up corporate wrong, we will continue to risk tossing out the board with the legislative bath.

Notes

1 A more academic treatment of the effect of legislated liabilities on Canadian corporate governance is provided in R. J. Daniels: "Must Boards Go Overboard?: An Economic Analysis of the Effects of Burgeoning Statutory Liability on the Role of Directors in Corporate Governance", (1994) 24 Can. Bus. L.J. 229.

2 In 1993, in response to mounting concern over the quality of the Canadian corporate governance regime, the Toronto Stock Exchange established a committee to consider corporate governance issues. The

committee was headed by former Ontario Securities Commission Chair Peter Dey. In 1994, the committee published its final report, "Where Were the Directors?". Among other matters, the report expressed concern with the growth of legislated directorial liabilities, especially those employee related liabilities that did not provide a due diligence defence. The committee called for a comprehensive governmental review of statutory liability provisions in order to ensure their necessity and effectiveness. The call to action was taken up by federal corporate regulators in their review of the CBCA, culminating in the introduction of a number of due diligence defences for what had before been offences of absolute liability.

8. OTHER STATUTORY DIRECTOR LIABILITIES IN CORPORATE LAW

Directors are subject to a variety of liabilities in corporate law other than the duty of loyalty (CBCA s. 122(1)(a), OBCA s. 134(1)(a)) and duty of care (CBCA s. 122(1)(b), OBCA s. 134(1)(b)). In particular, CBCA s. 118(1) and OBCA s. 130(1) make directors liable when the corporation sells shares for consideration other than money, "to make good any amount by which the consideration received is less than the fair equivalent of the money that the corporation would have received if the share had been issued for money on the date of the resolution". CBCA s. 118(2) (and OBCA s. 130(2)) prescribe further liabilities relating to various wrongful corporate payments. CBCA, s. 119 (OBCA, s. 131) renders directors jointly and severally liable to employees for all debts not exceeding six months' wages payable to each such employee for services performed for the corporation while they serve as directors. In order to bring a claim against directors, employees must have first obtained judgment against the corporation or have proved a claim against it. If this judgment or claim is not satisfied in full, then the employee is entitled to sue the directors personally for the amount of the shortfall. In the case of the CBCA, suit must be initiated against the directors within two years of the time that the director ceased to serve the corporation (s. 119(3)), while under the OBCA, the suit must be brought within six months (s. 131(2)(a)). These sections are further explored in *Mesheau v. Campbell* (1982), 39 O.R. (2d) 702, 1982 CarswellOnt 777 (C.A.) in Chapter 2.

You will note that both CBCA s. 118(6) and OBCA s. 130(6) allow the director to escape liability by proving that he "did not know and could not reasonably have known that the share was issued for a consideration less than the fair equivalent of the money that the corporation would have received if the share had been issued for money".

In addition, however, pursuant to the most recent round of amendments to the CBCA, directors have been given a due diligence defence with respect to all of the s. 118 and s. 119 liabilities (in addition to the pre-existing statutory defence of reliance on financial statements or expert reports (see CBCA s. 123(4)). By contrast, the OBCA does not contain a due diligence defence.

9. THE BUSINESS JUDGMENT RULE

In the United States, the duty of care standard has been subject to judicial modification by the so-called "business judgment rule". The rule may be stated as follows: When there is no evidence of fraud, illegality or conflict of interest in respect of a given corporate action involving business judgment, the directors are *presumed* to have acted in good faith and on a reasonable basis (*Shlensky v. Wrigley*, 95 Ill. App. 2d 173, 237 N.E.2d 776 (1968)). Thus, there will be no liability for breach of *either* the duty of loyalty (*e.g.* CBCA s. 122(1)(a)) or the duty of care (CBCA s. 122(1)(b)). It is important to note some common confusions that surround the business judgment rule. The correct way of stating the *US* rule is as an *onus* shifting device, and not a *burden* shifting device. The onus of proof determines who must prove their case — the plaintiff or the defence. Thus, in a civil case, the onus of proof is usually on the plaintiff. The burden of proof, on the other hand, describes the height of the evidentiary hurdle that the plaintiff must surmount to succeed. In a civil case, this is a balance of probabilities. By contrast, in a criminal case, the Crown must prove its allegations beyond a reasonable doubt. Under the US business judgment rule, the rule *shifts* the onus to the plaintiff and off the shoulders of the directors, tempering prior law stating that there is an onus on a person accused of having been a faithless fiduciary to demonstrate the entire fairness of the transaction. However, if the plaintiff can show some evidence of fraud, illegality, or conflict of interest, then under the US rule the onus of proof shifts onto the shoulders of the fiduciaries to demonstrate the entire fairness of the transaction.

By contrast, in Canada the initial onus of proof is *always* on the plaintiff. Thus, there is no need to shift the initial onus of proof off the shoulders of the directors. However, the question still remains whether the onus ought to shift onto the shoulders of the directors once the plaintiff has adduced evidence sufficient to raise an issue of fraud, illegality, or conflict of interest. The excerpt from *Schneider*, below, suggests that there will be *no* onus shifting (although the excerpt from *Brant* suggests that, as a practical matter, it may not make any difference). Thus, lacking the onus-shifting feature of the US "business judgment rule", the Canadian rule is somewhat *sui generis*.

In addition, you will note that the business judgment rule fuses the duty of care and the duty of loyalty. It gives directors a presumption of having acted *in good faith* and with due care. We will return to the business judgment rule in Chapter 6, and examine a special variant of the rule that applies in the context of takeover bids.

With respect to the US case of *Smith v. Van Gorkum*, note the emphasis that the court places on the *procedures* by which the decision was arrived at. This case is emblematic of one of the more important changes in corporate law jurisprudence in the past several decades — namely, the proceduralization of the duties of loyalty and care. That is, if all appropriate procedures are taken in corporate decision-making — and, in particular, referring the matter to an independent committee of the board, securing an outside valuation or other professional outside advice, and making sure that the board wrings its hands for a sufficient amount of time — liability becomes unlikely.

The basis for the business judgment rule is clear: the courts are reluctant to engage in extensive *ex post facto* review of the substantive merits of judgments made by directors. This reluctance is rooted in the concern that an environment characterized by the prospect of judicial "second-guessing" is inhospitable to effective business decision-making. Basically, obtrusive judicial scrutiny of decisions made, in good faith, by a board of directors is deemed inimical to the models of corporate governance upon which corporate law is constructed.

Why is judicial scrutiny of substantive decisions so incompatible with effective corporate governance? The most obvious concern is the gulf between the nature of managerial and judicial decision-making, and the implications of this divergence upon the institutional competence of the judiciary to undertake meaningful review of business decisions. Because there is no strong *a priori* basis for believing that the courts will be better able than the directors to make decisions that are in the best interests of the corporation, the role of the judiciary in reviewing complex business judgments, which are themselves the culmination of a host of complex judgments, is highly suspect. Even a seemingly straightforward judgment to expand a corporation's line of business into a new market may, in fact, be the culmination of a myriad discrete judgments regarding the capacity of the corporation to produce and market a new product, the anticipated reaction of rival corporations to the new product, the expected response of consumers to the new product, and the likely impact of macro-economic variables on the strength of market demand. In this respect, it is difficult to make a strong case that judges, with their background in legal analysis, are able to effectively assimilate the kinds of detail involved in a given business decision, and then to arrive at a decision that is clearly superior to the one generated by the directors.

But even if the judiciary were able to effectively evaluate the substantive merits of decisions made by directors, it is still not clear that they should do so. This is because of the inherent unfairness to directors that may result from *ex post* evaluation of *ex ante* decisions. Hindsight is twenty-twenty, and there is the danger that courts will dismiss the very real constraints that beset the process of business decision-making in reviewing directorial competence. Business decisions are, by their very nature, made in an environment where less-than-optimal information and time is available to decision-makers. In this environment of constrained decision-making, there is the real possibility that business decisions may be adopted that will, in time, prove to have been deeply flawed. Nevertheless, the fact that these decisions generate disappointing results does not necessarily implicate the legitimacy or the integrity of the decision-making that generated them. Whether courts are able to muster the expertise and sensitivity that will allow them effectively to simulate the impact of the constraints that impaired managerial foresight at the time that a decision was made is extremely unlikely. And, even if they could, how could judges possibly evaluate the appropriateness of *ex ante* decisions, given the inherent tradeoffs that have to be made by directors in choosing between risk and return? It is simply inconceivable that a court is equipped to decide whether a director is correct in selecting between two competing projects, one of which has a greater expected value and risk than the other. To say that a director erred in selecting either one of the projects is implicitly to impose a risk-return criterion on business decision-making that possesses only tenuous force.

Finally, apart from the capacity of courts to "second-guess" business judgments, it is clear that any dilution of the business judgment rule will have the effect of substantially increasing the level of care that directors must meet. This, in turn, will, because of the increased risk of personal liability, dissuade some directors from accepting board positions, and will deprive shareholders of the talents and experience of qualified individuals.

Smith v. Van Gorkom
488 A.2d 858 (Del. S.C. 1985)

Van Gorkom was the Chairman of Trans Union. Trans Union was entitled to certain tax credits and deductions under US tax law, but did not have enough income to take full advantage of them. In August, 1980, Trans Union's board of directors began to consider the sale of the company to a purchaser who had enough income to take advantage of Trans Union's deductions. Donald Romans, Chief Financial Officer for Trans Union, reported to the board that a rough feasibility investigation he had done as to whether a leveraged buy-out of Trans Union was possible suggested a price of $50 or $60 per share. Van Gorkom remarked that he would be willing to take $55 for his shares.

In September, Van Gorkom approached Pritzker, a corporate takeover specialist, to interest him in buying Trans Union for $55 per share. On September 18, Pritzker agreed to make such an offer. Trans Union's shares had a market value at the time of $37.25. On September 20, Van Gorkom met with Trans Union's senior management, of whom only two supported the takeover proposal. Nonetheless, Van Gorkom took the proposal to a meeting of Trans Union's directors the same day. He gave a twenty-minute presentation on the proposal, but did not explain how the figure of $55 per share had been arrived at. Copies of the drafted Merger Agreement arrived too late for the directors to study them. Romans explained to the board how he had looked at $50 and $60, and later $55 and $65, to see if a leveraged buy-out could be arranged at those prices, but that this did not amount to a valuation of the company. However, he told the board that $55 per share was in the fair price range, although at the beginning of it. Trans Union's attorney advised the board that they might be sued if they turned down Pritzker's offer, and that a fairness letter from an investment banker was not required by law for them to accept the offer. After two hours, the board approved the proposed Merger Agreement.

Five of Trans Union's directors were "inside" directors and five were "outside" directors. Of the five outside directors, four were corporate chief executive officers and one was the former Dean of the University of Chicago Business School.

The following excerpts deal with the actions of the directors at the meeting of September 20:

HORSEY, JUSTICE (for the majority): This appeal from the Court of Chancery involves a class action brought by shareholders of the defendant Trans Union Corporation ("Trans Union" or "the Company"), originally seeking rescission of a cash-out merger of Trans Union into the defendant New T Company ("New T"), a wholly-owned subsidiary of the defendant, Marmon Group, Inc. ("Marmon"). Alternate relief in the form of damages is sought against the defendant members of the Board of Directors of Trans Union, New T, and Jay A. Pritzker and Robert A. Pritzker, owners of Marmon.

Following trial, the former Chancellor granted judgment for the defendant directors by unreported letter opinion dated July 6, 1982. Judgment was based on two findings: (1) that the Board of Directors had acted in an informed manner so as to be entitled to protection of the business judgment rule in approving the cash-out merger . . . The plaintiffs appeal.

Speaking for the majority of the Court, we conclude that both rulings of the Court of Chancery are clearly erroneous. Therefore, we reverse and direct that judgment be entered in favor of the plaintiffs and against the defendant directors for the fair value of the plaintiffs' stockholdings in Trans Union . . .

We turn to the issue of the application of the business judgment rule to the September 20 meeting of the Board.

The Court of Chancery concluded from the evidence that the Board of Directors' approval of the Pritzker merger proposal fell within the protection of the business judgment rule. The Court found that the Board had given sufficient time and attention to the transaction, since the directors had considered the Pritzker proposal on three different occasions, on September 20, and on October 8, 1980 and finally on January 26, 1981. On that basis, the Court reasoned that the Board had acquired, over the four-month period, sufficient information to reach an informed business judgment on the cash-out merger proposal. The Court ruled:

> that given the market value of Trans Union's stock, the business acu-
> men of the members of the board of Trans Union, the substantial
> premium over market offered by the Pritzkers and the ultimate effect

on the merger price provided by the prospect of other bids for the stock in question, that the board of directors of Trans Union did not act recklessly or improvidently in determining on a course of action which they believed to be in the best interest of the stockholders of Trans Union.

* * *

Under Delaware law, the business judgment rule is the offspring of the fundamental principle, codified in 8 Del.C. §14(a), that the business and affairs of a Delaware corporation are managed by or under its board of directors . . .

In carrying out their managerial roles, directors are charged with an unyielding fiduciary duty to the corporation and its shareholders. *Loft, Inc. v. Guth*, Del.Ch., 2 A.2d 225 (1938), aff'd. Del.Supr., 5 A.2d 503 (1939). The business judgment rule exists to protect and promote the full and free exercise of the managerial power granted to Delaware directors. *Zapata Corp. v. Maldonado, supra* at 782. The rule itself "is a presumption that in making a business decision, the directors of a corporation acted on an informed basis, in good faith and in the honest belief that the action taken was in the best interests of the company." *Aronson, supra* at 812. Thus, the party attacking a board decision as uninformed must rebut the presumption that its business judgment was an informed one. *Id.*

The determination of whether a business judgment is an informed one turns on whether the directors have informed themselves "prior to making a business decision, of all material information reasonably available to them." *Id.*

Under the business judgment rule there is no protection for directors who have made "an unintelligent or unadvised judgment." *Mitchell v. Highland-Western Glass*, Del.Ch., 167 A. 831, 833 (1933). A director's duty to inform himself in preparation for a decision derives from the fiduciary capacity in which he serves the corporation and its stockholders. *Lutz v. Boas*, Del.Ch., 171 A.2d 381 (1961). See *Weinberger v. UOP, Inc., supra*; *Guth v. Loft, supra*. Since a director is vested with the responsibility for the management of the affairs of the corporation, he must execute that duty with the recognition that he acts on behalf of others. Such obligation does not tolerate faithlessness or self-dealing. But fulfillment of the fiduciary function requires more than the mere absence of bad faith or fraud. Representation of the financial interests of others imposes on a director an affirmative duty to protect those interests and to proceed with a critical eye in assessing information of the type and under the circumstances present here.

* * *

Thus, a director's duty to exercise an informed business judgment is in the nature of a duty of care, as distinguished from a duty of loyalty. Here, there were no allegations of fraud, bad faith, or self dealing, or proof thereof. Hence, it is presumed that the directors reached their business judgment in good faith, *Allaun v. Consolidated Oil Co.*, Del.Ch., 147 A. 257 (1929), and considerations of motive are irrelevant to the issue before us.

The standard of care applicable to a director's duty of care has also been recently restated by this Court. In *Aronson, supra*, we stated:

> While the Delaware cases use a variety of terms to describe the applicable standard of care, our analysis satisfies us that under the business judgment rule director liability is predicated upon concepts of gross negligence. (footnote omitted)

We again confirm that view. We think the concept of gross negligence is also the proper standard for determining whether a business judgment reached by a board of directors was an informed one.

In the specific context of a proposed merger of domestic corporations, a director has a duty under 8 Del.C. 251(b), along with his fellow directors, to act in an informed and deliberate manner in determining whether to approve an agreement of merger before submitting the proposal to the stockholders. Certainly in the merger context, a director may not abdicate that duty by leaving to the shareholders alone the decision to approve or disapprove the agreement. See *Beard v. Elster*, Del.Supr., 160 A.2d 731, 737 (1960). Only an agreement of merger satisfying the requirements of 8 Del.C. §251(b) may be submitted to the shareholders under §251(c) . . .

It is against those standards that the conduct of the directors of Trans Union must be tested, as a matter of law and as a matter of fact, regarding their exercise of an informed business judgment in voting to approve the Pritzker merger proposal.

* * *

The issue of whether the directors reached an informed decision to "sell" the Company on September 20, 1980 must be determined only upon the basis of the information then reasonably available to the directors and relevant to their decision to accept the Pritzker merger proposal. This is not to say that the directors were precluded from altering their original plan of action, had they done so in an informed manner. What we do say is that the question of whether the directors reached an informed business judgment in agreeing to sell the Company, pursuant to the terms of the September 20 Agreement presents, in reality, two questions: (A) whether the directors reached an informed business judgment on September 20, 1980; and (B) if they did not, whether the directors' actions taken subsequent to September 20 were adequate to cure any infirmity in their action taken on September 20. We first consider the directors' September 20 action in terms of their reaching an informed business judgment.

On the record before us, we must conclude that the Board of Directors did not reach an informed business judgment on September 20, 1980 in voting to "sell" the Company for $55 per share pursuant to the Pritzker cash-out merger proposal. Our reasons, in summary, are as follows:

The directors (1) did not adequately inform themselves as to Van Gorkom's role in forcing the "sale" of the Company and in establishing the per share purchase price; (2) were uninformed as to the intrinsic value of the Company; and (3) given these circumstances, at a minimum, were grossly negligent in approving the "sale" of the Company upon two hours' consideration, without prior notice, and without the exigency of a crisis or emergency.

As has been noted, the Board based its September 20 decision to approve the cash-out merger primarily on Van Gorkom's representations. None of the directors, other than Van Gorkom and Chelberg, had any prior knowledge that the purpose of the meeting was to propose a cash-out merger of Trans Union. No members of Senior Management were present, other than Chelberg, Romans and Peterson; and the latter two had only learned of the proposed sale an hour earlier. Both general counsel Moore and former general counsel Browder attended the meeting, but were equally uninformed as to the purpose of the meeting and the documents to be acted upon.

Without any documents before them concerning the proposed transaction, the members of the Board were required to rely entirely upon Van Gorkom's 20-minute oral presentation of the proposal. No written summary of the terms of the merger was presented; the directors were given no documentation to support the adequacy of $55 price per share for sale of the Company; and the Board had before it nothing more than Van Gorkom's statement of his understanding of the substance of an agreement which he admittedly had never read, nor which any member of the Board had ever seen.

Under 8 Del.C. §141(e), "directors are fully protected in relying in good faith on reports made by officers." . . .

The term "report" has been liberally construed to include reports of informal personal investigations by corporate officers, *Cheff v. Mathes*, Del.Supr., 199 A.2d 548, 556 (1964). However, there is no evidence that any "report," as defined under §141(e), concerning the Pritzker proposal, was presented to the Board on September 20. Van Gorkom's oral presentation of his understanding of the terms of the proposed Merger Agreement, which he had not seen, and Romans' brief oral statement of his preliminary study regarding the feasibility of a leveraged buy-out of Trans Union do not qualify as §141(e) "reports" for these reasons: The former lacked substance because Van Gorkom was basically uninformed as to the essential provisions of the very document about which he was talking. Romans' statement was irrelevant to the issues before the Board since it did not purport to be a valuation study. At a minimum for a report to enjoy the status conferred by §141(e), it must be pertinent to the subject matter upon which a board is called to act, and otherwise be entitled to good faith, not blind, reliance. Considering all of the surrounding circumstances — hastily calling the meeting without prior notice of its subject matter, the proposed sale of the Company without any prior consideration of the issue or necessity therefor, the urgent time constraints imposed by Pritzker, and the total absence of any documentation whatsoever — the directors were duty bound to make reasonable inquiry of Van Gorkom and Romans, and if they had done so, the inadequacy of that upon which they now claim to have relied would have been apparent.

The defendants rely on the following factors to sustain the Trial Court's finding that the Board's decision was an informed one: (1) the magnitude of the premium or spread between the $55 Pritzker offering price and Trans Union's current market price of $38 per share: . . . (3) the collective experience and expertise of the Board's "inside" and "outside" directors; and (4) their reliance on Brennan's legal advice that the directors might be sued if they rejected the Pritzker proposal. We discuss each of these grounds *seriatim*:

(1)

A substantial premium may provide one reason to recommend a merger, but in the absence of other sound valuation information, the fact of a premium alone does not provide an adequate basis upon which to assess the fairness of an offering price. Here, the judgment reached as to the adequacy of the premium was based on a comparison between the historically depressed Trans Union market price and the amount of the Pritzker offer. Using market price as a basis for concluding that the premium adequately reflected the true value of the Company was a clearly faulty, indeed fallacious, premise, as the defendants' own evidence demonstrates.

The record is clear that before September 20, Van Gorkom and other members of Trans Union's Board knew that the market had consistently undervalued the worth of Trans Union's stock, despite steady increases in the Company's operating income in the seven years preceding the merger. The Board related this occurrence in large part to Trans Union's inability to use its ITCs as previously noted. Van Gorkom testified that he did not believe the market price accurately reflected Trans Union's true worth; and several of the directors testified that, as a general rule, most chief executives think that the market undervalues their companies' stock. Yet, on September 20, Trans Union's Board apparently believed that the market stock price accurately reflected the value of the Company for the purpose of determining the adequacy of the premium for its sale.

In the Proxy Statement, however, the directors reversed their position. There, they stated that, although the earnings prospects for Trans Union were "excellent," they found no basis for believing that this would be reflected in future stock prices. With regard to past trading, the Board stated that the prices at which the Company's common stock had traded in recent years did not reflect the "inherent" value of the Company. But having referred to the "inherent" value of Trans Union, the directors ascribed no number to it. Moreover, nowhere did they disclose that they had no basis on which to fix "inherent" worth beyond an impressionistic reaction to the premium over market and an unsubstantiated belief that the value of the assets was "significantly greater" than book value. By their own admission they could not rely on the stock price as an accurate measure of value. Yet, also by their own admission, the Board members assumed that Trans Union's market price was adequate to serve as a basis upon which to assess the adequacy of the premium for purposes of the September 20 meeting.

* * *

Indeed, as of September 20, the Board had no other information on which to base a determination of the intrinsic value of Trans Union as a going concern. As of September 20, the Board had made no evaluation of the Company designed to value the entire enterprise, nor had the Board ever previously considered selling the Company or consenting to a buy-out merger. Thus, the adequacy of a premium is indeterminate unless it is assessed in terms of other competent and sound valuation information that reflects the value of the particular business.

Despite the foregoing facts and circumstances, there was no call by the Board, either on September 20 or thereafter, for any valuation study or documentation of the $55 price per share as a measure of the fair value of the Company in a cash-out context. It is undisputed that the major asset of Trans Union was its cash flow. Yet, at no time did the Board call for a valuation study taking into account that highly significant element of the Company's assets.

* * *

Here, the record establishes that the Board did not request its Chief Financial Officer, Romans, to make any valuation study or review of the proposal to determine the adequacy of $55 per share for sale of the Company. On the record before us: The Board rested on Romans' elicited response that the $55 figure was within a "fair price range" within the context of a leveraged buyout. No director sought any further information from Romans. No director asked him why he put $55 at the bottom of his range. No director asked Romans for any details as to his study, the reason why it had been undertaken or its depth. No director asked to see the study; and no director asked Romans whether Trans Union's finance department could do a fairness study within the remaining 36-hour period available under the Pritzker offer.

Had the Board, or any member, made an inquiry of Romans, he presumably would have responded as he testified: that his calculations were rough and preliminary; and, that the study was not designed to determine the fair value of the Company, but rather to assess the feasibility of a leveraged buy-out financed by the Company's projected cash flow, making certain assumptions as to the purchaser's borrowing needs. Romans would have presumably also informed the Board of his view, and the widespread view of Senior Management, that the timing of the offer was wrong and the offer inadequate.

The record also establishes that the Board accepted without scrutiny Van Gorkom's representation as to the fairness of the $55 price per share for sale of the Company — a subject that the Board had never previously considered. The Board thereby failed to discover that Van Gorkom had suggested the $55 price to Pritzker and, most crucially, that Van Gorkom had arrived at the $55 figure based on calculations designed solely to determine the feasibility of a leveraged buy-out. No questions were raised either as to the tax implications of a cash-out merger or how the price for the one million share option granted Pritzker was calculated.

We do not say that the Board of Directors was not entitled to give some credence to Van Gorkom's representation that $55 was an adequate or fair price. Under §141(e), the directors were entitled to rely upon their chairman's opinion of value and adequacy, provided that such opinion was reached on a sound basis. Here, the issue is whether the directors informed themselves as to all information that was reasonably available to them. Had they done so, they would have learned of the source and derivation of the $55 price and could not reasonably have relied thereupon in good faith.

None of the directors, Management or outside, were investment bankers or financial analysts. Yet the Board did not consider recessing the meeting until a later hour that day (or requesting an extension of Pritzker's Sunday evening deadline) to give it time to elicit more information as to the sufficiency of the offer, either from inside Management (in particular Romans) or from Trans Union's own investment banker, Salomon Brothers, whose Chicago specialist in merger and acquisitions was known to the Board and familiar with Trans Union's affairs.

Thus, the record compels the conclusion that on September 20 the Board lacked valuation information adequate to reach an informed business judgment as to the fairness of $55 per share for sale of the Company.

* * *

(3)

The directors' unfounded reliance on both the premium and the market test as the basis for accepting the Pritzker proposal undermines the defendants' remaining contention that the Board's collective experience and sophistication was a sufficient basis for finding that it reached its September 20 decision with informed, reasonable deliberation. Compare *Gimbel v. Signal Companies, Inc.*, Del. Ch., 316 A.2d 599 (1974), aff'd *per curiam*, Del.Supr., 316 A.2d 619 (1974). There, the Court of Chancery preliminary enjoined a board's sale of stock of its wholly-owned subsidiary for an alleged grossly inadequate price. It did so based on a finding that the business judgment rule had been pierced for failure of management to give its board "the opportunity to make a reasonable and reasoned decision." 316 A.2d at 615. The Court there reached this result notwithstanding the board's sophistication and experience; the company's need of immediate cash; and the board's need to act promptly due to the impact of an energy crisis on the value of the underlying assets being sold — all of its subsidiary's oil and gas interests. The Court found those factors denoting competence to be outweighed by evidence of gross negligence; that management in effect sprang the deal on the board by negotiating the asset sale without informing the board; that the buyer intended to "force a quick decision" by the board, that the board meeting was called on only one-and-a-half days' notice; that its outside directors were not notified of the meeting's purpose; that during a meeting spanning "a couple of hours" a sale of assets worth $480 million was approved; and that the Board failed to obtain a *current* appraisal of its oil and gas interests. The analogy of *Signal* to the case at bar is significant.

(4)

Part of the defense is based on a claim that the directors relied on legal advice rendered at the September 20 meeting by James Brennan, Esquire, who was present at Van Gorkom's request . . .

Several defendants testified that Brennan advised them that Delaware law did not require a fairness opinion or an outside valuation of the Company before the Board could act on the Pritzker proposal. If given, the advice was correct. However, that did not end the matter. Unless the directors had before them adequate information regarding the intrinsic value of the Company, upon which a proper exercise of business judgment could be made, mere advice of this type is meaningless; and, given this record of the defendants' failures, it constitutes no defense here.

We conclude that Trans Union's Board was grossly negligent in that it failed to act with informed reasonable deliberation in agreeing to the Pritzker merger proposal on September 20; and we further conclude that the Trial Court erred as a matter of law in failing to address that question before determining whether the directors' later conduct was sufficient to cure its initial error.

A second claim is that counsel advised the Board it would be subject to lawsuits if it rejected the $55 per share offer. It is, of course, a fact of corporate life that today when faced with difficult or sensitive issues, directors often are subject to suit, irrespective of the decisions they make. However, counsel's mere acknowledgement of this circumstance cannot be rationally translated into a justification for a board permitting itself to be stampeded into a patently unadvised act. While suit might result from the rejection of a merger or tender offer, Delaware law makes clear that a board acting within the ambit of the business judgment rule faces no ultimate liability. *Pogostin v. Rice, supra.* Thus, we cannot conclude that the mere threat of litigation, acknowledged by counsel, constitutes either legal advice or any valid basis upon which to pursue an uninformed course.

* * *

We hold, therefore, that the Trial Court committed reversible error in applying the business judgment rule in favor of the director defendants in this case.

* * *

McNEILLY, JUSTICE, dissenting: The majority opinion reads like an advocate's closing address to a hostile jury. And I say that not lightly. Throughout the opinion great emphasis is directed only to the negative, with nothing more than lip service granted the positive aspects of this case. In my opinion Chancellor Marvel (retired) should have been affirmed. The Chancellor's opinion was the product of well reasoned conclusions, based upon a sound deductive process, clearly supported by the evidence and entitled to deference in this appeal. Because of my diametrical opposition to all evidentiary conclusions of the majority, I respectfully dissent.

It would serve no useful purpose, particularly at this late date, for me to dissent at great length. I restrain myself from doing so, but feel compelled to at least point out what I consider to be the most glaring deficiencies in the majority opinion. The majority has spoken and has effectively said that Trans Union's Directors have been the victims of a "fast shuffle" by Van Gorkom and Pritzker. That is the beginning of the majority's comedy of errors. The first and most important error made is the majority's assessment of the directors' knowledge of the affairs of Trans Union and their combined ability to act in this situation under the protection of the business judgment rule.

Trans Union's Board of Directors consisted of ten men, five of whom were "inside" directors and five of whom were "outside" directors. The "inside" directors were Van Gorkom, Chelberg, Bonser, William B. Browder, Senior Vice-President-Law, and Thomas P. O'Boyle, Senior Vice-President-Administration. At the time the merger was proposed the inside five directors had collectively been employed by the Company for 116 years and had 68 years of combined experience as directors. The "outside" directors were A. W. Wallis, William B. Johnson, Joseph B. Lanterman, Graham J. Morgan and Robert W. Reneker. With the exception of Wallis, these were all chief executive officers of Chicago based corporations that were at least as large as Trans Union. The five "outside" directors had 78 years of combined experience as chief executive officers, and 53 years cumulative service as Trans Union directors.

The inside directors wear their badge of expertise in the corporate affairs of Trans Union on their sleeves. But what about the outsiders? Dr. Wallis is or was an economist and math statistician, a professor of economics at Yale University, dean of the graduate school of business at the University of Chicago, and Chancellor of the University of Rochester. Dr. Wallis had been on the Board of Trans Union since 1962. He also was on the Board of Bausch & Lomb, Kodak, Metropolitan Life Insurance Company, Standard Oil and others.

William B. Johnson is a University of Pennsylvania law graduate, President of Railway Express until 1966, Chairman and Chief Executive of

I.C. Industries Holding Company, and member of Trans Union's Board since 1968.

Joseph Lanterman, a Certified Public Accountant, is or was President and Chief Executive of American Steel, on the Board of International Harvester, Peoples Energy, Illinois Bell Telephone, Harris Bank and Trust Company, Kemper Insurance Company and a director of Trans Union for four years.

Graham Morgan is a chemist, was Chairman and Chief Executive Officer of U.S. Gypsum, and in the 17 and 18 years prior to the Trans Union transaction had been involved in 31 or 32 corporate takeovers.

Robert Reneker attended University of Chicago and Harvard Business Schools. He was President and Chief Executive of Swift and Company, director of Trans Union since 1971, and member of the Boards of seven other corporations including U.S. Gypsum and the Chicago Tribune.

Directors of this caliber are not ordinarily taken in by a "fast shuffle". I submit they were not taken into this multi-million dollar corporate transaction without being fully informed and aware of the state of the art as it pertained to the entire corporate panorama of Trans Union. True, even directors such as these, with their business acumen, interest and expertise, can go astray. I do not believe that to be the case here. These men knew Trans Union like the back of their hands and were more than well qualified to make on the spot informed business judgments concerning the affairs of Trans Union including a 100% sale of the corporation. Lest we forget, the corporate world of then and now operates on what is so aptly referred to as "the fast track". These men were at the time an integral part of that world, all professional business men, not intellectual figureheads . . .

At the time of the September 20, 1980 meeting the Board was acutely aware of Trans Union and its prospects. The problems created by accumulated investment tax credits and accelerated depreciation were discussed repeatedly at Board meetings, and all of the directors understood the problem thoroughly. Moreover, at the July, 1980 Board meeting the directors had reviewed Trans Union's newly prepared five-year forecast, and at the August 1980 meeting Van Gorkom presented the results of a comprehensive study of Trans Union made by The Boston Consulting Group. This study was prepared over an 18 month period and consisted of a detailed analysis of all Trans Union subsidiaries, including competitiveness, profitability, cash throw-off, cash consumption, technical competence and future prospects for contribution to Trails Union's combined net income.

* * *

I have no quarrel with the majority's analysis of the business judgment rule. It is the application of that rule to these facts which is wrong. An overview of the entire record, rather than the limited view of bits and pieces which the majority has exploded like popcorn, convinces me that the directors made an informed business judgment which was buttressed by their test of the market.

At the time of the September 20 meeting the 10 members of Trans Union's Board of Directors were highly qualified and well informed about the affairs and prospects of Trans Union. These directors were acutely aware of the historical problems facing Trans Union which were caused by the tax laws. They had discussed these problems *ad nauseam*. In fact, within two months of the September 20 meeting the board had reviewed and discussed an outside study of the company done by The Boston Consulting Group and an internal five year forecast prepared by management. At the September 20 meeting Van Gorkom presented the Pritzker offer, and the board then heard from James Brennan, the company's counsel in this matter, who discussed the legal documents. Following this, the Board directed that certain changes be made in the merger documents. These changes made it clear that the Board was free to accept a better offer than Pritzker's if one was made. The above facts reveal that the Board did not act in a grossly negligent manner in informing themselves of the relevant and available facts before passing on the merger. To the contrary, this record reveals that the directors acted with the utmost care in informing themselves of the relevant and available facts before passing on the merger . . .

Notes and Questions

1 Following the decision of the Delaware Supreme Court, the directors settled with the approval of the Delaware Chancery Court. According to Cary and Eisenberg, the settlement involved the payment of $23.5 million. Of this amount, $10 million was covered by the directors' insurance policies (Cary and Eisenberg, *Corporations, Cases and Materials*, 5th ed., 1987 Supplement, pages 102-103). The balance was, interestingly enough, paid by the Pritzker group on behalf of the Trans Union directors, even though the group was not a defendant to the action.

2 Is the judgment in the *Trans Union* case consistent with the rationale of the business judgment rule? Is the Court's conclusion that the directors breached the duty of care justified by the facts of the case? In particular, what impact should the premium over market price that the shareholders received on their Trans Union shares have had on the Court's conclusion? In view of the efficient capital markets hypothesis, what role should be accorded judicial determinations of "intrinsic value"? Should these values be permitted to trump prices generated by the market? Finally, what effect will the decision have on the incentive for managers to engineer transactions that facilitate shifts in corporate control? For a discussion of these issues, see Daniel Fischel, "The Business Judgment Rule and the *Trans Union Case*" (1985), 40 Business Lawyer 1437; Herzl and Katz, "*Smith v. Van Gorkom*: The Business of Judging Business Judgment" (1986), 41 Business Lawyer 1187; Chittur, "The Corporate Director's Standard of Care: Past, Present, and Future" (1985), 10 Del. J. Corp. L. 451.

3 In terms of the importance of certainty and predictability for business planning, what effect do you think the decision had and will have? See Bayless Manning, "Reflections and Practical Tips on Life in the Boardroom After *Van Gorkom*" (1985), 41 Business Lawyer 1 at 1, who states that the *Trans Union* case:

> exploded a bomb . . . Stated minimally, the court there pierced the business judgment rule and imposed individual liability on independent (even eminent) outside directors of Trans Union because (roughly) the court thought they had not been careful enough, and had not enquired enough, before deciding to accept and recommend to Trans Union's shareholders a cashout merger at a per-share that was less than the "intrinsic value" of the shares . . . The corporate bar generally views the decision as atrocious. Commentators predict dire consequences as directors come to realize how exposed they have become.

See also Macey and Miller, "*Trans Union* Reconsidered" (1988), 98 Yale L.J. 127.

4 Is the *Trans Union* court's faith in independent valuation of corporations via fairness opinions merited? Are these opinions clearly superior to the good faith review of an offer for shares of a corporation by the corporation's board of directors? In view of the fact that valuations are commissioned by the board of directors, do you think the exercise will contribute much information to shareholders? Fischel, *supra*, at page 1446, argues that:

> The benefit of comparing the price Pritzker was willing to pay with the trading price of Trans Union's shares is that both reflected market transactions — what willing buyers pay to willing sellers. The same cannot be said of the results of valuation studies . . . Indeed, anyone familiar with valuation techniques divorced from market transactions recognizes how uncertain, almost random, the whole process is: how slightly different estimates of future earnings or changes in the capitalization rate applied to such earnings can produce significantly different numbers; how different appraisers typically reach radically different conclusions.

In a similar vein, Manning, *supra*, argues that the *Trans Union* decision constituted "the Investment Bankers' Relief Act of 1985" (at 3).

5 The *Trans Union* judgment exhibits faith in the capacity of rigorous procedural review to ensure that substantively fair outcomes are generated. Is this assumption merited? In the realm of fiduciary duties, how much latitude should courts have to substitute procedural review for substantive review without compromising shareholder welfare?

6 Following the judgment of the Delaware Supreme Court in *Trans Union* the Delaware legislature responded by introducing the following provision into its corporate code:

> 102(b) . . . the certificate of incorporation may . . . contain any or all of the following matters . . .
>
> (7) A provision eliminating or limiting the personal liability of a director to the corporation or its stockholders for monetary damages for breach of fiduciary duty as a director, provided that such provision shall not eliminate or limit the liability of a director: (i) for any breach of the director's duty of loyalty to the corporation or its stockholders; (ii) for acts or omissions not in good faith or which involve intentional misconduct or a knowing violation of the law; (iii) under ss. 174 of this title [Liability of Directors for Unlawful Payment of Dividend or Unlawful Stock Purchase or Redemption]; or (iv) for any transaction from which the director derived an improper personal benefit. No such provision shall eliminate or limit the liability of a director for any act or omission occurring prior to the date when such provision becomes effective.

What effect will s. 102(b)(7) have on the performance of directors? Is the section consonant with the various models of corporate governance? Should a provision limiting the duty of care be a mandatory or permissive term in corporate articles? See: Coffee, "No Exit?: Opting Out, The Contractual Theory of the Corporation and the Special Case of Remedies" (1988), 53 Brooklyn Law Rev. 919; Schaffer, "Delaware's Limit on Director Liability: How the Market for Incorporation Shapes Corporate Law" (1987), 10 Harv. Journal of Law and Public Policy 665.

How extensive is the protection afforded by s. 102(b)(7)? First, the provision does not limit liability with respect to a breach of the director's duty of loyalty to the corporation. In view of the overlap that exists in the United States between the duty of care and the duty of loyalty, it is likely that plaintiffs will simply recast actions claiming breach of the former as actions for breach of the latter. Second, s. 102(b)(7) does not apply to acts or omissions not in good faith, or which involve intentional misconduct, or a knowing violation of the law, or for any transaction from which the director derived an improper personal benefit. It would seem therefore that the additional protection s. 102(b)(7) affords is limited to directorial negligence which, it can be argued, most directors would be indemnified against under the general indemnification provisions. Third, the provision only protects directors from monetary liability and preserves alternative remedies such as injunctive or declaratory relief. Furthermore, the section does not shield directors from liability for actions taken in their capacity as officers of the corporation. For an amplification of these issues, see: Veasey, Finkelstein, and Bigler, "Delaware Supports Directors with a Three Legged

Stool of Limited Liability, Indemnification, and Insurance" (1987), 42 Business Lawyer 399; Hanks, "Evaluating Recent State Legislation on Director and Officer Liability Limitation and Indemnification" (1988), 43 Business Lawyer 1207.

Interestingly, since 1986, half of the state legislatures in the United States have adopted legislative amendments that shield corporate directors from liability for breach of the duty of care. See: Investment Responsibility Research Center, IRRC Corporate Governance Bulletin, vol. IV, no. 5, (Sept./Oct. 1987), at 155.

Brant Investments Ltd. v. KeepRite Inc.
(1991), 3 O.R. (3d) 289, 1991 CarswellOnt 133 (C.A.)

In *KeepRite*, a parent corporation (Inter-City Manufacturing Ltd., or "ICM") had a number of subsidiaries. One of these, which was 65% owned by a subsidiary of the parent, was Keeprite. Keeprite was a publicly held corporation, and the balance of the shares were in the hands of public shareholders. ICM decided to use its powers of control to merge Keeprite with two of its wholly-owned subsidiaries. It struck an independent committee of the board of directors to review the proposed terms of the transaction and to determine whether the transaction was fair to the public shareholders of Keeprite. The committee indicated that it would not endorse the merger unless (*inter alia*) the price paid to the public shareholders was increased. The full board approved the transaction on the basis of the changes recommended by the committee. A group of minority shareholders nonetheless sued, claiming that the transaction was oppressive to the interests of the minority shareholders.

MCKINLAY J.A.:

* * *

Onus of proof

The appellants submit that, in an application for relief under s. 234 (now s. 241), once a dissenting shareholder has shown that an impugned transaction involves benefits to one group of shareholders in which dissenting shareholders do not share, and a corresponding detriment to the dissenting shareholders which the other group of shareholders do not suffer, then the burden of proof rests upon the majority shareholders to demonstrate that: (a) the impugned transaction is at least as advantageous to the company and to all shareholders as any available alternative transaction; (b) that no undue pressure was applied to the company, its officers and directors, to accept the impugned transaction as proposed; and (c) that the substance of the impugned transaction and the process of decision-making leading to its acceptance were intrinsically fair to the dissenting shareholders.

No case was cited to us that would substantiate such broad and onerous legal requirements. In any event, the learned trial judge in his very careful reasons dealt with each question raised. He did not consider that there were benefits to ICG which were not shared by the dissenting shareholders, nor did he consider that the dissenting shareholders suffered a detriment which ICG did not suffer. A review of the evidence and of the trial judge's decision makes it clear that there was substantial evidence on which he could base such findings. That being so, the burden of proof which the appellants would have shifted to the respondents on the above-mentioned bases does not arise.

Anderson J. pointed out that possible solutions to KeepRite's problems suggested by the dissenting shareholders were considered and rejected by KeepRite management and by the independent committee. To suggest that directors are required, when entering into a transaction on behalf of the corporation, to consider every available alternative transaction is unrealistic. Any number of considerations may be relevant, if not vital, to the carrying out of a particular transaction at a particular time. In many cases, there will not be obvious or immediate alternatives. The extent to which directors should inquire as to alternatives is a business decision, which, if made honestly in the best interests of the corporation, should not be interfered with.

The appellants also take the position that the single fact that this was a non-arm's-length transaction shifts the burden of proof to the respondent. The only example of such a shift of onus cited to us was in *Sinclair Oil Corp. v. Levien*, 280 A.2d 717 (1971). The facts in that case were much stronger than the facts in this case. Sinclair Oil Corporation allegedly caused damage to its subsidiary, Sinclair Venezuelan Oil Company (Sinven), as a result of numerous acts, including causing the subsidiary to pay substantial dividends, denying industrial development to the subsidiary and causing breach of contract between that subsidiary and a wholly owned subsidiary of Sinclair. The case involved a derivative action by minority shareholders of Sinven for losses suffered by it as a result of its parent's actions. In that case, the fiduciary duty owed by the parent to the subsidiary resulted in a shifting of the burden of proof to Sinclair to show "intrinsic fairness" in the dealings between it and its subsidiary.

As pointed out by the appellants, courts in this jurisdiction have held that where a party who owes a fiduciary duty deals with trust property to his own personal benefit, a burden of proof, the nature of which will depend on the circumstances of the case, will rest on the fiduciary. There are undoubtedly other cases where proof of basic preliminary facts would warrant a shift of onus. Whether or not this is one of those cases we need not decide since, as pointed out by Anderson J., the respondents in this case assumed from the outset the burden of adducing evidence as to the nature of the transaction, the manner in which it was carried out, and the result. It was not merely the non-arm's-length nature of the transaction that made it, in the trial judge's words, "tactically sound" to do so. As many of the

necessary facts were solely in the knowledge of the respondents, the burden
of adducing evidence on those facts would have been theirs in any event.

Independent committee

The appellants attack the role of the independent committee on the
basis, first, that it was not, in fact, independent, and second, that the advice
given by the committee to the directors of KeepRite was not in the best
interests of the company and its shareholders.

With respect to the makeup of the committee, the evidence discloses
that all of its members were outside members of the board of KeepRite.
None was an officer or director of ICG. The three-member committee
comprised H. Purdy Crawford and John Edison, both solicitors, and Ross
Hanbury, a former partner of Wood, Gundy. Mr. Crawford became involved
with KeepRite in the winter of 1979 when the Odette Group retained him
and the law firm in which he was a senior partner in connection with the
possible acquisition of KeepRite. That group eventually became owners of
approximately 50 per cent of the shares of KeepRite. It was at the request
of the Odette Group that Mr. Crawford became a director of KeepRite. His
first encounter with ICG was at the time of its failed take-over bid for
KeepRite. He continued as a member of the board after ICG acquired its
interest in KeepRite in 1981. Mr. Edison had acted as legal adviser to the
founder of KeepRite from its inception, and had also acted for the company
over a number of years. He was a long term member of the KeepRite board.
Mr. Hanbury had been involved with KeepRite since the 1960s, when Wood,
Gundy was involved in a public offering of KeepRite shares. There is no
evidence of any involvement with ICG by any of these individuals.

The trial judge found as a fact that the members of the committee were
truly independent in the sense that they "felt at all times free to deal with
the impugned transaction upon its merits" (*Brant Investments*, *supra*, at p.
756 O.R.). There was more than adequate evidence to substantiate such a
finding.

* * *

The real complaint of the appellants on this appeal is that, rather than making
his own assessment of the value to KeepRite of the transaction, the learned
trial judge relied on the decision of the independent committee that the
transaction was of value to KeepRite because of the synergies and economics of scale involved. The appellants argue that, although reliance on investigations carried out by such a committee may be appropriate in some cases,
it is not appropriate in this case where, they argue, the committee itself did
not adequately assess the benefits of the transaction to KeepRite. The appellants criticize work of the independent committee on the following bases:

(a) the committee did not consider whether there were alternative
transactions open to KeepRite;

(b) the committee approved the transaction based upon assurances that certain "synergistic" benefits could be achieved by combining the businesses — they were aware of the need for a strategic plan to realize these benefits but proceeded without obtaining one;

(c) the committee never received a final report from the consultants retained to review management's assumptions concerning the anticipated synergies; and

(d) the committee did not commission a valuation of the Inter-City businesses on a going concern basis.

(a) Possible alternative transactions

The appellants argue that there were a number of alternative transactions available to KeepRite which were not considered by the independent committee, and they point specifically to three. First, they say that Wood, Gundy, KeepRite's financial advisers, and Mr. McKay, KeepRite's chief executive officer, believed that equity could be raised in the absence of an asset purchase. Mr. S.A. Jarislowsky, called by the appellants, testified that the dissenting shareholders would have looked favourably at supporting such an offering. I do not consider that Mr. Jarislowsky's after-the-fact evidence of such a position is of assistance. There was some evidence that an alternative suggestion was made by Mr. Jarislowsky on behalf of the dissenting shareholders prior to the carrying out of the transaction. However, it is not for the minority shareholders to dictate to corporate officers the manner in which they should deal with corporate problems. Whether or not the directors or the independent committee looked favourably on any suggestion by Mr. Jarislowsky is irrelevant unless it could be shown that he presented an alternative which was definitely available and clearly more beneficial to the company than the chosen transaction. However, the suggestion made by Mr. Jarislowsky was nothing more than that — a mere suggestion.

[The court reviewed the specific suggestions and concluded that the independent committee had canvassed these.]

It is clear from the evidence that the independent committee did consider some alternative possibilities for solving KeepRite's problems. It did so, however, in the context of a concrete proposal for the purchase of assets from the ICG companies. The evaluation of that proposal was the purpose for which the committee was struck. I agree with the words of the trial judge where he stated at pp. 757-58 O.R.:

There is nothing inherently wrong in a parent company making such a proposal to a subsidiary. Any difficulty arises because the transaction, if carried forward, will not be at arm's length. It was because of that aspect of the transaction, and to protect against the vices which may be involved, that the Independent Committee was called into existence. In my view, the committee was not thereupon called to make a wide-ranging search for alternatives, or in other words, to determine whether the proposal which had been made was the best possible solution to the problem. Its function was to determine whether the proposed transaction was fair and reasonable and of benefit to KeepRite and its shareholders.

(b) Strategic plan

The appellants argue that, although the independent committee was aware of the need for a strategic plan to realize the synergistic benefits of the transaction, they proceeded without obtaining such a plan. First of all, the evidence referred to by the appellants on this point does not reveal that the committee considered that a comprehensive "strategic plan" to realize synergistic benefits was necessary. Mr. Purdy Crawford, a witness with broad experience in corporation matters, indicated in his evidence that it is not unusual for decisions to be made with respect to very substantial acquisitions without any previously existing strategic plan. However, in this case, the committee and the directors of KeepRite considered it absolutely necessary in the situation in which KeepRite found itself that some action be taken which would alleviate the concerns of KeepRite's bankers.

Early in 1983 a task force comprised of representatives of both KeepRite and ICG was appointed to study and report on the merits of combining the air-conditioning business of KeepRite and the heating business of the Inter-City companies. In the process of the work of that task force, a background financial paper was prepared which analyzed the financial impact of combining the businesses. This financial analysis was filed as an exhibit at trial. It analyzed the anticipated synergies from the integration of the two operations, and the anticipated effect on the resulting balance sheet of KeepRite — both of which were very important for the purposes of KeepRite's bankers.

It is clear from the evidence that KeepRite did have a plan to realize the proposed benefits of the transaction, which was reviewed by the independent committee. There does not appear to have been a minutely detailed plan setting out projected day-by-day actions to be followed after closing of the transaction, but no one suggests that such a detailed plan was necessary, or even desirable.

(c) Consultants' report

The independent committee retained the firm of Crosbie, Armitage as consultants to assess the benefits of the proposed transaction to KeepRite. Crosbie, Armitage did, in fact, make an assessment of the anticipated synergistic benefits of the transaction. Allan Crosbie presented a report dated March 23, 1983 to a meeting of the independent committee on that same date. His report contained an appendix setting forth the main elements of the proposed business plan arising out of the transaction and a reasonably detailed financial analysis of the proposed acquisition. He made it clear in his report that the assumptions on which it was based were developed by KeepRite and ICG senior operating personnel in several working sessions in which Crosbie, Armitage participated. Thus, the underlying assumptions used in the financial analysis represented a consensus view of the senior management of the two companies. On the basis of the information contained in the report, it was Mr. Crosbie's opinion that:

> Not only are there important cost savings as a result of rationalization of the businesses, but in addition there are substantial increased sales opportunities.

At the meeting of the independent committee, Mr. Crosbie informed its members that the transaction appeared to him and his associates to make business sense. Mr. McKay informed the committee that senior management could successfully carry out the integration and business plan as set out in the Crosbie, Armitage report.

The appellants criticize the independent committee because it did not obtain a further final report from Crosbie, Armitage establishing their confirmation of some of the assumptions on which their original report was based. In my opinion, the fact that the committee did not require such a report in no way invalidates the opinion contained in the original report and conveyed orally to the committee by Mr. Crosbie. The learned trial judge considered it completely appropriate that the assumptions on which the report was based were developed by senior operating personnel of KeepRite and ICG, along with personnel of Crosbie, Armitage. I agree. Those individuals were not only the persons who had access to and familiarity with the relevant information, but many of them were also the officers who would be implementing the integrated business plan after the completion of the transaction. There was no suggestion that any of the information presented was inaccurate or misleading.

(d) Valuation of the Inter-City business on a going-concern basis

The appellants complain that:

> The Committee did not commission a valuation of the Inter-City businesses on a going-concern basis, even though Mr. McKay expressed concern about their profitability. The Inter-City businesses had substantial losses in 1982, and budgeted further losses for 1983. They were reviewed by Inter-City, KeepRite and at least two members of the Committee as only marginally profitable, if at all.

None of these allegations is disputed by the respondents. The two Inter-City businesses, the major assets of which were to be purchased by KeepRite, had not recently been profitable. KeepRite itself had suffered substantial losses in the 1982 fiscal year, was experiencing a decrease in its share of the market in its field, and was under substantial pressure from its bankers to acquire new equity financing. It was not the profitability of the businesses as separate entities that was of concern to the independent committee, but the benefits to KeepRite of combining their operations. It is probably worth while at this point to quote from the summary business plan included in the Crosbie, Armitage report, since it very concisely indicates what the expected benefits to KeepRite would be:

1.   KeepRite would acquire the assets and liabilities of the businesses of ICG Manufacturing and ICG Energy respectively, exclusive of the St. Catharines facility and deferred taxes.

2.   ICG's sheet metal business would be wound up on an orderly basis.

3.   The significant portion of ICG's St. Catharines manufacturing business would be integrated into KeepRite's Brantford manufacturing facility.

4.   KeepRite and ICG's sales and distribution components would be rationalized. Also, as part of this rationalization, ICG would terminate its existing distribution business and sell direct or through other distributors in a manner similar to KeepRite. As part of the restructuring of ICG's sales and marketing network, this should enable reductions in sales personnel and the amounts of finished goods inventory that would have to be carried.

5.   With the rationalization of the KeepRite and ICG selling and distribution networks, it is anticipated that sales of certain product lines in Canada, the US and offshore markets would be expanded slightly. In particular, in Canada, with the rationalization of KeepRite's and ICG's sales forces, domestic sales increases are projected; in the US, utilizing KeepRite's existing sales and distribution network, sales increases of selected ICG products are projected.

6.   As part of this overall program, provision is to be made for establishing a senior marketing group.

7.   As part of the rationalization program, KeepRite and ICG Manufacturing and Engineering personnel requirements would be rationalized with attendant savings in costs.

8.   As part of the rationalization program, KeepRite and ICG corporate administration, finance and EDP departments would be rationalized with attendant savings in costs.

The independent committee retained Price, Waterhouse, KeepRite's auditors, to review the statement of net book values of ICG assets as at March 31, 1983. Price, Waterhouse held discussions with Coopers & Lybrand, who had completed an audit of the Inter-City companies as at December 31, 1982. Price, Waterhouse presented its opinion to the committee that the net book values were appropriate and appeared to have been arrived at in accordance with generally accepted accounting principles.

Since KeepRite was purchasing assets for the purpose of combining the two operations, the committee did not consider a going-concern valuation to be necessary.

The trial judge was satisfied that the independent committee was aware of its mandate, was at all times conscious that this was not an arm's-length transaction, and appropriately carried out its function of assessing the benefits of the transaction to KeepRite. He was completely satisfied on the evidence that the committee carried out its function in an appropriate and independent manner. I see no reason whatever to doubt the correctness of that finding. Neither the evidence nor the argument persuades me that his findings were anything other than appropriate.

Business judgment and the oppression remedy

The appellants argue strongly that since the enactment of s. 234 (now s. 241) of the CBCA, it is no longer appropriate for a trial judge to delegate to directors of a corporation, or to a committee such as that established in this case, judgment as to the fairness of conduct complained of by dissenting shareholders. This is particularly important, they argue, because the persons to whom that judgment is delegated are the very persons whose conduct is under scrutiny. They argue that the trial judge in this case erred in his approach to the exercise of his jurisdiction under s. 234, when he stated, at pp. 759-60 O.R.:

> the court ought not to usurp the function of the board of directors in managing the company, nor should it eliminate or supplant the legitimate exercise of control by the majority . . . Business decisions, honestly made, should not be subjected to microscopic examination.

This, they argue, indicates that the trial judge declined to exercise independent judgment with respect to the fairness of essential aspects of the impugned transaction. Such a submission is, in my view, patently unfounded. The portion of the trial judge's reasons quoted above should be placed in context. The relevant portion of the reasons is quoted below (pp. 759-60 O.R.):

> The jurisdiction is one which must be exercised with care. On the one hand the minority shareholder must be protected from unfair treatment; that is the clearly expressed intent of the section. On the other hand the court ought not to usurp the function of the board of directors in managing the company, nor should it eliminate or supplant the legitimate exercise of control by the majority. In *Re Bright Pine Mills*

Pty. Ltd., 1969 V.R. 1002 (Supreme Court of Victoria), analogous
legislation to s. 234 was under consideration. At p. 1011 O'Bryan J.,
writing for the full court, says:

> It is true to say, however, that it was not intended . . . to give
> jurisdiction to the Court (a jurisdiction the courts have always
> been loath to assume) to interfere with the internal management
> of a company by directors who in the exercise of the powers
> conferred upon them by the memorandum and articles of associ-
> ation are acting honestly and without any purpose of advancing
> the interests of themselves or others of their choice at the expense
> of the company or contrary to the interests of other shareholders.

Although the statute there under consideration was confined to "oppression", I consider the caveat there expressed to apply with equal
force to the wider language of s. 234. Business decisions, honestly
made, should not be subjected to microscopic examination. There
should be no interference simply because a decision is unpopular with
the minority.

There can be no doubt that on an application under s. 234 the trial
judge is required to consider the nature of the impugned acts and the method
in which they were carried out. That does not mean that the trial judge
should substitute his own business judgment for that of managers, directors,
or a committee such as the one involved in assessing this transaction. Indeed,
it would generally be impossible for him to do so, regardless of the amount
of evidence before him. He is dealing with the matter at a different time and
place; it is unlikely that he will have the background knowledge and expertise of the individuals involved; he could have little or no knowledge of the
background and skills of the persons who would be carrying out any proposed plan; and it is unlikely that he would have any knowledge of the
specialized market in which the corporation operated. In short, he does not
know enough to make the business decision required. That does not mean
that he is not well equipped to make an objective assessment of the very
factors which s. 234 requires him to assess. Those factors have been discussed in some detail earlier in these reasons.

It is important to note that the learned trial judge did not say that
business decisions honestly made should not be subjected to examination.
What he said was that they should not be subjected to microscopic examination. In spite of those words, the learned trial judge did, in fact, scrutinize,
in a very detailed and careful manner, the nature of the transaction in this
case and the manner in which it was executed. Having carefully reviewed
the major aspects of the appellants' criticisms of the transaction, he came
to the conclusion that it in no way, either substantively or procedurally,
offended the provisions of s. 234. Having carefully reviewed all of the
exhibits and transcribed evidence to which we were referred, I have no
hesitation in agreeing with the correctness of his assessment.

The appellants refer specifically to two areas where they say the trial judge declined to exercise independent judgment with respect to the fairness of essential aspects of the transaction. These were:

(1) whether the impugned transaction was, in fact, for the benefit of KeepRite as a whole, or rather beneficial to Inter-City and detrimental to KeepRite; and

(2) whether the "earnings dilution" caused by the disparity in historical earnings between KeepRite and the Inter-City businesses resulted in unfairness to the dissenting shareholders.

With respect to the first argument, I can only say that the reasons of the trial judge indicate exactly the reverse. If anything, he took an excess of care in exercising independent judgment with respect to the fairness of the transaction.

With respect to the second, the trial judge in his reasons dealt with the question of the disparity in historical earnings between the ICG subsidiaries and KeepRite. He stated that the members of the independent committee and the directors were aware of these problems and considered that they had been overcome. The learned trial judge was of the view that this was a matter of business judgment and he was not disposed to intervene. The appellants argue that the disparity in historical earnings would inevitably result in an earnings dilution to the shareholders of KeepRite. Such a result was by no means inevitable. A large proportion of the assets transferred consisted of inventory and accounts receivable, the book value of which were guaranteed by ICG, and no interest was payable on the note given by KeepRite to ICG covering payment of the purchase price. The cash resulting from realization of the receivables and inventory would have the effect of reducing the bank borrowings of KeepRite, and the transaction was very favourably viewed by KeepRite's bankers. If, in addition, the anticipated synergies were realized (which it appears in retrospect they were) there would likely be an earnings enhancement per share rather than the "earnings dilution" alleged by the dissenting shareholders.

Question

1 There are clearly contrasting elements in the degree of deference afforded the board in *Brant* and *Van Gorkom*. Which do you prefer?

Pente Investment Management Ltd. v. Schneider Corp.
(1998), 42 O.R. (3d) 177, 1998 CarswellOnt 4035 (C.A.)

[In *Pente Investment Management Ltd.,* Maple Leaf made a takeover bid for the Schneider Corp., which the directors of Schneider thwarted by entering into a lock-up arrangement with another bidder (with the express approval of the company's controlling shareholders). The court dealt the issue of the onus of proof as follows:]

WEILER J.A.: The duty of directors when dealing with a bid that will change control of a company is a rapidly developing area of law and, as I have indicated, Canadian authorities dealing with the question of the onus, or burden of proof, have not been uniform. In Brant Investments, *supra*, the issue whether the burden of proof is on the directors to justify their actions as being in the best interests of the company or on the shareholders challenging the actions of the company was also raised. McKinlay J.A., at pp. 311-12, found it unnecessary to decide the question because the trial judge had dealt with the issues on a substantive basis, and his decision did not turn on which party had the onus or burden of proof. The same is true in the present case. I would add, however, that it may be that the burden of proof may not always rest on the same party when a change of control transaction is challenged. The real question is whether the directors of the target company successfully took steps to avoid a conflict of interest. If so, the rationale for shifting the burden of proof to the directors may not exist. If a board of directors has acted on the advice of a committee composed of persons having no conflict of interest, and that committee has acted independently, in good faith, and made an informed recommendation as to the best available transaction for the shareholders in the circumstances, the business judgment rule applies. The burden of proof is not an issue in such circumstances.

10. INDEMNIFICATION AND INSURANCE

RONALD J. DANIELS AND SUSAN M. HUTTON,
**"The Capricious Cushion: The Implications of the
Directors' and Officers' Insurance Liability Crisis on
Canadian Corporate Governance"**
(1993), 22 Can. Bus. L.J. 182

* * *

In this article we explore the dynamics of the Canadian directors' and officers' insurance market by focusing on the crisis that afflicted that market in the mid-1980s (the "D&O crisis"). The crisis involved a dramatic and unanticipated contraction in the availability of D&O insurance. By understanding the roots of that crisis, one can make some informed predictions respecting the availability and pricing of directors' and officers' insurance in Canada. Our conclusions are somewhat troubling for enthusiasts of enhanced legal liabilities for directors. Close examination of the D&O crisis reveals that the market is vulnerable to cyclical industry-wide fluctuations in capacity and pricing that greatly undermine the ability of directors to insure against the future costs of legal liability. These problems are exacerbated by market conventions which limit the effective duration of coverage (short policy and post-policy discovery periods).

Although a number of different independent theories have been proffered to explain the occurrence of the mid-1980s crisis in liability insurance, following Romano's study of the American D&O crisis, we prefer a multi-factorial explanation that draws on an amalgam of endogenous (industry) and exogenous (legal and market) components. This approach is congenial to the determination of the extent to which linkages between the American and Canadian economies affected the Canadian crisis. While we find evidence that American trends are being used to inform risk prediction in the Canadian D&O market, we argue that this is not evidence of undue market power possessed by American insurers (essentially a story positing cross subsidies from Canadian to American consumers), but is simply the result of statistical imperatives which limit the predictive significance of the Canadian loss experience.

* * *

II. THE RATIONALE FOR AND STRUCTURE OF D&O LIABILITY INSURANCE

By and large, most liberal scholars are willing to support government intervention designed to internalize the non-negotiated external costs of a given activity pursuant to Kaldor-Hicks notions of efficiency. Typically, this intervention takes the form of either property rights or liability rules that attempt to reconstruct the allocation of resources that fully informed parties would conclude through their transaction-costs-free bargaining. However, when the party generating external costs is a corporation, special problems are posed for courts and legislatures in determining the extent to which individual parties within the corporation should be held legally responsible for this activity, and the way in which this responsibility should interact with enterprise liability.

The issue of the appropriate scope for enterprise and personal liability is heightened in the case of directors who may not have been directly responsible for ordering the corporation to engage in certain socially undesirable types of activity, but are nevertheless held legally responsible for the consequences of this activity by virtue of their corporate status. This liability is commonly referred to as "gatekeeper liability", and is found in the various common law and statutory duties that officers and directors owe to shareholders, employees, creditors, suppliers and communities. The rationale for gatekeeper liability is based on the belief that the existing array of traditional sanctions and rewards pinpointing liability on the enterprise and on the actual wrongdoer within the enterprise are incapable of reducing the level of corporate wrongdoing to socially optimal levels. It is therefore necessary to enlist the services of third-party monitors, albeit under the threat of personal liability, to score further reductions in corporate wrongdoing.

Like other forms of civil liability, gatekeeper liability for corporate delicts will affect both the care and activity levels of targeted individuals. This is both the intended and obvious effect of deterrence-based liability rules. However, there is a danger that the rules imposing this liability will be given overly zealous interpretation by the courts, resulting in excessive levels of deterrence. This is of particular concern in the corporate case given managerial risk aversion and the prospect that the application of gatekeeper liability will be governed by compensatory rather than deterrence objectives.

To temper excessive care and activity level reactions to potential gatekeeper liability, modern corporate law statutes permit a corporation to indemnify a director for any expense reasonably incurred in defending, settling or satisfying a judgment for any action, provided that the director's fiduciary duty to act "honestly and in good faith and with a view to the best interests of the corporation" has been fulfilled. For indemnity with respect to criminal or administrative actions enforceable by fines, there must also have been reasonable grounds for believing that the conduct was lawful. This option to indemnify becomes an obligation if the director is substantially successful on the merits of the defence to any action, again so long as he or she acted honestly and in good faith with a view to the best interests of the corporation; and had reasonable grounds for believing that his or her conduct was lawful. The quality of corporate governance is upheld by this obligation since winning on a technicality, such as the expiration of a limitation period barring the action in question, does not give rise to a mandatory duty for the corporation to indemnify the successful director.

Modern corporations statutes also permit a corporation to purchase insurance for the benefit of a director against any liability which may be incurred in his or her capacity as a director, provided always that such liability does not result from a failure to act honestly and in good faith with a view to the best interests of the corporation. Corporations can, therefore, purchase insurance for directors with coverage for a wider range of behaviour than that for which direct corporate indemnification is allowed. Actions which are insurable but not indemnifiable include those for which objectively reasonable grounds did not exist, but in respect of which the director none the less acted honestly and in good faith; an example would be a successful shareholders' derivative action for negligence where the court refuses to permit indemnification.

Due to the different coverages of indemnification and D&O insurance, corporations typically purchase two types of D&O liability insurance coverage: Corporate Reimbursement Coverage, to cover losses to the corporation arising from the corporation's indemnification of a director, and Personal Coverage to cover the liability of a director for which he or she is not indemnified by the corporation and would otherwise be personally responsible. In addition to coverage for legal liabilities not permitted at law to be covered through corporate indemnification, Personal Coverage assures directors that they will not be forced to bear costs for which the corporation may lawfully indemnify them, but owing to financial hardship (*e.g.*, insolvency) cannot. Such coverage will also protect the officer and director against the failure of the corporation to remit withheld taxes to Revenue Canada or to pay employee wages that are due.

The supply side of the D&O insurance market is two-tiered, with "primary" insurers writing the policies and then reselling the coverage in excess of a certain designated loss liability (the so-called "excess" layer) to what are known as "reinsurers". The reinsurers are liable for a particular claim only after the original insurer has paid a designated amount — this retained amount is known as the "primary" layer. The reinsurers receive a portion of the premium commensurate to their portion of the risk, but also pay what is known as a "ceding" commission to the insurer that brings them the business. The capacity of the reinsurance market to underwrite risks has a profound effect upon the capacity of the primary insurers, particularly for such large and specialized risks as D&O policies, since it is through reinsurance that insurers themselves spread their risks and limit their potential liability.

* * *

(3) Summary

When one considers the proliferation of non-corporate law directorial duties, it may be that there was a greater expansion of Canadian directors' and officers' liability during the "crisis" years of the mid-1980s than there was in the United States. However, there are simply not enough reported cases in Canada on which to form a statistically sound evaluation, and claims data is of only minor assistance. Thus, the lack of sufficient claims experience prevented the industry from forming a conclusion as to how D&O policies would be interpreted by Canadian courts in the early crisis year of 1985.

Therefore, while Romano argues that an "anti-insurance" bias on the part of U.S. courts when interpreting D&O policies led to non-diversifiable risk and uncertainty and undermined the insurance function, the very lack of opportunity to interpret such documents in Canadian courts meant that no independent analysis of the risks of that or any other bias could be formed. D&O insurers have no choice but to apply the U.S. example to Canada, tempered of course by Canadian claims experience and such judgments as are in fact generated by the Canadian courts. With the trends in the United States in 1985-86 towards a stricter application of the negligence and fiduciary standards applicable to directors, towards increased statutory duties of directors, and towards strict interpretations of D&O policies against the insurer, D&O insurers operating in Canada raised the premiums here in anticipation of a similar, albeit more "Canadian" (that is, subdued), judicial trend.

The foregoing analysis of the nature and causes of the most recent crisis in Canadian D&O liability insurance lays to rest any fears that the crisis was the artificial creation of collusion or of foreign insurers seeking to cross-subsidize their losses in foreign markets. Rather, the evidence corresponds with Winter's theory of competitive insurance cycles operating in a climate of restrictions on costless equity infusions. As Winter concludes:

> in general a crisis will be characterized by an increase in premiums that is greater — possibly much greater — than could be "justified" by any increase in expected claims. This increase and the consequent increase in profits is consistent with a competitive market. The market-wide increase in profits does not imply collusion.

The Canadian D&O liability insurance crisis can thus be seen in the context of a crisis in liability insurance generally. After years of surplus supply, the investment income underwriting, and cheap and abundant reinsurance, a trend towards higher tort awards and more stringent standards of care in the United States and several severe storms in Europe caused the global reinsurance market to contract — seemingly overnight. The severe contraction of the supply of reinsurance, and the inability of the Canadian capital markets to finance independently the larger risks such as D&O coverage, had the most severe impact on the most uncertain lines. As Winter says, "The most uncertain lines will bear the brunt of shocks to the capacity of the entire market, absorbing and releasing capacity over the cycle."

The small and undeveloped nature of the Canadian D&O market means that the law of large numbers is inoperative and Canadian D&O policies cannot be underwritten as a completely separate market. Thus, the uncertainty generated by the changing application of directors' negligence standards in the United States and the policy of interpreting D&O contracts against the interests of the insurer had a profound impact on expected claims in Canada and discouraged a uniquely Canadian expansion in reinsurance supply. This impact was in addition to the direct influence warranted by the trading and corporate links between the two countries. The failure to see the Canadian D&O market separately from that in the U.S. is not the result of investor or consumer myopia but of the statistical requirements of the insurance industry and the relative lack of applicable judicial precedents in Canada.

Questions

1 What difficulties might you foresee in arrangements that allow a corporation to furnish compensation for suits brought by or on behalf of the corporation against directors and officers without any judicial supervision?

2 If the rationale for indemnification and insurance arrangements is tied to the impact of lawsuits on legitimate business decisions, is it not more appropriate to recommend amendments to corporate law statutes and judicial doctrines that give rise to liability in such circumstances in the first place? Several jurisdictions have introduced amendments to their corporate statutes in an effort to circumscribe the scope of liability. See, for example, the discussion surrounding Delaware's adoption of s. 102(b)(7), *supra*.

Chapter 6

Fiduciary Duties Owed by Directors and Managers to the Corporation

1. INTRODUCTION TO FIDUCIARY DUTIES

Fiduciary duties are legal norms that are imposed on directors and managers in relation to their conduct with the corporation and shareholders. Fiduciary duties may also affect the relationship between different shareholders of the corporation or between the shareholders and the corporation. These duties ensure that the myriad corporate actors carry out their respective duties with the utmost good faith, do not put themselves in a position where their duty may conflict with self-interest, and do not derive a secret profit from their office. Under CBCA s. 122(1)(a) and OBCA s. 134(1)(a), directors and officers are required to "act honestly and in good faith with a view to the best interests of the corporation" in exercising their powers and discharging their duties.

What is the rationale for introducing fiduciary duties into corporate law? A number of commentators have pointed to the pervasive use of fiduciary norms in a range of legal contexts, and have asserted that their inclusion demonstrates certain community values, such as responsibility, fairness, and integrity that the law wishes to foster in individual relationships. The difficulty, however, is that this rationale does not provide any principled way of delineating the scope of the duty in the corporate context. Moreover, it raises the important issue of the transportability of fiduciary duties derived from trust, agency, partnership and family law to the corporate context. Must fiduciary duties in the corporate context be as rigorous as those duties imposed in other legal settings?

Other commentators have sought to justify fiduciary duties on the basis of the agency model of corporate law. In this framework, fiduciary duties are conceived merely as instruments that control agency costs. According to Easterbrook and Fischel, "Corporate Control Transactions" (1982), 91 Yale L.J. 698, at p. 702:

> [fiduciary] rules (should) approximate the bargain that investors and agents would strike if they were able to dicker at no cost. Such rules preserve the gains resulting from the delegation of authority and the

division of labor while limiting the ability of agents to further their own interests at the expense of investors.

Easterbrook and Fischel's conception of fiduciary duties has been strongly criticized by Victor Brudney ("Corporate Governance, Agency Costs, and the Rhetoric of Contract" (1985), 85 Col. L. Rev. 1403) and by Robert Clark ("Agency Costs Versus Fiduciary Duties," in Pratt and Zeckhauser, Eds., *Principals and Agents: The Structure of Business* (1985), Ch. 3).

In the following materials, you should consider the role of the courts in enforcing fiduciary duties. What is the rationale for the imposition of the duties? What sorts of standards should be used to evaluate these duties? Do courts have a comparative advantage in the enforcement of these duties? Is there any role (primary or residual) for markets in controlling the misconduct that is subject to penalty through fiduciary duties?

You should also consider the impact of procedural rights and remedies on an aggrieved party's ability to bring a complaint alleging a breach of fiduciary duty against a corporate actor. Although this subject is dealt with at length in Chapter 11 (Shareholders' Remedies), you should be aware of the two principal ways in which a fiduciary complaint can be brought:

(i) derivative action, i.e., an action brought in the name of the corporation for a wrong done to the corporation as a whole; and

(ii) personal action, i.e., an action to vindicate certain rights that are *personal* to the shareholder.

In addition to these traditional remedies, an aggrieved party may also vindicate her rights under various statutory remedies, i.e., oppression, application for winding-up, right of dissent and appraisal, investigations, and compliance orders.

Although these rights are formally distinct from the substantive fiduciary duties discussed herein, they do, in fact, give expression to similar underlying concerns and can be viewed as being "quasi-fiduciary" in nature.

2. BASIC SELF-DEALING TRANSACTIONS

(a) Introduction to Basic Self-Dealing

Examination of basic self-dealing transactions provides a useful starting point for studying the appropriate scope of fiduciary duties. Essentially, self-dealing transactions involve contracts or transactions concluded between the directors and officers of a corporation, either directly or through their interest in another entity, and the corporation itself. The dangers entailed by self-dealing transactions are obvious: whenever an insider contracts with the corporation, the risk of diversion of corporate wealth is clear. That is, insiders contracting with the corporation operate under a strong incentive to cause the corporation to enter into transactions on terms that favour the insider. Although requiring directors to hold a direct stake in the corporation will dull the incentive to appropriate wealth via self-dealing, it will not eradicate it. This is because when unfair self-dealing occurs, the loss that the director sustains on her investment in the corporation from an interested transaction is likely to be more than offset by the gains she realizes in her personal capacity.

The simplest form of self-dealing transaction is the sale of an asset to the corporation by a director or officer at a price that exceeds the asset's fair market value (or, its converse, the purchase of an asset from the corporation by an officer or director at a price that is below fair market value). The price differential at the corporation's expense constitutes an "unbargained for" diversion of wealth from shareholders to the interested party. As such, the costs occasioned by self-dealing transactions constitute a form of agency cost.

The materials that follow discuss the judicial response to self-dealing transactions. They indicate a movement of the courts and the legislature from reliance on categorical prohibitions against self-dealing transactions to more flexible rules that consider the procedural and substantive fairness of self-interested transactions. The current statutory provisions governing self-dealing transactions in the CBCA and OBCA enshrine judicial review of a procedural and substantive nature.

In considering the evolution of legal rules in this area, you should be sensitive to the arguments favouring the adoption of different legal rules. To the extent that retreat from a categorical rule against self-dealing transactions is predicated on a recognition that certain benefits may be derived from self-dealing transactions, what are those benefits? Are they likely to be concentrated in certain types of contexts or corporations, and, if so, can legal rules be structured and applied such that beneficial self-dealing transactions are upheld, while unfair self-dealing transactions are invalidated? What are the costs to corporate actors of employing a selective or differential rule to evaluate self-dealing transactions, in terms of predicting the legal status of self-dealing transactions? What differences are involved in the nature of the inquiry implicated by the adoption of different rules, and are all the rules equally compatible with judicial expertise? Finally, what role, if any, is there for market forces in controlling or evaluating self-dealing transactions?

(b) The Common Law

Aberdeen Railway Co. v. Blaikie Bros.
[1843-60] All E.R. Rep. 249, 2 Eq. Rep. 1281 (H.L.)

[The company entered into a contract to purchase a quantity of chairs from a partnership. At the time that the contract was concluded, a director of the company was a member of the partnership. The court held that the company was entitled to avoid the contract.]

LORD CRANWORTH L.C.: The directors are a body to whom is delegated the duty of managing the general affairs of the company. A corporate body can only act by agents, and it is, of course, the duty of those agents so to act as best to promote the interests of the corporation whose affairs they are conducting. Such an agent has duties to discharge of a fiduciary character towards his principal, and it is a rule of universal application that no one having such duties to discharge shall be allowed to enter into engagements in which he has or can have a personal interest conflicting or which possibly may conflict with the interests of those whom he is bound to protect. So strictly is this principle adhered to that no question is allowed to be raised as to the fairness or unfairness of a contract so entered into. It obviously is, or may be, impossible to demonstrate how far in any particular case the terms of such a contract have been the best for the *cestui que trust* which it was impossible to obtain. It may sometimes happen that the terms on which a trustee has dealt or attempted to deal with the estate or interests of those for whom he is a trustee have been as good as could have been obtained from any other person; they may even at the time have been better. But still so inflexible is the rule that no inquiry on that subject is permitted. . . .

Was, then, Mr. Blaikie so acting in the case now before us? If he was, did he, while so acting, contract, on behalf of those for whom he was acting, with himself? Both these questions must obviously be answered in the affirmative. Mr. Blaikie was not only a director, but, if that was necessary, the chairman of the directors. In that character it was his bounden duty to make the best bargains he could for the benefit of the company. While he filled that character, *viz.*, on February 6, 1846, he entered into a contract on behalf of the company with his own firm for the purchase of a large quantity of chairs at a certain stipulated price. His duty to the company imposed on him the obligation of obtaining these iron chairs at the lowest possible price. His personal interest would lead him in an entirely opposite direction — would induce him to fix the price as high as possible. This is the very evil against which the rule in question is directed; and I see nothing whatever to prevent its application here. I observe that Lord Fullerton seemed to doubt whether the rule would apply where the party whose act or contract is called in question, is only one of a body of directors, not a sole trustee or manager. But, with all deference, this appears to me to make no difference. It was Mr. Blaikie's duty to give to his co-directors, and through them to the company, the full benefit of all the knowledge and skill which he could bring to bear on the subject. He was bound to assist them in getting the articles contracted for at the cheapest possible rate. As far as related to the advice he should give them, he put his interest in conflict with his duty, and whether he was the sole director, or only one of many, can make no difference in principle. The same observation applies to the fact, that he was not the sole person trading with the company. He was one of the firm of Blaikie Brothers with whom the contract was made, and so was interested in driving as hard a bargain with the company as he could induce them to make. . . .

Transvaal Lands Co. v. New Belgium (Transvaal) Land and Development Co.
[1914] 2 Ch. 488, 84 L.J. Ch. 94 (C.A.)

SWINFEN EADY L.J. read the judgment of the Court (Lord Cozens-Hardy M.R., Swinfen Eady L.J., and Pickford L.J.): The first question raised by this appeal is whether the purchase by the plaintiffs from the defendants of a block of 3333 ordinary shares of the Lydenberg (Transvaal) Gold Exploration Company, Limited, for 999*l*. 18*s*. was voidable at the plaintiffs' option.

On February 1, 1911, there was a board meeting of the plaintiff company at which there were present Sir F. Young, in the chair (an old gentleman upwards of ninety and since deceased), Mr. James William Harvey, since deceased, and Henry Samuel. At this board meeting a suggestion was made by Samuel that the company should buy shares in the Lydenberg Company, and the matter was adjourned to a special board meeting on February 8. Harvey appears to have known very little if anything about this company, as the next day he wrote to Crake, the secretary of the company, asking for particulars about it, and referring to Samuel's proposal that the company should purchase 1000*l*. worth of shares. Crake in reply sent certain particulars taken from the Stock Exchange Official Intelligence, from which it appeared that the company was registered in October, 1894, but had never yet paid any dividend. On February 6 Harvey wrote again to Crake, the secretary, saying that he did not understand why Samuel proposed the purchase of the Lydenberg shares. It afterwards, however, transpired that Samuel was pecuniarily interested in the transaction, and that one half of the shares which he proposed that the plaintiff company should purchase belonged to himself.

On February 8 the board meeting was held at which the purchase was resolved upon. Sir F. Young was in the chair, and there were also present Messrs. Harvey and Samuel. [His Lordship read the minute of what took place at the meeting and continued:]

At this time the plaintiffs' cash resources were small, and they had to mortgage their uncalled capital to their bankers to raise the 1000*l*. required to pay for these Lydenberg shares.

It appears from the evidence that Samuel did not disclose on February 8 that he had any interest in the proposed purchase. He merely abstained from voting, on the ground that he was a director of the selling company, and the two directors forming the quorum who voted were Sir F. Young and Harvey. Harvey, however, held 1000 shares in the selling company, and was thus also interested in the sale of the shares, which as confidential agent of the plaintiff company he was instrumental in buying for them.

We should mention that Harvey held the 1000 shares of the defendant company as trustee under his father-in-law's will, and that Harvey's wife was beneficially interested in one tenth of the shares, subject to her mother's life interest therein.

The question thus arises, can a director of a company, on behalf of the company, buy shares or other property from himself, or from a company in which he is pecuniarily interested?

In our opinion, it is not material whether the interest which Harvey had in the 1000 shares was as trustee, or whether the shares belonged to him beneficially. As trustee it was his duty to do his best and make the most of the trust estate for his cestuis que trust, and as beneficiary his interest was to do the best he could for himself; but in either case his duty or interest, as the case might be, would conflict with the duty which he owed to the company of which he was director.

The law was thus stated by Sir Richard Baggallay, in the Privy Council, in *North-West Transportation Co. v. Beatty* (1): "A director of a company is precluded from dealing, on behalf of the company, with himself, and from entering into engagements in which he has a personal interest conflicting, or which possibly may conflict, with the interests of those whom he is bound by fiduciary duty to protect; and this rule is as applicable to the case of one of several directors as to a managing or sole director." . . .

Where a director of a company has an interest as shareholder in another company or is in a fiduciary position towards and owes a duty to another company which is proposing to enter into engagements with the company of which he is a director, he is in our opinion within this rule. He has a personal interest within this rule or owes a duty which conflicts with his duty to the company of which he is a director. It is immaterial whether this conflicting interest belongs to him beneficially or as trustee for others. He is bound to do as well for his cestuis que trust as he would do for himself. Again the validity or invalidity of a transaction cannot depend upon the extent of the adverse interest of the fiduciary agent any more than upon how far in any particular case the terms of a contract have been the best obtainable for the interest of the cestui que trust, upon which subject no inquiry is permitted. . . .

With regard to the plaintiff company, this matter is regulated by article 98.

This is the only provision in the plaintiff company's articles modifying what would otherwise be the rule of law applicable, and enabling a director of the plaintiff company to be interested as a member of a company with which the plaintiff company is contracting; but it requires that the director shall disclose the nature of his interest, and shall not vote in respect of any contract in which he is concerned.

The provisions of this article were not observed when the resolution to purchase the Lydenberg shares was carried, as Harvey voted in favour of it, and without his vote being counted there was no quorum, whereof the defendants, the other contracting party, had full notice. The result is that the contract was voidable, and has been duly avoided, and the plaintiffs are accordingly entitled to have the purchase-money repaid, but they must return the Lydenberg shares.

It was not disputed by the appellants that if the first transaction in Lydenberg shares is voidable, by reason of Harvey's vote having carried it, the second transaction in the partly paid shares of the plaintiff company stands in no better position and is voidable also, and the like result must follow. In our opinion the judgment appealed from was right, and the appeal fails and should be dismissed.

Questions

1 How far does Lord Cranworth's principle of "a personal interest . . . which may possibly conflict" go? Why should the court apply an "inflexible" rule when the context and merits of a decision are examined in other commercial cases? This question continues to divide commentators and is one that you should reconsider in light of the cases that follow in this chapter.

2 Articles and by-laws similar to Article 98 in *Transvaal* became common to avoid the strictness of the equitable rule. Such a development was inevitable, particularly in the closely-held company and small public companies, where the directors normally did business with their "own" company. A problem soon arose, however, with the ambit of such exculpatory clauses, which ran from requiring no notice of interest whatsoever to a requirement of notice and refraining from voting.

3 The rationale for the strict rule enunciated in *Aberdeen* is related not only to the substantial potential for conflict between the director's narrow self-interest and her overriding duty to the corporation, but also to the disabilities inherent in the capacity of non-interested directors to serve as effective safeguards against the adoption of abusive transactions. Non-interested directors may be directly or indirectly influenced by interested directors in deciding to approve or disapprove an interested transaction. The danger of these influences undermining the integrity of disinterested director review is enhanced when the review occurs after the transaction has been consummated, and a refusal to ratify the interested transaction will render the interested director or officer vulnerable to a lawsuit. Eisenberg argues that, while disinterested directors may be willing to vote against the adoption of an interested transaction when it is first proposed, they are much less inclined to vote against a self-interested transaction when a negative vote exposes interested directors to a lawsuit. (See Eisenberg, "Self-Interested Transactions in Corporate Law" (1988), 13 J. Corp. L. 997.)

The Liquidators of the Imperial Mercantile Credit Association v. Edward John Coleman and John Watson Knight
[1873] L.R. 7 E. & I. App. 189 (H.L.)

[Coleman and Knight was a stock-brokerage firm which underwrote a debenture for Peto to raise money for the extension of a railway line. The firm charged a commission of 5 per cent. Coleman was also a director of the Imperial Mercantile Credit Association and made a proposal to the Association for it to place the same debenture for a commission of 1 per cent. Before the Board approved this transaction, Coleman disclosed that he had a 1½ per cent interest in it.

The following extracts deal with Coleman's failure to make adequate disclosure of his interest in the transaction as required in the company's articles (by-laws), and his accountability for the profit made by him and his partnership.]

LORD CHELMSFORD: But it must be observed that the words of the article are not "to declare that he has an interest," but to "declare *his* interest," which seem to involve not merely the declaration of the existence of an interest but the nature of that interest. For surely when the directors are to determine whether they will enter into any contract, or order any work to be done for the company in which a brother director is interested, it may be a most important element in their consideration what the nature of the interest is which is required to be declared. For instance, in this case Mr. Coleman secures a commission of 5 per cent upon placing the debentures of the railway company. He conceals the fact at the time when it ought to be disclosed, and gets the directors to take the whole risk of placing the debentures upon the association for a commission of 1½ per cent, while for his own share of the transaction he is receiving a commission of 3½ per cent without any risk. If the directors had been fully informed of the real state of things, would they have accepted the proposal, and ought they to have done so as trustees for the shareholders?

It was, however, contended that Messrs. Knight & Coleman were known to be stockbrokers, and that, therefore, declaring that they had an interest in the transaction, conveyed all the requisite information that they were interested in that character. It was answered, however, that the commission of brokers upon placing shares and debentures varied considerably according to the varying character of each transaction; and, therefore, the knowledge that Messrs. Knight & Coleman were acting as stockbrokers afforded very scanty information as to the nature of their interest. Indeed, Mr. Coleman himself has given a complete answer to this suggestion, for in an affidavit made by him, to which I have already referred, he says: — "The undertaking such a liability as the placing of the debentures in question, amounting to £356,300, was a matter from its magnitude and character wholly beyond the ordinary business of stockbrokers, and for which there were and could be no ordinary or recognized terms of remuneration." He says "that the 'usual' broker's commission has no reference to such a matter, and it was and could necessarily only be a matter of contract between the brokers and principals engaged in such a transaction." There was, therefore, the more reason for disclosing the real nature of the transaction . . .

[LORD CHELMSFORD explained the basis of liability of the Respondent, Knight, Coleman's partner, as follows:] Mr. Knight had been ignorant that the money which was brought into the partnership was money obtained by his partner by a dereliction of duty, and that it was in law the money of the association, he might have had a good defence. But he was a party to and implicated in the breach of trust. He was acquainted with the whole transaction from first to last. He knew where the money which was brought into the partnership came from, and that it could not belong to his co-partner. With all this knowledge the liability of Mr. Knight cannot be separated from that of Mr. Coleman. They are, therefore, both of them liable to refund the sum of money which was carried to the account of the partnership, *minus* a sum of £1233 15*s*., being 3½ per cent on debentures amounting to £35,000 which were not placed nor guaranteed by the association, but which were sold on behalf of, and accounted for to, the railway company.

Question

Why did the court in *Imperial Mercantile* require more than a mere disclosure of a conflict of interest? Eisenberg argues that the mere disclosure of a conflict is often insufficient to alert the corporation to the prospect of abuse by the interested party. This is because the relationship between the corporation and its directors is predicated on trust and confidence. Explicit disclosure of the nature of an interested party's interest is necessary to "put the corporation on guard". Melvin Eisenberg, "Self-Interested Transactions in Corporate Law", *supra*.

Gray v. New Augarita Porcupine Mines Ltd.
[1952] 3 D.L.R. 1 (P.C.)

New Augarita Porcupine Mines Ltd. ("the Company") had no establishment of its own. Its business was conducted in the law office of Gray, who was vice-president, chairman of the Board, and the Company's solicitor. The by-laws required a Board of five directors, of whom three should form a quorum, and precluded a director from voting on any contract or arrangement in which he was interested. During the period in which Gray had self-dealings with the Company, there were only two other directors. One was an accountant and the other a typist, both employed by Gray's law office. The Company had an authorized capital of three million shares of one dollar each; all except five shares could be issued at a discount of ninety-nine per cent.

During the relevant period, Gray, among other transactions, issued shares to himself at a discount of eighty per cent; caused the Company to purchase from him, at a price determined by him, various mining claims in consideration of fully paid shares and sums of cash; caused the Company to purchase from him, for cash, holdings of speculative shares in other mining ventures in which he was interested; and made drawings upon the Company's bank account for his own purposes. Company records were not kept in a manner such that the extent of Gray's misappropriations could be determined. Shortly after the Ontario Securities Commission became interested in the activities of the Company, the accountant and the typist resigned as directors and four new directors were appointed. At a meeting of the new Board, Gray made a proposal to extinguish all his liabilities to the Company for a fixed sum. Gray's proposal was approved by the Board without the Board knowing the nature of Gray's interest in the agreement and the extent of his real liability to the Company. The effect of the agreement was that Gray stood to gain substantially from the settlement.

[The following extract from Lord Radcliffe's judgment discusses the degree of disclosure required of a director who enters into a contract with his own company.]

LORD RADCLIFFE: It is beyond dispute that there are certain special obligations upon a director who places himself in the position of contracting with his company. The general principle is that such a contract is not binding on the company, for a director is not entitled to place himself in a position in which his interest is in conflict with his duty. The company, it has been said, has a right to the services of its directors as an entire Board. Even if the contract is not avoided, whether because the company elects to affirm it or because circumstances have rendered it incapable of rescission, the director remains accountable to the company for any profit that he may have realized by the deal. Subject to any statutory requirements that cannot be dispensed with, it is open to companies to make such provisions as they please for the purpose of modifying the incidence of this general principle. By-laws 54 and 55 of the Company's by-laws are designed to achieve just such a modification: s. 94 of the *Companies Act* (R.S.O. 1937, c. 251) supplied the statutory requirements to which the by-laws were subjected. In the result Gray as a director was not precluded from entering into contracts or arrangements with the Company, but he was not permitted to vote upon a Board resolution dealing with such a contract or arrangement and he could only retain for himself any profit arising from the transaction if at the meeting which passed the resolution he had disclosed to his colleagues "the nature of his interest".

* * *

A director who wishes to keep for himself the benefit arising from some deal with his company has to establish that he has satisfied all necessary conditions. The onus is upon him. But it seems fairly plain that in this case Gray made no such disclosure as was required. He came to the meeting under very heavy liabilities towards the Company; he had been making large profits out of his transactions in the shares that he had allotted to himself, he had been making liberal use of the Company's funds for his own purposes. He left the meeting with all those liabilities extinguished for a secured payment of $18,765, a sum which charged him with the equivalent of no more than his ostensible issue price for the shares and which ignored altogether the benefits that he may have obtained from the use of the Company's funds. It was imperative that he should reveal to his colleagues before they voted the fact that to settle with him on the basis of 20 cents per share was to release him from liability at a price that was singularly favourable to himself. The nature of his interest in the agreement proposed consisted of just this fact that he stood to gain so much by the transaction and only he at the time had the means of knowing how much. There is no precise formula that will determine the extent of detail that is called for when a director declares his interest or the nature of his interest. Rightly understood, the two things mean the same. The amount of detail required must depend in each case upon the nature of the contract or arrangement proposed and the context in which it arises. It can rarely be enough for a director to say "I must remind you that I am interested" and to leave it at that, unless there is some special provision in a company's articles that makes such a general warning sufficient. His declaration must make his colleagues "fully informed of the real state of things" (see *Imperial Mercantile Credit Ass'n v. Coleman* (1873), L.R. 6 H.L. 189 at p. 201, *per* Lord Chelmsford). If it is material to their judgment that they should know not merely that he has an interest, but what it is and how far it goes, then he must see to it that they are informed (see Lord Cairns in the same case at p. 205). Tried by any test of this sort Gray's action falls short of what was required.

(c) Legislative Response

Section 120 of the CBCA is a legislative attempt to regulate contracts with directors or officers through a full disclosure mechanism. Compare s. 132 of the OBCA, especially ss. (7), (8) and (9). The legislation raises a number of issues, including the following:

(i) When is a contract "material"? What is a "material" interest? Who will make that determination? Should the legislation set guidelines, *e.g.*, a dollar amount, a percentage of sales, a percentage of shareholding?

(ii) Why is disclosure made only to one's fellow directors if ratification is not involved? Why should not the annual information circular inform shareholders of contracts or transactions in which the directors were interested?

(iii) What is the rationale for the single, general notice of s. 120(6)? Does it defeat the purpose of requiring disclosure of "the nature and extent of his interest" in s. 120(1)?

(iv) Section 120(5) prohibits an interested director from voting on any resolution to approve the contract except in the listed exceptions. May a director vote his shares as shareholder to ratify such a transaction under ss. (7.1)? If so, why?

(v) Section 57(s) of the CBCA Regulations (Management Proxy Circular) requires disclosure of transactions in which directors or officers were interested in the past year. Can you advise a client by reading s. 57(s) as to when disclosure must be made? Consider also s. 58 as to when disclosure of a transaction or interest may be omitted. Note s. 57(r)(i) with respect to disclosure of loans to directors.

3. CORPORATE OPPORTUNITIES

(a) Introduction to Corporate Opportunities

In the normal course of their activities, directors and managers of the corporation are required to evaluate a range of projects in order to determine whether the corporation should invest in them. In the normal course of affairs, a project will be recommended to the corporation if the project's benefits exceed its costs. The materials in the following section deal with the problems that arise when persons operating in a fiduciary relationship to the corporation independently invest in a project that could have been acquired by the corporation. Like self-dealing transactions, investment by a director or manager in such projects is problematic because valuable opportunities may be diverted from the corporation to directors and officers acting in a personal capacity.

One way to control such conduct is to impose fiduciary duties upon directors and officers that limit their ability to "take" opportunities belonging to the corporation. The difficulty, however, is that there is no clear agreement on the criteria that determine when a transaction "belongs" to the corporation. Must the project be in the corporation's line of business for a conflict to arise? Does an opportunity belong to the corporation solely on the basis of the profiteer having been made aware of the opportunity because of her connection with the corporation? What effect does a corporation's inability to exploit an opportunity (owing to financial, legal or managerial impediments) have on determining whether the project belongs to the corporation? Does an opportunity still "belong" to the corporation if it has been considered and rejected by the corporation? Finally, as in the case of self-dealing transactions, is there an argument for imposing different rules on directors and managers depending on the context in which the transaction arises?

The theory used to evaluate these cases is, of course, similar to the theory utilized to analyze other conflict transactions. At heart, the issue is simply one of determining whether the director or manager has usurped the authority granted to her by the shareholders of the corporation in order to acquire some "unbargained for" personal benefit. As such, corporate opportunities represent another instance of agency costs, and invite control through judicial sanction.

(b) The Common Law

Cook v. Deeks
[1916] 1 A.C. 554, 85 L.J.P.C. 161 (Ontario P.C.)

LORD BUCKMASTER L.C. (*per curiam*): The South Shore contract is the one which has given rise to the present dispute, and it is of the utmost importance to follow closely the circumstances under which it was obtained. The representative of the Canadian Pacific Railway Company was a Mr. Leonard, and it was he who arranged some, though it is impossible to say how many, of the contracts effected with the Toronto Construction Company on behalf of the railway company. His negotiations were always carried out either with Mr. Deeks or with Mr. Hinds. He never discussed any details with any other person, and he never saw the plaintiff in the office, though he sometimes saw him on the line. The management of Messrs. Deeks and Hinds of the affairs of the construction company was eminently satisfactory; but so far as railway construction was concerned the whole of their reputation for the efficient conduct of their business had been gained by them while acting as directors of the Toronto Construction Company. In 1911, and probably at an earlier date, the three defendants had settled that they would no longer continue business relationships with the plaintiff. It is unnecessary to seek the cause of the quarrel, or to determine whether they had good reason for the opinion that they had formed. There was nothing to compel them to work with or for the plaintiff, and it is impossible to see that they were bound to continue their relationship with him by any legal or moral consideration. They were, however, involved with him in different reciprocal duties, by reason of their relationship in connection with the Toronto Construction Company, and if they desired freedom to act, without regard to the restrictions that those relationships imposed, it was necessary that they should terminate their position as directors and shareholders in the company and place it in dissolution. This they could easily have accomplished owing to the fact that they held three-fourths of the share capital. It is suggested that they might also have resolved at a general meeting of the company that the company should no longer continue the work. This would have been all but equivalent to a resolution of voluntary liquidation; but even this step was not taken. While still retaining their position as directors, while still actually acting as managers of the company, and with their duties to the company of which the plaintiff was a shareholder entirely unchanged, they proceeded to negotiate with Mr. Leonard for the new Shore Line contract, in reality on their own behalf, but in exactly the same manner as they had always acted for the company, and doubtless with their claims enforced by the expeditious manner in which they, while acting for the company, had caused the last contract to be carried through.

The negotiations for this contract were opened by a telephone message sent through to Mr. Hinds at the Toronto Construction Company's office.

Upon receipt of that message certain units of price were prepared in the company's office, and, the prices being ultimately fixed, the defendant Hinds was informed by Mr. Leonard that, although the prices had been agreed to, the contract would not be then immediately let, as it was necessary that there should be an appropriation of the necessary cash made to authorize the contract by the Canadian Pacific Railway Company.

During the whole of this discussion, up till the time when these prices were fixed, it does not appear that at any moment the representatives of the Canadian Pacific Railway Company were told that this contract was in any way different from the others that had been negotiated in the same manner on behalf of the Toronto Construction Company, although it was plain that Mr. Leonard had been told by Mr. Deeks, when he was engaged on the Georgian Bay and Seaboard line, that when it was finished Messrs. Deeks and Hinds intended to go on their own account and leave Mr. Cook. But after all the necessary preliminaries of the contract had been concluded Mr. Hinds made to Mr. Leonard this statement: "Remember, if we get this contract it is to be Deeks and I, and not the Toronto Construction Company."

Two questions of law arise out of this long history of fact. The first is whether, apart altogether from the subsequent resolutions, the company would have been at liberty to claim from the three defendants the benefit of the contract which they had obtained from the Canadian Pacific Railway Company; and the second, which only arises if the first be answered in the affirmative, whether in such event the majority of the shareholders of the company constituted by the three defendants could ratify and approve of what was done and thereby release all claim against the directors.

It is the latter question to which the Appellate Division of the Supreme Court of Ontario have given most consideration, but the former needs to be carefully examined in order to ascertain the circumstances upon which the latter question depends.

It cannot be properly answered by considering the abstract relationship of directors and companies; the real matter for determination is what, in the special circumstances of this case, was the relationship that existed between Messrs. Deeks and Hinds and the company that they controlled. Now it appears plain that the entire management of the company, so far as obtaining and executing contracts in the east was concerned, was in their hands, and, indeed, it was in part this fact which was one of the causes of their disagreement with the plaintiff. The way they used this position is perfectly plain. They accelerated the work on the expiring contract of the company in order to stand well with the Canadian Pacific Railway when the next contract should be offered, and although Mr. McLean was told that the acceleration was to enable the company to get the new contract, yet they never allowed the company to have any chances whatever of acquiring the benefit, and avoided letting their co-director have any knowledge of the matter. Their Lordships think that the statement of the trial judge upon this point is well founded when he said that "it is hard to resist the inference that Mr. Hinds was careful to avoid anything which would waken Mr. Cook from his fancied security," and again, that "the sole and only object on the part of the defendants was to get rid of a business associate whom they deemed, and I think rightly deemed, unsatisfactory from a business stand-point." In other words, they intentionally concealed all circumstances relating to their negotiations until a point had been reached when the whole arrangement had been concluded in their own favour and there was no longer any real chance that there could be any interference with their plans. This means that while entrusted with the conduct of the affairs of the company they deliberately designed to exclude, and used their influence and position to exclude, the company whose interest it was their first duty to protect.

It is quite possible to enter into the speculation which form part of the examination of Mr. Leonard and Mr. Ramsay on behalf of the Canadian Pacific Railway. What might have happened if the railway company from the first considered Mr. Cook as a possible competitor, or considered the position of the Toronto Construction Company apart from Messrs. Deeks and Hinds, is a matter too conjectural to be brought into consideration. Their Lordships think that the Appellate Division of the Supreme Court of Ontario may have been misled in the attempts that they made to see whether this particular duty of the defendants had been the subject of previous judicial decision. Their Lordships see no reason to differ from the opinion which the Appellate Division extracted from careful consideration of the authorities, except so far as they were led by these conclusions to regard the transaction as a question of policy and a matter that lay entirely within the directors' individual discretion. But this reservation is important, for throughout the whole of the judgments, both of the learned judge who tried this case and of the Appellate Division, there is underlying rather the question as to whether the transaction was not one which, by virtue of their preponderating influence in the company, the defendants would be able ultimately to put right than the real question of whether it was one into which, consistently with their duty, they were at liberty to enter.

It is quite right to point out the importance of avoiding the establishment of rules as to directors' duties which would impose upon them burdens so heavy and responsibilities so great that men of good position would hesitate to accept the office. But, on the other hand, men who assume the complete control of a company's business must remember that they are not at liberty to sacrifice the interests which they are bound to protect, and, while ostensibly acting for the company, divert in their own favour business which should properly belong to the company they represent.

Their Lordships think that, in the circumstances, the defendants T.R. Hinds and G.S. and G.M. Deeks were guilty of a distinct breach of duty in the course they took to secure the contract, and that they cannot retain the benefit of such contract for themselves, but must be regarded as holding it on behalf of the company.

There remains the more difficult consideration of whether this position can be made regular by resolutions of the company controlled by the votes of these three defendants. The Supreme Court have given this matter the most careful consideration, but their Lordships are unable to agree with the conclusion which they reached.

In their Lordships' opinion the Supreme Court has insufficiently recognized the distinction between two classes of case and has applied the principles applicable to the case of a director selling to his company property which was in equity as well as at law his own, and which he could dispose of as he thought fit, to the case of a director dealing with property which, though his own at law, in equity belonged to his company. The cases of *North-West Transportation Co. v. Beatty* and *Burland v. Earle* both belonged to the former class. In each, directors had sold to the company property in which the company had no interest at law or in equity. If the company claimed any interest by reason of the transaction, it could only be by affirming the sale, in which case such sale, though initially voidable, would be validated by subsequent ratification. If the company refused to affirm the sale the transaction would be set aside and the parties restored to their former position, the directors getting the property and the company receiving back the purchase price. There would be no middle course. The company could not insist on retaining the property while paying less than the price agreed. This would be for the Court to make a new contract between the parties. It would be quite another thing if the director had originally acquired the property which he sold to his company under circumstances which made it in equity the property of the company. The distinction to which their Lordships have drawn attention is expressly recognized by Lord Davey in *Burland v. Earle* and is the foundation of the judgment in *North-West Transportation Co. v. Beatty*, and is clearly explained in the case of *Jacobus Marler Estates v. Marler*, a case which has not hitherto appeared in any of the well-known reports.

If, as their Lordships find on the facts, the contract in question was entered into under such circumstances that the directors could not retain the benefit of it for themselves, then it belonged in equity to the company and ought to have been dealt with as an asset of the company. Even supposing it be not *ultra vires* of a company to make a present to its directors, it appears quite certain that directors holding a majority of votes would not be permitted to make a present to themselves. This would be to allow a majority to oppress the minority. To such circumstances the case of *North-West Transportation Co. v. Beatty* and *Burland v. Earle* have no application. In the same way, if directors have acquired for themselves property or rights which they must be regarded as holding on behalf of the company, a resolution that the rights of the company should be disregarded in the matter would amount to forfeiting the interest and property of the minority of shareholders in favour of the majority, and that by the votes of those who are interested in securing the property for themselves. Such use of voting power has never been sanctioned by the Courts, and, indeed, was expressly disapproved in the case of *Menier v. Hooper's Telegraph Works*.

If their Lordships took the view that, in the circumstances of this case, the directors had exercised a discretion or decided on a matter of policy (the view which appears to have been entertained by the Supreme Court) different results would ensue, but this is not a conclusion which their Lordships are able to accept. It follows that the defendants must account to the Toronto Company for the profits which they have made out of the transaction. Their Lordships will therefore humbly advise His Majesty that the judgments of Middleton J. and of the Appellate Division be set aside, and that the case be referred back to the High Court Division of the Supreme Court of Ontario for the purpose of taking such account.

Note

Lord Buckmaster suggests that, as the defendants held three-fourths of the issued share capital, they could have secured their freedom to act by placing the company in dissolution. Would that have enabled them then to take up the South Shore contract free of any obligation to the plaintiff? What if, as suggested, they had caused the company to pass a resolution stating that it was no longer interested in work for the C.P.R.? Lord Buckmaster referred to the use of the majority's voting power in *Menier v. Hooper's Telegraph Works* (1874), 9 Ch. App. 350, 43 L.J. Ch. 330 (Ch. Div.). In that case, A held a controlling interest in B. In order to take for itself a contract in which B was interested, A used its votes to cause B to be placed in voluntary liquidation. James L.J. held as follows:

> The case made by the bill is very shortly this: The defendants, who have a majority of shares in the company, have made an arrangement by which they have dealt with matters affecting the whole company, the interest in which belongs to the minority as well as to the majority. They have dealt with them in consideration of their obtaining for themselves certain advantages. Hooper's Company have obtained certain advantages by dealing with something which was the property of the whole company. The minority of the shareholders say in effect that the majority has divided the assets of the company, more or less, between themselves, to the exclusion of the minority. I think it would be a shocking thing if that could be done, because if so the majority might divide the whole assets of the company, and pass a resolution that everything must be given to them, and that the minority should have nothing to do with it. Assuming the case to be as alleged by the bill, then the majority have put something into their pockets at the expense of the minority. If so, it appears to me that the minority have a right to have their share of the benefits ascertained for them in the best way in which the court can do it, and given to them.

Regal (Hastings) Ltd. v. Gulliver
[1942] 1 All E.R. 378 (H.L.)

The appellant company were the owners of a cinema in Hastings. With a view to the sale of the property of the company as a going concern they were anxious to acquire two other cinemas in Hastings. For this purpose they formed a subsidiary company with a capital of £50,000 in £1 shares. They were offered a lease of the two cinemas, but the landlord required a guarantee of the rent by the directors unless the paid-up capital of the subsidiary company was £5,000. The intention of the directors of the appellant company was that the appellant company should hold all the shares in the subsidiary company, and, since the appellant company at that time was unable to provide more than £2,000, it seemed that the directors would be obliged to give the required guarantee. The directors wished to avoid giving this guarantee, and the matter was arranged in this way. The appellant company was to take up 2,000 shares at par; the chairman of the directors promised to find £500; the other directors promised to do the same; and Garton, who was the solicitor to the appellant company, also promised to provide £500. This arrangement was made at a board meeting to which the directors and Garton were called by two notices, one of a board meeting of the appellant company and the other of a board meeting of the subsidiary company. Both meetings were to be held at the same time and place. In fulfillment of the arrangement 2,000 shares were allotted to the appellant company; 500 to each of the directors and Garton, but the shares in respect of the £500 "found" by the chairman of the directors were allotted to and paid for by two companies and one private individual, so that the companies and the individual took as beneficial owners and not as nominees of the chairman. At the same meeting, the board accepted a £92,500 offer for its interest in the three theatres, £77,500 being allocated to Regal's theatre and £5,000 to the leasehold interest in the other two. Ultimately the transaction was not carried through by the sale of the property of the company as a going concern, but by the sale of all the shares in the appellant company and in the subsidiary company. The 3,000 shares in the subsidiary company which were allotted to or on behalf of the directors of the appellant company and Garton were sold at a profit of £2 16s. 1d. per share. It was found as a fact that all the transactions were *bona fide*.

As a sequel to the sale of the shares in Regal, the company came under the management of a new board of directors, who caused to be issued the writ which initiated the litigation. By this action Regal sought to recover from its five former directors and its former solicitor a sum of £8,142, 10s. either as damages or as money had and received to the plaintiffs' use. The action was tried by Wrottesley J., who entered judgment for all the defendants with costs. An appeal by the plaintiffs to the Court of Appeal was dismissed with costs.

LORD RUSSELL OF KILLOWEN: The rule of equity which insists on those, who by use of a fiduciary position make a profit, being liable to account for that profit, in no way depends on fraud, or absence of *bona fides*; or upon such questions or considerations as whether the profit would or should otherwise have gone to the plaintiff, or whether the profiteer was under a duty to obtain the source of the profit for the plaintiff, or whether he took a risk or acted as he did for the benefit of the plaintiff, or whether the plaintiff has in fact been damaged or benefitted by his action. The liability arises from the mere fact of a profit having, in the stated circumstances, been made. The profiteer, however honest and well-intentioned, cannot escape the risk of being called upon to account.

The leading case of *Keech v. Sandford* is an illustration of the strictness of this rule of equity in this regard, and of how far the rule is independent of these outside considerations. A lease of the profits of a market had been devised to a trustee for the benefit of an infant. A renewal on behalf of the infant was refused. It was absolutely unobtainable. The trustee, finding that it was impossible to get a renewal for the benefit of the infant, took a lease for his own benefit. Though his duty to obtain it for the infant was incapable of performance, nevertheless he was ordered to assign the lease to the infant, upon the bare ground that, if a trustee on the refusal to renew might have a lease for himself, few renewals would be made for the benefit of *cestuis que trust*. Lord King L.C., said at p. 62:

> This may seem hard, that the trustee is the only person of all mankind who might not have the lease: but it is very proper that the rule should be strictly pursued, and not in the least relaxed . . .

One other case in equity may be referred to in this connection, *viz.*, *Ex p. James*, decided by Lord Eldon L.C. That was a case of a purchase of a bankrupt's estate by the solicitor to the commission, and Lord Eldon L.C., refers to the doctrine thus, at p. 345:

> This doctrine as to purchases by trustees, assignees, and persons having a confidential character, stands much more upon general principles than upon the circumstances of any individual case. It rests upon this: that the purchase is not permitted in any case however honest the circumstances; the general interests of justice requiring it to be destroyed in every instance; as no court is equal to the examination and ascertainment of the truth in much the greater number of cases.

Let me now consider whether the essential matters, which the plaintiff must prove, have been established in the present case. As to the profit being in fact made there can be no doubt. The shares were acquired at par and were sold three weeks later at a profit of £2 16s. 1d. per share. Did such of the first five respondents as acquired these very profitable shares acquire them by reason and in course of their office of directors of Regal? In my opinion, when the facts are examined and appreciated, the answer can only be that they did. The actual allotment no doubt had to be made by themselves and Garton (or some of them) in their capacity as directors of Amalgamated; but this was merely an executive act, necessitated by the alteration of the scheme for the acquisition of the lease of the two cinemas for the sole benefit of Regal and its shareholders through Regal's shareholding in Amalgamated. That scheme could only be altered by or with the consent of the Regal board. Consider what in fact took place on Oct. 2, 1935. The position immediately before that day is stated in Garton's letter of Sept. 26, 1935. The directors were willing to guarantee the rent until the subscribed capital of Amalgamated reached £5,000. Regal was to control Amalgamated and own the whole of its share capital, with the consequence that the Regal shareholders would receive their proportion of the sale price of the two new cinemas. The respondents then meet on Oct. 2, 1935. They have before them an offer to purchase the Regal cinema for £77,500, and the lease of the two cinemas for £15,000. The offer is accepted. The draft lease is approved and a resolution for its sealing is passed in anticipation of completion in five days. Some of those present, however, shy at giving guarantees, and accordingly the scheme is changed by the Regal directors in a vital respect. It is agreed that a guarantee shall be avoided by the six respondents bringing the subscribed capital up to £5,000. I will consider the evidence and the minute in a moment. The result of this change of scheme (which only the Regal directors could bring about) may not have been appreciated by them at the time; but its effect upon their company and its shareholders was striking. In the first place, Regal would no longer control Amalgamated, or own the whole of its share capital. The action of its directors had deprived it (acting through its shareholders in general meeting) of the power to acquire the shares. In the second place, the Regal shareholders would only receive a largely reduced proportion of the sale price of the two cinemas. The Regal directors and Garton would receive the moneys of which the Regal shareholders were thus deprived. This vital alteration was brought about in the following circumstances — I refer to the evidence of the respondent Garton. He was asked what was suggested when the guarantees were refused, and this is his answer:

Mr. Gulliver said "We must find it somehow. I am willing to find £500. Are you willing," turning to the other four directors of Regal, "to do the same?" They expressed themselves as willing. He said, "That makes £2,500," and he turned to me and said, "Garton, you have been interested in Mr. Bentley's companies; will you come in to take £500?" I agreed to do so.

My Lords, I have no hesitation in coming to the conclusion, upon the facts of this case, that these shares, when acquired by the directors, were acquired by reason, and only by reason of the fact that they were directors of Regal, and in the course of their execution of that office.

It now remains to consider whether in acting as directors of Regal they stood in a fiduciary relationship to that company. Directors of a limited company are the creatures of statute and occupy a position peculiar to themselves. In some respects they resemble trustees, in others they do not.

In some respects they resemble agents, in others they do not. In some respects they resemble managing partners, in others they do not . . .

[After reviewing the authorities:]

In the result, I am of opinion that the directors standing in a fiduciary relationship to Regal in regard to the exercise of their powers as directors, and having obtained these shares by reason and only by reason of the fact that they were directors of Regal and in the course of the execution of that office, are accountable for the profits which they have made out of them. The equitable rule laid down in *Keech v. Sandford* and *Ex p. James*, and similar authorities applies to them in full force. It was contended that these cases were distinguishable by reason of the fact that it was impossible for Regal to get the shares owing to lack of funds, and that the directors in taking the shares were really acting as members of the public. I cannot accept this argument. It was impossible for the *cestui que* trust in *Keech v. Sandford* to obtain the lease, nevertheless the trustee was accountable. The suggestion that the directors were applying simply as members of the public is a travesty of the facts. They could, had they wished, have protected themselves by a resolution (either antecedent or subsequent) of the Regal shareholders in general meeting. In default of such approval, the liability to account must remain. The result is that, in my opinion, each of the respondents Bobby, Griffiths, Bassett, and Bentley is liable to account for the profit which he made on the sale of his 500 shares in Amalgamated.

The case of the respondent Gulliver, however, requires some further consideration, for he has raised a separate and distinct answer to the claim. He says: "I never promised to subscribe for shares in Amalgamated. I never did so subscribe. I only promised to find others who would be willing to subscribe. I only found others who did subscribe. The shares were theirs. They were never mine. They received the profit. I received none of it". If these are the true facts, his answer seems complete. The evidence in my opinion establishes his contention. Throughout his evidence Gulliver insisted that he only promised to find £500, not to subscribe it himself. The £500 was paid by two cheques in favour of Amalgamated, one a cheque for £200 signed by Gulliver as director and on behalf of the Swiss company Seguliva, the other a cheque for £300 signed by Gulliver as managing director of South Downs Land Co., Ltd. They were enclosed in a letter of Oct. 3, 1935, from Gulliver to Garton, in which Gulliver asks that the share certificates be issued as follows, 200 shares in the name of himself, Charles Gulliver, 200 shares in the name of South Downs Land Co., Ltd., and 100 shares in the name of Miss S. Geering. The money for Miss Geering's shares was apparently included in South Down Land Co.'s cheque. The certificates were made out accordingly, the 200 shares in Gulliver's name being, he says, the shares subscribed for by the Swiss company . . .

There remains to consider the case of Garton. He stands on a different footing from the other respondents in that he was not a director of Regal.

He was Regal's legal adviser; but, in my opinion, he has a short but effective answer to the plaintiffs' claim. He was requested by the Regal directors to apply for 500 shares. They arranged that they themselves should each be responsible for £500 of the Amalgamated capital, and they appealed, by their chairman, to Garton to subscribe the balance of £500 which was required to make up the £3,000. In law his action, which has resulted in a profit, was taken at the request of Regal, and I know of no principle or authority which would justify a decision that a solicitor must account for profit resulting from a transaction which he has entered into on his own behalf, not merely with the consent, but at the request of his client . . .

One final observation I desire to make. In his judgment Lord Greene M.R. stated that a decision adverse to the directors in the present case involved the proposition that, if directors *bona fide* decide not to invest their company's funds in some proposed investment, a director who thereafter embarks his own money therein is accountable for any profits which he may derive therefrom. As to this, I can only say that to my mind the facts of this hypothetical case bear but little resemblance to the story with which we have had to deal . . .

LORD PORTER: My Lords, I am conscious of certain possibilities which are involved in the conclusion which all your Lordships have reached. The action is brought by the Regal company. Technically, of course, the fact that an unlooked for advantage may be gained by the shareholders of that company is immaterial to the question at issue. The company and its shareholders are separate entities. One cannot help remembering, however, that in fact the shares have been purchased by a financial group who were willing to acquire those of the Regal and the Amalgamated at a certain price. As a result of your Lordships' decision that group will, I think, receive in one hand part of the sum which has been paid by the other. For the shares in Amalgamated they paid £3 16s. 1d. per share, yet part of that sum may be returned to the group, though not necessarily to the individual share-holders by reason of the enhancement in value of the shares in Regal — an enhancement brought about as a result of the receipt by the company of the profit made by some of its former directors on the sale of Amalgamated shares. This, it seems, may be an unexpected windfall, but whether it be so or not, the principle that a person occupying a fiduciary relationship shall not make a profit by reason thereof is of such vital importance that the possible consequence in the present case is in fact as it is in law an immaterial consideration . . .

LORD SANKEY: As to the duties and liabilities of those occupying such a fiduciary position, a number of cases were cited to us which were not brought to the attention of the trial judge. In my view, the respondents were in a fiduciary position and their liability to account does not depend upon proof of *mala fides*. The general rule of equity is that no one who has duties of a fiduciary nature to perform is allowed to enter into engagements in which he has or can have a personal interest conflicting with the interests of those whom he is bound to protect. If he holds any property so acquired as trustee, he is bound to account for it to his *cestui que* trust. The earlier cases are concerned with trusts of specific property: *Keech v. Sandford*, per Lord King L.C. The rule, however, applies to agents, as, for example, solicitors and directors, when acting in a fiduciary capacity . . .

It is not, however, necessary to discuss all the cases cited, because the respondents admitted the generality of the rule as contended for by the appellants, but were concerned rather to confess and avoid it. Their contention was that, in this case, upon a true perspective of the facts, they were under no equity to account for the profits which they made. I will deal first with the respondents, other than Gulliver and Garton. We were referred to *Imperial Hydropathic Hotel Co., Blackpool v. Hampson*, where Bowen L.J., at p. 12, drew attention to the difference between directors and trustees, but the case is not an authority for contending that a director cannot come within the general rule. No doubt there may be exceptions to the general rule, as, for example, where a purchase is entered into after the trustee has divested himself of his trust sufficiently long before the purchase to avoid the possibility of his making use of special information acquired by him as trustee (see the remarks of Lord Eldon, in *Ex p. James* at p. 352) or where he purchases with full knowledge and consent of his *cestui que* trust. *Imperial v. Hampson* makes no exception to the general rule that a solicitor or director, if acting in a fiduciary capacity, is liable to account for the profits made by him from knowledge acquired when so acting.

It was then argued that it would have been a breach of trust for the respondents, as directors of Regal, to have invested more than £2,000 of Regal's money in Amalgamated, and that the transaction would never have been carried through if they had not themselves put up the other £3,000. Be it so, but it is impossible to maintain that, because it would have been a breach of trust to advance more than £2,000 from Regal and that the only way to finance the matter was for the directors to advance the balance themselves, a situation arose which brought the respondents outside the general rule and permitted them to retain the profits which accrued to them from the action they took. At all material times they were directors and in a fiduciary position, and they used and acted upon their exclusive knowledge acquired as such directors. They framed resolutions by which they made a profit for themselves. They sought no authority from the company to do so, and, by reason of their position and actions, they made large profits for which, in my view, they are liable to account to the company . . .

LORD MACMILLAN: The point was not whether the directors had a duty to acquire shares in question for the company and entered into the transaction lawfully, in good faith and indeed avowedly in the interests of the company. However, that does not absolve them from accountability for any profit which they made, if it was by reason and in virtue of their fiduciary office as directors that they entered into the transaction.

The equitable doctrine invoked is one of the most deeply rooted in our law. It is amply illustrated in the authoritative decisions which my noble and learned friend Lord Russell of Killowen has cited. I should like only to add a passage from *Principles of Equity*, by Lord James, which puts the whole matter in a sentence (3rd ed., 1778, Vol. 2, p. 87): "Equity", he says, "prohibits a trustee from making any profit by his management, directly or indirectly".

The issue thus becomes one of fact. The plaintiff company has to establish two things: (i) that what the directors did was so related to the affairs of the company that it can properly be said to have been done in the course of their management and in utilization of their opportunities and special knowledge as directors; and (ii) that what they did resulted in a profit to themselves. The first of these propositions is clearly established by the analysis of the whole complicated circumstances for which the House is indebted to my noble and learned friend who has preceded me. The second proposition is admitted, except in the case of Gulliver, in whose case I agree that, on the evidence, he is not proved to have made any profit personally. The conditions are, therefore, in my opinion, present which preclude the four directors who made a personal profit by the transaction from retaining such profit . . .

LORD WRIGHT: [The] question can be briefly stated to be whether an agent, a director, a trustee or other person in an analogous fiduciary position, when a demand is made upon him by the person to whom he stands in the fiduciary relationship to account for profits acquired by him by reason of his fiduciary position, and by reason of the opportunity and the knowledge, or either, resulting from it, is entitled to defeat the claim upon any ground save that he made profits with the knowledge and the assent of the other person. The most usual and typical case of this nature is that of principal and agent. The rule in such cases is compendiously expressed to be that an agent must account for net profits secretly (that is, without the knowledge of his principal) acquired by him in the course of his agency. The authorities show how manifold and various are the applications of the rule. It does not depend on fraud or corruption.

The Courts below have held that it does not apply in the present case, for the reason that the purchase of the shares by the respondents, though made for their own advantage, and though the knowledge and opportunity which enabled them to take the advantage came to them solely by reason of their being directors of the appellant company, was a purchase which, in the circumstances, the respondents were under no duty to the appellant to make, and was a purchase which it was beyond the appellant's ability to make, so that, if the respondents had not made it, the appellant would have been no better off by reason of the respondents abstaining from reaping the advantage for themselves. With the question so stated, it was said that any other decision than that of the Courts below would involve a dog-in-the-manger policy. What the respondents did, it was said, caused no damage to the appellant and involved no neglect of the appellant's interests or similar breach of duty. However, I think the answer to this reasoning is that, both in law and equity, it has been held that, if a person in a fiduciary relationship makes a secret profit out of the relationship, the Court will not inquire whether the other person is damnified or has lost a profit which otherwise he would have got. The fact is in itself a fundamental breach of the fiduciary relationship. Nor can the Court adequately investigate the matter in most cases. The facts are generally difficult to ascertain or are solely in the knowledge of the person who is being charged. They are matters of surmise; they are hypothetical because the inquiry is as to what would have been the position if that party had not acted as he did, or what he might have done if there had not been the temptation to seek his own advantage, if, in short, interest had not conflicted with duty . . .

It is suggested that it would have been mere quixotic folly for the four respondents to let such an occasion pass when the appellant company could not avail itself of it; but Lord King faced that very position when he accepted that the person in the fiduciary position might be the only person in the world who could not avail himself of the opportunity. It is, however, not true that such a person is absolutely barred, because he could by obtaining the assent of the shareholders have secured his freedom to make the profit for himself. Failing that, the only course open is to let the opportunity pass. To admit of any other alternative would be to expose the principal to the dangers against which James L.J. in the passage I have quoted uttered his solemn warning. The rule is stringent and absolute because "the safety of mankind" requires it to be absolutely observed in the fiduciary relationship. In my opinion, the appeal should be allowed in the case of the four respondents . . .

Notes and Questions

1 Do Lords Russell, Sankey, Macmillan and Wright all base their judgments on the same legal principles? Is there truly such a thing as "financial inability" when a corporation has the chance to invest in a profitable enterprise? If the purpose in *Regal* was to package the three properties for immediate resale, was that not a venture that could have been financed in the normal way?

2 Do you agree with Lord Russell's decision as to Gulliver? On what basis did he escape liability? Is there a case for treating the solicitor, Garton, differently?

3 The Supreme Court of Canada adopted the principle of *Regal* in *Zwicker v. Stanbury* (1953), [1954] 1 D.L.R. 257, [1953] 2 S.C.R. 438, 1953 CarswellNS 25, and in *Midcon Oil & Gas Co. v. New British Dominion Oil Co.*, [1958] S.C.R. 314, 12 D.L.R. (2d) 705, 1958 CarswellAlta 70.

4 Lord Porter's concern with the windfall that would be obtained by the new shareholders of Regal formed the basis of McDermid J.A.'s dissent in *Abbey Glen Property Corp. v. Stumborg*, 85 D.L.R. (3d) 35, [1978] 4 W.W.R. 28, 1978 CarswellAlta 236 (C.A.). He agreed that there had been a breach of fiduciary duty, but declined to give judgment for the

plaintiff corporation as it had paid a price for the shares calculated on an estimate of the corporation's assets and without reference to possible liability of former directors. Clement J.A., for the majority, held that "a change in shareholders of itself cannot diminish the rigour of the obligation to account to the company . . ." For a comment see Braith-waite, "Unjust Enrichment and Directors' Duties: Abbey Glen Property Corp. v. Stumborg" (1979), 3 Can. Bus. L.J. 210. See also s. 240(c) of the CBCA and s. 247(c) of the OBCA, which provide for payment of a judgment to former as well as present security holders rather than to the corporation itself in a shareholders' derivative action.

Phipps v. Boardman
[1965] 1 All E.R. 849 (C. A.), affirmed [1966] 3 All E.R. 721 (H.L.)

[The residuary estate of a testator, who had died in 1944, included eight thousand shares in a private company, which had an issued share capital of thirty thousand shares. The trustees of the testator's will were, in 1956, his widow (who was then senile), a married daughter, and an account-ant. The beneficial trusts of the testator's residuary estate were for its divi-sion, subject to an annuity to his widow, among his children, of whom the respondent was one and was entitled to five-eighteenths of the estate. At all material times the appellant, B., acted as solicitor for the trustees and for his co-appellant, P., a son of the testator. In 1956, B. and the accountant trustee decided that the position of the company was unsatisfactory and that something must be done to improve it. Towards the end of 1956 B. and P. attended the company's annual general meeting with proxies obtained from two trustees, the accountant and the daughter. They attended as representing the estate. Shortly after this meeting B. and P. decided, with the knowledge of the two trustees, to endeavour to obtain control of the company by themselves purchasing shares. The trustees had no power to invest trust monies in shares of the company. B., purporting to act on behalf of the trustees as shareholders, obtained information from the company concern-ing the price at which shares had changed hands. The negotiations for acquisition of shares were prolonged and passed through three phases. During the second phase, from April, 1957, to October, 1958, B. obtained much information from the company by purportedly acting on behalf of the trustees. In November, 1958, the widow trustee died. Ultimately, on March 10, 1959, (in the third phase of negotiations) an agreement for the sale of £14,567 shares of the company to B. and P. was signed, and by the end of July, 1959, they had acquired, with other purchases, 21,986 shares of the company. A considerable profit subsequently accrued from capital distri-butions on these shares. The appellants had acted honestly throughout. They appealed from a decision affirming an order declaring that they held five-eighteenths of the shares on trust for the respondent and directing an account of profits and an inquiry what should be allowed to B. and P. or either of them for their work and skill in obtaining the shares. On this appeal it was not contended that B. and P. had obtained the informed consent of the respondent beneficiary to their purchase of the shares of the company.]

LORD DENNING, M.R.: . . . Now the plaintiff brings this action claiming that Boardman and Tom Phipps ought not to be allowed to retain the profit they have made on the shares: and ought to account for it to the estate: and that he, the plaintiff, should have his 5/18ths. He does not suggest any dishonesty or bad faith on their part. He acknowledges that they have done a lot of hard work and are entitled to full and generous remuneration for what they have done; but he says they should not take the whole of this large profit for themselves.

. . . I think the judge put the position right when he said that "in 1956 they assumed the character of *self-appointed agents* for the trustees, for the purpose of extracting information as to the company's business from its directors." The word "self-appointed" was criticized by Mr. Bagnall, but its meaning is clear enough. These two gentlemen took upon themselves an authority which they did not truly possess: and, by virtue of this assumed authority, they obtained information and knowledge which they would not otherwise have got. This sort of thing has happened often enough before. There are many cases in the books where a person has assumed to have authority when in truth he has none. It has always been held that he is accountable just as if he had in fact the authority which he assumed. The classic instance is an executor de son tort. If a person intermeddles with the asset of an estate in such a way as to denote an assumption of the authority of an executor, he is accountable just as if he were an executor; see *Stamford's* case, *Read's* case. Likewise with a man who assumes to act as bailiff without authority. Thus in *Gawton v. Lord Dacres*, Anderson C.J. said: "If one become my bailiff of his own wrong, without my appointment, he is accountable to me." So with a person who assumes to act as trustee. In *Rackham v. Siddall*, Lord Cottenham L.C. held a lady who took on herself to act as trustee was just as liable as if she were in truth a trustee. Similarly in *Lyell v. Kennedy*, the House of Lords held that a person who took upon himself to receive the rents of property which to his knowledge belonged to others was chargeable in a fiduciary character with the rents he had received. In most of these cases the person had already some position or connection which gave him the opportunity of assuming authority to himself. So here Boardman was the solicitor to the estate. Tom Phipps was one of the chief beneficiaries. This gave them the opportunity of assuming authority to act as agents to the estate. They did assume it in their negotiations with Smith and are accountable just as if they were agents. That is how the judge regarded them. His finding was that "Boardman and Phipps were throughout in the position of agents for the trustees, for the purpose of using the trust shareholding to extract knowledge of the affairs of the company and ultimately to improve the company's profit-earning capacity." I am in complete agreement with that finding.

Treating them as agents, to what extent are they accountable? We have been through once again the cases where an agent makes a profit for himself out of his agency. It is quite clear that if an agent uses *property* with which he has been entrusted by his principal, so as to make a profit for himself out of it, without his principal's consent, then he is accountable for it to his principal, see *Shallcross v. Oldham*. So also if he uses a position of authority to which he has been appointed by his principal, so as to gain money by means of it for himself, then also he is accountable to the principal for it, see *Reading v. Attorney-General*. Likewise with *information or knowledge* which he has been employed by his principal to collect or discover, *or which he has other wise acquired*, for the use of his principal, then again if he turns it to his own use, so as to make a profit by means of it for himself he is accountable, see *Lamb v. Evans, Regal (Hastings) Ltd. v. Gulliver*, for such information or knowledge is the property of his principal, just as much as an invention is, see *Triplex Safety Glass Co. v. Scorah, Sterling Engineering Co. Ltd. v. Patchett*. It is otherwise when the information or knowledge is not the property of his principal. There are several cases which show that you cannot prevent an agent from taking advantage of an opportunity of earning money, even though it is an opportunity which comes his way in consequence of his employment, so long as he does not use his master's property, or break his contract by so doing, see *Whitney v. Smith, In re Corsellis, Lawton v. Elwes, Aas v. Benham*, per Bowen L.J. and the instance given by Lord Greene M.R. in *Regal (Hastings) Ltd. v. Gulliver*.

Once it is found that the agent has used his principal's property or his position so as to make money for himself, it matters not that the principal has lost no profits or suffered no damage, see *Parker v. McKenna*. Nor does it matter that the principal could have done the act himself, *Regal (Hastings) Ltd. v. Gulliver*. Nor do you have to find that the act, which brought about the profit, was one within the course of his employment, *Reading v. Attorney-General*. The reason is simply because it is money which the agent ought not to be allowed to keep. He gained an unjust benefit by the use of his principal's property or his position and must account for it.

In this case the judge found that the knowledge, of which profitable use was made, could properly be described as "the property" of the trust. He said that "the knowledge acquired, which was of a most extensive and valuable character . . . and which was the essential foundation upon which a decision could be taken, and was taken to buy the shares, was obtained exclusively by Boardman acting as agent for the trustees as holders of 8,000 shares. The correspondence shows this to a degree of clarity which would make demonstration in detail superfluous and tedious. As outsiders, desirous of buying their way into the company, one of this could be obtained. The directors would have flatly refused to deal with them as prospective purchasers had they not already been a substantial and threatening minority. This knowledge was (so far as the expression can be used) essentially the property of the trust."

This finding is decisive of the case. The appellants used this property of the trust so as to make a profit for themselves without the consent of the trustees. There was clearly no consent. The judge put it cogently: "One must not forget that Boardman, who throughout was the initiator of action, was the solicitor to the trust, the person to whom the trustees would look and did look for advice and for the protection of their interests. Before a person in his position would cease to be an agent and become a self-regarding principal, the clearest possible decision based on the clearest understanding of the position would be necessary."

It does not matter that the trustees could not themselves have invested in the shares of the company. But I must point out that they might have gone to the court and sought permission to exercise their pre-emptive rights. This would, if necessary, be another ground of liability on Boardman, for he placed himself in a position where there was a conflict between his duty to advise an application to the court and his interest to acquire the shares himself, see *Tornross v. Crocker* . . .

[Boardman and Phipps appealed to the House of Lords. The appeal was dismissed by a majority, Lords Guest, Cohen and Hodson, who expressed views similar to those of Lord Denning. Lord Upjohn and Viscount Dilhorne dissented.]

LORD UPJOHN (DISSENTING): . . . In these circumstances the respondent rather surprisingly seeks to hold the appellants accountable to him for his five-eighteenths share of the 21,986 shares so purchased, on the footing that the appellants are constructive trustees of these shares for and on behalf of the trust. So I turn to the relevant law on which this claim is based, but start by stating what is not in dispute, that the conduct of the appellants and each of them has never been anything except utterly honest and above board in every way. If they or either of them are accountable, it is because of the operation of some harsh doctrine of equity on consciences completely innocent in every way. . . .

The phrase "possibly may conflict" requires consideration. In my view it means that the reasonable man looking at the relevant facts and circumstances of the particular case would think that there was a real sensible possibility of conflict: not that you could imagine some situation arising which might, in some conceivable possibility in events not contemplated as real sensible possibilities by any reasonable person, result in a conflict.

Your lordships were referred at length to the decision of this House in *Regal (Hastings), Ltd. v. Gulliver.* That is a helpful case for its restatement of the well-known principles but the case itself bears no relation to the one before your lordships. . . .

[Lord Upjohn summarized the facts of *Regal*.]

This case . . . is one concerned not with trust property or with property of which the persons to whom the fiduciary duty was owed were contemplating a purchase but, in contrast to the facts in *Regal*, with property which was not trust property or property which was ever contemplated as the subject matter of a possible purchase by the trust.

There has been much discussion in the courts below and in this House on the observations of their lordships in the *Regal* case.

In my view, their lordships were not attempting to lay down any new view on the law applicable and indeed could not do so for the law was already so well settled. The whole of the law is laid down in the fundamental principle exemplified in Lord Cranworth's statement which I have already quoted. But it is applicable, like so many equitable principles which may affect a conscience, however innocent, to such diversity of different cases that the observations of judges and even in your lordships' House in cases where this great principle is being applied must be regarded as applicable only to the particular facts of the particular case in question and not regarded as a new and slightly different formulation of the legal principle so well settled. Therefore, as the facts in the *Regal* case to which alone their lordships remarks were directed were so remote from the facts in this case I do not propose to examine the *Regal* case further. . . .

. . . I shall refer to the judgment of Russell, L.J. which proceeded on a rather different basis. He said:

> The substantial trust shareholding was an asset of which one aspect was its potential use as a means of acquiring knowledge of the company's affairs, or of negotiating allocations of the company's assets, or of inducing other shareholders to part with their shares. That aspect was part of the trust assets.

My lords, I regard that proposition as untenable.

In general, information is not property at all. It is normally open to all who have eyes to read and ears to hear. The true test is to determine in what circumstances the information has been acquired. If it has been acquired in such circumstances that it would be a breach of confidence to disclose it to another, then courts of equity will restrain the recipient from communicating it to another. In such cases such confidential information is often and for many years has been described as the property of the donor, the books of authority are full of such references; knowledge of secret processes, "know-how", confidential information as to the prospects of a company or of someone's intention or the expected results of some horse race based on stable or other confidential information. But in the end the real truth is that it is not property in any normal sense, but equity will restrain its transmission to another if in breach of some confidential relationship.

With all respect to the views of Russell, L.J., I protest at the idea that information acquired by trustees in the course of their duties as such is necessarily part of the assets of trust property which cannot be used by the trustees except for the benefit of the trust. Russell, L.J. referred to the fact that two out of three of the trustees could have no authority to turn over this aspect of trust property to the appellants except for the benefit of the trust; this I do not understand, for if such information is trust property not all the trustees acting together could do it for they cannot give away trust property.

We heard much argument on the impact of the fact that the testator's widow was at all material times incapable of acting in the trust owing to disability. Of course trustees must act all of them and unanimously in matters affecting trust affairs, but they never performed any relevant act on behalf of the trust at all; I quoted Mr. Fox's answer earlier for this reason. At no time after going to the meeting in December, 1956, did Mr. Boardman or Tom rely on any express or implied authority or consent of the trustees in relation to trust property. They understood rightly that there was no question of the trustees acquiring any further trust property by purchasing further shares in the company, and it was only in the purchase of other shares that they were interested.

There is, in my view, and I know of no authority to the contrary, no general rule that information learnt by a trustee during the course of his duties is property of the trust and cannot be used by him. If that were to be the rule it would put the Public Trustee and other corporate trustees out of business and make it difficult for private trustees to be trustees of more than one trust. This would be the greatest possible pity for corporate trustees and others may have much information which they may initially acquire in connexion with some particular trust but without prejudice to that trust can make it readily available to other trusts to the great advantage of those other trusts.

The real rule is, in my view, that knowledge learnt by a trustee in the course of his duties as such is not in the least property of the trust and in general may be used by him for his own benefit or for the benefit of other trusts unless it is confidential information which is given to him (i) in circumstances which, regardless of his position as a trustee, would make it a breach of confidence for him to communicate to anyone, for it has been given to him expressly or impliedly as confidential; or (ii) in a fiduciary capacity, and its use would place him in a position where his duty and his interest might possibly conflict. Let me give one or two simple examples. A, as trustee of two settlements X and Y holding shares in the same small company, learns facts as trustee of X about the company which are encouraging. In the absence of special circumstances (such, for example, that X wants to buy more shares) I can see nothing whatever which would make it improper for him to tell his co-trustees of Y who feel inclined to sell that he has information that this would be a bad thing to do. Another example: A as trustee of X learns facts that make him and his co-trustees want to sell. Clearly he could not communicate this knowledge to his co-trustees of Y until at all events the holdings of X have been sold for there would be a plain conflict, reflected in the prices that might or might possibly be obtained.

My lords, I do not think for one moment that Lord Brougham in *Hamilton v. Wright*, quoted in the speech of my noble and learned friend, Lord Guest, was saying anything to the contrary; one has to look and see whether the knowledge acquired was capable of being used for his own benefit to *injure* the trust (my italics). That test can have no application to the present. There was no possibility of the information being used to injure the trust. The knowledge obtained was used not in connexion with trust property but to enhance the value of the trust property by the purchase of other property in which the trustees were not interested.

With these general observations on the applicable principles of law let me apply them to the facts of this case.

Chapter 1. At this stage the appellants went to the meeting with the object of persuading the shareholders to appoint Tom a director; admittedly they were acting on behalf of the trustees at that meeting. It is the basis of the respondent's case that this placed the appellants in a fiduciary relationship which they never after lost or, as it was argued, it "triggered off a chain of events" and gave them the opportunity of acquiring knowledge so that they thereafter became accountable to the trustees. From this it must logically follow that in acquiring the 2,025 shares they became constructive trustees for the trust.

My lords, I must emphatically disagree. The appellants went to the meeting for a limited purpose which failed. Then the appellants' agency came to an end. They had no further duties to perform. The discussions which followed showed conclusively that the trustee would not consider a purchase of further shares. So, when chapter 2 phase I opened, I can see nothing to prevent the appellants from making an offer for shares for themselves, or, for that matter, I cannot see that Mr. Boardman would have been acting improperly in advising some other client to make an offer for shares (other than the eight thousand) in the company. In the circumstances, the appellants' duties having come to an end, they owed no duty and there was no conflict of interest and duty, they were in no way dealing in trust property. Further, of course, they had the blessing of two trustees in their conduct in trying to buy further shares.

So had phase 1 of chapter 2 been successful I can see nothing to make them constructive trustees of the shares they purchased for the trust. Consider a simple example. Blackacre is trust property and next to it is Whiteacre; but there is no question of the trustees being interested in a possible purchase of Whiteacre as being convenient to be held with Blackacre. Is a trustee to be precluded from purchasing Whiteacre for himself because he may have learnt something about Whiteacre while acting as a trustee of Blackacre? I can understand the owner of Whiteacre being annoyed but surely not the beneficial owners of Blackacre, they have no interest in Whiteacre and their trustees have no duties to perform in respect thereof. . .

My lords, I believe the only conflict between the duty and interest of the appellants that can be suggested is that, having learnt so much about the company and realized that in the hands of experts like Tom the shares were a good buy at more than £3 a share, they should have communicated this fact to the trustees and suggested that they ought to consider a purchase and an application to the court for that purpose. This, so far as I can ascertain, was suggested for the first time in the judgment of Lord Denning, M.R. Had this been an issue in the action this might have been a very difficult matter, but it never was. There is no sign of any such case made in the pleadings: but what is much more important is that from start to finish in all three courts there was no suggestion of this in argument on behalf of the respondent; and what is most important of all, there is no suggestion in cross-examination of either of the trustees or of the appellants that the latter were under any such obligation. Mr. Fox must in fact have known all about these negotiations and the value of the shares at this time. In these circumstances can it really be asserted that by failure (if, indeed, they did so fail; we simply do not know) formally to tell the trustees that the shares were worth more than had previously been thought the appellants had placed themselves in a position where their interest might possibly conflict with their duty. . . . I cannot see that they have, from start to finish, in the circumstances of this case, placed themselves in a position where there was any possibility of a conflict between their duty and interest, except in respect of the one matter which I have considered and rejected on the facts of this case. While I have not answered my earlier analysis specifically, I think that I have done so in the course of this judgment except No. 4 which, in my view, does not arise.

I have dealt with the problems that arise in this case at considerable length but it could, in my opinion, be dealt with quite shortly. In *Barnes v. Addy*, Lord Selborne, L.C., said:

> It is equally important to maintain the doctrine of trusts which is established in this court, and not to strain it by unreasonable construction beyond its due and proper limits. There would be no better mode of undermining the sound doctrines of equity than to make unreasonable and inequitable applications of them.

That, in my judgment, is applicable to this case.

The trustees were not willing to buy more shares in the company. The active trustees were very willing that the appellants should do so themselves for the benefit of their large minority holding. The trustees, so to speak, lent their name to the appellants in the course of prolonged and difficult negotiations and, of course, the appellants thereby learnt much which would have otherwise been denied to them. The negotiations were in the end brilliantly successful. How successful Tom was in his reorganization of the company is apparent to all. They ought to be very grateful.

In the long run the appellants have bought for themselves with their own money shares which the trustees never contemplated buying and they did so in circumstances fully known and approved of by the trustees. To extend the doctrines of equity to make the appellants accountable in such circumstances is, in my judgment, to make unreasonable and inequitable applications of such doctrines.

I would allow the appeal and dismiss the action.

Notes

1 Lord Cohen, while accepting that "information is, of course, not property in the strict sense of that word," concluded that:

> Much of the information came the appellant's way when Mr. Boardman was acting on behalf of the trustees on the instructions of Mr. Fox and the opportunity of bidding for the shares came because he purported for all purposes except for making the bid to be acting on behalf of the owners of the 8,000 shares in the company.

Lord Hodson and Lord Guest were of the opinion that "confidential information" could properly be regarded as "the property of the trust" and Phipps and Boardman must account for what was earned through the use of that property.

According to Lord Upjohn the test of whether information is property is whether it has been acquired in circumstances in which it would be a breach of confidence to disclose it. In such circumstances equity will restrain its disclosure. It is important to note that breach of confidence and breach of fiduciary duty are separate equitable doctrines, although there can be cases in which they would overlap. A Canadian case which involved both breach of confidence and breach of fiduciary duty is *Bendix Home Systems Ltd. v. Clayton*, [1977] 5 W.W.R. 10, 33 C.P.R. (2d) 230 (B.C. S.C.). The breach of fiduciary duty alleged against the defendant, who was formerly president, a director and chief executive officer of the plaintiff company, was that he had used his position while still with the plaintiff to put in place a new company which took from the plaintiff many of its senior management personnel, and diverted the goodwill of dealers which it was his duty to attract for it. On this ground, the plaintiff succeeded. The breach of confidence alleged was the improper disclosure of proprietary information which the defendant had acquired in his capacity as president. The proprietary information concerned the company's net profit and return on sales, and information with respect to its dealer network. Finding that there was no breach of confidence, McFarlane J. held that all matters of a confidential nature which were pleaded were those which any company president in the particular industry would be expected to know and to take with him from job to job in the industry. For a comment on trade secrets and breach of confidence, see Braithwaite, "Trade Secrets: The Spring-Board Unsprung" (1979), 42 Mod. L. Rev. 94.

2 For contrasting views as to the appropriateness of the holding in *Phipps*, particularly on the "information as property" point, see: Stanley M. Beck, "The Quickening of Fiduciary Obligation: Canadian Aero Services v. O'Malley" (1975), 53 Can. Bar Rev. 771, 789–83, and Gareth Jones, "Unjust Enrichment and the Fiduciary's Duty of Loyalty" (1968), 84 Law Q. Rev. 472. Professor Jones expressed his opinion as follows:

To say that the fiduciaries' profit was made solely through the use of property (the information) received, *qua* fiduciaries, when the trust could not have utilized it and when the negotiations would have failed but for Boardman's business acumen and Boardman and Phipps' financial intervention, offends legal as well as common sense. To categorize confidential information as "property" or "equitable property" cannot solve the essential questions whether Boardman and Phipps were unjustly enriched, and whether policy demands that they should disgorge their enrichment even though they were not unjustly enriched. (at p. 485)

Jones argued that the decision in *Phipps* could only be justified on the ground that policy demands that Phipps and Boardman be shorn of their profits. He questioned the wisdom of such a policy on the following terms:

The wisdom of such a policy may be questioned. It may be more important to encourage than to punish the able and honest fiduciary. "There is a strong public interest in having persons and institutions ready and willing to be trustees [and agents] and there is a strong public interest in being fair" to them. *Phipps v. Boardman* will not encourage men of Boardman's ability and energy to devote themselves whole-heartedly to trust administration. Indeed many may think the House's decision an unreasonable and inequitable application of a stringent rule of equity. It has been said that the "safety of mankind requires that no [fiduciary] shall be able to put to his principal to the danger" of an inquiry as to whether the principal did or did not suffer any injury; and that "no court is equal to the examination and ascertainment of the truth in much the greater number of cases." But do not these dangers and difficulties disappear when the fiduciary's "integrity . . . is not in doubt," where the trust benefitted from the fiduciary's acts and where the fiduciary's profit has been made at the expense not of the fiduciary's principal but of those who had sold the shares. The stringency of a rule which guards against the possibility as well as the actuality of unjust enrichment should persuade the courts to apply it sensitively, not as a sledgehammer. It is proper that the courts should require the fiduciary to prove his honesty beyond doubt, and that if his enrichment is unjust he should be required to disgorge it to his principal. But if he can affirmatively show that he did act in what can reasonably be regarded as his principal's best interests and that the gain was not at the expense of a principal who suffered no loss, then he should be compelled to disgorge only if the court feels that it absolutely necessary, pour encourager les autres, to punish him. (at pp. 486-487).

3 A Privy Council decision in 1978 appeared to indicate a shift in sentiment towards the views of Lord Upjohn and Professor Jones. In *Queensland Mines Ltd. v. Hudson* (1978), 52 A.L.J.R. 399 (P.C.), Lord Scar-

man said that *Phipps v. Boardman* was the most recent statement by the House of Lords on fiduciary duties, but noted Lord Upjohn's caveat that "possibly may conflict" required consideration. In considering the facts as applied to the defendant director, Lord Scarman adopted Lord Upjohn's test. "In their Lordships' opinion, therefore, the facts have to be examined to determine whether Mr. Hudson acted in a way in which "there was a real sensible possibility of conflict" between his interests and the interest of Queensland Mines." The actual holding in the case was based on a finding of the fully informed consent of the plaintiff company to Hudson's exploitation of a mining license in his own name. Lord Scarman also expressed the opinion that in *Phipps* "their Lordships . . . differed in their analysis of the facts . . . [but] were agreed on the law." Do you agree? For critical comments, see (1979), 42 Mod. L. Rev. 711; (1978), 52 A.L.J. 574.

Peso Silver Mines Ltd. v. Cropper
[1966] 56 D.L.R. (2d) 117, 59 W.W.R. 329 (B.C. C.A.); affirmed, [1966] S.C.R. 673, 56 W.W.R. 641

[Peso Silver Mines Ltd. was incorporated as a private company in British Columbia in March, 1961, to take over a group of silver mining claims in the Yukon. The defendant Cropper, along with his associates Walker and Verity, was instrumental in incorporating Peso. Cropper, Walker and Verity were Peso's first directors, and Cropper was the managing director. In September, 1961, Peso was converted to a public company and shares were sold to the public, the proceeds being used to finance development of the claims. Peso acquired further claims and by March, 1962, held 362 claims covering 20 square miles, the purchase and development of which had put a considerable strain on its finances.

In late March, 1962, Peso, through Cropper and Verity, was offered three groups of claims (the Dickson claims), one of which was contiguous to its Yukon holdings. The Peso board, which by this time had been enlarged to six, turned the offer down because of strained finances and because it felt that Peso had enough ground under control. Approximately six weeks later, in May, 1962, Cropper, Walker, Verity and Dr. Aho, Peso's consulting geologist, formed a private company, Cross Bow, to take up the Dickson claims. Cross Bow was then converted to a public company with its shares being sold to finance development. Because of this, Walker, the President of Peso, wrote to the B.C. Superintendent of Brokers explaining the transaction. In the course of that letter, Walker explained that the Peso board was not interested in the company acquiring any more ground because of its financial position and because of the number of claims it already held. Walker went on to say that ". . . other parties however were interested in acquiring ground in this district, and we felt that some control might be maintained if we joined these groups. Our first interest is for the Peso shareholders and the continued and extensive development of the Peso ground, and it is to this end that our main interest must lie. We do feel, however, that if we do not become part of this new additional ground control, other people would be participating and acquiring regardless."

In December, 1963, control of Peso was purchased by Charter Oil. The president of Charter then demanded that Cropper, Walker and Verity turn over their interest in the company that held the Dickson claims to Peso. Walker and Verity agreed to do so but Cropper refused. The president of Charter then used his majority control position on the board of Peso to have Peso commence an action against Cropper for an accounting and declaration of trust and dismissed him as managing director.

Cropper claimed damages against the company for wrongful dismissal. The trial judge dismissed the company's claim and allowed Cropper's counterclaim for damages in the amount of $10,000.]

BULL, J.A.: . . . Notwithstanding, in this modern day and country when it is accepted as commonplace that substantially all business and commercial undertakings, regardless of size or importance, are carried on through the corporate vehicle with the attendant complexities involved by interlocking, subsidiary and associated corporations, I do not consider it enlightened to extend the application of these principles [of fiduciary duties] beyond their present limits. That the principles, and the strict rules applicable to trustees upon which they are based, are salutory cannot be disputed, but care should be taken to interpret them in the light of modern practice and way of life.

I now turn to the question of whether or not the acquisition by the respondent of the Cross Bow and Mayo shares in the one transaction and the Dayton shares in the other, fall within the first principle that no one who has fiduciary duties must be allowed to retain a profit from an engagement where his personal interest conflicts or may conflict with those of the principal to whom the duties are owed. There is no question whatsoever that the respondent as managing-director of the appellant was in a fiduciary relationship to it. Also there is no doubt that the respondent acted in the best of faith in both transactions and that there was no thought or intent on his part to profit himself at the expense of the appellant. The appellant had no interest in those of the Peso claims offered to it by Dickson before such offer was made, and, in fact, there is no evidence as to whether or not it knew the claims even existed. It did have a very definite interest in the properties while it was considering whether it could or would purchase them, but that interest ceased to exist when, by admittedly *bona fide* decision of its full board of directors made after professional advice was received, the offer was rejected by the appellant. It was only after this temporary interest of the appellant had ceased and after "it had been out of his mind", did the respondent participate in the impugned transaction. If the transaction had taken place when and as it did, but without the offer of these contiguous properties being before the appellant's directors for decision or during the time the appellant was considering the matter, the situation would have been entirely different, and the respondent might well have had to account to the appellant for his participation. But that is not the case here, and I cannot conclude that because offers of properties are continuously put before a mining company and rejected, henceforth any personal dealing with any of them by a director raises a conflict of personal interests with the interests of the company. On the contrary, it would seem that an out-and-out *bona fide* rejection by the company would be the best evidence that any later dealings with the property by anyone would not be against its interests. This is not a case like *Keech v. Sandford*, where a trustee took unto himself property that had been trust property but which was impossible, although desired, to be continued as such. Nor is the situation found in the *Regal (Hastings), Ltd.* case, where the full acquisition of the property was conceived and wanted by the company but other circumstances made it impossible to take that portion which the directors personally took. The interests of the trustee in the one case and of the directors in the other remained always in conflict with those of the principal. With regard to the second transaction involving the Dayton properties, the evidence is extremely unsatisfactory as to what these were, where they were, and whether or not they, or some of them, were rejects of the appellant. It does seem, however, that none of the claims were contiguous or adjacent to those of the appellant, and the evidence given by witnesses for the appellant would seem to show that the appellant was not interested in them for one reason or another. I do not think that the appellant has adduced evidence sufficient to support a finding that the interests of the appellant were in conflict at any time with the personal interests of the respondent so far as his holdings in Dayton are concerned.

It was the second principle of law as set out in the *Regal (Hastings), Ltd.* case that the appellant most strongly urged to support his submission that the respondent should be held accountable. It was said, with respect to the Cross Bow and Mayo transaction, that, as these properties were put up for sale to the appellant in the first instance the subsequent acquisition by the respondent and the two other directors was by reason of the fact that they acquired the knowledge of and about the properties *qua* directors and that therefore their personal transaction was one made by "reason of being directors" and "in the course of execution of that office". I cannot agree. I consider that the authorities require that to come within the rule, the impugned transactions must, as stated by Lord Russell, be by reason of the fact, and *only by reason* of the fact, that they were directors and in the *course of the execution* of that office. That clearly was the situation in the *Regal (Hastings), Ltd.* case where the whole transaction was implemented by the directors carrying out their duties as required by their company in a company transaction but in which they were personally involved. In the case of *Zwicker v. Stanbury, supra*, the directors were charged with the duty of and were carrying out a financial reorganization of a company which was in difficulties and took unto themselves in an allegedly private capacity securities which were or could form a very part of the refinancing processes being considered. In the case at bar, undoubtedly the knowledge of the Cross

Bow properties came to the respondent and others because they were directors of the appellant. Also it cannot be questioned that these directors were
acting only as such and in execution of that office when they considered
and rejected the offer to the company of the properties in question. But their
later negotiation for and acquisition of the mineral claims, although based
on such knowledge acquired as aforesaid, could not, in my respectful opinion, be said to have been done "only" in their capacity as directors and "in
the execution of that office". Once again, these properties were not something the appellant had brought within the ambit of its business or plans.
They, along with others, were simply offered to it and rejected. I cannot
think that the mere acquisition of knowledge in a directors' meeting qua
director in itself would bring any subsequent dealing with the subject matter
into the realm of being in the execution of that office.

In the *Regal (Hastings), Ltd.* case, Greene, M.R., said in the Court of
Appeal in his unreported judgment dated February 15, 1941 (and with which
Mackinnon, L.J., and du Parcq, L.J., agreed), that:

> To say that the Company was entitled to claim the benefit of those
> shares would involve this proposition: Where a Board of Directors
> considers an investment which is offered to their company and *bona
> fide* comes to the conclusion that it is not an investment which their
> Company ought to make, any Director, after that Resolution is come
> to and *bona fide* come to, who chooses to put up money for that
> investment himself must be treated as having done it on behalf of the
> Company, so that the Company can claim any profit that results to him
> from it. That is a proposition for which no particle of authority was
> cited; and goes, as it seems to me, far beyond anything that has ever
> been suggested as to the duty of directors, agents, or persons in a
> position of that kind.

Although the judgment of the Court of Appeal was reversed by the House
of Lords as cited above, the above-quoted hypothetical case suggested by
the Master of the Rolls did attract the comment of Lord Russell when he
said at p. 391:

> One final observation I desire to make. In his judgment Lord
> Greene, M.R., stated that a decision adverse to the directors in the
> present case involved the proposition that, if directors *bona fide* decide
> not to invest their company's funds in some proposed investment, a
> director who thereafter embarks his own money therein is accountable
> for any profits which he may derive therefrom. As to this, I can only
> say that to my mind the facts of this hypothetical case bear but little
> resemblance to the story with which we have had to deal.

As Greene, M. R., was found to be in error in his decision, I would think
that the above comment by Lord Russell on the hypothetical case would be

superfluous unless it was intended to be a reservation that he had no quarrel with the proposition enunciated by the Master of the Rolls, but only that the facts of the case before him did not fall within it. Apparently this view also has been taken by Denning, M.R., where, in *Phipps v. Boardman*, [1965] 1 All E.R. 849 at p. 856, [1965] 2 W.L.R. 839, a case involving the liability of trustees, he said:

> Likewise with *information or knowledge* which he has been employed by his principal to collect or discover, *or which he has otherwise acquired*, for the use of his principal, then again if he turns it to his own use, so as to make a profit by means of it for himself, he is accountable (see *Lamb v. Evans*, [1893] 1 Ch. 218 at pp. 226, 230, *Regal (Hastings), Ltd. v. Gulliver*, [1942] 1 All E. R. 378) for such information or knowledge is the property of his principal, just as much as an invention is (see *Triplex Safe Glass Co. v. Scorah*, [1937] 4 All E.R. 693 at p. 698; [1938] Ch. 211 at p. 217, *Sterling Engineering Co., Ltd. v. Patchett*, [1955] 1 All E.R. 369 at pp. 374, 376; [1955] A.C. 534 at pp. 544, 547). It is otherwise when the information or knowledge is not the property of his principal. There are several cases which show that you cannot prevent an agent from taking advantage of an opportunity of earning money, even though it is an opportunity which comes his way in consequence of his employment, so long as he does not use his master's property, or break his contract by so doing; see *Whitney v. Smith* (1869), L.R. 4 Ch. App. 513 at 521, *Re Corsellis, Lawton v. Elwes* (1883), (1887), 34 Ch. D. 675, *Aas v. Benham*, [1891] 2 Ch. 244 at p. 258 per Bowen, L.J., and the instance given by Lord Greene, M.R., in *Regal (Hastings), Ltd. v. Gulliver*.

Accordingly, I have come to the conclusion that the appellant cannot succeed upon the circumstances here present.

I would, therefore, dismiss the appeal from the judgment dismissing the appellant's action against the respondent.

[On appeal, the unanimous judgment of the Supreme Court was delivered by:]

CARTWRIGHT, J.: Counsel for the appellant founded his argument on the decision of the House of Lords in *Regal (Hastings), Ltd. v. Gulliver et al.*, in which the principles of equity relating to the liability of a person who acquires property in regard to which a fiduciary relationship exists are considered and the leading cases are reviewed. The judgment in *Regal* has been followed by this Court in *Zwicker v. Stanbury* and in *Midcon Oil & Gas Ltd. v. New British Dominion Oil Co. Ltd. et al.* Counsel for the respondent accepts the statements of the law contained in *Regal* and submits that their application to the facts of the case at bar does not result in imposing liability on the respondent.

It is not necessary to review the somewhat complicated facts of the *Regal* case. While each of the Law Lords stated his reasons in his own words, there was no difference in substance between their statements of the test to be applied in determining whether or not the directors were liable to account for the profit which they personally had made on the purchase and resale of shares in a subsidiary of *Regal*. It will be of assistance to consider the actual words which were used. . . .

[Cartwright, J. then quoted from the various opinions in *Regal*, most notably that of Lord Russell who stressed that the directors obtained these shares "by reason and only by reason of the fact that they were directors of Regal and in the course of execution of that office . . ."].

. . . The phrases which I have italicized in some of the passages quoted above appear to me to state in varying words the principle which Lord Russell of Killowen laid down, at p. 389 of the *Regal* judgment, in the passage quoted above which was adopted by Locke J. in the *Midcon* case.

On the facts of the case at bar I find it impossible to say that the respondent obtained the interests he holds in Cross Bow and Mayo by reason of the fact that he was a director of the appellant and in the course of the execution of that office.

If the members of the House of Lords in *Regal* had been of the view that in the hypothetical case stated by Lord Greene the director would have been liable to account to the company, the elaborate examination of the facts contained in the speech of Lord Russell of Killowen would have been unnecessary.

The facts of the case at bar appear to me in all material respects identical with those in the hypothetical case stated by Lord Greene and I share the view which he expressed that in such circumstances the director is under no liability. I agree with the conclusion of the learned trial judge and of the majority in the Court of Appeal that the action fails.

Notes and Questions

1   In a dissenting judgment in the Court of Appeal, Norris, J.A. looked to the principles set out in *Regal* to show that the intentions of the directors were irrelevant and that a strict application of the principles laid out in *Keech v. Sandford* was required. He then went on to discuss the policy upon which his decision was based, in contrast to the policy preference enunciated by Bull, J.A:

> Some argument was presented to the effect that because of the complexity of modern business, modern practice and the modern way of life, the strict rule laid down in the *Regal* and other cases should not be applied. . . . With the greatest respect, it seems to me that the complexities of modern business are a very good reason why the rule should be enforced strictly in order that such complexities may not be used as a smoke screen or shield behind which fraud might be perpetrated. The argument is purely and simply an irrelevant

argument of expediency as to what the law should be, not what it is. It might as well be said that such an argument if given effect to would open the door to fraud, and weaken the confidence which ordinary people should have in dealing with corporate bodies. In order that people may be assured of their protection against improper acts of trustees it is necessary that their activities be circumscribed within rigid limits. The language used and referred to with approval in the *Regal* case, e.g., "the inflexible rule", "the inexorable rule", "The rule is stringent and absolute, because 'the safety of mankind' requires it to be absolutely observed in the fiduciary relationship" indicate how strict the rule is. The history today of the activities of many corporate bodies has disclosed scandals and loss to the public due to failure of the directors to recognize the requirements of their fiduciary position. No great hardship is imposed on directors by the enforcement of the rule, as a very simple course is available to them which they may follow [approval by the shareholders].

2 Do you agree that *Peso* is different from *Regal* because the directors of *Peso* turned down the Dickson claims? In both *Peso* and *Regal* did not both companies want to acquire property (mining claims, a lease) which they could not afford? What decision might have been reached in *Regal* if the directors had taken the lease in their own names rather than purchase the shares themselves? Would it have been possible to have received the fully informed consent of an independent board in *Peso*, or should the directors have sought the permission of the shareholders? For an analysis and criticism of the case, see Stanley M. Beck, "The Saga of Peso Silver Mines: Corporate Opportunity Reconsidered" (1971), 49 Can. Bar Rev. 80; Note (1967), 30 Mod. L. Rev. 450.

A different approach to the question of a corporation's financial inability to pursue an opportunity was taken by the US Court of Appeals for the Second Circuit in the following case.

Irving Trust Co. v. Deutsch
73 F.2d 121 (2nd Cir., 1934)

[Acoustic Products Company ("Acoustic") dealt in phonographs, radios and related goods. In March 1928, Acoustic sought to acquire some needed patent rights from De Forest Radio Company ("De Forest"). Although De Forest was in receivership at the time, Reynolds & Co. ("Reynolds") controlled De Forest by virtue of an agreement it had to acquire all of the stock of De Forest, thereby allowing it to lift the receivership. Accordingly, Bell, an agent of Acoustic, was charged with the task of acquiring De Forest's patents from Reynolds. Ultimately, Reynolds refused to sell the patents outright to Acoustic, but agreed to allow Acoustic to acquire 1/3 of De Forest's stock and to negotiate a management contract with Acoustic. On April 3rd, the board of Acoustic approved a resolution empowering

Deutsch, the president of Acoustic, to secure funding to carry out the proposed agreement with Reynolds. On April 9th, Deutsch reported that funding had not been obtained for the transaction, but that "several individuals" were desirous of accepting the arrangement with Reynolds and conveying the benefits of the patents to Acoustic. A resolution was then approved by the board allowing another agent, Biddle, to accept the contract with Reynolds on behalf of Acoustic. On April 25th, several directors of Acoustic made an initial payment on the stock, and, one month later, after notifying Reynolds directly, they acquired the stock for themselves. Subsequently, an active market in the stock developed, and the directors sold their shares for a substantial profit. Acoustic became bankrupt, and the trustee in bankruptcy brought an action against the defendant directors to account for the profits on the stock.]

SWAN J.: The main defense asserted is that Acoustic by reason of its financial straits had neither the funds nor the credit to make the purchase and that the directors honestly believed that by buying the stock for themselves they could give Acoustic the advantage of access to the De Forest patents, while at the same time taking a stock speculation for their own benefit. In support of the proposition that the prohibition against corporate officers acting on their own behalf is removed if the corporation is itself financially unable to enter into the transaction. . . . The plaintiff cites *Wing v. Dillingham*, 239 F. 54 (5th Cir. 1917) as repudiating the above proposition. In *Wing v. Dillingham* a director of a corporation completed payments on timber land which the corporation had an option to purchase but was unable to pay for; the director taking title to the land and giving the corporation an option to acquire it by repaying his advances within six months. Long after the six months, and without repayment of the advances, the corporation's receiver was held entitled to avoid the transaction and require the director to account. The facts in the case at bar are even stronger against the defendant directors since here the directors absolutely bound Acoustic by contract to make the payments to Reynolds & Co., and thus subjected it to the risk of an action for damages for non-performance, without committing themselves to it to relieve it of this obligation if necessary when time for payment should arrive. The defendants' argument, contrary to *Wing v. Dillingham*, that the equitable rule that fiduciaries should not be permitted to assume a position in which their individual interests might be in conflict with those of the corporation can have no application where the corporation is unable to undertake the venture, is not convincing. If directors are permitted to justify their conduct on such a theory, there will be a temptation to refrain from exerting their strongest efforts on behalf of the corporation since, if it does not meet the obligations, an opportunity of profit will be open to them personally. . . . Indeed, in the present suit it is at least open to question whether a stronger effort might not have been made on the part of the management to procure for Acoustic the necessary funds or credit. Thus it appears that Deutsch owed Acoustic $125,000 on his note due February 2, 1928, and secured by collateral. No effort was made to collect it or to realize on the collateral. The directors contend that they took no action because Deutsch thought he had a defense to his note; but the validity of such defense, as well as whether the possibility of resorting to this asset was actually considered, is very doubtful. After April 9th no efforts appear to have been made to raise for Acoustic the $100,000 required for the De Forest stock. Moreover, Acoustic did have substantial banking accommodations on June 6th, and, if these had been made available a few weeks earlier, it would have been able to perform its contract with Reynolds & Co. While these facts raised some question whether Acoustic actually lacked the funds or credit necessary for carrying out its contract, we do not feel justified in reversing the District Court's finding that it did. Nevertheless, they tend to show the wisdom of a rigid rule forbidding directors of a solvent corporation to take over for their own profit a corporate contract on the plea of the corporation's financial inability to perform. If the directors are uncertain whether the corporation can make the necessary outlays, they need not embark it upon the venture; if they do, they may not substitute themselves for the corporation any place along the line and divert possible benefits into their own pockets. . . .

The defendant Bell was Acoustic's agent in the original negotiations with Reynolds, and it is urged by the plaintiff that as such agent he was a fiduciary precluded from making profits out of the subject-matter of his agency. On his behalf it is contended that his agency was ended when he delivered to Acoustic the written offer of Reynolds & Co. and that his participation in the Biddle syndicate was not by virtue of his former agency relationship nor because of any information he had obtained as Acoustic's agent; that he stands like any stranger to whom the syndicate might have offered a participation. But, even if the fact of his agency be disregarded, we think there is an applicable principle which requires him to account, namely, that one who knowingly joins a fiduciary in an enterprise where the personal interest of the latter is or may be antagonistic to his trust becomes jointly and severally liable with him for the profits of the enterprise. . . . Bell says that on April 7th or 9th he agreed with Mr. Deutsch that, if the latter was not successful in raising the purchase money for the stock from his own associates, he would join him to the extent of $25,000. This agreement, made at a time when the offer was still open for acceptance by the corporation, brings Bell within the principle above enunciated.

The defendant Stein was an employee of Acoustic, holding the position of chief engineer at the time he became a member of the Biddle syndicate. A mere employee of a corporation does not ordinarily occupy a position of trust or confidence toward his employer unless he is also an agent in respect to the matter under consideration. . . . Stein had no part, as did the directors, in binding the corporation to the contract to purchase the stock; nor can he be held on the principle applied to the defendant Bell. Shortly after the April 9th meeting Mr. Deutsch told him that the directors had decided that Acoustic did not have the funds to purchase the stock and that Deutsch, Biddle, Hammond, and others were to purchase it on their own account. Early in

May Stein was informed that one of the participants, Mr. Dows, had withdrawn and he was asked to take stock thus made available. He consented because it might assist Acoustic to get access to the De Forest patents. So far as appears, Stein did not see the minutes of the April 9th meeting, and may well have understood from his conversation with Deutsch that the company had rejected Reynolds & Co.'s offer, and that the individuals had then made an independent contract with Reynolds & Co. He is not shown to have had affirmative knowledge that the directors with whom he joined were pursuing a course which would make their personal interests antagonistic to those of Acoustic. . . .

. . . The plaintiff also argues that Reynolds & Co. knowingly participated with the directors of Acoustic in the breach of their fiduciary duty. However, Reynolds & Co. had the right to sell to whomever it could, and, on being informed that Acoustic was not able to perform, it was justified on that information in making the sale to the syndicate. No right of Acoustic was violated in so doing, as Acoustic could demand the stock only on fulfilling its own obligation. Reynolds & Co. was not obliged to prejudice this opportunity to dispose of the stock nor to investigate scrupulously the intracorporate affairs of Acoustic. Since it received no benefit from the transaction aside from completing the sale of the stock and there is no proof that it acted in a conspiracy to deprive Acoustic of a valuable asset, it cannot be held to an accounting. . . .

For the foregoing reasons, the decree of dismissal is reversed as against Bell, Biddle, Deutsch and Hammond; as to the other defendants, it is affirmed.

Questions

Would the decision (and should it) be the same if there was convincing evidence that Acoustic lacked the necessary funds? Are not the facts with respect to that essential question in the control of the directors/purchasers, e.g. Deutsch? What approach do you think Judge Swan would have taken in *Peso*?

Canadian Aero Services Ltd. v. O'Malley
(1973), [1974] S.C.R. 592, 40 D.L.R. (3d) 371

[The plaintiff-appellant company, Canaero, claimed that the defendants had improperly taken the fruits of a corporate opportunity in which the corporation had a prior and continuing interest. The main business of Canadian Aero (Canaero) was topographical mapping and geographical exploration. The defendants were assigned to Guyana for the purpose of developing and procuring a contract for the mapping of that country. The defendants thereafter resigned from Canaero, and unknown to the plaintiff, they incorporated a company (Terra Surveys Inc.) to perform identical work to that of their previous employer. Terra's proposal to map the terrain of

Guyana was accepted in competition with a proposal submitted by Canaero. Canaero alleged that O'Malley and Zarzycki had wrongfully taken the benefit of the corporate opportunity in breach of a fiduciary duty owed to the corporation.

In an action for an accounting and payment of profits, both the trial court and the Ontario Court of Appeal found against the plaintiff. However, the reasoning of the Court of Appeal was different from that of the trial judge in that the Court of Appeal was of the view that the relationship of the parties was that of employer and employee involving no fiduciary obligations.]

LASKIN, J.: . . . There are four issues that arise for consideration on the facts so far recited. There is, first, the determination of the relationship of O'Malley and Zarzycki to Canaero. Secondly, there is the duty or duties, if any, owed by them to Canaero by reason of the ascertained relationship. Thirdly, there is the question whether there has been any breach of duty, if any is owing, by reason of the conduct of O'Malley and Zarzycki in acting through Terra to secure the contract for the Guyana project; and, fourthly, there is the question of liability for breach of duty if established.

Like Grant, J., the trial judge, I do not think it matters whether O'Malley and Zarzycki were properly appointed as directors of Canaero or whether they did or did not act as directors. What is not in doubt is that they acted respectively as president and executive vice-president of Canaero for about two years prior to their resignations. To paraphrase the findings of the trial Judge in this respect, they acted in those positions and their remuneration and responsibilities verified their status as senior officers of Canaero. They were "top management" and not mere employees whose duty to their employer, unless enlarged by contract, consisted only of respect for trade secrets and for confidentiality of customer lists. Theirs was a larger, more exacting duty which, unless modified by statute or by contract (and there is nothing of this sort here), was similar to that owed to a corporate employer by its directors. I adopt what is said of this point by Gower, *Principles of Modern Company Law*, 3rd ed. (1969), at p. 518 as follows:

> . . .these duties, except in so far as they depend on statutory provisions expressly limited to directors, are not so restricted but apply equally to any officials of the company who are authorized to act on its behalf, and in particular to those acting in a managerial capacity.

The distinction taken between agents and servants of an employer is apt here, and I am unable to appreciate the basis upon which the Ontario Court of Appeal concluded that O'Malley and Zarzycki were mere employees, that is servants of Canaero rather than agents. Although they were subject to supervision of the officers of the controlling company, their positions as senior officers of a subsidiary, which was a working organization, charged them with initiatives and with responsibilities far removed from the obedient role of servants.

It follows that O'Malley and Zarzycki stood in a fiduciary relationship to Canaero, which in its generality betokens loyalty, good faith and avoidance of a conflict of duty and self-interest. Descending from the generality, the fiduciary relationship goes at least this far: a director or a senior officer like O'Malley or Zarzycki is precluded from obtaining for himself, either secretly or without the approval of the company (which would have to be properly manifested upon full disclosure of the facts), any property or business advantage either belonging to the company or for which it has been negotiating; and especially is this so where the director or officer is a participant in the negotiations on behalf of the company. . . .

[Laskin, J. then went on to discuss *Regal Hastings* and quote passages from the judgment.]

I need not pause to consider whether on the facts in *Regal (Hastings) Ltd. v. Gulliver* the equitable principle was over-zealously applied; see, for example, Gower, *op. cit.*, at pp. 535-7. What I would observe is that the principle, or, indeed, principles, as stated, grew out of older cases concerned with fiduciaries other than directors or managing officers of a modern corporation, and I do not therefore regard them as providing a rigid measure whose literal terms must be met in assessing succeeding cases. In my opinion, neither the conflict test, referred to by Viscount Sankey, nor the test of accountability for profits acquired by reason only of being directors and in the course of execution of the office, reflected in the passage quoted from Lord Russell of Killowen, should be considered as the exclusive touchstones of liability. In this, as in other branches of the law, new fact situations may require a reformulation of existing principle to maintain its vigour in the new setting.

The reaping of a profit by a person at a company's expense while a director thereof is, of course, an adequate ground upon which to hold the director accountable. Yet there may be situations where a profit must be disgorged, although not gained at the expense of the company, on the ground that a director must not be allowed to use his position as such to make a profit even if it was not open to the company, as for example, by reason of legal disability, to participate in the transaction. An analogous situation, albeit not involving a director, existed for all practical purposes in the case of *Boardman et al. v. Phipps*, [1967] 2 A.C. 46 which also supports the view that liability to account does not depend on proof of an actual conflict of duty and self-interest. Another, quite recent, illustration of a liability to account where the company itself had failed to obtain a business contract and hence could not be regarded as having been deprived of a business opportunity is *Industrial Development Consultants Ltd. v. Cooley*, [1972] 2 All E.R. 162, a judgment of a Court of first instance. There, the managing director, who was allowed to resign his position on a false assertion of ill health, subsequently got the contract for himself. That case is thus also illustrative of the situation where a director's resignation is prompted by a decision to obtain for himself the business contract denied to his company and where he does obtain it without disclosing his intention.

What these decisions indicate is an updating of the equitable principle whose roots lie in the general standards that I have already mentioned, namely, loyalty, good faith and avoidance of conflict of duty and self-interest. Strict application against directors and senior management officials is simply recognition of the degree of control which their positions give them in corporate operations, a control which rises above daily accountability to owning shareholders and which comes under some scrutiny only at annual general or at special meetings. It is a necessary supplement, in the public interest, of statutory regulation and accountability which themselves are, at one and the same time, an acknowledgement of the importance of the corporation in the life of the community and of the need to compel obedience by it and by its promoters, directors and managers to norms of exemplary behaviour. . . . [Laskin, J. went on to review case law from Australia, England, New Zealand and the United States to demonstrate his point.]

Submissions and argument were addressed to this Court on the question whether or how far Zarzycki copied Canaero's documents in preparing the Terra proposal. The appellant's position is that Zarzycki was not entitled to use for Terra what he compiled for Canaero; and the respondents contended that, although Zarzycki was not entitled to use for Terra the 1965 report or proposal as such that he prepared for Canaero, he was entitled to use the information therein which came to him in the normal course and by reason of his own capacity. It was the respondents' further submission that Zarzycki did not respond in 1966, on behalf of Terra on the basis of the 1965 report as an officer of and for Canaero; and they went so far as to say that it did not matter that O'Malley and Zarzycki worked on the same contract for Terra as they had for Canaero, especially when the project was not exactly the same.

In my opinion, the fiduciary duty upon O'Malley and Zarzycki, if it survived their departure from Canaero, would be reduced to an absurdity if it could be evaded merely because the Guyana project had been varied in some details when it became the subject of invited proposals, or merely because Zarzycki met the variations by appropriate changes in what he prepared for Canaero in 1965, and what he proposed for Terra in 1966. I do not regard it as necessary to look for substantial resemblances. Their presence would be a factor to be considered on the issue of breach of fiduciary duty but they are not a *sine qua non*. The cardinal fact is that the one project, the same project which Zarzycki had pursued for Canaero, was the subject of his Terra proposal. It was that business opportunity, in line with its general pursuits, which Canaero sought through O'Malley and Zarzycki. There is no suggestion that there had been such a change of objective as to make the project for which proposals were invited from Canaero, Terra and others a different one from that which Canaero had been developing with a view to obtaining the contract for itself.

Again, whether or not Terra was incorporated for the purpose of intercepting the contract for the Guyana project is not central to the issue of breach of fiduciary duty. Honesty of purpose is no more a defence in that respect than it would be in respect of personal interception of the contract by O'Malley and Zarzycki. This is fundamental in the enforcement of fiduciary duty where the fiduciaries are acting against the interests of their principal. Then it is urged that Canaero could not in any event have obtained the contract, and that O'Malley and Zarzycki left Canaero was an ultimate response to their dissatisfaction with that company and with the restrictions that they were under in managing it. There was, however, no certain knowledge at the time O'Malley and Zarzycki resigned that the Guyana project was beyond Canaero's grasp. Canaero had not abandoned its hope of capturing it, even if Wells was of opinion, expressed during his luncheon with O'Malley and Zarzycki on August 6, 1966, that it would not get a foreign aid contract from the Canadian Government. Although it was contended that O'Malley and Zarzycki did not know of the imminence of the approval of the Guyana project, their ready run for it, when it was approved at about the time of their resignations and at a time when they knew of Canaero's continuing interest, are factors to be considered in deciding whether they were still under a fiduciary duty not to seek to procure for themselves or for their newly-formed company the business opportunity which they had nurtured for Canaero.

Counsel for O'Malley and Zarzycki relied upon the judgment of this Court in *Peso Silver Mines Ltd. (N.P.L.) v. Cropper* (1966), 58 D.L.R. (2d) 1, [1966] S.C.R. 673, 56 W.W.R. 641, as representing an affirmation of what was said in *Regal (Hastings) Ltd. v. Gulliver* respecting the circumscription of liability to circumstances where the directors or senior officers had obtained the challenged benefit by reason only of the fact that they held those positions and in the course of execution of those offices. In urging this, he did not deny that leaving to capitalize on their positions would not necessarily immunize them, but he submitted that in the present case there was no special knowledge or information obtained from Canaero during their service with that company upon which O'Malley and Zarzycki had relied in reaching for the Guyana project on behalf of Terra.

There is a considerable gulf between the *Peso* case and the present one on the facts as found in each and on the issues that they respectively raise. In *Peso*, there was a finding of good faith in the rejection by its directors of an offer of mining claims because of its strained finances. The subsequent acquisition of those claims by the managing director and his associates, albeit without seeking shareholder approval, was held to be proper because the company's interest in them ceased. There is some analogy to *Burg v. Horn* because there was evidence that Peso had received many offers of mining properties and, as in *Burg v. Horn*, the acquisition of the particular claims out of which the litigation arose could not be said to be essential to the success of the company. Whether evidence was overlooked in *Peso* which would have led to the result reached in *Regal (Hastings) Ltd. v. Gulliver* (see the examination by Beck, "The Saga of Peso Silver Mines: Corporate Opportunity Reconsidered", 49 Can. Bar Rev. 80 (1971), at p.

101) has no bearing on the proper disposition of the present case. What is before this Court is not a situation where various opportunities were offered to a company which was open to all of them, but rather a case where it had devoted itself to originating and bringing to fruition a particular business deal which was ultimately captured by former senior officers who had been in charge of the matter for the company. Since Canaero had been invited to make a proposal on the Guyana project, there is no basis for contending that it could not, in any event, have obtained the contract or that there was any unwillingness to deal with it.

It is a mistake, in my opinion, to seek to encase the principle stated and applied in *Peso*, by adoption from *Regal (Hastings) Ltd. v. Gulliver* in the straight-jacket of special knowledge acquired while acting as directors or senior officers, let alone limiting it to benefits acquired by reason of and during the holding of those offices. As in other cases in this developing branch of the law, the particular facts may determine the shape of the principle of decision without setting fixed limits to it. So it is in the present case. Accepting the facts found by the trial Judge, I find no obstructing considerations to the conclusion that O'Malley and Zarzycki continued, after their resignations, to be under a fiduciary duty to respect Canaero's priority, as against them and their instrument Terra, in seeking to capture the contract for the Guyana project. They entered the lists in the heat of the maturation of the project, known to them to be under active Government consideration when they resigned from Canaero and when they proposed to bid on behalf of Terra.

In holding that on the facts found by the trial Judge, there was a breach of fiduciary duty by O'Malley and Zarzycki which survived their resignations I am not to be taken as laying down any rule of liability to be read as if it were a statute. The general standards of loyalty, good faith and avoidance of a conflict of duty and self-interest to which the conduct of a director or senior officer must conform, must be tested in each case by many factors which it would be reckless to attempt to enumerate exhaustively. Among them are the factor of position or office held, the nature of the corporate opportunity, its ripeness, its specificness and the director's or managerial officer's relation to it, the amount of knowledge possessed, the circumstances in which it was obtained and whether it was special or, indeed, even private, the factor of time in the continuation of fiduciary duty where the alleged breach occurs after termination of the relationship with the company, and the circumstances under which the relationship was terminated, that is whether by retirement or resignation or discharge. . . .

Liability of O'Malley and Zarzycki for breach of fiduciary duty does not depend upon proof by Canaero that, but for their intervention, it would have obtained the Guyana contract; nor is it a condition of recovery of damages that Canaero establish what its profit would have been or what it has lost by failing to realize the corporate opportunity in question. It is entitled to compel the faithless fiduciaries to answer for their default according to their gain. Whether the damages awarded here be viewed as an accounting of profits or, what amounts to the same thing, as based on unjust enrichment, I would not interfere with the quantum. The appeal is, accordingly, allowed against all defendants save Wells, and judgment should be entered against them for $125,000. The appellant should have its costs against them throughout. I would dismiss the appeal as against Wells with costs.

Questions

Has the Supreme Court implicitly overruled *Peso*? Does Laskin's judgment allow a lawyer to give a director viable guidelines for his conduct? Would the flexibility urged by Laskin C.J. in applying fiduciary standards cut both ways? That is, would it (should it) lead to a different result in *Phipps*? See also Beck, "The Quickening of Fiduciary Obligation: Canadian Aero Services v. O'Malley", *supra*.

Burg v. Horn
380 F.2d 897 (C.A. 2nd Cir., 1967)

[Plaintiff was a one-third shareholder and director of Darand Realty Corp. She sued derivatively the two other shareholder-directors, alleging that they took advantage of corporate opportunities by purchasing for themselves and for their profit several low-rent rooming and apartment buildings which should have been purchased for Darand. Prior to and after the formation of Darand by these three shareholders, the defendants were indirectly (through solely owned corporations) involved in the real estate business themselves. This was known to the plaintiff when she became a shareholder in Darand. There was no agreement or discussion as to whether defendants should continue their real estate business as before but plaintiff and her husband had "expected" the defendants to offer any low-rent properties they found in Brooklyn to Darand. While defendants were purchasing and selling real estate of this character on their own account, Darand was operating similarly. Plaintiff's action sought an accounting for receipts and expenditures and the imposition of a constructive trust on the alleged corporate opportunities over several years. The lower court found that defendants had failed to account for about $8,000 and held defendants liable for this but declined to hold them liable for taking advantage of corporate opportunities.]

LUMBARD, CHIEF JUDGE: Since the Horns are charged with breaching their fiduciary duty to a New York corporation doing business only in New York by acquiring properties located in New York, their liability is governed by New York law. . . . Under New York law, property acquired by a corporate director will be impressed with a constructive trust as a corporate opportunity only if the corporation had an interest or a "tangible expectancy" in the property when it was acquired. *Blaustein v.*

Pan Am. Petroleum & Transp. Co., 56 N.E. 2d 705, 713-714 (1944). Although some commentators have criticized the "interest or expectancy" test as vague and unhelpful, see, e.g., Walker, Legal Handles Used to Open or Close the Corporate Opportunity Door, 56 Nw. U.L. Rev. 608, 612-13 (1961), it clearly expressed the judgment that the corporate opportunity doctrine should not be used to bar corporate directors from purchasing any property which might be useful to the corporation, but only to prevent their acquisition of property which the corporation needs or is seeking, or which they are otherwise under a duty to the corporation to acquire for it.

Thus a director may not purchase for himself property under lease to his corporation, or draw away existing customers of the corporation. Nor may he purchase property which the corporation needs or has resolved to acquire, or which it is contemplating acquiring. He may not take advantage of an offer made to the corporation, or of knowledge which came to him as a director. None of these proscriptions aids the plaintiff, however, for there is no evidence that the properties she seeks for Darand were offered to or sought by Darand, came to the Horns' attention through Darand, or were necessary to Darand's success.

Plaintiff apparently contends that defendants were as a matter of law under a duty to acquire for Darand further properties like those it was operating. She is seemingly supported by several commentators, who have stated that any opportunity within a corporation's "line of business" is a corporate opportunity. E.g., Note, Corporate Opportunity, 74 Harv. L. Rev. 765, 768-69 (1961); Note, A Survey of Corporate Opportunity, 45 Geo. L.J. 99, 100-01 (1956). This statement seems to us too broad a generalization. We think that under New York law a court must determine in each case, by considering the relationship between the director and the corporation, whether a duty to offer the corporation all opportunities within its "line of business" is fairly to be implied. Had the Horns been full-time employees of Darand with no prior real estate ventures of their own, New York law might well uphold a finding that they were subject to such an implied duty. But as they spent most of their time in unrelated produce and real estate enterprises and already owned corporations holding similar properties when Darand was formed, as plaintiff knew, we agree with Judge Dooling that a duty to offer Darand all such properties coming to their attention cannot be implied absent some further evidence of an agreement or understanding to that effect. Judge Dooling's finding that there was no such understanding is not clearly erroneous.

Although we have found no New York case involving similar facts, our holding that the scope of a director's duty to offer opportunities he has found to his corporation must be measured by the facts of each case seems more consistent than any other with the holdings of New York courts applying the "interest or expectancy" test. Moreover, the decisions of other courts in analogous cases support our conclusion. The Supreme Court of Delaware held in *Johnston v. Greene*, 121 A. 2d 919 (1956), that a director of several corporations who was offered the patents and stock of a corporation engaged in an unrelated business and who arranged for the purchase of the stock by one of the corporations of which he was a director did not appropriate a corporate opportunity of that corporation by retaining the patents. The court recognized that a corporation's need to invest funds and a director's duty to seek investments for it might convert an investment opportunity offered to the director into a corporate opportunity, but held that "whether it does . . ., in any particular case, depends on the facts — upon the existence of special circumstances that would make it unfair for him to take the opportunity for himself." The court found especially persuasive against the existence of such special circumstances the fact that the director served on several boards. It has been urged that the reasoning of *Johnston v. Greene* is fallacious because the fact that a director may be under fiduciary obligations to more than one corporation should lead a court to find and enforce the strongest obligation, not to allow the director to disregard them all. Note, Corporate Opportunity, 74 Harv. L. Rev. 765, 770-771 (1961); Note, The Doctrine of Corporate Opportunity, 26 U. Cin. L. Rev. 104, 108-109 (1957). This criticism seems to us to miss the point underscored by the facts of this case, that a person's involvement in more than one venture of the same kind may negate the obligation which might otherwise be implied to offer similar opportunities to any one of them, absent some contrary understanding. Thus we affirm Judge Dooling's holding that the properties acquired by defendants were not corporate opportunities of Darand.

A director may be barred from competing with his corporation even though he does not by doing so appropriate a corporate opportunity. But the duty not to compete, like the duty to offer opportunities to the corporation, is measured by the circumstances of each case, so that the considerations which led us to hold that the properties acquired by the Horns were not corporate opportunities strongly suggest a finding that the Horns were free to compete by acquiring them. In any event, there is no evidence in the record suggesting that Darand has been harmed by the Horns' ownership and operation of the properties they acquired. Note, Fiduciary Duty of Officers and Directors Not to Compete With the Corporation, 54 Harv. L. Rev. 1191, 1197-99 (1941).

HAYS, CIRCUIT JUDGE (Dissenting):

My brothers hold that the scope of a director's duty to his corporation must be measured by the facts of each case. However, although they are unable to find any New York case presenting the same facts as those before us, they conclude that New York law does not support the imposition of liability in the circumstances of this case. I do not agree.

In an often quoted passage, the New York Court of Appeals laid down the principles of fiduciary conduct:

> Many forms of conduct permissible in a workaday world for those acting at arm's length, are forbidden to those bound by fiduciary ties. A trustee is held to something stricter than the morals of the market

place. Not honesty alone, but the punctilio of an honor the most sensitive, is then the standard of behavior. As to this there has developed a tradition that is unbending and inveterate. Uncompromising rigidity has been the attitude of courts of equity when petitioned to undermine the rule of undivided loyalty by the "disintegrating erosion" of particular exceptions.

Applying these standards to the instant case it seems clear that in the absence of a contrary agreement or understanding between the parties, the Horns, who were majority stockholders and managing officers of the Darand Corporation and whose primary function was to locate suitable properties for the company, were under a fiduciary obligation to offer such properties to Darand before buying the properties for themselves . . . That the Horns used Darand's funds to effectuate certain of these purchases reinforces the conclusion that their conduct was improper and failed to comport with the standards established by law.

Since the Horns were under a fiduciary duty imposed by law not to take advantage for themselves of corporate opportunities, it is irrelevant that, as the district court found, there was no agreement under which "the Horns would contract their real estate activities or offer every property they located to Darand." *A fortiori* the Horns were not free to select the best properties for themselves.

Questions

What was the likely expectation of both Burg and the Horns as to the Horns continuing to engage in other real estate ventures at the time they formed their venture? Is this the appropriate question to ask in the closely-held company situation? Who should bear the burden of proof of showing an agreement, understanding or acquiescence? Should there be a different (higher, lower) standard of duty applied in the closely held company situation? For comments critical of *Burg v. Horn* see (1968), 43 N.Y.U.L. Rev. 187, and (1967), 56 Geo. L.J. 381.

Notes on the US Cases

1 In his judgment in *Burg v. Horn*, Chief Judge Lumbard canvassed the three basic approaches taken by the US courts in corporate opportunity cases. The first is the "interest" or "expectancy" test, which is applied by asking whether the corporation needs or was seeking the opportunity in question. As Judge Lumbard notes, this test has been criticized as being vague and unhelpful, but is nonetheless the one most often applied. The second approach is to ask whether the opportunity is in the "line of business" of the corporation. The leading case is *Guth v. Loft, Inc.*, 5 A.2d 503 (S.C. Del., 1939), in which the Supreme Court of Delaware expressed the point as follows (at p. 514):

> Where a corporation is engaged in a certain business, and an opportunity is presented to it embracing an activity as to which it has fundamental knowledge, practical experience and ability to pursue . . . and is one that is consonant with its reasonable needs and aspirations. . . it may be properly said that the opportunity is in the line of the corporation's business.

This was the test argued for by the plaintiff in *Burg* but rejected by Judge Lumbard as "too broad a generalization." Rather, he said that the relationship between the director and his corporation had to be examined in each case to determine if all opportunities within its line of business had to be offered to it. The third test is the more general one of "fairness" — a test that finds echoes in Laskin C.J.'s judgment in *Canaero*. Judicial expression of this test is found in *Durfee v. Durfee & Canning*, 80 N.E.2d 522 (S.C. Mass., 1948), at p. 529:

> [T]he true basis of the doctrine [of corporate opportunity] should not be found in any expectancy or property interest concept, but in the unfairness on the particular facts of a fiduciary taking advantage of an opportunity when the interests of the corporation justly call for protection.

This is similar to Laskin C.J.'s statement in *Canaero* that he was "not to be taken as laying down any rule of liability to be read as if it were a statute." Rather, the general standards of loyalty and good faith "must be tested in each case by many factors . . ." To similar effect is the holding of the Delaware Supreme Court in the leading case of *Johnston v. Green*, 121 A.2d 919 (1956): "whether [an investment opportunity offered to a director becomes a corporate opportunity] in any particular case, depends on the facts — upon the existence of special circumstances that would make it unfair for him to take the opportunity for himself."

2 The burden of proof in corporate opportunity cases in the US is most often placed on the person taking the opportunity, by analogy to the "interested transaction" cases where the fiduciary has the burden of establishing the inherent fairness of the contract. The position of directors and senior officers, as well as of parent corporations, would seem to call for the inherent fairness standard in all corporate opportunity cases.

3 The court in *Burg v. Horn* has been criticized for allowing lower standards of fiduciary duties to govern directorial behaviour when directors enjoy multiple directorships. This is argued to be undesirable because it enhances the scope for unscrupulous conduct in settings where this danger is already high. See, for instance, "Note on Corporate Opportunity" (1968), 43 N.Y.U.L. Rev. 187, in which it was argued that the court erred in considering the fact of multiple directorships to be a

factor favouring the defendants in *Burg v. Horn*. The court was also criticized for failing to impose the burden of proof on the defendants:

> The *Burg* court . . . misplac(ed) the burden of proof, for the Horns were not required to show that they had fully disclosed all their acquisitions to Mrs. Burg, nor that they had offered Darand the opportunity of acquiring these properties. Rather than infer from the lack of an agreement that the Horns were free to acquire the properties, it would have been preferable for the court to have imposed upon the Horns a duty to fully disclose these properties and to offer them to Darand unless the Horns could prove an agreement with Mrs. Burg allowing them to operate independently of Darand (at 193).

VICTOR BRUDNEY AND ROBERT CHARLES CLARK, "A New Look at Corporate Opportunities"
(1981), 94 Harv. L. Rev. 997 at 998–1006 (footnotes deleted)

The law of corporate opportunities is among the least satisfactory limbs of doctrine in the corpus of corporate law. Not only are the common formulations vague, but the courts have articulated no theory that could serve as a blueprint for constructing meaningful rules. In part, this situation reflects the fact that the vast bulk of corporate opportunity cases have involved close corporations. Open-ended rules are often suitable for close corporations and the essentially contractual relationships of their investors and managers. But sharper doctrinal responses are called for by the claims of investors in public corporations against their executives, directors, and parent corporations. In this Article, we examine the theoretical underpinning of the corporate opportunity doctrine, and suggest relatively clear rules to implement it.

We begin by asking why there is any need for a corporate opportunity doctrine. According to the formulation of most courts, if a business opportunity is determined to be a corporate opportunity, then a corporate fiduciary — such as a director, officer, or controlling shareholder — may not take or "usurp" it for his own benefit, unless proper consent is given. Thus, a corporate opportunity is defined to be, as against fiduciaries, a corporate asset. The reasons for forbidding its appropriation are the same as those for generally forbidding corporate agents and fiduciaries from unilaterally taking corporate property for themselves. An essential reason is that a generalized fiduciary duty of loyalty is efficient . . .

In our examination of the problem of identifying corporate opportunities, we suggest what we think are relevant considerations and feasible rules. Our study rests upon two assumptions that are not generally reflected in the present doctrine. First, we submit that different considerations and rules should be employed for close corporations than for publicly held corporations. Second, we believe that in the latter case, rules should depend upon whether the appropriator is (1) a full-time officer or executive, (2) only an outside director or a part-time executive of more than one corporation, or (3) a parent corporation.

* * *

A. Relevant Differences Between Close and Public Corporations

The basic choice to be made when importing the fiduciary principle from the law of trusts to define the corporate opportunity doctrine is between a categorical approach and a selective approach. The former forbids all personal gains to the trustee from dealings relating to trust property, even if the transaction would deprive the beneficiary of nothing, and even if it might produce benefits for both him and the trustee. The latter forbids only behavior that in particular circumstances creates a serious probability of injury to the beneficiary; it would not prohibit transactions merely because the trustee as well as the beneficiary may gain from them. The categorical approach would define corporate opportunity in sweeping terms to include all possible active modes of making a profit, and would take a strict stance towards proposed exceptions and defenses. It would prohibit an officer or executive, for example, from taking any other active business opportunity — at least without the consent of the corporation. The selective approach would define corporate opportunity more narrowly, by criteria that relate each opportunity to the operations, needs, or expectations of the firm. It would require the fiduciary to show only that the opportunity he took does not fall within the criteria. On this approach, insiders would be denied some active business opportunities, but permitted to accept others.

In our view, it is desirable to use the selective approach for close corporations and the categorical approach for public corporations. Fundamentally, the stockholders of public corporations are more like the beneficiaries of trusts, for whom the stricter rule was fashioned, than are the participants in private ventures. Certainly this appears true when we consider stockholders in their role as selectors and monitors of their fiduciaries. And other relevant differences between the two types of enterprise also support our view.

The ability of the stockholders of private corporations to select the fiduciaries to whom they have entrusted their capital, and to police their management's contributions to (and diversions from) the enterprise is much greater than the selecting and monitoring capacities of shareholders in public corporations. Investors in public corporations are usually passive and widely scattered contributors of money to be managed by pre-selected officers to whom they effectively delegate full decision making power over operating matters. In contrast, investors in private ventures are fairly small in number and tend to know one another. They make more conscious choices when selecting managers from among themselves. They are likely to be active participants rather than merely passive contributors of funds. And they can consent in a more meaningful way to diversions of corporate assets by fellow participants, either when they form or join enterprises, or on the occasion of the diversion. Accordingly, such investors have less need of categorical strictures on such diversions.

Moreover, both the scope of the duties and the nature of the compensation of the managers differ between the two types of corporation. The duties of the executives of a public corporation normally require full-time application of their managerial talents and energies and leave no room for active participation in the development or operation of other businesses. Correspondingly, their compensation arrangements are such that neither equity nor efficiency requires them to be allowed to take covert indirect compensation as they see fit. But for many close corporations, other expectations may be more reasonable. The participants may sometimes agree, or assume in the initial arrangements, that their managing colleagues are not to work only for the particular corporation, but are free to engage in other activities. In any event, it is feasible in close corporations (as it is *not* in public corporations) to obtain the consent of all participants to such part-time employment by the managing participants. And such consent may well be inferred in close corporations when some participants are under compensated in relation to other participants. The formal compensation arrangements may not adequately separate the role of a participant's talents and efforts from the role of his capital contributions in determining his returns. In this context, a claim of under compensation might be plausible when the participants in the close corporation agreed or understood — or probably would have agreed, had they thought of the matter — that their financial rewards should reflect variations in their continuing active efforts as well as their initial capital contributions.

Finally, differences between the opportunity sets of the two types of enterprise imply different constraints on their managers. A publicly held enterprise may fairly be treated as large and flexible enough to accept any new investment opportunities that offer an appropriate return per unit of risk. Hence, its opportunity set embraces virtually any business in which its executives might want to invest and take an active role. The opportunity set of a close corporation is not nearly so broad. Market imperfections and transaction costs may preclude or impede such corporations' efforts to accept projects unrelated to their existing experience or talent or beyond their existing financial capacity. There may be many businesses that the officers of a closely held enterprise may seek to develop on their own time, but that would not deprive the enterprise of any opportunity it could reasonably hope to exploit.

All these differences between close and public corporations — in the investors' abilities to select and monitor managers and to contract with one another, in the managers' duties and compensation arrangements, and in the size of opportunity sets — are mainly a consequence of differences in size. They suggest that lawmakers *generally* ought to construct corporate law doctrines with a different jurisprudential orientation in the two contexts. As a rough but fair generalization, the basic characteristics of the corporate form of organization and the related statutory rules are best suited for large-scale enterprises owned by numerous public investors. In this context, legal rules can and should be uniformly applicable even when they are fairly precise and specific. The rules of corporate law, which define the relationships of stockholders to each other and to management, constitute something like a "standard contract" to which all the actors who play the standard roles of shareholder, director, and officer automatically agree merely by virtue of their assuming these roles. The outcome of legal disputes governed by public corporation law should leave little play for the vagaries of particular understandings and arrangements.

But the notion that corporate participants should be viewed as entering voluntarily into a "standard contract," or prefixed set of roles and relationships, has much less relevance to close corporations. The close corporation "deal" simply does not have to be the same for all close corporations. The roles of the investor and the manager are more likely to be mixed and shared by the participants, and the range of variations in the terms of participation is likely to be greater. As indicated, this is a straightforward consequence of size differences. The small number of players in the typical close corporation makes possible a far greater amount of real communication and agreement among all players about their particular situations and objectives. As the number of players increases, however, the number of communication channels needed to connect them all with each other increases astronomically. Publicly held corporations simply cannot have a meaningful system of "open" communications and particularized agreements among all their players.

Of course, commentators, courts, and lawmakers have long recognized that the special traits of close corporations made it desirable to modify some of the original formal rules in corporate statutes, at least with respect to such corporations. But our analysis of the differences between the two types of corporation also has implications for the judge-made fiduciary principle. It suggests that rules explicating the principle for specific recurring situations — rules like those governing corporate opportunities — should leave more room in the close corporation context for results to turn on the special facts, arrangements, and understandings of each situation. Lawmakers should assume that the parties in close corporations are better able than those in public ones to make individual bargains. Hence, less rigid rules than the categorical ones we shall propose in later Parts of this Article should govern participants in close corporations. What those less rigid rules should be is another question. In general, we believe that in this context only modest alterations are needed in the guidelines provided by existing law.

4. COMPETITION

Directors who sit on the boards of either vertically or horizontally interlocked companies are clearly in a conflict of interest situation, as often are parent corporations with respect to their subsidiaries. The cases in the previous sections on directors' contracts and transactions and corporate opportunities deal with such situations. A related problem is that of competition, either directly by engaging in a competing enterprise or indirectly by being interested in such an enterprise. The cases dealing with the proper limits of a fiduciary's conduct prior to leaving his present employment to engage in competition raise a different aspect of the same problem. For reasons which are not historically clear, the law has taken as lenient an attitude towards the issue of competing directors as it has taken a strict attitude towards other aspects of the duty of loyalty.

London and Mashonaland Exploration Company, Limited v. New Mashonaland Exploration Company, Limited
[1891] W.N. 165

CHITTY, J.: Motion on behalf of the plaintiff company to restrain the defendant company from publishing any announcement that Lord Mayo was one of its directors, and to restrain Lord Mayo from authorizing or permitting any such publication, and from acting as director of the defendant company.

The above-named companies were incorporated for the same object, and were rival companies. The plaintiff company was registered in March, 1891, and in the following month a resolution was passed at a meeting of the directors appointing Lord Mayo a director and chairman. The plaintiff company alleged that Lord Mayo accepted the appointment, and approved of a prospectus privately circulated, wherein his name appeared as director and chairman, and that numerous applications for shares had been received upon the faith of such prospectus. In July the prospectus of the defendant company was circulated with the name of Lord Mayo at the head of its list of directors. It was admitted that Lord Mayo had never acted as a director, nor attended any board meeting of the plaintiff company, and that he had never agreed, either expressly or by the articles of association, not to become a director of any similar company.

Chitty, J., said, even assuming that Lord Mayo had been duly elected chairman and director of the plaintiff company, there was nothing in the articles which required him to give any part of his time, much less the whole of his time, to the business of the company, or which prohibited him from acting as a director of another company; neither was there any contract express or implied to give his personal services to the plaintiff company and not to another company. No case had been made out that Lord Mayo was about to disclose to the defendant company any information that he had obtained confidentially in his character of chairman: the analogy sought to be drawn by the plaintiff company's counsel between the present case and partnerships was incomplete: no sufficient damage had been shown, and no case had been made for an injunction: the application was wholly unprecedented, and must be dismissed with costs.

Questions

1 Is Mr. Justice Chitty's judgment consistent with the earlier judgment of the House of Lords in *Aberdeen Railway v. Blaikie, supra*, and Lord Cranworth's "rule of universal application" that a fiduciary may not enter into engagements "in which he has or can have a personal interest conflicting or which may possibly conflict with the interests of those whom he is bound to protect?" Is the basis of Chitty J.'s judgment consistent with the basis of subsequent duty of loyalty cases? For a recent comment examining whether *London and Mashonaland* is still good law in the U.K., see Ross Grantham, "Can Directors Compete with the Company?" (2003), 66 Mod. L. Rev. 109.

Mr. Justice Chitty's brief judgment on a motion in *London and Mashonaland*, might never have been elevated into a judicial principle if it had not been picked up and repeated in the *dicta* of Lord Blanesburgh L.C. in *Bell v. Lever Bros. Ltd.*, [1932] A.C. 161 (H.L.):

> And this brings me to the position of a director in relation to contracts of the second class, with which we are here alone concerned. The principle will be found in the case usually cited in relation to it, although reported only in the Weekly Notes, of *London and Mashonaland Exploration Co. v. New Mashonaland Exploration Co.* where it was held that, it not appearing from the regulations of the company that a director's services must be rendered to that company and to no other company, he was at liberty to become a director even of a rival company, and it not being established that he was making to the second company any disclosure of information obtained confidentially by him as a director of the first company he could not at the instance of that company be restrained in his rival directorate. What he could do for a rival company, he could, of course, do for himself.

The "second class" of contract to which Lord Blanesburgh referred was one in which the director's company had no interest. Thus, the holding of *London and Mashonaland* that a director could become interested in a rival concern was used simply to emphasize the point in issue — that the director could be a party to a contract in which his company was not interested. Notwithstanding this use of *London and Mashonaland*, Lord Blanesburgh's *dicta* in *Bell v. Lever Bros. Ltd.* have been cited ever since as authority for the proposition that a director may engage in a competing business. For a case that ignores *Aberdeen Railway* and follows *London and Mashonaland*, see *Waite's Auto Transfer Ltd. v. Waite*, [1928] 3 W.W.R. 649 (president and director of one company allowed to set up a rival concern that canvassed customers of the first company). Would the holding in *Waite's Auto Transfer* survive the decision of the Supreme Court in *Canaero*?

2 A director who joins a rival concern and prefers its interests to those of the first company would likely face an application under s. 241 of the CBCA or s. 248 OBCA, with respect to the conduct of the first company. The use of the oppression remedy in such a case has been considered by the House of Lords. In *Scottish Co-Operative Wholesale Society Ltd. v. Meyer*, [1959] A.C. 324 (H.L.), Lord Denning was referred to Lord Blanesburgh's dicta in *Bell v. Lever Bros.* that a director could join the board of a rival company, to which he replied: "That may have been so at that time. But it is at the risk now of an application under s. 210 if he subordinates the interest of the one company to those of the other". (Section 210 is now s. 459 of the *Companies Act, 1985*.) Professor Gower, *Principles of Modern Company Law* (1997, 6th ed.), p. 622, comments as follows:

> it has been recognized that one who is a director of two rival concerns is walking a tight-rope and at risk if he fails to deal fairly with both.

3 In *Abbey Glen Property Corp. v. Stumborg*, [1976] 2 W.W.R. 1, McDonald J., in dealing with the defendant's argument that since the directors owed a fiduciary duty to another company they could not be in breach of their fiduciary duty to the plaintiff if what they did was in furtherance of their duty to the other company, indicated that he did not agree with the decision in *London and Mashonaland*. McDonald, J. said that although it was not strictly necessary to decide the point:

> I do not hesitate to express my opinion that the sweeping proposition for which the *London and Mashonaland* case and Lord Blanesburgh's dicta is cited is not the law. Even where there is no question of a director using confidential information, there may well be cases in which a director breaches his fiduciary duty to Company A merely by acting as a director of Company B. This will particularly be possible when the companies are in the same line of business and where acting as a director of Company B will harm Company A. Beyond that I need go no further than to say that the question whether there has been a breach of a director's duty to Company A must be determined upon the basis of the factors enumerated in *Canadian Aero Services v. O'Malley* and *Regal (Hastings) Ltd. v. Gulliver*, and a negative answer will not necessarily be produced by the mere fact that a director is also a director of Company B and owes it a like fiduciary duty.

4 In *Bendix Home Systems Ltd. v. Clayton* (1978), 33 C.P.R. (2d) 230, McFarlane J., held that there was a breach of fiduciary duty although there was no appropriation of a "maturing business opportunity" as there had been in *Canaero*. Rather, the defendants developed a plan, while still employed by the plaintiff, to enter into competition with their employer. What was objectionable was not that they intended to go into competition, which they had a perfect right to do:

> but that they put self-interest before their duty of loyalty and good faith to their employer whose interests were, during their employment, to be regarded as paramount to the defendants' personal ambitions. In this case the defendants . . . were entitled to leave Bendix, and to enter into competition with it in Canada. They were not entitled, however, to use their position of trust and influence in the Bendix organization, and to use the opportunities afforded by their employer during the course of their employment, to attempt to put in place a new company which would take from Bendix many of its senior management personnel in Canada, and to divert from Bendix the goodwill of dealers which it was the duty of the defendants to attract for Bendix.

The decision of Mr. Justice Clauson in a trust case, *In re Thomson*, is consistent with fiduciary principles and equally applicable to the corporate fiduciary.

In Re Thomson
[1930] 1 Ch. 203

CLAUSON J.: . . . The matter I have to decide is this. Is the defendant right or not in the submission which he makes in para. 16 of his defence:

> That at all times since the death of the testator or alternatively at all times since his ceasing to take any part in the conduct of the testator's said business the defendant has been and is lawfully entitled (subject to his observance of any restrictions imposed by the general law relative to his solicitation of customers of the testator or otherwise) to carry on or be concerned in the business of a yacht agent competing with that of the testator.

If he is right in that submission the action, so far as relates to this matter, ought not to have been started, and the plaintiffs must pay the costs with the further result that, if there was no cause of action, the injunction granted by the Court of Appeal would be one which, in such case, ought not to have been granted, and the defendant would be entitled to an inquiry as to damages for the injury sustained by the granting of the injunction. On the other hand, if the submission of the defendant is incorrect, it is obvious the action was properly started; and the defendant must pay the costs of the action with regard to this matter as well as the costs with regard to the other matter I have mentioned. There therefore arises for my decision this neat point. A testator carrying on the business of a yacht agent appoints an executor and directs him to carry on the business. The executor accepts the position of executor and in fact carries on the business; is that executor at liberty to sever his connection with the business, though it still remains a portion of the testator's estate, and himself start a competing yacht agent's business? The first thing to ascertain is what is a yacht agent's business, and what effect upon the interests of the beneficiary under the testator's will would result from the executor starting a competing business? For that purpose I am assisted by the statement in para. 14 of the defendant's defence, which is in these terms:

> The business of a yacht agent or broker is similar to that of a house agent i.e. the yacht agent receives or solicits the order or permission of yacht owners to place their yachts on his books and having ascertained by inquiry or advertisement a prospective purchaser of any particular yacht obtains and submits an offer to the owner and is paid a commission by him if a sale results. The greater part of the yachts for the time being on the market are therefore on the books of all yacht agents and that agent earns a commission on a sale who can first secure a purchaser. Every yacht agent consequently carries on a business which competes with that of every other yacht agent. The business of the testator was of the character of those of all other yacht agents in this paragraph described and the testator had no regular or exclusive connection.

I ought to say that in opening this case Mr. Gavin Simonds, for the plaintiffs, said he was not quite prepared to accept that statement as accurate, as he was not prepared to admit that the testator had no regular or exclusive connection. However, no evidence was given by the plaintiffs apart from the correspondence, and as against the defendant I am prepared to assume that para. 14 is an accurate statement. I do not think, for the purpose of my judgment, it is very material whether the testator had any regular or exclusive connection or not. Let me see what is involved in Mr. Allen starting a rival business of a yacht agent or broker on his own account. He will proceed to communicate with a yacht owner and he will enter into a contract with that yacht owner the effect of which will be that, if he, Mr. Allen, is fortunate enough to be the yacht agent who is the first to secure a purchaser for the owner of the yacht, he will obtain a benefit in the form of a commission. Now there is no question that as between Mr. Allen on the one hand and the beneficiaries under Mr. Thomson's will on the other, there was in existence, and as to this there is no dispute, a relation of a fiduciary nature; and the point I really have to consider is this: Would it or would it not have been a breach of Mr. Allen's fiduciary duty between himself and the beneficiaries under the will, if he had started at the time of the commencement of the action a new business of a yacht agent and had accordingly entered into such a contract as I have described with a yacht owner who might have entered into a similar contract with Mr. Thomson's executors which would have enabled Mr. Thomson's executors, should they have been the fortunate brokers who were the first to secure a purchaser for the owner of the yacht, to secure a commission?

In order to find the principle I have to apply I turn to the judgment of Cranworth L.C. in the House of Lords in the case of *Aberdeen Ry. Co. v. Blaikie Brothers. . . .*

I find the principle to be this. The rule of universal application is that an executor and trustee having duties to discharge of a fiduciary nature towards the beneficiaries under the will — in this particular case the duty of a fiduciary nature was to carry on the business of the testator to the best advantage of the beneficiaries — he shall not be allowed to enter into any engagement in which he has or can have a personal interest conflicting, or which possibly may conflict, with the interests of those whom he is bound to protect. Now if Mr. Allen had set up this competing business and had entered into such an engagement with a yacht owner as that to which I have referred, would he have been entering into an engagement in which he would have a personal interest conflicting or which possibly might conflict with the interests of those he was bound to protect? Having regard to the special nature of a yacht agent's business, it appears to me clear that I am bound to answer that question by saying that, by starting such a business and entering into such engagements, Mr. Allen would have been entering into engagements which would conflict, or certainly possibly might conflict with the interest of the beneficiaries under the will, because he would be obtaining for himself chances of earning a commission which, but for such competition, might be obtained for the beneficiaries under the will. It appears to me, therefore, that, if Mr. Allen had set up — he did not, because he was prevented by the injunction granted by the Court of Appeal — a competing business at the time in question, the commencement of the action, he would have been doing something which would have been a breach, as between himself and the beneficiaries, of the fiduciary duties he owed them. . . .

5. HOSTILE TAKEOVERS AND DEFENSIVE TACTICS BY TARGET MANAGEMENT

(a) Introduction to Hostile Takeovers and Defensive Tactics

The fifth, and by far the most contentious subject area for the study of fiduciary duties, relates to management defensive tactics in response to a hostile takeover bid. A hostile takeover bid enables an outside acquirer to obtain control of a target corporation without having to obtain the assent of target management. Simply put, an acquirer will make a bid (almost always at some premium above the market price of the shares) to the target shareholders for some or all of the voting shares of the target company. If, within the prescribed time period, the requisite number of shares are tendered by target shareholders into the bid, then the shares will be "picked up" by the acquirer and the bid completed.

It is the ability of a new owner to sidestep target management in obtaining control of the corporation that renders the hostile takeover bid so threatening to target management. According to the management discipline hypothesis, takeovers are motivated by the gains that an acquirer can realize from displacing opportunistic management with more dedicated and efficient managers, perhaps even the acquirer herself, once control is obtained. Under this hypothesis, the gains from the takeover of a corporation directly vary with the severity of agency problems besetting the target corporation. The more opportunistic target management has been, in terms of their levels of diversion and shirking, the greater the benefit, and corresponding incentive, to an acquirer to obtain control and oust target management.

If the management discipline hypothesis is accepted as being the exclusive, or even a contributory, motive for takeovers, the tendency for target management to fiercely resist takeovers is not surprising. Target management, fearing the loss of their jobs and reputational capital, will do their best to stave off a hostile takeover by using a range of defensive tactics. These tactics may make a control acquisition more expensive to an acquirer, or may even deter the takeover altogether. In either case, management resistance dulls the incentive for takeovers, and, because any reduction in the level of takeover activity will increase the scope for managerial opportunism, resistance by target management will harm target shareholders. As Henry Manne pointed out several decades ago, any constraint on the takeover market will exacerbate the problems occasioned by the separation of ownership and control in the modern corporation (Henry Manne, "Mergers and the Market for Corporate Control" (1965), 73 J. Pol. Econ. 110 at 113). This is because "[o]nly the takeover scheme provides some assurance of competitive affairs among corporate managers and thereby affords strong protection to the interests of vast numbers of small, non-controlling shareholders." (The management discipline hypothesis is currently most strongly associated with the work of Easterbrook and Fischel, *infra*.)

If the management discipline hypothesis is correct, then the analysis of defensive tactics falls neatly within the scope of fiduciary duty doctrine: since the spectre of self-interested behaviour is omnipresent when managers fend off takeovers, courts should, as in other conflict situations, enforce a blanket prohibition against such conduct. The first difficulty, however, is that it is far from settled that managerial discipline is always the sole or dominant motive for takeover activity. Commentators have claimed that a number of competing motives for takeovers exist, some of which will result in transactions that are entirely bereft of economic value. But once competing motives for takeovers are acknowledged to exist, the efficacy of employing a blanket prohibition against all defensive tactics becomes suspect. Arguably, defensive tactics should be permitted where transactions are harmful to shareholders or to society. Here again, the issue of categorical versus selective rules becomes important, as does the ancillary issue of the judiciary's ability to effectively delineate between "desirable" and "undesirable" takeovers.

Adding another layer of complexity to the determination of the appropriate scope of managerial defensive tactics is the issue of auctions. That is, even if it is assumed that takeovers are motivated by desirable goals, some scholars (like Gilson, *infra*), have argued that target management should be able to engage in certain types of conduct aimed at establishing an auction that will raise the price of target shares to the acquirer. Whether auctions should be permitted or, indeed, encouraged, must be considered at normative and positive levels. In terms of the former, a decision to promote auctions indicates a desire to confer much of the benefit from takeover transactions on target shareholders. But why should the law deliberately favour target shareholders over acquirers? What are the equitable arguments in support of this position? In terms of the latter, if it is agreed that target shareholders should be the principal beneficiaries of takeover activity, what are the costs to societal welfare (because of reduced takeover activity) that are entailed by this commitment?

The following materials canvass the issue of the appropriate scope of defensive tactics from a number of different perspectives. First, several different theoretical perspectives are presented on the takeover debate — in particular, the issues of competing takeover motives and the appropriate role of auctions is discussed. Second, empirical evidence relating to various theoretical motives for takeover bids is presented. Finally, the response of Anglo-Canadian and American courts to defensive tactics is documented.

One final comment: the extensive discussion of takeovers in this section reflects not merely the existence of a lively and interesting academic debate over the regulation of defensive tactics, but also the heightened level of activity that has occurred in the mergers and acquisition market in the recent past. Demott reports that in 1985, the dollar amount spent on mergers and acquisition activity in the United States was approximately $180–190 billion. During the same year, over 128 transactions were valued at more than $100 million. In Canada, the dollar value of mergers, adjusted for the smaller size of the Canadian economy, was 5 times as large as comparable values in the United States in the period 1975–79, and 2 times as large in the 1980–85 period. So significant has the effect of merger and acquisition activity been on Canadian capital markets, that the "float" (i.e., the shares not owned by controlling interests that are outstanding and available for trading) on the Toronto Stock Exchange has been reduced as a result of such activity. (Demott, "Comparative Dimensions of Takeover Regulation" (1987), 65 Washington Univ. L.R. 69 at 80-81.) These data buttress the characterization of takeover regulation as an issue of profound importance for Canadian courts, regulators, lawyers, and managers.

(b) Theoretical and Empirical Perspectives

JEFFREY MACINTOSH,
"The Poison Pill: A Noxious Nostrum for Canadian Shareholders"
(1993), 15 Canadian Business Law Journal, p. 276 (footnotes deleted)

The purpose of this article is straightforward. By reviewing the empirical literature on the effects of poison pills on shareholder wealth, I will construct an argument that poison pills are not in the best interests of shareholders. Shareholders would be well advised not to vote in favour of them. I will also suggest that courts and administrators should sanction such plans only when approved by shareholders. Securities regulators should block any attempt to put a pill in place when shareholders are asked to consider more than one issue in a single vote, as Inco shareholders were recently asked to do. Where shareholders approve poison pill plans, the courts should carefully supervise their deployment in order to enhance the likelihood that pills are used in the best interests of shareholders and not simply to entrench target managers.

2. What is the Function of Poison Pills?

There are two competing accounts of the function and purpose of poison pills. These may be described as the "shareholder interest" and "managerial entrenchment" hypotheses.

(1) Shareholder Interest Hypothesis

The germ of this explanation is that a hostile acquirer is able to employ coercive tactics that effectively force target shareholders to tender into a low bid, even though shareholders as a group would prefer to hold out for more. The poison pill is the antidote to this coercion. By making an acquisition prohibitively expensive without the co-operation of management, the pill enables holders. So empowered, management may either defeat a bid that is too low, force the acquirer to make a more generous offer, or shop the company around for a better bid. Alternatively, management may use the breathing space accorded them by the pill to put together a competing proposal, like a "self-tender" (issuer bid), recapitalization, divestiture of assets or the like resulting in greater value for the target shareholders. In this way, shareholders will receive "full and fair value" for their shares.

Proponents of this view typically identify two types of "coercive" activity by bidders. The first is the two-tier bid. A two-tier bid is a 100% share acquisition effected in two stages. The bidder initially makes a take-over bid for sufficient shares to give the acquirer control of the firm. Remaining shareholders are then forced out in a second step amalgamation or similar transaction. The second step cashout price is lower than that offered shareholders on the first step takeover bid. Although shareholders as a group may share the determination that the price offered is too low, this two-tier arrangement ostensibly offers each individual shareholder a powerful incentive to tender into the first step partial bid. If the shareholder fails to tender, and the bid is successful, that shareholder is struck with the lower second-tier price for all her shares. This element of compulsion may also result in a lower valued two-tier bid beating out a higher valued any-or-all bid.

The second form of compulsion is said to be a partial bid for less than all the shares of the corporation. By reducing the public float of shares available for trading, a partial bid creates a condition of illiquidity in the market for those shares remaining in public hands after the conclusion of the bid. This effectively transforms a partial bid into the equivalent of a two-tier bid, with a similar element of compulsion.

As noted, the poison pill is supposed to counter these coercive influences.

(2) The Management Entrenchment Hypothesis

When a successful hostile takeover bid occurs, the end result may be, and often is, loss of employment for the incumbent managers. This creates a potent conflict of interest for target managers, who may be more tempted to preserve their jobs at all costs than to act in the best interests of shareholders. Thus, the power given target management by the pill may be used abusively, rather than beneficially, to deter or thwart hostile bids and preserve managerial tenure. Because takeover bids usually result in the payment of large premiums to target shareholders, foreclosing a bid will result in a loss of potential takeover premiums with a corresponding diminution in share values. Moreover, incumbent managers will be insulated from the market for corporate control; shareholders may therefore find themselves stuck with inefficient managers, resulting in further losses in share value.

* * *

(8) Summary of the Empirical Evidence

The available evidence on the effects of poison pills, taken in its totality, is highly consistent with the managerial entrenchment hypothesis. On the announcement of the adoption of poison pill plans, share prices on average decline. The decline is more pronounced where the firm is already the subject of takeover speculation or an ongoing takeover battle. It is also greater where the pill in question has an ownership discrimination feature characteristic of the most form of flip in pill, like that adopted by Inco. Additional evidence supporting the management entrenchment hypothesis is garnered from the behaviour of stock prices around court decisions regarding poison pills. Decisions upholding pills lead to share price declines, and decisions striking them down lead to price increases, on average. Firms adopting pills typically have lower profitability than industry cohorts and lower average share holdings by managers, further supporting the management entrenchment hypothesis. Although managers often state that the pill is designed to thwart coercive two-tier and partial offers, the evidence points strongly away from any such coercive effect. In a majority of cases, the pill is used not against these supposedly coercive forms of offers, but against any-or-all offers, suggesting that managers may simply appeal to the coercion argument as a matter of convenience rather than conviction.

(c) Defensive Tactics and the Theory of Takeovers

EASTERBROOK AND FISCHEL,
"The Proper Role of a Target's Management in Responding to a Tender Offer"
(1982), 94 Harv. L. Rev. 1161

Tender offers are a method of monitoring the work of management teams. Prospective bidders monitor the performance of managerial teams by comparing a corporation's potential value with its value (as reflected by share prices) under current management. When the difference between the market price of a firm's shares and the price those shares might have under different circumstances becomes too great, an outsider can profit by buying the firm and improving its management. The outsider reduces the free riding problem because it owns a majority of the shares. The source of the premium is the reduction in agency costs, which makes the firm's assets worth more in the hands of the acquirer than they were worth in the hands of the firm's managers.

All parties benefit in this process. The target's shareholders gain because they receive a premium over the market price. The bidder obtains the difference between the new value of the firm and the payment to the old shareholders. Non-tendering shareholders receive part of the appreciation in the price of the shares.

More significantly for our purposes, shareholders benefit even if their corporation never is the subject of a tender offer. The process of monitoring by outsiders poses a continuous threat of takeover if performance lags. Managers will attempt to reduce agency costs in order to reduce the chance of takeover, and the process of reducing agency costs leads to higher prices for shares.

If the company adopts a policy of intransigent resistance and succeeds in maintaining its independence, the shareholders lose whatever premium over market value the bidder offered or would have offered but for the resistance or the prospect of resistance. This lost premium reflects a foregone social gain from the superior employment of the firm's assets.

* * *

II. THE ARGUMENTS SUPPORTING THE RIGHT OF TARGET MAN-AGEMENT TO ADOPT A DEFENSIVE STRATEGY

Our analysis cuts against the grain of many cases and a substantial amount of commentary. The rationales offered to support the right of target management to resist tender offers can be grouped in four categories: (1) tender offers do not increase welfare; (2) the target's shareholders benefit from price increases when tender offers are defeated; (3) the target's management has obligations to non-investor groups that may be adversely affected by a tender offer; and (4) the target's management is obligated to prevent unlawful conduct. In the sections that follow, we consider and reject each of these rationales as a basis for resistance.

A. The Arguments That Tender Offers Do Not Increase Welfare

Our argument relies on the premise that tender offers increase social welfare by moving productive assets to higher-valued uses and to the hands of better managers. Numerous commentators, however, have reached a contrary conclusion. It has been observed, for instance, that many target companies are "well run," have substantial amounts of cash from successful operations, and that the offeror retains the target's management after acquiring control. These observations are invoked to support an assertion that the acquired firms were not doing poorly; consequently, the argument concludes, tender offers do not move assets to better managers.

This is unpersuasive. It amounts to second-guessing the market. Unless the acquirer is giving away its money, the premium price paid for the shares indicates a real gain in the productivity of the assets. If General Motors is willing to bid $100 for a ton of steel owned by General Electric, and GE sells, we would count this as a value-increasing transaction despite the fact that GE otherwise would have put the steel to "good use" (perhaps $90 worth). The highly subjective observation that acquired firms are well run does not exclude the possibility that, in new hands, the firms would be better run. Only proof that markets are not efficient in pricing shares could support the argument that tender offers do not improve the use of resources.

That acquired firms often are cash rich, perhaps implying successful past operations, also does not demonstrate that takeovers are undesirable. To the contrary, that a firm holds a substantial cash position indicates agency costs. Cash can be invested. The acquirer usually invests the cash it obtains in the takeover, thus putting idle resources to work. The retention of the target's management after a takeover also is not significant. Although the management may keep their old titles, they often lose effective control to officers of the acquirer. Retention in office may be a form of bribe, paid to secure acquiescence in the takeover, rather than a signal of satisfactory performance.

Martin Lipton has advanced a related argument: Tender offers decrease social welfare because they "adversely affect long-term planning and thereby jeopardize the economy." But he fails to demonstrate how long-term planning is "adversely affected," let alone the economy jeopardized. The threat of takeovers does not prevent managers from engaging in long-range planning. If the market perceives that management has developed a successful long-term strategy, this will be reflected in higher share prices that discourage takeovers. To be sure, the risk of a tender offer ensures that corporate managers will be unable to assume that they can continue in office indefinitely. But this risk of displacement does not reduce welfare. Precisely the opposite is true; some insecurity of tenure is necessary to spur managers to their best performance. Society benefits from an active takeover market, therefore, because it simultaneously provides an incentive to all corporate managers to operate efficiently and a mechanism for displacing inefficient managers.

Harold Williams, former Chairman of the Securities and Exchange Commission, has argued that tender offers decrease welfare because they divert resources that otherwise could be used for capital investments and instead are used only to rear-range the ownership of existing corporate assets. The answer to this argument is that funds used to finance a tender offer are not necessarily diverted from investment to consumption. They are merely shifted from the acquiring corporation to the target's shareholders. The acquiring corporation could equally well have distributed these funds as dividends or put them to other non-investment uses. There is also no reason to assume that the target's shareholders will use these funds for consumption rather than capital investment. The shareholders may reinvest what they receive from the tender offeror. There is, therefore, no reason to conclude a priori that an active takeover market diverts funds from capital investment.

Tender offers have also been characterized as "raids" in which the offeror pays a premium for a working majority of the shares in order to loot the firm to the detriment of the minority shareholders. It is unlikely, however, that any tender offer for a substantial percentage of a company's shares will be motivated by a desire to loot the acquired corporation. A looter generates no new value, and thus cannot afford to pay a premium price for all shares. Even if a bidder seeks less than all shares, it cannot pay a significant premium for those it obtains. If, for example, the offeror acquires for $15 per share 70% of a firm whose shares had been trading for $10, it cannot hope to make a profit by looting. Also, looting from minority shareholders violates established rules, and a bidder would not be likely to escape detection if it violated these rules.

Another argument against tender offers portrays them as reducing the welfare of the shareholders of the acquirers by more than the premium paid to the target's shareholders. In this view, tender offers represent self-aggrandizing empire building by acquiring managers who err in deciding what firms to acquire or what price to pay. The difficulty with this view is its implicit assumption that product and labor market constraints (and the tender offer process itself) do not discipline managers. A corporation headed by an empire-building management team that did not maximize profits would fare poorly in the product market and would have lower share prices; its managers would fare poorly in the employment market. The corporation itself would become a takeover candidate.

Finally, it has been suggested that takeovers create monopolies. Profit increases that come about because of monopolization produce reductions in social welfare. This view, however, is contradicted by the evidence. Most tender offers raise no antitrust problems, and one careful study has shown that takeovers generally reduce concentration in the acquired firms' markets.

The raider, managerialist, and monopolist models of tender offers are also contradicted by data on stock price movements. Most of the movement in the price of a stock is correlated with movement in the market as a whole and depends on general economic conditions. But the movements in individual stock prices net of movements in the market give a rough picture of the fortunes of the issuing companies — called cumulative average residuals, or CARs — are powerful indicators of a company's performance.

* * *

B. The Argument That Share Price Increases Justify Resistance from Target's Management

Several commentators have noted that even if a tender bid fails, the share price of the target often rises, sometimes to more than the tender offer price. If shareholders so benefit, the argument goes, then management is justified in resisting tender offers. Although the data marshalled to support this point varies in quality, the premiums offered in unsuccessful offers appear to be less than the appreciation after the offer is defeated. This fact calls for explanation.

The most plausible reason for a price increase following the tender offer's defeat is that the market sees the defeat as simply one round in an extended auction. The market anticipates that in the future another offeror — one not saddled with the first offeror's higher costs of information — will acquire the target. Many management-induced withdrawals are followed by higher offers, and share prices increase as the eventual acquisition becomes more likely.

Another possible explanation for the price increase following a defeated tender offer is that the offer itself served to rouse the target's management to action. The offer warned management to improve its performance, and either the offer or the accompanying public disclosure may have provided the target's management with the information to do so.

Regardless of the cause of the price increase, shareholders in general have little cause for rejoicing. The price rise comes about because someone is taking a free ride on information generated by the first offeror. Free riding of this sort reduces the incentive to make the first offer, and, for the reasons we have developed earlier, decreases the amount of monitoring, decreases the number of offers, and harms shareholders in the long run.

* * *

C. Defensive Tactics and the Business Judgment Rule

In view of the recognized limits on the scope of the business judgment rule, it is surprising that courts have invoked the rule so freely as a basis for refusing to review the defensive conduct of managers faced with a hostile tender offer. A frequent consequence of a successful takeover attempt is the replacement of incumbent managers. For acquirers, replacement of target management is typically a significant motive for making the tender offer in the first place; for the target's shareholders, such offers present the most effective means of manifesting disapproval of management. Given the serious and unavoidable conflict of interest that inheres in any decision on one's own ouster, courts ought not to make available to a manager resisting a tender offer — and, in effect, fighting against his own replacement — the same deference accorded to the decisions of a manager in good standing.

Indeed, unlike transactions involving a conflict of managerial interest outside the realm of tender offers, efforts undertaken by target management primarily to resist a takeover bid should not even be susceptible of the justification that they happen to benefit the target. Such efforts to resist should instead be proscribed completely. Conflicts transactions outside the realm of tender offers are not similarly interdicted because they typically involve corporate decisions that shareholders, as a practical matter, simply cannot make. But in deciding whether to accept or reject a tender offer, managers enjoy no particular comparative advantage over shareholders. The decision does not involve management of the corporation's affairs in any meaningful sense and thus can be made by shareholders even though they are not involved in those affairs to any significant degree.

Moreover, the rationales underlying the policy of judicial restraint embodied in the business judgment rule in no way counsel against implementation of a rule of managerial passivity. The deference accorded managerial decisions under the business judgment rule reflects, in part, the inability of courts to make better business decisions than managers and, in part, the inefficiency that would result were managers encouraged to disregard the costs of gathering information and making decisions. A rule of managerial passivity does not require courts to make business decisions at all, let alone better decisions than managers. To implement a rule of passivity, all a court need do is determine whether managers were passive. It need not gather costly information nor induce managers to incur inefficiently large costs of decision making to stave off litigation. Under a rule of passivity, managerial decisions would be subject to attack only if designed to defeat takeover bids, and not for being inadequately researched.

* * *

D. The Meaning of Managerial Passivity

Although we have concluded that shareholders would want management to be passive in the face of a tender offer, we have not attempted to define precisely what we mean by passivity. Doubtless, managers must carry out the corporation's ordinary business. Perhaps, too, management should be able to issue a press release urging shareholders to accept or reject the offer. The offeror also will convey its views to the shareholders, who can act on these messages in light of the self-interest of both the management and the offeror. But almost any other defensive actions expend the target's resources and produce no gain to investors. Thus, management should not propose anti-takeover charter or bylaw amendments, file suits against the offeror, acquire a competitor of the offeror in order to create an antitrust obstacle to the tender offer, buy or sell shares in order to make the offer more costly, give away to some potential "white knight" valuable corporate information that might call forth a competing bid, or initiate any other defensive tactic to defeat a tender offer.

Our proposal for managerial passivity does not mean, however, that managers must go to sleep when they suspect an imminent tender offer. A requirement of managerial somnolence would deprive the corporation of valuable business opportunities and might give firms a device for hindering their competitors' operations. Yet many legitimate business decisions could have the effect of making the corporation less attractive to the bidder and thus could be called resistance. It is also possible, however, that many business decisions, ostensibly taken for the purpose of seizing valuable business opportunities, are actually undertaken for the purpose of defeating the tender offer. Distinguishing resistance from passivity will be simple in some cases and hard in others.

* * *

The timing of managerial action provides a useful, if imperfect, basis for resolving this dilemma. On the one hand, courts could simply presume, subject to rebuttal by a litigant who established the contrary, that any plans or programs set in motion before target managers had reason to believe that there would be a takeover attempt were not undertaken with a view to resisting the tender offer. Such plans would presumptively comply with the rule of passivity and would thus enjoy the freedom from judicial scrutiny otherwise available under the business judgment rule. On the other hand, if actions that materially hindered either the offer or the acquisition were taken immediately after management first had reason to know of an impending offer, then courts could presume that the actions were undertaken with a view to defeating the offer. The target's managers could be allowed to overcome the presumption, but only by a substantial demonstration that their actions were undertaken for the economic benefit of the target rather than for the purpose of defeating the offer.

This allocation of burdens places on the management — which has a clear conflict of interest and superior access to information about the reasons for and consequences of its deeds — the responsibility of justification. It meets two essential criteria: it does not incapacitate management from seizing profitable business opportunities just because another firm is attempting to acquire the target, and it also does not freely allow defensive stratagems.

GILSON, "A Structural Approach to Corporations"
(1982), 33 Stan. L.R. 819 at 870–872 (footnotes deleted)

While acknowledging that shareholders of a target company faced with an existing offer will benefit from management bargaining, a number of commentators argue that shareholders of all potential targets as a class, and the economy as a whole, are adversely affected by the potential for such conduct. The argument is that the threat of a tender offer constrains management's discretion to perform inefficiently or to self-deal. Thus, anything which reduces the incidence of tender offers reduces the power of the threat to constrain management and is detrimental to society.

The problem with competitive bidding in the face of an initial offer, it is argued, is that the initial offeror incurs sunk costs in identifying and evaluating the target company. These investment costs must be covered by expected profit on the takeover. A competing bidder does not incur these sunk information costs, since the target is already identified and target management will assist the competing bidder in evaluating the target's value. As a result, the transaction is profitable for the competing bidder at a higher price than for the initial bidder. This increases the risk associated with investment in takeover investigations and decreases the return associated with those investments. Not only do competitive bids increase the likelihood that a competitor will win, with the result that the sunk costs are entirely lost, but by increasing the price necessary for success, they reduce the potential profit associated with the investment. Therefore, the incentive to make initial offers, and hence the total number of offers, decrease.

I find the argument unpersuasive on a number of levels. First, the sunk cost argument seems to me significantly overstated. In any tender offer of substantial size the information costs associated with identifying and evaluating the target are a small proportion of the entire purchase price, and the white knight must also incur costs in verifying and assessing the significance of information provided by target management. One cannot help but suspect that success in most major transactions does not turn on differences of this magnitude.

More importantly, I suspect that the sunk costs are investments with a positive expected return even if the offeror is ultimately outbid. Increasingly, a potential bidder takes a substantial block position in the stock of a target before announcing its intentions. If the initial offeror is outbid, it will simply tender its target shares to its competitor, or sell them in the market, at a per-share profit approximately equal to the premium it initially offered plus the amount by which its offer was exceeded. McDermott, Inc.'s gross profit of approximately $15.5 million on shares purchased during its losing contest with Wheelabrator-Frye, Inc. for Pullman, Inc. is illustrative of the phenomenon.

This phenomenon reflects, of course, no more than that the risk of competitive bidding, like most financial risks, can be hedged. The sunk information costs are an investment in a risky asset whose return derives from successfully completing the acquisition and whose risk is that the bidder will lose the acquisition to a higher bidder. Purchase of target shares in the market prior to making the offer hedges that risk because the return on that asset varies inversely with the return on the investment in information. Indeed, if the initial offeror treats the returns associated with a successful acquisition as certain, the effect of the hedge is to allow the initial offeror to guarantee a risk-free return on its investment in information. Thus, it is not at all clear that the potential for competition should reduce the frequency of initial bids.

A second problem with the argument asserting the evils of soliciting competitive bids is that it ignores the efficiency-inducing effect of price competition. As a general principle, allocating resources among competing claimants by price is desirable because it places resources with the most efficient users. To assert that one should maximize the total number of tender offers without regard to the allocative benefits of price competition, one must assume that all offerors can make equally efficient use of target resources. This is unlikely. Indeed, one major explanation for the efficiency of mergers — synergy — assumes differing abilities to make use of target's assets. The theory ultimately turns upon the fit of the particular offeror, or the skills of the particular offeror's management, with the target company, and I see no basis for assuming these attributes are identical among competing bidders. Thus, even if competitive bidding reduces the overall number of offerors, the increase in efficiency from allocating target assets to their most efficient user must be balanced against the reduction in efficiency from fewer offers. While this balance cannot be easily identified, the greater the importance of synergy as an explanation for the acquiring company's gains, the more important the efficiency gain through price competition relative to the efficiency loss due to a lower frequency of tender offers.

ROBERTA ROMANO
"A Guide to Takeovers: Theory, Evidence and Regulation"
(1992), 9 Yale Journal on Regulation 119

I. Theories of Takeovers and Related Transactions

One important, and undisputed, datum about acquisitive transactions should be noted from the outset: acquisitions generate substantial gains to target company shareholders. All studies find that target firms experience statistically significant positive stock price responses to the announcement of takeover attempts or merger agreements. On average, there is a 20% increase over the pre-announcement market price for mergers and a 30% increase for tender offers in the period around the takeover announcement. Abnormal returns in going-private transactions (leveraged buyouts) are of similar magnitude, ranging across studies between 20% and 37%. Without question, the announcement of a bid is good news for target shareholders. The different explanations of acquisitions that will be examined are efforts at explaining the source of these gains.

The data are more ambiguous, however, concerning acquiring firms' returns. Depending on the sample and time period, acquirers experience positive, negative, or zero abnormal returns on a bid's announcement and completion. From the acquirer's perspective, there are two classes of explanations or motivations for a takeover: value-maximizing and non-value-maximizing ones. Value-maximizing explanations view takeovers as undertaken in order to increase the equity share price of the acquiring firm. Non-value-maximizing explanations consider takeovers in diametrically opposite terms, as transactions that maximize managers' utility rather than shareholder wealth. These two explanations therefore predict a different stock price reaction, positive and negative, respectively.

Value-maximizing explanations can be subdivided into efficiency, expropriation (wealth transfer), and market inefficiency explanations. This division is pivotal for policy analysis, but has no differential impact on the acquirer's expected return from the transaction. It will be positive in each case. Each non-value-maximizing explanation can be characterized as a distinct expropriation story, in which wealth is transferred from the acquiring firm's shareholders to the target firm (as well as to the managers). These transactions will thus have a negative stock price effect. To preview the classification schema, see Table 1.

There are, however, theoretically plausible reasons for not finding positive abnormal returns to bidders even when acquisitions are value-maximizing transactions. First, acquiring firms are typically much larger than target firms, making it more difficult to measure abnormal returns. Second, a bid may reveal information about the bidding firm unrelated to the particular acquisition, confounding the stock price effect. Third, if the takeover market is competitive, then bidders will earn only normal returns, as abnormal profits are competed away. Finally, for acquiring firms that have an active mergers and acquisitions program, the gain from a specific acquisition may have been anticipated in the bidder's stock price at the time the mergers and acquisitions program was announced.

Despite these interpretative subtleties concerning acquirers' stock price reactions, one may draw some generalizations from the data. The price movement for acquirers is small in percentage terms and less statistically significant than that for target firms. In addition, acquirers' returns have decreased over time and, in the 1980s, may have been negative. Moreover, even when acquirers earn negative returns, when their losses are aggregated with the targets' gains, acquisitions still net a positive abnormal return. Thus, because the division of the gain is skewed toward targets, takeovers that appear to be non-value-maximizing transactions for bidders may be socially beneficial (that is, aggregate wealth increases).

Studies of the performance of target firms after acquisition also shed light on whether acquisitions are value-maximizing or non-value-maximizing transactions. Here, stock price data are less reliable indicators for, as the interval over which the price is examined increases, changes can no longer be readily attributed to the event in question (the takeover) because it will be confounded with other events. Most of these studies therefore use accounting data to determine long-term changes in performance. As with event studies of the announcement effects on acquirers, the ex-post performance findings are also mixed. While earlier studies find no operating improvements in merged firms, more recent sophisticated studies find that performance improves post-merger.

One difficulty in assessing post-merger performance is in determining the appropriate comparison, which entails constructing a counterfactual benchmark — what the two firms' performances would have been had they not merged. In an important paper, Jarrell compares post-merger performance to analysts' pre-merger forecasts of the firms' performance. She finds that five years post-merger, the merged firms perform significantly better (9%) than the benchmark, although one to two years immediately after the merger the performance was worse than the benchmark. The capital market also accurately anticipates long-term performance: using regression analysis, Jarrell finds that the abnormal stock price effects upon a bid's announcement are significantly positively related to the merged firm's subsequent profitability. These data indicate that acquisitions are, indeed, value-maximizing, for the long-term performance of the combined firms improved. They also suggest that negative findings of earlier studies are, in all likelihood, the product of failure to use an appropriate benchmark.

* * *

A. Value-Maximizing Efficiency Explanations

There are two efficiency explanations of takeovers: to realize synergy gains and to reduce agency costs.

* * *

B. Value-Maximizing Expropriation Explanations

Expropriation explanations of takeovers focus on four distinct groups: taxpayers, bondholders, employees, and consumers.

* * *

3. Expropriation from Labor

The expropriation explanation of takeovers that attracts the most attention involves labor as the victim. The most sophisticated version of this explanation is Shleifer and Summers' breach of implicit contract explanation of hostile takeovers.

In Shleifer and Summers' scenario, shareholders initially hire trustworthy individuals as managers, in order to make credible long-term contract commitments to workers. The long-term commitments are implicit, rather than explicit contracts. After employees are hired, shareholders will want to breach the implicit contract, in order to increase their returns by lowering labor's share. A trustworthy management prevents them from doing so by honoring the informal agreements. A hostile takeover will, however, permit shareholders to behave opportunistically because, unlike trustworthy incumbents, a raider will not hesitate to break implicit contracts, cutting costs and releasing the pent-up value of the firm to shareholders.

* * *

Implicit contracts protect workers who have invested in transaction-specific human capital. By breaking these contracts, shareholders, through the raider, expropriate the quasi-rent value of the workers' investments. But, as shareholders benefit from workers who make such investments, the implicit contracts are ex ante efficient and it is hence undesirable that they be violated ex post. We then need a device to prevent the contracts from being broken, and trustworthy managers are posited to perform that function.

Shleifer and Summers' thesis is clever but not convincing. A key problem with their explanation is that it is questionable whether workers, particularly unionized workers, would opt to protect such extremely vulnerable investments as firm-specific capital through an implicit contract rather than some other explicit governance structure. As Williamson details, if contracts cannot be specified to avoid opportunism, other mechanisms will be devised to protect the vulnerable party's investment. The difficulty with the analysis is that Shleifer and Summers misuse the concept of an implicit contract. As Schwartz has observed, an implicit contract is a contract whose terms are observable to the contracting parties, but not to third parties, such as courts, and hence, not verifiable. An explicit contract is, correspondingly, one whose terms are both observable and verifiable. The choice of contact type depends upon the characteristics of the relevant contracting terms; if certain information is observable and verifiable, then it can be the basis of an explicit contract term, for performance of the contract can be conditioned on such a term and its breach can be enforced in court. The terms of concern to Shleifer and Summers — pension benefits, pension fund assets, wages, employment levels — are observable and verifiable. Thus they will be subject to explicit, and not implicit, contracting.

* * *

Finally, Shleifer and Summers offer no compelling reason why a hostile bidder can so easily do what incumbent management cannot, bargain for wage concessions. Many firms, including other airlines, engage in concession bargaining, and such efforts are typically independent of any hostile takeover threat. While it is not in the shareholders' interest to overpay workers, it is also not in their interest to underpay them.

Holmstrom suggests an alternative explanation to Shleifer and Summers' implicit contract story, which builds upon reputation. In this view, managers may be burdened with a reputation for weakness from past practices of capitulating to labor demands in order to make their jobs as managers more comfortable, and this reputation affects their credibility as bargainers in hard times. Thus, unlike raiders, who bring no such baggage to the negotiating table, incumbent management cannot obtain concessions. While interesting, I do not find this reputational explanation persuasive. It would be in labor's interest to grant concessions to the management it knows, rather than to a hardnosed raider, because past experience indicates that when financial conditions improve, the incumbents will be likely to seek comfort and return to the old regime of worker quasi-rents, whereas there is no basis to expect such favorable treatment from a raider.

* * *

Rosett tests Shleifer and Summers' breach of contract explanation more directly by examining union wage contracts before and after takeovers. He finds no support for their thesis: there is, in fact, a positive *gain* in union wealth levels after hostile acquisitions. Although there are losses after friendly acquisitions, even then the losses are insignificant relative to the premiums (when measured over 18 years after the takeover, the union losses in friendly acquisitions equal approximately 5% of the shareholders' gain). Bhagat, Shleifer, and Vishny also find that layoffs occur infrequently, affect high-level white collar workers, are higher when management successfully defeats a bid (either by remaining independent or by finding a white knight) than when a hostile bidder succeeds and, most important, result in losses that are small compared to takeover premiums (10-20%). In sum, while we would need counterfactual data to test the labor expropriation hypothesis fully — we need to know how many workers would have been laid off or what the wage profile would have looked like if the firm had not been acquired — what we do know suggests that expropriation from labor does not motivate takeovers.

* * *

C. Value-Maximizing Market Inefficiency Explanations

The final value-maximizing (that is, beneficial to acquirers' shareholders) explanation of takeover gains is premised on market inefficiency, the view that stock prices do not reflect firms' "fundamental value." According to this explanation, which is probably as widely-circulated in the popular press as the labor expropriation explanation, acquirers exploit market inefficiency by identifying undervalued firms, and presumably capture a large share of the gains by paying premiums below the correct valuation. There are two distinct market inefficiency explanations: general underpricing of stocks and myopia (overvaluation of current profits and excessive discounting of future profits).

* * *

D. Non-Value-Maximizing Expropriation Explanations

There are four non-value-maximizing explanations of takeovers. The first three are related, as they are all forms of managerialism: diversification, self-aggrandizement and free cash flow excesses by acquirers. The fourth, the hubris hypothesis, is a non-value-maximizing explanation ex post (once the bid is made) and not necessarily ex ante: managers may intend to maximize equity share prices by an acquisition but they overvalue the transaction's gains.

* * *

E. Summary and Conclusion

The preceding discussion — the explanations of takeovers and supporting empirical evidence — is summarized in Table 1. There is a substantial body of research that is consistent with agency cost reduction or synergy gain explanations of takeovers. There is, however, scant support for any of the expropriation explanations, whether the hypothetical victims are bondholders, labor, consumers or the government. There is even less support for market inefficiency explanations.

The data are more ambiguous regarding non-value-maximizing explanations. Manager-controlled firms engage in more diversifying mergers than owner-controlled firms and some acquirers earned negative abnormal returns in the 1980s. But these data can also be interpreted as consistent with value-maximization: firm-level diversification may lower executive compensation costs, and competition (auctions) reduces bidders' returns and may lead to overpayment (winner's curse). Most important, the net gains of acquisitions remain positive when bidder and target returns are matched. This finding undercuts the non-value-maximizing interpretation because it indicates that the gain from acquisitions is more than a simple transfer of wealth from acquirers to targets.

Table 1
Explanations of Takeovers

Explanation	Evidence
VALUE-MAXIMIZING	
Efficiency	
1. Synergy Gains	
a. Operating	- positive correlation between bidder and target returns in pure conglomerate and product extension mergers; smaller bidding banks experience higher returns than larger bidding banks; higher returns in bank mergers the smaller the target bank relative to the acquiring bank; related acquisitions more profitable than unrelated acquisitions; substantial portion of gains from hostile takeovers due to reallocation of target assets to purchasers in related industries.
b. Financial	- capital expenditure planning shifted to central headquarters; higher premiums when acquirer's cash flow rate higher than target's; increased capital outlays after acquisitions; accounting conventions have no stock price effects.
c. Diversification	- low stock return correlation bank mergers associated with significantly higher abnormal returns than high stock return correlation bank mergers; target bank stock return variability decreases after merger.
2. Reduced Agency Costs	
a. Inefficient Management	- high management turnover after takeover; bidders have higher rates of return than targets; targets have low Tobin's q ratios; hostile takeover targets are poor performers; targets whose managers are replaced had negative returns pre-takeover; bad bidders make good targets; significant cash flow improvements after both unrelated and related-firm acquisitions.

| b. Free Cash Flow | - probability of going private directly related to free cash flow and inversely related to growth; premiums correlated with free cash flow; targets have low Tobin's q ratios. |
| c. Improved Incentives from Ownership Increase (MBOs) | - productivity and operating improvements post-buyout; returns on going public (post-buyout value increase) directly related to management's equity stake. |

Expropriation

1. Taxes	- interest deduction explains significant portion of MBO premium, other tax benefits not important; net tax effect from MBO estimated as positive and debt shield value reduced by rapid repayment; post-buyout investors earn very high return in reverse buyouts.
2. Bondholders	- small negative or no significant impact on bondholder wealth; size of gain not correlated with amount of outstanding debt; protective covenants increasingly used in industries where LBOs more likely.
3. Labor	- no significant negative impact on employment levels, except for top and middle managers; some evidence that employment increases with control changes; no significant wage effect; overfunded pension reversions not significant factor.
4. Monopoly Power	- no effect on competitors' stock prices; unrelated acquisitions less profitable than related acquisitions in the 1980s; hostile takeovers reallocate assets to related buyers.

Market Inefficiency

| 1. Underpricing | - stock prices of targets that are not acquired return to pre-bid levels; event studies generally supportive of market efficiency. |

2. Market Myopia   - stock prices respond positively to increases in research and development (R&D) and capital investment expenditures; post-acquisition R&D expenditures do not decrease; targets in low intensity R&D industries and tend to spend less on R&D than industry; firms reduce R&D expenditures after adopting defensive charter amendments.

NON-VALUE-MAXIMIZING

1. Diversification   - manager controlled firms more likely to engage in diversifying mergers than owner-controlled firms.

2. Self-Aggrandizement   - bidder and target return correlations in pure conglomerate and product extension mergers are positive and not negative; positive relation between acquirers' abnormal returns and management stock ownership; bad bidders make good targets; acquirers' returns less negative when board is independent.

3. Free Cash Flow   - bad bidders are more likely to be acquired than good bidders; acquirers have positive abnormal returns before acquisition; acquirers have low Tobin's q ratios; free cash flow explains variance in returns across bidders; increases in free cash flow associated with decreases in bidders' gain from a takeover.

4. Hubris   - negative returns to acquirers in 1980s; bad bidders make good targets; bidders overpay in auctions.

I therefore read the literature as most consonant with the value-maximizing, efficiency-enhancing explanations of takeovers. However, different takeover theories each explain best only subsets of acquisitions and, though empirical studies might point in a particular direction, none are conclusive. There may be, then, instances of non-value-maximizing acquisitions as well as acquisitions which transfer wealth from particular groups to target shareholders, but these should be viewed as the exception, rather than the rule.

The theoretical problems involved in the protection of stakeholder concerns during change-of-control transactions are discussed in the following article by Daniels: "Stakeholders and Takeovers: Can Contractarianism be Compassionate?" (1993), 43 University of Toronto Law Journal 315.

RON DANIELS,
"Can Contractarianism Be Compassionate?"
(1993), 43 University of Toronto Law Journal 315

The issue of what, if any, purchase non-shareholder corporate constituencies (that is, employees, creditors, suppliers, customers, and communities) should have on the discretionary decisions of corporate management has proved to be one of the most durable, if not vexing, issues in modern corporate scholarship. Most recently, the issue has resurfaced in the context of the takeover wave of the 1980s, particularly during the latter part of the decade when control transactions became associated with high levels of leverage. At core, stakeholder advocates were riveted by the asymmetries involved in change-of-control transactions. While target shareholders earned consistent and sizeable returns from these transactions, stakeholders were left in the cold. Indeed, in some cases, control transactions were thought to be capable of inflicting highly focused losses on stakeholders. So severe were these losses that some commentators were led to conclude it was the gains from opportunistic breaching of stakeholder contracts that motivated the transactions in the first place.

As in the past, participants in the stakeholder and takeover debate generally array themselves into two distinct camps: one, which views any judicial or legislative attempt to protect stakeholders from harms not explicitly prohibited by corporate contracts as anathema ("non-protectionists"), and the other, which regards corporate responsibility for stakeholder harms as an innate and natural feature of the system of modern corporate governance ("protectionists"). In a perceptive article, Romano attributes part of the differences among scholars on divisive issues of corporate law to the starkly divergent normative beliefs that underlie each side. For non-protectionists, the underlying normative framework is individualistic liberalism, whereas for protectionists, it is usually communitarianism. Given the gulf that divides these underlying normative views, the hope for a principled and durable resolution to the stakeholder debate is indeed dim.

Recently, a small group of scholars working within the framework of law and economics (Coffee, Shleifer, and Summers) has attempted to bridge the chasm that separates the protectionist and non-protectionist positions by advancing a rationale for the protection of stakeholder interests on a takeover event that is based on implicit contract obligations. The genius of the implicit contract rationale is that it endorses the protectionists' claim for broad, humane assistance to stakeholders, but does so on the basis of the non-protectionists' autonomy-based contractarian paradigm. Equally important, the implicit contract rationale furnishes grounds for conferring special treatment on stakeholder harms in the takeover context.

Nevertheless, despite these virtues, close examination of the implicit contract rationale reveals that it is plagued by several serious infirmities, which undermine the potency and scope of the claim it can make in favour of providing distinctive relief to stakeholders on a takeover transaction. The most serious defect is the assumption that takeovers constitute a unique threat to stakeholder interests. As I will argue below, for most change-of-control transactions, this assumption lacks solid foundation. Ironically, despite the expectation that the implicit contract hypothesis would buttress efforts aimed at assisting stakeholders, the sad fact is that the rationale has obscured both an appreciation of how pervasive many of the problems occasioned by corporate restructuring are, as well as the broad range of instruments that can be used to address the harms suffered by the victims of economic change. Instead of invoking rationales for protection that are based on opportunistic cheating, a preferable way of thinking about stakeholder injury is through the prism of contractual failure, here the inability of parties to foresee future risks. So doing does more than merely provide greater conceptual clarity to the problem of stakeholder harm — it remits the problem to the realm of hypothetical bargains and opens the way for principled governmental intervention. I argue that this approach is desirable as, contrary to the antipathy to government intervention voiced by some law and economics scholars, state intervention expands the range and effectiveness of instruments that can be used to protect stakeholders and improve societal welfare.

* * *

IMPLICIT CONTRACTS — THE THIRD WAY

Charting a middle course between the Scylla of unaccommodating contractarianism and the Charybdis of quixotic communitarianism is the implicit contractual analysis. According to its proponents, implicit contractual analysis is able to furnish a rationale for protection of stakeholder interests upon a merger or acquisition event that is based on the parties' actual expectations. Hence, the paradigm's congeniality to both autonomy and welfare-based contractarianism. A further benefit alleged for the implicit contracting model is its ability to explain why change-of-control transactions are qualitatively more destructive to stakeholder interests than are other economic dislocations.

* * *

The implicit contractual claim in favour of stakeholder protection is not uncontroversial. To succeed, its supporters must first demonstrate that the corporation's shareholders, either explicitly or implicitly, made promises to stakeholders to allow them to share in the gains from a takeover. Having done so, they must then show that these promises were meant to be enforced by legal as opposed to non-legal sanctions. Each of these factors will be considered below.

1. Implicit contracts for gain sharing on a merger or acquisition event
Disregarding the mechanism for enforcement, the claim that shareholders
(or their proxies) and stakeholder actually concluded implicit contracts that
require gain sharing on a takeover transaction is controversial. However, it
is important to be clear about the precise source of controversy. It is not that
implicit promises are, as a general matter, implausible in the context of the
firm, just that the precise promise alleged by the advocates of the implicit
contractual paradigm is suspect. After all, given neoclassic economics'
reliance on command-based decision-making in explaining the comparative
advantage of firms over markets in organizing economic production, it
should not be surprising or controversial to expect that shareholders would
make implicit promises to stakeholders in exchange for agreement to perform certain tasks or duties. Otherwise, the benefits of flexible, discretionary
management would be lost.

To enthusiasts of the implicit contractarian model, the "wrong" of
takeovers is not that stakeholders lose, but that stakeholders lose while
shareholders gain. This asymmetrical sharing of gains and losses explains
why implicit contractarians are so critical of takeovers and more resigned
to the harms inflicted by a wide range of other dislocative transactions.

* * *

Despite its surface plausibility, the normative force of sharing symmetry cracks under close examination. To begin with, the empirical literature canvassed earlier does not support a clear link between shareholder
gains and stakeholder losses. If stakeholders lose following a takeover
transaction, the loss does not appear to be motivated primarily by redistributive goals. In other words, while shareholders may gain from a takeover,
this transactional gain is analytically distinct from the shareholder loss. In
most cases, both the shareholders and the stakeholders lost on the investment
made in the stakeholders' firm-specific capital. If a corporation is forced to
displace a stakeholder whose firm-specific capital has depreciated more
quickly than anticipated, this is a loss both for the corporation (that is,
shareholders) and the stakeholder. The reason why shareholders gain —
despite the loss related to obsolete stakeholder firm-specific capital — is
that there are other unrelated gains (synergies, improved management, monopoly profits, tax benefits) from a takeover that are split between acquiring
and target shareholders. And since these gains lack any causal nexus to the
stakeholder loss, there is no reason to force gain sharing.

Second, even if one assumes that part of the shareholders' gain on a
takeover derives from redistributions from stakeholders, it is not at all clear
that this situation is in any way distinct from a wide range of other non-
control transactions or events that impose losses on stakeholders.

* * *

In these terms, the only real difference between rationalization that occurs
in a takeover and non-takeover context may well be the degree of crystal-

lization of shareholder gain: in the takeover setting, it is up-front and visible, whereas in the non-takeover case, it may occur more slowly and is, therefore, less transparent.

A third and final point goes to the actual symmetry in nature of stakeholder and shareholder losses. Even if shareholders suffer losses prior to the implementation of a rationalization programme that will then inflict losses on stakeholders, there is no reason to expect that the losses suffered by each will actually be commensurate with one another. Shareholder losses could be fairly shallow and short-lived, while stakeholder losses are likely to be higher and more protracted. To be a valid criterion for determining the degree of stakeholder protection, it is not sufficient merely to demonstrate that both groups have suffered losses, but that the losses are actually parallel. Otherwise, management could simply contort accounting data to show a paper loss to shareholders, which would then insulate the company from having to provide any further redress to stakeholders.

* * *

2. Implicit promises enforced by legal sanctions

Even if one assumes that stakeholders actually expected distinctive protection from shareholders on a takeover transaction, the question then emerges as to how that expectation is to be enforced. To enlist the state's assistance in enforcing these implicit promises, stakeholders must demonstrate that the parties relied on legal, as opposed to self-enforcing, non-legal, sanctions.

The role and operation of non-legal sanctions has been closely considered by David Charny. In the tradition of Klein and Leffler and Williamson, Charny argues that commercial parties utilize a variety of non-legal sanctions to bond non-simultaneous obligations emanating from implicit contractual undertakings. These sanctions are based on the desire of the promisor "to maintain reputation or profitable relationships, the concern for standing among peers, and the force of conscience."

Charny's analysis of the role of non-legal sanctions raises vexing problems for Coffee's claim that takeovers invite special treatment for stakeholders because of opportunistic breaching of implicit contracts. Assuming that stakeholders are capable of negotiating rationally with the corporation at the time of their initial contract (or even subsequently upon modification), what grounds are there for legal enforcement of implicit contractual undertakings? In order to have enticed the corporation's stakeholders to agree to perform some service in exchange for an implicit contractual undertaking, a credible performance bond would have to be posted. If, at a later stage, the corporation's shareholders decide to forgo that bond and suffer whatever non-legal sanction is specified, then the stakeholder should not be able to invoke the judicial process to seek redress. Quite simply, the stakeholder's contract was only for performance conditioned upon a non-legal sanction, and, to the extent that a takeover causes shareholders to suffer these sanctions, then there is little in the parties' actual ex ante expectations that supports intervention. In these terms, a shareholder decision to sever stakeholder ties to the corporation, and suffer whatever non-legal sanctions were constructed, can hardly be deemed opportunistic. Rather, as in the case of any other right protected by a liability rule, shareholders have simply decided to exercise their right to breach the implicit contract by paying the specified price.

* * *

CONCLUSION

In the previous discussion, I identified the defects in the claims of both non-protectionist and protectionists. In essence, the non-protectionist argument failed for its unwillingness to take seriously the presence of conventional contracting failures, while the protectionist position failed for its reluctance to consider either the actual expectations of the contracting parties, or the efficiency consequences of across the board protection. Against this backdrop, I then considered in detail the implicit contractual claim in favour of distinctive treatment for stakeholders following a takeover transaction. Close inspection of this argument, however, revealed several serious infirmities. Of these, the most important relate to the implausibility of special promises for stakeholder protection following a takeover event and the difficulties in knowing whether these promises, even if they exist, are meant to be enforced by legal as opposed to non-legal sanctions. Close evaluation of these arguments suggests that the specific properties of takeover transactions do not appear to support distinctive treatment for stakeholders.

Notes

The debate over takeover policy and the appropriate scope of management defensive tactics is dealt with in the following articles. The argument for complete managerial passivity in response to a takeover bid is made in: Easterbrook and Fischel, "The Proper Role of a Target's Management in Responding to a Tender Offer", *supra*; Easterbrook and Fischel, "Auctions and Sunk Costs in Tender Offers" (1982), 35 Stan. L.R. 1; and Schwartz, "The Fairness of Tender Offer Prices in Utilitarian Theory" (1988), 18 Jour. Legal Studies 165.

Critical evaluation and modification of Easterbrook and Fischel's argument from within an economic analysis paradigm is found in : Bebchuk, "The Case for Facilitating Competing Tender Offers" (1982), 95 Harv. L.R. 1028; Bebchuk, "The Case for Facilitating Competing Tender Offers: A Reply and Extension" (1982), 35 Stan. L. Rev. 23; Coffee, "Regulating the Market for Corporation Control: A Critical Assessment of the Tender Offer's Role in Corporate Governance" (1985), 84 Colum. L. Rev. 1145; Gilson, "A Structural Approach to Corporations: The Case Against Defensive Tactics in Tender Offers", *supra*; Gilson, "The Case Against Shark Repellent Amendments: Structural Limitations on the Enabling Concept" (1982), 34 Stan. L. Rev. 775; Gilson, "Seeking Competitive Bids Versus Pure Passivity in Tender Offer Defense" (1982), 35 Stan. L. Rev. 51; Roll,

"The Hubris Hypothesis of Corporate Takeovers" (1986), 59 J. Bus. 197. Analysis and criticism from outside the economic paradigm is found in: Lipton, "Takeover Bids in the Target's Boardroom" (1979), 35 Bus. Law. 101; Lipton, "Takeover Bids in the Target's Boardroom: An Update After One Year" (1980), 36 Bus. Law. 1017; Lipton, "Takeover Bids in the Target's Boardroom: A Response to Professors Easterbrook and Fischel" (1980), 55 N.Y.U.L. Rev. 1231; Lowenstein, "Pruning Deadwood in Hostile Takeovers: A Proposal for Legislation" (1983), 83 Colum. L. Rev. 249.

Canadian evidence on the gains from corporate control transactions is considered by: B. Espen Eckbo, "Mergers and the Market for Corporate Control: The Canadian Evidence" (1986), 19 Cdn. Jour. of Econ. 236.

(d) The Common Law

(i) Canadian Jurisprudence on Defensive Tactics

The directors have a broad range of powers vested in them through legislation, by-laws and articles of association that may be used to react to a hostile takeover bid. The most sweeping and important, as discussed in Chapter 4, is the power to manage or supervize management. Other significant powers are the power to issue shares, CBCA, s. 25, OBCA, s. 23 and BCCA, s. 41; the power to purchase shares of the corporation, CBCA, s. 34 and OBCA, s. 30; the power, as part of the power to manage, to declare dividends, to initiate a takeover or amalgamation, or to sell major assets (which might, however, require a shareholder vote in some circumstances, CBCA s. 189(3), OBCA s.184(3)); and the power, in a private company, to refuse to register a share transfer if such a power is conferred in the articles of association, CBCA, s. 6(1)(d), OBCA, s. 5(1)(d) and BCCA, s. 58. Clearly, directors' acts may be challenged if they act beyond the authority conferred. And they may be challenged if the power has been exercised without due care and in a negligent fashion. We are concerned in this Part with abuse of power — with an exercise of power that, as a matter of equitable supervision by the courts, is said to be for an improper purpose. Initially, the English and Canadian courts used the phrase "improper purpose" in a sense that was somewhat different than, but an adjunct to a breach of fiduciary duty. Virtually all of these cases involve an issuance of shares for the purpose of influencing the control of the company. Thus, for example, in *Bonisteel v. Collis Leather Co.* (1919), 45 O.L.R. 195 (H.C.)), the court found that an issuance of shares was in good faith and in what the directors perceived to be the best interests of the company. Nonetheless, the court held that the issuance was made with an improper purpose — the purpose of defeating the intended acquisition of a control block by a shareholder that the board did not approve of. Thus, while in *Bonisteel* the directors did not, strictly speaking, violate their fiduciary duty to the company, they nonetheless acted in an illegal manner. While in *Bonisteel* the court held that the issuance was void, in most other improper purpose cases, the courts have held that an issuance of shares for the purpose of influencing control of the company was merely voidable.

Despite being a lower court holding, the following case is a watershed in Canadian takeover jurisprudence. Berger J.'s fusion of the improper purpose doctrine with the directors' and officers' fiduciary duty is now the doctrinally standard approach to cases involving target resistance to a hostile takeover bid.

Teck Corp. Ltd. v. Millar
33 D.L.R. (3d) 288, [1973] 2 W.W.R. 385 (B.C. S.C.)

Afton Mines Ltd. was a junior mining company that was incorporated in B.C. in 1965 by a group led by Millar, a geological engineer. Its principal asset was some copper claims near Kamloops, B.C. As is common in the mining business, Millar sought to interest a major mining company in the claims to finance an extensive drilling program. (In mining parlance, a deal with a "major", by which the major takes over possession, exploration and development of the property in return for an equity interest by way of shares in the junior is termed an "ultimate deal".)

Afton financed preliminary drilling itself with very encouraging results. Further financing was necessary but Millar thought it was too early for Afton to negotiate an ultimate deal. Accordingly, he sought to sell shares to a major to raise the needed capital. After discussions with a number of majors, Millar approached Canadian Explorations Ltd. (Canex), a subsidiary of Placer Developments Ltd., one of the world's largest mining concerns. Canex proposed an ultimate deal which Millar rejected. After some negotiation, an agreement was signed in March, 1972 whereby Canex purchased 100,000 shares at $3.00 per share and received a right of first refusal on any future financing, including any ultimate deal submitted to Afton.

Teck Corporation Limited (Teck) had become interested in the Afton property in late 1971. Millar met with Keevil of Teck who sought an ultimate deal which was rejected, as was an offer to buy all the shares of Millar and his associates. Teck then offered to buy 100,000 shares at $4.00 per share. However, Millar and his fellow directors preferred to deal with the Placer subsidiary Canex, even though it was offering only $3.00 per share, because of Placer's excellent reputation in the industry and because it had developed a number of successful mines in B.C. Teck had not brought a mine into production in B.C. and Millar accepted a lower price because he wanted Placer involved in the property. Berger J. found it of importance that long before Teck began buying Afton shares in the market, Millar dealt with Placer rather than Teck because he believed it was better for Afton to do so.

Teck then began to purchase Afton's shares in the market and by the end of May, 1972 they had obtained a majority of the shares at a cost of some $16,000,000, an average price of $13 per share. During this period (April-May) Millar held many meetings with Placer and Teck representatives, as well as with officials of two other majors, concerning an ultimate deal. Towards the end of May, Millar knew that Teck was close to acquiring control — as did Placer. Millar then proposed a 70% (Afton) — 30% (Placer) ultimate deal to Placer which was accepted on May 30th and signed on June 1st, after approval by Placer's board. Under the terms of the contract, Placer was to receive 30% of Afton's outstanding share capital if it chose to put the property into production after further exploration and development work.

Teck meanwhile was concerned that Afton would make an ultimate deal with another major and sent a letter on May 29th to the Afton directors saying that no ultimate deal should be made yet and that Teck could arrange better terms than anyone else. On May 30th, Teck requisitioned a shareholders' meeting of Afton. On May 31st Teck delivered a letter to Millar and the Afton directors saying no ultimate deal should be made without consultation and legal action would be taken if a deal was made involving the issuance of shares. On the same day, Teck's solicitors delivered a letter to Afton's solicitors stating that Teck owned a controlling position and that Afton should take no action outside the ordinary course of business until the requisitioned shareholders' meeting was held. Despite the letter, Afton's solicitor advised the board that they could enter into the deal with Placer provided they genuinely thought such action to be in the best interests of Afton. The ultimate deal was signed on June 1st and Teck launched its action on June 2nd.

BERGER, J.: . . . Now counsel for Teck does not accuse the defendant directors of a crass desire merely to retain their directorships and their control of the company. Teck acknowledges that the directors may well have considered it to be in the best interests of the company that Teck's majority should be defeated. Even so, Teck says, the purpose was not one countenanced by the law. Teck relies upon *Hogg v. Cramphorn Ltd.*, [1967] Ch. 254. In that case the directors of Cramphorn Ltd. established a trust for the benefit of the company's employees and allotted shares to the trust, nominating themselves as trustees to enable them to purchase the shares. Buckley, J. (as he then was), found that the directors had done so to ensure that a Mr. Baxter, who was seeking to acquire control of the company, could not achieve a majority. Buckley, J., was persuaded that the directors had acted in good faith, believing they were serving the best interests of the company.

[Berger J. then went on to quote the relevant portions of the judgment by Buckley J. in *Hogg v. Cramphorn*.]

. . .thus Buckley, J., takes the view that the directors have no right to exercise their power to issue shares, in order to defeat an attempt to secure control of the company, even if they consider that in doing so they are acting in the company's best interests.

Counsel for Teck says the reasoning in *Hogg v. Cramphorn Ltd.*, *supra*, is applicable in the case at bar. He says the defendant directors believed Teck would use its dominant position to compel Afton to give Teck the ultimate deal. They believed that under Teck's management the property would not be developed as profitably as it would under Placer's management. They also believed that the value of Afton's shares, including their own, would decline, under Teck's management. Therefore, the argument goes, the defendant directors entered into the contract with Canex so that shares would be alloted under the contract to defeat Teck's majority. The case then is on all fours with *Hogg v. Cramphorn Ltd.*

Counsel for Teck says that *Hogg v. Cramphorn Ltd.* offers an elaboration of the rule that directors may not issue shares for an improper purpose. If their purpose is merely to retain control, that is improper. So much may be taken for granted. Counsel then goes on to say that *Hogg v. Cramphorn Ltd.* lays it down that an allotment of shares, and any transaction connected with it, made for the purpose of defeating an attempt to secure a majority is improper, even if the directors genuinely consider that it would be deleterious to the company if those seeking a majority were to obtain control.

This, it seems to me, raises an issue of profound importance in company law. Lord Greene, M. R., expressed the general rule in this way in *Re Smith & Fawcett Ltd.*, [1942] Ch. 304 at p. 306, [1942] 1 All E.R. 542: "They [the directors] must exercise their discretion bona fide in what they consider — not what a court may consider is in the interests of the company, and not for any collateral purpose." Yet, if *Hogg v. Cramphorn Ltd.*, *supra*, is right, directors may not allot shares to frustrate an attempt to obtain control of the company, even if they believe that it is in the best interests of the company to do so. This is inconsistent with the law as laid down in *Re Smith & Fawcett Ltd.* How can it be said that directors have the right to consider the interests of the company, and to exercise their powers accordingly, but that there is an exception when it comes to the power to issue shares, and that in the exercise of such power the directors cannot in any circumstances issue shares to defeat an attempt to gain control of the company? It seems to me this is what *Hogg v. Cramphorn Ltd.* says. If the general rule is to be infringed here, will it not be infringed elsewhere? If the directors, even when they believe they are serving the best interests of the company, cannot issue shares to defeat an attempt to obtain control, then presumably they cannot exercise any other of their powers to defeat the claims of the majority or, for that matter, to deprive the majority of the advantages of control. I do not think the power to issue shares can be segregated, on the basis that the rule in *Hogg v. Cramphorn Ltd.* applies only in a case of an allotment of shares.

Neither can it be distinguished on the footing that the power to issue shares affects the rights of the shareholders in some way that the exercise of other powers does not. The Court's jurisdiction to intervene is founded on the theory that if the directors' purpose is not to serve the interest of the company, but to serve their own interest or that of their friends or of a particular group of shareholders, they can be said to have abused their power. The impropriety lies in the directors' purpose. If their purpose is not to serve the company's interest, then it is an important purpose. Impropriety depends upon proof that the directors were actuated by a collateral purpose, it does not depend upon the nature of any shareholders' rights that may be affected by the exercise of the directors' powers. . . .

The classical theory is that the directors' duty is to the company. The company's shareholders are the company: Boyd, C., in *Martin v. Gibson* (1907), 15 O.L.R. 623, and therefore no interests outside those of the shareholders can legitimately be considered by the directors. But even accepting that, what comes within the definition of the interests of the shareholders? By what standards are the shareholders' interests to be measured?

In defining the fiduciary duties of directors, the law ought to take into account the fact that the corporation provides the legal framework for the development of resources and the generation of wealth in the private sector of the Canadian economy: Bull, J.A., in *Peso Silver Mines Ltd. (N.P.L.) v. Cropper* (1966), 56 D.L.R. (2d) 117 at pp. 154-5, affirmed 58 D.L.R. (2d) 1.

> . . .the corporation has become almost the unit of organization of our economic life. Whether for good or ill, the stubborn fact is that in our present system the corporation carries on the bulk of production and transportation, is the chief employer of both labor and capital, pays a large part of our taxes, and is an economic institution of such magnitude and importance that there is no present substitute for it except the State itself.

Jackson J., in *State Tax Commission v. Aldrich et al.* (1942), 316 U.S. 174 at p. 192.

A classical theory that once was unchallengeable must yield to the facts of modern life. In fact, of course, it has. If today the directors of a company were to consider the interests of its employees no one would argue that in doing so they were not acting *bona fide* in the interests of the company itself. Similarly, if the directors were to consider the consequences to the community of any policy that the company intended to pursue, and were deflected in their commitment to that policy as a result, it could not be said that they had not considered *bona fide* the interests of the shareholders.

I appreciate that it would be a breach of their duty for directors to disregard entirely the interests of a company's shareholders in order to confer a benefit on its employees: *Parke v. Daily News Ltd.*, [1962] Ch. 927. But if they observe a decent respect for other interests lying beyond those of the company's shareholders in the strict sense, that Will not, in my view, leave directors open to the charge that they have failed in their fiduciary duty to the company. In this regard, I cannot accept the view expressed by Professor E. E. Palmer in *Studies in Canadian Company Law*, c. 12, "Directors Power and Duties", pp. 371-2.

So how wide a latitude ought the directors to have? If a group is seeking to obtain control, must the directors ignore them? Or are they entitled to consider the consequences of such a group taking over? In *Savoy Corp. Ltd.*

v. Development Underwriting Ltd. (1963), N.S.W.R. 138 at p. 147, Jacobs, J., said:

> It would seem to me to be unreal in the light of the structure of modern companies and of modern business life to take the view that directors should in no way concern themselves with the infiltration of the company by persons or groups which they bona fide consider not to be seeking the best interests of the company.

My own view is that the directors ought to be allowed to consider who is seeking control and why. If they believe that there will be substantial damage to the company's interests if the company is taken over, then the exercise of their powers to defeat those seeking a majority will not necessarily be categorized as improper.

I do not think it is sound to limit the directors' exercise of their powers to the extent required by *Hogg v. Cramphorn Ltd.*, [1967] Ch. 254. But the limits of their authority must be clearly defined. It would be altogether a mistake if the law, in seeking to adapt itself to the reality of corporate struggles, were to allow the directors any opportunity of achieving an advantage for themselves at the expense of the shareholders. The thrust of companies legislation has brought us a long way since *Percival v. Wright*, [1902] 2 Ch. 421.

If the directors have the right to consider the consequences of a takeover, and to exercise their powers to meet it, if they do so *bona fide* in the interests of the company, how is the Court to determine their purpose? In every case the directors will insist their whole purpose was to serve the company's interest. And no doubt in most cases it will not be difficult for the directors to persuade themselves that it is in the company's best interests that they should remain in office. Something more than a mere assertion of good faith is required.

How can the Court go about determining whether the directors have abused their powers in a given case? How are the Courts to know, in an appropriate case, that the directors were genuinely concerned about the company and not merely pursuing their own selfish interests? Well, a similar task has been attempted in cases of conspiracy to injure. There the question is whether the primary object of those alleged to have acted in combination is to promote their own interests or to damage the interests of others: *Crofter Hand Woven Harris Tweed Co. v. Veitch*, [1942] A.C. 435.

I think the Courts should apply the general rule in this way: The directors must act in good faith. Then there must be reasonable grounds for their belief. If they say that they believe there will be substantial damage to the company's interests, then there must be reasonable grounds for that belief. If there are not, that will justify a finding that the directors were actuated by an improper purpose. . . .

In the United States the whole question of directors' exercise of their powers to defeat an attempt to take over a company has been considered in the State of Delaware. In the United States the law allows a company to purchase its own shares, and the cases have usually arisen where directors have sought to deal in the company's shares. Of course, directors in the exercise of such a power must *bona fide* consider the best interests of the company. The Delaware Courts have held that they cannot exercise their power merely for the purpose of retaining control: *Bennett v. Propp* (1962), 187 A. 2d 405 (Supreme Court of Delaware). But in *Kors v. Carey* (1960), 39 Del. Ch. 47, 158 A. 2d 136 (Court of Chancery of Delaware), it was held that directors were entitled to exercise their power to deal in the company's shares for the purpose of defeating an attempt to take over the company that they believed would not be in the best interests of the company. The Delaware Courts regard the presence of reasonable grounds for the directors' exercise of their powers as the test of good faith. The directors must have considered the consequences of a transfer of control, and must have acted upon reasonable grounds: *Cheff v. Mathes* (1964), A. 2d 548 (Supreme Court of Delaware).

   If there are no reasonable grounds for the directors' alleged belief, but their purpose is merely to freeze out a group of shareholders, the transaction will be set aside: *Condec Corp. v. Lukenheimer Co.* (1967), 230 A. 2d 769 (Court of Chancery of Delaware). What extent of damage must the directors anticipate to justify the exercise of their powers to defeat those seeking a majority? In both *Kors v. Carey* and *Cheff v. Mathes* the directors anticipated a change in policy, though in each case a fundamental change. That change was in each case one that would have had profound consequences to the company's whole way of doing business, and one that the directors believed would damage the company's interests. It was held that constituted reasonable grounds for the exercise of the directors' powers.

   I am not prepared therefore to follow *Hogg v. Cramphorn Ltd., supra*. I think that directors are entitled to consider the reputation, experience and policies of anyone seeking to take over the company. If they decide, on reasonable grounds, a take-over will cause substantial damage to the company's interests, they are entitled to use their powers to protect the company. That is the test that ought to be applied in this case.

The directors' purpose in the case at bar

   The whole case, in my view, turns on the question of Millar's motivation. His was the dominant mind on the board, his purpose was the board's purpose. Teck, in support of its contention that Millar was primarily concerned to defeat Teck's majority, relies upon the evidence that I have already outlined in this judgment. Then Teck goes further, and says that the terms of the contract of June 1st itself show that the defendant directors could only have signed it to frustrate Teck's attempt to obtain control. . . .

   I think that Millar's position is one that can be understood. He was considering bringing the project through to the completion of feasibility, and he told all of the majors that approached him that he intended to. But, he says, and I accept it, that he was prepared throughout to enter into an ultimate deal with Placer, or even with another major for that matter, before feasibility, if a deal were offered that he found acceptable. . .

. . .The plaintiff relies on Millar's statement, made at Kamloops on May 27th, that Price was running around trying to dilute Teck down. I accept the evidence that Millar made the statement. It reveals he was aware that Teck was concerned that if Afton signed a contract providing for the issuance of shares, Teck's position would be jeopardized. It shows that Millar was well aware that Teck's whole purpose would be frustrated if further shares were issued pursuant to a contract. But does that mean that was Millar's purpose, to dilute Teck's share interest? Or was his purpose to sign a contract that he considered to be in the best interests of the company? Millar, after all, said he did not think he approved of what Price was doing, and then he laughed. I do not think this establishes any Machiavellian intent on Millar's part. He knew that what he had said would consternate the Keevils. It was, I think, to some extent an expression of his personality, and to some extent a matter of deliberate calculation. Does it show that Millar was primarily actuated by a desire to frustrate Teck's attempt to gain control? Millar gave evidence that he was by that time resigned to Teck obtaining control. He did not think he could prevent that. Indeed he could not. Teck did obtain its majority. It now controls the company. I do not think the evidence shows that Millar was willing to make any deal so long as it would lead to the issuance of shares in sufficient numbers to frustrate Teck. . . .

. . . So what conclusions ought to be drawn? Now I think Millar was to a great extent acting intuitively. He did not weigh the alternatives and consider the implications on a finely balanced scale. People usually do not make decisions in that way. Most important decisions in life contain an intuitive element. That is why it is quite mistaken to think that Millar's thinking can be entirely reconstructed. I am not convinced that he himself — or anyone else in the like position — would be capable of that.

This question of motive has been canvassed exhaustively with the defendant directors since these proceedings were begun. When Teck brought its application for an injunction back in June, the directors made affidavits and they were cross-examined before Mr. Justice Anderson. Then examinations for discovery of all concerned, including all the directors, were held. The directors have given evidence in this trial and have been cross-examined at length, and what they said in their affidavits and on discovery has been canvassed with them. It would not be surprising if inconsistencies emerged, and some have. Despite this, I think their evidence regarding their motives and purposes ought to be accepted. . . .

I find their object was to obtain the best agreement they could while they were still in control. Their purpose in that sense was to defeat Teck. But, not to defeat Teck's attempt to obtain control, rather it was to foreclose Teck's opportunity of obtaining for itself the ultimate deal. That was, as I view the law, no improper purpose. In seeking to prevent Teck obtaining the contract, the defendant directors were honestly pursuing what they thought was the best policy for the company. . . .

I have put the defendants' purpose in a negative way, that is, I have said they wanted to foreclose Teck's opportunity of obtaining the development contract. But in a larger sense their purpose was a positive one. They wanted to make a contract with Placer while they still had the power to do so. But not at any price. Millar stood firm in his rejection of Placer's 60-40 offer of May 19th, even when he knew that Teck's share position was eroding his control of the company. He was not prepared to concede 40% equity simply in order to sign a contract providing for the issuance of shares to Placer. He held out for a better contract, and he got it. Now I suppose it is possible that if Millar had held out even longer, if he had carried on with his drilling programme he would have been able to negotiate a contract even more favourable to Afton than the contract of June 1st, but I do not think there was any reasonable basis for him to think he could have. The odds were against it. Teck would soon be in a position to compel Afton to sign a contract with them, and Millar did not believe that Canex's first right of refusal offered Afton any real protection against such an eventuality. He knew that time was short. At the same time, Placer knew that if it was going to obtain the contract, it would have to reach agreement with Millar before Teck had an opportunity of replacing the directors. So all things conspired to bring about the signing of the contract. Teck was the catalyst. Millar, Price and Haramboure were, in my view, acting in the best interests of the company. And the evidence shows that they had reasonable grounds for that belief.

Now Teck, of course, was a shareholder. And it is said that it was no part of Millar's purpose to protect Teck's interests. I think it is fair to say that Millar's primary purpose was to make the most advantageous deal he could for Afton. That is as far as the Court ought to go in seeking to analyze his motivation. And, in my view, in trying to make the best deal he could for Afton, Millar was acting in the best interests of the general body of shareholders, including Teck, because once Teck's interest in acquiring control is put to one side, its interest, like that of the other shareholders, was in seeing Afton make the best deal available. I find Millar's purpose was to serve that interest.

The defendant directors were elected to exercise their best judgment. They were not agents bound to accede to the directions of the majority of the shareholders. Their mandate continued so long as they remained in office. They were in no sense a lame duck board. So they acted in what they conceived to be the best interests of the shareholders, and signed a contract which they knew the largest shareholder, holding a majority of the shares, did not want them to sign. They had the right in law to do that. When a company elects its board of directors and entrusts them with the power to manage the company, the directors are entitled to manage it. But they must not exercise their powers for an extraneous purpose. That is a breach of their duty. At the same time, the shareholders have no right to alter the terms of the directors' mandate except by amendment of the articles or by replacing the directors themselves.

The purpose of the directors in their negotiations with Placer was from the beginning a legitimate one. The purpose was to make a favourable deal for Afton. That purpose continued throughout. Did it become an improper purpose because Teck acquired large shareholdings? Did it become an improper purpose because the directors made a deal with Canex knowing that they had to before Teck acquired the power to stop them? I think on the evidence the answer must be no.

The onus of proof is on the plaintiff: see *Australian Metropolitan Life v. Ure* (1923), A.L.J.R. 199 at p. 219, Isaacs, J. Applying what I conceive to be the proper test for determining whether the defendant directors acted in good faith within the meaning of *Re Smith & Fawcett, Ltd.*, [1942] Ch. 304, the plaintiff has failed to show the directors had no reasonable grounds for believing that a take-over by Teck would cause substantial damage to the interests of Afton and its shareholders. Indeed, I am satisfied that it has been affirmatively shown that the directors did have reasonable grounds for such belief.

I find here that the directors had a sufficient knowledge of Teck's reputation, its technical and managerial capacity, and its previous experience, to consider the consequences of a take-over. They decided to make a deal with Placer while they still had the power to do so. They wanted to see the company's principal asset, its copper property, developed efficiently and profitably. They believed, and they had reasonable grounds for such belief, that the property would not be developed efficiently and profitably for the benefit of the shareholders, if Teck got control of it.

If I am wrong in rejecting *Hogg v. Cramphorn Ltd.*, [1978] Ch. 254, it is not applicable here in any event. In *Hogg v. Cramphorn Ltd.* the primary purpose of the directors was to frustrate an attempt to obtain control of the company. In the case at bar the primary purpose of the directors was to make the best contract they could for Afton. I find that the primary purpose of the directors was to serve the best interests of the company. Their primary purpose was to see that the ultimate deal the company made was a deal with Placer, not Teck. They were not motivated by a desire to retain control of the company. They may have thought the issuance of shares under the contract with Canex would enable them, if they had Canex's support, to regain control from Teck. If they did, that was a subsidiary purpose. On any view of the law, therefore, no allegation of improper purpose can be sustained against the defendant directors. . . .

Notes

1 On defensive tactics, see generally see Frank Iacobucci, "Planning and Implementing Defences to Take-Over Bids: The Directors' Role", (1981), 5 Can. Bus. L.J. 131.

2 In *Exco Corp. v. Nova Scotia Savings & Loan Co.* (1987), 35 B.L.R. 149 (N.S. T.D.), Richard J. declined to follow *Teck* in condemning the conduct of the directors of Nova Scotia Savings and Loan Company who had distributed treasury stock to friendly parties in an effort to defeat an unwelcome takeover bid by Exco. In the course of his reasons, he distinguished *Teck* on the basis that "what was under consideration there was a very unusual set of facts which must be somewhat unique to the mining industry". He also stated that:

> the test laid out by Berger J., in the *Teck* case requires further refinement if it [is] to be applied generally. When exercising their power to issue shares from treasury the directors must be able to show that the considerations upon which the decision to issue was based are consistent not only with the best interests of the company and inconsistent with any other interests. This burden ought be on the directors once a treasury share issue has been challenged. I am of the view that such a test is consistent with the fiduciary nature of the director's duty . . .

As will be seen from other Canadian cases explored below, however, the general approach followed by Berger J. has now been adopted across the country, and the competing *Exco* test has been widely rejected. The prime difficulty with *Exco* is that the directors' action in response to a takeover bid can easily be consistent not only with the best interests of the company, but also the interests of the directors themselves. Thus, for example, where the directors believe that the takeover bid is not in the best interests of the company, they might take defensive measures that have the effect of defeating the bid. Thus, they would be acting consistently not only with the company's interests, but their own personal interests, in violation of *Exco*. Conversely, a takeover bidder might offer some of the inside directors (i.e., senior officers) lucrative opportunities to stay with the company following a successful bid. Once again, should directors believe that the bid is in the best interests of the company, under the *Exco* test, they would not be able to facilitate the bid because it would be consistent with their personal interest as well as the company's.

3 The core of Berger J.'s test is that:

> [t]he directors must act in good faith. Then there must be reasonable grounds for their belief. If they say that they believe there will be substantial damage to the company's interests, then there must be reasonable grounds for that belief. If there are not, that will justify a finding that the directors were actuated by an improper purpose . . .

By comparison, the statutory fiduciary duty in the CBCA and other cognate statutes require that the directors "act honestly and in good faith with a view to the best interests of the corporation." One curiosity about *Teck* and its progeny is that while the statutory test makes no mention of "reasonable grounds" for the directors' belief, the courts have nearly uniformly imported the requirement for reasonable grounds into the test for the propriety of directors' conduct on the occurrence of a takeover bid. Is there any warrant for a court to disregard a statutory test in favour of a common law test?

4 Berger J. drew extensively upon American authority in crafting the standard to be applied to directors. In particular, he cited with approval the approach taken in *Cheff v. Mathes*, 199 A.2d 548 (Del. S.C., 1964) and *Kors v. Carey*, 158 A.2d 136 (Del. Ch., 1960). These cases not only specify the standard of behaviour applicable to directors, but represent the first application of the "business judgment rule" in the context of contested takeovers. You will recall that we introduced the business judgment rule in Chapter 5 (dealing with the duty of care). In the United States, the business judgment rule is both a rule of deference to managerial expertise *and* an onus-shifting device. It arose out of the fact that in the United States, the courts had held that when a fiduciary was sued for an alleged breach of fiduciary duty, an onus fell on the defendant directors to show the intrinsic fairness of the transaction. Feeling that this was too onerous, the courts fashioned the business judgment rule, pursuant to which an initial onus lay on the plaintiff to show facts suggesting that the action in question involved fraud, illegality, dishonesty of purpose, self-dealing or, more generally, a conflict of interest. Only then would an onus shift to the directors to show the fairness of the transaction. However, beginning with *Cheff v. Mathes*, and more fully expressed in the American cases explored below, the American courts' takeover jurisprudence has been coloured by the fact that the case of contested takeover bids is inherently different from many other cases involving an allegation of breach of fiduciary duty. When a takeover bid occurs, a potent conflict of interest arises. The duty of the directors is to act in the best interest of the shareholders. This may well involve accepting a premium takeover bid. However, hostile takeovers often result in directors and senior officers losing their jobs. Thus, the directors (and particularly the inside directors) will often be tempted to fend off a hostile takeover bid that is in the shareholders' best interests, in order to preserve their jobs. For this reason, the American courts have held that in cases involving hostile takeovers, an initial onus of proof (described in the *Unocal* case which immediately follows) falls upon the directors. They may then shift the onus back to the plaintiff by satisfying the *Unocal* test.

You will note that, in contrast to the onus-shifting that is an intrinsic part of the American business judgment rule, in *Teck*, Berger J. stated that the onus of proof was on the plaintiff throughout. Keep the issue of the onus of proof in mind in reading the Canadian takeover cases that follow the American authorities below, to see whether the Canadian cases have now come into line with US authority.

5 In any case involving allegations of director and/or officer misconduct, and extending well beyond the issue of hostile takeover bids, it is a virtual certainty that the plaintiff will allege not only that there has been a breach of fiduciary duty under CBCA s. 122 (or its equivalent in other jurisdictions), but also that there has been oppressive conduct under CBCA s. 241 (or its equivalent elsewhere). You will note that a suit alleging director or officer misconduct is a suit of a derivative nature. That is, the nature of the alleged wrong is one done to the entire body of shareholders, and not merely some subset of shareholders (which would ground only a personal action: see Chapter 11 for further details). While on its face it is not entirely clear that the oppression remedy was intended to embrace suits of an inherently derivative nature, the balance of authority favours the view that a derivative-type suit may be commenced under the oppression remedy. See Jeffrey G. MacIntosh, "The Oppression Remedy: Personal or Derivative?" (1991) 70 Can. Bar Rev. 29. In particular, the courts have not balked at allowing oppression claims in cases involving hostile takeovers. See, *e.g., Canada (Director appointed under s. 253 of Canada Business Corporations Act) v. Royal Trustco Ltd.* (1984), 6 D.L.R. (4th) 682, 1984 CarswellOnt 90 (C.A.), appeal dismissed by Supreme Court, [1986] 2 S.C.R. 537, 1986 CarswellOnt 1010, 1986 CarswellOnt 1488, and the *Schneider* case, below. There are certain advantages and potential disadvantages to claiming oppression. One possible advantage is that an oppression suit may be begun by the "application" procedure, rather than as a full blown "action". The application procedure involves affidavit rather than *viva voce* evidence, and dispenses with potentially expensive discovery proceedings. However, in most cases this potential advantage is more illusion than reality. If there are contested facts (as there almost invariably are in cases involving alleged breaches of fiduciary duty or oppression), then the court will convert the application into an action involving the normal trial procedures. The real advantages of an oppression suit are two-fold. First, the substantive standard ("fairness") is broader than either the common law or statutory fiduciary duty standard. For example, even if the directors act honestly and in good faith, with a view to the best interests of the corporation, they may act in a manner that yields a *result* that is unfair and, therefore, oppressive. See, *e.g., Ferguson v. Imax Systems Corp.* (1983), 43 O.R. (2d) 128, 150 D.L.R. (3d) 718, 1983 CarswellOnt 926 (C.A.), leave to appeal to the Supreme Court of Canada refused (1983) 52 N.R. 317n, (1983) 2 O.A.C. 158n; and see generally Jeffrey G. MacIntosh, Janet Holmes and Steve Thompson, "The Puzzle of Shareholder Fiduciary Duties" (1991), 19 Can. Bus. L.J. 86; Jeffrey G. MacIntosh, "Minority Shareholder Rights in Canada and England: 1860–1987" (1989) 27 Osgoode Hall L.J. 561. In addition, the oppression provisions give the court a much wider remedial jurisdiction than is available under either common law or equitable principles. See, *e.g.,* CBCA s. 241(3). In addition, as explored in Chapter 7, the oppression remedy gives the plaintiff more freedom to draw the conduct of a controlling shareholder into the action. For these reasons, prudent counsel will almost always allege oppression in any case involving alleged breach of fiduciary duty.

6 In *Bernard v. Valentini* (1978), 18 O.R. (2d) 656, 83 D.L.R. (3d) 440 (H.C.), Cory J. held that on an application for an interim injunction to restrain the directors of a company from issuing shares for the alleged purpose of maintaining control, it was not incumbent upon an applicant to establish a strong *prima facie* case:

> It is sufficient if the applicant satisfies the court that the case is not a frivolous one and that there are substantial issues to be tried. Once the applicant has satisfied that prerequisite, then the granting of relief will be dependent upon a consideration of other matters, including the threatened harm to the applicant which might not be adequately compensated by way of damages, the preponderance of convenience and the effect of the injunction upon the parties.

On the facts, Cory J. held that it was a proper case to issue an injunction conditional upon the plaintiff giving the usual undertaking as to damages. The shares in fact had been issued and the injunction restrained the individual defendants from exercising any rights that flowed from the shares.

See also *Shield Development Co. v. Snyder* (1975), [1976] 3 W.W.R. 44 (B.C. S.C.) and *Exco Corp. v. Nova Scotia Savings & Loan Co.* (1987), 35 B.L.R. 149 (N.S. S.C.).

7 Under s. 34 of the CBCA, s. 30 of the OBCA and s. 259 of the BCCA, a corporation is given power to purchase its own shares. Should the same considerations apply to a repurchase of shares as to an allotment? Does it make a difference that on a repurchase, shareholders may not be able to sell their shares at an increased price as they would on a takeover? Is there greater potential for abuse of fiduciary duty on a repurchase? The *Ontario Securities Act (1990)* specially regulates issuer bids in Part XX and in Part X of the Regulations.

8 In *Sparling v. Royal Trustco* (1984), 6 D.L.R. (4th) 682, appeal dismissed by Supreme Court, [1986] 2 S.C.R. 537, Cory J.A. of the Ontario Court of Appeal held that the oppression remedy in the CBCA can be invoked by the Director (the administrative official who oversees the application of the Act) to protect minority shareholders. In *Royal Trustco*, the directors of the target company (Royal Trustco) were not informed of defensive tactics being used by their management to fend off a takeover bid. In particular, the directors failed to inform shareholders that they had arranged for shares to be purchased on the open market by investors that were "friendly" to management (thereby greatly lowering the likelihood that the bidder, Campeau Corporation, would be able to amass enough stock to gain control of Royal Trustco).

This was a material omission in the information circular sent to shareholders regarding the bid. This omission allowed the Director to seek
damages from the company and its directors under the oppression
remedy. The Court rejected the argument that the Director was precluded from bringing such an action as it would amount to the creation
of a new remedy, i.e., a class action on behalf of aggrieved shareholders
for which there was insufficient statutory authority. The Court held that
failing to allow the Director to bring the action would deny shareholders
a remedy that Parliament sought to confer under the Act. In support of
its conclusion, the Court held that "[i]n the C.B.C.A. there is a clear
indication that the Director is a protector of the public's interest in
corporate affairs."

9 Because Canadian takeover jurisprudence is in some respects derivative
of American takeover jurisprudence, in the following section we examine the American situation. We then compare other Canadian cases
to see the ways in which Canadian takeover cases have tracked this US
jurisprudence, and the ways in which they have not.

(ii) American Jurisprudence on Defensive Tactics

As noted above, *Cheff v. Mathes*, 199 A.2d 458, 41 Del. Ch. 494 (1964),
is the beginning of modern American jurisprudence regarding the response
of directors to a takeover bid. *Cheff* involved a share re-purchase by a
corporation at a premium above market price, from a shareholder who
threatened to acquire control of the corporation. The re-purchase was held
to be a permissible exercise of directorial discretion. In the course of his
reasons, Carey J. stated that the test for evaluating the conduct of directors
was

> whether or not defendants satisfied the burden of proof of showing
> reasonable grounds to believe a danger to corporate policy and effect-
> iveness existed by the presence of . . . (the potential acquirer's) . . .
> stock ownership. It is important to remember that the directors satisfy
> their burden by showing good faith and reasonable investigation; the
> directors will not be penalized for an honest mistake of judgment, if
> the judgment appeared reasonable at the time the decision was made.

The test developed in *Cheff* underwent modification in *Unocal Corp.
v. Mesa Petroleum Co.*, 493 A.2d 946 (Del. S.C. 1985). In *Unocal*, a third
party made a two-tier tender offer for Unocal. In a two-tier offer, the acquirer
(in this case Mesa Petroleum) begins with a "partial" takeover bid for a
stated percentage of the target firm's equity. A partial bid will typically
involve the intended acquisition of 20–40% of the target's shares — just
sufficient to give the acquirer *de facto* control (shares that are tendered into
the bid are taken up *pro rata* by the acquirer until it reaches its acquisition
target). Once the bid has been completed and the acquirer has control, it

will then use its power of control to effect a "second step" transaction in which the remaining public shareholders are forced out of the company (i.e., a "going private", "squeezeout", "freezeout" or "force out" transaction). The squeezeout transaction will be effected at a lower price than that which was offered in the first step (i.e., the takeover bid), and it is for this reason that the two steps taken together are referred to as a "two-tier" offer. In order to defend against the two-tier bid, Unocal management offered to repurchase shares of Unocal at a premium price from all shareholders *except* Mesa Petroleum. This gave shareholders an alternative transaction at a higher price than the Mesa bid, and had the effect of stopping Mesa's attempt to gain control of Unocal. As noted above, the test applied to assess the propriety of the directorial conduct was based on a standard of review that was more onerous than the business judgment rule that usually applies in cases alleging breach of fiduciary duty, but less demanding than a full-blown fairness test. The following extract from the case discusses this "intermediate standard", in the context of a takeover bid found by the court to be highly coercive.

Unocal Corp. v. Mesa Petroleum Co.
493 A.2d 946 (Del. S.C. 1985)

MOORE J.:

II.

The issues we address involve these fundamental questions: Did the Unocal board have the power and duty to oppose a takeover threat it reasonably perceived to be harmful to the corporate enterprise, and if so, is its action here entitled to the protection of the business judgment rule?

Mesa contends that the discriminatory exchange offer violates the fiduciary duties Unocal owes it. Mesa argues that because of the Mesa exclusion the business judgment rule is inapplicable, because the directors by tendering their own shares will derive a financial benefit that is not available to *all* Unocal stockholders. Thus, it is Mesa's ultimate contention that Unocal cannot establish that the exchange offer is fair to *all* shareholders, and argues that the Court of Chancery was correct in concluding that Unocal was unable to meet this burden.

Unocal answers that it does not owe a duty of "fairness" to Mesa, given the facts here. Specifically, Unocal contends that its board of directors reasonably and in good faith concluded that Mesa's $54 two-tier tender offer was coercive and inadequate, and that Mesa sought selective treatment for itself. Furthermore, Unocal argues that the board's approval of the exchange offer was made in good faith, on an informed basis, and in the exercise of due care. Under these circumstances, Unocal contends that its directors properly employed this device to protect the company and its stockholders from Mesa's harmful tactics.

III.

We begin with the basic issue of the power of a board of directors of a Delaware corporation to adopt a defensive measure of this type. Absent such authority, all other questions are moot. Neither issues of fairness nor business judgment are pertinent without the basic underpinning of a board's legal power to act.

The board has a large reservoir of authority upon which to draw. Its duties and responsibilities proceed from the inherent powers conferred by 8 *Del. C.* §141(a), respecting management of the corporation's "business and affairs". Additionally, the powers here being exercised derive from 8 *Del. C.* § 160(a), conferring broad authority upon a corporation to deal in its own stock. From this it is now well established that in the acquisition of its shares a Delaware corporation may deal selectively with its stockholders, provided the directors have not acted out of a sole or primary purpose to entrench themselves in office.

* * *

Finally, the board's power to act derives from its fundamental duty and obligation to protect the corporate enterprise, which includes stockholders, from harm reasonably perceived, irrespective of its source.

* * *

Thus, we are satisfied that in the broad context of corporate governance, including issues of fundamental corporate change, a board of directors is not a passive instrumentality.

* * *

When a board addresses a pending takeover bid it has an obligation to determine whether the offer is in the best interests of the corporation and its shareholders. In that respect a board's duty is no different from any other responsibility it shoulders, and its decisions should be no less entitled to the respect they otherwise would be accorded in the realm of business judgment. *See also Johnson v. Trueblood*, 629 F.2d 287, 292-293 (3d Cir. 1980). There are, however, certain caveats to a proper exercise of this function. Because of the omnipresent spectre that a board may be acting primarily in its own interests, rather than those of the corporation and its shareholders, there is an enhanced duty which calls for judicial examination at the threshold before the protections of the business judgment rule may be conferred.

This Court has long recognized that: We must bear in mind the inherent danger in the purchase of shares with corporate funds to remove a threat to corporate policy when a threat to control is involved. The directors are of necessity confronted with a conflict of interest, and an objective decision is difficult.

In the face of this inherent conflict directors must show that they had reasonable grounds for believing that a danger to corporate policy and effectiveness existed because of another person's stock ownership.

* * *

However, they satisfy that burden "by showing good faith and reasonable investigation. . . ."

* * *

Furthermore, such proof is materially enhanced, as here, by the approval of a board comprised of a majority of outside independent directors who have acted in accordance with the foregoing standards.

* * *

In the board's exercise of corporate power to forestall a takeover bid our analysis begins with the basic principle that corporate directors have a fiduciary duty to act in the best interests of the corporation's stockholders.

* * *

As we have noted, their duty of care extends to protecting the corporation and its owners from perceived harm whether a threat originates from third parties or other shareholders. But such powers are not absolute. A corporation does not have unbridled discretion to defeat any perceived threat by any Draconian means available.

* * *

A further aspect is the element of balance. If a defensive measure is to come within the ambit of the business judgment rule, it must be reasonable in relation to the threat posed. This entails an analysis by the directors of the nature of the takeover bid and its effect on the corporate enterprise. Examples of such concerns may include: inadequacy of the price offered, nature and timing of the offer, questions of illegality, the impact on "constituencies" other than shareholders (i.e., creditors, customers, employees, and perhaps even the community generally), the risk of nonconsummation, and the quality of securities being offered in the exchange.

* * *

While not a controlling factor, it also seems to us that a board may reasonably consider the basic stockholder interests at stake, including those of short term speculators, whose actions may have fueled the coercive aspect of the offer at the expense of the long term investor. Here, the threat posed was viewed by the Unocal board as a grossly inadequate two-tier coercive tender offer coupled with the threat of greenmail.

Specifically, the Unocal directors had concluded that the value of Unocal was substantially above the $54 per share offered in cash at the front end. Furthermore, they determined that the subordinated securities to be exchanged in Mesa's announced squeeze out of the remaining shareholders in the "back-end" merger were "junk bonds" worth far less than $54. It is now well recognized that such offers are a classic coercive measures designed to stampede shareholders into tendering at the first tier, even if the price is inadequate, out of fear of what they will receive at the back end of the transaction. Wholly beyond the coercive aspect of an inadequate two-tier tender offer, the threat was posed by a corporate raider with a national reputation as a "greenmailer".

In adopting the selective exchange offer, the board stated that its objective was either to defeat the inadequate Mesa offer or, should the offer still succeed, provide the 49% of its stockholders, who would otherwise be forced to accept "junk bonds", with $72 worth of senior debt. We find that both purposes are valid.

However, such efforts would have been thwarted by Mesa's participation in the exchange offer. First, if Mesa could tender its shares, Unocal would effectively be subsidizing the former's continuing effort to buy Unocal stock at $54 per share. Second, Mesa could not, by definition, fit within the class of shareholders being protected from its own coercive and inadequate tender offer.

Thus, we are satisfied that the selective exchange offer is reasonably related to the threats posed. It is consistent with the principle that "the minority stockholder shall receive the substantial equivalent in value of what he had before."

* * *

This concept of fairness, while stated in the merger context, is also relevant in the area of tender offer law. Thus, the board's decision to offer what it determined to be the fair value of the corporation to the 49% of its shareholders, who would otherwise be forced to accept highly subordinated "junk bonds", is reasonable and consistent with the directors' duty to ensure that the minority stockholders receive equal value for their shares.

V.

Mesa contends that it is unlawful, and the trial court agreed, for a corporation to discriminate in this fashion against one shareholder. It argues correctly that no case has ever sanctioned a device that precludes a raider from sharing in a benefit available to all other stockholders. However, as we have noted earlier, the principle of selective stock repurchases by a Delaware corporation is neither unknown nor unauthorized.

* * *

Thus, while the exchange offer is a form of selective treatment, given the nature of the threat posed here the response is neither unlawful nor unreasonable. If the board of directors is disinterested, has acted in good faith and with due care, its decision in the absence of an abuse of discretion will be upheld as a proper exercise of business judgment.

* * *

VI.

In conclusion, there was directional power to oppose the Mesa tender offer, and to undertake a selective stock exchange made in good faith and upon a reasonable investigation pursuant to a clear duty to protect the corporate enterprise. Further, the selective stock repurchase plan chosen by Unocal is reasonable in relation to the threat that the board rationally and reasonably believed was posed by Mesa's inadequate and coercive two-tier tender offer. Under those circumstances the board's action is entitled to be measured by the standards of the business judgment rule. Thus, unless it is shown by a preponderance of the evidence that the directors' decisions were primarily based on perpetuating themselves in office, or some other breach of fiduciary duty such as fraud, overreaching, lack of good faith, or being uninformed, a Court will not substitute its judgment for that of the board.

In this case that protection is not lost merely because Unocal's directors have tendered their shares in the exchange offer. Given the validity of the Mesa exclusion, they are receiving a benefit shared generally by all other stockholders except Mesa. In this circumstance the test of *Aronson v. Lewis*, 473 A.2d at 812, is satisfied. *See also Cheff v. Mathes*, 199 A.2d at 554. If the stockholders are displeased with the action of their elected representatives, the powers of corporate democracy are at their disposal to turn the board out.

* * *

With the Court of Chancery's findings that the exchange offer was based on the board's good faith belief that the Mesa offer was inadequate, that the board's action was informed and taken with due care, that Mesa's prior activities justify a reasonable inference that its principle objective was greenmail, and implicitly, that the substance of the offer itself was reasonable and fair to the corporation and its stockholders if Mesa were included, we cannot say that the Unocal directors have acted in such a manner as to have passed an "unintelligent and unadvised judgment".

* * *

The decision of the Court of Chancery is therefore REVERSED, and the preliminary injunction is VACATED.

Note

The *Unocal* case is now one of two leading US cases for testing the propriety of directorial resistance to a takeover bid. The *Revlon* case, which follows, is the other leading case.

Revlon Inc. v. MacAndrews & Forbes Holdings Inc.
506 A.2d 173 (Del. S.C., 1985)

[*Revlon Inc. v. MacAndrews & Forbes Holdings Inc.*, 506 A.2d 173 (Del. Super, 1985) plays a special role among the cases announcing Delaware's "intermediate standard" of review. In addition to contributing to the development of the proportionality test, the opinion also sets out the limits of the test's application. Once the company's sale has become "inevitable",

Revlon decrees that resistance under the aegis of *Unocal*'s proportionality test must end, and management's duty shifts from canvassing alternatives to a sale to determining how the sale should take place.

In this case, the court determined that the Revlon directors had breached their duty of care by entering into a series of transactions with Forstmann Little & Co. that had the effect of thwarting the efforts of Pantry Pride Inc. to acquire Revlon. These transactions included an option granted Forstmann to purchase certain assets (the lock-up option), a promise by Revlon to deal exclusively with Forstmann (the no-shop option) and the payment of a $25 million cancellation fee to Forstmann if the transaction was aborted. The court analysed the genesis of these transactions in light of the history of the Pantry Pride takeover bid, and determined that they represented unwarranted concessions granted to Forstmann in an attempt by the directors to avoid liability for debt incurred during a previous round of defensive tactics designed to thwart Pantry Pride's bid. The following extract from the case describes the history of this deal, and demonstrates the point at which defensive tactics fail the *Unocal* test].

MOORE J.: On August 19, the Revlon board met specially to consider the impending threat of a hostile bid by Pantry Pride. At the meeting, Lazard Freres, Revlon's investment banker, advised the directors that $45 per share was a grossly inadequate price for the company. Felix Rohatyn and William Loomis of Lazard Freres explained to the board that Pantry Pride's financial strategy for acquiring Revlon would be through "junk bond" financing followed by a break-up of Revlon and the disposition of its assets. With proper timing, according to the experts, such transactions could produce a return to Pantry Pride of $60 to $70 per share, while a sale of the company as a whole would be in the "mid 50" dollar range. Martin Lipton, special counsel for Revlon, recommended two defensive measures: first, that the company repurchase up to 5 million of its nearly 30 million outstanding shares; and second, that it adopt a Note Purchase Rights Plan. Under this plan, each Revlon shareholder would receive as a dividend one Note Purchase Right (the Rights) for each share of common stock, with the Rights entitling the holder to exchange one common share for a $65 principal Revlon note at 12% interest with a one-year maturity. The Rights would become effective whenever anyone acquired beneficial ownership of 20% or more of Revlon's shares, unless the purchaser acquired all the company's stock for cash at $65 or more per share. In addition, the Rights would not be available to the acquirer, and prior to the 20% triggering event the Revlon board could redeem the rights for 10 cents each. Both proposals were unanimously adopted.

Pantry Pride made its first hostile move on August 23 with a cash tender offer for any and all shares of Revlon at $47.50 per common share and $26.67 per preferred share, subject to (1) Pantry Pride's obtaining financing for the purchase, and (2) the Rights being redeemed, rescinded or voided.

The Revlon board met again on August 26. The directors advised the stockholders to reject the offer. Further defensive measures also were planned. On August 29, Revlon commenced its own offer for up to 10 million shares, exchanging for each share of common stock tendered one Senior Subordinated Note (the Notes) of $47.50 principal at 11.75% interest, due 1995, and one-tenth of a share of $9.00 Cumulative Convertible Exchangeable Preferred Stock valued at $100 per share. Lazard Freres opined that the notes would trade at their face value on a fully distributed basis. Revlon stockholders tendered 87 percent of the outstanding shares (approximately 33 million), and the company accepted the full 10 million shares on a pro rata basis. The new Notes contained covenants which limited Revlon's ability to incur additional debt, sell assets, or pay dividends unless otherwise approved by the "independent" (non-management) members of the board.

At this point, both the Rights and the Note covenants stymied Pantry Pride's attempted takeover. The next move came on September 16, when Pantry Pride announced a new tender offer at $42 per share, conditioned upon receiving at least 90% of the outstanding stock. Pantry Pride also indicated that it would consider buying less than 90%, and at an increased price, if Revlon removed the impeding Rights. While this offer was lower on its face than the earlier $47.50 proposal, Revlon's investment banker, Lazard Freres, described the two bids as essentially equal in view of the completed exchange offer.

The Revlon board held a regularly scheduled meeting on September 24. The directors rejected the latest Pantry Pride offer and authorized management to negotiate with other parties interested in acquiring Revlon. Pantry Pride remained determined in its efforts and continued to make cash bids for the company, offering $50 per share on September 27, and raising its bid to $53 on October 1, and then to $56.25 on October 7.

In the meantime, Revlon's negotiations with Forstmann and the investment group Adler & Shaykin had produced results. The Revlon directors met on October 3 to consider Pantry Pride's $53 bid and to examine possible alternatives to the offer. Both Forstmann and Adler & Shaykin made certain proposals to the board. As a result, the directors unanimously agreed to a leveraged buyout by Forstmann. The terms of this accord were as follows: each stockholder would get $56 cash per share; management would purchase stock in the new company by the exercise of their Revlon "golden parachutes"; Forstmann would assume Revlon's $475 million debt incurred by the issuance of the Notes; and Revlon would redeem the Rights and waive the Notes covenants for Forstmann or in connection with any other offer superior to Forstmann's.

When the merger, and thus the waiver of the Notes covenants, was announced, the market value of these securities began to fall. The Notes, which originally traded near par, around 100, dropped to 87.50 by October 8. One director later reported (at the October 12 meeting) a "deluge" of telephone calls from irate noteholders, and on October 10 the Wall Street Journal reported threats of litigation by these creditors.

Pantry Pride countered with a new proposal on October 7, raising its $53 offer to $56.25, subject to nullification of the Rights, a waiver of the Notes covenants, and the election of three Pantry Pride directors to the Revlon board. On October 9, representatives of Pantry Pride, Forstmann and Revlon conferred in an attempt to negotiate the fate of Revlon, but could not reach agreement. At this meeting Pantry Pride announced that it would engage in fractional bidding and top any Forstmann offer by a slightly higher one. It is also significant that Forstmann, to Pantry Pride's exclusion, had been made privy to certain Revlon financial data. Thus, the parties were not negotiating on equal terms.

Again privately armed with Revlon data, Forstmann met on October 11 with Revlon's special counsel and investment banker. On October 12, Forstmann made a new $57.25 per share offer, based on several conditions. The principal demand was a lock-up option to purchase Revlon's Vision Care and National Health Laboratories divisions for $525 million, some $100-$175 million below the value ascribed to them by Lazard Freres, if another acquirer got 40% of Revlon's shares. Revlon also was required to accept a no-shop provision. The Rights and Notes covenants had to be removed as in the October 3 agreement. There would be a $25 million cancellation fee to be placed in escrow, and released to Forstmann if the new agreement terminated or if another acquirer got more than 19.9% of Revlon's stock. Finally, there would be no participation by Revlon management in the merger. In return, Forstmann agreed to support the par value of the Notes, which had faltered in the market, by an exchange of new notes. Forstmann also demanded immediate acceptance of its offer, or it would be withdrawn. The board unanimously approved Forstmann's proposal because: (1) it was for a higher price than the Pantry Pride bid, (2) it protected the noteholders, and (3) Forstmann's financing was firmly in place. The board further agreed to redeem the rights and waive the covenants on the preferred stock in response to any offer above $57 cash per share. The covenants were waived, contingent upon receipt of an investment banking opinion that the Notes would trade near par value once the offer was consummated.

Pantry Pride, which had initially sought injunctive relief from the Rights plan on August 22, filed an amended complaint on October 14 challenging the lock-up, the cancellation fee, and the exercise of the Rights and the Notes covenants. Pantry Pride also sought a temporary restraining order to prevent Revlon from placing any assets in escrow or transferring them to Forstmann. Moreover, on October 22, Pantry Pride again raised its bid, with a cash offer of $58 per share conditioned upon nullification of the Rights, waiver of the covenants, and an injunction of the Forstmann lock-up.

On October 15, the Court of Chancery prohibited the further transfer of assets, and eight days later enjoined the lock-up, no-shop, and cancellation fee provisions of the agreement. The trial court concluded that the Revlon directors had breached their duty of loyalty by making concessions to Forstmann, out of concern for their liability to the noteholders, rather than maximizing the sale price of the company for the stockholders' benefit.

A.

We turn first to Pantry Pride's probability of success on the merits. The ultimate responsibility for managing the business and affairs of a corporation falls on its board of directors.

* * *

In discharging this function the directors owe fiduciary duties of care and loyalty to the corporation and its shareholders.

* * *

These principles apply with equal force when a board approves a corporate merger . . . and of course they are the bedrock of our law regarding corporate takeover issues.

* * *

While the business judgment rule may be applicable to the actions of corporate directors responding to takeover threats, the principles upon which it is founded — care, loyalty and independence — must be satisfied.

If the business judgment rule applies, there is a "presumption that in making a business decision the directors of a corporation acted on an informed basis, in good faith and in the honest belief that the action taken was in the best interests of the company."

* * *

However, when a board implements anti-takeover measures there arises "the omnipresent specter that a board may be acting primarily in its own interests, rather than those of the corporation and its shareholders . . ."

* * *

This potential for conflict places upon the directors the burden of proving that they had reasonable grounds for believing there was a danger to corporate policy and effectiveness, a burden satisfied by a showing of good faith and reasonable investigation. . . . In addition, the directors must analyze the nature of the takeover and its effect on the corporation in order to ensure balance — that the responsive action taken is reasonable in relation to the threat posed.

* * *

The Revlon directors concluded that Pantry Pride's $47.50 offer was grossly inadequate. In that regard the board acted in good faith, and on an informed basis, with reasonable grounds to believe that there existed a harmful threat to the corporate enterprise. The adoption of a defensive measure, reasonable in relation to the threat posed, was proper and fully accorded with the powers, duties, and responsibilities conferred upon directors under our law.

D.

However, when Pantry Pride increased its offer to $50 per share, and then to $53, it became apparent to all that the break-up of the company was inevitable. The Revlon board's authorization permitting management to negotiate a merger or buyout with a third party was a recognition that the company was for sale. The duty of the board had thus changed from the preservation of Revlon as a corporate entity to the maximization of the company's value at a sale for the stockholders' benefit. This significantly altered the board's responsibilities under the *Unocal* standards. It no longer faced threats to corporate policy and effectiveness, or to the stockholders' interests, from a grossly inadequate bid. The whole question of defensive measures became moot. The directors' role changed from defenders of the corporate bastion to auctioneers charged with getting the best price for the stockholders at a sale of the company.

III.

This brings us to the lock-up with Forstmann and its emphasis on shoring up the sagging market value of the Notes in the face of threatened litigation by their holders. Such a focus was inconsistent with the changed concept of the directors' responsibilities at this stage of the developments. The impending waiver of the Notes covenants had caused the value of the Notes to fall, and the board was aware of the noteholders' ire as well as their subsequent threats of suit. The directors thus made support of the Notes an integral part of the company's dealings with Forstmann, even though their primary responsibility at this stage was to the equity owners.

The original threat posed by Pantry Pride — the break-up of the company — had become a reality which even the directors embraced. Selective dealing to fend off a hostile but determined bidder was no longer a proper objective. Instead, obtaining the highest price for the benefit of the stockholders should have been the central theme guiding director action. Thus, the Revlon board could not make the requisite showing of good faith by preferring the noteholders and ignoring its duty of loyalty to the shareholders. The rights of the former already were fixed by contract.

* * *

The noteholders required no further protection, and when the Revlon board entered into an auction-ending lock-up agreement with Forstmann on the basis of impermissible considerations at the expense of the shareholders, the directors breached their primary duty of loyalty.

The Revlon board argued that it acted in good faith in protecting the noteholders because *Unocal* permits consideration of other corporate constituencies. Although such considerations may be permissible, there are fundamental limitations upon that prerogative. A board may have regard for various constituencies in discharging its responsibilities, provided there are rationally related benefits accruing to the stockholders. *Unocal*, 493 A.2d at 955. However, such concern for non-stockholder interests is inappropriate when an auction among active bidders is in progress, and the object no longer is to protect or maintain the corporate enterprise but to sell it to the highest bidder.

Revlon also contended that . . . it had contractual and good faith obligations to consider the noteholders. However, any such duties are limited to the principle that one may not interfere with contractual relationships by improper actions. Here, the rights of the noteholders were fixed by agreement, and there is nothing of substance to suggest that any of those terms were violated. The Notes covenants specifically contemplated a waiver to permit sale of the company at a fair price. The Notes were accepted by the holders on that basis, including the risk of an adverse market effect stemming from a waiver. Thus, nothing remained for Revlon to legitimately protect, and no rationally related benefit thereby accrued to the stockholders. Under such circumstances we must conclude that the merger agreement with Forstmann was unreasonable in relation to the threat posed.

A lock-up is not *per se* illegal under Delaware law. . . . Options can entice other bidders to enter a contest for control of the corporation, creating an auction for the company and maximizing shareholder profit. Current economic conditions in the takeover market are such that a "white knight" like Forstmann might only enter the bidding for the target company if it receives some form of compensation to cover the risks and costs involved.

* * *

However, while those lock-ups which draw bidders into the battle benefit shareholders, similar measures which end an active auction and foreclose further bidding operate to the shareholders' detriment.

* * *

The Forstmann option had a similar destructive effect on the auction process. Forstmann had already been drawn into the contest on a preferred basis, so the result of the lock-up was not to foster bidding, but to destroy it. The board's stated reasons for approving the transactions were: (1) better financing, (2) noteholder protection, and (3) higher price. As the Court of Chancery found, and we agree, any distinctions between the rival bidders' methods of financing the proposal were nominal at best, and such a consideration has little or no significance in a cash offer for any and all shares. The principal object, contrary to the board's duty of care, appears to have been protection of the noteholders over the shareholders' interests.

While Forstmann's $57.25 offer was objectively higher than Pantry Pride's $56.25 bid, the margin of superiority is less when the Forstmann price is adjusted for the time value of money. In reality, the Revlon board ended the auction in return for very little actual improvement in the final bid. The principal benefit went to the directors, who avoided personal liability to a class of creditors to whom the board owed no further duty under the circumstances. Thus, when a board ends an intense bidding contest on an insubstantial basis, and where a significant by-product of that action is to protect the directors against a perceived threat of personal liability for consequences stemming from the adoption of previous defensive measures, the action cannot withstand the enhanced scrutiny which *Unocal* requires of director conduct.

* * *

V.

In conclusion, the Revlon board was confronted with a situation not uncommon in the current wave of corporate takeovers. A hostile and determined bidder sought the company at a price the board was convinced was inadequate. The initial defensive tactics worked to the benefit of the shareholders, and thus the board was able to sustain its *Unocal* burdens in justifying those measures. However, in granting an asset option lock-up to Forstmann, we must conclude that under all the circumstances the directors allowed considerations other than the maximization of shareholder profit to affect their judgment, and followed a course that ended the auction for Revlon, absent court intervention, to the ultimate detriment of its shareholders. No such defensive measure can be sustained when it represents a breach of the directors' fundamental duty of care. . . . In that context the board's action is not entitled to the deference accorded it by the business judgment rule. The measures were properly enjoined. The decision of the Court of Chancery, therefore, is
AFFIRMED.

Paramount Communications Inc. v. QVC Network Inc.
637 A.2d 34 (Del. S.C., 1994)

VEASEY CHIEF JUSTICE:

II. APPLICABLE PRINCIPLES OF ESTABLISHED DELAWARE LAW

The General Corporation Law of the State of Delaware (the "General Corporation Law") and the decisions of this Court have repeatedly recognized the fundamental principle that the management of the business and affairs of a Delaware corporation is entrusted to its directors, who are the duly elected and authorized representatives of the stockholders.

* * *

Under normal circumstances, neither the courts nor the stockholders should interfere with the managerial decisions of the directors. The business judgment rule embodies the deference to which such decisions are entitled.

Nevertheless, there are rare situations which mandate that a court take a more direct and active role in overseeing the decisions made and actions taken by directors. In these situations, a court subjects the directors' conduct to enhanced scrutiny to ensure that it is reasonable. The decisions of this Court have clearly established the circumstances where such enhanced scrutiny will be applied. . . . The case at bar implicates two such circumstances: (1) the approval of a transaction resulting in a sale of control, and (2) the adoption of defensive measures in response to a threat to corporate control.

* * *

A. The Significance of a Sale or Change of Control

* * *

Because of the intended sale of control, the Paramount-Viacom transaction has economic consequences of considerable significance to the Paramount stockholders. Once control has shifted, the current Paramount stockholders will have no leverage in the future to demand another control premium. As a result, the Paramount stockholders are entitled to receive, and should receive, a control premium and/or protective devices of significant value. There being no such protective provisions in the Viacom-Paramount transaction, the Paramount directors had an obligation to take the maximum advantage of the current opportunity to realize for the stockholders the best value reasonably available.

B. The Obligations of Directors in a Sale or Change of Control Transaction

The consequences of a sale of control impose special obligations on the directors of a corporation. In particular, they have the obligation of acting reasonably to seek the transaction offering the best value reasonably available to the stockholders. The courts will apply enhanced scrutiny to ensure that the directors have acted reasonably. The obligations of the directors and the enhanced scrutiny of the courts are well-established by the decisions of this Court. The directors' fiduciary duties in a sale of control context are those which generally attach. In short, "the directors must act in accordance with their fundamental duties of care and loyalty." . . .

It is basic to our law that the board of directors has the ultimate responsibility for managing the business and affairs of a corporation. In discharging this function, the directors owe fiduciary duties of care and loyalty to the corporation and its shareholders. This unremitting obligation extends equally to board conduct in a sale of corporate control.

* * *

In determining which alternative provides the best value for the stockholders, a board of directors is not limited to considering only the amount of cash involved, and is not required to ignore totally its view of the future value of a strategic alliance. . . . Instead, the directors should analyze the entire situation and evaluate in a disciplined manner the consideration being offered. Where stock or other non-cash consideration is involved, the board should try to quantify its value, if feasible, to achieve an objective comparison of the alternatives. In addition, the board may assess a variety of practical considerations relating to each alternative including: [an offer's] fairness and feasibility; the proposed or actual financing for the offer, and the consequences of that financing; questions of illegality; . . . the risk of non-consummation; . . . the bidder's identity, prior background and other business venture experiences; and the bidder's business plans for the corporation and their effects on stockholder interests.

. . . These considerations are important because the selection of one alternative may permanently foreclose other opportunities. While the assessment of these factors may be complex, the board's goal is straightforward: Having informed themselves of all material information reasonably available, the directors must decide which alternative is most likely to offer the best value reasonably available to the stockholders.

C. Enhanced Judicial Scrutiny of a Sale or Change of Control Transaction

Board action in the circumstances presented here is subject to enhanced scrutiny. Such scrutiny is mandated by: (a) the threatened diminution of the current stockholders' voting power; (b) the fact that an asset belonging to public stockholders (a control premium) is being sold and may never be available again: and (c) the traditional concern of Delaware courts for actions which impair or impede stockholder voting rights.

* * *

The key features of an enhanced scrutiny test are: (a) a judicial determination regarding the adequacy of the decisionmaking process employed by the directors, including the information on which the directors based their decision; and (b) a judicial examination of the reasonableness of the directors' action in light of the circumstances then existing. The directors have the burden of proving that they were adequately informed and acted reasonably.

Although an enhanced scrutiny test involves a review of the reasonableness of the substantive merits of a board's actions, a court should not ignore the complexity of the directors' task in a sale of control. There are many business and financial considerations implicated in investigating and selecting the best value reasonably available. The board of directors is the corporate decisionmaking body best equipped to make these judgments. Accordingly, a court applying enhanced judicial scrutiny should be deciding whether the directors made a reasonable decision, not a perfect decision. If a board selected one of several reasonable alternatives, a court should not second-guess that choice even though it might have decided otherwise or subsequent events may have cast doubt on the board's determination. Thus, courts will not substitute their business judgment for that of the directors, but will determine if the directors' decision was, on balance, within a range of reasonableness.

D. Revlon and Time-Warner Distinguished

The Paramount defendants and Viacom assert that the fiduciary obligations and the enhanced judicial scrutiny discussed above are not implicated in this case in the absence of a "break-up" of the corporation, and that the order granting the preliminary injunction should be reversed. This argument is based on their erroneous interpretation of our decisions in Revlon and Time-Warner.

* * *

The decisions of this Court following reinforced the applicability of enhanced scrutiny and the directors' obligation to seek the best value reasonably available for the stockholders where there is a pending sale of control, regardless of whether or not there is to be a break-up of the corporation.

* * *

Under Delaware law there are, generally speaking and without excluding other possibilities, two circumstances which may implicate Revlon duties. The first, and clearer one, is when a corporation initiates an active bidding process seeking to sell itself or to effect a business reorganization involving a clear breakup of the company. However, Revlon duties may also be triggered where, in response to a bidder's offer, a target abandons its long-term strategy and seeks an alternative transaction involving the breakup of the company.

* * *

The Paramount defendants' position that both a change of control and a break-up are required must be rejected. Such a holding would unduly restrict the application of Revlon, is inconsistent with this Court's decisions in Barkan and Macmillan, and has no basis in policy. There are few events that have a more significant impact on the stockholders than a sale of control or a corporate break-up. Each event represents a fundamental (and perhaps irrevocable) change in the nature of the corporate enterprise from a practical standpoint. It is the significance of each of these events that justifies: (a) focusing on the directors' obligation to seek the best value reasonably available to the stockholders; and (b) requiring a close scrutiny of board action which could be contrary to the stockholders' interests.

Accordingly, when a corporation undertakes a transaction which will cause: (a) a change in corporate control; or (b) a break-up of the corporate entity, the directors' obligation is to seek the best value reasonably available to the stockholders. This obligation arises because the effect of the Viacom-Paramount transaction, if consummated, is to shift control of Paramount from the public stockholders to a controlling stockholder, Viacom. Neither Time-Warner nor any other decision of this Court holds that a "break-up" of the company is essential to give rise to this obligation where there is a sale of control.

Notes

1 The *Unocal* test has been applied in so many cases that they are now too numerous to mention. In some of these cases, defensive tactics have been found to be reasonable under the *Unocal* test: see, *e.g.*, *Polk v. Good*, 507 A.2d 531 (Del. S.C. 1986); *Moran v. Household International Inc.*, 500 A.2d 1346 (Del. S.C. 1985); *Newmont Mining Corp. v. Pickens*, 831 F.2d 1448 (9th Cir. 1987); *Grand Metropolitan PLC v. Pillsbury Co.*, Civ. No. 10323 (Del. Ch., 1988); *Desert Partners, L.P v. USG Corp.*, 686 F. Supp. 1289 (N.D. Ill, 1988). In other cases, defensive tactics have been found to be unreasonable under the *Unocal* test: see, *e.g.*, *Phillips v. Instituform of North America, Inc.*, C.A. No 9173 (Del. Ch. Aug. 27, 1987); *AC Acquisition Corp. v. Anderson, Clayton & Co.*, 519 A.2d 103 (Del. Ch. 1986); *Dynamics Corp. of America v. CTS Corp.*, 637 F. Supp. 406 (N.D. Ill. 1986), aff'd, 794 F.2d 250 (7th Cir. 1986), rev'd on other grounds, 107 S. Ct. 1637 (1987); *Robert M. Mass Group, Inc. v. Evans*, Fed. Sec. L. Rep. (CCH) para. 93,924 (Del. Ch. July 14, 1988); *City Capital Associates Ltd. Partners v. Interco Inc.*, Civ. No. 10105 (Del. Ch. Nov. 1, 1988).

2 The *Unocal* test is analyzed by Ronald J. Gilson and Reinier H. Kraakman in "Delaware's Intermediate Standard for Defensive Tactics: Is There Substance to the Proportionality Review?" (1989), 44 The Bus. Law. 247. The authors argue that the proportionality test enunciated in *Unocal* is more than a "threshold test", i.e., once a threat is established, any response by target management is justified. Rather, the test is seen to be "regulatory" in nature; i.e., management must justify its choice of defensive actions by reference to the magnitude of the threat posed by a particular bid. The authors then proceed to develop a taxonomy of threats and discuss responses that are commensurate with these threats. The analysis proposed by Gilson and Kraakman was expressly relied upon by the Delaware Chancery Court in the *Interco* decision, *supra*.

3 For a Canadian discussion of developments in the American case law respecting takeovers, see John Howard, "Takeover Battles and the Business Judgment Rule: Recent American Case Law Development" (1986), 11 Can. Bus. L.J. 445.

(iii) Recent Developments in Canadian Jurisprudence After *Unocal* and *Revlon*

Pente Investment Management Ltd. v. Schneider Corp.
(1998), 42 O.R. (3d) 177, 1998 CarswellOnt 4035 (C.A.)

WEILER J.A.: Schneider is a 108 year-old company now governed by the *Business Corporations Act (Ontario)* ("OBCA") which went public three decades ago. The Family, consisting of the third and fourth generations, through Holdings retained control through a two class share structure. The Family held 70.5% of the voting common shares representing 7.6% of the total equity of Schneider and 17.2% of the non-voting A Shares representing 15.3% of the equity; thus the Family held 22.9% of the equity but a control block of the votes that was sufficient to pass a special majority if only the common shares were taken into account. However, in the tradition of fair dealing espoused by the founder J.M. Schneider, when the sharing of pre-mium previously attributable to multiple voting shares as opposed to single shares became an issue in the Canadian Tire case (*Re Canadian Tire Corp.* (1987), 35 B.L.R. 117 (Ont. Div. Ct.)), the Family was instrumental in adopting a coattails provision in amending Schneider articles of incorpo-ration in 1988 even though it was not required to do so at that time as it was not issuing any further shares then. There were pronouncements made that the A shareholders would be treated equally and equitably as if they were partners with the common shareholders.

[In order to ensure the fair treatment of the non-voting A shares, the Schneider family took the initiative in proposing that a "coattail" provision be inserted in the company's articles, and this was duly passed by the requisite majority of shareholders. The coattail aimed at ensuring equal treatment of the voting shares and the non-voting A shares in the event of a takeover bid, and it did so in the following manner: Suppose that an acquirer sought to gain control of Schneiders. It need only make a takeover bid for the voting common shares, and not for the Class A shares, since holding Class A shares will add nothing to its power to control the company. The coattail, however, specified that on the occurrence of an offer for the voting shares alone (an "exclusionary" offer), the Class A shareholders would have the right to convert their shares into voting common shares. That way, an acquirer would effectively be forced to extend the takeover bid to the Class A shares. If it did not, then it could not be sure of gaining control of the company, since presumably on the making of an "exclusionary offer" for the common shares, all Class A shares would be converted into common shares, and the acquirer would hold only a small percentage of the total votes.

However, the Schneider family was concerned to retain a veto over any takeover bid that occurred. The coattail was thus drafted so that if there was an exclusionary offer for the common shares, the Class A shares would *not* be convertible into common shares *if* the holders of 50 per cent or more of the common shares filed a certificate with the company's transfer agent and secretary indicating that they would not accept an exclusionary offer. This certificate could even be filed as a "standing certificate" before any offer was made, and the Schneider family duly filed a standing certificate. This effectively gave the Schneider family a veto over any takeover bid. While an acquirer might still make an exclusionary bid for the common shares, it could never gain control of a majority of the common shares, since the family held a majority block and could simply decide not to tender. In addition, it could not gain control of the company by buying up Class A shares, making an "exclusionary offer" for the common shares, and converting its Class A shares into common shares, because the anti-conversion certificate would prevent the Class A shares from being converted into common shares. Despite these protections, Maple Leaf Foods believed that it could acquire control of Schneiders by making simultaneous takeover bids that were not entirely identical for the two classes of shares, thus making an "exclusionary offer" that would trigger the coattail provision, giving all of the Class A shares a vote. The court continued:]

On November 5, 1997, Maple Leaf, a competitor of Schneider, announced its intention to make an unsolicited take-over bid for [Schneider's common shares] at $19 a share, through its holding company SCH. In response, the Board established a special committee consisting of the independent non-family directors to review the Maple Leaf offer and to consider other alternatives. Subsequently Maple Leaf itself made an offer of $22 a share, but this offer was rejected by the Family. Ultimately, the Family told the special committee that the only offer it would accept was an offer made by Smithfield Foods, an American company that, at the time, was equal to $25 a share. In order for the Family to accept the Smithfield offer, which would have had the effect of enabling Smithfield to "lock-up" control of Schneider, the Board had to take certain steps which, on the advice of the special committee, it took. Despite this, and after the Family had agreed to the Smithfield offer, on December 22, 1997, Maple Leaf made a further offer of $29 a share to Schneider's common and Class A shareholders.

[Despite this, the Schneider family continued to refuse to lift its certificate of anti-conversion for any bid other than the Smithfield bid. The family apparently had mixed motives for favouring the Smithfield bid. Mr. Justice Farley, the trial judge, observed that: "In particular, the Schneider Family advised the Board of Directors that it had reviewed the various proposals in terms of three factors: financial value, continuity of the Corporation in a manner consistent with the Schneider family's desires, and the effect of any transaction on the Corporation's various stakeholders, including shareholders, employees, suppliers, and customers." However, as indicated in the Court of Appeal judgment, the consideration offered in the three different bids had different tax consequences — and, hence, different value — in the hands of the Schneider family. In particular, the Maple Leaf and Booth Creek offers were cash offers, and the Smithfield offer was a share exchange offer. Smithfield's share exchange offer would yield a tax saving to the Schneider family of $4 per share. Weiler J.A. continued:]

While the appellants have challenged Farley J.'s finding that the Family would not sell to Maple Leaf, there is ample evidence to support this finding. Even at $29 a share, when tax considerations were factored in, the Maple Leaf offer was only as advantageous as the Smithfield offer to the Family, not more advantageous. Apart from financial criteria, Maple Leaf did not meet the Family's expressed concern about the effect of a change of control on the continuity of employment for Schneider's employees, the welfare of suppliers, and the relationship with its customers, whereas Smithfield did . . .

At a subsequent meeting of the Special Committee that night, Nesbitt Burns advised that while the Smithfield proposal was within the $25–29 fair price range, the risk associated with adverse share price movement and exchange rate movement during the short period until the offer could be formally accepted should be reflected by applying a 6% discount to the offer so that its present value was $23.50. Nesbitt Burns also told the Special Committee that, in its view, if the Smithfield offer were permitted to expire and no other change of control transaction involving Schneider were consummated, the shares of Schneider would settle in a trading range between $18 and $20 a share.

The Special Committee then recessed and Dodds [the CEO] made enquiries of Smithfield as to whether it would raise its offer. Smithfield refused to pay more but Dodds was successful in negotiating a slight improvement in the exchange rate aspect of the offer.

The original proposal, as submitted by Smithfield, contemplated that the transaction would proceed by way of a plan of arrangement or merger. That is, the Board would approve of the Family entering into a lock-up agreement for its shares with Smithfield, then the merger proposal would be voted upon by all shareholders and approved by the court. Before asking the shareholders and the court to approve the merger the Board would have had to provide an opinion that the transaction was fair. In light of Nesbitt Burns' discounted valuation of the Smithfield proposal, the Board was unwilling to do so.

To avoid the Board having to issue an opinion that the proposed transaction was fair, Smithfield made offers by way of take-over bids to acquire any and all common voting shares and all Class A shares of Schneider on the condition that the Family agree to tender its shares. The shares of Schneider were to be exchanged for .5415 of a share in a newly incorporated, wholly-owned Canadian subsidiary of Smithfield. Each whole exchangeable share would then be exchangeable for one common share in Smithfield. The structure of this second transaction meant that Smithfield might not be able to acquire two-thirds of the Class A shares and, therefore, might not be able to take Schneider private.

In order for the Family to accept the offer from Smithfield, it was still necessary for the Board to waive the standstill provision in the confidentiality agreement Smithfield signed and to remove the rights plan. The Family asked the board to do this. Upon the recommendation of the special committee, the Board did so. On December 18, 1997, the Family entered into the lock-up agreement.

On December 22, 1997, Maple Leaf announced that, despite the Family's lock-up agreement with Smithfield, it was increasing its offer to $29 per share, cash, conditional on obtaining two-thirds of each class of share. Prior to this, Maple Leaf entered into deposit agreements with two funds to buy Maple Leaf's shares at $29, no matter what the outcome of its latest bid was. On December 30, 1997, five Class A shareholders, holding in aggregate 675,000 shares, representing more than 10 per cent of the total Class A shares outstanding, wrote a letter to Schneider's Board of Directors complaining that "the actions or inaction of the Special Committee, together with those of the Schneider family have in effect, contaminated the value maximization process outlined by the board in its directors' circular and in its public statements".

Determining Whether the Directors Have Acted in the Best Interests of the Corporation

The mandate of the directors is to manage the company according to their best judgment; that judgment must be an informed judgment; it must have a reasonable basis. If there are no reasonable grounds to support an assertion by the directors that they have acted in the best interests of the company, a court will be justified in finding that the directors acted for an improper purpose: *Teck Corp. v. Millar* (1973), 33 D.L.R. (3d) 288 (B.C.S.C.) at pp. 315-16, adopted as the law in Ontario by Montgomery J. in *Olympia & York Enterprises Ltd. v. Hiram Walker Resources Ltd.* (1986), 59 O.R. (2d) 255, 37 D.L.R. (4th) 194 (H.C.J.), affirmed (1986), 59 O.R. (2d) 254, 37 D.L.R. (4th) 193 (Div. Ct.).

One way of determining whether the directors acted in the best interests of the company, according to Farley J., is to ask what was uppermost in the directors' minds after "a reasonable analysis of the situation": *820099 Ontario Inc. v. Harold E. Ballard Ltd.* (1991), 3 B.L.R. (2d) 123 at p. 176 (Ont. Gen. Div.), affirmed (1991), 3 B.L.R. (2d) 113 (Ont. Div. Ct.); *CW Shareholdings Inc. v. WIC Western International Communications Ltd.*, No. 98-CL-2821 (May 17, 1998), Toronto (Gen. Div.) [reported 39 O.R. (3d) 755, 160 D.L.R. (4th) 131]. It must be recognized that the directors are not the agents of the shareholders. The directors have absolute power to manage the affairs of the company even if their decisions contravene the express wishes of the majority shareholder: *Teck Corp. Ltd. v. Millar, supra*, at p. 307. However, acting in the best interests of the company does not necessarily mean that the directors must act in the best interests of one of the groups protected under s. 234. There may be a conflict between the interests of individual groups of shareholders and the best interests of the company: *Brant Investments Ltd. v. Keep Rite Inc.* (1987), 60 O.R. (2d) 737, 42 D.L.R. (4th) 15 (H.C.J.), affirmed (1991), 3 O.R. (3d) 289 at p. 301, 3 O.R. (3d) 289 (C.A.). Provided that the directors have acted honestly and reasonably, the court ought not to substitute its own business judgment for that of the Board of Directors: *Brant Investments v. Keep Rite Inc., supra*, which deals with the analogous section of the *Canadian Business Corporations Act*, R.S.C. 1985, c. C-44. If the directors have unfairly disregarded the rights of a group of shareholders, the directors will not have acted reasonably in the best interests of the corporation and the court will intervene: *820099 Ontario Inc. v. Harold E. Ballard Ltd., supra.*

The appellants have urged this court to consider the actions of the directors pursuant to a standard which is derived from statute law in the State of Delaware known as "enhanced scrutiny". The key features of the enhanced scrutiny test are a judicial determination of the adequacy of the decision-making process employed by the directors and a judicial examination of the reasonableness of the directors' actions in light of the circumstances then existing: *Paramount Communications v. QVC Network Inc.,* 637 A.2d 34 at p. 45 (Del. 1934). The directors have the onus of satisfying the court that they were adequately informed and acted reasonably. Some Canadian authorities such as *Exco Corp. v. Nova Scotia Savings & Loan Co.* (1987), 35 B.L.R. 149, 78 N.S.R. (2d) 91 (S.C.) and *347883 Alberta Ltd. v. Producers Pipelines Inc.* (1991), 80 D.L.R. (4th) 359, 92 Sask. R. 81 (C.A.) have adopted a proper purpose test, which is similar to enhanced scrutiny in that it shifts the burden of proof to the directors to show that their acts are consistent only with the best interests of the company and inconsistent with any other interests. These cases recognize that there may be a conflict between the directors who manage the company and the interests of certain groups of shareholders, particularly those s. 248 is designed to protect, and have espoused shifting the burden of proof as a method of overcoming the potential conflict.

The law as it has evolved in Ontario and Delaware has the common requirements that the court must be satisfied that the directors have acted reasonably and fairly. The court looks to see that the directors made a reasonable decision, not a perfect decision. Provided the decision taken is within a range of reasonableness, the court ought not to substitute its opinion for that of the board even though subsequent events may have cast doubt on the board's determination. As long as the directors have selected one of several reasonable alternatives, deference is accorded to the board's decision: Paramount, *supra*, at p. 45; *Brant Investments, supra*, at p. 320; *Themadel Foundation v. Third Canadian General Investment Trust Ltd.* (1998), 38 O.R. (3d) 749 at p. 754 (C.A.). This formulation of deference to the decision of the Board is known as the "business judgment rule". The fact that alternative transactions were rejected by the directors is irrelevant unless it can be shown that a particular alternative was definitely available and clearly more beneficial to the company than the chosen transaction: *Brant Investments, supra*, at pp. 314-15.

A common method used to alleviate concerns that a conflict of interest exists between directors, who may be major shareholders, and the interests of a minority or non-voting group of shareholders, is the creation of a special committee from among the independent members of a board who do not have a conflict. The purpose of a special committee is to advise the Directors and to make a recommendation as to what the Board should do. It appears that under the law of Delaware, where a Board acts on the recommendation of a special committee, the decision will be accorded respect under the business judgment rule, provided that the special committee has discharged its role independently, in good faith, and with the understanding that in a situation where a change of control transaction is contemplated, the special committee can only agree to a transaction that is fair in the sense of being the best available in the circumstances: *In re First Boston, Inc. Shareholders Litigation*, [1990] Fed. Sec. L. Rep., para. 95, 322 (Del. 1990).

The duty of directors when dealing with a bid that will change control of a company is a rapidly developing area of law and, as I have indicated, Canadian authorities dealing with the question of the onus, or burden of proof, have not been uniform. In *Brant Investments, supra*, the issue whether the burden of proof is on the directors to justify their actions as being in the best interests of the company or on the shareholders challenging the actions of the company was also raised. McKinlay J.A., at pp. 311-12, found it unnecessary to decide the question because the trial judge had dealt with the issues on a substantive basis, and his decision did not turn on which party had the onus or burden of proof. [See Note 3 at end of document.] The same is true in the present case. [See Note 4 at end of document.] I would add, however, that it may be that the burden of proof may not always rest on the same party when a change of control transaction is challenged. The real question is whether the directors of the target company successfully took steps to avoid a conflict of interest. If so, the rationale for shifting the burden of proof to the directors may not exist. If a board of directors has acted on the advice of a committee composed of persons having no conflict of interest, and that committee has acted independently, in good faith, and made an informed recommendation as to the best available transaction for the shareholders in the circumstances, the business judgment rule applies. The burden of proof is not an issue in such circumstances.

The members of the committee acted in good faith in the sense that they acted honestly. The committee's decision was also informed, in the sense that the committee was aware that any offer for Schneider's shares might be bettered by Maple Leaf, and that the Family would not sell to Maple Leaf. While the appellants have challenged Farley J.'s finding that the Family would not sell to Maple Leaf, there is ample evidence to support this finding. Even at $29 a share, when tax considerations were factored in, the Maple Leaf offer was only as advantageous as the Smithfield offer to the Family, not more advantageous. Apart from financial criteria, Maple Leaf did not meet the Family's expressed concern about the effect of a change of control on the continuity of employment for Schneider's employees, the welfare of suppliers, and the relationship with its customers, whereas Smithfield did. Once again, the real questions are whether the committee was independent and whether the process undertaken by the special committee was in the best interests of Schneider and its shareholders in the circumstances. While *Paramount, supra*, indicates that non-financial considerations have a role to play in determining the best transaction available in the circumstances, here it was conceded that the court should only have regard to financial considerations.

The Special Committee

* * *

(ii) Should members of Schneider's senior management, particularly Dodds, have been permitted to have a significant role in the sale negotiations with potential bidders?

The appellants submit that Dodds had a conflict of interest because he had an interest in continued employment with Schneider and a further conflict arising out of his loyalty to the Family.

A potential conflict of interest arises because as a director of a target company, the senior executive has a duty to act in the best interests of the shareholders, but as a member of senior management the executive retains an interest in continued employment. In actively negotiating with a potential bidder the executive is negotiating with his potential boss or executioner. The appellants rely on the decision of Blair J. in *CW* Shareholdings Inc., supra, for the proposition that no senior executive of a company being sold should be permitted to have a significant role in the sale process.

The *raison d'être* of a special committee independent of management and the controlling shareholder is to protect the interests of minority shareholders and to bring a measure of objectivity to the assessment of bids. If, as was the case in *CW Shareholdings*, senior management in the target company is a member of the special committee, the purpose in setting up the special committee might be compromised and less reliance placed on its assessment of a particular bid than if the committee were truly independent. Blair J. recognized this and he was critical of the role played by senior management in *CW Shareholdings*. In the end, however, he concluded that the involvement of management in the special committee did not so taint its approval of the Shaw Communications bid as to undermine the transaction. He also found that the committee had conducted itself in a fashion that enabled the directors to carry out their objective of maximizing shareholder value. In that case, Blair J. upheld the Board's decision, based upon the special committee's recommendation to enter into an agreement with Shaw that provided for a break fee and asset agreement in the event that its bid was not accepted.

A major distinction between the *CW Shareholdings* decision and this case is that senior management, including Dodds, was not part of the special committee that was set up, and consequently had no vote as to whether to recommend a bid. A potential conflict of interest still existed, however, because of the active role Dodds played in negotiating with the bidders.

Farley J. recognized that in allowing Dodds and, to a lesser extent, Hooper, the chief financial officer of Schneider, to deal with bidders directly, a potential conflict of interest existed but that this had to be balanced against the benefits to be obtained. He stated:

It would be appropriate, however, to comment as well [th]at the use of the two management directors, Dodds and Hooper, in dealing with the bidders and advisors directly, would not seem inappropriate. Potentially there could be conflict, but that must be balanced against the reasonable benefits to be obtained. They knew the operations of the business — what the bidders would be interested in and they were guided by the advisors. They reported to the special committee which could make the "final" decisions and give directions. Potential conflict was minimized by the bail-out packages granted them. From the material before me it would not appear that these management persons acted or behaved inappropriately overall. It would be undesirable to subject each step they took to isolated microscopic inspection. I note in passing that Dodds would have received approximately $1,000,000 in stock and options value extra if the Maple Leaf $29 offer had been accepted as opposed to the Smithfield one; of course no one but Maple Leaf knew how much it would have offered if it had been solicited on December 17.

[Weiler J.A. held that, on the facts, Dodd not have a significant conflict of interest, since Maple Leaf Foods had promised to treat him generously if the Maple Leaf bid was successful (and for a number of other reasons).]

Process Arguments

(i) Should the special committee have been created?

The appellants submit that by creating a special committee, hiring advisers, and setting up a data room, the Family used Schneider's money to better the offer from Maple Leaf, which it was not entitled to do. In addition to being rejected by Farley J., a similar argument was rejected by Montgomery J. in *Olympia & York, supra*, at p. 272. The reason is obvious: the appointment of a special committee is intended to ensure that the interests of those the oppression remedy is intended to protect are not unfairly disregarded or prejudiced. It is clearly in the interests of a company, and of all shareholders, for alternatives to an unsolicited takeover offer to be explored. It might give the shareholders a higher price for their shares. The creation of a special committee was part of the process undertaken by the Board to obtain the best transaction available in the circumstances.

(ii) Should the special committee have created a data room?

The appellants' submission that proprietary confidential information obtained from the data room was a valuable corporate asset that was either given away to the acquiring company or dissipated must also fail. As Farley J. pointed out, access to the data room was essential in order to conduct a market canvass for alternative offers. Other bidders, particularly those who had not operated in the Canadian market, needed to gain an appreciation of market conditions, and of Schneider's business. That could only be obtained with access to Schneider's confidential information. No alternative bid would have been elicited without access to Schneider's confidential information. Maple Leaf, as a competitor of Schneider for many years, had an appreciation of market conditions and of Schneider's business and did not require further information in order to make its bid.

The decision to establish a data room at the company's expense was that of the special committee, made with full knowledge of the Family's position that it was not committed to selling. The Board did not seek the approval or the consent of the Family to establish the data room for the use of information or for the nature of the confidentiality agreements that were signed with prospective bidders.

In creating a data room the special committee acted independently and reasonably. The creation of a data room made confidential information available to all bidders as part of a process to get the best transaction available to the shareholders in the circumstances. I see no merit in this ground of appeal.

(iii) Flawed committee process

The appellants submit that the trial judge ignored or failed to appreciate the evidence given by Ruby, the chairman of the special committee, to the effect that the special committee had no involvement in any negotiations with prospective bidders, that Dodds conducted the negotiations, and that the special committee did not consider whether Dodds had any conflict of interest. After considering the circumstances under which Dodds acted, I have already concluded that Dodds did not have a conflict of interest.

The special committee had no prior experience in dealing with a take-over bid and did not have the in-depth knowledge of Schneider that Dodds did. It was therefore appropriate for the special committee not to conduct the negotiations with potential bidders directly. Farley J. found that although the special committee did try to determine the views of the Family "recognizing its gatekeeper and veto role", there was no evidence that the approval of the Family was sought with respect to any decision taken by the special committee. The evidence supports the conclusion that the members of the special committee acted independently in the sense that they were free to deal with the impugned transaction on its merits. This ground of appeal also fails.

(iv) Should the special committee have insisted that Maple Leaf and any other interested party be given an opportunity to make their best and final offer prior to the board of directors of Schneider taking the steps that it did on December 17, 1997 to commit its shares to Smithfield?

The appellants submit that the Board was obliged to keep the bidding process alive by going back to Maple Leaf after it received the Smithfield bid on December 17. This submission has two alternative premises: (1) the directors could only discharge their duty to act in the best interests of the corporation by conducting an auction of the shares of Schneider; (2) a public expectation had been created by the comments made by the Schneider family that an auction would be held and, therefore, both the Family and the Board were under a duty to ensure that an auction was conducted.

The appellant's first premise is wrong in law. The second is contrary to Farley J.'s findings of fact and those findings are supported by the evidence.

(v) Was there a duty to conduct an auction of the shares of Schneider?

The decision in *Revlon v. McAndrews & Forbes Holdings, Inc.*, 506 A.2d 173 (Del. 1986), stands for the proposition that if a company is up for sale, the directors have an obligation to conduct an auction of the company's shares. *Revlon* is not the law in Ontario. In Ontario, an auction need not be held every time there is a change in control of a company.

An auction is merely one way to prevent the conflicts of interest that may arise when there is a change of control by requiring that directors act in a neutral manner toward a number of bidders: *Barkan v. Amsted Industries Inc.*, 567 A.2d 1279 at p. 1286 (Del. 1989). The more recent *Paramount* decision in the United States, *supra*, at pp. 43–45 has recast the obligation of directors when there is a bid for change of control as an obligation to seek the best value reasonably available to shareholders in the circumstances. This is a more flexible standard, which recognizes that the particular circumstances are important in determining the best transaction available, and that a board is not limited to considering only the amount of cash or consideration involved as would be the case with an auction: *Paramount*, *supra*, at p. 44. There is no single blueprint that directors must follow. Although the decision in *Paramount* and the other decisions of the courts in Delaware to which I have referred are not the law of Ontario, they can offer some guidance.

When it becomes clear that a company is for sale and there are several bidders, an auction is an appropriate mechanism to ensure that the board of a target company acts in a neutral manner to achieve the best value reasonably available to shareholders in the circumstances. When the board has received a single offer and has no reliable grounds upon which to judge its adequacy, a canvass of the market to determine if higher bids may be elicited is appropriate, and may be necessary: *Barkan*, *supra*, at p. 1287, citing *In re Fort Howard Corp. Shareholders Litig.*, Del. Ch., C.A. No. 991, 1988 WL 83147.

The Family did not seek to sell its controlling interest in Schneider. The Board received an offer from Maple Leaf that it felt was inadequate, but, in the final analysis, the best way to judge its adequacy was to determine if higher bids could be elicited through a market canvass. The fact that a market canvass was conducted did not mean that the Family would agree to sell its stake. Indeed, Farley J. found as a fact that the Family's decision to sell was highly conditional on a satisfactory offer being received.

The appellant submits that there was considerable evidence indicating that the Schneider Family had by December 17, if not before, concluded that a sale of its shares was inevitable. Having undertaken a market canvass, however, there was no obligation on the special committee to turn this canvass into an auction, particularly because to do so was to assume the risk that the competing offers that the market canvass had generated might be withdrawn. There was no obligation on the special committee or the Board to go back to Maple Leaf on December 17 and ask it to make another offer. A market canvass and not an auction was being conducted; the special committee and the Board only had a short time within which to consider Maple Leaf's offer; Maple Leaf had already been asked to make an appropriate offer, and there was no certainty it would make a higher bid. There was an obligation on the special committee and the directors to consider the bids which their market canvass had realized in addition to Maple Leaf's bid. Farley J. found Maple Leaf knew, or should have known, that the bidding process was almost over when it made its $22 per share bid. Maple Leaf's board had authorized the issuance of enough Maple Leaf shares to finance a $29 a share bid for Schneider before the bidding process entered its final stage. Maple Leaf was nonetheless content to let its $22 bid stand despite knowing that there were competing bids that might be accepted in preference to its own, and despite the fact that Maple Leaf's board had authorized a higher $29 bid. This was a risk Maple Leaf chose to assume.

Was there a public expectation created by the Family that an auction would be held?

While s. 248 protects the legitimate expectations of shareholders, those expectations must be reasonable in the circumstances, and reasonableness is to be ascertained on an objective basis. [Find Note 5 at end of document.] The interests of the shareholders of a company are intertwined with the expectations that have been created by the company's principals: *Naneff v. Con-Crete Holdings Ltd.* (1995), 23 O.R. (3d) 481, 23 B.L.R. (2d) 286 (C.A.). Therefore, the question is whether the statements made by the Family, and widely reported in press releases issued in response to Maple Leaf's bids, created a reasonable expectation that an auction would be held. Whether or not a reasonable expectation has been created is a question of fact: *Arthur v. Signum Communications Ltd.*, [1993] O.J. No. 1928 (Div. Ct.), Campbell J., for the court, at paras. 6-7. After examining the press releases and the evidence, Farley J. found that any expectations of the claimants, who were non-Family shareholders, were not reasonable or founded in fact.

A summary of his findings on this point is as follows:

• The Family's position on selling its controlling shareholding in Schneider was always conditional to a high degree. The Family only said that they "might consider" selling. The conditional nature of the Family's position was always clearly expressed by the Board in its public statements.

- It was inappropriate for Maple Leaf to ignore the plain meaning of the public statements made by the Family and the Board. Maple Leaf "wished" that there was an unrestricted auction for Schneider but in fact there never was.

- The claimants had not proved that their reasonable expectations were thwarted. "When the gatekeeper shareholder merely indicates that it 'might consider' accepting a more financially attractive offer, then the shareholders are speculating that a deal on that basis may come to pass in which they could participate".

There was more than adequate evidence to support these findings and they cannot be disturbed.

In as much as there was no reasonable expectation on the part of the non-Family shareholders that an auction would be held after receiving the last Smithfield bid, the special committee was not obliged to give Maple Leaf an opportunity to make a third bid for Schneider's shares.

[The court then discussed allegations that the special committee had favoured the family rather than non-family shareholders. The court held that the special committee did what it could do given that the Schneider family refused to tender into any bid other than the Smithfield bid. The passage that deals with this issue may be found in Chapter 7.]

I would dismiss the first main ground of appeal.

Note

1 A further aspect of the judgment deals with the coattail provision attached to the non-voting shares. Weiler J.A. described the function of a coattail as follows:

> Coattail provisions are designed to ensure that if the common voting shareholders wish to accept an offer that will lead to a change in control and if the price or terms offered to the common voting shareholders are more favourable than those offered to the holders of non-voting shares, the non-voting shareholders get an equal opportunity to participate in any change of control premium.

> The provisions work in the following way. If the holders of restricted shares, such as non-voting shares, are excluded from participating in the common voting share takeover bid, they will then be given a right of conversion of their restricted or non-voting shares into common voting shares. Coattail provisions are intended to encourage non-exclusionary bids. When triggered, the non-voting shareholders then have the opportunity to participate in the take-over bid.

> The articles of Schneider Corp. defined the coattail in the following terms:

"Exclusionary Offer" means an offer to purchase common shares of the Corporation that . . . is not made concurrently with an offer to purchase Class A Non-Voting shares that is identical to the offer to purchase common shares in terms of price per share and percentage of outstanding shares to be taken up exclusive of shares owned immediately prior to the offer by the Offeror and in all other material respects and that has no condition attached other than the right not to take up and pay for shares tendered if no shares are tendered pursuant to the offer for common shares.

Weiler J.A. noted that:

If the word acquired or purchased had been used in the definition of "exclusionary offer" instead of tendered there would not have been a problem with coattail provision. But Maple Leaf's lawyers recognized the problem. Maple Leaf's offer to purchase the common shares of Schneider was made concurrently with its offer to purchase the Class A shares. The offer to the Class A shareholders contained a condition entitling Maple Leaf not to take up and pay for any Class A shares deposited if Maple Leaf did not acquire any common shares pursuant to the offer to purchase common voting shares. This was not the condition permitted under the coattail provisions. The coattail provisions gave the right not to take up and pay for Class A shares if no common shares were tendered. Because the condition attaching to its Class A shares was different, Maple Leaf submits that its offer to the common shareholders was an exclusionary one.

Thus, Maple Leaf hoped that no one would notice that that it was making an exclusionary offer that would trigger the coattail — least of all the Schneider family, who could then file an anti-conversion certificate to cause the coattail *not* to be activated. Maple Leaf's hope was thus that they would receive a large number of Class A shares in their takeover bid for the Class A's, that the Class A shares would become voting shares, and that they would then have enough votes to displace the Schneider family as controllers of Schneiders.

Despite the wording of the coattail, both the lower court and the court of appeal held that the coattail was *not* triggered. Weiler J.A. held that:

The words of a statute to be interpreted are to be read in their entire context and in their grammatical and ordinary sense harmoniously with the scheme of the Act, the object of the Act, and the intention of Parliament: *Rizzo v. Rizzo Shoes Ltd.*, [1998] 1 S.C.R. 27, 154 D.L.R. (4th) 193. (This decision holds that although the literal reading of the words in the *Employment Standards Act* entitling an employee to severance, termination, or vacation pay upon termination by the employer would not include the employer's bankruptcy, when the words are examined in their entire context they must be interpreted to include a termination resulting from the bankruptcy of the employer.) So, too, here, the wording of the coattail provision must be given an interpretation which accords with its object and the intention of the framers of the provision.

The interpretation of a coattail provision must be viewed objectively and as a reasonably prudent business person would view it: *Saunders v. Cathton Holdings Ltd.* (1997), 88 B.C.A.C. 264 at p. 272, 36 B.L.R. (2d) 151.

When the public interest is involved, evidence with respect to the understanding and intention of the provision is admissible to assist in determining whether a proposed interpretation is consistent with the public interest: *Re Canadian Tire Corp.* (1987), 35 B.L.R. 117 (Ont. Div. Ct.) at pp. 143-44.

The purpose of adopting a coattail provision is to discourage exclusionary offers, whereas a literal reading of Schneider's coattail provision gives the opposite effect. Certainty of meaning is of paramount importance in commercial transactions that affect the public. Those considering whether or not to tender to an offer to purchase their shares must know what investment decision they are making: see *Saunders, supra*, at pp. 272-73. In this instance, it appeared to the shareholders that the offers were the same because the amount to be paid to both classes of shareholders was the same. Maple Leaf understood how its offers would be perceived. If, instead, Maple Leaf was of the opinion that its offer was exclusionary, it could have said in its offering circular that it intended to apply to the appropriate authorities to have the issue of whether or not the offer was exclusionary determined in court as was done in *CW Shareholdings, supra*. Maple Leaf did not.

The interpretation of Maple Leaf's offers adopted by Farley J. is consistent with the way a reasonably prudent business person would construe the offer. The outcome he reaches is consistent with public expectations and is commercially sound. It employs a purposive approach. Farley J. did not err in holding that the Maple Leaf offer for common shares was not an "exclusionary offer" and that the coattail provisions in Schneider's articles had not been triggered.

(iv) The Powers of the Toronto Stock Exchange in Connection With A Share Issuance: A Note on the *Torstar* and *Canada Malting* Cases

The Toronto Stock Exchange Company Manual, Part VI.A (para. 601) ("Changes In Capital Structure of Listed Companies"), reads as follows:

(a) Every company having securities listed on the Exchange shall give immediate notice to the Exchange of each proposed option, underwriting, sale or issue of treasury securities (other than debt securities which are not convertible into equity securities), or of securities held for the benefit of the treasury or to be created for the treasury and shall furnish promptly to the Exchange a copy of each option, underwriting or sales agreement entered into with respect to any such securities. The Exchange shall have the right either to accept or not accept the notice for filing and in case of such non-acceptance the proposal shall not be proceeded with; otherwise the securities of the company may be suspended from trading or delisted.

(b) The Exchange may require shareholder approval as a condition of acceptance of a notice under subsection (a) if, in the opinion of the Exchange, the proposed transaction:

(i)   may materially affect control of the company;

(ii) has not been negotiated at arm's length; or

(iii) is of such a nature as to make shareholder approval desirable, having regard to the interests of the company's shareholders and the investing public.

(c) If the notice is accepted for filing, the Exchange shall give prompt notice thereof to each Participating Organization and may give notice thereof to the press.

(d) Every such company which has made such proposal or entered into such agreement shall give immediate notice to the Exchange of each payment or default thereunder and of each proposed extension, assignment or other material change therein and no such proposed extension, assignment or other material change shall be proceeded with unless notice thereof is accepted for filing by the Exchange.

Notes on Para. 601 (formerly By-Law 19.06)

The consequences of failing to comply with para. 601 of the Company Manual range from a temporary suspension of trading of the stock over the Exchange to a permanent "delisting" of the stock. The Exchange is loath to apply these sanctions, however, because they disadvantage shareholders and the trading public as much as or more than the company itself. The *Torstar* case (below) involves deliberate non-compliance with para. 601 (formerly by-law 19.06) and indicates the response of the Securities Commission. The *Canada Malting* case involves an attempt by a group of minority shareholders to have the OSC reverse the decision of the TSE "filing committee" to "accept notice" of a share issuance without requiring a majority of the minority shareholder approval.

(1) In *Torstar Corp.*, Re (1986), 9 O.S.C.B. 3088 (Securities Comm.) (June 3, 1986) the Southam family held the largest block of Southam Inc. (the

large publishing concern) and apparently exercised a measure of *de facto* control over the company. However, the Southam family holdings (somewhere on the order of 10%) were far too small to block a hostile takeover bid for the shares of Southam. In July of 1985, rumours began to circulate that there was a takeover bid in the offing for the shares of Southam Inc. There was active trading in the shares of Southam and the price began to rise. The company had also received advice from Dominion Securities Pitfield that the company might be worth more with part of it split off and sold. Alarmed at the threat to their control over the company, the family first responded by spearheading an effort to have stiff "shark repellent" provisions put in the company's articles to ward off any hostile takeover. When institutional investors objected, the amendments to the articles were so watered down as to still leave the company open to a takeover.

In a very short space of time (three or four days, including a Sunday), Southam Inc. arrived at an arrangement with Torstar Corp. whereby Southam issued sufficient voting common shares to Torstar to give Torstar 20% of the voting equity of Southam, and Torstar issued to Southam a block of nonvoting common and preference shares giving them a combined total of about 30% of these two classes of shares. In addition, an agreement was entered into between Torstar and the Southam family, under which Torstar agreed to vote the shares issued to it for directors nominated by the Southam board of directors "after consultation with members of the Southam Group [i.e., family]". Torstar also agreed to a "standstill" under which they would not acquire further shares of Southam within a ten-year period. The directors of the two companies were advised about by-law 19.06 but deliberately decided not to give the Exchange notice. In its reasons, the OSC found as a fact that the reason for failing to notify the Exchange was a fear that Exchange might delay approval long enough so that a hostile bidder would have time to succeed, as well as a concern that the Exchange might require shareholder approval and such approval might not be forthcoming. The purpose of the share issuance was clearly to frustrate any potential takeover bid.

When the Exchange was subsequently apprised of the issuance, it retroactively accepted notice of the issuance (i.e., approved the issue), stating that it saw no reason for requiring shareholder approval of the issue. Nonetheless, miffed that the Torstar and Southam directors had failed to give advance notice to the Exchange, the Exchange asked the OSC to deny all trading exemptions to Torstar and Southam directors for a period of time to punish them for non-compliance (without trading exemptions, an individual cannot buy or sell securities in Ontario). The OSC agreed, and denied all trading exemptions for the Torstar and Southam directors for a period of six months. In so doing, the OSC found that the effect of the share exchange was "to deny Southam shareholders the possibility of receiving a takeover bid at a price in excess of the then-current market price". The OSC stressed that it must be left up to shareholders whether or not to accept or reject a takeover bid. Whether or not management thought they were acting in the

best interests of the corporation, what they did removed the decision from
the hands of shareholders. The OSC did not think, however, that it would
be appropriate to unwind the exchange, since "investments have been made
on the basis of the transaction", and to do so would "possibly unfairly
prejudice innocent shareholders, both directly and indirectly".

How serious a sanction is a denial of exemptions? Many securities
which are traded on the TSX are also traded on other Canadian or American
exchanges. Technically, trading over another exchange would violate the
order, since "trade" is defined in the *Securities Act* to include any act in
furtherance of a trade. However, as a practical matter, a trade over the New
York Stock Exchange will not come to the attention of the OSC, so the
denial of exemptions is all but unenforceable. Even if obeyed to the letter,
do you think that a six-month denial of exemptions is a serious or effective
sanction?

(2) The facts behind *Canada Malting* Co., Re (1986) 9 O.S.C.B. 3566, 1986
CarswellOnt 151 (Securities Comm.) (27 June, 1986) are similar to the
Torstar case. Molson and Labatt's were the largest shareholders of Canada
Malting company ("Malting"), holding 14.17% each, for a combined total
of 28.3%. These two companies were also Malting's biggest customers,
accounting for 80% of domestic sales and 50% of worldwide sales of malt.
On Oct. 1, 1985, a V.P of Malting received a phone call from a Toronto
brokerage house indicating that a takeover bid for Malting was in the works.
The board of directors was immediately notified. Dominion Securities Pitfield was hired as an advisor, and they suggested that shares be issued to
Molson and to Labatt's to derail the possibility of a bid. Molson and Labatt's
indicated their willingness, and the issuance was made, boosting the combined holdings of the two companies to just under 40%. Unlike the *Torstar*
case, however, proper advance notice was given to the Exchange. The
Exchange approved the issuance without requiring that a majority of disinterested shareholders approve the issue. The filing committee of the
Exchange proceeded on the basis that this was indeed a non-arm's length
transaction; however, in their reasons for not requiring shareholder approval,
the committee stated that the issuance was no different from many other
run-of-the-mill private placements which the Exchange had routinely approved in the past without requiring shareholder approval. The committee
felt that to require shareholder approval, it would in effect be saying that all
non-arm's length transactions required shareholder approval. The committee was undoubtedly influenced in its decision by the fact that the issuance
was made at a price 15% higher than the price at which Malting's stock had
traded in the month before the issuance.

In this case, the applicants before the OSC were minority shareholders
of Malting who felt aggrieved at the TSE's decision not to require minority
shareholder approval. Section 22(3) of the *Ontario Securities Act* allows
any person "directly affected" by a TSE decision to apply to the OSC for a
hearing and review. The Act allows the OSC to "confirm such decision

under review or make such other decision as the Commission considers proper". The gist of the complaint was that because the issuance had achieved its intended purpose of fending off any takeover bid, minority shareholders had lost the premium they would have received for their shares on such a bid.

The OSC found as a fact that, although Malting had acted from mixed motives in making the issuance (there was some support for the company's claim that the issuance was made to fund a diversification program), the prime motive at the time was to derail any takeover bid. Nonetheless, the OSC declined to exercise its statutory powers to reverse the decision of the TSE not to require shareholder approval of the issuance. The OSC held that the Commission would only intervene in the "extremely infrequent" event where:

i)   the TSE proceeded on some incorrect principle;
ii) the TSE erred in law;
iii) the TSE overlooked material evidence;
iv) new and compelling evidence was presented to the OSC that was not presented to the TSE; and
v)   the TSE's perception of the public interest conflicts with that of the OSC.

On the facts, it found no reason to interfere, although the Commission stated that this was not the same as actually agreeing with the TSE's decision. In the interest of certainty of the capital markets, it would be best not to make the OSC's review powers into a review of the merits of the decision. The TSE had a reasonable basis upon which to approve the issuance without requiring shareholder approval.

In dissent, Director Charles Salter suggested that the Exchange had overlooked s. 2(a) of by-law 19.06. In his view:

The Committee did not appreciate as it should have appreciated that to increase Labatt's and Molson percentage ownership from about 29% to almost 40% was a substantial alteration and improvement in their position and materially affected their ability to control Canada Matting . . . It is a fact of corporate life that minority control at the 28% level is vulnerable to hostile take-over attempts in a way that minority control at the 40% level is not.

Which reasons do you prefer: that of the majority (Beck and Blain), or the dissent of Salter?

(v) The Toronto Stock Exchange Requirement for Coattail Provisions

Section 1.09 — Take-over Protection

The Exchange will not accept for listing classes of Non-Voting or Subordinate Voting Shares that do not have take-over protective provisions ("coattails") meeting the criteria set out below. This requirement does not apply to classes of Restricted Shares that were listed on the Exchange prior to August 1, 1987 but if any listed company proposes to remove, add or change coattails attaching to listed Restricted Shares, the proposal must be pre-cleared with the Exchange and must fit within the criteria set out below.

The following are criteria only; the actual wording of a coattail is the responsibility of the issuer, subject to pre-clearance by the Exchange. The Exchange will be pleased to discuss proposed coattails at any stage in the drafting process.

The applicable criteria depend on whether there is a published market for the company's Common Shares, as follows:

(1) If there is a published market for the Common Shares, the coattails must provide that if there is an offer to purchase Common Shares that must, by reason of applicable securities legislation or the requirements of a stock exchange on which the Common Shares are listed, be made to all or substantially all Common shareholders who are in a province of Canada to which the requirement applies, the holders of Restricted Shares will be given the opportunity to participate in the offer through a right of conversion, unless:

(a) an identical offer (in terms of price per share and percentage of outstanding shares to be taken up exclusive of shares owned immediately prior to the offer by the offeror, or associates or affiliates of the offeror, and in all other material respects) con-currently is made to purchase Restricted Shares, which identical offer has no condition attached other than the right not to take up and pay for shares tendered if no shares are purchased pursuant to the offer for Common Shares; or

(b) less than 50% of the Common Shares outstanding immedi-ately prior to the offer, other than Common Shares owned by the offeror, or associates or affiliates of the offeror, are deposited pursuant to the offer.

(The purpose of clause (b) is to prevent the mere making of a bid from triggering the conversion privilege if holders of more than 50% of the Common Shares do not tender to the bid. Note that clause (b) refers to shares deposited as opposed to shares taken up.)

(2) If there is no published market for the Common Shares, the holders of at least 80% of the outstanding Common Shares will generally be required to enter into an agreement with a trustee for the benefit of the holders of Restricted Shares from time to time, which agreement will have the effect of preventing transactions that would deprive the hold-ers of Restricted Shares of rights under applicable take-over bid leg

islation to which they would have been entitled in the event of a take-over bid if the Common Shares had been Restricted Shares.

In the rare cases where there is a material difference between the equity interests of the Common and Restricted shares, or in other special circumstances, the Exchange may permit or require appropriate modifications to the above criteria.

The criteria are designed to ensure that the fact that Common Shares are not of the same class as Restricted Shares will not prevent the holders of Restricted Shares from participating in a take-over bid on an equal footing with the Common shareholders. If, in the face of these coattails, a take-over bid is structured in such a way as to defeat this objective, the Exchange may take disciplinary measures against any person or company under the jurisdiction of the Exchange who is involved, directly or indirectly, in the making of the bid. The Exchange may also seek intervention from other regulators in appropriate cases.

Where a company has an outstanding class of shares that carry more than one vote per share but are not Common Shares, coattails will be considered on an individual basis. Coattails may also be required by the Exchange in the case of a company that has more than one outstanding class of voting securities but no shares that fall within the definition of Non-Voting or Subordinate Voting Shares.

Pertinent definitions are as follows:

(a) "Common Shares" means Residual Equity Shares that are fully franchised, in that the holder of each such share has a right to vote each share in all circumstances calling for a vote under the applicable corporate legislation, irrespective of the number of shares owned, that is not less, on a per share basis, than the right to vote attaching to any other share of an outstanding class of shares of the company;

(b) "Non-Voting Shares" means Restricted Shares which do not carry the right to vote at shareholders' meetings except for a right to vote in certain limited circumstances (e.g., to elect a limited number of directors or to vote in circumstances where the applicable corporate legislation provides the right to vote for shares which are otherwise non-voting);

(c) "Preference Shares" means shares to which there is attached a genuine and non-specious preference or right over any class of Residual Equity Shares of the company;

(d) "Residual Equity Shares" means shares which have a residual right to share in the earnings of the company and in its assets upon liquidation or winding up;

(e) "Restricted Shares" means Residual Equity Shares which are not Common Shares;

(f) "Restricted Voting Shares" means Restricted Shares which carry a right to vote which is subject to some limit or restriction on the number or percentage of shares which may be voted by a person or company or group of persons or companies (except where the restriction or limit is applicable only to persons who are not Canadians or residents of Canada); and

(g) "Subordinate Voting Shares" means Restricted Shares which carry a right to vote at shareholders' meetings but another class of shares of the same company carries a greater right to vote, on a per share basis.

(vi) The Powers of the Securities Regulators in Policing Defensive Tactics

The securities regulators have the power to make orders "in the public interest." For example, the Ontario *Securities Act* (R.S.O. 1990, c. S-5) provides that:

127. (1) The Commission may make one or more of the following orders if in its opinion it is in the public interest to make the order or orders:

1. An order that the registration or recognition granted to a person or company under Ontario securities law be suspended or restricted for such period as is specified in the order or be terminated, or that terms and conditions be imposed on the registration or recognition.

2. An order that trading in any securities by or of a person or company cease permanently or for such period as is specified in the order.

3. An order that any exemptions contained in Ontario securities law do not apply to a person or company permanently or for such period as is specified in the order.

4. An order that a market participant submit to a review of his, her or its practices and procedures and institute such changes as may be ordered by the Commission.

5. If the Commission is satisfied that Ontario securities law has not been complied with, an order that a release, report, preliminary prospectus, prospectus, return, financial statement, information circular, take-over bid circular, issuer bid circular, offering memorandum, proxy solicitation or any other document described in the order,

      i. be provided by a market participant to a person or company,

      ii. not be provided by a market participant to a person or company, or

      iii. be amended by a market participant to the extent that amendment is practicable.

6. An order that a person or company be reprimanded.

7. An order that a person resign one or more positions that the person holds as a director or officer of an issuer.

8. An order that a person is prohibited from becoming or acting as a director or officer of any issuer.

9. If a person or company has not complied with Ontario securities law, an order requiring the person or company to pay an administrative penalty of not more than $1 million for each failure to comply.

10. If a person or company has not complied with Ontario securities law, an order requiring the person or company to disgorge to the Commission any amounts obtained as a result of the non-compliance.

These powers give the securities regulators a great deal of discretion to regulate takeover bids. In particular, s. 127(2), the so-called "cease trade" power, allows the Ontario Securities Commission ("OSC") to effectively enjoin any transaction that it finds contrary to the public interest. Thus, for example, the Ontario Securities Commission issued a cease trade order to enjoin a takeover bid in *Canadian Tire Corp. v. C.T.C. Dealer Holdings Ltd.* (1987), 35 B.L.R. 56, 10 O.S.C.B. 857, 1987 CarswellOnt 128 (Securities Comm.), affirmed (1987), 59 O.R. (2d) 79, 23 Admin. L.R. 285, 35 B.L.R. 117, 37 D.L.R. (4th) 94, 21 O.A.C. 216, 1987 CarswellOnt 1733 (Div. Ct.), leave to appeal to Ont. C.A. refused (1987), 35 B.L.R. xx (Ont. C.A.), which appears in the chapter immediately following.

The regulators have issued National Policy 62-202 (which has been adopted in concert by all the various Canadian regulatory authorities) that indicates the manner in which regulatory discretion will be exercised in relation to defensive tactics associated with takeover bids.

NATIONAL POLICY 62-202: TAKE-OVER BIDS — DEFENSIVE TACTICS

PART 1 DEFENSIVE TACTICS

1.1 Defensive Tactics

(1) The Canadian securities regulatory authorities recognize that take-over bids play an important role in the economy by acting as a discipline on corporate management and as a means of reallocating economic resources to their best uses. In considering the merits of a take-over bid,

there is a possibility that the interests of management of the target company will differ from those of its shareholders. Management of a target company may take one or more of the following actions in response to a bid that it opposes:

1. Attempt to persuade shareholders to reject the bid.

2. Take action to maximize the return to shareholders including soliciting a higher bid from a third party.

3. Take other defensive measures to defeat the bid.

(2) The primary objective of the take-over bid provisions of Canadian securities legislation is the protection of the *bona fide* interests of the shareholders of the target company. A secondary objective is to provide a regulatory framework within which take-over bids may proceed in an open and even-handed environment. The take-over bid provisions should favour neither the offeror nor the management of the target company, and should leave the shareholders of the target company free to make a fully informed decision. The Canadian securities regulatory authorities are concerned that certain defensive measures taken by management of a target company may have the effect of denying to shareholders the ability to make such a decision and of frustrating an open take-over bid process.

(3) The Canadian securities regulatory authorities have determined that it is inappropriate to specify a code of conduct for directors of a target company, in addition to the fiduciary standard required by corporate law. Any fixed code of conduct runs the risk of containing provisions that might be insufficient in some cases and excessive in others. However, the Canadian securities regulatory authorities wish to advise participants in the capital markets that they are prepared to examine target company tactics in specific cases to determine whether they are abusive of shareholder rights. Prior shareholder approval of corporate action would, in appropriate cases, allay such concerns.

(4) Without limiting the foregoing, defensive tactics that may come under scrutiny if undertaken during the course of a bid, or immediately before a bid, if the board of directors has reason to believe that a bid might be imminent, include

(a) the issuance, or the granting of an option on, or the purchase of, securities representing a significant percentage of the outstanding securities of the target company,

(b) the sale or acquisition, or granting of an option on, or agreeing to sell or acquire, assets of a material amount, and

(c) entering into a contract other than in the normal course of business or taking corporate action other than in the normal course of business.

(5) The Canadian securities regulatory authorities consider that unrestricted auctions produce the most desirable results in take-over bids and they are reluctant to intervene in contested bids. However, they will take appropriate action if they become aware of defensive tactics that will likely result in shareholders being deprived of the ability to respond to a take-over bid or to a competing bid.

(6) The Canadian securities regulatory authorities appreciate that defensive tactics, including those that may consist of some of the actions listed in subsection (4), may be taken by a board of directors of a target company in a genuine attempt to obtain a better bid. Tactics that are likely to deny or limit severely the ability of the shareholders to respond to a take-over bid or a competing bid may result in action by the Canadian securities regulatory authorities.

(7) As a general rule, the Canadian securities regulatory authorities will not advise parties as to the propriety of proposed action in a particular case except in the context of a meeting or proceeding of which interested parties have been given notice.

PART 2 EFFECTIVE DATE

2.1 Effective Date — This National Policy comes into force on August 4, 1997.

Note

The issue of poison pills has come before the securities regulators in a number of cases. The following case is representative of the attitude of the regulators toward pills.

Chapters Inc., Re
(2001), 24 O.S.C.B. 1657, 2001 CarswellOnt 903 (Securities Comm.)

ONTARIO SECURITIES COMMISSION: In March 2000, a principal of Trilogy, Mr. Gerald Schwartz, informed Chapters' CEO, Mr. Lawrence Stevenson, of his interest in a friendly acquisition of Chapters. On April 16, 2000 Chapters' Board of Directors adopted a shareholder rights plan that was confirmed by Chapters' Shareholders on September 13, 2000. The Rights Plan included a "permitted bid" feature requiring a permitted bid to remain open for a minimum period of 45 days. To be a permitted bid under the Rights Plan, a bid must have been made to all Chapters shareholders of record and no Shares could be taken up unless more than 50% of the aggregate of outstanding Shares held by independent shareholders (as defined in the Rights Plan) had been deposited and not withdrawn. In addition, once there had been a deposit of more than 50% of the Shares, this had to be publicly announced and the bid had to remain open for at least a further 10 business days.

On November 28, 2000, Trilogy announced an unsolicited partial bid to acquire 4,888,000 Shares of Chapters for a cash consideration of $13.00 per share (the "Trilogy Offer"). This represented approximately 43% of the outstanding Shares. On November 28, 2000, a total of 1,082,200 Shares, representing approximately 9.5% of the outstanding Shares, were held by Trilogy. If the bid were successful, Trilogy would own approximately 53% of the Shares and have control of Chapters. Upon a successful completion of the bid, Trilogy indicated that it intended to propose a merger plan between Chapters and Indigo.

On December 11, 2000, Trilogy mailed the Trilogy Offer to Chapters' shareholders. The Trilogy Offer was initially open for acceptance until January 3, 2001, however, the expiry date was extended to January 24, 2001.

[The Commission indicated that the board had initiated a search for alternative acquirers.]

The search for alternatives culminated in the announcement on January 18, 2001 of an offer from Future Shop (the "Proposed Offer") which the Chapters Board recommended to shareholders. Chapters waived its Rights Plan in respect of the Future Shop Proposed Offer. Future shop expected to mail the Proposed Offer to Chapters shareholders by mid-February and closing was expected by mid-March.

As a result of the Future Shop Proposed Offer, the Chapters Board announced on January 18, 2001 that it had entered into a support agreement (the "Support Agreement") with Future Shop under which Future Shop would be making the Future Shop Proposed Offer. The Proposed Offer was conditional upon the continuation of the Rights Plan and Chapters could not remove the pill without breaching the Support Agreement.

Under the Future Shop Proposed Offer, Chapters shareholders had the option to elect to receive consideration equal to (a) $16.00 in cash; or (b) two Future Shop common shares for each Chapters Share. The Proposed Offer was subject to a maximum aggregate cash consideration of $100 million and a maximum aggregate number of Future Shop shares issuable of up to 12 million shares. Assuming all Chapters shareholders elect all cash or all shares, each shareholder could have expected to be prorated so that they would have received approximately 50% shares.

Shareholders in a position to tender approximately 30% of Chapters' Shares had agreed to lock-up (the "Lock-Up Agreement") to the Proposed Offer and only tender to a "superior bid" if one were made before January 25, 2001. In the Lock-Up Agreement, a superior bid was defined as an offer with a value of $17.50 or more that was received by 4 p.m. Toronto time on Wednesday January 24, 2001.

The Support Agreement contained a number of noteworthy terms and conditions. Firstly, the agreement contained a covenant requiring Chapters to support the Future Shop Proposed Offer and also provided for a break fee of approximately 5% of the aggregate transaction price. Secondly, it contained a term that the Rights Plan would remain in place in order that the proposed offer by Future Shop could be prepared and mailed, and that the Rights Plan be waived in respect of the Future Shop Proposed Offer at a point in time when Future Shop was in a position to take up and pay for the Shares. Thirdly, the Support Agreement contained a non-solicitation term, commonly known as a "no-shop provision", whereby Chapters would not participate in or encourage any unsolicited written acquisition proposal by a third party. Finally, the Support Agreement also precluded Chapters from releasing any third party, aside from Future Shop, from confidentiality obligations.

Additionally, the Rights Plan included a provision which provided that, in general terms, the plan would terminate with respect to all bids upon the waiver of the Plan for any one bid (the "waive-for-one-waive-for-all" clause). Also, in the Support Agreement, Chapters agreed not to waive the Plan until Future Shop was ready to take-up and pay for the shares subject to its bid.

On January 10, 2001, Trilogy amended its offer by increasing the price payable for the Chapters Shares to $15.00 cash per share (the "Amended Offer"). Additionally, Trilogy announced on January 20, 2001, one day before the hearing, its intention to once again enhance its offer if the Commission cease traded the Rights Plan. The proposed enhancement (the "Proposed Enhancement") consisted of $17 per share for all of the outstanding common shares less the locked-up Shares under the Lock-Up Agreement and the Shares already owned by Trilogy.

III. Analysis

The Shareholder Rights Plan

This Rights Plan poison pill hearing is somewhat unique. The nature and effect of the Lock-Up and Support Agreements, the "waive-for-one-waive-for-all" clause and the contention that shareholders should have both offers open for acceptance at the same time raise substantial questions for the Commission.

Our analysis should be considered against the background of the following brief summary. Chapters has had nearly two months since the Trilogy unsolicited cash bid, to secure the emergence of Future Shop — colloquially a white knight. Not only have management shares of approximately thirty percent (30%) of the target shareholders, including management, locked up to the white knight, but the target has also entered into a support agreement with Future Shop providing for a five percent (5%) break fee and a no-shop clause. The target has also waived the pill with respect to Future Shop but to no other bidder. In this context, Chapters sought to keep the shareholder Rights Plan in place, at least until mid-march, despite the above efforts to end the auction. We cannot agree with Chapter's position in this regard.

[The Commission quoted extensively from National Policy 62-202, indicating that shareholders must ultimately decide the fate of competing takeover bids.]

The authority of the Canadian securities administrators to exercise this mandate has resulted in a series of decisions that serve to guide the Commission's approach with respect to defensive tactics. The starting point is the decision in *Re Canadian Jorex Ltd.* (1992), 15 O.S.C.B. 257.

In *Jorex*, the Commission established the overriding principle governing the consideration of poison pills, that is "there comes a time when the pill has to go". As a result of *Jorex*, the question becomes not whether, but "when does the pill go."

In order to make this determination, the Commission is guided by the decision in *Re Consolidated Properties* (2000), 23 O.S.C.B. 7981. In Consolidated, the Commission referred to the test used in *Re MDC Corporation and Regal Greetings & Gifts Inc.* (1994), 17 O.S.C.B. 4971, to determine whether or not the pill should go:

> As the Commission said in the *Matter of MDC Corporation and Regal Greetings & Gifts Inc.* . . .
>
> > If there appears to be a real and substantial possibility that, given a reasonable period of further time, the board of the target corporation can increase shareholder choice and maximize shareholder value, then, absent some other compelling reason requiring the termination of the plan in the interests of shareholders, it seems to us that the Commission should allow the plan to function for such further period, so as to fulfil their fiduciary duties.
>
> On the basis of the decisions since Regal, "reasonable possibility" would appear to us to be a more appropriate description than "real and substantial possibility", although both may in practice amount to the same thing.

Implicit in this assessment is a balancing of interests. When applying the Regal test, the Commission must consider and balance the duties of management against the interests of shareholders. This approach was adopted in *Argentina Gold Corp.*, [1999] 6 B.C.S.C. Weekly Summary 23, where the British Columbia Securities Commission stated:

> In determining whether a poison pill should stay or go, there is a natural tension between the objectives of letting the shareholders decide for themselves, as described in *Jorex*, and of letting management and the board fulfil what they see as their fiduciary duties, as set out in *Regal*. Striking a balance between these objectives in any particular case is highly dependent on the specific facts.

As recognized by the Commission in *Argentina Gold*, the individual result of a poison pill case depends on the specific facts. All relevant factors must be considered when determining whether or not the pill has outlived its purpose. *Royal Host Real Estate Investment Trust* (1999), 22 OSCB 7819, a decision of the Alberta, British Columbia and Ontario Securities Commissions, provides the following list of factors:

While it would be impossible to set out a list of all of the factors that might be relevant in cases of this kind, they frequently include:

• whether shareholder approval of the rights plan was obtained;

• when the plan was adopted;

• whether there is broad shareholder support for the continued operation of the plan;

• the size and complexity of the target company;

• the other defensive tactics, if any, implemented by

• the number of potential, viable offerors;

• the steps taken by the target company to find an alternative bid or transaction that would be better for the shareholders;

• the likelihood that, if given further time, the target company will be able to find a better bid or transaction;

• the nature of the bid, including whether it is coercive or unfair to the shareholders of the target company;

• the length of time since the bid was announced and made;

• the likelihood that the bid will not be extended if the rights plan is not terminated.

This is the approach that was taken in *Jorex* and that served as the starting point for the analysis in the subsequent decisions.

The principal factors which, in our view, were relevant to the determination that it was time for the Chapters pill to go are as follows:

(a) The Rights Plan was adopted on April 16, 2000, by Chapters' Board of Directors and was confirmed by Chapters' Shareholders on September 13, 2000. Although the pill is not strictly tactical, it was adopted subsequent to the March 2000 meeting between Gerald Schwartz and Larry Stevenson where Mr. Schwartz expressed an interest in a friendly merger of Chapters and Indigo.

When shareholders approve a pill it does not mean that they want the pill to continue indefinitely. A company's board of directors is not permitted to maintain a shareholder rights plan indefinitely to prevent a bid's proceeding, but may do so as long as the board is actively seeking alternatives and if there is a real and substantial possibility that the board can increase shareholder choice and maximize shareholder value. It was submitted by counsel for Trilogy that the Support Agreement confirmed that Chapters is no longer seeking alternative bids.

(b) Outside of the Shares locked-up by the Future Shop Support Agreement, there has been no demonstration of broad shareholder support for the continuance of the pill. Moreover, counsel for Trilogy has provided support from two institutional shareholders indicating that they wanted to be free to tender to the offer.

(c) Chapters is neither large in size, nor complex in nature. As such, a potential bidder should be able to assess the company in a relatively short period of time.

(d) As a result of the Trilogy Offer, Chapters has engaged in a number of defensive tactics. On January 18, 2001, the Chapters Board announced that it had entered into a support agreement with Future Shop under which Future Shop would be making an offer. The Support Agreement waives the pill with respect to Future Shop and disallows Chapters the ability to remove the pill for competitive bids without breaching the Support Agreement.

The Support Agreement contained a number of typical terms and conditions. Firstly, the agreement contained a covenant requiring Chapters to support the Future Shop Proposed Offer and also provided for a break fee of approximately 5% of the aggregate transaction price. Secondly, the Support Agreement contained a non-solicitation term, commonly known as a "no-shop provision", whereby Chapters would not participate in or encourage any unsolicited written acquisition proposal by a third party. Thirdly, the Support Agreement also precluded Chapters from releasing any third party, aside form Future Shop, from confidentiality obligations.

The Support Agreement also contained some not so typical terms. One of such terms required the Rights Plan to remain in place in order that the proposed offer by Future Shop could be prepared and mailed, and that the Rights Plan be waived in respect of the Future Shop Proposed Offer at a point in time when Future Shop is in a position to take up and pay for deposited Shares. In effect, this term equalizes the timing of all bids and is discussed below.

Additionally, the Rights Plan included a provision under which the plan would terminate with respect to all bids upon the waiver of the rights plan (the "waive-for-one-waive-for-all" clause). The traditional use for such a clause is to remove management's ability to use discretionary powers in a manner that waives the application of a pill to a bid that it is prepared to recommend, while requiring a competing bid to wait out the full permitted bid period.

Under a typical "waive-for-one-waive-for-all" clause, once management waives the pill for one bid, the pill is automatically waived for all bids. These clauses are used to accentuate the auction process. The Chapters Board, however, has agreed to include a clause in the Future Shop Support

Agreement so that the pill is only waived for competing bids upon the take-up of Chapters Shares by Future Shop. This places a significant amount of control in the hands of Future Shop.

It is highly unlikely that a competing bidder, such as Trilogy, would continue an offer for such an extended period of time and assume the risks associated with the modified clause in the Future Shop Support Agreement. The longer the bid is open increases the bid's sensitivity to market risks and the time value of money. Also, as it stands, if shareholders, other than the locked-up shareholders, chose to tender to a competing bid, Future Shop could frustrate that choice by declining to take up any shares under its bid and therefore avoid triggering the deemed waiver clause. The use of the clause in this manner eliminates shareholder choice and subverts the very purpose for which a deemed waiver clause was intended.

Finally, Chapters has entered into an agreement with Future Shop not to waive the pill in favour of any other bid. While the parties are free to enter into a support agreement, its terms cannot trump a determination by the Commission that it is in the public interest that the pill be cease traded.

(e) Chapters and Indigo are the major players in the Canadian retail book industry. The likely absence of synergies with companies outside the book industry result in the existence of few potential, viable offerors.

(f) The plan was firmly in place on November 28, 2000 when Trilogy announced its bid to acquire the Chapters Shares. During the 54 days the plan has been in effect, Chapters commenced a search for alternatives that resulted in the emergence of a proposed offer from Future Shop on January 18, 2001, 51 days after the announcement of the Trilogy Offer.

(g) Given the Lock-Up and Support Agreements that now exist between Chapters and Future Shop, it is unlikely that extending the pill will result in a competing bid.

(h) The current offer by Trilogy is a $15.00 all cash bid for 4,888,000 of the 11,374,704 outstanding Shares of Chapters. This represents a significant premium over the market value of the stock at the time of the bid. The bid is also partial in that it is for only 43% of the outstanding Shares of Chapters. As such, it was argued that it was coercive. If one factors out the shares subject to the Lock-Up Agreement, each non-locked up Chapters shareholder who tenders would receive a 75.4 percent take-up, translating into $11.31 in cash per share.

Moreover, the Proposed Enhancement announced on January 20, 2001 is also an all cash offer at $17.00 per share for all of the Shares outstanding less the locked-up Shares and the Shares already owned by Trilogy.

(i) The Rights Plan has been in effect for 54 days. This time period is significantly longer than the minimum 21-day period currently required in the Act.

(j) Trilogy submitted that it had no intention of extending its current bid beyond the January 24, 2001, expiration date unless the pill was cease traded by the Commission. Although counsel for Chapters submitted that in many cases where this assertion has been made, the bid was nevertheless extended, we prefer the approach adopted by the British Columbia Securities Commission in *Argentina Gold, supra,* as follows:

> Although an offeror's assertions in these circumstances that it will not extend must be assessed with caution, we could not discount the possibility that Barrick would decide to stand back and see what happened on the property with a view to returning with a lower bid or abandoning its interest altogether if exploration results turned out to be less promising than they appeared.
>
> Argentina Gold's shareholders might well have been willing to take the risk of letting the Barrick bid fall away (indeed later events showed they were), but that was a decision for them to make "without undue hindrance from defensive tactics that may have been adopted by the target board with the best of intentions" (to quote *Jorex*).
>
> We do not consider it unreasonable that Trilogy might have withdrawn its offer. Mr. Wright testified as to the costs and risks associated with keeping an offer outstanding for a longer period of time. As a result, it was unlikely that an extension of the pill would lead to an increase in either the Future Shop Proposed Offer, or the Trilogy bid. In fact, the evidence demonstrated that the maintenance of the pill was precisely the obstacle preventing Trilogy from increasing its offer. Consequently, Trilogy chose not to amend its offer unless the pill was removed. Instead, Trilogy announced its intention to enhance its offer if and when the Commission cease traded the shareholders rights plan.
>
> Accordingly, we conclude that there was no reasonable possibility that, given a reasonable period of time, the Chapters Board would be able to increase shareholder choice or value. Indeed we were satisfied that shareholders would not receive the benefit of the Proposed Enhancement unless the pill was cease traded.

6. SANCTION BY SHAREHOLDERS OF FIDUCIARY BREACH

(a) Introduction to Ratification

One of the most troubled areas in company law is that of shareholder approval — ratification — of an act by the board or individual directors that constitutes a breach of fiduciary duty. In such disparate areas as the issuance of shares, self-interested contracts, corporate opportunity, duty of care, and compensation, the question of legitimation through shareholder sanction arises. In particular, which breaches of duty may be ratified and which may not, and what is the logic of the distinction? Assuming that a given fiduciary breach is subject to ratification, what form of ratification, i.e., unanimous, supra-majority, or bare majority, is required? Does the form of required ratification differ across contexts? What impact does interested shareholder voting have on the effect of ratification? What is the effect of properly executed ratification — i.e., validation of the transaction, immunization of the transaction from judicial review on certain grounds, or a shift in the burden for establishing some defect in the transaction to the plaintiff? The treatment in the cases of these issues is far from satisfactory.

Arguably, any attempt to deal on a principled basis with ratification must begin with a realization that shareholder ratification is subject to many of the same "collective action" problems that beset shareholder voting in other more benign situations, i.e., election of directors. These collective action problems emanate from the free rider problems that are endemic to shareholder voting in the corporation. Because there is little reason to expect that shareholders of widely held corporations will examine ratification issues any more closely than other corporate action requiring their approval (i.e., voting for directors in the normal course of affairs), the value of ratification, especially when it is in the form of a bare shareholder majority, is suspect.

If shareholder ratification in the form of simple or bare shareholder majorities is vulnerable, should the rules governing ratification be altered? An obvious and extreme cure for shareholder apathy would be a rule of unanimity. Under such a rule, the vote of even a shareholder with a single share is important because she retains the power to "hold-up" any proposed action by her refusal to vote in favour of it. Consequently, the shareholder will find that, given that she has clear causal impact on corporate activity, it is in her rational interest to invest in information generation and assimilation activities to the extent of the pro-rated value of the proposed corporate activity on her particular shareholding. Whether a more stringent voting rule is desirable turns on a comparison of the costs and benefits it occasions. For it is indeed possible that the benefits from more widespread and active shareholder voting on ratification are eclipsed by the costs that accompany a more stringent rule in terms of delay and minority shareholder opportunism. These costs may be so high as to effectively bar a corporation from concluding an interested transaction, irrespective of its intrinsic merits. Therefore, in considering the materials in this section, you should bear in mind the consequences entailed by the adoption of different ratification regimes, and, in particular, the effects on a corporation's capacity to adopt transactions that are only available to the corporation on the basis that they are accompanied by a self-interested element.

Finally, in considering the following materials, you should be cognizant of the roots of the ratification power: the power is derived from memorandum corporate law jurisdictions, where shareholders hold residual power in the corporation. Does this feature work to render the ratification power somewhat incongruous with the regime developed under the CBCA and its cognate legislation?

(b) The Common Law

North-West Transportation Company, Limited v. Beatty
(1887), 12 App. Cas. 589 (P.C.)

SIR RICHARD BAGGALLAY: The action, in which this appeal has been brought, was commenced on the 31st of May, 1883, in the Chancery Division of the High Court of Justice of Ontario. The plaintiff, Henry Beatty, is a shareholder in the North-West Transportation Company, Limited, and he sues on behalf of himself and all other shareholders in the company, except those who are defendants. The defendants are the company and five shareholders, who, at the commencement of the action, were the directors of the company. The claim in the action is to set aside a sale made to the company by James Hughes Beatty, one of the directors, of a steamer called the *United Empire*, of which previously to such sale he was sole owner.

The general principles applicable to cases of this kind are well established. Unless some provision to the contrary is to be found in the charter or other instrument by which the company is incorporated, the resolution of a majority of the shareholders, duly convened, upon any question with which the company is legally competent to deal, is binding upon the minority, and consequently upon the company, and every shareholder has a perfect right to vote upon any such question, although he may have a personal interest in the subject-matter opposed to, or different from, the general or particular interests of the company.

On the other hand, a director of a company is precluded from dealing, on behalf of the company, with himself, and from entering into engagements in which he has a personal interest conflicting, or which possibly may conflict, with the interests of those whom he is bound by fiduciary duty to protect; and this rule is as applicable to the case of one of several directors as to a managing or sole director. Any such dealing or engagement may, however, be affirmed or adopted by the company, provided such affirmance or adoption is not brought about by unfair or improper means, and is not illegal or fraudulent or oppressive towards those shareholders who oppose it.

The material facts of the case are not now in dispute. . . .

At a meeting of the directors held on the 10th of February, 1883, and at which all the directors except the defendant William Beatty were present, it was resolved that a by-law, which was read to the meeting, for the purchase of the *United Empire*, should pass. It is unnecessary to refer in detail to the terms in which this by-law was expressed; it is sufficient to state that, after reciting an agreement between the company and the defendant James Hughes Beatty, that the company should buy and the defendant should sell the steamer *United Empire* for the sum of $125,000, to be in part paid in cash and in part secured, as therein mentioned, it was enacted that the company should purchase the steamer from the defendant upon those terms, with various directions for giving effect to the terms of the contract.

The agreement recited in the by-law was executed at the same meeting.

At a meeting of shareholders, held, as arranged, on the 16th of February, 1883, the by-law which had been enacted by the directors was read by the secretary, and, after being modified in its terms, with respect to the price, was adopted by a majority of votes.

The *United Empire*, on her completion, was delivered to the company, and has ever since been employed in the ordinary business of the company.

. . .

It is proved by uncontradicted evidence, and is indeed now substantially admitted, that at the date of the purchase the acquisition of another steamer to supply the place of the *Asia* was essential to the efficient conduct of the Company's business; that the *United Empire* was well adapted for that purpose; that it was not within the power of the Company to acquire any other steamer equally well adapted for its business; and that the price agreed to be paid for the steamer was not excessive or unreasonable.

. . . Had there been no material facts in the case other than those above stated, there would have been, in the opinion of their Lordships, no reason for setting aside the sale of the steamer; it would have been immaterial to consider whether the contract for the purchase of the *United Empire* should be regarded as one entered into by the directors and confirmed by the shareholders, or as one entirely emanating from the shareholders; in either view of the case, the transaction was one which, if carried out in a regular way, was within the powers of the company; in the former view, any defect arising from the fiduciary relationship of the defendant James Hughes Beatty to the company would be remedied by the resolution of the shareholders, on the 16th of February, and, in the latter, the fact of the defendant being a director would not deprive him of his right to vote, as a shareholder, in support of any resolution which he might deem favourable to his own interests.

There is, however, a further element for consideration, arising out of the following facts, which have been relied upon in the arguments on behalf of the plaintiff, as evidencing that the resolution of the 16th of February was brought about by unfair and improper means. . . .

[Sir Richard Baggallay went on to show that the by-law which adopted the Beatty contract was passed by votes which Beatty himself either possessed or controlled.]

. . . it follows that the majority of votes in favour of the confirmation of the by-law was due to the votes of the defendant J.H. Beatty.

These last-mentioned facts were stated by the plaintiff in his claim in the action, and he not only insisted that the defendant J.H. Beatty was in such a fiduciary relation to the company that it was not competent for him, under any circumstances, to enter into the contract for the sale of his steamer to the company, but he made various charges of fraud and collusion against the defendant directors, other than the defendant J.D. Beatty, who was also the secretary of the company.

These charges of fraud and collusion were abandoned at the trial of the action, but the facts before referred to were pressed upon the judges, before whom, in succession, the action came, and afforded to those judges who were of opinion that the sale should be set aside the substantial grounds for their decisions.

The action first came on to be heard before the Chancellor of Ontario, who, on the 6th of May, 1884, ordered the sale to be set aside, with the usual consequential directions. All charges of fraud and collusion being discarded, the Chancellor treated the question as one of "purely equitable law," and held that the threefold character of director, shareholder, and vendor, sustained by the defendant J. H. Beatty, involved a conflict between duty and interest, and that, being so circumstanced, he could not be permitted, in the conduct of the company's affairs, to exercise the balance of power which he possessed, to the possible prejudice of the other shareholders.

The defendants appealed against the order of the Chancellor, and, on the 17th of April, 1885, the Court of Appeal of Ontario allowed the appeal, and ordered that the plaintiff's bill should be dismissed, with costs. In the opinion of the members of that Court, the resolution to purchase the steamer was a pure question of internal management, and the shareholders had a perfect right, either to ratify the act of the directors, or to treat the matter as an original offer to themselves, and to assent to and complete the purchase.

From the order of the Court of Appeal the plaintiff appealed to the Supreme Court of Canada, and on the 9th of April, 1886, the Supreme Court reversed the order of the Court of Appeal, and affirmed that of the Chancellor. It appears to have been the opinion of the judges of the Supreme Court that the case turned entirely on the fiduciary character of the defendant J. H. Beatty as a director: that, if the acts or transactions of an interested director were to be confirmed by the shareholders, it should be by an exercise of the impartial, independent, and intelligent judgment of disinterested shareholders and not by the votes of the interested director, who ought never to have departed from his duty; that the course pursued by the defendant J. H. Beatty was an oppressive proceeding on his part; and that, consequently, the vote of the shareholders, at the meeting of the 16th of February, 1883, was ineffectual to confirm the by-law which had been enacted by the directors. The nature of the transaction itself does not appear to have been taken into consideration by the judges in their decision of the case.

From this decision of the Supreme Court of Canada the appeal has been brought with which their Lordships have now to deal. The question involved is doubtless novel in its circumstances, and the decision important in its consequences; it would be very undesirable even to appear to relax the rules relating to dealings between trustees and their beneficiaries; on the other hand, great confusion would be introduced into the affairs of joint stock companies if the circumstances of shareholders, voting in that character at general meetings, were to be examined, and their votes practically nullified, if they also stood in some fiduciary relation to the company.

It is clear upon the authorities that the contract entered into by the directors on the 10th of February could not have been enforced against the company at the instance of the defendant J.H. Beatty, but it is equally clear that it was within the competency of the shareholders at the meeting of the 16th to adopt or reject it. In form and in terms they adopted it by a majority of votes, and the vote of the majority must prevail, unless the adoption was brought about by unfair or improper means.

The only unfairness or impropriety which, consistently with the admitted and established facts, could be suggested, arises out of the fact that the defendant J.H. Beatty possessed a voting power as a shareholder which enabled him, and those who thought with him, to adopt the by-law, and thereby either to ratify and adopt a voidable contract, into which he, as a director, and his co-directors had entered, or to make a similar contract, which latter seems to have been what was intended to be done by the resolution passed on the 7th of February.

It may be quite right that, in such a case, the opposing minority should be able, in a suit like this, to challenge the transaction, and to shew that it is an improper one, and to be freed from the objection that a suit with such an object can only be maintained by the company itself.

But the constitution of the company enabled the defendant J.H. Beatty to acquire his voting power; there was no limit upon the number of shares which a shareholder might hold, and for every share so held he was entitled to a vote; the charter itself recognized the defendant as a holder of 200 shares, one-third of the aggregate number; he had a perfect right to acquire further shares, and to exercise his voting power in such a manner as to secure the election of directors whose views upon policy agreed with his own, and to support those views at any shareholders' meeting; the acquisition of the *United Empire* was a pure question of policy, as to which it might be expected that there would be differences of opinion, and upon which the voice of the majority ought to prevail; to reject the votes of the defendant upon the question of the adoption of the by-law would be to give effect to the views of the minority and to disregard those of the majority.

The judges of the Supreme Court appear to have regarded the exercise by the defendant J.H. Beatty of his voting power as of so oppressive a character as to invalidate the adoption of the by-law; their Lordships are unable to adopt this view; in their opinion the defendant was acting within his rights in voting as he did, though they agree with the Chief Justice in the views expressed by him in the Court of Appeal, that the matter might have been conducted in a manner less likely to give rise to objection.

Questions

1 Did the Privy Council substitute its view of the merits of the transaction for that of the minority? Why would the minority vote against the transaction if it was so clearly in the interest of the company? What did Sir Richard Baggallay mean when he said that the Supreme Court of

Canada did not appear to consider the nature of the transaction? What is the case for allowing a fiduciary, in his capacity as shareholder, to judge his own actions? Does the law allow other fiduciaries — principals, trustees, lawyers, guardians — a similar privilege? Is the case for shareholder ratification, in which the interested party votes, stronger or weaker in the public company or the private company? Note that s. 120(7) of the CBCA and s. 132(8) of the OBCA require a director's or officer's contract to be "reasonable and fair" whether or not approved by the directors or shareholders.

Marsh argues that shareholder ratification of an interested transaction should not be able to immunize a transaction from judicial review because shareholders cannot negotiate effectively on behalf of the corporation with interested directors. (Harold M. Marsh, "Are Directors Trustees?" (1966), 22 Bus. Lawyer 35.) According to Marsh, shareholders "are, they must be, limited to rejecting, or accepting the deal formulated by interested directors. Even if it be assumed that the deal is fair, that is not what the shareholders are entitled to. They are entitled to have someone negotiate the best deal obtainable for their corporation, fair or unfair" (at 49).

2 The Privy Council in *North-West Transportation* scrutinized the constitution of the company to see if there was any explicit provision that would restrict the capacity of the majority shareholder to ratify the sale. As a general matter, what impact should provisions in the constating documents of the corporation have on the effect of ratification? If a provision in the article or by-laws of a corporation stipulates that a simple majority vote is sufficient to validate the transaction, should an affirmative majority vote bar the courts from reviewing the fairness of a transaction?

3 In *Wedge v. McNeill* (1981), 126 D.L.R. (3d) 596 (P.E.I. S.C.), Mr. Justice Large held that it was "contrary to law for the defendants to vote . . . in the circumstances of unfair and inequitable contracts with a failure to disclose exorbitant profits" where the defendant directors had used their votes as shareholders to approve a contract with another company in which they were the majority shareholders. The Prince Edward Island Court of Appeal reversed (1982), 142 D.L.R. (3d) 133 (P.E.I. C.A.), on the basis that "not sufficient facts were set out for the trial judge to come to a proper conclusion". Chief Justice Nicholson did note that there could be circumstances "which would prohibit them [the directors] from voting [as shareholders]." Denying interested directors their vote as shareholders "in the circumstances of unfair and inequitable contracts" effects a result that is consistent with Sir Richard Baggallay's holding in *North-West Transportation* that minority shareholders should be able to challenge such a transaction "and to show that it is an improper one." It is also consistent with the requirement of "reasonableness" and "fairness" in s. 120(7) and (7.1) of the CBCA (s. 132(7) and (8) OBCA).

Bamford v. Bamford
[1970] Ch. 212 (C.A.)

HARMAN L.J.: This appeal from Plowman, J., is concerned with a popular modern subject — the subject of take-overs.

. . . It was eventually decided to set the matter down and an order was made; and the preliminary point of law was argued on 4th April 1968.

The preliminary point was in these terms:

> On the assumption (which is made solely for the purpose of the hearing of this preliminary point of law) that the allotment by the board of [Bamfords] of 500,000 shares at par to [Burgesses] on 20th November, 1967, was not made bona fide in the interests of [Bamfords], because it was a tactical move in a battle for control of [Bamfords], having as its primary purpose to make it more difficult for [Excavators] to obtain such control.
>
> Where as a matter of law and on the true construction of the Memorandum and Articles of Association of [Bamfords] such allotment was capable of being effectively ratified and/or approved by an ordinary resolution of a general meeting of [Bamfords].

The learned judge decided that point of law in this way:

> Declare that as a matter of law and on the true construction of the memorandum and articles of association of [Bamfords] such allotment was capable of being effectively ratified and approved or approved by an ordinary resolution of a general meeting of [Bamfords].

If that is right, that is an end of the action, as has been recognized by the fact that the order goes on to order both actions to be consolidated and to stand dismissed. Now there is an appeal to this court.

The notice of appeal gives as its grounds these:

> (i) That on the true construction of the articles of association of [Bamfords] the power to allot the shares purported to be allotted to [Burgesses] on 20th November, 1967, was vested in the directors of [Bamfords] in them alone and that the company in general meeting had no residual power to make or ratify or approve an allotment of the said shares. (ii) That an allotment not made bona fide in the interests of [Bamfords] is void and thus incapable of ratification or approval.

Now to me from the very start that sounded odd, and I shall be forgiven if, after all the eloquence which we have had in this case, I am expressing the view which I have held throughout — that this is a tolerably plain case. It is trite law, I had thought, that if directors do acts, as they do every day, especially in private companies, which, perhaps because there is no quorum, or because their appointment was defective, or because sometimes there are no directors properly appointed at all, or because they are actuated by improper motives, they go on doing for years, carrying on the business of the company in the way in which, if properly constituted, they should carry it on, and then they find that everything has been, so to speak, wrongly done because it was not done by a proper board, such directors can, by making a full and frank disclosure and calling together the general body of the shareholders, obtain absolution and forgiveness of their sins; and provided the acts are not ultra vires the company as a whole everything will go on as if it had been done all right from the beginning. I cannot believe that is not a commonplace of company law. It is done every day. Of course, if the majority of the general meeting will not forgive and approve, then the directors must pay for it.

It will be remembered that in the well-known case, *Regal (Hastings), Ltd. v. Gulliver*, decided in the House of Lords, Lord Russell of Killowen in the course of his speech made a very significant observation about this. In that case certain directors had acquired some shares by reason of the fact that they were directors of a certain company. They afterwards sold those shares at a profit. It was held that they must account for the profit because it had been obtained as a result of their directorships and therefore was in the nature of trust property of the company. Lord Russell said this:

> The suggestion that the directors were applying simply as members of the public is a travesty of the facts. They could, had they wished, have protected themselves by a resolution (either antecedent or subsequent) of the Regal shareholders in general meeting. In default of such approval, the liability to account must remain.

So that Lord Russell considers it obvious that they could, either by getting a previous approval or a subsequent ratification, retain the profit, which otherwise they must disgorge.

So it seems to me here that these directors, on the assumptions which we have to make, made this allotment in breach of their duty — *mala fide*, as it is said. They made it with an eye primarily on the exigencies of the take-over war and not with a single eye to the benefit of the company, and therefore it is a bad allotment; but it *is* an allotment. There is no doubt that the directors had power to allot these shares. There is no doubt that they did allot them. There is no doubt that the allottees are on the register and are for all purposes members of the company. The only question is whether the allotment, having been made, as one must assume, in bad faith, is voidable and can be avoided at the instance of the company — at their instance only and of no one else, because the wrong, if wrong it be, is a wrong done to the company. If that be right, the company, which had the right to recall the allotment, has also the right to approve of it and forgive it; and I see no difficulty at all in supposing that the ratification by the decision of 15th December in the general meeting of the company was a perfectly good "whitewash" of that which up to that time was a voidable transaction; and that is the end of the matter. Unfortunately, so it seems to me, the matter has been bedevilled by the course that the case has taken. The learned judge delivered a very long and elaborate judgment in which he went through the whole line of cases to show that the general meeting of the company by ordinary resolution cannot override or usurp the authority of the directors where the conduct of the business is entrusted to them. I see no quarrel with any of those cases and I do not see that anybody can say there is any question about it. I will only mention one of them because it has an observation or so which may be useful. It is *North-West Transportation Co., Ltd. v. Beatty*, a Privy Council case. The decision of the Board was delivered by Sir Richard Baggallay. The point, as stated in the headnote, was that a voidable contract, fair in its terms and within the powers of the company, had been entered into by its directors with one of their number as sole vendor. It was, therefore, of course, voidable; but it was said, and said quite properly, that the general meeting could set that right. Sir Richard Baggallay said this:

> The general principles applicable to cases of this kind are well established. Unless some provision to the contrary is to be found in the charter or other instrument by which the company is incorporated, the resolution of a majority of the shareholders, duly convened, upon any question with which the company is legally competent to deal, is binding upon the minority, and consequently upon the company, and every shareholder has a perfect right to vote upon any such question, although he may have a personal interest in the subject-matter opposed to, or different from, the general or particular interests of the company. On the other hand, a director of a company is precluded from dealing, on behalf of the company, with himself, and from entering into engagements in which he has a personal interest conflicting, or which possibly may conflict, with the interests of whose whom he is bound by fiduciary duty to protect; and this rule is as applicable to the case of one of several directors as to a managing or sole director. Any such dealing or engagement may, however, be affirmed or adopted by the company, provided such affirmance or adoption is not brought about by unfair or improper means, and is not illegal or fraudulent or oppressive towards those shareholders who oppose it.

So that Sir Richard Baggallay had no doubt that a voidable transaction of that sort could be set right by the company in general meeting if the matter was properly explained to the shareholders.

The learned judge, having gone through these cases at great length, came to the conclusion that though it was true that the general meeting could not override the directors it could affirm that which they had done;

but he arrived at this result by what to my mind is a curiously inapt process. He said that the right to allot shares if not delegated to anybody else is in the company in general meeting: in this case by art. 12 that power has been delegated to the directors: but in the present instance the directors, having regard to their equivocal position, cannot exercise the power: it therefore remains to the company and the company can do what it has done, and it has what is termed in the notice of appeal a "residual" power. That might be all very well if the company in general meeting had ever made in allotment. It never did anything of the sort. It merely ratified that which the directors had already done and prevented its being undone. Therefore it seems to me that to talk of "residual" power is entirely beside the mark, with all respect to those who think otherwise.

The learned judge supported his view about "residual" power with two cases. I will only mention one of them and that is *Grant v. United Kingdom Switchback Rys. Co.* I cite that because of certain observations both of Cotton and Lindley, L.JJ. There, there was a limitation on the powers of the directors to borrow; they overstepped those powers and were affirmed by a general meeting. It was said that could not be done because there was an article which gave a special resolution as necessary to a future authority to exceed the borrowing power. Cotton, L.J., said:

> A majority of a meeting called with due notice of the object for which it was called could make this a contract of this company, and it would be wrong for the Court to interfere with the proceedings of a general meeting as to an act within the powers of the company. It is clear that a contract of this nature [that is to say borrowing money] was within the objects of the company, and the appeal, in my opinion, fails.

Lindley, L.J., said:

> The Appellant contends that the company could not ratify this contract except by special resolution. In my opinion that contention is unfounded. There is a broad distinction between altering the articles and merely saying this act was not authorized by the articles, but we will ratify it'. The shareholders can ratify any contract which comes within the powers of the company, and this contract clearly does, for the articles expressly authorize selling any part of the undertaking of the company.

It was said by counsel for the plaintiffs that the company in general meeting could not ratify this transaction for it was not a power within the power of the general meeting and therefore it could not ratify it. I think that is a fallacy. The power to allot shares is clearly something within the powers of the company and it is therefore an intra vires power and one which the company can ratify.

Lastly there has been a very recent case, *Hogg v. Cramphorn, Ltd.*, before Buckley, J., which is very like the present and which the learned judge purported to follow though he did not exactly do so. That also was a question of a take-over. Buckley, J., came to the conclusion that certain shares were not properly issued by the directors because they were issued as part of the take-over war and not with a single eye to the company's benefit: he therefore said the issue was bad: but it could be ratified by a general meeting. He said:

> Counsel for the plaintiff says, no doubt rightly, that the company in general meeting could not by ordinary resolution control the directors in the exercise of the powers under art. 10. He goes on to say, I think, with less justification, that what they could not ordain a majority could not ratify. There is, however, a great difference between controlling the directors' exercise of a power vested in them and approving a proposed exercise by the directors of such a power, especially where the proposed exercise of the power is of a kind which might be assailed if it had not the manifest approval of the majority. Had the majority of the company in general meeting approved the issue of the . . . shares before it was made
>
> I do not think that any member could have complained of the issue being made; for in these circumstances, the criticism that the directors were, by the issue of the shares, attempting to deprive the majority of their constitutional rights would have ceased to have any force. It follows. . . that a majority in a general meeting of the company at which no votes were cast in respect of the . . . shares could ratify the issue of those shares

and he proposed, therefore, as he said, to stand that action over until it was seen whether a general meeting would ratify the transaction - which it did, as the report shows, and therefore the complaint fell to the ground.

The present case is very much on a parallel with that, apart from the timing. Here, the approving resolution had been passed before the preliminary point came before the judge and, that having been done, the act, wrong as it was in its inception, was ratified and approved, and validly ratified and approved. That in my opinion was the end of the matter, and the learned judge, though not for reasons with which I altogether sympathize, came to the right conclusion. I would dismiss this appeal.

RUSSELL L.J.: This case depends solely on the mooted point of law and the assumptions on which it is based. It is to be artificially assumed that the board, to whose decision by the articles the disposal of unissued shares was confided, allotted to Burgesses these 500,000 shares as a tactical move in a battle for control of the company, having as its primary purpose to make it more difficult for Excavators to obtain such control. It is further to be assumed that the effect of such assumption is that the allotment was not made by the board bona fide in the interests of the company. No other facts or assumptions are relevant to our consideration of this appeal; and whether the assumptions are correct is not, of course, for present decision. The question of law is whether the allotment in those circumstances was capable of being effectively ratified and/or approved by an ordinary resolution of the company in general meeting.

There is no doubt that the allotment (on the given assumptions) would be voidable as against the allottee without such a resolution at least if the allottee was aware of the improper purpose, and that the directors could be issued in appropriate proceedings for misfeasance; but unless the allotment is avoided in proceedings it is effective. The question basically is whether the company in general meeting can waive the voidability by an ordinary resolution or whether a special resolution would be required.

A great deal of discussion below and here has centred on the question whether the company has some residual power to allot shares. I do not myself see the problem in that light at all. The company by such a resolution would not be alloting shares at all. They have already been allotted. The question is whether such a resolution can prevent the shares being recalled. It is argued that this can only be done by special resolution because the resolution would alter or contradict the articles. I cannot see that it would, nor that any authority cited leads to that conclusion. The board had the power to allot, and allotted, albeit for an improper motive, and albeit that they were thereby guilty of a misfeasance; but I see no provision of the articles that is altered or contradicted or disobeyed by the resolution envisaged. In *Salmon v. Quin & Axtens, Ltd.* the express term of the articles giving the plaintiff a veto on the proposed transaction could not be overridden either by the directors or by ordinary resolution of the company: but that was quite different from a case in which a power given to the board was undoubtedly exercised but with an improper motive.

It is argued that under the articles allotment can only be: (a) by the board (which is true); and (b) by the board acting in good faith, and that a resolution by the company waiving the defect in mala fide and therefore voidable allotment infringes the articles and must be a special resolution. I do not accept this argument, which seems to me to run counter to the general situation that impropriety by directors in the exercise of their undoubted powers is a proper matter for waiver or disapproval by ordinary resolution. Basically the argument treats an allotment by directors otherwise than bona fide in the interests of the company as a nullity, which it is not. In truth the allotment of shares by directors not bona fide in the interests of the company is not an act outside the articles: it is an act within the articles but in breach of the general duty laid on them by their office as directors to act in all matters committed to them bona fide in the interests of the company.

The point before us is not an objection to the proceedings on *Foss v. Harbottle* grounds; but it seems to march in step with the principles that underlie the rule in that case. None of the factors that admit exceptions to that rule appear to exist here. The harm done by the assumed improperly

motivated allotment is a harm done to the company of which only the
company can complain. It would be for the company by ordinary resolution
to decide whether or not to proceed against the directors for compensation
for misfeasance. Equally, assuming that the allottee could not rely on *Royal
British Bank v. Turquand*, it would be for the company to decide whether
to institute proceedings to avoid the voidable allotment: and again this
decision would be one for the company in general meeting to decide by
ordinary resolution. To litigate or not to litigate, apart from very special
circumstances, is for decision by such a resolution. If, as I consider, the
company could validly decide by ordinary resolution not to institute proceedings to avoid the voidable allotment — a resolution which could not
possibly be said to contradict or alter the articles — it seems to me to support
entirely the view that an ordinary resolution in the terms posed in the point
of law would be effective, having as it would in substance the same purpose
and effect as a resolution not to bring proceedings to avoid the allotment.

In the end, however, the contention of the plaintiffs that the suggested
resolution would be a resolution to allot shares, or a resolution to alter or
contradict any provision of the articles, is in my judgment quite unfounded;
and I also would dismiss the appeal.

Notes and Questions

1 What is Harman L.J.'s justification for saying that a *mala fide* act by
the directors may be ratified? Does *Hogg v. Cramphorn, supra*, stand
for that proposition? Was he simply characterizing all breaches of duty
as *mala fide*? If so, what of the judgment of the Privy Council in *Cook
v. Deeks, supra*, where an attempt by the majority to sanction their own
acts was strongly disapproved? Might not *Hogg* and *Bamford* possibly
be considered cases of the directors taking an advantage that belongs
to the company — the right to issue new shares? Is it every case of
acting for a "collateral purpose" that will be capable of ratification?
Are *Piercy v. Mills*, [1920] 1 Ch. 77 (Ch. D.) (directors issued sufficient
new shares to turn the majority into a minority and thus ensured their
continued dominance of the board) and *Punt v. Symons*, [1903] 2 Ch.
506 (Ch. D.) (directors issued shares for the purpose of creating a
majority sufficient to enable them to pass a special resolution to deprive
other shareholders of special rights conferred on them by the articles)
the same "type" of improper purpose case as *Hogg* and *Bamford*? For
a discussion of *Bamford* see Note, (1969) 32 Mod. Rev. 563.

2 It is important to note that the newly issued shares were not voted in
either *Hogg* or *Bamford*. In *Hogg*, Buckley J. required an undertaking
from the directors not to exercise the votes on the new shares. In
Bamford, the new shares were issued to another company and on the
ratification vote that company voluntarily refrained from voting. Is there
a distinction between allowing the interested director to vote his majority holdings as shareholder to ratify in *North-West Transportation*

and not allowing the newly issued shares to be voted to confirm that very issue as in *Hogg*?

The extent of the power of the majority to ratify directors' acts is raised in the judgment of Mahoney J.A. in *Winthrop Investments Ltd. v. Winns Ltd.*, [1975] 2 N.S.W.R. 666. The main issue in the case was the ability of the shareholders of Winns to ratify a purchase of property and consequent issue of shares in part-payment to defeat a takeover. An injunction was granted to the plaintiff on the basis that full and accurate disclosure had not been made to Winn's shareholders. In the course of their judgments, the judges of the New South Wales Court of Appeal approved the holding in *Bamford*. Mahoney J. A., however, expressed some concerns as to the extent of the majority's power.

Winthrop Investments Ltd. v. Winns Ltd.
[1975] 2 N.S.W.R. 666 (C.A.)

MAHONEY J.A.: . . . The relationship between the powers of directors and the powers of the company in general meeting has been determined authoritatively, for this court, by the decision in *Ngurli Ltd. v. McCann* (1953), 90 CLR 425. Their Honours held, (1953) 90 CLR 425 at 438, that "voting powers conferred on shareholders and powers conferred on directors by the articles of association of companies must be used bona fide for the benefit of the company as a whole". Citing the well known passage in the judgment of Evershed MR in *Greenhalgh v. Arderne Cinemas Ltd.* [1951] Ch 286 at 291, their Honours pointed out ((1953), 90 CLR 425 at 438) that "for the benefit of the company as a whole" does not mean for the benefit of the company as a commercial entity, but for the benefit of "the corporators as a general body". Their Honours said ((1953) 90 CLR 425 at 439):

> The court is more ready to interfere in the second (the case of directors) than it is in the first instance (the case of the company in general meeting). Shareholders even where they are also directors are not trustees of their votes and as individuals in general meetings can usually exercise their votes for their own benefit. But there is a limit even in general meetings to the extent to which the majority may exercise their votes for their own benefit. That limit is expressed in the classic passage from the judgment of Lindley MR in *Allen v. Gold Reefs of West Africa* [1900] 1 Ch 656 at 67 1. The power of a three-fourths majority to alter articles of association must, Lord Lindley said, "like all other powers, be exercised subject to those general principles of law and equity which are applicable to all powers conferred on majorities and enabling them to bind minorities. It must be exercised, not only in the manner required by law, but also bona fide for the benefit of the company as a whole, and it must not be exceeded." . . .
Nor can the majority of shareholders exercise their voting powers in

general meeting so as to commit a fraud on the minority. They must not exercise their votes so as to appropriate to themselves or some of themselves property, advantages or rights which belong to the company.

There is a difference in the restrictions imposed upon the exercise of directors' powers and those imposed upon the exercise of the powers of a general meeting in that, whereas the former cannot be exercised so as to result in a benefit to the directors, the latter may be exercised in a particular way, even though it is clear that a benefit will accrue to the majority shareholders. Contrast the position where the majority use their voting power "to make a present to themselves": *Cook v. Deeks* [1916] 1 AC 554 at 564; *Peters American Delicacy Co Ltd v. Heath* (1939) 61 CLR 457 at 506. But, the question remains whether, subject to such difference, the powers of the company in general meeting are in this regard less restricted than those of directors; in particular, the question remains whether, for example, the powers of the company in general meeting may be exercised solely for what, in respect of directors' powers, is assumed to be a collateral purpose, in the defeat of a take-over.

I do not think that this question was decided by the Court of Appeal in *Bamford v. Bamford* [1970] Ch 212. Plowman J had, as I have pointed out, accepted that the shareholders in general meeting were not subject to such a limitation. But the Court of Appeal did not decide that question. The Court was asked to assume that the allotment of shares by the directors was made for a collateral purpose, and was asked to determine whether the allotment "was capable of being effectively ratified and/or approved" by the general meeting. The Court was not asked to accept, nor did it so do, that the postulated general meeting would be acting with any particular purpose, whether that of advancing the interests of the company as a whole, or of achieving a collateral purpose. It would be possible to envisage a general meeting which, having been properly informed as to the collateral purposes of the directors, yet determined to affirm the proposed transaction, merely because it was for, and for the object of achieving the benefit of the company as a whole . . . .

Counsel did not refer the Court to any case which finally determines the power of shareholders so to act. It is established that resolutions of shareholders in general meeting would not be effective in this way, if the purpose of the majority at the meeting was otherwise than for the purposes of the company as a whole, as explained in *Ngurli Ltd v McCann* (1953) 90 CLR 425. It has not yet been settled whether, if the purpose of that majority be that which the directors are here assumed to have, viz the defeating of the Winthrop take-over, that will be an improper purpose of that majority within the principles adverted to in *Ngurli Ltd v. McCann* (1953) 90 CLR 425. *Bamford v. Bamford* [1970] Ch 212 decides that, in an exercise by the shareholders of the power of the company to avoid a transaction on that ground, a resolution may be valid to affirm the transaction; it decides, as I have previously pointed out, nothing as to whether that resolution may be ineffective, because the majority had the same purpose. Therefore, if Winthrop, at the hearing of the proceeding in this case, can show that the majority passed the resolution for the same purpose that the directors had, to defeat the take-over, a serious question remains to be argued whether the resolutions in any way assist the defendants: compare *Miles v. Sydney Meat-Preserving Co (Ltd)* (1913) 17 CLR 639 at 644 . . .

Notes and Questions

1 The extent of the power of the majority to confirm has not yet been settled in Anglo-Canadian company law. In American jurisprudence the rule is clear that shareholders may ratify acts of the board, and directors may vote their stock in their own self-interest "so long as there is no fraud, overreaching or attempt to intentionally dissipate the corporation's assets . . . ." *Smith v. Brown-Borhek Co.*, 200 A.2d 398 at 402 (Pa. S.C., 1964). While the law may well be the same in Canada, particularly in light of s. 242(1) CBCA and s. 249(1) OBCA, which treat ratification merely as a piece of evidence to be taken into account by the court in either a derivative action under s. 239 (CBCA) or an application re oppression under s. 241 (CBCA), some *dicta* in *Bamford, Regal (Hastings)* and *Peso Silver Mines* have raised difficult questions.

   In *Bamford* Harman L.J. quoted Lord Russell in *Regal (Hastings)* to the effect that the directors could "have protected themselves by a resolution (either antecedent or subsequent) of the Regal shareholders in general meeting . . ." Norris J.A., in his dissent in *Peso*, followed Lord Russell's dicta and stated that Cropper and his colleagues should have obtained the approval of the shareholders prior to their purchase. The difficulty with Lord Russell's *dicta* in *Regal (Hastings)* is that in *Cooks v. Deeks* the Privy Council, following *Menier v. Hoopers Tele graph Works*, said that although shareholders may vote as they please and in their own self-interest, the majority cannot act to take corporate assets for themselves and to the exclusion of the minority. Nor may the majority give away corporate assets to a third party, as in *Parke v. Daily News, supra.* But *Regal* and *Peso* are clearly corporate property cases. In *Regal* the directors were required to account for their profit on the sale of the shares. If they had not sold the shares, they would have held them as constructive trustees for the company. In *Peso*, if the plaintiff company had succeeded, Cropper would have been required to transfer his holdings to it. It remains for the courts to settle the ambit of shareholder ratification, most likely in the context of sections 239 and 241 of the CBCA. See generally, Stanley M. Beck, "The Saga of Peso Silver Mines: Corporate Opportunity Reconsidered", *supra*, p.114 *et seq.*

2 As noted above, the American courts follow *North-West Transportation v. Beatty, supra*, but have worked out limitations in a number of situations. For instance, simple majority ratification is found to be incapable

of ratifying transactions involving fraud, overreaching and waste. In *Schreiber v. Bryan*, 396 A.2d 512 (1978), the Delaware Chancery Court held that waste of corporate assets is incapable of ratification without unanimous shareholder consent. The Court stated that:

> Where waste of corporate assets is alleged and sufficient facts to support the allegation are present in the record to require an inquiry into the transaction, the Court is charged with the responsibility of examining all the facts surrounding the acts, notwithstanding independent stockholder ratification.

The concept of waste in American jurisprudence has proved itself particularly elastic in permitting the courts to strike down any transaction in which there is a taking of corporate assets. For instance, ratification has not saved a stock-option plan when the court has determined that there was no consideration, or inadequate consideration, for the benefits granted (*(Kerbs v. California-Eastern Airways, Inc.*, 33 Del. Ch. 69, 90 A.2d 652 (1952)). Nor will ratification cure the appropriation of a corporate opportunity (*Schreiber v. Bryan, supra.*)

If ratification is incapable of dispositively validating an interested transaction, what is its exact effect? By and large, the modern view of ratification in the United States is that ratification will not insulate a transaction from fairness scrutiny by the courts, but it can shift the burden of proving the intrinsic fairness of the transaction from defendant to plaintiff.

In *Gottlieb v. Heyden Chemical Corp.*, 91 A.2d 57 (Del. S.C., 1952), the Court held that ratification by less than a unanimous vote will work to shift the burden of proof to an objecting shareholder to demonstrate that the terms are so unequal as to amount to a gift or waste of corporate assets. This is because:

> the entire atmosphere is freshened and a new set of rules invoked where formal approval has been given by a majority of independent, fully informed [share] holders. (At p. 59.)

Several ancillary questions arise logically from this rule, however. For instance, what is the effect of majority shareholder ratification when interested directors participate in the vote? In *Fliegler v. Lawrence*, 361 A.2d 218 (1976), the Delaware Supreme Court held that a ratification by a majority of shareholders would fail to shift the burden of proof when the interested directors held a majority of shares and they voted these shares in favour of the transaction. The Court stated that the ratification was insufficient to bring the transaction within the rule propounded in *Gottlieb* because only a third of the disinterested shareholders voted on the transaction, and it was unclear whether the non-voting shareholders would sanction the transaction. Although the case seems to indicate that a vote by a majority of disinterested shareholders in favour of an interested transaction is sufficient to shift the burden to the plaintiff, there have been cases in which it was held that even a disinterested majority vote affirming an interested transaction is incapable of shifting the burden to the plaintiff. See *Pappas v. Moss*, 393 F.2d 865 (3rd Cir., 1968).

Another question arising from the Court's decision in *Gottlieb* concerns the capacity of interested directors to vote proxies obtained from disinterested shareholders in favour of an interested transaction. In *Smith v. Brown-Borhek Company, supra*, Bell, C.J. held that

> The vote of a proxy is binding on the stockholder who gives it, provided it is not exercised in bad faith . . . In the instant case the stockholders were fairly and fully informed . . . [that the interested transaction was] . . . to come before the annual meeting for consideration and approval. There was no fraud or concealment. The stockholders were on notice that this question and an appropriate resolution would be presented at the meeting.

The Court was, no doubt, influenced by the fact that, even if the shares owned by the defendants and the shares held in trust by the defendants were not voted in favour of the transaction, the transaction would still have been approved by a majority of shareholders.

3 The importance of s. 242 of the CBCA or s. 249 of the OBCA with respect to the treatment of ratification in a derivative suit under s. 239 (CBCA) or s. 246 (OBCA) or an oppression application under s. 241 (CBCA) or s. 248 (OBCA), is illustrated by *Pavlides v. Jensen*, [1956] Ch. 565 (Ch. D.). The plaintiff alleged gross negligence in the sale of a mine for £182,000 which he alleged was worth £1,000,000. The trial judge held that the action was not maintainable as fraud had not been pleaded and the shareholders could ratify the directors' acts. In *Daniels v. Daniels*, [1978] 2 W.L.R. 73 (Ch. D.), Templeman J. refused to follow *Pavlides* on similar facts — an allegation of negligence in the sale of property at less than market value — and allowed the action to proceed notwithstanding no allegation of fraud. Sections 239 and 241 now sweep away distinctions between fraud and negligence and if the court is persuaded that the case is a proper one to proceed, the issue will be tried with ratification being a matter to be considered in the ultimate disposition. Thus, if *Smith v. Brown-Borhek Co.*, had arisen under the CBCA, the matter would have been heard on its merits with ratification being an important item of evidence.

4 Apart from ratification of directors' acts, may the shareholders relieve the directors and officers from personal liability for breach of duty? The potential for abuse of such a general relieving power is obvious given the rule of *North-West Transportation* and the reality of directorial control over the proxy machinery. Accordingly, s. 122(3) CBCA and s. 134(3) OBCA prohibit in broad terms any relief from liability under the Act. In this regard, it is important to note that the sections

codify and enlarge the common law duties of care and loyalty. Thus, a resolution which is a usual feature of many annual corporate meetings "that actions of the officers and directors during the past corporate year shall be ratified, approved and confirmed" is of little, if any, legal effect. Moreover, ratification is only of effect if the shareholders have been fully and accurately informed of the details of what it is they are ratifying. See *Atlas Coal Co. v. Jones*, 61 N.W.2d 663 at 672 (Iowa S.C., 1953).

5 The extent to which a company may indemnify a director or officer against liability or other expenses is dealt with comprehensively in s. 124 of the CBCA and s. 136 of the OBCA. The costs for which one may be indemnified include an amount paid to settle an action and include any civil, criminal or administrative action. The general limitations with respect to indemnification are set out in s. 136(1) of the OBCA and s. 124(3) of the CBCA: the director or officer must have acted honestly and in good faith with a view to the best interest of the corporation, and in the case of a criminal or administrative proceeding that is enforced by a monetary penalty, he or she must have had reasonable grounds for believing that his or her conduct was lawful. Under s. 136(3) of the OBCA, a director or officer is entitled to be indemnified against all costs, charges and expenses reasonably incurred in the defence of an action, provided that he or she is "substantially successful" in that defence and that the conditions set out in subsection (1) are fulfilled. This mandatory indemnification is also provided for under s. 124(5) of the CBCA, provided that the director or officer seeking indemnification "was not judged by the court or other competent authority to have committed any fault or omitted to do anything that the individual ought to have done". Whether the director is sued by his own corporation, either derivatively or directly, indemnification is subject to court approval. Under s. 136(4) of the OBCA and s. 124(6) of the CBCA, a corporation may purchase and maintain insurance for the benefit of directors and officers against any liability incurred by an individual in that capacity. Insurance protection may not be provided if the fiduciary was not acting honestly and in good faith.

Chapter 7

Regulating the Exercise of Power by Controlling Shareholders

1. THE CONCEPT OF "CONTROL"

Controlling shareholders fall into two camps; those with "*de jure*" control and those with "*de facto*" control. Shareholders with *de jure* control hold (or have the power to vote) 50% plus 1 of the votes and are thus able to secure the passage of an ordinary resolution without the cooperation of any other shareholder. A shareholder possessing *de jure* control is also referred to as a "majority" shareholder. The concept of *de facto* control arises out of the fact that, under our corporate statutes, only those shares that are actually voted (whether in person or by proxy) count in determining whether corporate resolutions are passed. Thus, for example, under the CBCA, "ordinary resolution" means "a resolution passed by a majority of the votes cast by the shareholders who voted in respect of that resolution" (CBCA, s.2(1)). Typically, in a public corporation, not all shareholders will vote (many consign their forms of proxy to the "circular file" — i.e., the waste bin). Thus, a shareholder holding perhaps 20%, or even 10% or less, can be confident of securing the passage of an ordinary resolution. Such a shareholder possesses the power of *de facto* control, and is thus a "controlling" (although not a "majority") shareholder. Below, we use the phrase "controlling shareholder" to refer to *all* shareholders possessing *de jure* or *de facto* control.

(Note, however, that while *de facto* control is usually defined in terms of the votes necessary to secure an ordinary resolution without the cooperation of any other shareholder, it may also be defined as the power to secure a *special* resolution (two-thirds of the votes cast).)

We sometimes also speak of the power of "negative" control — that is, the power to *block* the passage of a special resolution. A shareholder (or coalition of shareholders) can possess either a *de jure* or a *de facto* power of negative control. Thus, a shareholder holding 34% of the shares possesses the *de jure* power to block a special resolution, while a shareholder holding perhaps 10% of the shares might have sufficient shares, as a practical matter, to block a special resolution (and therefore has a *de facto* power of negative control).

2. WHY SHOULD WE WORRY ABOUT THE EXERCISE OF POWER BY CONTROLLING SHAREHOLDERS?

JEFFREY G. MACINTOSH,"Corporations"
Law Society of Upper Canada, Special Lectures,
1990: Fiduciary Duties, 189, at xx (footnotes omitted)

Fiduciary duties are commonly imposed in situations in which one person — who for convenience I will refer to as the "agent" — undertakes to perform a task on behalf of another, who for convenience I will refer to as the "principal". The agent upon whom fiduciary duties are imposed will typically have incentives to act at odds with her duty to further the interests of the principal. There will thus be a "conflict of interest". Moreover, through the exercise of discretionary powers ceded to her by the principal, the agent will have the ability to favour her interests over those of the principal. It is this combination of incentives and power to effect the economic welfare of another that are the impetus for the imposition of fiduciary duties.

Corporate directors and officers (who I will refer to collectively as "managers") furnish an obvious example. Directors and officers are essentially agents of the corporation's shareholders. Although their *legal* duty is formally owed to *the corporation*, the courts have often said that "the corporation" means, in effect, the body of shareholders as a whole, and indeed creditors and other fixed claimants who one might have thought of as an integral part of "the corporation" have no standing at common law to enforce the fiduciary duties of the managers. Although it may not be doctrinally accurate to think of shareholders as principals, it is an analytically helpful construct in the sense that directors and officers are charged with the task of maximizing corporate value, and the achievement of this objective will also maximize shareholder wealth. But whether we think of "the corporation" or the shareholders as the principal matters not. What is important is that fiduciary duties are imposed on corporate managers both because they have incentives to favour their own interests at the expense of those whom they serve, and because they have wide-ranging powers that can be used to achieve this end. For example, the directors set their own remuneration, and might easily be tempted to siphon off the corporation's assets by setting an extraordinary level of remuneration. Corporate officers might use the corporation's funds to buy an unneeded company jet, rather than using the money for new investments. There are innumerable other ways in which the managers might divert corporate funds to serve their own purposes, rather than those of the firm.

All of this seems rather obvious. But if this is so, then certainly the case in favour of imposing fiduciary duties on controlling shareholders must be equally obvious. They too have incentives to favour themselves at the expense of other corporate claimants — including minority shareholders. Equally importantly, majority or controlling shareholders will have the ability to accomplish this objective. The primary means for effecting such harm is through the exercise of the voting powers ceded shareholders both by the corporation's constating documents and by the governing legislation. For example, the controllers might vote to amend the articles to expropriate minority shareholders at an undervalue. Or, they might vote to transfer the corporation's assets to themselves at an undervalue. Given the wide range of matters upon which shareholders are empowered to vote, the controllers will not lack for opportunities to elevate their own interests over those of the minority.

It is clear, however, that shareholders need not always resort to exercise of their voting powers to accomplish the objective of favouring themselves at the expense of the minority. Where the controlling shareholders and the managers are the same (or substantially the same) persons, the controllers may use their managerial powers as the instrumentality for effecting a transfer of wealth from minority to majority. But even without an identity of controlling shareholders and managers, the controllers' power to appoint and dismiss directors and officers is certain to result in a management that is highly attentive to the wishes of the controller. Thus, the ability to work harm to minority interests arises whether or not controlling shareholders themselves formally participate in the management of the company.

For a further exegesis of some of the problems that can arise as between controlling and minority shareholders, see Ronald J. Daniels and Jeffrey G. MacIntosh, "Toward a Distinctive Canadian Corporate Law Regime" (1992) 29 Osgoode Hall L. J. 863; David Strangeland, Ronald J. Daniels and Randall Morck, in "In High Gear: A Case Study of the Hees-Edper Corporate Group", in Ronald J. Daniels and Randall Morck, Eds., *Corporate Decision-Making in Canada* (1995). Indeed, Daniels and MacIntosh suggest that because Canadian capital markets are heavily dominated by corporations that have a controlling shareholder (including many that are part of extended corporate empires controlled by extremely wealthy families), the question of controlling shareholder conduct is one of the central issues in the regulation of Canadian capital markets.

While, however, a good *prima facie* case exists for imposing a fiduciary duty on controlling shareholders or regulating controlling shareholder conduct by other means, there is another side to the story. While in many cases benefits will result either from impressing controlling shareholders with duties to other shareholders (or otherwise constraining their conduct), we must always weigh these benefits against the *costs* of regulation. For example, impressing controlling shareholders with a fiduciary duty may deter some transactions that are purely redistributive (i.e., that transfer wealth from minority to majority shareholders) and which are therefore wasteful from a social perspective. Moreover, creating such duties will create new costs associated with litigating disputes about the propriety of shareholder conduct. While such suits may reduce the probability of opportunistic share-holder conduct, not all suits will be meritorious. Those that are not will not only create direct costs that are a deadweight social loss, but also opportunity costs associated with tying up various shareholders and corporate personnel in the litigation process. We further examine the costs and benefits of controlling shareholders at the end of the chapter.

3. THE STRONGLY MAJORITARIAN TEMPERAMENT OF EARLY ANGLO-CANADIAN COMMON LAW

The strongly majoritarian temperament of early English and Canadian company law is described by Jeffrey G. MacIntosh, "Minority Shareholder Rights in Canada and England: 1860–1987" (1989) 27 Osgoode Hall L.J. 561 (footnotes omitted):

> The wellspring of the principle of majoritarianism in company law is undoubtedly the 1843 holding in the case of *Foss v. Harbottle* [(1843), 2 Hare 461]. In that case it was decided that in respect of any wrong done to the company, the decision of whether or not to undertake an action was a matter for the majority of shareholders to decide. Thus, an individual shareholder could not sue in respect of a wrong done *to the corporation* if a majority of shareholders either *had* ratified the wrong, or simply *could* ratify the wrong (whether or not such ratifi-cation had actually occurred). [Note: In *Foss*, the company had pur-chased land from some of its directors at an inflated price, and minority shareholders sought to overturn the transaction.]
>
> The holding clearly suggests that, within the sphere in which a majority of shareholders is competent to act, the will of the majority is absolute.
>
> The holding in *Foss v. Harbottle* is not only a rule about the decision making structure of the corporation and the relative positions of majority and minority; it is also a statement of the jurisdictional limits of judicial intervention in corporate affairs. Thus, according to Lord Davey in *Burland v. Earle* [[1902] A.C. 83 (P.C.), at 93]:
>
>> it is an elementary principle of the law relating to joint stock companies that the Court will not interfere with the internal man-agement of companies acting within their powers, and in fact has no jurisdiction to do so.
>
> The rule can be justified on a number of grounds: the prevention of a multiplicity of shareholder actions; the avoidance of futile litigation (where

an individual shareholder suit is derailed by subsequent shareholder ratification); or the impropriety of judicial interference in matters which involve
business or investment judgment and which are properly within the province
of shareholders to decide. However, this ostensibly procedural rule is clearly
not without substantive effect: it creates a significant danger (particularly
where the directors are majority or controlling shareholders) of the diversion
of corporate resources by majority shareholders without minority shareholder redress. The obvious dangers of the rule in *Foss v. Harbottle* generated exceptions to the rule. One of these exceptions was more or less
mechanical in its application: an individual shareholder could sue in respect
of matters requiring the assent of some special majority of shareholders. A
second exception allowed a shareholder to sue to restrain an act *ultra vires*
the corporation. Two other exceptions were anything but mechanical; a
shareholder could sue in respect of matters which constituted a "fraud on
the minority" of shareholders (where the wrongdoers were in control) or in
respect of those harms which were a wrong to the shareholder *personally*,
rather than merely *derivatively*. The exceptions to the rule are tied together
by a common thread; in none of these cases could a majority of shareholders
ratify the wrong. The exceptions to the rule are in a sense the obverse of
those matters which are in essence matters relating to the internal management of the company. If, for example, a corporate act constituted a fraud on
the minority, it could not be said to constitute merely a matter of internal
management to be resolved according to the will of a majority of shareholders.

As has been pointed out by a number of commentators, the substance
of what constituted a "fraud on the minority" was limited essentially to
appropriation of corporate assets or the grossest sort of overreaching by
majority shareholders. As the famous case of *Northwest Transportation Co.
v. Beatty* made clear, a mere conflict of interest was insufficient, by itself,
to call the fraud principle into action. What was required was a truly egregious interference with clearly defined minority shareholder rights. The
courts adopted the posture that shareholders owed no duties of a fiduciary
character — either to the company, or to fellow shareholders.

At least part of the reason for the reluctance to impose fetters on the
exercise of majority power appears to have been the result of the nineteenth
century conception of the nature of the property interest represented by
holding shares in a company. Shares are a species of property. And, as was
said by Jessel M.R. in *Pender v. Lushington* [(1877), 6 Ch. D. 70 (C.A.)]:

> where men exercise their rights of property, they exercise their rights
> from some motive adequate or inadequate, and I have always consid-
> ered the law to be that those who have the rights of property are entitled
> to exercise them, whatever their motives may be for such exercise.

Therefore, a shareholder might vote as he please, though he be "actuated in giving his vote by interests entirely adverse to the interests of the company as a whole."

For Lord Jessel, the vote which accompanies the share is an inseparable incident of the property entitlement; *ergo*, there must be as few fetters on its exercise as possible. This conclusion is far from inevitable; indeed, it is fundamentally tautological. The unspoken (and unsupported) premise is that once the characterisation of "property" has been established, the right must be as nearly absolute as possible. Reasoning from first principles, it is just as easy to imagine that the voting right accompanying share ownership is impressed with duties of a fiduciary character owed to fellow shareholders or to the company. Lord Jessel's essentially question-begging definition of the nature of the property interest associated with share ownership, however, no doubt had an intuitive appeal to nineteenth century jurists more used to dealing with "property" rights as *a priori* constructs than as mere instrumentalities.

This relatively unencumbered spirit of majoritarianism which had gained ascendency by the turn of the century, invaded all the cracks and recesses of company law, including jurisprudence dealing with corporate fundamental changes. So far as the minority shareholder was concerned, a sort of corporate *caveat emptor* was the rule of the day.

Few passages illustrate the position of the minority shareholder quite so graphically as this quotation from a 1928 judgment of Middleton J.A. in respect of a minority shareholder's winding-up application, holding that:

> [the plaintiff] is a minority shareholder and must endure the unpleasantness incident to that situation. If he choose to risk his money by subscribing for shares, it is part of his bargain that he will submit to the will of the majority. In the absence of fraud or transactions *ultra vires*, the majority must govern, and there should be no appeal to the Courts for redress.

The following case (referred to in the above excerpt) is a good illustration of just how far the courts were prepared to defer to the will of the majority.

North-West Transportation Company, Limited v. Beatty
(1887), 12 App. Cas. 589 (PC.)

SIR RICHARD BAGGALLAY: The action, in which this appeal has been brought, was commenced on the 31st of May, 1883, in the Chancery Division of the High Court of Justice of Ontario. The plaintiff, Henry Beatty, is a shareholder in the North-West Transportation Company, Limited, and he sues on behalf of himself and all other shareholders in the company, except those who are defendants. The defendants are the company and five shareholders, who, at the commencement of the action, were the directors of the company. The claim in the action is to set aside a sale made to the company by James Hughes Beatty, one of the directors, of a steamer called the *United Empire*, of which previously to such sale he was sole owner.

The general principles applicable to cases of this kind are well established. Unless some provision to the contrary is to be found in the charter or other instrument by which the company is incorporated, the resolution of a majority of the shareholders, duly convened, upon any question with which the company is legally competent to deal, is binding upon the minority, and consequently upon the company, and every shareholder has a perfect right to vote upon any such question, although he may have a personal interest in the subject-matter opposed to, or different from, the general or particular interests of the company.

On the other hand, a director of a company is precluded from dealing, on behalf of the company, with himself, and from entering into engagements in which he has a personal interest conflicting, or which possibly may conflict, with the interests of those whom he is bound by fiduciary duty to protect; and this rule is as applicable to the case of one of several directors as to a managing or sole director. Any such dealing or engagement may, however, be affirmed or adopted by the company, provided such affirmance or adoption is not brought about by unfair or improper means, and is not illegal or fraudulent or oppressive towards those shareholders who oppose it.

The material facts of the case are not now in dispute . . .

At a meeting of the directors held on the 10th of February, 1883, and at which all the directors except the defendant William Beatty were present, it was resolved that a by-law, which was read to the meeting, for the purchase of the *United Empire*, should pass. It is unnecessary to refer in detail to the terms in which this by-law was expressed; it is sufficient to state that, after reciting an agreement between the company and the defendant James Hughes Beatty, that the company should buy and the defendant should sell the steamer *United Empire* for the sum of $125,000, to be in part paid in cash and in part secured, as therein mentioned, it was enacted that the company should purchase the steamer from the defendant upon those terms, with various directions for giving effect to the terms of the contract.

The agreement recited in the by-law was executed at the same meeting.

At a meeting of shareholders, held, as arranged, on the 16th of February, 1883, the by-law which had been enacted by the directors was read by the secretary, and, after being modified in its terms, with respect to the price, was adopted by a majority of votes.

The *United Empire*, on her completion, was delivered to the company, and has ever since been employed in the ordinary business of the company . . .

It is proved by uncontradicted evidence, and is indeed now substantially admitted, that at the date of the purchase the acquisition of another steamer to supply the place of the *Asia* was essential to the efficient conduct of the Company's business; that the *United Empire* was well adapted for that purpose; that it was not within the power of the Company to acquire any other steamer equally well adapted for its business; and that the price agreed to be paid for the steamer was not excessive or unreasonable . . .

Had there been no material facts in the case other than those above stated, there would have been, in the opinion of their Lordships, no reason for setting aside the sale of the steamer; it would have been immaterial to consider whether the contract for the purchase of the *United Empire* should be regarded as one entered into by the directors and confirmed by the shareholders, or as one entirely emanating from the shareholders; in either view of the case, the transaction was one which, if carried out in a regular way, was within the powers of the company; in the former view, any defect arising from the fiduciary relationship of the defendant James Hughes Beatty to the company would be remedied by the resolution of the shareholders, on the 16th of February, and, in the latter, the fact of the defendant being a director would not deprive him of his right to vote, as a shareholder, in support of any resolution which he might deem favourable to his own interests.

There is, however, a further element for consideration, arising out of the following facts, which have been relied upon in the arguments on behalf of the plaintiff, as evidencing that the resolution of the 16th of February was brought about by unfair and improper means . . .

[Sir Richard Baggallay went on to show that the by-law which adopted the Beatty contract was passed by votes which Beatty himself either possessed or controlled.]

[I]t follows that the majority of votes in favour of the confirmation of the by-law was due to the votes of the defendant J.H. Beatty.

These last-mentioned facts were stated by the plaintiff in his claim in the action, and he not only insisted that the defendant J.H. Beatty was in such a fiduciary relation to the company that it was not competent for him, under any circumstances, to enter into the contract for the sale of his steamer to the company, but he made various charges of fraud and collusion against the defendant directors, other than the defendant J.D. Beatty, who was also the secretary of the company.

These charges of fraud and collusion were abandoned at the trial of the action, but the facts before referred to were pressed upon the judges, before whom, in succession, the action came, and afforded to those judges who were of opinion that the sale should be set aside the substantial grounds for their decisions.

The action first came on to be heard before the Chancellor of Ontario, who, on the 6th of May, 1884, ordered the sale to be set aside, with the usual consequential directions. All charges of fraud and collusion being discarded, the Chancellor treated the question as one of "purely equitable law", and held that the threefold character of director, shareholder, and vendor, sustained by the defendant J.H. Beatty, involved a conflict between duty and interest, and that, being so circumstanced, he could not be permitted, in the conduct of the company's affairs, to exercise the balance of power which he possessed, to the possible prejudice of the other shareholders.

The defendants appealed against the order of the Chancellor, and, on the 17th of April, 1885, the Court of Appeal of Ontario allowed the appeal, and ordered that the plaintiff's bill should be dismissed, with costs. In the opinion of the members of that Court, the resolution to purchase the steamer was a pure question of internal management, and the shareholders had a perfect right, either to ratify the act of the directors, or to treat the matter as an original offer to themselves, and to assent to and complete the purchase.

From the order of the Court of Appeal the plaintiff appealed to the Supreme Court of Canada, and on the 9th of April, 1886, the Supreme Court reversed the order of the Court of Appeal, and affirmed that of the Chancellor. It appears to have been the opinion of the judges of the Supreme Court that the case turned entirely on the fiduciary character of the defendant J.H. Beatty as a director: that, if the acts or transactions of an interested director were to be confirmed by the shareholders, it should be by an exercise of the impartial, independent, and intelligent judgment of disinterested shareholders and not by the votes of the interested director, who ought never to have departed from his duty; that the course pursued by the defendant J.H. Beatty was an oppressive proceeding on his part; and that, consequently, the vote of the shareholders, at the meeting of the 16th of February, 1883, was ineffectual to confirm the by-law which had been enacted by the directors. The nature of the transaction itself does not appear to have been taken into consideration by the judges in their decision of the case.

From this decision of the Supreme Court of Canada the appeal has been brought with which their Lordships have now to deal. The question involved is doubtless novel in its circumstances, and the decision important in its consequences; it would be very undesirable even to appear to relax the rules relating to dealings between trustees and their beneficiaries; on the other hand, great confusion would be introduced into the affairs of joint stock companies if the circumstances of shareholders, voting in that character at general meetings, were to be examined, and their votes practically nullified, if they also stood in some fiduciary relation to the company.

It is clear upon the authorities that the contract entered into by the directors on the 10th of February could not have been enforced against the company at the instance of the defendant J.H. Beatty, but it is equally clear that it was within the competency of the shareholders at the meeting of the 16th to adopt or reject it. In form and in terms they adopted it by a majority of votes, and the vote of the majority must prevail, unless the adoption was brought about by unfair or improper means.

The only unfairness or impropriety which, consistently with the admitted and established facts, could be suggested, arises out of the fact that the defendant J.H. Beatty possessed a voting power as a shareholder which enabled him, and those who thought with him, to adopt the by-law, and thereby either to ratify and adopt a voidable contract, into which he, as a director, and his co-directors had entered, or to make a similar contract, which latter seems to have been what was intended to be done by the resolution passed on the 7th of February.

It may be quite right that, in such a case, the opposing minority should be able, in a suit like this, to challenge the transaction, and to shew that it is an improper one, and to be freed from the objection that a suit with such an object can only be maintained by the company itself.

But the constitution of the company enabled the defendant J.H. Beatty to acquire his voting power; there was no limit upon the number of shares which a shareholder might hold, and for every share so held he was entitled to a vote; the charter itself recognized the defendant as a holder of 200 shares, one-third of the aggregate number; he had a perfect right to acquire further shares, and to exercise his voting power in such a manner as to secure the election of directors whose views upon policy agreed with his own, and to support those views at any shareholders' meeting; the acquisition of the *United Empire* was a pure question of policy, as to which it might be expected that there would be differences of opinion, and upon which the voice of the majority ought to prevail; to reject the votes of the defendant upon the question of the adoption of the by-law would be to give effect to the views of the minority and to disregard those of the majority.

The judges of the Supreme Court appear to have regarded the exercise by the defendant J.H. Beatty of his voting power as of so oppressive a character as to invalidate the adoption of the by-law; their Lordships are unable to adopt this view; in their opinion the defendant was acting within his rights in voting as he did, though they agree with the Chief Justice in the views expressed by him in the Court of Appeal, that the matter might have been conducted in a manner less likely to give rise to objection.

Note

1 The Supreme Court of Canada would have created what we now refer to as a "majority of the minority" requirement for the approval of transactions like those in *North-West Transportation*. That is, they would have required that the votes of the directors who had an interest in the steamship not be counted for purposes of determining whether shareholders had ratified the corporation's conduct. How persuasive was the Privy Council's argument that the Supreme Court of Canada was wrong in its approach? As we detail further below, the majority of the minority voting principle rejected by the Privy Council has recently gained ascendance in many areas of corporate and securities law.

4. EARLY ENGLISH JUDICIAL ATTEMPTS TO CREATE A FIDUCIARY DUTY

While early company law was strongly majoritarian in flavour, there is ample evidence of a constant rearguard action on the part of a non-trivial number of judges to impress at least *majority* shareholders with a fiduciary duty. While these attempts ultimately proved abortive, the seeds of the duty that these cases *would have* planted in the common law have now become important in understanding the nature of the quasi-fiduciary duty that the courts have created under the oppression remedy.

JEFFREY G. MACINTOSH,
"Minority Shareholder Rights in Canada and England: 1860–1987"
(1989) 27 Osgoode Hall L.J. 561 (footnotes omitted)

The first tentative steps towards a generalized fiduciary duty of shareholders can be seen in those cases which impressed upon shareholders a duty to exercise their voting powers in good faith. This duty of good faith, enunciated around the turn of the century, was substantially toothless for the first fifty years of its existence: nonetheless, it provided a toehold for later important developments.

The grandfather of all these cases is *Allen v. Gold Reefs of West Africa, Limited* [[1900] 1 Ch. 656 (C.A.)]. Zuccani, a shareholder, held large quantities of both partly and fully paid shares. [NOTE: At the time when *Allen* was decided, when shareholders purchased shares from the company, they were not required to pay the full price (as they are today). Only part of the price could be paid, with the balance being a debt owed to the company. In this case, it was said that the shareholder held "partly paid" shares.] The articles allowed the directors to make calls on the partly paid shares [i.e., the directors could require that shareholders holding partly paid shares pay off some or all of their debt to the company], and also furnished the company with a lien in respect of unpaid calls, extending to the partly paid, but not the fully paid shares. When Zuccani died, he left a large sum owing in respect of unpaid calls on his partly paid shares. When it appeared that the assets of the estate would be insufficient to pay all claimants, the shareholders passed a special resolution amending the articles so that the fully paid shares, in addition to the partly paid shares, were subject to the lien. As Zuccani was the only holder of fully paid shares, there can be little doubt that the action of the company was aimed at the shares held by Zuccani's estate; indeed, counsel for the company admitted as much. Zuccani's estate argued that the alteration was oppressive, in bad faith and amounted to a retrospective alteration of the articles of the company.

In a holding which echoes decisions canvassed earlier as to the defeasible nature of shareholders' rights, Lindley M.R. noted that the statute appeared to allow for any type of variation of the articles, and held that "[t]he power thus conferred on companies to alter the regulations contained in their articles is limited only by the provisions contained in the statute and the conditions contained in the company's memorandum of association". The "contractual" rights of shareholders bestowed by the articles were said to be "limited as to their duration by the duration of the articles which confer them". Nevertheless, Lindley M.R. also held that:

Wide, however, as the language of s. 50 is, the power conferred by it must, like all other powers, be exercised subject to those general principles of law and equity which are applicable to all powers conferred on majorities and enabling them to bind minorities. It must be exercised, not only in the manner required by law, but also *bona fide for the benefit of the company as a whole*, and it must not be exceeded. [Emphasis added.]

The Court of Appeal was, however, not persuaded that the modification had been undertaken in bad faith: the amendment was allowed to stand.

The outcome by itself might be enough to persuade an observer of average perception that the good faith principle did not, at its inception, have very sharp teeth.

Note carefully how closely the *Allen* duty parallels the fiduciary duty owed by directors and officers. In the CBCA, s. 122 states:

122. (1) Every director and officer of a corporation in exercising their powers and discharging their duties shall
        (a) act honestly and in good faith with a view to the best interests of the corporation . . .

In *Allen*, the court would have impressed shareholders with the duty to act "*bona fide for the benefit of the company as a whole*".

Nonetheless, MacIntosh indicates two ways in which the courts substantially eviscerated this fiduciary duty. First, in *Shuttleworth v. Cox Brothers*, [1927] 2 K.B. 9 (C.A.), the English Court of Appeal held that the issue of whether the shareholders had acted in good faith was to be judged, subject to strict limits, from the viewpoint of the shareholders themselves. In the words of Bankes L.J.:

the test is whether the alteration of the articles was *in the opinion of the shareholders* for the benefit of the company. By what criterion is the Court to ascertain the opinion of the shareholders upon this question? The alteration may be so oppressive as to cast suspicion on the honesty of the persons responsible for it, or so extravagant that no reasonable men could really consider it for the benefit of the company. In such cases . . . the alteration of the company's articles shall not stand . . .

This sharply circumscribed the *Allen* principle. Second, as noted by MacIntosh:

The *Allen* court had suggested not only that shareholders must act in good faith, but that they must act *for the benefit of the company as a whole.* In *Greenhalgh v. Arderne Cinemas (No.2)* [[1951] 1 Ch. 286 (C.A.)], Evershed M.R. said,

> the phrase "the company as a whole", does not (at any rate in such a case as the present) mean the company as a commercial entity, distinct from the corporators: it means the corporators as a general body, that is to say the case may be taken of an individual hypothetical member and it may be asked whether what is proposed is in the honest opinion of those who voted in its favour, for that person's benefit.

In the view of Lord Evershed, this is the functional equivalent of a principle of non-discrimination:

> I think that the matter can, in practice, be more accurately and precisely stated by looking at the converse and by saying that a special resolution of this kind would be liable to be impeached if the effect of it were to discriminate between the majority shareholders and the minority shareholders, so as to give to the former an advantage of which the latter were deprived.

However, as MacIntosh notes, *Greenhalgh* and other decisions interpreted the meaning of "discriminate" very narrowly. As long as a change in the articles affected all shareholders in a *formally* equal manner, the resolution would not be interpreted to be discriminatory. This is illustrated by the facts of *Allen* itself; the majority clearly acted in a manner that was "discriminatory" insofar as the resolution in that case was passed only to get more money out of Zuccani's estate. It was aimed at affecting, and did in fact affect, only a single shareholder. Since most shareholder resolutions are crafted to have the same legal impact on all shareholders of a class or classes, this restrictive definition of "discrimination" severely circumscribed the good faith principle.

In addition, as noted above, in *Pender v. Lushington* Lord Jessel M.R. held that "a shareholder may vote his shares from whatever motive, though he be 'actuated in giving his vote by interests entirely adverse to the interests of the company as a whole.'" As noted by MacIntosh, this is simply inconsistent with the anti-discrimination principle in *Allen*.

To summarize, the *Allen* principle — which seems to be essentially a fiduciary duty — was substantially eviscerated by subsequent judicial developments. However, as discussed below, *Allen* is nonetheless important, as it has recently been revived under the oppression remedy. The oppression remedy thus substantially incorporates the typically statutory fiduciary standard (acting in good faith and in the best interests of the company) and, as we shall see, extends this duty to include a duty of *fairness*.

5. MORE RECENT CANADIAN JUDICIAL ATTEMPTS TO CREATE A FIDUCIARY DUTY

The courts' schizophrenic attitude toward the issue of shareholders fiduciary duties is evident in the Canadian cases. Writing in 1990, MacIntosh noted that:

> In four lower court holdings in three different provinces (one affirmed by the Ontario Court of Appeal), the principle that shareholders owe no fiduciary duty has been reaffirmed. And in *Wotherspoon v. Canadian Pacific Ltd.* [(1981), 35 O.R. (2d) 449, 129 D.L.R. (3d) 1 (C.A.)], the Ontario Court of Appeal in *obiter* has suggested that if shareholders owe any fiduciary duty, it would be owed only to the company, and not to other shareholders.

See Jeffrey G. MacIntosh, "Corporations", in *Law Society of Upper Canada, Special Lectures, 1990: Fiduciary Duties*, 189 (footnotes omitted). However, MacIntosh also noted:

> But to go no further than these cases would be a grave mistake, for the adventurous researcher can discover a solid handful of cases that insist that shareholders do owe fiduciary duties, either to the company or to other shareholders. There are no less than three lower court holdings in Ontario of this ilk. Perhaps even more astonishing, there are five (or perhaps even six) Ontario Court of Appeal judgments that support the existence of shareholder fiduciary duties.

The most commonly cited of these is *Goldex Mines Ltd. v. Revill* (1975), 7 O.R. (2d) 216, 54 D.L.R. (3d) 672 (C.A.). As summarized by MacIntosh (*ibid.*):

> In *Goldex Mines Ltd. v. Revill* the Court of Appeal again appears to have signalled the existence of shareholder fiduciary duties. A struggle for control of Probe Mines Limited led (*inter alia*) to charges that the directors of the company had violated the proxy rules governing public corporations. A key issue before the Court of Appeal was whether a violation of the proxy rules constituted a derivative action (for which leave of the court would be necessary) or a personal action. The court held that any misrepresentation or failure to make proper disclosure to shareholders would give rise to *both* a derivative and a personal action. It is in this context that the court stated that:
>
> > The principle that the majority governs in corporate affairs is fundamental to corporation law, but its corollary is also important — that the majority must act fairly and honestly. Fairness is the touchstone of equitable justice, and when the test of fairness is

not met, the equitable jurisdiction of the Court can be invoked to prevent or remedy the injustice which misrepresentation or other dishonesty has caused. The category of cases in which fiduciary duties and obligations arise is not a closed one.

The action contemplated by the Court of Appeal was a personal action. Thus, the fiduciary duty posited by the court would flow from the "majority" of shareholders to minority shareholders, rather than to the company.

6. THE CURRENT CANADIAN POSITION WITH RESPECT TO FIDUCIARY DUTIES OF SHAREHOLDERS AT COMMON LAW

Brant Investments Ltd. v. KeepRite Inc.
(1991), 3 O.R. (3d) 289, 80 D.L.R. (4th) 161 (C.A.)

The important facts of *Brant* are fairly simple. Inter-City Gas Corporation (ICG, incorporated in Manitoba) stood atop the pyramid of companies involved in the transactions in question. ICG owned all of the shares in Inter-City Manufacturing Ltd. (ICM, also incorporated in Manitoba). In turn, ICM owned all of the shares of ICG Energy Products Ltd. (Energy Products), a federally incorporated company. ICM also owned 65% of the shares of Keeprite Inc. Thus, Keeprite, ICM, and Energy Products were all under common control. It was decided by ICG that it would be useful to integrate the operations of Keeprite, ICM and Energy Products. Thus, the board of Keeprite was approached with a view to approving a purchase of substantially all of assets of the other two companies. The board of Keeprite set up a committee of independent directors (i.e., directors who were not officers of Keeprite and not otherwise connected with Keeprite) to investigate the fairness of the transaction to Keeprite. The committee met a number of times and recommended a substantial reduction in the purchase price, from $24 million to about $20 million. This was done, and the transaction was approved by the full board and the asset purchase was completed.

Certain minority shareholders of Keeprite commenced an oppression action, arguing that the asset purchases were oppressive to the interests of the minority interests of Keeprite. This action failed at trial and was appealed to the Ontario Court of Appeal.

Note that in order to raise the money to effect the asset purchases, Keeprite made a "rights" offering (rights are securities which entitle the holder to purchase further shares in the company, at some future date) to its shareholders. Because exercise of the rights would result in the issuance of more common shares than the articles permitted, the articles of incorporation had to be amended to accommodate the rights offering. This required shareholder approval by a special resolution, and also allowed shareholders voting against the amendment to the articles to dissent and claim the "fair value" of their shares, under what is now CBCA s. 190. The plaintiff shareholders dissented and asked the court to fix a fair value for their shares. While the following excerpts deal only with the issue of oppression, the plaintiffs are referred to below as the "dissenting shareholders".

The judgment of the Court was delivered by McKinlay J.A.:

MCKINLAY J.A.: The learned trial judge dismissed the oppression action on the basis that the record did not establish any of the grounds on which an oppression remedy may be granted pursuant to s. 234(2), and that no prejudicial effect on or disregard of the interests of the minority had been shown. The appellants argued three grounds of appeal:

(a) the trial judge erred in concluding that there is no fiduciary duty owed by a majority shareholder to the minority, particularly in respect of a transaction in which the majority shareholder has a clear conflict of interest with the minority;

(b) the trial judge misdirected himself with respect to the onus of proof of oppression; and

(c) the trial judge erred in failing to apply an objective test of fairness in considering whether the impugned transaction consisted of or resulted in oppression of the dissenting shareholders, and in particular:

   (i) he erred in concluding that some "want of probity" or bad faith of the respondents is requisite to a finding of oppression; and

   (ii) he erred in suggesting that allegations of oppressive corporate conduct can be disposed of on the basis of judicial deference to the business judgment of corporate officers and directors.

* * *

The trial judge, while recognizing that the categories of fiduciary relationships are not closed and have recently been broadened, was of the view that majority shareholders owe no fiduciary duty to minority shareholders, first, because no such duty is currently recognized by Canadian authority or learned opinion and, second, because the relationship between the majority and the minority lacks any of the *indicia* which have traditionally led courts of equity to find such a duty.

The appellants cite three Ontario cases to support their position that the common law recognizes a fiduciary duty owed by a majority shareholder to the minority: *Goldex Mines Ltd. v. Revill* (1974), 7 O.R. (2d) 216, 54 D.L.R. (3d) 672 (C.A.), at pp. 223-24 O.R.; *Ontario (Ontario Securities Commission) v. McLaughlin*, Ont. H.C.J., Henry J., December 20, 1987 [summarized at 10 A.C.W.S. (3d) 270]; and *Re Canadian Tire Corp.* (1987), 35 B.L.R. 56, 10 O.S.C.B. 857 (Securities Commission), affirmed (1987), 59 O.R. (2d) 79 sub nom. *Re C.T.C. Dealer Holdings Ltd. and Ontario Securities Commission*, 23 Admin. L.R. 285, 35 B.L.R. 117, 37 D.L.R. (4th) 94, 21 O.A.C. 216 (Div. Ct.) [leave to appeal to Ont. C.A. refused (1987), 35 B.L.R. xx].

In *Goldex Mines*, the Ontario Court of Appeal dismissed an appeal from the Divisional Court which had set aside the writs in two actions because, in the opinion of the Divisional Court [*Probe Mines Ltd. v. Goldex Mines Ltd.*, [1973] 3 O.R. 869, 38 D.L.R. (3d) 513], the actions were derivative in nature and the requisite leave had not been granted prior to the issuing of the writs. The proposed actions were based on allegedly false and misleading information disseminated by the company to shareholders. In the process of dismissing the appeal, the Court of Appeal made the following comment at p. 224 [O.R.]:

> The principle that the majority governs in corporate affairs is funda-mental to corporation law, but its corollary is also important — that the majority must act fairly and honestly. Fairness is the touchstone of equitable justice, and when the test of fairness is not met, the equitable jurisdiction of the Court can be invoked to prevent or remedy the injustice which misrepresentation or other dishonesty has caused. The category of cases in which fiduciary duties and obligations arise is not a closed one: *Laskin v. Bache & Co. Inc.*, [1972] 1 O.R. 465 at p. 472, 23 D.L.R. (3d) 385 at p. 392.

The Court of Appeal in that case did not hold that a fiduciary duty was owed by directors or majority shareholders to the minority shareholders, but merely commented that the category of cases in which fiduciary duties arise is not closed.

[McKinlay J.A. then noted that in *Laskin v. Bache* (referred to immediately above) the Ontario Court of Appeal held that "[s]uch a special [fiduciary] duty may arise from the circumstances and relations of the parties. These may give rise to an implied contract at law or to a fiduciary obligation in equity." She thus implied that the holding in *Goldex* stands for no more than that relatively modest proposition.]

Ontario (Ontario Securities Commission) v. McLaughlin, supra, involved motions by the defendants pursuant to rules 20.01 and 21.01 of the Rules of Civil Procedure, O. Reg. 560/84, for orders striking out statements of claim as showing no triable issue. The plaintiffs, in their statements of claim, had asserted an alternative claim for injuries they suffered as minority shareholders, through diminution of the value of their shares by reason of an alleged breach of fiduciary duty owed to them by the majority share-holders. In considering whether or not to strike this claim, Henry J. referred to the Court of Appeal decision in the *Goldex* case and also to the decision of Anderson J. in the case at bar. He concluded that there were differing views on this issue requiring legal clarification, and that the matter should be left to the trial judge. Consequently, he refused to strike the claim based on breach of fiduciary duty.

The last case cited by the appellants on this issue was *Re Canadian Tire Corp., supra*, in which the Ontario Securities Commission decided to issue, pursuant to the provisions of s. 123 of the *Securities Act*, R.S.O. 1980, c. 466, a cease-trading order on a take-over bid and on the trade in common shares owned by the majority shareholders. In its reasons, the Commission stated that the vendors on the take-over bid were "in a fiduciary position in at least two categories — as directors of Tire and as Tire's controlling shareholders" (at p. 954 [O.S.C.B.], p. 110 [B.L.R.]), but did not explain to whom the fiduciary duty was owed. In its comments, the Commission purported to rely on the decision of the Ontario Court of Appeal in the *Goldex Mines* case. However, the Commission stated that its decision to impose a cease-trading order did not depend on finding a fiduciary duty, and that the Commission was not the proper forum "particularly in a s. 123 proceeding, to determine the question of whether or not there has been a breach of fiduciary duty" (at p. 955 O.S.C.B., p. 111 [B.L.R.]). What the Commission did determine in its reasons in that case was that the majority shareholders failed to act fairly and honestly and that their unfair and dishonest conduct supported facts which in themselves would have been sufficient to warrant a cease trading order under s. 123. On appeal, the Divisional Court quite properly rejected the appellant's argument that the Commission had usurped the functions of a court in finding a breach of fiduciary duty on the part of the selling shareholders, since the Commission did not so find.

It is clear that none of the foregoing authorities imposes a fiduciary duty on majority shareholders or directors in favour of minority shareholders. The case that comes closest to doing so is the *Goldex Mines* case, which was decided prior to the coming into force of the CBCA in December of 1975, and involved facts which, if they arose at the present time, would appropriately lead to an application under s. 234 of the CBCA or its counterpart, s. 247(2) of the *Ontario Business Corporations Act*, 1982, S.O. 1982, c. 4 (the OBCA). The enactment of these provisions has rendered any argument for a broadening of the categories of fiduciary relationships in the corporate context unnecessary and, in my view, inappropriate.

QUESTION

1 Did the court canvass the full range of available precedent? Are you persuaded by the court's reading of the *Goldex* case?

7. DUTIES OWED BY SHAREHOLDERS UNDER THE OPPRESSION REMEDY

While *Brant* appears to completely foreclose the issue of a shareholder fiduciary duty, the last paragraph from the above excerpt from *Brant* arguably gives back what the court purports to take away. The court appears to suggest that if a shareholder fiduciary duty need be crafted, then this can be done under the oppression remedy. The following section indicates that courts have, in fact, fashioned a fiduciary duty under the oppression remedy, although they have more commonly styled the duty as one of "equitable rights" or simply "fairness" (the overarching general standard under the oppression remedy). The grandfather of all these cases — the *Ebrahimi* case that follows — is arguably the most important corporate law decision in modern times. It not only holds that shareholders may owe each other equitable duties, but that such duties are grounded in shareholder *expectations* (although as subsequent holdings have made clear, these expectations must be reasonable). You will note that *Ebrahimi* is not an oppression case, but a case arising under an English statutory provision that allows a court to wind up a company if it is "just and equitable" to do so. Nonetheless, as indicated further below, the "equitable rights" and "expectations" principles from *Ebrahimi* have been imported into scores of Canadian oppression cases.

Ebrahimi v. Westbourne Galleries Ltd.
(1972), [1972] 2 All E.R. 492, [1973] A.C. 360 (H.L.)

LORD WILBERFORCE: My Lords, the issue in this appeal is whether the respondent company, Westbourne Galleries Ltd., should be wound up by the court on the petition of the appellant who is one of the three shareholders, the personal respondents being the other two. The company is a private company which carries on business as dealers in Persian and other carpets. It was formed in 1958 to take over a business founded by the second respondent (Mr. Nazar). It is a fact of cardinal importance that since about 1945 the business had been carried on by the appellant and Mr. Nazar as partners, equally sharing the management and the profits. When the company was formed, the signatories to its memorandum were the appellant and Mr. Nazar and they were appointed its first directors. Of its issued share capital, 500 shares of £1 each were issued to each subscriber and it was found by the learned judge, after the point had been contested by Mr. Nazar, that the appellant paid up his shares out of his own money. Soon after the company's formation the third respondent (Mr. George Nazar) was made a director, and each of the two original shareholders transferred to him 100 shares, so that at all material times the appellant held 400 shares, Mr. Nazar 400 and Mr. George Nazar 200. The Nazars, father and son, thus had a majority of the votes in general meeting. Until the dispute all three gentlemen remained directors. The company made good profits, all of which were distributed as directors' remuneration. No dividends have ever been paid, before or after the petition was presented.

On 12th August 1969 an ordinary resolution was passed by the company in general meeting, by the votes of Mr. Nazar and Mr. George Nazar, removing the appellant from the office of director, a resolution which was effective in law by virtue of s. 184 of the *Companies Act 1948* and art. 96 of Part I of Table A. Shortly afterwards the appellant presented his petition to the court.

This petition was based in the first place on s. 210 of the *Companies Act 1948*, the relief sought under this section being an order that Mr. Nazar and his son be ordered to purchase the appellant's shares in the company.

In the alternative it sought an order for the winding-up of the company. The petition contained allegations of oppression and misconduct against Mr. Nazar which were fully explored at the hearing before Plowman J. The learned judge found that some were unfounded and others unproved and that such complaint as was made out did not amount to such a course of oppressive conduct as to justify an order under s. 210. However, he made an order for the winding-up of the company under the "just and equitable" provision. I shall later specify the grounds on which he did so. The appellant did not appeal against the rejection of his case under s. 210 and this House is not concerned with it. The company and the individual respondents appealed against the order for winding-up and this was set aside by the Court of Appeal. The appellant now seeks to have it restored.

My Lords, the petition was brought under s. 222(f) of the *Companies Act 1948*, which enables a winding-up order to be made if "the court is of opinion that it is just and equitable that the company should be wound up". This power has existed in our company law in unaltered form since the first major Act, the *Companies Act 1862*. Indeed, it antedates that statute since it existed in the *Joint Stock Companies Winding-up Act 1848*. For some 50 years, following a pronouncement by Lord Cottenham LC in 1849, the words "just and equitable" were interpreted so as only to include matters *ejusdem generis* as the preceding clauses of the section, but there is now ample authority for discarding this limitation. There are two other restrictive interpretations which I mention to reject. First, there has been a tendency to create categories or headings under which case must be brought if the clause is to apply. This is wrong. Illustrations may be used, but general words should remain general and not be reduced to the sum of particular instances. Secondly, it has been suggested, and urged on us, that (assuming the petitioner is a shareholder and not a creditor) the words must be confined to such circumstances as affect him in his capacity as shareholder. I see no warrant for this either. No doubt, in order to present a petition, he must qualify as a shareholder, but I see no reason for preventing him from relying on any circumstances of justice or equity which affect him in his relations with the company, or, in a case such as the present, with the other shareholders.

One other signpost is significant. The same words "just and equitable" appear in the *Partnership Act 1892*, s. 25, as a ground for dissolution of a partnership and no doubt the considerations which they reflect formed part of the common law of partnership before its codification. The importance of this is to provide a bridge between cases under s. 222(f) of the *Companies Act 1948* and the principles of equity developed in relation to partnerships.

The winding-up order was made following a doctrine which has developed in the courts since the beginning of this century. As presented by the appellant, and in substance accepted by the learned judge, this was that in a case such as this, the members of the company are in substance partners, or quasi-partners, and that a winding-up may be ordered if such facts are shown as could justify a dissolution of partnership between them. The

common use of the words "just and equitable" in the company and partnership law supports this approach. Your Lordships were invited by the respondents' counsel to restate the principle on which this provision ought to
be used; it has not previously been considered by this House. The main line
of his submission was to suggest that too great a use of the partnership
analogy had been made; that a limited company, however small, essentially
differs from a partnership; that in the case of a company, the rights of its
members are governed by the articles of association which have contractual
force; that the court has no power or at least ought not to dispense parties
from observing their contracts; that, in particular, when one member has
been excluded from the directorate or management, under powers expressly
conferred by the *Companies Act 1948* and the articles, an order for winding-
up whether on the partnership analogy or under the just and equitable
provision, should not be made. Alternatively, it was argued that before the
making of such an order could be considered the petitioner must show and
prove that the exclusion was not made *bona fide* in the interests of the
company.

My Lords, I must first make some examination of the authorities in
order to see how far they support the respondents' propositions and, if they
do not, how far they rest on a principle of which this House should disapprove. I will say at once that, over a period of some 60 years, they show a
considerable degree of consistency, and that such criticism as may be made
relates rather to the application of accepted principle to the facts than to the
statements of principles themselves . . .

[Lord Wilberforce then reviewed several authorities, and continued:]

My Lords, in my opinion these authorities represent a sound and rational development of the law which should be endorsed. The foundation
of it all lies in the words "just and equitable" and, if there is any respect in
which some of the cases may be open to criticism, it is that the courts may
sometimes have been too timorous in giving them full force. The words are
a recognition of the fact that a limited company is more than a mere judicial
entity, with a personality in law of its own: that there is room in company
law for recognition of the fact that behind it, or amongst it, there are
individuals, with rights, expectations and obligations inter se which are not
necessarily submerged in the company structure. That structure is defined
by the *Companies Act 1948* and by the articles of association by which
shareholders agree to be bound. In most companies and in most contexts,
this definition is sufficient and exhaustive, equally so whether the company
is large or small. The "just and equitable" provision does not, as the respondents suggest, entitle one party to disregard the obligation he assumes
by entering a company, nor the court to dispense him from it. It does, as
equity always does, enable the court to subject the exercise of legal rights
to equitable considerations; considerations, that is, of a personal character
arising between one individual and another, which may make it unjust, or
inequitable, to insist on legal rights, or to exercise them in a particular way.

It would be impossible, and wholly undesirable, to define the circumstances in which these considerations may arise. Certainly the fact that a company is a small one, or a private company, is not enough. There are very many of these where the association is a purely commercial one, of which it can safely be said that the basis of association is adequately and exhaustively laid down in the articles. The superimposition of equitable considerations requires something more, which typically may include one, or probably more, of the following elements: (i) an association formed or continued on the basis of a personal relationship, involving mutual confidence — this element will often be found where a pre-existing partnership has been converted into a limited company; (ii) an agreement, or understanding, that all, or some (for there may be "sleeping" members), of the shareholders shall participate in the conduct of the business; (iii) restriction on the transfer of the members' interest in the company — so that if confidence is lost, or one member is removed from management, he cannot take out his stake and go elsewhere.

It is these, and analogous, factors which may bring into play the just and equitable clause, and they do so directly, through the force of the words themselves. To refer, as so many of the cases do, to "quasi-partnerships" or "'in substance partnerships" may be convenient but may also be confusing. It may be convenient because it is the law of partnership which has developed the conceptions of probity, good faith and mutual confidence, and the remedies where these are absent, which become relevant once such factors as I have mentioned are found to exist: the words "just and equitable" sum these up in the law of partnership itself. An in many, but not necessarily all, cases there has been a pre-existing partnership the obligations of which it is reasonable to suppose continue to underlie the new company structure. But the expressions may be confusing if they obscure, or deny, the fact that the parties (possibly former partners) are now co-members in a company, who have accepted, in law, new obligations. A company, however small, however domestic, is a company not a partnership or even a quasi-partnership and it is through the just and equitable clause that obligations, common to partnership relations, may come in.

My Lords, this is an expulsion case, and I must briefly justify the application in such cases of the just and equitable clause. The question is, as always, whether it is equitable to allow one (or two) to make use of his legal rights to the prejudice of his associate(s). The law of companies recognizes the right, in many ways, to remove a director from the board. Section 184 of the *Companies Act 1948* confers this right on the company in general meeting whatever the articles may say. Some articles may prescribe other methods, for example a governing director may have the power to remove (*cf. Re Wondoflex Textiles Pty Ltd.*). And quite apart from removal powers, there are normally provisions for retirement of directors by rotation so that their re-election can be opposed and defeated by a majority, or even by a casting vote. In all these ways a particular director-member may find himself no longer a director, through removal, or non-re-election: this situation he must normally accept, unless he undertakes the burden of proving fraud or *mala fides*. The just and equitable provision nevertheless comes to his assistance if he can point to, or prove, some special underlying obligation of his fellow member(s) in good faith, or confidence, that so long as the business continues he shall be entitled to management participation, an obligation so basic that if broken, the conclusion must be that the association must be dissolved. And the principles on which he may do so are those worked out by the courts in partnership cases where there has been exclusion from management (see *Const v. Harris*) even where under the partnership agreement there is a power of expulsion (see *Blisset v. Daniel* and *Lindley on Partnership*).

I come to the facts of this case. It is apparent enough that a potential basis for a winding-up order under the just and equitable clause existed. The appellant after a long association in partnership, during which he had an equal share in the management, joined in the formation of the company. The inference must be indisputable that he, and Mr. Nazar, did so on the basis that the character of the association would, as a matter of personal relation and in good faith, remain the same. He was removed from his directorship under a power valid in law. Did he establish, a case which, if he had remained in a partnership with a term providing for expulsion, would have justified an order for dissolution? This was the essential question for the judge. Plowman J. dealt with the issue in a brief paragraph in which he said:

> while no doubt the petitioner was lawfully removed, in the sense that he ceased in law to be a director, it does not follow that in removing him the respondents did not do him a wrong. In my judgment, they did do him a wrong, in the sense that it was an abuse of power and a breach of good faith which partners owe to each other to exclude one of them from all participation in the business on which they have embarked on the basis that all should participate in its management. The main justification put forward for removing him was that he was perpetually complaining, but the faults were not all on one side and, in my judgment, this is not sufficient justification. For these reasons, in my judgment, the petitioner therefore has made out a case for a winding-up order.

Reading this in the context of the judgment as a whole, which had dealt with the specific complaints of one side against the other, I take it as a finding that the respondents were not entitled, in justice and equity, to make use of their legal powers of expulsion and that, in accordance with the principles of such cases as *Blisset v. Daniel*, the only just and equitable course was to dissolve the association. To my mind, two factors strongly support this. First, Mr. Nazar made it perfectly clear that he did not regard the appellant as a partner; but did regard him as an employee. But there was no possible doubt as to the appellant's status throughout, so that Mr. Nazar's refusal to recognize it amounted, in effect, to a repudiation of the relationship. Secondly, the appellant, through ceasing to be a director, lost his right to share in the profits through directors' remuneration, retaining only the chance of receiving dividends as a minority shareholder. True that an assurance was given in evidence that the previous practice (of not paying dividends) would not be continued, but the fact remains that the appellant was henceforth at the mercy of the Messrs. Nazar as to what he should receive out of the profits and when. He was, moreover, unable to dispose of his interest without the consent of the Nazars. All these matters lead only to the conclusion that the right course was to dissolve the association by winding-up.

I must deal with one final point which was much relied on by the Court of Appeal. It was said that the removal was, according to the evidence of Mr. Nazar, *bona fide* in the interests of the company, that the appellant had not shown the contrary, that he ought to do so or to demonstrate that no reasonable man could think that his removal was in the company's interest. This formula, "*bona fide* in the interests of the company" is one that is relevant in certain contexts of company law and I do not doubt that in many cases decisions have to be left to majorities or directors to take which the courts must assume had this basis. It may, on the other hand, become little more than an alibi for a refusal to consider the merits of the case, and in a situation such as this it seems to have little meaning other than "in the interests of the majority". Mr. Nazar may well have persuaded himself, quite genuinely, that the company would be better off without the appellant but the appellant disputed this, or thought the same with reference to Mr. Nazar, what prevails is simply the majority view. To confine the application of the just and equitable clause to proved cases of mala fides would be to negative the generality of the words. It is because I do not accept this that I feel myself obliged to differ from the Court of Appeal.

I would allow the appeal and restore the judgment of Plowman J. I propose that the individual respondents pay the appellant's costs here and in the Court of Appeal.

Appeal allowed.

Note

1 The "just and equitable" ground for winding up is a common statutory provision that appears, for example, in the CBCA (s.214(1)(b)(ii)). As noted by Lord Wilberforce, the courts have fashioned a number of doctrinal categories that justify a "just and equitable winding up": "loss of substratum", "justifiable lack of confidence", "deadlock" and "the partnership analogy". In *Ebrahimi*, Lord Wilberforce granted the winding up on the basis of the partnership analogy.

2 You will note that while Lord Wilberforce recognizes that in small or private corporations "equitable considerations" may arise that alter the strict legal bargain of the parties, he is careful to confine this to the

context of a just and equitable winding up. Canadian courts have simply ignored this limitation and have transposed the expectations principle holus bolus to the oppression remedy, although mostly with respect to *private* rather than *public* companies.

3 Lord Wilberforce also suggested that to invoke the expectations principle, "the superimposition of equitable considerations" will typically require that the association be formed or continued on the basis of a personal relationship involving mutual confidence, an agreement that some or all of the shareholders participate in the conduct of the business, and restrictions on the transferability of the shares. While Canadian courts will typically take these and similar factors into account in deciding whether there has been oppression in the case of a private company, they are not regarded as essential *indicia* of oppression.

4 The following case indicates the extent to which early judicial attempts to create a fiduciary duty for shareholders have been revived under the oppression remedy.

Ferguson v. Imax Systems Corp.
(1983), 150 D.L.R. (3d) 718 (Ont. C.A.)

BROOKE J.A.: The appellant seeks relief under s. 234 of the *Canada Business Corporations Act*, 1974-75-76 (Can.), c. 33. She alleges that Imax Corporation (the company), in attempting by a special resolution to amend its articles to reorganize its capital, is acting in a manner that is oppressive, unfairly prejudicial, or that unfairly disregards her interests as a security holder. She alleges that the powers of the directors of the company have been exercised in a similar fashion with the same results.

As a result the appellant sought an injunction to restrain the company from holding a special meeting to vote on the resolution, or failing that, other similar relief. She contends that the effect of the resolution would be the redemption of her class B non-redeemable shares and that the resolution was designed to, and would, in fact, put her out of the company because she was the only holder of class B shares without any other share interest through which she could participate in the company's growth which now seems certain.

Hollingworth J. dismissed her application: see 12 B.L.R. 209. He reviewed the evidence, made few findings of fact, and dismissed the application holding that a case of oppression had not been made out. However, pursuant to s. 184(4) of the Act he appointed an appraiser to assist the court in fixing fair value for the class B shares. Both parties appealed. The company appealed to the Divisional Court from the order appointing the appraiser and the appellant cross-appealed from the order dismissing her application for injunction.

On a motion to quash the cross-appeal on the grounds that it was brought in the wrong court, the Divisional Court adjourned that appeal to this court: see 34 O.R. (2d) 298, 130 D.L.R. (3d) 280. The Divisional Court allowed the company's appeal on the grounds that on a motion under s. 234 of the Act there was no jurisdiction to make an order under s. 184(4): see 38 O.R. (2d) 59, 134 D.L.R. (3d) 519, 28 C.P.C. 290. Leave to appeal to this court from that judgment was granted and the matter is before us. However, in view of the conclusion which I have reached, it will be unnecessary to deal with that appeal.

There was no trial of the issues below, rather the parties proceeded offering their evidence by way of affidavit and the transcripts of the cross-examination on the affidavits.

The facts are as follows. The company was incorporated in 1967 to exploit a patented film projection system. On the evidence, the promoters of the company were Ivan Graeme Ferguson, R. Kerr, R. Kroiter, and Betty June Ferguson, the appellant, who was the wife of Ivan Graeme Ferguson. The first shareholders were three couples, Mr. and Mrs. Ferguson, Mr. and Mrs. Kroiter, and Mr. and Mrs. Kerr. Mrs. Kroiter was Mr. Ferguson's sister and Mr. Kerr had been Mr. Ferguson's friend from school days.

Shares were issued and allotted equally among the three couples so that each family's holdings were the same. Each husband received 700 shares of the common stock of the company and each wife received 700 shares of the class B stock of the company. The shares of the class B stock were nonredeemable and entitled the holder to receive in priority to the common shares a non-cumulative cash dividend at the rate of 5¢ per share per year and thereafter the class B shares participated equally as to dividends with the common shares and in the event of liquidation, dissolution or winding-up. However, the class B shares were non-voting unless the company failed to pay the 50 dividend for two consecutive years. The capital structure of the company also provided for class A preference shares, none of which was ever issued.

It is of some importance to the appellant that, unlike the other two wives who apparently at no time did any work for the company, she worked hard in the company's interest and was one of its founders together with the three men. It is really not disputed that in the early days of the company the three men were each employed in other endeavors and could not devote their full time to the company.

The appellant was a film editor and had knowledge of the film business. Her evidence is that she took part with the three men in the decision to buy the patent and after the company was incorporated, participated in its management and administration. During those years, unlike the other two wives, the appellant participated in the day-to-day administration of the business. Indeed, she assumed full responsibility for an office that the company operated in New York City from the date of the company's incorporation until that office was closed in 1970. To a large extent she was not compensated for her work and efforts but carried on to help the company in which she had an ownership-interest.

During those years there were apparently agreements entered into between the members of the three families. The effect of the agreements was that in the event that a wife predeceased her husband her shares would pass to him, and in the event of his death that his shares and those of his wife would be sold to the surviving male shareholders. The appellant said that she signed the agreement because her husband told her that the company was near bankruptcy and that the agreement was needed to satisfy financiers. However, the agreements also secured the control of the company within the three families.

After the office in New York was closed, some of its records were moved to the appellant's home here and thereafter she did some of the company's business from there and, at the same time, worked as a film editor on a feature film produced by the company.

About this time each of the husbands and the wives agreed to reduce their shareholding and each transferred 70 shares of his or her stock to a valued employee, Mr. William Shaw, as an incentive for him to remain with the company. During that period Mrs. Kerr transferred her shares to her husband and the company issued further shares to some small investors but significantly each investor, as in the case of each family, held an equal number of both common and class B shares. The result was that at the time material to these proceedings, the company had issued an outstanding 2,069.57 shares of both classes of stock. The list of shareholders was as follows:

SHAREHOLDERS	COMMON SHARES		CLASS "B" PREFERENCE SHARES	
	No.	Percent	No.	Percent
Graeme Ferguson	630	24.14%		
B. Ferguson			630	24.14%
R. Kroiter	563	21.57%		
J. Kroiter			563	21.57%
R. Kerr	630	24.14%	630	24.14%
W. Shaw	340	13.03%	340	13.03%
S. Daymond	89	3.14%	89	3.14%
C.W. Breukelman	22	.84%	22	.84%
Executronics Limited	111	4.25%	111	4.25%
S. Daymond, C.W. Breukelman, Executronics Limited	1	.04%	1	.04%
Canmount Investment Corp. Ltd.	33.5	1.28%	33.5	1.28%
Forden Investments Ltd.	33.5	1.28%	33.5	1.28%
J. Chaplin	156.57	6.00%	156.57	6.00%

In 1972 the appellant and her husband separated. In 1974 they were divorced. At that time the company was emerging from its financial difficulties and in 1974 made a profit of some $72,000. In the years that followed the respondent agrees that the net income of the company was improved and the respondent's figures show its progress to be as follows:

1975: $104,263
1976: $51,432
1977: $132,935
1978: $210,775 (this figure was calculated in accordance with different accounting policies than those used previously)
1979: $165,696 ($454,647 had the respondent continued to follow its pre-1978 accounting policies in this year)

The appellant contends that the company is enjoying good profits. She relies on the evidence of an expert called for the purpose of making an evaluation of the Class B shares and contends that the accounting principles used in 1979 were changed and resulted in lower profits than would have been shown had the principles used in previous years been applied on a consistent basis. The expert had expressed the opinion that the compensation offered at the rate of $175 for each class B share was premised on an overly conservative capitalization rate. Moreover, the evaluation assumed a cash flow for 1979 or approximately $190,000 whereas the actual figure in the financial statement of the company for the year showed a cash flow of approximately $1,000,000 or over five times the amount assumed for the purpose of the evaluation.

Mr. Justice Hollingworth was obviously left in some doubt as to the proper value of the shares and ordered that an appraiser be appointed to determine the issue. However, one thing that clearly emerges is that the company had turned the corner after 1974 and now was a profitable organization, with its position improving each year. In addition, the evidence disclosed that substantial salaries and expenses were paid to the three men who now ran the company to the exclusion of the appellant.

It is the appellant's contention that from the time of her separation Mr. Ferguson set out to put her out of the company, to get her shares and to see to it that she did not participate in any benefits from the growth of the company. He was unwilling to permit her to continue as a shareholder and, she contends, as the dominant person in the control group and as the company's president and a director, he put pressure on the others in the group and the directors to squeeze her out.

The fact is that shortly after Ms. Ferguson separated from her husband she was discharged by the company. It is her evidence that during negotiation of their separation agreement her husband tried to get her to sell or transfer her shares to him but she refused. She said, and it is not denied, that he took the position in negotiations that it would not be in the interests of the company to have non-working shareholders. The contention was obviously untenable having regard to the share position of each of Mrs. Kroiter and Mrs. Kerr at that time.

It was the appellant's evidence that Mr. Ferguson put heavy pressure on the company not to declare dividends and that by virtue of his close friendship with his fellow officers, directors and shareholders, Mr. Kerr, Mr. Shaw, and Mr. Kroiter, he was able to prevent the declaration of dividends and so her participation in the financial growth of the company. It is a fact that, save for the 50 per share preferred dividend on the class B shares, no dividends were declared or paid by the company down to the date that the notice of the meeting to alter the corporation's share structure was delivered although, on the evidence of its earnings and the financial statements, it seems probable that the company was in a position to pay dividends.

It was the appellant's evidence, and it was uncontested, that in 1977 she was told by Mr. Kerr, who was then a director, that the company would not declare dividends because Mr. Ferguson refused to have her share equally with him in corporate distributions. Subsequently, in 1978, she says she was told by Mr. Breukelman and Mr. Kerr that she should sell her shares as her husband would prevent a declaration of dividends so long as she remained a shareholder. On being pressed on this issue in cross-examination she said:

Q. Can you recall anything else that occurred at that conversation?
A. Yes, it was a very long conversation.
Q. What else can you recall?
A. Well, I told him, I did not want to sell my shares and I said, did I have to in order for William to get more percentage of the company. He said, no, that the company could issue more shares, which they have done. It was very long. Do you want to hear it all, the whole conversation. It went on for a very long time. I'd be happy to go through it. Anyway, he said, that the company — he wanted the company to issue dividends because there were people that did not work in the company, for instance his close friend Jim Chaplin who had invested in the company, and the company wanted to issue dividends, but they couldn't because I would share equally in the same amount of money that Graeme got. That made him very unhappy.
Mr. Manes: Made who unhappy?
The Deponent: Graeme Ferguson, unhappy that I would get equal amount of dividends that he got. Therefore, he was putting pressure on Robert and everybody not to issue dividends. That they wanted to issue dividends because people like Daymond and his close friend Jim Chaplin were not getting anything out of the company for their investments because they were not paying dividends. He said, he didn't personally care about the difference between class B and Preference Shares because he held both Class B and Common Shares and everybody else in the company also held both Class B and Common Shares. Graeme's sister held only Class B, Preferred Shares, but her husband held the Common Shares so everybody else in that company it does

not effect what happens to the Class B shares because they will get the money out of the company through the Common Shares. And he said, you know, if we don't pay dividends we can take it out in salaries or expense accounts, but that it wasn't — he felt badly about Jim Chaplin not getting any money for his investment in the company, if the company would not pay dividends and that is why they wanted me to sell my shares.

By Mrs. Block:

Q. Are you saying, that in order to sell, in order to give Shaw more shares, Kerr was proposing that you sell all of your 630 shares to Shaw?

A. He did not put it that way, no. He said, would I sell my Imax Shares and the gist of the conversation was, would I sell because Graeme would not allow the company to pay dividends. You know, he said they could issue more shares to Bill Shaw and they could, but they didn't need my shares in order to give Bill Shaw more shares. The reason they wanted me to sell out was because they wanted to be able to pay dividends and Graeme did not want any dividends being paid because I would share equally with him. He worked in the company. He felt he worked very hard in the company. I was no longer working in the company. I said, "Look Robert, when I divorced Graeme", and I had to divorce him. He brought a young woman home and committed adultery in my living room and it was damaging to my children.

Mr. Manes: I don't think we have to go through that.

The Deponent: That's why I had to divorce him and them I'm not loose, I'm forced from the company for divorcing him. Now they're saying I'm not entitled to dividends because I'm not working in the company, but you know Jim Chaplin doesn't work in the company and they want to see him get dividends. Roman Kroiter is at the film board. You know, his shares are in, what do you call it, escrow or they're being held because he works for the government, but they don't mind him getting a part of the company, it's only me that isn't. That they don't want to pay dividends to.

By Mrs. Block:

Q. In respect of the contribution of shares to Shaw, what did Kerr say to you about giving some of your shares to Shaw? Was he talking about giving all of your shares or some of your shares to Shaw?

A. He didn't say anything about giving shares to Bill Shaw.

Q. I mean selling.

A. He said, would I sell my Imax shares, that they wanted to issue Bill Shaw some more shares in the company and I said, "Well do I have to sell my shares in order for Bill to get more shares in the company", and he said, no that the company could issue more shares, and they have as far as I understand it. You can look that up, it's right in there that they issued him more shares.

Q. So you say that you were never asked to sell part of your shares as
the other shareholders were willing to do to give Bill Shaw participation?
A. I was never told that other shareholders were willing to do that. I
was asked if I would sell my shares. I said, no I absolutely did not want
to sell my shares. I would not.

This evidence is not denied. Having regard to the whole of the cross-
examination and the affidavit material, I am satisfied that what she says is
true. The company could pay dividends. Mr. Ferguson set out to stop the
payment because he did not want Mrs. Ferguson to share in the benefits in
the growth of the company and wanted to force her to sell her shares to him
or to one of the other men in the company. It was argued that he was but
one shareholder and one director and alone could not stop the company
from the payment of dividends. But the fact is that he did so. Mr. Kerr, Mr.
Shaw, and Mr. Kroiter were his friends and close to him and from the
evidence of Mrs. Ferguson it is clear that they yielded to the pressure that
he brought on them to bring about this result. In my opinion this conduct
was oppressive and unfair to her.

The event leading to this litigation was the delivery of a notice of a
special meeting of shareholders which the plaintiff received on November
16, 1979. The resolution proposed to be voted on at the special meeting was
one that in effect would cancel and convert all of the class B non-redeemable
shares into class A shares. Those shares would, until 1984, be non-voting
and limited to 9% cumulated dividends. Thereafter the shares would be
redeemed by the company at a designated value of $175 per share plus any
unpaid cumulated dividends. That value was set as of November 9, 1979,
and was based on an evaluation prepared for the company. The resolution
also provided for removing the limitation on the number of shares that might
be issued by the company.

In the notice of the meeting the company explained the purpose of the
resolution and said in an information circular that the purpose of the change
was:

The amendment of the Corporation's articles as contemplated by the
special resolution is being proposed in order to enable the Corporation
to more effectively plan for future growth, through the provision of a
simpler equity structure, while providing to the holders of preference
shares of the Corporation a predictable and substantial cash flow —
both by way of cumulative cash dividends and by way of redemption
of shares — over the period through to February 29, 1984. The share
provisions will also afford the holders of preference shares the opportunity to sell such shares to the Corporation at a specified price in the
event of certain changes in control of the Corporation.

There was no evidence by way of affidavit or otherwise from the president or a director of the company or anyone as to why the resolution had been put before the shareholders. However, there was an affidavit by an expert in corporation management finance who said that five benefits which might flow from such a resolution were:

(a) it removes limits on the number of common shares which may be issued and the consideration for which they may be issued resulting in increased financing flexibility;

(b) it provides the Respondent with "a cleaner capital structure";

(c) it provides Class B Preference shareholders with a certain and very attractive return on their investment;

(d) it permits the orderly retirement of non-participating shares, assuring new investors that their equity participation will be equal to their voting power;

(e) the new capital structure facilitates the use of equity participation incentives as a means of attracting middle and upper management people to the Respondent.

This evidence, although giving a possible explanation for the corporate reorganization, does not give the reasons that motivated those in management and so does not refute the inference of unfairness.

A review of the finances of the company as revealed by the evidence indicates that it is profitable and should continue to be so and that it may be timely for the company to redeem some of its equity holding. Nevertheless, in my opinion, these facts do not insulate the company from dealing fairly with the appellant who is a minority shareholder.

The policy of the law to ensure just and equitable treatment of minorities can be traced back to early cases. In *Allen v. Gold Reefs of West Africa, Ltd.*, [1900] 1 Ch. 656 at p. 671, Lindley M.R., speaking of the powers of a corporation to amend its articles, said:

it must, like all other powers, be exercised subject to those general principles of law and equity which are applicable to all powers conferred on majorities and enabling them to bind minorities. It must be exercised, not only in the manner required by law, but also *bona fide* for the benefit of the company as a whole, and it must not be exceeded.

In *Goldex Mines Ltd. v. Revill et al.* (1974), 7 O.R. (2d) 216 at p. 224, 54 D.L.R. (3d) 672 at p. 680, Arnup J.A. for this court, after considering the earlier cases, said:

The principle that the majority governs in corporate affairs is fundamental to corporation law, but its corollary is also important —

that the majority must act fairly and honestly. Fairness is the touchstone of equitable justice and when the test of fairness is not met, the equitable jurisdiction of the court can be invoked to prevent or remedy the injustice which misrepresentation or other dishonesty has caused.

But s. 234 must not be regarded as being simply a codification of the common law. Today one looks to the section when considering the interests of the minority shareholders and the section should be interpreted broadly to carry out its purpose: see the *Interpretation Act*, R.S.C. 1970, c. I-23, s. 11. Accordingly, when dealing with a close corporation, the court may consider the relationship between the shareholders and not simply legal rights as such. In addition, the court must consider the *bona fides* of the corporate transaction in question to determine whether the act of the corporation or directors effects a result which is oppressive or unfairly prejudicial to the minority shareholder. Counsel has referred us to a number of decisions. They establish primarily that each case turns on its own facts. What is oppressive or unfairly prejudicial in one case may not necessarily be so in the slightly different setting of another.

Here we have a small close corporation that was promoted and is still controlled by the same small related group of individuals. The appellant's part in that group and her work for the corporation is important. Further, the attempt to force her to sell her shares through non-payment of dividends was not simply the act of Mr. Ferguson, but was also the act of the others in the group including the present director, in concert with him. Having regard to the intention of that group to deny the appellant any participation in the growth of the company I think the resolution authorizing the change in the capital of the company is the culminating event in a lengthy course of oppressive and unfairly prejudicial conduct to the appellant. In my opinion the company has not acted *bona fides* in exercising its powers to amend. By the payment of moneys now as a capital payment, which moneys on the evidence ought to have been by way of dividends over the years the appellant's non-redeemable shares are now to be redeemed and those in control of the company will be rid of her. She is the only one so affected. All of the other class B shareholders hold an equal number of common shares personally or through their spouses. The appellant cannot be considered like someone who came to the company lately and took a minority position in one of several classes of stock. Like the Kroiters and the Kerrs, her investment must be regarded as being in the shares which she and her husband held. The agreements as to the disposition of family shares in the event of the death of the husband or the wife confirm that this was really a family venture not only in the case of the Fergusons but for each of the three couples.

Viewed in this way, and as all of the other class B shareholders held an equal number of common shares either personally or with their spouses, it is idle to suggest that the vote on the resolution would be anything other than a means to get moneys which they had eagerly sought by way of dividends but were denied because of the appellant's presence and as a means to end her presence as an obstacle to further payment. I doubt if any corporate purpose would enter the minds of the class B shareholders when the resolution was put to them to vote on. The resolution was a final solution to the problem of the ex-wife shareholder.

In my opinion the appellant satisfied the onus upon her when relying on s. 234 of the Act and she was entitled to the relief sought in the first instance. We have been advised that a motion to prohibit the company from proceeding with the meeting of shareholders to vote on the resolution was dismissed by Holland J. and accordingly the vote was held and its outcome was as predicted. In the circumstances the appeal is allowed. The order of Hollingworth J. dismissing the appellant's claim and appointing an assessor pursuant to s. 184(4) of the Act is set aside and an order will go forever prohibiting the company from implementing the resolution.

The appellant will have her costs in this court and in all of the proceedings below.

Appeal allowed.

Notes

1 One of the difficulties that courts have encountered under the oppression remedy has been how to fit majority or controlling shareholders into a section that deals nominally only with the conduct of "the corporation" and "the directors". *Ferguson* is illustrative of one of the ways in which courts have finessed this issue. While, strictly speaking, a shareholder resolution does not amount to *corporate* conduct, once the corporation acts upon that resolution, it converts shareholder conduct into corporate conduct — which falls squarely within the purview of the oppression remedy. This device is implicitly used in *Ferguson*. While the court consistently refers to the unfair conduct that occurred as conduct of the *company*, it is clear that the court is effectively discussing the conduct of the coalition of shareholders that comprised a controlling interest.

2 Note also that, however the court arrives at its finding of oppression, the oppression remedy specifically allows the court to make orders against a controlling shareholder. See, *e.g.*, CBCA s.241(3)(f), (g). In fact, the commonest remedy given under the oppression remedy is an order that a controlling shareholder purchase the shares of the complaining minority. See, *e.g.*, *Miller v. F. Mendel Holdings Ltd.* (1984), 26 B.L.R. 85 (Sask. Q.B.); *National Building Maintenance Ltd. v. Dove*, [1972] 5 W.W.R. 410 (B.C. C.A.). Since "the court may make any interim or final order it thinks fit", a judge may make other orders against controlling shareholders as well. See generally Jeffrey G. MacIntosh, "Corporations", in *Law Society of Upper Canada, Special Lectures, 1990: Fiduciary Duties*, 189.

3 Under the oppression provision, a complainant may complain about conduct not only of the corporation, but "of any of its affiliates". Thus, *corporate* controllers that possess *de jure* control (and, hence, qualify as "affiliates") fall directly within the purview of the oppression remedy.

4 As an exercise, work through the interlocking set of definitions in the CBCA defining the term "affiliate", to see how they restrict the concept of affiliate to *de jure* controlling corporations.

5 Corporations that are not *de jure* controllers (and, hence, affiliates) can be brought within the oppression provision by any of the other means indicated in these cases and notes. However, the case that immediately follows these notes suggests yet another way in which controlling shareholder conduct can be attacked — via the conduct of interlocking directors.

6 Note also how *Ferguson* relies on both *Allen v. Gold Reefs of West Africa* and *Goldex Mines v. Revill* in holding that Betty Ferguson had been treated *unfairly*. This demonstrates the extent to which the courts have used the oppression remedy to revive doctrines that *Brant v. Keeprite* otherwise appears to have put to rest. More generally, the oppression remedy has served the function of breaking the old pro-majoritarian paradigm of shareholder relations and substituting a new, more balanced view of controller/minority relations. See generally Jeffrey G. MacIntosh, Janet Holmes and Steve Thompson, "The Puzzle of Shareholder Fiduciary Duties" (1991) 19 Can. Bus. L.J. 86.

7 Under the oppression remedy, however, *Allen* has been revived with a twist. Recall that in *Allen*, the court imposed a duty of "good faith" on the majority shareholder. In *Ferguson*, the court found that the company had not acted in good faith and so had breached the *Allen* duty. However, the balance of authority favours the view that a showing of bad faith is not a prerequisite to demonstrating oppression. All that is required that the conduct in question *effect a result* that is unfair. See, *e.g.*, *Brant v. Keeprite*, *supra*. Thus, the same result that is achieved in *Ferguson* could be reached even without a finding of bad faith conduct. However, *Ferguson* suggests that a showing of *bad faith* is almost certain to lead to a finding of oppression. See generally Jeffrey G. MacIntosh, "Bad faith and the Oppression Remedy: Uneasy Marriage or Amicable Divorce?" (1990) 69 Can. Bar Rev. 276.

8 Note also how in *Ferguson* the court sidesteps the limitations (noted above in the excerpt from MacIntosh) that the courts had placed on the good faith principle in *Allen*. The first was that the court was to decide the issue of whether the shareholders had acted in good faith from the point of view of the shareholders themselves, unless the conduct was "so oppressive as to cast suspicion on the honesty of the persons responsible for it, or so extravagant that no reasonable men could really consider it for the benefit of the company". By contrast, it is now clear that the fairness standard under the oppression remedy is to be judged objectively, from the court's perspective (hence, the absence of a need

to show bad faith). As the Ontario Court of Appeal stated in *Pente Investment Management Ltd. v. Schneider Corp.* (1998), 42 O.R. (3d) 177, 1998 CarswellOnt 4035 (C.A.), "[w]hile s. 248 protects the legitimate expectations of shareholders, those expectations must be reasonable in the circumstances and reasonableness is to be ascertained on an objective basis".

9 Note also that after *Allen*, the idea that shareholder "discriminatory" conduct could be set aside was restricted to situations in which there was some *legal* difference in the manner in which the controller and the majority were treated. However, in *Imax*, Betty Ferguson was affected in precisely the same *legal* manner as every other shareholder — even though the economic effect on her of the change in the articles was unique. The court thus effectively adopts a definition of discrimination that parallels that in the human rights cases, i.e., formally identical legal treatment may amount to illegal discrimination if it has a disparate impact on different individuals or groups.

10 *Ferguson* also imports the idea from *Ebrahimi* that (in Mr. Justice Brooks' words) "when dealing with a close [i.e., private] corporation, the court may consider the relationship between the shareholders and not simply legal rights as such". In essence, *Fersuson* fuses Lord Wilberforce's "equitable considerations" with the idea of "fairness" under the oppression remedy. This fusion is made even more explicit in the decision of the Ontario Court of Appeal in *Pente Investment Management Ltd. v. Schneider Corp.* (1998), 42 O.R. (3d) 177, 1998 CarswellOnt 4035 (C.A.). The court stated:

> Conduct which disregards the interests of any shareholder and not simply a shareholder's legal rights will infringe s. 248 of the OBCA [the oppression remedy]. This is because the oppression remedy is basically an equitable remedy and the court has jurisdiction to find an action is oppressive, unfairly prejudicial, or unfairly taken in disregard of the interests of a security holder if it is wrongful, even if it is not actually unlawful: *Westfair Foods Ltd. v. Watt* (1990), 4 W.W.R. 685 (Alta. Q.B.), aff'd (1991) 4 W.W.R. 695 (Alta. C.A.), leave to appeal refused [1991] 2 S.C.R. viii.

Scottish Co-operative Wholesale Society Ltd. v. Meyer
(1958), [1959] A.C. 324, [1958] 3 All E.R. 66 (H.L.)

Scottish Co-operative, the parent company, formed a subsidiary to enter the rayon business. In organizing the business, the parent employed Meyer, making him managing director of the subsidiary and one of its substantial stockholders in order to have the benefit of his expertise and business contacts. The parent, however, retained fifty-one percent of the shares and control of the board of directors. At the end of five years, Meyer was no longer needed for the successful operation of the business, and the parent, in an effort to force him out, established its own department to perform the subsidiary's tasks. At the same time, the parent's nominees on the subsidiary's board passively supported the parent by allowing the subsidiary's traditional activities to decline.

LORD DENNING: My Lords, I had myself prepared a summary of the material facts in this case but, in view of the comprehensive statement by my noble and learned friend, Lord Keith of Avonholm, I will not burden your Lordships with what I had written. I would only say that I am sorry that the events of 1952 were excluded as irrelevant. Dr. Meyer and Mr. Lucas from the very beginning put those events in the forefront of their complaints. They did so in the first letter of their solicitors dated February 19, 1953, and in the original petition lodged on July 14, 1953. The burden of their complaints was that, when there was a recession in 1952 in the rayon trade, they — Dr. Meyer and Mr. Lucas — tried, on behalf of the textile company, to develop trade in other goods: particularly in the export of woollen materials to Germany (where they had valuable trade connections) and in a large export order for £60,000: but that they were thwarted in their efforts by the actions of two of the nominee directors, who tried to get the trade for the Scottish Co-operative Wholesale Society itself. Whether these complaints be true or not your Lordships cannot know — because these allegations were excluded from probation. But your Lordships have, I think, sufficient material to decide the case on the other facts which were proved.

The complaints which were established were, I think, these: The co-operative society set up a competing business. It established its own merchant converting department, engaged in the rayon trade itself, and quoted more favorable terms to its own department than it did to the textile company. It is said that the co-operative society did this with intent to injure the textile company — to depress the value of its shares so that the co-operative society could get them cheap — but I would not myself go as far as this. It seems to me that the co-operative society all the time was seeking to promote its own interests. It was ready in 1946 to enlist the co-operation of Dr. Meyer and Mr. Lucas when they were useful to it — so as to get an introduction into the rayon trade — but it was ready to throw them over when they were no longer useful. By which I mean that it was ready to withdraw all support from them. That was, I think, the state of mind of the co-operative society right from the moment in November, 1951, when Dr. Meyer and Mr. Lucas refused to realign the shares at par. At that time the rayon trade was in a recession and Dr. Meyer and Mr. Lucas were not of so much use to the society as they had been. By the time the rayon trade revived, the controls were off and the co-operative society was able to engage in rayon production itself — and it had no further need of Dr. Meyer and Mr. Lucas or of the textile company. It had its own department for rayon. So the textile company could go to the wall. It had "served its purpose" — or rather the purpose of the co-operative society — and could be let go into liquidation. The co-operative society had not the voting power to put it into voluntary liquidation. But liquidation might come about by sheer inanition. So it came about that, when Dr. Meyer and Mr. Lucas in January, 1953, offered to sell their shares to the co-operative society at a price to be negotiated (mentioning 96s.), the co-operative society refused "at the present time." The co-operative society thought, perhaps, that, if they waited, sooner or later liquidation would come about, or that terms of purchase would be arranged later more favorable to the co-operative society than paying 96s. a share.

Such being "the matters complained of" by Dr. Meyer and Mr. Lucas, it is said: "Those are all complaints about the conduct of the co-operative society. How do they touch the real issue — the manner in which the affairs of the textile company were being conducted?" The answer is, I think, by their impact on the nominee directors. It must be remembered that we are here concerned with the manner in which the affairs of the textile company were being conducted. That is, with the conduct of those in control of its affairs. They may be some of the directors themselves, or, behind them, a group of shareholders who nominate those directors or whose interests those directors serve. If those persons — the nominee directors or the shareholders behind them — conduct the affairs of the company in a manner oppressive to the other shareholders, the court can intervene to bring an end to the oppression.

What, then, is the position of the nominee directors here? Under the articles of association of the textile company the co-operative society was entitled to nominate three out of the five directors, and it did so. It nominated three of its own directors and they held office, as the articles said, "as nominees" of the co-operative society. These three were therefore at one and the same time directors of the co-operative society — being three out of 12 of that company — and also directors of the textile company — three out of five there. So long as the interests of all concerned were in harmony, there was no difficulty. The nominee directors could do their duty by both companies without embarrassment. But, so soon as the interests of the two companies were in conflict, the nominee directors were placed in an impossible position. Thus, when the realignment of shareholders was under discussion, the duty of the three directors to the textile company was to get the best possible price for any new issue of its shares (see *per* Lord Wright in *Lowry v. Consolidated African Selection Trust Ltd.*), whereas their duty to the co-operative society was to obtain the new shares at the lowest possible price — at par, if they could. Again, when the co-operative society determined to set up its own rayon department, competing with the business of the textile company, the duty of the three directors to the textile company was to do their best to promote its business and to act with complete good faith towards it; and in consequence not to disclose their knowledge of its affairs to a competitor, and not even to work for a competitor, when to do so might operate to the disadvantage of the textile company (see *Hivac Ltd.*

v. Park Royal Scientific Instruments Ltd.), whereas they were under the self-same duties to the co-operative society. It is plain that, in the circumstances, these three gentlemen could not do their duty by both companies, and they did not do so. They put their duty to the cooperative society above their duty to the textile company in this sense, at least, that they did nothing to defend the interests of the textile company against the conduct of the co-operative society. They probably thought that "as nominees" of the co-operative society their first duty was to the co-operative society. In this they were wrong. By subordinating the interests of the textile company to those of the co-operative society, they conducted the affairs of the textile company in a manner oppressive to the other shareholders.

It is said that these three directors were at most only guilty of inaction — of doing nothing to protect the textile company. But the affairs of a company can, in my opinion, be conducted oppressively by the directors doing nothing to defend its interests when they ought to do something — just as they can conduct its affairs oppressively by doing something injurious to its interests when they ought not to do it.

The question was asked: "What could these directors have done?" They could, I suggest, at least on behalf of the textile company, have protested against the conduct of the co-operative society. They could have protested against the setting up of a competing business. But then it was said: "What good would that have done?" Any protest by them would be sure to have been unavailing, seeing that they were in a minority on the board of the cooperative society. The answer is that no one knows whether it would have done any good. They never did protest. And it does not come well from their mouths to say it would have done no good, when they never put it to the test. See the decision of this House in *Morison, Pollexfen & Blair Ltd. v. Walton*, as described by Scrutton L.J. in *Coldman v. Hill.* Even if they had protested, it might have been a formal gesture, ostensibly correct, but not to be taken seriously.

Your Lordships were referred to *Bell v. Lever Brothers Ltd.*, where Lord Blanesburgh said that a director of one company was at liberty to become a director also of a rival company. That may have been so at that time. But it is at the risk now of an application under s. 210 if he subordinates the interests of the one company to those of the other.

So I would hold that the affairs of the textile company were being conducted in a manner oppressive to Dr. Meyer and Mr. Lucas. The crucial date is, I think, the date on which the petition was lodged — July 14, 1953. If Dr. Meyer and Mr. Lucas had at that time lodged a petition to wind up the company compulsorily, the petition would undoubtedly have been granted. The facts would plainly justify such an order on the ground that it was "just and equitable" that the company should be wound up: see *In re Yenidje Tobacco Co. Ltd.* But such an order would unfairly prejudice Dr. Meyer and Mr. Lucas because they would only recover the break-up value of their shares. So instead of petitioning for a winding-up order, they seek to invoke the new remedy given by s. 210 of the *Companies Act 1948.* But what is the appropriate remedy? It was said that s. 210 only applies as an alternative to winding up and that an order can only be made under s. 210 if the company is fit to be kept alive: whereas in this case the business of the company was virtually at an end when the petition was lodged, and there was no point in keeping it alive. If the co-operative society were ordered, in these circumstances, to buy the shares of Dr. Meyer and Mr. Lucas, this would amount, it was said, to an award of damages for past misconduct — which is not the remedy envisaged by s. 210.

Now, I quite agree that the words of the section do suggest that the legislature had in mind some remedy whereby the company, instead of being wound up, might continue to operate. But it would be wrong to infer therefrom that the remedy under section 210 is limited to cases where the company is still in active business. The object of the remedy is to bring "to an end the matters complained of", that is, the oppression, and this can be done even though the business of the company has been brought to a standstill. If a remedy is available when the oppression is so moderate that it only inflicts wounds on the company, whilst leaving it active, so also it should be available when the oppression is so great as to put the company out of action altogether. Even though the oppressor by his oppression brings down the whole edifice — destroying the value of his own shares with those of everyone else — the injured shareholders have, I think, a remedy under s. 210.

One of the most useful orders mentioned in the section — which will enable the court to do justice to the injured shareholders — is to order the oppressor to buy their shares at a fair price: and a fair price would be, I think, the value which the shares would have had at the date of the petition, if there had been no oppression. Once the oppressor has bought the shares, the company can survive. It can continue to operate. That is a matter for him. It is, no doubt, true that an order of this kind gives to the oppressed shareholders what is in effect money compensation for the injury done to them: but I see no objection to this. The section gives a large discretion to the court and it is well exercised in making an oppressor make compensation to those who have suffered at his hands.

True it is that in this, as in other respects, your Lordships are giving a liberal interpretation to s. 210. But it is a new section designed to suppress an acknowledged mischief. When it comes before this House for the first time it is, I believe, in accordance with long precedent — and particularly with the resolution of all the judges in *Heydon's* case — that your Lordships should give such construction as shall advance the remedy. And that is what your Lordships do today.

I would dismiss the appeal.

Appeal dismissed.

Notes and Questions

1 In his judgment, Viscount Simmonds would appear to be willing to go even farther than Lord Denning in applying the oppression remedy to the conduct of shareholders. He said that:

> it is not possible to separate the transactions of the society [the majority shareholder] from those of the company. Every step taken by the latter was determined by the former . . . [I]t appears to me incontrovertible that the society behaved to the minority shareholders of the company in a manner which can justly be described as "oppressive". They had the majority power and they exercised their authority in a manner "burdensome, harsh and wrongful" — I take the dictionary meaning of the word.

See also *Re H.R. Harmer Ltd.*, [1959] 1 W.L.R. 62 (C.A.). The English Court of Appeal has also applied the oppression remedy quite explicitly to the conduct of shareholders, as evidenced by the following passage from *Re Jermyn Street Turkish Baths Ltd.*, [1971] 3 All E.R. 184 (C.A.). Buckley L.J. held that:

> In our judgment, oppression occurs when shareholders having a dominant power in a company, either (1) exercise that power to procure something that is done or not done in the conduct of the company's affairs or (2) procure by an express or implicit threat of an exercise of that power that something is not done in the conduct of the company's affairs . . .

Thus, it may be quite unnecessary to use the device employed by Lord Denning (the interlocking dictatorships) to bring shareholder conduct within the oppression remedy.

8. THE DUTY OF A CONTROLLING SHAREHOLDER WHEN TENDERING INTO A TAKEOVER BID

Pente Investment Management Ltd. v. Schneider Corp.
(1998), 40 B.L.R. (2d) 244, 1998 CarswellOnt 2156 (Gen. Div.
[Commercial List]), affirmed (1998), 42 O.R. (3d) 177, 1998 CarswellOnt
4035 (C.A.)

[In *Maple Leaf*, Maple Leaf Foods wished to acquire a controlling interest in Schneider Corp. However, Schneider Corp. had been set up with two classes of shares — the common shares, which were voting, and the Class A shares, which were essentially identical to the common shares except that they did not vote. The Schneider family held 70.5% of the common shares and therefore controlled the company (even though they held only 7.6% of the total equity of the company when the Class A shares were factored in). The Schneider family thus effectively held a veto over any takeover bid for Schneider Corp. The articles of Schneider Corp., however, contained a "coattail" provision that allowed the Class A shareholders to convert their shares into common shares on the occurrence of an "exclusionary offer" for the common shares (i.e., an offer to the common shareholders alone). However, the articles also allowed shareholders holding 50% or more the common shares to file a "non-conversion" certificate, indicating that they would refuse to tender their shares into a takeover bid. If such a certificate was filed, then even if there was an "exclusionary offer" for the common shares, the Class A shareholders could not convert their shares into common shares. This certificate could be filed as a "standing certificate" that applied to *any* takeover bid that might occur, and the family duly filed a standing certificate. This effectively gave them a veto over any takeover bid that occurred. Despite this, Maple Leaf Foods made simultaneous takeover bids for *both* the common shares and the Class A shares, taking the view that they had made an exclusionary offer for the common shares, because their bid for the Class A shares contained slightly different conditions than the bid for the common shares. If the offer was indeed "exclusionary", it would trigger the coattail, and by triggering the coattail, Maple Leaf hoped to acquire a controlling interest in Schneider Corp. via their holdings of Class A shares, which, pursuant to the exclusionary offer, they thought would all be converted into voting common shares, diluting the family's control position. The Maple Leaf bid prompted Schneider Corp. to look for other offers, and two were forthcoming — from Booth Creek and Smithfield. The family ultimately decided that it only would tender its shares into the Smithfield bid. Why did the family favour the Smithfield bid? According to Farley J.:]

FARLEY J.: In particular, the Schneider Family advised the Board of Directors that it had reviewed the various proposals in terms of three factors: financial value, continuity of the Corporation in a manner consistent with the Schneider family's desires, and the effect of any transaction on the Corporation's various stakeholders, including shareholders, employees, suppliers and customers . . .

At the Board meeting which commenced approximately one hour later, Fontana, as the spokesperson for the Family, read the following statement, apparently verbatim:

The family has supported the effective process that the Board and the Special Committee have pursued in response to the original MLF bid that came unexpectedly six weeks ago. We believe that not it would be important to that process for the family to state its opinion at this time.

We also think that it is important to reiterate that we as a family did not seek to sell this company but that through the process of the last 6 weeks we have come to the conclusion that now is the time to sell the control of the company.

During the last six weeks we have recognized the following points.

1. The 108 year history of this company results in a strong feeling with this family. It always has been and we hope that it can continue in the future.

2. We recognize that the meat packing industry has been evolving into larger players that can withstand the financial vagaries of commodity markets and that have the financial resources to invest in the business.

3. For a Canadian company to takeover our company we believe that there would have to be significant rationalization of our company and that J.M. Schneider Inc. would essentially disappear and that the Schneider brands may be eroded over the long term.

4. We would like to see Schneiders grow and take advantage of the opportunities that we believe are available to the pork industry and that J.M. Schneiders tried to take advantage of on their own in their business plans.

5. We would like to see a healthy pork industry evolve with several large players in Canada. This would be good for the many stake-holders of the Canadian pork industry.

These general issues are important to the family but all offers must be considered from a financial perspective as well.

There are essentially three offers on the table:

The $22 MLF offer has been rejected by the Family but we recognize that why (it) will top any bid [*sic*].

The Gillett deal at $25.50 is a straight cash offer. We believe that this deal could satisfy many of the other issues that we have raised but for the family there are tax considerations that make this offer less attractive than the other offers. In addition the conditions of the offer are such that it amounts to option [*sic*] to decide later rather than commit now to the company and the pork industry. Only the family is required to commit now. These conditions are on the extreme end in favour of the buyer rather than the seller.

The last offer is from Smithfield. It offers the family the ability to take all shares therefore allowing us to continue to participate in the growth of the pork industry. It also allows the family to take advantage of tax considerations. These conditions are available in the MLF offer but we, as a family, believe that the following points support the Smithfield offer:

1. The opportunity for share growth and value enhancement is greater with the Smithfield share.

2. For family shareholders wanting to diversity [*sic*] in the future, the liquidity of this stock is attractive.

3. Smithfield/JMS company will be a dominant North American player that is growing in international markets.

4. The family will have a representative in the Smithfield board.

5. There is greater opportunity in the Smithfield offer for the Schneider brands and the company to grow.

6. We know that Smithfield has been active in the past purchasing other companies. We understand that after these purchases, they have allowed the companies to continue to operate and grow relatively independently.

In conclusion, the family has unanimously agreed that we will support the Smithfield bid. (Emphasis added.)

[The case raises three issues of interest for the purposes of this chapter; 1. did the Schneider family, as shareholders, owe the company or the other shareholders a fiduciary duty in deciding to whom to tender, or could they act solely out of selfish self-interest? 2. can shareholders consider the best interests of constituencies other than shareholders in deciding how to tender? 3. does the existence of a controlling shareholder change the role of the board of directors?

Farley J. addressed the first of these issues as follows:]

It must be appreciated that the Family as controlling shareholders did not have to sell to anyone or to any bid, no matter how lucrative that bid may be seen on any objective basis. They could say at any time "Thank you but NO!" or words to that equivalence. They could act in what they perceived as their interests (and logically even against their interests if they chose to do so). Did the Family at any time do anything — or omit to do something which they ought to have done — which would preclude them from maintaining that position — or preclude them from selling to someone else on a basis that may not be as financially attractive a deal as a third party may be offering? While this latter concept may jar against the view that persons should act in their best financial interests — that is, that one should be rational in a dollar sense — there is, to my view, no obligation to do so in these circumstances.

[In so holding, however, Farley J. appears to have drawn a distinction between a shareholder's decision about whether to tender into a takeover bid, and a shareholder's decision about how to vote. In respect of the latter, Farley J. embraces the *Allen* good faith limitation in the following passage:]

I pause to note that if one however gets into a situation where one is voting in a corporate situation and the vote effects the class within which one is voting, then Viscount Haldane in *British America Nickel Corp. v. M.J. O'Brien Ltd.*, [1927] A.C. 369 (Ontario P.C.) would appear to place a restriction on a shareholder's discretion to act in his own interests when he observed at pp. 371-3:

> They must be exercised subject to a general principle, which is applicable to all authorities conferred on majorities of classes enabling them to bind minorities; namely, that the power given must be exercised for the purpose of benefiting the class as a whole, and not merely individual members only. Subject to this, the power may be unrestricted. It may be free from the general principle in question when the power arises not in connection with a class, but only under a general title which confers the vote as a right of property attaching to a share . . .
>
> But their Lordships do not think that there is any real difficulty in combining the principle that while usually a holder of shares or debentures may vote as his interest directs, he is subject to the further principle that where his vote is conferred on him as a member of a class he must confirm to the interest of the class itself when seeking to exercise the power conferred on him in his capacity of being a member.

[The second issue noted above — may shareholders take non-shareholder interests into account when deciding how to tender — was not explicitly addressed by the court. However, by necessary implication, Farley J.'s decision suggests that this is permissible. For this and other reasons, Farley J. ultimately held in favour of the defendants and dismissed the suit.]

Note

1 In upholding Farley J.'s decision, the Court of Appeal did not comment on the above-noted aspects of Farley J.'s judgment. See *Pente Investment Management Ltd. v. Schneider Corp.* (1998), 42 O.R. (3d) 177, 1998 CarswellOnt 4035 (C.A.) (other aspects of which are explored in the following section).

9. THE DUTY OF THE BOARD OF DIRECTORS WHEN THERE IS A CONTROLLING SHAREHOLDER

Pente Investment Management Ltd. v. Schneider Corp.
(1998), 42 O.R. (3d) 177, 1998 CarswellOnt 4035 (C.A.)

[NOTE: In view of the fact that the Schneider family refused to tender into any bid except the Smithfield bid, as discussed in the preceding judgment, the board of Schneider Corp. took certain measures to favour the Smithfield bid over the other bids. In particular, Smithfield and Booth Creek had been required, as a condition for reviewing the firm's books, to enter into a "standstill" agreement whereby they agreed not to make an offer for Schneider Corp. within two years except with the written consent of the board of Schneider Corp. In order to allow the Smithfield (but not the Booth Creek) bid to proceed, the board waived the standstill agreement in favour of Smithfield. The board had also put in place a poison pill, which it also withdrew in favour of Smithfield. This allowed the Schneider family to enter into a contractual "lock-up" arrangement in which the Schneider family agreed to tender into the Smithfield bid and no other bid.]

WEILER J.A.: It must be recognized that the directors are not the agents of the shareholders. The directors have absolute power to manage the affairs of the company even if their decisions contravene the express wishes of the majority shareholder: *Teck Corporation Ltd. v. Millar et al.* (1973), 33 D.L.R. (3d) 288 (B.C. S.C.) at 307 . . .

The appellants allege that the advice given by the special committee to the Board of Schneider was not in Schneider's best interests or those of its shareholders. They submit that the special committee should have refused to waive the standstill provisions in the confidentiality agreement with Schneider, thereby preventing the agreement between the Family and Smithfield. The appellants also submit that if the Board of Schneider could not enter into a share exchange with Smithfield because of fairness concerns it could not agree to a takeover bid. These submissions are really alternative ways of saying that the transaction with Smithfield was unfair to the non-Family shareholders, that it was not in the best interests of the company.

If the Smithfield offer can reasonably be considered to be the best available offer in the circumstances, then the Smithfield offer was not unfair or contrary to the best interests of the company. This is also essentially a fact driven question on which Farley J. made the following findings:

- The Smithfield offer was solicited by Schneider. Smithfield, a reluctant suitor, had to be "coaxed" to make a bid. Smithfield imposed a "no-shop" condition on its offer to the Schneider Family and did not want to haggle.

- There was no breach of confidence in the communications between Smithfield, and the Schneider Board and the Family. The spirit of the standstill provision between Smithfield and Schneider was honoured. Confidential information was used appropriately in the best interests of the shareholders. At all times the Schneider Board remained in control of the process dealing with the Smithfield offer.

- It was reasonable for the Board to accommodate a transaction between Smithfield and the Family by waiving the standstill provision contained in the Smithfield confidentiality agreement in view of advice received that the share price of Schneider would fall back to a range of $18 to $20 per share in the absence of a change of control transaction.

• Maple Leaf could not have made an offer that would have been satisfactory to the Schneider Family at that time.

• The Board exercised their powers and discharged their duties honestly and in good faith.

• The Board pursued all available opportunities to maximize shareholder value and achieved reasonable results for all of the shareholders of Schneider.

• It was unfair to say that the special committee had the Family's interests uppermost in its mind not those of the shareholders generally, or the non-Family shareholders specifically. It was beyond the power of the special committee to insist that the Family give up its veto power and the special committee realized this.

As Farley J. emphasized, one of the particular circumstances having a bearing on a board of directors' attempts to obtain the best deal available in the circumstances is whether the company has a controlling shareholder. For example, in *Paramount, supra*, control of the corporation was not vested in a single person, entity, or group, but was widely held by a number of unaffiliated shareholders. In that case, the proposed sale of shares represented a premium for the change and consolidation of control of the company in a group that would have the power to materially alter the interests of the widely dispersed shareholders. In *Pente*, the control premium for the shares of Schneider belonged to the Family. By contrast, the unaffiliated shareholders do not own, and are not giving up, the power to control the company's future.

Notes

1 The Court of Appeal's judgment indicates that while the existence of a controlling shareholder does not alter the board's duty to act in the best interests of the company (i.e., *all* of the shareholders), it might well condition the options that are available to the board. On the facts, the board simply could not force the Schneider family to tender into any particular bid. It had to accept this reality, and do what was in the best interest of all of the shareholders, given this constraint. On the facts, it did so. A very similar holding is found in *Benson v. Third Canadian General Investment Trust Ltd.* (1993), 14 O.R. (3d) 493, 1993 CarswellOnt 166 (Gen. Div. [Commercial List]).

2 The board of Schneider Corp. convened a special committee of the board of directors (often simply called an "independent committee") to report to the full board on the various takeover bids. In general, the convening of a special committee, *especially one that is made up of*

independent directors, is now a standard board procedure and one that is given a good deal of weight by the courts in deciding whether the directors acted appropriately. In any case in which there is a controlling shareholder, failing to appoint an independent committee to opine on major transactions will seriously raise the probability of director liability. The greater the extent to which the committee has independent directors (or, better still, "unrelated" directors — i.e., those who have no relationship to the corporation other than as directors) will significantly influence the degree of deference that the courts will accord the committee. Further excerpts from *Schneider* in Chapter 6, however, indicate that there is no absolute requirement that *all* committee members be independent. See also *CW Shareholdings Inc. v. WIC Western International Communications Ltd.* (1998), 39 O.R. (3d) 755, 1998 CarswellOnt 1891 (Gen. Div. [Commercial List]).

10. "MAJORITY OF THE MINORITY" VOTING

Imposing fiduciary or fiduciary-like duties on controlling is not the only way to protect minority interests against the over-reaching of controlling shareholders. Another way is by "majority of the minority" voting. The term is not a term of art. However, the general idea is to condition corporate action on the approval of shareholders, *excluding* either the controlling shareholder(s), any shareholder that stands to benefit from the corporate action or both. Majority of the minority voting is explored in Chapter 9 ("Shareholders' Rights").

11. THE ROLE OF THE SECURITIES REGULATORS

As noted earlier, the securities regulators have the power to make orders "in the public interest." For example, the *Ontario Securities Act* (R.S.O. 1990, c. S-5) provides that:

> 127. (1) The Commission may make one or more of the following orders if in its opinion it is in the public interest to make the order or orders:
>
> 1. An order that the registration or recognition granted to a person or company under Ontario securities law be suspended or restricted for such period as is specified in the order or be terminated, or that terms and conditions be imposed on the registration or recognition.
>
> 2. An order that trading in any securities by or of a person or company cease permanently or for such period as is specified in the order.
>
> 3. An order that any exemptions contained in Ontario securities law do not apply to a person or company permanently or for such period as is specified in the order.

4. An order that a market participant submit to a review of his, her or its practices and procedures and institute such changes as may be ordered by the Commission.

5. If the Commission is satisfied that Ontario securities law has not been complied with, an order that a release, report, preliminary prospectus, prospectus, return, financial statement, information circular, take-over bid circular, issuer bid circular, offering memorandum, proxy solicitation or any other document described in the order,
    i.   be provided by a market participant to a person or company,
    ii. not be provided by a market participant to a person or company, or
    iii. be amended by a market participant to the extent that amendment is practicable.

6. An order that a person or company be reprimanded.

7. An order that a person resign one or more positions that the person holds as a director or officer of an issuer.

8. An order that a person is prohibited from becoming or acting as a director or officer of any issuer.

9. If a person or company has not complied with Ontario securities law, an order requiring the person or company to pay an administrative penalty of not more than $1 million for each failure to comply.

10. If a person or company has not complied with Ontario securities law, an order requiring the person or company to disgorge to the Commission any amounts obtained as a result of the non-compliance.

Subsection 127(2), the so-called "cease trade" power, allows the Ontario Securities Commission ("OSC") the power to effectively enjoin any transaction that it finds contrary to the public interest, at least if the transaction involves "trading" (a term that is very broadly defined in the legislation to include acts in furtherance of a trade, even if there is no consummated trade). A wide variety of transactions that may involve improper conduct on the part of a controlling shareholder involve trading. These include a takeover bid, an "issuer bid" (in which the corporation makes a public offer to repurchase its own securities), an amalgamation (which involves the cancellation of existing securities and the issuance of new securities to take their place), and a "going-private" transaction, pursuant to which public shareholders are effectively evicted from the corporation, turning the corporation from a public to a private corporation. Similarly, if the transaction involves the use of an exemption under the securities legislation, s.127(3) allows the OSC to bar access to the exemption, again effectively enjoining the transaction. This can be used, for example, to prevent a controlling shareholder from adding to its shareholdings, if the share-holder's acquisition of shares will either drive its holdings above the 20% ownership threshold, or add to its holdings, if it started out with more than 20%. The OSC might also use its power to order that a person resign one or more positions that the person holds as a director or officer of an issuer, to loosen the grip that a controlling shareholder might exercise by virtue of a directorial or management position. The discretionary powers also give the OSC the muscle to deter transactions before they ever come to fruition, simply be threatening to convene a hearing to determine whether one or more of the discretionary powers will be exercised.

The following case is an example of a transaction that was stopped not by the courts, but by the Ontario Securities Commission using its cease trade power.

Re Canadian Tire
(1987), 10 O.S.C.B. 857 (Securities Comm.), affirmed by Divisional Court (1987), 10 O.S.C.B. 1771 (Div. Ct.)

[Canadian Tire had two classes of shares — voting common shares and "Class A" non-voting common shares that were essentially identical to the voting shares save for the absence of a vote. The voting common shares constituted only 4% of the total equity of the company. This so-called "dual class" share structure is common in Canada, because of the large number of family-controlled corporations; the dual class structure enables the family to control the company by holding only a small part of the total equity. Indeed, in 1983, the Billes family had used its control to cause the company to enter into a reorganization pursuant to which the existing common shares were divided into two parts — the voting commons and the non-voting Class A shares. Existing shareholders were given fixed proportions of each. The Billes family subsequently sold off its non-voting shares and used the proceeds to purchase additional voting commons, allowing them to sell a substantial fraction of their equity while remaining in control of the com-pany. In the end, three children of the founding shareholders of Canadian Tire — Fred, David, and Martha Billes — owned 60.9% of the outstanding voting common shares of Canadian Tire. Both the voting common shares and the Class A shares traded on the Toronto Stock Exchange.

In order to secure shareholder and regulatory approval of the reorgan-ization, the Billes family agreed to attach a coattail provision to the Class A shares. This coattail stated that if there was a takeover bid for the voting common shares, *and* a majority of the voting shares were tendered into the takeover bid, then the Class A shares would become voting shares. This would give any acquiror an incentive to make a takeover bid for *both* the voting shares and the Class A shares.

The coattail was leaky, however, insofar as there could be a premium takeover bid for the voting shares that would *not* trigger the coattail as long as fewer than 50% of the voting shares were tendered into a bid. Because the Billeses owned more than 50% of the Class A shares, they could effectively keep the coattail from being triggered by refusing to tender some or all of their shares into a takeover bid.

As it turned out, some years later Fred and David (but not Martha) decided that they wanted to sell their voting shares, but only if they could get an average of $100 for them. In order to do this, they made a deal with the independently owned dealers of Canadian Tire (which were not owned by Canadian Tire, but which purchased all of their goods from Canadian Tire, as well as support services). Under the deal, the independent dealers would make a bid for the voting common shares at $160 per share (when the shares were trading for about $25 in the public market). However, so as not to trigger the coattail, the bid would be a "partial" takeover bid for only 49% of the common shares. The brothers would tender all of their shares into the takeover bid and (under applicable securities laws) would have 49% of their shares taken up and paid for at the premium price, and the rest returned to them. Following the takeover bid, they planned to sell off the remaining 51% of their holdings into the public market, thus disposing of all of their shares. Since under this arrangement the coattail would not be triggered, the Class A shareholders would fail to participate in the takeover premium. The Class A shares (which, prior to the takeover bid, had traded at about a 25–30% discount to the voting shares) were mostly held by institutional shareholders. These institutional shareholders prompted the Ontario Securities Commission to call a hearing into whether a cease trade order should be issued (effectively enjoining the transaction), in order to protect the interests of the Class A shareholders.]

Ontario Securities Commission:

C. The Public Interest

In these circumstances, we have no hesitation in saying that this transaction is contrary to the public interest, as that term is used in section 123 of the Act. When the public market is sold some $100 million of Class A non-voting shares consequent upon a reorganization that, among other things, provides takeover protection to those shares and the controlling shareholders, some three years later, devise a scheme in conjunction with those who wish to obtain control of the Corporation, to circumvent the coattail while, in effect, receiving the full price for their shares, regulatory intervention to stop an abusive transaction is called for. A transaction such as is proposed here is bound to have an effect on public confidence in the integrity of our capital markets and on public confidence in those who are the controllers of our major corporations. If abusive transactions such as the one in issue here, and this is as grossly abusive a transaction as the Commission has had before it in recent years, are allowed to proceed, confidence in our capital markets will inevitably suffer and individuals will be less willing to place funds in the equity markets. That can only have a deleterious effect on our capital markets and, in that sense, it is in the public interest that this Offer be cease traded along with the Billeses' tendering of their common shares to the Offer.

* * *

E. The Proper Forum

Counsel for the Billeses and the Dealers also argued that the Commission is not the proper forum for this case. The contention was that this is a private matter between the Class A shareholders and the controlling shareholders. Accordingly, the Class A shareholders should pursue their remedies in the courts where the issues can more properly be sorted out through the trial process. This contention is supported by the fact that the Notice of Hearing in para. 14 alleges breaches of fiduciary duty, and such breaches are properly matters to be tried in the courts, either under the oppression remedy or in a derivative action.

The contention that the issue here is a private one between two classes of shareholders is far wide of the mark. A purported sale of control in the circumstances set out above, where the rights of the holders of some 83 million Class A shares are concerned, is not a private matter, although individual rights in terms of a particular shareholding are involved. This is demonstrably a public matter involving a major public company and one that concerns and impacts on the public marketplace. In the sense in which counsel were using the idea of a private *lis*, any takeover bid would, according to their analysis, be a private matter between shareholders. Yet it is well known that takeover bids, the rules applying to them and how they are conducted, are very much a public matter in the sense of their concern to, and impact on the marketplace and its perceived integrity. The Commission, accordingly, has always played a major role in overseeing such transactions.

Moreover, the argument that this matter more properly belongs before the courts, mistakes the respective roles of the courts and the Commission in overseeing the management and actions of public companies and protecting shareholders' interests. The Commission is vested with the power to regulate the capital markets in the public interest and is given broad powers to do so. The power to intervene includes the power to cease trade and to do so, at least initially, without a public hearing if satisfied of the necessity. In carrying out its regulatory function, the Commission necessarily impacts on the rights and obligations of companies, directors and shareholders. But it does so from the perspective of the regulation of the public markets and their fair and efficient operation. The subjecting of takeover bids to an elaborate code of rules and regulations, backed by the power to issue a cease trade order, if conduct during the course of a bid calls for it, is perhaps the best known example of this regulatory function.

The courts, on the other hand, adjudicate rights between shareholders and their companies. In so doing, the judicial process has the advantage of the refinement of issues provided by pleadings, examinations for discovery and the trial process. Moreover, the courts are able to provide remedies appropriate to the individual case. What the courts are not structured to do, is to move quickly to regulate public markets through regulating shareholder and/or corporate conduct. To be sure, the injunction remedy is available in the proper case, but it is not a remedy designed to be used as a regulatory tool.

The line between when Commission action or judicial process is appropriate in shareholder and corporate matters is, of course, not so clearly marked as the foregoing comments would indicate. There is bound to be overlap as there is no clear line between securities and corporate matters and many issues before the Commission involve the conduct of fiduciaries. But the role of the Commission is not to determine breaches of fiduciary duty, or to deal with a breach of a corporate statute, in order to provide a private remedy. Rather, it is to regulate shareholder and corporate conduct in the context of, and for the purpose of, regulating the public securities markets. Again, the line will not always be clear as intervention in matters that from one aspect are of a private nature will, from another aspect, be seen to have public market implications. If the Commission should mistake its role in a particular case, or act beyond the jurisdiction granted, the courts can rectify the matter and set out a new balance through the appeal procedure granted under s. 9 of the Act [allowing for appeal of any Commission decision to the Divisional Court].

F. Breach of Fiduciary Duty

As to the allegations of breach of fiduciary duty here, we agree that in most cases, that is a matter best left to the courts to determine. Indeed, we declined to hear evidence on the allegation in para. 14(v) of the Notice of Hearing on just that basis. Our decision to impose a cease trading order does not depend on a finding of breach of fiduciary duty. However, an allegation of breach of fiduciary duty, and evidence which clearly concerns the conduct of those who are fiduciaries, can be important in supporting facts which otherwise would support a s. 123 [public interest] order. That is the case here. The Billeses are in a fiduciary position in at least two categories; as directors of Tire and as Tire's controlling shareholders.

While the law in Canada is still developing with respect to the fiduciary duty that controlling shareholders owe to the minority, the courts in Ontario have clearly signalled that duty of fairness to the minority is imposed upon those who are in a controlling shareholder position. The judgment of the Ontario Court of Appeal in *Goldex Mines Ltd. v. Revill* (1974), 54 D.L.R. (3d) 672 (Ont. C.A.) is much in point. In dealing with the developing jurisprudence with respect to fiduciary duties, the Court made the following statement:

> The principle that the majority governs in corporate affairs is fundamental to corporation law, but its corollary is also important, that the

majority must act fairly and honestly. Fairness is the touchstone of equitable justice, and when the test of fairness is not met, the equitable jurisdiction of the Court can be invoked to prevent or remedy the injustice which misrepresentation or other dishonesty has caused. The category of cases in which fiduciary duties and obligations arise is not a closed one: *Laskin v. Bache & Co., Inc.*, [1972] O.R. 465 at p. 472, 23 D.L.R. (3d) 385 at p. 392.

That statement by the Court of Appeal provides guidance to the Commission with respect to the conduct of controlling shareholders when that conduct is in question in a case where Commission staff seeks a cease trade order. To repeat, the Commission is not the proper forum, particularly in a s. 123 proceeding, to determine the question of whether or not there has been a breach of fiduciary duty. But an allegation and a *prima facie* showing of such a breach can be useful evidence to support facts which otherwise call for intervention by the Commission under s. 123.

Here, the relationship of the Billeses as controlling shareholders to the minority is clear. And it is equally clear that their conduct, particularly seen in light of the events of 1983, in seeking now to avoid the takeover bid protection that was inserted for the protection of the Class A shareholders is a failure on their part to act fairly and honestly. In that sense, their conduct supports the facts here which otherwise call for the invocation of a cease trade under s. 123.

Notes

1   The Class A shares consistently traded in the market at a substantial (25–30%) discount to the voting common shares. It has been argued that the price of a share consists of two components — the first reflecting the value of the company under current management and the second reflecting the likelihood that an acquirer will make a takeover bid for the shares at a premium above market. See Frank H. Easterbrook and Daniel R. Fischel, "The Proper Roles of a Target's Management in Responding to a Tender Offer" (1981), 94 Harv. L. Rev. 1161. If so, the difference in price between voting and non-voting shares that are otherwise substantially identical results from the likelihood that any takeover bid will be made only for the voting shares. In similar fashion, if a non-voting shares are protected by an airtight coattail, voting and non-voting shares should trade at similar prices. Thus, if the market regarded the Canadian Tire coattail as binding in all situations, presumably the price of the voting shares and the Class A shares would have been much closer than it was. This suggests that the institutional Class A shareholders were quite aware that they were buying shares with questionable takeover bid protection and the receipt of a takeover premium by the Class A shares would have been a windfall. There was indeed testimony before the Commission to the effect that the market

was well aware of the leaky nature of the coattail. Indeed, while an investment banker from one large firm had testified that the market had not been aware of the terms of the coattail, it turned out that his own firm had sent clients a memorandum detailing the deficiency in the Canadian Tire coattail (i.e., the fact that it could be circumvented by a bid for less than 50% of the voting common shares). Thus, both theory and evidence cast some doubt on the wisdom of the *Canadian Tire* ruling.

2 Regardless of whether the Commission got it right, however, the effect of the *Canadian Tire* decision (upheld by the Divisional Court) is clear — the securities regulators will apply fiduciary standards of conduct in determining whether controlling shareholders have breached the public interest. Thus, the situation is something like this. First, the courts have held that controlling shareholders owe no fiduciary duty either to other shareholders or to the corporation. Second, nonetheless, the courts appear to have created a quasi-fiduciary duty (if not an outright fiduciary duty) under the oppression remedy. Third, the securities regulators will apply fiduciary standards of conduct in determining whether to apply their public interest powers. Since securities regulators are not bound by judicial precedent, however, (and are not bound by their own prior rulings) these fiduciary standards may differ materially from those applied by the courts.

12. ARE CONTROLLING SHAREHOLDERS GOOD FOR CANADIAN CAPITAL MARKETS?

It is very common for Canadian corporations to have a controlling shareholder. For example, R. Morck and D. Strangeland, in "Corporate Performance and Large Shareholders: An Empirical Analysis", in D. Strangeland, Ph.D. Thesis, Faculty of Business, University of Alberta, 1995, found that fewer than 16% of the largest 550 Canadian corporations had no shareholder holding 20% or more of the stock. Someshwar Rao and Clifton R. Lee-Sing, in "Governance Structure, Corporate Decision-Making and Firm Performance in North America", in Ronald J. Daniels and Randall Morck, Eds., *Corporate Decision-Making in Canada* (Calgary: University of Calgary Press, 1995), 43, found that 55.5% of a very large sample of Canadian firms had a *de jure* controller, 21.4% had a *de facto* controller (defined as having a shareholder with 20–49.9% ownership), and 23.1% were widely held (defined as having no shareholder with as much as 20% ownership). Comparable figures are reported in Ronald J. Daniels and Jeffrey G. MacIntosh, "Toward a Distinctive Canadian Corporate Law Regime" (1992) 29 Osgoode Hall L. J. 863, and Rafael La Porta, Florencio Lopez-de-Silanes and Andrei Shleifer, "Corporate Ownership Around the World" (1999) 54 J. Fin. 471. This is not atypical of relatively small capital markets like Canada's. By contrast, large capital markets like those in the United States are dominated by "manager controlled" or "widely held" companies; i.e., companies lacking a controlling shareholder. This divergence of corporate type between Canada and the US prompted Daniels and MacIntosh ("Toward a Distinctive Canadian Corporate Law Regime" (1992) 29 Osgoode Hall L. J. 863) to suggest that in Canada, corporate disputes will more often consist of minority/controlling shareholder disputes than shareholder/manager disputes. This is because a controlling shareholder will tend to closely monitor managers but may be tempted to engineer transactions or corporate payouts in a manner that favours its interests over those of the minority. This speculation now has some empirical footing. In particular, MacIntosh and Schwartz (Jeffrey G. MacIntosh and Lawrence P. Schwartz, "Do Institutional and Controlling Shareholders Increase Corporate Value?", in Ronald J. Daniels and Randall Morck, Eds., *Corporate Decision-Making in Canada* (Calgary: University of Calgary Press, 1995, 303) found that:

> [t]here is fairly strong support for the hypothesis that the presence of a controlling shareholder resulted in a lower price to book ratio. However, there is even stronger support for the hypothesis that the presence of a controlling shareholder resulted in both higher return on assets and return on equity, although there was no discernible effect on sales growth.
>
> Save for the absence of an affect on sales growth, however, these results are consistent with our hypotheses about the effect of a controlling shareholder on firm value. We earlier hypothesized that the presence of a controlling shareholder should result in better monitoring of managers. This in turn should result in higher ROA [return on assets] and ROE [return on equity] (which we assume are not as likely to be affected by redistributive transactions as price to book). However, in an efficient market, where controllers regularly engage in some redistribution of profits at the expense of non-controlling interests, the price of firms with controlling shareholders will be discounted to reflect this risk. The fact that the price to book ratio is less when there is a controlling shareholder thus suggests that, even though such corporations generate higher profits, these profits are siphoned off by controlling shareholders.

This does not mean, however, that we can expect all shareholder-controlled enterprises to be run more efficiently than non-shareholder controlled companies. The above study looked at *averages*. As in any statistical population, there will be considerable variation around the average. In particular cases, the controlling interest may adopt policies that lead to *lower* corporate value. A case study on point is provided by David Strangeland, Ronald J. Daniels and Randall Morck, in "In High Gear: A Case Study of the Hees-Edper Corporate Group", in Ronald J. Daniels and Randall Morck, Eds., *Corporate Decision-Making in Canada* (Calgary, University of Calgary Press, 1995), 223. The authors of this study examined what was once an extremely large corporate conglomerate controlled by a single family (the Bronfmans) — the "Hees-Edper" group of companies. At its height, this conglomerate consisted of over 100 companies that comprised approximately 15% of the value of the companies traded on the Toronto Stock Exchange. In order to motivate the managers of the various companies in the conglomerate, managers were given low salaries but were required to borrow money from their companies in order to buy company stock. In addition, the companies were organized in a pyramidal structure, such that the parent company would own 51% of another company, which would own 51% of another company, which would own 51% of another company, and so on. Many of the subsidiary companies were public companies. Using this technique, the Bronfmans were able to command a vast empire of companies even though their indirect ownership of firms in the middle and bottom of the pyramid was extremely small. Strangeland *et al.* compared the performance of these companies with those that were not part of a similar corporate group. They found that their performance was, at best, no better than these other companies. Indeed, there were indications that the Hees-Edper group of companies experienced inferior performance despite having higher levels of risk.

This study should be used with caution in interpreting the effect of a controlling shareholder on firm performance, however. The authors attributed the poor performance of the conglomerate companies to the practice of paying senior managers small salaries coupled with mandatory share ownership. This encouraged the managers to take inefficient risks with their companies in order to cause the stock price to appreciate. In addition, the use of conglomerate structure, now widely discredited (because it spreads management expertise too thin), appears to have played a role in the poor performance. The authors speculate that the conglomerate structure both contributed to, and facilitated the taking of inefficient risks. Finally, it should also be noted that while the later performance of the Hees-Edper group was not particularly impressive, judging from the early success of the conglomerate, a very high level of management expertise was presumably applied at earlier stages.

Another study that shows a more ambiguous effect of control on performance than the MacIntosh/Schwartz study is Vijay Jog and Ajit Tulpule, "Control and Performance: Evidence from the TSE 300", in Ronald J. Daniels and Randall Morck, Eds., *Corporate Decision-Making in Canada* (Calgary: University of Calgary Press, 1995), 105. The authors summarize their findings as follows:

> This analysis allows us to draw some reasonably robust conclusions based on the overall results and associated statistical tests. First, it is clear that the relationship between control and stock market performance is sector-specific, with the non-manufacturing sector being more sensitive to the effects of control than the manufacturing sector. In the manufacturing, an investor would have been better off simply

investing in large Canadian manufacturing firms — which did better than the overall manufacturing sector portfolio. There was little, if any, use in investing in securities, based on the degree of control of a firm within that sector or within a specific size group. However, in the non-manufacturing sector, investment based on control does have performance implications . . . [A]ccounting-based measures fail to detect any differences in firm performance based on the associated degree of control, either for a given year or over the entire time period. Overall, none of our results shows any consistent differences between widely held firms and closely held firms belonging to the TSE 300.

Someshwar Rao and Clifton R. Lee-Sing, in "Governance Structure, Corporate Decision-Making and Firm Performance in North America", in Ronald J. Daniels and Randall Morck, Eds., *Corporate Decision-Making in Canada* (Calgary: University of Calgary Press, 1995) 43, also found no relationship between either the rate of return in equity or the return on assets and concentration of corporate ownership. However, the rate of return was higher for firms with a *de facto* controller.

The results in these studies may be a product of the fact (as suggested by the MacIntosh/Schwartz study) that controlling shareholders have both positive and negative effects on corporate value. While controlling shareholders police management more efficiently, increasing corporate value, they are also frequently able to use their powers of control to favour their interests over those of the minority. There is in fact an abundance of other evidence that is consistent with this proposition. See Ronald J. Daniels and Paul Halpern, "Too Close for Comfort: The Role of the Closely Held Public Corporation in the Canadian Economy and the Implications for Public Policy" (1996), 26 Can. Bus. L. J. 11.

One particular case of ownership concentration merits discussion. Studies have been conducted to examine the effect of *managerial* ownership on corporate performance. The seminal theoretical work in this regard is that by Michael Jensen and William Meckling, "Theory of the Firm: Managerial Behavior, Agency Costs and Ownership Structure" (1976), 3 J. of Fin. Econ. 305. Jensen and Meckling speculated that as manager ownership increases, the value of the firm should also monotonically increase. This is because the interests of the managers are more fully aligned at high levels of managerial ownership. For example, when a manager own 75% of a company with no debt, for every dollar she takes out of the company in the form of perquisite consumption and/or shirking, she indirectly bears (through diminution in the value of her equity claims) 75% of the cost. However, if the manager owns 1% of the firm, for every dollar she takes out of the company, she indirectly bears only 1% of the cost. Thus, managerial incentives to consume perquisites and to shirk diminish as ownership increases.

This view of the "agency costs" of the separation of ownership and control, however, overlooks the fact that as managers accrue larger ownership interests, they become harder to displace through the mechanism of a hostile takeover or a proxy contest. They can therefore consume private benefits of control (such as enjoying the prestige that accompanies control of a major public corporation) without fear of being displaced.

Empirical investigations on the value of managerial share ownership have yielded interesting results. Randall Morck, Andrei Schliefer and Robert W. Vishny, in "Management Ownership and Market Valuation: An Empirical Analysis" (1988), 20 J. of Fin. Econ. 293, found that as ownership rises from 0 to 5%, market valuation increases. However, from 5% to 25%, market valuation decreases. From 25% upwards, it increases again. This changing relationship may well reflect the trade-off of the alignment effect of higher ownership with the entrenchment effect. However, looking at a sample of much smaller companies, J.J. McConnell and H. Servaes, in "Additional Evidence on Equity Ownership and Corporate Value" (1990) 27 J. Fin. Econ. 595 found that there was an increase in corporate value up to about 40–50% ownership, and a decrease thereafter. Both of these studies, however, strongly suggest that *managerial* ownership is an important determinant of corporate value.

Both the causes of concentrated ownership in Canada and other potential problems associated with concentrated ownership are examined in detail in Ronald J. Daniels and Paul Halpern, "Too Close for Comfort: The Role of the Closely Held Public Corporation in the Canadian Economy and the Implications for Public Policy" (1996), 26 Can. Bus. L. J. 11; Randall K. Morck, in "On the Economics of Concentrated Ownership" (1996), 26 Can. Bus. L. J. 63; and Ronald J. Daniels and Edward M. Iacobucci, "Some of the Causes and Consequences of Corporate Ownership Concentration in Canada", in R. Morck, Ed., *Concentrated Corporate Ownership* (Chicago: University of Chicago Press, 2000), 81. These include: market power and protectionism, the effect of concentrated ownership on corporate growth, efficiency consequences associated with control by founders and subsequently by their heirs, and effects on banking regulation and investment rules.

Interestingly, in a study of the 49 largest economies in the world, La Porta *et al.* find that the kind of concentrated ownership structure that prevails in Canada is the norm, rather than the exception. See Rafael La Porta, Florencio Lopez-de-Silanes and Andrei Shleifer, "Corporate Ownership Around the World" (1999) 54 J. Fin. 471. Controlling shareholders often accentuate their control through the use of pyramidal ownership structures in which the controlling shareholder controls corporation A, which owns a controlling interest in corporation B, which owns a controlling interest in corporation C, and so on (just as in the Hees-Edper group of companies, *supra*). Through this device, the ultimate controller can control a huge empire of companies via an equity interest at the top of the pyramid that is small compared to the total assets under control. While the study found that there were pyramidal ownership structures in Canada, the number of such structures was not disproportionate to other developed countries in the sample. The most significant finding of this study is that when shareholder rights are strong, ownership tends to be *less* concentrated. This is because when shareholder rights are weak, the private benefits of control escalate. That is, when controlling shareholder conduct is relatively unchecked, the controller can divert more of the corporation's earnings stream into its own pocket. This creates a potent incentive for those with the means to acquire — and exploit — control.

In a companion piece also examining corporations with controlling shareholders, La Porta *et al.* find that when shareholder rights are weak, corporations had lower valuations. Thus, the expropriation effected by controlling shareholders does more than simply transfer wealth from minority shareholders to controlling shareholders; it also impairs the efficiency of the corporate sector. See Rafael La Porta, Florencio Lopez-De-Silanes, Andrei Shleifer and Robert Vishny, "Investor Protection and Corporate Valuation" (2002) 57 J. Fin. 1147.

Chapter 8

Insider Trading

1. INTRODUCTION

Let's state it clearly, and in the unambiguous terms that it deserves: Insider trading is legally forbidden. It's morally wrong. And it's economically dangerous.

> — Arthur Levitt (former Chairman of the US Securities and Exchange Commission), "A Question of Integrity: Promoting Investor Confidence by Fighting Insider Trading" (1998).

A variety of laws prohibit or otherwise regulate insider trading in Canada. Of particular interest in a course on corporate law are the provisions contained in federal and provincial corporations statutes, such as s. 131 of the CBCA, s. 138 of the OBCA and s. 192 of the BCBCA. These provisions do not prohibit insider trading, but create civil liability on the part of the inside trader to the corporation and to people with whom the inside trader transacted. In addition, however, insider trading is dealt with under the laws enacted by the provinces pursuant to their jurisdiction over transactions in securities. Securities legislation tends to prohibit insider trading outright, and violators face fines or imprisonment. Section 382.1 of the *Criminal Code*, added in 2004, contains a new indictable offence of "prohibited insider trading", carrying a maximum penalty of 10 years' imprisonment.

Despite the clear message sent by federal and provincial law as to the illegality and impropriety of insider trading, the regulation of insider trading presents something of a mystery in academic circles, where a thirty-year debate has failed to yield a consensus view as to whether insider trading should be regulated at all.

We therefore begin our examination of insider trading by exploring the question "Why should insider trading be unlawful?"

2. WHY SHOULD INSIDER TRADING BE UNLAWFUL?

It may be helpful to explain, at the outset, what is meant by "insider trading". Insider trading usually refers to the purchase or sale of securities of a corporation by particular categories of persons (known as "insiders") on the basis of material non-public information. Important theoretical and practical questions arise, for example, as to:

- Who should be considered to be an insider: directors and officers are obviously insiders, but what about shareholders, employees, outside attorneys, consultants, potential business partners, family members of all of the foregoing and complete strangers who happen to receive inside information?

- What it means for information to be "material" and "non-public". Does information need to be published in a particular way in order for it to cease to be inside information, or is it sufficient that it not be confidential? (The CBCA, OBCA and BCBCA use the term "confidential".) Must it have been acquired in the course of the insider's duties in order to be inside information? Must the information be "specific" (the OBCA and BCBCA use this term) in order to be material inside information?

- Whether the mere knowledge of inside information ought to disqualify an insider from trading or whether the information must have been a significant factor in the insider's decision to trade.

Of course, before we can provide good answers to these questions, we must first articulate what, if anything, is wrong with insider trading. Let us therefore return to the question at hand, namely, why trading by insiders (however defined) on the basis of material non-public information (however defined) should be unlawful.

The wrongfulness of insider trading is differently conceptualized depending on whether one approaches the problem from the perspective of corporate law and its concern for relationships within the corporation or from the perspective of securities law and its concern for investor protection and the fairness and efficiency of the capital markets. From a corporate law perspective, the element of wrongfulness that most readily comes to mind is, perhaps, the apparent inconsistency of the insider's conduct with her fiduciary duties. From a securities law perspective the foremost concerns are the actual or perceived unfairness of the insider's informational advantage over other investors and the impact of insider trading on investor confidence and the functioning of the capital markets.

(a) Insider Trading as Breach of Fiduciary Duty

Is insider trading inconsistent with insiders' fiduciary duties? We have seen, in the materials on corporate opportunities, that the information acquired by a director or officer by virtue of her office belongs, in some sense, to the corporation, and the director or officer might well be restricted in her subsequent personal use of the information: consider *Boardman v. Phipps*;

Peso Silver Mines Ltd. v. Cropper; and *Canadian Aero Services Ltd. v. O'Malley (supra)*. The Supreme Court of Canada expressed the view in *Multiple Access v. McCutcheon (infra)* that the insider trading provisions of the CBCA are based on this rationale:

> I agree with the submission of counsel for the Attorney General of Canada that the impugned provisions of the *Canada Corporations Act* are directed at preserving the integrity of federal companies and protecting the shareholders of such companies; they aim at practices, injurious to a company or to shareholders at large of a company, by persons who because they hold positions of trust or otherwise are privy to information not available to all shareholders. . . . Insiders should not benefit, either at the expense of the company or at the expense of other shareholders, from their access to confidential information intended to be available only for a corporate purpose and not for the personal benefit of anyone. Information so acquired is at the expense of the enterprise. Confidential company information is a corporate asset the benefit of which is intended to benefit the company, its shareholders and creditors. (Per Dickson C.J.)

Of course, if the basis for the wrongfulness of insider trading is that information is a corporate asset, it would suggest that insider trading should not be prohibited outright; rather, the critical question in any case should be whether adequate consent was given by the corporation to the director or officer's use of that asset.

A second possible argument from fiduciary duty might be that the director or officer's use of her informational advantage to earn profits in transactions with the corporation's shareholders — her exploitation of the ignorance of her own corporation's shareholders — is at odds with fiduciary duties owed to them. As the cases excerpted later in the chapter indicate, Canadian and Commonwealth courts have not been particularly amenable to this argument. It may be that the effect of s. 131 of the CBCA and its analogues in provincial corporate law statutes is to create a fiduciary-type duty where the common law had not recognized one. However, the definition of "insider" is very broad in s. 131 of the CBCA and within the OBCA and BCBCA, and it is not clear why all, or even most, of the people covered by the definitions should be considered to owe special duties of a fiduciary character to the corporation's shareholders.

Moreover, a theory of insider trading based on fiduciary duties owed to the shareholders with whom the insider transacts could only explain a prohibition against insider trading involving *purchases* of stock by insiders. A different theory would be need to explain why there would be anything objectionable in withholding information while *selling* stock to non-shareholders or while buying or selling other securities of the corporation, such as bonds.

Despite these difficulties, both of these arguments from fiduciary duty have been successful in the United States, where they form the foundation of the so-called "classical theory" of insider trading discussed in cases such as *Cady Roberts* and *Chiarella v. U.S.*, *infra*.

(b) Insider Trading and Unfairness

From a securities law perspective, different concerns account for the prohibition against insider trading. One of the principal concerns is the actual or perceived unfairness of the insider's informational advantage over other investors in the stock market.

The concern for informational equality was, for a time, an important rationale offered by securities regulators in the United States for the prohibition against insider trading: see, for example, *Securities & Exchange Commission v. Texas Gulf Sulphur Co.*, 401 F.2d 833 (2nd. Cir. N.Y., 1968), referring to "the justifiable expectation of the securities marketplace that all investors trading on impersonal exchanges have relatively equal access to material information" and *In the Matter of Cady Roberts & Co.*, 40 S.E.C. 907 (1961), referring to "the inherent unfairness involved where a party takes advantage of [inside information] knowing it is unavailable to those with whom he is dealing".

The idea that a fair securities market requires a degree of informational equality has been controversial. Two puzzles presented by the informational equality argument are:

- What differentiates the superior informational access that directors, officers, significant shareholders, employees and other insiders have from other sources of inequality in the stock market, such as greater wealth (and with it a greater ability to bear risk) or superior training in the interpretation of financial data?

- If unequal access to information is unfair, why should only insider *trading* be prohibited? Insiders exploit their informational advantage not only when they buy on undisclosed good news and sell on undisclosed bad news, but also when they use inside information in making a decision *not* to trade (for example, in deciding to defer a planned purchase of stock by a week because disclosure of a piece of bad news is pending).

The following excerpts explore the debate over informational equality.

VICTOR L. BRUDNEY,
**"Insiders, Outsiders and Informational Advantages under the
Federal Securities Laws"**
(1979), 93 Harv. L. Rev. 322

Another — indeed the essential — element which makes an informational advantage unusable by those who possess it in dealing with those who do not is the inability of the latter to overcome it lawfully, no matter how great may be their diligence or large their resources. This notion is sometimes cast in terms of a rule seeking to effect equal access to material information for persons trading with each other. The meaning of the concept of "equal access" is not self-evident. But viewed most broadly it does not extend so far as to require actual equality or sharing of information. Viewed more narrowly it would presumably deny an informational advantage to those who seek to use otherwise nonpublic information which they are precluded by legal restrictions from disclosing to public investors. And it may appropriately extend to those who, while not precluded by law from waiving their informational advantage, derive it from sources who will not make it public, so that the public cannot lawfully obtain it.

The rationale of the rule based on limiting the trading privileges available to such an exclusive possessor of information, as explained in *Cady, Roberts*, rests on a conception of "inherent unfairness" in the use of the informational advantage. Whether the "unfairness" of allowing exploitation of such informational advantages reflects "felt" or "inherent" investor expectations, or expectations created by the rule, there is a sound functional basis for the rule. That basis is not confined to expectations of investors about their entitlement to corporate information in transactions with fiduciaries. If one transactor, by reason of his profession or regular occupational interests or otherwise, acquires material nonpublic information which he is not lawfully permitted to disclose to other transactors or which public transactors cannot lawfully acquire, use of that information by the former to his advantage and the latter's disadvantage is likely to be counterproductive in economic effect. A rational buyer (or seller) in a market, who knows that the person with whom he is dealing has material information about the value of the product being exchanged which he could not lawfully acquire, will either refrain from dealing with that transactor or demand a risk premium. If the market is thought to be systematically populated with such transactors some investors will refrain from dealing altogether, and others will incur costs to avoid dealing with such transactors or corruptly to overcome their unerodable informational advantages. None of those responses is socially useful. All raise the cost of capital. And some are simply unlawful attempts to obtain information corruptly from those who are forbidden from disclosing it.

Nor is the ability to exploit such privileged possession of information so beneficial as a stimulus to producing the information as to be worth imposing those costs. Information about the value of securities that is legitimately acquired in circumstances that preclude the acquirer from disclosing it or suggest that his source will not disclose it to others is not generally accumulated for use by its possessor in personal trading in securities. Whether it is inside corporate information or market information or any other imaginable relevant information, it is sought — and made available to a select few — in the course of fulfilling other purposes, such as rendering services or selling goods to the source of the information or others; and therefore the incentive for personal gains from trading is not necessary to induce those few to pursue it. It will be produced without that stimulus, and be useful for the other purposes for which it was generated. Nor can any acceptable gain be urged from a rule allowing such exploitation of material information. On the contrary, any such use of the information is, as we have seen in the case of corporate insiders (or the corporation), likely to be at the expense of the enterprise or some of its public investors in whose service or for whose benefit it was accumulated. And any such use of market information by those most likely to have it — that is, those who obtain it as a product of their occupation or position in the securities markets — will also often be at the expense of the person in whose service or for whose benefit they acquired it.

FRANK H. EASTERBROOK, "Insider Trading, Secret Agents, Evidentiary Privileges, and the Production of Information"
1981 Sup. Ct. Rev. 309

The last concept of fairness I consider here is that it is unfair for one person to trade with another unless the two are equally knowledgeable about the subject of the deal . . . [But] if information must be equalized, there will be precious little to go around. Indeed, the fact that some people can reap rewards by creating and using information provides a great benefit to the ignorant. The informed traders will buy and sell stock until its price is appropriate in light of its risk. They cannot manipulate the price for long. If it goes too high, some informed traders will start selling short, and if it goes too low they will start buying. Solid evidence suggests that this process of equilibration is completed in a few minutes after new information becomes available. The informed traders thus protect the uninformed. Because the price is set by the knowledgeable, it is quite safe to buy stock in ignorance. It would be a colossal waste if the information, so conveniently and cheaply embedded in prices, had to be extracted and presented to everyone who executed a trade on the market.

[The author next considers the argument that "trading becomes unfair if one person lacks access to information known to another".]

People do not have or lack "access" in some absolute sense. There are, instead, different costs of obtaining information. An outsider's costs are high; he might have to purchase the information from the firm. Managers have lower costs (the amount of salary foregone); brokers have relatively low costs (the value of the time they spent investigating); Sherlock Holmes also may be able to infer extraordinary facts from ordinary occurrences at low cost. The different costs of access are simply a function of the division of labor. A manager (or a physician) always knows more than a shareholder (or patient) in some respects, but unless there is something unethical about the division of labor, the difference is not unfair.

What argument can be offered in support of Easterbrook's contention that "if information must be equalized, there will be precious little to go around"? What is Brudney's counterargument?

As Easterbrook suggests, transactions between more-informed and less-informed people take place every day, and are not usually thought of as unfair. Such transactions occur, for example, whenever a homeowner hires a plumber or a student hires a tutor or a client consults a lawyer. Do you agree that there is no difference between such transactions and transactions for a product (or stock) where the buyer or seller has, but does not disclose, information about the product (or stock) which would be material to other party's decision? See Michael J. Trebilcock, *The Limits of Freedom of Contract*, Ch. 5 (discussing informational asymmetry) (1993), and Ian B. Lee, "Fairness and Insider Trading", 2002 Colum. Bus. L. Rev. 120, at p. 172.

(c) Insider Trading, Investor Confidence and Market Liquidity

Another concern from the perspective of securities law is that, whether or not insider trading is actually unfair, it reduces investor confidence and thus impairs the liquidity of the securities markets.

> Our markets are strong because investors are confident of their basic fairness. Trading on inside information damages the entire structure of our markets, because it deeply shakes this vital investor confidence.
> — Arthur Levitt, *loc. cit.*

ROBERT B. THOMPSON,
"Insider Trading, Investor Harm and Executive Compensation"
(1999) 50 Case W. Res. L. Rev. 291 (footnotes omitted)

Even if there is no loss or little individual effect as a result of insider trading, investors may still want the conduct regulated. There may be a parallel to preferences revealed in various experimental settings of the ultimatum game. In the ultimatum game, two parties are given a sum of money to divide. One of the parties is to propose the division;

the other can then choose either to accept or reject. If accepted, the parties get to keep the proceeds as divided; if rejected, neither gets anything. Traditional rational choice economics and game theories based on similar assumptions of self-interested behavior would predict a small amount to be offered to the second party (so that the second party would be better off than if there were no transaction) but the disproportionate portion to the first party. Instead of such a split, many experiments find "offers typically average about 30-40 percent of the total, with a 50-50 split often the mode. Offers of less than 20 percent are frequently rejected". Thus in some settings, players depart from the equilibrium predicted by rational self-interest and instead propose a division that is closer to equal sharing. Similarly, shareholders may prefer to limit insider trading even if the harm is not immediately visible. Part of the attraction of the investor confidence argument for insider trading is likely a manifestation of the choices said to be evidenced by the outcome of the ultimatum game.

In addition to its possible impact on investor confidence, insider trading may also increase the transaction costs associated with stock market transactions. Transactions over the stock market generally do not take place between identifiable investors but through "market-makers". A market-maker quotes a "bid price" (the price at which someone can sell a particular security to the market-maker) and an "asked price" (the price at which someone can purchase the security from the market-maker). The bid price is always lower than the asked price. How much lower depends on the market-maker's cost of doing business. As Macey explains in the following extract, market-makers systematically lose in their trades with insiders and must recoup these losses by increasing the spread between the bid and asked prices they quote. These increases, in turn, can be expected to adversely affect market liquidity.

JONATHAN R. MACEY,
"Securities Trading: A Contractual Perspective"
(1999) 50 Case W. Res. L. Rev. 269 (footnotes omitted)

Another effect that must be taken into account when gauging the effects of insider trading . . . is its effect on transaction costs that such trading imposes on market participants. As David Haddock and I observed in earlier work, all traders bear a share of the increased costs to market makers that are associated with insider trading. The logic behind this observation is simple. The bid-asked spread, quoted by exchange specialists and other market makers, represents a transaction cost for market participants. In turn, from the perspective of the market makers, this bid-asked spread represents the risks, as well as the carrying costs and other expenses associated with holding an inventory of securities and maintaining a continuous two-sided market. Increases in the incidence of insider trading cause, in turn, an increase in the expected losses that market makers experience as a result of maintaining an inventory and making a two-sided market in a firm's stock. This is because market professionals systematically profit — by difference, or "spread" between the bid price and the offered price — in trades to outsiders. However, because insiders will never buy on the basis of inside information unless the offered price is too low, and because they will never sell unless the bid price is too high, market makers and other market professionals, such as exchange specialists, will systematically lose in their trading interactions with insiders.

Consequently, holding all else equal, as the percentage of insiders among the entire population of traders in the shares of a particular firm goes up, expected losses to market-makers and other liquidity providers will concomitantly increase. In order to compensate themselves for these expected losses to insiders, providers of liquidity must increase their bid-asked spread.

Macey argued that these costs did not justify a mandatory prohibition against insider trading, since insider trading might also produce some benefits for investors. We shall see in the following sections that the claimed benefits of insider trading include improved stock price accuracy and entrepreneurial compensation. In Macey's view, the question whether, in a particular case, these benefits were sufficient to outweigh the increased transaction costs associated with insider trading in the corporation's securities ought to be left to contract: at p. 279.

3. ARGUMENTS FOR DEREGULATION

Henry Manne launched the modern debate over insider trading in 1966 when he published a book, *Insider Trading and the Stock Market*, contesting the then-orthodox view that insider trading is inherently wrongful. In a recent op-ed piece, Manne reprised some of his main arguments for the deregulation of insider trading.

HENRY MANNE,
"The Case for Insider Trading"
Wall St. Journal, Mar. 17, 2003, p. A14

There have been three primary economic arguments [in defense of insider trading] (not counting the show-stopper that the present law simply cannot be effectively enforced). The first and generally undisputed argument is that insider trading does little or no direct harm to any individual trading in the market, even when an insider is on the other side of the trades.

The second argument in favor of allowing insider trading is that it always (fraud aside) helps move the price of a corporation's shares to its "correct" level. Thus insider trading is one of the most important reasons we have an "efficient" stock market. While there have been arguments about the relative weight to be attributed to insider trading and to other devices also performing this function, the basic idea that insider trading pushes stock prices in the right direction is largely unquestioned today.

The third economic defense of insider trading has been that it is an efficient and highly desirable form of incentive compensation, especially for corporations dependent on innovation and new developments. This argument has come to the fore recently with the spate of scandals involving stock options. These are the closest substitute for insider trading in managerial compensation, but they suffer many disadvantages not found with insider trading. The strongest argument against insider trading as compensation is the difficulty of calibrating entitlement and rewards.

Critics of insider trading have responded to these arguments principally with two aggregate-harm theories, one psychological and the other economic. The first, the faraway favorite of the SEC, is the "market confidence" argument: If investors in the stock market know that insider trading is common, they will refuse to invest in such an "unfair" market. Thus investment and liquidity will be seriously diminished. But there is no evidence that publicity about insider trading ever caused a significant reduction in aggregate stock market activity. It is merely one of many scare arguments that the SEC and others have used over the years as a substitute for sound economics.

The more responsible aggregate-harm argument is the "adverse selection" theory. This argument is that specialists and other market makers, when faced with insider trading, will broaden their bid-ask spreads to cover the losses implicit in dealing with insiders. The larger spread in effect becomes a "tax" on all traders, thus impacting investment and liquidity. This is a plausible scenario, but it is of very questionable applicability and significance. Such an effect, while there is some confirming data, is certainly not large enough in aggregate to justify outlawing insider trading.

Manne's article touches on three common arguments against the regulation of insider trading: that it causes no harm, that it serves a useful function in improving the accuracy of stock prices and that insider trading privileges might be a useful form of executive compensation.

The following readings deal with the points raised by each of these arguments.

(a) Does Insider Trading Harm Investors?

Proponents of deregulation argue that insider trading cannot be shown to harm investors. According to this argument, non-insiders trading contemporaneously with an insider are approximately equally likely to be on the same side of the market as the insider (*e.g.*, to be buying when the insider is buying) as they are to be on the opposite side (*e.g.*, to be selling when the insider is buying). The gains of those trading in the same direction as the insider cancel out the losses of those trading in the opposite direction. Accordingly, non-insiders, as a group, ought to be indifferent to insider trading. Another argument first articulated by Manne and often repeated is that the non-insiders who turn out to have been on the opposite side of the market from the insider would have traded anyway, even if the insider had abstained from trading. The following extract is representative of academic commentary arguing that insider trading causes no significant harm to investors.

STEPHEN BAINBRIDGE,
"The Insider Trading Prohibition: A Legal and Economic Enigma"
(1986) 38 U. Fla. L. Rev. 35 (footnotes omitted)

An individual investor who trades in a security while material information is undisclosed is injured if he sold at the wrong price. However, it is unclear whether non-insiders as a group are injured. For example, if a firm's stock currently sells at $10 per share, but after disclosure of the new information will sell at $15, a shareholder who sells at the current price has suffered a $5 loss. The insider who purchases the share obtains a corresponding $5 gain. Yet, any outsider who buys stocks on the day the investor sells also gets a $5 gain per share.

If insider trading causes the price of the stock to rise to $12, the outsiders who buy at $12 are injured because they receive only a $3 gain instead of the $5 gain they would have received, but the shareholders receive a $2 gain instead of no gain. In either case, as a group, non-insider transactions essentially wash unless the insider's trade constitutes a significant percentage of total trading . . .

The second argument [that insider trading causes harm] is that inside trading generates price movements which induce investors to buy or sell at the wrong time. Assuming insider trading has an effect on prices, this inducement argument still raises a number of questions. The initial issue is the extent to which investors consider price in making investment decisions. Manne argues investors should be divided into two categories: investors, "whose market decisions will be a function of time", and traders, "whose decisions will be a function of the price of the security". He argues investors make investment decisions based on factors including dividend history, corporate growth, or management reputation, while traders make decisions entirely upon recent price fluctuations . . . [T]hose most likely to be sensitive to price fluctuations are sophisticated traders. They know full well that price changes may be attributable to insider trading and thus are least in need of protection.

Is there any argument that the losses suffered by the outsiders who trade in the opposite direction from insiders are unfair, even though other outsiders have coincidentally obtained gains in the same aggregate amount? Bainbridge also considers this argument: see 38 U. Fla. L. Rev. at p. 59. Do you agree with Bainbridge that it is primarily sophisticated traders who take price into account in making investment decisions and that unsophisticated traders and long-term investors are less likely to suffer any harm as a result of insider trading?

(b) Insider Trading and the Accuracy of Market Prices

DENNIS W. CARLTON AND DANIEL R. FISCHEL
"The Regulation of Insider Trading"
(1983) 35 Stan. L. Rev. 857 (footnotes omitted)

The social gains from efficient capital markets are well known. The more accurately prices reflect information, the better prices guide capital investment in the economy. From the perspective of an individual firm, however, efficient capital markets are a public good, unless private, as opposed to social, gains accrue to the firm when the prices of its own securities convey accurate information. Why, then, does a firm disclose information about itself?

One reason is that disclosure can reduce wasteful expenditures on search and reduce investor uncertainty about the firm. This may make the firm more valuable to investors. Investors expend resources to identify overvalued or undervalued securities until the next dollar they spend on information no longer produces an additional dollar of return. If the firm can produce information about itself at the lowest cost, disclosure of information by the firm will save resources by reducing the amount of expenditures on search and will lead to less investor uncertainty about the firm.

A second reason is that disclosure of information by the firm also may enable the firm's current investors to sell their shares to outsiders at a higher price, on average. If the firm discloses no information, outsiders may assume the worst and discount the price they are willing to pay for shares by a factor that reflects their uncertainty. Because every firm has an incentive to distinguish itself from those firms about which the worst is true, so that outsiders will pay a higher price for its shares, information will be produced.

Finally, accurately priced securities will enable firms to observe more accurately when corporate managers are successful. Thus, markets for managerial services and for corporate control will function more effectively. Also, the better managers will signal their quality by their willingness to tie a higher proportion of their compensation to stock performance. Accurate prices then enable these managers to receive the rewards for their superior performance. For these reasons, shareholders would want managers to disclose information about the value of the firm.

Complete disclosure, however, would not be optimal. Disclosure is costly, and at some point the costs will outweigh the benefits of increased disclosure. Moreover, in some cases, disclosure might destroy the information's value. It would not be in the investors' interest to disclose, for example, that a confidential study revealed the presence of valuable mineral ore deposits on land the firm intends to purchase.

Since the firm's shareholders value the ability to control information that flows to the stock market, they may also value insider trading because it gives the firm an additional method of communicating and controlling information. If insiders trade, the share price will move closer to what it would have been had the information been disclosed. How close will depend on the amount of "noise" surrounding the trade. The greater the ability of market participants to identify insider trading, the more information such trading will convey. At the extreme, trading by insiders is as fully revealing as complete disclosure. But since insiders will limit the size of their positions because of risk aversion and will camouflage their trading to some degree, they convey less information by trading than that conveyed by (credible) full disclosure.

Several reasons explain why communicating information through insider trading may be of value to the firm. Through insider trading, a firm can convey information it could not feasibly announce publicly because an announcement would destroy the value of the information, would be too expensive, not believable, or — owing to the uncertainty of the information — would subject the firm to massive damage liability if it turned out *ex post* to be incorrect. Conversely, firms also could use insider trading to limit the amount of information to be reflected in price. Controlling the number of traders who have access to information may be easier than controlling how much information gets announced over time. In other words, announcement of information need not be continuous, while trading on inside information can be. Thus, insider trading gives firms a tool either to increase or to decrease the amount of information that is contained in share prices.

R. GILSON AND R. KRAAKMAN,
"The Mechanisms of Market Efficiency"
(1984), 70 Va. L. Rev. 549 (citations omitted)

Those who advocate relaxing the prohibitions against insider trading typically argue that such trading is not merely harmless, but is actually beneficial in a number of respects. Our particular concern here is the assertion that insider trading has desirable effects on the market price of the security being traded. For example, sell orders by insiders with unfavorable private information are said to drive the price of the security down toward its "true" value, the price at which it would trade if the inside information were disclosed. A buyer of the security thereby pays a lower and more accurate price than he or she would have paid in the absence of insider trading. For our purposes, the argument's most interesting feature is its unstated assumption about the market dynamic by which insider trading alters the price of the security. It seems clear that the decline in price is generally believed to be caused by the increase in supply resulting from the insider's sell order. The problem, however, is that this critical assumption concerning the operative market dynamic is wrong.

The error in this supply-based explanation for the price effect of insider trading lies in its misspecification of the relevant supply. Capital asset pricing theory teaches that a security represents only a particular combination of expected return and systematic risk, for which there is a vast number of substitutes. Thus, the relevant supply for purposes of determining the impact of insider trading is not the "float" in the particular security, but rather the total of all other investment opportunities with a similar relationship between risk and return. The increase in the correctly specified supply caused by an insider's sell order is simply too small to have any but a transitory, and probably insignificant, impact on the price of the security.

Our approach to the concept of market efficiency and the capital market mechanisms that underlie it allows us to identify the manner in which insider trading alters security prices. The price of a security changes as a result of new information that alters investors' expectations about the security's risk and return. Insiders trade because private information alters their expectations. But their trading will change the market's expectations about the security, and hence its price, only if their private information is somehow transmitted to the market. [By] deducing the content of private information from transitory price fluctuations or the identity of traders . . . the market "learns" the relevance of the insiders' private information from their own trading activity, and the price of the security changes to reflect the market's new information.

Identifying the mechanism that underlies the price effects of insider trading is critical because it focuses attention on the relative efficiency of these price adjustments. Comparatively speaking, derivatively informed trading is an inefficient capital market mechanism. Insider trading, then, often causes prices to move in the 'right' direction, just as proponents of deregulation argue. But because derivatively informed trading functions slowly and sometimes only sporadically, encouraging it is unlikely to have much effect on the efficiency of securities prices. If we stipulate for the moment that our sole concern is market efficiency, it hardly follows that deregulating insider trading without more is the most promising of possible reforms.

. . .

Consider how a discussion of insider trading might proceed if it selected market efficiency as its chief aim and built upon analysis of the derivatively informed trading mechanism. Recall that price decoding, the chief source of the price effects of insider trading, is also a poor transmitter of derivative information in comparison to trade decoding. Minor fluctuations in price and volume are inherently ambiguous or subject to noise; observations on the activity of individual traders are much more informative. It follows that the greater the number of uninformed traders who are able to learn the identity of insider traders, the size of their trades, and other derivative information, the more effectively the derivatively informed trading mechanism will operate and the greater will be the market's relative efficiency with respect to the inside information. Thus, making the derivatively informed trading mechanism more effective requires wider distribution of the information on which the critical deductions are based, and the issue becomes how to disclose the fact that insiders are trading and the size of the trades. But while certain insiders are currently required by Section 16(a) of the *Securities Exchange Act* to disclose their trading, disclosure is required only some ten to forty days after the trade, hardly an aid to efficient operation of the derivatively informed trading mechanism. Understanding the mechanism by which insider trading alters market price thus suggests that a serious argument for lifting the prohibition on insider trading based on information effects must also consider a recommendation that the insider be required to disclose, at some period before trading, his identity and the size of the intended trade.

(c) Insider Trading and Executive Compensation

R. GILSON AND R. KRAAKMAN,
"The Mechanisms of Market Efficiency"
(1984), 70 Va. L. Rev. 549 (citations omitted)

Another common justification for insider trading, also originating with Henry Manne, is that it represents a form of compensation bargained for by insiders. According to this view, prohibition of insider trading simply shifts the form but not the amount of managerial compensation — a result that, without more, hardly seems worth the cost. And while our requirement of pre-trade disclosure does not prohibit insider trading, it would tend to reduce the profit available from such trading precisely because the derivatively informed trading mechanism would be more efficient. Thus, the increase in informational efficiency from disclosure comes at the cost of an arguably unnecessary shift in the form of managerial compensation. This is not the place to evaluate the overall desirability of insider trading, but even a brief consideration suggests that restricting the use of insider trading as a form of management compensation may be beneficial in itself.

One concern is the relative lack of effective market checks on the payment of excessive compensation through insider trading as compared to more traditional methods. Because excessive insider trading does not alter the firm's cash flows, it need not affect firm performance in the product or capital market in ways that will significantly constrain managerial self-interest. Nor would the market for corporate control pose a sufficient check. If a target's managers earn excessive compensation by insider trading, its attraction to potential acquirers may rest in part on the possibility that their managers stand to gain the same opportunity after acquisition. Eliminating insider trading might benefit the shareholders through an increase in share price, but the acquiring company managers, by foregoing the opportunity for insider trading, would bear the entire cost. Thus, for this purpose, the market for corporate control may operate only to shift the opportunity for excessive compensation between managers, rather than to eliminate it. Reinforcing the lack of market checks on insider trading is the difficulty of monitoring such trading. Although more traditional methods of compensation necessarily appear in the accounting records of the firm, levels of insider trading cannot easily be determined for precisely the same reasons that prevent effective enforcement of the current prohibition.

In addition to the greater potential for excessive payments, the use of insider trading as a method of compensation also raises problems of perverse incentives. The literature on insider trading has long recognized that incentives concerning whether and when to disclose new company information may be affected by the opportunity for insiders to trade before disclosure. But the availability of insider trading also has a perverse effect on managers' risk preferences in connection with firm investments. Giving managers the right to trade on inside information, even if only on positive information, has the effect of giving them an option that will be exercised only if positive information is produced. We know, however, that the value of an option increases as the risk of the company's business — the variability of return — increases. Thus, managers who can trade on inside information have an incentive to increase the risk of the business by making more risky investments. This is not so troublesome in itself as it might, however inexactly, balance the risk aversion resulting from the managers' undiversified human capital investment in the firm. The problem, however, is that the incentive extends to making negative net present value investments: investments for which the increase in risk is not matched by a commensurate increase in expected return. In this setting, managers share in the gain if the risky investments pay off, but the shareholders bear all of the cost if they do not.

ROBERT B. THOMPSON,
"Insider Trading, Investor Harm and Executive Compensation"
(1999) 50 Case W. Res. L. Rev. 291 (footnotes omitted)

[Of Manne's assertions,] the one that provoked most of the uproar in the 1960s . . . was that insider trading constitutes the most appropriate device for compensating entrepreneurs in the large corporation. [With few exceptions,] the defendants in the visible insider trading cases have not been entrepreneurs — the group for whom the compensation was seen as necessary. More illustrative is the lawyer, James O'Hagan, for whom takeover information provided a needed source of funds [see *U.S. v. O'Hagan*, below], or Keith Loeb in the Chestman case, two generations and one marriage removed from the entrepreneur. [Loeb had traded on the basis of non-public information communicated to him by his wife, who had received the information from her mother, who was the sister of the president of the company: see *U.S. v. Chestman*, 947 F.2d 551 (2d. Cir., 1991).]

More fundamentally, executive compensation has changed in a way that makes this prong of the insider trading argument less compelling. At the time of writing his book in 1966, Manne based part of his assertion for insider trading as executive compensation on his comparative analysis of the various alternatives for compensating entrepreneurs. Salary, bonus, profit-sharing plans, and stock options failed to meet the conditions for appropriately compensating entrepreneurs. Since 1966, changes in insider compensation have come closer to filling the need that Manne described. Not only has there been growth in executive compensation generally, but there is a richer array of forms that are regularly used. The experience of venture capital financing has produced compensation agreements aimed directly at compensating start-up entrepreneurs and balancing their return with others who contribute to the enterprise. Options need not require that money already be invested, as concerned Manne in 1966, and there is a greater willingness to make differential awards that permit payment for entrepreneurial services.

These various forms of compensation have some advantages over insider trading as entrepreneurial compensation. First, they seem less likely to reward the wrong people. Defining the target group is direct, although not perfect; information leakage is less likely. Second, this compensation is not secret, which makes it easier to monitor. [Securities laws require ongoing disclosure of executive compensation for all public companies.] In addition, these other forms of compensation typically require a corporate governance process prior to their initial availability, such as action by the directors or shareholders, as opposed to insider trading, which is triggered by the insider's actions. Compensation is often a volatile issue and has been so for much of this century. Currently, executive compensation is higher than in past periods, and higher in the United States than in other countries. In that setting, the disclosure and governance framework that governs non-insider trading compensation likely has a comparative advantage as compared to insider trading as compensation.

The academic debate as to whether or not insider trading should be regulated has no clear victor, as illustrated by the fact that Manne's 2003 article (excerpted, *supra*) repeats arguments he first made nearly 30 years prior. Are you persuaded by the arguments for deregulation, or by the arguments offered in support of the prohibition?

As we turn to the case law and statutory law on insider trading, it is worth keeping in mind the underlying academic debate and trying to understand:

(a) on what theory or theories of insider trading the various rules seem to rest, and what they are trying to accomplish; and

(b) to what extent they are vulnerable to the criticisms raised by the proponents of deregulation;

in addition, of course, to mastering the details of the cases and legislation themselves.

4. COMMON LAW

Percival v. Wright
[1902] 2 Ch. 421, 71 L.J. Ch. 846

[This was an action to set aside a sale of shares in a limited company on the ground that the purchasers, being directors, ought to have informed their vendor shareholders of certain pending negotiations for the sale of the company's undertaking.]

The shares of the company, which were in a few hands and were transferable only with the approval of the board of directors, had no market price and were not quoted on the Stock Exchange.

On 8 October 1900, the plaintiffs' solicitors wrote to the secretary of the company asking if he knew of any one disposed to purchase shares.

On 15 October 1900, in answer to the secretary's inquiry as to what price they were prepared to accept, the plaintiffs' solicitors wrote stating that the plaintiffs would be disposed to entertain offers of £12 5s per share. This price was based on a valuation which the plaintiffs had obtained from independent valuers some months previously.

On 17 October 1900, the chairman of the company wrote to the plaintiffs' solicitors stating that their letter of 15 October had been handed to him, and that he would take the shares at £12 5s.

On 20 October 1900, the plaintiffs' solicitors having taken a fresh valuation, replied that the plaintiffs were prepared to accept £12 10s per share.

On 22 October 1900, the chairman wrote accepting that offer, and stating that the shares would be divided into three lots.

On 24 October 1900, the chairman wrote stating that 85 shares were to be transferred to himself and 84 shares apiece to two other named directors.

The transfers having been approved by the board, the transaction was completed.

The plaintiffs subsequently discovered that, prior to and during their own negotiations for sale, the chairman and the board were being approached by one Holden with a view to the purchase of the entire undertaking of the company, which Holden wished to resell at a profit to a new company. Various prices were successively suggested by Holden, all of which represented considerably over £12 10s per share; but no firm offer was ever made which the board could lay before the shareholders, and the negotiations ultimately proved to be abortive. The Court was not in fact satisfied on the evidence that the board ever intended to sell.

The plaintiffs brought this action against the chairman and the two other purchasing directors, asking to have the sale set aside on the ground that the defendants as directors ought to have disclosed the negotiations with Holden when treating for the purchase of the plaintiffs' shares . . .

SWINFEN EADY J.: It is urged that the directors hold a fiduciary position as trustees for the individual shareholders, and that, where negotiations for sale of the undertaking are on foot, they are in the position of trustees for sale. The plaintiffs admitted that this fiduciary position did not stand in the way of any dealing between a director and a shareholder before the question of sale of the undertaking had arisen, but contended that as soon as that question arose the position was altered. No authority was cited for that proposition, and I am unable to adopt the view that any line should be drawn at that point. It is contended that a shareholder knows that the directors are managing the business of the company in the ordinary course of management, and impliedly releases them from any obligation to disclose any information so acquired. That is to say, a director purchasing shares need not disclose a large casual profit, the discovery of a new vein, or the prospect of a good dividend in the immediate future, and similarly a director selling shares need not disclose losses, these being merely incidents in the ordinary course of management. But it is urged that, as soon as negotiations for the sale of the undertaking are on foot, the position is altered. Why? The true rule is that a shareholder is fixed with knowledge of all the directors' powers, and has no more reason to assume that they are not negotiating a sale of the undertaking than to assume that they are not exercising any other power. It was strenuously urged that, though incorporation affected the relations of the shareholders to the external world, the company thereby becoming a distinct entity, the position of the shareholders inter se was not affected, and was the same as that of partners or shareholders in an unincorporated company. I am unable to adopt that view. I am therefore of opinion that the purchasing directors were under no obligation to disclose to their vendor shareholders the negotiations which ultimately proved abortive. The contrary view would place directors in a most invidious position, as they could not buy or sell shares without disclosing negotiations, a premature disclosure of which might well be against the best interests of the company. I am of opinion that directors are not in that position.

There is no question of unfair dealing in this case. The directors did not approach the shareholders with the view of obtaining their shares. The shareholders approached the directors, and named the price at which they were desirous of selling. The plaintiffs' case wholly fails, and must be dismissed with costs.

Notes and Questions

1 *Percival v. Wright* can be read narrowly or broadly. Taken narrowly, the ratio might simply be that there is no duty on corporate directors to disclose privileged corporate information to persons in the plaintiffs' position (whether sellers or buyers). The case has often been cited for the much broader proposition that directors owe shareholders no fiduciary duties in any circumstances. More recent cases have qualified this proposition in Canada.

2 The undisclosed sale of the company's undertaking did not actually go through; one might well ask, therefore, what their complaint was. Consider the following argument, however: What was important to the plaintiffs was that, at the time when the sale of shares was consummated, the directors were in possession of information that, if known to the plaintiffs, might well have resulted in a sale on different terms (i.e., the plaintiffs would have insisted on receiving more for their shares). Therefore, the failure to complete the sale of the company's undertaking is completely immaterial. Indeed, the very fact that a purchaser was willing to contemplate buying the undertaking at a high price revealed to the plaintiffs that their shares were probably worth more than their prior expectation (and this is probably why they sought rescission in this case).

3 Should it matter that the sellers approached the directors, rather than the other way around? If the basis of our concern about insider trading is inequality of information, does it matter who approaches whom?

Coleman v. Myers
[1977] 2 N.Z.L.R. 225 (S.C.)

[The defendants, a son and his father, were the managing director and chairman of a private company in which other family members, individually or through trusts, were shareholders. The company had realty, shares and cash to a value of over $5 million. The son devised a plan to buy out all the other shareholders at $4.80 per share by ultimately using the company's assets — the cash and proceeds from sale of the realty — to be financed initially by short-term bank credit and repaid through capital dividends. The son formed a new company to make the takeover offer, which when it had nine-tenths of the shares could then compulsorily acquire the remaining ten percent. The plan worked with the plaintiff being a reluctant seller when he learned the defendant had acquired 90% of the shares. In the result, the defendant was left sole owner of a company that held shares in another company worth millions of pounds. When the plaintiffs learned these facts, they sued, alleging, *inter alia*, fraud and breach of fiduciary duty in that the son had not disclosed his plans and the magnitude of the potential gains (the realty was sold for $3.5 million, and the son knew its true value was far above book value through consulting property valuators), that he represented that he intended to keep the realty and that the company needed the cash in the business and it was not available for capital dividends. The plaintiffs claimed rescission and, alternatively, damages.

Mahon J. found for the defendant on the basis of no misrepresentation. In the course of his judgment he held that there was a duty on the directors to disclose information to the shareholders and that *Percival v. Wright* was wrongly decided.

The Court of Appeal reversed Mahon J. holding that there had been a failure to make adequate disclosure to allow shareholders to assess the takeover bid. The comments of Woodhouse and Cooke JJ. with respect to *Percival v. Wright* are of importance.]

WOODHOUSE J.: For the respondents it is denied at the outset that any fiduciary duty was owed to the shareholders. Then it is said that even if there were such a duty it had been discharged by the provision of all facts which would reasonably affect the value of the shares. It was contended also that the appellants had independently acquired all the material information; that the proposals of Mr. Douglas Myers to use C & E funds to finance the take-over offer were irrelevant; that the price paid for the shares was a fair one; and that the claim by appellants as minority shareholders was based upon the misconception that they were entitled to share in the assets of the undertaking.

In this area of the case a good deal of attention was focussed on a decision of Swinfen Eady J. in *Percival v. Wright*, [1902] 2 Ch. 421. It involved a purchase of shares by the directors of a company at a time when they had knowledge of a likely and favourable sale of the whole undertaking. The vendor shareholders later brought proceedings against the directors claiming that the latter were in a fiduciary position towards them at the time of the sale. The judge disagreed and some textbook writers have regarded the decision as authority for the proposition that a company director, while owing a fiduciary duty to his company, will never have such a duty in respect of the shareholders. Not unnaturally the respondents have sought to rely upon the case which they submit should be regarded as having decided the law upon the point in New Zealand. I do not think that it does.

The restricted nature of the argument addressed to the court in *Percival v. Wright* and the surprising nature of a concession deliberately associated with it needs to be appreciated in order to understand the true implications of the decision. It was submitted that the directors held a fiduciary position for the shareholders where negotiations for a sale of the whole undertaking of the company were on foot; but not otherwise. The argument was that in such circumstances the directors were in the position of trustees for sale. And there was a further concession: it was accepted that there had been no unfair dealing by the directors or a purchase of the shares at an undervalue. So the very limited point put to the court was simply that fortuitous negotiations for the sale of the undertaking altered the whole position. That, in my view, could not possibly be the test and, with respect, the decision of the judge in that particular case, restricted as I think it was to that one point, was inevitable.

In my opinion it is not the law that anybody holding the office of director of a limited liability company is for that reason alone to be released from what otherwise would be regarded as a fiduciary responsibility owed to those in the position of shareholders of the same company. Certainly their status as directors did not protect the defendants in a Canadian case which finally made its way to the Privy Council: see *Allen v. Hyatt* (1914), 30 T.L.R. 444. The decision in that case turned upon the point that the directors of the company had put themselves in a fiduciary relationship with some of their shareholders because they had undertaken to sell shares of the shareholders in an agency capacity. But there is nothing in the decision to suggest that in the case of a director the fiduciary relationship can arise only in an agency situation. On the other hand, the mere status of company director should not produce that sort of responsibility to a shareholder and in my opinion it does not do so. The existence of such a relationship must depend, in my opinion, upon all the facts of the particular case.

When dealing with this part of the present case Mahon J. himself came to the conclusion that *Percival v. Wright* had been wrongly decided. Then he expressed his opinion generally upon the point in the following way:

> The essential basis of breach of fiduciary duty is the improper advantage taken by the defendant of a confidence reposed in him either by, or for the benefit of, the plaintiff. When one considers the legal relationship between the shareholder in a limited liability company and the director entrusted with the management of that company, it appears to me that in any transaction involving sale of shares between director and shareholder, the director is the repository of confidence and trust necessarily vested in him by the shareholder, or by his legal status, in relation to the existence of information affecting the true value of those shares.

He then qualified that conclusion by restricting it to those holding office as directors in private companies. It may be that he intended some qualification beyond that but if he did not then, with respect, I think myself the conclusion is too broadly stated.

As I have indicated it is my opinion that the standard of conduct required from a director in relation to dealings with a shareholder will differ depending upon all the surrounding circumstances and the nature of the responsibility which in a real and practical sense the director has assumed towards the shareholder. In the one case there may be a need to provide an explicit warning and a great deal of information concerning the proposed transaction. In another there may be no need to speak at all. There will be intermediate situations. It is, however, an area of the law where the courts can and should find some practical means of giving effect to sensible and fair principles of commercial morality in the cases that come before them; and while it may not be possible to lay down any general test as to when the fiduciary duty will arise for a company director or to prescribe the exact conduct which will always discharge it when it does, there are nevertheless some factors that will usually have an influence upon a decision one way or the other. They include, I think, dependence upon information and advice, the existence of a relationship of confidence, the significance of some particular transaction for the parties and, of course, the extent of any positive action taken by or on behalf of the director or directors to promote it. In the present case each one of those matters had more than ordinary significance and when they are taken together they leave me in no doubt that each of the two directors did owe a fiduciary duty to the individual shareholders. The reasons are implicit in the account I have given of the C & E company and those associated with it together with the depth of knowledge and experience on the one side when contrasted with the relative lack of it on the other and the careful development of the takeover proposals . . .

COOKE J.: Swinfen Eady J. did not say that directors can never be in a fiduciary position *vis-a-vis* shareholders with whom they are dealing. The actual outcome of that case certainly does not shock the conscience. As has been seen, major concessions were made in argument. It was a decision of a single judge at first instance. Apparently it has never been considered in any reported New Zealand case . . . It was distinguished in non-committal language by the Privy Council in *Allen v. Hyatt* (1914), 30 T.L.R. 444. In so far as it might be thought to lay down a general proposition that no fiduciary duty is owed by a director dealing with individual shareholders to disclose particular inside information acquired by him, that proposition was criticized in England by the Cohen Committee in 1945 (Cmnd 6659, para 86) and by the Jenkins Committee in 1962 (Cmnd 1749, para 89) and in New Zealand by the Macarthur Committee in 1973 (para. 312). While the result of *Percival v. Wright* may have been correct on its facts, the judgment can carry little authority for any general proposition in this country; and with respect, I do not find it of much help in the present case . . .

On one interpretation the first of the passages I have quoted from Mahon J.'s judgment might be understood to propound a general rule applicable to directors of private companies with unlisted shares and to certain kinds of transactions in public company shares. But such may not have been the learned judge's intention. At all events, in the present case it is not necessary to go as far as attempting to lay down any general rule, nor have counsel for the appellants invited the court to do so. On the other hand Mr. Williams, who argued this part of the case for the respondents, acknowledged that even if *Percival v. Wright* were accepted as undoubted law in New Zealand, it would merely exclude any automatic fiduciary duty, leaving open the possibility of such a duty failing on a director in particular circumstances.

In the particular circumstances of this case it seems to me obvious that each of the respondent directors did owe a fiduciary duty to the individual shareholders. To that extent I fully agree with Mahon J. Broadly, the facts giving rise to the duty are the family character of this company; the positions of father and son in the company and the family; their high degree of inside knowledge; and the way in which they went about the take-over and the persuasion of shareholders.

Dusik v. Newton
(1985), 62 B.C.L.R. 1, 1985 CarswellBC 86 (C.A.)

[Newton owned 90% of Fletcher's Ltd., a company formed under the *Company Act*, R.S.B.C. 1979, c. 59. Dusik's wholly owned subsidiary owned the other 10%. Dusik also carried on another business, Willowbrook, which had run up large debts with the Bank of British Columbia and which was on the verge of failing. Dusik had pledged his shares in Fletcher's to the bank and the bank had appointed a receiver for Willowbrook. Dusik was anxious to refinance Willowbrook to get it out of debt and make a new start. Among the debts was a debt of $66,000 owed to the Alberta Pork Producers Marketing Board (the "Board"). Dusik had been engaged in negotiations not only for the settlement of this debt, but for the sale of his shares to the Board as well. Unbeknownst to Dusik, the Board had also approached Newton to buy his shares. Initially, the Board offered Newton three options: (i) sale of all the assets of Fletcher's for $15 million; (ii) sale of all the shares in Fletcher's for $15 million (with Newton first acquiring Dusik's 10%); (iii) sale of Newton's 90% share of Fletcher's for $13.5 million, with the Board acquiring Dusik's 10% on its own. At least the first, and arguably the third of these options contemplated a *pro rata* division of the proceeds of sale between Dusik and Newton, with Dusik receiving $1.5 million. However, Newton and the Board apparently realized that it was to both their advantages that Dusik receive less than his *pro rata* share of the purchase price. Newton would then receive proportionately more of the sale price, and the Board would keep Dusik from being financially able to resurrect Willowbrook (a company in competition with Fletcher's) using the sale proceeds. Thus, the Board eventually purchased Newton's shares for $14.16 million, and Dusik's for $450,000. Although Dusik had requested financial statements for 1980, Newton had deliberately withheld these statements and also held no shareholders' meeting in 1980. The sale of Dusik's shares was consummated under extreme pressure from the Board, who threatened that if Dusik did not sell, it would purchase the shares directly from the Bank of B.C. (to whom the shares were pledged). Only after the sale of Dusik's shares did Dusik find out that Newton had also sold his shares — for $14.16 million. Dusik sued, claiming that Newton's failure to disclose to Dusik the negotiations between himself and the Board, and what the Board was willing to pay for the shares, constituted a breach of a fiduciary duty owed by Newton to Dusik. Dusik was successful at trial, and the decision was upheld upon appeal to the B.C. Court of Appeal.]

CARROTHERS J.A.: We begin with the principles derived from the cases. In Gower's *Principles of Modern Company Law*, 4th ed. (1979)

the text says in discussion of the fiduciary duties of directors (at p. 573):

> Secondly, the fiduciary duties are owed to the company and to the company alone. The difficulties which may be caused by treating a metaphysical entity as the beneficiary, in whose interests the directors must act, are referred to later. Here it suffices to emphasize that, in general, the directors owe no duties to the individual members as such, or, a fortiori, to a person who has not yet become a member — such as a potential purchaser of shares in it. This principle is regarded as firmly established by the much-criticized decision in *Percival v. Wright* ([1902] 2 Ch. 421), where directors purchased shares from their members without revealing that negotiations were in progress for a sale of the undertaking at a favourable price. This, however, does not mean that directors can never stand in a fiduciary relationship to the members; they well may if they are authorized by the letter to negotiate on their behalf with, for example, a potential take-over bidder *Allen v. Hyatt*. But far less than the establishment of an agency relationship may suffice, particularly, as a recent important New Zealand decision *Coleman v. Myers* illustrates, in the case of a family company, "depending upon all the surrounding circumstances and the nature of the responsibility which in a real and practical sense the director has assumed towards the shareholder". Nor, as we shall see, does it necessarily follow that if they make a personal profit as a result of the use of inside information in dealings in the company's securities they will not break their fiduciary duty to the company and be liable to account to it.

[Carrothers J.A. then quoted from the opinions of Woodhouse and Cooke JJ. in *Coleman v. Myers* and from decisions of the Ontario Court of Appeal, including *Goldex Mines Ltd. v. Revill* (1975), 54 D.L.R. (3d) 672, discussed in Chapter 7, *supra*, on the subject of fiduciary duties owed to minority shareholders.]

Counsel for Newton says that the general rule is that laid down in *Percival v. Wright*, that a director does not owe a fiduciary duty to minority shareholders and only three exceptions have emerged. They are where a director acts as an agent of a minority shareholder; where a director buys shares from a minority shareholder; and where a director has been dishonest with or has misled a minority shareholder. In our view the law is no longer that restrictive. The correct approach is stated in the passages we have quoted from *Coleman v. Myers* and the Ontario cases.

We go now to the area of fact and the question whether there is a basis for interference by this Court with the finding of the judge that Newton, as a director, was in breach of a fiduciary duty to Dusik, minority shareholder, causing him loss. The background and general circumstances are significant. Fletcher's was a company of two shareholders. There was a special relationship between the two. In 1968, upon acquiring 90% of the shares of Fletcher's, Newton hired Dusik as general manager. He was looking for the best available salesman and induced Dusik to leave his employment with Pacific Meats, in part, by the option to purchase Fletcher's shares. The two men worked together to build up the company.

In considering breach of duty in connection with the sale of Fletcher's shares to the board the difference in views of the parties as to the law is not significant. The essence of Dusik's complaint is that Newton failed in his duty to inform him of matters. The argument for Newton recognizes that under the third exception to the *Percival v. Wright* rule, a director is under a duty not to mislead a minority shareholder. And the argument recognizes that there can be misleading in a negative way by failure to inform.

We have no doubt that apart from two factors that we will turn to immediately, Newton as director owed Dusik the duty of disclosing to him that the board was proposing to acquire all of Fletcher's shares for the price of $15 million. The first factor is Newton's alleged belief that Dusik had already made his own bargain with the board, and, effectively, was no longer a shareholder. But the judge decided that he did not hold that belief and we have already concluded that he did not err in that finding. The second factor pertains to Fletcher's 1980 financial statements. Dusik alleged that they were deliberately withheld from him and if he had seen them he would have been aware that his shares were worth far more than he thought when he dealt with the board . . .

No annual general meeting of Fletcher's was held in 1980. Dusik never received the 1980 financial statements. The statements were released by Fletcher's auditors May 2, 1980. Bradley testified that Newton specifically instructed him to withhold them. He testified further that there was no justification for withholding the statements from Dusik apart from concern about the tax audit. He agreed that they could have been given to him with a caution about the tax audit and further agreed that if he had been in Dusik's position he would have wanted the statements. The tax audit took place in June or July and by September Newton was advised that there would be no reassessment. Examined for discovery Newton said he provided Dusik with the 1980 financial statements. But, at trial he admitted that he had not done so. Newton's evidence was that he deliberately withheld the statements from everybody, because of the tax audit, although he knew that Dusik was endeavouring to sell his shares in the summer of 1980 and that the financial results would be critical to him . . .

In our view the judge did not err in concluding that Newton deliberately kept Dusik in the dark thus making himself liable for the consequent loss.

Bell v. Source Data Control Ltd.

(February 12, 1986), Doc. 14581/81, [1986] O.J. No. 621 (H.C.), affirmed (1998), 66 O.R. (2d) 78, 1988 CarswellOnt 113 (C.A.).

[Three minority shareholders, each holding 10% of the shares of the company, approached the majority shareholder, Hood, seeking to sell their shares. Each stated that he sought a price of $200,000 for his shares, and authorized Hood (who held 60% of the company) to find a third-party purchaser willing to buy his shares at that price. Unbeknownst to the minority shareholders, Hood (who untruthfully told the minority shareholders that his shares were not for sale) was already in negotiations with McLean-Hunter to sell his shares. McLean-Hunter had, in fact, indicated a desire to purchase the whole company. An impasse developed when Hood indicated that he wanted $2.1 million for his share of the company, and McLean-Hunter indicated that it was not willing to pay more than $3 million for the entire company. Hood's demand of $2.1 million could not be satisfied if the other shareholders were to participate *pro rata* according to their holdings. The impasse was broken when a deal was struck between Hood and McLean-Hunter whereby the latter would purchase the minority interests of the three shareholders willing to sell for $200,000 each (the remaining minority shareholder refused to sell), and would pay Hood $2.1 million for his 60% share. The minority shareholders concluded the sale without knowing the consideration paid to Hood or even the identity of the purchaser of their shares. When they found out what Hood had received for his shares, they sued, alleging breach of fiduciary duty owed both as shareholder and director. The following excerpt is taken from Eberle J.'s comments on the allegation of breach of fiduciary duty.]

The notion that it requires more than the mere capacity of shareholder and perhaps more than the capacity of director to fasten a fiduciary duty upon a person who holds shares in a company was further developed in . . . *Coleman v. Myers* (1977), 2 N.Z.L.R. at page 225 for the trial decision, and at page 297 for the Court of Appeal decision. In the Court of Appeal's decision, at page 324 there is a useful comment on *Allen v. Hyatt* . . . The quotation is as follows:

But there is nothing in the decision to suggest that in the case of a director the fiduciary relationship can arise only in an agency situation. On the other hand, the mere status of company director should not produce that sort of responsibility to a shareholder and in my opinion it does not do so. The existence of such a relationship must depend, in my opinion, upon all the facts of the particular case.

Finally, it may be useful on this aspect of the case to refer to *Pelling v. Pelling*, (1982) 2 W.W.R. 185. In that case, at page 187, Berger J. said:

> Dealing first with the claim at common law: there is no fiduciary obligation as between shareholders, and no general fiduciary obligation owed by a director to shareholders.

That statement may be over-simplified, and should properly be read subject to the proviso that I have just quoted from *Coleman v. Myers* that simply the relationship of shareholder to shareholder does not import any fiduciary element. A shareholder may so conduct himself *vis-à-vis* another shareholder, such as becoming an agent for that other, that he takes on a fiduciary character towards that other shareholder. As I have found in this case, there is nothing in the circumstances of it by which Hood adopted, or should have fastened upon him, a fiduciary character.

Weiss v. Schad

(1999), [1999] O.J. No. 4356, 1999 CarswellOnt 3649 (S.C.J.), affirmed (2002), [2002] O.J. No. 1599, 2002 CarswellOnt 1498 (C.A.)

GARTON J.: The plaintiff Heinrich Weiss ("Weiss") . . . may be described as a sophisticated businessman whose companies conduct business all over the world, including Europe, Asia and North America. The conglomerate has about 1.8 billion dollars in sales annually. The plaintiff Siemag Rosenkaimer Grundstucksgesellschaft GbR ("Siemag") is a partnership established pursuant to the laws of (West) Germany, with its head office located in the Town of Hilchenbach. It is a holding company for the Weiss family investments.

The defendant Robert Schad ("Schad") is the president, director and majority shareholder of Husky Injection Molding Systems Ltd. ("Husky"), which is incorporated pursuant to the laws of Ontario . . . Schad owns and controls the defendant numbered company, 864062 Ontario Limited ("864062").

At the time that this action arose, the defendant Peter Hall ("Hall") was a Husky director, shareholder and the vice president of finance . . .

Following two years of negotiations, which commenced in September 1987, the plaintiffs, who held a 15% shareholding interest in Husky, agreed to sell their shares to the defendant numbered company, 864062, for $28.50 per share. The deal closed on October 31, 1989.

Unbeknownst to the plaintiffs, the defendants began discussions in November 1988 with a Japanese company, Komatsu Ltd. ("Komatsu"), with a view to forming a partnership or strategic alliance. An agreement between Husky and Komatsu was eventually reached on December 5, 1989. The transaction closed on February 15, 1990, about three and a half months after the sale of the plaintiffs' shares. The Komatsu agreement involved the purchase of 26% of Husky's shares for $28,000,000 in American currency, or approximately $73.00 per share. Komatsu was also given three years within which to exercise an option to increase its shareholding in Husky to 50%. There was a further provision whereby Komatsu, if it did not exercise this option, could require that Husky repurchase its shares at the same price, with some provision for interest. This unwinding agreement was in fact exercised in 1993, with Husky reacquiring the Komatsu shares in three annual installments . . .

The position of the plaintiffs is that Schad and Hall owed a fiduciary duty to them to disclose that they were engaged in discussions with another company about investing in Husky. It was submitted that by not making this disclosure, they breached their fiduciary duty.

The plaintiffs acknowledge that the defendants were not obliged to reveal the identity of the potential investor; they did not have to tell them specifically that they were dealing with Komatsu. However, it was argued that Schad and Hall, as directors, had a fiduciary duty to advise the plaintiffs that they were negotiating with a company for the sale of a significant equity interest in Husky. It was argued that had the plaintiffs been made aware of this fact, they would have suspended their own negotiations with the defendants until the arrangement with the potential investor had been determined. If a deal were reached, it would, in Weiss' view, probably establish a higher market value for the shares than he could bargain for in his own negotiations with the defendants. There was no evidence before the court as to the value of Husky's shares after the closing of the Komatsu deal. However, in May 1989, Citibank had provided a preliminary estimate of $57.00 per share based on the enhanced value of a strategic alliance.

As a general rule, directors and controlling shareholders do not owe fiduciary duties to minority shareholders. They are fiduciaries in relation to the company and not in relation to individual shareholders. This principle was first set out in *Percival v. Wright*, [1902] 2 Ch. 421 . . .

In *McKinlay Transport Ltd. v. Motor Transport Industrial*, [1996] O.J. No. 461 (Ont. Ct. Gen. Div.), Lane J. . . . states:

> In my opinion, the plaintiff goes too far when it submits that *Percival* is no longer the law. The cases show that no general duty, fiduciary or otherwise, arises between a director and shareholders simply because of the fact of directorship. There must be something more; something to engage the equitable jurisdiction of the court . . . It may be that the directors have in effect engaged to act as agents for the shareholder as in *Allen* or were acting outside the scope of normal directors' duties in seeking to sell all the shares of the company, as in *Tongue* [*Tongue v. Vencap Equities Alberta Ltd.* (1994), 17 Alta. L.R. (3d) 103 (Q.B.)] and

in *Gadsden v. Bennetto* (1913), 9 D.L.R. 719 (Man. C.A.); or were conspiring with a creditor to put the company into receivership so they might buy it at a good price, as was alleged in *Vladi Vladi Private Islands Ltd. v. Haase* (1990), 96 N.S.R. (2d) 323 (N.S.C.A.). The common thread is that the acts complained of are not simply the normal acts of directors in the operation of the company.

· · ·

As I am not prepared to find that a share transaction between a director and a shareholder automatically gives rise to a fiduciary relationship, the issue to be determined in the present case is whether the surrounding circumstances are such as to engage the equitable jurisdiction of the court. In my view, the dynamics of the relationship between the defendants and the plaintiffs do not justify the imposition of a fiduciary duty.

It cannot be said that the defendants, at any point in the negotiating process, relinquished their self-interest in dealing with the plaintiffs. There was no trust placed by Weiss in either Schad or Hall and no expectation on his part that they would act in his best interest. What occurred is best described as a commercial negotiation between two sophisticated parties who at all times dealt with each other at arms-length.

Weiss had no personal interest whatsoever in Schad's plans for Husky. Through a joint venture in the early seventies, he found himself the owner of shares in the company, but he was a passive investor throughout. He was content to sell the shares if he could get a good return on his investment or the price that "hurts". He wanted to receive a certain multiple of his original investment. The bargaining process then commenced. Hall's opening offer was $14.00 per share; Wirke [general manager of the Weiss companies and the person responsible for negotiating on behalf of Weiss] was aiming for $34.00. Wirke understood that the defendants, as purchasers, would bargain for the lowest possible price and that his role was to get the highest price.

The plaintiffs did not rely on the defendants for any advice. Wirke retained Price Waterhouse to assist him. His instructions were to find out certain information from the defendants "without disclosing an interest on our part" . . .

The plaintiffs were not peculiarly vulnerable, but were sophisticated and experienced in business and in making investment decisions. They operated in Europe, Canada and the United States. They were familiar with the business sector in which Husky operated, and had access to information in that industry through Husky's competitor, Battenfeld, which they controlled. Their shares in Husky represented a minor investment for them. Like any deal he might make on the stock market, Weiss wanted to make a good profit. If he could get a certain price, he was prepared to sell.

Although it was the defendants who first approached Weiss with respect to the purchase of his shares, it cannot be said that any unfair or undue pressure was exerted by them in order to persuade him to sell. The defendants were eager to purchase the shares, but it was the plaintiffs who controlled the pace of the negotiations. Wirke deliberately took his time in returning messages. Aware of the defendants' eagerness to buy the shares, he employed delay as part of his negotiating strategy in order to get a better price. Wirke's tactics, much to the frustration of the defendants, resulted in the bargaining process dragging on for two years . . .

In my view, having regard to all of the circumstances, the plaintiffs have failed to establish that they were peculiarly vulnerable or at the mercy of the defendants. The bargaining positions of the parties were equal. The plaintiffs were experienced in business and had access to information in the plastic injection industry. They had their own resources and professional advisors, including their own legal counsel as well as Price Waterhouse. They had been advised to obtain further information in order to arrive at an accurate valuation of their shares. They rejected that advice. They knew the price that they wanted for the shares and, through skilful negotiating, managed to close the deal at a price very close to their intended target. They controlled the pace of the discussions. Weiss, an able and experienced businessman, would have been well aware of the fact that Schad and Hall, as directors of Husky, were privy to information which he did not have. He could not be said to have been "caught off guard" or to have failed to see the risks inherent in selling his shares to Schad. Certainly the plaintiffs' advisors at Price Waterhouse knew that the directors would have all kinds of information potentially relevant to value and which the plaintiffs would not have unless they asked for it . . .

In the absence of any special circumstances and it not having been established that Schad and Hall were acting outside the scope of their normal duties as directors, I conclude that there was no fiduciary duty owed to the plaintiffs by the defendants to disclose the fact that there were discussions taking place with a potential investor.

Note

In *Tongue v. Vencap Equities Alberta Ltd.* (1994), [1994] A.J. No. 115, 1994 CarswellAlta 35 (Q.B.), McBain J. reviewed *Dusik v. Newton* and concluded that "it is clear that where a director buys shares from a minority shareholder, a fiduciary duty arises". The Alberta Court of Appeal allowed an appeal from McBain J.'s ruling on other grounds, without commenting on the fiduciary duty claim: see *Tongue v. Vencap Equities Alberta Ltd.*

(1996), [1996] A.J. No. 435, 1996 CarswellAlta 384 (C.A.). In *Weiss v. Schad*, Garton J. disagreed with McBain J.'s reading of *Dusik*.

5. STATUTORY LAW

In Canada, provisions prohibiting or regulating insider trading can be found in the federal and provincial corporations statutes, such as the CBCA or the OBCA, and in provincial securities legislation, such as the *Ontario Securities Act*. The validity of co-existing federal corporate and provincial securities legislation relating to insider trading was upheld by the Supreme Court of Canada in the following 1982 case.

Multiple Access Ltd. v. McCutcheon,
[1982] 2 S.C.R. 161, 1982 CarswellOnt 128, 1982 CarswellOnt 738
(per Dickson C.J.)

> This appeal raises the issue of the constitutionality of provincially, and federally, enacted "insider trading" legislation, and, more specifically, very similar sections in provincial and federal statutes which deal with the use of confidential information by insiders . . .
>
> The power of Parliament in relation to the incorporation of companies with other than provincial objects has not been narrowly defined. The authorities are clear that it goes well beyond mere incorporation. It extends to such matters as the maintenance of the company, the protection of creditors of the company and the safeguarding of the interests of the shareholders. It is all part of the internal ordering as distinguished from the commercial activities. . . . Insider malfeasance affects, directly and adversely, corporate powers, organization, internal management. It affects also financing because shareholders and potential shareholders must be assured the company's affairs will be scrupulously and fairly conducted; otherwise the raising of capital, clearly an element of company law, will be inhibited . . . Providing safeguards against the malfeasance of the managers is strictly within what might properly be called the constitution of the company . . .
>
> I agree with the submission of counsel for the Attorney General of Canada that the impugned provisions of the *Canada Corporations Act* are directed at preserving the integrity of federal companies and protecting the shareholders of such companies; they aim at practices, injurious to a company or to shareholders at large of a company, by persons who because they hold positions of trust or otherwise are privy to information not available to all shareholders . . . Insiders should not benefit, either at the expense of the company or at the expense of other shareholders, from their access to confidential information intended to be available only for a corporate purpose and not for the personal benefit of anyone. Information so acquired is at the expense of the enterprise. Confidential company information is a corporate asset the

benefit of which is intended to benefit the company, its shareholders and creditors . . .

It is true that the net cast by s. 100.4 of the *Canada Corporations Act* is a broad one but it must be broad if it is to be effective. Section 100.4 speaks of insiders, employees, associates, and affiliates. It may catch more than just directors or managers. There is no reason in principle why this should be fatal to constitutional integrity. Practical considerations no doubt dictated that the net be broad if confidential information, vital to the financial integrity of the company, were to be adequately protected from those unprincipled insiders who were in a position to be privy to such information.

[Dickson C.J. then turned to the challenge to the validity of the insider trading provisions of the *Ontario Securities Act*.]

The argument against the validity of ss. 113 and 114 of the *Ontario Securities Act* is that they are beyond the legislative power of the Province in that they purport to apply to companies incorporated under the laws of Canada; these sections are not in pith and substance enactments regulating the securities business; in actuality they define critical corporate relationships; it is beyond the power of a province to enact laws that regulate the corporate relationships of a federally-incorporated company.

I do not think this argument is tenable. It is well established that the provinces have the power, as a matter of property and civil rights, to regulate the trade in corporate securities in the province, provided the statute does not single out federal companies for special treatment or discriminate against them in any way. There must be no impairment of status or of the essential power to raise capital for corporate purpose. But federal incorporation does not render a company immune from securities regulation of general application in a province . . .

Federally-incorporated companies are subject, with one important exception, to provincial regulations with respect to trading in securities. The legislative powers of the Province are restricted so that "the status and powers of a Dominion Company as such cannot be destroyed: . . . and legislation will be invalid if a Dominion Company is "sterilized in all its functions and activities" or "its status and essential capacities are impaired in a substantial degree" . . . Subject to that exception, a federal company empowered to carry on a particular business in a province is subject to the competent legislation of the province as to that business. If it wishes to raise capital through the sale of securities there is no reason why it should not be subject to the laws of the province applicable to all those in the province who wish to raise capital through security sales, and subject thereafter to rules requiring honest dealings in securities, so that the public be not defrauded.

(a) Corporate Law

CBCA

(i) Short-Selling and Options

In a nutshell, short-selling is a way of speculating on a stock price decline consisting of borrowing shares from a broker and selling them on the open market. When and if the stock price declines, the investor buys shares on the open market to return to the broker. Her profit consists of the difference between the proceeds she received from the initial short sale (less transaction costs), less her cost of buying the shares back on the open market (including transaction costs). While her short position is "open", i.e., after she has borrowed and sold the shares but before she has bought replacement shares, part or all of the proceeds of the initial short sale generally sit in an account with the broker as collateral for the share borrowing. Some or all of the interest that would otherwise be earned on the account is retained by the broker as compensation for the loan of shares.

Section 130(1) of the CBCA prohibits an insider from "knowingly selling, directly or indirectly, a security of a distributing corporation or any of its affiliates" unless the insider owns and has fully paid for the security. There is an exception for sales where the insider "owns another security convertible into the security sold or an option or right to acquire the security sold" under the circumstances set forth in that subsection.

Section 130(2) prohibits an insider from "selling a call or buying a put in respect of a security of the corporation or any of its affiliates".

A call is an option to buy shares from the seller of the option, while a put is an option to sell shares to the seller of the option, in each case at a fixed "strike price" and during a given period.

Buying a call option is a way of speculating on a stock price *increase*, since the option will be valuable to the extent that the stock price when the option is exercised is greater than the previously agreed strike price. For example, if someone buys a call option on 100 shares of a particular company with a strike price of $10 and an exercise period of three months and at some point during the three months the stock price increases to $12 and the option-holder decides to exercise the option, she will have earned a profit of $2 per share: she will buy 100 shares from the seller of the option at the agreed price of $10 per share, and immediately resell the shares on the market for $12 per share, pocketing the difference. Her net profit is $2 per share less transaction costs and less whatever she paid the seller for the call option in the first place. If, on the other hand, the stock price does not go above $10 during the exercise period, the option-holder will not exercise the option and it will expire, worthless.

Buying a put option is a way of speculating on a stock price *decrease*, since the option will be valuable to the extent that the stock price at the time of exercise is less than the strike price. Buying a put option is also a way of protecting an existing stock holding from future price declines. For example, if someone owns 100 shares of a company which are currently worth $100 per share, and she purchases a 3-month put option on the shares of that company with a strike price of $100 per share, she knows she will be able to sell her shares for $100 per share for the next three months, even if the market price of the shares declines, simply by exercising the put option.

Selling a call option is another way of speculating on a stock price *decrease*. Do you see why? Do you also see why *selling a put option* is a way of speculating on a stock price *increase*?

Why should insiders be prohibited from short-selling, and from selling call options or buying put options on, securities of their corporation or its affiliates?

You should carefully review the definitions of "insider" and "affili-ates", noting, in particular, that the definition of "insider" for purposes of s. 130 differs from the definition for purposes of s. 131.

For more on the mechanics of short-selling and options, students may wish to refer to R.W. Hamilton and R.A. Booth, *Business Basics for Law Students* (3d) (2002), §§14.19, 15.2.

(ii) Liability for Use of Confidential Information and for Tipping

Insiders of CBCA corporations who purchase or sell a security of the cor-poration with knowledge of "confidential information that, if generally known, might reasonably be expected to affect materially the value of any of the securities of the corporation" are liable to compensate their counter-party in the transaction (s. 131(4)), and must disgorge to the corporation any "benefit or advantage received or receivable by the insider as a result of" the transaction (s. 131(5)).

As an exception to ss. 131(4) and (5), the insider is not liable to compensate her counterparty or to disgorge any benefit to the corporation if she reasonably believed the information had been generally disclosed (s. 131(4)(a)). In addition, the insider is not liable to compensate her counter-party under s. 131(4), but is not exempted from the disgorgement require-ment of s. 131(5), if the counterparty knew or should have known the information (s. 131(4)(b)) or the transaction took place in the circumstances prescribed in s. 42 of the Regulations (s. 131(4)(c)), such as where the purchase or sale was in fulfillment of a contractual obligation entered into before the insider acquired the confidential information (CBC Regs, s. 42(c)).

Liability is also incurred by an insider who engages in tipping, i.e., in the words of s. 131(6), "who discloses to another person confidential infor-mation with respect to the corporation that has not been generally disclosed and that, if generally known, might reasonably be expected to affect mate-rially the value of any of the securities of the corporation". Pursuant to ss. 131(6) and (7), which run parallel to ss. 131(4) and (5), an inside "tipper" is liable to compensate outsiders who were the counterparties of anyone who received the information, and to disgorge to the corporation any benefit or advantage received or receivable by the tipper as a result of the disclosure.

As with ss. 131(4), there are defences to the insider tipping liability provisions, including the insider's reasonable belief that the information had been generally disclosed (s. 131(6)(a)), which precludes both liability to compensate trading counterparties of the tippee and liability to the corporation; and the actual or constructive knowledge of the information by the person alleging damages (s. 131(6)(b)), which precludes only liability to counterparties but not liability to the corporation. In addition, there is no liability if the disclosure of the information was necessary in the course of the insider's business, except where the insider is a proposed takeover bidder or business combination partner (or an insider, affiliate or associate of such a person), in which case the disclosure must have been necessary to effect the takeover bid or business combination.

Section 131(8) provides that the court, in assessing damages for insider trading or tipping, "must consider" the difference between the price paid or received by the plaintiff and the average market price of the security over the twenty trading days immediately following general disclosure of the information. What do you think is the purpose of this provision?

The definitions are, as always, very important and should be carefully studied. The definition of "insider" set forth in s. 131(1) is critical to the scope of the provision, and it refers both to other defined terms (such as "affiliate") and to the Regulations. Some important classes of persons who are included in the definition are directors, senior officers, employees, tippees, people involved in a professional activity or engaged in business with the corporation, shareholders owning 10% or more of a class of voting securities, and directors and senior officers of affiliates. Also included are those who acquire inside information as a result of a proposed business combination with the corporation.

It is also important to note that the definition of "security" includes not only securities of the corporation, but securities of "another entity, the market price of which varies materially with the market price of the securities of the corporation". Why do you think this was added?

Looking back to the policy discussion with which this chapter began, what appears to be the theoretical basis for s. 131 of the CBCA? The insider's liability to account to the corporation for any benefit or advantage received or receivable (ss. 131(5) and (7)) is consistent with the idea that insider trading amounts to misappropriation of a corporate asset. But how can the insider's liability to compensate transaction counterparties (ss. 131(4) and (6)) be explained?

Practically speaking, in a transaction over a securities exchange, it may be difficult or impossible to identify the particular investors who were on the opposite side of an insider's trade for purposes of the insider's liability under ss. 131(4) and (6). Even if the insider's counterparties could be identified, what is the justification for awarding damages to them, but not to the other outside investors who traded in the same direction, at the same time?

Can there be penal liability for insider trading under the CBCA? While s. 241 of the CBCA makes it a summary conviction offence to fail, without reasonable cause, to comply with any provision of the CBCA, it is doubtful whether insider trading as described in s. 131 amounts to non-compliance with the Act, since s. 131 (unlike s. 130 of the CBCA or s. 76 of the OSA) does not explicitly prohibit the practice; it merely attaches civil liability to it.

(iii) Ontario and British Columbia

Like s. 131 of the CBCA, the insider trading provisions of the OBCA and BCBCA make the insider liable to compensate counterparties and to account to the corporation for any benefit or advantage received or receivable (OBCA, s. 138(5); BCBCA, s. 192(2)) from an insider trade.

However, there is no provision in either the OBCA or the BCBCA analogous to s. 130 of the CBCA, prohibiting insider short-selling.

Moreover, the wording of the liability provisions differs significantly between the OBCA and BCBCA, on the one hand, and the CBCA, on the other hand. While liability under s. 131 of the CBCA arises from having engaged in a transaction "with knowledge of confidential information. . .", s. 138(5) of the OBCA imposes liability where the insider, "in connection with a transaction in a security of the corporation . . ., *makes use* of any *specific* confidential information *for the insider's own benefit or advantage*. . ." (emphasis added). Like the Ontario provision. the B.C. provision also contains concepts of "making use" of the information, of the information being "specific", and of the use being "for the benefit or advantage of the insider".

The following are a few other noteworthy differences between the OBCA and BCBCA, on the one hand, and the CBCA, on the other:

- There is no provision in the OBCA or BCBCA explicitly creating liability for tipping. Could a tipper be said to be a person who "in connection with a transaction in a security of the corporation, makes use of any specific confidential information for the insider's own benefit or advantage . . ." within the meaning of s. 138(5) of the OBCA? See also the similarly worded s. 192(2) of the BCBCA.

- The Ontario provision applies only to corporations that are not "offering corporations", i.e., generally speaking, the Ontario provision applies to corporations whose securities are not publicly traded (s. 138(1), definition of "corporation"). The BCBCA contains a similar limitation, applying only to "private companies". The CBCA provision contains no such limitation.

- The Ontario and B.C. provisions do not contain language expanding the definition of "security" to include securities of other entities the value of which is correlated to the corporation's securities. Might this difference be insignificant in practice, given that the Ontario and B.C. provisions are in any event limited to non-publicly-traded corporations?

- The exceptions are more limited in the Ontario and B.C. statutes. The OBCA provision, for example, contains no exception for the insider's reasonable belief that the information was generally known.

- The B.C. provision can be waived by contract: s. 192(5). It is, of course, not sufficient for the insider and outside buyer or seller of the securities to agree to waive s. 192; the private corporation must also agree to waive the section, otherwise the insider would still be liable under s. 192(3)(b) to account to the corporation for any benefit received from the transaction. What is the justification for allowing parties to contract out of insider trading liability?

The following cases illustrate, among other things, the application of the concepts of "making use", "specific confidential information", and "for the insider's benefit or advantage". The first case, *Green v. Charterhouse*, was decided under the *Ontario Securities Act*, which contained these concepts until it was amended in 1979. The second case, *Tongue v. Vencap*, was decided under the CBCA, which also contained these concepts until s. 131 was amended in 2001 to bring it into line with provincial securities legislation.

Green v. Charterhouse Group Canada Ltd.
(1976), 12 O.R. (2d) 280, 68 D.L.R. (3d) 592, 1976 CarswellOnt 832
(C.A.)

The following facts are taken from Johnston, "Green v. Charterhouse Group Canada Ltd. et al." (1973), 51 Can. Bar Rev. 676 at pp. 678–80 (footnotes omitted).

Green was a director and senior officer of Imbrex Ltd. and of one of its subsidiaries Green Ltd. until December, 1967. He then resigned from both offices in both companies under a negotiated severance agreement. Imbrex was a federally incorporated company listed on the Toronto and Canadian and Vancouver Stock Exchanges. It was formed in 1965 to merge Green's carpet distributorship company in Ontario with two similar companies in Quebec and the Maritime provinces.

Green and the principal shareholders of the Quebec, Maritime and Western constituent companies in the amalgamation which gave birth to Imbrex, along with Charterhouse Group Canada Ltd., a venture capitalist which had supplied equity financing, were parties to a shareholders' buy-sell agreement. Under the terms one party was obliged to give the others a right of first refusal before selling his shares. All these parties were insiders of Imbrex and all but the Maritime group and Green himself were subsequently defendants in the insider suit.

Commencing in the spring of 1967 Green gave notice of his desire to sell 20,000 of his approximately 100,000 Imbrex shares. When the parties to the shareholders' agreement failed to exercise their rights he sold the 20,000 through the market at prices of $5.25 to $6. At the time of his severance from Imbrex in December, 1967 he indicated his desire to dispose of the remaining 80,000. Negotiations with the other parties to the agreement commenced culminating in Green's offer to sell all at $6 a share on May 3rd, 1968 and his acceptance of a counter offer to purchase all at $5.7/8 on May 6th, the transaction which spawned this suit.

At the time of his severance from Imbrex, Green had unsuccessfully offered his shares to Harding Carpets Ltd. Imbrex's President, Godbout, early in January, 1968 began discussions with Harding officers with a view to a merger of the two companies. After several meetings, they concluded by mid-February that each company should consider its position and renew discussions on April 1st. This they did and Godbout notified Imbrex directors that Harding welcomed a merger but how and when to do it was subject to further consideration. On May 1st Harding postponed a meeting with Godbout proposed for the same day to May 21st. It was further postponed until Godbout told Harding on June 9th of another potential acquirer of Imbrex and the next day Godbout offered all Imbrex shares to Harding at $8.50-$8.75. Harding refused. Godbout concluded that the possibilities of merger with Harding were very slim, believing that Harding was angered at Godbout's apparent desire for Imbrex to acquire control of Harding through the merger and at his discussions with a potential acquirer which had a wide variety of product lines. Godbout then knew that Harding would almost certainly sever the franchise arrangement which was Imbrex' principal asset.

Godbout immediately contacted Neon Products Ltd., a Vancouver based conglomerate, and they quickly agreed on a Neon share exchange take over bid for Imbrex which at the then market price for Neon valued Imbrex at $12 per share. The Neon-Imbrex relationship had its birth in an investment dealer's exploratory letter to Godbout in late February, 1968 followed by several meetings in March and April, with Neon suggesting on April 29th that Imbrex was worth $10 a share in Neon stock and Godbout countering he would only consider reporting a price of $12.50 a share to the Imbrex board. Neon's analysts were permitted access to Imbrex to make an appraisal on the promise that Neon would make an offer by May 16th if satisfied. The Neon discussions were reported to the Imbrex board with some concern expressed that Neon stock was inflated in price.

Green had been advised by several of the Imbrex directors of the possibility of an offer for Imbrex. He interpreted that the offerer was Harding. On April 30th, six days before the disposition of his 80,000 shares, the Imbrex board authorized the advice to be crystallized in a confidential letter from one of its directors to Green. It stated "that preliminary discussions have taken place which conceivably might result in an offer being made for Imbrex shares at a price in excess of their current market price" and concluding "it is expected that the matter will be resolved within the next two weeks".

The Imbrex shares ranged in price from $4 to $5 in March, 1968 trading, reached a peak of $5? for April on the last day of the month with heavier trading in May peaking at $6 2/8. By June 10th the price reached $7 and following the announcement of the Neon offer on June 12th gradually increased to a high of $16? on June 28th. Neon's high was $16 1/2 in January, 1968 remaining stable until it reached peaks of $25 in April and $26 in May. In June its high was $43? and its low $231/2 and for the rest of 1968 its high ranged between $361/4 and $443/4. It declined through 1969 with a high at year end of $21 dropping to $7.40 in 1970 and reviving somewhat to a high of $10 2/8 and a low of $8.80 at the end of 1972.

ARNUP J.A.: The claim under s. 113 of the *Securities Act*.

In considering the applicability of s. 113, nothing turns on the definition of "insider". It is true that Jordans Rugs Limited, which made the purchase of 40,000 shares from Green, did not prior to the purchase own equity shares of Imbrex carrying more than 10% of the voting rights attached to all equity shares of Imbrex for the time being outstanding, within the meaning of s. 109(1)(c)(ii) of the Act. It would appear, however, that Jordans Rugs Limited is an "associate" of the two Jordan-Knoxes, who were themselves insiders, as directors of Imbrex.

Leaving aside for the time being the phrase "make use of", did the defendants possess "specific confidential information . . . that, if generally known, might reasonably be expected to affect materially the value of" Imbrex shares? The trial Judge was of the view that while the information was "confidential" (which was not disputed by anyone in this Court), it was not specific". Taking the case of Godbout, who obviously had more information than anyone else, it is my view that the information he had on April 30, 1968, as to the first quarter earnings, and as to the state of the negotiations with Neon was in each case "specific". (Since Mr. Weir does not rely on Godbout's knowledge of the Harding discussions, it is not necessary to characterize that information.)

The facts Godbout had concerning Neon might have been unbelievable to other directors, or the proposals which were being made to him might have been totally unacceptable to them or some of them. The information may not have been worthy of credence or of sufficient weight to justify any positive action by the board of Imbrex. Nevertheless, in my view the information was specific"; the word is used by the section in contradistinction to "general", or not specific". A useful illustration of the difference between what is specific and what is not is the state of the information possessed by Godbout following the meetings with Pattison in Vancouver on April 16th. The two men met because Pattison had made an inquiry concerning the circumstances under which all of the Imbrex shares might be for sale. Pattison talked about Neon and its "goals and ambitions". When they talked later in the day, Pattison again talked of Neon, but made no offers or overtures concerning Imbrex shares. Without attaching undue significance to Godbout's evidence at trial describing their conversation as "general", the information Godbout had on April 16th was "general", and not "specific".

The heart of the s. 113 issue is whether the defendants or some of them "made use of" specific confidential information for his or their own benefit or advantage. The issue is illustrated by the opposing arguments. Mr. Weir submits that if an insider has the information, and makes a purchase of shares from a shareholder who does not have the information, s. 113 at once comes into play, without more. The argument of the defendants was that it is not enough to have the information. To "make use of" it, they submit, the information must be a "factor" in the insider's participation in the transaction which the insider carries out with the person alleged to be aggrieved, "either by inducing him to enter into it or by assisting him or otherwise influencing him in the manner in which he performs it" (the quotation is from Mr. Genest's factum).

The trial judge accepted this argument but attached to it a proviso that once it is proven that an insider had specific confidential information, and had bought shares from a shareholder who did not have such information, an "onus of explanation" devolves upon the insider to establish that he did not make use of the information.

I would also accept the proposition that a plaintiff invoking s. 113 must show that there was specific confidential information, which the insider had, and that it was a factor (in the sense stated) in the action the insider took whereby the plaintiff suffered loss. The proviso or corollary I would link to this principle is that once it is shown that the insider had such information, and entered into a transaction involving the purchase of shares of a shareholder who did not have it, the burden of proof is thereafter upon the insider to show that in fact he did not make use of the information in the transaction, that is, that the information was not a factor in what he did. This is more than an "onus of explanation"; it is a burden of proof that rests on the insider to the end of the case. It is of course one that is satisfied by a preponderance of credible evidence, on a balance of probabilities — the standard burden of proof in civil cases.

This difference between my statement and that of the trial Judge does not affect the result in this case, because his findings of fact are clear and unequivocal, and amply satisfy the burden of proof which rested upon the defendants. We are therefore not involved in any semantic niceties concerning the difference between an "onus of explanation" and a "burden of proof", and in whether the trial Judge misdirected himself in using the former expression instead of the latter.

In my view it is a question of fact in each case, and with respect to each individual in a case, whether the individual made use of specific confidential information. In this case there are clear findings of fact with respect to each of the individuals that he or they did not "make use of" the information. Particularly with respect to Godbout, this is a finding which we are all persuaded we must approach with caution. Godbout knew a great deal; it was specific and confidential. The fact is that he gave evidence to show why it could not be said of him that he made use of the confidential information that he had. He was cross-examined at great length. The trial Judge, approaching this evidence with a healthy skepticism, might well have disbelieved it. In fact he chose to accept it. On this particular issue, the trial Judge's disbelief of Green is not a correlative of his affirmation of the credibility of Godbout. That latter finding must stand by itself. It is one which it was quite open for the trial Judge to make, and after considering all of the important documents in the case, as well as all of the evidence at trial to which we were referred (and much more), we are not prepared to disturb his finding.

The case against the other defendants is considerably less strong than that against Godbout. Without recapitulating the evidence led against each one of them, there are specific findings that Sinclair (on behalf of Charterhouse) did not make use of the information that he had, which was considerably less than that possessed by Godbout, and similar findings were made with respect to the other insiders.

An experienced trial Judge such as Grant J., without doubt would approach with skepticism the evidence of Godbout that he did not tell the other listeners on the conference call of the discussions with Pattison which had taken place so recently. The fact that Godbout did not tell them is corroborated by the other parties to the call, and of course is sworn to by Godbout himself. Again, it was open for the trial Judge to disbelieve Godbout but he chose to accept his evidence. Similarly, the trial Judge found that Sinclair did not know of the Pattison-Godbout discussions of April 29th until after the contract with Green had been made. There is no reason to upset this finding. The same conclusions must be reached with regard to the findings concerning Pouliot and Charles Jordan-Knox.

I should comment upon Sinclair's so-called "warning letter" of April 30, 1968. Whatever may be said of this letter as being a discharge of the "moral obligations" which Godbout thought Green's former associates owed to Green, the letter was not the disclosure which may provide a defence to an action under s. 113(1) of the *Securities Act*. While the letter does not say so, the writer is really saying that "confidential information exists which might be of substantial significance to you but which I am not at liberty to disclose". Once the necessary ingredients of a cause of action against an insider under s. 113(1) are shown to exist, then the resulting obligation is discharged by disclosure of "such information". It is not discharged by disclosing it exists, without saying what it is.

Writing the letter to Green was a decent thing to do. The writing of it, and what it said, were of the greatest significance in a case involving allegations of conspiracy and fraud against its writer and those associated with him in the transaction which shortly followed its writing. Its legal effect in the action as presented on this appeal is minimal.

No doubt the Ontario legislation was influenced by the American provisions, particularly s. 10(b) of the *Securities Exchange Act* of 1934 and Rule 10b-5, which have been discussed in several cases involving Texas Gulf Sulphur Co. Inc. (as its name then was), and in *Re Cady, Roberts & Co.* (1961), 40 S.E.C. 907 at p. 912. While in very broad and general terms the underlying purpose of s. 10(b) and Rule 10b-5 and of the Ontario Act are the same, in trying to impose limitations upon insiders of corporations and in laying down standards of disclosure by the company and its directors, the plain fact is that the language of the Ontario Act is not the same as the American. The trial Judge was right in saying he did not need to look at American cases to interpret plain words in an Ontario statute. The American law prior to 1934 was not the same as our inherited principles of *Percival v. Wright* Nor have I found it necessary to resort to any canons of construction based on "enactments restrictive of common law rights". Like the trial Judge, I have taken the Legislature's words as I found them.

Some misgivings have been expressed as to the trial Judge's reference to information "acquired for corporate purposes": Prof. Johnston's commentary, *supra*, at p. 683. With respect I would not so confine "confidential information" (assuming the trial Judge intended thus to qualify or limit the section). The probabilities doubtless are that the insider acquired his information through participation in the company's affairs, but there is not a sine qua non to the operation of the section. The insider may learn something that no one else knows, but which fulfils all the attributes of specific, confidential information found in s. 113(1).

I should mention also the argument raised by Mr. Genest on behalf of those defendants who were at all times outside Ontario. On their behalf it was submitted that the *Securities Act* had no application to transactions occurring outside this Province. Interesting as this argument was, it fails on the facts. It is clear on the evidence that the agreement with Green was made by Sinclair, and that his communications to and from Green all occurred in Ontario. It is further clear from the evidence, and that of Sinclair in particular, that in making the counter-offer of $5?, he was acting for those who had by that time agreed to take down Green's shares, in agreed proportions . . .

We heard argument at length on the difficult question of the measure of damages under s. 113 . . .

We were invited to consider such questions as whether the wrongdoer is entitled to take the position that the measure of his obligation is the loss that would have been suffered by a reasonable person if disclosure as required by law had in fact been made to the plaintiff. There are unresolved questions as to what is a "direct loss suffered": the expression in s. 113(1).

The situation is complicated by the fact that Green, if he had held his shares, could have accepted Neon's offer; he might have decided to hold Neon's shares thus acquired; he might have sold them, at the right time, at a substantial profit; or if he had elected to hold them to the date of the trial, he would have suffered a substantial loss. Furthermore, are all of the joint parties liable to the same degree? Is Mr. Pouliot, who became (with his firm) a holder of 5,000 shares solely because of other pressure put upon him by Godbout, now to find himself liable to Green for $1,000,000? Should the "New York rule", well recognized in the United States (for a recent example, see *Reynolds v. Texas Gulf Sulphur Co.* (1970), 309 F. Supp. 548 at p. 563) be applied in Ontario where liability is found under s. 113? The New York rule is really a more sophisticated application of the broad rule enunciated in the several Roman cases; it fixes as a terminal point of the period within which the market price of shares is relevant, the end of a reasonable period after due disclosure within which the aggrieved shareholder can protect his interests.

I do not propose to deal with these very difficult questions of damages, in view of my conclusion that there is no liability to the plaintiff on the part of any of the defendants.

I would dismiss the appeal with costs, those of Imbrex to be taxed on the basis already stated.

Tongue v. Vencap Equities Alberta Ltd.
(1996), [1996] A.J. No. 435, 1996 CarswellAlta 384 (C.A.)

KERANS, IRVING and RUSSELL JJ.A.: This is an appeal by the unsuccessful defendants against a judgment against them after trial in Queen's Bench.

The appellants and defendants are directors and shareholders in a company called Synerlogic Inc. The respondents and plaintiffs were shareholders in that company who sold their shares, directly or indirectly, to the appellants. The basis of the suit is that, during the negotiation of this sale, the appellants made use of confidential information not known to the plaintiffs. The trial judge accepted that complaint and gave judgment to the plaintiffs for the difference between the sale price of their shares and the sale price they would have gained had they known the confidential information.

The full details of the facts are in the trial decision, which is now reported at (1994) 17 Alta. L.R. (3d) 103. The plaintiffs sold their shares for roughly one-third their actual value. They had made an offer to sell to the appellants in early June, 1988 at 60 cents a share, which was roughly the price of the last recorded sale share in this closely held corporation. The appellants accepted that offer. When they accepted the offer, they were aware of a serious expression of interest by a major company which would, if it proceeded with the purchase, pay more than three times that price. That transaction was in fact firmed up about the same time that the sale to the plaintiffs was completed, and at a considerable profit to the appellants.

The plaintiffs alleged, and the trial judge accepted, that the appellants were . . . in breach of the provision of s. 131(4) of the *Canada Business Corporations Act* [the wording of which, at the time, was identical to s. 138(5) of the OBCA].

The learned trial judge concluded, after a careful review of the evidence, that the appellants had specific confidential information, namely the expression of interest just mentioned, which, if generally known, would reasonably affect materially the value of the security. He also found that they made use of this information in the sense that they decided to purchase the shares of the plaintiffs and profit from that purchase and the subsequent resale. He also found that the sale price could not have been discovered by the plaintiffs through the exercise of reasonable diligence. Lastly he found that a formal release executed by the plaintiffs in connection with completion of the purchase was not effective to bar this suit. He gave judgment accordingly for the advantage received.

On appeal, four grounds are raised.

First, it is said that the learned trial judge erred in finding that the appellants or any of them made use of any specific confidential information for their own benefit or advantage. There are two aspects to this ground. First, it is said that there is no liability under s. 131(4) if the non-insider is told by the insider the substance, but not the details, of the insider's knowledge and the non-insider decides to carry on without further enquiry. Alternatively, it is argued that there is no liability on the part of an insider for any advantage gained where the insider's motivation for the transaction is something other than to take advantage.

As to the second, the learned trial judge explicitly found as a fact that the intention of the appellants when they entered into this transaction was to make the profit that was available to them. It is argued for the appellants that this was an unreasonable finding, because the true and primary purpose of the appellants when they purchased these shares was to eliminate the nuisance of these troublesome minority shareholders. It is said that there was no evidence that the purpose for which the transaction was completed was to make a profit.

We do not agree. On the one hand, to be sure, there are the protestations as to purpose uttered from the witness box and in memoranda by the appellants. On the other hand, there was the evidence of the hard fact that they all knew about the prospect for huge profits when they agreed to this purchase. A key memorandum to directors, dated June 17, 1988, said:

> Accordingly, we could, at worse, purchase additional shares of Synerlogic Inc. at an attractive earnings multiple, or acquire the shares and sell them at more than three times acquisition cost if the proposed sale proceeds.

Ascribing motive to any human act is almost always a matter of inference, and we cannot say that the inference drawn by the learned trial judge here was unreasonable. In any event, it is not correct to say that there is no evidence that the profit motive played no part in deliberations. For example, the minutes of the board meeting of the appellant Vencap indicate that the profit motive was one matter discussed.

It is said by Mr. Redmond that the taking of the advantage must be the dominant motive. In this regard, he relies upon the decision of the Ontario Court of Appeal in *Green v. Charterhouse Group Canada Ltd. et al.*, [1973] 2 O.R. 677. In that case, Arnup J.A. said that the phrase "make use of" connotes "some positive act on behalf of the insider to take advantage of the information that he possesses to profit in the marketplace". We agree. If a profit is a truly minimal and incidental aspect of a transaction, s. 131 may not apply. In any event, we also agree with Arnup, J.A. that the onus of demonstrating that profit was not a key motive lies with the inside trader. In this case, this onus was not met.

Returning to the first argument, we agree with the trial judge that the limited disclosure in this case was not adequate compliance with the requirements of s. 131. The appellants took great care to document the degree of disclosure made. They demanded that the plaintiffs formally acknowledge that they were told this:

> We have been informed . . . that offers to acquire the company may be forthcoming in the near future on financial terms that might prove more advantageous to the shareholders than we are prepared to accept by selling now. We understand that expressions of interest have been received from potential suitors and that by tendering our shares on the terms offered, we risk realizing any potential additional gain.

It is said that this is enough advice to put any reasonable investor on notice of the existence of other offers of other information.

The learned trial judge rejected this argument. He said that, in the circumstances of this case, where there had been some rumours and some share dealings in the recent past, the two critical facts were (1) that the person who expressed interest was a major, international firm of considerable substance and (2) that the expression of interest hinted at a price that was more than triple any sale price in the recent past. These were the two facts that were carefully suppressed in the vague statements just quoted. The learned trial judge concluded that the appellants had deprived the plaintiffs of precisely the information needed that materially affected the value of the security. We agree.

Before us, it was said that the appellants were not at liberty to disclose any more information because the third party had requested confidentiality. With respect, imposition of confidentiality does not release the inside trader of its obligations. On the contrary, the section is all about dealing in confidential information.

Moreover, as Mr. Macleod argued, s. 131 does not require any disclosure in breach of any confidence. What it does require is that the inside trader not rely on the confidential information if it decides to enter a transaction. This obligation left the appellants with three choices in this case: (1) refuse to treat with the plaintiffs because of the delicate situation; (2) seek permission from the third party to disclose the details to the plaintiffs; or (3) make an offer at a price that obviated the issue.

In passing, we observe that the proposal from the third party involved the acquisition of shares. As a result, it was inevitable that all shareholders sooner or later be told about it. It is not at all clear that the third party, in the circumstances, intended that its interest be reported only to shareholders who were friendly with management.

In any event, the appellants chose a fourth option: to limit disclosure to generalities. The risk of this approach is that it may be misunderstood. It leaves the other party in a position where she must guess at the true state of affairs. That is exactly what happened here. The plaintiffs guessed that the references were to the renewal of earlier offers by other third parties at share prices that were not so exciting. As a result of this mistaken guess, they resolved to complete the purchase.

In our respectful view, the very purpose of the insider trading regulation is to prevent the insider from putting the outsider into a guessing game with the insider holding a sure hand.

Moreover, it is obvious here that the plaintiffs were under some pressure to sell out. They were a significant minority interest but they had had a major falling-out with the majority interest, were very unhappy, and anxious to get out of the company. In our view, the appellants took advantage of that situation to force their hands. This is not the level playing field intended by s. 131.

We are of the view in the result that the learned trial judge was right to say that the disclosure made was not adequate compliance with the requirements of the statute.

The next ground of appeal is that the plaintiffs failed to exercise reasonable diligence to acquire the critical information, and, as a result, the saving provision in (a) of s. 131 was triggered. The learned trial judge rejected this argument on the basis that, as a matter of fact, the plaintiffs had nowhere else to go for added information, and would be refused the information by the appellants on the grounds of confidentiality. These are reasonable findings, supportable on the evidence.

It was said before us, and we agree, that the requirement for reasonable diligence can require a degree of persistence in a demand for information. The learned trial judge accepted that, but said that the plaintiffs acted reasonably in not persisting with any demands because of the pre-existing bad relationship between them and the controlling interests. He said that the plaintiffs honestly believed that they had been "stone-walled" for some time by the company in respect of many matters, and he was of the opinion that this was a factor that made their failure to persist reasonable.

In our view, these are all reasonable findings. It was said that the refusal of the appellants to be co-operative is not an answer to a failure of the plaintiffs to be persistent. We do not agree. The attitude of the appellants, and the record of dealings between them, are factors that are relevant on the question of what amounts to reasonable diligence.

The next ground of appeal is that, in any event, the plaintiffs should be bound by a release they gave in connection with the sale of the shares. The terms of this release, which were negotiated between the solicitors for the two parties, contains an absolute general release for any outstanding claim of any kind on the part of the plaintiffs against the appellants. It makes no specific reference to non-disclosure or to s. 131.

In the ordinary course, a release cannot be effective, notwithstanding its wording, if it purports to waive a cause of action not known to the releasor: *Athabasca Realty Co. Ltd. v. Foster* (1982), 18 Alta. L.R. (2d) 385 (C.A.).

In some cases, one may be able to argue that, if the releasor has before him sufficient material that puts him on his inquiry whether he has a cause of action but he makes no inquiry and instead signs a waiver or release, then the release is effective notwithstanding that the releasor does not have precise knowledge of the cause of action. In this case, one could fairly argue that these plaintiffs were not prudent in executing a release after having received a refusal to supply meaningful details of the inside information.

That argument, however, is not available to the appellants in this case by reason of s. 122 of the *Business Corporations Act* which provides:

122(3) Subject to subsection 146(5), no provision in a contract, the articles, the bylaws or a resolution relieves a director or officer from the duty to act in accordance with this Act or the regulations or relieves him from liability for a breach thereof.

In our view, the learned trial judge was correct to say that this provision renders unenforceable any attempt by contract to have a releasor waive or release his right to be dealt with fairly under s. 131 in a case where he does not know that he was not dealt with fairly. As Mr. Macleod said, any other view would reduce the insider trading rule to a travesty. One could have a token exemption clause in every share purchase agreement.

The situation might be otherwise if, after a breach and with full knowledge of the breach details, a person executes a waiver and release. A release may be effective also if it contained an exclusive acknowledgment of the fact of non-disclosure and an explicit acknowledgment of the duty, but without any knowledge of the particulars. In any event, it is not necessary to pass comment on that for the purposes of this case.

In the light of these conclusions, we need not consider the findings about a fiduciary relationship. We would accordingly dismiss the appeal.

The following case is noteworthy for its treatment of the issue of "direct loss", which is relevant to the measure of compensation under the OBCA and BCBCA provisions.

Roberts v. Pelling
(1981), 130 D.L.R. (3d) 761, 1981 CarswellBC 620 (S.C.)

BERGER J.: The defendant Pelling, who controlled the majority of shares in Strataco Management Ltd., obtained a firm offer of $200,000 from a Mr. Thom, for the shares of the company. The defendant had 52 shares. Thom at first offered $150,000 for the defendant's shares, but then he offered $200,000 for all the outstanding shares. Then the defendant approached the plaintiff Roberts and, without disclosing Thom's offer, negotiated the redemption of Roberts' 24 shares by Strataco Management Ltd. for $21,500. Another shareholder, who, like Roberts, had 24 shares, agreed to the redemption of his shares for $24,000.

The plaintiff says that this was an insider transaction under s. 152 of the *Companies Act, 1973* (B.C.), c. 18 (now s. 153 of the *Company Act*, R.S.B.C. 1979, c. 59). Section 152 reads:

152. Every insider or affiliate of an insider of a corporation who, in connection with a transaction relating to any share of the corporation or any debt obligation of the corporation, makes use of any specific confidential information for the benefit or advantage of himself or of any associate or affiliate of himself, that, if

generally known might reasonably be expected to affect materially the value of the share or the debt obligation, is

(a) liable to compensate any person for any direct loss suffered by the person as a result of the transaction, unless the information was known or ought reasonably to have been known to the person at the time of the transaction; and

(b) accountable to the corporation for any direct benefit or advantage received or receivable by the insider or his affiliate, as the case may be, as a result of the transaction.

In the alternative, the plaintiff says that the defendant is liable for breach of fiduciary duty.

The plaintiff says that since he held 24% of the shares, he should have received 24% of the sale price, i.e., $48,000. So the relief claimed, whether as "direct loss" under s. 152 or damages at common law, is $26,500, that is, $48,000 less $21,500.

Dealing first with the claim at common law: there is no fiduciary obligation as between shareholders, and no general fiduciary obligation owed by a director to shareholders. A director's duty is to the company; he has no fiduciary obligation to the shareholders. There are some exceptions to this rule (Gower, Principles of Modern Company Law, 4th ed. (1979), p. 573) but the plaintiff has been unable to persuade me that the case at bar falls within any of them. The common law has not thus far provided a remedy in a case such as this. [page763]

Turning then to s. 152: the defendant says that "specific confidential information" means corporate information (for instance, information about oil discovered on company property) and not information coming to a shareholder *qua* shareholder. I am not prepared to hold that the application of s. 152 is thus limited. . . . The information that the defendant made use of was not merely information relating to an offer to buy the defendant's shares, but was, in effect, an offer to buy the company. It should have been disclosed . . .

But there is still the question of how s. 152 should be applied. The defendant, relying on the evidence of Mr. Martin Linsley, a chartered accountant, says there was no loss to the plaintiff, that $21,500 was as much, or more than, the plaintiff's shares were worth. This is because, as he claims, Strataco Management Ltd. had a fair market value of no more than $60,000 to $70,000.

The best evidence of the market value of Strataco Management Ltd. and its shares is what a willing, informed purchaser, dealing at arm's length, would be prepared to pay. Mr. Linsley said that Thom was all of these things, but that he was imprudent. I am not persuaded of this. Although the defendant testified that he would not have paid $200,000 for the shares of Strataco Management Ltd., the fact is that he had let it be known to the plaintiff and others, for some time before the sale to Thom, that he would sell his controlling interest for

$150,000. I think this would have been a fair price for his controlling interest; it was, in fact, the very price he negotiated at first with Thom for his own shares.

The plaintiff says that the intent of s. 152 is that the minority shareholders should have enjoyed the benefit of a deal, such as the one Thom made with the defendant, on a pro rata basis with the defendant. But "direct loss" cannot be construed as meaning, in a case such as this, losses on a sale of shares on a pro rata basis, that is, it cannot be construed as excluding a control block premium. Putting the matter another way: there is nothing in s. 152 that excludes a minority discount
. . .

I think that the value to be assigned to Roberts' minority share-holder's interest ought to be $25,000. He is therefore entitled to judg-ment for $3,500.

Given that there has been divided success, there should be no costs to any party.

Judgment for plaintiffs.

(b) Securities Law

In addition to giving rise to liability under the company law of the jurisdiction of incorporation of the corporation, insider trading is also regulated by securities legislation in every province except New Brunswick and Prince Edward Island.

(i) Insider Reporting

The cornerstone of the regulatory scheme recommended by the Kimber Committee was "full and public disclosure of all transactions effected by insiders in the securities of their companies. The insider who knows that his trading will become public knowledge will be less likely to engage in improper trading". Section 107 of the *Ontario Securities Act* ("OSA") re-quires insiders to file a report within 10 days of becoming an insider, and within 10 days of any change in her ownership, control, or direction over securities. See also s. 87 of the *B.C. Securities Act*. The idea behind this requirement is that a shareholder who trades through an impersonal stock exchange transaction can ascertain whether an insider traded at the same time.

The definition of "insider" for purposes of the insider reporting provisions is typically limited to directors, senior officers (of the corporation, its sub-sidiaries, or significant shareholders), persons or groups beneficially owning 10% or more of the corporation's voting securities, and the corporation itself: see, *e.g.*, s. 1(1) of the OSA.

If you work your way carefully through the network of definitions that apply to the concept of "insider", you will see that the reporting requirements can become a major headache for large corporate groups with scores of associated or controlled corporations. The difficulties are illustrated in *Re*

British American Oil Corporation Limited, [June 1967] O.S.C. Bulletin 9. The applicant's parent corporation in the US, Gulf Oil, controlled some 140 subsidiaries throughout the world, and the applicant had 75 controlled subsidiaries. Each of the companies, and the directors and officers of each, were insiders of each other and required to report. In granting an exemption from the reporting requirements, the Commission indicated that it would only require reports from those whose connection with the applicant was such that they were likely to have access to confidential information concerning it, or whose activities were likely to have a substantial impact on the applicant. This position is formalized in National Instrument 55-101, which exempts an insider from the requirement to file an insider report if she neither holds securities of the issuer in a significant amount nor is in a position to acquire knowledge of undisclosed material information.

(ii) Civil Liability for Insider Trading

The *Ontario Securities Act,* like federal and provincial companies legislation, imposes civil liability for insider trading or, in the words of the statute, where a "person or company in a special relationship with a reporting issuer . . . purchases or sells securities of the reporting issuer with knowledge of a material fact or material change with respect to the reporting issuer that has not been generally disclosed": s. 134(1). The definition of "special relationship", found in s. 76(5), covers many of the same categories of persons as the definition of "insider" under s. 131 of the CBCA.

   Indeed, since the 2001 amendments to the insider trading provisions of the CBCA were intended, in part, to conform them substantially to provincial securities legislation, it is not surprising that the OSA provisions are comparable to those in s. 131 of the CBCA. For instance:

- The OSA provision refers to "knowledge" of the information and does not require that the person have "made use" of the information "for [her] advantage or benefit".

- There is liability for tipping: OSA s. 134(2).

- The inside trader is liable both to compensate counterparties and to account to the corporation for any benefit or advantage received or receivable as a result of the transaction or tipping: OSA ss. 134(1), (2), (4).

- There is a provision concerning the measure of damages analogous to s. 131(8) of the CBCA: s. 134(6).

- The definition of "security" includes securities of other entities, the market price of which varies materially with the market price of the securities of the insider's corporation: s. 134(8)(b).

   Other provinces' securities legislation contains provisions similar to s. 134 of the *Ontario Securities Act.* See, for example, s. 136 of the *B.C. Securities Act.*

(iii) Prohibited Insider Trading

Provincial securities legislation also typically expressly prohibits insider trading. For example, in Ontario, s. 76(1) of the *Securities Act* provides that "no person or company in a special relationship with a reporting issuer shall purchase or sell securities of the reporting issuer with the knowledge of a material fact or material change with respect to the reporting issuer that has not been generally disclosed". There is a defence where the person or company can prove that it "reasonably believed that the material fact or material change had been generally disclosed": s. 76(4). The *Ontario Securities Act* also prohibits tipping: ss. 76(2), (3). See, by way of comparison, ss. 86(1) and (2) of the *B.C. Securities Act*.

Violators are liable to the penal sanctions applicable generally to violations of securities legislation. For example, in Ontario, the penalty for contraventions of securities law is a fine of up to $1,000,000 or up to two years' imprisonment, or both: see s. 122(1) of the *Ontario Securities Act*.

6. FEDERAL CRIMINAL LAW

In 2004, Parliament adopted Bill C-13, creating a new indictable offence of "prohibited insider trading" and a new hybrid offence of tipping. C-13 has added the following section to the *Criminal Code*:

382.1 (1) A person is guilty of an indictable offence and liable to imprisonment for a term not exceeding ten years who, directly or indirectly, buys or sells a security, knowingly using inside information that they

(a) possess by virtue of being a shareholder of the issuer of that security;

(b) possess by virtue of, or obtained in the course of, their business or professional relationship with that issuer;

(c) possess by virtue of, or obtained in the course of, a proposed takeover or reorganization of, or amalgamation, merger or similar business combination with, that issuer;

(d) possess by virtue of, or obtained in the course of, their employment, office, duties or occupation with that issuer or with a person referred to in paragraphs (a) to (c); or

(e) obtained from a person who possesses or obtained the information in a manner referred to in paragraphs (a) to (d).

(2) Except when necessary in the course of business, a person who knowingly conveys inside information that they possess or obtained in a manner referred to in subsection (1) to another person, knowing that there is a risk that the person will use the information to buy or

sell, directly or indirectly, a security to which the information relates, or that they may convey the information to another person who may buy or sell such a security, is guilty of

(a) an indictable offence and liable to imprisonment for a term not exceeding five years; or

(b) an offence punishable on summary conviction.

(3) For greater certainty, an act is not an offence under this section if it is authorized or required, or is not prohibited, by any federal or provincial Act or regulation applicable to it.

(4) In this section, "inside information" means information relating to or affecting the issuer of a security or a security that they have issued, or are about to issue, that

(a) has not been generally disclosed; and

(b) could reasonably be expected to significantly affect the market price or value of a security of the issuer.

Note that, by virtue of s. 382.1(3), insider trading is an offence under the section only if it is prohibited by a federal or provincial Act or regulation, such as a provincial Securities Act. Of what significance is the fact that s. 131 of the CBCA is not worded as a prohibition?

Does any other federal *Criminal Code* provision apply to insider trading? *R. v. Littler* (1974), 65 D.L.R. (3d) 443 (Que. C.A.) and (1975), 65 D.L.R. (3d) 467 (Que. C.A.), is often cited as an example of the potential for an insider trader to be convicted of fraud under the *Criminal Code*, although the case appears to have involved affirmative misrepresentations and not merely non-disclosure.

7. THE US POSITION

Although some US courts have held that insider trading violates fiduciary duties as a matter of state corporate law — see, for example, *Diamond v. Oreamuno, infra* — the primary legal vehicle for the regulation of insider trading in the United States is federal securities law.

(a) Federal Securities Law

(i) Rule 10b-5

Perhaps surprisingly, US securities legislation does not explicitly prohibit insider trading. Rather, the prohibition has emerged by way of judicial interpretation of a general "anti-fraud" rule adopted by the Securities and

Exchange Commission under s. 10(b) of the *Securities Exchange Act* of 1934. The relevant rule, Rule 10b-5, reads as follows:

> It shall be unlawful for any person, directly or indirectly, by the use of any means or instrumentality of interstate commerce, or of the mails, or of any facility of any national securities exchange:
>
> > (a) to employ any device, scheme or artifice to defraud,
> >
> > (b) to make any untrue statement of a material fact or to omit to state a material fact necessary in order to make the statements made, in the light of the circumstances under which they were made, not misleading, or
> >
> > (c) to engage in any act, practice, or course of business which operates or would operate as a fraud or deceit upon any person,
>
> in connection with the purchase or sale of any security.

Violation of Rule 10b-5 can result in both civil liability for damages to purchasers and sellers of the securities and, if the violation was wilful, in criminal prosecution by the SEC.

In *Cady, Roberts & Co.*, 40 S.E.C. 907 (1961), the SEC interpreted Rule 10b-5 as requiring corporate insiders having knowledge of material non-public information to either disclose the information or abstain from trading. It rested the requirement on two rationales: equality of access ("the inherent unfairness involved where a party takes advantage of [inside information] knowing it is unavailable to those with whom he is dealing") and the insider's relationship to the corporation ("the existence of a relationship giving access, directly or indirectly, to information intended to be available only for a corporate purpose and not for the personal benefit of anyone").

The so-called "disclose-or-abstain" rule was upheld by the Second Circuit Court of Appeals in a famous 1968 decision, an excerpt from which follows.

Securities & Exchange Commission v. Texas Gulf Sulphur Co.
401 F.2d 833 (2nd Cir. N.Y., 1968), cert. den. sub nom. *Coates v. S.E.C.*, 394 U.S. 976 (1969).

The following facts are summarized from Waterman C.J.'s opinion. The case involves the exploratory activities of Texas Gulf Sulphur ("TGS"), a mining company on the Canadian Shield. In October, 1963, a very promising core sample ("K-55-1") was drilled. On the basis of this sample, TGS decided to buy adjoining land and TGS's president instructed the exploration group to keep the test results confidential so as not to jeopardize the land acquisition program. Between October, 1963, and March, 1964, several of the defendants — TGS employees who knew about the core sample — bought TGS shares and call options and tipped outsiders who also bought TGS shares and call options. On April 12, 1964, to deflate media rumours of a major ore strike, TGS published a press release stating that "the work done to date has not been sufficient to reach definite conclusions and any statement as to size and grade of ore would be premature and possibly misleading".

Drilling operations continued, and TGS officials began to plan ultimate disclosure of the discovery. On April 16, *The Northern Miner*, a Canadian mining industry journal, published an article, prepared on the basis of interviews with several of the defendant officials of TGS, confirming a 10 million ton ore strike. TGS also provided an official statement to the Ontario Minister of Mines which was released to the Canadian media at 9:40 a.m. on April 16. Another official statement, announcing a strike of at least 25 million tons of ore was read to representatives of American financial media from 10:00 a.m. to 10:10 or 10:15 a.m. on April 16 and appeared over Merrill Lynch's private wire at 10:29 a.m. and over the Dow Jones ticker tape at 10:54 a.m.

Between April 12 and April 16, three of the defendants, Clayton (a TGS engineer), Crawford (TGS's corporate secretary) and Coates (a TGS director) engaged in transactions in TGS stock. Clayton bought 200 shares of TGS stock on April 15, and Crawford bought 300 shares at the opening of the Midwest Stock Exchange on April 16. Coates left the TGS press conference and called his broker shortly before 10:20 a.m. on the 16th, buying 2,000 shares for family trust accounts of which he was a trustee but not a beneficiary; Coates' broker and his customers also purchased 1,500 additional shares.

During the period of drilling in Timmins, the market price of TGS stock gained, moving from 17 3/8 on November 8 to 30 7/8 at the close of trading on April 13. On April 16, the day of the official announcement of the Timmins discovery, the price climbed to a high of 37 and closed at 36 3/8. By May 15, TGS stock was trading at 58 1/4.

WATERMAN C.J.:

A. Introductory

Rule 10b-5 was promulgated pursuant to the grant of authority given the SEC by Congress in Section 10(b) of the *Securities Exchange Act of 1934* (15 U.S.C. § 78j(b)). By that Act Congress purposed to prevent inequitable and unfair practices and to insure fairness in securities transactions generally, whether conducted face-to-face, over the counter, or on exchanges. The Act and the Rule apply to the transactions here, all of which were consummated on exchanges. ... [T]he Rule is based in policy on the justifiable expectation of the securities marketplace that all investors trading on impersonal exchanges have relatively equal access to material information. The essence of the Rule is that anyone who, trading for his own account in the securities of a corporation has "access, directly or indirectly, to information intended to be available only for a corporate purpose and not for the personal benefit of anyone" may not take "advantage of such information knowing it is unavailable to those with whom he is dealing", i.e., the investing public. Insiders, as directors or management officers are, of course, by this Rule, precluded from so unfairly dealing, but the Rule is also applicable to one possessing the information who may not be strictly termed an "insider" within the meaning of Sec. 16(b) of the Act. Thus, anyone in possession of material inside information must either disclose it to the investing public, or, if he is disabled from disclosing it in order to protect a corporate confidence, or he chooses not to do so, must abstain from trading in or recommending the securities concerned while such inside information remains undisclosed. So, it is here no justification for insider activity that disclosure was forbidden by the legitimate corporate objective of acquiring options to purchase the land surrounding the exploration site; if the information was, as the SEC contends, material, its possessors should have kept out of the market until disclosure was accomplished.

B.   Material Inside Information

An insider is not, of course, always foreclosed from investing in his own company merely because he may be more familiar with company operations than are outside investors. An insider's duty to disclose information or his duty to abstain from dealing in his company's securities arises only in "those situations which are essentially extraordinary in nature and which are reasonably certain to have a substantial effect on the market price of the security if (the extraordinary situation is) disclosed".

Nor is an insider obligated to confer upon outside investors the benefit of his superior financial or other expert analysis by disclosing his educated guesses or predictions. The only regulatory objective is that access to material information be enjoyed equally, but this objective requires nothing more than the disclosure of basic facts so that outsiders may draw upon their own evaluative expertise in reaching their own investment decisions with knowledge equal to that of the insiders . . .

"The basic test of materiality . . . is whether a reasonable man would attach importance . . . in determining his choice of action in the transaction in question. This, of course, encompasses any fact . . . which in reasonable and objective contemplation might affect the value of the corporation's stock or securities" . . . Such a fact is a material fact and must be effectively disclosed to the investing public prior to the commencement of insider trading in the corporation's securities.

The speculators and chartists of Wall and Bay Streets are also "reasonable" investors entitled to the same legal protection afforded conservative traders. Thus, material facts include not only information disclosing the earnings and distributions of a company but also those facts which affect the probable future of the company and those which may affect the desire of investors to buy, sell, or hold the company's securities.

In each case, then, whether facts are material within Rule 10b-5 when the facts relate to a particular event and are undisclosed by those persons who are knowledgeable thereof will depend at any given time upon a balancing of both the indicated probability that the event will occur and the anticipated magnitude of the event in light of the totality of the company activity. Here, notwithstanding the trial court's conclusion that the results of the first drill core, K-55-1, were "too 'remote' to have had any significant impact on the market, i.e., to be deemed material", knowledge of the possibility, which surely was more than marginal, of the existence of a mine of the vast magnitude indicated by the remarkably rich drill core located rather close to the surface (suggesting mineability by the less expensive openpit method) within the confines of a large anomaly (suggesting an extensive region of mineralization) might well have affected the price of TGS stock and would certainly have been an important fact to a reasonable, if speculative, investor in deciding whether he should buy, sell, or hold. After all, this first drill core was "unusually good and . . . excited the interest and speculation of those who knew about it" . . .

Our survey of the facts found below conclusively establishes that knowledge of the results of the discovery hole, K-55-1, would have been important to a reasonable investor and might have affected the price of the stock. On April 16, The Northern Miner, a trade publication in wide circulation among mining stock specialists, called K-55-1, the discovery hole, "one of the most impressive drill holes completed in modern times". Roche, a Canadian broker whose firm specialized in mining securities, characterized the importance to investors of the results of K-55-1. He stated that the completion of "the first drill hole" with "a 600 foot drill core is very very significant . . . anything over 200 feet is considered very significant and 600 feet is just beyond your wildest imagination". He added, however, that it "is a natural thing to buy more stock once they give you the first drill hole". Additional testimony revealed that the prices of stocks of other companies, albeit less diversified, smaller firms, had increased substantially solely on the basis of the discovery of good anomalies or even because of the proximity of their lands to the *situs* of a potentially major strike.

Finally, a major factor in determining whether the K-55-1 discovery was a material fact is the importance attached to the drilling results by those who knew about it. In view of other unrelated recent developments favourably affecting TGS, participation by an informed person in a regular stock-purchase program, or even sporadic trading by an informed person, might lend only nominal support to the inference of the materiality of the K-55-1 discovery; nevertheless, the timing by those who knew of it of their stock purchases and their purchases of short-term calls — purchases in some cases by individuals who had never before purchased calls or even TGS stock — virtually compels the inference that the insiders were influenced by the drilling results. This insider trading activity, which surely constitutes highly pertinent evidence and the only truly objective evidence of the materiality of the K-55-1 discovery, was apparently disregarded by the court below in favor of the testimony of defendants' expert witnesses, all of whom "agreed that one drill core does not establish an ore body, much less a mine". Significantly, however, the court below, while relying upon what these defense experts said the defendant insiders ought to have thought about the worth to TGS of the K-55-1 discovery, and finding that from November 12, 1963, to April 6, 1964, Fogarty, Murray, Holyk, and Darke spent more than $100,000 in purchasing TGS stock and calls on that stock, made no finding that the insiders were motivated by any factor other than the extraordinary K-55-1 discovery when they bought their stock and their calls. No reason appears why outside investors, perhaps better acquainted with speculative modes of investment and with, in many cases, perhaps more capital at their disposal for intelligent speculation, would have been less influenced, and would not have been similarly motivated to invest if they had known what the insider investors knew about the K-55-1 discovery.

Our decision to expand the limited protection afforded outside investors by the trial court's narrow definition of materiality is not at all shaken by fears that the elimination of insider trading benefits will deplete the ranks of capable corporate managers by taking away an incentive to accept such employment. Such benefits, in essence, are forms of secret corporate compensation, derived at the expense of the uninformed investing public and not at the expense of the corporation which receives the sole benefit from insider incentives. Moreover, adequate incentives for corporate officers may be provided by properly administered stock options and employee purchase plans of which there are many in existence. In any event, the normal motivation induced by stock ownership, i.e., the identification of an individual with corporate progress, is ill-promoted by condoning the sort of speculative insider activity which occurred here; for example, some of the corporation's stock was sold at market in order to purchase short-term calls upon that stock, calls which would never be exercised to increase a stockholder equity in TGS unless the market price of that stock rose sharply.

The core of Rule 10b-5 is the implementation of the Congressional purpose that all investors should have equal access to the rewards of participation in securities transactions. It was the intent of Congress that all members of the investing public should be subject to identical market risks — which market risks include, of course, the risk that one's evaluative capacity or one's capital available to put at risk may exceed another's capacity or capital. The insiders here were not trading on an equal footing with the outside investors. They alone were in a position to evaluate the probability and magnitude of what seemed from the outset to be a major ore strike; they alone could invest safely, secure in the expectation that the price of TGS stock would rise substantially in the event such a major strike should materialize, but would decline little, if at all, in the event of failure, for the public, ignorant at the outset of the favorable probabilities would likewise be unaware of the unproductive exploration, and the additional exploration costs would not significantly affect TGS market prices. Such inequities based upon unequal access to knowledge should not be shrugged off as inevitable in our way of life, or, in view of the congressional concern in the area, remain uncorrected.

We hold, therefore, that all transactions in TGS stock or calls by individuals apprised of the drilling results of K-55-1 were made in violation of Rule 10b-5. Inasmuch as the visual evaluation of that drill core (a generally reliable estimate though less accurate than a chemical assay) constituted material information, those advised of the results of the visual evaluation as well as those informed of the chemical assay traded in violation of law.

C.   When May Insiders Act?

Appellant Crawford, who ordered the purchase of TGS stock shortly before the TGS April 16 official announcement, and defendant Coates, who placed orders with and communicated the news to his broker immediately after the official announcement was read at the TGS-called press conference, concede that they were in possession of material information. They contend, however, that their purchases were not proscribed purchases for the news had already been effectively disclosed. We disagree.

Crawford telephoned his orders to his Chicago broker about midnight on April 15 and again at 8:30 in the morning of the 16th, with instructions to buy at the opening of the Midwest Stock Exchange that morning. The trial court's finding that "he sought to, and did, 'beat the news'", is well documented by the record. The rumors of a major ore strike which had been circulated in Canada and, to a lesser extent, in New York, had been disclaimed by the TGS press release of April 12, which significantly promised the public an official detailed announcement when possibilities had ripened into actualities. The abbreviated announcement to the Canadian press at 9:40 a.m. on the 16th by the Ontario Minister of Mines and the report carried by The Northern Miner, parts of which had sporadically reached New York on the morning of the 16th through reports from Canadian affiliates to a few New York investment firms, are assuredly not the equivalent of the official 10 to 15 minute announcement which was not released to the American financial press until after 10:00 a.m. Crawford's orders had been placed before that. Before insiders may act upon material information, such information must have been effectively disclosed in a manner sufficient to insure its availability to the investing public. Particularly here, where a formal announcement to the entire financial news media had been promised in a prior official release known to the media, all insider activity must await dissemination of the promised official announcement.

Coates was absolved by the court below because his telephone order was placed shortly before 10:20 a.m. on April 16, which was after the announcement had been made even though the news could not be considered already a matter of public information. [However, the] reading of a news release, which prompted Coates into action, is merely the first step in the process of dissemination required for compliance with the regulatory objective of providing all investors with an equal opportunity to make informed investment judgments. Assuming that the contents of the official release could instantaneously be acted upon, at the minimum Coates should have waited until the news could reasonably have been expected to appear over the media of widest circulation, the Dow Jones broad tape, rather than hastening to insure an advantage to himself and his broker son-in-law.

In *Chiarella v. U.S.* and *Dirks v. SEC* the US Supreme Court rejected the "equal access" theory advanced by the SEC and the Second Circuit, adopting instead a theory of insider trading based on a "fiduciary or other similar relation of trust and confidence" between the insider and the corporation's shareholders (the "classical theory"). We have seen, above, the conceptual puzzles posed by this theory.

Chiarella v. U.S.,
445 U.S. 222 (1980)

Mr. Justice POWELL delivered the opinion of the Court . . .

The question in this case is whether a person who learns from the confidential documents of one corporation that it is planning an attempt to secure control of a second corporation violates §10(b) of the *Securities Exchange Act* of 1934 if he fails to disclose the impending takeover before trading in the target company's securities.

Petitioner is a printer by trade. In 1975 and 1976 he worked as a "markup man" in the New York composing room of Pandick Press, a financial printer. Among documents that petitioner handled were five announcements of corporate takeover bids. When these documents were delivered to the printer, the identities of the acquiring and target corporations were concealed by blank spaces or false names. The true names were sent to the printer on the night of the final printing.

The petitioner, however, was able to deduce the names of the target companies before the final printing from other information contained in the documents. Without disclosing his knowledge, petitioner purchased stock in the target companies and sold the shares immediately after the takeover attempts were made public. By this method, petitioner realized a gain of slightly more than $30,000 in the course of 14 months. Subsequently, the Securities and Exchange Commission (Commission or SEC) began an investigation of his trading activities. In May 1977, petitioner entered into a consent decree with the Commission in which he agreed to return his profits to the sellers of the shares. On the same day, he was discharged by Pandick Press.

In January 1978, petitioner was indicted on 17 counts of violating §10(b) of the *Securities Exchange Act* of 1934 (1934 Act) and SEC Rule 10b-5. [Chiarella was convicted and his appeal to the Second Circuit Court of Appeals was dismissed.]

[O]ne who fails to disclose material information prior to the consummation of a transaction commits fraud only when he is under a duty to do so. And the duty to disclose arises when one party has information "that the other [party] is entitled to know because of a fiduciary or other similar relation of trust and confidence between them". In its *Cady, Roberts* decision, the Commission recognized a relationship of trust and confidence between the shareholders of a corporation and those insiders who have obtained confidential information by reason of their position with that corporation. This relationship gives rise to a duty to disclose because of the "necessity of preventing a corporate insider from . . . tak[ing] unfair advantage of the uninformed minority stockholders".

The federal courts have found violations of §10(b) where corporate insiders used undisclosed information for their own benefit. [Citing *Texas Gulf Sulphur, supra*.] The cases also have emphasized, in accordance with the common-law rule, that "[t]he party charged with failing to disclose market information must be under a duty to disclose it". Accordingly, a purchaser of stock who has no duty to a prospective seller because he is neither an insider nor a fiduciary has been held to have no obligation to reveal material facts.

The Court of Appeals affirmed the conviction by holding that "[a]nyone — corporate insider or not — who regularly receives material nonpublic information may not use that information to trade in securities without incurring an affirmative duty to disclose". Although the court said that its test would include only persons who regularly receive material, nonpublic information, its rationale for that limitation is unrelated to the existence of a duty to disclose. The Court of Appeals, like the trial court, failed to identify a relationship between petitioner and the sellers that could give rise to a duty. Its decision thus rested solely upon its belief that the federal securities laws have "created a system providing equal access to information necessary for reasoned and intelligent investment decisions". The use by anyone of material information not generally available is fraudulent, this theory suggests, because such information gives certain buyers or sellers an unfair advantage over less informed buyers and sellers.

This reasoning suffers from two defects. First not every instance of financial unfairness constitutes fraudulent activity under §10(b). Second, the element required to make silence fraudulent — a duty to disclose — is absent in this case. No duty could arise from petitioner's relationship with the sellers of the target company's securities, for petitioner had no prior dealings with them. He was not their agent, he was not a fiduciary, he was not a person in whom the sellers had placed their trust and confidence. He was, in fact, a complete stranger who dealt with the sellers only through impersonal market transactions.

We cannot affirm petitioner's conviction without recognizing a general duty between all participants in market transactions to forgo actions based on material, nonpublic information. Formulation of such a broad duty, which departs radically from the established doctrine that duty arises from a specific relationship between two parties should not be undertaken absent some explicit evidence of congressional intent. [N]o such evidence emerges from the language or legislative history of § 10(b) . . .

In its brief to this Court, the United States offers an alternative theory to support petitioner's conviction. It argues that petitioner breached a duty to the acquiring corporation when he acted upon information that he obtained by virtue of his position as an employee of a printer employed by the corporation. The breach of this duty is said to support a conviction under §10(b) for fraud perpetrated upon both the acquiring corporation and the sellers . . . The jury was not instructed on the nature or elements of a duty owed by petitioner to anyone other than the sellers. Because we cannot affirm a criminal conviction on the basis of a theory not presented to the jury, we will not speculate upon whether such a duty exists, whether it has been breached, or whether such a breach constitutes a violation of §10(b) . . .

Reversed.

Dirks v. SEC
463 U.S. 646 (1983)

The following facts are summarized from the Court's opinion. Raymond Dirks, a securities analyst, received information from a former insurance company officer that the company's assets were vastly overstated as the result of fraudulent corporate practices and that various regulatory agencies had failed to act on similar charges made by company employees. Dirks investigated these allegations by speaking with current and former employees of the insurance company. While his investigation was ongoing, he openly discussed the information he had obtained with a number of clients and investors, some of whom sold their holdings in the company. *The Wall Street Journal* declined to publish a story on the fraud allegations, as urged by Dirks. After the price of the insurance company's stock fell during petitioner's investigation, the New York Stock Exchange halted trading in the stock. State insurance authorities then impounded the company's records and uncovered evidence of fraud. Only then did the Securities and Exchange Commission file a complaint against the company, and only then did *The Wall Street Journal* publish a story based largely on information assembled by Dirks.

The SEC found that Dirks had aided and abetted violations of Rule 10b-5, by repeating the allegations of fraud to members of the investment community who later sold their stock in the insurance company. However, because of his role in bringing the fraud to light, however, the SEC only censured him. Upon review, the D.C. Court of Appeals entered judgment against Dirks.

Justice POWELL delivered the opinion of the Court:

> We were explicit in *Chiarella* in saying that there can be no duty to disclose where the person who has traded on inside information "was not [the corporation's] agent, . . . was not a fiduciary, [or] was not a person in whom the sellers [of the securities] had placed their trust and confidence". Not to require such a fiduciary relationship, we recognized, would "depar[t] radically from the established doctrine that duty arises from a specific relationship between two parties" and would amount to "recognizing a general duty between all participants in market transactions to forgo actions based on material, nonpublic information". This requirement of a specific relationship between the shareholders and the individual trading on inside information has created analytical difficulties for the SEC and courts in policing tippees who trade on inside information. Unlike insiders who have independent fiduciary duties to both the corporation and its shareholders, the typical tippee has no such relationships. In view of this absence, it has been unclear how a tippee acquires the *Cady, Roberts* duty to refrain from trading on inside information.
>
> The SEC's position, as stated in its opinion in this case, is that a tippee "inherits" the *Cady, Roberts* obligation to shareholders whenever he receives inside information from an insider:
>
> > Tippees such as Dirks who receive non-public material information from insiders become "subject to the same duty as [the] insiders"

This view differs little from the view that we rejected as inconsistent with congressional intent in *Chiarella*. In effect, the SEC's theory of tippee liability in both cases appears rooted in the idea that the antifraud provisions require equal information among all traders. This conflicts with the principle set forth in *Chiarella* that only some persons, under some circumstances, will be barred from trading while in possession of material nonpublic information. Judge Wright correctly read our opinion in *Chiarella* as repudiating any notion that all traders must enjoy equal information before trading: "[T]he 'information' theory is rejected. Because the disclose-or- refrain duty is extraordinary, it attaches only when a party has legal obligations other than a mere duty to comply with the general antifraud proscriptions in the federal securities laws". We reaffirm today that "[a] duty [to disclose] arises from the relationship between parties ... and not merely from one's ability to acquire information because of his position in the market".

Imposing a duty to disclose or abstain solely because a person knowingly receives material nonpublic information from an insider and trades on it could have an inhibiting influence on the role of market analysts, which the SEC itself recognizes is necessary to the preservation of a healthy market. It is commonplace for analysts to "ferret out and analyze information", and this often is done by meeting with and questioning corporate officers and others who are insiders. And information that the analysts obtain normally may be the basis for judgments as to the market worth of a corporation's securities. The analyst's judgment in this respect is made available in market letters or otherwise to clients of the firm. It is the nature of this type of information, and indeed of the markets themselves, that such information cannot be made simultaneously available to all of the corporation's stockholders or the public generally.

. . .

The conclusion that recipients of inside information do not invariably acquire a duty to disclose or abstain does not mean that such tippees always are free to trade on the information. [However,] the tippee's duty to disclose or abstain is derivative from that of the insider's duty. As we noted in *Chiarella*, "[t]he tippee's obligation has been viewed as arising from his role as a participant after the fact in the insider's breach of a fiduciary duty". Thus, some tippees must assume an insider's duty to the shareholders not because they receive inside information, but rather because it has been made available to them improperly. [A] tippee assumes a fiduciary duty to the shareholders of a corporation not to trade on material nonpublic information only when the insider has breached his fiduciary duty to the shareholders by disclosing the information to the tippee and the tippee knows or should know that there has been a breach.

But to determine whether the disclosure itself "deceive[s], manipulate[s], or defraud[s]" shareholders, the initial inquiry is whether there has been a breach of duty by the insider. This requires courts to focus on objective criteria, i.e., whether the insider receives a direct or indirect personal benefit from the disclosure, such as a pecuniary gain or a reputational benefit that will translate into future earnings. There are objective facts and circumstances that often justify such an inference. For example, there may be a relationship between the insider and the recipient that suggests a quid pro quo from the latter, or an intention to benefit the particular recipient. The elements of fiduciary duty and exploitation of nonpublic information also exist when an insider makes a gift of confidential information to a trading relative or friend. The tip and trade resemble trading by the insider himself followed by a gift of the profits to the recipient.

Under the inside-trading and tipping rules set forth above, we find that there was no actionable violation by Dirks. It is undisputed that Dirks himself was a stranger to Equity Funding, with no pre-existing fiduciary duty to its shareholders. He took no action, directly or indirectly, that induced the shareholders or officers of Equity Funding to repose trust or confidence in him. There was no expectation by Dirk's sources that he would keep their information in confidence. Nor did Dirks misappropriate or illegally obtain the information about Equity Funding. Unless the insiders breached their *Cady, Roberts* duty to shareholders in disclosing the nonpublic information to Dirks, he breached no duty when he passed it on to investors as well as to the Wall Street Journal.

It is clear that neither Secrist nor the other Equity Funding employees violated their *Cady, Roberts* duty to the corporation's shareholders by providing information to Dirks. The tippers received no monetary or personal benefit for revealing Equity Funding's secrets, nor was their purpose to make a gift of valuable information to Dirks. As the facts of this case clearly indicate, the tippers were motivated by a desire to expose the fraud. In the absence of a breach of duty to shareholders by the insiders, there was no derivative breach by Dirks. Dirks therefore could not have been "a participant after the fact in [an] insider's breach of a fiduciary duty".

We conclude that Dirks, in the circumstances of this case, had no duty to abstain from use of the inside information that he obtained. The judgment of the Court of Appeals therefore is reversed.

The "alternative theory" advanced by the US Government in *Chiarella*, but not considered by the US Supreme Court because it had not been submitted to the jury, came to be called the "misappropriation theory" because it held that the basis for insider trading liability was the use of the information in a manner inconsistent with duties owed to the source of the information — in essence, a misappropriation of the information. This alternative basis for insider trading liability under Rule 10b-5 was adopted and applied by the Supreme Court in *O'Hagan v. U.S.*

O'Hagan v. U.S.
521 U.S. 642 (1997).

JUSTICE GINSBURG delivered the opinion of the Court.

Respondent James Herman O'Hagan was a partner in the law firm of Dorsey & Whitney in Minneapolis, Minnesota. In July 1988, Grand Metropolitan PLC (Grand Met), a company based in London, England, retained Dorsey & Whitney as local counsel to represent Grand Met regarding a potential tender offer for the common stock of the Pillsbury Company, headquartered in Minneapolis. Both Grand Met and Dorsey & Whitney took precautions to protect the confidentiality of Grand Met's tender offer plans. O'Hagan did no work on the Grand Met representation. Dorsey & Whitney withdrew from representing Grand Met on September 9, 1988. Less than a month later, on October 4, 1988, Grand Met publicly announced its tender offer for Pillsbury stock.

On August 18, 1988, while Dorsey & Whitney was still representing Grand Met, O'Hagan began purchasing call options for Pillsbury stock. Each option gave him the right to purchase 100 shares of Pillsbury stock by a specified date in September 1988. Later in August and in September, O'Hagan made additional purchases of Pillsbury call options. By the end of September, he owned 2,500 unexpired Pillsbury options, apparently more than any other individual investor. O'Hagan also purchased, in September 1988, some 5,000 shares of Pillsbury common stock, at a price just under $39 per share. When Grand Met announced its tender offer in October, the price of Pillsbury stock rose to nearly $60 per share. O'Hagan then sold his Pillsbury call options and common stock, making a profit of more than $4.3 million.

[According to the subsequent indictment, O'Hagan's motive had been to use these profits to conceal his previous embezzlement and conversion of unrelated client trust funds.

O'Hagan was indicted and convicted of securities fraud under various federal laws, including Sec. 10(b) and Rule 10b-5, and was sentenced to a 41-month term of imprisonment. The Court of Appeals for the Eighth Circuit reversed all of the convictions, holding that liability under Sec. 10(b) and Rule 10b-5 could not be grounded on the "misappropriation theory".]

Under the "traditional" or "classical theory" of insider trading liability, §10(b) and Rule 10b-5 are violated when a corporate insider trades in the securities of his corporation on the basis of material, nonpublic information. Trading on such information qualifies as a "deceptive device" . . . because "a relationship of trust and confidence [exists] between the shareholders of a corporation and those insiders who have obtained confidential information by reason of their position with that corporation". That relationship, we recognized, "gives rise to a duty to disclose [or to abstain from trading] because of the 'necessity of preventing a corporate insider from . . . tak[ing] unfair advantage of . . . uninformed . . . stockholders.'" [citation omitted]. The classical theory applies not only to officers, directors, and other permanent insiders of a corporation, but also to attorneys, accountants, consultants, and others who temporarily become fiduciaries of a corporation.

The "misappropriation theory" holds that a person commits fraud "in connection with" a securities transaction, and thereby violates §10(b) and Rule 10b-5, when he misappropriates confidential information for securities trading purposes, in breach of a duty owed to the source of the information. Under this theory, a fiduciary's undisclosed, self-serving use of a principal's information to purchase or sell securities, in breach of a duty of loyalty and confidentiality, defrauds the principal of the exclusive use of that information. In lieu of premising liability on a fiduciary relationship between company insider and purchaser or seller of the company's stock, the misappropriation theory premises liability on a fiduciary-turned-trader's deception of those who entrusted him with access to confidential information.

The two theories are complementary, each addressing efforts to capitalize on nonpublic information through the purchase or sale of securities. The classical theory targets a corporate insider's breach of duty to shareholders with whom the insider transacts; the misappropriation theory outlaws trading on the basis of nonpublic information by a corporate "outsider" in breach of a duty owed not to a trading party, but to the source of the information. The misappropriation theory is thus designed to "protec[t] the integrity of the securities markets against abuses by 'outsiders' to a corporation who have access to confidential information that will affect th[e] corporation's security price when revealed, but who owe no fiduciary or other duty to that corporation's shareholders".

In this case, the indictment alleged that O'Hagan, in breach of a duty of trust and confidence he owed to his law firm, Dorsey & Whitney, and to its client, Grand Met, traded on the basis of nonpublic information regarding Grand Met's planned tender offer for Pillsbury common stock. This conduct, the Government charged, constituted a fraudulent device in connection with the purchase and sale of securities.

We agree with the Government that misappropriation, as just defined, satisfies §10(b)'s requirement that chargeable conduct involve a "deceptive device or contrivance" used "in connection with" the purchase or sale of securities. We observe, first, that misappropriators, as the Government describes them, deal in deception. A fiduciary who "[pretends] loyalty to the principal while secretly converting the principal's information for personal gain", "dupes", or defrauds the principal . . .

[F]ull disclosure forecloses liability under the misappropriation theory: Because the deception essential to the misappropriation theory involves feigning fidelity to the source of information, if the fiduciary discloses to the source that he plans to trade on the nonpublic information, there is no "deceptive device" and thus no §10(b) violation — although the fiduciary-turned-trader may remain liable under state law for breach of a duty of loyalty . . .

We turn next to the §10(b) requirement that the misappropriator's deceptive use of information be "in connection with the purchase or sale of [a] security". This element is satisfied because the fiduciary's fraud is consummated, not when the fiduciary gains the confidential information, but when, without disclosure to his principal, he uses the information to purchase or sell securities. The securities transaction and the breach of duty thus coincide . . .

The theory is . . . well tuned to an animating purpose of the *Exchange Act*: to insure honest securities markets and thereby promote investor confidence. Although informational disparity is inevitable in the securities markets, investors likely would hesitate to venture their capital in a market where trading based on misappropriated nonpublic information is unchecked by law. An investor's informational disadvantage *vis-a-vis* a misappropriator with material, nonpublic information stems from contrivance, not luck; it is a disadvantage that cannot be overcome with research or skill.

In sum, considering the inhibiting impact on market participation of trading on misappropriated information, and the congressional purposes underlying §10(b), it makes scant sense to hold a lawyer like O'Hagan a §10(b) violator if he works for a law firm representing the target of a tender offer, but not if he works for a law firm representing the bidder. The text of the statute requires no such result. The misappropriation at issue here was properly made the subject of a §10(b) charge because it meets the statutory requirement that there be "deceptive" conduct "in connection with" securities transactions . . .

The judgment of the Court of Appeals for the Eighth Circuit is reversed, and the case is remanded for further proceedings consistent with this opinion.

It is so ordered.

Notes and Questions

1 Although the *O'Hagan* decision has generally been welcomed by commentators, one question raised by the decision is why the US federal securities laws should be concerned with the protection of property rights in information which are traditionally a state law concern, just as

they would be a provincial concern in Canada: see, *e.g.*, Roberta S. Karmel, "Outsider Trading on Confidential Information — A Breach in Search of a Duty" (1998) 20 Cardozo L. Rev. 83, at p. 95.

2 In 2000, the SEC adopted Rules 10b5-1 and 10b5-2 to clarify certain uncertainties left unresolved by *O'Hagan*:

   a. Rule 10b5-1 specifies that a trade is "on the basis of" material non-public information if the insider had knowledge of the information at the time of the trade. Recall that under ss. 131(4) and (5) of the CBCA and ss. 76(1) and 134(1) of the *Ontario Securities Act*, insider trading is established if the transaction was made "with knowledge" of the confidential information, whereas under s. 138(5) of the OBCA and s. 192(2) of the BCBCA, the plaintiff must show that the insider "made use of" the information. Rule 10b5-1 also creates a series of affirmative defences analogous to those referred to under s. 131(4)(c) of the CBCA, for example, performance under a previously entered-into binding contract and transactions under a pre-set investment plan.

   b. Rule 10b5-2 provides that a "duty of trust or confidence" is presumed to exist, within the meaning of *O'Hagan*, where the recipient of the information (a) agrees to maintain information in confidence, (b) ought reasonably to know, based on past practice, that the person communicating the information expects the information to be kept in confidence, or (c) received it from her spouse, parent, child, or sibling.

3 As the case law stands, insider trading liability under Rule 10b-5 can be based on either the "classical theory" articulated in *Chiarella* or on the "misappropriation theory" articulated in *O'Hagan*. If the trader discloses to her source that she intends to trade on non-public information, there is no deception and, therefore, no violation of Rule 10b-5 under the misappropriation theory. However, if the trader owed a duty to disclose the information by virtue of a fiduciary relationship to shareholders there could still be a violation of Rule 10b-5 under the classical theory.

4 How would the facts in *Chiarella*, *Dirks* and *O'Hagan* be analyzed under s. 131 of the CBCA?

(ii) Section 16

Section 16 of the *Securities Exchange Act* of 1934 contains three provisions that are of interest to us.

The first, s. 16(a), requires any director, officer or shareholder owning more than 10% of the equity of any reporting issuer to file a statement of her beneficial ownership, and to update the statement each month with any changes. The purpose of this provision was similar to that of the insider reporting requirements of the *Ontario Securities Act*, namely to deter insider trading by requiring disclosure of trades: see Steve Thel, "The Genius of Section 16: Regulating the Management of Publicly Held Companies" (1991) 42 Hastings L.J. 391, at p. 419.

The second provision of interest, s. 16(b), requires any person covered by s. 16(a) to disgorge to the corporation any profit earned on the corporation's equity securities from in-and-out transactions separated by less than six months. The provision is explicitly directed at the possibility that the insider might have made improper use of inside information, since s. 16(b) opens with the statement that its purpose is "preventing the unfair use of information which may have been obtained by such beneficial owner, director, or officer by reason of his relationship to the issuer", yet the rule in s. 16(b) applies strictly, regardless of whether or not any inside information was used by (or even known to) the insider, so long as the purchase and sale, or sale and purchase, were separated by less than six months. Conversely, transactions separated by six months or more escape the section, even if inside information was used. If the corporation fails to bring suit to enforce its right under s. 16(b), any shareholder may sue on its behalf. The great virtue of the short-swing approach taken in s. 16(b) is its administrability; no complex issues of fact cloud the question of liability. The cost of easy enforcement is the rule's inefficiency in identifying those who actually violate the policy behind the statute. Some will be caught who did not have any intention of trading on inside information; others who do, will not.

Finally, s. 16(c), which prohibits persons covered by s. 16(a) to sell their corporation's stock short, is comparable to s. 130 of the CBCA.

(b) State Corporate Law

Diamond v. Oreamuno
248 N.E.2d 910 (N.Y. C.A., 1969)

FULD C.J.: Upon this appeal from an order denying a motion to dismiss the complaint as insufficient on its face, the question presented — one of first impression in this court — is whether officers and directors may be held accountable to their corporation for gains realized by them from transactions in the company's stock as a result of their use of material inside information.

The complaint was filed by a shareholder of Management Assistance, Inc. (MAI) asserting a derivative action against a number of its officers and directors to compel an accounting for profits allegedly acquired as a result of a breach of fiduciary duty. It charges that two of the defendants — Oreamuno, chairman of the board of directors, and Gonzalez, its president — had used inside information, acquired by them solely by virtue of their positions, in order to reap large personal profits from the sale of MAI shares and that these profits rightfully belong to the corporation. Other officers and directors were joined as defendants on the ground that they acquiesced in or ratified the assertedly wrongful transactions.

MAI is in the business of financing computer installations through sale and lease back arrangements with various commercial and industrial users. Under its lease provisions, MAI was required to maintain and repair the computers but, at the time of this suit, it lacked the capacity to perform this function itself and was forced to engage the manufacturer of the computers, International Business Machines (IBM), to service the machines. As a result of a sharp increase by IBM of its charges for such service, MAI's expenses for August of 1966 rose considerably and its net earnings declined from $262,253 in July to $66,233 in August, a decrease of about 75%. This information, although earlier known to the defendants, was not made public until October of 1966. Prior to the release of the information, however, Oreamuno and Gonzalez sold off a total of 56,600 shares of their MAI stock at the then current market price of $28 a share.

After the information concerning the drop in earnings was made available to the public, the value of a share of MAI stock immediately fell from the $28 realized by the defendants to $11. Thus, the plaintiff alleges, by taking advantage of their privileged position and their access to confidential information, Oreamuno and Gonzalez were able to realize $800,000 more for their securities than they would have had this inside information not been available to them. Stating that the defendants were "forbidden to use [such] information . . . for their own personal profit or gain", the plaintiff brought this derivative action seeking to have the defendants account to the corporation for this difference . . .

In reaching a decision in this case, we are, of course, passing only upon the sufficiency of the complaint and we necessarily accept the charges contained in that pleading as true.

It is well established, as a general proposition, that a person who acquires special knowledge or information by virtue of a confidential or fiduciary relationship with another is not free to exploit that knowledge or information for his own personal benefit but must account to his principal for any profits derived therefrom. This, in turn is merely a corollary of the broader principle, inherent in the nature of the fiduciary relationship, that prohibits a trustee or agent from extracting secret profits from his position of trust.

In support of their claim that the complaint fails to state a cause of action, the defendants take the position that, although it is admittedly wrong for an officer or director to use his position to obtain trading profits for himself in the stock of his corporation, the action ascribed to them did not injure or damage MAI in any way. Accordingly, the defendants continue, the corporation should not be permitted to recover the proceeds. They acknowledge that, by virtue of the exclusive access which officers and directors have to inside information, they possess an unfair advantage over other shareholders and, particularly, the persons who had purchased the stock from them but, they contend, the corporation itself was unaffected and, for that reason, a derivative action is an inappropriate remedy.

It is true that the complaint before us does not contain any allegation of damages to the corporation but this has never been considered to be an essential requirement for a cause of action founded on a breach of fiduciary duty . . . This is because the function of such an action, unlike an ordinary tort or contract case, is not merely to compensate the plaintiff for wrongs committed by the defendant but, as this court declared many years ago, "to prevent them, by removing from agents and trustees all inducement to attempt dealing for their own benefit in matters which they have undertaken for others, or to which their agency or trust relates". (Emphasis supplied.)

Just as a trustee has no right to retain for himself the profits yielded by property placed in his possession but must account to his beneficiaries, a corporate fiduciary, who is entrusted with potentially valuable information, may not appropriate that asset for his own use even though, in so doing, he causes no injury to the corporation. The primary concern, in a case such as this, is not to determine whether the corporation has been damaged but to decide, as between the corporation and the defendants, who has a higher claim to the proceeds derived from the exploitation of the information. In our opinion, there can be no justification for permitting officers and directors, such as the defendants, to retain for themselves profits which, it is alleged, they derived solely from exploiting information gained by virtue of their inside position as corporate officials.

In addition, it is pertinent to observe that, despite the lack of any specific allegation of damage, it may well be inferred that the defendants' actions might have caused some harm to the enterprise. Although the corporation may have little concern with the day-to-day transactions in its shares, it has a great interest in maintaining a reputation of integrity, an image of probity, for its management and in insuring the continued public acceptance and marketability of its stock. When officers and directors abuse their position in order to gain personal profits, the effect may be to cast a cloud on the corporation's name, injure stockholder relations and undermine public regard for the corporation's securities. As Presiding Justice Botein aptly put it, in the course of his opinion for the Appellate Division, "[t]he prestige and good will of a corporation, so vital to its prosperity, may be undermined by the revelation that its chief officers had been making personal profits out of corporate events which they had not disclosed to the community of stockholders".

The defendants maintain that extending the prohibition against personal exploitation of a fiduciary relationship to officers and directors of a corporation will discourage such officials from maintaining a stake in the success of the corporate venture through share ownership, which, they urge, is an important incentive to proper performance of their duties. There is, however, a considerable difference between corporate officers who assume the same risks and obtain the same benefits as other shareholders and those who use their privileged position to gain special advantages not available to others. The sale of shares by the defendants for the reasons charged was not merely a wise investment decision which any prudent investor might have made. Rather, they were assertedly able in this case to profit solely because they had information which was not available to any one else — including the other shareholders whose interests they, as corporate fiduciaries, were bound to protect.

Although no appellate court in this State has had occasion to pass upon the precise question before us, the concept underlying the present cause of action is hardly a new one . . . for example, it is conclusively presumed that, when a director officer or 10% shareholder buys and sells securities of his corporation within a six-month period, he is trading on inside information. The remedy which the Federal statute provides in that situation is precisely the same as that sought in the present case under State law, namely, an action brought by the corporation or on its behalf to recover all profits derived from the transactions.

In providing this remedy, Congress accomplished a dual purpose. It not only provided for an efficient and effective method of accomplishing its primary goal — the protection of the investing public from unfair treatment at the hands of corporate insiders — but extended to the corporation the right to secure for itself benefits derived by those insiders from their exploitation of their privileged position. The United States Court of Appeals for the Second Circuit has stated the policy behind section 16(b) in the following terms (*Adler v. Klawans*, 267 F.2d 840, 844):

> The undoubted congressional intent in the enactment of § 16(b) was to discourage what was reasonably thought to be a widespread abuse of a fiduciary relationship — specifically to discourage if not prevent three classes of persons from making private and gainful use of information acquired by them by virtue of their official relationship to a corporation.

Although the provisions of section 16(b) may not apply to all cases of trading on inside information, it demonstrates that a derivative action can be an effective method for dealing with such abuses which may be used to accomplish a similar purpose in cases not specifically covered by the statute . . .

In the present case, the defendants may be able to avoid liability to the corporation under section 16(b) of the Federal law since they had held the MAI shares for more than six months prior to the sales.

Nevertheless, the alleged use of the inside information to dispose of their stock at a price considerably higher than its known value constituted the same sort of "abuse of a fiduciary relationship" as is condemned by the Federal law. Sitting as we are in this case as a court of equity, we should not hesitate to permit an action to prevent any unjust enrichment realized by the defendants from their allegedly wrongful act.

The defendants . . . maintain [that] the Federal legislation constitutes a comprehensive and carefully wrought plan for dealing with the abuse of inside information and that allowing a derivative action to be maintained under State law would interfere with the Federal scheme. Moreover, they urge, the existence of dual Federal and State remedies for the same act would create the possibility of double liability.

An examination of the Federal regulatory scheme refutes the contention that it was designed to establish any particular remedy as exclusive. [The Court notes that even Federal securities law contains two separate provisions concerning insider trading: section 16(b) of the *Exchange Act* and Rule 10b-5 under section 10(b) of the *Exchange Act*, as interpreted by the SEC and Federal courts.] . . .

The remedies which the Federal law provides for [a] violation [of Rule 10b-5], however, are rather limited. An action could be brought, in an exceptional case, by the SEC for injunctive relief. This, in fact, is what happened in the *Texas Gulf Sulphur* case (401 F.2d 833, *supra*). The purpose of such an action, however, would appear to be more to establish a principle than to provide a regular method of enforcement. A class action under the Federal rule might be a more effective remedy but the mechanics of such an action have, as far as we have been able to ascertain, not yet been worked out by the Federal courts and several questions relating thereto have never been resolved. These include the definition of the class entitled to bring such an action, the measure of damages, the administration of the fund which would be recovered and its distribution to the members of the class . . . Of course, any individual purchaser, who could prove an injury as a result of a Rule 10b-5 violation can bring his own action for rescission but we have not been referred to a single case in which such an action has been successfully prosecuted where the public sale of securities is involved. The reason for this is that sales of securities, whether through a stock exchange or over-the-counter, are characteristically anonymous transactions, usually handled through brokers, and the matching of the ultimate buyer with the ultimate seller presents virtually insurmountable obstacles. Thus, unless a section 16(b) violation is also present, the Federal law does not yet provide a really effective remedy.

In view of the practical difficulties inherent in an action under the Federal law, the desirability of creating an effective common-law remedy is manifest . . . There is ample room in a situation such as is here presented for a "private Attorney General" to come forward and enforce proper behavior on the part of corporate officials through the medium of the derivative action brought in the name of the corporation. Only by sanctioning such a cause of action will there be any effective method to prevent the type of abuse of corporate office complained of in this case . . .

The order appealed from should be affirmed with costs, and the question certified answered in the affirmative.

Notes and Questions

1 Does Diamond follow principles laid down in *Regal (Hastings)* and in *Canaero*? Is Judge Fuld clear as to whether his decision would have been the same if there clearly would have been double liability? Do you think it should be? Suppose Oreamuno had not traded but had informed a friend who traded. Should Oreamuno (the tipper) be liable to the corporation for the friend's (the tippee) profits?

2 Considerable doubt has been cast on the holding on *Diamond*. The Florida Supreme Court, in *Schein v. Chasen*, 313 So. 2d 739 (1975), on the basis that there was no allegation of injury to the corporation, and the Seventh Circuit Court of Appeals, in *Freeman v. Decio*, 584 F.2d 186 (1978), have declined to follow the holding in *Diamond*. In *Freeman*, the Court raised the question of whether the insider-director had truly been unjustly enriched *vis-a-vis* the corporation when the corporation could not have used the information for profit, questioned any damage to corporate goodwill as being speculative and expressed concern about potential double liability. See Highberger, "Common Law Corporate Recovery for Trading on Non-Public Information" (1974), 74 Colum. L. Rev. 269. In *Fankel v. Slotkin*, 795 F. Supp. 76 (E.D.N.Y., 1992), a federal district court again questioned the relevance of *Diamond*, noting that the case had been decided at a time when class actions under Rule 10b-5 had not yet developed into an effective shareholder remedy.

Chapter 9

Shareholders' Rights

1. INTRODUCTION

This chapter will begin a focus on the role of shareholders in the corporation. Canadian corporation statutes reflect an enabling philosophy in that the formation and activities of corporations have been encouraged by placing very few hurdles to achieving incorporation. Indeed society generally has provided many inducements in support of corporations, such as preferential income tax treatment. As a subject, corporation law is a form of constitutional law that is set against this enabling philosophy and that attempts to regulate the rights and duties of those who participate in the corporation and, to a limited degree, those who relate to or are greatly affected by it. In this respect, normative rules of corporation law are in many cases difficult to prescribe or articulate on many of the various issues that are studied in this book.

Many popular generalizations or assumptions that have been made about shareholders are especially in need of re-examination in the light of the major social, economic and political changes that have occurred in Western societies generally and in Canadian society in particular. One of the general assumptions is that shareholders are the owners of the corporation, but this statement begs further analysis to ask what does ownership mean in this context, and compared to what; or put another way, what property or rights are owned by the shareholder? It is also said that shareholders are primarily if not exclusively interested in the growth or return on their investment. Is this in fact the case? What, if anything, happens to this assertion of shareholder expectations when the state becomes the sole or dominant shareholder of the corporation or when religious or charitable institutions are the shareholders?

Numerous significant developments have taken place in the size and type of corporation and the nature of the shareholder constituency. The vast majority of corporations in Canada are closely held and it is often said that the needs and expectations of shareholders in these entities differ materially from those of their counterparts in widely held corporations. As a result, many argue for correspondingly different statutory and judicial rules. Indeed, some aspects of the closely held corporation will receive special attention in the next chapter.

At the same time, the mix of shareholders has become extremely complicated and varied. The emergence of institutional shareholdings has been profound when one thinks of the portfolio investments of mutual funds, pensions, insurance companies, credit unions and other financial intermediaries. It is most appropriate to ask whether corporation law has kept properly abreast of these developments. In this connection, the role of provincial securities commissions under securities legislation is very relevant since these bodies have greatly affected, and in turn have been influenced by, shareholder concerns on various issues traditionally left to corporation law. As evidenced by the introduction of the *Sarbanes-Oxley Act* of 2002 in the US and the corresponding Canadian response, securities regulators are increasingly regulating in the area of corporate governance. See discussion, *infra*.

Against this background, we examine briefly what rights are or should be given to shareholders by corporation statutes in the modem context. To the extent there are rights assigned, there must also be means of enforcing these rights through effective remedies, and this subject is explored in a following chapter.

At this stage, it might be concluded that as long as shareholders have reasonable protection for their interests, they are content to leave to others the management of the business affairs of the corporation. As this argument goes, shareholders, at least in the widely held corporation, have neither the expertise nor the interest to run the corporation. The reasonable protection will, *inter alia*, include the imposition of duties of care and skill and fiduciary fair dealing on corporate management as outlined in previous chapters. However, where the matter under consideration by the corporation comes closer to affecting the nature of the shareholders' investment or is a decision on who will run the corporation, it is more likely the shareholders will wish to have a voice on the matter. (See generally an analysis of the criteria for shareholder involvement in corporate decision making in Eisenberg, "The Legal Roles of Shareholders and Management in Modern Corporate Decision Making", (1969), 57 Cal. L. Rev. 1; Iacobucci, Pilkington and Pritchard, *Canadian Business Corporations* (1977), 132–48).

The next issue is how such shareholder opinion gets expressed. Here the pervasive majority rule of corporation law is directly encountered. In the context of examining shareholder rights, one has to determine what rights are individually conferred and what are subject to majority support. A further question relates to the specific majority required to approve particular transactions or issues. Needless to say, checks and balances exist to prevent abuse of minorities in Canadian constitutional law, and the need for similar protection in corporation law has been recognized by courts and legislators for some time. Whether they have been effectively recognized is another question.

2. PRE-EMPTIVE RIGHTS

Where a "pre-emptive right" exists, the corporation must offer existing shareholders the opportunity to subscribe for a new share offering in the proportion that their shareholdings bear to the total number of shares issued and outstanding. We have already seen that the company's managers may be tempted (whether for good or bad motives) to issue shares to defeat a current or anticipated takeover bid, or to alter the distribution of control. See *supra*, Chapter 6. The existence of a pre-emptive right makes it very much more difficult for the managers to do so, since all shareholders must be offered their *pro rata* allotment.

A pre-emptive right can serve another function. Share issuance at an undervalue will result in the "dilution" of the interests of current shareholders, with concomitant diminution in the value of their investments. Suppose, for example, that there are 100 shares in ABC Inc., a company with a steady net profit of $1,000 per year, which is paid out annually as dividends on the shares. Earnings per share are $10, and hence the annual dividend amounts to $10 per share. Based on a price/earnings ratio (or "multiplier") of 10, each share will trade for $100. (Note that in practice, this price/earnings ratio is determined by the market.) The total value of the company is $10,000 (100 shares worth $100 each). Suppose now that the controlling shareholder in the company causes 50 shares to be issued to herself at $40 each (i.e., at a $60 discount from actual value). This will result in $2000 flowing into the corporate treasury, which the company will then invest. We will make the assumption that net profits rise in proportion to the cash infusion; that is, they go to $1200 per year. Now what are the shares worth? There are 150 shares outstanding, and net profits of $1200 to be divided among them. This means that earnings per share are $8 per annum. Using the same price/earnings ratio as before, each share is now worth only $80. Every minority shareholder loses $20 per share held. While the value of the holdings of the majority shareholder decreases by an identical amount, she nonetheless gains overall by virtue of having purchased the shares issued at an undervalue. The share issuance at an undervalue has resulted in a transfer of wealth from the minority shareholders to the majority shareholder. A pre-emptive right would have given every minority shareholder the opportunity to purchase the underpriced shares, resulting in protection from dilution.

In the United States, prior to the enactment of statutory provisions dealing with the matter, the courts recognized the pre-emptive right as a means of shareholder protection against dilution of their interests without their consent (see Drinker, "The Pre-emptive Right of Shareholders to Subscribe to New Shares" (1930), 43 Harv. L. Rev. 586).

Under Canadian common law, the issuance of shares by a corporation does not give rise to a pre-emptive right. See *Harris v. Sumner* (1909), 39 N.B.R. 204 (C.A.). However, under the older "improper purpose" test (still current in England) an issuance of shares designed to alter or influence control could be struck down as a breach of the fiduciary duty of the directors. See *Bonisteel v. Collis Leather Co. Ltd., supra*, at Chapter 6. It would appear that the Canadian courts have jettisoned this test in favour of the test of acting honestly on reasonable grounds enunciated by Berger J. in *Teck v. Millar, supra*, at Chapter 6. The *Teck* test was adopted by the Manitoba Court of Appeal in *Olson v. Phoenix Industrial Supply Ltd. et al.*, noted, *supra,* in Chapter 6, and has also been adopted by the lower courts of several provinces, including Ontario. You will recall that in that case, an issuance of shares designed expressly to deprive the majority shareholder of control was approved on the grounds that the evidence established that the directors were acting honestly, in good faith and in the best interests of the company in issuing shares, and that they did so on reasonable grounds. See also *Hiram Walker, supra*, at Chapter 6.

It is no longer sufficient to have regard only to the common law; the enactment of the oppression remedy has brought about wholesale change in the law of business corporations, and there are at least three cases that have considered the question of pre-emptive rights. The English case *Re a Company*, [1985] B.C.L.C. 80 (Ch. D.) involved a small corporation with only two shareholders; Lewis owned 1/3 of the shares, and the Boltons owned 2/3. When disagreements arose between the parties, a resolution was brought forward by the Boltons to increase the capital of the company and to give the directors authority to issue shares. Lewis sought an injunction under the English oppression provision to prevent the Boltons from voting their shares in favour of the resolution. The Boltons testified that it was their intention to issue shares only on the basis of a *pro rata* rights offering ("rights" are securities that entitle the holder to purchase shares; a rights offering is usually made to the company's shareholders on a *pro rata* basis). The court granted the injunction, holding that even a *pro rata* offering could operate in an unfairly prejudicial manner

> if it could be shown, for example, that it was known that although the offer would be *pro rata* yet the member would be unable by reason of his own circumstances to take it up, and that the knowledge was a factor leading to the making of an offer which was in truth illusory because it could never be accepted. (*Ibid.*, at 82.)

Similarly, in *Re Sabex Int. Ltee* (1979), 6 B.L.R. 65 (Que. S.C.), a corporation was formed through the combination of one business owned by the applicants and another owned by the respondents. The respondents held 54% of the shares and the applicants 44%. The corporation sought further funds to expand operations; however, its bankers insisted that an additional $100,000 of share equity be invested before they would expand the company's line of credit. In order to satisfy this requirement, the company put forward a rights offering to all shareholders. The applicants objected under s. 234 of the CBCA (the oppression provision, now CBCA s. 241) on the ground that the offering was oppressive because it forced them to participate in order to avoid diluting their interests. Acknowledging the legitimate need for additional equity, the fact that the plan treated all shareholders in a formally equal manner and the presence of good faith, the court nonetheless granted an injunction apparently because the effect of the rights offering was to dilute the minority's interest if it did not subscribe. Do you think this is an appropriate result? See also *Mazzotta v. Twin Gold Mines* (1987), 37 B.L.R. 218 (Ont. H.C.) (reaching a similar result).

The Ontario Securities Commission has taken steps to combat the potential abuses associated with non-*pro rata* share offerings. OSC National Instrument 45-101, which deals with rights offerings, provides (in part):

Part 7 Additional Subscription Privilege

7.1

Additional Subscription Privilege — An issuer shall not grant an additional subscription privilege to a holder of a right unless the issuer grants the additional subscription privilege to all holders of rights.

7.2

Stand-by Commitment — If there is a stand-by commitment for a rights offering, the issuer will grant an additional subscription privilege to all holders of rights.

7.3

Number or Amount of Securities
   (1) Under an additional subscription privilege, each holder of a right shall be entitled to receive, on exercise of the additional subscription privilege, the number or amount of securities that is equal to the lesser of
   (a) the number or amount of securities subscribed for by the holder under the additional subscription privilege; and
   (b) $x(y/z)$ where
      x the aggregate number of securities available through unexercised rights,
      y the number of rights previously exercised by the holder under the rights offering, and
      z the aggregate number of rights previously exercised under the rights offering by holders of rights that have subscribed for securities under the additional subscription privilege.

   (2) Any exercised rights shall be exercised on a *pro rata* basis to holders who subscribed for additional securities based on the additional subscription privilege up to the number of securities subscribed for by a particular holder.

7.4

Price of Securities — The subscription price under an additional subscription privilege or a stand-by commitment shall be the same as the subscription price under the basic subscription privilege.

A "stand-by commitment" is an agreement to purchase all the rights not taken up by shareholders on the rights offering. The National Instrument recognizes the fact that not all shareholders will purchase rights even where the offering is below market price; thus, if a party related to (and acting in concert with) a major or controlling shareholder gives a stand-by commitment, the major or controlling shareholder will be able to increase its proportionate ownership in the company, and hence its ability to control the company.

Section 26 of the OBCA, which is broadly similar in this respect to section 28 of the CBCA, expressly allows a pre-emptive restriction to be written into the company's constitution.

The U.K. *Companies Act*, 1980 introduced pre-emptive rights because of the European Common Market directives on company law harmonization (see now *Companies Act*, 1985, s. 89). For a discussion of the U.K. provisions, see Daniel D. Prentice, *Companies Act1980* (Toronto: Butterworths 1980), pp. 23–31. The statutory treatment in the US is even more varied: denying pre-emptive rights in some jurisdictions, denying them unless expressly granted, expressly granting them and authorizing limitations on them. (See Iacobucci, Pilkington and Prichard, *Canadian Business Corporations* (1977), 147–150).

Which approach do you prefer?

3. SHAREHOLDER VOTING

(a) Introduction

The separation of ownership and control in the modern corporation gives rise to potential problems that have already been alluded to; managers may not pay attention to the interests of shareholders so much as their own interests. There are three main ways in which managers may favour their own interests over those of the shareholders. First, they may consume excessive perquisites, such as large interest-free loans from the corporation, the payment of excessive salaries and fees, the furnishing of excessively lavish offices, *etc.* Second, they may simply pay insufficient attention to running the firm (*e.g.*, too much time on the golf course). Third, they may choose investment projects that are less risky than the shareholders would choose. This is because managers are underdiversified; that is, a great portion of the typical (senior) manager's personal wealth will be tied to the firm, not only in the form of stock and stock options, but in the form of the manager's salary. By comparison, shareholders usually hold diversified portfolios of securities and are less concerned about the risk of any single investment as they are about the riskiness of the portfolio as a whole. As a result, the managers may select investment projects that are not terribly promising, but which tend to minimize the probability of financial distress or bankruptcy (pursuant to which the managers might conceivably lose their jobs).

So long as the managers own less than 100% of the firm, then the costs of perquisite consumption, careless management and risk-shifting are borne in part by public shareholders, creating an incentive for the managers to engage in the forms of self-interested behaviour indicated above.

In a now very famous work written in 1932 (*The Modern Corporation and Private Property*), Adolf Berle and Gardiner Means suggested that the separation of ownership and control in the modern public corporation spelled the end of effective shareholder oversight of corporate managers. Since, in their view, management had become a virtually autonomous organ of the corporation, it was inevitable that managers would engage in a significant level of non-profit maximizing behaviour.

Aside from legal controls over the behaviour of the corporate managers, there are a variety of market mechanisms that serve to constrain managerial behaviour and ensure that managers do not depart too far from profit maximizing behaviour. These have already been alluded to, and include the market for corporate control, the market for managers, and the product markets in which the firm sells its wares.

One type of legal restraint has already been examined; managerial (and, to the extent that they exist in Canadian law shareholder) duties of a fiduciary character.

Shareholder voting, which we look at in this chapter, is both a device for controlling managerial diversion, slack and risk-shifting, as well as for registering shareholder preferences relating to important business decisions in the life of the corporation. Shareholders are statutorily empowered to vote for directors and also in respect of an enumerated set of transactions that are often referred to as corporate "fundamental changes". These are transactions like amalgamations that fundamentally alter the structure (and/or the business) of the corporation (a more complete enumeration may be found below).

Shareholder voting seems a natural answer to the problems of managerial excess, ineptitude and risk-shifting. If the managers fail to perform adequately, then the shareholders may replace the directors (and through them, the managers appointed by the board of directors). The efficacy of shareholder voting as an oversight device has frequently been questioned, however. Since in the typical case few shareholders will actually be able to attend the shareholders' meeting at which directors will be elected, most shareholders who vote do so by "proxy"; that is, they nominate someone else (the proxyholder) to vote for them at the meeting by means of a written instrument (the form of proxy). Under the CBCA and OBCA, the management of most corporations is required to send shareholders a form of proxy on which management designates its nominations for directors (the reasons for the requirement are discussed briefly below). The form of proxy allows the shareholder to endorse management's slate of candidates by simply nominating as proxyholder a person indicated on the form of proxy (designated by management) who will vote for management's choices. It will be beyond the reach of most shareholders to nominate alternate candidates for directors before the meeting, since both the CBCA and OBCA allow only shareholders holding 5% of the shares or 5% of a class of shares entitled to vote at the meeting to make nominations for directors (CBCA s. 137(4); OBCA s. 99(4)). Although shareholders may make nominations at the meeting itself, such nominations will almost always be doomed to failure where management has solicited proxies for its nominees in advance. Thus, in the usual case (unless a shareholder or group of shareholders has mounted a proxy battle) the slate of candidates nominated by management will run unopposed — and will be elected to office.

Further, there is the problem of "rational shareholder apathy" (a phrase coined by Robert Clark in his article "Vote Buying and Corporate Law" (1979), 29 Case West. L. Rev. 776). In the modern public corporation share ownership is often fragmented amongst a large number of shareholders. The costs of becoming sufficiently informed to vote effectively are quite large. Shareholders must familiarize themselves with the records of those standing for election, and such information may be difficult to come by, if available at all. For the average shareholder, the benefits are tenuous; the prospect that the votes wielded by the shareholder will influence the outcome is small. Further, to the extent that benefits accrue from using one's votes carefully, the benefits are distributed amongst all shareholders, creating a classic "free rider" effect. Each shareholder has an incentive to let someone else do the work, knowing that they and all other shareholders will enjoy the fruits of the efforts made by the knowledgeable few. As a result, many shareholders simply fail to return the proxy material sent to them by management. Many others who choose to exercise their voting franchise will do so by endorsing without investigation management's team of nominees. See *The Proxy System, infra,* and see generally Raymond Crete, *The Proxy System in Canadian Corporations* (1986), Clark, *supra,* and Easterbrook and Fischel, "Voting in Corporate Law" (1983), 26 J. Law & Econ. 395.

Shareholder voting is far from costless; there are considerable costs that attend the preparation and mailing of proxy materials to shareholders, especially in very large public corporations, not to mention the cost of the meeting itself. Since the benefits of shareholder voting (at least in the larger public corporation) appear to be minimal, is shareholder voting an anachronism that ought to be done away with? The answer appears to be clearly in the negative. Enfranchising shareholders can lead to oversight of management in a number of important ways. First, there may be shareholders with large blocks of shares, particularly institutional investors like insurance companies, pension and mutual funds, banks and other financial intermediaries. A very high percentage of all shares traded in the market are now controlled by such investors. These investors will have much better incentives to use their voting power (and powers of suasion) effectively to ensure that only competent individuals with proven track records are elected as directors. The old "Wall Street" (or "Bay Street") rule under which institutional investors simply sold their holdings if dissatisfied with management is on its way to becoming an anachronism. See Jeffrey G. MacIntosh, "The Role of Institutional and Retail Investors in Canadian Capital Markets" (1993), 31 Osgoode Hall L.J. 371; and Brian R. Cheffins, "Michaud v. National Bank of Canada and Canadian Corporate Governance: A 'Victory' for Shareholder Rights?" (1998), 30 C.B.L.J. 20.

Second, the existence of a voting class of security holders facilitates replacement of inefficient management through the mechanism of the "hostile" takeover bid (i.e., one that is not sanctioned by management). Where management has become too self-indulgent or lazy, the share price of the company will fall as corporate profits sag. It will become profitable for an acquiror to mount a takeover bid for the company's voting equity and if successful, use its aggregated voting power to appoint a new managerial team. This could not occur but for the existence of a class of security holders possessing the power to elect directors.

Lastly, the existence of a voting class of security holders facilitates the replacement of inefficient management by means of a proxy battle. In such a contest, a dissident shareholder (or, more frequently, group of shareholders) attempts to replace management by securing the proxies of shareholders and using these proxies to vote for an alternate slate of directors nominated by the dissidents.

Thus, empowering at least one class of security holders to elect directors serves as a powerful check on the nearly inevitable tendency of management to depart, at least to a degree, from their assigned role of maximizing corporate profits.

As we have indicated, in addition to voting for directors, shareholders vote on so-called "fundamental changes" in the life of the corporation. These include (*inter alia*) amalgamation (CBCA s. 183, OBCA s. 176); sale of all or substantially all the assets of the corporation (CBCA ss. 189(3)–(8), OBCA ss. 184(3)–(8)); continuance in another jurisdiction (CBCA s. 188, OBCA s. 181); and changes to the corporation's articles of incorporation (CBCA s. 173, OBCA s. 168). Can you supply a rationale for shareholder voting on corporate fundamental changes? Are the reasons different from or similar to those that suggest a role for voting for directors?

(b) Note on Statutory and Judicial Voting Entitlements

The right to vote is a fundamental right of shareholders and is one feature that distinguishes shares from debt obligations. Voting rights are enshrined in the corporate legislation of each Canadian jurisdiction. Section 24 of the CBCA provides that at least one class of shares must be voting, entitled to receive dividends, and to receive the assets remaining on dissolution. To a similar effect is section 22(3) of the OBCA, except that this section requires only that there be a class of shares having voting rights and the entitlement to receive the remaining property of the corporation upon dissolution. In each statute, if the articles are silent about voting rights, then each share carries one vote (CBCA s. 140(1), OBCA s. 102(1)).

Since only one class of the corporation's shares must have the right to vote, and since it is possible to create a capital structure with many different classes of shares, it is clear under the CBCA and OBCA (and the legislation of the other provinces) that shares may be created with no voting rights at all. It is usual, for example, to create preferred shares that do not vote (although preferred shares may have a contingent vote that comes into play if, say, preferred dividends are not paid for 6 of any 8 consecutive quarters). It became increasingly common in the 1980s to create "common" shares that do not possess the right to vote. Sometimes these common shares are identical in all respects save voting rights to a class of voting common shares. More often, they will possess a higher dividend rate or a preferential dividend as a "sweetener" to induce purchase of the shares.

Where one or more classes of shareholders do not vote (either for directors or to approve corporate fundamental changes) clear dangers of opportunistic behaviour are created. For example, suppose holders of the voting class of shares resolved to amend the articles of incorporation to remove a preferential dividend attaching to a class of preferred shares. There is nothing, save perhaps a suit for breach of fiduciary duty or an oppression action that would prevent this from occurring. There are two distinct forms of statutory response to the dangers of abuse that arise from the unequal distribution of voting rights. One is to mandatorily enfranchise shares that would not otherwise carry the right to vote. This is done in the CBCA, for example, in connection with an amalgamation (s. 183(3)), sale of all or substantially all the assets of the corporation (s. 189(6)) and continuance in another jurisdiction (s. 188(4)). Another form of response also seen in the CBCA is the requirement that certain fundamental transactions be approved separately by every class of shareholders, whether or not the class would otherwise carry the right to vote. This is done, for example, in connection with an amalgamation (s. 183(4)), sale of all or substantially all the assets of the corporation (s. 189(7)) and amendments to the articles of incorporation (s. 176) (in each case, note the limitations imposed upon the furnishing of a class vote). The OBCA employs only the latter technique. See, *e.g.*, OBCA ss. 170, 176(3), 184(6).

It is important to realize that class rights may be altered not only directly, but indirectly. For example, instead of removing a preferential dividend attaching to a class of preferred shares (a direct alteration of the terms of the preferred shares) the common shareholders might create a new class of preferred shares having an entitlement to dividends that is preferential to the existing class of preferreds. They might then issue this class to new security holders or perhaps even to themselves as a "stock dividend". In either case, this would affect the relative claim of the original preferred shareholders to the earnings stream of the company, reducing the value of these preferreds. In *Greenhalgh v. Arderne Cinemas Ltd.*, [1946] 1 All E.R. 512 (C.A.), the terms of issue of the preferred shares had been drafted so as to allow the preferreds to vote separately as a class on any change in the articles of the company that had the effect of "varying" the rights of the preferred shareholders. The English Court of Appeal held that this clause protected the preferreds only in the case of a direct, and not an indirect modification of rights of the preferreds. It is for this reason that the drafters of the CBCA crafted s. 176 (cf. OBCA s. 170) to include events modifying class rights both directly and indirectly.

There is at least one other situation where voting rights can serve as a check on opportunistic behaviour. Recall the facts of *Northwest Transportation v. Beatty* (*supra*, Chapter 6). A major shareholder in the company sold a steamship to the company. That same shareholder then used his votes to "ratify" the sale to the company. Clearly, a ratification secured only by the votes of an interested shareholder is not a very effective means of ensuring the fairness of the transaction. One would have a much higher degree of confidence in the fairness of the transaction if it was ratified by at least a majority of the uninterested shareholders (that is, shareholders having no particular interest in the subject matter of the transaction). The same applies to shareholder approval of fundamental transactions.

There are as yet few statutory requirements for approval of transactions by a majority of disinterested shareholders (or a "majority of the minority"). Such a requirement is found in the OBCA in section 190, however (dealing with "going private"; that is, evicting the "public" shareholders and concentrating ownership in the hands of a relative few shareholders). Moreover, there appears to be a growing trend at common law to require that shareholder approvals or ratifications be given by a majority of the minority of shareholders. See, *e.g.*, *Wedge v. McNeil* (1981), 126 D.L.R. (3d) 596 (P.E.I. S.C.), reversed on evidentiary grounds by (1982), 142 D.L.R. (3d) 133 (P.E.I.C.A.); *Re Northwest Forest Products Ltd.*, *infra*, Chapter 11; *Clemens v. Clemens Bros. Ltd.*, [1976] 2 All E.R. 268 (Ch. D.). See generally, *supra*, Chapter 6.

Increasingly, the securities regulators of the various provinces are requiring approval of certain transactions either by a majority of shareholders or, in some cases, by a majority of the minority. Where, for example, an existing class of voting equity securities is broken up into voting and non-voting (or restricted voting) components by a change in the articles or otherwise, the Ontario Securities Commission requires approval of the transaction by a majority of shareholders, not counting any shareholders who form part of a controlling group. See OSC Rule 56-501. Similarly, OSC Rule 61-501 requires that a majority of the minority vote be held to approve transactions with interested parties, including going private transactions and "related party transactions" (major transactions involving interested parties).

The stock exchanges are also involved. The Toronto Stock Exchange, for example, may require approval of an issuance of shares where a substantial block of shares is issued or where the issuance materially affects the control of the issuer. The required approval may be of all shareholders, or of a majority of the minority. See TSE Policy 3.5. But see also *Re Torstar Corporation and Southam Inc.* [6 June 1986] O.S.C.B. 3033 and *Re Canada Malting*, [27 June 1986] O.S.C.B. 3565.

(c) Note on Classification of Shares

Rule 56-501 of the Ontario Securities Commission, noted above, creates a scheme for the classification of shares according to their voting rights. The purpose of the scheme is to ensure that buyers and sellers of publicly traded securities fully understand the nature of the voting rights attaching to the securities being traded.

1.1 Definitions

In this Rule

. . .

"class" includes a series of a class;

"common shares" means equity shares to which are attached voting rights exercisable in all circumstances, irrespective of the number or percentage of shares owned, that are not less, on a per share basis, than the voting rights attaching to any other shares of an outstanding class of shares of the issuer, unless the Director makes a determination under section 4.1 that the shares are restricted shares;

. . .

"equity shares" means shares of an issuer that carry a residual right to participate in the earnings of the issuer and, upon the liquidation or winding up of the issuer, in its assets;

. . .

"non-voting shares" means restricted shares that do not carry the right to vote generally, except for a right to vote that is mandated in special circumstances by law;

"preference shares" means shares to which are attached a preference or right over the shares of any class of equity shares of the issuer, but does not include equity shares;

. . .

"restricted share term" means each of "non-voting shares", "subordinate voting shares", "restricted voting shares" and every other term designated by the Director under subsection 4.1(2);

"restricted shares" means
(a) equity shares that are not common shares, and
(b) equity shares determined to be restricted shares under subsection 4.1(1);

"restricted voting shares" means restricted shares that carry a right to vote subject to a restriction on the number or percentage of shares that may be voted by a person, a company or any combination of persons and companies, except to the extent the restriction or limit is permitted or prescribed by statute and is applicable only to persons or companies that are not citizens or residents of Canada or that are otherwise considered as a result of any law applicable to the issuer to be non-Canadians;

. . .

"subject securities" means shares that have the effect, or would have the effect if and when issued, of changing a class of outstanding equity shares into restricted shares;

"subordinate voting shares" means restricted shares that carry a right to vote, if there are shares of another class of shares outstanding that carry a greater right to vote on a per share basis

Under this Rule, if an issuer has restricted shares, or securities that are convertible, exchangeable, or exercisable into restricted shares, then the shares must be described using the classification scheme. The appropriate term must be used in documents sent by the issuer to its shareholders.

(d) Permissible Limitations on the Right to Vote in the Corporation's Constitution

Jacobsen v. United Canso Oil & Gas Ltd.
11 B.L.R. 313, [1980] 6 W.W.R. 38 (Alta. Q.B.)

FORSYTH J.: This matter came before me for determination of a preliminary point of law on a peremptory basis to determine the following question:

Does the Defendant's By-Law (By-Law No. 6) which provides that no person shall be entitled to vote more than 1,000 shares of the Defendant notwithstanding the number of shares actually held by him contravene the provisions of the *Canada Business Corporations Act*;

The determination of this issue involves not only consideration of the present provisions of the *Canada Business Corporations Act*, 1974-75-76 (Can.), c. 33, but also the provisions of the applicable legislation at the time the by-law was enacted.

The defendant United Canso Oil & Gas Ltd. (hereinafter referred to as "United Canso") was incorporated by letters patent on April 13, 1954, pursuant to the *Companies Act*, R.S.C. 1952, c. 53, By-law No. 1, the general by-law of the company, was duly enacted on April 15, 1954, and provided, *inter alia*, as follows:

> Upon a show of hands each shareholder present in person shall have one vote and upon a poll each shareholder present in person or by proxy shall have one vote for each share held by such shareholder unless the letters patent, supplementary letters patent or by-laws of the Company otherwise provide in respect of the shares of any particular class.

I would note that there is no dispute between the parties that at the time of incorporation and up to the present time United Canso has had only one class of shares, the present capitalization being 12 million common shares.

By-law No. 6 of the company was duly enacted on March 19, 1964, and provided, *inter alia*, as follows:

> With respect to any matter to be voted upon at any meeting of shareholders called after the final adjournment of the meeting at which this By-Law Number 6 is ratified, any one person as hereinafter defined shall be entitled to vote:
>
> (i) with respect to shares registered in his name on the books of the Company which are beneficially owned by him, the number of such shares, but in no event more than 1,000;
>
> (ii) with respect to shares registered in his name on the books of the Company which he holds as a trustee other than as a nominee, the number of such shares but in no event more than 1,000; and
>
> (iii) with respect to shares registered in his name as nominee and on instructions from each one person who is the owner thereof a number of shares owned by each such one person but in no event more than 1,000 with respect to each such one person, provided that no such one person shall vote or give instructions as to the voting of more than 1,000 shares in the aggregate.

The relevant legislation applicable at the time that by-law was enacted was again the *Companies Act* [superseded by the *Canada Corporations Act*, S.C. 1964-65, c. 52 [now R.S.C. 1970, c. C-32]. This change of by-law with respect to voting procedure, however, was not reflected in any supplementary letters patent until July 25, 1974, when supplementary letters of patent were issued to United Canso amending the letters patent of the company by adding thereto the voting limitations contained in By-law No. 6. These supplementary letters patent were issued by the Minister of Consumer and Corporate Affairs by virtue of the powers vested in him by the *Canada Corporations Act*, which Act replaced the *Companies Act*. The *Canada Corporations Act* itself was subsequently replaced by the *Canada Business Corporations Act*.

It might be useful to note at this time that s. 4 of the *Canada Business Corporations Act* provides as follows:

4. The purposes of this Act are to revise and reform the law applicable to business corporations incorporated to carry on business throughout Canada, to advance the cause of uniformity of business corporation law in Canada and to provide a means of allowing an orderly transference of certain federal companies incorporated under various Acts of Parliament to this Act.

In keeping with the provisions of s. 4 of the *Canada Business Corporations Act* the Act makes provision for what is referred to as a continuance of corporations incorporated under previous federal legislation to bring them within the provisions of the *Canada Business Corporations Act*. Section 261(3) which is applicable to United Canso provides as follows:

(3) A body corporate to which Part I of the *Canada Corporations Act* applies, other than a body corporate in respect of which an order has been made under the *Winding-Up Act* before this Act comes into force, shall apply for a certificate of continuance under s. 181 within five years after this Act comes into force.

(8) A body corporate referred to in subsection (3) that does not make an application to obtain a certificate of continuance within the period specified in that subsection is dissolved upon the expiry of that period.

United Canso, in fact, made an application for continuance under s. 181 of the *Canada Business Corporations Act* within the time period set out and a certificate of continuance was issued on October 24, 1979. I would note that the articles of continuance contain attached as Sched. 11 in effect a repeat of the provisions of By-law No. 6 setting forth the voting restrictions of a maximum of 1,000 votes regardless of the number of shares beneficially held.

The position of the plaintiff is that the voting limitation was invalid when first established by By-law No. 6 as it contravened the provisions of the *Companies Act*, then in force, was invalid when incorporated by way of supplementary letters patent as it contravened the provisions of the *Canada Corporations Act*, then applicable, and was invalid when it was purportedly brought forward by virtue of the articles of continuance as it contravened the provisions of the *Canada Business Corporations Act*. In addition, the plaintiff argues that, in any event, even if the voting limitation was initially valid under the provisions of the *Companies Act* and the *Canada Corporations Act*, it clearly violates the provisions of the *Canada Business Corporations Act* and that what may have been valid in 1964 or even 1974, is clearly not valid under the new Act regardless of continuance.

The defendant takes the position that the voting limitations were properly authorized initially, were properly incorporated into supplementary letters patent, are authorized and contemplated by the *Canada Business*

Corporations Act, either expressly, or in any event by virtue of the *Interpretation Act*, S.C. 1967-68 (Can.), c. 7 [now R.S.C. 1970, c. I-23], and the rights of shareholders as they were before the *Canada Business Corporations Act* came into force are continued.

The issue before the Court raises certain fundamental questions with respect to the rights of shareholders of a corporation. It was argued by the plaintiff that there is a presumption of equality between shareholders and the voting restriction in question contravenes this presumption. In this regard reference was made to *Palmer's Company Law* (22nd ed., 1976), vol 1, p. 334, where the learned author states:

> Prima facie the rights carried by the shares rank *pari passu i.e.*, the shareholders participate in the benefits of membership equally. It is only when a company divides its share capital into different classes with different rights attached to them that the prima facie presumption of equality of shares must be displaced.

Gower, on *Modern Company Law* (3rd ed., 1969) at p. 349, expresses a similar sentiment where the learned author states:

> The typical company — one limited by shares — must issue some shares, and the initial presumption of the law is that all shares confer equal rights and impose equal liabilities. As in partnership equality is assumed in the absence of evidence to the contrary. Normally the shareholders' rights will fall under three heads: (i) dividends, (ii) return of capital on a winding up (or authorised reduction of capital), and (iii) attendance at meetings and voting, and unless there is some indication to the contrary all the shares will confer the like rights to all three. So far as voting is concerned this is a comparatively recent development, for, on the analogy of the partnership rule, it was long felt that members' rights to control through voting should be divorced from their purely financial interests in respect of dividend and capital, so that the equality should be between members rather than between shares. . . It is now recognised that *if voting rights are to vary, separate classes of shares must be created so that the different number of votes can be attached to the shares themselves and not to the holder*. (The italics are mine.)

It is to be noted that the learned author of course was dealing with the development of company law in England, but nevertheless there are many parallels to be drawn between the evolution of company law in England and that in Canada.

As already mentioned, United Canso was incorporated pursuant to the provisions of the *Companies Act*. It is interesting to note that By-law No. 1 of the company enacted at the time of incorporation provides with respect to the voting of shares in part as follows: [See *supra*] . . .

It appears to me clear on a reading of the by-law that it was contemplated that it was only when different classes of shares were created that a change in the voting rights of one vote for each share might be established. It does not follow, however, that that by-law in effect in itself restraints the corporation from subsequently duty passing the amending By-law No. 6 containing the restriction of voting rights in respect of the one class of shares. I would note here that there was no argument advanced and indeed it was conceded that that by-law was properly passed insofar as the formalities are concerned, that is, notice to shareholders and the requisite number of shareholders being present.

The first question to be addressed is, however, whether By-law No. 6, although duly ratified by the shareholders of United Canso, was nevertheless passed in accordance with the then provisions of the *Companies Act*.

At first blush, ss. 102 and 103 of the *Companies Act*, as they then were, would seem to support the validity of a by-law limiting the number of votes a shareholder might have regardless of the number of shares held. Sections 102 and 103 as they read at the time of enactment of By-law No. 6, provided in part as follows:

> 102. Subject to the provisions of any by-law of the company duly enacted under the provisions of this Act, each share of the capital stock of any company issued and allotted, shall, subject to the provisions of this Part, carry voting rights and entitle the shareholder to one vote for each such share owned by him.

> 103. In the absence of other provisions in that behalf in the letters patent, supplementary letters patent or by-laws of the company.

> . . .

> (b) at all meetings of shareholders every shareholder is entitled to give one vote for each share then held by him; . . .

However, those sections must be read in the context of the Act as a whole and not in isolation. As was stated by Lord Reid in *Inland Revenue Commrs. v. Hinchy*, [1960] A.C. 748 at 766, [1960] 1 All E.R. 505 (H.L.):

> It is no doubt true that every Act should be read as a whole, but that is, I think, because one assumes that in drafting one clause of a Bill, the draftsman had in mind the language and substance of other clauses, and attributes to Parliament a comprehension of the whole Act.

In considering the issues to be determined in the relevant provisions of the *Companies Act*, it is important to remember that United Canso has only one class of shares, these being par value shares.

Part I of the Act, and in particular those sections dealing with formation of new companies, sets forth, inter alia, the information to be set forth in an application for letters patent including the nature and number of shares, including classes of shares it is proposed to issue. Section 12 deals with different classes of shares and subs. (1) of s. 12 provides in part as follows:

> 12.(1) The letters patent or supplementary letters patent of a company may provide for shares of more than one class and for any preferred, deferred or other special rights, restrictions, conditions or limitations attaching to any class of shares; . . .
>
> (2) The shares of all series of the same class carrying voting rights shall not carry the right to more than one vote for each share, and when any fixed cumulative dividends or amounts payable on a return of capital are not paid in full, the shares of all series of the same class shall participate rateably in respect of such dividends including accumulations, . . .
>
> (5) The authorized capital of a company having shares with a nominal or par value shall, with respect to those shares, be the total nominal amount of those shares.
>
> . . .
>
> (8) Each share of the capital stock without nominal or par value shall be equal to every other such share of the capital stock subject to the preferred, deferred or other special rights or restrictions, conditions or limitations attached to any class of shares.

As already noted the one class of shares of United Canso are par value shares and accordingly the provisions of subs. (8) are not directly applicable, but only no doubt due to the ramifications which flow from the issuance of par value rather than non-par value shares including the provisions of subs. (5) previously quoted.

> (14) In no case shall shares of a public company of any class or any subdivision of any class, whether with or without par value, be issued and allotted to which shall attach any exclusive right to control the management of the business or affairs of the company by the election or removal of the board of directors thereof or otherwise.
>
> (15) Nothing in subsection (14) shall be deemed to prevent the issue, under authority of provision therefor either by letters patent or by-law, of any preferred shares to which are attached preferential voting rights, exercisable in a stated event only, although, in the stated event, an exclusive right to control or manage is attached to or is an incident to such preferred shares.

In short, s. 12 recognizes the establishment of different classes of shares which may contain restrictions, conditions or limitations attaching to such classes of shares. There is no comparable section in the Act suggesting such restrictions, conditions or limitations where there is only one class of shares.

Section 33(4) of the *Companies Act* is interesting in that it states:

(4) Where the capital stock of the company consists of more than one class of shares every certificate of each class shall contain a statement of the rights and conditions attaching to such class of shares.

Surely Parliament could not have intended that where there was only one class of shares that class could contain rights and conditions which need not be evidenced on the share certificate itself and that the holder would be presumed to know the by-laws or the provisions of the letters patent of the company and that it is only when there are several classes of shares that such rights and conditions must be set forth in the statement on the certificate.

Section 59 of the *Companies Act* also seems to be supportive of this position. Section 59(1) provides in part as follows:

59.(1) When no provision is made by the letters patent or supplementary letters patent for shares of more than one class, the directors of a company may from time to time make by-laws.

(a) for the creating and issuing of any shares as preferred shares with such preferred or other special rights, restrictions, conditions or limitations, whether in regard to dividend, voting, return of capital, or otherwise as may be set out in any such by-law, but no limitations shall be imposed upon the right to vote;

In short, I am satisfied that the provisions of ss. 102 and 103 previously quoted relating to the altering of the one vote for one share provision must be read, in considering the Act as a whole, as contemplating the issuance of different classes of shares carrying rights and restrictions, and conditions including voting restrictions with respect to such class of shares. In my view, the *Companies Act* in force at the time of the enactment of the by-law recognized the presumption of law quoted by the authorities previously referred to that all shares confer equal rights and impose equal liabilities and that if voting rights are to vary separate classes of shares must be created so that the different numbers of votes can be attached to the shares by themselves and not to the holder. It follows that By-law No. 6 at the time it was first enacted, contravened the provisions of the *Companies Act* and was invalid.

However, as noted, supplementary letters patent for United Canso were issued on July 25, 1974, amending the letters patent of United Canso by adding thereto the voting limitations contained in By-law No. 6. These supplementary letters patent were issued under the provisions of the *Canada Corporations Act* which Act replaced the *Companies Act*. The *Canada Corporations Act* while replacing the *Companies Act* nevertheless contains substantially the same provisions previously referred to in the *Companies*

Act. Section 13 of the *Canada Corporations Act* is equivalent to s. 12 of the *Companies Act*, s. 13(1) providing as follows:

> 13.(1) The letters patent or supplementary letters patent of a company may provide for shares of more than one class and for any preferred, deferred or other special rights, restrictions, conditions or limitations attaching to any class of shares.

Subsection (4) of s. 13 is identical to subs. (2) of s. 12 of the *Companies Act* and the other provisions of s. 12 of the *Companies Act* referred to previously have their counterparts set forth in s. 13 of the *Canada Corporations Act*. The provisions of s. 33(4) of the *Companies Act* previously quoted has its counterpart somewhat expanded in s. 36(4) of the *Canada Corporations Act* which provides as follows:

> (4) Where a company has more than one class of shares
>
> (a) the preferences, rights, conditions, restrictions, limitations or prohibitions attaching to any class of shares shall be stated in legible characters
> >   (i) on every share certificate representing that class of shares, or
> >   (ii) by a writing permanently attached to the share certificate; or
> (b) there shall be inscribed on each such share certificate, in legible characters, a statement that there are preferences, rights, conditions, restrictions, limitations or prohibitions attached to such class of shares, and that the full text thereof is obtainable on demand, and without fee, from the secretary of the company.

In addition, subs. (5) of s. 36 contemplates the obtaining of the full particulars of any preferences, rights, conditions, *etc.*, attaching to any particular class of share. That subsection provides as follows:

> (5) Where a statement referred to in paragraph (4)(b) is inscribed on the share certificate, the secretary of the company shall furnish, without fee, to the shareholder on demand the full text of any preferences, rights, conditions, restrictions, limitations or prohibitions attached to such class of shares.

At the time of the enactment of the *Canada Corporations Act*, s. 104 [re-en. R.S.C. 1970 (1st Supp.), c. 10, s. 8] of that Act read as follows:

> 104. Subject to the provisions of any by-law of the company duly enacted under this Act, each share of the capital stock of a company issued and allotted, shall, subject to this Part, carry voting rights and entitle the shareholder to [one] vote for each share owned by him.

That section was [re-enacted] however, to read as follows:

> 104. Subject to section 105, and in the absence of other provisions in that behalf in the letters patent or supplementary letters patent, at all meetings of shareholders every shareholder is entitled to give one vote for each share then held by him, but no shareholder in arrears in respect of any call is entitled to vote at any meeting.

Thus, it became necessary if a change was contemplated with respect to voting rights for shares to obtain such change by applying for and obtaining supplementary letters patent rather than simply by amending the by-laws of the company. However, again bearing in mind the provisions of the *Canada Corporations Act* previously referred to which carried forward from the *Companies Act*, it appears this section, referring to a change in the basic provision of one share one vote, can only have been contemplated to come into effect where more than one class of shares was established and not, as in the case of United Canso, where there is only one class of shares.

The question arises as to whether or not the fact that supplementary letters patent were in fact issued changes this situation. I do not see how the administrative act of having caused the supplementary letters patent to issue can validate and render enforceable a provision which appears to be clearly contrary to the intent of the Act under which the supplementary letters patent were issued.

Section 4 of the *Canada Corporations Act* should be noted which provides as follows:

> 4. The provisions of this Part relating to matters preliminary to the issue of the letters patent or supplementary letters patent are directory only, and no letters patent of supplementary letters patent issued under this Part shall be held void or voidable on account of any irregularity or insufficiency in respect of any matter preliminary to the issue of the letters patent or supplementary letters patent.

I do not think, however, that this provision in any way changes that position as clearly as what was being dealt with here was not an irregularity or insufficiency but rather a fundamental provision attaching to the one class of shares of United Canso which as already mentioned clearly appears to be contrary to the overall provisions of the *Canada Corporations Act*.

I am, accordingly, satisfied notwithstanding the issuance of supplementary letters patent incorporating By-law No. 6 and limiting the right of a holder of shares to no more than 1000 votes regardless of the number of shares that such by-law and the supplementary letters patent issued in 1974 were invalid.

This does not end the matter. A certificate of continuance for United Canso was issued on October 24, 1979, pursuant to s. 181 of the *Canada*

Business Corporations Act and the articles of continuance contained, attached as Sched. 2, the same voting restriction previously set forth in By-law No. 6. Accordingly, it is necessary to consider the provisions of the *Canada Business Corporations Act* and, in particular, whether or not by virtue of the fact that the limitation was contained in the articles of continuance, that limitation became effective on the issuance of the certificate of continuance and is, accordingly, still in force.

It should be first noted that the authority for continuance of United Canso under the *Canada Business Corporations Act* is contained in s. 261.

Section 181 [am. 1978-79, c. 9, s. 57] of the *Canada Business Corporations Act* provides in part as follows: [subsections 1.1, 2, 3, 4(a)(c), 7]
. . .

Subsection (7) [of s. 181] is quoted, as it was referred to in argument on several occasions, but it would appear clear that the relevancy of that subsection would only come into play if it had been found that By-law No. 6 or the supplementary letters patent issued relating to By-law No. 6 were in fact valid. Having found to the contrary in that regard it is difficult to see that subs. (7) renders any assistance in the consideration of this matter. It is to be noted, however, that it is clear pursuant to sub s. (1.1) of s. 181 that an amendment to the letters patent can be effected in the articles of continuance with respect to any corporation applying for continuance under the *Canada Business Corporations Act*, if the amendment is an amendment a corporation incorporated under this Act may make to its articles. Does the *Canada Business Corporations Act* contemplate an amendment of the nature set forth in the articles of continuance?

. . . Again it is to be noted that particular provisions come into play where there are two or more classes of shares requiring the setting forth of rights, privileges, *etc.*, attaching to such shares. Thus, the distinction is clearly made between that situation and the situation where there is only one class of shares where it must be assumed there are no rights, restrictions, *etc.*, attaching to such shares. Section 134(1) is similar to the previously quoted provisions of the *Canada Corporations Act* and the *Companies Act* and provides as follows:

134.(1) Unless the articles otherwise provide, each share of a corporation entitles the holder thereof to one vote at a meeting of shareholders.

However, that section must [be] read in relation to s. 24 [am. 1978-79, c. 9, s. 9] of the Act which provides as follows [subss. (3), (4)]:

(3) Where a corporation has only one class of shares, the rights of the holders thereof are equal in all respects and include the rights.

(a) to vote at any meeting of shareholders of the corporation;

(b) to receive any dividend declared by the corporation; and

(c) to receive the remaining property of the corporation on dissolution.

(4) the articles may provide for more than one class of shares and, if they so provide,

(a) the rights, privileges, restrictions and conditions attaching to the shares of each class shall be set out therein; and

(b) the rights set out in subsection (3) shall be attached to at least one class of shares but all such rights are not required to be attached to one class.

It seems abundantly clear on a reading of s. 24(3) as well as the reading of the entire Act that again Parliament has even more clearly specified that it is only when there is more than one class of shares that different rights, privileges, restrictions and conditions attaching to shares may arise.

It is argued that subs. (3) of s. 24 must be read as being subject to subs. 168(5)(c) of the Act which reads as follows:

(5) Subject to subsections 254(2) and (3), the Governor in Council may make regulations with respect to a corporation that constrains the issue or transfer of its shares prescribing

. . .

(c) the limitations on voting rights of any shares held contrary to the articles of the corporation;

In short, s. 24(3) must not be read in the absolute sense but is subject to other provisions in the Act which may change the basic position established by s. 24. Section 168(5)(c), however, clearly has a very restricted application and only applies to corporations which constrain the issue or transfer of their shares for the particular purposes as set out in s. 168.

It is also argued that s. 24(3) is not inconsistent with the provisions of Bylaw No. 6 as continued under the articles of continuance of United Canso in that it deals with the right to vote but not in any way with the number of votes. The voting limitations in the articles of continuance clearly do not affect the right of a shareholder to vote and apply equally to all shareholders. It is only when their shareholdings exceed 1,000 shares that they are restricted from voting any shares in excess of 1,000. I am not satisfied this is an interpretation which can be put on s. 24(3). In effect it is argued that the rights of the holders of the shares are equal in that all shareholders can only vote a maximum of 1,000 shares regardless of the number of shares held. It might similarly be argued that they would be equal if all shareholders could only receive dividends to a maximum of 1,000 shares regardless of the number of shares held or receive the remaining property of the corporation on the basis of a 1,000 share maximum regardless of the number of shares held. It seems to me reading s. 24 as a whole, each shareholder has the right to vote at any meeting of shareholders on the basis of the number of shares held where the corporation only has one class of shares and that this presumption can only be upset where there are more [than] one class of shares established in which case the provisions of subs. (4) come into play. That position in this regard is in my opinion fortified by the provisions of subs. (4)(b) of s. 24 which makes it clear that all of the rights set forth in subs. (3) must, where there is more than one class of shares, be attached to at least one class of shares.

In the result for the reasons aforesaid the answer to the preliminary point of law put before the Court is that the defendant's By-law No. 6 which provides that no person shall be entitled to vote more than 1,000 shares of the defendant notwithstanding the number of shares actually held by him does, in fact, contravene the provisions of the *Canada Business Corporations Act* and is invalid. . . .

Order accordingly.

Notes

1 Immediately before the decision in *Jacobson* was released, United Canso was continued as a Nova Scotia company. See *Jacobsen v. United Canso Oil & Gas Ltd.* (1980), 12 B.L.R. 113, 40 N.S.R. (2d) 692, 1980 CarswellNS 28 (T.D.), where the Court declined to rule on the validity of the voting restriction.

2 Why do you think the company's managers wished to have the 1000 vote restriction? What do you expect would be the effect of the restriction on the value of the company's shares? Why do you suppose a majority of shareholders apparently supported the change?

Bowater Canadian Limited v. R.L. Crain and Craisec Ltd.
(1987), 62 O.R. (2d) 752 (C.A.)

The judgment of the court was delivered orally by

HOULDEN J.A.: The appellant Bowater Canadian Limited ("Bowater") filed an application in weekly court before McRae J. challenging the voting provisions contained in the respondent R.L. Crain Inc.'s ("Crain") articles of incorporation. McRae J. held that the voting provisions offended the *Canada Business Corporations Act*, S.C. 1974-75-76, c. 33 ("CBCA"), as amended, to the extent that the special common shares held by the respondent Craisec Ltd. ("Craisec") carry ten votes per share in the hands of Craisec, but only one vote per share in the hands of a potential transferee. However, having regard to the knowledge and intentions of the parties and in light of the general principles of contract and corporate law, he held that the "step-down" provision of the special common shares was severable with the result that the special common shares carry ten votes irrespective of whether they are held by Craisec or by a transferee.

The following are the provisions of the articles of amalgamation dealing with the capital of Crain:

> The Corporation is authorized to issue two million four hundred thousand (2,400,000) common shares and four hundred and seventy-one thousand (471,000) special common shares.
>
> The special common shares carry and are subject to the following terms, conditions and restrictions: -
>
> (1) The said special common shares shall carry and the holder thereof shall be entitled to ten (10) votes per share at all meetings of the shareholders of the Corporation so long as such special common shares shall be held by the person or corporation to whom such shares were issued originally by the Corporation. In the event any such special common shares cease to be held by the corporation to whom such shares were issued originally by the Corporation, then such special common shares shall carry and the holder thereof shall be entitled to one (1) vote only per share at all meetings of the shareholders of the Corporation.
>
> (2) Such special common shares may at any time be converted, either in whole or in part, into common shares of the Corporation on the basis of one (1) common share for each special common share held. Following any such conversion as aforesaid, the special common shares so converted shall be cancelled and shall not be reissued. In the event any such special common shares are presented for conversion as aforesaid the Corporation shall take all such steps as may be necessary, including, if necessary, the obtaining of Articles of Amendment, to effect such conversion.
>
> (3) In the event of the liquidation, dissolution, or winding-up of the Corporation, whether voluntary or involuntary, or in the event of any other distribution of assets among the Shareholders for the purpose of winding-up its affairs, the holders of the common shares and the special common shares shall be equally entitled, share for share, to receive the remaining property of the Corporation.

It will be noted that on liquidation, dissolution or winding-up of the corporation the holders of the special common shares share equally with the other shareholders. Furthermore, we were informed by counsel for Crain that all shareholders, regardless of class, share equally in the distribution of dividends.

On the argument of this appeal all counsel were agreed that although the step-down provision was created at a time when the *Companies Act*, R.S.C. 1952, c. 53, was in force, the appeal could be decided on the basis of the CBCA, this being the procedure followed by McRae J.

There is no doubt, as McRae J. pointed out, that Bowater was not misled by the voting provisions of the Crain shares. Mr. Thomson conceded that Bowater, when it purchased its shares, was fully cognizant of the restrictions and conditions attaching to the two classes of shares.

In his reasons for judgment, McRae J. held that although there was no express prohibition in the CBCA against a step-down provision, s. 24(4) of the Act should be interpreted in accordance with the general principles of corporation law with the result that the rights which are attached to a class of shares must be provided equally to all shares of that class, this interpretation being founded on the principle that rights, including votes, attach to the share and not to the shareholder. Subsections (3) and (4) of s. 24 of the CBCA, as amended by S.C. 1978-79, c. 9, s. 9, provide:

> 24(3) Where a corporation has only one class of shares, the rights of the holders thereof are equal in all respects and include the rights
>
> (a) to vote at any meeting of shareholders of the corporation;
>
> (b) to receive any dividend declared by the corporation; and
>
> (c) to receive the remaining property of the corporation on dissolution.
>
> (4) The articles may provide for more than one class of shares and, if they so provide,
>
> (a) the rights, privileges, restrictions and conditions attaching to the shares of each class shall be set out therein; and
>
> (b) the rights set out in subsection (3) shall be attached to at least one class of shares but all such rights are not required to be attached to one class.

Counsel for the appellant did not, of course, challenge McRae J.'s interpretation of s. 24(4). It was, however, challenged by counsel for the respondents; but, notwithstanding the able arguments that have been addressed to us, we are not persuaded that it is wrong. In our opinion if there was not equality of rights within a class of shareholders, there would be great opportunity for fraud, even though that is not a problem in this case. Section 24(5) of the Alberta *Business Corporations Act*, S.A. 1981, c. B-15, reflects what we take to be the applicable principle of corporate law, it provides:

> 24(5) Subject to section 27, if a corporation has more than one class of shares, the rights of the holders of the shares of any class are equal in all respects.

Mr. Garrow contended that even if the step-down provision violates the provision of the CBCA, it was saved by s. 181(8) of the Act which reads:

181(8) Subject to subsection 45(8), a share of an extra-provincial corporation issued before the extra-provincial corporation was continued under this Act is deemed to have been issued in compliance with this Act and with the provisions of the articles of continuance irrespective of whether the share is fully paid and irrespective of any designation, rights, privileges, restrictions or conditions set out on or referred to in the certificate representing the share, and continuance under this section does not deprive a holder of any right or privilege that he claims under, or relieve him of any liability in respect of, an issued share.

With respect, we do not agree with Mr. Garrow's submission. We do not think that the subsection was intended to protect "rights, privileges, restrictions or conditions" that are unlawful.

Having held that the step-down provision of the special common shares was invalid, McRae J. turned his attention to the issue of severability. After a careful review of the submissions of counsel, he concluded that the step-down provision was severable, with the result, as we have stated, that special common shares now carry ten votes each regardless of whether they are held by Craisec or a transferee. Again, we agree with this ruling. In this connection, we are particularly impressed with the minutes of a meeting of shareholders of Crain held January 19, 1959. This is the meeting which authorized the creation of the special common shares. The portion of the minutes dealing with the special common shares reads as follows:

On motion duly made by Mr. MacTavish and seconded by Mr. Plummer, it was resolved that the shareholders sanction, ratify and confirm By-law number 80 being a By-law sub-dividing the present 100,000 Common Shares into 400,000 Common shares, creating an additional 400,000 Common shares ranking pari passu in all respects with the existing Common shares as sub-divided and creating 167,000 Special Common Shares which shall carry the right to ten votes per share, and authorizing an application to the Secretary of State of Canada for Supplementary Letters Patent confirming such changes.

It will be noted that no mention is made of the step-down provision, only that each special common share is to carry the right to ten votes per share.

When the special common shares were created, Crain was making a very advantageous purchase of a majority interest in a company known as Business Systems Limited ("BSL"). Under the purchase agreement the vendors were to receive either four common shares of Crain or $40 cash. At the time of the purchase Craisec had effective control of Crain. Craisec agreed to exchange 41,750 common shares of Crain for BSL common and Class "C" preferred shares in consideration for which it received 167,000 special common shares of Crain enabling it to maintain control of Crain.

The provisions for ten votes per share have now been in force for almost 30 years and, prior to this application, have not been questioned by shareholders, although the share capital of Crain has been rearranged on several occasions, the last being August, 1986.

Mr. Thomson contended that because the step-down provision was invalid, the whole of cl. 1 of the articles of amalgamation was also invalid so that the special common shares and the subordinate voting shares would all carry only one vote. We do not agree. Rather, as we have said, we agree with McRae J. that the step-down provision can be severed without affecting the validity of the provision for ten votes for each special common share. We believe that this accords with the intention of the parties at the time that the shares were created.

In the result, the appeal is dismissed with costs. The cross-appeals are also dismissed but in the circumstances without costs.

Appeal and cross-appeals dismissed.

Notes and Questions

1 Before the lower court, Craisec had proposed an amendment to the company's articles that it requested the court put in place under the authority given it in current s. 241 . Under the proposed amendment, should Craisec desire to sell special common shares, it would be able to do so by means of first converting the shares into ordinary common shares, and then transferring the shares to the third party. This proposal was designed to get around the problems identified by the court in the holding, *supra*. Calling this proposal a "conversion shuffle", McRae J. held that this was an impermissible attempt to do indirectly what it could not do directly. See *Bowater Canadian Ltd. v. R.L. Crain Ltd. and Craisec Ltd. (No. 2)*, unreported, Sup. Ct. Ont.

At the same hearing, Bowater argued that the step down was not severable from the provision in the articles dealing with shareholder voting. Therefore, the entire provision in the articles dealing with voting was void, resulting in the invalidation of the multiple votes attaching to the special common shares. Bowater further argued that, per current CBCA s. 140 (formerly s. 134) each share would therefore carry one vote. McRae J. rejected this submission as well, holding that the multiple voting rights were severable from the step down.

Bowater also argued that to strike down the step down while allowing the special common shares to retain their weighted voting rights would confer a windfall on Craisec, since Craisec would then be able to sell shares with ten votes per share (such shares presumably being worth more on the market than shares with one vote each). McRae J. rejected this argument, holding that it was Bowater that would be unjustly enriched if the multiple voting rights were invalidated. According to McRae J., "[t]he essence of this application is an effort by the takeover offerer, Bowater, to acquire control of Crain at a bargain basement price." He held that Bowater was never misled as to the rights of the shares, and knew at all times that the voting arrangement was designed to keep control in the Crain family.

2 The plaintiff in the Bowater case proceeded by way of application under the oppression remedy, seeking relief under that provision. The lower court held that the step down did not violate the CBCA oppression provision, but nonetheless violated s. 24 of the Act (a finding affirmed in the appeal judgment, *supra*). Having determined that there was no oppression, what jurisdiction did the Court have to determine that there was a violation of another provision of the CBCA? In giving Bowater relief, did the Court also give substantive effect to the merely procedural rules of court (which it relied on, in addition to s. 24)?

3 Suppose that Crain had initially incorporated into its articles the conversion provision that it asked the Court to insert in Crain's articles in the lower court (see note 1, *supra*), rather than the step down. Do you think that the Court would have upheld the provision?

4 As noted in note 1, *supra*, one reason for not invalidating the multiple voting arrangement was that this would result in the unjust enrichment of Bowater. Suppose that Bowater had been complaining about a directors' resolution that gave the directors and officers clearly exorbitant remuneration, or perhaps a charter provision giving the directors unfettered power to cause the forfeiture of shares, without giving reasons. Would Bowater be unjustly enriched by allowing a suit for breach of fiduciary duty (or oppression) to succeed? Should only those who were shareholders at the time of the action complained about have standing to sue? If not, then on what principled basis can we distinguish between those cases in which there is unjust enrichment and those in which there is not? Put somewhat differently, when should a shareholder be allowed to purchase a potential lawsuit when buying shares?

5 Many companies that trade publicly in Canada (and many that do not) are controlled by families, as in the Bowater case. It is very common in such enterprises to see two classes of shares; voting (or multiple voting) shares held or controlled by the family, and non-voting (or inferior voting) shares held by public shareholders. This enables the key shareholders to control the enterprise by holding a relatively small portion of the total equity in the company. For example, after a 1983 reorganization of the capital structure of Canadian Tire, the controlling family (the Billeses) were able to control the company by virtue of holding about 62% of the voting shares of the company, even though this constituted only about 2.5% of the total equity of the company. It is clear that this type of bifurcated share structure makes it very difficult, and in many cases impossible, for a potential acquiror to obtain control of the company through the mechanism of a "hostile" takeover bid (i.e., one not sanctioned by the existing controllers). Is this a good or a bad

thing? Are there good reasons why we observe this kind of capital structure? In the same vein, what are the policy arguments for and against a step-down provision? Does it serve a useful estate planning function? See Stephanie Ben-Ishai and Poonam Puri, "Dual-Class Share Ownership in Canadian Family-Controlled Corporations: Evidence of Canadian Corporate and Securities Law Failures?" (Osgoode Hall Law School, 2004).

(e) Protection of Non-Voting Shares in Takeover Bids

When a takeover bid is made, it is usually made for the *voting* shares of a target corporation. This is because the acquiror can only exercise control if it has the power to replace the directors, and it is the voting class of shares that confers this power. Takeover bids are almost always made at a premium to the current market price to induce shareholders to tender; hence, those who hold the voting equity receive a premium for their shares, while non-voting shareholders are most often left out in the cold. Since one of the important policies underlying modern takeover legislation is equality of treatment for all shareholders of the target company, it has been suggested by some that this "unequal treatment" is unfair. This was the position adopted by the Ontario Securities Commission in a 1984 Position Paper entitled "Draft and Interim Policy on Restricted Shares and Request for Comments" (March 2, 1984). To overcome this unequal treatment, the Commission included in Interim Policy 1.3 a requirement that non-voting or restricted voting shares carry "coattail" provisions. Such provisions are designed to ensure that the non-voting equity will share in the fruits of any takeover bid. One of the most common coattails, for example, automatically converts the non-voting shares into voting shares if any takeover bid is made for the company. This effectively forces the acquiror to bid for the non-voting equity as well as the voting in order to secure control. The Commission received a considerable amount of unfavourable comment on this feature of the Interim Policy, based (ostensibly) not on any objection to the principle of equal treatment, but on practical difficulties in implementing the Policy. See "OSC Statement Concerning Restricted Shares", [12 Oct. 1984] O.S.C.B. 4295. Thus, the requirement for coattails was omitted from the final version of the policy.

The argument about coattails was revived in 1987 with the takeover bid by the "independent dealers" of Canadian Tire for 49% of the voting shares of Canadian Tire. The non-voting Class A shares contained a coattail that converted the Class A shares into voting shares should there be a takeover bid for "a majority" of the voting shares. The bid was thus structured in a manner that would secure control for the dealers, but would avoid triggering the coattail. The Ontario Securities Commission issued a cease trade order to halt the transaction on the grounds that it was "grossly abusive" of the capital markets and the minority (Class A) shareholders. The OSC held that the transaction was "artificial" in that it would effect a change in control without triggering the coattail, when (in the OSC's view) investors had expected that any change in control would trigger the coattail. The OSC further held that the spirit, if not the letter of the coattail protection had been violated. See *Re Canadian Tire Corporation Limited and C.T.C. Dealer Holdings Limited* (1987), 35 B.L.R. 56. The Ontario Divisional Court affirmed; see (1987), 35 B.L.R. 117. The Ontario Court of Appeal declined to hear an appeal.

Following *Canadian Tire*, the Toronto Stock Exchange decided to step in where the OSC had feared to tread. On July 30, 1987, the Exchange issued a "Notice to Members, Listed Companies and Securities Lawyers" entitled "Exchange Policy on Take-over Protection for Holders of Non-voting and Subordinate Voting Shares". The TSE indicated that it would refuse to list any newly created restricted voting shares that lacked coattail protection.

As noted, a concern that shareholders be treated "equally" underlies the coattail requirement. Would permitting unequal treatment tend to foster more changes of control, and, if so, would both majority and minority shareholders be better off as a result? For differing views on this question, see Andrews, "The Shareholder's Right to Equal Opportunity in the Sale of Shares" (1965), 78 Harv. L. Rev. 505 and Easterbrook and Fischel, "Corporate Control Transactions" (1982), 91 Yale L.J. 698.

Note that determining what "equal treatment" entails may involve more than a simple mechanical exercise where the classes of shares to be equally treated differ in more respects than simply voting rights. Establishing what is equal treatment may therefore involve a costly administrative and/or judicial proceeding, especially if the rule leads minority shareholders to litigate purely in order to grab a larger share of the pie. Is this another reason for dispensing with an "equal treatment" rule in some or all situations? See *Palmer v. Carling O'Keefe Breweries of Canada Limited, and Elders IXL Limited* (1988), 37 B.L.R. 316 (Ont. S.C.), rev'd (1989), 67 O.R. (2d) 161 (Div. Ct.) (the Court of Appeal declined to hear the appeal).

(f) Cumulative Voting for Directors

Section 107 of the CBCA provides for cumulative voting and sets out detailed rules for how such voting is to be carried out. Section 120 of the OBCA adopts the CBCA's approach to cumulative voting procedure. Section 65 of the NBBCA requires that cumulative voting be used in the election of directors. The BCBCA, SCA and NSCA do not expressly provide for cumulative voting.

For an explanation of the mechanics of cumulative voting, see MacKinnon, "The Protection of Dissenting Shareholders" in Ziegel (Ed), *Studies in Canadian Company Law*, Volume 1, p. 507, at pp. 540–43 (1967).

Report of the Ontario Select Committee on Company Law
pp. 71–73 (1967)

The Right to Cumulative Voting.

8.2.1 In view of the fact that management of an Ontario company is firmly in the hands of its board of directors, probably the most important individual shareholder's right accruing to the shareholder of an Ontario company is his right to elect the board of directors. Section 64 of the Ontario Act states that where the charter or by-laws of a company so provides, every share-holder entitled to vote at an election of directors has the right to cast a number of votes equal to the number of votes attached to the shares held by him multiplied by the number of directors to be elected and that he may cast all such votes in favour of one candidate or distribute them among the candidates in such manner as he sees fit. This system of voting is known as "cumulative voting", a right which is not given shareholders in the United Kingdom *Companies Act* or by common law although it has gained wide-spread acceptance, in various forms, in the United States.

8.2.2 The 1952 Select Committee seemed to recognize the merits of the cumulative voting system but recommended deferment of enacting provisions which would make cumulative voting mandatory until an opportunity had been given to canvass the views of other Canadian jurisdictions on this innovation. That Committee accordingly recommended the enactment of Section 64 which put cumulative voting on a permissive rather than on a mandatory basis. The question which this Committee is therefore required to resolve is whether or not, on grounds of public policy, the cumulative voting system should be mandatory. So long as the system is permissive only. experience has shown that it is highly unlikely that provision will be made for cumulative voting either in the charter or by-laws of a company.

8.2.3 Normally, each voting share carries the right of one vote per share. As a result, shareholders who collectively hold in the aggregate more than 50% of the votes can elect all of the directors of the company. For example, in the case of a company with 10,000 common shares outstanding carrying one vote per share, at a meeting of shareholders called to elect, say, 9 directors, those shareholders who hold shares in the aggregate entitling them to 5,100 votes would, by casting such votes, elect 9 directors of their choice. An opposition group of shareholders with shares aggregating 4,900 votes could muster only 4,900 votes for each candidate for election and, of course, could therefore elect none. Under the cumulative voting system, by contrast, the shareholders' group with 5,100 shares would be entitled to a total of 45,900 votes, i.e. 5,100 multiplied by 9 (the number of directors) and the shareholders' group with 4,900 shares would be entitled to 44,100 votes, i.e. 4,900 x 9. By distributing its 44,100 votes among only 4 candidates for election as directors, the minority shareholder group could give each of the 4 candidates 11,025 votes. No matter how the majority distributes the votes available to it, it can elect no more than 5 directors since it cannot give its sixth man as many as 11,025 votes.

8.2.4 Cumulative voting is unknown in the United Kingdom and the subject was not even dealt with by the Jenkins Committee. Cumulative voting is not provided for in any of the other Provinces except Manitoba which adopted permissive but not mandatory cumulative voting in the *Companies Act* passed in 1964. So far as the Committee is able to ascertain, cumulative voting for corporations originated at the Illinois Constitutional Convention in 1870 and the theory supporting the system was developed by analogy to democratic political organizations designed to uphold the position of minority representation in government. This origin of the cumulative voting system is, in itself, a factor which should be closely scrutinized since there are obvious differences in principle between incorporated business organizations and governmental or law making bodies of any kind. It should also be noted that at the time cumulative voting was introduced in Illinois it "was a very wild and ruthless period of development in American industrial history where there were few limitations on what corporate managers did . . . since then we have developed many means of control". ["Should Cumulative Voting for Directors be Mandatory? A Debate," (1955), 11 The Business Lawyer 9.] Cumulative voting is provided for either in the general corporation statute, or State constitutions of all of the United States except four. In over one-half of the States cumulative voting is mandatory rather than permissive. The trend in the United States, however, appears to be away from mandatory cumulative voting. Of the 11 States that have adopted cumulative voting since 1950, all but one state have chosen to put it on an optional basis. In addition, the *Model Business Corporation Act* was amended in 1955 to put cumulative voting in effect, on an optional basis whereas prior to that time the *Model Act* provided for mandatory cumulative voting.

8.2.5 Impressive arguments can be made for and against mandatory cumulative voting. Of the arguments in favour of the system, the most persuasive is that based on the "democratic necessity" or "fairness" concept, that is, that the cumulative voting system is equitable and consistent with acceptable democratic principles and therefore should be compulsory. However, this argument depends upon the aptness of the analogy drawn between the incorporated business organization and the political body, an analogy which is inherently defective. The most persuasive argument against cumulative voting is that it encourages the election of directors representing particular interest groups who, by virtue of their partisan role, encourage disharmony in the management of the affairs of the company. An American author who made a comprehensive study of cumulative voting established that cumulative voting, in the States in which it was available, was rarely used by shareholders. [Williams, *Cumulative Voting for Directors*.] The author attributed this disinterest to the fact that the typical shareholder, at least in publicly-held companies, has long since come to regard himself as an investor rather than a proprietor and is apparently content to leave management in the hands of the professional managers.

8.2.6 In view of the uncertainties which surround the true value of the cumulative voting system, the Committee does not recommend that cumulative voting be made mandatory for Ontario companies. The many recommended legislative changes outlined in this Report will significantly strengthen the position of the minority shareholder in Ontario and until those recommendations have been implemented and put into practice, it is difficult to know whether or not mandatory cumulative voting would be a necessary or desirable feature of Ontario law.

Proposals for a New Business Corporations Law for Canada
pp. 73-74 (1971)

207. The right to cumulate may be effectively defeated by a variety of devices such as rotating directorships and reduction in the number of directors. The former is precluded by paragraph (f) which requires the annual retirement of the entire body of directors, and the latter by paragraph (h) which limits the right to reduce the number of directors of corporations in which cumulation is permitted. Paragraphs (c) and (d) of s. [107] introduce a procedure for the election of directors that is novel in Canadian legislation. Under this provision, which is based upon comparable legislation in the United Kingdom — *Companies Act*, 1948, s. 183 — and South Africa — Act 46 of 1926, s. 96 — the election of every director must be the subject of a separate resolution, unless the shareholders first pass a resolution allowing more than one director to be elected by a single resolution. The purpose of this requirement is to prevent shareholders from being confronted with the necessity to vote upon an entire slate of nominees for office, of only some of whom they may approve. This is a necessary part of the cumulative voting provisions. Paragraph (e) is designed to deal with a problem that may arise under this system if there is a greater number of candidates than there are offices to be filled. The procedure prescribed here is simply that the candidates receiving the lowest number of votes are eliminated, and the remaining candidates are declared elected.

Question

In view of the foregoing, what conclusion do you draw with respect to the matter of cumulative voting? Should it be required for all corporations? What factors should be considered in deciding the matter?

(g) The Right to Appoint a Proxy

(i) Background to Present Legislation

The case summarized below was decided before the enactment of the modern legislation on the subject of proxy voting and deals with some aspects of the common law regarding use of proxy. The common law is still important in the case of a corporation which is exempt from the proxy information requirements under the relevant statute.

In *Garvie v. Axmith*, [1962] O.R. 65, 31 D.L.R. (2d) 65, the directors of the defendant company gave notice of a special meeting of shareholders to approve an agreement by the company to purchase the assets and undertaking of a second company and an application for supplementary letters patent to permit refinancing of the company under a new name. The material sent out with the notice, including financial statements of the two companies, made it apparent that the net worth of the two companies as shown in their balance sheets did not form the basis of comparative valuation for the purposes of the proposed refinancing, but no information as to valuation was in fact given. In addition, since many shares were held by several brokers in the form of "street" certificates (that is, in the names of nominees on behalf of the beneficial share owners) some shareholders received no notice of the meeting.

The resolutions were passed by the shareholders with the directors casting a substantial number of proxy votes, many of which were declared invalid. Spence J. held that it was the right of each shareholder to receive with notice of a meeting, sufficient information to permit him to come to an intelligent conclusion whether he should vote in favour of the proposal to be put to the meeting or against it. The court also held that, although the use of a proxy form with the names of the proxy printed therein and without the provision of a blank form of proxy is not good corporate practice, it does not vitiate the notice of a meeting.

The Report of the Attorney General's Committee on Securities Legislation in Ontario (the "Kimber Report", (1965)) noted the importance of proxies in large public companies with numerous shareholders and argued that, since management most always solicits proxies on its own behalf in a way which invites shareholders to appoint management nominees, it therefore tends to perpetuate itself in office.

Neither Canadian law nor the legislation of the United Kingdom contained provisions as to the manner of soliciting proxies. Certain abuses in the United States had, however, led to the passing of section 14(a) of the *Securities Exchange Act* of 1934 which governs the form of proxy and the information which must be sent with it when proxies are solicited. The Committee focused its attention on three areas: the contents of the form of proxy itself, the information which should accompany any solicitation of proxies, and the question of whether or not solicitation of proxies should be mandatory before shareholder meetings of a public company. As to the form of proxy, the Committee recommended that it contain space to nominate a person of the shareholder's choice, as well as the management nominee. Further, the Committee recommended that the form of proxy be designed so as to be able to specify by ballot a choice on each separate matter to be voted on at the meeting, and that the form indicate clearly if the proxy is solicited on behalf of management.

The Committee adopted the US view concerning the importance of accompanying proxies. For this reason, the Report recommended that an "information circular", with prescribed contents, should accompany each proxy when mailed to the shareholders. The standard of disclosure in the information circular was aimed at ensuring that the circular would reveal as much information as would be revealed by attending the meeting in person.

Finally, the Committee recommended that solicitation of proxies by the management of all public companies be made mandatory, but that it not be required that the proxy or the information circular be filed with or reviewed by any governmental agency prior to mailing.

(ii) The Proxy Legislation

IACOBUCCI, PILKINGTON AND PRICHARD
Canadian Business Corporations
pp. 181–183, (footnotes omitted)

The legislation dealing with proxies and proxy solicitation serves at least three important purposes. It provides a means of participation for shareholders in company decisions, disclosure of sufficient information in order that the shareholders may evaluate proposed company initiatives, and disclosure of information which adequately depicts the financial position of the company and which is vital to the investing public.

Loss wrote of the comparable and precursory American proxy legislation as a means of participation:

> Corporate practice has come a long way from the common law's nonrecognition of the proxy device. The widespread distribution of corporate securities with the concomitant separation of ownership and management, puts the entire concept of the stockholders' meeting at the mercy of the proxy instrument. This makes the corporate proxy a tremendous force for good or evil in our economic scheme. Unregulated, it is an open invitation to self-perpetuation and irresponsibility of management. Properly circumscribed, it may well turn out to be the salvation of the modern corporate system.

The *Kimber Report* emphasized the importance of disclosure to the investing public as it "provides the capital market with the information necessary" to achieve its principal economic functions which are "to assure the optimum allocation of financial resources in the economy, to permit maximum mobility and transferability of those resources, and to provide facilities for a continuing valuation of financial assets."

Canada has recently seen substantial reform of the proxy legislation. Following the recommendations of the *Kimber Report*, the Ontario, Alberta, British Columbia and Federal Acts have all adopted similar proxy provisions which have resulted in a comprehensive and basically sound set of requirements recognizing the important purposes described above. The legislation was a response to the common law by which shareholders had no right to vote by proxy. The right to vote by proxy had to be granted by special authority in the corporate constitution and, in a memorandum jurisdiction, "there seemed to be no limit so the extent to which the right, if granted, could be contractually circumscribed." Moreover, since management determined the form and use of the proxy, various practices developed which favoured the directors' ability to accumulate voting support unfairly. Further, the only obligation upon those calling company meetings was to give adequate notice:

> The contents of the notice were left to be regulated by the articles of the company and by the rules of equity and the common law. It is true that in those cases in which judicial approval was essential to the validity of some corporate act, the courts as a matter of practice insisted upon full fair disclosure, generally by means of an explanatory circular, of all relevant facts but there was no statutory obligation to follow this procedure.

The statutory provisions that deal with proxies are found in the CBCA at sections 147 to 154, and sections 32 to 43 of the Regulations; see also sections 175 to 181 of the BCCA and sections 109 to 114 of the OBCA. The OBCA sections have been based on the CBCA provisions with some important variations. For example, section 110(2) of the OBCA provides that a proxy ceases to be valid one year from its date with respect to meetings of shareholders of offering corporations. The implication is that a proxy with respect to a non-offering corporation continues to be valid until duly revoked. In comparison, section 148(3) of the CBCA provides that a proxy is valid only at the meeting for which it is given or any adjournment thereof.

There have been some decisions which have emphasized the importance of adherence to the proxy legislative requirements. In *Charlebois et al. v. Bienvenu et al.*, [1967] 2 O.R. 635, 64 D.L.R. (2d) 683 (H.C.) [rev'd on another point, [1968] 2 O.R. 217, 68 D.L.R. (2d) 578 (C.A.)], Fraser, J. held that the management of a corporation committed a constructive fraud on the minority shareholders by soliciting proxies without complying with the provisions of the Corporations Act as to proper notice. In the result, an interlocutory injunction was ordered restraining the board of directors which had been purportedly elected from acting. In *Babic et al. v. Milinkovic* (1972), 22 D.L.R. (3d) 732 (B.C. S.C.), Kirke Smith, J. granted an interim injunction restraining the directors of a company from acting on resolutions

because of the failure of the corporation's officers to provide each shareholder with proxies prior to or with each notice of the corporation's meeting
as provided by the B.C. Companies Act, thereby rendering the decisions
purportedly taken at that meeting incurable nullities. The decision was
affirmed: (1972), 25 D.L.R. (3d) 752 (B.C. C.A.).

(iii) The Form of Proxy

Reproduced on the following two pages is a sample form of proxy.

RBC

Computershare

Computershare Trust Company of Canada
9th Floor, 100 University Avenue
Toronto, Ontario M5J 2Y1
Telephone 1-866-586-7635
514-982-8875
Facsimile 1-866-249-7775
416-263-9524
www.computershare.com

Security Class

Holder Account Number

Use a <u>black</u> pen. Print in CAPITAL letters inside
the grey areas as shown in this example.

| A B C | 1 2 3 | X |

Form of Proxy - Common Shares - Annual Meeting to be held on February 27, 2004

Notes to Proxy

1. This Form of Proxy should be dated and signed by the shareholder or shareholder's attorney authorized in writing. If the shareholder is a corporation, the Form of Proxy should be signed by its duly authorized officer or officers. If not dated, it shall be deemed to bear the date of January 27, 2004.

2. This Form of Proxy should be read in conjunction with the accompanying Notice of Annual Meeting of Common Shareholders and Management Proxy Circular.

3. THE SHAREHOLDER MAY APPOINT A PROXYHOLDER, OTHER THAN EITHER OF THE PERSONS DESIGNATED IN THE FORM OF PROXY, TO ATTEND AND ACT ON THE SHAREHOLDER'S BEHALF AT THE MEETING, AND MAY DO SO EITHER BY DELETING THE NAMES OF THE DESIGNATED PERSONS AND INSERTING THE NAME OF THE PERSON THE SHAREHOLDER WISHES TO APPOINT IN THE SPACE PROVIDED IN THE FORM OF PROXY, OR BY COMPLETING ANOTHER PROPER FORM OF PROXY. THE PROXYHOLDER IS NOT REQUIRED TO BE A SHAREHOLDER OF ROYAL BANK.

4. THIS PROXY IS SOLICITED BY THE MANAGEMENT OF ROYAL BANK AND THE SHARES REPRESENTED BY THIS PROXY WILL BE VOTED FOR OR AGAINST OR WITHHELD FROM VOTING IN ACCORDANCE WITH THE INSTRUCTIONS GIVEN BY THE SHAREHOLDER.

5. IN THE ABSENCE OF ANY CONTRARY INSTRUCTIONS, THE SHARES REPRESENTED BY PROXIES RECEIVED BY MANAGEMENT WILL BE VOTED "FOR" ITEMS 1 AND 2 AND IN FAVOUR OF MANAGEMENT'S PROPOSALS GENERALLY, AND "AGAINST" ITEMS 3, 4, 5 AND 6.

6. Information contained in or otherwise accessible through the Web sites mentioned in this Form of Proxy does not form a part of this Form of Proxy. All references in this Form of Proxy to the Web sites are inactive textual references only.

METHOD OF VOTING

To Vote by Mail	To Vote by Fax
• Complete, sign and date the reverse hereof.	• Complete, sign and date the reverse hereof.
• Return this Proxy in the envelope provided.	• Forward it by fax to (416) 263-9524 or toll-free to 1-866-249-7775 for calls within Canada and the U.S.
	• Forward it by fax to (416) 263-9524 for calls outside Canada and the U.S.

Signed and completed Forms of Proxy should be received at the Toronto office of Computershare Trust Company of Canada by 5:00 p.m. (Eastern Standard Time) on February 25, 2004, or hand-delivered at the registration table on the day of the meeting prior to the commencement of the meeting.

THANK YOU

002END

This Form of Proxy is solicited by and on behalf of Management.

Appointment of Proxy

The undersigned holder of Common Shares of **ROYAL BANK OF CANADA** ("Royal Bank") hereby appoints: **GUY SAINT-PIERRE**, failing whom **GORDON M. NIXON**

OR

Print the name of the person you are appointing if this person is someone instead of the foregoing

as the proxyholder of the undersigned, to attend and act on behalf of the undersigned at the **ANNUAL MEETING OF COMMON SHAREHOLDERS OF ROYAL BANK TO BE HELD ON THE 27TH DAY OF FEBRUARY 2004**, and at any adjournment thereof, with the power of substitution and with all the powers that the undersigned could exercise with respect to the said shares if personally present and with authority to vote at the said proxyholder's discretion except as herein otherwise specified and to vote and act in said proxyholder's discretion with respect to amendments or variations to matters referred to in the accompanying Notice of Annual Meeting of Common Shareholders and with respect to other matters that may properly come before the meeting.

The said proxyholder is hereby directed to vote for or against or withhold from voting as indicated below:

The Board of Directors and management recommend that shareholders VOTE FOR items 1 and 2 below:

1. Election of Directors

The proposed nominees named in the accompanying Management Proxy Circular are:

W.G. Beattie; G.A. Cohon; D.T. Elix; J.T. Ferguson; L.Y. Fortier; P. Gauthier; J. Lamarre; B.C. Louie; J.E. Newall; G.M. Nixon; D.P. O'Brien; C.R. Otto; R.B. Peterson; J.P. Reinhard; C.W. Sewell, Jr.; K.P. Taylor; V.L. Young

☐ **VOTE FOR** all nominees listed above (except for the following nominees from whom I withhold my vote): _____

☐ **WITHHOLD** my vote from all nominees

2. Appointment of Auditors   VOTE FOR ☐   WITHHOLD VOTE ☐

Shareholder Proposals   The Board of Directors and management recommend that shareholders VOTE AGAINST items 3 to 6 below:

	FOR	AGAINST			FOR	AGAINST
3. Shareholder Proposal No.1	☐	☐		5. Shareholder Proposal No.3	☐	☐
4. Shareholder Proposal No.2	☐	☐		6. Shareholder Proposal No.4	☐	☐

The four Shareholder Proposals are set out in Schedule 'D' to the accompanying Management Proxy Circular.

PLEASE SEE THE NOTES ON THE REVERSE SIDE, WHICH ARE PART OF THIS FORM OF PROXY.

Authorized Signature(s) - Sign Here - This section must be completed for your instructions to be executed.

Signature(s)

Day   Month   Year

Quarterly Financial Statements Request

ROYAL BANK OF CANADA'S quarterly reports to shareholders are available at rbc.com/investorrelations, but if you wish to receive the 2004 quarterly reports by mail please mark this box. If you do not mark the box, or do not return this form, you will NOT receive these reports by mail.   ☐

Minutes of Meeting Request

Mark this box if you would like to receive the minutes of this Annual Meeting of Common Shareholders. If you do not mark the box, or do not return this form, you will NOT receive these minutes by mail.   ☐

■ RYCQ

002EOE

+

(iv) The Concept of Solicitation

The concept of "solicitation" is central to the proxy system. For the definition of solicitation, see OBCA s. 109; CBCA s. 147. The BCBCA is silent on proxy solicitation, as well as form of proxy and information circular requirements, leaving the matter to the British Columbia *Securities Act.*

Brown v. Duby
(1980), 11 B.L.R. 129, 28 O.R. (2d) 745 (S.C.)

CRAIG J.: I have two motions before me in this matter. I will deal first with the application for an interlocutory injunction restraining the defendants from soliciting proxies from shareholders of United Canso Oil & Gas Ltd. without the dissident proxy circular required by the *Canada Business Corporations Act*, S.A. 1974-75-76, c. 33 (the Act).

The plaintiff United Canso Oil & Gas Ltd., (Canso) is a company incorporated under the laws of Canada; it has its head office in the city of Calgary in the province of Alberta. Its co-plaintiff is a shareholder and officer of Canso.

The defendants, except for D.E King & Co. Inc., are all shareholders of the company. They are also members of a Shareholders' Committee (dissident shareholders) formed in December 1979. This committee is opposed to the present management of the company. The defendant D. E King & Co. Inc. is a limited company carrying on business in New York City. Part of its business is the solicitation of proxies on behalf of companies and individuals.

Canso is engaged in the exploration for and development of oil and gas properties and mineral deposits, located principally in Western Canada, the United States of America and Australia. It is publicly owned and its common shares are listed for trading in Canada on the Toronto and Montreal Stock Exchanges. They are traded in the United States of America on the Boston and Pacific Stock Exchanges.

The majority of the shareholders holding the majority of shares reside in the United States of America. I was informed by counsel that the largest number of Canadian shareholders are resident in Ontario and that they hold a majority of the Canadian shares. For reasons which I need not repeat I have dismissed the defendants' motion to dismiss this application upon the ground of lack of jurisdiction.

The plaintiffs claim that the individual defendants caused two letters to be sent by D.E King & Co. Inc. to certain shareholders and stockbrokers. The first letter was dated March 7th, 1980, and was sent only to the shareholders of Canso resident in the United States of America. The second letter was dated March 30th, 1980, and was sent to all shareholders. The plaintiffs claim that both letters constitute a solicitation of proxies within the meaning of s. 144(1) of, and in breach of, the Act which provides in part as follows:

[s. 144.(1)(b), which is now ss. 150.(1)(b), is omitted] I will return to the "dissident's proxy circular" in a moment. Section 141 provides in part:

[s. 141 (a), (b), (c), which are now in s. 147, are omitted]

In my opinion the letter of March 30th is not a solicitation for proxies within the meaning of s. 144(1) but is directed to requesting the shareholders to sign a requisition requiring the calling of a meeting of shareholders "for the election of directors" pursuant to s. 137 which provides:

[s. 137.(1), now s. 143.(1), is omitted]

Turning now to the letter of March 7th, I quote it in full (except for the proxy circular" attached to it giving the names, addresses, principal occupations and shareholdings of the Shareholders' Committee):

UNITED CANSO OIL & GAS LTD.	SHAREHOLDERS COMMITTEE
335-8th Avenue	2810 Glenda Avenue
Calgary, Alberta	Forth Worth, Texas
T2P IC9	76117
(403) 269-8221	(817) 831-0761

March 7, 1980

DEAR FELLOW UNITED CANSO SHAREHOLDER:

We believe it's time for a change in the management of your Company.

As substantial shareholders of United Canso Oil & Gas Ltd. we have formed this Committee because of our serious concern about your Company's past operating record and its future prospects under a board of directors led by the incumbent president, John W. Buckley.

In our view, the Buckley-headed management has failed to achieve the Company's potential for growth. The history of your Company's management, as we see it, has been marked by conflicts of interest and little progress. Your Company lost $272,079 for the fiscal year ended September 30, 1979 and $1,056,533 for the quarter ended December 31, 1979. Instead of a record of earnings growth, the Buckley management - as it has done in the past - offers you promises for the future.

We intend to solicit proxies at the next meeting of shareholders for the election of an entirely new Board of Directors, committed to managing the Company for the benefit of all its shareholders.

The members of the Committee together own more than 394,000 shares - over twenty times the amount owned by the present board, which together owns fewer than 18,000 shares, or less than one-third of 1% of your Company. We believe we share with you a common interest in the Company and its future.

We are writing to you now to introduce the Committee. We enclose a description of the Committee members, including their present principal occupations and their shareholders [sic] in United Canso.

We are not requesting proxies at this time. The Shareholders Committee will ask for your proxy only after we have prepared a definite proxy statement, which cannot be done for the next shareholders' meeting until the incumbents' materials have been sent out. At present, we do not know the date of the meeting, the incumbent slate, or, indeed, what matters are to be considered at the meeting.

If the experience of the past two shareholder meetings is any guide, the present management will mail their materials to you not more than 30 days before the meeting date. *We urge you not to send in any management proxy before you have received and considered or proxy materials.*

In their proxy materials, management may well attempt to win your vote by attacking the Committee and its members, We also expect that the incumbents will attempt to divert your attention from their record in recent years by promises of future growth. You should know that Mr. Buckley has already begun to make vague promises for the future: "record fiscal 1980 operating revenues" and a "turnaround in profitability". We ask you to consider what these promises really mean. Operating revenues are not necessarily any measure of profitability: remember fiscal 1979, a year in which, despite record operating revenues, your Company suffered a sizeable loss. Moreover, any profit - however small - would fulfill Mr. Buckley's promise of a "turnaround in profitability", after the loss the Company sustained last year.

Management may also attempt to point with pride to the recent rise in the price of United Canso stock - even though the stock has only recently sold at the levels it reached in 1974.

Do not be misled by these tactics. We ask you not to sign any proxy for the Buckley slate of directors, but to consider, in your own best interests, the information we will be reporting to you.

If you are undecided, we suggest you consult your broker, banker or investment advisor.

We Welcome Your Comments

We hope you, as an owner of United Canso, will share with us your concerns about the Company, and your hopes and thoughts for the Company's future.

Please write us at either of the addresses shown on our letterhead, or call us collect at the numbers shown there.

For those of you whose stock is held of record by a broker, bank or other nominee, we enclose a postage prepaid card which will enable you to furnish your name, address and telephone number so that we may contact you directly should you so desire.

We took forward to hearing from you and to working together toward a new management for United Canso.

Sincerely yours

UNITED CANSO OIL & GAS LTD.
SHAREHOLDERS COMMITTEE

It is my view that, while this letter states that "we are not requesting proxies at this time", it appears to be a solicitation within the meaning of the definition of "solicit" or "solicitation" in s. 141(b) and (c) in that it is a "request not to execute a form of proxy" for management and/or a "withholding" of proxies from management.

The proxy circular giving a description of the committee members, including occupations and their shareholders [sic] in Canso, does not meet the requirements of a "dissident's proxy circular" referred to in s. 144(b).

The requirements of a dissident's proxy circular are provided for by s. 38 of the regulations, SOR/79-316. I quote only those parts of s. 38 that are relied on by counsel for the plaintiff in this case:

38. A dissident's proxy circular shall contain the following information:

. . .

(c) details of the identity and background of each dissident, including

. . .

(iii) all material occupations, offices or employments during the preceding 5 years, with starting and ending dates of each and the name, principal business and address of the body corporate or other business organization in which each such occupation, office or employment was carried on,

. . .

(v) convictions in criminal proceedings during the preceding 10 years for which a pardon has not been granted, other than in respect of traffic violations and similar offences, and the date and nature of the conviction, the name and location of the court and the sentence imposed;

(d) the circumstances under which each dissident became involved in the solicitation and the nature and extent of his activities as a dissident;

. . .

(f) details of the interest of each dissident in the securities of the corporation to which the solicitation relates, including

. . .

(ii) the dates on which securities of the corporation were purchased or sold during the preceding 2 years, the amount purchased or sold on each date and the price at which they were purchased or sold,

(iii) if any part of the purchase price or market value of any of the securities specified in subparagraph (ii) is represented by funds borrowed or otherwise obtained for the purpose of acquiring or holding the securities, the amount of the indebtedness as of the latest practicable date and a brief description of the transaction including the names of the parties,

. . .

(i) details of any contract, arrangement or understanding, including the names of the parties, between a dissident or his associates and any person with respect to

(i) future employment by the corporation or any of its affiliates, or

(ii) future transactions to which the corporation or any of its affiliates will or may be a party.

It is my opinion that the background information required by the above quoted regulation is obviously important material to be considered by shareholders along with other information in deciding whether to support management or the dissidents; and that the regulation was framed with that in mind.

Because the shares of Canso are listed for trading on certain U.S. exchanges, Canso is required to meet certain requirements of the *Securities Exchange Act* of 1934 (U.S.) (SEC), including its proxy provisions. The evidence before me indicates that the March 7th letter was also sent to the SEC and to the Boston and Pacific Stock Exchanges pursuant to the requirements of the SEC.

There is evidence before me that United States counsel for the Shareholders' Committee advises that the March 7th letter complied in full with the SEC requirements.

The letter of March 7th was sent from the United States and it was not sent to Canadian shareholders. It is suggested by counsel for the defendants that the provisions of the Act relating to proxy solicitation do not have extraterritorial effect in this situation. I disagree. The status of a corporation is to be determined by the law of the incorporating jurisdiction; see Cheshire's *Private International Law* (8th ed.), p. 191, and 20 C.J.S. 12, s. 1788. The general rules are stated in *Corpus Juris Secundum*.

> 1802. Every corporation necessarily carries its charter wherever it goes, for that is the law of its existence. Whatever disabilities are thereby placed upon the corporation at home it retains abroad, and whatever legislative control is it subject to at home must be recognized and submitted to by those who deal with it elsewhere with knowledge of such limitations . . .
>
> Apart from burdens which may be imposed upon them by the laws of a state which a foreign corporation enters and in which it undertakes to do business . . . the rights and liabilities of stockholders and directors are determined by the charter and governing laws of the state in which the corporation is created. (pp. 21, 22, 23)

The general rules stated above are subject to exceptions. Upon principles of comity, a corporation which establishes or seeks to establish a business domicile in a state other than that of its creation takes that domicile subject to the responsibilities and burdens imposed by the laws in force there; it becomes amenable to the laws of the latter state. See 20 C.J.S. 27, s. 1807. In the absence of this last-mentioned rule, the principles of comity could invite abuse from individuals choosing to incorporate a company in a country having lax corporation laws and then carrying on the corporation's business in a jurisdiction having stricter corporation laws, all the while shielded by the cloak of the law of the corporation's domicile: Gower, *The Principles of Modern Company Law* (3rd ed., 1969), p. 669. To prevent or at least discourage such abuse, the host state very often prescribes certain terms and conditions upon which foreign corporations will be permitted to carry on business in the host state. However, a corporation remains subject to the law of its incorporating jurisdiction notwithstanding that its business and centre of administration may be in another jurisdiction: *cf.* Gower, p. 668; 9 Hals. (4th ed.) 732, para. 1227. Thus a corporation which carries on operations outside the jurisdiction in which it was incorporated will be subject to the requirements of its incorporating statute as well as those imposed by the laws of the host state.

In the instant case, as a condition of registration of its shares in the United States, Canso is obliged to comply with the trading rules and regulations of the SEC. These rules and regulations apply irrespective of the incorporating statute but these do not supplant the Canadian Act and its requirements. That is, the provisions of the Act relating the proxy solicitation apply to Canso and its shareholders wherever Canso carries on business; even though they are also required to comply with the laws of the host jurisdiction. Therefore if the letter of March 7th is interpreted as a solicitation of proxies then it was written in contravention of the Act and its regulations. In my opinion the plaintiffs have established a *prima facie* case of solicitation, or at least there is a serious question to be tried as to that issue: *Yule Inc. v. Atlantic Pizza Delight Franchise* (1968) Ltd. (1977), 17 O.R. (2d) 505, 35 C.P.R. (2d) 273, 80 D.L.R. (3d) 725 (Div. Ct.).

In my opinion the object of the Act and the provisions in question are for the benefit of the shareholders and to protect them from possible harm. The Act provides for offences and penalties for breach. It is my view that these penalties are not the sole remedies available; but that this legislation gives rise to rights enforceable by action: *Direct Tpt. Co. v. Cornell*, [1938] O.R. 365, [1938] 3 D.L.R. 456 (C.A.); also the comments of Duff J. in *Orpen v. Roberts*, [1925] S.C.R. 364, [1925] 1 D.L.R. 1101 at 1105-6; and *Cunningham v. Moore* [1972] 3 O.R. 369, 28 D.L.R. (3d) 277, affirmed [1973] 1 O.R. 357, 31 D.L.R. (3d) 149 (H.C.). Also the action is based on the alleged tort of conspiracy; that is an agreement of two or more shareholders to breach the provisions of the statute: *Posluns v. Toronto Stock Exchange*, [1964] 2 O.R. 547, 46 D.L.R. (2d) 210, affirmed [1966] 1 O.R. 285, 53 D.L.R. (2d) 193, affirmed [1968] S.C.R. 330, 67 D.L.R. (2d) 165.

Upon the application in this action the question of the appropriateness of interlocutory injunction remains. There is very little Canadian jurisprudence in matters involving proxy solicitation disputes between shareholders of a corporation. Undoubtedly the next meeting of shareholders will be held before the trial of the action, so that an interlocutory injunction is almost tantamount to a final judgment after trial. The annual meeting is required by law to be held within 15 months of the last annual meeting — which now means that it must be held on or before June 28th, 1980; counsel for the plaintiffs advises me that an undertaking has been given to the Toronto Stock Exchange that it will be held on or before that date.

In my view damages in lieu of injunction would not be an adequate remedy to either side in this case, so that the question of balance of convenience arises. Also injunction is an extraordinary remedy and in my view it ought not to be ordered in this case solely because of the breach mentioned unless it can be said that is clearly required to protect the shareholders in the circumstances. I was referred to American authorities which indicate that United States Courts are generally unwilling to tip the scales toward one shareholders group or the other in a proxy contest: *Cook United Inc. v. Stockholders' Protective Committee of Cook United Inc.* (1979), Fed. Sec. L. Rep. (C.C.H.) 95,576 (S.D.N.Y); *McConnell v. Lucht* (1970), 320 F. Supp. 1162 (S.D.N.Y); and *Kennecott Copper Corpn. v. Curtiss-Wright Corpn.* (1978), 584 F.2d 1195 (U.S.C.A., 2nd Cir.).

In *Gen. Time Corpn. v. Talley Indust. Inc.* (1968), 403 F. 2d 159 the United States Court of Appeals, Second Circuit, dealt with a case involving use of proxies allegedly obtained in violation of the SEC regulations including allegations of false or misleading statements with respect "to any material fact, or which omits to state any material fact contrary to regulation." Judge Friendly stated at p. 162:

The standard of materiality is somewhat more elusive in relation to statements issued in a contested election than in regard to a prospectus or other representation designed to induce the purchase or sale of securities, or a proxy statement seeking approval of a proposed corporate transaction — the situation in *Borak* . . . No one knows just what motivates stockholders in choosing between slates. Those experienced in contested elections are likely to doubt whether proxy statements are read with much precision, and determination of the influence of a particular omission or even misstatement is almost sheer guesswork. The past record of the management, the market performance of the stock, the lustre of the opposition, and the recommendations of brokers and investment advisors based on such considerations, are likely to be much more influential than tired-eye scrutiny of the proxy statements. Still, issuers of such statements should be held to the fair accuracy even, in the hurly-burly of election contests.

The test, we suppose, is whether, taking a properly realistic view, there is a substantial likelihood that the misstatement or omission may have lead a stockholder to grant a proxy to the solicitor or to withhold one from the other side, whereas in the absence of this he would have taken a contrary course. This latter circumstance — that there is another side — has a bearing on materiality in a case where, as here, the facts have been disclosed to it in ample time for comment.

The case of *Twentieth Century Fox Film Corpn. v. Lewis* (1971), 334 F. Supp. 1398 (S.D.N.Y), dealt with an application, among other things, to a U.S. District Court, New York, for a preliminary injunction restraining the defendants from soliciting proxies until certain statements were filed in compliance with the SEC rules and until a written proxy statement also complying with the SEC rules was forwarded to the shareholders. In dismissing the application the Court stated at p. 1402:

It may be that whatever defects alleged here may be cured by the final material submitted to the shareholders and no one may be mislead (sic). Additionally in view of the active nature of the contest here, it seems unlikely to this court that the shareholders will not be fully exposed to the issues involved.

In the instant case there is some (but not much) evidence that some shareholders have already decided to support the dissidents; but it is not shown that it would be otherwise but for the breach. In the light of my decision the defendants will be required to comply with the solicitation rules of the Act. Here the letter of March 7th, 1980, was critical of management; also the material before me alleges specific instances of mismanagement. The dissident shareholders are entitled to be critical and to communicate their criticisms to other shareholders. Here, however, their letter of March 7th, 1980, gives rise to a *prima facie* case that it solicits proxies contrary to

s. 144. It might be said that the real breach was one of omission to provide the required background information as to the members of the committee by way of "dissidents proxy circular". It is apparent to me (as in the *Twentieth Century Fox Film* case, *supra*) that there will be an active proxy contest. Ample time remains with which to make full presentation of the relevant information and conflicting contentions of both sides; and the shareholders will have the particulars omitted from the March 7th letter. It seems unlikely to this Court that the shareholders will not be fully exposed to the issues involved.

Counsel for the defendants submits that the defendants will be seriously harmed by an interlocutory injunction far more than the plaintiffs will be aided. The balance of convenience element in a proxy battle was considered in *D-Z Invt. Co. v. Holloway* (1974), Fed. Sec. L. Rep. (C.C.H.) 96,057 (S.D.N.Y.), at p. 96,061:

> Additionally, and in balancing the hardships, the Court finds that the equities of the present situation tip decidedly in defendants' favor, rather than that of the plaintiff. If a preliminary injunction were to issue, no matter how such was explained to the shareholders by the present management, a substantial number of shareholders would regard its issuance as a determination of the alleged *Securities Act* violations on the merits and a finding that the incumbent management had acted improperly with regard to the Trust Again, as this Court had opportunity to state in *Sherman v. Posner, supra*:
>
> > Conversely, if the preliminary injunction were granted at this time, irreparable injury would accrue to the defendants. Beyond a peradvanture, the issuance of an injunction would come to the attention of the stockholders. . . And no matter how clearly it was indicated otherwise, the issuance of the injunction undoubtedly would be viewed by some as a favourable adjudication of the claims of the plaintiff. This would be tantamount to a determination of wrongdoing on the part of the [present] management.
>
> *Just how this result could be remedied in the event it was found at a full hearing that the claims of the plaintiff were unfounded is not readily perceptible to this Court.* (The italics are mine.)

See also *Kass v. Arden-Mayfair Inc.* (1977), 431 F. Supp. 1037 (C.D. Calif.) where the Court stated (at p. 1041):

> In addition, the issuance of a preliminary injunction now would undoubtedly come to the attention of all stockholders. No matter how clearly it was indicated that the issuance was in no way an adjudication on the merits, it would be inevitable that at least a substantial number of stockholders would reach the conclusion that such a holding was tantamount to final determination of wrong-doing on the part of man-

agement. *Kauder v. United Board and Carton Corp.*, 199 F. Supp. 420, 423 (S.D.N.Y., 1961).

For these reasons it is my opinion that the balance of convenience favours the defendants; the extraordinary remedy of injunction is not appropriate. The application is dismissed. Having reached this decision it is unnecessary for me to deal with any of the other interesting points raised by counsel on this application.

Both motions dismissed.

Note

For a comment on an unreported case involving the definition of "solicitation", namely, *Western Mines Ltd. v. Sheridan*, see Getz, "Proxies — The meaning of Solicitation" 1 Can. Bus. L.J. 472 (1976).

(v) Critique of the Proxy Provisions

Much criticism has been heard of the proxy legislation. Recall that the motivating purpose behind the proxy rules is to foster shareholder democracy by ensuring that management's nominees for directors (and proposed fundamental changes) are exposed to scrutiny and that shareholders have an adequate opportunity to vote. It has been argued that the proxy rules have had exactly the opposite effect. In particular, as the *Duby* case makes clear, there is a risk that relatively informal communications between shareholders may be construed as proxy "solicitations" requiring the assembly (at great expense) of a dissidents' proxy circular. While the court in *Duby* took a very pragmatic view of the situation, and refused to penalize the dissident shareholders' conduct, how many shareholders would be willing to risk a lawsuit (and one with perhaps a less favourable outcome than *Duby*) by engaging in informal communications that might be construed to be solicitations?

This issue has drawn much more attention in the United States than in Canada. One of the largest US public pension funds (the California Public Employees Retirement System, often referred to simply as "CalPERS") was instrumental in bringing the issue to the attention of the Securities and Exchange Commission (or "SEC", which administers the federal proxy legislation). A number of academic commentators have also been influential in bringing the issue to prominence. See, *e.g.*, Bernard S. Black, "Shareholder Passivity Reexamined" (1990), 89 Mich. L. Rev. 520; John Pound, "Proxy Voting and the SEC: Investor Protection Versus Market Efficiency" (1991) 29 J. Fin. Econ. 241. In the result, the SEC sought and received from Congress changes to the proxy legislation that are designed to exempt informal shareholder communications from the full rigours of the proxy rules. In "The Role of Institutional and Retail Investors in Canadian Capital Markets" (1993), 32 Osgoode Hall L.J. 370, Jeffrey MacIntosh proposed similar changes to the Canadian legislation. In 2001, some of the risk of shareholder communications being construed as proxy "solicitations" has been mitigated by exceptions that were added to the requirement to assemble a dissident's proxy circular under s. 150 of the CBCA. A shareholder may now solicit proxies without a dissident's proxy circular in the case of a targeted solicitation to 15 or fewer shareholders (s. 150(1.1)), or if the solicitation is by public broadcast, speech or publication (s. 150(1.2)). As well, the definition of "solicitation" in s. 147 has been narrowed to exclude a public announcement by a shareholder on how he or she intends to vote.

Prior to the amendments, it is true that many institutional investors (pension funds, mutual funds, insurance companies, banks, trust companies, *etc.*) had made a fairly regular habit of informally discussing management initiatives amongst themselves; however, the targeted solicitation exception now expressly authorizes such activity. Taking advantage of the narrower definition of "solicitation", the Ontario Teachers Pension Plan, for example, now makes publicly available on its website how it intends to vote at upcoming corporate meetings.

(vi) Proxy Solicitation Expenses

There is very little statutory guidance relating to proxy solicitation expenses or expenses relating to the costs of holding shareholders' meetings. Although s. 105(6) of the OBCA deals with this to a certain extent, it is still the common law to which we must turn for guidance. Unfortunately, there is not much Anglo-Canadian case law on the matter, although see *Peel v. London and North Western R.R. Co.*, [1907] 1 Ch. Div. 5 (C.A.), which held that management could expend funds to make its position known to shareholders.

In *Levin v. Metro-Goldwyn-Mayer Inc.*, 264 F. Supp. 797 (S.D.N.Y. 1967) the action arose from a conflict for corporate control of MGM between two groups, one of which included the plaintiff. The plaintiffs sought an injunction to stop the current management from soliciting proxies for an upcoming shareholders' meeting by means of public relations firms, proxy soliciting organizations and the like. The plaintiffs argued that the costs of such allegedly extravagant means of proxy solicitation should be borne by the directors themselves. The plaintiffs were contesting seats on the board of directors and undoubtedly felt that their own campaign resources could not stretch the company's funds which were being used for the management solicitation. The court held that the proper question to be determined was whether or not illegal or unfair means of communication were being employed by management, and contended that they were not and so denied the injunctive relief. The court also refused to enjoin the use of corporate employees for proxy solicitation, the use of more than one proxy solicitation firm by management, the use of persons in business relationships with MGM (actors, directors, *etc.*) in the solicitation of proxies for management, the employment by the corporation of a public relations firm, and the use of Louis Nizer's law firm in the solicitation process.

Rosenfeld v. Fairchild Engine & Airplane Corp.
309 N.Y. 168, 128 N.E. 2d 291 (N.Y.C.A. 1955)

FROESSEL J.: In a stockholder's derivative action brought by plaintiff, an attorney, who owns 25 out of the company's over 2,300,000 shares, he seeks to compel the return of $261,522, paid out of the corporate treasury to reimburse both sides in a proxy contest for their expenses. The Appellate Division, 284 App. Div. 201, 132 N.Y. S. 2d 273, has unanimously affirmed a judgment of an Official Referee, Sup., 116 N.Y.S. 2d 840, dismissing plaintiff's complaint on the merits, and we agree. . . .

Of the amount in controversy $106,000 was spent out of corporate funds by the old board of directors while still in office in defense of their position in said contest; $28,000 were paid to the old board by the new board after the change of management following the proxy contest, to compensate the former directors for such of the remaining expenses of their unsuccessful defense as the new board found was fair and reasonable; payment of $127,000, representing reimbursement of expenses to members of the prevailing group, was expressly ratified by a 16 to 1 majority vote of the stockholders.

. . .The Appellate Division found that the difference between plaintiff's group and the old board "went deep into the policies of the company", and that among these Ward's contract was one the "main points of contention." The Official referee found that the controversy "was based on an understandable difference in policy between the two groups, at the very bottom of which was the Ward employment contract."

By way of contrast with the findings here, in *Lawyers' Advertising Co. v. Consolidated Ry., Lighting & Refrigeration Co.*, 187 N.Y. 395, at page 399, 80 N.E. 199, at page 200, which was an action to recover for the cost of publishing newspaper notices not authorized by the board of directors, it was expressly found that the proxy contest there involved was "by one faction in its contest with another for the control of the corporation . . . a contest for the perpetuation of their offices and control." We there said by way of *dicta* that under such circumstances the publication of certain notices on behalf of the management faction was not a corporate expenditure which the directors had the power to authorize.

Other jurisdictions and our own lower courts have held that management may look to the corporate treasury for the reasonable expenses of soliciting proxies to defend its position in a *bona fide* policy contest. . . .

It should be noted that plaintiff does not argue that the aforementioned sums were fraudulently extracted from the corporation: indeed, his counsel conceded that "the charges were fair and reasonable," but denied "they were legal charges which may be reimbursed for." This is therefore not a case where a stockholder challenges specific items, which, on examination, the trial court may find unwarranted, excessive or otherwise improper. Had plaintiff made such objections here, the trial court would have been required to examine the items challenged.

If directors of a corporation may not in good faith incur reasonable and proper expenses in soliciting proxies in these days of giant corporations with vast numbers of stockholders, the corporate business might be seriously interfered with because of stockholder indifference and the difficulty of procuring a quorum, where there is no contest. In the event of a proxy contest, if the directors may not freely answer the challenges of outside groups and in good faith defend their actions with respect to corporate policy for the information of the stockholders, they and the corporation may be at the mercy of persons seeking to wrest control for their own purposes, so long as such persons have ample funds to conduct a proxy contest. The test is clear. When the directors act in good faith in a contest over policy, they have the right to incur reasonable and proper expenses for solicitation of proxies and in defense of their corporate policies, and are not obliged to sit idly by. The courts are entirely competent to pass upon the *bona fide* and any given case, as well as the nature of their expenditures when duly challenged.

It is also our view that the members of the so-called new group could be reimbursed by the corporation for their expenditures in this contest by affirmative vote of the stockholders. With regard to these ultimately successful contestants, as the Appellate Division below has noted, there was, of course, "no duty . . . to set forth the facts, which corresponding obligation of the corporation to pay for such expense." However, where a majority of the stockholders chose — in this case by a vote of 16 to 1 — to reimburse the successful contestants for achieving the very end sought and voted for by them as owners of the corporation, we see no reason to deny the effect of their ratification nor to hold the corporate body powerless to determine how its own moneys shall be spent.

The rule then which we adopt is simply this: In a contest over policy as compared to a purely personal power contest, corporate directors have the right to make reasonable and proper expenditures, subject to the scrutiny of the courts when duly challenged, from the corporate treasury for the purpose of persuading the stockholders of the correctness of their position and soliciting their support for policies which the directors believe, in all good faith, are in the best interests of the corporation. The stockholders, moreover, have the right to reimburse successful contestants for the reasonable and *bona fide* expenses incurred by them in any such policy contest, subject to like court scrutiny. That is not to say, that corporate directors can, under any circumstances, disport themselves in a proxy contest with the corporation's moneys to an unlimited extent. Where it is established that such moneys have been spent for personal power, individual gain or private advantage, and not in the belief that such expenditures are in the best interests of the stockholders and the corporation, or where the fairness and reasonableness of the amounts allegedly expended are duly and successfully challenged, the courts will not hesitate to disallow them. . . .

VAN VOORHIS J. (dissenting): . . . The Appellate Division held that stockholder authorization or ratification was not necessary to reasonable expenditures by the management group, the purpose of which was to inform the stockholders concerning the affairs of the corporation, and that, although these incumbents spent or incurred obligations of $133,966 (the previous expenses of annual meetings of this corporation ranging between $7,000 and $28,000), plaintiff must fail for having omitted to distinguish item by item between which of these expenditures were warranted and which ones were not; and the Appellate Division held that the insurgents also should be reimbursed, but subject to the qualification that "The expenses of those who were seeking to displace the management should not be reimbursed by the corporation except upon approval by the stockholders." It was held that the stockholders had approved.

No resolution was passed by the stockholders approving payment to the management group. It has been recognized that not all of the $133,966 in obligations paid or incurred by the management group was designed merely for information of stockholders. This outlay included payment for all of the activities of a strenuous campaign to persuade and cajole in a hard-fought contest for control of this corporation. It included, for example, expenses for entertainment, chartered airplanes and limousines, public relations counsel and proxy solicitors. However legitimate such measures may be on behalf of stockholders themselves in such a controversy, most of them do not pertain to a corporate function but are part of the familiar apparatus of aggressive factions in corporate contests. . . .

The Appellate Division acknowledged in the instant case that "It is obvious that the management group here incurred a substantial amount of needless expense which was charged to the corporation," but this conclusion should have led to a direction that those defendants who were incumbent directors should be required to come forward with an explanation of their expenditures under the familiar rule that where it has been established that directors have expended corporate money for their own purposes, the burden of going forward with evidence of the propriety and reasonableness of specific items rests upon the directors. . . .

The second ground assigned by the Appellate Division for dismissing the complaint against incumbent directors is stockholder ratification of reimbursement to the insurgent group. Whatever effect or lack of it this resolution had upon expenditures by the insurgent group, clearly the stockholders who voted to pay the insurgents entertained no intention of reimbursing the management group for their expenditures. The insurgent group succeeded as a result of arousing the indignation of these very stockholders against the management group; nothing in the resolution to pay the expenses of the insurgent group purported to authorize or ratify payment of the campaign expenses of their adversaries, and certainly no inference should be drawn that the stockholders who voted to pay the insurgents intended that the incumbent group should also be paid. Upon the contrary, they were removing the incumbents from control mainly for the reason that they were charged with having mulcted the corporation . . .

There is no doubt that the management was entitled and under a duty to take reasonable steps to acquaint the stockholders with essential facts concerning the management of the corporation, and it may well be that the existence of a contest warranted them in circularizing the stockholders with more than ordinarily detailed information. . . .

What expenses of the incumbent group should be allowed and what should be disallowed should be remitted to the trial court to ascertain, after taking evidence, in accordance with the rule that the incumbent directors were required to assume the burden of going forward in the first instance with evidence explaining and justifying their expenditures. Only such as were reasonably related to informing the stockholders fully and fairly concerning the corporate affairs should be allowed. The concession by plaintiff that such expenditures as were made were reasonable in amount does not decide this question. By way of illustration, the costs of entertainment for stockholders may have been, and it is stipulated that they were, at the going rates for providing similar entertainment. That does not signify that entertaining stockholders is reasonably related to the purposes of the corporation. . . .

Regarding the $127,556 paid by the new management to the insurgent group for the campaign expenditures, the question immediately arises whether that was for a corporate purpose. . . . If unanimous stockholder approval had been obtained and no rights of creditors or of the public intervened, it would make no practical difference whether the purpose were *ultra vires* — i.e., not a corporate purpose. . . . Upon the other hand, an act which is *ultra vires* cannot be ratified merely by a majority of the stockholders of a corporation. . . .

In considering this issue, as in the case of the expenses of the incumbents, we begin with the proposition that this court has already held that it is beyond the power of a corporation to authorize the expenditure of mere campaign expenses in a proxy contest. *Lawyers' Advertising Co. v. Con solidated Ry., Lighting & Refrigeration Co.* . . . In that case, and in all of the other decisions which have been cited with the single exception of a Federal district court decision, *Steinberg v. Adams*, D.C., 90 F. Supp. 604, 606, the question concerned reimbursement of a management group. Moreover, with the exception of an English decision, *Peel v. London & North Western R.R. Co.*, [1907] 1 Ch. Div. 5, all of the appellate court cases which have been cited, and *Steinberg v. Adams*, were decided under the law of the State of Delaware. The Delaware law contains more latitude than in New York. . . .

The case most frequently cited and principally relied upon from among these Delaware decisions is *Hall v. Trans-Lux Daylight Picture Screen Corp.*, 20 Del. Ch. 78, 171 Atl. 336 (1934). There the English case was followed . . . which distinguished between expenses merely for the purpose

of maintaining control, and contests over policy questions of the corporation. In the *Hall* case the issues concerned a proposed merger, and a proposed
sale of stock of a subsidiary corporation. These were held to be policy
questions, and payment of the management campaign expenses was upheld.

In our view, the impracticability of such a distinction is illustrated by
the statement in the *Hall* case . . . that "It is impossible in many cases of
intracorporate contests over directors, to sever questions of policy from
those of persons." This circumstance is stressed [in] Judge Rifkind's opinion
in the *Steinberg* case: . . . "The simple fact, of course, is that generally
policy and personnel do not exist in separate compartments. A change in
personnel is sometimes indispensable to a change of policy. A new board
may be the symbol of the shift in policy as well as the means of obtaining
it."

That may be all very well, but the upshot of this reasoning is that
inasmuch as it is generally impossible to distinguish whether "policy" or
"personnel" is the dominant factor, any averments must be accepted at their
face value that questions of policy are dominant. Nowhere do these opinions
mention that the converse is equally true and more pervasive, that neither
the "ins" nor the "outs" ever say that they have no program to offer to the
shareholders, but just want to acquire or to retain control, as the case may
be. In common experience, this distinction is unreal. It was not mentioned
by this court in *Lawyers' Advertising Co. v. Consolidated Ry., Lighting &
Refrigeration Co.* . . . As in political contests, aspirations for control are
invariably presented under the guise of policy or principle. A valiant effort
was made in the English case . . . to conserve the distinction in the opinion
by Buckley, L.J., who said: "Those who are conversant with the affairs of
joint stock companies are well aware that cases often arise in which the
board in power are anxious to maintain themselves in power, to procure
their own re-election, or to drive a policy not really in the interests of the
corporation, but for some private purpose of their own, down the throats of
the corporators at a general meeting, and in which they issue at the expense
of the company circulars and proxy papers for the purpose of attaining that
object. When a case of that kind comes before the Court, I sincerely trust
that the decision of this Court in this case will not be cited as any authority
for justifying the action of the directors."

The main question of "policy" in the instant corporate election, as is
stated in the opinions below and frankly admitted, concerns the long-term
contract with pension rights of a former officer and director, Mr. J. Carlton
Ward, Jr. The insurgents' chief claim of benefit to the corporation from
their victory consists in the termination of that agreement, resulting in an
alleged actuarial saving of $350,000 to $825,000 to the corporation, and the
reduction of other salaries and rent by more than $300,000 per year. The
insurgents had contended in the proxy contest that these payments should
be substantially reduced so that members of the incumbent group would not
continue to profit personally at the expense of the corporation. If these
charges were true, which appear to have been believed by a majority of the

shareholders, then the disbursements by the management group in the proxy contest fall under the condemnation of the English and the Delaware rule.

These circumstances are mentioned primarily to illustrate how impossible it is to distinguish between "policy" and "personnel," as Judge Rifkind expressed it, but they also indicate that personal factors are deeply rooted in this contest. That is certainly true insofar as the former management group is concerned. It would be hard to find a case to which the careful reservation made by the English Judge in the Peel case, *supra*, was more directly applicable.

Some expenditures may concededly be made by a corporation represented by its management so as to inform the stockholders, but there is a clear distinction between such expenditures by management and by mere groups of stockholders. The latter are under no legal obligation to assume duties of managing the corporation. They may endeavor to supersede the management for any reason, regardless of whether it be advantageous or detrimental to the corporation but if they succeed, that is not a determination that the company was previously mismanaged or that it may not be mismanaged in the future.

* * *

Insofar as a management group is concerned, it may charge the corporation with any expenses within reasonable limits incurred in giving widespread notice to stockholders of questions affecting the welfare of the corporation. . . . Expenditures in excess of these limits are *ultra vires*. The corporation lacks power to defray them. The corporation lacks power to defray the expenses of the insurgents in their entirety. The insurgents were not charged with responsibility for operating the company. No appellate court case is cited from any jurisdiction holding otherwise. No contention is made that such disbursements could be made, in any event, without stockholder ratification; they could not be ratified except by unanimous vote if they were *ultra vires*. The insurgents, in this instance, repeatedly announced to the stockholders in their campaign literature that their proxy contest was being waged at their own expense. If reimbursement of such items were permitted upon majority stockholder ratification, no court or other tribunal could pass upon which types of expenditure were "needless," to employ the characterization of the Appellate Division in this case. Whether the insurgents should be paid would be made to depend upon whether they win the stockholders election and obtain control of the corporation. It would be entirely irrelevant whether the corporation is "benefitted" by their efforts or by the outcome of such an election. The courts could not indulge in a speculative inquiry into that issue. That would truly be a matter of business judgment. . . The losers in a proxy fight may understand the interests of the corporation more accurately than their successful adversaries, and agitation of this character may ultimately result in corporation advantage even if there be no change in management. Nevertheless, under the judgment which is appealed from, success in a proxy contest is the indispensable condition upon which disbursement of the insurgents depend. . . . The way is open and will be kept open for stockholders and groups of stockholders to contest corporate elections, but if the promoters of such movements to choose to employ the costly modern media of mass persuasion, they should look for reimbursement to themselves and to the stockholders who are aligned with them. If the law be that they can be recompensed by the corporation in case of success, and only in that event, it will operate as a powerful incentive to persons accustomed to taking calculated risks to increase this form of highpowered salesmanship to such a degree that, action provoking reaction, stockholders' meetings will be very costly. To the financial advantages promised by control of a prosperous corporation, would be added the knowledge that the winner takes all insofar as the campaign expenses are concerned. To the victor, indeed, would belong the spoils.

The questions involved in this case assume mounting importance as the capital stock of corporations becomes more widely distributed. To an enlarged extent the campaign methods consequently come more to resemble those of political campaigns, but, as in the latter, campaign expenses should be borne by those who are waging the campaign and their followers, instead of being met out of the corporate or the public treasury. Especially is this true when campaign promises have been made that the expenses would not be charged to the corporation. . . .

Appeal dismissed.

Questions

1 What considerations should be taken into account in deciding whether insurgent shareholders' expenses should be reimbursed? Is success determinative or relevant? Would it be a boon to shareholder democracy to routinely reimburse dissident shareholder proxy expenses and thus encourage shareholders to enter into proxy battles? Or would this simply tend to attract cranks and persons with an ax to grind with management (such as dismissed employees)? Is there some middle ground that would encourage meritorious proxy battles while weeding out the frivolous or vexatious proxy challenges?

2 Should the fact of shareholder approval or disapproval of the expenses be conclusive of the matter?

3 Should an insurgent group be required to disclose whether it will seek reimbursement? Should a stated intention not to seek reimbursement bar the insurgents from later seeking reimbursement?

4 Would it make sense to allow reimbursement of expenses on the basis of the proportion of shareholder votes obtained by the insurgents compared to the expenses and votes obtained by management?

(vii) Remedies for Breach of Proxy Legislation

A right is only as effective as the remedies to secure enforcement of the right. Thus, a crucial question in relation to the rights created by proxy legislation is the means by which aggrieved parties may secure their enforcement. A number of bases for such enforcement are explored in this note.

(A) Implied Civil Right of Action

Sometimes a statute will mandate, regulate or prohibit certain activity without indicating if any civil (or in some cases, either civil or criminal) consequences arise from breach of the statutory provisions. In these cases, the courts are sometimes willing to "imply" a private right of action arising in favour of at least some private parties. *Brown v. Duby, supra,* which involved a dissident's proxy circular that failed to comply with the CBCA regulations, is such a case. The court held that the criminal penalties that the CBCA prescribed for breach of the statute were not exclusive of civil liability, and that a private right of action arose for breach of the proxy legislation. The plaintiff in favour of whom the action arose was both an officer of United Canso as well as a shareholder, and it is not entirely clear in which of these capacities the right of action arose, although the court recognized such a right in the corporation as well.

The existence of an implied private right of action has also been recognized by the Ontario Court of Appeal in *Goldex Mines v. Revill, infra.* The statute under consideration (the forerunner to the current OBCA) contained nothing that would expressly allow the corporation or an aggrieved shareholder to sue for breach of the statutory provisions. Nevertheless, the court held that misleading or deficient disclosure to shareholders in connection with a proxy solicitation could give rise to both a derivative and a personal cause of action. Although we have not yet explored in detail the difference between these two types of actions, a derivative action arises where the corporation is the injured party, and shareholders are hurt only indirectly, as a consequence of the harm to the corporation. A personal action generally arises where the harm to the shareholder is not merely incidental to the harm to the corporation, but is particular to a shareholder or group of shareholders. Breaches of fiduciary duty owed to the corporation give rise to derivative actions; breaches of duties owed directly to shareholders give rise to personal actions. Can you logically articulate how an action for breach of proxy legislation (or in respect of any other matter) could give rise to both a personal and a derivative action? How can the injury be at once one that harms the corporation and grounds a derivative action (and therefore one in respect of which all shareholders suffer indirectly and in equal measure) and one in respect of which the complainant shareholders suffer special harm?

No discussion of an implied private right of action would be complete without reference to *Canada v. Saskatchewan Wheat Pool*, [1983] 1 S.C.R. 205, 143 D.L.R. (3d) 9. In *Saskatchewan*, the Supreme Court of Canada held that there was no independent tort of breach of a statutory provision. Rather, breach of a statutory provision might serve as evidence of the breach of a duty owed by the defendant. *Saskatchewan* thus appears to call into question all of those cases which have held that breach of a statute might by itself ground a civil action. Despite *Saskatchewan*, however, at least one court has implied a private right of action in the securities law context. In *Jones v. Deacon Hodgson* (1986), 34 B.L.R. 1 (Ont. H.C.), the court recognized the existence of an implied right of action for failure to prepare and file a prospectus as required by the Ontario *Securities Act*. More recently, however, see *Roman Corp. v. Peat Marwick Thorne* (1992), 8 B.L.R. (2d) 43, 11 O.R. (3d) 248, 1992 CarswellOnt 149 (Gen. Div. [Commercial List]), holding that breach of statute cannot by itself ground an action.

Would such a right of action (if it exists) support a claim for damages? In *Brown*, the Court suggested that damages would not be an adequate remedy. The difficulties associated with calculating damages are further explored below.

(B) Statutory Liability

CBCA

Section 154 of the CBCA provides a statutory means for ensuring that the proxy legislation is complied with. An "interested person" or the Director may apply to a court which may make "any order it thinks fit", including a restraining order, a mandatory injunction and an order adjoining the meeting. The section applies where "a form of proxy, management proxy circular or dissident's proxy circular contains an untrue statement of a material fact or omits to state a material fact required therein or necessary to make a statement contained therein not misleading in light of the circumstances in which it was made . . ." An interested person would certainly include a shareholder. Who else might the phrase include (*e.g.*, a director or officer of the company; an outside party)? Note that the Director's power to sue allows him to commence an action not unlike a class action in favour of minority shareholders: see *Sparling v. Royal Trustco Ltd.* (1984), 24 B.L.R. 145 (Ont. C.A.), affirmed [1986] 2 S.C.R. 537.

One curiosity surrounding the *Brown* case, *supra*, is that the Court felt compelled to recognize a private right of action to ground the suit. Can you think of a reason why s. 154 of the CBCA (the applicable statute) would not have been a sufficient basis upon which to ground the suit?

If the holding in *Goldex* (discussed, *supra*) applies to s. 154, then is it necessary to obtain leave of the court under CBCA s. 239 before suing under s. 154? Or is there perhaps some argument that s. 154 is restricted to personal causes of action? In *Goldhar v. Quebec Manitou Mines Ltd.* (1976),

9 O.R. (2d) 740, 61 D.L.R. (3d) 612 (Ont. Div. Ct.), *infra*, the court held that the general compliance and restraining order provision of the former OBCA could not be used in relation to derivative causes of action. *Prima facie*, the holding applies to s. 154 as well.

While we have not yet explored the statutory oppression remedy in detail, you should keep in mind the possibility of resorting to the oppression remedy in any case involving breach of the disclosure requirements. The question of whether the oppression provision can be used in relation to causes of action which are essentially derivative in nature is explored, *infra*.

OBCA

Section 253(2) of the OBCA is drafted in a manner broadly similar to s. 154 of the CBCA. However, notice that the provision allows only the Ontario Securities Commission to apply to a court for an order. Could a shareholder nonetheless apply under s. 253(1) for an order restraining a management solicitation where there has been a material misrepresentation in a management proxy circular? Could management apply to restrain a solicitation by a dissident shareholders' group in a case involving a misrepresentation in a dissident proxy circular? Look carefully at the statutory definition of "complainant" in s. 245(b).

(C) Injunctions

Whether the action arises by way of an implied right of action or statutory provision, one of the most effective remedies for breach of the proxy legislation is the injunction (or "restraining order"). Despite the reluctance to issue an injunction against dissident shareholders evident in *Brown v. Duby*, the courts have not been shy to use the injunction in a number of cases involving misleading or incomplete proxy materials sent to shareholders by management. For example, in *Garvie v. Axmith*, [1962] O.R. 65, 31 D.L.R. (2d) 65 (H.C.), the court issued an injunction to prevent the corporation from acting on resolutions where shareholders were sent a deficient notice of meeting. Similarly, in *Alexander v. Westeel Rosco Ltd.* (1978), 22 O.R. (2d) 80, 75 D.L.R. (3d) 16 (H.C.), the court issued an interim injunction to prevent the consummation of an amalgamation because of, *inter alia*, a deficient proxy circular mailed to shareholders under the CBCA. The injunction is a flexible tool that can be used to prevent a solicitation from occurring, a meeting from being held, or resolutions passed at a meeting from being acted upon. A mandatory injunction (or "compliance order") may also be issued requiring correction of deficient or misleading proxy material or other action.

You should note the functional similarity between the grant of an injunction and an order rescinding corporate action. See, *e.g.*, *Babic v. Milinkovic* (1972), 22 D.L.R. (3d) 732 (B.C. S.C.), affirmed 25 D.L.R. (3d) 752 (B.C. C.A.).

(D) Damages

It is conceivable that a shareholder or other aggrieved party may wish to pursue a claim for damages rather than injunctive relief in connection with a violation of proxy legislation. Such a claim may be relatively difficult to make out. The courts have preferred injunctive relief; indeed, there is not a single case in Canada where damages have been awarded in connection with false, misleading or deficient proxy disclosure to shareholders. Given the difficulties associated with making an award of damages, this is perhaps not surprising. Suppose, for example, that shareholders elected the slate of directors nominated by management. If it could be shown that the management proxy circular was misleading in some material respect, what would the measure of damages be? If the action was constituted as a derivative action in favour of the corporation, then presumably the nature of the damage alleged would be the harm resulting to the company by reason of having an improperly elected (and perhaps incompetent or otherwise unsuitable) board of directors. By what metric could this damage be measured? Indeed, could it even be shown that the harm was actually caused by the misrepresentation? Without the misrepresentation, the same board of directors might have been elected anyway. Similar comments might be made in relation to the adoption of corporate fundamental changes by shareholders. Nor is there reason to believe that the calculation of damages in relation to personal actions commenced by shareholders would be any easier. On the issue of causation, see *Harris v. Universal Explorations Ltd.* (1982), 17 B.L.R. 135, 37 A.R. 35 (C.A.). See generally Crête, *The Proxy System in Canadian Corporations*, at 324–330, 348-349. Despite the fact that Canadian courts have not yet awarded damages in connection with a proxy violation, there may be cases where a court anxious to give relief is forced to award damages because it is too late to apply injunctive relief. See, for example, *Norcan Oils Ltd. v. Fogler*, [1965] S.C.R. 36, 49 W.W.R. 321, 46 D.L.R. (2d) 630, where the Supreme Court held that it was beyond the jurisdiction of the court under the legislation in question to unwind an already consummated amalgamation. In such a case, damages would be the only available remedy.

Another question worth pondering: would a court in fact have jurisdiction to award damages under s. 154? Are the words "any order it thinks fit" to be given a broad reading, or are these words limited *ejusdem generis* by the more specific enumerations which follow?

Question

We have already referred to a number of problems that imperil the efficacy of shareholder oversight of management, like shareholder "collective action" problems and the domination of the proxy machinery by management. The proxy rules are designed to ensure that shareholder oversight through the mechanism of the shareholder meeting is truly meaningful. Now that you know something about the design of these rules, we invite you to conduct your own evaluation of the effectiveness of these rules in achieving that objective.

4. SHAREHOLDER MEETINGS

(a) Introduction

The shareholder meeting is (or at least is intended to be) a key instrument of managerial accountability to shareholders. There are two types of shareholder meetings: annual and special. The company must have an annual meeting each year (within 15 months of the last annual meeting): CBCA s. 133(a), OBCA s. 94(a). At least three items of business must be transacted at an annual meeting. These are the election of directors (see CBCA s. 106(3), OBCA s. 119(4)) (although since directors may hold office for as long as three years, there may be no directors to elect in any given year), the appointment of auditors (see CBCA s. 162(1), OBCA s. 149(1)) and the presentation of financial statements and auditor's report to the shareholders (CBCA s. 155(1), OBCA s. 154(1). Other specific items of business may be transacted as well.

There may be important business that arises between annual meetings. In this case, the directors may call a special meeting of shareholders (CBCA s. 133(b), OBCA s. 94(b)). Special meetings will typically be held when management is contemplating a fundamental change in the corporation that requires shareholder approval (*e.g.*, an amalgamation, continuance in another jurisdiction, *etc.*), although they may be held for other reasons.

The directors are not the only group with the power to call a shareholders' meeting. Both the CBCA and OBCA provide that the holders of not less than 5% of the issued shares that carry the right to vote at a meeting sought to be held may "requisition" a shareholders' meeting (CBCA s. 143, OBCA s. 105) to transact the business stated in the requisition. See *Re Goldhar and D'Aragon Mines Ltd.* (1977), 15 O.R. (2d) 80, 75 D.L.R. (3d) 16 (H.C.).

You should also note that the CBCA and OBCA both have provisions relating (*inter alia*) to the place where meetings may be held (CBCA s. 132, OBCA s. 93), notice of meetings (CBCA s. 135, OBCA s. 96) and the requisite quorum to hold a meeting (CBCA s. 139, OBCA s. 101).

Aside from allowing shareholders to vote on such important matters as the election of directors and fundamental corporate changes, the shareholders' meeting is designed, at least in theory, to provide a forum for shareholders to discuss matters relating to the business and affairs of the corporation. Thus, shareholders have a right of discussion and a right to submit proposals to be discussed at shareholders' meetings. These rights are explored further, *infra*.

(b) Unanimous Shareholders' Resolutions

Eisenberg (formerly Walton) v. Bank of N.S.
[1965] S.C.R. 681, 7 C.B.R. (N.S.) 264

SPENCE J.: This is an appeal from the judgment of the Court of Appeal for Ontario pronounced on March 16, 1964, affirming the judgment at trial pronounced on March 15, 1963.

The action was brought by the appellant as trustee in bankruptcy of Ridout Real Estate Limited to recover from the respondent bank certain sums realized by the bank from assets which the said company had pledged to the bank as security for a loan to one George H. Ridout and his brother Ernest Ridout.

George Ridout was a director and president and was the sole beneficial owner of all the issued shares in the said Ridout Real Estate Limited. Ernest Ridout had been such sole beneficial owner but had transferred his shares to George Ridout and at all relevant times was neither a director nor shareholder of the Ridout Real Estate company.

On July 18, 1955, the said Ernest Ridout arranged with an officer of the defendant bank that it should loan to George Ridout and to him the sum of $100,000 for the purpose of permitting the said Ernest Ridout to obtain a release of his guarantee of the bonds of Taylor Forbes Limited which were then in default. As security for the loan, the bank was given a hypothecation of eleven promissory notes made by the Irmac Construction Company Limited in favour of Ridout Real Estate Limited and an assignment of the interest of Ridout Real Estate Limited in a partnership known as the Town and Country Development. One McIntosh, the supervisor of the Toronto branches of the respondent bank, was directed to carry out the transaction on behalf of the bank.

On the next day, July 19, 1955, Mr. McIntosh met Ernest Ridout and talked over the matter arranging for completion of certain documents which the bank required. After lunch, on the same day, Mr. McIntosh met, by appointment, Miss M.E. MacDonald, who delivered to him an envelope containing the following documents:

(1) Note for $95,000 signed by George Ridout and Ernest Ridout.

(2) Assignment of the interest of Ridout Real Estate Limited in Town and Country Development, executed on behalf of the Ridout company by George Ridout and bearing the corporate seal.

(3) Copy of a resolution authorizing the Ridout company to assign its interest in Town and Country Development as security and authorizing George Ridout to sign the assignment, certified by Miss M.E. MacDonald under the Ridout company's seal, to be a true copy of a resolution of the board of directors of the Ridout company, passed at a meeting of directors on July 19, 1955.

(4) Hypothecation Agreement executed on behalf of the Ridout company by George Ridout and Miss M.E. MacDonald under the seal of the Ridout company, by which hypothecation agreement Ridout Real Estate Limited hypothecated "all notes, cheques, drafts and other bills of exchange now lodged and/or which may hereafter be lodged with the bank and any resultant proceeds".

(5) Copy of a resolution authorizing the Ridout company to pledge the eleven Irmac notes of $10,000 each, and authorizing George Ridout to sign such hypothecation, certified by Miss MacDonald under the seal of the Ridout company to be a true copy of a resolution of the board of directors of the Ridout company, passed at a meeting of the directors.

(6) Direction from George Ridout requesting the bank to issue the cheque for $100,000 to M.H. Roebuck.

(7) The eleven notes of the Irmac company.

(8) Cheque of the Ridout company in favour of the Bank of Nova Scotia for $5,000 signed by George Ridout and Miss M.E. MacDonald.

Mr. McIntosh was familiar with the signatures of George Ridout and Ernest Ridout and was satisfied with their signatures on the document. Miss MacDonald represented that she was the secretary of Ridout Real Estate and was entitled under the by-laws to execute the said documents. She was not such secretary but she was the head office manager and was a signing officer of the Ridout company in connection with its business with its ordinary bank which was not the respondent. The secretary-treasurer of the company was one Mr. Muir who was then absent on holidays.

The first three Irmac notes becoming due in August, September and October, were paid and were credited against the loan of $95,000, that is, the $100,000 less the $5,000 cheque.

In November 1955, $45,000 was received in respect of the Ridout Real Estate interests in the Town and Country Development and the respondent bank was also paid a cheque of the Ridout Real Estate Limited for $10,000. This cheque was signed by George Ridout and Mr. Muir. These payments reduced the loan to $10,000. The bank then made a further advance of $70,000 to George Ridout and took another promissory note signed by George Ridout and Ernest Ridout for that amount. This increased the total loan to $80,000 and the bank issued a cheque for the amount of $70,000 to George Ridout who deposited it to the credit of the trust account of Ridout Real Estate Limited in its regular bank. The loan in the sum of $80,000 was discharged by applying against it the proceeds from the eight Irmac notes, and the final payment was on June 5, 1956.

On December 1, 1956, Ernest Ridout deposited to the credit of the trust account of the Ridout company in its regular bank the sum of $58,416.25. A receiving order was made on January 3, 1957. The appellant was appointed trustee in bankruptcy of Ridout Real Estate Limited.

The appellant commenced this action by a writ issued on June 3, 1959.

At trial, the action was dismissed by King J. and the appeal from the judgment of the learned trial judge was dismissed in the unanimous judgment of the Court of Appeal.

In this Court, able argument was made by counsel for both the appellant and the respondent bank, counsel for the third parties adopting the latter argument. Counsel for the appellant took the firm position that he was not alleging that the transaction was ultra vires the real estate company but on the other hand admitted that the transaction was one which could bind the company if it had been unanimously approved by shareholders in meeting duly called for such purpose.

It is admitted that no resolution of directors was passed and that no meeting of directors took place. However, the "inside management rule" enunciated inter alia in *The Royal British Bank v. Turquand*, would apply to protect an innocent third party dealing with Ridout Real Estate Ltd., without notice of those facts and that Miss MacDonald was not the secretary of the company.

In the Court of Appeal for Ontario, Schroeder J.A. said:

> Since I have come to the decision that the doctrine of estoppel operates in favour of the defendant it follows that I also take the view that the defendant comes within the protection of the principle of *The Royal British Bank v. Turquand* (1856), 6 El. & B1. 327, and *William Augus tus Mahony v. The East Holyford Mining Company (Limited)* (1875), L. R. 7 H.L. 869.

I have come to the conclusion that, in this Court, it is not necessary to investigate whether the respondent bank is entitled to rely on the "inside management rule". Whether or not it were able to do so it is plain that the transactions were not only approved by the sole beneficial owner but he was the chief instigator of the transactions and directed them throughout. It is true that no meeting of shareholders was ever held to approve the transactions. If there had been a directors' meeting, fully attended, the directors were George Ridout, Mr. Muir and two other employees. None of the latter three held any shares beneficially, and all were mere nominees of George Ridout. Therefore, the result of either the shareholders' meeting or the directors' meeting would have been a foregone conclusion. If any director had seen fit to oppose George Ridout's wishes, he could be removed from his position as director with the utmost celerity and, of course, George Ridout was the sole beneficial owner of all the shares and his wishes would have been the unanimous decision of the shareholders' meeting.

Under these circumstances, the problem of what kind of unanimous authorization of shareholders is sufficient becomes important. . . . [Mr. Justice Spence then reviewed several authorities and concluded:]

Therefore, upon a consideration of the above authorities, I have been led to the conclusion that a corporation, when a matter is ultra vires of the corporation, cannot be heard to deny a transaction to which all the shareholders have given their assent even when such assent be given in an informal manner or by conduct as distinguished from a formal resolution at a duly convened meeting. Since, of course, George Ridout not only assented to the transaction but instigated it, his assent being, as admitted, that of the sole beneficial shareholder therefore binds the company.

Before parting with the matter, I wish to make it clear that I am not deciding that the transaction between Ridout Real Estate Limited, hereafter referred to as "the Company", and the respondent bank was one which it was lawful for the company to enter into. It is unnecessary to express an opinion on this question because it was conceded that the transaction was one within the powers of the company and capable of ratification by the shareholders in general meeting. I have already indicated my view that in such circumstances the unanimous consent of all the shareholders given in fact is as effective to validate the transaction as if given in a formal meeting.

It was also conceded (i) that George Ridout was the beneficial owner of every issued share of the capital stock of the company, and (ii) that the appellant did not stand in any position different from that of the company in regard to this transaction. I mention this to make it plain that we were not called upon to decide either of these matters. . . .

Appeal dismissed with costs.

Notes and Questions

1 Both the CBCA and OBCA now provide that the shareholders may dispense with shareholders' meetings and do all those matters normally required to be dealt with at a shareholders' meeting (or other business) by unanimous shareholder resolutions (CBCA s. 142, OBCA s. 104); be careful to distinguish these from unanimous shareholder agreements, discussed, *infra.* Since shareholders' meetings are both expensive and time consuming, these provisions are especially useful for smaller private corporations with few shareholders (particularly family corporations), at least where little disagreement arises about the conduct of the business. Such shareholder resolutions are also very useful where the shareholders reside in widely disparate locations, or if there is but a single shareholder in the corporation. Note that the holding in *Eisenberg v. Bank of Nova Scotia* goes further in that it validates corporate actions "to which all the shareholders have given their assent even where such assent be given in an informal manner or by conduct . . ." Given that the statutory provisions cited above post-date *Eisenberg*, do they replace the common law by virtue of the principle of *expressio unius exclusio alterius*? Or does the *Eisenberg* decision continue to have force?

2 Note that not only was there no shareholders' meeting to authorize the transaction in *Eisenberg*, there was no directors' meeting either (although the company submitted documents to the bank which purported

to be true copies of directors' resolutions). Was it necessary for the Supreme Court to hold as they did in order to protect the bank? More specifically, could the court have simply invoked principles of agency law (explored in Chapter 4) to achieve the same result? What does the *Eisenberg* decision add to these principles of agency law?

(c) The Use of Directors' Powers in Relation to Meetings

Schnell v. Chris-Craft Industries Inc.
285 A.2d 430 (Del. Ch. 1971), rev'd. 437 (S.C. Del.)

The plaintiffs were dissatisfied with Chris-Craft's recent performance, and along with other dissident shareholders of Chris-Craft formed a shareholders' committee. On October 16, 1971, the committee filed with the SEC their intention to wage a proxy contest for the purpose of electing new directors. Two days later at a directors' meeting, the company's bylaws in respect of its annual meeting were amended. Previously, the annual meeting was to be held on the second Tuesday in January; the new bylaw allowed the directors to hold the meeting any day in December or January. That year's meeting was then rescheduled for December 8, 1971. The plaintiffs sought a preliminary injunction against the corporation carrying out the change in date, and an order reinstating the former meeting date. They argued that the change in meeting date was entered into to handicap the efforts of the shareholders' committee to adequately prepare for the proxy battle. The defendants claimed that the new meeting date was chosen to take advantage of better weather conditions and to avoid the necessity of mailing notices to shareholders during the rush of Christmas mail. The Delaware Court of Chancery found that management's intention was to hamper the efforts of the shareholder committee. However, as management's actions were legal under Delaware law, and because the plaintiffs had already had adequate time to present their views to other shareholders, a preliminary injunction was deemed to not be warranted. The plaintiffs appealed.

Appeal Judgment:

HERRMANN J. (for the majority of the Court): This is an appeal from the denial by the Court of Chancery of the petition of dissident stockholders for injunctive relief to prevent management from advancing the date of the annual stockholders' meeting from January 11, 1972, as previously set by the bylaws, to December 8, 1971.

The opinion below is reported at 285 A.2d 430. This opinion is confined to the frame of reference of the opinion below for the sake of brevity and because of the strictures of time imposed by the circumstances of the case.

It will be seen that the Chancery Court considered all of the reasons stated by management as business reasons for changing the date of the meeting; but that those reasons were rejected by the Court below in making the following findings:

> I am satisfied, however, in a situation in which present management has disingenuously resisted the production of a list of its stockholders to plaintiffs or their confederates and has otherwise turned a deaf ear to plaintiffs' demands about a change in management designed to lift defendant from its present business doldrums, management has seized on a relatively new section of the Delaware Corporation Law for the purpose of cutting down on the amount of time which would otherwise have been available to plaintiffs and others for the waging of a proxy battle. Management thus enlarged the scope of its scheduled October 18 directors' meeting to include the by-law amendment in controversy after the stockholders committee had filed with the S.E.C. its intention to wage a proxy fight on October 16.
>
> Thus plaintiffs reasonably contend that because of the tactics employed by management (which involve the hiring of two established proxy solicitors as well as a refusal to produce a list of its stockholders, coupled with its use of an amendment to the Delaware Corporation Law to limit the time for contest), they are given little chance, because of the exigencies of time, including that required to clear material at the S.E.C., to wage a successful proxy fight between now and December 8. . . .

In our view, those conclusions amount to a finding that management has attempted to utilize the corporate machinery and the Delaware Law for the purpose of perpetuating itself in office; and, to that end, for the purpose of obstructing the legitimate efforts of dissident stockholders in the exercise of their rights to undertake a proxy contest against management. These are inequitable purposes, contrary to established principles of corporate democracy.

The advancement by directors of the by-law date of a stockholders' meeting, for such purposes, may not be permitted to stand. Compare *Condec Corporation v. Lunkenheimer Company*, 43 Del.Ch. 353, 230 A.2d 769 (1967).

When the by-laws of a corporation designate the date of the annual meeting of stockholders, it is to be expected that those who intend to contest the reelection of incumbent management will gear their campaign to the by-law date. It is not to be expected that management will attempt to advance that date in order to obtain an inequitable advantage in the contest.

Management contends that it has complied strictly with the provisions of the new Delaware Corporation Law in changing the by-law date. The answer to that contention, of course, is that inequitable action does not become permissible simply because it is legally possible.

Management relies upon *American Hardwater Corp. v. Savage Arms Corp.*, 37 Del.Ch. 10, 135 A.2d 725, aff'd 37 Del.Ch. 59, 136 A.2d 690

(1957). That case is inapposite for two reasons: it involved an effort by stockholders, engaged in a proxy contest, to have the stockholders' meeting adjourned and the period for the proxy contest enlarged; and there was no finding there of inequitable action on the part of management. We agree with the rule of American Hardware that, in the absence of fraud or inequitable conduct, the date for a stockholders' meeting and notice thereof, duly established under the by-laws, will not be enlarged by judicial interference at the request of dissident stockholders solely because of the circumstances of a proxy contest. That, of course, is not the case before us.

We are unable to agree with the conclusion of the Chancery Court that the stockholders' application for injunctive relief here was tardy and came too late. The stockholders learned of the action of management unofficially on Wednesday, October 27, 1971; they filed this action on Monday, November 1, 1971. Until management changed the date of the meeting, the stockholders had no need of judicial assistance in that connection. There is no indication of any prior waning of management's intent to take such action; indeed, it appears that an attempt was made by management to conceal its action as long as possible. Moreover, stockholders may not be charged with the duty of anticipating inequitable action by management, and of seeking anticipatory injunctive relief to foreclose such action, simply because the new Delaware Corporation Law makes such inequitable action legally possible.

Accordingly, the judgment below must be reversed and the cause remanded, with instructions to nullify the December 8 date as a meeting date for stockholders; to reinstate January 11, 1972 as the sole date of the next annual meeting of the stockholders of the corporation; and to take such other proceedings and action as may be consistent herewith regarding the stock record closing date and any other related matters.

WOLCOTT C.J. (dissenting): I do not agree with the majority of the Court in its disposition of this appeal. The plaintiff stockholders concerned in this litigation have, for a considerable period of time, sought to obtain control of the defendant corporation. These attempts took various forms.

In view of the length of time leading up to the immediate events which caused the filing of this action, I agree with the Vice Chancellor that the application for injunctive relief came too late.

I would affirm the judgment below on the basis of the Vice Chancellor's opinion.

Appeal Allowed.

Notes and Questions

1 Note that the majority of the Supreme Court of Delaware suggested that the Delaware statute made the conduct undertaken by management "legally possible", but nonetheless held that the court could intervene (as it did in this case) to enjoin "fraud or inequitable conduct". An

important question for you to consider is by what legal theory a Canadian court might intervene to achieve the same result. Consider the "improper purpose" cases explored in Chapter 6. Could these be applied to "read down" the authority given the directors to set the meeting date (you should also consider if these cases are still good law, given their fate in the *Teck*, *Hiram Walker* and *Olson* cases considered earlier (see Chapter 6))? If not, could a court simply invoke principles of fiduciary duty now given statutory force (see, *e.g.*, CBCA s. 122) or the statutory oppression remedy? What other decisions might the directors make in relation to meetings which would be subject to the same judicial oversight?

2   Note also that the majority in *Schnell* held that "[i]t is not to be expected that management will attempt to advance the date [of the meeting] in order to obtain an inequitable advantage in the contest". To what extent do the cases explored thus far suggest that a Canadian court would feel free to invoke an expectations principle in order to limit the authority given the directors? You should keep this question in mind when reading cases on the oppression remedy and winding up in Chapter 11.

(d) The Conduct of Meetings and the Right of Discussion

Wall v. London and Northern Assets Corp.
[1898] 2 Ch. 469 (C.A.)

The London and Northern Assets Corporation (referred to in the excerpt from the report's statement of facts below as "the Assets Company") was registered as a limited company. This action arose from, among other things, a meeting convened by the company in order to approve of a sale of assets.

An extraordinary general meeting of the Assets Company was held on February 22, 1898, at which a resolution approving of the agreement of the 11th was moved and seconded. The meeting was adjourned to March 22, when, after the chairman had addressed the meeting Mr. Wall entered into an explanation of his objections to the scheme. Mr. Parker pointed out the advantages of the scheme, and the objections to the schemes outlined in a circular of Mr. Wall. A Mr. Rowley was speaking against the schemes, both of the directors and of Mr. Wall, but was interrupted by cries of "Vote." The chairman then, supported by others, put a motion that the debate should then close, and there voted 24 in favour of the motion and 2 against it. The chairman then put the resolution, which was carried by 35 to 3. Mr. Wall expressed his wish for a poll, but could not obtain the support of four other members present for demanding it, and the chairman declared the meeting closed. The above is the substance of what appears in the minutes of the meeting. Mr. Wall deposed that, "Shortly after the discussion of the scheme had begun, and while I and other shareholders were desirous of addressing the meeting, the chairman put a resolution to the meeting that the discussion should be terminated. This resolution was carried, and those shareholders who were desirous of speaking were thus prevented from so doing."

On April 6 an extraordinary general meeting was held for the purpose of confirming the resolution. The chairman referred to a notice of amendment received from Mr. Wall, which was as follows: "That the following be added to the resolution confirming contract — 'Subject to the purchaser agreeing to allow any individual or any body of dissentient shareholders to have their share of the assets agreed to be sold in lieu of the London and Northern debenture shares due to them.' " The chairman ruled that the amendment could not be put, and moved that the resolution of March 22 should be confirmed. This motion was seconded. The minute of the meeting proceeded as follows:

> Mr. Rowley expressed his views against the resolution, and also against the suggestions made by Mr. Wall in his circulars. Mr. Timmis moved the adjournment of the meeting for a fortnight or three weeks. Major Baker objected to any adjournment, pointing out that the resolution had been before the shareholders since February 22, and pressed for the vote of the shareholders to be taken at once. Mr. Wall spoke in favour of adjournment, when certain shareholders suggested that further discussion on the question of adjournment should be terminated, and the voting on the motion for adjournment taken at once. The chairman left this to the meeting to decide, and 16 members voted that the discussion be terminated, and 8 against. Thereupon a demand for a poll was handed in by Mr. Wall, who claimed that discussion on the question should not be suppressed. The chairman ruled that no poll could be demanded. Mr. Wall, having protested against the decision of the chairman, continued his remarks at some length upon the desirability of an adjournment, and seconded the motion of Mr. Timmis. The chairman put to the meeting the motion for the adjournment, when there voted 8 in favour of the adjournment, and 19 against. The chairman thereupon declared the motion for the adjournment lost. The chairman then put the original resolution, of which notice had been given, as moved by him, when there voted 20 for the resolution, and 5 against, and the chairman declared the resolution carried.

Mr. Wall handed in a demand for a poll signed by himself and four other parties present, and it was fixed for April 13.

The result of the poll was:

For the resolution.	Persons.	Votes.
Voting in person	10	2,243
Voting by proxies	178	23,350
	188	25,593

Against.

Voting in person	7	1,936
Voting by proxies	59	8,930
	66	10,866

On April 15 Mr. Wall commenced an action, on behalf of himself and all other shareholders in the Assets Company except those who had voted for the resolution, against the Assets Company and its directors, asking a declaration that the special resolution which the company purported to pass on March 22, 1898, and to confirm on April 13, 1898, and the agreement therein referred to, were *ultra vires*, void, and invalid, and an injunction to restrain the defendants from acting upon the resolution. The plaintiff moved for an injunction.

[The trial Judge, Stirling J., held, *inter alia*, that there had been no such irregularities in the meeting as to vitiate the resolution. The plaintiff appealed to the Court of Appeal.]

SIR NATHANIEL LINDLEY M.R.: . . . Then Mr. Cozens-Hardy raised various points of irregularity, which I shall dispose of very shortly, because I think they mostly are not points with which this Court has anything to do. The only new one is the point about the closure. It appears that there was a discussion about this matter at a meeting of shareholders of the Assets Company, and, after having heard the views — I do not say of all those who opposed, but of one or two of them — the meeting came to the conclusion that they had heard enough, and did not want to hear any more, and thereupon the chairman declared the discussion closed. That is said to be a matter calling for the interference of this Court. I do not think so. I think it would be a very bad precedent that we should interfere in such a case. I am aware of the importance of the observations made by Lord Eldon in *Const v. Harris*, in which he said, "I call that the act of all" (he was speaking of the meeting of large companies), "which is the act of the majority, provided all are consulted, and the majority are acting bona fide, meeting, not for the purpose of negativing, what any one may have to offer, but for the purpose of negativing, what, when they are met together, they may, after due consideration, think proper to negative: For a majority of partners to say, We do not care what one partner may say, we, being the majority, will do what we please, is, I apprehend, what this Court will not allow." I think that principle is as important, and, perhaps, more important, to bear in mind now than it was sixty or seventy years ago; but Lord Eldon does not mean that a minority who are bent on obstructing business and resolved on talking for ever should not be put down. He means that the majority are not to be tyrannical. After hearing what is to be said, they may say, "We have heard enough. We are not bound to listen till everybody is tired of talking and has sat down." There is no reason for supposing that there was any terrorism in this matter, and this appeal must be dismissed with costs.

CHITTY L.J.: As to the closure, I think if we laid down that the chairman, supported by a majority, could not put a termination to the speeches of those who were desirous of addressing the meeting, we should allow a small minority, or even a member or two, to tyrannize over the majority. The case has been put by Mr. Cozens-Hardy as the terrorism of the majority. If we accepted his proposition we should put his weapon into the hands of the minority, which might involve the company in all- night sittings. That seems to me to be an extravagant proposition, and in this particular case there seems to have been nothing arbitrary or vexatious on the part of the chairman or of the majority. I am not, of course, saying that the majority must not listen to reasonable arguments for a reasonable time. I will advert only to one other point, and must be excused for not going into the other "irregularities" which Mr. Cozens-Hardy has mentioned. He said that it was wrong of the chairman to refuse to put to the meeting, merely held for the confirmation of the original resolution passed by three-fourths of the proprietors, another resolution by way of amendment. His refusal, in my opinion, was right, because that meeting was called for one purpose only, and that was to confirm or reject the original resolution which had been passed, and any amendment would be wholly irrelevant, because the single purpose of the meeting was to say Aye or Nay, is the original resolution to stand or fall?

COLLINS L.J.: . . . I am of the same opinion.

Appeal Dismissed.

National Dwellings Society v. Sykes
[1894] 3 Ch. 159

[By the articles of the National Dwellings Society, the business of the society was to be managed by a council invested with all the usual powers of directors. The articles of the society provided that every general meeting would be led by a member of the council, but if one was not present, the members present could choose one of their own rank to preside. The articles also allowed any ordinary meeting to, without notice, receive the accounts, balance sheets, and reports of council and the auditors, and accept or reject them.

At the annual general meeting on April 12, 1894, the chair was taken by Sykes, a council member, who moved a resolution that the report and accounts be received. The resolution was put to a vote and defeated with six votes in favour and 28 against. Sykes declared the resolution lost, declared the meeting dissolved, and left the room with his supporters, though the election of directors and auditors had not been disposed of. The remaining members elected another chairman and passed a resolution to adjourn the meeting for six weeks. At that meeting, unattended by Sykes, an investigation committee was appointed to look into the society's affairs. The committee commenced an action against the council. At issue in the case was the legality of Sykes' conduct as chairman of the April 12 meeting.]

CHITTY J.: A question of some importance has been mooted in this case, with regard to the powers of the chairman over a meeting. Unquestionably it is the duty of the chairman, and his function, to preserve order, and to take care that the proceedings are conducted in a proper manner, and that the sense of the meeting is properly ascertained with regard to any question which is properly before the meeting. But, in my opinion, the power which has been contended for is not within the scope of the authority of the chairman — namely, to stop the meeting at his own will and pleasure. The meeting is called for the particular purposes of the company. According to the constitution of the company, a certain officer has to preside. He presides with reference to the business which is there to be transacted. In my opinion, he cannot say, after that business has been opened, "I will have no more to do with it; I will not let this meeting proceed; I will stop it; I declare the meeting dissolved, and I leave the chair." In my opinion, that is not within his power. The meeting by itself (and these articles certainly apply to what I have said) can resolve to go on with the business for which it has been convened, and appoint a chairman to conduct the business which the other chairman, forgetful of his duty or violating his duty, has tried to stop because the proceedings have taken a turn which he himself does not like. I think perhaps what I have said is sufficient for the present purpose, and I need say no more except that the other questions raised by this application will stand adjourned till after the general meeting has been held as arranged.

Notes

1 Subsection 137(1)(b) of the CBCA and s. 99(1)(b) of the OBCA now provide for a shareholder right of discussion. The CBCA provides that: "A shareholder entitled to vote at an annual meeting of shareholders may (b) discuss at the meeting any matter in respect of which he would have been entitled to submit a proposal." This section thus statutorily enshrines a right of discussion only at annual meetings. By contrast, the OBCA extends such right to every shareholder "entitled to vote at a meeting of shareholders", thus including special as well as annual meetings. Does the CBCA provision exclude by implication a right of discussion at special meetings? Or is there a common law right of discussion? If so, does the common law right allow the shareholder to discuss the same range of matters as the statute provides in respect of an annual meeting?

2 Note that the CBCA and OBCA extend the right of discussion to any shareholder entitled to vote at a meeting. A shareholder may be so entitled because the shareholder holds voting shares. As we saw in the preceding section, the statutes may also create an entitlement to vote, either in a group with other classes of shareholders or separately as a class, whether or not the shares normally carry the right to vote. If these statutory provisions are not called into play, however, there is nothing in the corporate legislation that gives the non-voting shareholders a

right either to attend shareholders' meetings or to ask questions. Out of a concern that the voice of non-voting (or restricted voting) shareholders should be heard, the Ontario Securities Commission has issued Rule 56-501 and the TSX has issued Policy 3.5 that require that "reporting issuers" (public corporations) send non-voting shareholders all material sent to voting shareholders in connection with meetings, to allow these shareholders to attend shareholders' meetings and to ask questions.

3 An Ontario case arising under the CBCA followed the holding in the *National Dwelling Society* case and reaffirmed the right of shareholders to be heard at an annual shareholders' meeting, without discussion of s. 137. In *Re Bomac Batten Ltd. and Pozhke* (1983), 43 O.R. (2d) 344 (Ont. H.C.) the chairman (Pozhke) had ruled that a proxy deposited with the company was invalid because the shareholder, a partnership, had not complied with the corporate by-law requiring that a proxy be "authorized by a resolution of the board of directors or governing body of the body corporate or association . . ." He then ruled that, because of the invalidity of the proxy, there was no quorum present at the shareholders' meeting and declared the meeting adjourned. The prox-yholder whose proxies were declared invalid immediately protested, requesting that the validity of the proxies be discussed, asserting that the partnership was not an "association" within the by-laws, and rep-resenting that if a resolution was necessary it had in fact been passed. The chairman refused to entertain any discussion and left the meeting. The remaining shareholders present elected a new chairman who ac-cepted the proxies in question; the meeting then proceeded to elect a new board of directors. The newly elected board of directors sought (*inter alia*) a declaration from the court that the meeting had been improperly adjourned, that the proxies were valid, and that the new board was validly elected. Cromarty J. found that a partnership of the character in question was not a "body corporate" or "association", and hence the by-law in question did not apply, and the proxies were valid. He also held that the meeting had been improperly adjourned, that the shareholders had properly continued the meeting, and that the new board of directors was validly elected. In the course of his judgment, he stated:

> In *Gray v. Yellowknife Gold Mines Ltd. et al.*, [1946] O.W.N. 938, Mr. Lennox, the learned Assistant Master of the Supreme Court who had been directed by the Court of Appeal to ascertain "who are the duly elected directors of Yellowknife Gold Mines Ltd. at present holding office", said of the chairman of a meeting at p. 942:
>
> > Mr. Gale classifies the position of chairman as quasi-judicial. That may be placing the standard too high when matters in which the chairman is actually interested are being debated but in the exercise of the discretion vested in him, and in making rulings in the course of his conduct of the meeting, the position at least

approximates that of a person occupying a quasijudicial position. Due, no doubt, to the high standard required of a chairman, he is afforded some protection in the performance of his duty.

and at p. 945:

The principle upon which the decisions are based is that a chairman should not be permitted to defeat the purpose for which the meeting was called by stopping the meeting or clogging the procedure provided for the transaction of the business before the meeting.

Mr. Pozhke failed in his duty to act quasi-judicially since it is a fundamental error by a presiding officer to fail to hear both sides of an argument before coming to a conclusion. He also failed in duty in leaving a meeting with a quorum present.

The Ontario courts were given a chance to revisit these issues in a series of cases involving litigation between Michael Blair and Canadian Express Limited (a member of the Bronfman group of companies). The facts were as follows. Blair was a director, chief executive officer and substantial shareholder in Consolidated Enfield Corporation ("Enfield"). Canadian Express was the largest shareholder in Enfield, and in the months leading up to the annual shareholders' meeting, considerable tension had developed between Blair and Canadian Express. Nonetheless, Canadian Express had indicated that it would support management's slate of nominees for director, including Blair, at the meeting. Fearing that Canadian Express might change its mind, Blair consulted Enfield's lawyers on the night before the meeting with a view to determining what he should do if a nomination for directors was made from the floor. He was told that Canadian Express had used the form of proxy sent to shareholders by management, and that because of a note on the back of the form of proxy, the form of proxy gave the proxyholders no discretion to vote for candidates other than the management slate. Just before the annual meeting, Canadian Express did indeed change its mind and decided to nominate Timothy Price as a director, rather than Blair. The Canadian Express proxyholders voted for Price. Had their votes been counted, there would have been enough votes to elect Price in Blair's stead. As Chairman of the meeting, however, Blair again consulted with Enfield's lawyers, who again advised him that the proxies could only be voted for the management slate of directors. Blair then returned to the floor, indicated that a number of proxies had been held invalid, and declared the management slate of directors elected. When a representative of Canadian Express indicated that he wished to be heard, Blair declined to give him the floor. Canadian Express subsequently sued both Blair and Enfield seeking a declaration that Price, and not Blair, had been validly elected as a director. In *Canadian Express Ltd. v. Blair* (1989), 46 B.L.R. 92 (Ont. H.C.),

Holland J. held that on the proper construction of the proxies, they had been properly voted for Price. In so holding, he stated that:

> In coming to this conclusion, I have accepted the evidence of Professor Crête, recognized by both sides as a leading authority in this country on proxies, which evidence dealt with the policies underlying the proxy solicitation process and particularly the importance of enabling shareholders to freely exercise their voting rights in accordance with their intentions. I have also accepted the evidence of King, DaCosta and Norris as establishing a generally accepted industry practice and particularly their evidence that shareholder designees who hold blank proxies as here submitted are recognized as having full discretion to vote as they see fit, just as the shareholders in person at the meeting could vote . . . There is no doubt on the evidence that the proxyholders intended to and did cast their votes for Price and not for Blair.

Holland J. also held that Canadian Express's challenge succeeded because Blair had failed to meet the quasi-judicial standard of behavior expected of the Chair of the meeting:

> In any event, I find that Blair failed to meet the quasi-judicial standard of conduct demanded of a Chairman: *Re Bomac Batten Ltd. and Pozhke et al.* (1983), 43 O.R. (2d) 344 (H.C.) . . . Based on the evidence as to the completion and filing of the disputed proxies and the events leading up to the July 20th meeting, which included the meeting on July 19 attended by Blair, the scrutineers and counsel for Enfield, the exchange at the directors' meeting on July 20th in the morning and the nomination of Price from the floor, it can be reasonably inferred that Blair was alerted to the fact that the election of directors would be contentious and that he was likely to be in a position of conflict. It took approximately 1 1/2 hours after the balloting until Blair reconvened the meeting to announce the results of the balloting. At that time, Blair, reading from a statement prepared by his legal advisors, stated that Price had received no votes and that he, Blair, had been elected. This, I am satisfied, was in accordance with the plan conceived by Blair to protect his personal interests.

Holland J. also held that Blair had failed to accord dissenting shareholders the right to be heard following his ruling on the validity of the proxies:

> At the very least, he had an obligation to allow those affected by his ruling on the disputed ballots an opportunity to be heard. He chose to act as judge in his own cause and it is properly inferred from the evidence that he had determined to act in this way, at least at the time of the July 19th meeting, and, until the announcement of the voting results. In view of Blair's conduct alone and quite apart from the true construction of the proxies, his ruling cannot stand.

He held that reliance on legal advice was no excuse, holding that "it was his responsibility to conduct himself quasi-judicially throughout the proceedings. Holland J. awarded costs jointly and severally against Blair and Enfield. Canadian Express, however, now had control of Enfield, and decided to collect the costs (of about $165,000) solely from Blair. Blair then requested Enfield to indemnify him as to costs. When Enfield refused, Blair sued. In *Blair v. Consolidated Enfield Corp.*, unreported, Ont. Gen. Div., October 28, 1992, Carruthers J. held that Blair was not entitled to an indemnity under s.136 of the OBCA (nor under the similarly worded by-law of Enfield). He held that, whether or not Blair had acted in good faith, he had not acted in the best interests of Enfield in defending the litigation begun by Canadian Express. The following is the appeal from this judgment. Although the central issue is the entitlement to an indemnity, this turns on the propriety of Blair's conduct as Chairman of the shareholders' meeting.

Blair v. Consolidated Enfield Corp.
(1993), 15 O.R. (3d) 783, 1993 CarswellOnt 165 (C.A.), affirmed [1995] 4 S.C.R. 5

CARTHY J.A.: [Carthy J.A. reviewed the facts, as recounted above, and continued:]

The single issue before this court is the proper application to the facts of the company by-law which grants rights of indemnity in the terms authorized by s. 136(1) of the Ontario *Business Corporations Act*. I will refer throughout to the Act because the by-law of the company reads to the same effect.

[Carthy J.A. then quoted s. 136 of the OBCA. He also noted that the trial judge in this proceeding, Carruthers J., had concluded that Blair could not be acting in the best interests of Enfield in defending the litigation against him unless it could be shown that he was a better director than the director who replaced him. Addressing this last point, Carthy J.A. stated:]

There are implicit errors in this reasoning. First, the best interest of the corporation in this case centres not upon the choice of particular directors, but upon the integrity of the voting procedure and the validity of corporate acts of the directors following the vote. The company is in the hands of its voting shareholders to choose the persons to manage it. The sole interest of Enfield in the election of directors, and the sole proper concern of those advising and representing it, was to be assured of the propriety of the procedure. Second, it is in the interest of a corporation to defend its corporate acts, if defence is justified, for the same reason that it is concerned with the validity of those acts when performed. Finally, I read s. 136(1)(a) and the language "acted . . . with a view to the best interests of the corporation" as referring back to, in this case, the conduct of the vote for directors — not to the conduct of the litigation. The litigation that is contemplated by s.

136(1)(a) is against the director personally and the indemnity is against personal liability. There is no purpose in a requirement that personal litigation be conducted in the best interests of the corporation. The costs of litigation are dealt with separately in s. 136(1) and must be "reasonably incurred".

[Carthy J.A. reviewed the events leading up to the shareholders' meeting of Enfield giving rise to this litigation. These events showed that serious animosity and mistrust had arisen between Blair and Canadian Express, which was the largest single shareholder in Enfield. He held that these events could not be determinative of the issue of Blair's good faith; at best, they supplied a "motive for improper conduct at the meeting," a motive which existed even without reference to these preceding events given that Blair's tenure with the company was at stake at the meeting. He then reviewed what had taken place at the meeting, and noted that Canadian Express's nominee had not been given the opportunity to speak following the vote for directors and declaration that Canadian Express's proxies had been ruled invalid. He continued:]

[T]he respondent says that if Blair had been acting in a *bona fide* fashion in keeping with his quasi-judicial duties as chairman he would, once it was recognized that a "mistake" had been made, have given Walt and Boultbee [the representatives of Canadian Express] an opportunity to correct the proxies or, at least, give them an opportunity to make representations concerning the interpretation with another disinterested chairperson appointed to make a ruling. Blair's answer is that he asked indisputably competent lawyers to advise him in the broadest of terms, and he followed their advice. Further, he argues that the vote had been taken and the chairman owed a duty to all shareholders to rule upon its legal effect. Nor could he simply accept the word of the proxyholder that the shareholder intended to proffer an open discretion and that a mistake had been made in filling out the proxies. While Walt, as president of Canadian Express, could speak for the company, Boultbee could not speak for the shareholders he represented and thus, given the legal opinion, he would be countermanding their written instructions.

Issue

Should Carruthers J. have held that Blair satisfied the onus of bringing himself within the language of s. 136 of the Ontario *Business Corporations Act*? Has he demonstrated that on July 20 he acted honestly and in good faith with a view to the best interests of the corporation?

Good Faith Reliance on Legal Advice

At issue is his ruling on the overall balloting, and to conclude that his ruling was *male fide* because the result favoured him is to conclude that he was compelled to rule the other way, or give up the chair, no matter what advice he received. Aside from the question of giving up the chair, the real test should be whether the ruling was made with the *bona fide* intent that the company have a lawfully elected board of directors.

There is thus little guidance in the Canadian authorities on the extent to which legal advice affects the assessment of good faith conduct. Nor have we been directed to any settled views expressed in other jurisdictions. I have already concluded that, on a proper reading of ss. 130 to 136 of the Ontario *Business Corporations Act*, legal advice does not automatically sanctify conduct based upon it as honest and in good faith for purposes of claiming indemnity under s. 136. It is, however, an ingredient to be considered and one should not be dismissive of it simply because it favours the election of the chairperson or, as in many such situations, because it comes from a law firm whose own retainer is at stake. It must be considered in the context in which it was given and alongside the duty of the chairperson to act fairly.

The authorities referred to above generally describe the chairperson's duty as quasi-judicial without defining what that means in this context. It is confusing to me to use, and seek to define, the word judicial or quasi-judicial in this context because an adjudicator or judge can never have a personal interest in the issue. A chairperson who is more than a nominal shareholder of a public company, on the other hand, always has a personal interest in everything that affects the company, which includes all of the rulings of the chair. If that distinction is not recognized the reflex reaction is to assume that a decision which benefits the chair personally is non-judicial and thus not *bona fide*. In my view, it is preferable to describe the duty as one of honesty and fairness to all individual interests, and directed generally toward the best interests of the company.

The events that lead up to the meeting of July 20 created an aggressively competitive atmosphere. Blair felt very strongly that the shareholders as a whole should be fully informed of a change in control. He undoubtedly resented the surprise nomination of Price and was pleased with Osler's advice. That makes him very much a protagonist in the duel for control. However, that is the position of any chairperson dependent for his position upon proxy support and threatened by contrary votes.

The ballots cast were in accordance with the instructions in the proxies or they were not. An experienced team of lawyers gave an opinion the evening before and, broadening their inquiries to even more lawyers when the event occurred, they remained of the same view. They also told Blair that it was his duty to make the ruling despite his interest in the outcome. Following this sequence of events I do not see that he had a choice. It would have appeared more fair if he had not closed debate, but the result could not have been different. If lawyers for Canadian Express had expressed a contrary view, he would then have two opinions on a complicated legal problem. Given the necessity of determining who the legal directors of the company were, so that business could be carried on in a regular fashion, some decision had to be made. Even if a disinterested chairperson could have been found in the room, he or she would, in these circumstances, have had to look to the corporation's solicitors for an answer to this purely legal issue of interpretation.

Counsel for Canadian Express focused on the lack of fairness shown by Blair in knowing that a mistake had been made and giving no opportunity to correct it. They argue that when the nomination of Price was made from the floor that Blair, in fairness, should have alerted Walt and Boultbee that they would not be able to vote for Price. Presumably, Walt would then have executed a new proxy on behalf of Canadian Express but Boultbee would have had to return to the shareholders he represented to obtain new proxies, on the assumption that it would be their desire to change them. It must be remembered that there is another faction deserving fairness from the chairman — the 15 per cent of shareholders who decided not to be represented on the basis of what they read in the management information circular, or for whatever other reason. If the meeting was to be adjourned to accommodate Walt and Boultbee, should these shareholders not be informed that a battle for control was on and that their votes could determine the result? In my view it goes too far to say that the duty of fairness means that Blair must selectively assist those who attend to vote in the process leading to the vote. His duty of fairness relates to the decision-making process and the conduct of a proper corporate meeting. His taunting remark to Timothy Price did not distinguish him, but I am satisfied that the evidence shows that he properly performed his duty as chairman of the meeting.

The Conduct of the Litigation

The respondent relies on *Balestreri v. Robert*, [1985] Que. S.C. 1038, 30 B.L.R. 283, affirmed March 30, 1992 by the Quebec Court of Appeal, for the proposition that Blair disentitled himself to indemnification by not pursuing the litigation in good faith. That case was dealing with a similar by-law under the federal counterpart of the Ontario *Business Corporations Act* and the court found that a director's participation in an inquiry into the affairs of a corporation was not conducted in good faith. The director's participation was found to be solely directed to obstructionism on behalf of a large shareholder, and thus it was held that indemnity should be denied.

As I said earlier when dealing with the reasons of Carruthers J., on my reading of the Ontario *Business Corporations Act*, good faith is related to the ruling on July 20 and the expenses of the litigation are limited by s. 136(1) to those which are reasonably incurred. To the extent that my reasoning differs from that in *Balestreri*, there is no difference in the result. Litigation that is pursued in bad faith is not likely to involve "reasonably incurred" expenses. My analysis will be as to whether Blair acted reasonably in his defence of the litigation.

[Carthy J.A. found that Blair J. had acted reasonably in defending the litigation. Indeed, on July 24 he had requisitioned a shareholders' meeting to conduct a fresh election for directors.]

Blair added nothing to the costs of the proceedings, his requisition of an annual meeting made it possible for the board to hold one before the litigation reached the courtroom, and his conduct was consistent with his protestations throughout that he had no interest in leading the company if voted out by a majority of informed shareholders. That was precisely the challenge in the requisition of July 24.

In conclusion, I would allow the appeal, set aside the dismissal of the application, and in its place grant judgment against Enfield requiring it to indemnify Blair for any costs payable by Blair to Canadian Express arising out of application No. RE1730/89 and requiring it to pay Blair the amount of costs he incurred in contesting the assessment of costs in that litigation. If the amount is contested those costs are to be assessed.

The costs of this appeal and of the application before Carruthers J. should be paid by the respondent to the appellant forthwith after assessment.

Appeal allowed.

Questions

1 Given that the Court of Appeal did not overrule Holland J.'s judgment that Price was elected director rather than Blair, what is the status of Holland J.'s finding that Blair had failed to meet the quasi-judicial standard of behavior expected of him?

2 Whose reasoning do you prefer on the issue of Blair's conduct? That of Holland J. and Carruthers J. or that of the Court of Appeal?

(e) Shareholder Proposals

Normally, matters like nominations for directors, proposed changes to the company's articles and by-laws, and proposals relating to other matters (like the adoption of fundamental changes) originate with the managers of the corporation. Certainly in larger public companies, most shareholders are entirely divorced from the management of the company and content to leave matters in the hands of the professional managers.

Out of a concern to foster shareholder democracy, however (see *Proposals for a New Business Corporations Law for Canada*, Vol. 1, Ottawa, 1971, paras. 273–279), the CBCA (and provincial acts, see below) allows shareholders to make proposals to be considered at shareholders' meetings (CBCA s. 137, OBCA s. 99, BCBCA s. 188).

There are four categories of proposals that a shareholder might make. First, shareholders may make a proposal that the articles be amended (CBCA ss. 175(1), OBCA ss. 169(1)); second, that a by-law be made, amended or repealed (CBCA s. 103(5), OBCA s. 116(5)); third, shareholders holding at least 5% of the shares or 5% of a class of voting shares may make nominations for the election of directors (CBCA s. 137(4), OBCA s. 99(4)). The last category is a residual category of somewhat uncertain dimensions. Broadly speaking, if the proposal does not relate to the business or affairs of the corporation, the managers may refuse to circulate it Thus, the fourth category consists of those proposals that fall outside of this limit (and that do not run afoul of the more technical limitations in CBCA s. 137(5),OBCA s. 99(5)). The proposal is circulated at the corporation's expense with the management proxy circular; the shareholder may also request that management circulate a supporting statement of not more than 200 words under the OBCA (s. 199), 500 words under the CBCA (Regulations s. 49), and 1000 words under the BCBCA (s. 188).

The CBCA's shareholder proposals provisions were reformed in 2001. The changes were influenced by two major cases arising out of the similar shareholder proposals sections of the *Bank Act*: *Verdun v. Toronto Dominion Bank*, [1996] 3 S.C.R. 550; and *Michaud c. Banque Nationale du Canada*, [1997] R.J.Q. 547 (Que.S.C.), both of which will be discussed below. Proposals may be made by registered or beneficial shareholders. To be eligible to submit a proposal, a shareholder must continuously hold a prescribed minimum number of shares for a prescribed amount of time before submitting a proposal. The current requirement is a six-month hold period on shares worth $2,000 or comprising 1% of the total number of outstanding voting shares, whichever is less (CBCR s. 47). Support from other shareholders can be counted toward meeting these eligibility requirements (CBCA s. 137(1.1)(b)). The corporation has the right to demand proof that the shareholder meets the eligibility requirements (s. 137(1.4)), which may be necessary if a beneficial shareholder is making the proposal.

Management must circulate a shareholder proposal to shareholders, except in certain circumstances where they may refuse to do so. While the CBCA previously allowed management to refuse to circulate a proposal that was "primarily for the purpose of promoting general economic, political, racial, religious, social or similar causes" (old s. 137(5)(b)), the CBCA now uses much more general wording, allowing management to omit a proposal that "does not relate in a significant way to the business or affairs of the corporation". Does the latter formulation give management and/or the court a freer hand in defining what shareholders may include in a proposal, given the comparative vagueness of the "business or affairs of the corporation"? If the phrase is defined narrowly to mean only those matters relating to corporate profitability (in conformity with cases like *Dodge v. Ford* and *Parke v. Daily News*, considered earlier in Chapter 4) then perhaps there is little difference in the scope of the exception between the old CBCA provision and the new one. But if a broader meaning is accepted (as per

Berger J. in *obiter* in the *Teck* case, *supra*, Chapter 6) then might the new CBCA provision permit shareholder proposals that the prior CBCA provision would not have?

One question that arises in connection with shareholder proposals is the effect of the proposal. Is it binding on management? Is it merely a recommendation to management? This question must be examined separately in relation to the four categories of shareholder proposals. The answer is straightforward in relation to nominations for the election of directors. A nomination for the election of directors is simply that — nothing more and nothing less.

In relation to a proposal to change the by-laws, the OBCA explicitly answers the question of the effect of the proposal in s. 116(5), by indicating that: "If a shareholder proposal to make, amend or repeal a by-law is made in accordance with section 99 and is adopted by shareholders at a meeting, the by-law, amendment or repeal is effective from the date of its adoption and requires no further confirmation." The OBCA contains no such provision in relation to a shareholder proposal to change the articles (see s. 169(1)). Does this mean that such a proposal has no binding effect? If so, it would be a curious result: the directors, if they concurred in the recommendation, would presumably then have to convene another shareholders' meeting at which a second vote would be taken to actually pass the change to the articles. The reason for the difference in drafting appears to be because s. 116(3) requires shareholder confirmation of a by-law where initiated by a director. In other words, the wording of s. 116(5) is designed merely to emphasize that no shareholder confirmation of a by-law is necessary where the by-law initiates with shareholders as a proposal (rather than with the directors) and the proposal is passed by the shareholders. Moreover, s. 169(2) suggests by implication that if the proposal is passed, it is effective; otherwise, no dissent right would arise, and notice about such right would be unnecessary.

The CBCA does not deal explicitly with the effect of a shareholder proposal relating to the articles either. Again, however, it would seem rather curious if the proposal, duly passed by a resolution of shareholders, were merely a recommendation to management rather than a completed act. You might note that the predecessor statute to the CBCA (the *Canada Corporations Act*, R.S.C. 1970, c. C-32, s. 13(6)) required all amendments to the articles to begin with a directors' resolution. The CBCA omits this requirement (as does the OBCA) suggesting the no directors' resolution is necessary to complete a change in the articles. Further, in the case of an amendment to the articles, s. 175(2) of the CBCA suggests by clear implication that a properly passed proposal to amend the articles is binding.

Perhaps the greatest difficulties arise in connection with determining the effect of a proposal failing in the fourth category. Both the CBCA (s. 102) and the OBCA (s. 115) give the directors the power to manage (or, in the OBCA, to supervise the management of) the corporation. If a shareholder made a proposal to amalgamate the corporation with another corporation, and this was passed by a special resolution (as required to effect an amalgamation), would that trench on the authority of the directors to manage the corporation if it were considered binding? Or, if a shareholder made a proposal to discontinue the manufacture of a certain product (as in the *Medical Committee* case, briefly recounted, *infra*) would that be an impermissible interference with the power to manage and would the proposal therefore assume the status of a recommendation only? What it is that is encompassed within the power to manage is not entirely self-defining. In the normal course of events, the directors (and their appointed managers) will make a decision to amalgamate, and will then submit this decision to shareholders for approval. Thus, the decision to amalgamate will involve activity that would normally be considered to fall within management's prerogative to manage as well as the exercise of shareholder powers of approval. A decision to abandon a particular product would appear to more clearly fall within the exclusive domain of management decision-making. What in your view is the effect of a shareholder proposal in each of these cases? Could it perhaps even be argued that, because these matters fall within management's domain, management would be justified in refusing to entertain the proposal?

Should there be a requirement for management to report on any follow-up action it has taken in relation to a proposal that was approved by a majority of shareholders?

Notes

1 The American framework governing shareholder proposals in publicly traded companies is set out in Rule 14-a8 of the *Securities Exchange Act* of 1934. As in Canada, a shareholder may deliver a proposal and request that management circulate it in the corporation's proxy materials. There are 13 grounds under which management may refuse to circulate a shareholder proposal. A proposal can be refused, for example, on procedural grounds, for dealing with the ordinary business operations of the corporation, for relating to the election to an office or for being motivated by general political and moral concerns. If management refuses a shareholder proposal, it must notify the shareholder and the SEC and provide reasons for the refusal. If the SEC rules that the refusal is unjustified, it will send a letter recommending that the proposal be included in the proxy materials. To obtain a legally binding ruling, a shareholder must commence an action in the courts or appeal to the SEC for a decision binding the corporation.

   Medical Committee for Human Rights v. SEC, 139 U.S. App. D.C. 226, 432 F.2d 659 (D.C., 1970), deals with management's right to refuse to circulate a shareholder proposal on the ground that it deals with the ordinary business of the corporation. The Medical Committee for Human Rights wrote to the Board of Dow Chemical Company requesting that it include a proposal in the corporation's proxy materials. The proposal was to the effect that Dow stop selling napalm to buyers who could not give reasonable assurance that it would not be used on human beings. Dow refused to include this proposal in the 1968 proxy statement on the ground that it had arrived too late, and again refused to include it in the 1969 proxy statement, on the grounds that it was motivated by general political and moral concerns and related to the conduct of Dow's ordinary business operations. The SEC agreed with Dow's position, and the Medical Committee initiated an action to force the SEC to reconsider its claim and furnish adequate reasons for its decision. Tamm C.J., said:

> The management of Dow Chemical Company is repeatedly quoted in sources which include the company's own publications as proclaiming that the decision to continue manufacturing and marketing napalm was made not because of business considerations but in spite of them; that management in essence decided to pursue a course of activity which generated little profit for the shareholders and actively impaired the company's public relations and recruitment activities because management considered this action morally and politically desirable. (App. 40a-43a; see also *id.* at 33.) The proper political and social role of modern corporations is, of course, a matter of philosophical argument extending far beyond the scope of our present concern; the substantive wisdom or propriety of particular corporate political decisions is also completely irrelevant to the resolution of the present controversy. What is of immediate concern, however, is the question of whether the corporate proxy rules can be employed as a shield to isolate such managerial decisions from shareholder control. After all, it must be remembered that "[t]he control of great corporations by a very few persons was the abuse at which Congress struck in enacting Section 14(a)." *SEC v. Transamerica Corp., supra.* We think that there is a clear and compelling distinction between management's legitimate need for freedom to apply its expertise in matters of day-to-day business judgment, and management's patently illegitimate claim of power to treat modern corporations with their vast resources as personal satrapies implementing personal political or moral predilections. It could scarcely be argued that management is more qualified or more entitled to make these kinds of decisions than the shareholders who are the true beneficial owners of the corporation; and it seems equally implausible that an application of the proxy rules which permitted such a result could be harmonized with the philosophy of corporate democracy which Congress embodied in section 14(a) of the *Securities Exchange Act* of 1934.

Note that the result of this case was not an order that the company circulate the proposal, but rather that the SEC reconsider the petitioner's claim and furnish adequate reasons for its decision. As such, the holding in the Medical Committee case can be interpreted as somewhat less far reaching than might at first appear.

Is the holding consistent with holdings in cases like *Dodge v. Ford* (*supra*, Chapter 4)? Is it consistent with the purpose and intention of the SEC regulation in question?

Varity Corp. v. Jesuit Fathers of Upper Canada
(1987), 59 O.R. (2d) 459, 1987 CarswellOnt 145 (H.C.), affirmed (1987),
60 O.R. (2d) 640, 1987 CarswellOnt 2264 (C.A.)

AUSTIN J.: This is an application by Varity Corporation, formerly Massey-Ferguson, for an order permitting Varity not to include in its mailing to shareholders for the annual general meeting, a proposal that the company end its investments in South Africa.

The proposal is put forward by two shareholders, the Jesuit Fathers of Upper Canada and the Ursuline Religious of the Diocese of London in Ontario.

Varity is a federal company. Section 131 of the Canada *Business Corporations Act*, S.C. 1974-75, c. 33 [now s. 137], applies, and it provides that the shareholders may require the company to circulate proposals and supporting statements. There are exceptions based on shareholder status, timing, and content. Varity admits that these shareholders have status, no issue was raised as to timing, and the only objection raised involved the content of the proposal.

The proposal reads as follows:

WHEREAS the Commonwealth Eminent Persons Group concluded in June 1986 that the South African government was not prepared to negotiate the dismantling of apartheid, and that economic measures to compel change "may offer the last opportunity to avert what could be the worst bloodbath since the Second World War";

WHEREAS the South African Council of Churches, and the Confederation of South African Trade Unions (COSATU), as well as black leaders such as Bishop Desmond Tutu, now support the call for disinvestment by foreign enterprises from South Africa in an effort to achieve peaceful elimination of apartheid;

WHEREAS many corporations have concluded that their social programs to improve the lives of blacks within and outside the workplace no longer justify the continued presence of foreign investment within the persisting structure of apartheid; and the author of the U.S. Sullivan Code of Conduct for companies in South Africa, the Rev. Leon Sullivan, has called for disinvestment if apartheid is not dismantled by May, 1987;

WHEREAS present conditions in South Africa make continued viable economic investments risky;

WHEREAS Varity Corporation has an 18.95% investment in Fedmech Holdings Limited, a South African corporation, which produces farm implements, tractors and accessories, harvesting machinery, trailers, industrial loaders and transport systems;

WHEREAS Varity, through its subsidiary Perkins Diesel Engines (UK), has a license agreement for the production of diesel engines with Atlantis Diesel Engines Co. (ADE), established by the South African government to ensure South African self-sufficiency in diesel engines for agricultural, commercial and military needs;

WHEREAS Varity recently argued before the Parliamentary Standing Committee on Human Rights that it is "a positive force for peaceful progress" in South Africa, but at the same time

— cited its lack of decision-making power as a minority shareholder in responding to questions about sub-standard wages paid for a period of time at Fedmech;

— revealed that it had terminated donations to assist black South African development in 1983 because of "hard times",

— reported that the declared policy of Atlantis Diesel Engines (ADE) is "completely nondiscriminatory", when in fact ADE is located in a "coloured only" area and employs no blacks;

WHEREAS Varity has been unable to make any commitment that the equipment that it assists in producing in South Africa will not be used by government agencies in the enforcement of apartheid laws;

WHEREAS Varity's license agreement with Atlantis Diesel Engines (ADE) involves it in an industry of sufficient strategic importance to the South African government that ADE has been declared a Key Point Industry, which by order of the Minister of Defence must establish a private plant-based militia, subject to government takeover in the event of civil unrest;

THEREFORE BE IT RESOLVED that the shareholders ask the Board of Directors to:

— take immediate steps to terminate Varity's investments in South Africa;

— take immediate steps to terminate Varity's license agreement with Atlantis Diesel Engines, and if there are legal obstacles, provide a report and a plan of action to the shareholders within ninety days;

— announce publicly to the South African government Varity's plans to leave South Africa as soon as possible.

In support of that proposal is a "supporting statement" which reads as follows:

> Varity Corporation is among Canada's largest transnational corporations. As a result of refinancing assistance to the company, the Government of Canada and the Government of Ontario are among its shareholders. Thus, the presence of Varity in South Africa is of particular significance, since it represents an investment by Canadian taxpayers in South Africa.
>
> We believe that a meaningful process of disinvestment involves the termination of all business which might provide support to the South African government, including sales and technology transfers. A meaningful process of disinvestment should also include the provision of full information to representatives of black workers, and consultation with them about the terms of withdrawal. In addition, in consultation with the workers and other anti-apartheid groups, the Company should establish, or continue, corporate financial contributions to projects for the enhancement of black welfare and in support of anti-apartheid activities.

Section 131(5)(b) of the Act provides that a corporation is not required to comply with a shareholder's request if

> (b) it clearly appears that the proposal is submitted by the shareholder primarily for the purpose of enforcing a personal claim or redressing a personal grievance against the corporation or its directors, officers or security holders, or primarily for the purpose of promoting general economic, political, racial, religious, social or similar causes . . .

Varity applies for exemption from the mailing requirement upon the basis that the proposal has been submitted primarily for the purpose of promoting general economic, political, racial, religious, social, or similar causes and in particular the abolition of apartheid in South Africa.

The application was opposed by the Jesuit Fathers and the Ursuline Religious. Their position was that:

(a) the onus was on the applicant;

(b) apartheid is not only socially and morally wrong, it contributes to the maintenance of an unstable and undesirable business climate from which Varity should withdraw;

(c) most shareholders of companies such as Varity do not attend company meetings, so one of the obstacles to reaching and activating shareholders is the cost of communication;

(d) s. 131 was designed to permit shareholders to communicate with other shareholders on matters concerning the company at the company's expense;

(e) to succeed, the applicant has to persuade the court that the proposal was submitted primarily for the purpose of promoting general economic, political, racial, religious, social, or similar causes;

(f) the present proposal relates not to any such general purpose but to the specific business affairs of Varity in South Africa.

I agree with propositions (a) through (e). In so far as (f) is concerned, the respondents point out that their resolution is directed at Varity's involvement in South Africa and that their desire is to have Varity terminate that involvement. They argue that this is a specific goal or purpose and that while it may be an economic, political, racial, religious, or social purpose, it remains specific and accordingly does not fall within the reach of s. 131(5)(b).

I agree that the proposal has a specific purpose and that that purpose is directly relevant to Varity. It is argued that because of this, s. 131(5)(b) has no application even if the respondents have as their general over-all goal the abolition of apartheid in South Africa. It is argued that if s. 131(5)(b) were to apply, it would prevent the taking of the first step towards that goal.

The language of the proposal and the supporting statement leave me in no doubt that the primary purpose of the proposal is the abolition of apartheid in South Africa. As I read the legislation, the fact that there may be a more specific purpose or target does not save the proposal. That more specific purpose here is the withdrawal of Varity. The legislation makes it clear that if the primary purpose is one of those listed, however commendable either the specific or the general purpose may be, the company cannot be compelled to pay for taking the first step towards achieving it. In other words, the company cannot be compelled to distribute the proposal.

In my view, the applicant is entitled to the order asked for. It indicated at the outset that it would not ask for costs in any event so I make no order as to costs.

Order accordingly.

Notes and Questions

1 Did the Court pay adequate attention to the assertion in the Jesuit Fathers' proposal (an assertion accepted as fact by the Court) that apartheid results in an "unstable and undesirable business climate . . ."? If the Jesuit Fathers had framed their proposal around this single assertion, would (or should) the company have failed in its attempt to omit the proposal? Would the result be any different under the new CBCA provision?

2 Note that the Court puts the onus of proof on the "applicant" to make out its case. In this case, the company was applying for an order to omit

the proposal from the management proxy circular, pursuant to what is now CBCA s. 137(9). But suppose the company had simply decided to omit the proposal and the Jesuit Fathers had sought an order under s. 137(8) that the proposal be included in the management proxy circular. Would the onus of proof still be on the "applicant" (i.e., the Jesuit Fathers)? Would (or should) it be on the company? Does it make any sense to shift the onus of proof depending on who makes the application?

3 In *Greenpeace Foundation of Canada v. Inco Ltd.* (February 23, 1984), Montgomery J., [1984] O.J. No. 274 (H.C.), a proposal was submitted to limit sulphur dioxide emissions at Inco's Sudbury operations to 274 tonnes per day. Inco refused to circulate the proposal, leading Greenpeace to apply to the court. The court rejected Greenpeace's application, in part because a proposal to reduce emissions to 43 tonnes per day had been voted on the previous year and had only received 1.6% of the votes cast. The court found these proposals to be substantially the same, thus running afoul of OBCA section 99(5)(d). Almost unquestionably the earlier proposal, involving a much more drastic reduction in sulphur dioxide emissions, would be much more costly for the company to implement. If you were a shareholder voting on these proposals, would you regard them as interchangeable, especially considering this undoubted difference in cost?

4 An important recent shareholder proposal case in Canada is *Michaud c. Banque nationale du Canada*, [1997] R.J.Q. 547, 1997 CarswellQue 3831 (S.C.). Mr. Michaud was a registered shareholder of National Bank who was qualified to make proposals under the shareholder proposal provisions in the *Bank Act*, which are equivalent to those under the CBCA. He sent resolutions to the National Bank, the Royal Bank (after purchasing a single registered share to qualify) and the other major Canadian banks. The proposals related to various aspect of corporate governance, including: capping the overall compensation of the highest-ranking bank executives to twenty times the average salary of bank employees; separating the role of the chair of the board of directors from the CEO of the bank; prohibiting providers of services to the bank from serving as directors; and increasing the number of women nominated for election as directors. The banks declined to submit Michaud's resolutions, and Michaud sought an order that the banks circulate the proposals under section 144(2) of the *Bank Act*.

The banks argued in court that since Michaud had only a small amount invested in each bank, he was not sufficiently aggrieved to have standing. They also argued that Michaud's proposals could be excluded under the *Bank Act* for being submitted primarily to redress a personal grievance; to secure publicity; and to promote general economic, political and social causes. Rayle J. rejected all of these arguments, finding that Michaud had standing and was not abusing the shareholder proposal right. She stated that a civilized discussion of Michaud's proposals would benefit the banks and their shareholders. The banks were ordered to include Michaud's proposals in their proxy materials and allow his proposals to go to a vote at the annual general meetings. Ultimately, the resolutions were defeated at the meetings.

Another noteworthy recent case is *Verdun v. Toronto Dominion Bank*, [1996] 3 S.C.R. 550, 1996 CarswellOnt 3943, 1996 CarswellOnt 3944. Verdun, with his wife, was the beneficial owner of over 2000 shares of Toronto-Dominion Bank. He submitted 11 proposals relating to the structure and make-up of the board of directors and procedures at the annual shareholders' meetings. Management refused to circulate the proposals, arguing that they were submitted to address a personal grievance and that Verdun was seeking to gain publicity, running afoul of section 143(5) of the *Bank Act*. As well, they argued that since Verdun was not a registered shareholder, he was not a "shareholder entitled to vote" under the meaning of section 143 of the *Bank Act* and therefore not entitled to submit proposals. The Ontario Court (General Division) dismissed Verdun's application, finding his proposals to have been submitted to secure publicity. The Court of Appeal found that it was unnecessary to consider section 143(5), as Verdun was not a "shareholder entitled to vote". The Supreme Court agreed with the Court of Appeal.

Compare the facts of *Michaud* and *Verdun*. Michaud was the registered owner of a single share of Royal Bank, purchased only in order to qualify to make a proposal, and was entitled to do so. Verdun was beneficial co-owner of over 2000 shares of Toronto-Dominion Bank, but was not entitled to make a proposal. Note that both *Verdun* and *Michaud* would have been treated differently under the post-2001 CBCA: Michaud would not have met the ownership requirement to make a proposal, while Verdun would not have been barred from making a proposal on the basis of being a beneficial shareholder. Are the new ownership requirements more fair in restricting the right to make proposals to those shareholders with a significant investment in the corporation?

5 Suppose a shareholders' meeting is requisitioned and a shareholder proposal made to make a fundamental change in the corporation (*e.g.*, removal of the present board, as authorized by, *e.g.*, CBCA s. 109(1), or an amalgamation, *etc.*). What, if anything, can the current board do to frustrate the purpose for which the meeting is called? *Cf. Shield Development Co. v. Snyder* (1975), [1976] 3 W.W.R. 44, 1975 CarswellBC 227 (S.C.) and *Carrington Viyella Overseas (Holdings) Ltd. v. Taran* (February 24, 1983), Doc. Montreal 500-05-022164-824, 500-022164-824, Applications 2–4 (Que. S.C.).

6 Are shareholder proposals truly useful in promoting corporate democracy? Schwartz, "The Public Interest Proxy Contest: Reflections on

Campaign G.M." (1970-71), 69 Michigan L.R. 419 recounts the efforts undertaken by the Project on Corporate Responsibility, a Washington-based non-profit corporation formed to "promote corporate responsibility and to educate management and the public about the social role of corporations." The goals of the Project were to carry on a proxy contest which would gain public attention and to obtain support for several resolutions including the enlargement of the GM Board of Directors so that public interest directors might be elected and the creation of a Shareholders' Committee for Corporate Responsibility to act as a commission and submit a report on the corporation and its role in modern society.

The campaign succeeded in getting the Courts to order the inclusion of two of its resolutions in the circular mailed by GM to all its shareholders with the management proxy solicitation package. As well, Campaign GM mailed its own solicitation to a selected 5000 institutions and brokers. The Campaign culminated at the GM Annual Meeting in 1970, which was mostly taken up with Campaign GM issues. In the final result, however, the two Campaign proposals were overwhelmingly defeated, receiving under 3% of the votes cast. Even so, the leader of the Campaign announced victory for having created a national debate on the subject of corporate responsibility.

In a mid-1980s survey of Canadian corporations conducted by Raymonde Crête, 84 of 93 firms (or 90.3%) indicated that they had never received a request to include a shareholder proposal in the management proxy materials. Only three companies had actually included the proposal in the proxy materials. Of the votes cast, only 0.1%, 1.3%, and 6.7% of shareholders voted in favour of the proposal. According to Crête:

> These figures suggest that, at least in the cases of the respondents, the shareholder proposal mechanism is rarely used and that, even when it is used, few of the proposals submitted thereby are finally included in the firms' proxy materials. Furthermore, it is important to note that the responses to the questionnaire do not reflect the situation for a particular year. Rather they indicate the total number of occasions upon which shareholder proposals have been submitted to the respondents, as far back as their records show.

Raymonde Crête, *The Proxy System in Canadian Corporations* (1986), at 387.

Do shareholder proposals thus serve no useful function? Perhaps they do, even though they routinely fail. Consider the following passage from Jeffrey G. MacIntosh, "The Role of Institutional and Retail Investors in Canadian Capital Markets" (1993), 31 Osgoode Hall L.J. 371, at 411-412:

[T]he shareholder proposal provisions have not been extensively used in Canada. It has been suggested that a practical reason for this non-use is the fact that most public corporations have a controlling shareholder, and the prospects of success are typically not great. While this is undeniably true, the shareholder proposal mechanism is nonetheless important and useful. While the prospects for success may be poor in an individual case, shareholder proposals can nonetheless serve an educative function by putting issues of concern to . . . investors on the public agenda. This can have the salutary effect of creating pressure on corporate managers not to adopt wealth-reducing measures. By generating public debate, shareholder proposals can also cause normally passive shareholders to rethink their sometimes unthinking support of management.

7 While shareholder proposals are becoming more frequently used in Canada, most of them have little chance of being successfully passed. The majority of publicly traded Canadian companies are controlled either legally or effectively by an individual or small group, making it impossible for a minority shareholder to get enough votes to pass a proposal. The most likely avenue for success for a shareholder proposal is in winning enough support that management decides to take notice and make changes to avoid alienating investors. For more discussion on this subject and the *Michaud* case, see Brian R. Cheffins, "Michaud v. National Bank of Canada and Canadian Corporate Governance: A 'Victory' for Shareholder Rights?" [1998] 30 C.B.L.J. 20–72.

(f) Judicially Ordered Meetings

The corporation statutes also contain provisions which enable the court to order a meeting of shareholders where it is "impracticable" to convene a meeting. See, *e.g.*, CBCA, section 144; OBCA, section 106.

The case law on these provisions falls into two categories. First, there are cases in which the "impracticability" arises from some technical cause, such as the impossibility of obtaining a quorum. As an example, in *Re Edinburgh Workmen's Houses Improvement Co. Ltd.*, [1934] S.L.T 513, the articles required a quorum of 13 members personally present. At meetings held to consider certain resolutions to reduce capital, only two members were present, and when an application was made to court for confirmation of these resolutions, it appeared that only 14 of the 54 members lived in or near Edinburgh, the site of the head office. It was concluded that great difficulty would be experienced in obtaining the personal attendance of the necessary quorum, and the court ordered a meeting to be held with a quorum of five members personally present. See also *Re Beckers Pty Ltd.* (1942), 59 W.N. (N. S.W.) 206; and *Re Noel Tedman Holdings Pty Ltd.*, [1967] Qd. R. 561, where the only two shareholders and directors of the company were killed in the same motor accident. There is another category of cases, however, in which the impracticability, while superficially technical in character, is in fact a reflection of an underlying dispute over policy or control. The leading cases are discussed in Getz, "Court Ordered Company Meetings" (1969), 33 The Conveyancer and Property Lawyer (N.S.) 399. Getz states that the applicants for a court ordered meeting need not show that the directors have breached their duties to the corporation, but rather that the shareholders have been deprived of their rights "to have an account of the conduct of the company's affairs and an opportunity to express their views on Corporate policy". He concludes:

> If this view is correct, then, in principle, and contrary to the impression that may be gained from a reading of the decided cases, the provision for a court-ordered meeting is not simply a majority share-holders' remedy. If there is any opportunity to which a minority share-holder is entitled, it is the opportunity to persuade his fellows of the wisdom of his view, and the unwisdom of their view of corporate policy. The only chance he gets to do this is at company meetings, and for them to deprive him of it by exercising their undoubted right as shareholders not to attend must be a sufficient ground for invoking the section. While they have the right, they must pay the price of its exercise.

> There is one important limitation upon the scope of section 135 [empowering the court to order a meeting]: the purpose for which the meeting is sought to be ordered must be one that is constitutionally proper having regard to the powers of the general meeting under the *Companies Act* and the articles. This proposition is clearly illustrated by the decision of the Ontario Court of Appeal in *Re British International Finance (Canada) Ltd.*, *Charlebois v. Bienvenu*. Two factions were fighting for control of a company, and each claimed to be the duly elected board. The matters in dispute between the parties were the subject of a pending court action, but the practical difficulty was that until the issues in that action were decided, "no one would know who was entitled to control the affairs of the company." An application was made seeking a court-ordered meeting "for the purpose of electing directors." The trial judge granted the order, and on appeal, the Court of Appeal agreed that the impracticability of calling or conducting a meeting had been made out.

> But the real issues on appeal were, first, whether the court could order a meeting "to achieve some purpose thereat beyond the power of shareholders at a meeting called in any other manner," and secondly, whether the election of directors was, in the circumstances, such a lawful purpose. On the first question Aylesworth J., delivering the opinion of the court, held that:

>> the section is aimed at and limited to the removal of difficulties militating against the conduct of business which may lawfully come before the meeting. Once such difficulties have been re-

moved by the provisions of the order, however, it is open to the shareholders present at the meeting to conduct only such business thereat which could have been conducted at a meeting legally called in any other manner.

As to the second question, the court held that under the Ontario *Corporations Act* the election of directors was an annual affair. If, in the pending action, it was decided that the insurgent board had been improperly elected, the original board would remain in office. If, on the other hand, the contested election had resulted in the valid election of a new board, that would be the duly constituted board of directors. In either event, however, it was not competent for the company "to hold what in effect amounts to a second election of an entire board of directors within one year." Consequently, the appeal was allowed and the application dismissed.

If the view advanced above as to the true scope of s. 135 is sound, then what provision may represent a significant weapon in the armoury available to shareholders to secure accountability for managerial conduct. It is a view, moreover, that is especially attractive in the light of the limitations that seem to have become encrusted upon s. 210 [the former English oppression provision]. So long as English company law remains committed to the chimera of shareholder rights as a vehicle for the enforcement of managerial responsibilities, the wider interpretation suggested for s. 135 seems desirable.

Canadian Javelin Ltd. v. Boon-Strachan Coal Co.
(1976), 69 D.L.R. (3d) 439 (Que. S.C.)

This case arose out of a dispute between two factions in management of Canadian Javelin Ltd. John Doyle was the beneficial owner, directly and indirectly, of 18% of the stock of Canadian Javelin. He had been a director of the company, and its driving force in management, since its inception in 1951. However, he had become a figure of controversy, with charges laid against him in Newfoundland. One of the factions contended that at a directors' meeting on January 29, 1976, Doyle had offered to resign as director if the directors decided his presence was detrimental to the company.

On March 3, 1976, notice of a directors' meeting was forwarded to each director. The meeting was to be held on March 6, and although four directors, including Doyle, were not in the Montreal area, the meeting was not postponed. At the meeting, the directors that were present accepted Doyle's earlier offer of resignation, elected and appointed new officers, changed the signing authority at the company's banks, and appointed new legal counsel. On March 15, a meeting was held with five directors present, including those who had been unable to attend the Montreal meeting. Those directors found that the directors of the March 6 meeting were no longer directors, and appointed their own directors and officers. There was also extensive litigation undertaken between the two groups. As a result of the dispute, the company's line of credit with the Banque Nationale de Paris was terminated, putting the company's financial outlook in doubt. Boon Strachan Coal Co. Ltd., a shareholder of Canadian Javelin owned by Doyle, requested that the court order a general special meeting of shareholders.

COLAS J.: There is no doubt from the evidence that the situation is not only abnormal but detrimental to the best interests of the Company and of its shareholders. The role of directors is to act in a fiduciary capacity for the benefit of the Company. They must spend all their efforts and energy to study all the problems that are related with the good management and to take the most appropriate decision that will safeguard the assets and promote the development of the Company. Directors should not try to take over the control of the Company for their own personal advantage and with the hope that they will consolidate their power by creating a climate of uncertainty that places the Company in a suspicious position.

On April 22, 1976, a letter (ex. P-7) was sent by petitioner Boon-Strachan asking that a special general meeting of the shareholders be called. No response has been given to said petitioner. An explanation was given at the hearing for not calling the said general meeting of the shareholders in that the financial statements were not ready. The Court is of the opinion that the mere fact of the financial statements not being ready is not a valid reason to preclude the holding of a special meeting of the shareholders. In *Re El Sombrero Ltd.*, [1958] Ch. 900 at pp. 906-7, Mr. Justice Wynn-Parry of the Chancery Division states that:

> There is a clear statutory duty on the directors to call the meeting whether or not the accounts, the consideration of which is only one of the matters to be dealt with at an annual general meeting, are ready or not. It cannot possibly serve as an excuse for failing to perform that statutory duty. It is quite obvious that the only reason why the respondents refuse to call an annual general meeting is because the inevitable result of convening and holding that meeting would be that they would find that they had ceased to be directors.

Although the facts in this motion differ considerably from those of the *El Sombrero* case, the Court can apply a similar conclusion in that it is quite evident that the March 6th board and management of the *mis-en-cause* does not feel ready to ask the shareholders for a renewal of their mandate.

Much has been said about the requirements of the S.E.C. This Court is not compelled by the regulations of the S.E.C. but may direct the person to be named as chairman of the proposed meeting to call and hold it in conformity with such regulations as far as is practicable.

Section 106 of the *Canada Corporations Act* reads as follows:

106. Where for any reason it is impracticable to call a meeting of shareholders of the company in any manner in which meetings of shareholders may be called, or to conduct the meeting in manner prescribed by the letters patent, supplementary letters patent, the by-laws or this Part, the court in the province in which the head office of the company is situated, may, either of its own motion, or on the application of any director or any shareholder who would be entitled to vote at the meeting, order a meeting to be called, held and conducted in such manner as the court thinks fit and, where any such order is made, may give such ancillary or consequential directions as it thinks expedient; and any meeting called, held and conducted in accordance with any such order shall for all purposes be deemed to be a meeting of shareholders of the company duly called, held and conducted.

The Court has examined thoroughly the jurisprudence cited by the attorneys of both parties and has studied the relevant doctrines and like Mr. Justice Bell, in *Re Zimmerman and Commonwealth Int'l Leverage Fund Ltd. et al.* (1966), 56 D.L.R. (2d) 709, 52 M.P.R. 87, along with Chief Justice Campbell, who heard the appeal of said case reported in 58 D.L.R. (2d) 160, M.P.R. *loc. cit.*, the Court has found out that there is a meagre number of cases that may apply to this motion. Mr. Justice Bell in his said judgment quotes [at p. 714] Mr. Justice Wynn-Parry in the English case of *Re El Sombrero Ltd.* above-cited, that is:

It is to be observed that the section opens with the words "If for any reason," and therefore it follows that the section is intended to have, and, indeed, has by reason of its language, a necessarily wide scope. The next words are ". . . it is impracticable to call a meeting of the company . . ." The question then arises, what is the scope of the word "impracticable"? It is conceded that the word "impracticable" is not synonymous with the word "impossible"; and it appears to me that the question necessarily raised by the introduction of that word "impracticable" is merely this: examine the circumstances of the particular case and answer the question whether, as a practical matter, the desired meeting of the company can be conducted, there being no doubt, of course, that it can be convened and held. Upon the face of the section there is no express limitation which would operate to give those words "is impracticable" any less meaning than that which I have stated, and I can find no good reason in the arguments which have been addressed to me on behalf of the respondents for qualifying in any way the force of that word "impracticable" or the interpretation which I have placed upon it, and therefore upon that point I am in favour of the applicant.

In *Dumart Packaging Co. Ltd. v. Dumart*, [1928] 1 D.L.R. 640 at p. 641, 61 O.L.R. 478, Mr. Justice Middleton states:

Motions of this kind are somewhat frequent in company cases in which there is some internecine warfare between factions in the company, each claiming to be entitled to represent the company. In these cases the practice of the Court is to direct that the proceedings be stayed until a meeting of the shareholders of the company can be called so as to enable the will of the shareholders, or of the majority, to be ascertained. These cases are collected in *Buckley's Companies Acts*, 9th ed., p. 614, and in *1928 Yearly Practice*, p. 46.

CONSIDERING that the evidence has shown that it is urgent that a general meeting of the shareholders be called and held in order to stop the damage that may be caused to the assets of the Company at the detriment of the shareholders, on account of the contradictory decisions that are taken by the two parallel boards of directors presently purporting to act on behalf of the company and on account of the uncertainty as to the control of the management of the company;

CONSIDERING that the Company will be in default of holding an annual general meeting after June 30, 1976, and the Company has not prepared and is not in preparation of any notice and proxy statements and other relevant documents for such an annual meeting and it is obvious that the present management does not intend to call a meeting in the near future;

CONSIDERING that in view of the tactics adopted by certain of the directors of the Company and the evident animosities existing, certain shareholders and directors of the company cannot hope to be fairly treated if the meeting is conducted by any one of the present officers and directors of the Company and thus the Court is of the opinion that in the present case it is obvious that there are no means available to the petitioners which will provide any assurance that the business of the meeting will be properly conducted except under an order of this Court (*cf. Re Routley's Holdings Ltd.* (1960), 22 D.L.R. (2d) 410 at p. 415, [1960] O.W.N. 160);

CONSIDERING that it is in the best interest of the Company that a special general meeting of the shareholders be called as soon as possible for the purpose of giving a clear mandate to those persons whom the shareholders wish to manage the Company;

CONSIDERING that in order to put an end to the litigations presently pending and any future litigation and to have the decision of the shareholders accepted by all factions, it is necessary that the meeting be conducted by a disinterested person of high repute;

CONSIDERING that Mr. Michel Robert, the past Bâtonnier Général of the Province of Quebec, being a disinterested person of high repute has manifested his readiness to act as chairman of such meeting and to cause notices to be sent to the shareholders;

CONSIDERING that the Court, when ordering the calling of the meeting or directing the conduct of the meeting, has to be careful to do as little violence as possible to the corporate articles or regulations and should in fact be careful to see that any meeting ordered to be held should be called and conducted in conformity with such articles or regulations as far as practicable;

CONSIDERING that the attorneys of petitioners have mentioned that if a date is chosen for the holding of the meeting, it should be at the end of the month of July so as to give sufficient time for the preparation of the required documentation and of the meeting;

FOR THESE REASONS, THE COURT:

(i) DOTH ORDER that a special general meeting of the shareholders of the *mis-en-cause*, Canadian Javelin Limited be held in Montreal, Canada, at the Windsor Hotel, on Thursday, July 29, 1976, or if more convenient to the chairman of the meeting, on Friday, July 30, 1976, at the cost of the Company, and order Mr. Michel Robert to cause notice of such meeting of the shareholders to be sent to all shareholders of record as of July 2, 1976, at least five clear days prior to the date fixed for such meeting;

(ii) DOTH ORDER that all shareholders of record on the books of the transfer agent and Registrar of the Company as of July 2, 1976, be conclusive evidence of eligibility to vote at said meeting;

(iii) DOTH ORDER that all brokerage companies and partnerships or individuals, holding shares of the Company as nominees for beneficial owners, forward all material concerning the meeting, inclusive but not exclusive of notice of meeting, proxy forms and materials, to the beneficial owners, and that such brokerage companies, partnerships and individuals be allowed to vote only if a signed direction of the beneficial owners accompanies the proxies submitted in their names;

(iv) DOTH ORDER that, where a brokerage company holding shares in its name as nominee, is no longer active as a stock exchange member, or as a licensed active broker or broker-dealer, such shares may be voted by proxy through description of the shares by number and quantity as attestation as to beneficial ownership before a Commissioner of Oaths or any other person authorized to receive affidavits in the jurisdiction where it is given, such document to be conclusive evidence of their right to vote by proxy or in person;

(v) DOTH ORDER that banks and trust companies, acting in a fiduciary capacity, sign an appropriate form as to their authority to direct the proxy in favour of whom they wish to vote for and the signing by such banks or trust companies of this form, will be conclusive evidence of the right to vote;

(vi) DOTH ORDER that the notice of the meeting be accompanied by a proxy form of conforming with the rules and regulations of the *Canada Corporations Act* and as far as is practicable, in the opinion of Mr. Michel Robert, with the S.E.C. regulations;

(vii) DOTH ORDER that no proxy solicitation be made by any group or persons representing themselves as management of the Company and that any solicitation of proxies be made under the rules and regulations of *Canada Corporations Act* and as far as is practicable, in the opinion of Mr.

Michel Robert, with the S.E.C. regulations and that any solicitor of such proxies present itself as a dissident;

(viii) DOTH ORDER and appoint the said Michel Robert, to preside over the special general meeting of shareholders and doth order that his decisions be final and binding over all parties concerned;

(ix) DOTH ORDER and authorize Michel Robert, to appoint two independent scrutineers for the purpose of counting and preparing proxies for voting and the further counting of votes of shareholders appearing in person at the meeting;

(x) DOTH ORDER that the directors elected at the special general meeting of shareholders hold office until the next annual general meeting of shareholders of the Company and their qualification and duties be governed by the by-laws of the Company;

(xi) DOTH ORDER that no additional new shares or convertible debentures or share options of the company be issued or allotted or transacted by the Company until after the next annual general meeting of shareholders;

(xii) DOTH ORDER that all costs, charges and fees of the special general meeting of shareholders be at the expense of the Company;

(xiii) DOTH RESERVE to petitioners a right to seek such other conclusions as may in the circumstances be necessary;

(xiv) DOTH ORDER and grant provisional execution of this judgment notwithstanding any appeal. . . .

Order accordingly.

Notes

1 Did the Court have jurisdiction to order a meeting in the *Javelin* case, given that one or the other of the contending boards was likely a properly elected board? Should the Court have instead simply determined who the properly elected board was, making it unnecessary for the company to go to the trouble and expense of calling a new shareholders' meeting? *Cf. Re British International Finance (Canada) Ltd., Charebois v. Bienvenu,* referred to in the excerpt from the Getz article, *supra.*

2 See also *FTS Worldwide Corp v. Unique Broadband Systems Inc.,* [2001] O.T.C. 938, 2001 CarswellOnt 4557 (S.C.J.); *Atkinson, Re* (2002), [2002] A.J. No. 1306, 2002 CarswellAlta 1549 (Q.B.); *Croation Peasant Party of Ontario, Canada v. Zorkin* (1981), 38 O.R. (2d) 659, 1981 CarswellOnt 725 (H.C.); and *Athabaska Holdings Ltd. v. ENA Datasystems Inc.* (1980), 30 O.R. (2d) 527, 1980 CarswellOnt 1391 (H.C).

See, generally, on shareholders' meetings, Getz "The Structure of Shareholder Democracy", in Ziegel (Ed.), *Studies in Canadian Company Law,* Vol. 2, p. 239 (1973); *Athabaska Holdings Ltd. v. ENA Datasystems Inc.* (1980), 30 O.R. (2d) 527, 116 D.L.R. (3d) 318 (H.C.).

Barsh v. Feldman
(1986), 54 O.R. (2d) 340 (H.C.)

VAN CAMP J.: This is an application under s. 106(1) of the *Business Corporations Act*, 1982 (Ont.), c. 4, for the following:

1. an order requiring a meeting of the shareholders of the corporation;

2. an order to vary the requirements of a quorum as set out in By-law I so that only two shareholders, holding at least 51% of the issued shares, are required to be present instead of the present requirement of the three share-holders who each hold one share.

Section 106 of the *Business Corporations Act*, 1982 is as follows:

106(1) If for any reason it is impracticable to call a meeting of share-holders of a corporation in the manner in which meetings of those shareholders may be called or to conduct the meeting in the manner prescribed by the by-laws, the articles and this Act, or if for any other reason the court thinks fit, the court, upon the application of a director or a shareholder entitled to vote at the meeting, may order a meeting to be called, held and conducted in such manner as the court directs and upon such terms as to security for the costs of holding the meeting or otherwise as the court deems fit.

(2) Without restricting the generality of subsection (1), the court may order that the quorum required by the by-laws, the articles or this Act be varied or dispensed with at a meeting called, held and conducted under this section.

(3) A meeting called, held and conducted under this section is for all purposes a meeting of shareholders of the corporation duly called, held and conducted.

Under s. 94 of the *Business Corporations Act, 1982* the directors are required to call an annual meeting of shareholders not later than 15 months after holding the last preceding annual meeting and may, at any time, call a special meeting of shareholders. The last meeting of shareholders and of directors was held on April 8, 1966. On May 27, 1985, Barsh, holding one of the three shares, requisitioned the directors under s. 105 of the *Business Corporations Act, 1982* to call a meeting of shareholders for the certain purposes stated. Under s. 105, the directors were required to call the meeting of shareholders. No such meeting has been called.

Feldbar Construction Company was incorporated in November, 1954, as a private company with restrictions on the transfer of shares. Hyman Feldman, Benjamin Barsh and his son, Harvey Samuel Barsh, each sub-scribed for one common share. Hyman Feldman and Benjamin Barsh each invested $20,000. Harvey Samuel Barsh made no investment of capital, but was to perform services for the corporation in lieu of a capital investment. The services were to be those of a builder and developer.

The corporation carried on the business of acquiring real property and building houses on portions thereof. The two tracts of land that it now owns are vacant parcels which were acquired over 20 years ago. Some 40 houses were built and sold on one parcel of land between 1960 and 1966. At that time, the corporation became relatively inactive and ceased to hold meetings.

Benjamin Barsh died in 1983. His son, Harvey Samuel, exercised an option under the will to purchase his father's share. He now holds his father's share in the corporation as a bare trustee for S. & E. Consultants Limited as to a one-half interest and each of Stella Rudolph, his sister, and Joseph Barsh, his brother, as to a one-quarter interest. The shares of S. & E. Consultants Limited are owned by him and his wife.

Since 1983, Harvey Samuel Barsh has wished to see the two tracts of land developed and has formed certain plans to this effect. Mr. Feldman had shown little, if any, interest in these plans until at least August, 1985. In late 1984, Barsh proposed buying out Feldman's interest. Feldman did not return to Barsh the resolutions to effect the transfer of the share of the deceased or the resolution of the shareholders electing the corporate solicitor as a director. It was at this time that Barsh requisitioned the special meeting of shareholders. Negotiations continued for the purchase of Feldman's interest and for the amendment of By-law 1 which would have the effect of eliminating the need for his attendance or vote at a meeting of shareholders and directors and his removal as a signing officer. A new general by-law is required to conform with the requirements of the *Business Corporations Act, 1982*. Although Feldman states that he is now willing to meet with the applicants to formulate a joint policy for the development or disposition of these properties, the prior delay makes it doubtful that the parties can agree. However, Feldman has given an undertaking through his counsel to sign a resolution for the annual meeting, approving the annual financial statements, electing the officers, appointing a director to replace the deceased and to approve the transfer of the share of the deceased to Barsh, in trust. This obviates the necessity of the meeting of shareholders.

I am of the opinion that the facts do not support the exercise of discretion to change the quorum. The result would be that one of three equal shareholders was effectively locked into a company in which he had no control. The quorum here was not to permit attendance of a shareholder, but to ensure that there would be no corporate action, except on the consent of all. Each shareholder has an equal interest. If there is no such consent obtainable, then there are provisions for the winding-up of the Corporation. None of the shareholders wish a winding-up, but unless they can agree it is the only alternative. The corporation was carefully structured so that no shareholder could control it. The affidavit of Feldman shows that because the other two shares were held by father and son, to give Feldman protection all decisions of directors and shareholders would require his consent and all cheques drawn on the corporate account would require his signature. That agreement was reflected in the provisions of ss. 3 and 4 of By-law 1 providing for a quorum of three persons at meetings of shareholders and directors. The banking resolution of the directors was enacted to require the signature of Feldman on the company cheques. The letters patent give one vote for each share held, but there can be no meetings unless all are present, that is, unless all agree. The obligation to have a general meeting can be met by an agreed agenda.

The answer to the problem of disagreement among the shareholders is not to compel a meeting whereby two of the three equal shareholders may outvote the third. The answer is the winding-up of the corporation. When none of them wish that winding-up, they can find a compromise.

I find the respondent, Feldman, not unreasonable in refusing to call or to attend a meeting which would have resulted in loss of sharing of control for him and effective transfer of complete control to Barsh. I have been referred to several decisions, but each depends upon its own facts. I note the quotation from *Re Morris Funeral Service Ltd.*, [1957] O.W.N. 161 at p. 164, 7 D.L.R. (2d)642:

> The powers of the Court under s. 309 [the predecessor section] are, of course, discretionary. It is to be noted that in none of the reported decisions was the Court requested by one faction among the shareholders to intervene as against some other faction; on the contrary, in each case the Court was requested to remove some obstacle making it impracticable for the shareholders as a whole, or for an overwhelming majority thereof to call or conduct a meeting in accordance with the requirements in that behalf of the Company's Articles of Association. It is further to be observed, as illustrated in [*Re Pall Mall Building Society's Deed of Dissolution*, [1947] W.N. 143], that the Court, when ordering the calling of a meeting or directing the conduct of a meeting, was careful to do as little violence as possible to the corporate articles or regulations and, in fact, was careful to see that any meeting ordered to be held should be called and conducted in conformity with such articles or regulations as far as practicable.

The corporation in this application was carefully structured to require agreement of the three equal shareholders. This court should not intervene to effectively remove the need for agreement by the third shareholder. The application is dismissed. In the circumstances, there should be no costs.

Application dismissed.

Note

For a contrasting holding on the issue of quorum variation, see *Re Pizza Pizza Limited*, unreported, Sept. 14, 1987, Ont. S.C., per Sutherland J.

(g) Shareholder-Requisitioned Meetings

Shareholders may requisition directors to call meetings under CBCA section 143. (see also, *e.g.*, OBCA s. 105). This right is limited to shareholders of not less than 5% of the issued voting shares of a corporation. When a proper requisition is received, directors must, subject to certain exemptions, call a shareholders' meeting (s. 143(3)) as soon as possible (s. 143(5)). If directors do not call a meeting within 21 days of receipt of a requisition, any shareholder who signed the requisition may call the meeting. While the OBCA specifically makes this subject to the listed exemptions, the CBCA does not (*cf.* OBCA s.105(4) with CBCA s. 143(4)). Does this mean that under the CBCA a shareholder may call a requisitioned meeting regardless of whether the proposed meeting runs afoul of the exemptions?

The business that can be conducted at shareholder-requisitioned meetings is limited in the same way that shareholder proposals are (CBCA s.102). However, these meetings are often used to remove current directors and elect new ones, and because directors may be reluctant to call a meeting designed to remove them from power, shareholder-requisitioned meetings make it easier to remove directors before their terms end. Shareholder requisitioning of meetings can be particularly significant in the context of a takeover bid. As an acquirer often can not afford to wait until the annual meeting, and the board of directors will often be reluctant to call a special meeting, it may be necessary for the acquirer, through its shares in the target, to call the meeting.

Airline Industry Revitalization Co. v. Air Canada
(1999), 45 O.R. (3d) 370, 1999 CarswellOnt 3020 (S.C.J. [Commercial List]) (footnotes removed)

[Airline Industry Revitalization Co. (hereinafter "AirCo") was a corporation used by Onex Corp. and American Airlines to acquire and merge Air Canada and Canadian Airlines. To this end, AirCo sought to take over Air Canada. AirCo acquired 3.1% of Air Canada's common shares and 6.6% of Air Canada's Class A non-voting shares. In order to put the takeover into effect, AirCo considered it necessary for Air Canada to implement changes to its articles. On August 30, 1999, the Air Canada Board called a special shareholders meeting for January 7, 2000. On August 31, AirCo and other shareholders comprising over 5% of Air Canada's voting shares requisitioned the Board to call a special meeting between November 4 and November 8 to approve the takeover bid, implement the suggested changes to the articles, and alter control of the Board. The Board rejected the requisition, and AirCo brought an application for an order requiring the directors to call the meeting, or for the court to call the meeting. It should be noted that the federal government, by making an order under the *Canada Transportation Act*, had created a 90 day window for Air Canada, Canadian, and other parties to negotiate a merger without violating the *Competition Act* and that the 90 day period was to end on November 10, 1999.]

R.A. Blair J.: The narrow issue on this application, however, is whether or not Air Canada should be required to hold a meeting in response to the AirCo requisition and, if so, when that meeting should be held. While the foregoing background helps provide an understanding of the context in which this issue must be determined, not all of the rhetoric which has accompanied the battle as a whole is pertinent to the resolution of what is presently before this court.

As I see it, the application stands to be determined upon a consideration of the following matters:

1.   Whether Air Canada's Board of Directors is required by s. 143(3) of the *Canada Business Corporations Act*, R.S.C. 1985, c. C-44, as amended (the "CBCA") to call and hold a special meeting of shareholders pursuant to the requisition;

2.   If not, does the applicant nonetheless have the right to call such a meeting on its own, by virtue of the provisions of s. 143(4) of the CBCA, and should it be left to do so without court intervention if such is the case?

3.   If the answer is "No" in either case, should the court exercise its discretion under s. 144 of the CBCA to order that a meeting of the type requested by the applicant be held, and fix the date for such a meeting within the time parameters sought by the applicant?

On behalf of AirCo, Mr. Finkelstein submits that, in spite of all "the sound and fury", these considerations revolve around a simple issue. He defines that issue as whether the shareholders of Air Canada should be deprived of their opportunity to consider the AirCo offers before they expire on November 9 and before the s. 47 order expires on November 10. The shareholders cannot consider the AirCo offers effectively without a special meeting prior to those dates, he contends, because one of the conditions of the offers is that such a meeting be held and that the steps contemplated to be taken at that meeting be taken. The Air Canada Board has arrogated to itself the right to say "No" to the AirCo bid by refusing to hold a meeting until after the bid expires and the s. 47 order lapses, and they are not entitled to do so, the argument concludes. He relies upon the decision of this court in *RioCan Real Estate v. Realfund*, [1999] O.J. No, 1349 (Gen. Div.).

On behalf of Air Canada, on the other hand, Mr. Dunphy submits that s. 143 of the CBCA does not apply at all in the circumstances of this case because:

(a) "a record date" had been set for a meeting by the Air Canada Board and, accordingly, the Board is not required to respond to the requisition because of the exception provided for in s. 143(3)(a) of the CBCA;

(b) a shareholder is not entitled to call a meeting for the amendment of articles of incorporation by way of requisition and, accordingly, the business to be transacted at the requisitioned meeting is not business that can validly be considered by the shareholders at such a meeting; and

(c) the 10 per cent ownership restraint imposed by the *Air Canada Act* — which remains the law of Canada — insulates Air Canada from a take-over bid attempt and the AirCo proposal, including the business to be transacted at the meeting to give effect to it, is simply a cleverly contrived mechanism to circumvent that law, and is, accordingly, not something which can validly be considered by the shareholders at such a meeting.

If there is no right on the part of AirCo to resort to s. 143, Mr. Dunphy submits, and the applicant is left to rely upon the exercise of the court's discretion under s. 144, such discretion should be exercised very sparingly and only with great deference to the exercise of business judgment on the part of the Board of Directors. There is no basis for the exercise of such discretion on the facts of this case, he contends.

Law and Analysis

I have come to the conclusion that the AirCo requisition is a valid requisition in the proper form, for the purposes of this application, and that the Air Canada directors were obliged to call a meeting of the shareholders to transact the business stated in the requisition in accordance with s. 143 of the CBCA. In my opinion, the "record date" exception of s. 143(3)(a) does not apply on the facts of this case, and it cannot be said for the purposes of this application that the subject matter of the requisition is not the proper subject matter of such a meeting. Accordingly, it is open for AirCo to call the requisitioned meeting of the shareholders, pursuant to s. 143(4) of the CBCA, and they are at liberty to do so. That being the case, and AirCo having a corporate remedy of its own, it would not be wise in my view for the court to intervene at this stage and exercise its discretion under s. 144 of the CBCA to call the meeting itself.

My reasons for coming to this conclusion are the following.

[R.A. Blair J. examined the statutory framework of shareholder-requisitioned meetings and continued:]

The Record Date

At the directors' meeting held on August 30, 1999, Air Canada set a record date for a special meeting of shareholders to be held on January 7, 2000. The record date is November 18, 1999. Notice of the record date was given early the next morning, August 31, and published in the *National Post* of that date. It is conceded that the AirCo requisition was not made until later that day. Thus, it is clear on the facts that Air Canada had fixed "a record date" and given notice thereof, prior to receipt of the requisition.

In my opinion, however, the record date which was fixed is not a "record date" which qualifies as an exception under s. 143(3)(a) of the CBCA. Air Canada announced in its press release dated August 31, 1999, that the January 7 meeting was called, amongst other things, "to consider valid proposals, including the proposal of Onex Corporation and American Airlines, that may be presented". However, Air Canada now appears to have resiled from that position. In its factum, filed in response to this application, Air Canada states that "the [Air Canada] Board has not to date agreed to place the proposed AirCo amendments on the January 7 agenda" (para. 24), and that "the Air Canada Board has never agreed to hold a meeting to transact the business set out in the requisition" (para. 37). In argument, Mr. Dunphy made it clear that Air Canada does not consider the January 7 meeting to be a meeting called to deal with the business stated in the AirCo requisition.

That being the case, I do not see how the "record date" which was fixed by Air Canada can be a "record date" that qualifies as an exception under s. 143(3)(a). Section 143 contemplates that shareholders who meet the 5 per cent threshold are entitled to requisition a meeting. The directors shall call the meeting, unless the circumstances meet one of the exceptions articulated in s. 143(3). Although there appears to be no jurisprudence on the point, it seems to me that a "record date" as contemplated in s. 143(3)(a) must be a "record date" for a meeting at which there is some reasonable chance that the business stated in the requisition will be considered. It is one thing to say that if a meeting is requisitioned, and there is already a meeting pending at which the matters in question can be considered, then the directors are not obliged to call another meeting. There is no point in duplicating meetings, and the directors generally are vested with the power to call meetings of shareholders and to determine the timing and place of such meetings. It is quite another thing, however, to say that even though the required percentage of shareholders have requisitioned a meeting, their statutory right to have their business considered at a meeting may be thwarted by the simple expedient of the directors having already fixed a record date for a meeting on other matters. I interpret "record date" in para. 143(3)(a) of the CBCA to refer to a record date for a meeting having been fixed prior to receipt of the requisition but at which the requisitioners' business may nonetheless be considered. Likewise, I interpret "meeting of shareholders" in para. 143(3)(b) in the same way: the directors are obligated to call a validly requisitioned meeting, unless the directors have called a meeting of shareholders, and given notice thereof, and the requisitioners' business may be considered at that meeting.

Such is not the case here. Had Air Canada continued with its announced intention to have the Onex proposal (i.e., the AirCo bid) considered at the January 7 meeting, the decision of this court in *RioCan v. RealFund, supra,* would have been directly relevant.

In *RioCan*, the court was faced with a situation where certain unit-holders of a trust fund, who were making a take-over bid for the fund, had requisitioned a meeting of the unitholders for the purpose of dealing with a proposed merger which was to form part of the take-over process. The trustees of the fund — who were in an analogous position to the Air Canada directors in this case — agreed to call a meeting in response to the requisition, but they called the meeting for a date which was significantly beyond the date when the bid in question would expire. Thus the issue in *RioCan* was not whether a meeting would be called to consider the business stated in the requisition, but when that meeting should take place.

By adopting its stance that the pending January 7 shareholders' meeting is not a meeting to deal with the business stated in the AirCo requisition, Air Canada has removed from this application the argument that this is simply a case of determining whether the timing set by the Board for the meeting is reasonable or whether it should be interfered with because it has rendered consideration of the imminent business opportunity academic. On Air Canada's own view of the landscape, the AirCo proposal is not to be considered at all.

I shall return to the *RioCan* decision later in these reasons.

The Right to Requisition a Meeting to Amend Articles

Mr. Dunphy submits that deficiencies in the AirCo requisition made it "a dead letter" upon its delivery and, therefore, that the directors had no obligation to call the meeting sought. This submission is premised upon the argument that amendments to articles of incorporation may only be initiated by shareholders at an annual meeting of shareholders and that such amendments cannot be put forward by a shareholder at a special meeting.

I do not accept this submission.

Section 175 of the CBCA states:

175(1) Subject to subsection (2), a director or a shareholder who is entitled to vote at an annual meeting of shareholders may, in accordance with s. 137, make a proposal to amend the articles.

(2) Notice of a meeting of shareholders at which a proposal to amend the articles is to be considered shall set out the proposed amendment and, where applicable, shall state that a dissenting shareholder is entitled to be paid the fair value of his shares . . .

Section 137 is the provision which enables a shareholder entitled to vote at an annual meeting to submit notice of any matter the shareholder proposes to raise at the meeting. It requires that such a proposal be included in a management proxy circular, subject to certain legislative exceptions, and establishes a procedural remedy in the form of an application to court for shareholders claiming to be aggrieved by a refusal of the corporation to include the proposal.

I do not read the foregoing provisions as limiting to an annual meeting of shareholders the right of a shareholder to propose an amendment to articles of the corporation. The reference in s. 175(1) of the CBCA to a shareholder "who is entitled to vote at an annual general meeting of shareholders" is in my view descriptive of the type of share held rather than of the occasion on which the right to vote may be exercised. I observe that ss. (2) refers to notice of a meeting of shareholders at which a proposal to amend the articles is to be considered. It does not specify that the meeting is to be an annual meeting. Moreover, there is nothing whatsoever in the language of s. 143, which gives rise to the power to requisition a meeting, that in any way purports to limit the scope of matters which may properly be the subject matter of the requisition.

I can see no reason why proposed amendments to articles cannot be the subject matter of a requisitioned meeting. Mr. Dunphy argues that the implications of amendments to articles can be very significant — not the least of which is the creation of dissenting shareholder rights — and, accordingly, that such important considerations should not be ousted from the directors' general authority to govern the affairs of the corporation, including the question of determining the timing of such consideration. I have difficulty in understanding the substantive difference between dealing with amendments to articles at an annual meeting and doing so at a special meeting called by requisition, however. There is nothing in the nature of the two types of meetings, or in the ability of the directors and the corporation to prepare for or respond to the proposed amendment, that makes one form of meeting qualitatively different from the other in those respects. All business transacted at a special meeting of shareholders or at an annual meeting, except consideration of financial statements, auditor's reports, the election of directors and the reappointment of the incumbent auditor, is deemed to be "special" business: CBCA s. 135(5). It was held in *Austin Mining Co. v. Gemmel* (1886), 10 O.R. 697 at p. 703, that a special meeting may be called to perform the work of a general meeting if the work to be done or object of the meeting is clearly defined and specified in the notice calling the meeting. Furthermore, as I have indicated, there is nothing in the language of s. 175, or s. 137 or, more particularly, s. 143, which precludes the requisitioning of a meeting to amend articles.

Accordingly, I am not prepared to give effect to the argument that AirCo has no right to requisition the meeting in question because it is not open for such a meeting of shareholders to consider an amendment to articles of incorporation.

[R.A. Blair J. then analyzed whether AirCo's proposal ran afoul of the *Air Canada Public Participation Act*, finding that there were arguments for and against the proposal. As it did not clearly violate the Act, it should be available for shareholders to decide whether or not to accept it.]

Conclusions Respecting Section 143

I am therefore of the view that the AirCo requisition is a valid requisition pursuant to s. 143 of the CBCA, in the sense that the requisition is signed by the holders of at least 5 per cent of the voting shares of Air Canada and is in the proper form, and that the business to be transacted, as stated in the requisition, is business which may properly be put before a requisitioned meeting of the shareholders. Further, I am satisfied that the only exception under s. 143(3) which was relied upon by Air Canada in argument, namely the fact that Air Canada had set a record date for a meeting to be held on January 7, 2000, has no application on the facts of the case as they were put to the court. It follows, then, that the Air Canada directors were obliged to call a meeting of the shareholders to transact the business stated in the requisition. They have chosen not to do so, taking the position instead that the meeting called for January 7 is not a meeting called to deal with the business stated in the requisition.

AirCo, however, is not without a remedy in the circumstances. Section 143(4) of the CBCA provides that if the directors do not call a meeting within 21 days of receipt of the requisition, any shareholder who signed the requisition may call the meeting. Moreover, even if I am in error in my conclusions above with respect to the application of the "record date" exception under s. 143(3)(a) or with respect to the ability of shareholders to requisition a meeting to consider amendments to articles of incorporation, I am of the view that AirCo would still be entitled to rely upon the provisions of s. 143(4). Having regard to the purpose of s. 143 — which, as I see it, is to ensure that shareholders who can garner sufficient support to meet the 5 per cent threshold are able to get the business which they wish to have transacted before a meeting of shareholders, notwithstanding their minority position and an actual or potentially unwilling board of directors — I am satisfied that the right of the requisitioning shareholder to call the meeting under s. 143(4), where the directors have declined to do so, applies even where the directors have correctly concluded that one of the exceptions of s. 143(3) applies. The difference is that the onus is on the shareholder and not on management to call the meeting "as nearly as possible in the manner in which meetings are to be called pursuant to the by-laws [and Parts XII and XIII of the CBCA]."

The language of s. 143(4) is straightforward. If the directors do not call the meeting within 21 days, "any shareholder who signed the requisition may call the meeting". Nothing indicates that if the directors have properly exercised their right not to call a meeting because of the applicability of one of the s. 143(3) exceptions, the meeting may not be held. Interestingly, the comparable provision of the Ontario *Business Corporations Act*, R.S.O. 1990, c. B.16, as amended (the "OBCA") — s. 105(4) — is identical in wording to that of s. 143(4) of the CBCA, except that it is prefaced with the words "subject to subsection (3)". This difference in wording suggests that under the OBCA regime, a requisitioned meeting which the directors are properly exempted from calling may not be called by the requisitioning shareholder, whereas under the CBCA regime the opposite is the case.

In any event, for the reasons I have articulated above, I do not think the Air Canada directors were entitled to rely on one of the exceptions of s. 143(3) of the CBCA on the facts of this case. I am therefore of the view that AirCo is entitled to rely upon the provisions of s. 143(4) and that it may, accordingly, "call the meeting". Moreover, I am of the view that it should be left to exercise its own statutory remedy to that effect, if it should choose to do so. . . .

The Section 144 Discretion

Section 144 of the CBCA — which is cited in full earlier in these reasons — provides that if for any reason it is impracticable to call a meeting in the normal way or if for any other reason a court thinks fit, the court may order that a meeting be held. This provision gives the court a broad discretion to order that a shareholders' meeting be called and held, and to determine the manner in which the meeting shall be conducted. In my opinion, it is a discretion which should be exercised cautiously, however, given the general scheme of the CBCA, which is to repose in the directors of a corporation the general power to manage its business and affairs, including the primary responsibility for determining when shareholders will be consulted and asked to act at meetings. I agree with Mr. Dunphy that corporations are not run by plebiscite and that shareholders do not have a general power to call shareholders' meetings as and when they feel like it. The requisition provisions of s. 143 and the jurisdiction given to the court under s. 144 are exceptions to the primary role of directors in this regard.

Where there is a "corporate" remedy still open to a shareholder under the legislative scheme — as there is here for AirCo, by virtue of s. 143(4) of the CBCA — the court should be reluctant to step into the fray and impose its own solution to the "meeting" problem by exercising its discretion under s. 144, in my view: see, *Streit v. Swanson*, [1946] O.R. 565, [1946] 4 D.L.R. 107 per McRuer C.J.H.C., at p. 572. The bare-knuckled skirmishes of corporate restructuring warfare are best resolved by the combatants themselves to the extent possible, in their own boardrooms and meeting rooms and — where, as is the case here, there are political dimensions as well — in the public domain, rather than in the courtroom. The court's role is to decide issues of a procedural or substantive nature which need to be determined to enable the process to proceed in a proper and timely fashion, but otherwise to remain apart from the battle.

For these reasons, I am unwilling in the circumstances presented here to exercise the court's discretion to impose its own meeting with its own format and its own timing on the parties. This is not a case where it is "impracticable" to call the meeting in the manner in which meetings of the Air Canada shareholders may be called: s. 144. AirCo may call the requisitioned meeting of the shareholders itself. It should do that, if so advised.

Conclusion

I am not prepared, therefore, to grant the main relief sought by the applicant, namely an order requiring the Air Canada directors to call a meeting of the corporation's shareholders on a date between November 4 and November 8, 1999, for the purpose of transacting the business stated in the AirCo requisition. I am satisfied and declare, however, that the AirCo requisition is a valid one in the proper form under s. 143 of the CBCA and that AirCo is entitled, if so advised, to call the requisitioned meeting itself, having regard to the failure of the Air Canada directors to do so within 21 days of receipt of the requisition by virtue of the provisions of s. 143(4) of that Act. In doing so, AirCo will call the meeting, as nearly as possible, in the manner in which meetings of Air Canada shareholders are to be called pursuant to the by-laws of the corporation and Parts XII and XIII of the CBCA.

Application dismissed.

5. RIGHT TO CORPORATE INFORMATION: ACCESS TO CORPORATE RECORDS

Note

Corporate statutes require corporations to maintain specified records and to allow access to these records by shareholders and other designated persons. See ss. 19 to 22 and 138 of the CBCA and ss. 139 to 147 of the OBCA. In addition to corporate records, the statutes also require the preparation of and accessibility to prescribed financial information relating to the corporation and this will be briefly referred to in the next section dealing with the appointment of auditors.

IACOBUCCI, PILKINGTON AND PRICHARD,
Canadian Business Corporations
(1977), pp. 178–181 (footnotes omitted)

The shareholders' access to corporate information has long been held to be of great importance; indeed Gower has described disclosure as the "fundamental principle underlying the *Companies Act*". But the *Kimber Report* found that despite this early recognition of the importance of disclosure, "what was considered adequate disclosure at one given time has proven to be inadequate in a subsequent period." Information is important for at least two basic reasons. First, it allows the shareholders and the securities market as a whole to evaluate the relative strengths and weaknesses of the enterprise so that they can make informed decisions as to whether or not to invest or continue to invest in the company. Second, only with adequate information are the shareholders able to evaluate effectively the performance of the corporation's directors and officers and to exercise their rights to have the directors and officers accountable for their misdeeds. In a dispute between a dissenting shareholder and those in control, the accessibility of information becomes a key factor as management's ready access to the records of the company and other inside information gives it a distinct advantage over the individual shareholder who may be unable to substantiate his suspicions of wrongdoing with documentary proof.

The statutory response has been on four fronts, the last three of which have been dealt with elsewhere in this book: (i) provisions giving shareholders the right to inspect company records, (ii) provisions allowing specified numbers of shareholders to requisition general meetings and circulate proposals, (iii) provisions requiring disclosure of financial and insider trading information, and (iv) provisions giving the right to have inspectors and auditors appointed to investigate the affairs of the corporation . . .

The provisions giving the shareholders the right to inspect company records are similar in all Canadian companies legislation. Each shareholder is entitled to copies of the memorandum, articles and any ordinary or special resolutions at a nominal charge. He is also entitled to inspect the register of members and may obtain copies of the register or any part thereof at a nominal charge. A shareholder has similar rights with regard to the register of mortgages, and the minutes of general meetings of the company.

Each of these provisions is important and worthy of retention. It may be useful, however, to specify in the statute that shareholder lists obtained from the register must only be used for purposes connected with the corporation. Such a provision will help to avoid any potential misuse of the lists for the purposes of sending a shareholder advertising for other securities or unrelated matters. Also, the memorandum and articles should be available without charge to the shareholders rather than at the present fee since the statute should encourage shareholders to be aware of their rights and to participate in the corporation's affairs and such a provision, although perhaps largely symbolic, would be a small step in this direction.

The combined impact of the various mechanisms in each of the four classes of response to the need for information appears to be adequate in relation to specific transactions. However, they do not cover the case of the shareholder who wants information about the company's affairs when no specific transaction is contemplated. For example, should shareholders have the right to demand the identity of customers and suppliers and the volume of business with each, if they feel, and have some grounds to suspect, that one particular ethnic or racial group is being privileged or discriminated against? Although obviously an unlimited right to demand information cannot be provided since it could be damaging to the firm's competitive position and lead to harassment of corporate management, it may be that more information than is available at present could be provided without reaching these damaging limits. Serious consideration should be given to designing a mechanism with the appropriate safeguards . . .

Note

The company's directors also have both common law and statutory rights to inspect the books of the company. In *Conway v. Petronius Clothing Co. Ltd.*, [1978] 1 All E.R. 185, [1978] 1 W.L.R. 72 (Ch. D.), the Court held that the U.K. *Companies Act* did not confer a statutory right on a director to inspect the company's books of account but that there was a common law right to do so. In *Healy v. Healy Homes Ltd.*, [1973] I.R. 308, it was held that a director is entitled to the assistance of an accountant in exercising his right of inspection.

With respect to the shareholder's rights of inspection, see *Johnston v. West Fraser Timber Corp.* (1980), 22 B.C.L.R. 337,18 C.P.C. 219 (S.C.), where the Court upheld the shareholder's right under the B.C. corporation statute to inspect the corporate records and said that the shareholder is not disentitled to this right because of some alleged improper purpose in getting the information.

Under the CBCA and OBCA, directors have a statutory entitlement to inspect certain records of the directors. CBCA s. 20(2) requires the corporation to "prepare and maintain adequate accounting records and records containing minutes of meetings and resolutions of the directors and any committee thereof." Section 20(4) requires that such records "at all reasonable times be open to inspection by the directors." Look carefully at 20(4) and 20(2); do the directors have a statutory right to inspect those records referred to in s. 20(1) (i.e., are these "records described in subsection (2)", via the reference in subsection (2) to "the records described in subsection (1)")? Why do you suppose the shareholders do not also have an entitlement to look at the accounting records and records of directors' meetings?

6. RIGHT TO APPOINT AN AUDITOR: FINANCIAL DISCLOSURE, AUDITOR'S LIABILITY AND THE AUDIT COMMITTEE

(a) Introduction

Corporation statutes uniformly confer upon the shareholders the right to appoint and to remove the auditor. As to appointment, see, *e.g.*, OBCA s. 149 and CBCA s. 162. The function of the auditor is to assess the financial statements which the corporation proposes to place before the shareholders and to report on the preparation and accuracy of those statements. Since the

availability and reliability of financial information is vital to the efficiency
and integrity of the corporation, the auditor, to be useful, must be guaranteed
appropriate access to records, must be independent, and must be properly
qualified. The legislation attempts to ensure that these requirements are met.

Of direct relevance to the role of the auditor is the nature and extent of
the financial disclosure required by the particular corporation statute because, as previously noted, the auditor must review the corporation's financial statements. The provisions of the corporation statutes dealing with
financial statements are extremely important and reference should be made
generally to ss. 155 to 172 of the CBCA, ss. 154 to 160 of the OBCA and
ss. 197 to 201 of the BCBCA. It is beyond the scope of this book to discuss
these requirements in any detail but what will be highlighted are some
specific issues relating to auditors.

Not all corporations require the appointment of an auditor. The various
sections dealing with exemption and waiver (CBCA s. 163; OBCA s. 148;
BCBCA s. 197) speak mainly of non-reporting companies or those whose
gross revenues do not exceed certain limits or may, in the case of s. 148 of
the OBCA, combine both criteria. The propriety of exempting companies
other than those which are small and closely held and where none of the
shareholders believes such safeguard is necessary has been questioned by
Iacobucci, Pilkington and Prichard in *Canadian Business Corporations*
(1977), at page 396:

> The exemption should not be available to a wide range of companies.
> The requirement of an audit not only helps to ensure the reliability of
> financial statements but also has the effect of encouraging compliance
> with statutory requirements, checking corporate mismanagement, and
> developing standardized financial reporting. The costs involved are
> justified by these benefits, and therefore only small closely held cor-
> porations should be exempted from auditor requirements.

(b) Qualifications and Independence

The statutes uniformly impose qualifications upon eligibility for appointment as auditor. The BCBCA, for example, prescribes certain professional qualifications (s. 205). All the statutes disqualify persons from acting
as auditors who are not "independent" (CBCA, s. 161; BCBCA, s. 206; and
OBCA, s. 152) and, directly or indirectly, provide definitions of what does
and does not constitute "independence".

(c) Functions

The OBCA, CBCA, BCBCA and other provincial acts all require that
the auditor make such examination as will enable him to report on the
financial statements on an annual basis. The CBCA, for instance, in s. 170
gives the auditor a right to demand information and explanation from the

directors, officers, employees or agents of the corporation and he is also given access to records, documents, books, accounts and vouchers of the corporation or any of its subsidiaries that are, in his opinion, necessary to enable him to make the examination and give the report that is required by statute. The auditor must state whether the statement is in accordance with generally accepted accounting principles consistent with that period. (see OBCA s.153; CBCA s.169) Generally accepted accounting principles are set by the Canadian Institute of Chartered Accountants, which is the self-regulatory body for chartered accountants in Canada. Indeed, the CBCA so states in s. 70 of the Regulations. Does compliance with generally accepted accounting principles necessarily meant that the financial statements fairly present the financial position of a company? See Janne Chung, Poonam Puri and Linda Thorne, "Factors Influencing Auditor Liability in Canada" (June 2004), (unpublished manuscript on file with the authors) for a discussion of *Kripps v. Touche Ross & Co.*, [1998] B.C.J. No. 1670, 1998 CarswellBC 1540 (S.C.) in which the British Columbia Court of Appeal stated in obiter that the appropriate standard of care of an auditor is to ensure that financial statements are fair, not to merely ensure that they conform to GAAP.

In addition to his or her reporting duties, the auditor, as part of his general function of informing and reporting to shareholders, is under a duty to attend certain shareholders' meetings and answer any questions. It is worth noting that under s. 168(2) of the CBCA a director, as well as a shareholder, has the right to require the auditor to attend a shareholders' meeting (see also OBCA s. 151(2)).

One final point with regard to the duties of the auditor is significant. Under s. 247 of the CBCA, s. 253 of the OBCA and s. 228 of the BCBCA — the duties of the auditor, as set out in the statute, regulations, articles, by-laws or unanimous shareholder agreement can be enforced by application to the court. A present or former security holder, a director, an officer, the Director (under the CBCA), a creditor and any other person to whom the court grants standing may apply to the court for an order directing the auditor to comply with, or restraining him or her from acting in breach of his duties.

Certain rights have been conferred on the auditor to enable him to carry out his statutory duties. Not only is the auditor to have access to information required and such explanations as will enable him to make his report on the financial statements (CBCA, s. 170, OBCA, s. 153), but he also has the right to attend any general meeting and to be heard on any matter which concerns him (OBCA, s. 151(1); CBCA, s. 168(1)). In addition, corporate law statutes have codified the common law by awarding qualified privilege to any written statement or report which the auditor makes pursuant to his duties under the act (CBCA s.172and OBCA s.151(7)).

(d) Removal

There are two ways in which an auditor may be removed under the corporate law statues. An "interested party" may apply to the court for an order to disqualify or remove the auditor, or the shareholders may pass an ordinary resolution at a special or general meeting which has been called for the purpose of removing the auditor (CBCA ss. 161(4), 165(1); OBCA ss. 149(4), 152(4)). If the corporation is a reporting company, notice of removal must be given in the information circular, with the name of the management's new nominee placed on the proxy form (see CBCA ss. 168(5), (6); OBCA s. 149(5)). This is done in order to protect the independence of the auditor by providing him or her with an opportunity to place before the shareholders any explanation he feels they should have in order to evaluate a proposal to replace him. Consequently, management would not continuously seek to replace a questioning auditor with one who is more amenable to management interests.

(e) Oversight

Under National Instrument 52-108, there is an external oversight of auditors by the Canadian Public Accountability Board (CPAB). Every public accounting firm that issues auditors' reports with respect to the financial statements of reporting issuers must enter into an agreement with the CPAB. If CPAB is not satisfied with the audit firm's quality, the firm may cease to be a "participant in good standing", thus being prohibited from issuing auditor's reports. As you read the section on auditors' liability, keep in mind that there is now an oversight system in place to help ensure the quality of auditor's reports.

(f) Liability of Auditors

IACOBUCCI, PILKINGTON, AND PRICHARD,
Canadian Business Corporations
(1977), pp. 410–414 (footnotes omitted)

Although the Alberta, British Columbia, Ontario and Federal Acts impose several duties on an auditor, many of which depend upon his exercising professional judgment, they do not specify any standard of care and skill according to which those duties must be fulfilled, nor do they specify to whom the duties are owed. Case law on the nature and extent of an auditor's liability to third parties for negligent mis-statement is still developing as the principle in *Hedley Byrne v. Heller* is elaborated and applied. It may be that this common law development should not be cut short by premature codification. However, the question of an auditor's liability to third parties who rely on his report may be left open without precluding the establishment of standards which an auditor must meet in performing his duties.

Though Anglo-Canadian companies statutes specify the auditor's general duties, they do not, as Lord Justice Warrington pointed out in *Re City Equitable Fire Insurance Co., Ltd.*:

> . . . lay down any rule at all as to the amount of care, or skill, or investigation, or anything of that kind, which is to be brought to bear by the auditors in performing the duties which are imposed upon them. . . . That is left to be determined by the general rules which, in point of law, are held to govern the duties of the auditors, whether those rules are to be derived from the ordinary law, or from the terms under which the auditors are to be employed.

The standard of care which an auditor must meet may be specified in the company's articles, or in his contract, otherwise, the common law governs.

It can be argued that the judicial decisions governing an auditor's standard of care do not go far enough to ensure that an auditor provides shareholders with the kind of independent assessment which alone is useful to them. The traditional judicial formulation of an auditor's duty was propounded prior to the establishment of statutory requirements of corporate financial disclosure and prior to the requirement that companies appoint auditors. Even though in modern times the corporate context has changed and there has been improvement in accounting standards and increased concern about the need for accurate and full disclosure of financial information to shareholders, the traditional formulation of auditor's duties is still applied. The issue is whether the auditor is bound only to verify information presented by management or whether he is also under a duty to investigate and ensure that the information is reliable — that is, in the traditional catch-phrase, whether he must be a watchdog or a bloodhound.

Traditionally the auditor has been required to be merely a watchdog, as Lord Justice Lopes stated in the oft-quoted case of *Re Kingston Cotton Mill Co. (No. 2)*:

> It is the duty of an auditor to bring to bear on the work he has to perform that skill, care, and caution which a reasonably competent, careful, and cautious auditor would use. What is reasonable skill, care and caution must depend on the particular circumstances of each case. An auditor is not bound to be a detective, or, as was said, to approach his work with suspicion or with a foregone conclusion that there is something wrong. He is watch dog, but not a bloodhound. He is justified in believing tried servants of the company in whom confidence is placed by the company. He is entitled to assume that they are honest, and to rely upon their representations, provided he takes reasonable care. If there is anything calculated to excite suspicion he should probe

it to the bottom; but in the absence of anything of that kind he is only bound to be reasonably cautious and careful.

It would appear from this test and its application in subsequent cases, that unless an auditor comes across something which arouses his suspicion, he is not obliged to undertake investigations to substantiate whether the information before him is in fact reliable. In an obiter statement in *Fomento (Sterling Area), Ltd. v. Selsdon Fountain Pen Co. Ltd.*, Lord Denning challenged this traditional formulation of an auditor's responsibility:

> What is the proper function of an auditor? It is said that he is bound only to verify the sum, the arithmetical conclusion, by reference to the books and all necessary vouching material and oral explanations; and that it is no part of his function to inquire whether an article is covered by patents or not. I think this is too narrow a view. An auditor is not to be confined to the mechanics of checking vouchers and making arithmetical computations. He is not to be written off as a professional "adder-upper and subtractor". His vital task is to take care to see that errors are not made, be they errors of computation, or errors of omission or commission, or downright untruths. To perform this task property, he must come to it with an inquiring mind — not suspicious of dishonesty, I agree — but suspecting that someone may have made a mistake somewhere and that a check must be made to ensure that there has been none.

Lord Denning's formulation of the auditor's responsibility gives effect to the modern purpose of the audit requirement and the report of the auditor to the shareholders. As one commentator asks:

> . . . why should this discretion be limited to cases where the clues appear before his eyes? What great burdens would be thrown on him if his duties included those Lord Denning suggested flow from his appointment? In what sense does he fulfil his obligation of conducting an independent check if he is to rely "blindly" (or subject to a formal check) on the word and work of those in control of the company? A shareholder must expect and receive an unbiased and uninfluenced assessment by his expert of the financial position of his company. It is only the auditor who can fulfil the role expected of him.

In the recent Supreme Court of Canada case of *Haig v. Bamford*, Dickson, J. in an *obiter* statement emphasized the importance of the auditor's responsibility:

> The increasing growth and changing role of corporations in modern society has been attended by a new perception of the societal role of the profession of accounting. The day when the accountant served

only the owner-manager of a company and was answerable to him alone has passed. The complexities of modern industry combined with effects of specialization, the impact of taxation, urbanization, the separation of ownership from management, the rise of professional corporate managers, and a host of other factors, have led to marked changes in the role and responsibilities of the accountant, and in the reliance which the public must place upon his work. The financial statements of the corporations upon which his reports can effect the economic interests of the general public as well as of shareholders and potential shareholders.

With the added prestige and value of his services has come, as the leaders of the profession have recognized, a concomitant and commensurately increased responsibility to the public. It seems unrealistic to be oblivious to these developments.

However, it has not yet been established in the case law that, in the absence of suspicious circumstances, an auditor is under any obligation to examine into the reliability of the statements on which he reports.

Since it is arguable that the case law has not established adequate standards for auditors, and since the duties of other corporate personnel, namely directors, officers and trustees under indentures, are specified in reformed corporations legislation, it may well be that the standards required of auditors should also be delineated. The fact that standards of care and skill are not specified is the more significant in light of the fact that directors may be relieved of liability if they rely and act in good faith on statements contained in an auditor's report. If the shareholders are expected to rely on auditors' reports and the directors are exempted from liability if they have relied upon them, then auditors ought to be under a duty to conduct their work in a manner which can be relied upon with confidence.

In addition to establishing a standard according to which an auditor must exercise his duty, it would also be useful if corporations legislation specified to whom the duty is owed. Though an auditor's contractual relationship is with the corporation, his duty is to report not to the corporation but to the shareholders. Whether it can be implied from this that the auditor owes a duty of care to the shareholder, a breach of which would give the shareholder a cause of action in his own right, is far from clear.

Notes and Questions

1 The issue of the liability of auditors has been addressed in different ways throughout the commonwealth. In *Scott Group Ltd. v. McFarlane*, [1978] 1 N.Z.L.R. 553 (C.A.), the New Zealand Court of Appeal found that the auditors of a corporation owed a duty of care to a plaintiff who had acquired the corporation through a takeover bid. In his majority judgement, Woodhouse J. found that there was a sufficient relationship to ground liability for four reasons. 1. The auditors were professionals

who were in the business of providing expert advice for a reward. 2. Auditors of a public company must be taken to have accepted not only a duty to shareholders but also to those whom they can "reasonably forsee . . . will need to use and rely upon [the accounts] when dealing with the company or its members in significant matters affecting the Company assets and business." 3.The auditors had no direct knowledge that a takeover bid was contemplated, but they knew that the accounts would become a matter of public record under the *Companies Act* of 1955 and that concerned persons, such as the Scott Group, would have direct access to them. 4. There is no opportunity in the ordinary case for any intermediate examination of the underlying authenticity of a company's accounts.

In *Caparo Industries plc v. Dickman*, [1990] 2 W.L.R. 358 (U.K. H.L.), Camparo Industries Ltd. purchased a controlling interest in Fidelity plc on the strength of an unqualified auditor's report on Fidelity's financial statements. Once it acquired control, it discovered that there were material mistakes in the financial statements, and a reported £1.3 million profit should have been a £400,000 loss. Caparo sued the auditor, alleging negligence in the audit of Fidelity's financial statements. The case went all the way to the House of Lords on the issue of whether the auditor owed Caparo a duty of care either as an auditor or a potential acquiror. The House of Lords held that the auditor owed no duty of care to Caparo in either capacity. In general, their Lordships held that in order to establish tortuous liability, the plaintiff must show foreseeability of damages, proximity of relationship and circumstances that would make it just and equitable to impose liability. Perhaps more importantly, the Lords held that any cause of action against the auditors for breach of duty belonged to the company. Thus, if auditors were negligent, only the company could sue the auditors, and not an individual shareholder. In essence, *Caparo* stands for the proposition that no individual shareholder has an action either in negligence nor for breach of contract against the firm's auditors. *Caparo* thus greatly restricts the class of persons to whom the auditors owe a *Hedley Byrne* duty.

For a comment on *Caparo*, see Brian R. Cheffins, "Auditors' Liability in the House of Lords: A Signal Canadian Courts Should Follow" (1991), 18 Can. Bus. L. J. 118. Professor Cheffins argues that *Caparo* was rightly decided. He notes that the common argument in favour of tortuous liability for negligence is that it will induce a higher degree of care in potential tortfeasors, as they will do their audits more carefully out of fear of being found liable for mistakes. Cheffins disputes this argument. He notes that while auditor's liability in tort has historically been circumscribed, it is nonetheless possible for a user of the financial statements to contract with the auditor to establish liability should the audit be negligently performed. This is in fact rarely done. Cheffins argues that if tort liability was a cost-effective tool for inducing adequate care, we would in fact observe more instances in which such contracts were struck. Professor Cheffins argues that it is often in fact more cost-effective for, say, a potential acquiror to hire its own financial experts "to evaluate the corporation being acquired to assess the regulatory and market impact of the acquisition," rather than to contract with the auditor. He further argues that imposing liability to third parties who rely on financial statements would in fact have a minimal effect on the degree of care taken by auditors, since auditors are already liable to the companies with whom they contract to perform audits. In net, he argues that imposing additional liability would likely increase the costs of an audit without yielding additional benefits in the form of a higher degree of care. Do you agree?

2 In *Hercules Management Ltd. v. Ernst & Young*, [1997] 2 S.C.R. 165, 1997 CarswellMan 198, 1997 CarswellMan 1999, Ernst & Young was hired in 1971 by Northguard Acceptance Ltd. (NGA) and Northguard Holdings Ltd. (NGH) to audit their financial statements and to provide audit reports to the companies' shareholders. In 1984 NGA and NGH went into receivership. In 1988 shareholders and investors in NGA and NGH brought an action against Ernst & Young, claiming the audit reports for 1980, 1981 and 1982 were negligently prepared and seeking damages in tort and contract. Ernst & Young brought a motion in the Manitoba Court of Queen's Bench seeking to have the plaintiffs' claims dismissed. The motions judge granted the motion with respect to four plaintiffs. An appeal to the Manitoba Court of Appeal was dismissed. La Forest J., in addressing whether the appellants were owed a duty of care by the respondents, reiterated the two-part test for determining such a duty and stated that the test applies to negligent misrepresentation:

> In Kamloops, *supra*, at pp. 10-11, Wilson J. restated Lord Wilberforce's test in the following terms:
>
> (1) is there a sufficiently close relationship between the parties (the [defendant] and the person who has suffered the damage) so that, in the reasonable contemplation of the [defendant] carelessness on its part might cause damage to that person? If so,
>
> (2) are there any considerations which ought to negative or limit (a) the scope of the duty and (b) the class of persons to whom it is owed or (c) the damages to which a breach of it may give rise?
>
> As will be clear from the cases earlier cited, this two-stage approach has been applied by this Court in the context of various types of negligence actions, including actions involv-

ing claims for different forms of economic loss. Indeed, it was implicitly endorsed in the context of an action in negligent misrepresentation in *Edgeworth Construction Ltd. v. N. D. Lea & Associates Ltd.*, [1993] 3 S.C.R. 206, at pp. 218-19. The same approach to defining duties of care in negligent misrepresentation cases has also been taken in other Commonwealth courts. In *Scott Group Ltd. v. McFarlane*, [1978] 1 N.Z.L.R. 553, for example, a case that dealt specifically with auditors' liability for negligently prepared audit reports, the *Anns* test was adopted and applied by a majority of the New Zealand Court of Appeal.

I see no reason in principle why the same approach should not be taken in the present case. Indeed, to create a "pocket" of negligent misrepresentation cases (to use Professor Stapleton's term) in which the existence of a duty of care is determined differently from other negligence cases would, in my view, be incorrect; see: Jane Stapleton, "Duty of Care and Economic Loss: a Wider Agenda" (1991), 107 L.Q. Rev. 249. This is not to say, of course, that negligent misrepresentation cases do not involve special considerations stemming from the fact that recovery is allowed for pure economic loss as opposed to physical damage. Rather, it is simply to posit that the same general framework ought to be used in approaching the duty of care question in both types of case.

La Forest J. held that the first branch of the test depends upon whether there is a close enough relationship between the plaintiff and defendant to constitute a relationship of proximity. He then examined how proximity would be found in a negligent misrepresentation case:

> To my mind, proximity can be seen to inhere between a defendant-representor and a plaintiff-representee when two criteria relating to reliance may be said to exist on the facts: (a) the defendant ought reasonably to foresee that the plaintiff will rely on his or her representation; and (b) reliance by the plaintiff would, in the particular circumstances of the case, be reasonable. To use the term employed by my colleague, Iacobucci J., in *Cognos*, *supra*, at p. 110, the plaintiff and the defendant can be said to be in a "special relationship" whenever these two factors inhere.

As well, the plaintiff's reliance on the defendant's statements must be reasonable. However, La Forest J. rejected the additional requirements that the House of Lords apply in cases of negligent misrepresentation, as not being relevant to the existence of a *prima facie* duty of care:

As should be evident from its very terms, the reasonable foreseeability/reasonable reliance test for determining a *prima facie* duty of care is somewhat what broader than the tests used both in the cases decided before *Anns*, *supra*, and in those that have rejected the *Anns* approach. Rather than stipulating simply that a duty of care will be found in any case where reasonable foreseeability and reasonable reliance inhere, those cases typically require (a) that the defendant know the identity of either the plaintiff or the class of plaintiffs who will rely on the statement, and (b) that the reliance losses claimed by the plaintiff stem from the particular transaction in respect of which the statement at issue was made. This narrower approach to defining the duty can be seen in a number of the more prominent English decisions dealing either with auditors' liability specifically or with liability for negligent misstatements generally. (See, *e.g.*: *Candler v. Crane, Christmas & Co.*, [1951] 2 K.B. 164 (C.A.), at pp. 181-82 and p. 184, per Denning L.J. (dissenting); *Hedley Byrne & Co. v. Heller & Partners Ltd.*, [1964] A.C. 465; *Caparo*, *supra*, per Lord Bridge, at p. 576, and per Lord Oliver, at pp. 589.) It is also evident in the approach taken by this Court in *Haig v. Bamford*, [1977] 1 S.C.R. 466.

While I would not question the conclusions reached in any of these judgments, I am of the view that inquiring into such matters as whether the defendant had knowledge of the plaintiff (or class of plaintiffs) and whether the plaintiff used the statements at issue for the particular transaction for which they were provided is, in reality, nothing more than a means by which to circumscribe — for reasons of policy — the scope of a representor's potentially infinite liability. As I have already tried to explain, determining whether "proximity" exists on a given set of facts consists in an attempt to discern whether, as a matter of simple justice, the defendant may be said to have had an obligation to be mindful of the plaintiff's interests in going about his or her business. Requiring, in addition to proximity, that the defendant know the identity of the plaintiff (or class of plaintiffs) and that the plaintiff use the statements in question for the specific purpose for which they were prepared amounts, in my opinion, to a tacit recognition that considerations of basic fairness may sometimes give way to other pressing concerns. Plainly stated, adding further requirements to the duty of care test provides a means by which policy concerns that are extrinsic to simple justice — but that are, nevertheless, fundamentally important — may be taken into account in assessing whether the defendant should be compelled to compensate the plaintiff for losses suffered. In other words, these further requirements serve a policy-based limiting function with respect to the ambit of the duty of care in negligent misrepresentation actions.

These policy-based requirements are, La Forest J. held, more appropriately considered under the second branch of the test. Regarding policy, La Forest examined the concerns that exposing auditors to negligent misrepresentation claims would lead to indeterminate liability and much higher costs faced by auditors in the form of insurance premiums, resources expended on avoiding liability and litigation:

> In applying the two-stage *Anns/Kamloops* test to negligent misrepresentation actions against auditors, therefore, policy considerations reflecting those repercussions should be taken into account. In the general run of auditors' cases, concerns over indeterminate liability will serve to negate a *prima facie* duty of care. But while such concerns may exist in most such cases, there may be particular situations where they do not. In other words, the specific factual matrix of a given case may render it an "exception" to the general class of cases in that while (as in most auditors' liability cases) considerations of proximity under the first branch of the *Anns/Kamloops* test might militate in favour of finding that a duty of care inheres, the typical concerns surrounding indeterminate liability do not arise. This needs to be explained.
> As discussed earlier, looking to factors such as "knowledge of the plaintiff (or an identifiable class of plaintiffs) on the part of the defendant" and "use of the statements at issue for the precise purpose or transaction for which they were prepared" really amounts to an attempt to limit or constrain the scope of the duty of care owed by the defendants. It the purpose of the *Anns/Kamloops* test is to determine (a) whether or not a *prima facie* duty of care exists and then (b) whether or not that duty ought to be negated or limited, then factors such as these ought properly to be considered in the second branch of the test once the first branch concerning "proximity" has been found to be satisfied. To my mind, the presence of such factors in a given situation will mean that worries stemming from indeterminacy should not arise, since the scope of potential liability is sufficiently delimited. In other words, in cases where the defendant knows the identity of the plaintiff (or of a class of plaintiffs) and where the defendant's statements are used for the specific purpose or transaction for which they were made, policy considerations surrounding indeterminate liability will not be of any concern since the scope of liability can readily be circumscribed. Consequently, such considerations will not override a positive finding on the first branch of the *Anns/Kamloops* test and a duty of care may quite properly be found to exist . . .

The foregoing analysis should render the following points clear. A *prima facie* duty of care will arise on the part of a defendant in a negligent misrepresentation action when it can be said (a) that the defendant ought reasonably to have foreseen that the plaintiff would rely on his representation and (b) that reliance by the plaintiff, in the circumstances, would be reasonable. Even though, in the context of auditors' liability cases, such a duty will often (even if not always) be found to exist, the problem of indeterminate liability will frequently result in the duty being negated by the kinds of policy considerations already discussed. Where, however, indeterminate liability can be shown not to be a concern on the facts of a particular case, a duty of care will be found to exist.

Turning to the facts of the case, La Forest J. found that while the respondent owed the plaintiffs a *prima facie* duty of care, the second part of the test was not met. While the respondent had knowledge of the plaintiffs, the purpose of the auditor's report is to assist the shareholders as a group in scrutinizing the conduct of the company's affairs and to protect the company from the consequences of incorrect financial statements. The purpose is not to assist individual shareholders in making investment decisions. He rejected the appellants' claims that the respondents had agreed to prepare reports aimed at aiding them in protecting their individual investments, and dismissed the appeal.

3 The narrowing of auditor liability brought about by *Hercules* was closely followed by an amendment to the CBCA from joint and several liability of defendants to proportionate liability in situations where there is a financial loss that arises out of an error, omission or misstatement in financial information (CBCA s. 237.3(1)). Under the old scheme of joint and several liability, if the auditors were responsible for, e.g., 5% of the plaintiff's losses, with the company and any other defendants being 95% responsible, the auditor could still be liable for 100% of the plaintiff's losses. Under the new scheme, with some exceptions, the auditors would be liable only to the extent that they were responsible for the losses. See P. Puri and S. Ben-Ishai, "Proportionate Liability Under the CBCA in the Context of Recent Corporate Governance Reform: Canadian Auditors in the Wrong Place at the Wrong Time?" (2003) 39 C.B.L.J. 1. Professors Puri and Ben-Ishai argue that the threat of shareholder litigation acts as an incentive for auditors to perform their function effectively, and in light of recent corporate governance and accounting scandals that have reduced investor confidence in auditors, the reduction in the scope of auditor's liability is not a favourable development.

(g) Evaluation

Poonam Puri, in her article "Converging Numbers: Harmonization of Accounting Standards in the Context of the Role of the Auditor in Corporate Governance" (in A. Anand and W. Flanagan, Eds., Responding to Globalization: Queen's Annual Business Law Symposium 2001 (Toronto: Carswell, 2001)), raises some serious questions about the credibility of the auditor's role in the corporate governance of public corporations, in light of the recent financial collapse of Enron and the demise of accounting firm Arthur Andersen. Puri notes that accounting standards provide broad principles and argues that they allow management the ability to posture and afford auditors too much discretion in determining whether management's financial statements fairly present the financial picture of the company. While some may consider the flexibility in GAAP a strength, Puri argues that the wide scope of discretion afforded to auditors assists in creating an environment where auditors are more likely to succumb to pressure by management to report financial data in ways favourable to management. If an accounting principle is generally accepted in that sense, and if it has been used in past financial statements, then an auditor may certify a company's financial statements notwithstanding that the particular principle chosen might not result in the fairest presentation of the company's results for the past year.

Puri is also concerned about the manner in which accountants are appointed and dismissed. Notwithstanding that the corporations statutes may require that this is to be done by shareholders, the reality is that management controls who the accountant is to be and also decides when an accountant is to be dismissed. As we have seen, the accountant is given independent rights of audience and explanation before the shareholders if he is dismissed. But it may be queried how often one of the major national accounting firms will take advantage of these statutory rights with respect to the audit of a large public corporation.

Responding to the financial collapse of Enron and Worldcom and the demise of accounting firm Arthur Andersen, US Congress passed the *Sarbanes-Oxley Act* of 2002 (SOX) which required the US Securities and Exchange Commission (SEC) to, *inter alia*, strengthen its rules on auditor independence and clarify the relationship between the auditor and a company's audit committee. SOX and related SEC rules clarify auditor independence requirements by creating bright line prohibitions against certain non-audit activities, by requiring audit partner rotation and by playing restrictions on audit partner compensation and employment relationships. As required by SOX, the SEC also promulgated Rule 10A-3 which makes it clear that the audit committee, not management, is responsible for appointing, compensating and overseeing the company's relationship with its auditors. The audit committee is also charged with resolving any disputes between the auditors and management over financial statement reporting. Finally, SOX created the Public Companies Accountability Oversight Board

(PCAOB), which regulates public accounting firms, including non-US accounting firms, that audit the financial statements of SEC reporting companies.

In light of the competition and convergence in corporate governance and global capital markets, Canadian regulatory reform largely mirrored the US changes. The Canadian Institute of Chartered Accountants created new independence standards for auditors in 2003. Canadian securities regulators released Multi-lateral Instrument 52-110, discussed below, which defines the audit committee's role and composition. As noted earlier, the Canadian Public Companies Accountability Board has been created, with similar functions as PCAOB, its US counterpart. In May 2004, proposals were also released to strengthen the corporate governance provisions in the CBCA.

(h) The Audit Committee

The CBCA, s. 171, and the OBCA, s. 158, require the appointment of an audit committee in large or widely held corporations. In each case, the audit committee is to be composed of not fewer than three directors, a majority of whom shall not be officers or employees of the company. The essential task of this "independent" audit committee is to review the company's financial statements before they are signed by the directors and presented to the shareholders. In each case the auditor is given the right to appear before any meeting of the audit committee and may be required to appear before the audit committee when it so requests. The auditor is also given an independent right to call a meeting of the audit committee to consider any matter that the auditor believes should be brought to the attention of the directors or the shareholders.

Stricter rules regarding audit committee independence are prescribed by securities law. Multilateral Instrument 52-110, adopted in 2004 by all Canadian securities jurisdictions save British Columbia, requires every member of the audit committee of an issuer to be independent (with some exceptions). MI52-110 applies a more restrictive definition of "independence" than corporate statutes. At the time of publication of this book, corporate statutes only require that the majority of audit committee members not be officers or employees of the company, while Multilateral Instrument 52-110 disallows any "material relationship" which could interfere with a member's independent judgement (s. 1.4). The Instrument also requires that audit committee members be "financially literate", a requirement not currently present in the corporate statutes (s. 3.1(4)). Under MI 52-110, audit committees are now responsible for overseeing the work of the external auditor, for preapproving all non-audit services to be conducted by the auditor for the company or its subsidiaries and for reviewing the financial reporting documents before they are publicly released. For a comment on the audit committee's composition and responsibilities, see Poonam Puri and Stephanie Ben-Ishai, "Proportionate Liability Under the CBCA in the Context of Recent Corporate Governance Reform: Canadian Auditors in the Wrong Place at the Wrong Time?" (2003) 39 C.B.L.J. 1.

Chapter 10

Special Aspects of the Closely Held
or Private Corporation

1. INTRODUCTION

Although the vast majority of Canadian corporations are closely held or private corporations, there has been relatively little attention paid by the courts or the legislatures to devising special legal rules for their treatment. It is not easy to point to a widely accepted definition of the closely held corporation, but there are some features of such corporations that are generally discernible. Shareholders of such corporations are few in number and usually take an active part in the corporation's business. The shares of the corporation are not publicly traded and generally the resources of the corporation, both in terms of its invested capital and ability to attract additional capital, are limited. However, there are notable exceptions such as the Jim Pattison Group, the PCL Construction Group and Ellis-Don Inc.

In many respects the closely held corporation can be viewed as an incorporated partnership which, *inter alia*, emphasizes the consensual relationship among the shareholders. As such, they will want to determine who will become a shareholder to ensure they can get along with the individual and will often insist on unanimity of decisions, thereby rejecting the majority rule of corporation law. Because they often depend on the corporation for their livelihood, shareholders of closely held corporations will normally want to play an effective role in management and may reinforce this, if necessary or desirable, by seeking a veto power over major decisions.

Before dealing with some of the ways that shareholders of such corporations arrange their affairs and deal with control of the corporation, we will take a brief look at the historical development of the closely held or private corporation.

The following is extracted from Iacobucci and Johnston, "The Private or Closely Held Corporation", in Zeigel, Ed., *Studies in Canadian Company Law*, Vol. 2 (1973) 68, at pp. 72–80 (footnotes omitted).

LEGISLATIVE TREATMENT OF THE PRIVATE
OR CLOSELY-HELD CORPORATION

1. Survey of Corporation Statutes

(a) The United Kingdom

In the light of modern legislative developments concerning the private corporation, it is interesting to trace the origin of the private corporation under Anglo-Canadian law. As with so much of Canadian company law doctrine, the private corporation originated in the United Kingdom and was adopted subsequently by Canadian jurisdictions.

Although a term of usage in the 18th century, the private corporation did not enter the statute books formally until the 1907 *Companies Act* and reappeared in the *Companies (Consolidation) Act* 1908 with the three basic conditions found in its definition today. The 1908 Act introduced the distinction between the private and public company and required only the latter to file publicly with the registrar a financial statement in the form of a balance sheet. The reasons for the introduction of the private company appear to be, first, to allow the small partnership (indeed, the "family" company after *Salomon v. Salomon & Co.*) to become an incorporated entity and, second, to permit such entity to enjoy certain advantages. The immediate benefit for the small enterprise, in addition to limited liability of its members notwithstanding their full participation in the affairs of the company, was the conferral of specified privileges and immunities, the most notable of which has become the relief from publicly filing copies of its financial statements.

Although the private corporation was primarily invented for the small concern or family business, it was widely used by the large enterprise through, for example, the incorporation of subsidiaries. Consequently, as a result of the recommendation of the 1945 Report of the Committee on Company Law Amendment (the Cohen Report), a new revision of the definition of private company was enacted to exempt more precisely only the small family company from the requirement of public filing of financial statements. This revision introduced the "exempt private company" which appeared in the 1948 *Companies Act*. Although its basic purpose was simply to exempt only genuine private companies from the obligation to file statements, in practice the new definition proved unworkable so that the cure was apparently worse than the disease.

The next round commenced with the recommendation of the 1962 Report of the Company Law Committee (The Jenkins Report) to abolish the distinctions between (a) the exempt and non-exempt private company, and (b) the private company and public company. However, only the former recommendation was followed by the *Companies Act*, 1967, which eliminated the troublesome exempt private company with the result that the public-private distinction remains in the United Kingdom. If the other recommendation of the Jenkins Report on abolishing private companies had been adopted, the legislation would have gone full circle in about 60 years.

In summary then, the United Kingdom position is as follows:

(1) There is a private-public company distinction recognized by statute.

(2) The definition of the private company is one which
    (a) by its articles restricts the right to transfer its shares,
    (b) limits the number of its members to 50 with certain modifications, and
    (c) prohibits any offer of its shares or debentures to the public.

(3) The main advantages of the private company over the public company are
    (a) a private company may be formed and start business more easily and cheaply than the public company, and
    (b) a private company is free from several formalities and enjoys special privileges unavailable to the public company.

[The foregoing summary of the U.K. position was materially altered by the U.K. *Companies Act, 1980* (now consolidated in the U.K. *Companies Act, 1989*), which, instead of defining private company, contains a definition of public company only, thereby making the private company the residual type of company under the statute. This was necessitated by the Common Market directive on company law harmonization. For a full discussion of the matter, see Prentice, *Companies Act 1980,* 4-19 (1980).]

* * *

(c) United States

In the United States, statutory recognition of the private company, or closely-held corporation or close corporation [C.H.C.] as it is called in that country, has come rather late compared to other countries. In fact, it was not until the 1940's that pressure for special legislation governing close corporations developed. Furthermore, the number of states which have adopted legislative changes since the pressure for reform was initiated is not great. However, several jurisdictions in the United States have adopted special provisions dealing with the C.H.C. or, going further, adopted a separate chapter of the corporation statute for the close corporation. It is interesting to note that in some of the relatively recent United States statutes the C.H.C. is defined in basically the same terms as the United Kingdom definition of a private company of 1908. . .

[A]t this juncture that the United States statutory developments on the C.H.C., although later in starting, appear to have caught up and indeed surpassed Anglo-Canadian treatment of the subject in many respects; the approach of conferring limited privileges on the C.H.C. has been supplemented by a more fundamental examination of the nature of the C.H.C. with a view to endowing it with increased flexibility of operation.

(d) Canada

The federal *Canada Corporations Act* and the corporations legislation of all the provinces of Canada, except Newfoundland, Nova Scotia, Ontario, and Quebec, specifically provide for the private company distinction. There are differences among the various jurisdictions of Canada in the treatment of several aspects of the private company, but the legislation is basically similar to and is modelled on the 1908 United Kingdom statute. Although the Canadian jurisdictions did not suffer the agony of the United Kingdom "exempt private company" experiment, Ontario and the federal legislators have recently shown signs of undergoing some pains of change in their recent attempts at reforms of their corporation statutes.

Under the *Canada Corporations Act*, the definition of private company again is based on the 1908 United Kingdom statute. In the 1970 amendments to the *Canada Corporations Act*, certain important changes were made to the statute, including the introduction of the "constrained share company". The rationale for this type of company is to allow federal public companies to restrict the number of shares which can be held by persons who are not Canadian citizens where such a restriction is imposed by other legislation. In addition certain provisions were introduced for the mandatory disclosure of financial information for all companies, whether private or public, under certain financial conditions.

The most recent Canadian developments relating to the private company, indeed to company law generally, are the Federal Proposals and the *Draft Canada Act* prepared in connection therewith. Basically, the approach taken in the *Draft Canada Act* is that there is no single specific definition which establishes a private-public company distinction. Instead the corporation is defined functionally in various parts of the *Draft Canada Act* where it is deemed desirable to treat a C.H.C. differently from a widely-held corporation. Consequently, corporations under the *Draft Canada Act* in effect may be "private" or "public" depending on the particular function or activity dealt with in the statute. Furthermore, where separate treatment is necessitated, appropriate criteria for differentiating between the types of companies have been provided. Other changes, some of which are of an extremely fundamental nature in the treatment of a private company, have been made by the *Draft Canada Act* and these will be discussed under separate topics throughout this chapter.

[The *Canada Corporations Act* is the predecessor statute to the CBCA. The "*Draft Canada Act*" is now the CBCA. Under the CBCA, public corporations are distinguished from private on the basis that they are corporations that have made a "distribution to the public" or are "distributing corporations". For details of this distinction and its implications see, *infra*, Chapter 3, section 4(a).

(e) Ontario Corporation Legislation

(1) The Select Committee Recommendation

The Ontario Select Committee on Company Law in its 1967 Report noted the principal reasons for the original introduction of the private company distinction:

(a) as a relief from publicity of accounts of the company; and
(b) to reinforce the prohibition against private companies offering their securities to the public.

The Select Committee pointed out that these reasons did not apply in Ontario because, first, Ontario corporate legislation never did require companies incorporated under it to file, and make public, annual financial statements; and second, the securities laws of Ontario have offered protection to the public in the sale of corporate securities, so that to require companies to have charter prohibitions against public offerings of their securities was unnecessary. Consequently the Select Committee concluded that the distinction between the private company and public company should be abolished, and recommended appropriate amendments to the provisions of the corporation statute which gave private companies certain privileges and rights, none of which, in the view of the Committee, were worth retaining.

(2) The Basic Distinction in the B.C.A.

Ironically, while the Federal Proposals have followed the Select Committee's recommendation, the Ontario B.C.A. has not. The distinction made in the B.C.A. — between those companies offering their securities to the public ("offering corporations") and those which do not ("non-offering corporations") represents a compromise with some attendant difficulties.

[The "Select Committee" report referred to above (frequently referred to as the "Lawrence Report", after its chairman), resulted in the enactment of the predecessor statute to the current OBCA. The current OBCA, enacted in 1982 and proclaimed on July 29, 1983, makes periodic distinctions between public and private corporations, as in the CBCA. For details of this distinction and its implications see, *infra*, Chapter 3, section 4(a).

The *Securities Act* (Ontario), R.S.O. 1990, c. S.5 ("OSA") formerly distinguished between public and private corporations on a different basis from the OBCA, defining a "private company" as a corporation having fewer than 50 shareholders, imposing restrictions on the transferability of shares, and not offering its securities for sale to the public. This "private company" concept has been replaced by a "closely held issuer" exemption under OSC Rule 45-501 — *Exempt Distributions*. Closely held issuers are required to impose restrictions on the transferability of shares and have no more than 35 beneficial shareholders (exclusive of investors entitled to purchase securities under certain other exemptions and employees). Another important definition in the OSA is "reporting issuer". Reporting issuers (as defined in s. 1(1) of the Act) are basically companies that have offered their shares to the public or that trade on a stock exchange. Reporting issuers are subject to (*inter alia*) restrictions relating to the issuance and trading of their securities, takeover bids and insider trading.

For a discussion of whether there should be separate legislation for private corporations, in view of the differences between private and public corporations, see Brian R. Cheffins, "U.S. Close Corporations Legislation: A Model Canada Should Not Follow" (1990), 35 McGill L. J. 160.]

2. RESTRICTIONS ON THE TRANSFER OF SHARES

(a) Statutory and Contractual Provisions

The major provisions concerning restrictions on the transfer of shares are found in CBCA ss. 6(1)(d), 49(8) and (9) and OBCA ss. 5(1), 56(3) and (8)–(10).

COATES, "Share Transfer and Transmission Restrictions in the Close Corporation"
(1968), 3 U.B.C.L. Rev. 96 at pp. 98–104 (footnotes omitted)

Why Restrictive Provisions Are Needed

Share transfer and transmission restrictions are needed for many reasons, some of the main ones being: (i) to prevent intrusion of undesirable business associations; (ii) to preserve the relative interests of the owners; (iii) to resolve deadlock (or as a control device); (iv) to comply with [the definition of private company in legislation]; (v) to anticipate and prevent unnecessary conflict; (vi) to ensure continuity of the business; (vii) to provide a market at an acceptable price for the shares. The emphasis to be placed on any one of the above reasons will of course depend on the specific corporation.

In a public company or a private company other than a close corporation the transfer of shares in the company will normally have no effect on the operation or management of the business. In a close corporation, however, a transfer of shares may result in financial loss to the shareholders and to the company. If the new shareholder wishes to participate actively in the business it is often found that his personality, business skills, honesty, and energy do not correspond to those of the retiring shareholder and are not compatible with those of the remaining shareholders. Participants in a partnership or close corporation often associate originally because of their complementing skills and talents. If the new shareholder wishes merely to invest and not work in the business, friction will almost inevitably arise as to the mode and amount of distribution of income. In a close corporation profits are normally distributed by means of salaries. The active shareholders would normally be unwilling to pay an inactive shareholder a salary. Also, they would feel that they were entitled to take up the amount of the salary formerly paid to the shareholder who has just left because they have probably assumed most of his responsibilities and work. The problems become more acute if the new shareholder has purchased a controlling interest.

It is undesirable that the proportionate shareholders be altered except by unanimous consent. When the enterprise is initiated the owners agree on the control and profit division and it is usually desirable that this initial arrangement is not altered. This could be done by one shareholder buying all or a part of the holdings of another. This problem is especially serious in the United States where stock redemption plans (i.e., the corporation purchases the stock from the retiring shareholder) are used. For example, if A holds forty per cent (40%), B thirty per cent (30%) and C thirty per cent (30%), and B's stock is redeemed, A would then have complete control.

The use of share transfer restrictions as control devices and as a means of resolving deadlocks is a very important but often forgotten reason for the use of comprehensive transfer restrictions. Transfer restrictions are considered to be the basis of an effective control system. Variations of the buy-out agreement such as a "Russian Roulette" arrangement is an example of this. One shareholder should not be able to threaten to sell his shares to an undesirable person or to a competitor in order to force his will on other members. Since corporate assets are often not capable of being divided up and have little liquidation value, dissolution may not be the most desirable method of resolving deadlock. . . .

[Certain statutes] require that the right to transfer shares be restricted as a condition of being a private company, however, there is no minimum restriction specified which will satisfy the requirements of the Acts. For example, would a stipulation that shares could not be transferred to anyone with blue eyes be sufficient and satisfactory? Most of the restrictions which are adopted in the articles are a simple consent restriction.

Often the only potential purchasers for shares in a close corporation are the other shareholders and so in the absence of a binding buy-out agreement, stipulating a valuation price of formula, the selling shareholder is at the mercy of the remaining ones. Transfer restrictions in the form of buy-out agreements provide a market in the event of certain contingencies. Closely related to the problem of marketability of shares is the necessity of the minority preventing squeeze-outs by the majority, a situation which is becoming more frequent.

Transfer restrictions may even be desirable on preferred shares and on shareholders' loans or debentures, depending on the various rights attached such as voting, dividends or interest. In a joint venture corporation involving equal shareholders, a transfer restriction is essential because the purchaser of either party's fifty per cent (50%) obtains an automatic veto over the entire affairs of the corporation.

Comprehensive and sophisticated transfer and transmission restrictions are a necessity in a close corporation.

Nature of the Restriction and Some Preliminary Considerations

There are some things of importance which should be noted generally now even though they are discussed in more detail later in the paper. First, it is generally recognized that there is a difference between a transfer and transmission. A transfer is a voluntary change of ownership of the shares, *e.g.*, a normal sale. A transmission is a non-voluntary change of ownership by operation of law. A transfer or transmission restriction could be defined as any condition or limitation which qualifies the right of a shareholder or anyone acting through or on behalf of him to alienate his interest in a corporation. There is no limit as to the variety of restrictions which may be employed, and the events upon which they may be contingent. The rationale of restrictive provisions was succinctly stated by Mr. Justice Holmes in the case of *Barret v. King*.

> Stock in a corporation is not merely property. It also creates a personal relation analogous otherwise than technically to a partnership. [Hence] . . . there seems no greater objection to retaining the right of choosing one's associates in a corporation than in a firm.

The basic drafting problem is to anticipate all possible contingencies, not just the normal ones. The basic legal problem is whether by careful drafting one can block all transfers and transmissions.

Planning and preparing share transfer and transmission restrictions involves many general considerations such as the legality of the proposed restrictions, under what law the legality is determined, the efficacy of the restrictions in achieving the desired results, the instruments in which the restrictions should be placed, tax considerations, and the specific needs of each corporation and each shareholder. Examples of the latter are the number of shareholders, whether all of them participate in the affairs of the company, health, estate, and family of each of the shareholders, the kind of business they are involved in, the value of the business and its annual income. When preparing that part of the corporate paper which involves transfer restrictions, the lawyer must keep all these considerations in mind and not be enticed into accepting a standard form buy-sell or combined buy-sell and first option agreement which may be offered by the client's insurance advisor or a precedent text. It is an area where he must be imaginative and flexible.

Types of Restrictions, Their Advantages, Disadvantages and Validity

Variations of the main types of restrictions are almost infinite, but the main types utilized are: absolute prohibitions on share transfer limited in time, consent restraints requiring up to one hundred per cent (100%) approval of the directors or the shareholders; a first option provision or some variation such as a Russian Roulette arrangement; special time or event buy-out arrangements or options; and the buy-sell agreement contingent on death. There are many contingencies upon which a transfer or transmission restriction may be operative, and so the specific provision must be chosen carefully.

Absolute restrictions. In certain enterprises an absolute prohibition on share transfer unlimited in time would be the most advantageous but this has always been held invalid. However, it would seem that an absolute restraint limited in time may be valid but the time limit must be reasonable and necessary in the circumstances. Five years would probably be the longest period available regardless of the circumstances. Such a restriction may be necessary to ensure that certain skills or assets are guaranteed during the formative stages. Again, the joint venture corporation would be the most likely and frequent user of the absolute restriction. In any event an absolute restraint can be virtually ensured indirectly. A shareholders' agreement may provide that each party provide certain assets for a specific period of time, or the capital structure may be devised with a minimum amount in share capital and a maximum number of dollars in the form of a loan or debentures which are not repayable for a specified number of years. In either case a shareholder would be reluctant to sell his shares and leave all his original investment tied up in a business in which he is not a member and over which he has no control. An effectively drafted consent restriction will achieve almost the same result.

Consent restrictions. In practice, the consent restriction is adopted almost universally, probably because it appears in the Table A articles [a standard form set of articles appended to legislation in memorandum jurisdictions]. The mechanics of it are that no transfer is valid or effective until it has been approved by the directors, or the shareholders, or both, or a certain proportion of either or both. The main advantage of it is that the remaining shareholders can prevent the sale of shares to an undesirable outsider without tying up their own capital to purchase such shares. But this advantage would seem to be more than outweighed by the disadvantage that anyone wishing to sell is virtually at the mercy of the remaining shareholders and is very vulnerable to a "squeeze-out". The parties having the right of refusal do not have to give reasons for their refusal to transfer, the only requirement being that the refusal must be *bona fide* in the best interests of the company. The court will assume that the directors have acted *bona fide* even when reasons are not given. The directors do not have to give reasons and an examination for discovery to determine the reasons or grounds will be refused. Occasionally the court will infer *mala fides* from the circumstances or from the refusal to give reasons. If reasons are given, however, they can be examined by the court and declared wrong. Consent may be inferred from an entry in the share register and where the restriction is such that the directors have a power to refuse a transfer, inability to exercise this power of refusal due to deadlock will entitle the transferee to demand registration of the transfer. As is obvious, the consent restriction has always been accepted as valid in Canadian and English jurisdictions and has been held to bind an executor, a sheriff seizing under a writ of execution, and a trustee in bankruptcy.

First option restrictions. This is probably the best and most equitable *inter vivos* restriction. The mechanics of it are that any shareholder desiring to sell his shares must offer them to the other shareholders by a specified procedure and at a specified price before he can sell them to an outsider. There is no express or implied covenant that the remaining shareholders will purchase the shares so offered and no obligation to do so. Preciseness in drafting such a restriction is particularly vital. It must be stated whether the whole block has to be taken and if not what procedure of allocation is to be adopted. It also must be stated whether the restriction applies to transfers to both shareholders and outsiders obviously it must be in most cases. The first option overcomes the main disadvantage of the consent restriction in that it balances the relative positions of the buying and selling shareholders since the seller is no longer at the mercy of the remaining shareholders. But this may not solve his problems in that there may be no outside market for the shares, a situation which is not abnormal when dealing with a close corporation, especially if his interest is a minority one. The disadvantage to the remaining shareholders is that they have to produce the necessary cash to purchase the shares within, normally, ninety days. If they do not have the funds available they may find themselves forced to accept as a fellow shareholder an undesirable outsider. Again, this is even more crucial if the interest being sold is a majority one. This could be overcome to a certain extent by providing that the purchase price is to be paid off in either fixed annual instalments or as a percentage of gross or net profit. There are many useful variations of the normal first option provision such as the Russian Roulette arrangement or the similar restricted auction. The mechanics of the Russian Roulette arrangement are as follows: X offers to buy Y's shares for a certain price. Y then has the choice of accepting the offer or buying X's shares at the same price. The restricted auction eliminates some of the risk inherent in such a plan by providing that all the shares shall be sold at an auction with the present shareholders being the only allowable bidders. The advantage of both of these schemes is that they have a built in valuation mechanism eliminating one of the most difficult problems.

Event options. These are actually only an extension of the first option arrangement. They merely provide that at a special time or on the happening of a special event one party shall offer his shares to the other by a certain procedure and at a specified price. The following are examples of the special times or events which may trigger such an option: if one corporation isn't able to provide essential services, if one shareholder does not contribute a specified minimum amount of capital within a certain time period, bankruptcy, seizure of shares by writ of execution, termination of employment and retirement.

Buy-out arrangements. These provisions are usually made contingent on the same events as the ones listed above. The fact that there is a binding obligation on the remaining shareholders to purchase may make them more appropriate in certain circumstances such as retirement from employment or from the board of directors. There is a problem which will be discussed later of whether such provisions can bind a trustee in bankruptcy, a sheriff acting under a writ of execution, and any person taking from either of them. It is often desirable in connection with such provisions to provide for some kind of funding, possibly by arrangements that the price be paid off in instalments.

Buy-sell agreement. This is an agreement between all shareholders which provides that on the death of a shareholder his executors are obligated to sell his shares to the remaining shareholders at a specified price and the remaining shareholders are likewise obligated to purchase such shares when offered. There appears to be no question as to the validity of such an agreement, it being accepted that such is not a testamentary disposition and that each shareholder has an insurable interest in the life of the others. The advantages of such an agreement are obvious — ready cash is provided to the estate for estate taxes, succession duties, and normal living expenses, and, as suggested earlier, it being essential in a close corporation that the membership be selected and restricted, this agreement ensures continuity of the business and harmony among the shareholders. The arrangement may become unwieldy, however, if there are more than four shareholders or if there are significant differences in age, health and financial resources of the shareholders. It is essential that the buy-sell agreement be funded with life insurance.

(b) Judicial Interpretation of Restrictions

Smith & Fawcett Ltd., Re
[1942] 1 All E.R. 542, [1942] 1 Ch. 304 (C.A.)

The articles of association of Smith & Fawcett Ltd. provided that "the directors may at any time in their absolute and uncontrolled discretion refuse to register any transfer of shares." The appellant, as executor of his father, claimed to be registered in respect of 4,001 shares. The directors refused to register a transfer unless he was willing to sell 2,000 of the shares to a named director at a certain price, in which case they would register a transfer of the remainder.

LORD GREENE M.R.: The principles to be applied in cases where the articles of association of a company confer a discretion on directors with regard to the acceptance of transfers of shares are, for the present purposes, free from doubt. They must exercise their discretion *bona fide* in what they consider — not what a court may consider — to be in the interests of the company, and not for any collateral purpose. They must have regard to those considerations, and those considerations only, which the articles upon their true construction permit them to take into consideration. In construing the relevant provisions in the articles, it is to be borne in mind that one of the normal rights of a shareholder is the right to deal freely with his property and to transfer it to whomsoever he pleases. When it is said, as it has been said more than once, that regard must be had to this last consideration, it means, I apprehend, nothing more than this: that the shareholder has such a *prima facie* right, and that right is not to be cut down by uncertain language or doubtful implications. The right, if it is to be cut down, must be cut down with satisfactory clarity. It certainly does not mean that articles, if appropriately framed, cannot be allowed to cut down the right of transfer to any extent which the articles on their true construction permit.

There is also another consideration which I think is worth bearing in mind when one comes to examine the construction of any article that falls for consideration, and that is that this type of article is one which is for the most part confined to private companies. Private companies are, of course, separate entities in law just as much as are public companies, but from the business and personal point of view they are much more analogous to partnerships than to public corporations. Accordingly, it is to be expected that, in the articles of such a company, the control of the directors over the membership may be very strict indeed. There are very good business reasons, or there may be very good business reasons, why those who bring such companies into existence should give them a constitution which gives to the directors powers of the widest description.

In the present case the article is as follows:

The directors may at any time in their absolute and uncontrolled discretion refuse to register any transfer of shares.

As I have said, it is beyond question that that is a fiduciary power, and the directors must exercise it *bona fide* in what they consider to be the interests of the company. The language of the article does not point to any particular matter as being the only matter to which the directors are to pay attention in deciding whether or not they will allow the transfer to be registered. The article does not, for instance, say, as is to be found in some articles, that they may refuse to register any transfer of shares to a person not already a member of the company, nor does it say that they may refuse to register any transfer of shares to a transferee of whom they do not approve. In cases where articles are framed with some such limitation on the discretionary power of refusal as I have mentioned in the two examples which I have given, it follows on plain principle that, if they go outside the matters which the articles say are to be the only matters to which they are to have regard, the directors will have exceeded their powers.

Counsel for the appellant maintained that, whatever language was used in the articles, the power of the directors to refuse to register a transfer must always be limited to matters personal to the transferee, and he points out that in the present case there can be no personal objection to his client becoming a member of the company, for the simple reason that the directors are prepared to accept him as the holder of 2,000 of the shares which have come to him as legal personal representative of his father. Counsel therefore says that there is no personal objection to the transferee here, and that is the only matter which directors are entitled to take into account. He relies for that proposition upon observations in several authorities where that is laid down, but on examination of those authorities it becomes quite clear that the judges who delivered the judgments in them were dealing with the particular form of article which happened to be before them, and the form of article was one which by its express language confined the directors to the consideration of the desirability of admitting the proposed transferee to membership on grounds personal to him.

I cannot put the point, which I am endeavouring to make, with greater clearness than it is put by Warrington L.J., in *Re Bede Steam Shipping Co.* In that case the articles empowered the directors:

> . . . in their discretion and without assigning any reasons therefor [to] refuse to register the transfer of any shares (not being a fully paid up share) to any person of whom they do not approve as transferee and may decline to register the transfer of any fully paid up share or shares on certifying that in their opinion it is contrary to the interests of the company that the proposed transferee should be a member thereof.

That was the precise limitation on the directors' power to refuse the transfer which was in issue in that case. Warrington L.J., says this at p. 136:

> The article gives them one ground, and one ground only, for refusing to register the transfer of a fully-paid share, namely, that in their opinion it is contrary to the interests of the company that the proposed transferee should be a member.

It is perfectly clear from that observation that the court was not laying down some general rule to be applied to all forms of article, but was coming to a decision upon the particular article before it, the nature of which was such as to confine the directors to the consideration of one particular matter.

There is nothing, in my opinion, in principle or in authority to make it impossible to draft such a wide and comprehensive power to directors to refuse to transfer as to enable them to take into account any matter which they conceive to be in the interests of the company, and thereby to admit or not to admit a particular person and to allow or not to allow a particular transfer for reasons not personal to the transferee but bearing on the general interests of the company as a whole — such matters, for instance, as whether by passing a particular transfer the transferee would obtain too great a weight in the affairs of the company or might even perhaps obtain control. The question, therefore, is simply whether, on the true construction of the particular article, the directors are limited by anything except their *bona fide* view as to the interests of the company. In the present case the article is drafted in the widest possible terms, and I decline to write into that clear language any limitation other than a limitation, which is implicit by law, that a fiduciary power of this kind must be exercised *bona fide* in the interests of the company. Subject to that qualification, an article in this form appears to me to give the directors what it says, namely, an absolute and uncontrolled discretion.

That being my view on the question of law in this case, it only remains to consider the issue of fact which has been raised. It is said that on the evidence before us we ought to infer that the directors here were purporting to exercise their power to refuse a transfer, not *bona fide* in the interests of the company, but for some collateral purpose-namely, the desire of the leading director to acquire part of the shares for himself at an under-value. Speaking for myself, I strongly dislike being asked on affidavit evidence alone to draw inferences as to the *bona fides* or *mala fides* of the actors. In the present case the principal director has sworn an affidavit which, if accepted, makes it clear that, whether rightly or wrongly, the directors have *bona fide* considered the interests of the company and come to the conclusion that it would be undesirable to register the transfer of the totality of these shares.

We are invited to say that that does not represent the fact and that the real motive which influenced the deponent was not a consideration for the interests of the company but a consideration for his own personal interests. I for one, except in a clear case, am strongly opposed to drawing an inference of that kind from mere affidavit evidence. If it is desired to charge a deponent with having given an account of his motives and his reasons which is not the true account, then the person on whom the burden of proof lies should, in my judgment, take the ordinary and obvious course of requiring the deponent to submit himself to cross-examination. That does not, of course, mean that it is illegitimate to draw such inferences in a proper case. There may be on the face of the affidavit sufficient justification for doing so, but where you have the oath of the deponent, as we have it here, and the only grounds on which the court is asked to disbelieve it are matters of inference, many of them of a doubtful character, I for one must decline to give to those suggestions the weight which it is desired to give to them.

Accordingly, on the evidence I am satisfied, as the judge was satisfied, that there is no ground shown here for saying that the directors' refusal has been due to anything but a *bona fide* consideration of the interests of the company as the directors see them. That being so, and that being on the true construction of the article the only matter to which the directors have to pay regard, I am of opinion that the judge was perfectly right in the conclusion to which he came, and that this appeal fails and must be dismissed with costs.

Luxmoore L.J.: I agree.

Asquith J.: I agree.

Appeal dismissed.

Note

Smith & Fawcett Ltd., Re remains one of the leading cases on the scope of directors' discretion. For other cases, see *Lyle & Scott Ltd. v. Scott's Trustees & British Invt. Trust Ltd.*, [1959] A.C. 763, [1959] 2 All E.R. 661 (H.L.); *Re Shoal Harbour Marine Service Ltd.* (1956), 19 W.W.R. (N.S.) 670, (1956), 20 W.W.R. (N.S.) 312, 448 (B.C. S.C.); *Charles Forte Invt. Ltd. v. Amanda*, [1963] 2 All E.R. 940 (C.A.); and *Re Swaledale Cleaners, Ltd.*, [1968] 3 All E.R. 619, [1968] 1 W.L.R. 1710 (C.A.).

Edmonton Country Club Ltd. v. Case
[1975] S.C.R. 534

[The appellant company was incorporated under the Alberta *Companies Act* in 1945. In 1963 the articles of association were altered to impose a minimum annual fee and to give a right of forfeiture or forced sale of shares in the event of default. In 1969 further changes in the articles of association were approved by which the owner of a common or preferred share of the company was required to pay to the company an "annual minimum fee to be established by the Directors" unless he or his nominee exercised playing privileges and paid the playing fee, failing which his common and preferred shares became subject to a lien or charge in favour of the company enforceable by sale of the shares. Also in that year article 17 was altered to permit the directors to set the amount of a transfer fee for the registration of share transfers. In 1970 a special resolution was passed stipulating that "each shareholder, whether playing or non-playing, shall be required to pay the annual club fees as levied by the Board for the then current year."

A challenge to the validity of the 1963, 1969 and 1970 resolutions was brought by the respondent, who in 1966 inherited one common and one preferred share of the company from his father. The trial judge found that the resolutions were *ultra vires* the company and void *ab initio*. He also found that article 20A, which gave the directors the right to refuse to register any transfer of shares, was *intra vires* and valid. An appeal and cross-appeal were dismissed by the Appellate Division of the Supreme Court of Alberta. With leave, the company then appealed to this Court and the shareholder cross-appealed. The Supreme Court of Canada dismissed the appeal and the cross-appeal. On the major issue relating to the levying of an annual fee, the Supreme Court held the resolutions *ultra vires* because they offended the basic principle of limited liability, namely, that a shareholder who has paid for his shares is thereafter free of further pecuniary obligations with respect to those shares. The Supreme Court split on the issue relating to article 20A with Dickson J. speaking for the majority upholding the validity of the provision and Laskin J. for the minority denying the validity of the provision. The excerpts from the judgment deal with this issue.]

DICKSON J.: . . . The other aspect of the transferability problem concerns the validity of art. 20A of the articles of association. This provision appeared in the articles as originally drafted and has remained unaltered:

> 20A. No shares in the Company whether or not paid up shall be transferred to any person without the consent of a majority of the Directors, who may refuse such consent whether such shares are or are not paid up, in their unfettered discretion.

The effect is to vest in the directors a power, exercisable without stated criteria, to restrict or even veto the transfer of a fully paid share of the company. The question which must be answered is whether a company incorporated under *The Companies Act* of Alberta can give its directors such a power. The trial judge and the Court of Appeal answered this question in the affirmative and Mr. Case has cross-appealed.

A private company must, by its memorandum or articles, restrict or prohibit the right to transfer any of its shares, and a public company, other than one whose shares are listed for trading on a stock exchange, may include in its articles restrictions on the right of transfer. In *Canada National Fire Insurance Co. v. Hutchings*, the Privy Council held that a company incorporated by letters patent under the *Companies Act*, R.S.C. 1906, c. 79, could not validly make a by-law giving the directors an unrestricted power to disapprove transfers but Sir Walter Phillimore said in the course of the judgment, p. 456:

> There is . . . for the present purpose no analogy between companies in the United Kingdom which are formed by contract, whether it be under deed of settlement or under memorandum and articles of association to which the Registrar of Joint-Stock Companies necessarily assents if the documents are regular in form, and Canadian companies which are formed under the Canadian *Companies Act*, either by letters patent or by special Act.

and at p. 459, referring to the power of veto given the directors, he said:

There are decided cases in the English Courts which show that such a power may be lawfully reserved on the occasion of the constitution of the company, and a sufficient number of such cases to show that the power has been found convenient in use.

Re Gresham Life Assur. Society; *Ex p. Penney*; *Re Bell Bros, Ltd.*; *Ex p. Hodgson*; *Re Coalport China Company*; and *Re Smith and Fawcett, Limited* might be cited as examples.

The right of a shareholder to transfer his shares is undoubtedly one of the incidents of share ownership, assured by *The Companies Act* of Alberta, s. 61, "The shares or other interest of any member in a company are personal estate, transferable in the manner provided by the articles of the company . . .", as it is by the *Companies Act*, 1948 (U.K.), s. 73, but the right is not absolute. We find in 6 Halsbury, 3rd ed., p. 252, the statement:

> A restriction on the right to transfer shares is not repugnant to absolute ownership of the shares, but is one of the original incidents of the shares attached to them by the contract contained in the articles.

and:

> There is apparently no limit to the restriction on transfer which may be so imposed . . .

The same thought is expressed, more positively, in Palmer's *Company Law*, 21st ed., p. 340:

> It is common for articles to provide that the directors shall have the power of declining to register a transfer without assigning any reason therefor; or in their absolute and uncontrolled discretion; or in some equally sweeping terms . . .

and in Gower's *Modern Company Law*, 3rd ed., p. 392:

> These restrictions may take any form, but in practice they normally either give the existing members a right of pre-emption or first refusal, or confer a discretion on the directors to refuse to pass transfers.

This footnote follows:

> The latter restriction is commonly found in conjunction with the former. In the U.S.A. it is generally held that restrictions, being restraints on the alienability of personal property, must be reasonable. In England it is clear that there is no such rule except, perhaps, when the restrictions are imposed after the shares have been issued.

I have concluded that art. 20A is not *ultra vires* the company and that the cross-appeal must fail. The power to refuse to consent to a transfer of shares was reserved to the directors upon incorporation of the company, by the contract contained in the articles, and is not something now sought to be imposed upon unwilling shareholders. Before we move to strike down such a power on the ground that it is unreasonable, we should, in my view, have some factual support for that conclusion. There is no evidence before us, nor is it alleged, that the directors have at any time in the almost 30-year history of the company acted in bad faith or arbitrarily or otherwise abused the power.

I would accordingly dismiss the appeal with costs and dismiss the cross-appeal without costs.

The judgment of Spence and Laskin JJ. was delivered by

LASKIN J.(*dissenting in part*): I am in agreement with my brother Dickson that the appeal fails for the reasons that he has given. The cross-appeal respecting the validity of art. 20A of the articles of association gives me more pause, but, on balance, I am of the opinion that the article should be struck out.

My brother Dickson has fairly assessed it as vesting in the directors "a power exercisable, without stated criteria, to restrict or even veto the transfer of a fully paid share of the company". The difference between us is whether this arbitrary power, not related to any standard for the exercise of an unfettered discretion, should be controlled only in the context of a particular case requiring its exercise (as he would have it), or whether it should be struck out simply because it is on its face utterly arbitrary (as I would have it).

The considerations which move me to strike it out are easily stated. What the company has in effect done is to turn itself into a private club, despite the fact of its incorporation as a public company. I am not persuaded that persons, knowing of the arbitrary power of the directors to control shareholdings, would, or should be expected to submit themselves to whatever obloquy may be involved in the possible rejection of their application for a transfer of shares. If the company is unwilling to establish criteria upon which to enable a measure of reasonable exercise of discretion to be considered in advance, it ought not to be permitted to have the cover of incorporation as a public company.

The relevant *Companies Act* of Alberta, R.S.A. 1942, c. 240, does not confer any express power upon a public company to restrict the transfer of fully paid shares. Any such power must be drawn inferentially from s. 65 which provides that "the shares . . . of any member in a company shall be personal estate, transferable in the manner provided by the articles of the company . . .". In so far as this may be thought to confer some authority to restrict transfer, I would read it, as I would read a similar power in a municipal Act or in legislation establishing a statutory agency, as requiring some standard which would be amenable to judicial control, if need be. The

standard articles of association set out in Table A of the First Schedule of
the Act include s. 17 which provides that "the directors may decline to
register any transfer of shares, not being fully paid shares, to a person of
whom they do not approve, and may also decline to register any transfer of
shares on which the Company has a lien". This is hardly a telling provision
one way or another, but, so far as it is indicative of policy, it militates against
a conclusion that an absolute restriction of the transfer of fully paid shares
may be introduced into the articles of association of a public company.
Restrictions on transfer are, of course, part of the very being of a private
company, as is evident from s. 2(z) of the Act.

It is said, however, and certainly there is case law to support this view,
that in memorandum and articles of association companies, albeit incorporated as public companies, the contractual aspect of the memorandum
and articles supports the power to include drastic restrictions on transfer.
This has been also referred to as part of the general law governing such
companies.

There are two comments that I would make on this submission. The
first is that, although originating in contract, shares in a public company are
a species of property and as such are entitled to the advantage of alienability
free from unreasonable restrictions unless there is statutory warrant otherwise. The second comment concerns the so-called contractual aspect of
memorandum of association companies. The memorandum of association
is but a method of incorporation, under which its contractual aspect is
submerged in a statutory regime subjecting the company to public regulation. I cannot, in such circumstances, and in the absence of express power
in the memorandum, subscribe to the proposition that there is a contractual
warrant for adopting an article of association which confers an unlimited
discretion to refuse a transfer of shares.

My brother Dickson has referred to the judgment of the Judicial Committee in *Canada National Fire Insurance Co. v. Hutchings*, where a distinction was drawn, in respect of the matter under consideration, between a
letters patent company or one incorporated under a special Act and a memorandum of association company. I cannot be persuaded that the form of
incorporation can have such a remarkable effect upon the permissible scope
of a power to regulate or prescribe conditions for the transfer of stock in a
public company.

I am not concerned here to examine how far restrictions on transfer
may go in a public company before courting invalidity. In *Ontario Jockey
Club Ltd. v. McBride*, the Judicial Committee, dealing with a letters patent
company, said that it is permissible to give a right of pre-emption but that
"a restriction which precludes a shareholder altogether from transferring
may be invalid" (at p. 923). I would not be so equivocal and, certainly, the
Judicial Committee was not equivocal on this very point in the *Hutchings*
case.

The pre-emption or first option type of restriction is a common one in
the United States and it has generally been held valid. But the position there

is otherwise in respect of restrictions of the kind found in art, 20A, particularly where there is no limitation of time on the restriction. The law in the United States appears to have sought reconciliation of the contractual and property aspects of shares, so far as restrictions on transfers are concerned, by applying a test of reasonableness. *Ballantine on Corporations*, rev. ed., 1946, at p. 778, states the position as follows:

> It has been held in numerous cases that restrictions which prohibit transfers except upon the approval and consent of the directors or other shareholders are invalid as contrary to public policy and as imposing undue restraints upon the alienation of property. But a requirement of consent by directors or shareholders has sometimes been upheld, especially when imposed by charter or by an agreement of the shareholders of a closed corporation.

I should note that the closed corporation is similar to the private company in Canadian law: see Gower: "Some Contrasts Between British and American Corporation Law" (1955), 69 Harv. L. Rev. 1369, at pp. 1375-6. Oleck, *Modern Corporation Law*, vol. 3, 1959, deals with the same point in a more modified way than Ballantine in two passages at pp. 286 and 300 respectively, as follows:

> Take a restriction, not uncommon, which declares that a shareholder shall not transfer his shares unless he first obtains the consent of the directors, or of the shareholders, or of a certain proportion of the directors or the shareholders. Generally speaking, this type of restriction is considered an unreasonable one and is thought to contravene public policy, and it is held, on this ground, that a mere by-law restriction of this character is "void" and unenforceable. On the other hand, a restriction of this kind inserted in the original articles of incorporation has been sustained in two cases.
>
> A less common restraint is the "consent" restriction, whereunder the consent of the board of directors or of the remaining shareholders is a prerequisite to the transfer of the stock. While these restrictions have been upheld they operate virtually to bar the alienation of the shares and are more likely to be considered unreasonable and therefore void.

A test of reasonableness commends itself to me, especially in view of the emphasis on the property aspect of shares indicated by s. 65 of the Alberta *Companies Act* already referred to. On this view, it is my opinion that art. 20A is bad. I am reinforced in this view by the fact that it would *ex facie* preclude even involuntary transfers, although it appears in the present case that the plaintiff who acquired the shares under his father's will did get the approval of the directors for their effective transfer to him.

I would, accordingly, allow the cross-appeal with costs.

Appeal dismissed.

Note

For some cases dealing with questions arising from restrictions on the transfer of shares, see *Assoc. Finance Co. Ltd. v. Webber and Dixon*, [1972] 4 W.W.R. 131, 28 D.L.R. (3d) 673 (B.C. S.C.); *Nadeau v. Nadeau and Nadeau Ltd.* (1973), 6 N.B.R. (2d) 512 (N.B. S.C.); *Harvey v. Harvey*, [1979] 2 W.W.R. 661 (B.C. C.A.); and *Carter v. Roy M. Lawson Ltd.* (1982), 36 N.B.R. (2d) 353, 129 D.L.R. (3d) 214 (Q.B.).

3. SHAREHOLDERS' AGREEMENTS

(a) Introductory Note

One of the most important rights of a shareholder is the right to vote. Just as important can be the right to join with other shareholders to combine voting rights. Such combinations can be effected by separate agreements which may also contain many other provisions, for example, a right of first refusal or other restriction on the transfer of shares. These agreements are usually found in closely held companies reflecting a partnership approach to the corporation, but they can also be useful for those large corporations which have one or two dominant shareholders who wish to combine their voting power in some way. As will be discussed below, this objective can be achieved by a variety of means: voting agreements, voting trusts or, pursuant to the CBCA or OBCA, by a unanimous shareholder agreement.

At common law, agreements among shareholders as to the manner in which they will vote their shares are lawful (*Ringuet v. Bergeron*, [1960] S.C.R. 672, 24 D.L.R. (2d) 449; *Greenwell v. Porter*, [1902] 1 Ch. 530). See, generally, Pickering, "Shareholders' Voting Rights and Company Control" (1965), 81 L.Q.R. 248.

CBCA s. 145.1 and OBCA s. 108(1) provide that agreements among two or more shareholders as to how shares shall be voted are permitted.

However, this rule is generally stated as subject to the qualification that the agreements must be for a lawful purpose (*Motherwell v. Schoof*, [1949] 2 W.W.R. 529, [1949] 4 D.L.R. 812 (Alta. S.C.)). This is an important qualification where the agreement purports to bind the shareholders *qua* directors since such an agreement is unlawful as an invalid attempt to fetter the exercise of the directors' discretion. There is authority that this limitation applies even to unanimous shareholder agreements (*Atlas Dev. Co. Ltd. v. Calof and Gold* (1963), 41 W.W.R. 575 (Man. Q.B.) and *Alder v. Dobie* (1999), [1999] B.C.J. No. 808, 1999 CarswellBC 758 (S.C.)).

(b) Voting Agreements

Clark v. Dodge
269 N.Y. 410; 199 N.E. 641 (1936) (citations omitted)

CROUCH J.: The action is for the specific performance of a contract between the plaintiff Clark and the defendant Dodge, relating to the affairs of the two defendant corporations. To the complaint a joint answer by the three defendants was interposed, consisting of denials and a separate defense and counterclaim. To the separate defense and counterclaim a reply was made. The defendant then moved under rule 112 of the Rules of Civil Practice, and under sections 476, 96 and 279 of the *Civil Practice Act*, to dismiss the complaint. The motion was made "on the pleadings in this action and the admissions of the plaintiff" in two affidavits submitted by him on a prior motion in the action. The alleged admissions are equivocal at best, and clearly were not "intended to be treated as a part of a pleading or made to avoid some question arising on the pleadings." . . .

We shall deal, therefore, with the questions here presented in the light of the facts most favorable to plaintiff appearing in the pleadings only.

Those facts, briefly stated, are as follows: The two corporate defendants are New Jersey corporations manufacturing medicinal preparations by secret formulae. The main office, factory and assets of both corporations are located in the State of New York. In 1921, and at all times since, Clark owned twenty-five per cent and Dodge seventy-five per cent of the stock of each Corporation. Dodge took no active part in the business, although he was a director and, through ownership of their qualifying shares, controlled the other directors of both corporations. He was the president of Bell & Company, Inc., and nominally general manager of Hollings-Smith Company, Inc. The Plaintiff Clark was a director and held the offices of treasurer and general manager of Bell & Company, Inc., and also had charge of the major portion of the business of Hollings-Smith Company, Inc. The formulae and methods of manufacture of the medicinal preparations were known to him alone. Under date of February 15, 1921, Dodge and Clark, the sole owners of the stock of both corporations, entered into a written agreement under seal, which after reciting the stock ownership of both parties, the desire of Dodge that Clark should continue in the efficient management and control of the business of Bell & Company, Inc., so long as he should "remain faithful, efficient and competent to so manage and control the said business;" and his further desire that Clark should not be the sole custodian of a specified formula but should share his knowledge thereof and of the method of manufacture with a son of Dodge, provided, in substance, as follows: That Dodge during his lifetime and, after his death, a trustee to be appointed by his will, would so vote his stock and so vote as a director that the plaintiff (a) should continue to be a director of Bell & Company, Inc. and (b) should continue as its general manager so long as he should be "faithful, efficient and competent;" (c) should during his life receive one-fourth of the net income of the corporations either by way of salary or dividends; and (d) that no unreasonable or incommensurate salaries should be paid to other officers or agents which would so reduce the net income as materially to affect Clark's profits. Clark on his part agreed to disclose the specified formula to the son and to instruct him in the details and methods of manufacture; and further, at the end of his life to bequeath his stock-if no issue survived him to the wife and children of Dodge.

It was further provided that the provisions in regard to the division of net profits and the regulation of salaries should also apply to the Hollings-Smith Company.

The complaint alleges due performance of the contract by Clark and breach thereof by Dodge in that he has failed to use his stock control to continue Clark as a director and as general manager, and has prevented Clark from receiving his proportion of the income, while taking his own, by causing the employment of incompetent persons at excessive salaries, and otherwise.

The relief sought is reinstatement as director and general manager and an accounting by Dodge and by the corporations for waste and for the proportion of net income due plaintiff, with an injunction against further violations.

The only question which need be discussed is whether the contract is illegal as against public policy within the decision in *McQuade v. Stoneham* (263 N.Y. 323), upon the authority of which the complaint was dismissed by the Appellate Division.

"The business of a corporation shall be managed by its board of directors" (General Corporation Law [Cons. Laws, Ch. 23], 27). That is the statutory norm. Are we committed by the *McQuade* case to the doctrine that there may be no variation, however slight or innocuous, from that norm, where salaries or policies or the retention of individuals in office are concerned? There is ample authority supporting that doctrine . . . and something may be said for it, since it furnishes a simple, if arbitrary, test. Apart from its practical administrative convenience, the reasons upon which it is said to rest are more or less nebulous. Public policy, the intention of the Legislature, detriment to the corporation, are phrases which in this connection mean little. Possible harm to *bona fide* purchasers of stock or to creditors or to stockholding minorities have more substance; but such harms are absent in many instances. If the enforcement of a particular contract damages nobody-not even, in any perceptible degree, the public-one sees no reason for holding it illegal, even though it impinges slightly upon the broad provision of section 27. Damage suffered or threatened is a logical and practical-test, and has come to be the one generally adopted by the courts.

Where the directors are the sole stockholders, there seems to be no objection to enforcing an agreement among them to vote for certain people as officers. There is no direct decision to that effect in this court, yet there are strong indications that such a rule has long been recognized. The opinion in *Manson v. Curtis* closed its discussion by saying: "The rule that all the stockholders by their universal consent may do as they choose with the corporate concerns and assets, provided the interests of creditors are not affected, because they are the complete owners of the corporation, cannot be invoked here." That was because all the stockholders were not parties to the agreement there in question. So, where the public was not affected, "the parties in interest, might, by their original agreement of incorporation, limit their respective rights and powers," even where there was a conflicting statutory standard. (*Ripin v. U.S. Woven Label Co.*) Such corporations were little more than (though not quite the same as) chartered partnerships.

In *Lorillard v. Clyde* (86 N.Y. 384) and again in *Drucklieb v. Harris* (200 N.Y. 211), where the questioned agreements were entered into by all the stockholders of small corporations about to be organized, the fact that the agreements conflicted to some extent with the statutory duty of the directors to manage the corporate affairs was thought not to render the agreements illegal as against public policy, though it was said they might not be binding upon the directors of the corporation when organized. (*Cf.* Lehman J., dissenting opinion in the *McQuade* case.) The rule recognized in *Manson v. Curtis*, and quoted above, was thus stated by Blackmar J., in *Kassel v. Empire Tinware Co.*:

> As the parties to the action are the complete owners of the corporation, there is no reason why the exercise of the power and discretion of the directors cannot be controlled by valid agreement between themselves, provided that the interests of creditors are not affected.

Fells v. Katz, where all the stockholders were parties to the agreement, is no authority to the contrary. The decision there merely construed the agreement and found that plaintiff had breached it, thereby justifying his removal. "The agreement of the stockholders to continue a man in the directorate must be construed as an obligation to retain him only so long as he keeps the agreement on his part faithfully to act as a trustee for the stockholders". Indeed, the case may be regarded as applying the test of damage above referred to. Any other construction would have caused damage to the corporation and its stockholders and would have been illegal.

Except for the broad dicta in the *McQuade* opinion, we think there can be no doubt that the agreement here in question was legal and that the complaint states a cause of action. There was no attempt to sterilize the board of directors, as in the *Manson* and *McQuade* cases. The only restrictions on Dodge were (a) that as a stockholder he should vote for Clark as a director — a perfectly legal contract; (b) that as director he should continue Clark as general manager, so long as he proved faithful, efficient and competent — an agreement which could harm nobody; (c) that Clark should always receive as salary or dividends one-fourth of the "net income." For the purposes of this motion, it is only just to construe that phrase as meaning whatever was left for distribution after the directors had in good faith set aside whatever they deemed wise; (d) that no salaries to other officers should be paid unreasonable in amount or incommensurate with services rendered — a beneficial and not a harmful agreement.

If there was any invasion of the powers of the directorate under that agreement, it is so slight as to be negligible; and certainly there is no damage suffered by or threatened to anybody. The broad statements in the *McQuade* opinion, applicable to the facts there, should be confined to those facts.

The judgment of the Appellate Division should be reserved and the order of the Special Term affirmed, with costs in this court and in the Appellate Division.

Crane C.J., Lehman, O'Brien, Hubbs, Loughran, and Finch JJ., concur.

Judgment accordingly.

Ringuet v. Bergeron
[1960] S.C.R. 672, 24 D.L.R. (2d) 449

Abbott and Ritchie JJ. concur with Judson J.
Taschereau J. concurs with Fauteux J. (dissenting)

JUDSON J.: The respondent sued the appellants for a declaration that against each of them, he was entitled to certain shares of the St. Maurice Knitting Mills Ltd. registered in their names. In the Superior Court the learned trial Judge dismissed the action. The Court of Queen's Bench (Appeal Side) [[1958] Que. Q.B. 222] allowed the appeal and maintained the action. The two unsuccessful shareholders now appeal to this Court.

The action was brought on an agreement dated August 3, 1949, between the respondent and the appellants. At that time these parties and four other persons each held 50 shares of the St. Maurice Knitting Mills Ltd., a company incorporated by letters patent under Part I of the Quebec *Companies Act*, R.S.Q. 1941, c. 276. These shares constituted all the issued capital stock of the company. The purpose of the agreement was to provide for the acquisition of 50 shares from one Frank Spain and the division of these shares among the parties. With these 50 shares divided among them the parties then had control of the company and they agreed, among other matters, to vote for their election to the Board of Directors; to ensure the election of the appellant Ringuet as president of the company, of the appellant Pagé as vice-president and general manager, and of the respondent Bergeron as secretary-treasurer and assistant general manager of the company, all at stated and agreed salaries. They also agreed to vote unanimously at all meetings of the company and provided for a penalty for breach of the contract in the following terms:

> 11. *Dans toutes assemblées de la dite Compagnie, les parties aux présentes s'engagent et s'obligent à voter unanimement sur tout objet qui nécessite un vote. Aucune des parties aux présentes ne pourra différer d'opinion avec ses coparties contractantes en ce qui concerne*

le vote. Le vote préponderant du Président devra toujours être en faveur des deux parties contractantes.

12. Si l'une des parties ne se conforme à la présente convention, ses actions seront cédées et transportées aux deux autres parties contractantes en parts égales, et ce gratuitement.

Telle est la sanction de la non exécution d'aucune des clauses de la présente convention par l'une des parties contractantes.

Two or three months later the parties also purchased the shares of another shareholder Robert Sevigny and divided them among themselves in accordance with the agreement. On the completion of this purchase, there remained only five shareholders in the company: the two appellants, the respondent, the *mise-en-cause* Gerard Jean, and Zénon Bachand. On February 3, 1950, the three parties to the first agreement entered into another agreement and included in this one the *mise-en-cause* Gerard Jean. The purpose of this agreement was to provide for the admission of Gerard Jean into the controlling group and for the acquisition of the shares of Zénon Bachand, the last of the minority shareholders. Two shares were issued from the treasury and the total issued shares were equally divided among the four individuals with the result that each held 88 shares. The contract of February 3, 1950, to which Jean was a party, contains no provision corresponding to cl. 12 of the contract of August 3, 1949. It does not purport to replace or alter the earlier contract, which remains in full force and effect.

From August 3, 1949 to June 14, 1952 the three parties to the first contract observed its terms. There had during this period been certain increases in salary which were properly authorized and fixed by mutual consent. On June 14, 1952 the appellant Maurice Pagé, at a directors' meeting, began to take steps to oust the respondent from the management of the company, and at a shareholders' meeting held on July 21, 1952, the appellants and Jean voted themselves in as a new board of directors. The respondent says that he had no notice of this meeting and did not attend. He was not nominated and no votes were cast for his election as director of the company. The new board of directors held a meeting following the shareholders' meeting. Ringuet was elected president, Pagé was elected vice-president and Jean, secretary-treasurer. The respondent was thus completely excluded from the management of the company. He brought his action alleging that the appellants in failing to vote for his election to the board of directors and in not ensuring that he be appointed assistant general manager and secretary-treasurer, had violated the contract of August 3, 1949, and that he was entitled to enforce the penalty provided in cl. 12 of the agreement. He claimed a transfer of 88 shares from each defendant. The facts were admitted in the pleadings and the sole defence was that the contract was contrary to public order.

The Superior Court rejected the action on the very narrow ground that cl. 12 had no application when one party was suing the other two. No opinion delivered in the Court of Queen's Bench accepted this interpretation of cl. 12 and no attempt was made in this Court to support the judgment at trial on this ground. In the Court of Queen's Bench the learned Chief Justice and Mr. Justice Owen found for the respondent, with Mr. Justice Pratte dissenting. The Chief Justice found nothing illegal in the agreement and decided that it should be given its full effect. The ratio of the dissenting opinion is to be found in the distinction drawn between the rights of a shareholder and the obligations assumed on becoming a director. While majority shareholders may agree to vote their shares for certain purposes, they cannot by this agreement tie the hands of directors and compel them to exercise the power of management of the company in a particular way. This appears in the following extract from the reasons of Pratte J. [p. 236]:

> *Mais la situation des directeurs est bien différente de celle des actionnaires. Le directeur est designé par les actionnaires, mais il n'est pas à proprement parter leur mandataire; il est un administrateur charge par la loi de gérer un patrimoine qui n'est ni le sien, ni celui de ses codirecteurs, ni celui des actionnaires, mais celui de la compagnie, une personne juridique absolument distincte à la fois de ceux qui la dirigent et de ceux qui en possèdent le capital-actions. En cette qualité, le directeur doit agir en bonne conscience, dans le seul interet du patrimoine confié à sa gestion. Cela suppose qu'il a la liberté de choisir, au moment d'une decision à prendre, celle qui lui parait la plus conforme aux intérêts sur lesquels la loi lui impose le devoir de veiller.*

There can be no objection to the general principle stated in this passage, but, in my view, it was not offended by this agreement. However, the conclusion of Pratte J. was that a director who has bound himself as this contract bound the parties has rendered himself incapable of doing what the law requires of him and that cl. 11 requiring unanimity at all meetings had that effect. He also held that cl. 11 was not severable and that therefore the agreement was invalidated in its entirety.

Owen J. agreed that the undertaking of unanimity at directors' meetings which he considered was required by cl. 11 might be contrary to public order but that it was not necessary to decide this since the clause was severable from the other provisions of the agreement to which he gave full effect. The defendants had failed to comply with other clauses in the contract — the voting of Bergeron's salary, the election of Bergeron as a director of the company and his appointment as secretary-treasurer and assistant general manager.

The point of the appeal is therefore whether an agreement among a group of shareholders providing for the direction and control of a company in the circumstances of this case is contrary to public order, and whether it is open to the parties to establish whatever sanction they choose for a breach of such agreement.

Did the parties to this agreement tie their hands in their capacity as directors of the company so as to contravene the requirements of the Quebec *Companies Act*, which provides (s. 80) that "the affairs of the company shall be managed by a board of not less than three directors"? I agree with the reasons of the learned Chief Justice that this agreement does not contravene this or any other section of the Quebec *Companies Act*. It is no more than an agreement among shareholders owning or proposing to own the majority of the issued shares of a company to unite upon a course of policy or action and upon the officers whom they will elect. There is nothing illegal or contrary to public order in an agreement for achieving these purposes. Shareholders have the right to combine their interests and voting powers to secure such control of a company and to ensure that the company will be managed by certain persons in a certain manner. This is a well-known, normal and legal contract and one which is frequently encountered in current practice and it makes no difference whether the objects sought are to be achieved by means of an agreement such as this or a voting trust. Such an arrangement is not prohibited either by law, by good morals or public order.

It is important to distinguish the present action, which is between contracting parties to an agreement for the voting of shares, from one brought by a minority shareholder demanding a certain standard of conduct from directors and majority shareholders. Nothing that can arise from this litigation and nothing that can be said about it can touch on that problem. The fact that this agreement may potentially involve detriment to the minority does not render it illegal and contrary to public order. If there is such injury, there is a remedy available to the minority shareholder who alleges a departure from the standards required of the majority shareholders and the directors. The possibility of such injurious effect on the minority is not a ground for illegality.

I think that this litigation can be decided on the simple ground that cl. 11 has no reference to directors' meetings. Clause 11 refers to meetings of the company, that is, shareholders' meetings, and not to meetings of the board of directors. On this point I agree with the Chief Justice, who stated his opinion in the following terms [pp. 230-1]:

> *Au surplus, y a-t-il quelque chose qui répugne à la loi, à l'ordre public et aux bonnes moeurs qu'un groups d'actionnaires s'entendent pour controler et diriger une compagnie, pour devenir ses administrateurs, ses principaux officiers? Il n'était surement pas besoin d'un contrat écrit pour pareille entente qui intervient chaque jour dans le monde des compagnies. Il est notoire qu'un grand nombre d'entre elles sont contrôlées par un groupe d'actionnaires qui souvent même ne représentent pas la majorité des actions.*
>
> *L'engagement des cocontractants à voter unanimement leurs actions dans les assemblées de la compagnie ne saurait lui-même, à mon avis, être invalide; après tout, chacun des comparants d'a pas renoncé à la délibération, à la discussion, au droit de faire triompher son*

opinion avant de se ranger à l'avis de la majorité qui en principe doit gouverner.

I have the greatest difficulty in seeing how any question of public order can arise in a private arrangement of this kind. The possibility of injury to a minority interest cannot raise it. If this were not so, every arrangement of this kind would involve judicial enquiry. Minority rights have the protection of the law without the necessity of invoking public order. This litigation is between shareholders of a closely held company. The agreement which the plaintiff seeks to enforce damages nobody except the unsuccessful party to the agreement. No public interest or illegality is involved. . . .

Appeal dismissed.

For a discussion of this decision, see K.S. Howard, (1959), 37 Can. Bar Rev. 490; and R.A. Harris, "Note" (1961), U.T. Fac. L. Rev. 149.

(c) Voting Trusts

PICKERING, "Shareholders' Voting Rights and Company Control"
(1965), 81 L.Q.R. 248 at pp. 257–260 (footnotes omitted)

The voting trust. A voting trust is created when the voting rights of some or all of the shares in a company are settled upon trust. The trust in this context, as in others, can be a very flexible instrument. It may be comprised of all or only some of the shares with voting rights. The powers of the trust may give the trustees an absolute and unfettered discretion to act as they wish or their authority may be restricted. The objects which they are empowered to fulfil may be general or, usually in combination with capital structures conferring appropriate class rights, they may be confined to certain specific matters. In effect a voting trust confers a joint irrevocable proxy with general or restricted powers. It is a more formal device for concentrating control than the voting agreement and usually will have wider effect.

The voting trust in some ways has similar effects to the use of non-voting and "loaded" shares as a means of concentrating control in relatively few hands. Together with other inter-member devices it has been widely used in the United States of America, but relatively neglected in the United Kingdom where in general the constitutional devices have been preferred. In contrast to the extensive litigation which has taken place in the United States on problems arising from the use of voting trusts, and their regulation by statute in many cases, there is apparently no reported case in English law dealing expressly with issues arising from a corporate voting trust, nor are there statutory provisions specifically applicable to them.

There are perhaps three situations where voting trusts may have special usefulness. First, particular circumstances may make the intervention of outside or independent trustees desirable. For example, where there is a close association of members and directors each individually having a comparable status within the company the existence of independent trustees with powers to appoint or supervise the appointment of directors and managing directors may prevent undesirable internecine strife. Secondly, where a company is incorporated for objects which require for their proper implementation the continued control of persons holding certain beliefs or opinions a voting trust may be one way of achieving this. Thirdly, in very large companies where the membership is both great in number and dispersed in area the interests of the shareholders may be more effectively and continuously safeguarded by trustees acting on their behalf than by the efforts of individual members in general meeting. In addition, it can be argued forcefully that such trustees could more appropriately exercise the power of appointing directors than what are, in effect, often self-perpetuating boards of directors, and similarly that they might exercise a valuable independent role in deciding such questions as directors' remuneration and terms of appointment. These are very contentious points and in practice voting trusts established for this latter purpose are extremely rare or non-existent among larger companies in England.

Apart from such specific functions voting trusts may be employed as a straightforward device by which a relatively small group of individuals within a company can acquire majority control. Under it shareholders may surrender more of their legal rights and remedies than under almost any other means of concentrating control, except perhaps the management contract, but the questions raised by its use have not yet been decided by the courts in England. Ballantine has described the issues of principle involved in the following terms:

> In general, the power to control the election of directors and so to manage and control the property, business and patronage of a great corporation, to direct its policies and the expenditure of vast sums of money, indirectly to appoint and fix the compensation of its officials and executives, is a power of great value, even if the corporation is not in a position to pay dividends on its shares. But this power of control is not properly regarded as a species of property which may be reserved or split off, and bought and sold, apart from the beneficial interests in the shares of stock. Voting power is an ancillary or protective right, not an independent species of property which may be used to give dominion over the investments of others.

Note on US Position

The United States has developed extensive case and statute law to deal with the problem of abuse of control by trustees. Among the devices used by American courts are limitation periods (the most common being 10 years); cancellation provisions requiring the agreement either of all beneficiaries or of a simple majority of them; notice provisions whereby the voting trust, to be valid, must be registered on the company books so that it becomes subject to the general notice provisions; and the requirement of "proper purpose" for the existence of the trust (the securing of control as an end in itself may not be a proper purpose). See *Painter on Close Corporations* (3d ed. 1998), s. 3.2.

(d) Unanimous Shareholder Agreements

IACOBUCCI, **"Canadian Corporation Law: Some Recent Shareholder Developments"**
in *The Cambridge Lectures 1981*
(N. Eastham and B. Krivy, Eds., 1982) 88 at pp. 92–95.

One of the exceptions to the general statement made earlier about the legislative emphasis on proposals for public or widely-held corporations and their shareholders is the introduction of the unanimous shareholder agreement (u.s.a.) for closely-held corporations. The u.s.a. is predicated on the assumption that the dominant interests to be served by decision-making in the private or closely-held corporation are the expectations and needs of its shareholders. It is argued that the promotion of economic efficiency, which is the underlying interest of social policy in this respect, is best met by enabling the shareholders to arrange the organization of their enterprise as they choose.

At common law, shareholders were able to enter shareholders' agreements which could contain covenants, *inter alia*, as to the voting of the shares of the parties to the agreement, and these undertakings were specifically enforceable. However, there was some murky jurisprudence on the extent to which shareholders could agree to fetter or interfere with the discretion of the directors even if all the shareholders of the corporation were parties to the agreement. Consequently statutory intervention was needed to allow shareholders to choose their corporate control and management structure.

To meet these specifications and needs, the u.s.a. device was introduced into Canada by section 149 [now s. 146] of the CBCA, and has been adopted by many provincial statutes, with substantial modifications made by Alberta and Ontario in their recent statutory revisions. I would like to make a few comments about each of the federal, Alberta and Ontario provisions.

What to me is most interesting about unanimous shareholder agreements is that they are constitutional documents akin to the company's articles of incorporation and by-laws, yet they are contractual in nature so that they can govern shareholders' personal or individual rights as well. Numerous provisions of the CBCA are made subject to the u.s.a., notably:

(1) the management of the business and affairs of the company (subsection 97(1)) [now s. 102];

(2) the passing of by-laws (section 98) [now s. 103];

(3) the appointment of officers and the delegation of powers to them (section 116 and see also section 110) [now s. 121];

(4) the power to borrow and give security (subsection 183(1)) [now s. 189]; and

(5) the situations in which a complaining shareholder can request dissolution of the company (paragraph 207(i)(b)) [now s. 214(1)(b)].

Subsection 140(2) [now s. 146(1)] of the CBCA simply declares as valid a written agreement which is entered into by all the shareholders of a corporation, or all the shareholders and a person who is not a shareholder, and which restricts the powers of the directors to manage the business and affairs of the corporation. Subsection 140(4) [now s. 146(5)] provides that the shareholders are, to the extent they have taken on directors' duties and powers, liable as directors would be. The CBCA also specifies that a transferee of shares is deemed to be a party to the u. s. a. if he has actual knowledge of it or if a reference to it is conspicuously noted on the certificate representing the shares. In addition, under the CBCA the court can order the company and its directors and officers to comply with a u.s.a. and restrain any of such persons from acting in breach of it. This remedial provision is most noteworthy in that it highlights the constitutional character of the u.s.a. in that the company and its officers and directors need not be parties to the agreement, yet the undertakings contained in the agreement can be enforced against them.

The new Alberta *Business Corporations Act* adopts and extends the u.s.a. concept [now s. 146]. After acknowledging that the primary approach of the CBCA u.s.a. provisions reflected a desire to have shareholders rather than directors manage a closely-held company, the designers of the Alberta statute felt that the u.s.a. should be expanded in scope to make the device even more useful and to clarify some of the problems which were felt to be present in the CBCA provisions.

With respect to the expanded scope of the u. s. a., the Alberta section allows the entrenchment of any provision concerning the internal affairs and organization of the corporation. The Alberta definition of a u.s.a. includes an agreement which does any one of the following:

(1) regulates the rights and liabilities of shareholders, as shareholders, among themselves or between themselves and any other party to the agreement;

(2) regulates the election of directors;

(3) provides for the management of the business and affairs of the corporation, including the restriction or abrogation, in whole or in part, of the powers of the directors;

(4) includes any other matter that may be contained in a u.s.a. pursuant to any of other provision of the Alberta *Business Corporations Act*.

With respect to clarifying problems in the CBCA, the Alberta section contains rather detailed provisions dealing with the consequence of acquiring, through transfer or issuance by the company, shares subject to a u.s.a.

The Alberta section makes some drafting improvements, and adds a curious provision in subsection 140(9) [146(9)] which allows shareholders to exclude the application of all but not a part of section 140 [146]. It has been stated that the exclusion "would leave the agreement as a mere personal agreement among the parties to it", presumably meaning that such an agreement does not have the constitutional character that would accompany a u.s.a. subject to section 140 [146]. Finally, subsection 140(8) [146(8)] of the Alberta provision stipulates that a u.s.a. can be amended only with the written consent of all those who are shareholders at the effective date of the amendment. In view of the flexible approach taken by the Alberta draftsmen to expand the concept of the u.s.a., it is surprising to find a rigid rule requiring unanimity. Interestingly, the proposed Ontario approach is an opposite one in that paragraph 108(6)(a) of the new OBCA states that any amendment of the u.s.a. may be effected in the manner specified in the u.s.a.

Speaking of Ontario, its proposed statute also makes some changes to the CBCA treatment of the u.s.a., but they are not so extensive as the Alberta changes just discussed. Subsection 108(5) of the proposed Ontario Act makes it clear that a shareholder inherits all the rights, powers, duties and liabilities of a director, whether arising under the Act or otherwise, to ensure that common law as well as all statutory liabilities are included when the shareholder assumes the role of a director. Paragraph 108(6)(b) allows shareholders also to provide for the arbitration of differences or disputes, thereby removing an obstacle which faces directors under the common law.

Understandably, a number of criticisms have been levelled at the u.s.a. provisions. Some of these are: the provisions are uncertain as to their meaning, especially as to the extent of liability imposed on the shareholders; they are a loophole for avoiding the Canadian residency requirement for directors by permitting a nominee director with the foreign shareholder or shareholders entering a u.s.a. to exercise all management powers; they are not clear as to the number of votes which can be cast (for example, does each shareholder get one vote or as many votes as he has shares?). However, despite the uncertainties and criticisms, I regard the provisions as sensible and welcome since they allow parties to form basically what amounts to an incorporated partnership that has statutory basis and force.

It may be that colleagues from the United Kingdom will observe that so much fuss about the u.s.a. is puzzling, since their company statute and those statutes in Canada which followed it (for example, B.C.) have for some time permitted a flexible contractual approach to the company's constitution which might in substance be analogized to the u.s.a.; but this approach has not been without uncertainty and difficulty.

Notes and Questions

1　A key difference between public and private corporations relates to the process of incorporation and constitutional structure. Both because of the small number of participants involved, and the often idiosyncratic needs of particular capital contributors, the structure of the corporation is established by elaborate bargaining between prospective shareholders. As a consequence of this bargaining process, a significant part of the relationship of the parties is embodied in shareholder agreements, and not merely the articles and by-laws. Through a shareholder agreement, the parties will frequently wish to allocate day-to-day powers of control by designating which of their number will serve as directors and officers of the corporation. A shareholder agreement will also very often indicate how the profits of the corporation shall be paid out. The choice between paying out profits as salary and directors' fees or as dividends can have profound and often differential tax consequences for the participants and will be something the shareholders will wish to settle in advance. Other important matters may be dealt with in shareholders' agreements. It is far from infrequent that disputes arise between shareholders of private corporations relating to the means and ends to be pursued by the corporation; thus, an important feature of many shareholder agreements will be elaborate dispute resolution mechanisms. Similarly, because of the close working relationship between the corporate constituents and the need for trust and mutual compatibility, restrictions on the transferability of shares are a common feature of shareholder agreements (note that CBCA s. 6(1)(d) requires that any restrictions on transfer be put into the articles; these will often be replicated in the shareholders' agreement). Shareholder agreements also very often require a demanding super-majority voting approval for the undertaking of fundamental changes like an amalgamation, a sale of the corporation's assets, *etc.* Sometimes, unanimity will be required, effectively giving each shareholder a power of veto.

As noted above, the enactment of the statutory unanimous shareholder agreement was a response to difficulties at common law associated with fettering the powers of the directors. Since the passage of these provisions, unanimous shareholder agreements have become the most important planning tool available to participants in private corporations in arranging mutual rights and entitlements. Such agreements will often embody contractual provisions of the variety discussed in Coates, "Share Transfer and Transmission Restrictions in the Close Corporation", *supra.*

2 The statutory provisions relating to unanimous shareholder agreements are found in ss. 2(1) and 146 of the CBCA, and ss. 1(1) and 108 of the OBCA. Note that the distinguishing feature of a "unanimous shareholder agreement" in the statutes is that it "restricts, in whole or in part, the powers of the directors to manage or [to supervize the management of] the business and affairs of the corporation". Suppose an agreement between all the shareholders of the corporation restricts the authority of the directors, but also contains other agreements, relating to such matters as buy-sell arrangements, requisite shareholder votes on the undertaking of fundamental changes, shareholder voting agreements, *etc.* Is the whole agreement a "unanimous shareholder agreement", or only that part that relates to the authority of the directors? Do the words "in whole or in part" in CBCA s. 146(1) and (2) and OBCA s. 108(2) refer to the "written agreement", or do they refer to the restriction of the powers of directors? The distinction may be important. For example, a transferee of shares with notice of a common law voting agreement is not bound by the agreement (because of the absence of privity of contract); see *Greenhalgh v. Mallard*, [1943] 2 All E.R. 234 (C.A.). However, a transferee of shares subject to a u.s.a. is bound by the u.s.a.; see CBCA s. 146(3), OBCA s. 108(4) (although note the limitation contained in CBCA s. 49(8), OBCA s. 56(3)).

3 Suppose that shares subject to a u.s.a. were transferred to a third party in circumstances under which that third party is not bound by the u.s.a. (see CBCA s. 49(8), OBCA s. 56(3)). What happens to the u.s.a., since it is no longer an agreement between all the shareholders of the corporation? Does it cease to have effect (at least in relation to those parts restricting the authority of the directors)?

4 Note that where there is a u.s.a. CBCA s. 146(5) and OBCA s. 108(5) give each shareholder the "rights, powers, duties and liabilities of a director of the corporation, whether they arise under this Act or otherwise". What is the scope of the "or otherwise"? It would appear that this phrase was intended to ensure that common law liabilities would be transferred from directors to shareholders. But what else? For example, the *Income Tax Act* fixes each director of the corporation with liability for failure of the corporation to remit employee source deductions to the government. Can a provincial enactment transfer to shareholders a federal liability specifically attaching to the directors of the corporation? If it cannot, then the directors might find themselves in the unenviable position of not actually managing the company, but being liable for the managerial dereliction of the shareholders.

5 What is the function and status of directors where the u.s.a remits all authority to manage to the shareholders? Is there any point in retaining the requirement to have directors in such circumstances?

6 Note that the CBCA fails to specifically provide how a u.s.a. may be amended, while OBCA s. 108(6)(a) provides that "any amendment of the unanimous shareholder agreement may be effected in the manner specified therein". Would it be possible under the CBCA for a u.s.a. to specify a non-unanimous amendment procedure? Note also that there is common law authority that directors may not refer disputes amongst themselves to arbitration, as this would constitute a fettering of their discretion; see *Atlas Developments v. Calof and Gold* (1963), 41 W.W.R. 575 (Man. Q.B.). This limitation may apply to shareholders as well under a u.s.a. This is why OBCA s. 108(6)(b) specifically provides that disputes arising under the u.s.a. may be referred to arbitration.

7 Note that it is standard practice for the corporation to be made a party to a u.s.a., even where the agreement imposes no specific obligations upon the corporation. Can you think of why this might be done?

8 The court has authority under the oppression remedy to make an order "creating or amending a unanimous shareholder agreement". See CBCA s. 241(3)(c), OBCA s. 248(3)(c). The following case illustrates that the broad discretion given the court under the oppression remedy may also be used to constrain the exercise of powers granted under a u.s.a. As you read the case, you might pause to reflect on the manner in which the oppression remedy allows a court to import notions of contractual "unconscionability" into the law of corporations. Is this a good or a bad development?

Bury v. Bell Gouinlock Ltd.
(1984), 48 O.R. (2d) 57 (H.C.), affirmed (1985), 49 O.R. (2d) 91
(Div. Ct.)

EBERLE J.: The applicant was a shareholder and employee of the respondent. He left the employ of the respondent on May 9, 1984, in order to better himself and almost immediately began working for another brokerage house in Toronto. The shareholders of the respondent had a shareholders' agreement which provided that a shareholder who left the employ of the company was required to sell his shares to the company at prices and on terms spelled out in the agreement. It is the interaction of the terms of that agreement concerning the sale of the shares and s. 247 [now 248] of the Ontario *Business Corporations Act, 1982* S.O. 1982, c. 4, which gives rise to this application.

There seem to be three areas of difficulty. The first is whether s. 247 [248] of the Act may be utilized to give relief in face of a valid contract between the parties dealing with the very matters in issue. The second area is whether it is shown that the actions of the respondent fall within the type of conduct described in s. 247(2) [248(2)]. The third area is what relief may properly be given within the bounds of an originating motion and without the trial of an issue.

As to the first area, no case has been cited where the activities giving rise to the litigation were also the subject-matter of a written contract between the parties — a written contract the validity of which has not been questioned in the argument in this case. However, the reported cases cited to me do not contain any language suggesting that relief cannot be given in a case such as the present.

Indeed, s. 247(3)(c) [248(3)(c)] expressly provides that the court may make any order it thinks fit including, without limiting the generality of the foregoing:

> (c) an order to regulate a corporation's affairs by amending the articles or by-laws or creating or amending a unanimous shareholder agreement;

This is a far-reaching provision. Since the court has been given power to remodel a shareholders' agreement, it seems to me that the court must also have authority under the section to set limits to the exercise of a power given by a shareholders' agreement, if the court finds that a particular exercise of such power has the effect aimed at by s. 274(2) [248(2)]. The appropriate canon of interpretation has been stated in *Re Ferguson and Imax Systems Corp.* (1983), 43 O.R. (2d) 128 at p. 137, 150 D.L.R. (3d) 718 at p. 727, as follows, ". . . and the section should be interpreted broadly to carry out its purpose". Those words were said in relation to a section of the *Canada Business Corporations Act*, S.C. 1974-75-76, c. 33 [s. 241], which is to substantially the same effect as s. 247 [248] of the Ontario Act.

Accordingly, I am of the view that s. 247 [248] may give relief in fact of a provision in a contract valid between the parties.

That is particularly so in the present case where the applicant seeks not to invalidate any provision in the shareholders' agreement, but takes the position that the exercise by the company of the right given to it by para. 16 of the agreement to extend from six months to twelve months the period within which the company will pay for the applicant's shares is oppressive or unfairly prejudicial or unfairly disregards the interests of the applicant in the circumstances of this case.

This brings me to the second area of problem: is that decision of the company in the circumstances of this case oppressive to the applicant or otherwise within the concluding words of s. 247(2) [248(2)]?

The relevant facts are these. The company and the other shareholders were, as was the applicant, fully aware of the fact that in the securities business, because of by-laws of the Investment Dealers Association and of the Toronto Stock Exchange, an individual cannot be a shareholder of two brokerage houses at the same time. Accordingly, the invocation by the company of the 12 months provision in para. 16 of the agreement has the effect of preventing the applicant from becoming a shareholder in his new employer and thus prevents him from obtaining dividend income or other income accruing only to a shareholder. It is evident that since the applicant was a shareholder of the respondent company it would be expected that he would likely become, or wish to become, a shareholder in any new employer. His status in the securities business is evidently one in which that would be expected.

For what reason has the respondent chosen so to penalize the applicant? None whatever has been advanced. The respondent argued that the onus is on the applicant to show that the respondent's decision is not properly based. In my view, since the basis for the respondent's action lies peculiarly within the knowledge of the respondent, any onus on the applicant is met where, as here, no ground is advanced to justify the decision. The deprivation to the applicant is sufficient to raise a *prima facie* case of oppression or unfairness. It is particularly striking that the respondent does not advance the ground that a requirement that it pay the applicant within six months would cause the respondent any financial difficulty.

If a payment within the initial six months period will not cause the respondent any financial difficulty, why has it chosen to rely on the provision in para. 16 to extend the payment period to 12 months? The only reasonable inference that comes to mind is that it is designed merely to punish the applicant. I do not mean to suggest that financial hardship would be the only justifiable ground for a 12-month payment period under the terms of the shareholders' agreement. There may be many other good grounds relevant in other cases. In the present case, no other justification is advanced, nor even suggested, beyond the bare legal right contained in para. 16.

There are, in my view, other relevant circumstances. For instance, the agreement provides that no interest shall be paid on the purchase price; accordingly, the company has the free use of the applicant's money for 12 months. Yet the applicant is deprived of his status as shareholder in the respondent company as and from the date of his departure from that company; and he is further deprived of any dividends paid on those shares during the 12-month period; yet, as observed above, he is unable to become a shareholder in his new employer. In the absence of some good reason for so acting, it seems to me that the result of the respondent's action is oppressive to the applicant. In addition, para. 12 of the agreement requires the company to notify the departing shareholder of the share price which the company will pay "forthwith" after the determination of the price. The price is to be determined according to a formula set out in the agreement and ought to have been done by the company as soon as it received the audited financial statements for the previous year. These were received, I am told, in February, 1984. Apparently no determination was made at that time but, more importantly, the company did not comply with the combined effect of paras. 11(3) and 12 of the agreement by notifying the applicant forthwith after his termination of the price at which the company would buy his shares according to the formula. Although on several occasions, the applicant sought this information from the president of the company, the company did nothing until July 20th, when it responded to a letter from the applicant's solicitors. On that occasion, for the first time, the company notified the applicant of the prices at which he was required to sell his shares. In my view, that is not "forthwith" after his departure from the company.

* * *

It is to be noted that it was not until September 6, 1984, the last day allowed for filing affidavit material pursuant to the order of McKinley J. of August 1, 1984, that an affidavit was filed by the company. In this affidavit is to be found the only evidence that the company made any decision to invoke the 12-month provision in para. 16 of the agreement.

While that agreement does not establish any time-limit for the company to give notification of such a decision, nevertheless, in my view, the actions of the company throughout exhibit a consistent policy of delaying the applicant at every step. This course of conduct, when viewed with the unexplained decision of the company to avail itself of the 12-month period for payment to the plaintiff for his shares, leads me to the conclusion that it would be contrary to the provisions of s. 247(2) [248(2)] of the Ontario *Business Corporations Act, 1982* to permit the company to invoke that 12-month period.

I have now reached the third problem area, namely, what relief may properly be granted.

* * *

The company could easily have notified the applicant on May 9th of the prices of his shares in accordance with the financial statement of December 31, 1983, and was required to do so "forthwith". Accordingly, I think the appropriate relief to be given is that the company be required to pay the applicant on November 9, 1984, the appropriate amount for his shares and, of course, the applicant must deliver his shares duly endorsed in blank for transfer on that date. The amount to be paid is $60,000 for the B shares plus $70,600 for the A shares. This is arrived at based on a price of $35.30 for each of 2,000 A shares. The total is $130,600.

Judgment for Plaintiff

An appeal to the Ontario Divisional Court was dismissed, the Court concluding that s. 247(1) [248(1)] of the OBCA gives the Court a wide discretion and that Eberle J. had not improperly exercised his discretion. (49 O.R. (2d) 91.)

Questions

1 Consider and evaluate the following arguments:

a. The Court in *Bury* overstepped the acceptable limits of judicial intervention by effectively re-making a contract freely entered into by two consenting and fully informed parties. Bury was under no compulsion to work for Bell Gouinlock. By voluntarily entering into the contract (the u.s.a.) with full knowledge of all its terms, he thereby agreed to accept the exercise of powers vested in Bell even where the consequences of such exercise might place him in a disadvantageous position. There was no requirement in the contract for Bell to give any reason for exercising its option to extend the payout period to 12 months. Had the parties wished to constrain Bell's ability to exercise this contractual power, and/or to require Bell to state reasons for exercise of the power, then terms to this effect could easily have been included in the agreement. The absence of such constraint strongly suggests that the choice of whether or not to extend the payout period was left by the parties to Bell's unfettered discretion. The result of the case is to confer an unearned windfall on Bury.

b. There are good economic reasons for a contractual provision that allows the employer to inflict a hardship on departing employees. The employer (Bell) may invest a substantial amount of time, effort and money in training its employees. The skills acquired by its employees are highly transferable, however, and there is a significant danger that once the employee has acquired these skills another employer will steal the employee away with a more attractive offer. The firm's investment in the employee will be irretrievably lost. The result will be that brokerage firms will be very reluctant to hire and train "new blood", to the detriment not only of the industry and the investing public, but aspiring brokers as well. The clause in question is therefore simply a rational and reasonable response to a very real problem, and one that ultimately operates in favour of both the employer and employee.

c.   The Court reached the right result. Contractual silence regarding the limits of the exercise of an apparently unconstrained power does not incontestably confirm that such power was intended to be totally without boundaries. The parties might well have, and probably did expect that the power conferred upon Bell would only be exercised for some good reason. Such good reason might include the inability of Bell to raise the necessary funds, or the financial hardship caused Bell in paying out Bury immediately. It is not reasonable to expect the parties to formulate complete contracts that spell out what is to happen in every possible eventuality; greater economy of drafting (and not a great deal less certainty) will result from according broadly drafted contractual provisions the meaning that the parties would reasonably have expected. On these facts, it is probable that Bell extended the payout period for one reason only: to punish Bury for leaving the firm. That is not a good reason, and not one to which the Court ought to lend its *imprimatur*.

2 It is fair to say that the oppression remedy has revolutionized the law of private companies. Majority/minority relations (both in relation to public and private companies) were once characterized by the following quotation from *Re Jury Gold Mine Dev. Co.*, [1928] 4 D.L.R. 735 (Ont. C.A.):

> [the plaintiff] is a minority shareholder and must endure the unpleasantness incident to that situation. If he choose to risk his money by subscribing for shares, it is part of his bargain that he will submit to the will of the majority. In the absence of fraud or transactions *ultra vires*, the majority must govern, and there should be no appeal to the Courts for redress.

The oppression remedy is designed to give minority shareholders significantly more power to challenge the actions of majority or controlling shareholders than they have at common law. Indeed, almost all of the cases decided under the statutory oppression remedy have involved private companies, although this is now starting to change. See generally Jeffrey G. MacIntosh, "Minority Shareholder Rights in Canada and England: 1860–1987" (1989), 27 Osgoode Hall L.J. 561.

3 Suppose third parties have acquired rights against the corporation when one of the signatories to a u.s.a. acts in a manner contrary to the agreement. What is the legal position of the third party? The following case may shed some light on this question.

Re 609940 Ontario Inc. (Five Star Auto); Cicco v. Trustee, 609940 Ontario Inc., 609940 Ontario Inc. and Bertucci
Ontario Supreme Court [In Bankruptcy] September 19, 1985

HENRY J. (orally): The bankrupt company made an assignment in bankruptcy on 18th June 1985 pursuant to a director's resolution. A shareholder moves for an order declaring the assignment a nullity. The important issue raised is whether the resolution contravenes a "unanimous shareholder agreement" made under s. 108 of the *Business Corporations Act, 1982*, S.O., c. 4 and if so whether the resolution is unauthorised and the assignment void.

The bankrupt, 609940 Ontario Inc., trading as Five Star Auto, is in effect an incorporated partnership carrying on the business of automobile repair and used car sales. It was incorporated on 4th January 1985. The principals are Mr. Raphaele Bertucci and Peter Cicco. Each held 50 per cent of the shares and were the only officers and directors. On 4th January 1985, the two shareholders and the company made an agreement expressed to be in contemplation of the unanimous shareholder agreement provision in s. 108 of the *Business Corporations Act*, which provides in part:

(2) A written agreement among all the shareholders of a corporation or among all the shareholders and one or more persons who are not shareholders may restrict in whole or in part the powers of the directors to manage or supervise the management of the business and affairs of the corporation.

The shareholder agreement provided that:

1. The Chairman presiding at a meeting of Directors or Shareholders shall not have a casting or deciding vote in the case of an equality of votes, it being understood that all decisions affecting the Corporation shall be made only with the consent of both Bertucci and Cicco.

By May 1985 differences had arisen between the two shareholders and Mr. Cicco decided to withdraw. An agreement was made to settle their differences which was incorporated in a letter dated 22nd May 1985; Mr. Bertucci was to continue to operate the business, would assume personal responsibility for and pay the debts of the company. Assets contributed by Mr. Cicco were to be returned to him; he was to receive certain indemnities and mutual releases were to be given. Mr. Cicco agreed to transfer his shares to Mr. Bertucci and/or the company; to deliver all books and records of the company to Bertucci and to resign as an officer and director of the company. The transaction was to be completed or closed by 31st May 1985; in the meantime the formal documents were executed by Mr. Cicco and delivered into escrow including the transfer of his shares, the release and indemnity agreement and his resignation as secretary and director. By 31st May Mr. Bertucci had not performed his undertakings. Mr. Cicco is currently suing for specific performance or damages.

Mr. Cicco ceased to be a director of the company on 4th June 1985 leaving Mr. Bertucci as the sole director and president. On 7th June 1985 without Mr. Cicco's consent he adopted a director's resolution that the company make an assignment in bankruptcy and authorized himself as president to execute the necessary documents. The assignment for the general benefit of creditors was filed by him on 18th June 1985 under the *Bankruptcy Act*. Mr. Cicco's documents held in escrow were returned to his solicitor on 24th June and the bankruptcy was then disclosed.

The first meeting of creditors was called for 11th July 1985 but it aborted for lack of a quorum. At that time Mr. Cicco's solicitors objected to the assignment as being unauthorized and void and his solicitor again challenged the assignment by letter to the trustee on 2nd July. It is fair to say on the evidence before me that the trustee was on notice that the director's resolution and the assignment were challenged as being in contravention of the unanimous shareholder agreement at least by 2nd July, and it had the means of discovering the situation earlier as the books and records of the company were in its hands before 25th June. The trustee proceeded to administer the estate taking the position that he could not do otherwise unless the court annulled the assignment.

Mr. Cicco . . . moves for annulment of the assignment. The grounds stated are simple: that by reason of the unanimous shareholder agreement the director was not authorized to adopt the enabling resolution without the consent of Mr. Cicco; the *Business Corporations Act* requires directors to comply with the shareholder agreement and to manage the affairs of the corporation subject to its provisions; therefore the assignment is void.

The relevant provisions of the *Business Corporations Act* are as follows [the court sets out OBCA ss. 108(2) and (5), 1(1)48, 115 and 134(2)] . . .

The court may annul an assignment in bankruptcy under s. 151(1) of the *Bankruptcy Act* [now 181(1) of the *Bankruptcy and Insolvency Act*, R.S. 1985, c.B-3] which provides:

151.(1) [181(1)] Where, in the opinion of the court, a receiving order ought not to have been made or an assignment ought not to have been filed, the court may by order annul the bankruptcy.

To annul the assignment the court must therefore conclude that the assignment ought not to have been made. This is a wide ranging and flexible test. There is no simple or universal principle prescribed. It is a case by case decision which imports the exercise of discretion. In the past the bankruptcy courts have annulled an assignment on the ground of mistake, lack of proper notice of the directors' meeting adopting the enabling resolution and a clear sufficiency of assets to pay all creditors' claims. Counsel have referred me to a number of judicial decisions in bankruptcy cases which I have considered although none is directly in point. These are *Re Trail Bldg. Supply Ltd.* (1957), 36 C.B.R. 100, 21 W.W.R. 270 (B.C. S.C.); *Re Assoc. Colour Laboratories Ltd.* (1970), 14 C.B.R. (N.S.) 35, 73 W.W.R. 566, 12 D.L.R. (3d) 338 (B.C. S.C.); *Re Prince Albert Beef Producers Ltd.* (1979), 32 C.B.R. (N.S.) 301, 1 Sask. R. 138 (Q.B.); and *Re London, New York & Paris Assoc. of Fashions Ltd.* (1982), 40 C.B.R. (N.S.) 127, 131 D.L.R. (3d) 653, 36 Nfld. & P.E.I.R. 517, 101 A.P.R. 517 (Nfld. T.D.).

The sections cited from the *Business Corporations Act* were enacted for the first time in 1982. As I see it the new sections override the former common law rule that shareholders could not fetter the power and discretion of directors by agreement among themselves: see, for example, *Motherwell v. Schoof*, [1949] 2 W.W.R. 529, [1949] 4 D.L.R. 812 (Alta. T.D.). That rule has been altered by the statutes so that a unanimous shareholder agreement may restrict the powers of the directors and they are subject to that agreement in managing the affairs of the corporation. A new rule of internal management was thus created.

The shareholder agreement of 4th January 1985 is in my opinion a unanimous shareholder agreement as defined by the Act. It binds the directors but does it bind a third party dealing with the company who has no notice of the restrictive authority of its directors? In the case at least of the trustee in bankruptcy the answer is "no". The assignment is for the benefit of the creditors and the function of the trustee is to protect their interest. It is the policy of the Act that assets of an insolvent company are to be distributed to the creditors according to the scheme of priorities there described; a debtor or a creditor may set the machinery in motion.

Here the sole director has done so. The trustee, who has started his administration, in his affidavit deposes that at the date of the assignment the company was insolvent. There is a deficiency of assets; it is expected that some preferred creditors will be paid but that there will be nothing for the unsecured creditors. In these circumstances, the director made the decision to invoke the Act, justifiably so in my opinion. There is no question that the resolution and assignment are regular on their face; the director was duly appointed and qualified to act. The effect of the unanimous shareholder agreement is to limit his authority but in my opinion that is an entirely internal matter between the director and the shareholders. He may be accountable to them for failure to comply with the agreement and the statute but that does not render the assignment void or disentitle the trustee to rely on the assignment and supporting resolution. To hold otherwise would have the result that no trustee could safely act under a corporate assignment in bankruptcy without enquiring into the internal (and unpublished) fetters on the authority of the duly appointed directors convened in a regular meeting. In my opinion that cannot have been the intention of the legislature.

Although it is not conclusive, I have derived assistance from the judgment of Batshaw J. in *Re Deziel; Miller v. McKechnie* (1962), 4 C.B.R. (N.S.) 215 (Que. S.C.).

I have not dealt with the issues raised as to whether Mr. Cicco ceased to be a shareholder when he agreed to transfer his shares or whether that act terminated the unanimous shareholder agreement or whether the applicant has standing to bring this motion. I prefer to base my decision on the fundamental issue.

The application will therefore be dismissed.

Application dismissed.

Chapter 11

Shareholders' Remedies

1. INTRODUCTION

In Chapter 9, we examined various methods by which a shareholder may participate in the governance of the corporation through the bundle of rights that the corporation statute generally assigns to shareholders. These rights can be contractually embellished or supplemented, especially in the context of the private or closely held corporation as was briefly explored in Chapter 10. It is obvious that if the rights given to shareholders, whether by the statute or by contract, are to be worthwhile, correspondingly effective remedies must also be available to cure their breach.

The broad distinction between a right and a remedy can be stated easily enough. Remedies, generally speaking, are the means for ensuring that shareholders are given the rights to which they are entitled. For example, a shareholder may have the right to vote her shares, either by statute or under the articles of the company. Should the company deny this right, then some means must exist to protect the right. The shareholder might commence a personal action, a derivative action, or an oppression action. A court could then order that the company accord the shareholder the right to which she is entitled.

The distinction between a right and a remedy is not always crystal clear in practice, however. Consider the oppression provision; although commonly referred to as the oppression "remedy", it is clear that this provision augments the substantive rights of shareholders by expanding upon the range of matters that would be actionable at common law (or under CBCA s. 122, OBCA s. 134) for breach of fiduciary duties. It is also clear that the oppression remedy provides a new, more expeditious procedure for defending rights the denial of which would have been actionable at common law. Thus, it has the characteristics of both a right and a remedy. See, *e.g.*, *Sparling v. Javelin International Ltd. et al.*, [1986] R.J.Q. 1073, *infra*.

Our main task in this chapter is to understand the differences between derivative actions, personal actions, and oppression actions. As we have already indicated, a derivative action may be commenced where all shareholders are affected equally by the impugned conduct, and the real plaintiff is "the corporation"; i.e., normally any remedy will be given in favour of the corporation, rather than an individual shareholder or shareholders. A personal action may be commenced where a shareholder or shareholders have some grievance that is peculiar to herself or themselves, and not shared equally by all other shareholders. In such an action, the remedy would issue in favour of the shareholder(s). The oppression remedy, once again, straddles the line. At the date of publication, it would appear that a shareholder can commence an action of either a personal or derivative nature under the oppression remedy, although the authority on this question is somewhat divided (see *infra*).

As you read the following materials, which focus on the descriptive aspects of shareholder remedies, you should not lose sight of the normative questions. For example, how far-reaching are the rights and remedies that the legislation ought to accord shareholders? Shareholders rights and remedies have both costs and benefits. The oppression remedy may be beneficial if it protects shareholders against actions that are little more than redistributions of wealth in favour of managers or a constituency of shareholders. As we have seen, there are many ways in which this can occur, and the common law of fiduciary duties will not always prove adequate to the task of thwarting such unproductive redistributions. The oppression remedy also is potentially costly in that it may invite meritless shareholder claims ("nuisance suits", or in the US, "strike suits") launched solely with the intention of extorting a costly settlement from the company. A widely drawn oppression remedy (or other shareholder rights or remedies) also creates uncertainty about legal rights which we can predict will result in a greater amount of litigation. Litigation is costly in a number of ways. Most obviously, there is the direct cost to the participants. There is also a cost to the state, which provides courtrooms, pays judges' salaries, *etc.* In many cases, there is a cost to the company as well, even should it ultimately prevail. Executives of the company may have to spend time with company lawyers planning strategy, collecting evidence, or testifying in court. An oppression suit may delay or even abort a value-generating transaction, to the ultimate detriment of all corporate constituents.

Other arguments, however, can be marshalled in favour of widely drawn shareholder remedies. All shareholder-initiated litigation suffers from a "free rider" problem. Litigation alleging breach of fiduciary duty or oppression is potentially costly to the litigants (particularly so with the "costs follow the event" rule). However, the benefits of a successful suit (particularly if the action is derivative in character) are likely to be realized by some or all of the shareholders. Thus, the incentive of each shareholder is to lie in the grass hoping someone else will expend the time and expense and take the risk of suing. This is particularly true where the shares are widely held and most shareholders have small holdings and stand to gain relatively little from successful litigation. Where the substantive rights of shareholders are broadly drawn, there is a greater incentive to sue, overcoming to a degree the free rider problem. There are more direct solutions to the free rider problem, however, which involve an appropriate casting of the rules on costs. These are discussed, *infra* (can you think of what they might be?).

Another key question is that of standing to sue. At common law, it was clear that creditors could not sue corporate managers alleging breach of fiduciary duty. However, creditors are given standing under the oppression remedy. Is there a principled basis upon which we can decide who should be able to sue, and for what wrongs?

We turn our attention first to the derivative action.

2. THE DERIVATIVE ACTION

(a) Introduction

Where a corporation has been injured by some wrongdoing, a shareholder of the corporation arguably also has been injured through the diminution in value of his or her shares that is traceable to the corporate injury. As we will examine, the courts followed by legislatures developed a derivative action whereby a shareholder was permitted to bring an action to rectify a wrong committed against the corporation for which management did not seek redress, often because they or one of their members were the alleged wrongdoers. Under the derivative action, a shareholder on behalf of the corporation brings an action which derives from the corporation's cause of action. This indirect or derivative action is in contrast to the personal or direct action whereby a shareholder enforces his own rights as distinct from those of the corporation.

The positive aspects of the derivative action are that it can be an effective private remedial instrument to ensure and enhance management accountability. On the other hand, the US "strike suit" action, i.e., litigation having little merit that seeks to extract gains from the nuisance value of claims for high damages, is ample evidence of potential abuse. This abuse has led to procedural reforms and responses in the US and Canada to prevent or minimize the adverse aspects of derivative actions. As will be seen, the derivative action has many facets and debates about its utility continue.

A brief examination will first be made of the situation that existed in Anglo-Canadian common law. We then will turn to the special legislative provisions that create a statutory derivative action which has received a number of interpretations by Canadian courts. Some of these cases will also be briefly studied.

(b) At Common Law: The Rule in *Foss v. Harbottle*

BECK, "The Shareholders' Derivative Action"
(1974), 52 C.B.R. 159 at 164–168 (footnotes omitted)

1. A Recapitulation of *Foss v. Harbottle*

In order to understand and evaluate the reform of the derivative suit it is necessary to set out briefly the substantive and procedural problems spawned by the rule. The decision in *Foss v. Harbottle* was premised on the separate legal personality of the corporation and on majority rule in internal corporate affairs. If the corporation is a legal person separate from its members, it follows that for a wrong done to it the corporation itself is the only proper plaintiff. The two shareholders who appeared as plaintiffs in *Foss v. Harbottle* alleged, *inter alia*, a sale by the directors of their own property at inflated values to the company. The wrong alleged was thus a wrong to the company and the Vice-Chancellor ruled that the plaintiffs had no standing to sue on behalf of the corporation.

As to the transaction itself and bringing suit for damages for the injury caused by it, those were both matters to be decided upon by the company in general meeting. The purchase of their own lands for the corporation by the directors was a transaction that was voidable at the option of the corporation. The corporate pleasure was to be determined by the shareholders in general meeting and as the plaintiffs did not represent a majority, or allege that the will of the majority had been determined, they had no standing to sue in the name of the company. The court was not going to be put in the position of ruling on a breach of trust that the principal might elect to confirm. Moreover, the decision whether or not to bring suit in the company name belongs at common law to the general meeting where, once again, the majority rules. In short, the will of the majority had not been ascertained and the plaintiffs were non-suited. Thus in 1843, one year before the first modern companies Act, the Court of Chancery applied its rule of non-interference in the internal affairs of a partnership to the incorporated company. Internal affairs were a matter for the majority and the majority was thus firmly established in a pivotal position and has remained there ever since. Two other judicial extensions to the rule in *Foss v. Harbottle* soon increased the power of the majority even more.

In *Mozley v. Alston* two shareholders brought a personal action for a declaration that the board of directors was holding office illegally and in contravention of the terms of the company's Act of incorporation. James L.J. was of the opinion that the rule applied. An usurpation of the office of director was a wrong done to the company and the company was the only proper complainant. His Lordship did not consider the argument that the plaintiffs were asserting a personal right to have the internal governmental affairs of the company conducted in accordance with its terms of incorporation and according to which terms they had subscribed their capital.

This "irregularity" branch of the rule was further settled in 1875 in *MacDonald v. Gardiner*. The articles provided for the taking of a poll upon the demand of five members. When a poll was demanded on a motion to adjourn, the chairman ruled there could be no poll on that question. The Court of Appeal said that the matter was an internal dispute and for the majority to decide — the rule applied. The court did not advert to the section that has been in the English *Companies Act* since 1856 which constitutes the memorandum and articles a contract between the members and the company and thus to the fact that the plaintiff could be considered as suing to enforce his personal right to have his contract enforced according to its terms. This irregularity branch of the rule has been approved by the Privy Council and applied in many cases:

> . . . no mere informality or irregularity which can be remedied by the majority will entitle the minority to sue, if the act when done regularly would be within the powers of the company and the intention of the majority of shareholders is clear.

The second extension of the rule came with the decision of the Privy Council in *North-West Transportation Co. v. Beatty* in 1887. What the Vice-Chancellor had said in *Foss v. Harbottle* must be done, was done in the *North-West* case. The controlling director who had purchased his own property for the company submitted the contract to the general meeting for its approval. Approval was given but only by reason of Mr. Beatty's votes *qua* shareholder. The Supreme Court of Canada held that an interested director could not use his shareholder's votes to confirm his own contract. The Privy Council disagreed and ruled that Mr. Beatty was entitled to vote to approve the transaction. Moreover, as a general proposition, a shareholder was said to be entitled to exercise his vote "from motives or promptings of what he considers his own individual interest".

Subsequent companies Acts amendments and corporate draughtsmanship have added further complexity to the rule and have changed majority control from what it was in 1843. At common law a director could not submit a contract in which he was interested to the board for approval as he himself was disqualified from voting and the company was entitled to have the disinterested opinion of every director. Thus all such contracts had to go to the general meeting. This inconvenience was soon remedied by statutory amendment, now common to nearly all companies Acts, whereby the board could approve such transactions if the interested director declared his interest and refrained from voting. There was no longer any need to inform the shareholders of such transactions, much less seek their approval.

The power of the directors (and thus of the majority shareholders) was further increased by corporate draughtsmanship which, through the articles of association, vested management in the boards of directors. In the five Canadian letters patent jurisdictions and in Ontario, where incorporation is now by articles of incorporation, management power is vested in the board by statute. The power to manage includes the power, probably the exclusive power, to use the corporate name in litigation. Thus the two matters of majority control that were at the heart of the judgement in *Foss v. Harbottle*, the possibility of shareholder approval of the contract in which the directors were interested, and the decision to sue in the corporate name, no longer belong to the majority and reside, almost exclusively, in the board of directors. This has not, however, prevented the directors themselves from resorting to the shareholders for ratification of their actions as a sort of safety-valve protection, a manoeuvre which, as we shall see, has introduced a new complication into an already complex area of the law.

Taken in its purest form the rule, along with the additional corporate facts noted above, would allow the directors — majority shareholders to ride roughshod over the majority. Thus a number of exceptions have been worked out in an attempt to give shareholders who are aggrieved by an unremedied wrong to the company access to the courts to sue on behalf of the company. The exceptions to the rule are those listed by Jenkins L.J. in *Edwards v. Halliwell*.

1. *Ultra Vires* Act: ". . . in cases where the act complained of is wholly ultra vires the company or association the rule has no application because there is no question of the transaction being confirmed by any majority."

2. Fraud on the Minority: ". . . where what has been done amounts to what is generally called in these cases a fraud on the minority and the wrongdoers are themselves in control of the company, the rule is relaxed in favour of the aggrieved minority who are allowed to bring what is known as a minority shareholders action on behalf of themselves and all others."

3. Special Majorities: "An individual member is not prevented from suing if the matter is one which could be validly done or sanctioned not by a simple majority of the members . . . but only by some special majority."

4. Personal Rights: Where "the personal and individual rights of membership of the plaintiff have been invaded", the rule "has no application at all".

The *ultra vires* and special majorities exceptions are straightforward and pose few problems. But in the areas of fraud on the minority and personal rights the shareholder is up against the procedural maze of the rule. The line between personal and derivative actions is neither clear nor settled and the shareholder who brings his suit believing he has a personal right of action may be met by a ruling that the wrong of which he complains is not to him but to the company and he must comply with the rule — which may well mean that his grievance will go unremedied.

The fraud on the minority exception is the one most often invoked by the aggrieved minority shareholder. But although the courts have used such broad language as "the court will prevent the management of companies being so conducted as to produce injustice or injury to any of the members", and the court will interfere if the conduct of the majority is "oppressive" or "harsh" or, even more generally, if no adequate remedy remained except that of a suit by individual corporators "the claims of justice would be found superior to any difficulties arising out of technical rules respecting to the mode in which corporations are required to sue" [*Foss v. Harbottle, supra*] the path to an actual remedy has proved extremely narrow and hazardous. Indeed it is difficult, if not impossible, despite the generous sentiments of the judicial language, to find judicial interference to halt conduct that falls short of an expropriation of corporate assets. The narrowness of the fraud exception is shown by *Pavlides v. Jensen* ([1956]] Ch. 565) a case in which the directors were accused of negligence for selling an asset for £182,000 which it was alleged was worth £1,000,000. A personal action was not maintainable as no shareholders' individual right *qua* shareholder had been interfered with. Fraud was not pleaded as the sale of assets at an alleged £800,000 undervalue was not a fraudulent expropriation of corporate assets, but was mere negligence.

The rule was therefore applied as the general meeting had power to ratify the directors' acts, or to decide not to take action for negligence. Even if fraud is involved the shareholder is always faced with the uncertain procedural hurdles of determining who has control, who are the wrongdoers, which corporate organ may take action in the company name, upon whom the demand to sue must be made, and whether or not the transaction is ratifiable.

It was to remedy these problems and to open the door to a wider range of shareholders' derivative actions that section 99 [now section 246] was included in the Ontario Act and section 229 [now section 239] in the federal Act.

Note

The common law derivative action remains in use in the U.K., though it has been somewhat overshadowed by the creation of a statutory "unfair prejudice" remedy similar to the Canadian oppression remedy. For recent U.K. cases that have discussed the exceptions to the rule in *Foss v. Harbottle*, see *Prudential Assurance Co. v. Newman Industries Ltd. (No. 2)* (1981), [1982] 1 All E.R. 354 (C.A.); *Smith v. Croft (No. 2)*, [1988] Ch. 114; and *Barrett v. Duckett*, [1995] 1 B.C.L.C. 243.

(c) The Statutory Derivative Action

The Federal Act

The CBCA creates a statutory derivative action in s. 239. Section 239(1) allows a complainant to "apply to a court for leave to bring an action in the name and on behalf of a corporation or any of its subsidiaries, or intervene in an action to which any such body corporate is a party, for the purpose of prosecuting, defending or discontinuing the action on behalf of the body corporate". "Complainant" is defined in s. 238 as (a) a current or former registered holder or beneficial owner of a security of a corporation or any of its affiliates, (b) a current or former director or officer of a corporation or any of its affiliates, (c) the Director or (d) anyone else who the court considers a proper person to make an application.

Section 239(2) provides that several conditions that must be satisfied for the court to allow a derivative action to be brought. First, the complainant must give the directors notice of intent to apply to the court at least fourteen days before the application is made, and therefore allow the directors of the corporation to bring the action. Second, the complainant must be acting in good faith. Third, the bringing of the action must appear to be in the interests of the corporation.

Section 240 sets out specific orders that a court may make in connection with a derivative action. These include, but are not limited to: (a) an order allowing a person to control the action, (b) an order directing the conduct of the action, (c) an order that payment to a defendant go to security holders rather than the corporation and (d) an order requiring the corporation to pay the complainant's legal fees.

Section 242(1) indicates that shareholder approval of an alleged wrong-doing is not conclusive, but may be taken into account. Section 242(2) requires the court's approval of any settlement or discontinuation of an action. Section 242(4) allows the court to order the corporation to pay the interim costs of the complainant.

A striking feature of the statutory derivative action is the importance of the court. Leave of the court is required to commence the action, and the grounds on which leave may be granted lend themselves to a large degree of judicial discretion. As noted by Iacobucci, Pilkington and Prichard in *Canadian Business Corporations*:

> a paramount role is given to the court [in respect of statutory derivative actions]. This approach has no doubt been influenced by largely un-regulated (to Canadian observers) shareholder actions in the United States about which Canadian draftsmen were most apprehensive. Leave of the court appears to be the compromise struck by the drafts-man to allay the fears of those who thought imminent tragedy was approaching by the conferral of a derivative action right.

The Provincial Acts

Most of the provincial acts have statutory derivative action legislation sim-ilar to that in the CBCA. Sections 245–7 of the OBCA do not differ signif-icantly from their CBCA counterparts. The statutory derivative actions of Manitoba (MCA ss. 231–3), Newfoundland (NCA, ss. 368–70), Saskatch-ewan (SBCA ss. 231–3), and Nova Scotia (NSCA, Third Schedule s. 4) differ from that of the CBCA only in that their notice requirements do not set a time limit but instead require "reasonable notice". Unlike other acts, Alberta (ABCA ss. 239–41) and New Brunswick (NBBCA ss. 163–5) also specifically include "a creditor of the corporation" in their definitions of "complainant".

In 2004, the *Company Act* in British Columbia was replaced by the *Business Corporations Act*. Sections 232 and 233 of the new BCBCA deal with the derivative action. While the old BCCA granted the right to seek leave to a "member or director", the BCBCA grants the right to a shareholder or director. The criteria for leave to commence a derivative action are listed in section 233(1) of the BCBCA, and include reasonable efforts by the complainant to cause the directors to commence the action, notice, good faith and the requirement that the legal proceeding appears to the court to be in the best interests of the company. The old BCCA had required that the action be "*prima facie* in the interests of the company". The BCBCA does not contain an equivalent to CBCA s. 240(c), which specifically allows the court to make an order such that damages be paid to shareholders rather than the corporation. However, a court could fashion such an order under the BCBCA s. 233(4) because the court may make any order it deems appropriate.

Note

> Review the derivative action provisions in the CBCA and the provincial corporate law statutes with respect to the following points:
>
> (i) the class of persons who may launch the action;
> (ii) grounds for court approval to proceed and the role of the court generally;
> (iii) the treatment of costs; and
> (iv) the range of orders and relief that may be granted by the court.

(d) Judicial Interpretation of the Derivative Action

Re Northwest Forest Products Ltd.
[1975] 4 W.W.R. 724 (B.C. S.C.)

[Northwest was 51% owner of Fraser Valley Pulp and Timber Ltd. Assets of Fraser Valley were sold to another company at what appeared to be a great undervaluation. The directors of Northwest were petitioned by its shareholders to vote the company's shares of Fraser Valley to set aside the sale, but did not respond. The complainants sought leave to commence a derivitave action.]

CASHMAN L.J.S.C.: Mr. McConnell submits that when viewed as a whole the affidavit and material in support of the motion does not disclose a *prima facie* case and furthermore that the directors were never informed of the specific action they were requested to take prior to this motion and indeed he questions whether the motion itself discloses an action.

As I understand his submission it appears that while he does not necessarily agree that the applicants are acting in good faith as required by subs. (3)(b) or that both were members of the company within the meaning of subs. (3)(d) he does not seriously contend that these things are not so.

Accordingly I find that the applicants have satisfied the requirements of s. 222(3)(b) and (d).

He does however submit that while the applicants did make a reasonable effort to cause the directors to commence an action the applicants failed to specify the precise nature of the action. In making this submission he relies upon the United States case of *Halprin v. Babbit* (1962), 303 E 2nd 138 at 14 1. He submits that there is no evidence that the directors had full knowledge of the basis of the claim.

It is my view that this is the correct interpretation of the requirement of s. 222(3)(a). The directors could hardly bring any action whether by their own initiative or on the requisition of a minority shareholder without knowing the specific cause of action. However I would think that no more would be required than that sufficient to found an endorsement on a generally endorsed writ of summons.

Mr. McConnell submits that there is difference between the relief sought in the motion and that set out in the requisition, the two paragraphs of which read as follows:

1. To pass a resolution that the Company take action against the persons who were directors of the Company during the time when certain shares of Fraser Valley Pulp & Timber Ltd. owned by the Company were voted for a special resolution to sell the assets of Fraser Valley Pulp & Timber Ltd. to Green River Log Sales Ltd., and against the person who held the proxy for the said shares and cast them for such special resolution.

2. To pass a resolution that the directors of the Company cause the shares of Fraser Valley Pulp & Timber Ltd., held by the Company be voted at a meeting of Fraser Valley Pulp & Timber Ltd., to bring action to set aside the sale by Fraser Valley Pulp & Timber Ltd., to Green River Log Sales Ltd., on the ground that the assets of Fraser Valley Pulp & Timber Ltd., in such sale were so grossly undervalued to the knowledge of the directors of both Fraser Valley Pulp & Timber Ltd. and Green River Log Sales Ltd., as to amount to a fraud on the shareholders of Fraser Valley Pulp & Timber Ltd.

In my view that notice sufficiently specifies the cause of action and contains sufficient information to found an endorsement on a writ.

While there are some differences between the wording of the requisition and that relief sought in the motion, which is conceded by Miss Southin, I do note that Mr. Ross's letter of 3rd April 1974 sets out the relief sought in substantially the same words as contained in the motion. Those words I have set out heretofore in this judgment.

Furthermore the relief sought is in the nature of equitable relief and there is in my view no substantial difference between the requisition and the motion as both refer to fraud. Furthermore there is no evidence that the directors refused to commence the action in the terms specifically set out in either the letter or the requisition. All the directors did was defeat the motion.

Accordingly I find that the applicants have satisfied the requirements of s. 222(3)(a).

The real question here is whether in the circumstances of this case "it is *prima facie* in the interests of the company that the action be brought" (s. 222(3)(c)). It will be noted that the Legislature has said that it is sufficient to show that the action sought is *prima facie* in the interests of the company and does not appear to require that the applicants prove a *prima facie* case. Presumably the authors of that legislation had in mind that a minority shareholder being in a real sense on the outside is often not in a position to obtain evidence such as that the Crown would be expected to put forward to found a *prima facie* case in a criminal matter.

In a criminal case the Crown is not required to do more than produce evidence which if unanswered and believed is sufficient to raise a *prima facie* case upon which the jury might be justified in finding a verdict: *Girvin v. The King* (1911), 45 S.C.R. 167, 20 W.L. R. 130; *Rex v. Scott*, [1919] 2 W.W.R. 227, 14 Alta. L.R. 439, 31 C.C.C. 399 (C.A.).

The words "*prima facie*" are not defined in any statute of which I am aware.

"*Prima facie*" is defined as "at first sight", "on the face of" in *Jowitt's Dictionary of English Law* and *Black's Law Dictionary*. The latter volume also contains the definition "so far as can be judged from the first disclosure".

It should be borne in mind that an application such as this is in the nature of an interlocutory application because it decides nothing more than that an action may or may not be commenced.

That being so then the various civil cases set out in *Cross on Evidence*, 2nd ed., at pp. 24–26, and *Phipson on Evidence*, 11th ed., p. 103, are of small assistance. The cases set out in these volumes are concerned with "*prima facie* evidence" upon the trial of an issue. The definition of "*prima facie* evidence" when used in English statutes usually has that meaning attributed to it by Statford J. A. in *Regina v. Jacobson and Levy*, [1931] App. D. 466 at 478 (South Africa), where he said this:

> ... "*prima facie* evidence" in its usual sense is used to mean *prima facie* proof of an issue, the burden of proving which is upon the

party giving that evidence. In the absence of further evidence from the other side, the *prima facie* proof becomes conclusive proof and the party giving it discharges his onus.

It will be seen that that definition is not particularly helpful because such a criterion must be for proof upon trial. This application decides nothing more than whether the applicant has adduced sufficient evidence which on the face of that evidence discloses that it is, so far as can be judged from the first disclosure, in the interests of the company to pursue the action.

Adopting that definition one must then consider what disclosures are contained in the evidence which might warrant a Court exercising its discretion to allow the minority shareholders here to commence an action against the directors for fraud in the name of and on behalf of the company.

The principal matters relied upon by the applicants are:

1. The sale to Green Valley of the entire undertaking of Fraser Valley for a price of approximately $91,700 less than its apparent value for lending purposes, both transactions having been concluded on the same day.

2. The apparent failure of the directors to seek out any bids from other persons, bearing in mind that Louis Clarke as a director of both companies appears on the face of the documents to have derived a benefit from this transaction.

3. The apparent failure of the directors to find out the current market value of the lands sold as it appears in the notes of Mr. Ross that the directors did not rely upon the appraisal made 31st December 1971 when consummating the sale to Green River.

4. The possible loss of diminution of the water lot.

5. The question as to the authority of the directors to make the sale to Green River in the absence of any evidence as to voting authority or the presence or absence of sufficient members to pass the resolutions.

6. The acceptance of a promissory note in substitution for a debenture and an account receivable.

In my view these are matters which concern the interests of the company as the major shareholders of Fraser Valley within the meanings of s. 222(3)(c). These may also be matters of moment and concern to the individual shareholders of the company, but that, in my view, does not detract from the derivative nature of the action sought to be commenced.

Miss Southin submits that the question is whether there is evidence that discloses a case that should be dealt with. Mr. McConnell who relies in his argument essentially on majority rule points out that a court must give careful consideration to the possible consequences of such an order. There can be no question but that that is an important consideration.

The standard of care required of a director of a company is that set out in 6 Hals. (3d) 309, para. 619:

A director is liable for negligence if he fails to exercise such degree of care as a reasonable man might be expected to take in the circumstances on his own behalf, and the company in consequence suffers loss.

Bearing that standard in mind it is my view that the applicants have put forward sufficient evidence which on the face of it discloses a failure on the part of the directors to take that degree of care required of them and accordingly I grant leave to the applicants to bring the action set out in the motion in the name of and on behalf of Northwest Forest Products Ltd. against the five persons named in the motion.

The motion also claims security for costs and disbursements. It is conceded that that application is premature and cannot as appears by s. 222(4) be brought until the action is commenced.

The costs of the motion will be costs in the cause.

Application Granted.

Re Marc-Jay Investments Inc. and Levy
(1974), 5 O.R. (2d) 235, 50 D.L.R. (3d) 45 (H.C.)

O'LEARY J.: This is an application under s. 99(2) of the *Business Corporations Act*, R.S.O. 1970, c. 53, for an order permitting a shareholder to commence a representative action under s. 99(1) of the said Act.

I understand it to be agreed that the applicant was the beneficial owner of approximately 12.9% of the shares of Levy Industries Limited at the time of the purchase by it on November 15, 1972, of Premium Forest Products Limited, which transaction the intended action is designed to set aside. The applicant was not at the time the registered owner of any shares in Levy Industries Limited. I am satisfied on the reasoning to be found in *Re Great West Permanent Loan Co. and Winding-up Act*, [1927] 2 W.W.R. 15, and *Goodbun v. Mitchell et al.*, [1928] 1 W.W.R. 495, that the beneficial owner of a share has the status to bring an action under s. 99(1) even though he is not the registered owner of the share.

I am also satisfied that the applicant has made reasonable efforts to cause Levy Industries Limited to commence such an action and that Levy Industries Limited refused to do so.

I am likewise satisfied that the shareholder, in bringing this application and in regard to his expressed intention to commence that contemplated action, is acting in good faith. Levy Industries Limited purchased Premium from Seaway Multi-Corp Limited. At the time of the purchase, Levy's board of directors and Seaway's board of directors were identical, that is to say the 12 directors of Seaway were also the 12 directors of Levy.

On the contemplated action the applicant intends to allege, *inter alia*, that the purchase by Levy of Premium was an improvident transaction to the knowledge of Levy's directors and was therefore fraudulent, at least in so far as it affected the minority shareholders, and that in any event the material provided to the shareholders under Item No. 10 of Form 15 of the Regulations, R.R.O. 1970, Reg. 78, under the *Business Corporations Act* was so deficient, that it did not permit the shareholders to form a reasoned judgment concerning the transaction in question, when a meeting was called to approve of the purchase under s. 134(5) of the said Act.

Since the transaction involving the purchase of the shares of Premium was between companies with the same directors it is argued that a constructive fraud occurred and the purchase would be set aside even without proof that the transaction was in fact improvident. It is not my function to decide whether such contemplated action will succeed at trial, but simply to decide whether there is *prima facie* merit to it. It is argued by the applicant that if the transaction was in fact fraudulent on the shareholders it would be in the interest of the shareholders that it be set aside and I accept that proposition.

While Levy has tendered evidence in opposition to the allegations made against it, it appears that some information was not disclosed in the material sent to the shareholders which may have been essential for them to make a reasoned judgment in deciding whether or not to confirm the action of the directors in buying Premium.

It further appears that the applicant is of the belief that Levy paid far too much for Premium and the appellant points to some evidence in support of that belief.

It is obvious that a Judge hearing an application for leave to commence an action, cannot try the action. I believe it is my function to deny the application if it appears that the intended action is frivolous or vexatious or is bound to be unsuccessful. Where the applicant is acting in good faith and otherwise has the status to commence the action, and where the intended action does not appear frivolous or vexatious and could reasonably succeed; and where such action is in the interest of the shareholders, then leave to bring the action should be given.

The respondent has not shown that the intended action would be either frivolous or vexatious. It is beyond question that if the allegations of the applicant are correct it would be in the interest of the minority shareholders that the action be brought. The main position of the respondent was that the material filed by it should convince me that the purchase of Premium was not improvident for the shareholders of Levy. To reach that conclusion I would have to weigh the affidavit material filed on this application. I agree that I have to weigh it to determine whether it shows that the intended action is without merit or is frivolous or vexatious. Having weighed the evidence I am not of the opinion that the contemplated action is without merit or is frivolous or vexatious. I believe, however, that is the extent to which I am entitled to weigh the evidence. I am not to deny leave to bring an action simply because on a weighing of the evidence I should decide it is unlikely that the action will be successful. I might say I have not reached any such conclusion in this case.

I feel, therefore, that I must give the applicant leave to bring its intended action. Such leave is granted with costs to the applicant in the cause.

Application granted.

Note

For a case following *Marc-Jay*, see *Armstrong v. Gardner* (1978), 20 O.R. (2d) 648 (Ont. H.C.). Cory J., in granting leave to commence an action under s. 99 of the predecessor to the present OBCA, made some useful observations on the requirements for getting leave. For example, he stated that an application for leave under the section could be based on the information and belief of others since first-hand evidence would not usually be available.

Re Bellman and Western Approaches Ltd.
(1981), 33 B.C.L.R. 45, 130 D.L.R. (3d) 193 (C.A.).

[This case arose from a dispute between two groups of shareholders of Western Approaches Ltd., a CBCA corporation. The petitioners, the Bellman group, were minority shareholders, whose control of the "investors' common shares" allowed them to select three of the corporation's eight directors. The Duke group controlled the "founders' common shares", entitling them to select the other five directors. They also held 25% of the investors' common shares. The Duke group and their controlled companies entered into a loan agreement with a bank, which enabled them to purchase the majority of the investors' common shares and control the election of all of Western's directors. The loan agreement included a provision providing for disclosure of confidential information about Western to the bank, and a requirement that the directors use their powers to cause Western to go public. The complainants sent a letter to the company, alleging wrongdoing on the part of the directors, and requesting that the corporation seek relief. The board sought outside advice from a law firm and an accounting firm, and was advised that the corporation should not take any action. Western was advised to execute a supplemental agreement reinforcing the overriding obligation of the directors to act in the best interests of the corporation. The complainants sought leave to bring a derivative action, which was granted by the lower court.]

NEMETZ C.J.B.C.: Mr. Goldie's submission may be summarized by saying that the alleged error relating to each of the three conditions precedent set out in s. 232(2) of the federal Act. I will deal with these subsections *seriatim*:

(a) Notice

This subsection requires that reasonable notice be given to the directors of the corporation, in this case, Western. It was pointed out to us that one of the grounds in the petition (para. l(b)) concerning take-over bids was not contained in the notice letter. Price Waterhouse and Bull Housser proceeded with their investigations as set out in the notice letter. Accordingly, it is said that the directors decided not to sue without having an opportunity of considering this allegation. It is to be noted that the Federal Act only requires the giving of "reasonable notice" of intention to apply to commence a derivative action. A perusal of the notice letter of June 26, 1980, when read together with the response of January 16, 1981, leads me to conclude that the directors were reasonably notified of the Bellman group's intention to apply to commence a derivative action. Failure to specify each and every cause of action in a notice does not, in my opinion, invalidate the notice as a whole.

(b) Good faith

Mr. Goldie agreed that it is possible for both a personal and a derivative action to proceed on the same set of facts: *cf. Goldex Mines Ltd. v. Revill et al.* (1974), 54 D.L.R. (3d) 672, 7 O.R. (2d) 216 (Ont. C.A.); *Borak v. J.I. Case Co.* (1963), 317 F. Supp. 2d 838; *Johnson v. American General Ins. Co.* (1969), 296 F. Supp. 802 at p. 808. However, he argued, where the relief requested in both actions is substantially the same, that is evidence of a lack of good faith since it is vexatious to seek the same relief in two actions. However, after examining the relief sought in each action, I conclude that the relief is not the same. Damages for breach of fiduciary duty are not available in the personal action, nor have such damages in that action been sought. Damages are being sought in the derivative action. That distinction, among others, is sufficient to justify the initiation of the derivative action under this heading.

(c) Interests of the corporation

In my view this is the key section for consideration in this case. The section does not say that the Court must be satisfied that it is in the interests of the corporation. It says that no action may be brought unless the Court is satisfied that it appears to be in the interests of the corporation to bring the suit. I take that to mean that what is sufficient at this stage is that an arguable case be shown to subsist. This is quite different from the rules established at common law. [Nemetz C.J.B.C. examined the common law rule in *Foss v. Harbottle* and its exceptions, the state of the American common law, and the American statutory derivative action.]

Presumably it was the intention of the drafters of our federal Act to remove the common law barriers which I have described. Section 235(i) clearly eliminates the ratification procedure. An alleged breach of duty, ratification of which is approved by the shareholders, no longer provides a sole reason to dismiss an application for leave to proceed derivatively. Sections 232 and 233 set out a summary procedure by way of an application before a Chambers Judge to have a quick determination of where a complainant may institute a derivative suit. The conditions precedent, although bearing a resemblance to the prerequisites of the common law, have significant differences.

Because of my views in relation to (a) and (b), I will allude only to (c) regarding which we are informed no Canadian case law exists.

How is a Court to exercise its discretion in coming to a determination that it is satisfied that "it appears to be in the interests of the corporation" to allow the derivative action to be brought? The discretion is a wide one. However, despite its breadth, nowhere does Parliament say, nor, in my opinion, was it intended, that the logic of the common law in cases of this kind be disregarded. One must first look to the decision of the directors who, having been given reasonable notice by a complainant in good faith, decide not to assert a corporate right of action. In this case they refused. Can it be said that this refusal was given impartially? It was submitted that the resolution not to sue was passed by four independent directors since the Duke group and Asper did not vote. It was also submitted that the decision of these "independent" directors was based upon the reports of their accountants and outside lawyers and that in any event they could reasonably conclude that the disadvantages to the company outweighed the advantages. How do I conclude that these four directors were not independent? Messrs. Milroy, Dewar, Shier and Atkinson were nominated by the Investors Group on January 16, 1980, at a time when the Duke group held a majority of the investors' shares. More important is the effect upon their independence of cls. 3.03 and 3.04 of the guarantor's agreement where the borrowers covenanted to use their powers as directors to assert control over the directors nominated by the investors group to act and vote in ways favorable to the lender.

It is also curious that the instructions of the directors to the investigators, i.e., Price Waterhouse, were limited to certain periods of time in respect only of legal expenses, expenses charged to the company and contra account settlements. Since the legal opinion of January 15, 1981, was based on this limited report it can hardly be said to have been conclusive of the substantive issues raised by the complainants, namely, the breach of fiduciary duty.

Considering the whole of the evidence before the Chambers Judge, she could have come to the conclusion that at the time when they came to the decision not to sue, the directors did stand in a dual relation which prevented them from exercising an unprejudiced judgment. While it is true that a quantifiable loss was not proven, nevertheless, it was sufficient to have adumbrated a potential loss resulting from the covenant in the guarantor's agreement requiring the borrowers to pay a fee to the guarantor in the event that they were not able to cause the company to go public. Since the fee was based on gross revenue, it might place the directors in a position of conflict in deciding whether it is in their interest to keep revenues down in order to reduce the potential fee or to maximize revenues in the interest of all of the shareholders. However, this would be a matter for the trial Court to consider. It is sufficient that it appears to be in the interest of the company that the action be brought.

I would, accordingly, dismiss the appeal.

Appeal dismissed.

Notes

1 There is much American jurisprudence on the effect of the directors of
the defendant corporation seeking outside advice with respect to the
substance of the grieving shareholder's complaints, and the desirability
of an action being brought by the corporation against the wrongdoers.
There are two lines of authority on the question of how much deference
to give to a litigation committee's findings. Courts in some jurisdictions
refuse to question the business judgment of a litigation committee, so
long as it is disinterested and performed an adequate investigation.
Therefore, the use of an independent litigation committee acts as a
defence to derivative actions in these jurisdictions. See *Auerbach v.
Bennett*, 419 N.Y.S.2d 920 (1979); *Hirsch v. Jones Intercable, Inc.*,
984 P.2d 629 (Colo., 1999); and *Cuker v. Mikalauskas*, 692 A.2d 1042
(Pa., 1997). In other jurisdictions, the litigation committee must be
independent and conduct a fair investigation in order for its decision to
be considered, but the court may also question whether or not the
committee's decision was reasonable. See *Zapata v. Maldonado*, 430
A.2d 779 (Del., 1981); *Abramowitz v. Posner*, 672 F.2d 1025 (2nd Cir.
N.Y., 1982); and *Strougo ex rel. Brazilian Equity Fund, Inc. v. Bassini*,
112 F.Supp.2d 355 (S.D.N.Y., 2000).

For a detailed set of guidelines on the question of independent
committee recommendations in the context of derivative actions, see
Principles of Corporate Governance (American Law Institute, 1994).
The recommendations attempt to balance the right of the corporation,
as seen by the drafters, to seek termination of an action for business
reasons and the need for careful judicial review of the reasons so offered
because those in control of the corporation may wish to justify dismissal
for self-serving motives.

What importance should a Canadian court attach to such an independent review in a derivative action? For a discussion of independent reviews in the context of a hostile takeover bidder allegeing oppression, see *Pente Investment Management Ltd. v. Schneider Corp.*
(1998), 42 O.R. (3d) 177; and *C.W. Shareholding Ltd. v. WIC Western
International Communications Ltd.* (1998), 39 O.R. (3d) 755 (Gen.
Div.). Do you think special statutory provisions should be enacted to
deal with the issue?

2 Shareholder approval of an alleged breach of a right or duty does not
automatically disallow a derivative action. The CBCA provides:

> 242 (1) An application made or an action brought or intervened in
> under this part shall not be stayed or dismissed by reason only that
> it is shown that an alleged breach of a right or a duty owed to the
> corporation or its subsidiary has been or may be approved by the

shareholders of such body corporate, but evidence of approval by the shareholders may be taken into account by the court in making an order under section 214, 240, or 241.

See *Schadegg* v. *Alaska Apollo Resources Inc.* (1994), [1994] B.C.J. No. 1100, 1994 CarswellBC 2132 (S.C.), where a financing scheme of a widely held company was approved of by over 80% of the shareholders. This overwhelming approval and corresponding scant support for the complainant's petition, while not a bar to an action, was taken as evidence that a derivative action would not be in the company's interests. What evidence should a court examine beyond shareholder approval in assessing the merits of a derivative action?

3 The good faith of the applicant is one of the criteria for leave to bring a derivative action. To what extent must good faith be demonstrated and to what extent may it be assumed? See *Tremblett v. S.C.B. Fisheries Ltd.* (1993), 116 Nfld. & P.E.I.R. 139, 1993 CarswellNfld 52 (T.D.); *Primex Investments Ltd. v. Northwest Sports Enterprises Ltd.* (1995), 13 B.C.L.R. (3d) 300, 1995 CarswellBC 958 (S.C. [In Chambers]), reversed (1996), 26 B.C.L.R. (3d) 357, 1996 CarswellBC 2505 (C.A.), leave to appeal to S.C.C. dismissed [1998] S.C.C.A. No. 406; and *Discovery Enterprises Inc. v. Ebco Industries Ltd.* (1997), 40 B.C.L.R. (3d) 43, 1997 CarswellBC 1586 (S.C.), affirmed (1998), 50 B.C.L.R. (3d) 195, 1998 CarswellBC 1225 (C.A.), leave to appeal to S.C.C. dismissed [1997] S.C.C.A. No. 4. In *Discovery,* Williams C.J.S.C. said (at 59):

> The test for good faith in this type of case was dealt with in Primex, where the court considered the requirement under s. 225 of the B.C. *Company Act*. Mr. Justice Tysoe in finding the applicant acted in good faith appears to tie the requirement of "good faith" to the test of the "interest of the company". He states that where there is an arguable case, the applicant cannot be said to be acting in bad faith because he wants the company to pursue what he genuinely considers to be a valid claim. In that case, there was no evidence the applicant was using the prospect of a derivative action as a threat in order to extract some advantage from the company. Tysoe J. also indicates that an applicant advancing self-interest is not necessarily acting in bad faith.

The onus of showing good faith rests upon the applicant, but it appears that it will be assumed if the applicant seems to have a good claim. The result is that the fate of the good faith requirement may depend upon whether the action is in the best interests of the corporation.

4 May a creditor be granted leave to bring a derivative action? A creditor may be a "proper person" to bring an action under s. 238 of the CBCA

or an equivalent. See *First Edmonton Place Ltd. v. 315888 Alberta Ltd.* (1988), 40 B.L.R. 28, 1988 CarswellAlta 103 (Q.B.) [appeal adjourned (1989), 45 B.L.R. 110, 1989 CarswellAlta 181 (C.A.)] (at 63):

> In the case of a creditor who claims to be a "proper person" to make a s.232 application, in my view the criterion would be whether, even if the applicant did not come within s. 231 (b)(i) or (ii), he or it would nevertheless be a person who could reasonably be entrusted with the responsibility of advancing the interests of the corporation by seeking a remedy to right the wrong allegedly done to the corporation. The applicant would not have to be a security holder (as I have defined that notion), director or officer of the corporation.

Note, however, that *First Edmonton* examined this issue in the context of an oppression claim. See also *Daon Development Corp., Re* (1984), 10 D.L.R. (4th) 216, 1984 CarswellBC 175 (S.C.); and *Royal Trust Corp. of Canada v. Hordo* (1993), 10 B.L.R. (2d) 86, 1993 CarswellOnt 147 (Gen. Div. [Commercial List]). Are there valid reasons for a broader characterization of a "proper person" to be a complainant in the context of an oppression action as compared to a derivative action? Does it make a difference to the analysis that the New Brunswick and Alberta Acts specifically include a creditor in their definitions of a complainant?

5 May a person who does not fall within the definition of "complainant" at the time of the wrongdoing buy shares of the corporation, thereby purchasing the right to bring a derivative action? See *Richardson Greenshields of Canada Ltd. v. Kalmacoff* (1995), 22 O.R. (3d) 577, 1995 CarswellOnt 324 (C.A.), leave to appeal to S.C.C. dismissed [1995] S.C.C.A. No. 260, which concerned an application for leave to commence a derivative action under the *Trust and Loan Companies Act*, S.C. 1991, c. 45. The definition of "complainant" under this Act is substantially similar to the CBCA. Robins J.A. found that acquisition of securities after the wrongdoing did not bar the person from being a proper complainant (at 583-4):

> Farley J. was of the view that Richardson Greenshields did not qualify under cl. (a) of this definition section and, therefore, in so far as this clause is concerned, failed to meet the threshold requirement entitling it to proceed under s. 339. Relying on his decision in *Royal Trust Corp. of Canada v. Hordo* (1993), 10 B.L.R. (2d) 86, he concluded that in a derivative action, as in an oppression action, "persons who acquire shares after the facts which were the subject of the complaint were known should not be treated as a complainant".

> The respondents do not seek to support this conclusion. They acknowledge, properly, in my opinion, that the appellant is a complainant for the purposes of s. 339. Although its shares were acquired

after the roll-down had been announced and for the express purpose of launching a derivative action, it is now common ground that this does not in itself preclude the appellant from being a complainant. The Act does not impose a condition of ownership contemporaneous with the acts complained of and, in any event, it may be noted that the breaches complained of are of an ongoing nature. It is sufficient that Richardson Greenshields is "a registered holder . . . of a security of [the] company" at the time it brings the application. As such, it meets the requirements of cl. (a). It follows that the judge erred in restricting the term "complainant" to persons who were shareholders at the time the facts which gave rise to the complaint occurred and in holding that the appellant did not have the necessary status by virtue of cl. (a) of the defining section to invoke s. 339.

This raises the possibility of an entrepreneurial plaintiff "buying-in" to a right to recovery by purchasing stock in a wronged corporation and bringing a derivative action. How, if at all, does this differ from buying-in to any other form of litigation, which is generally not permitted? See Poonam Puri, "Financing of Litigation by Third Party Investors: A Share of Justice?" 36(3)(1998) O.H.L.J. 515.

6   Is the common law derivative action still available despite the existence of the statutory derivative action? In *Farnham v. Fingold*, [1973] 2 O.R. 132, 33 D.L.R. (3d) 156, 1973 CarswellOnt 840 (C.A.), *infra*, which dealt with Ontario's old derivative actions provisions, Jessup J.A. said for the court (at 135):

> Section 99 of the *Business Corporations Act*, R.S.O. 1970, c. 53 provides . . . All forms of derivative actions purporting to be brought on behalf of and for the benefit of the corporation come within it, and therefore s-s. (2) applies to all such actions.

(e) Costs In Derivative Actions

As previously mentioned, the prevailing costs rules are absolutely pivotal to an assessment of the efficacy of shareholder rights and remedies. Costs can be staggering in complex corporate-commercial litigation, and the average shareholder with a small stake will have neither the resources nor appropriate incentives (due both to the free rider problem and small stake) to commence litigation. Larger shareholders may have both the resources and the incentives, but too often these shareholders will be part of the control group accused of wrongdoing. Although institutional shareholders, like pension funds, banks, trust and insurance companies and the like might also sue, these shareholders will frequently be loath to sue rather than simply sell their holdings if dissatisfied with management. Fortunately, this attitude (sometimes referred to as the "Wall Street Rule") is rapidly changing, and institutional shareholders are now willing to adopt a more confrontational stance *vis-à-vis* management and controlling shareholders. In any case, there are ways in which costs rules can be cast that will greatly attenuate the free rider problem facing shareholders. One of these is to allow recovery of costs by the plaintiff from all those who stand to benefit from a favourable judgment. Where the action is derivative in character, and the award is made in favour of the corporation, a convenient way of avoiding costly collection problems while indirectly distributing the costs of litigation amongst all those who benefit is to have the corporation pay the costs of the litigation. While this seems an ideal solution to the free rider problem, it unfortunately creates another, equally vexing problem. Where the corporation automatically pays all the costs of the action, shareholders may be encouraged to commence nuisance or "strike" suits lacking any merit. Even when commencing an action in good faith, shareholders have an incentive to sue if there is any possibility, however remote, of success. This is almost certain to result in excessive litigation. One balancing mechanism is to presumptively require the corporation to pay the costs of the litigation, subject to a demonstration that the plaintiff has not commenced the action in good faith and/or the action has some reasonable possibility of success. *Cf.* OBCA s. 105(6). Are there any other solutions?

Note that a number of provisions in the CBCA deal with the issue of costs. The Act provides that a complainant is not required to give any security for costs (s. 242(3)), that the court may make an interim order as to costs (s. 242(4)), and that the court may also order an indemnity as to costs (s. 240(d) and s. 242(4)). Similar provisions may be found in the OBCA (see ss. 249(3), 249(4), 247(d)).

The following case considers the question of when an indemnity for costs will be ordered.

Turner et al. v. Mailhot et al.
(1985), 28 B.L.R. 222 (Ont. H.C.)

[The Plaintiff and his wife owned 30% of the common shares of the corporation; the balance of the shares were owned by the defendant and his wife. A disagreement arose between the parties, which led to the plaintiff and his wife being locked out of the company's premises and the termination of their employment and of Turner's position as director and officer of the company. The plaintiff sought and obtained leave to bring a derivative action seeking return to the company of lost income diverted to the defendant. He then applied for indemnity for the costs of the action, under s. 246 [now 242(4)] of the CBCA.]

REID J.: . . . The situation here may be compared with that before the English Court of Appeal in *Wallersteiner v. Moir (No. 2)*. That was a carefully considered decision which justifies close scrutiny and extensive reference. Each of the Judges, Denning M.R. and Buckley and Scarman L.JJ, wrote separate reasons which although not entirely in agreement with each other produced a common agreed result.

In that case Moir was acting as the representative of the minority shareholders in litigation equivalent to a derivative action under the *Business Corporations Act*. An order was made indemnifying him against his fees and costs. The gist of the Court's decision was that the order rested upon equity and the Court's discretion, the Court having concluded that the action was reasonable and prudent in the company's interest, was brought in good faith and, as well, in Denning M.R.'s view was also in the public interest.

It was observed that Moir had exhausted his own funds in fighting the litigation for over ten years and contributions from other minority shareholders had as well been exhausted. As Denning M.R. said Moir had "come to the end of his tether" (p. 856 [All E.R.]) yet the litigation was not finished. Moir had "not any money left with which to pay the costs in further matters" and was fearful of the prospect of having to pay personally costs if he should lose (pp. 856-57). On that basis there is a clear distinction between that case and this for I have already observed that Turner make no such claim.

Another distinction exists. The company on whose behalf Moir was suing was "a substantial public company of long standing" (p. 853) (sometimes referred to in the judgments as "the companies"). Moir was a minority shareholder holding only a few shares. We are not told how many, or what relation their number bore to the number of issued shares of the company but comments made in the judgments are revealing. Denning M. R. referred at p. 857 to Moir's "few shares which might appreciate a little in value" if he were successful in the litigation. At p. 860 he observed further:

> It would appear that any advantage to Mr. Moir himself would be trivial, seeing that he holds so few shares . . .

In contrast, Turner and his wife, are the only minority shareholders, in the defendant company. It is not realistic here to say, as was said in *Wallersteiner*, that if Turner "wins all the way through no part will redound to his own benefit" (p. 860). If Turner is successful in this litigation the monetary benefit to the company could be in the millions. That, in turn, would greatly increase the book value of Turner's shares. Whether he would be capable of forcing the reluctant majority to turn that into a realizable benefit for him and his wife is certainly open to question at this point. Yet, that aside, this action more closely resembles a struggle between Turner and Mailhot over their own advantage with the company used as a vehicle than an attack by an almost lone altruist (Moir) upon an entrenched and devious miscreant (Wallersteiner) for the advantage of the company involved.

[Reid J. quoted from the *Wallersteiner* case and continued:]

If that reasoning were applied here it would suggest strongly that Turner, having obtained leave of this Court to bring the action, had established a *prima facie* claim to indemnity. There is nothing in the *Business Corporations Act* which would indicate to me that the views expressed in *Wallersteiner* would not form a reasonable basis for the interpretation of

the sections of the Act governing the application before me. The section of our Act that governs applications for leave to bring a derivative action simply states in statutory language the gist of what the Judges of the Court of Appeal said in *Wallersteiner*. Thus, it must be established that directors of the relevant company refused to bring the action, that the complainant is acting in good faith, and that the action appears to be in the interests of the company. Section 245 is the relevant provision. It states:
[s. 245 omitted]

Since an applicant, in order to obtain leave under s. 245 must, in effect, fulfil the conditions laid down in *Wallersteiner*, he or she could reasonably be taken to have established a *prima facie* right to indemnity.

* * *

Yet the right is merely *prima facie*. There may, in my opinion, be considerations arising out of the circumstances of particular cases that might affect the question whether that *prima facie* right should be turned into a proven right. I would think, for instance, that financial inability to carry on an action would weigh heavily in favour of a grant of indemnity and may well overbear any considerations raised by a respondent.

In the absence of such an element, however, other factors might predominate. I have already said that Turner makes no claim of financial inability and the beneficiaries of a successful outcome would not so much be the company as the two minority shareholders. I do not think that the financial ability to carry on an action should necessarily deprive a plaintiff in a derivative action of indemnification: that would be contrary to the principle that the plaintiff is the agent of the company for the purposes of the action. Yet the fact that the benefit sought is more for plaintiff than the company is a consideration that weighs with me.

In the result I do not think that, at this stage anyway, an order for complete indemnity should be made. I therefore direct that Turner is entitled to indemnity to the extent of one-half of his incurred and reasonable future fees and costs. That direction is made without prejudice to any future application that Turner might be advised to make for more complete indemnification as would be the case, for instance, if the day arrived when he was financially incapable of sustaining the litigation.
[The court noted that $40,000 had been paid by the company towards Mailhot's costs of defending the action.]

In my opinion it was inappropriate to pay out company funds for the defence of Mailhot. Similarly, it would be inappropriate to pay out further funds for that purpose. Since the funds were paid out essentially for Mailhot's benefit and at his direction an order shall go directing Mailhot to pay into court the sum of $40,000 for the purpose of furnishing indemnification for Turner in accordance with the order that I have made or with any future order of this Court.

Notes and Questions

1 Note that to the extent that the corporation is ordered to pay all or part of the costs of the action, then the costs are indirectly spread to all the shareholders in the proportion of their shareholdings (at least, assuming there are no significant creditors; see note 2, *infra*). If the corporation is ordered to pay half the costs of the action, and the plaintiffs own approximately half the shares (as in *Turner*) then the indemnity is, in effect, as to only one-quarter of the costs of the action. A full indemnity from the corporation is still only an indemnity as to half the costs, from the plaintiff shareholder's point of view. Is there any reason for awarding an indemnity as to only half the costs in the *Turner* case? Should the court be able to award a partial or full indemnity against the accused wrongdoers, rather than the corporation?

2 Where a costs award is made against the corporation, at least part of the burden of the award is shouldered by the corporation's fixed claimants, including creditors, trade creditors and employees. This is because any depletion of the assets of the corporation jeopardizes, to at least some degree, the corporation's ability to meet its fixed claims as they come due. Does this strengthen the case in favour of an indemnity against the accused wrongdoers, rather than the corporation?

3 Should the rules regarding the awarding of an indemnity be different in relation to private corporations and public corporations? If so, why?

4 The relevant corporate legislation, unlike the CBCA and OBCA, may not provide for an indemnity as to costs. In such a case a court may still be able to draw upon relatively recent common law to order an indemnity. In *Wallersteiner v. Moir (No. 2)*, [1975] 1 All E.R. 849, [1975] Q.B. 373 (C.A.), Lord Denning ordered such an indemnity in a case involving apparently meritorious litigation by an impecunious plaintiff, basing his award on principles of equity. The circumstances in which such an award will be made have most recently been discussed by the English Chancery Court in *Watts v. Midland Bank PLC.*, [1986] B.C. L.C. 15, and by the English Court of Appeal in *Smith v. Croft*, [1986] 2 All E.R. 551.

In the United States, there has been considerable controversy surrounding the payment of plaintiff's counsel fees and expenses in derivative actions. See Cole, "Counsel Fees in Stockholders' Derivative and Class Actions — Hornstein Revisited" (1972), 6 U. Rich. L. Rev. 259; Mowrey, "Attorney Fees in Securities Class Action and Derivative Suits" (1978), 3 J. Corp. Law 267; Herzel and Hagan, "Plaintiff's Attorneys' Fees in Derivative and Class Actions" [Winter, 1981] Litigation 25. For detailed recommendations on the topic, see s. 7.17 of *Principles of*

Corporate Governance: Analysis and Recommendations, Discussion Draft No. 1 (American Law Institute, 1985).

5 For a case considering the issue of an award of interim costs (rather than an indemnity) under the oppression remedy, see *Alles v. Maurice, infra.*

(f) The Relationship Between the Complainant and the Corporation

While a derivative action is brought "in the name of and on behalf of a corporation", the representative nature of the action raises the question: What is the relationship between the complainant, who is acting in the name of the corporation, and the corporation? Is the complainant required to look after all of the corporation's interests in the derivative action?

In *Discovery Enterprises Inc. v. Ebco Industries Ltd.* (1998), 41 B.L.R. (2d) 207, 1998 CarswellBC 2539 (C.A.), Discovery was pursuing an oppression action against Ebco and had obtained leave to bring a derivative action in Ebco's name against its creditors. Ebco sought to enjoin Discovery's law firm, which was representing it in both actions, from participating in the derivative action, arguing that it was a conflict of interest to have it acting both on Ebco's behalf and against it. Newbury J.A. held that while Discovery was acting in Ebco's name, did not mean that Discovery was acting *for* Ebco (at 212):

> The fact that the company's name is used as plaintiff, presumably to ensure that it receives any damages or other sums ultimately awarded to it, should not obscure the substance of the litigation, which is a contest between the Class D and majority shareholders. Since Discovery has conduct of the action, it will be instructing its counsel as plaintiff's counsel — they will not take instructions from Ebco, and Ebco should not seek advice from them.

Ebco also argued that the representative acting on behalf of a company in a derivative action assumes a fiduciary duty to that company, and that it is the representative's duty to look after that company's interests. Newbury J.A. disagreed with this, saying that the relationship between the parties could not be simultaneously adversarial and fiduciary. Ebco's interests in the litigation process in matters such as document discovery and privilege were not to be looked after by Discovery but by Ebco's board. Further protection would be offered by the court's overall supervisory powers in a derivative suit.

3. THE PERSONAL ACTION

BECK, **"The Shareholders' Derivative Action"**
(1974), 52 C.B.R. 159 at 169–179 (footnotes omitted)

A. The Personal Action

The ownership of stock in a corporation carries with it a number of personal rights. A partial list of the most common are the right to receive timely and informative notice of company meetings, the right to vote at such meetings, the right to have a properly executed proxy accepted and the right to inspect certain of the corporation's records. Some of these rights arise out of the companies Acts (the right to inspect books), some out of the articles or bylaws (number of days before meeting by which notice must be given) and some out of judicial legislation to make the requirements of the statute or corporation contract meaningful (truly informative notice). As to a right that can be truly classified as personal, the individual shareholders may have had similar rights infringed and may join in the action for redress in which case the action will be representative in form, but the substance remains the assertion of a personal right by each shareholder. The *locus classicus* is the judgment of Jessel M.R., in *Pender v. Lushington*:

> This is an action by Mr. Pender for himself. He is a member of the company, and whether he votes with the majority or the minority he is entitled to have his vote recorded — an individual right in respect of which he has a right to sue. That has nothing to do with the question like that raised in *Foss v. Harbottle* and that line of cases.

It might be thought that the line between personal rights and corporate rights would be well and clearly drawn. There is after all not much confusion between being denied the right to vote and a taking of property which depletes the corporate treasury. Between those two poles, however, there is uncertain ground and it is suggested that the personal rights category is in fact much broader than has been thought to be the case.

The reason for the confusion and for limiting personal actions stems from the idea that all wrongs committed by corporate directors and officers, and all duties owed by them, run exclusively to the corporation. The fictional legal entity is viewed by the courts as an unbreachable barrier behind which the directors are safe from personal shareholder attack. Moreover, acts by the directors which could readily be construed as their own personal acts are invariably seen as corporate acts. All of which is a natural result of the fact that a company acts only through its board of directors and, occasionally, its shareholders. But a director acts in a variety of capacities — as an agent of the company, as the company itself, and as an appointed officer to carry out such formal functions as running the proxy machinery and calling and conducting meetings. If a functional analysis were given to the directors' actions in each case it is suggested that it would lead to a result that would accord more with reality while widening the ambit of the shareholders' personal action. The matter was well stated by Judge Fuld in *Gordon v. Elliman*. At issue in the Gordon case was the alleged failure of the corporation to pay dividends in fraud of the minority shareholders in order to squeeze them out. It was argued, successfully, that the action was derivative and that New York's security for expenses provision applied. Fuld J. dissented:

> The action, is, in short, brought against the corporation as a legal entity and, if successful, will require the corporation to part with some of its assets in favour of its stockholders. I am, therefore, unable to follow the legal alchemy by which a breach of duty by the corporation — a corporate wrong is transmitted into a corporate right.
>   The vice of the test [is the action open to compel the performance of corporate acts which good faith requires the directors to take in order to perform a duty which they owe to the corporation?] is that it presupposes that every duty owed by corporate directors runs exclusively to the corporation as such and never directly to the stockholders in their personal and individual right. The law is otherwise. . . . In a very real sense all suits against corporation — which must of necessity act through directors and officers — involve the action of the directors or of officers responsible to the directors. . . . In short, it simply is not the law that an attack on directors' conduct is, *ipso facto*, the assertion of a corporate right of action. The mere fact that the power to declare dividends resides in the directors and that a suit to compel a dividend payment challenges directors' action has no bearing on the question of whose right is involved in such a suit. We must seek elsewhere to ascertain the manner of the "right" that a court enforces when it overrules the decision of corporate directors. . . .

The confusion in Anglo-Canadian company law over whether a personal action is possible when the directors act for an improper purpose, other than taking corporate property, would be cleared up by the type of functional analysis that Judge Fuld advocated. Directors' fiduciary duties are said to be "owed to the company and to the company alone", and "to redress a wrong done to the company. . . . the action should *prima facie* be brought by the company itself". In issuing shares, for example, the directors are exercising a fiduciary power which must be performed *bona fide* for the general advantage of the company. If they use the power to keep themselves in control, or to turn a minority into a majority, or to defeat the wishes of the majority, or to discriminate between groups of shareholders, they will have breached their fiduciary duty and an action will lie. But an action by whom? The answer to that question is best approached by asking who, in reality, is the aggrieved party and not by the mechanistic application of the formula that the director is an agent, the company is the principal and therefore action for fraud, negligence or irregularity lies only at the suit of the company. Most cases of fraud will clearly involve a taking by the director to the detriment of the company and the company is the only proper complainant. But a variety of other cases in which the directors act improperly involve not a breach of duty by the agent but a causing of the company to perform a corporate act in an improper or irregular manner to the direct detriment of the shareholders and for which they ought personally to be able to sue.

No doubt a company may be said to have a vital interest in having its affairs conducted in a proper manner and in accordance with the law and its internal regulations. But how, to ask Judge Fuld's question, is a wrongful issuance of shares by the company truly turned into a wrong to the company for which only the company may seek redress? Only in the most theoretical sense may the company be said to have been injured by its directors' misuse of the power granted to them. A more realistic analysis is that by the misuse of their powers the directors have caused the company to issue shares to the detriment of one group of shareholders and to the advantage of another — including, most likely, themselves. It should follow, therefore, that the shareholders that have been injured have a personal right of action against the company and the directors for a declaration that the issue and allotment is void and for an injunction to restrain the voting of such shares if they are about to be used at a general meeting. This is the American position and it is suggested that it is in fact what has occurred in similar cases in England and in Canada.

In *Condec Corporation v. Lunkenheimer* the directors of the defendant company caused it to enter into a merger agreement with a third company that involved the issuance of a large block of defendant's shares to the third company. The issue was large enough to prevent the plaintiff from exerting the voting control which it had just acquired through a cash tender offer. In declaring the issue void, the Delaware court observed:

> Finally, we are not here concerned with the need of proving corporate injury as has been held to be the case when a stockholder attacks derivatively the spending of corporate funds for the purchase of his corporation's own stock. This rather is a case of a stockholder with a contractual right being deprived of such control by what is virtually a corporate legerdemain.

There was no doubt in the Vice-Chancellor's mind that the directors had breached their fiduciary duty which they owed "to the company and to the shareholders". But breach of fiduciary duty did not necessarily mean that a corporate right was being asserted. There is no need for the Anglo-Canadian courts to take the step that the American courts have long since taken and hold that the directors owe a fiduciary duty to the shareholders (and the majority shareholders, on occasion, to the minority) to allow a personal right of action in such cases. The reference above by the Vice-

Chancellor to the shareholder's "contractual right" is presumably a reference to the right to vote that goes with each share. A tainted allotment to shift control deprives the shareholder of his votes which, in the aggregate, give him control. Seen in this light, the reasoning is the same as in *Pender v. Lushington* — the shareholder's personal rights have been interfered with.

The line of cases from *Piercy v. Mills* and *Punt v. Symons* deal with an invalid issuance of shares do not give any clear guide as to whether they were considered to be personal or derivative actions. The form of the action was usually representative (as it may be when personal rights are being asserted, and as it must be in a derivative suit) and the company and the wrong doing directors were joined as defendants, so an argument for either cause of action is plausible. With one exception, however, there is no discussion in all these cases of the procedural necessities of the derivative action, or indeed any mention of the derivative action as there invariably is in the true derivative suit. In fact, *Piercy v. Mills* was an individual shareholder's action and it is submitted that each of the other cases were also personal actions brought in representative form. Moreover, analogous leading cases in which the directors were alleged to have breached their fiduciary duty by exercising their powers for an improper purpose have also been personal actions. *Smith v. Fawcett* was a personal action by the executor of a deceased shareholder alleging that the directors were exercising their unrestricted power to refuse transfers in bad faith. As there was no showing of bad faith the action failed, but there was no question of the standing of the individual plaintiff to challenge the directors' action. Similarly in *Galloway v. Hale Concerts Society*, two individual shareholders successfully alleged that the directors had breached their fiduciary duty in causing the company to levy calls on their shares to the exclusion of the other shareholders.

What is occurring in these cases is an interference by the company with the rights of certain of the shareholders and is the same type of conduct that occurs in similar cases where the right of a shareholder to take personal action is firmly established. These cases involve such matters as varying or abrogating class rights, depriving a member of some right conferred upon him by the articles or by-laws, altering the internal corporate structure in a manner that amounts to a fraud on the minority, and depriving a member of his right to vote. A personal action may be more readily granted in such cases because one group of shareholders is more clearly seen to be taking action that deprives another of their rights. But this is also the case where the directors, while acting for a collateral purpose, cause the corporation to act in a manner that deprives a group of shareholders of their rights. In such cases as *Piercy, Smith and Galloway*, the judicial reasoning, although it is not clearly expressed as such, is that in causing the company to do certain acts which are primarily of an internal nature and which primarily affect the shareholders (issue shares, make calls, refuse transfers, solicit proxies) the directors assume a fiduciary obligation toward the company as a whole, that is to the shareholders as a general body, to act with an even hand and in good faith. If they breach that duty the shareholders may sue in their individual capacities for a declaration of their rights or to restrain the company from acting. Some observations of Russell L.J., in *Bamford v. Bamford* may seem to clash with this argument. *Bamford* was, once again, an allotment of shares to fend off a takeover bid. The articles of association of the Bamford Company vested the power to issue shares in the directors. The question in the case was not whether the directors had exceeded their powers, (it was assumed by Plowman J. that they had), but whether the shareholders might ratify such directorial excess and thus validate the issue. That was the point of law set down for argument, and on that basis Plowman J. treated the action as a personal one by the two individual plaintiffs to enforce the contract in the articles between the members and the company created by section 20(1) of the English *Companies Act, 1948*. In short, the plaintiffs argued that the terms of their contract required that only the directors could issue shares and to allow the shareholders to ratify an unlawful issue would be, in effect, to allow them a power of issuance.

In the Court of Appeal, in the course of discussing the ratification point, Russell J.A. said:

> The point before us is not an objection to the proceedings on *Foss v. Harbottle* grounds. But it seems to me to march in step with the principles that underlie the rule in that case.

After thus implicitly recognizing that the action was personal and not derivative, but expressing the opinion that some of the same principles applied, His Lordship then observed:

> None of the factors that admit exceptions to that rule appear to exist here. The harm done by the assumed improperly motivated allotment is a harm done to the company, of which only the company can complain. It would be for the company by ordinary resolution to decide whether or not to proceed against the directors.

Russell L.J. then expressed the opinion that the decision whether or not to litigate was the equivalent of a decision on ratification. It is suggested that the analogy, and that was clearly all that it was, to *Foss v. Harbottle* for the purpose of deciding the ratification point was unfortunate. There is little, if any precedent for his Lordship's dictum that only the company can complain of an improper allotment. For the reasons advanced above it is suggested that an individual shareholder has standing to complain of such an allotment, or of any other corporate act which the directors cause the company to take for a collateral purpose.

The Australian courts have clearly treated an improper allotment of shares as giving rise to a personal action, although the reasoning in the leading cases is rather confused. In *Ngurli v. McCann* the High Court held that in failing to consider the interests of the company as a whole in issuing new shares the directors had breached their fiduciary duty and ". . . the plaintiffs have a clear right to sue in their own names to remedy the breach of trust". In so holding, the High Court relied on the decisions of the Privy Council in *Burland v. Earle* and *Cook v. Deeks* to the effect that where the acts complained of are of a fraudulent character the minority can sue when the wrongdoers are in control. The High Court then reasoned that the right to issue new capital is an advantage which belongs to the company and the appropriation of a corporate advantage for the benefit of the majority to the exclusion of the minority is a fraudulent act. The difficulty with applying this reasoning to *Ngurli* (apart from the novel idea that the right to issue new shares is a corporate asset) is that both *Burland* and *Cook* were share-holders' derivative actions and what was clearly being referred to was the right of the minority to personally bring suit or, behalf of the company when the wrongdoers are in control — the fraud exception to *Foss v. Harbottle*.

In *Provident International Corporation v. International Leasing Cor poration*, Helsham J. relied on *Ngurli* and held that the rule ". . . does not apply in the case of a fraud on the powers of directors, at any rate where the abuse of power concerns a purported issue of shares, and I am of the opinion that this is so where the fraud consists of no dishonesty but a mere attempt to use the power for purposes other than that for which it is given". But here again the non-applicability of the rule has reference to the ability of the minority to sue in a derivative and not a personal capacity. However, Heis-ham J. went on to use language that could be taken to be a holding that the directors owe fiduciary duties directly to the shareholders.

> The reason why the rule in *Foss v. Harbottle* does not apply in a case of fraud on a power such as the present no doubt resides in the fiduciary nature of the duty owed and the fact that it is owed to all the corporators of the company. A breach of duty owed to an individual shareholder as one of the corporators could not be ratified by a majority of share-holders; any attempt by a majority to ratify a breach of fiduciary duty by directors would be no less a fraud qua that shareholder than was the case in the acts of the directors.

It is certainly the accepted position in the United States that directors, and majority shareholders in certain cases, stand in direct fiduciary relationship to the shareholders. But there is no case in the Commonwealth that so holds and as much as such a development is desirable and inevitable, it is not clear that that is what Heisham J. meant. *Provident International Corp.* is simply based on the proposition, elaborated above, that it is the shareholders who are directly affected when an improper allotment of shares is made and they therefore have a personal right to sue, have the corporate act declared void and to have the share register rectified. The directors who authorized the allotment may, but need not be, joined as co-defendants with the com-pany. Heisham J. also relied on the more recent High Court judgment in *Harlowe's Nominees Pty. Ltd. v. Woodside Oil Co.* which was a personal action to set aside an improper allotment and for rectification of the share register. There was no question either at trial or in the High Court of the plaintiff's right to maintain a personal action.

It may be, as in threatened *ultra vires* or illegal acts, that there is both a personal and corporate right of action. The shareholder may properly sue to restrain the company, or the company may proceed against the directors to restrain them from taking the proposed action. "But the fact that this second alternative is a possible one is no reason for refusing to allow a member to sue the company if he has an independent right to do so". So too in collateral purpose cases; the shareholders are the ones most directly concerned, and injured, in such cases and the fact that the corporation, in an indirect way, may also be injured by the failure of the directors to stay within their powers should not prevent the shareholders from asserting their personal rights.

Securities legislation provides the clearest example of both personal and corporate rights of action arising from the same wrongful act. Both the Ontario *Securities Act* and the Ontario *Business Corporations Act* provide for individual and corporate recovery when an insider trades in a company's securities with knowledge of material, confidential information. Such a statutory provision is necessary for a personal action because of the holding in *Percival v. Wright*. But even if the statute were silent as to a corporate right of action it is suggested that one would exist, in addition to the personal right, by extension of the principles in *Regal (Hastings) Ltd. v. Gulliver*, particularly as recently elaborated by the Supreme Court of Canada in *Canadian Aero Services Ltd. v. Terra Surveys Ltd.* This result was reached recently in the United States where a common law derivative action was allowed both in cases of insider trading by directors and by directors and "tippees".

The courts in the United States have recognized, particularly in the context of securities legislation, that the same allegations of fact can support both a derivative and personal action. The leading case is *J.I. Case Co. v. Borak* in which the Supreme Court indicated that violation of the proxy solicitation requirements of the *Securities Exchange Act* of 1934 gave rise to a private as well as a derivative action. In the Court of Appeals the plaintiff had, *inter alia*, appealed from a trial holding that the cause of action in the first count in the complaint, which related to a denial of pre-emptive rights, was derivative and that Wisconsin's security for expenses statute applied. In reversing, the court held that the security for expenses statute was not applicable, saying:

> . . . we think the trial court failed to recognize the principle that the same allegations of fact might support either a derivative suit or an individual cause of action by shareholders.

It is fairly clear that breaches of the proxy solicitation legislation in Canada give rise to a personal action. The analogy is to the notice cases in which it has consistently been held that every shareholder is entitled to truly informative notice of matters proposed for decision. Mandatory proxy solicitation and the information circular that must accompany it, is an attempt to provide fuller corporate disclosure on a continuing, consistent basis — it is simply notice in the modern form. If the statutory provisions have not been complied with, or if the material is inadequate or misleading, a shareholder has a personal right to sue for a declaration that the meeting and all acts done at it are void. It may also be, as the United States Supreme Court thought in Borak, that deceptive proxy solicitation also give rise to a derivative action. It tells nothing against the right to bring a personal action for a declaration to agree with Justice Clark that: [(1964), 377 U.S. at 432.]

> The injury which a stockholder suffers from a corporate action pursuant to a deceptive proxy solicitation ordinarily flows from the damage done to the corporation, rather than from the damage inflicted directly upon the stockholder. The damage suffered results not from the deceit practiced on him alone but rather from the deceit practiced in the stockholders as a group.

In *Charlebois v. Bienvenu*, Fraser J. also seemed to be of the opinion that the sending of a misleading proxy statement could support a derivative suit but on somewhat different grounds than those expressed in Borak: [(1967), 64 D.L.R. (2d) 683 at 694.]

> The defendants were also in breach of duty owed to the company quite apart from the requirements of the *Corporations Act*. The relationship of directors to a company is fiduciary and to hold an annual meeting and election of directors after sending out a misleading information circular . . . would seem *prima facie* to be a breach of that duty.

Farnham v. Fingold
[1973] 2 O.R. 132, 33 D.L.R. (3d) 156 (C.A.)

JESSUP J.A. (for the Court): This is an appeal from the order of Morand J. dismissing, *inter alia* three motions of various of the defendants to strike out the statement of claim on the grounds that the claims therein set forth disclose no reasonable cause of action and that the plaintiff has no status to maintain the claims in a class action. The appellants ask for an order dismissing the plaintiff's action without prejudice to the plaintiff's right to commence a fresh and properly constituted action, alternatively for an order striking out the statement of claim with leave to amend the writ of summons and to deliver a fresh statement of claim, and, alternatively for an order striking out specific paragraphs of the statement of claim.

The judgment of Morand, J., is reported in [1972] 3 O.R. 688, 29 D.L.R. (3d) 279, and it sets forth the facts alleged to give rise to the action and its nature so that it is unnecessary to repeat them. The prayer for relief reads:

37. The plaintiff therefore claims:

(a) damages in the amount of $25 million against the defendant for conspiracy to injure the plaintiff and other shareholders and former shareholders of Slater Steel Industries Limited;

(b) damages in the amount of $25 million as against the defendants J. Paul Fingold, David B. Fingold, Ralph W. Cooper, Harvey Fingold, Marvin Gerstein, Sidney Fingold, Fobasco Limited, for breach of their fiduciary duty as directors and/or officers and/or insiders of Slater Steel Industries Limited to the plaintiff and other shareholders of Slater Steel Industries Limited in the sale of shares of Slater Steel Industries Limited to Stanton Pipes Limited;

(c) damages in the amount of $25 million against all the defendants for breach of the provisions of The Securities Act and The Business Corporations Act of Ontario in the sale of shares of Slater Steel Industries Limited to Stanton Pipes Limited;

(d) damages in the amount of $25 million against the defendant Stanton Pipes Limited for inducing a breach by the other defendants of their fiduciary duties to the shareholders of Slater Steel Industries Limited and breach of The Securities Act and The Business Corporations Act of Ontario, in the sale of shares of Slater Steel Industries Limited to Stanton Pipes Limited;

(e) a declaration that the controlling shareholders hold any premium obtained upon the sale of their shares in Slater Steel Industries Limited to Stanton Pipes Limited over the market price of those shares for the benefit of Slater Steel Industries Limited and/or its general shareholders and/or the vendors of such shares to them;

(f) an accounting of all sums paid or to be paid by Stanton Pipes Limited to the other defendants except Slater Steel Industries Limited and McDonald Currie & Co. on account of the sale of shares of Slater Steel Industries Limited to Stanton Pipes Limited by such defendants, a reference to the Master at Toronto for the taking of such accounting and directions for the payment of any such sums as may have been or may be received by such defendants;

(g) damages in the amount of $25 million against the defendants Henderson and Morris;

(h) an interlocutory and permanent injunction restraining the defendants and each of them from entering into or completing any sale of shares or purported sale of shares of Slater Steel Industries Limited to Stanton Pipes Limited;

(i) his costs of this action;

(j) such further and other relief as to this Court may seem just.

The claims made in the statement of claim are completely novel. Their success may depend on the trial Court applying or extending the principle followed in *Perlman v. Feldmann* (1955), 219 F. 2d 173, and *Brown v. Halbert* (1969), 76 Cal. Rptr. 781, or on the trial Court holding that a breach of the provisions of Part IX of the *Securities Act*, R.S.O. 1970, c. 426, constitutes an actionable civil wrong. As I appreciate the appellants' argument, they do not now challenge Morand, J.'s decision that the difficult question of law raised by the novelty of the plaintiff's claims should not be determined in interlocutory proceedings, and their attack on the form of the action and the statement of claim is confined to matters not specifically dealt with in the judgment below.

The defendants Barney Morris and Ralph Henderson are claimed to be members of the alleged conspiracy. However, in addition, it is separately alleged with respect to them alone:

> 30. With regard to the defendants Ralph Henderson and Barney Morris, the plaintiff states the Bache & Co. and in particular the defendants Ralph Henderson and Barney Morris recommended the shares of Slater Steel Industries Limited to their customers for a long period of time and encouraged the plaintiff and other persons to invest in such shares. Relying upon the recommendations of the defendants Henderson and Morris, the plaintiff and other shareholders purchased shares in Slater Steel Industries Limited. The plaintiff states that the defendants Henderson and Morris, in concert with and/or upon the inducement of the controlling shareholders, have acted in breach of their obligations to the plaintiff and to other shareholders of Slater Steel Industries Limited who have purchased shares through or upon the recommendations of such defendants and/or Bache & Co., in arranging for the sale of shares owned by the defendants Henderson and Morris, and their friends and relations to the exclusion of other shareholders of Slater Steel Industries Limited including the plaintiff and at a premium price not available to such shareholders.

In my view, the relief claimed against Morris and Henderson based on this para. 30 is not, in the words of Rule 66, "in respect of or arising out of the same transaction or occurrence, or series of transactions or occurrences", as those which may give rise to liability of the other defendants. In the result, I think the claims so made against them are not properly joined in the action. In addition, the shareholders who dealt with Morris and Henderson or Bache & Co. constitute a separate class whose interest would seem to be antagonistic to those of some other members of the class on whose behalf the plaintiff brings the action.

Certain parts of the statement of claim and in particular all or parts of paras. 22, 23, 29, 32, 34, 36 and 37E are concerned with rights, duties or obligations owed to the defendant Slater Steel Industries Limited or with damage alleged to be suffered by that corporation as a result of the actions of the other defendants. Such matters are properly the subject of a derivative action rather than a class action. Morand, J., said it was "crucial" to distinguish between the two types of action, but found this action to be entirely a class action. I respectfully disagree.

Section 99 of the *Business Corporations Act*, R.S.O. 1970, c. 53, provides in part:

> 99(1) Subject to subsection 2, a shareholder of a corporation may maintain an action in a representative capacity for himself and all other shareholders of the corporation suing for and on behalf of the corporation to enforce any right, duty or obligation owed to the corporation under this Act or under any other statute or rule of law or equity that could be enforced by the corporation itself, or to obtain damages for any breach of any such right, duty or obligation.
>
> (2) An action under subsection 1 shall not be commenced until the shareholder has obtained an order of the court permitting the shareholder to commence the action.

Counsel for the respondent argues that the type of derivative action exemplified by *Foss v. Harbottle* (1843), 2 Hare 461, 67 E.R. 189, and succeeding cases continues to be maintainable in this Province apart from s. 99 and that the section only applies to plaintiffs who wish to take advantage of ss. (4) and (5) which provide:

> (4) At any time or from time to time while an action commenced under this section is pending, the plaintiff may apply to the court for an order for the payment to the plaintiff by the corporation of reasonable interim costs, including solicitor's and counsel fees and disbursements, for which interim costs the plaintiff shall be accountable to the corporation if the action is dismissed with costs on final disposition at the trial or on appeal.
>
> (5) An action commenced under this section shall be tried by the court and its judgement or order in the cause, unless the action is dismissed with costs, may include a provision that the reasonable costs of the action are payable to the plaintiff by the corporation or other defendants taxed as between a solicitor and his own client.

However, in my opinion, the very broad language of s. 99(1) embraces all causes of action under any statute or law or in equity, that a shareholder may sue for on behalf of a corporation. All forms of derivative actions purporting to be brought on behalf of and for the benefit of the corporation come within it, and therefore s-s. (2) applies to all such actions. Furthermore, I think it is clear that the interests of the corporation would be antagonistic to at least a part of the class the plaintiff represents with respect to the other claims in the action, i.e., to the sub-class of former shareholders. . .

[Jessup J.A. discussed the law surrounding class actions under the old Rule 75.]

In so far as the action is founded upon s. 150 of the *Business Corporations Act*, Mr. Garrow submitted that such a claim, if not brought by the corporation, could be brought only by the Ontario Securities Commission "in the name of and on behalf of the corporation", by virtue of s. 151. Section 150 creates a liability to "any person" who suffers a direct loss as a result of a transaction by insiders that falls within the section. it also creates an obligation on the insider to account to the corporation. Section 151, in my view, relates only to the obligation to the corporation and does not affect the cause of action of "any person who suffered any direct loss". The same conclusion must be reached with respect to ss. 113 and 114 of the *Securities Act*.

It was also argued that in so far as the plaintiff's cause of action is founded upon s. 113 of the *Securities Act* and s. 150 of the *Business Corporations Act* it cannot be maintained because the loss claimed is not "direct loss" within the meaning of those sections. I agree with Morand J., that this is not a question that should be decided in interlocutory proceedings.

Besides those mentioned, the statement of claim is prejudicial or embarrassing in the following respects:

(1) Special damages and not the conspiracy is the gist of an action for conspiracy and the special damages of each member of the class should be pleaded. As I understand the respondent's argument, those special damages will be pleaded as the pro rata share of each member of the class of the gross premium I have mentioned.

(2) The class on behalf of which the action is maintained is not clearly and specifically defined and facts are not alleged to show the plaintiff is a member of that class. As I understand the respondent's factum, the class comprises all shareholders and former shareholders of Slater Steel Industries Limited who were shareholders at the time of the sale of control to Stanton Pipes Limited. I see no antagonism between the interests of the members of such a class but it should be so defined in the statement of claim.

(3) Paragraphs 34 and 35 are embarrassing in that they do not allege facts but rather possible future wrongs.

(4) Paragraphs 37(b) to (e) both inclusive are evidently alterative claims and should be pleaded as such. Moreover, the plaintiff's claim is not for 25 million dollars but rather for whatever is shown to be the amount of the gross premium I have mentioned.

In the result, I would allow the appeal with costs here and below, set aside the order of Morand, J., and in its place direct an order:

A. Dismissing the action with costs against the defendants Morris and Henderson in so far as the action against them is based on the allegations of fact made in para. 30 of the statement of claim, without prejudice to the right to commence a separate action against such defendants;

B. Dismissing the action with costs against all defendants in so far as the action is derivative in nature, without prejudice to the right to commence such separate action for which leave may be granted in the future under s. 99(2) of the *Business Corporations Act*;

C. Striking out the statement of claim with liberty to amend the writ of summons and deliver a fresh amended statement of claim within 20 days.

Appeal allowed.

Note

Perlman v. Feldman, reproduced in Chapter 6, *supra*, was brought as a derivative action. Do you agree that where a minority shareholder brings an action alleging that the majority has appropriated a control premium on the sale of its shares that the action is derivative rather than personal? As to this, it is interesting to note that the Court in *Perlman* gave a personal remedy (ordering that the premium be held in trust for those who were shareholders at the time the company was sold). Both the OBCA, s. 247(c), and the CBCA, s. 240(c), expressly allow such a "personal" remedy in a derivative action, but s. 233 of the BCBCA does not.

Goldex Mines Ltd. v. Revill
(1975), 7 O.R. (2d) 216, 54 D.L.R. (3d) 672 (C.A.)

[Goldex Mines was a shareholder of Probe Mines Ltd. This decision culminated from the fifth round of proceedings stemming from a dispute among Probe's directors and over a proposed purchase of gypsum claims from a company controlled by a former Probe director. Goldex alleged breaches of duties by directors and defendant shareholders, but did not specify whether these duties were owed to Probe or to its shareholders.]

BY THE COURT: The right to sue.

With the foregoing questions dealt with, there remains the real and important issue: does Goldex have the right to maintain this (second) action without first obtaining the leave of the Court under s. 99 of the Act? Haines J., would have left this question to the trial Judge, as he suggested was done by Morand, J. in *Farnham v. Fingold et al.*, [1972] 3 O.R. 688, 29 D.L.R. (3d) 279.

His decision was given before the judgment of this Court in that case, reported in [1973] 2 O.R. 132, 33 D.L.R. (3d) 156. Our judgment was not only considered by the Divisional Court but in the end formed the basis on which the writs were set aside, since that Court concluded that the action was "wholly derivative in nature" and no leave to bring it had been obtained under s. 99. Its judgment sets out the entire endorsement of the writ ([1973] 3 O.R. at pp. 880-4, 38 D.L.R. (3d) at pp. 524-8) and we need not repeat it.

In broad terms the issue is whether the Divisional Court was right in its conclusion. We think the issue can be confined in narrower terms. It is this: Where the same acts of directors or of shareholders cause damage to the company and also to shareholders or a class of them, is a shareholder's cause of action for the wrong done to him derivative?

It is well to draw attention to the appropriate terminology which should be employed. The point is well taken by Professor Stanley M. Beck in his thorough and useful article "The Shareholders' Derivative Action", 52 Can. Bar Rev. 159 (1974) (see pp. 185-6). Where a legal wrong is done to shareholders by directors or other shareholders, the injured shareholders suffer a personal wrong, and may seek redress for it in a personal action. That personal action may be by one shareholder alone, or (as will usually be the case) by a class action in which he sues on behalf of himself and all other shareholders in the same interest (usually, all other shareholders save the wrongdoers). Such a class action is nevertheless a personal action.

A derivative action, on the other hand, is one in which the wrong is done to the company. It is always a class action, brought in representative form, thereby binding all the shareholders. This was so at common law, as s. 99 recognizes (see Beck, *op. cit.*, at p. 185).

The distinction, therefore, as Professor Beck points out, is not between a class action and a derivative action, but between a personal action (whether or not a class action) and a derivative action. The action here is a class action. No one suggests that on that ground alone it is open to objection. The objection is that it is derivative, and cannot be brought without leave.

In *Farnham v. Fingold, supra,* this Court was not required, on the facts of that case, to consider a situation where the same wrongful act is both a wrong to the company and a wrong to each individual shareholder. In one sense every injury to a company is indirectly an injury to its shareholders. On the other hand, if one applies the test: "Is this wrongful act one in respect of which the company could sue?", a shareholder who is personally and directly injured must surely be entitled to say, as a matter of logic, "the company cannot sue for my injury; it can only sue for its own".

These distinctions have been considered in several American cases, usually in States where a shareholder bringing a derivative action may be required to put up security for costs. Some of these cases are discussed by Professor Beck, *op. cit.* It has not been necessary in Ontario heretofore to draw such a fine dividing line, but the enactment of s. 99 makes some distinction essential, because leave of the Court is required for all those parts of a claim that are derivative. (Once leave is obtained, personal and derivative claims may be joined, subject to the Rules, i.e., if the claims arise out of the same transaction or occurrence.)

It would not be difficult to reach the conclusion that a shareholder's action is personal where one group of shareholders, by their own non-representative activities (i.e. not as directors) acts in such a way as to deprive another group of shareholders of their rights, where those rights are derived from the letters patent (or articles of incorporation), the company's by-laws, or from statutory provisions enacted for the protection of shareholders as such. The more difficult case arises where the directors, whose shareholdings are controlling or merely substantial, for a collateral purpose of their own, cause the company to act in a manner that deprives a group of shareholders of their rights (Beck, *op. cit.*, at p. 174). To cause the company to act to serve personal objectives of directors would clearly be a breach of the directors' fiduciary duty to the company. Beck suggests that it is also a breach of the directors' fiduciary duty to shareholders as a whole — the duty "to act with an even hand and in good faith"; he also asserts that this principle has been indicated (if not always clearly expressed) in the decided cases.

The line of demarcation between a derivative action and a personal action was discussed by Traynor C.J., in *Jones v. H.F. Ahmanson & Co. et al.* (1969), 460 Pac. Rep. 2d 464 at p. 470 *et seq.*, 81 Cal. Rptr. 592. The argument that the directors, officers and controlling shareholders owe a duty only to the corporation was rejected. The plaintiff was held entitled to bring her action without complying with s. 7616 of the California Financial Code, requiring a prior determination by a commissioner that a proposed derivative action complied with certain statutory prerequisites.

One phrase used in the judgment of Traynor C.J., requires comment. At pp. 470-1, referring to *Shaw v. Empire Savings & Loan Ass'n*, 186 Cal. App. 2d 401 at p. 407, he said:

> the court [in *Shaw*] noted the "well established general rule that a stockholder of a corporation has no personal or individual right of action against third persons, including the corporation's officers and directors, for a wrong or injury to the corporation which results in the destruction or depreciation of the value of his stock, since the wrong thus suffered by the stockholder is merely incidental to the wrong suffered by the corporation and affects all stockholders alike." From this the court reasoned that a minority shareholder could not maintain an individual action unless he could demonstrate the injury to him was somehow different from that suffered by other minority shareholders. In so concluding the court erred. The individual wrong necessary to support a suit by a shareholder need not be unique to that plaintiff. The same injury may affect a substantial number of shareholders. If the injury is not incidental to an injury to the corporation, an individual cause of action exists.

What limitation on the general principle is intended by the words in the last sentence: ". . . not incidental to an injury to the corporation"?

In the context of the whole judgment, we believe Traynor, C.J. meant by this phrase: ". . . not arising simply because the corporation itself has been damaged, and as a consequence of the damage to it, its shareholders have been injured".

In *Charlebois et al. v. Bienvenu. et al.*, [1967] 2 O.R. 635 at p. 644, 64 D.L.R. (2d) 683 at p. 692, Fraser J., held that the holding of an annual meeting and election of directors after the sending out of a misleading information circular by the directors was a breach of the directors' fiduciary duty to the company. We hold that such an act is also a breach of duty to the other shareholders. If the directors of a company choose, or are compelled by statute, to send information to shareholders, those shareholders have a right to expect that the information sent to them is fairly presented, reasonably accurate, and not misleading.

The proposition that a shareholder is entitled to adequate information from which he can form an intelligent judgment on the matters he is entitled to vote on was enunciated by Spence J., in *Garvie v. Axmith et al.*, [1962] O.R. 65 at pp. 82-7, 31 D.L.R. (2d) 65 at pp. 82-7. It was supported by quotations of opinion by Roach J., in *Re National Grocers Co. Ltd.*, [1938] O.R. 142 at p. 154, [1938] 3 D.L.R. 106 at p. 116, and LeBel J., in *Re N. Slater Co. Ltd.*, [1947] O.W.N. 226 at p. 227, [1947] 2 D.L.R. 311 at pp. 313-4, 28 C.B.R. 31. We accept the proposition and hold that it is not confined to cases under s. 33 of the *Corporations Act*, R.S.O. 1960, c. 71 [now R.S.O. 1970, c. 89, s. 35] (special resolutions; see now s. 189(2) of the Act).

Examples of statutory directions respecting the sending of information to shareholders are found in ss. 106(i)(a), 115 to 120, 134(5)(b), 169, 184 and 194(2) and (3) of the Act. Section 256 provides that every person who makes or assists in making a statement in any document required by or for the purposes of the Act or the Regulations that, at the time and in the light of the circumstances under which it was made, is false or misleading in respect of any material fact or that omits to state a material fact the omission of which makes the statement false or misleading, is guilty of an offence.

It has long been the law that minority shareholders can sue, even where there is a clear wrong to the company, where there has been "an oppressive and unjust exercise of the powers of the majority shareholders for the promotion of an advantage to themselves to the peculiar detriment of the minority": *Henderson v. Strang et al.* (1919), 60 S.C.R. 201 at p. 202, 54 D.L.R. 674 at p. 675, [1920] 1 W.W.R. 982, followed in *Gray v. Yellowknife Gold Mines Ltd. et al. (No. 1)*, [1947] O.R. 928 at p. 963, [1948] 1 D.L.R. 473 at p. 498. With the legislative trend obviously towards greater protection of shareholders by seeing that they receive certain information, truthfully and fairly presented, we see no difficulty in holding that shareholders are injured if they do not receive it, apart altogether from any breach of duty owed to the company itself. Where information is sent to shareholders that is untrue or misleading, the duty to shareholders is breached, whether the senders were required by statute to send out that class of information, or whether they simply chose to do so.

The principle that the majority governs in corporate affairs is fundamental to corporation law, but its corollary is also important — that the majority must act fairly and honestly. Fairness is the touchstone of equitable justice, and when the test of fairness is not met, the equitable jurisdiction of the Court can be invoked to prevent or remedy the injustice which misrepresentation or other dishonesty has caused. The category of cases in which fiduciary duties and obligations arise is not a closed one: *Laskin v. Bache & Co. Inc.*, [1972] 1 O.R. 465 at p. 472, 23 D.L.R. (3d) 385 at p. 392.

Turning to the way the plaintiff's case is pleaded in the extensive endorsement on the writ, set out in full in the reasons of Hughes J., there is no clear allegation anywhere that that plaintiff sues in respect of wrongs to shareholders personally. On the contrary — as Hughes J., pointed out: [1973] 3 O.R. at p. 885, 38 D.L.R. (3d) at p. 529 — cls. E, G and I all give grounds for the injunctions sought therein, and in each case the concluding ground is that "the Defendant Directors are in breach of their fiduciary duty to Probe" (giving reasons for the allegation). The grounds are expressed cumulatively and not in the alternative. Thus, on their face, these three clauses assert claims to relief which are founded on a breach of duty to Probe and which Probe itself could assert.

Clause E(1) asserts that the defendants

> . . . circulated to all shareholders of the corporation a communication dated the 29th day of September, 1972 which was calculated to result in the procurement of proxies in favour of the personal defendants and the withholding of proxies in favour of the plaintiff, thereby effecting a solicitation without appendixing thereto or delivering as a separate document accompanying such solicitation an information circular as prescribed by section 118 of The *Business Corporations Act* . . .

If this passage stood alone, it could be interpreted as a pleading of wrongful acts causing damage to the plaintiff and other shareholders, and thus disclosing a cause of action which we have earlier said is not derivative, and which is therefore outside s. 99.

Similarly, cl. E(2) alleges that the information circular dated October 5, 1972, approved by the defendant directors and sent out with the notice calling the annual meeting of Probe for October 31, 1972, in conjunction with a solicitation of proxies by the defendant directors, was false and misleading in three respects. This subcl. (2), while not framed as an allegation of wrongful acts causing damage to the plaintiff and other shareholders, as shareholders, could also be interpreted as meaning that in substance.

The allegations with respect to the annual report of Probe to its shareholders dated September 25, 1972, pose more difficult problems. They occur:

(1) in clause C. of the endorsement, claiming that the resolution of the directors approving the annual report is a nullity;

(2) in clause D., claiming that all proxies obtained by the defendant directors "in response to the solicitation of proxies accompanied by the Information Circular . . . and the Annual Report . . ." are null and void;

(3) in clause E(3), which, in support of the claim for an injunction restraining the personal defendants from voting their proxies, alleges that the Annual Report is false and misleading.

There is also an oblique reference to the annual report in cl. L, which seeks to prevent the defendant directors from engaging in any renewed solicitation of proxies "until a corrected and complete Information Circular and Annual Report are provided to shareholders".

While the preparation, approval and circulation to shareholders of a "false and misleading" annual report is undoubtedly a wrong to the company, the circulation of such a report to shareholders, accompanied by a solicitation on behalf of the directors of the shareholders' proxies, is in our view also a wrong to shareholders as such, affecting their own personal rights. An action attacking such a report, seeking a declaration or an injunction, or both, is not derivative, and leave of the Court to bring it is not required.

The allegations in the endorsement respecting the Mountain Gypsum agreement with Probe, as now framed, all raise causes of action which are really Probe's, although the carrying out of them could affect shareholders of Probe and possibly solidify or change the control of Probe's shares. This portion of the claim, referred to in cls. E(2)(a), (3), (4), F, G, H, I and K, is in substance derivative. The same applies to the underwriting agreement of June 21, 1972, with W.D. Latimer Co. Ltd. which is tied to cl. E(2)(b) and (c).

The trouble with the endorsement is that it discloses no attempt to differentiate between claims personal to shareholders and claims which are derivative. As already indicated, the subclauses of claims E and G intermingle "grounds" that are clearly derivative in nature with some that are not. We do not think it is our function to suggest a redraft of the endorsement so as to bring it into conformity with the principles enunciated herein.

The Divisional Court decided that all of the claims made were derivative, and set aside the writ and interlocutory orders made on the basis of it. We have concluded that the facts set out in the material would support an endorsement making some claims for relief that are personal and not derivative, if properly pleaded, but they are inextricably woven in to the derivative claims, in the present endorsement.

We considered whether it would be appropriate merely to strike out the endorsement on the writ, with leave to amend, rather than strike out the writ itself, as the Divisional Court did. We have decided against doing so, for two reasons. No limitation period is involved, and a new writ can be issued. In addition, the plaintiff may decide to apply for leave under s. 99, and if it obtains leave, it can add to the derivative claims thus permitted such personal claims as it sees fit (subject, of course, to the Rules).

The Divisional Court was asked to grant leave *nunc pro tunc* under s. 99(2), if it concluded that the claims made were derivative. It declined to do so: [1973] 3 O.R. at pp. 886-7, 38 D.L.R. (3d) at pp. 530-1. The same request was made to this Court. We agree with the reasons for refusing leave given by the Divisional Court, which apply with even greater force to the application for leave made to us. We refuse leave also.

There was considerable discussion before us as to our directing the calling of an annual meeting, with a neutral chairman. With the writ struck out, there is nothing left on which we can act.

Section 111 of the Act empowers the Court to order a meeting to be called if it is "impracticable" to call a meeting in the regular way. If it is not impracticable for the present directors to call a new meeting, which is now long overdue.

Clause M of the endorsement seeks "an order removing the Defendant Directors as officers and directors of Probe". We have no jurisdiction to order this. It is a matter for the shareholders, either under s. 140 [am. 1972, c. 138, s. 37(2)] of the Act, or at an annual meeting.

Appeal dismissed.

Hercules Management Ltd. v. Ernst & Young
[1997] 2 S.C.R. 165, 1997 CarswellMan 198, 1997 CarswellMan 199

[The appellants were shareholders of two related corporations. The respondent was an accounting firm that was hired by the two corporations to perform annual audits of their financial statements and provide audit reports to their shareholders. After the corporations went into receivership, the appellants brought an action claiming that the audit reports were negligently prepared, and that they had lost money in reliance on them. Much of the judgment focused on procedural matters and the issue of whether the respondents owed a duty of care under the law of negligence to the appellants.]

LA FOREST J.: . . . All the participants in this appeal — the appellants, the respondents, and the intervener — raised the issue of whether the appellants' claims in respect of the losses they suffered in their existing shareholdings through their alleged inability to oversee management of the corporations ought to have been brought as a derivative action in conformity with the rule in *Foss v. Harbottle* rather than as a series of individual actions. The issue was also raised and discussed in the courts below. In my opinion, a derivative action — commenced, as required, by an application under s. 232 of the Manitoba *Corporations Act* — would have been the proper method of proceeding with respect to this claim. Indeed, I would regard this simply as a corollary of the idea that the audited reports are provided to the shareholders as a group in order to allow them to take collective (as opposed to individual) decisions. Let me explain.

The rule [in *Foss v. Harbottle*] provides that individual shareholders have no cause of action in law for any wrongs done to the corporation and that if an action is to be brought in respect of such losses, it must be brought either by the corporation itself (through management) or by way of a derivative action. The legal rationale behind the rule was eloquently set out by the English Court of Appeal in *Prudential Assurance Co. v. Newman Industries Ltd. (No. 2)*, [1982] 1 All E.R. 354, at p. 367, as follows:

> The rule [in *Foss v. Harbottle*] is the consequence of the fact that a corporation is a separate legal entity. Other consequences are limited liability and limited rights. The company is liable for its contracts and torts; the shareholder has no such liability. The company acquires causes of action for breaches of contract and for torts which damage the company. No cause of action vests in the shareholder. When the shareholder acquires a share he accepts the fact that the value of his investment follows the fortunes of the company and that he can only exercise his influence over the fortunes of the company by the exercise of his voting rights in general meeting. The law confers on him the right to ensure that the company observes the limitations of its memorandum of association and the right to ensure that other shareholders observe the rule, imposed on them by the articles of association. If it is right that the law has conferred or should in certain restricted circumstances confer further rights on a shareholder the scope and consequences of such further rights require careful consideration.

To these lucid comments, I would respectfully add that the rule is also sound from a policy perspective, inasmuch as it avoids the procedural hassle of a multiplicity of actions.

The manner in which the rule in *Foss v. Harbottle*, *supra*, operates with respect to the appellants' claims can thus be demonstrated. As I have already explained, the appellants allege that they were prevented from properly overseeing the management of the audited corporations because the respondents' audit reports painted a misleading picture of their financial state. They allege further that had they known the true situation, they would have intervened to avoid the eventuality of the corporations' going into receivership and the consequent loss of their equity. The difficulty with this submission, I have suggested, is that it fails to recognize that in supervising management, the shareholders must be seen to be acting as a body in respect of the corporation's interests rather than as individuals in respect of their own ends. In a manner of speaking, the shareholders assume what may be seen to be a "managerial role" when, as a collectivity, they oversee the activities of the directors and officers through resolutions adopted at shareholder meetings. In this capacity, they cannot properly be understood to be acting simply as individual holders of equity. Rather, their collective decisions are made in respect of the corporation itself. Any duty owed by auditors in respect of this aspect of the shareholders' functions, then, would be owed not to shareholders *qua* individuals, but rather to all shareholders as a group, acting in the interests of the corporation. And if the decisions taken by the collectivity of shareholders are in respect of the corporation's affairs, then the shareholders' reliance on negligently prepared audit reports in taking such decisions will result in a wrong to the corporation for which the shareholders cannot, as individuals, recover.

This line of reasoning finds support in Lord Bridge's comments in *Caparo, supra*, at p. 580:

> The shareholders of a company have a collective interest in the company's proper management and in so far as a negligent failure of the auditor to report accurately on the state of the company's finances deprives the shareholders of the opportunity to exercise their powers in general meeting to call the directors to book and to ensure that errors in management are corrected, the shareholders ought to be entitled to a remedy. But in practice no problem arises in this regard since the interest of the shareholders in the proper management of the company's affairs is indistinguishable from the interest of the company itself and any loss suffered by the shareholders . . . will be recouped by a claim against the auditor in the name of the company, not by individual shareholders. [Emphasis added.]

It is also reflected in the decision of Farley J. in *Roman I, supra*, the facts of which were similar to those of the case at bar. In that case, the plaintiff shareholders brought an action against the defendant auditors alleging, *inter alia*, that the defendant's audit reports were negligently prepared. That negligence, the shareholders contended, prevented them from properly overseeing management which, in turn, led to the winding up of the corporation and a loss to the shareholders of their equity therein. Farley J. discussed the rule in *Foss v. Harbottle* and concluded that it operated so as to preclude the shareholders from bringing personal actions based on an alleged inability to supervise the conduct of management.

One final point should be made here. Referring to the case of *Goldex Mines Ltd. v. Revill* (1974), 7 O.R. (2d) 216 (C.A.), the appellants submit that where a shareholder has been directly and individually harmed, that shareholder may have a personal cause of action even though the corporation may also have a separate and distinct cause of action. Nothing in the foregoing paragraphs should be understood to detract from this principle. In finding that claims in respect of losses stemming from an alleged inability to oversee or supervise management are really derivative and not personal in nature, I have found only that shareholders cannot raise individual claims in respect of a wrong done to the corporation. Indeed, this is the limit of the rule in *Foss v. Harbottle*. Where, however, a separate and distinct claim (say, in tort) can be raised with respect to a wrong done to a shareholder *qua* individual, a personal action may well lie, assuming that all the requisite elements of a cause of action can be made out.

The facts of *Haig, supra*, provide the basis for an example of where such a claim might arise. Had the investors in that case been shareholders of the corporation, and had a similarly negligent report knowingly been provided to them by the auditors for a specified purpose, a duty of care separate and distinct from any duty owed to the audited corporation would have arisen in their favour, just as one arose in favour of Mr. Haig. While the corporation would have been entitled to claim damages in respect of any losses it might have suffered through reliance on the report (assuming, of course, that the report was also provided for the corporation's use), the shareholders in question would also have been able to seek personal compensation for the losses they suffered *qua* individuals through their personal reliance and investment. On the facts of this case, however, no claims of this sort can be established.

Appeal dismissed with costs.

Notes

1 In *Kraus v. J.G. Lloyd Pty. Ltd.*, [1965] V.R. 232 (Vict. S.C.) the plaintiff shareholder asked for an injunction to restrain the first defendant from acting as a director after being called upon by a majority of shareholders of a closely held company to retire. The plaintiff complained that the defendants were running the affairs of the company without a proper quorum of directors and that they had refused to allow the plaintiff and other shareholders to appoint other directors. The court held that the individual rights of the plaintiff as a member of the company had been invaded and that the rule in *Foss v. Harbottle* presented no obstacle to her claim for relief. The court declared the first defendant no longer entitled to serve as a director and granted the injunction. Also the court ordered the one remaining director to convene a general meeting within 21 days for the election of directors.

2 In *Jones v. H.F Ahmanson & Co.*, 460 P. 2d 464 (Cal. 1969); 81 Ca. 3d 592, Traynor C.J. said (at pp. 598-9):

> Analysis of the nature and purpose of a shareholders' derivative suit will demonstrate that the test adopted in the Shaw case does not properly distinguish the cases in which an individual cause of action lies.
>
> A shareholder's derivative suit seeks to recover for the benefit of the corporation and its whole body of shareholders when injury is caused to the corporation that may not otherwise be redressed because of failure of the corporation to act. Thus, "the action is derivative, i.e., in the corporate right, if the gravamen of the complaint is injury to the corporation, or to the whole body of its stock or property without any severance or distribution among individual holders, or if it seeks to recover assets for the corporation or to prevent the dissipation of its assets."
>
> A stockholder's derivative suit is brought to enforce a cause of action which the corporation itself possesses against some third

party, a suit to recompense the corporation for injuries which it has suffered as a result of the acts of third parties. The management owes to the stockholders a duty to take proper steps to enforce all claims which the corporation may have. When it fails to perform this duty, the stockholders have a right to do so. Thus, although the corporation is made a defendant in a derivative suit, the corporation nevertheless is the real plaintiff and it alone benefits from the decree; the stockholders derive no benefit therefrom except the indirect benefit resulting from a realization upon the corporation's assets. The stockholder's individual suit, on the other hand, is a suit to enforce a right against the corporation which the stockholder possesses as an individual.

It is clear from the stipulated facts and plaintiff's allegations that she does not seek to recover on behalf of the corporation for injury done to the corporation by defendants. Although she does allege that the value of her stock has been diminished by defendants' actions, she does not contend that the diminished value reflects an injury to the corporation and resultant depreciation in the value of the stock. Thus the gravamen of her cause of action is injury to herself and the other minority stockholders.

In *Shaw v. Empire Savings & Loan Assn.*, the court noted the "well established general rule that a stockholder of a corporation has no personal or individual right of action against third persons, including the corporation's officers and directors, for a wrong or injury to the corporation which results in the destruction of depreciation of the value of his stock, since the wrong thus suffered by the stockholder is merely incidental to the wrong suffered by the corporation and affects all stockholders alike."

From this the court reasoned that a minority shareholder could not maintain an individual action unless he could demonstrate the injury to him was somehow different from that suffered by other minority shareholders.

In so concluding the court erred. The individual wrong necessary to support a suit by a shareholder need not be unique to that plaintiff. The same injury may affect a substantial number of shareholders. If the injury is not incidental to an injury to the corporation, an individual cause of action exists. To the extent that *Shaw v. Empire Savings & Loan Assn.* is inconsistent with the opinion expressed herein, it is disapproved.

3 Assuming certain wrongs can give rise to both derivative and personal actions, what rules should be followed? Should the rules on, and distinctions between, derivative and personal actions apply where a small closely held corporation is involved? See *Watson v. Button*, 235 F. 2d 235 (9th Cir. 1956) and *Thomas v. Dickson*, 250 Ga. 772 (S.C., 1983).

In *Thomas* the plaintiff, the sole shareholder of a corporation, was allowed to bring a personal action for a wrong done to the corporation. Bell J. said (at 774-5):

> The general rule is that a shareholder seeking to recover misappropriated corporate funds may only bring a derivative suit . . . However, exceptions to this rule have been recognized, including an exception which looks to the reasons requiring derivative actions to determine if they are applicable . . .

> In the instant case, the reasons requiring derivative suits do not exist. The reasons underlying the general rule are that 1) it prevents a multiplicity of lawsuits by shareholders; 2) it protects corporate creditors by putting the proceeds of the recovery back in the corporation; 3) it protects the interests of all shareholders by increasing the value of their shares, instead of allowing a recovery by one shareholder to prejudice the rights of others not a party to the suit; and 4) it adequately compensates the injured shareholder by increasing the value of his shares . . .

> We will now examine this case to see if these reasons are applicable. First, Mrs. Dickson is the *only* injured shareholder; consequently, there can be no multiplicity of lawsuits, and there is no concern that a recovery by her will prejudice the rights of other shareholders. In addition, Mrs. Dickson would not be adequately compensated by a corporate recovery. For a shareholder, the potential benefit of a corporate recovery in such cases is the increase in the value of his or her shares. See, Note, "Distinguishing Between Direct and Derivative Shareholder Suits", 110 U. of Penn. L. Rev. 1147 (1962). There would be no such benefit to Mrs. Dickson, however, since, in a closely held corporation, there is no ready market for her shares.

> The final consideration underlying the general rule, the protection of creditors, is also not present in this case. The audit reports of Trio introduced below indicate that for the fiscal years 1976 through 1980, Trio was paying its debts as they came due, and that there was no outstanding or dissatisfied creditor. Additionally, neither Thomas nor Akin offered evidence of any creditor in need of protection . . .

> Because Mrs. Dickson was *the sole injured* shareholder and because the reasons underlying the general rule calling for corporate recovery do not exist in this case, we find that Mrs. Dickson was properly allowed to bring this direct action.

Should this line of reasoning be followed in Canada?

4. RELIEF FROM OPPRESSION

(a) Introduction: The Mischief and Response

As we have seen a basic principle of corporation law is majority rule, a concept which has many ramifications. At one level, it means that the majority shareholders decide who will be the directors of the corporation who in turn determine how the corporation will be run. At another level, the majority shareholders will also determine the outcome of questions that are required to be referred to shareholders for approval. In each case, whether a decision by the directors or approval by shareholders, the interests of minority shareholders are recognized through the duties owed by directors, and the equitable restraints imposed on majority shareholder action to ensure fair treatment of the minority.

However, notwithstanding these restraints on directors and majority shareholder action, the case law offers a number of examples where shareholders were being unfairly or improperly treated and courts were reluctant to interfere. This was especially the case in private or closely held corporations. Recall, for example, the circumstances in *Donahue v. Rodd Elec trotype Co. of New England, Inc.* 328 N.E. 2d 505 (Mass. 1975), discussed *supra*, in Chapter 6. Many U.K. cases, however, are also cited as examples where the court ought to have recognized more effectively the plight of minority shareholders: see *e.g. Greenhalgh v. Arderne Cinemas Ltd.*, [1951] 1 Ch. 286, [1950] 2 All E.R. 1120 (C.A.), which is discussed briefly, *infra*.

One immediate response to this minority shareholder problem was to resort to the court for a winding-up order. However, this remedy could well result in a disadvantage to the minority shareholder who wished to continue his investment and maintain the business enterprise as a viable entity. Moreover, the proceeds from dissolution might not in any way reflect the damage already allegedly inflicted upon the shareholder's investment; and the proceeds could also be small compared to the earnings potential of the business especially where the only buyers for the shares are the alleged oppressors.

Against this background, the 1945 U.K. Cohen Committee recommended giving the court power to put an end to an act of oppression and this was enacted in section 210 of the U.K. *Companies Act*, 1948. In 1962, the U.K. Jenkins Committee recommended substantial amendments to overcome what turned out to be a number of judicially constructed limitations on the scope and application of the remedy. In particular, these committees highlighted four situations where the remedy would be appropriate: (1) where controlling directors unreasonably refuse to register transfers of the minority's holdings to force a reduced sale price for them to take advantage of; (2) where directors award themselves excessive remuneration that diminishes the funds available for distribution as dividends; (3) to prevent the issuing of shares to directors and others on special or advantageous terms; and (4) to prevent the refusal to declare non-cumulative preference dividends on shares held by the minority. It does not take an abundance of imagination to envision many other circumstances in which the oppression remedy would be an appropriate response.

The Canadian jurisdictions slowly adopted and improved on the U.K. provision, which in turn was significantly altered by section 75 of the 1980 U.K. *Companies Act* (now s. 459 of the U.K. *Companies Act*, 1985). An increasing number of decisions have been rendered by Canadian courts that already indicate that the oppression remedy may be the most significant one in the shareholder arsenal.

(b) The Canadian Statutory Provisions

IACOBUCCI, PILKINGTON AND PRICHARD,
Canadian Business Corporations
(1977) pp. 204–208 (footnotes omitted)

Federal

Section 234 [now s. 241] is the Federal Act's equivalent of the United Kingdom section 210 [now s. 459 of U.K. *Companies Act*, 1985]. It is supplemented by the provisions of section 235 [s. 242] and is in essence section 210 [s. 459] plus the changes recommended by the Jenkins Committee.

A "complainant" may apply to a court for an order and where the court is satisfied that (a) any act or omission of the corporation or its affiliates effects a result, or (b) the business or affairs of the corporation or its affiliates are or have been carried on or conducted in a manner, or (c) the powers of the directors of the corporation or any of its affiliates are or have been exercised in a manner that is "oppressive or unfairly prejudicial to or that unfairly disregards the interests of any security holder, creditor, director or officer", the court may make an interim or final order it thinks fit and subsection 234(3) [s. 241(3)] without limiting the generality of this power, gives examples including: orders (i) restraining the conduct complained of, (ii) appointing a receiver or receiver-manager, (iii) amending the articles or by-laws or a unanimous shareholder agreement, (iv) directing an issue or exchange of securities, (v) directing changes in directors, (vi) directing the purchase of the securities of a security holder, (vii) directing payment to a security holder, (viii) varying or setting aside a transaction to which the corporation is a party and compensating any other parties, (ix) directing production of any financial statement or accounting, (x) compensating any aggrieved person, (xi) directing rectification of the corporate records or registry, (xii) liquidating or dissolving the corporation, (xiii) directing an investigation, or (xiv) requiring the trial of any matter. If the order directs amendments of the articles or by-laws, the directors shall comply forthwith and paragraph 234(4)(b) [s. 241(4)(b)] prevents any further amendments without the court's approval. Any such amendments ordered by the court do not give rise to a dissenting shareholders' right of appraisal under section

184 [s. 190]. Subsection 234(6) [s. 241(6)] prevents the court from ordering the corporation to purchase securities of a security holder or pay to a security holder any part of the moneys paid by him for securities if there are reasonable grounds for believing that after the payment the corporation would be unable to meet its liabilities or the realizable value of its assets would thereby be less than the aggregate of its liabilities.

Section 235 [s. 242] adds four procedural and evidentiary qualifications to a section 234 [s. 241] application. First, the fact that the complained of conduct has been approved by the shareholders of the corporation is not sufficient grounds to stay or dismiss the application for relief; it is merely a factor that the court may take into account in making an order. Second, court approval is required for any stay, discontinuance or dismissal under section 234 [s. 241], and if the court determines that any complainant may be substantially affected by such stay, discontinuance or dismissal, it may order any party to the application to give notice to the complainant. Third, a complainant is not required to give security or costs when making his application. Fourth, the court may order the corporation to pay the complainant's interim costs, including legal fees and disbursements, but the complainant is accountable for these costs upon the final disposition of the application.

Section 234 [s. 241] has incorporated the six major recommendations of the Jenkins Report, each of which was designed to strip away the self-imposed judicial qualifications that have limited the application of section 210 [s. 459]. First, under section 210 [s. 459] the petitioner was required to show that the corporation's conduct was sufficiently poor so as to provide just and equitable grounds to wind-up the corporation. This requirement has now been omitted by section 459 of the 1985 U.K. *Companies Act*. This duty, which often prevented successful actions, has been criticized as too difficult an onus:

> It was the view of the Northern Ireland Committee on Company Law Reform that the section imposed too heavy an onus on the petitioner because the requirement that the company should be wound-up necessitated proof of a lack of probity akin to fraud. Shareholders, it is said, are entitled to relief long before this point is reached.

Section 234 [s. 241] abrogates this standard. It merely requires that the applicant show that the conduct is "oppressive or unfairly prejudicial to" or that it "unfairly disregards the interests of any security holder, creditor, director, or officer". It is not necessary to establish that grounds for winding-up the corporation exist.

Second, the courts have interpreted section 210 [s. 459] as requiring the petitioner to show a "course of conduct" which is oppressive, and it therefore does not cover isolated acts of the corporate body. The wording of section 234 [s. 241] clearly applies to isolated acts and does not require a continuing course of conduct. [Note that s. 459 of the U.K. *Companies Act*, 1985 no longer requires a "course of conduct".]

Third, the sole criterion in the original section 210 [s. 450] was "in a manner oppressive". The Jenkins Committee felt that this was too narrow a basis for protection and that the section should be expanded to include affairs which were being conducted "in a manner unfairly prejudicial to the interests of those members". Section 234 [s. 241] incorporated these broader grounds.

Fourth, the Jenkins Committee recommended that "section 210 [s. 450] should be amended to make clear that legal personal representatives and others to whom shares are transmitted by process of law, but who are not registered as members, are entitled to present a petition or seek an injunction under that section". Section 234 [s. 241] not only incorporated this recommendation but goes considerably further. By extending the availability of the section to "complainants", the section gives discretion to the court to entertain applications by the registered or beneficial owners, present and former, the Minister's representative and "any other persons who, in the discretion of a court, is a proper person to make an application".

Fifth, the Jenkins Committee recommended that the court have an express power to restrain the continuation or commission of any act which would suffice to support a petition under section 210. Paragraph 243(3)(a) [s. 241(3)(a)] includes this as a particular power of the court: "an order restraining the conduct complained of".

Sixth, section 234 [s. 241] incorporates the recommendation that the court be given the express power to authorize the bringing of proceedings in the name of the company against a third party on such terms as the court may direct. This power must be seen as complementary to the derivative action under section 233 [now s. 240].

Note

The oppression remedies of the corporate Acts of Alberta (ABCA s. 242), Saskatchewan (SBCA s. 234), Manitoba (MCA s. 234), New Brunswick (NBBCA s. 166), Nova Scotia (NSCA Third Schedule, s. 5) and Newfoundland (NCA s. 371) are substantially similar to that of the CBCA. Ontario's s. 248 differs in that it allows the applicant to seek relief from "threatened" acts of the company, and thus has a prospective aspect. In addition, in the case of an offering corporation, the Ontario Securities Commission may apply to the court for a remedy. British Columbia's s. 227 also offers protection from threatened acts, but does not list the ground of "unfairly disregards" and is arguably narrower in scope than the other oppression remedies.

(c) Overlap Between Oppression Remedy and Fiduciary Duties

What is the distinction between conduct that constitutes a breach of a director or officer's fiduciary duty, and conduct that is oppressive, unfairly prejudicial, or that unfairly disregards (collectively referred to below simply as conduct that is "oppressive")? The answer is that there is a significant overlap between common law and statutory fiduciary duties and the oppression remedy. For example, the oppression provision explicitly makes actionable any conduct that results in the powers of the directors having been exercised in an oppressive manner. The substantive ground for invoking the oppression section is "unfairness", and this substantive trigger is almost always broader than the substantive trigger for the invocation of fiduciary duties. What this means in practice is that the courts have routinely characterized directorial conduct that is a breach of fiduciary duty as oppressive.

What if an officer who is not a director acts in breach of fiduciary duty? Although the conduct of officers is not explicitly countenanced by the oppression provision, the provision does embrace any conduct of the corporation that is oppressive. The acts of senior officers are, in effect, acts of the corporation. Thus, acts of officers that are breaches of fiduciary duty are also drawn into the oppression remedy.

It may have occurred to you that a breach of a director's or officer's fiduciary duty will normally give rise to a derivative action, since the fiduciary duty is owed to the company. What about the oppression remedy? Does it embrace derivative actions? This question is explored further below. For now it will suffice to say that, although the drafters of the oppression remedy appear to have intended that oppression actions have a personal character, most courts have allowed actions of a derivative character to go forward under the oppression remedy. This development has further confounded the action for breach of fiduciary duty and the action alleging oppression.

It is not therefore surprising that it has become common in any action alleging breach of fiduciary duty to also allege oppression. Indeed, it is probably easiest to think of the oppression remedy as simply creating an expanded fiduciary duty (keeping in mind that the oppression remedy does in fact embrace some actions that will be purely personal in character) — although for some reason the courts have shied away from characterizing the substantive duties created by the oppression remedy as fiduciary in nature. In fact, as noted above, the oppression provision was designed precisely to circumvent limitations in the common law of fiduciary duties that denied minority shareholders a remedy where it was thought just that one should be available. This makes all the more curious the courts' continuing reluctance to characterize the oppression remedy as creating duties of a fiduciary character, although one explanation for why the courts have done so is offered in Jeffrey G. MacIntosh, Janet Holmes and Steve Thompson, "The Puzzle of Shareholder Fiduciary Duties" (1991), 19 Can. Bus.

L.J. 86. MacIntosh *et al.* argue that the conservative precedent-bound Anglo-Canadian legal tradition resulted in a situation in which judges could offer minority shareholder few remedies against abuse by majority or controlling shareholders. It was widely felt, however, that the common law was excessively restrictive. The oppression remedy has served the function of allowing judges wedded to a doctrine of precedent (and hence unable without legislative intervention to subvert the old paradigm of virtually unchecked majority rule) to fashion a new definition of majority-minority relations in corporation law. If this theory is correct, then it makes some sense that the courts have continued to treat fiduciary duties and the oppression remedy as two related, but distinct legal doctrines. Confounding the oppression remedy with fiduciary duties might result in judges feeling that they could do no more under the oppression remedy than under the law of fiduciary duties. This would defeat the very reason for having an oppression remedy that is designed to allow judges to voyage into hitherto unchartered territory.

Because (i) any breach of fiduciary duty (by a director or officer, or even, as explored below, by a controlling shareholder) is almost certain to be characterized as oppression, (ii) the oppression remedy offers a broader substantive cause of action ("fairness", and no requirement that *mala fides* be shown: see *infra*) than does the law of fiduciary duties, (iii) the remedies available under the oppression remedy are broader than those available in an action for breach of fiduciary duty, (iv) the courts have allowed derivative-type actions to proceed under the oppression provision, the oppression remedy is, little by little, swallowing up the law of fiduciary duties. The danger that this creates is that the broad fairness standard for intervention under the oppression remedy creates so much judicial discretion that it undermines the comparatively greater certainty created by the law of fiduciary duties. Perhaps this danger is self-correcting; as new cases are decided under the oppression remedy, new paradigms will be fashioned and a new jurisprudence will emerge that will channel judicial decision-making much as the older fiduciary cases did. What do you think?

In any case, the important lesson to keep in mind is that the oppression provision is probably the most important innovation in corporate law in the twentieth century, and one that stands to transform the relationship between corporate directors, officers, and shareholders. Having said this, you should also keep in mind, however, that the majority of cases decided under the oppression provision involve private companies; fewer cases apply the remedy to public companies. As you read through the materials in this section, you should ask yourself whether the broad judicial discretion that is given to judges under the oppression remedy is as appropriate for public corporations as it is for private corporations.

(d) Judicial Interpretation of the Action

(i) Standing to Bring an Oppression Action

The statutory definition of "complainant" for an oppression action is the same as in an application for leave to commence a derivative action. They are both defined under s. 238 of the CBCA. The action is open to shareholders, directors and officers of the corporation, as well as those the court considers "proper persons". The next case is an important one for the meaning of "proper person" within the context of an oppression action, and the issue of whether a creditor may bring an oppression action.

First Edmonton Place Ltd. v. 315888 Alberta Ltd.
(1988), 40 B.L.R. 28, 1988 CarswellAlta 103 (Q.B.)

D.C. McDonald J.: In order to obtain leave to bring an action under either of these sections, the applicant must be found to be a "complainant" as defined in s. 231, As the applicant is clearly not within s. 231(b)(ii), First Edmonton Place can satisfy this requirement only if it can come within s. 231(b)(i) or (iii).

Is the applicant a "complainant" within the meaning of s. 231(b)(i)?

It will be recalled that s.231(b)(i) defines a "complainant" as "a registered holder or beneficial owner, or a former registered holder or beneficial owner, of a security of a corporation or any of its affiliates". On behalf of First Edmonton Place it is contended that the lease is a security of the corporation and that the lessor is the beneficial owner of the security. To repeat the definition of "security" as found in s. 1(u), that word includes a "debt obligation of a corporation and includes the certificate evidence in such a share or debt obligation". We have seen also that under s. 1(g.1) "debt obligation," is defined as meaning "a bond, debenture, note or other evidence of indebtedness or guarantee of a corporation, whether secured or unsecured". The report of the Institute of Law Research and Reform of Alberta, made the following observations concerning this definition of "complainant" (at p, 149): The definition of "complainant" in CBCA s. 231 includes a present and former registered holder of a "security" of a company or its affiliates. The definition of "security" in CBCA s. 2 includes a "debt obligation of a corporation," and ,a certificate evidencing such a . . . debt obligation." The reference to the certificate in CBCA s. 2 and the reference to a registered holder in CBCA s. 231 Probably restricts the definition of "complainant" to those creditors who are entitled to have certificates and who are to be entered in the securities register.

In my opinion, that is a correct interpretation of CBCA s. 231 and of the definition of "complainant" found in s. 231(b)(i) of the ABCA. In other words, a creditor can be a "complainant" under s. 231(b)(i) only if it holds or is the beneficial owner of a security of the corporation, and if the security is of a type which is capable of being registered under s. 88.2(2) or (5) with the Registrar of Corporations, and in the register of mortgages specifically affecting property of the corporation, which is to be kept by the corporation pursuant to s. 88.5(1). Those provisions apply, according to the definitions contained in s. 88.1 to any "mortgage", and the word "mortgage" includes a "charge", so that the provisions in s. 88.2 relating to the filing of "debentures containing any charge" require the registration of such debentures as well as mortgages. Section 88.2 thus creates a scheme for the registration of mortgages and debentures. Such written evidence of a debt obligation is in my view a certificate evidencing . . . a . . . debt obligation".

Thus, it is clear that, by reference to the clear implication on the face of s. 231(b)(i), the word "complainant" includes only the registered holders or beneficial owners of a mortgage issued by the corporation or a debenture creating a charge, issued by the corporation. It is therefore not necessary to turn to the Institute's report to justify that result, but it is nonetheless worth quoting the rationale which was given by the Institute for the inclusion of holders of debt security as complainants (at p, 150):

> the holders of debt securities are in much the same position as, and virtually indistinguishable from, the holders of non-voting preference shares, and should have similar treatment in the interests of fairness and of maintaining the attractiveness of debt securities as investments.

That rationale could, however, apply equally to lessors and to creditors who have extended credit to the corporation, for it could be argued that they too, like the holders of non-voting preference shares, should be treated fairly, and that there is an interest in encouraging the commercial liability of corporations by making it attractive to extend credit to them. Whether such a logical extension of the rationale would be justified is, however, a matter that need not be considered further because of the plain meaning of the statute.

This plain meaning reflects the meaning of "bonds, debentures and notes" in the world of corporate financing. In *Securities Law and Practice* (Vol, 1, 1984) by V.P, Alboini, bonds and debentures are stated to be the "traditional debt instruments issued by corporations" while notes are "issued by any issuer including individuals" (at pp, 0-33, 0-34).

Is the applicant a "complainant" under s. 231(b)(iii)?

Under s. 231(b)(iii), a person may be a complainant" if he is a person "who, in the discretion of the court, is a proper person to make an application under this Part".

This is not so much a definition as a grant to the court of a broad power to do justice and equity in the circumstances of a particular case, where a person, who otherwise would not be a "complainant", ought to be permitted to bring an action under either s. 232 or s. 234 to right a wrong done to the corporation which would not otherwise be righted, or to obtain compensation himself or itself where his or its interests have suffered from oppression by the majority controlling the corporation or have been unfairly prejudiced or unfairly disregarded, and the applicant is a "security holder, creditor, director or officer".

The report of the Institute of Law Research and Reform of Alberta had some reservations about the inclusion of such a broad power to permit a person to complain. It is stated, at p. 150: "We have some reservations about legislation which confers broad statutory discretions without guidelines". Here, however, we think such a discretion appropriate. The specific listed classes appear to us to cover all cases in which the derivative and personal remedies should be available, but foresight is necessarily imperfect, and the general discretion would allow the courts to make up for the imperfections of foresight. We think also that the courts can be relied upon to allow only proper applications. Section 231(b)(iv) of the *Draft Act* therefore follows CBCA s. 231(d).

(It should be noted that what was s. 231(b)(iv) in the *Draft Act* became s. 231(b)(iii) in the ABCA.) The Institute's report thus recommended that the question of who is a "proper person" be left to the discretion of the court. Even accepting that the s. 232 and s. 234 remedies should be given a liberal interpretation, the circumstances in which a person who is not a security holder (as I have interpreted that phrase), or a director or officer should be recognized as a proper person to make an application must show that justice and equity clearly dictate such a result.

In the case of a creditor who claims to be a "proper person," to make a s. 232 application, in my view the criterion to be applied would be whether, even if the applicant did not come within s. 231(b)(i) or (ii), he or it would nevertheless be a person who could reasonably be entrusted with the responsibility of advancing the interests of the corporation by seeking a remedy to right the wrong allegedly done to the corporation. The applicant would not have to be a security holder (as I have defined that notion), director or officer of the corporation. The applicant could be a creditor. The applicant might even be a person who at the time of the act or conduct complained of was not a creditor but was a person toward whom the corporation might have a contingent liability. No good purpose would be served in saying more than that now.

I turn now to an application by a person who claims to be a "proper person" to make an application under s. 234, As in the case of an application made under s. 232, an applicant for leave to bring an action under s. 234 does not have to be a security holder, director or officer. The applicant could be a creditor, or even a person toward whom the corporation had only a contingent liability at the time of the act or conduct complained of. However, it is important to note that he would not be held to be a "proper person" to make the application under s. 234 unless he satisfied the court that there was some evidence of oppression or unfair prejudice or unfair disregard for the interests of a security holder, creditor, director or officer.

Having said that, assuming that the applicant was a creditor of the corporation at the time of the act or conduct complained of, what criterion should be applied in determining whether the applicant is, a "proper person" to make the application? Once again, in my view, the applicant must show that in the circumstances of the case justice and equity require him or it to be given an opportunity to have the claim tried.

There are two circumstances in which justice and equity would entitle a creditor to be regarded as "a proper person", (There may be other circumstances; these two are not intended to exhaust the possibilities.) The first is if the act or conduct of the directors or management of the corporation, which is complained of, constituted using the corporation as a vehicle for committing a fraud upon the applicant. (In the present case there is no evidence suggesting such fraud, although there is some evidence of the directors having used the money paid as a cash inducement for their own personal investment purposes, and that, as I shall later explain, may constitute fraud against the corporation: see *infra* where *R. v. Olan, Hudson and Hartnett* is cited.)

Second, the court might hold that the applicant is a "proper person to make an application," for an order under s, 234 if the act or conduct of the directors or management of the corporation, which is complained of, constituted a breach of the underlying expectation of the applicant arising from the circumstances in which the applicant's relationship, with the corporation arose. For example, where the applicant is a creditor of the corporation, did the circumstances, which gave rise to the granting of credit, include some element which prevented the creditor from taking adequate steps when he or it entered into the agreement, to protect his or its interests against the occurrence of which he or it now complains? Did the creditor entertain an expectation that, assuming fair dealing, its chances of repayment would not be frustrated by the kind of conduct which subsequently was engaged in by the management of the corporation? Assuming that the evidence established the existence of such an expectation, the next question would be whether that expectation was, objectively, a reasonable one . . .

In the case of the application under s. 234, leave to bring an action in regard to either claim is denied because the applicant was not a creditor at the time of the act or conduct complained of.

Notes

1 Professors Ben-Ishai and Puri's empirical study of the oppression remedy in Canada found that while the remedy's wording suggests that it is not exclusively for shareholders, shareholders constituted the largest class of complainants, accounting for 80% of all complainants, with a 53% success rate. Creditors accounted for only 8% of all complainants in Professors Ben-Ishai and Puri's study but had a tremendously high success rate of 83%. Given the high rate of success for actions that were brought by creditors, combined with recent jurisprudence and com-

mentary and the current economic climate, Professors Puri and Ben-Ishai predict that of all non-shareholder complainants, we will see more claims and a higher success rate for creditors against both widely held and closely held corporations. See Stephanie Ben-Ishai and Poonam Puri, "The Canadian Oppression Remedy Judicially Considered: 1995–2001", (2004) 30:1 Queen's Law Review (forthcoming).

In the trial decision of *Peoples Department Stores Inc. v. Wise*, (1998), 23 C.B.R. (4th) 2000 (Que. S.C.), Justice Greenberg held that because only creditors have a meaningful stake in the assets of an insolvent corporation, directors have an obligation to ensure that an insolvent corporation is properly administered and its assets are not dissipated in a manner that is prejudicial to the creditors. Justice Pelletier, writing for the Quebec Court of Appeal, overturned Justice Greenberg's decision holding that "by importing this theory into Canadian law the trial judge was usurping the intervention role of the legislator by establishing a general regime for liability of directors favouring third parties who find themselves prejudiced by the management acts of directors . . .". See (2003), 41 C.B.R. (4th) 225. Leave to appeal from the Quebec Court of Appeal's decision has been granted to the Supreme Court of Canada ([2003] S.C.C.A. No. 133).

Following the lower court decision in *Peoples*, many commentators were swift in pointing out the difficulties of extending a fiduciary duty to creditors and expressed a preference for the development of the oppression remedy to deal with the treatment of creditor stakeholders: see, for example, Edward A. Sellers, Natasha J. MacParland and F. James Hoffner, "Governance of the Financially Distressed Corporation in Global Capital Markets: Selected Aspects of the Financing and Governance of Canadian Enterprises in Cross-Border Workouts" in Janis Sarra, Ed., *Corporate Governance in Global Capital Markets* (Vancouver: UBC Press, 2003) 297 at 307. See also Edward M. Iacobucci and Kevin E. Davis, "Reconciling Derivative Claims and the Oppression Remedy" (2000) 12 Sup. Ct. L. Rev. (2d) 86.
How should the Supreme Court of Canada address the issues raised by the *Peoples* case?

2 Is a wrongfully dismissed employee a proper person to bring an oppression action? If, for example, an employee-shareholder is dismissed, the oppression remedy may be available if the loss of employment is intrinsically linked to his or her status as a shareholder. See *Naneff v. Con-Crete Holdings Ltd.* (1993), 11 B.L.R. (2d) 218, 1993 CarswellOnt 157 (Gen. Div. [Commercial List]), varied (1994), 19 O.R. (3d) 691, reversed (1995), 23 O.R. (3d) 481, 1995 CarswellOnt 1207 (C.A.); *Flatley v. Algy Corp.* (2000), [2000] O.J. No. 3787, 2000 CarswellOnt 3734 (S.C.J. [Commercial List]); and *Krynen v. Bugg* (2003), 2003

CarswellOnt 1138 (S.C.J.). Free-standing employees have not been successful in bringing oppression actions. Why do you think that is? See Stephanie Ben-Ishai and Poonam Puri, "The Canadian Oppression Remedy Judicially Considered: 1995–2001", (2004), 30:1 Queen's Law Review (forthcoming).

3 Other applicants who have been deemed "proper persons" to bring an oppression action include the widow of a deceased shareholder (see *Lenstra v. Lenstra* (1995), 1995 CarswellOnt 2678 (Gen. Div.)), a trustee in bankruptcy (see *Olympia & York Developments Ltd. (Trustee of) v. Olympia & York Realty Corp.*, [2001] O.T.C. 646, 2001 CarswellOnt 2954 (S.C.J. [Commercial List]), additional reasons at (2001), 2001 CarswellOnt 4739 (S.C.J. [Commercial List]) and a custodian of funds set up for immigrant investors (see *HSBC Capital Canada Inc. v. First Mortgage Alberta Fund (V) Inc.* (1999), 47 B.L.R. (2d) 180, 1999 CarswellAlta 458 (Q.B.)). Also of interest is *Gainers Inc. v. Pocklington* (1992), 7 B.L.R. (2d) 87, 1992 CarswellAlta 277 (Q.B.), in which the court held that in special circumstances the corporation itself may be a proper person to bring an oppression action. Finally, some cases have held that an applicant need not have actually been affected by the alleged oppression to have standing, but may have standing in the interests of righting a wrong done to others. When might this be the case? See *PMSM Investments Ltd. v. Bureau* (1995), 24 B.L.R. (2d) 295, 1995 CarswellOnt 1394 (Gen. Div. [Commercial List]); and *Joncas v. Spruce Falls Power & Paper Co.*, [2000] O.T.C. 339, 6 B.L.R. (3d) 109, 2000 CarswellOnt 1689 (S.C.J.), affirmed by 15 B.L.R. (3d) 1 (O.C.A.).

4 As a practical matter, why might an aggrieved party who is not a shareholder prefer commencing an oppression action over an ordinary civil claim? Professors Ben-Ishai and Puri suggest that from the litigation strategy perspective of an advocate initiating an action, the oppression remedy may be preferable to the ordinary civil action for three reasons. First, the oppression remedy may be commenced by way of application, without pleadings or discovery, and as a result it may proceed more quickly if there are no significant factual issues in dispute. Second, the relief that a court can provide under the oppression remedy is broader and more flexible than can be provided under an ordinary civil action. Third, the blurry state of Canadian law on the nature and type of fiduciary duties owed to non-shareholder stakeholders has created the need for an alternative flexible remedial option. See S. Ben-Ishai and P. Puri, "The Canadian Oppression Remedy Judicially Considered: 1995–2001)", (2004), 30:1 Queen's Law Review (forthcoming).

5 As a matter of corporate law theory, should non-shareholder stakeholders who may have recourse against the corporation under common law, statutory and/or contract law remedies be allowed to utilize the oppression action? What implications does an expansionary interpretation of the definition of "complainant" have for the purposes for which a corporation is said to exist?

(ii) The Substantive Scope of the Oppression Action

Note

The English Act of 1948 that introduced the oppression remedy to Anglo-Canadian jurisprudence made actionable corporate conduct that was "oppressive". Thus, in defining the substantive scope of the oppression remedy, the early English jurisprudence dealt solely with the meaning of "oppressive" conduct, rather than the broader formulation found in the CBCA and OBCA. The word "oppression" has a common law lineage that predates the oppression remedy; see, *e.g.*, *Northwest Transportation Company, Limited v. Beatty*. However, what was "oppressive" or a "fraud on the minority" at common law was essentially restricted to takings of property or other clearly egregious interferences with minority shareholder rights or expectations. See Beck, "The Shareholders' Derivative Action", *supra*, this chapter. The English courts accorded the statutory concept of "oppression" a much wider ambit than at common law. Two definitions are widely cited. In *Elder v. Elder & Watson Ltd.*, [1952] S.C. 49, Lord Cooper said that "the essence of the matter seems to be that the conduct complained of should at the lowest involve a visible departure from the standards of the fair dealing and a violation of the conditions of fair play on which every shareholder who entrusts his money to a company is entitled to rely." In *Scottish Co-operative Wholesale Society Ltd. v. Meyer*, [1959] A.C. 324, [1958] 3 All E.R. 66 (H.L.), a number of the judgments considered the meaning of "oppressive" conduct. Lord Simmonds adopted the dictionary meaning of "burdensome, harsh and wrongful" and the outcome of the case indicates that "wrongful" includes conduct that falls short of actual illegality or invasion of legal rights but that can nonetheless be described as reprehensible.

In the CBCA and the OBCA, the oppression remedy is triggered not only by actions that are "oppressive", but also by any action that is "unfairly prejudicial or that unfairly disregards the interests of any security holder, creditor, director or officer". As can be seen from the following cases, the Canadian courts have used this expanded definition to widen the scope of conduct covered by the original English provision, moving towards a broadly based definition of "fairness" as the substantive standard. The first case, *Ferguson v. Imax*, is also helpful in exploring the relationship between the oppression remedy and the common law of fiduciary duties.

Ferguson v. Imax Systems Corp.

(1983), 150 D.L.R. (3d) 718, 1983 CarswellOnt 926 (C.A.), leave to
appeal refused (1983), 2 O.A.C. 158 (note), 52 N.R. 317 (note) (S.C.C.)

[Imax Systems Corp. was incorporated to exploit a film projection system.
The founding shareholders were the appellant, her then-husband, and two
other couples. Upon incorporation the husbands each received seven hundred shares of the common shares of the company, while the wives each
received 700 shares of the class B shares. The class B shares were non-
voting and paid a dividend of five cents per share in priority to the common
shares, sharing equally in dividends and liquidation thereafter. The appellant
had knowledge of the film business and participated in the management and
administration of the company. Following Ferguson's separation and subsequent divorce, the company, acting under pressure from her ex-husband,
tried to squeeze her out. She was discharged by Imax, and the company
refused to declare dividends beyond those required by the class B shares.
The company also proposed to cancel and convert all class B shares to non-
voting, limited-dividend shares. Ferguson sought relief under s. 234 of the
CBCA alleging that the company and its directors were acting in a manner
that was oppressive, unfairly prejudicial, or that unfairly disregarded her
interests as a security holder.]

BROOKE J.A.: . . . The policy of the law to ensure just and equitable
treatment of minorities can be traced back to early cases. In *Allen v. Gold
Reefs of West Africa, Ltd.*, [1900] 1 Ch. 656 at p. 671, Lindley M.R.,
speaking of the powers of a corporation to amend its articles, said:

> it must, like all other powers, be exercised subject to those general
> principles of law and equity which are applicable to all powers con-
> ferred on majorities and enabling them to bind minorities. It must be
> exercised, not only in the manner required by law, but also *bona fide*
> for the benefit of the company as a whole, and it must not be exceeded.

In *Goldex Mines Ltd. v. Revill et al.* (1974), 7 O.R. (2d) 216 at p. 224,
54 D.L.R. (3d) 672 at p. 680, Arnup J.A. for this court, after considering
the earlier cases, said:

> The principle that the majority governs in corporate affairs is
> fundamental to corporation law, but its corollary is also important —
> that the majority must act fairly and honestly. Fairness is the touchstone
> of equitable justice and when the test of fairness is not met, the equitable
> jurisdiction of the court can be invoked to prevent or remedy the
> injustice which misrepresentation or other dishonesty has caused.

But s. 234 must not be regarded as being simply a codification of the
common law. Today one looks to the section when considering the interests

of the minority shareholders and the section should be interpreted broadly to carry out its purpose: see the *Interpretation Act*, R.S.C. 1970, c. I-23, s. 11. Accordingly, when dealing with a close corporation, the court may consider the relationship between the shareholders and not simply legal rights as such. In addition, the court must consider the *bona fides* of the corporate transaction in question to determine whether the act of the corporation or directors effects a result which is oppressive or unfairly prejudicial to the minority shareholder. Counsel has referred us to a number of decisions. They establish primarily that each case turns on its own facts. What is oppressive or unfairly prejudicial in one case may not necessarily be so in the slightly different setting of another.

Here we have a small close corporation that was promoted and is still controlled by the same small related group of individuals. The appellant's part in that group and her work for the corporation is important. Further, the attempt to force her to sell her shares through non-payment of dividends was not simply the act of Mr. Ferguson, but was also the act of the others in the group including the present director, in concert with him. Having regard to the intention of that group to deny the appellant any participation in the growth of the company I think the resolution authorizing the change in the capital of the company is the culminating event in a lengthy course of oppressive and unfairly prejudicial conduct to the appellant. In my opinion the company has not acted *bona fides* in exercising its powers to amend. By the payment of moneys now as a capital payment, which moneys on the evidence ought to have been by way of dividends over the years the appellant's non-redeemable shares are now to be redeemed and those in control of the company will be rid of her. She is the only one so affected. All of the other class B shareholders hold an equal number of common shares personally or through their spouses. The appellant cannot be considered like someone who came to the company lately and took a minority position in one of several classes of stock. Like the Kroiters and the Kerrs, her investment must be regarded as being in the shares which she and her husband held. The agreements as to the disposition of family shares in the event of the death of the husband or the wife confirm that this was really a family venture not only in the case of the Fergusons, but for each of the three couples.

Viewed in this way, and as all of the other class B shareholders held an equal number of common shares either personally or with their spouses, it is idle to suggest that the vote on the resolution would be anything other than a means to get moneys which they had eagerly sought by way of dividends but were denied because of the appellant's presence and as a means to end her presence as an obstacle to further payment. I doubt if any corporate purpose would enter the minds of the class B shareholders when the resolution was put to them to vote on. The resolution was a final solution to the problem of the ex-wife shareholder.

In my opinion the appellant satisfied the onus upon her when relying on s. 234 of the Act and she was entitled to the relief sought in the first instance. We have been advised that a motion to prohibit the company from proceeding with the meeting of shareholders to vote on the resolution was dismissed by Holland J. and accordingly the vote was held and its outcome was as predicted. In the circumstances the appeal is allowed. The order of Hollingworth J. dismissing the appellant's claim and appointing an assessor pursuant to s. 184(4) of the Act is set aside and an order will go forever prohibiting the company from implementing the resolution.

The appellant will have her costs in this court and in all of the proceedings below.

Appeal allowed.

Note

Reread *Ebrahimi v. Westbourne Galleries Ltd.* (1972), [1972] 2 All E.R. 492, [1973] A.C. 360 (H.L.), which is is set out in Chapter 7, *supra*. It is not, in fact, an oppression case at all. It arises pursuant to a motion to wind up the corporation, on the ground that it is "just and equitable" to do so (such actions are dealt with, *infra*, this chapter). And indeed, you will notice that Lord Wilberforce is careful to confine the scope of the decision to actions seeking a winding up on the just and equitable ground. Why is the decision important to consider in the context of the oppression remedy? The answer is that the Canadian courts have ignored Lord Wilberforce's attempt to confine the scope of the "equitable rights" enunciated in the case. There are now literally scores of cases applying the concept of equitable rights in the context of suits arising under the oppression remedy. In other words, *Ebrahimi* has had a huge impact on the way in which the Canadian courts have applied the oppression remedy.

Ebrahimi is arguably one of the most important company law cases decided in the twentieth century. It evinces an attitude to resolving corporate disputes that is very different from prior cases. Instead of confining minority interests to the rights they had explicitly "contracted" for (whether pursuant to the articles, by-laws, or any shareholder agreement), *Ebrahimi* indicates that shareholder expectations may be a source of rights as well. This greatly broadens the grounds upon which a disgruntled minority may challenge the actions of majority or controlling shareholders.

One of the first cases in which a Canadian judge called upon Lord Wilberforce's "equitable rights" to resolve an oppression suit was *Diligenti v. RWMD Operations Kelowna Ltd.* (1976), 1 B.C.L.R. 36, 1976 CarswellBC 3 (S.C.). In *Diligenti*, Diligenti was one of four "partners" (owning equal 25% shareholdings) in a business that was formed to operate a Keg and Cleaver restaurant in Kelowna; they latter acquired a second franchise in Prince George. As in *Ebrahimi*, Diligenti was entitled to remuneration for his managerial duties; he claimed to have done the main work in obtaining the franchises and getting them going. Disagreements arose between the shareholders and Diligenti was ousted from management. He was removed as a manager and also, at a shareholders' meeting, as a director. The other three shareholders then formed a management company and charged the restaurants a 2 1/2% management fee for managing the business. Diligenti sued under the oppression remedy in the B.C. legislation, which created a cause of action in relation both to conduct that is "oppressive" and to conduct that is "unfairly prejudicial". While Diligenti alleged oppressive acts other than his removal from management, the court dealt mainly with the issue of his ouster from management. The court held that "unfairly prejudicial" is broader in its meaning than that which is "oppressive". Conduct that is oppressive would include only an interference with the strict legal rights of the petitioner. However, the "unfairly prejudicial" ground allows the court to import Lord Wilberforce's notion of equitable rights into the oppression remedy and thus to inquire into whether the petitioner's equitable rights have been violated. On the facts, the court held that Diligenti's equitable rights had indeed been interfered with in his removal as a director, and that this constituted unfair prejudice. In the course of his judgment, Fulton J. stated that:

> On the face of it it would appear to me that, particularly in a company of the nature of those involved here — private companies, closely held, formed to take over the operations of four individuals who have been equal founders and proprietors of a venture and in which companies each of the four holds the same number of shares — each of its members has a very real interest and concern in the management of the affairs of the company.

However, it was Diligenti's removal as a director, rather than simply as a manager, which constituted the unfair prejudice:

> I am referring here to management generally in the sense that management of the affairs of the company is in the hands of the directors and policy decisions and general business decisions affecting the future of the companies are made by them, as distinct from a particular managerial position to which a director — or a member — may be appointed. In my view, as such shareholder he would have a very real interest in being and remaining a director so as to have a voice and a vote in the shaping of the policies and the general business decisions which the board, in its over-all responsibilities, will make on behalf of the company. This is not solely a matter of protection of his interest in the narrow sense — for being one of four he can always be out-voted: it is a matter of whether or not he has a right, in the circumstances, to the opportunity for a continued voice and vote in shaping policies.

Importantly, there was no explicit agreement for all the shareholders to participate in management. Indeed, there was no longstanding partnership between the shareholders (one of the facts referred to by Lord Wilberforce in *Ebrahimi* as giving rise equitable rights). Fulton J. was prepared to infer the existence of an agreement to participate in management from the circumstances of the partnership and the nature of the relationship between the parties:

> [I]t is clear from the material I have reviewed that the whole concept commenced on a joint venture-partnership basis, with each of the four partners sharing equally in the continuing management and direction of affairs. This is borne out by the fact that the properties in question where the operations were to be carried on were acquired in the names of the four partners jointly, and that the shares in the companies formed to take over the operations were held in equal proportions, and that each of the partners became a director of those companies.

Thus, his removal as a director constituted unfair prejudice:

> First, in circumstances such as exist here there are "rights, expectations and obligations *inter se*" which are not submerged in the company structure, and these rights are enjoyed by a member as part of his status as a shareholder in the company which has been formed to carry on the enterprise: amongst these rights are the rights to continue to participate in the direction of that company's affairs. Second, although his fellow members may be entitled as a matter of strict law to remove him as a director, for them to do so in fact is unjust and inequitable, and is a breach of equitable rights which he in fact possesses as a member. And third, although such breach may not "oppress" him in respect of his proprietary rights as a shareholder, such unjust and inequitable denial of his rights and expectations is undoubtedly "unfairly prejudicial" to him in his status as member.

Fulton J. also held that complaints of diversion of profits might also fit within the oppression provision:

> [T]here is evidence that substantial sums were and are still being so diverted to a company owned by the three majority shareholders, and in my view in the circumstances here — the exclusion of the applicant from all enjoyment of such moneys and the diversion of them to those three shareholders — there is thus *prima facie* evidence of an act at least unfairly prejudicial to the applicant, if not indeed of conduct oppressive to him.

The end result of the case was to refuse a motion to dismiss for failure to state a cause of action.

The concept of reasonable expectations has been extremely important to the judicial consideration of the oppression remedy. The next case deals with this concept.

Westfair Foods Ltd. v. Watt
(1991), 79 D.L.R. (4th) 48, 1991 CarswellAlta 63 (C.A.)

[The appellant was a public corporation that had two classes of shares. The class A shares carried a $2 dividend in priority to the common shares, and all dividends beyond those going to the class A shares went to the common shares. In the event of liquidation, the class A shares shared equally with the common shares. The corporation had a long-standing policy of paying a regular dividend to its shareholders while retaining much of its earnings. In 1985 the corporation adopted a policy of distributing its net annual earnings as dividends. At trial the new policy was found to be oppressive to holders of class A shares, who had an interest in retained earnings. It was also found to be oppressive on the basis of procedural shortcomings surrounding the change in policy. The trial judge ordered that the corporation purchase the class A shares.]

KERANS J.A.: I turn then to the substantial rights conferred by the provision. Obviously, they turn on effect not intent. Equally obviously, they govern all the activities of the corporation. The rights conferred upon shareholders are that they, at any time and in any way during their relationship with the company, are to be insulated from anything oppressive, unfairly prejudicial, or that unfairly disregards their interests. For the relations among shareholders, this is a major modification of majority rule.

In my view, the provisions were and remain a compendious way for Parliament to say to the courts that the classes mentioned in the Act are to be treated fairly in the sense of justly by corporations. For example, both parties cite and rely on *Ebrahimi v. Westbourne Galleries*, [1973] A.C. 360. Lord Wilberforce there said at p. 379:

> [T]here is room in company law for recognition of the fact that behind it, or amongst it, there are individuals with rights, expectations and obligations *inter se* which are not necessarily submerged in the company structure.

I agree with a similar sentiment by McDonald J. in *First Edmonton Place v. 315888 Alberta Ltd.* (1988), 40 B.L.R. 28 at pp. 59-60, 60 Alta. L.R. (2d) 122, 10 A.C.W.S. (3d) 268 (Q.B.).

I cannot put elastic adjectives like "unfair", "oppressive", or "prejudicial" into watertight compartments. In my view, this repetition of overlapping ideas is only an expression of anxiety by Parliament that one or the other might be given a restrictive meaning. I am grateful for the history in the *First Edmonton Place* case. Recent changes adding words like "unfairly disregard" reflect just that concern: see Dickerson *et al.*, *Proposals for a New Business Corporations Law for Canada* (Ottawa: Information Canada, 1971), p. 163, where the mischief was reported to be:

the self-imposed judicial qualifications that have limited the application. . . . and. . . . cast considerable doubt upon the effectiveness of the
original provisions.

The irony is that too much repetition encourages rather than eliminates
narrowing arguments. For example, in Peterson, *Shareholder Remedies in
Canada* (Butterworths, 1989), para. 18.60, the author contends that "unfairly
disregards" implies that some "disregarding" is fair! I reject that kind of
parsing. The original words, like the new additions, command the courts to
exercise their duty "broadly and liberally", as this court has already said
about the nearly identical Alberta law in *Keho Holdings Ltd. v. Noble* (1987),
38 D.L.R. (4th) 368, 52 Alta. L.R. (2d) 195, 78 A.R. 131 (C.A.).

Having concluded that the words charge the courts to impose the
obligation of fairness on the parties, I must admit that the admonition offers
little guidance to the public, and Parliament has left elucidation to us. I have
elsewhere said that I take this sort of indirection as legislative delegation:
see *Transalta Utilities Corp. v. Alberta Public Utilities Board* (1986), 43
Alta. L.R. (2d) 171 at p. 180, 68 A.R. 171, 36 A.C.W.S. (2d) 376 (C.A.).

We fail in that duty of elucidation, I think, if we merely say "this is
fair" or "that is not fair" without ever explaining why we think this or that
is fair. Thus I, and I dare say others, am not much helped by cases and
comments that simply announce that I am to enforce "fair play" or "fair
dealing": see, for example, Dickerson, *op. cit.*, para. 48.

On the other hand, I do not understand that the delegation of this duty
permits a judge to impose personal standards of fairness. Let me illustrate
what is probably obvious by two extreme examples. A judge who firmly
believes in the virtues of unrestricted private enterprise might say that
fairness requires that people protect themselves to their best capacity and
that the courts not protect those who fail to protect themselves. On the other
hand, a judge who firmly believes that private property is a trust held for
the benefit of society as a whole might say that what is fair is what best
benefits society.

The role of a judge in our society limits the impulses of both my
mythical judges. We must not make rules unless we can tie them to values
that seem to have gained wide acceptance. We do that largely by testing
any proposed rule against other legal rules, which by long tradition seem
accepted. In short, we seek precedent, or we seek to argue from what we
consider to be principles adopted in precedent. So, in *Keho*, this court relied
upon precedent in other situations where courts were asked to decide what
was "just and equitable".

I will not attempt to catalogue all the rules generated by the words in
the statute. For example, the courts have imposed the duty on directors to
protect the interests of all shareholders, not just those who elect them. I will
later deal with that rule. The authorities also impose upon the majority
interest the obligation not to use their electoral power to profit themselves
at the expense of minority shareholders. The principal complaint here does

not engage that rule. The complaint is not by a minority who has been outvoted. It is by an entire class of shares in competition with another class of shares.

It is said for the shareholders that yet another rule exists. This is that the directors must have due regard for, and deal fairly with, the "interests" of all shareholders. I have concern about over-use of the word interests. This example serves to express it: a thief is very interested in my watch, and will get it if he can. A law about fairness will not, however, show any respect for his interest. The real question is whether the law should accept his obvious interest in financial gain as, in all the circumstances, one that deserves protection. I do not accept that all ambition to acquire property deserves protection. I do accept that our tradition is that a hope for profit, as opposed to a mere desire, sometimes deserves protection.

One deserving case is where the person to whom the profit will go has nourished that hope. The company and the shareholders entered voluntarily, not by duty or chance, into a relationship. Our guides are the rules in other contexts, such as contract law, equity, and partnership law, where the courts have also considered just rules to govern voluntary relationships. In very general terms, one clear principle that emerges is that we regulate voluntary relationships by regard to the expectations raised in the mind of a party by the word or deed of the other, and which the first party ordinarily would realize it was encouraging by its words and deeds. This is what we call reasonable expectations, or expectations deserving of protection. Regard for them is a constant theme, albeit variously expressed, running through the cases on this section or its like elsewhere. I emphasize that all the words and deeds of the parties are relevant to an assessment of reasonable expectations, not necessarily only those consigned to paper, and not necessarily only those made when the relationship first arose.

I do not for a moment suggest that that analysis about expectations deserving protection is the sole basis for rules under the statute. I think, for example, of totally unforeseen windfalls or calamities. This is not such a case, but I dare say that even in those cases the expectations of the parties are a sound starting point. And the test will always be helpful in cases where mere interests collide.

The test then is always facts-specific, and cases decided on other facts offer only a limited guide. Unfortunately, no other reported case offers the same facts as this. The closest is *International Power Co. v. McMaster University*, [1946] 2 D.L.R. 81, [1946] S.C.R. 178, 27 C.B.R. 75. That case is about the distribution of a surplus from the winding-up of a company. Even after reimbursement of the par value of both common and preferred shares, a large surplus remained. The court decided that the by-laws, properly interpreted, awarded that exclusively to the common shares. No "fairness" rule was invoked, but the court strayed into those areas. In a dissent, the Chief Justice proposed that both classes share equally after an adjustment for the capitalized value of preferential dividends. In response, Kerwin J., for the majority, quoted this statement from *Will v. United Lanket Planta-tions*, [1914] A.C. 11 (H.L.), at p. 19:

> [T]he people who took the preference shares . . . knew perfectly well that they were taking shares with a preferential dividend of 10 per cent. I think they would have been rather surprised, although no doubt they would have been gratified, if they had been told that they are about to receive the almost boundless additional advantages which have been held out to them in the arguments we have been hearing.

During argument before us, both parties dwelt at length with two US cases: *Burton v. Exxon Corp.*, 583 F. Supp. 405 (1984) (U.S.D.C.), and *Jedwab v. MGM Grand Hotels Inc.*, 509 A. 2d 584 (1986) (Delaware Chancery Court). Both are trial level decisions. Both consider and apply the rule earlier established in *Sinclair Oil Corp. v. Levien*, 280 A.2d 717 (1971) (Del. Supr.), that decisions by the board of directors about matters of conflict between shareholders may, if the board is dominated by one party to the conflict, be vacated unless the board shows that the decision was "inherently fair".

In *Burton*, the court pronounced upon the distribution as dividends of funds suddenly available to a moribund company that had operated in Hungary, but had been caught first by World War II and then by the Iron Curtain. In a slight twist on this case, the controlling interests caused the entire amount to be paid on outstanding and unpaid dividends to one class of shares, the first preferred shares, which were held by them. The holders of second preferred shares protested that this was unfair because the funds could be reinvested, and some day produce a return to all shareholders. The court disagreed, saying that the result "may be unfortunate" (p. 418) but not unfair. I do not find either the decision or the discussion very helpful.

In *Jedwab* the common shareholders proposed a corporate merger that would convert all the assets of the corporation to cash and distribute them. The preferred shares protested that the distribution proposal was unfair, and sought interim injunctive relief. On the application the judge had to assess the chance of success. This turned in part on whether there was an arguable conflict and in part on what possible claims a preferred share might make. On that latter point, he concluded that the relations between classes of shares were "essentially contractual" but the right of equal distribution raised "may be measured by equitable as well as legal standards" (p. 594). I do not disagree with either statement, but find neither of much help.

I conclude that what is appropriate in this case is to assess the facts found by the learned Chief Justice on the scales of "reasonable expectations" to see if that offers a fair solution. In my view, it does but not one of assistance to the shareholders here on the principal issue.

The learned Chief Justice held that the new dividend policy [48 B.L.R. at p. 75]:

already diminishes the value of the Class A Shares in relation to the common shares and alters the relationship between them in the marketplace. There can be little doubt that this unfairly prejudices the interests of the class A shareholders who purchased the shares with the expectation that they would share in the business success or failure of the corporation.

Moreover, he observed sternly that the company did not take a broad view of the issue [at p. 78]:

> Throughout these proceedings, counsel for Westfair made no argument with respect to the interests of the class A shareholders, relying solely on a definition and interpretation of their rights as expressed in the shareholders agreement of 1946. Repeatedly, in written argument, the language of rights, not interests, is utilized, further reinforcing this impression. On the basis of the evidence presented before me, I am satisfied that the directors of Westfair and, specifically the sole common shareholder, Kelly Douglas, relied upon the narrowest definition of the rights of the class A shareholders to achieve, by means of the trailing dividend and borrowing policies, what they were unable to achieve with the consent of the class A shareholders in the 1980 proxy resolution.

If it did not do so before, the company through its counsel certainly took a different view before us. It accepted that the current law requires a company to respect both rights and interests. But, it contended that respect for the interests of both common and preferred shareholders produces the same result here as would having regard merely for their rights. The need for fairness to both remains, and can only be resolved fairly by the traditional means.

My disagreement with the learned Chief Justice, while of great significance, can be simply stated. In the passage quoted, he said that the right to share in distribution of the assets on liquidation created an expectation by class A shareholders that they would share in the "success or failure" of the company. In my view, any expectation that they would share in the future success (as opposed to failure) of the company in a measure beyond the dividend promised them was not a reasonable expectation . . .

Counsel also said that the board of directors of the company, even if it did not make a decision adverse to the legitimate interests of the shareholders, did not adequately address the issue. The submissions were that they did not consult or inform the shareholders, did not arrange independent review, did not do a careful study, and did not even address their minds to the position of the shareholders. These were what Mr. Haigh called "procedural" complaints, as opposed to the "substantial" complaint about the new dividend policy.

The burden of the argument is that, if they correctly decided the "substantial" issue as I have held they did, they did so from good luck, not good and fair management. In fairness to them, I should add that the directors did take counsel on that point.

The shareholders complained that the directors also paid them insufficient heed in other respects. It must have been particularly galling to see the auditors describe the company in the financial statements as a "wholly owned subsidiary", thus expunging the shareholders from the face of the globe with the stroke of an accountant's pen. Like the learned Chief Justice, I am not impressed with the explanation that the reference is about control, not ownership. A non-fact remains so whatever an accountant says. But I cannot see what harm this did, other than to give understandable offence.

Other examples exist. The Toronto Stock Exchange wrote to the company to propose a de-listing of the class A shares. The company did not even trouble to respond to the letter. I cannot, with respect, raise this event to class higher than insensitivity. The number of outstanding class A shares falls well below the latest TSX standards. When this court proposed an injunction to use best efforts to relist, Mr. Crawford expressed no interest, and one reason was that there was no hope of success.

I acknowledge that the learned Chief Justice judged some "procedural" complaints as well-founded. I will accept that the company viewed the shareholders as a nuisance. No doubt the failure of the management to agree with the shareholders about retained earnings is the main reason for a loss of confidence, but other events exacerbated this. These other matters exemplify an unfair disregard for the shareholders.

Also, forced purchase is an appropriate remedy. No doubt it would be best for all if the shares were to be sold. I therefore would let the order of the learned Chief Justice stand.

Appeal Dismissed

Notes

1 For an exhaustive summary of the role of reasonable expectations in the oppression remedy, see *820099 Ontario Inc. v. Harold E. Ballard Ltd.* (1991), 3 B.L.R. (2d) 113, 1991 CarswellOnt 141 (Div. Ct.). See also *Naneff v. Con-Crete Holdings Ltd.* (1993), 11 B.L.R. (2d) 218, 1993 CarswellOnt 157 (Gen. Div. [Commercial List]), reversed (1995), 23 O.R. (3d) 481, 1995 CarswellOnt 1207 (C.A.); and *C.I. Covington Fund Inc. v. White* (2000), 10 C.P.R. (4th) 49, 2000 CarswellOnt 4680 (S.C.J.), affirmed (2001), 15 C.P.R. (4th) 144, 2001 CarswellOnt 3527.

2 The English House of Lords has recently reviewed the role of reasonable expectations, referred to as "legitimate expectations", in the oppression remedy. See *O'Neill v. Phillips*, [1999] 1 W.L.R. 1092, [1999] 2 All E.R. 961 (H.L.). The court advocated using two ways to define the

scope of legitimate expectations. The first is to base intervention in company affairs on equitable principles that have evolved from the law of partnership. The second is to interpret the contract between the parties in light of their real intentions, including promises that arose later in the relationship. How different is this equity/contract approach from the approach of the Canadian courts?

(iii) Does the Oppression Remedy Require a Showing of Bad Faith?

A very important issue arising under the oppression provision is whether success requires a showing that the defendant acted without *bona fides*. Are bad intentions essential, or can a court find that well-intentioned conduct is nonetheless actionable if it effects a result that is oppressive?

This issue is particularly important because breach of the statutory fiduciary duty would appear to require an absence of *bona fides*. For example, the CBCA states that every director and officer must "act honestly and in good faith with a view to the best interests of the corporation". See CBCA s.122(1)(a). Thus, if the oppression remedy is based on the results of conduct rather than motive or intentions, its substantive scope is that much broader than the law of fiduciary duties.

As demonstrated in Jeffrey G. MacIntosh, "Bad faith and the Oppression Remedy: Uneasy Marriage or Amicable Divorce?" (1990), 69 Can. Bar Rev. 276, the courts have given remarkably inconsistent answers to this question. Professor MacIntosh argues that bad faith might be seen either as a necessary condition for finding liability, or as a sufficient condition. Under the former, there can be no liability without a showing of bad faith. Under the latter, an unfair result might by itself ground liability, but a showing of bad faith will also ground liability. Conversely, it might be the case that bad faith is neither necessary nor sufficient to ground liability: i.e., the issue is only whether an unfair result has been effected. Or, one could take the view that both bad faith and unfair result are necessary to ground liability. Professor MacIntosh classifies the cases and finds that cases can be found to support all four views of the role of bad faith in the oppression remedy.

Professor MacIntosh argues, however, that the origins and construction of the oppression provision suggest that it was never intended that bad faith be a necessary part of the cause of action. He argues that the question of unfair result should be at the centre of the inquiry (although cases in which there is bad faith but no unfair result should probably also be actionable in order that the plaintiff be able to prevent future conduct that achieves an unfair result):

> If the jurisprudential foundation of the "bad faith" school is exceedingly weak, the fundament upon which the "unfair result" school rests is correspondingly strong. In this section I will argue that statutory interpretation points strongly to the absence of a bad faith requirement. I will also suggest that a bad faith requirement would be inconsistent

with the general drift of corporate law towards protection of the reasonable expectations of shareholders.

Subsection 122(1) of the CBCA and similar provisions of cognate statutes require that "[e]very director and officer of a corporation in exercising his powers and discharging his duties shall (a) act honestly and in good faith with a view to the best interests of the corporation . . .". This is a subjective test that makes bad faith the central element of a breach of fiduciary duty. By contrast, the . . . oppression provision makes no reference at all to acting in "good faith", "honestly", or *"with a view* to the best interests of the corporation" (emphasis added). Rather, it creates liability for conduct that is "oppressive" or unfairly prejudicial to or that unfairly disregards the interests of "the complainant." This suggests that, while bad faith may be a key element of breach of the statutory fiduciary duty, it forms no part of the oppression action. This conclusion is fortified by reference to the Dickerson Report [which gave rise to the current federal legislation]. In drafting the fiduciary duty provision of the CBCA, the Dickerson Committee left no doubt of its intention to eliminate the proper purpose doctrine (which required no showing of bad faith) and substitute a single test for liability with "an emphasis on good faith". Having done so in a conscious and deliberate manner, it does not seem tenable that the Committee would forget to include a requirement to show bad faith in the oppression provision if it was their intention that such a requirement be an intrinsic and indispensable part of the cause of action. Moreover, the Committee adopted Lord Cooper's definition of oppression (*supra*, focusing on the question of fairness), rather than Lord Keith's definition (*supra*, requiring "lack of probity" to make out a cause of action). All of these facts point to the omission of a bad faith requirement under the oppression provision.

One of the most significant recent trends in Canadian corporate law is the recognition that legal rights may derive from the reasonable expectations of shareholders regarding their relationship to other corporate constituents. This trend can, in no small measure, be traced to the [judgment of Lord Wilberforce in the signal case *Ebrahimi v. Westbourne Galleries Ltd.*].

This reasoning was largely adopted by the Ontario Court of Appeal in *Brant Investments Ltd. v. KeepRite Inc.* (1991), 80 D.L.R. (4th) 161, 45 O.A.C. 320, 1 B.L.R. (2d) 225, 1991 CarswellOnt 133 (C.A.), in which Madame Justice McKinlay stated:

I have concluded that evidence of bad faith or want of probity in the actions complained of is unnecessary in an application under s. 234. I should have been content to arrive at that conclusion merely on the basis of a literal reading of the provision coupled with an application of the statutory objective articulated in s. 4, "to revise and reform the law applicable to business corporations incorporated to carry on business throughout Canada", had it not been for the substantial body of conflicting opinion on this issue cited to us, involving the application of s. 234 or similarly worded provisions in provincial or Commonwealth statutes.

In considering whether conduct is "oppressive" one can appropriately look to the English cases decided before 1980 which defined that word in a similar context. Adopting the definition applied by Lord Simonds in the *Scottish Co-Operative* case — namely, "burdensome, harsh and wrongful" — it is unlikely that an act could be found to be oppressive without there being an element of bad faith involved. However, in considering the alternative question of whether any act is unfairly prejudicial to, or unfairly disregards the interests of one of the protected persons or groups, I am of the view that a requirement of lack of *bona fides* would unnecessarily complicate the application of the provision and add a judicial gloss that is inappropriate given the clarity of the words used. Of course, there may be many situations where the rights of minority shareholders have been prejudiced or their interests disregarded, without any remedy being appropriate. The difficult question is whether or not their rights have been prejudiced or their interests disregarded "unfairly". In testing the facts in a given case against the word "unfairly", evidence of bad faith as to motive could be relevant, but there may be other cases where particular acts effect an unfair result, but where there has been no bad faith whatsoever on the part of the actors.

For recent cases following this aspect of *Brant*, see *Sidaplex-Plastic Suppliers Inc. v. Elta Group Inc.* (1998), 40 O.R. (3d) 563, 1998 CarswellOnt 2819 (C.A.); and *Krynen v. Bugg* (2003), 2003 CarswellOnt 1138 (S.C.J.). Note, however, that some British Columbia cases have held that in the absence of some illegal act, bad faith is required: see *Mahoney v. Taylor* (1996), [1996] B.C.J. No. 1479, 1996 CarswellBC 1441 (S.C.); and *Saarnok-Vuus v. Teng* (2003), [2003] B.C.J. No. 353, 2003 CarswellBC 342 (S.C.). Can this difference be explained by the absence of protection against unfair disregard of interests in the BC Act?

(iv) Is the Oppression Remedy Personal or Derivative?

Note

A question of even greater importance than whether a showing of bad faith is required is the question of whether the oppression remedy embraces actions of a derivative character. As noted above, if it does, then the overlap between the action for breach of fiduciary duty and the oppression remedy becomes virtually complete, since breaches of fiduciary duty will almost always involve derivative actions. As noted further below, the cases have not been consistent on this issue. The case which follows, however, expresses the point of view which appears now to be the dominant one.

Sparling v. Javelin International Ltd
[1986] R.J.Q. 1073

The following facts are condensed from a 72-page judgment that followed a 66-day trial. John C. Doyle was the moving force behind Javelin, a company started in 1949 and continued under the CBCA on March 10, 1980. He was originally the controlling (but not majority) shareholder and, until 1976, a director as well. The company had been public since 1951; it became widely held; of record, about 10,000 were US residents or citizens. Doyle became a fugitive in Canada based on criminal fraud charges laid by the R.C.M.P He also became a fugitive in the United States after failing to present himself to the authorities to serve a three-year term for securities fraud. He lived outside Canada (in Panama, which has no extradition treaty with either Canada or the United States) from 1964 onwards. From Panama, Doyle incorporated a subsidiary of Javelin called Pavonia, although the share certificates representing Javelin's sole ownership of Pavonia were never sent to the parent, Javelin. Doyle had control of the company, through ownership of a control block of shares, since the company was founded, with the sole exception of about 4 months during which a group of dissident directors attempted to seize power (an event referred to in the report as the "palace revolt"); see *Re Canadian Javelin Ltd. and Boon-Strachan Coal Co. Ltd.*, *supra*, Chapter 9. Following the palace revolt, and the judicially-ordered meeting of shareholders that followed, Doyle resumed control of the company by means of using his control block to elect a sympathetic board of directors. He appears to have had an absolute grip on the company, appointing directors who were neither inquisitive about his actions nor reluctant to do his bidding. An earlier oppression action commenced by the Director of the CBCA, Frederic Sparling, resulted in a finding that certain actions of Doyle were oppressive towards the minority shareholders. Rothman J. of the Quebec Superior Court (in a judgment rendered April 7, 1982) ordered the suspension of the powers of the board of directors and the appointment of a receiver-manager to run the company.

In this follow-up case, the Director commenced an oppression action on behalf of the minority shareholders of Javelin seeking additional findings of oppression relating to past conduct and alleging that Doyle had continued to act oppressively towards the interests of the minority shareholders. The Director also sought a new remedy — namely, a winding-up of the company. The action alleged that Doyle had, *inter alia*, arranged phony transactions paid for by Javelin the benefit of which flowed back to Doyle personally. Doyle had also been paid hefty "consulting" fees that the Director alleged were unearned. Javelin had paid Doyle's personal legal expenses to fight about a dozen and a half shareholder suits that had been commenced against him (mostly in the U.S.). He had also arranged the affairs of the company so that the subsidiary, Pavonia, effectively acquired control of the parent, disenabling the receiver-manager from removing the oppressive effects of Doyle's control. The Court found in favor of the Director in respect of all substantial allegations.

Doyle nonetheless argued that the wrongs alleged by the Director and found by the Court to have occurred were all derivative in character, and not a suitable matter for an oppression application. The Court ruled as follows:

GOMERY J.: . . . Counsel for Mr. Doyle submit that the Court has no jurisdiction to adjudicate upon a claim directed against their client for restitution of money since such a claim is of the nature of a derivative action and may only be exercised in conformity with the rules and procedure provided in section 232 C.B.C.A.; since no preliminary permission to bring such an action was granted by the Court, conclusions of the nature being requested by the Director are illegal.

It is not contested that the claims brought by the Director could have been exercised by way of derivative action under section 232. The question is whether or not they may also be made by way of an application under section 234.

A series of decided cases seems at first glance to support the proposition made on behalf of Mr. Doyle, but care must be taken in reading these Judgments because they were decided before the relevant provincial and federal laws enacted the oppression remedy as it is now expressed in section 234. Thus *Re Goldhar and Quebec Manitou Mines Ltd.*, *Goldex Mines Ltd. v. Revill*, and *Farnham v. Fingold* should be read with caution: in none of these decisions is the question the same as what must be decided here.

Be that as it may, the headnote in the *Goldex Mines Ltd.* case states flatly:

Any action by a shareholder seeking relief against a wrong done to a corporation is a derivative action . . . leave of the Court is required for its commencement. Where an action is commenced without leave it is improperly constituted . . .

Similar decisions have been rendered in two British Columbia cases but the fact situation in each instance is distinguishable from the circumstances here.

The only reported case where the issue is addressed directly is *Re Peterson and Kanata Investments Ltd.*, a decision of the British Columbia Supreme Court. Under B.C. legislation very similar if not identical to the C.B.C.A., minority shareholders applied to the court for relief on the ground that the affairs of the company were being conducted in a manner oppressive to them, in that the controlling shareholder had abused his control in order to profit at the company's expense. Counsel for the controlling shareholder argued that the applicants should have proceeded by way of derivative action. This submission was not accepted, Mr. Justice Toy stating:

> In my view, the new rights created by s. 222 (the B.C. equivalent of s. 234 C.B.C.A.) are in addition to whatever other rights or remedies the three members have either by statute or at common law.

Some distinguished scholars are of the same opinion. In *Canadian Business Corporations* the authors state:

> There will be no clear dividing line between cases where this remedy for relief from oppression will be available and cases where the derivative action will be available and appropriate. Actually, there will be some middle ground where both will be available and the aggrieved person will be able to select the remedy which best resolved his problem. The object of a derivative action is to remedy a wrong done to the corporation. The usual object of a section 234 application is to remedy a wrong done to a minority shareholder or other aggrieved person. For example, diversion of corporate profits is clearly a wrong done to the corporation and would normally be remedied by a derivative action. On the other hand, a refusal to declare dividends in order to squeeze out minority shareholders would be remedied by an application for relief from oppression of that minority. But the payment of excessive salaries to dominant shareholders who appoint themselves as officers is a borderline case; it may constitute a wrong to the corporation and at the same time it may have as its specific goal the squeezing out of a minority group. In this case the aggrieved persons would be free to select either remedy. We do not foresee any difficulty with this overlap, particularly since the court maintains full discretion over both of them.

And Professor Mary Anne Waldron, in an article entitled "Corporate Theory and the Oppression Remedy" says:

> All corporate statutes in Canada that provide for oppression remedies also provide for corporate derivative actions brought by shareholders with the consent of the court on behalf of their corporation for wrongs done to the corporation. However, if an oppression application rather than a derivative action is used to seek relief from directors' misconduct, no court approval is needed to commence the action.

The Court is of the same view. The intent of Parliament in enacting section 234 was to include in its ambit all shareholders' recourses, on the condition that a finding of oppression or unfairness first opens the door to the exercise of the Court's jurisdiction. Nothing in the wording of section 234 suggests that the recourses foreseen in section 232 may not be included in a section 234 application. Indeed, some of the orders suggested by section 234(3) encompass derivative recourses; in particular subsection (h) foresees an order compensating the corporation and subsection (j) foresees an order compensating an aggrieved person; the corporation itself may be the aggrieved person.

To decide that any right belonging to the corporation may only be exercised by way of derivative action would be to deny the fundamental nature of the reform which enactment of section 234 represents. Such an interpretation would also require a multiplicity of proceedings in a case such as this. There is a decided advantage to a simplified procedure whereby all demands to enforce the rights of minority shareholders can be dealt with in one application.

The derivative action will continue to apply in cases where the applicant does not choose to scale the barrier that section 234(2) represents, but in our view it may be combined with other recourses if the applicant is able to overcome that obstacle.

Notes and Questions

1 One thing that seems absolutely clear about the oppression remedy is that it achieves one aim envisioned by the drafters and expands the range of actionable wrongs as compared to the common law of fiduciary duties. See generally MacIntosh, "Minority Shareholder Rights in Canada and England, 1860–1987" (1988), 27 O.H.L.J. 1. The derivative action provision in the statute is purely procedural in nature; in order to succeed in a derivative action, the plaintiff must show that there has been a breach of a fiduciary duty owed to the corporation. Thus, the substantive hurdle in s. 241(2) is easier, not more difficult to scale than the substantive hurdle required to commence a derivative action. In the face of this, it seems odd for the court to say in *Sparling* that "[t]he derivative action will continue to apply in cases where the applicant does not choose to scale the barrier that section 241(2) represents . . .".

If the oppression remedy can be resorted to in any case involving a derivative type of action, this appears, as a practical matter, to render the derivative action completely obsolete. Who would risk failing to comply with the procedural strictures applying in the case of a derivative action when they can be entirely circumvented by commencing an oppression action? One might argue that a derivative action affords procedural protections not found in an oppression action. However, although the oppression action is commenced by summary procedure (i.e., by application rather than an action), without pleadings and discoveries, the court will almost routinely order the trial of complex issues involving factual disputes, converting the oppression application into a regular action with pleadings and discoveries, and putting it on a par to the type of action that results when the suit is brought derivatively. If the oppression action can be used in this way, then why did the drafters of the CBCA (and OBCA) not simply remove the provisions relating to derivative actions? Also, why should they be so solicitous to prevent abuses connected with derivative actions by requiring leave of the court to commence the action (and to discontinue it), but provide such an easy way around this requirement (and the other procedural hurdles)? Perhaps the problem was that the drafters simply failed to adequately consider the relationship between the two provisions. Interestingly enough, the situations cited by the Cohen and Jenkins committees in England as showing the need for an oppression remedy consist of conduct that would give rise to both personal and derivative actions at common law. How do you think this dilemma should be resolved? For an argument that derivative actions should be allowed to proceed only with leave of the court under the statutory derivative action provisions, see Jeffrey G. MacIntosh, "The Oppression Remedy: Personal or Derivative?" (1991), 70 Can. Bar Rev. 29. However, see also Edward M. Iacobucci and Kevin E. Davis, "Reconciling Derivative Claims and the Oppression Remedy" (2000), 12 S.C.L.R. (2d).

2 Not all judicial authority on the question is in agreement with the *Sparling* holding. For example, in *Re Goldstream Resources Ltd.* (1986), 2 B.C.L.R. (2d) 244 (S.C.), the B.C.S.C. held that an action of a derivative character can be commenced only with the leave of the court under the provision relating to derivative actions. Cases on both sides of the issue are canvassed in Jeffrey G. MacIntosh, "The Oppression Remedy: Personal or Derivative?" (1991), 70 Can. Bar Rev. 29. Professor MacIntosh notes that many judges have allowed derivative-type actions to proceed under the oppression remedy, without the appropriateness of this ever being raised. This has become even more pronounced in recent years. See Poonam Puri and Stephanie Ben-Ishai, "The Canadian Oppression Remedy Judicially Considered: 1995–2001", (2004), 30:1 Queen's Law Review (forthcoming). In general, the weight of judicial opinion seems to lie on the side of the *Sparling*, rather than *Goldstream.*

3 Very often in a private corporation, a wrong that is formally a wrong to "the company" is in fact simply symptomatic of a dispute between various parties in the corporation. The *Diligenti* case, discussed *supra*, falls into this camp. Diligenti, you will recall, went into business with three other shareholders, and when there was a falling out the other three ganged up on him and diverted profits to a corporation that they controlled (similar to the *Remillard-Dandini* case explored in Chapter 6). Formally, this is a derivative wrong, since the wrong was done to the corporation. In substance, however, the wrong was symptomatic of a dispute between the shareholders. This argument has sometimes been used to justify allowing derivative types of actions to proceed under the oppression remedy. Note, however, that this argument only applies to

private corporations, and not public. Further, what if not all shareholders are part of the dispute? If the action does not proceed derivatively, then these other parties will be forced to become parties to the litigation. Moreover, where the remedy is one of favour of the company (as it will normally be in a derivative proceeding) the interest of these shareholders is protected whether or not they are parties to the litigation. Indeed, where all shareholders are similarly harmed by the impugned conduct (*e.g.*, by the taking of excessive remuneration), there is no easy or fair way to institute a personal remedy in favour of some shareholders but not others. Thus, even in the case of the private corporation where the wrong to the corporation is symptomatic of an underlying dispute between shareholders, there are good arguments for forcing the action to proceed derivatively.

This is to say nothing of the interests of creditors. A personal remedy in a derivative type of suit (*e.g.*, an award of damages directly to aggrieved shareholders in a case in which there is excessive managerial compensation) trumps the interests of creditors in the corporation's assets and earnings stream. This is another reason for forcing all derivative types of proceedings to go forward only as properly constituted derivative actions. These are other arguments are made in MacIntosh, *supra*.

Yet another complication that arises where derivative types of actions are allowed to proceed under the oppression provision is highlighted by *Alles v. Maurice* (1992), 9 C.P.C. (3d) 49, 5 B.L.R. (2d) 154 (Ont. Gen. Div.), per Austin J. In *Alles*, the plaintiff sued under the oppression remedy claiming, *inter alia*, payment of excessive remuneration and other derivative-type wrongs by other shareholder/director/managers in a number of related corporations. The corporations in question, as well as the individual managers were named as defendants. The issue arose, however, of who would instruct the lawyers for the corporation. On the facts, the alleged wrongdoers had hired and instructed lawyers. The dangers of this are obvious. Assuming that real harms had been perpetrated on the corporation, the wrongdoers were hardly the best people to instruct the corporation's lawyers as to how they should best defend the corporation's interests. On the other hand, assuming that there has not been any harm to the corporation, the plaintiff is no better a person to instruct the lawyers for the corporation. The difficulty is that there is no unbiased person to instruct the lawyers acting for the corporation, and we therefore should have little confidence that the corporation's best interests (and thus the interests of all of those who have some claim on the corporation but are not represented in the proceeding) will be properly represented. By contrast, where the action proceeds derivatively, the plaintiff appointed by the court to prosecute the action in the name of and on behalf of the corporation must demonstrate to a court that the action is *prima facie* in the best interests of the corporation.

In *Alles*, Austin J. granted the plaintiff's motion that the solicitors appointed (by the defendants) to represent the corporation be removed. He further ordered that the parties agree upon a solicitor, and indicated that if they could not agree, the court would select one.

(v) Can the Oppression Action be Applied to the Conduct of Shareholders of the Corporation?

Whether the oppression remedy applies to the conduct of shareholders is one of the most difficult, but important, questions that arise under the oppression remedy. One must of course start out by looking at the statute. Section 241(2) indicates that the oppression remedy will apply in cases where:

(a) any act or omission of the corporation or any of its affiliates are or have been carried on or conducted in a manner, or

(b) the business or affairs of the corporation or any of its affiliates are or have been carried on or conducted in a manner, or

(c) the powers of the directors of the corporation or any of its affiliates are or have been exercised in a manner that is oppressive . . .

At first glance, this formulation seems to allow little room to attack the conduct of a shareholder. However, you will note that the remedy applies not only to conduct of the corporation, but also to that of any "affiliate" of the corporation. Look at the definition of "affiliate" in CBCA s. 2(2), and the definition of "control" in s. 2(3). These definitions include a parent corporation that owns at least 50% of the shares of the subsidiary (and see *Sparling v. Javelin International Ltd. et al.*, [1986] R.J.Q. 1073 at 1130, suggesting that it is possible to "control" within the meaning of the statute with fewer than 50% of the shares). Thus, any action by a parent holding a majority of the shares of the corporation may be brought under the umbrella of the CBCA oppression provision (and, if *Sparling* is correct, which can be doubted from the strict conjunctive wording of the two tests in s. 2(3), any parent holding *de facto* control in the corporation). (You should check the comparable provisions in the OBCA to see if the situation is the same.)

The following case supplies another avenue for drawing the conduct of a majority or controlling shareholder within the scope of the oppression remedy. Note the crucial importance of the interlocking directorships to the holding.

Scottish Co-operative Wholesale Society Ltd. v. Meyer
[1959] A.C. 324, [1958] 3 All E.R. 66 (H.L.)

Scottish Co-operative, the parent company, formed a subsidiary to enter the rayon business. In organizing the business, the parent employed Meyer, making him managing director of the subsidiary and one of its substantial stockholders in order to have the benefit of his expertise and business contacts. The parent, however, retained fifty-one percent of the shares and control of the board of directors. At the end of five years, Meyer was no longer needed for the successful operation of the business, and the parent, in an effort to force him out, established its own department to perform the subsidiary's tasks. At the same time, the parent's nominees on the subsidiary's board passively supported the parent by allowing the subsidiary's traditional activities to decline.

LORD DENNING: My Lords, I had myself prepared a summary of the material facts in this case but, in view of the comprehensive statement by my noble and learned friend, Lord Keith of Avonholm, I will not burden your Lordships with what I had written. I would only say that I am sorry that the events of 1952 were excluded as irrelevant. Dr. Meyer and Mr. Lucas from the very beginning put those events in the forefront of their complaints. They did so in the first letter of their solicitors dated February 19, 1953, and in the original petition lodged on July 14, 1953. The burden of their complaints was that, when there was a recession in 1952 in the rayon trade, they — Dr. Meyer and Mr. Lucas — tried, on behalf of the textile company, to develop trade in other goods: particularly in the export of woollen materials to Germany (where they had valuable trade connections) and in a large export order for £60,000: but that they were thwarted in their efforts by the actions of two of the nominee directors, who tried to get the trade for the Scottish Co-operative Wholesale Society itself. Whether these complaints be true or not your Lordships cannot know — because these allegations were excluded from probation. But your Lordships have, I think, sufficient material to decide the case on the other facts which were proved.

The complaints which were established were, I think, these: The co-operative society set up a competing business. It established its own merchant converting department, engaged in the rayon trade itself, and quoted more favorable terms to its own department than it did to the textile company. It is said that the co-operative society did this with intent to injure the textile company — to depress the value of its shares so that the co-operative society could get them cheap — but I would not myself go as far as this. It seems to me that the co-operative society all the time was seeking to promote its own interests. It was ready in 1946 to enlist the co-operation of Dr. Meyer and Mr. Lucas when they were useful to it — so as to get an introduction into the rayon trade — but it was ready to throw them over when they were no longer useful. By which I mean that it was ready to withdraw all support from them. That was, I think, the state of mind of the co-operative society right from the moment in November, 1951, when Dr. Meyer and Mr. Lucas refused to realign the shares at par. At that time the rayon trade was in a recession and Dr. Meyer and Mr. Lucas were not of so much use to the society as they had been. By the time the rayon trade revived, the controls were off and the co-operative society was able to engage in rayon production itself — and it had no further need of Dr. Meyer and Mr. Lucas or of the textile company. It had its own department for rayon. So the textile company could go to the wall. It had "served its purpose" — or rather the purpose of the co-operative society — and could be let go into liquidation. The co-operative society had not the voting power to put it into voluntary liquidation. But liquidation might come about by sheer inanition. So it came about that, when Dr. Meyer and Mr. Lucas in January, 1953, offered to sell their shares to the co-operative society at a price to be negotiated (mentioning 96s.), the co-operative society refused "at the present time." The co-operative society thought, perhaps, that, if they waited, sooner or later liquidation would come about, or that terms of purchase would be arranged later more favorable to the co-operative society than paying 96s. a share.

Such being "the matters complained of" by Dr. Meyer and Mr. Lucas, it is said: "Those are all complaints about the conduct of the co-operative society. How do they touch the real issue — the manner in which the affairs of the textile company were being conducted?" The answer is, I think, by their impact on the nominee directors. It must be remembered that we are here concerned with the manner in which the affairs of the textile company were being conducted. That is, with the conduct of those in control of its affairs. They may be some of the directors themselves, or, behind them, a group of shareholders who nominate those directors or whose interests those directors serve. If those persons — the nominee directors or the shareholders behind them — conduct the affairs of the company in a manner oppressive to the other shareholders, the court can intervene to bring an end to the oppression.

What, then, is the position of the nominee directors here? Under the articles of association of the textile company the co-operative society was entitled to nominate three out of the five directors, and it did so. It nominated three of its own directors and they held office, as the articles said, "as nominees" of the co-operative society. These three were therefore at one and the same time directors of the co-operative society — being three out of 12 of that company — and also directors of the textile company — three out of five there. So long as the interests of all concerned were in harmony, there was no difficulty. The nominee directors could do their duty by both companies without embarrassment. But, so soon as the interests of the two companies were in conflict, the nominee directors were placed in an impossible position. Thus, when the realignment of shareholders was under discussion, the duty of the three directors to the textile company was to get the best possible price for any new issue of its shares (see *per* Lord Wright in *Lowry v. Consolidated African Selection Trust Ltd.*), whereas their duty to the co-operative society was to obtain the new shares at the lowest possible price — at par, if they could. Again, when the co-operative society determined to set up its own rayon department, competing with the business of the textile company, the duty of the three directors to the textile company was to do their best to promote its business and to act with complete good faith towards it; and in consequence not to disclose their knowledge of its affairs to a competitor, and not even to work for a competitor, when to do so might operate to the disadvantage of the textile company (see *Hivac Ltd. v. Park Royal Scientific Instruments Ltd.*), whereas they were under the self-same duties to the co-operative society. It is plain that, in the circumstances, these three gentlemen could not do their duty by both companies, and they did not do so. They put their duty to the cooperative society above their duty to the textile company in this sense, at least, that they did nothing to defend the interests of the textile company against the conduct of the co-operative society. They probably thought that "as nominees" of the co-operative society their first duty was to the co-operative society. In this they were wrong. By subordinating the interests of the textile company to those of the co-operative society, they conducted the affairs of the textile company in a manner oppressive to the other shareholders.

It is said that these three directors were at most only guilty of inaction — of doing nothing to protect the textile company. But the affairs of a company can, in my opinion, be conducted oppressively by the directors doing nothing to defend its interests when they ought to do something — just as they can conduct its affairs oppressively by doing something injurious to its interests when they ought not to do it.

The question was asked: 'What could these directors have done? They could, I suggest, at least on behalf of the textile company, have protested against the conduct of the co-operative society. They could have protested against the setting up of a competing business. But then it was said: "What good would that have done?" Any protest by them would be sure to have been unavailing, seeing that they were in a minority on the board of the cooperative society. The answer is that no one knows whether it would have done any good. They never did protest. And it does not come well from their mouths to say it would have done no good, when they never put it to the test. See the decision of this House in *Morison, Pollexfen & Blair Ltd. v. Walton*, as described by Scrutton L.J. in *Coldman v. Hill*. Even if they had protested, it might have been a formal gesture, ostensibly correct, but not to be taken seriously.

Your Lordships were referred to *Bell v. Lever Brothers Ltd.*, where Lord Blanesburgh said that a director of one company was at liberty to become a director also of a rival company. That may have been so at that time. But it is at the risk now of an application under section 210 if he subordinates the interests of the one company to those of the other.

So I would hold that the affairs of the textile company were being conducted in a manner oppressive to Dr. Meyer and Mr. Lucas. The crucial date is, I think, the date on which the petition was lodged — July 14, 1953. If Dr. Meyer and Mr. Lucas had at that time lodged a petition to wind up the company compulsorily, the petition would undoubtedly have been granted. The facts would plainly justify such an order on the ground that it was "just and equitable" that the company should be wound up: see *In re Yenidje Tobacco Co. Ltd.* But such an order would unfairly prejudice Dr. Meyer and Mr. Lucas because they would only recover the break-up value of their shares. So instead of petitioning for a winding-up order, they seek to invoke the new remedy given by section 210 of the *Companies Act, 1948*. But what is the appropriate remedy? It was said that section 210 only applies as an alternative to winding up and that an order can only be made under section 210 if the company is fit to be kept alive: whereas in this case the business of the company was virtually at an end when the petition was lodged, and there was no point in keeping it alive. If the co-operative society were ordered, in these circumstances, to buy the shares of Dr. Meyer and Mr. Lucas, this would amount, it was said, to an award of damages for past misconduct — which is not the remedy envisaged by section 210.

Now, I quite agree that the words of the section do suggest that the legislature had in mind some remedy whereby the company, instead of being wound up, might continue to operate. But it would be wrong to infer therefrom that the remedy under section 210 is limited to cases where the company is still in active business. The object of the remedy is to bring "to an end the matters complained of," that is, the oppression, and this can be done even though the business of the company has been brought to a standstill. If a remedy is available when the oppression is so moderate that it only inflicts wounds on the company, whilst leaving it active, so also it should be available when the oppression is so great as to put the company out of action altogether. Even though the oppressor by his oppression brings down the whole edifice — destroying the value of his own shares with those of everyone else — the injured shareholders have, I think, a remedy under section 210.

One of the most useful orders mentioned in the section — which will enable the court to do justice to the injured shareholders — is to order the oppressor to buy their shares at a fair price: and a fair price would be, I think, the value which the shares would have had at the date of the petition, if there had been no oppression. Once the oppressor has bought the shares, the company can survive. It can continue to operate. That is a matter for him. It is, no doubt, true that an order of this kind gives to the oppressed shareholders what is in effect money compensation for the injury done to them: but I see no objection to this. The section gives a large discretion to the court and it is well exercised in making an oppressor make compensation to those who have suffered at his hands.

True it is that in this, as in other respects, your Lordships are giving a liberal interpretation to section 210. But it is a new section designed to suppress an acknowledged mischief. When it comes before this House for the first time it is, I believe, in accordance with long precedent — and particularly with the resolution of all the judges in *Heydon's* case — that your Lordships should give such construction as shall advance the remedy. And that is what your Lordships do today.

I would dismiss the appeal.

Appeal dismissed.

Notes and Questions

1 In his judgment, Viscount Simmonds would appear to be willing to go even farther than Lord Denning in applying the oppression remedy to the conduct of shareholders. He said that "it is not possible to separate the transactions of the society [the majority shareholder] from those of the company. Every step taken by the latter was determined by the former . . . [I]t appears to me incontrovertible that the society behaved to the minority shareholders of the company in a manner which can justly be described as 'oppressive'. They had the majority power and they exercised their authority in a manner 'burdensome, harsh and wrongful' — I take the dictionary meaning of the word." See also *Re H.R. Harmer Ltd.*, [1959] 1 W.L.R. 62 (C.A.). The English Court of Appeal has also applied the oppression remedy quite explicitly to the conduct of shareholders, as evidenced by the following passage from *Re Jermyn Street Turkish Baths Ltd.*, [1971] 3 All E.R. 184 (C.A.). Buckley L.J. held that:

> In our judgment, oppression occurs when shareholders having a dominant power in a company, either (1) exercise that power to procure something that is done or not done in the conduct of the company's affairs or (2) procure by an express or implicit threat of an exercise of that power that something is not done in the conduct of the company's affairs . . .

Thus, it may be quite unnecessary to use the device employed by Lord Denning (the interlocking directorships) to bring shareholder conduct within the oppression remedy. You should review *Ferguson v. Imax, supra*, with an eye to how carefully the Ontario Court of Appeal distinguished (or failed to distinguish between) "the corporation" and those shareholders who controlled the corporation. Is *Ferguson* in the same mold as *Harmer* and *Jermyn*?

2 In many cases, it is not necessary to characterize the acts of shareholders as oppressive, unfairly prejudicial *etc.* in order to bring oneself within the oppression remedy. For example, if an oppressive shareholder resolution is passed and the company acts on the resolution, then it can be said that the corporation has committed the act of oppression. Having found oppression, it is clear that the court may then make orders that have affect or are directed against shareholders. For example, it is common for the court to order that a majority or controlling shareholder buy the shares of the complainant minority shareholder. See, *e.g., Wind Ridge Farms Ltd. v. Quandra Group Investments Ltd.* (1999), 178 D.L.R. (4th) 603, 1999 CarswellSask 592 (C.A.); *Miller v. F. Mendel Holdings Ltd.* (1984), 26 B.L.R. 85 (Sask. Q.B.). This is another way of, in effect, bringing shareholder conduct within the purview of the

oppression remedy. See generally MacIntosh, "Minority Shareholder Rights in Canada and England, 1860-1987" (1988), 27 O.H.L.J. 1.

(vi) The Oppression Remedy and the Duties of Directors in the Context of Corporate Transactions

Note

Illustrating the sprawling nature of the oppression remedy, shareholders and defeated take-over bidders have attempted to utilize the oppression action against the target company in the context of hostile take-over bids. However, the use of the oppression remedy against public companies has not been met with much success in Canada. Professor Puri and Ben-Ishai's empirical study, *supra*, found that of the 8% of cases that dealt with public companies, the success rate was 33% as compared to a success rate of 54% for closely held corporations. See for example *Pente Investment Management Ltd. v. Schneider Corp.* (1998), 42 O.R. (3d) 177, 1998 CarswellOnt 4035 (C.A.); and *CW Shareholdings Inc. v. WIC Western International Communications Ltd.* (1998), 39 O.R. (3d) 755, 1998 CarswellOnt 1891 (Gen. Div. [Commercial List]). In both *Pente* and *WIC*, the judicians determined whether the case for oppression had been made out on the basis of whether the directors discharged their fiduciary duties to the corporation. In this regard, the business judgement rule has become very important. In cases involving alleged oppression in the context of a takeover bid, it has become standard practice for the target company to form a committee of independent directors to judge the merits of the bid and to attempt to solicit other bids. Courts have generally deferred to the judgements of such committees. Also reread *Brant Investments Ltd. v. KeepRite Inc.*, *supra*, Chapter 7, in which the court was faced with the application of the oppression remedy in the context of a related party transaction. What is the appropriate level of review by the courts in an oppression action given the deference generally afforded to corporate decisions under the business judgement rule?

(vii) Costs Orders Under the Oppression Remedy

The costs provisions relevant to oppression actions are dealt with in part (a), *supra*. One of the powers granted to the court is the power to award interim costs (payable by the corporation). See, *e.g.*, CBCA s.242(4). *Alles v. Maurice* (1992), 9 C.P.C. (3d) 42, 5 B.L.R. (2d) 146 (Ont. Gen. Div.), per Blair J., deals with the issue of when an award of interim costs will be made. The plaintiff in the oppression action accused a number of participants in a number of related corporations of taking excessive remuneration, charging personal expenses to the companies, and making incomplete disclosure to shareholders. She had spent a great deal of money on valuators and lawyers in attempting to fulfill her obligations as director of two of the companies in question, and in determining the financial position of these companies. Some $45,000 had already been spent, and some $68,000 worth of work remained unbilled. The plaintiff indicated that she could not continue with the action if the company did not pay her interim costs. Blair J. noted that in *Wilson v. Conley* (1990) 1 B.L.R. (2d) 220, 46 C.P.C. (2d) 85 (Ont. Gen. Div.) it had been held that there were three requisites to the award of interim costs: 1) that the Applicant be in financial difficulty; 2) that the financial difficulty arise out of the alleged oppressive actions of the Respondents; and 3) that the Applicant has made out a strong *prima facie* case. Blair J. expressly declined to follow the second and third of these criteria, stating that:

> [The plaintiff's] inability to finance lawsuit is every bit as real, [even where the cause is not the alleged oppressive conduct]. In my view it is this inability to fund an otherwise meritorious lawsuit and the advantage which such a situation gives to an "oppressive" majority that the power given under s. 248(4) [of the OBCA] to order costs is directed. There is nothing in the language of the statute or in its purpose which, to my mind, requires that the applicant demonstrate a cause and effect relationship between the conduct of the respondents and the need for funding . . .

> In the end, I would prefer to say simply that an applicant for relief under s. 248(4) need establish that there is a case of sufficient merit to warrant pursuit and that the applicant is genuinely in financial circumstances which but for an order under s. 284(4) would preclude the claim from being pursued.

(viii) Remedies Under the Oppression Remedy

STEPHANIE BEN-ISHAI AND POONAM PURI
The Canadian Oppression Remedy Judicially Considered: 1995–2001
(Osgoode Hall Law School, 2003)

E. Remedy

Professors Ben-Ishai and Puri's empirical study on the oppression remedy, *supra*, found that the Canadian judiciary has shown a willingness to be innovative in granting remedies for a successful oppression application. The most common remedy granted by the court was a share purchase, at 32% of all remedies granted. A share purchase involves an order directing the corporation (or any other person) to purchase securities from a security holder. This remedy was most commonly granted in the context of a closely held corporation where a minority shareholder was successful in showing oppression by the majority shareholder. The Canadian judiciary had found the share purchase remedy appropriate where shareholders have lost confidence in each other and accordingly could not continue to work together.

On the other hand, their results indicate that the Canadian judiciary did not find the share purchase remedy appropriate where the corporation or the majority shareholders did not have sufficient funds to make a share purchase. In such situations, the Canadian judiciary found it more appropriate to grant a winding-up order. In 6% of the remedies granted the winding-up order was granted. Their results indicate that Canadian courts are open to using this remedy but do so in limited cases and reluctantly. This reluctance can be traced back to the reluctance of the English courts to impose the winding-up remedy because of the drastic consequence of terminating the existence of a company, which as discussed in an earlier section of this article, ultimately pushed the English legislature to develop the oppression remedy.

After the share purchase remedy, their results indicate that the most common remedy in 17% of the remedies granted was the residual remedy, which included remedies such as specific performance, constructive trusts, ordering a directors' meeting, and valuation of assets. In 21% of the remedies granted compensation of an aggrieved person was ordered, which included current and former shareholders, employee-shareholders, but more often, creditors as complainants.

The following case is a good example of oppression arising in the context of a smaller, closely held corporation. It is in the this context that the oppression remedy has had its greatest impact.

Naneff v. Con-Crete Holdings Ltd.
(1995), 23 O.R. (3d) 481, 1995 CarswellOnt 1207 (C.A.)

[Mr. Naneff built a successful family business. In 1977 he made his two sons, Alex and Boris, equal holders of all of the equity in the business, while retaining control through redeemable voting preference shares. In 1990, angry about his lifestyle, Alex's family threw him out of the family home. They also removed him as an officer of all of the companies of the family business, excluded him from participation in the management of the business and cut off most of his income from the business. At trial, the family's conduct was found to be oppressive to Alex, and the trial judge ordered that the family business be sold publicly with any of (or a combination of) Alex, Boris and Mr. Naneff entitled to purchase it.]

GALLIGAN J.A.: The judgment at trial contained a number of specific remedies. The fundamental and most important remedy, contained in para. 9, was that the business, i.e., those corporations which comprise it, be sold publicly as a going concern with each of or any combination of Mr. Naneff, Alex and Boris being entitled to purchase it. There were remedies contained in paras. 4 to 7, inclusive, of the judgment which set aside certain changes in corporate structure and other corporate arrangements which were made after Alex was ejected. Those remedies were ordered in an effort to restore the corporate arrangements to the state which they were in at the time of Alex's ejection. One remedy ordered the payment to Alex of his outstanding shareholder's loans to two of the corporations together with interest. There were two other ancillary remedies which I will mention later. I propose to discuss those remedies and give my opinion with respect to their validity.

1.   Public Sale of the Companies Forming the Business as a Going Concern

Before discussing the merits of the challenge to this remedy, I wish to make brief reference to the principles which guide an appellate court in its review of a remedy ordered under s. 248(3) of the O.B.C.A. Section 248(3) empowers a court upon a finding of oppression to make any order "it thinks fit". When that broad discretion is given to a court of first instance, the law is clear that an appellate court's power of review is quite limited. In *Mason v. Intercity Properties Ltd.* (1987), 59 O.R. (2d) 631 at p. 636, 38 D.L.R. (4th) 681 (C.A.), Blair J.A. set out the governing principle:

> The governing principle is that such a discretion must be exercised judicially and that an appellate court is only entitled to interfere where it has been established that the lower court has erred in principle or its decision is otherwise unjust.

I approach this issue, therefore, keeping in mind that this court can only interfere with the remedy if it concludes that there was an error in principle on the part of Blair J. or if the remedy in all of the circumstances is an unjust one. It cannot be interfered with, as Carruthers J. said (at p. 701) when giving the judgment of the Divisional Court, "simply because someone else might prefer a different way of going about things". With great deference to Blair J., who is a distinguished jurist with extensive commercial law experience, I regret to say that I have concluded, in the circumstances of this case, that the remedy of public sale of this business amounts to an error in principle and is unjust to Mr. Naneff.

At the outset I think it is important to keep in mind that this is not a normal commercial operation where partners make contributions and share the equity according to their contributions or where persons invest in a business by the purchase of shares. This is a family business where the dynamics of the relationship between the principals are very different from those between the principals in a normal commercial business. As the courts below have correctly held, the fact that this is a family business cannot oust the provisions of s. 248 of the O.B.C.A. Nevertheless, I am convinced that the fact that this is a family matter must be kept very much in mind when fashioning a remedy under s. 248(3), as it bears directly upon the reasonable expectations of the principals.

I have come to that conclusion after considering certain observations made by Lord Wilberforce during the course of his speech in *Ebrahimi v. Westbourne Galleries Ltd.*, [1973] A.C. 360, [1972] 2 All E.R. 492 (H.L.). The statute under consideration, the *Companies Act, 1948*, s. 222, authorized the court to wind up a company if it was "just and equitable" to do so. In my opinion, the words "just and equitable" convey the same meaning as the word "fit" in s. 248(3) of the O.B.C.A. Lord Wilberforce explained that when this jurisdiction is being exercised, the relationship between the principals should not be looked at from a technical legal point of view; rather the court should examine and act upon the real rights, expectations and obligations which actually exist between the principals. He said at p. 379:

> The words are a recognition of the fact that a limited company is more than a mere legal entity, with a personality in law of its own: that *there is room in company law for recognition of the fact that behind it, or amongst it, there are individuals, with rights, expectations and obligations inter se which are not necessarily submerged in the company structure.* That structure is defined by the *Companies Act* and by the articles of association by which shareholders agree to be bound. In most companies and in most contexts, this definition is sufficient and exhaustive, equally so whether the company is large or small. The "just and equitable" provision does not, as the respondents suggest, entitle one party to disregard the obligation he assumes by entering a company, nor the court to dispense him from it. *It does, as equity always does, enable the court to subject the exercise of legal rights to equitable considerations; considerations, that is, of a personal character arising between one individual and another*, which may make it unjust, or inequitable, to insist on legal rights, or to exercise them in a particular way. (Emphasis added.)

Thus, I think any remedy granted under s. 248(3) in this case had to be fashioned so that it was just, having regard to the considerations of a personal character which existed among Mr. Naneff, Alex, and Boris.

The provisions of s. 248(3) give the court a very broad discretion in the manner in which it can fashion a remedy. Broad as that discretion is, however, it can only be exercised for a very specific purpose; that is, to rectify the oppression. This qualification is found in the wording of s. 248(2) which gives the court the power, if it finds oppression or certain other unfair conduct, to "make an order to rectify the matters complained of". Therefore, the result of the exercise of the discretion contained in s. 248(3) must be the rectification of the oppressive conduct. If it has some other result, the remedy would be one which is not authorized by law. I agree with the opinion expressed by Professor J.G. MacIntosh in his paper "The Retrospectivity of the Oppression Remedy" (1987-88), 13 Can. Bus. L.J. 219 at p. 225:

> The private law character of the enactment strengthens the argument, for in seeking to redress equity between private parties the provision *does not seek to punish but to apply a measure of corrective justice.* (Emphasis added.)

That opinion was referred to with approval by Glube C.J.T.D. in *Mathers v. Mathers* (1992), 113 N.S.R. (2d) 284 (N.S.T.D.) at p. 304, 309 A.P.R.

284, reversed on other grounds (1993), 123 N.S.R. (2d) 14, 340 A.P.R. 14 (C.A.).

My analysis of s. 248(2) indicates that there is another limit imposed by law upon the apparently unlimited discretionary powers contained in s. 248(3). Section 248(2) provides that when the court is satisfied that in respect of a corporation there is certain specified conduct "that is oppressive, or unfairly prejudicial to or that unfairly disregards the interest of any security holder, creditor, director, or officer of the corporation, the court may make an order to rectify the matters complained of". The expression "security holder" includes a shareholder. Thus, the provision only deals with the interest of a shareholder, creditor, director or officer. It follows from a plain reading of the provision that any rectification of a matter complained of can only be made with respect to the person's interest as a shareholder, creditor, director or officer.

In *Stone v. Stonehurst Enterprises Ltd.* (1987), 80 N.B.R. (2d) 290, 202 A.P.R. 290 (Q.B.), Landry J. was called upon to interpret s. 166(2) of the New Brunswick *Business Corporations Act*, S.N.B. 1981, c. B-9.1, whose provisions are the same as s. 248(2) of the O.B.C.A. The company in question was a family company run as a family business. The company decided to sell its assets. A minority shareholder in his personal capacity wanted to buy the assets and bid for them. When the majority shareholder exercised her controlling interest and sold the assets to someone else, the minority shareholder attacked the transaction as being oppressive to him as a shareholder. Landry J. held that the Act protected a person's interest as a shareholder "as such". Basing his opinion on the judgment of Jenkins L.J. in *Re H.R. Harmer Ltd.*, [1958] 3 All E.R. 689 at p. 698, [1959] 1 W.L.R. 62 (C.A.), Landry J. said at p. 305:

> It must be remembered, and it is very important in this case, that it is only the interest of a shareholder *as such*, or of a director or officer *as such* that is protected by this section.

> The applicant must establish that his interest *as a shareholder* has been affected. He may of course have other interests, such as being a pro-spective purchaser of the assets of the company. But it is only the applicant's interest as a shareholder which we must be concerned with in applying s. 166. (Emphasis in original.)

I agree with and adopt Landry J.'s analysis as a correct statement of the law. Persons who are shareholders, officers and directors of companies may have other personal interests which are intimately connected to a transaction. However, it is only their interests as shareholder, officer or director as such which are protected by s. 248 of the O.B.C.A. The provisions of that section cannot be used to protect or to advance directly or indirectly their other personal interests

I conclude, therefore, that the discretionary powers in s. 248(3) O.B.C.A. must be exercised within two important limitations:

(i) they must only rectify oppressive conduct;

(ii) they may protect only the person's interest as a shareholder, director or officer as such.

The law is clear that when determining whether there has been oppression of a minority shareholder, the court must determine what the reasonable expectations of that person were according to the arrangements which existed between the principals. The cases on this issue are collected and analyzed by Farley J. in *820099 Ontario Inc. v. Harold E. Ballard Ltd.* (1991), 3 B.L.R. (2d) 113 at p. 123 (Ont. Gen. Div.), affirmed (1991), 3 B.L.R. (2d) 113 (Ont. Div. Ct.). I agree with his comment at pp. 185-86:

> Shareholder interests would appear to be intertwined with shareholder expectations. It does not appear to me that the shareholder expectations which are to be considered are those that a shareholder has as his own individual "wish list". They must be expectations which could be said to have been (or ought to have been considered as) part of the compact of the shareholders.

The determination of reasonable expectations will also, in my view, have an important bearing upon the decision as to what is a just remedy in a particular case.

The finding made by Blair J. that Alex expected ultimately to be an equal co-owner of the business with his brother cannot be challenged. However, it must be interpreted in the light of two other important and intertwined considerations. The first consideration is that Alex fully understood that until death or voluntary retirement his father retained ultimate control over the business even to the extent of deciding what dividends would be paid and what would be done with any of those dividends. The second consideration is that this was a family business which had been built by his father.

The importance of the first of those considerations is that Alex knew that until his father died or retired he could under no circumstances have any right to have or even to share absolute control of the business. Therefore, under no circumstances could Alex's reasonable expectations include the right to control the family business while his father was alive and active. The second consideration is important because, while Alex expected that his father would give him an equal share in the control of the business upon his death or retirement, that expectation was based upon his belief that his father would continue to be bountiful to him in the future. It should have been apparent to Alex that he could not expect that paternal bounty to continue if his father for good reason or bad no longer considered him to be a dutiful son. It would have been quite unrealistic of Alex to expect that his father would continue to be bountiful to him if his family ties were severed. Alex knew that the reason for his father giving him one-half of the equity in the family business was his father's desire for his sons to work with him in his business. He must also have known that it would be impossible for him, Mr. Naneff, and Boris to work together in the business as a family if the family bonds ceased to exist. It is for those reasons that Alex's reasonable expectation must be looked at in the light of the family relationship.

It is my view that the first error in principle in this remedy is that it did more than simply rectify oppression. As I noted above, the O.B.C.A. authorizes a court to rectify oppressive conduct. I think the words of Farley J. in Ballard, *supra*, at p. 197 are very appropriate in this respect:

> The court should not interfere with the affairs of a corporation lightly. I think that where relief is justified to correct an oppressive type of situation, the surgery should be done with a scalpel, and not a battle axe. I would think that this principle would hold true even if the past conduct of the oppressor were found to be scandalous. *The job for the court is to even up the balance, not tip it in favour of the hurt party.* I note that in *Explo Syndicate v. Explo Inc.*, a decision of the Ontario High Court, released June 29, 1989], Gravely L.J.S.C. stated at p. 20:
>
> In approaching a remedy the court, in my view, should interfere as little as possible and *only to the extent necessary to redress the unfairness.* (Emphasis added.)

The order of Blair J. gave Alex something which he knew he could never have while his father was alive and active — the opportunity to obtain full control of the family business. A remedy that rectifies cannot be a remedy which gives a shareholder something that even he never could have reasonably expected.

Moreover, I am unable to view the remedy as anything other than a punitive one towards Mr. Naneff. There was never any doubt among the three men that Mr. Naneff would exercise ultimate control of the family business until he died or retired. Mr. Naneff solidified his right of complete control by the corporate arrangements he put in place at the time of the estate freeze and which he kept in place to the knowledge of his sons throughout the time that the three of them worked together. It is not the task of any court of law to judge the family dispute or to rule upon the justice of the expulsion of Alex from the family. However, I am unable to accept as anything other than punitive a remedy which puts at risk the very condition upon which Mr. Naneff exercised his bounty in favour of his sons — his total control of the business during his active life. The O.B.C.A. authorizes a court to rectify oppression; it does not authorize the court to punish for it.

The second error in this remedy is that it attempts to protect Alex's interest in the family business as a son and family member, in addition to protecting his interest as a shareholder as such. As I mentioned above, it is my view that Alex's expectation of ultimately obtaining an equal share of the control of the business with Boris was based upon his expectation of being the continuing object of his father's bounty. That in turn depended upon him remaining in his father's favour and remaining in his father's eyes a member of the family. The remedy of public sale, which gives Alex the opportunity to buy the company, enables him to obtain that control while out of his father's favour. This appears to protect much more than his interest as a shareholder as such; it protects, indeed it advances, his interest as a son.

It is my view, therefore, that the remedy imposed in this case constituted an error in principle in that it did more than rectify oppression, and it did more than protect Alex's interest as a shareholder as such in the companies.

As well as concluding that the remedy granted to Alex was wrong in principle, it is my view that the remedy was unjust to Mr. Naneff. By the time of Alex's ouster from the business, Mr. Naneff had devoted almost 40 years of his life to creating, nurturing and building the business into a very significant enterprise. Instead of using profits from the business to acquire other personal assets, he used them to finance the growth and expansion of the business. There was never any doubt in the minds of his sons that their father gave them their equity positions upon the understanding that he would retain ultimate control as long as he wanted to exercise it. No one can disparage the productive and devoted work which Alex put into the business. But his nine years of contribution pales to almost insignificance when compared with that of his father's contribution.

The effect of the relief granted to Alex is to put Mr. Naneff in the position where he is just another person, equal to Alex, who is entitled to buy the business which he had himself founded and built from nothing. The remedy jeopardizes something which Alex knew was always to be his father's, the right to ultimate control of the business. The remedy gives to Alex the possibility of taking control of the business, something he knew he could never have during his father's lifetime. Having regard to the circumstances of this case this remedy, which jeopardizes the right which everyone knew belonged to Mr. Naneff and which gives Alex the opportunity to take away that right, strikes me as unjust.

At trial there were three possible fundamental remedies suggested to the trial judge. One of them was properly rejected out of hand. No more need be said about it. The alternative remedy to public sale of the business as a going concern was that Mr. Naneff and Boris acquire Alex's shares of the companies at fair market value, without minority discount. In my view that was the just remedy in this case. While I find that Mr. Naneff's oppressive conduct should not endanger his right to control the business, neither should he be able to take away what he had given to Alex, or to take away what Alex had contributed to the business. This remedy, together with certain of the other remedies ordered by Blair J., would have had the effect of fully compensating Alex for the value of the equity given to him by his father and for his own contributions to the business. The value of his shares would reflect the success of the business and Alex's contribution toward that success, as well as the value of the gift of equity which he had received from his father. When I discuss the remedy respecting the shareholders' loans, it will be seen that when the business was ordered to repay Alex the amounts of his loans, in fact he was receiving his share of the operating profits of the business over previous years.

This remedy would be just because it will put Alex, in so far as money can, in the position which he would have been in had he not been ejected. It would not give him an opportunity to which he had no reasonable expectation. It would not put at risk Mr. Naneff's right to ultimate control which Alex knew was a condition of his father's gift of equity. The remedy would protect Alex's interest as a shareholder as such.

It is my opinion that para. 9 of the trial judgment, which provides for the sale of the appellant companies on the open market as a going concern, cannot be sustained. In its place, I would order that the appellants acquire Alex's shares of the companies at fair market value fixed as of the date of his ouster, December 25, 1990. It is conceded on behalf of the appellants that it would not be fair to apply a minority discount to the market value of Alex's shares. I agree and would order that there be no minority discount when fixing the fair market value of his shares. Alex is also entitled to prejudgment interest on the value of his shares as provided in the *Courts of Justice Act*, R.S.O. 1990, c. C.43, from December 25, 1990.

In the event that the parties cannot agree upon the value of the shares or to having the value of them fixed in some other way, I would direct a new trial restricted to fixing the value of Alex's shares in the appellant companies as of December 25, 1990. In my view the costs of such a new trial ought to be in the discretion of the judge presiding at it.

Appeal allowed.

Note

Disputes of the Naneff variety do not always end up in court if counsel for each of the parties has planned appropriately for the possibility of irreconcilable differences. Contractual devices like buyout arrangements, arbitration clauses and the like can go a long way to resolving difficulties without resort to the courts, if only by allowing one disputant to buy out the other(s). The courts are often asked to intervene in cases where adequate buyout arrangements would have ended the difficulties. As noted above, the most common remedy dispensed by the courts under the oppression remedy is an order that one party (or parties) buy out the other (or others). Such a court-ordered buyout accomplishes the same result as a privately negotiated buyout provision. Unfortunately, the lawyer as planner will frequently confront two pressing difficulties. First, a number of parties commencing a small business — very likely members of the same family, or close friends — will not seek separate legal advice upon incorporating and capitalizing the business. Rather, even when apprised of the conflict of interest, they will insist that one lawyer act for all. A lawyer asked to do so should reflect very carefully both on the rules of ethics governing his conduct in acting in the face of a clear conflict of interest and the further possibility of civil liability should the relationship fall apart (which it will

do in a non-trivial number of cases) and one or more of the parties claim
that their interests were not adequately provided for. A second difficulty is
client resistance. Family members and good friends will not always be
terribly receptive to the idea of incorporating dispute resolution procedures
in a unanimous shareholder agreement. They would prefer to believe that
disharmony is an impossibility, and will want to avoid communicating to
the other participants even the suggestion that they think a falling out is a
likelihood. As a solicitor, however, you omit such arrangements only at
your peril (and that of your clients).

5. COMPLIANCE AND RESTRAINING ORDERS

As is pointed out in Chapter 3, s. 19 of the BCBCA provides that the
memorandum and articles, when registered, shall bind the company and its
members as though they had respectively been signed and sealed by each
member and had contained covenants on the part of each member to observe
all of them.

There is some authority in memorandum jurisdictions to the effect that
each shareholder has a general contractual right to have the company's
affairs managed in accordance with the terms of the memorandum of association and articles of association (*Re H.R. Harmer Ltd.*, [1959] 1 W.L.R.
62, [1958] 3 All E.R. 689 (C.A.)). Shareholders have been allowed to
challenge the wrongful appointment of directors and conduct of the company's affairs by an improperly constituted board of directors (*Catesby v.
Burnett*, [1916] 2 Ch. 325; *The Theatre Amusement Co. v. Stone* (1915), 50
S.C.R. 32, at 36-7, 6 W.W.R. 1438). Somewhat of an obstacle, however, is
the principle from *Foss v. Harbottle* (1843), 2 Hare 461, 67 E.R. 189, stating
that the corporation is the proper plaintiff to bring an action to rectify
irregularities in the conduct of the corporation's affairs.

Several of the Canadian corporation statutes have distinct sections
enforcing compliance with the rules governing the corporation. Section 247
of the CBCA allows a complainant (as defined in s. 238) or creditor to seek
a compliance or restraining order against a variety of persons relating to
abrogations of the statute, regulations, articles, by-laws, or a unanimous
shareholder agreement. To similar effect is s. 253 of the O.B.C.A., but
noteworthy is the addition of "shareholder" to the list of persons against
whom a compliance or restraining order may be obtained. See also ABCA
s. 248, MCA s. 240, NBBCA s. 172, NCA s. 378, NSCA Third Schedule,
s. 6 and SBCA s. 240. Of these, only the Alberta Act includes "shareholder"
in the list of persons against whom such an order may be obtained.

The BCBCA has a most interesting compliance provision in s. 229
that allows for the correction of a "corporate mistake". On the motion of
the court itself or the application of any interested person, the court may
make an order to correct an omission, defect, error or irregularity in the
conduct of the company that leads to a breach of the Act, causes non-

compliance with the memoranda or articles or renders ineffective a share-holders' or directors' meeting. The court is given wide powers to rectify such a mistake.

Goldhar v. Quebec Manitou Mines Ltd.
(1975), 9 O.R. (2d) 740, 61 D.L.R. (3d) 612 (Div. Ct.)

REID J. (for the court): A question of such importance arises on the threshold of this appeal that it demands our first attention.

The appeal is from the dismissal by a Judge of the High Court sitting in Chambers of an application based on s. 261 of the *Business Corporations Act*, R.S.O. 1970, c. 53, as amended. The relevant part of that section reads:

261(1) Where a corporation or a director, officer or employee of a corporation does not comply with any provision of this Act, the articles or the by-laws of the corporation, a shareholder or a creditor of the corporation, notwithstanding the imposition of any penalty in respect of such non-compliance and in addition to any other rights he may have, may apply to the court for an order directing the corporation, director, officer or employee, as the case may be, to comply with such provision, and upon such an application the court may make such order or such other order as the court thinks fit.

Applicant seeks an order for compliance with s. 144. It reads:

144. Every director and officer of a corporation shall exercise the powers and discharge the duties of his office honestly, in good faith and in the best interests of the corporation, and in connection therewith shall exercise the degree of care, diligence and skill that a reasonably prudent person would exercise in comparable circumstances.

The relief requested is:

(i)   an order declaring void the delegation by the board of directors of Quebec Manitou Mines Ltd. (Quebec) to three of themselves the ca-pacity to vote shares of Quebec;
(ii) an order declaring void the proxy of Quebec purportedly exercised by the respondent McDonald at the shareholders' meeting of Manitou-Barvue Mines Ltd. held on December 6, 1974;
(iii) an order directing that the votes cast at that shareholders' meeting be recounted with the exception of the shares represented by the proxy of Quebec voted by the respondent McDonald.

A difficulty is immediately apparent in that an order is sought against Manitou-Barvue Mines Ltd., but it is not and has never been party to these proceedings.

There are other problems with the relief asked. The relief now requested in applicant's factum differs from that requested from the Judge of first instance. Still other relief was requested during the course of the argument from that set out in the *factum*.

These are, however, peripheral problems. On the merits of the application, a detailed and complicated set of facts has been laid before us. They raise a question of obvious novelty; one clearly of importance to the parties and perhaps beyond them to the corporate world. The question may be stated in general terms. Suppose corporations A and B are public companies whose shares are listed on a stock exchange. May the directors of A properly maintain themselves in positions of influence and advantage in B by virtue of A having "working control", through share ownership of B, which has, in turn, working control of A? It is argued that as a practical matter the directors of A, unless the Court intervenes, will be able to maintain perpetual control of both A and B and, in effect, stultify the votes of the "outside" shareholders of both companies.

The breach, or breaches, of s. 144 alleged, stem from this curious situation. In the course of defining and developing the issues, counsel directed our attention to numerous corporate minutes, resolutions, and to lengthy depositions and transcripts. Argument was correspondingly elaborate.

Basically, it is submitted that for the directors of Quebec to use that company's control of Manitou-Barvue to their personal advantage and that of their friends and, in effect, to stultify the votes of other Quebec shareholders, is a breach of s. 144, and of a trust obligation the directors owe to the shareholders of Quebec which can only properly be met by the directors causing Quebec to refrain from voting the shares of Manitou-Barvue owned by Quebec. (We are asked as well on the same grounds to nullify the voting of those shares at a recent shareholders' meeting of Manitou-Barvue.)

These observations reveal the novel nature of the issues raised and of the relief sought.

Section 144 was introduced in 1970. It is a broad statement of obligations of directors. Its underlying concept is not new; the obligations owed by directors to corporations, and through them to shareholders, has been the subject of much litigation over many years. Prior to 1970, those issues had to be decided on the basis of common law. A glance at the reports of such cases reveals that they tended to be lengthy and difficult. A recent example of an attempt by shareholders to assert common law derivative rights in another Province is *Teck Corporation Ltd. v. Millar et al.* . . . The casting of directors' obligations into a statutory form in Ontario holds no promise that their enforcement will be any easier if two recent examples, *Farnham et al. v. Fingold et al.*, . . . and *Goldex Mines Ltd. v. Revill et al.*; *Probe Mines Ltd. v. Goldex Mines Ltd.*, . . . are any guide. When a directors' observance of his duty to a corporation under s. 144 is on trial, the inquiry is into questions of honesty and good faith; whether acts done were in the best interests of the corporation and whether the skill, care and diligence exercised were such as could be expected of a reasonably prudent person in comparable circumstances. These can be and usually are questions of nicety and complication.

Respondents argue that s. 261 was not intended to provide a summary means of trying the kinds of questions described above and should be confined to the rectification of simple "mechanical" omissions of a type that lend themselves to summary disposition. An instance might be failure to furnish a list of shareholders pursuant to s. 164. Others of the type are reflected in s-s. (2) which permits the Ontario Securities Commission to apply to Court for orders where there has been a failure to send proxies or information circulars to shareholders before a meeting or a failure to file an insiders' report. It is obvious that omissions of this type might easily be dealt with on motion and that s. 261 could be of particular value to shareholders where no other remedy is readily at hand. Beyond such simple matters, it is argued, s. 261 should not be stretched.

With that proposition we are inclined to agree. The difficulty of passing judgment on the honesty and good faith of directors in respect of decisions made sometimes of necessity hurriedly in sophisticated and complicated factual settings, or upon the credibility of witnesses when the directors as well as the witnesses are revealed only through affidavits and transcripts, needs no illustration. Suffice to say that these questions may be difficult enough to weigh fairly even after a full trial where the appearance and demeanor of witnesses has been experienced, and the testimony of directors tested against pre-trial discovery.

Support for the respondents' position is as well implied by the decisions in *Farnham v. Fingold* and *Goldex v. Revill, supra,* for a different reason.

In both of those cases, s. 99 of the *Business Corporations Act,* introduced at the same time as s. 144, was construed. Section 99 reads in part:

> 99(1) Subject to subsection 2, a shareholder of a corporation may maintain an action in a representative capacity for himself and all other shareholders of the corporation suing for and on behalf of the corporation to enforce any right, duty or obligation owed to the corporation under this Act or under any other statute or rule of law or equity that could be enforced by the corporation itself, or to obtain damages for any breach of any such right, duty or obligation.
>
> (2) An action under subsection 1 shall not be commenced until the shareholder has obtained an order of the court permitting the shareholder to commence the action.
>
> (3) A shareholder may, upon at least seven days notice to the corporation, apply to the court for an order referred to in subsection 2, and, if the court is satisfied that,

(a) the shareholder was a shareholder of the corporation at the time of the transaction or other event giving rise to the cause of action;

(b) the shareholder has made reasonable efforts to cause the corporation to commence or prosecute diligently the action on its own behalf; and

(c) the shareholder is acting in good faith and it is *prima facie* in the interests of the corporation or its shareholders that the action be commenced,

the court may make the order upon such terms as the court thinks fit, except that the order shall not require the shareholder to give security for costs.

In *Farnham*, Jessup J.A., speaking for the Court of Appeal, said at p. 135 O.R., p. 159 D.L.R.:

However, in my opinion, the very broad language of s. 99(1) embraces all causes of action under any statute or in law or in equity, that a shareholder may sue for [and] on behalf of a corporation. All forms of derivative actions purporting to be brought on behalf of and for the benefit of the corporation come with it, and therefore s-s. (2) applies to all such actions.

Of the decision in *Farnham*, Hughes J., for the Divisional Court [in *Goldex Mines Ltd., supra*], observed at pp. 876-7 O.R., pp. 520-1 D.L.R.:

If I may venture therefore to summarize the effect of this decision, I think it stands for two propositions: (1) no matter how the action is framed, if relief is sought against a wrong alleged to be done to a corporation it is derivative, and (2) that all derivative actions are embraced by the provisions of s. 99 of the *Business Corporations Act* which provides an exclusive code for their conduct in Ontario.

It is true that in neither case was s. 144 directly raised. It is clear, however, that s. 144 states the obligations owed by directors to a corporation. Directors must act "in the best interests of the corporation", not the shareholders. The section is a restatement, with perhaps some variation, of the common law which has been the source of shareholders' derivative rights for many years. The rights conferred on shareholders under s. 144 being derived from rights owed to the corporation, are therefore the "derivative" rights spoken of in s. 99. It is such rights that appellant seeks to assert by way of motion. An action to enforce them would fall within s. 99. The strong implication of the above decisions is that only through s. 99 could such rights be enforced.

The question may be tested in yet another way. A glance at s. 261 discloses that the rights conferred upon shareholders by s. 261 are direct rather than derivative. It is not corporations that are entitled to apply for their enforcement; it is shareholders under s-s. (1) and the Ontario Securities Commission under s-s. (2). The instances in s-s. (2) of s. 261 are examples of non-derivative rights. The obligation to send out proxies is an obligation owed by the managers of a corporation to its shareholders, not by the directors to the corporation. An obligation to file an insider's report may or may not fall on a director but even if it did, it creates no obligation to a corporation. There is thus nothing in s. 261 to suggest that a shareholder obtains the rights conferred by s-s. (1) indirectly through a corporation, or that under s-s. (2) the Securities Commission is asserting derivative rights on behalf of shareholders. It can be fairly said therefore that s. 261 appears to have no relevance to derivative rights and was never intended as a vehicle for their enforcement.

It was argued that s. 261 was at least complementary to s. 99 and necessarily so because no summary relief could be obtained under s. 99. This argument was developed in the following way.

No action under s. 99 may be commenced without leave or without seven days' notice. These conditions precedent create the disturbing impression that the traditional right of shareholders to apply for an *ex parte* interim injunction in a derivative action has now been lost. The right to such relief has proven over the years to be a valuable protection for shareholders, particularly when facing an imminent shareholders' or directors' meeting. It is argued that the Legislature should not lightly be assumed to have swept away this relief; and that s. 261, which provides for "such order as the court deems fit", should be read large so as to furnish the means to an *ex parte* injunction not available under s. 99. If this is so, and injunctions may be granted on summary application under s. 261, there is no reason why other relief obtainable under s. 99 in an action should not be obtainable summarily under s. 261.

This amounts to saying that the Legislature intended to provide not only complementary but concurrent vehicles for the assertion of shareholders' derivative claims, one by action under s. 99, the other by motion under s. 261.

It has already been observed that s. 261 does not, on its face, appear to have any relevance to derivative claims. But even if this were not as plain as it is, one would experience difficulty in accepting that the Legislature intended to provide explicitly for derivative rights to be asserted in an action maintainable only with leave and in the same breath provide impliedly for the same to be done on a motion without leave. I see nothing that requires, or even justifies, the acceptance of legislative inconsistency on this scale, and I reject the argument.

For these reasons, I must reluctantly conclude that s. 261 does not confer alternative, concurrent or complementary rights to those conferred by s. 99. Shareholders who seek to enforce upon directors the obligations imposed by s. 144 must do so in an action brought pursuant to s. 99. This application is dismissed. The novelty and importance of the jurisdictional question raised justifies no order as to costs.

I have commented on the apparent disservice done to shareholders by the Legislature in depriving them of the time-honored right to an *ex parte* interim injunction. It may be that in appropriate circumstances in an action under s. 99 an order for leave could be granted *nunc pro tunc* and the seven-day notice period abridged. That possibility was scanned by Hughes J., in *Goldex* (see report pp. 886-7 O.R., pp. 530-1 D.L.R.), but as he pointed out, "there are no words [in the section] such as 'unless otherwise ordered' to suggest that the requirement in this respect should be in any way abridged". And, even if such an order could be made, it could not be made *ex parte*; there is nothing in the section contemplating that possibility and no external authority to support it. The point is not directly before us, but the dilemma of shareholders is, for we were given to understand that an application for an interim injunction made concurrently with the application under s. 261 failed for want of leave. I respectfully draw this awkward situation to the attention of the Legislature. It may well have been created by inadvertence and could be cured by a simple amendment. [See section 246(3)(4) of the O.B.C.A.]

Application dismissed.

Notes and Questions

1 McIntyre J., in interpreting s. 248 of the ABCA (then s. 240), departed from Goldhar. See *Caleron Properties Ltd. v. 510207 Alberta Ltd.* (2000), 9 B.L.R. (3d) 218, 2000 CarswellAlta 1155 (Q.B.) (at p.225 [B.L.R.]):

> [B]ased on the plain meaning of s. 240 in the context of the ABCA as a whole, I can see no justification for restricting its application to the rectification of simple mechanical omissions. Furthermore, because the right conferred on a complainant by s. 240 is in addition to any other right the complainant may have, I can see no justification for restricting its application based on whatever other standing that person may have. A complainant is not precluded from relying on s. 240 merely because that complainant may have concurrent standing pursuant to other sections of the ABCA. Indeed, as D.H. Peterson comments at para. 10.14, [*Shareholder Remedies in Canada* (Markam: Butterworths, 2000, 2nd edition)]: "[t]o strictly require that the wrongdoing be remedied through the traditional remedies, such as the oppression remedy and derivative and personal actions, can be overkill in many cases."

Which line of reasoning do you agree with?

2 There is also a compliance order provision in the *Ontario Securities Act*, R.S.O. 1990, c.S.5. Section 128 reads:

> 128.(1) The Commission may apply to the Ontario Court (General Division) for a declaration that a person or company has not complied with or is not complying with Ontario securities law. 1994, c. 11, s. 375.
>
> (3) If the court makes a declaration under subsection (1), the court may, despite the imposition of any penalty under section 122 and despite any order made by the Commission under section 127, make any order that the court considers appropriate against the person or company, including, without limiting the generality of the foregoing, one or more of the following orders:
>
> > 1. An order that the person or company comply with Ontario securities law.

3 The statutory restraining and compliance order provisions allow the court to make not only a restraining order, but "any further order it thinks fit". Could this conceivably involve an award of damages? An order that the articles of the corporation be changed, or that directors be removed? Any other remedy that a court might grant under the oppression remedy? If not, what would be the warrant for reading down the apparently clear words of the statute?

4 As an exercise, you should determine which statutory provisions bear on the question of awarding costs in connection with an application for a compliance and restraining order. Is the category of persons who are covered by the relevant costs provisions the same as those who may apply for a restraining order?

5 Note that the CBCA and O.B.C.A. both contain other restraining order provisions relating to specific subject matters. See, *e.g.*, CBCA ss. 154 (proxy solicitations), 243(3)(b) (holding of shareholder meetings). *Cf.* O.B.C.A. ss. 253(2), 250(2)(b). See generally Dennis H. Peterson, *Shareholder Remedies in Canada* (Markham: Butterworths, 2000).

6. RECTIFICATION ORDERS

The following comments are based on the discussion found in Iacobucci, Pilkington and Prichard, *Canadian Business Corporations* (1977), pp. 219–223.

General corporation statutes provide that the register of members of a company is *prima facie* evidence of the matters entered in it and hence of the fact of membership and the extent of holdings. Despite the fact that it is not conclusive and that in some cases there is theoretically no obligation on a person improperly entered to have himself removed, in practice such a person will be ill-advised to refrain from taking action. The courts have placed great importance on the need for speedy removal of a name from the register since its presence may act as an inducement to others to subscribe for shares or allow the company credit.

The alleged shareholder should take steps to have his name removed from the register. This can be achieved by bringing an action against the company for rescission or by applying to the court under the appropriate statutory provisions . . .

Under the CBCA if the name of a person is alleged to be or has been wrongly entered or retained in, or wrongly deleted or omitted from, the register or other records of a corporation, the corporation, a security holder of the corporation or any aggrieved person may apply to a court for an order that the register or record be rectified (s. 243). The Director must be given notice of any application under this section and he is entitled to appear to be heard. The court may make any order it thinks fit including, without limiting the generality of the foregoing, an order (a) requiring the register or record to be rectified, (b) restraining the corporation from calling or holding a meeting of shareholders or paying a dividend before such recti- fication, (c) determining the right of a party to the proceedings to have his name entered or retained in, or deleted or omitted from the register or record whether the issue arises between two or more security holders or alleged security holders, or between the corporation and any security holders or alleged security holders and (d) compensating a party who has incurred a loss. To a similar effect is s. 250 of the O.B.C.A. which is based on s. 243 of the CBCA, but the Ontario section does not require notice to the Director of an application.

Notes and Questions

1   Section 230 of the BCBCA allows for the rectification of information wrongly entered into or omitted or deleted from a company's basic records. The company, a shareholder or any other aggrieved party may apply to the court, and the court may make any order it sees fit, including an order requiring the records be corrected. The court may also order compensation for a party who has suffered a loss as a result of the incorrect information. This section seems to be quite broad, as "infor- mation" could encompass anything in the records.

2   You should determine which costs provisions of the statutes apply when a rectification order is sought. Compare the coverage of these provisions with the class of persons who has standing to seek a rectification order. Is a statutory amendment justified?

3 A rectification order may be made in connection with an oppression action. See CBCA s. 241(3)(k) and O.B.C.A. s. 248(3)(k). Other provisions of these statutes provide for correction of documents other than the registers of records of the corporation. See, *e.g.*, CBCA s. 154(1)(b) (correction of misleading form of proxy or proxy circular), 205(3)(b) (correction of misleading documents issued in connection with a take-over bid). *Cf.* O.B.C.A. s. 253(2)(b).

7. INVESTIGATIONS

The effective exercise of shareholder remedies will frequently depend on possessing the relevant information. An important statutory aid for shareholders in this respect is the court-ordered investigation of the corporation's affairs where the shareholder-applicant can satisfy the court that there are circumstances which warrant the court order. These court-ordered investigations should be distinguished from the shareholder-appointed investigations which are mounted by a shareholders' resolution appointing an inspector who has the same powers as one appointed by the court (see s. 250 of the BCBCA).

The report of the inspector carrying out the court-ordered investigation could provide the basis for further remedies in the form of a derivative action, relief from oppression application, compliance order or winding-up order. Such a report could even have a more beneficial result by encouraging the wrongful party to rectify the matter voluntarily.

The provisions in the BCCA, O.B.C.A. and CBCA relating to investigations vary as to the terms and conditions under which an application for an investigation may be brought, by whom, and against whom. The powers of the court also vary. Compare ss. 248–255 of the BCBCA, ss. 161–167 of the O.B.C.A. and ss. 229–237 of the CBCA.

The Report of the Dickerson Committee succinctly stated the rationale for the investigation provisions:

464. The system of inspection is designed to serve two purposes. First, it is a valuable weapon in the armory available to shareholders as a protection against mismanagement. Although Part 19.00 of the *Draft Act* [relating to Remedies, Offenses and Penalties] greatly extends and improves the means of redress open to individual shareholders in the courts, it will almost certainly be true in many cases that even the most sophisticated litigative weapons will be valueless for lack of information as to the details of suspected mismanagement. That information is, by its very nature, likely to be known by the suspected wrongdoers and unlikely to be known or voluntarily disclosed to those seeking to complain of the suspected wrongdoing. Accordingly, we have provided in [s. 222(2)] that if an applicant can satisfy the court that there are circumstances suggesting wrongdoing, an investigation order may be made in aid of litigation.

465. Moreover, there is a public interest in the proper conduct of corporate affairs, and while the protection of the public interest may be a byproduct of the protection of shareholder interests, we are not persuaded that it is a necessary by-product. Accordingly, [s. 222(2)] provides for an application by the [Director].

The main role of an inspector is to discover facts. Does the inspector also have the power to determine that the law has been violated? The question arose in *Re First Investors Corp. (No. 1)*, unreported, Alta. Q.B., March 19, 1988, No. 8703-16333, in which Berger J. held that:

the inspector shall report his opinion as to whether any individual, corporation or government agency has committed fraud or any other illegal act or is liable for acts of negligence, wrongdoing or illegality. As a necessary corollary of his fact-finding role, he shall consider and apply existing law in reporting to the court whether he has discovered evidence "tending to show" [that the legal grounds for commencing the investigation are supported]; he will set out his findings of fact together with the evidence in support of those findings: he will delineate the legal framework that guided his investigation.

The legal status of the investigator's report in subsequent proceedings is not entirely clear. In *Re Pergamon Press Ltd.*, [1970] 3 All E.R. 535 (C.A.), the English Court of Appeal held that the report cannot form the foundation of subsequent proceedings. As succinctly put by Middleton J.A. in *Re Shell Castle Fire Place Ltd.* (1927), 33 O.W.N. 195 (C.A.):

The report merely gives the minority shareholders information of greater or less value. It may not be accurate, binds no one, and determines nothing.

However, in *Abraham v. Inter Wide Investments Ltd.* (1985), 51 O.R. (2d) 460 (H.C.), an inspector's report supplied the key facts relied upon by the Court in finding oppressive conduct under the oppression remedy (see also *Re Ferguson and Imax Systems Corporation* (1984), 44 C.P.C. 17 (Ont. Div. Ct.), in which an inspector's report was also admitted as evidence in an oppression action). What status should an inspector's report have? Consider the following arguments:

(i) The powers of an inspector or investigator are administrative in nature, rather than judicial or quasi-judicial. See, *e.g.*, *Doyle v. Restrictive Trade Practices Commission* (1985), 60 N.R. 218 (Fed. C.A.); *Re First Investors Corp. (No. 1)*, unreported, Alta. Q.B., March 18, 1988. It is not entirely clear that all the requirements of both procedural fairness and natural justice must be adhered to. *Cf. Doyle, supra, Re Pergamon Press Ltd., supra* and *First Investors, supra*. Thus, it is unfair for the report to be accorded weight in a civil proceeding when the evidence contained therein has been compiled without all the procedural protections available in a trial. The investigation is not rendered useless if it cannot be introduced as evidence; facts uncovered therein can tell potential litigants if their fears were well grounded or not. As well, if litigation follows, the report can point counsel in the right direction in making inquiries in the discovery process. This way, the same facts may be introduced into the trial process, but with appropriate procedural protections.

(ii) The whole point of conducting an investigation is to assist shareholders in uncovering facts that may support litigation. The rationale for authorizing an investigation is dealt a severe blow if evidence unearthed in the course of the investigation cannot be used in subsequent proceedings. It is a costly waste of resources to insist that litigants to go the trouble of unearthing the same information already uncovered by the investigation.

Moreover, it is not clear that the procedural protections afforded under the investigation procedure are inadequate; the inspector may be authorized by a court under both the CBCA and O.B.C.A. to conduct hearings and to examine witnesses under oath, as well as to command production of documents. At any hearing conducted by an inspector, it is likely that requirements of both procedural fairness and natural justice will come into play. See *Doyle, supra*. At any hearing, any person being investigated or being examined at a hearing has a right to be represented by counsel (see CBCA s. 232(2); O.B.C.A. s. 164(2)). There are other protections built into the statutes in anticipation that some or all of the evidence adduced before the inspector and/or the inspector's report may subsequently be introduced as evidence in judicial proceedings (see, *e.g.*, CBCA ss. 233, 234, 236; O.B.C.A. ss. 165, 166). Thus, there is no reason to exclude the inspector's report from judicial proceedings.

Before you commit yourself to either of the above views (or some other view) you should think about the relationship of the investigation procedure to pre-trial discovery. We already have elaborate discovery procedures designed both to furnish litigating parties with information about the relative strengths of their cases and to facilitate settlement. In *Aftex Products (Western) Ltd. v. Rothman (No. 2)*, (April 28, 1982), per Maclaughlin J. (B.C.S.C.), the plaintiff commenced an oppression action alleging that certain unauthorized personal expenses had been charged to the company. The plaintiff also sought an investigation to determine the nature and amounts of the unauthorized personal expenses. In refusing the request, the Court held that:

> A major purpose for which the order is sought is to obtain information to be used in the final determination of this action at the expense of the company . . . If pre-trial discovery is necessary, it can be obtained by converting this proceeding to an action and proceeding as one would

upon a writ. In view of the differences between the parties on the facts and how they interpret them, this may be a more economical and more efficient manner of proceeding.

Did the plaintiff in this action make a tactical mistake in commencing the oppression action contemporaneously with the request for an investigation? Would (or should) the result have been different if the plaintiff had simply requested an investigation, not in the contest of an ongoing oppression action? Did the Court overlook the statement of the Dickerson Committee that "an investigation order may be made in aid of litigation"? The *Aftex* case squarely raises the question of the relationship between an investigation and pre-trial discovery. It is always possible (barring impecuniosity) for the plaintiff to undertake litigation at his/her own expense and use the discovery process to test the merits of the case. Should the investigation procedure (usually paid for by the company: see *infra*) therefore be limited to cases involving impecunious plaintiffs? Consider the following alternative view: "An investigation should be ordered by the courts when there are allegations of non-trivial improprieties in the conduct of the affairs of the company, but the known facts are sufficiently unclear that it would be an undue burden to insist that the plaintiff commence an action (with attendant risk and expense) in order to discover whether an action is merited."

The courts have traditionally been reluctant to order an investigation, especially where it appears that some other source of information is available. For example, in *Re Baker and Paddock Inn Peterborough Ltd.* (1977), 16 O.R. (2d) 38, 2 B.L.R. 101 (H.C.), Galligan J. stated that the power of the court to intervene in the affairs of a private corporation should be exercised with caution and held that the shareholders desirous of the court order did not establish that they could not get the information privately and hence an investigation was not ordered. Another example is *Royal Trustco Ltd. (No. 3), Re* (1981), 14 B.L.R. 307, 1981 CarswellOnt 120 (H.C.), which refused an investigation because there was already enough material information available. Eberle J. said (at p.314 [B.L.R.]):

> However I am unable to conclude that any substantial area of factual investigation is now required. There is already on the table ample material on which any shareholder or other aggrieved party may decide whether or not take legal proceedings. If there were not, that might be sufficient justification to order an investigation, i.e., to ascertain facts in a manner and to an extent that might be beyond the capabilities of an ordinary shareholder to do. There may well be other grounds of justification, for I do not mean to suggest that the one I have indicated is the only one. The turning point in the present case is that the issues raised in this case, which are legal ones, or mixed legal and factual ones, are better disposed of in litigation between parties, where rights

can be determined, than in an investigation which cannot determine rights.

See also *Budd v. Gentra Inc.* (1997), 53 O.T.C. 154, 1997 CarswellOnt 5226 (Gen. Div. [Commercial List]).

Notes and Questions

1 Note that there is no requirement in the statutory provisions noted above (re investigations) for the applicant to be acting in good faith. Nonetheless, at least one court has imposed such a requirement. In *Hendin v. Cadillac Fairview*, unreported, Jan. 31, 1983, S.C.D., No. 18-0206, the applicant was a real estate agent who alleged that he had not been paid his commission on the controversial sale of over 10,000 apartment units in Toronto. The Court held that the applicant's true purpose in bringing the application was to assist him in his claim to collect the real estate commission. Finding that he was not acting in good faith, the Court therefore denied the request for an investigation. See also *Balestreri v. Robert (receiver-manager); Sparling et al. (mis-en-cause)* (1985), 30 B.L.R. 283. Is there any warrant for this super-added condition, given that there is no such requirement in the statute (contrast the derivative action provisions, which expressly require that the applicant be acting in good faith)?

2 An investigation may be authorized in connection with an oppression action. See CBCA s. 241(3)(m); O.B.C.A. s. 248(3)(m).

3 Note that an investigation may also be authorized under the Ontario *Securities Act*, R.S.O. 1980, c. 466, Part VI. You might have a look at these provisions and compare them to those in the CBCA and O.B.C.A.

4 A case of potentially great impact is *Consolidated Enfield Corp. v. Blair* (1994), 19 B.L.R. (2d) 9, 1994 CarswellOnt 249 (Gen. Div.), per Logan J. In *Blair*, Blair applied to the Ontario court for an order of investigation order under s.161 of the O.B.C.A. respecting Consolidated Enfield ("Enfield"), a company of which he had formerly been a director and the Chief Executive Officer. When Enfield was taken over by Canadian Express (and Blair resigned as CEO and was removed as director), Blair alleged that Enfield had made insufficient disclosure to shareholders of transactions with related corporations for shareholders. Canadian Express is part of a large empire of companies under the control of the Bronfman family. As explained by the court (at paras. 8-9):

> Briefly Blair maintains security transactions and accounting irregularities have occurred in the management of Enfield's treasury since July 20, 1989. Enfield is a subsidiary to other corporations which he

refers to as "the Edper Group". The irregularities pertain to transfer of securities between related corporations.

He pointed out that these corporations have the power to exercise control over the financial decisions made on behalf of Enfield. The corporations are subject to common supervision, but the financial statements and other disclosed material do not adequately describe the relationship or give meaningful information which records the proportion of Enfield's activities involved between related parties. What the financial information does mention cannot be easily understood. Tax returns show the total income from securities, but do not list a schedule of securities with income earned.

The transactions in question involved purchases of securities by Enfield in companies related to Canadian Express. Blair and another shareholder of Enfield (Algonquin, of which Blair was then CEO) sued alleging that the failure to disclose was oppressive or unfairly prejudicial to shareholders, and that this justified an investigation. He also alleged that the manner in which related party transactions were approved was oppressive (at para. 24):

> In [Blair's] view the information disclosed is unfairly prejudicial to, or unfairly disregards his interests as a security holder. The information is confusing and not informative. In addition to improper disclosure the recent management of Enfield conducts the affairs of the corporation in a manner that is oppressive. It unfairly disregards the interests of Algonquin and himself. The approval method it uses for related party security transactions is unfairly prejudicial to them.

Logan J. held that, although it was not necessary that all related party transactions be approved by shareholders, inadequate disclosure to the auditor about related party dealings might nonetheless constitute unfair prejudice to a shareholder. (Note, however, that Logan J. deliberately refrained from saying anything about whether Ontario Securities Commission Policy 9.1 had been complied with.) Noting the "tremendous financial haemorrhage that has taken place in Enfield after the month of July 1989", he further held that there must be some special approval mechanism for related party transactions, and that the procedure adopted by Enfield was not adequate (at para. 87):

> The proportion of related party transactions to total assets of Enfield is too great [for related party transactions to be subjected to close scrutiny]. The need for fast decisions does not out weigh the need for precaution.

It certainly appears to myself that an inference may be drawn from the examination comments such as the ones made by Mr. Lawson and from the affidavits that the approval structure within Enfield which provides for a decision process for non-arms length investments does not always function or if it does, it is very loose. A strong impression exists of justification after the fact by current management. I find that Blair and Algonquin have satisfied the burden of proof required under section 161 of the O.B.C.A.

It appears to myself that a structural deficiency exists in Enfield when it comes to the approval process for related party security transactions. The system used does not appear to be adequate. Even though directors may act honestly, the approval process does not operate in a fashion which allows the directors to act at all times in the best interests of the corporation. It is not fair and just. In my view it appears to unfairly disregard the interests of Blair and Algonquin as minority security holders in Enfield.

It further appears that the inadequate approval system for related party transactions causes a lack of proper or sufficient communication of information by the officers of Enfield to the auditors about the nature and extent of related party transactions, the description of the relationship in all such transactions along with an accurate break down of amounts involved. The lack of communication that eventually results causes inappropriate disclosure to security holders about the proportion of Enfield's activities which involve related parties. It appears that the insufficiency of such information is unfairly prejudicial to Blair and Algonquin. It appears that the form of the existing structure means that partiality and deception may exist . . .

I order an investigation to be made by a person to be named by myself after receiving the submissions of counsel and Blair. The person so named shall investigate and report on the actual system employed by the current management of Enfield to independently review related party security transactions and the manner and method by which the approval process functions with individual settlements.

The person shall report on the manner by which related party information reaches the directors of the corporation and is processed by them. I further order that the person investigate whether sufficient information is given by management in the financial statements with respect to related security transactions which would allow a security holder to know the proportion of related party activities made by Enfield within the accounting year.

The *Blair* case has far-reaching implications, given that there are many Canadian corporations that are part of extended corporate empires and which frequently enter into related party transactions with other corporations in the same group.

7 As in the case with all shareholder rights and remedies, the issue of costs is crucially important in determining the efficacy of the right.

Note that as in the case of derivative actions and oppression actions, the applicant is not required to give security for costs (CBCA s. 229(4); O.B.C.A. s. 161(4)). Other than this, the statutes say nothing about costs except that the court may order the corporation to pay the costs of the investigation (CBCA s. 230(1)(1); O.B.C.A. s. 162(1)(1)). In *Re Ferguson and Imax Systems Corp.* (1984), 47 O.R. (2d) 225 (Ont. D.C.) (a follow-up case to *Re Ferguson and Imax Systems Corp.* (1983), 150 D.L.R. (3d) 718 (Ont. C.A.), *supra*), the plaintiff sought an investigation into alleged continuing acts of oppression. The trial judge had ordered that the investigation proceed without permitting cross-examination on the plaintiff's affidavits, apparently taking the earlier Court of Appeal finding of oppression as *res judicata* of the issue of ongoing oppression. Further, the inspector appointed by the Court (Laventhol and Horwath) had sworn an affidavit in favor of the plaintiff before the motions court judge, raising the appearance of bias. The District Court held that the trial judge had erred in two ways: first, he could not know if the statutory standard for an investigation ("it appears that" there is oppressive behavior) had been satisfied, owing to the absence of cross-examination and the incorrect taking of the earlier holding as *res judicata*. Second, an inspector other than Laventhol and Horwath should have been appointed in order to avoid the appearance of partiality. Nonetheless, the Court ordered that the company pay the costs of the already completed investigation, holding that the inspector had a right to be able to expect payment from somebody who would be able to pay. The Court nonetheless gave the trial judge in the further oppression proceedings that were to follow the authority to allow the company a claim over against Mrs. Ferguson for the costs of the investigation.

In *Re Teperman & Sons Ltd.* (1984), 29 B.L.R. 1 (Ont. H.C.J.) the Court held that it had a wide discretion under the statute to order costs in connection with an investigation. An order was made that the company pay the costs of the investigation, because (*inter alia*) the investigation had been of benefit to the company and stockholders in the company. An order also issued that the directors (whose conduct in paying generous and apparently unjustified remuneration had been called into question) should be jointly and severally liable should the company have insufficient funds to pay the costs. In *Consolidated Enfield Corp. v. Blair* (1996), 28 O.R. (3d) 714, 1996 CarswellOnt 455 (Div. Ct.), leave to appeal refused by 63 A.C.W.S. (3d) 1271, 1996 CarswellOnt 2291 (C.A.), the Court held that costs of an investigation were to be paid in most cases by the corporation. There could be cases where costs would be ordered a different way, but this would depend upon material before the judge other than the investigator's report.

8. APPRAISAL REMEDY

IACOBUCCI, PILKINGTON AND PRICHARD,
Canadian Business Corporations
(1977), pp. 168–171 (footnotes omitted)

Introduction

An appraisal right is the right of a shareholder to require the company to purchase his shares at an appraised price if the company takes certain "triggering" actions from which he dissents. The right works as a device to reconcile the majority's need to adjust to changing economic conditions with the right of the members of the minority to refuse to participate in ventures beyond their initial contemplation. Such a right of appraisal is intended to avoid the common law difficulties of trying to restrict an abuse of power detrimental to minority shareholders by the directors or by majority shareholders where shareholder approval is required. As a rule, it will arise only in situations involving major structural changes, often described as "fundamental changes", and while the enterprise is continuing. Next to dissolution it is the most drastic step for the shareholder to take and will therefore likely be used sparingly but, as we argue below, its existence is essential and may lead not only to minority relief but also to more diligent efforts by management and the controlling shareholders.

The appraisal remedy exists in some form in all of the states of the United States except West Virginia. The Ontario, British Columbia, and Federal Acts all grant appraisal rights as do the proposed statutes for New Brunswick and Prince Edward Island. There is an extensive body of literature on the appraisal right in the United States which surveys the arguments for and against and the *Select Committee Merger Report* recently examined these same issues.

The leading critic of the appraisal right is Manning, who makes a twofold criticism. First, he says that it ill-serves the shareholder who uses it since the legal technique is laborious, slow, technical and expensive and the awards are unpredictable. Each of these criticisms is valid to some extent but they are equally applicable to many types of litigation. They do not assess the validity of the concept as an integral part of the protection of the minority. Second, Manning argues that the corporation is ill-served by an appraisal right because it creates a drain on cash flow at a critical time (but if the remedy is slow then the award will likely be made after the enterprise survives its critical period), it frightens creditors and suppliers (no evidence is offered to support this), and uncertainty is created by the unknown number of dissenters.

Some writers suggest that the appraisal right should be limited to the private company because of the alternative means available for dissent in the public company. In a private company there may be no or only very limited opportunities for the dissenter to sell his shares to anyone except the majority. In a publicly-held corporation, the market offers a potentially viable alternative. Further, shareholder expectations in the publicly-held firm may be more closely related to the market rather than the enterprise itself. The viability of the market alternative is directly related to the depth and transactions costs of the market. If the market is thin the dissenter's sale, particularly if he owns a large block of stock, may have a depressing effect on the available price. Further, the news of the structural change from which the shareholder dissents may have a depressing effect on the price before he has an opportunity to sell if securities analysts agree that the change is unwise.

There is, however, another consideration which makes a strong case for maintaining the appraisal right even in the publicly-held corporation. This is the function which the appraisal right serves as a check on management:

> Appraisal rights . . . have, in the past, served as a countervailing power to force the insiders to tailor their plans to minimize the number of dissenters by getting the best deal possible . . . when [the appraisal right] is removed, the insiders lack the real self-interest to fashion a plan acceptable to a sufficient number of shareholders.

By retaining his check, a check to be used only as a last resort by the dissenting shareholders who feel the decision was so improvident that the market no longer offers a fair alternative, it may be that it will produce extra care on the part of management and the majority when making such a decision.

Once the appraisal right is adopted in principle, the most difficult remaining task is to define the appropriate class of triggering events in a manner that is consistent with the normative model discussed above and which recognizes the competing interests of the majority and minority. . . .

Each of the B.C., Ontario, and Federal corporation statutes provide for a dissenting shareholder's appraisal right: see section 238 of the BCBCA, section 185 of the OBCA, and section 190 of the CBCA. Review the above sections with respect to:

a)   the events giving rise to the appraisal right;
b)   the procedure to be followed;
c)   the exclusiveness or non-exclusiveness of the right;
d)   the treatment of costs arising from exercising the appraisal rights; and
e)   the conditions under which the appraisal right can be withheld (see section 185(29) of the OBCA), withdrawn, or deferred.

One of the most important questions arising under these sections is the determination of the value of the dissenting shareholder's shares. The following case discusses some of the approaches that have been developed to ascertain the appropriate value. (See generally, Campbell, *The Principles and Practice of Business Valuation* (1975).)

Domglas Inc. v. Jarislowsky, Fraser & Co.
13 B.L.R. 135, [1980] C.S. 925, 1980 CarswellQue 51 (S.C.), affirmed (1982), 138 D.L.R. (3d) 521, 1982 CarswellQue 32 (C.A.)

Generally accepted and recognized valuation principles and theory have postulated four approaches to the valuation of corporate shares. They are:

A. The quoted market price on the stock exchange: the market value approach.
B. The valuation of the net assets of the company at fair market value: the assets approach.
C. The capitalization of maintainable earnings: the earnings or investment value approach.
D. Some combination of the preceding three approaches.

In the *Libby* case, cited above, the Court wrote at pp. 59 and 60:

> The cases indicate that there is no definite rule for determining "fair value", but that the proper results in each case will depend upon the particular circumstances of the corporation involved. Among other jurisdictions with valuation statutes similar to our own, we do find, however, a consensus that the component elements to be relied upon in determining "fair value" are stock market price, investments value, and net asset value.
> While it is generally agreed that the process of stock appraisal involves consideration of all three of those elements of value, "the weight to be given to these factors depends upon the circumstances of each individual case. The courts have consistently declined to lay down hard and fast rules" . . .
> All three components of "fair value" may not influence the result in every valuation proceeding, yet all three should be considered. "Compelling the consideration of all of them, including those which may turn out to be unreliable in a particular case, has the salutary effect of assuring more complete justification . . . of the conclusion . . . reached."

A. The Market Value Approach

Professor Bonbright stated:

> "Market Value" itself imports no idea either of a justified price, or of an enduring price, and the ridiculously inflated prices prevailing during

a boom, like the panicky prices prevailing during a depression, are just as true market values as are the prices that are supposed to reflect both normal conditions and intrinsic values. One of the most true things about market values in that they are likely to be crazy values.

In *Untermyer v. British Columbia* (1928), 1928 CarswellBC 103, [1929] S.C.R. 84 , the Supreme Court of Canada was called upon to establish the fair market value of shares, as to the date of death, for purposes of estate taxes. Mignault J. wrote at p. 91 [S.C.R.]:

> We are favoured by counsel with several suggested definitions of the words "fair market value". The dominant word here is evidently "value", in determining which the price that can be secured on the markets — if there be a market for the property (and there is a market for shares listed on the stock exchange) — is the best guide. It may, perhaps, be open to question whether the expression "fair" adds anything to the meaning of the words "market value", except possibly to this extent that the market price must have some consistency and not be the effect of a transient boom or a sudden panic on the market. The value with which we are concerned here is the value at Untermeyer's death, that is to say, the then value of every advantage which his property possessed, for these advantages, as they stood, would naturally have an effect on the market price. Many factors undoubtedly influence the market price of shares in financial or commercial companies, not the least potent of which is what may be called the investment value created by the fact — or the prospect as it then exists — of large returns by way of dividends, and the likelihood of their continuance or increase, or again by the feeling of security induced by the financial strength or the prudent management of a company. The sum of all these advantages control the market price, which, *if it be not spasmodic or ephemeral, is the best test of the fair market value of property of this description.* (The italics are mine.)

In the case of *National System of Baking of Alberta Ltd. v. R.* (1977), 1977 CarswellNat 430, [1978] C.T.C. 30 (Fed. T.D.) , cited above, Mahoney J. cited the above excerpt from the *Untermeyer* case, and then added [(at p. 34 [C.T.C.]):

> I take it that in referring to a spasmodic or ephemeral market price, Mignault J. was postulating a special circumstance in which prices quoted in the market would not be a proper measure of fair market value.

The definitions of "ephemeral" and "spasmodic" in the *Shorter Oxford Dictionary* are:

Ephemeral: Beginning and ending in a day; existing only for a day or a few days; shortlived, transitory.

Spasmodic: Occurring or proceeding by fits and starts; irregular, intermittent; not sustained.

In *Henderson v. Minister of National Revenue*, 1975 CarswellNat 188, [1975] C.T.C. 485 (Fed. C.A.), the Federal Court of Appeal appears to have extended the principle enunciated by the Supreme Court in the *Untermeyer* case to embrace the market as well as the market price. Mignault J. had limited his comments to the market price. In *Henderson*, the Court stated at p. 492 [C.T.C.]:

> Given a consistent market in the sense of a market that is not "the effect of a transient boom or a sudden panic" or that is "not spasmodic or ephemeral", to adopt the terms used by Mignault J. in the *Untermeyer* case, the stock market is the best evidence of fair market value.

In the light of those cases, the market for Domglas's shares on the Stock Exchanges was clearly "spasmodic", in the sense in which Mignault J. used that term. It was "irregular, intermittent and not sustained"; what is referred to in stock market parlance as a "thin market".

The total number of approximately 15,500 Domglas common shares traded during the period from January 1, 1976 to February 21, 1978, the date of the first public, announcement of the proposed amalgamation, represented only 0.65 of 1 per cent of the total issued and outstanding shares, and approximately 15 per cent of the minority shares. Hardly a sustained and regular market!

Considering the facts and circumstances in the present case, and in the light of the jurisprudence above, the stock market value approach is totally inappropriate and is rejected. The stock market prices of Domglas common shares will play no part in the fixing of a fair value by the Court.

Professor Bonbright expressed it admirably when he wrote at p. 811 of vol. II of his textbook:

> (Valuation of a business enterprise) . . . requires concepts of value distinct from that of current market price. The verdict of the market place must give way to the verdict of a fair-minded and intelligent appraiser.

B. The Assets Approach

It will be recalled that in the *Amer. Gen.* and *Roessler* cases, cited above, the assets approach was employed. However, *American General* was an investment holding company, and the later cases, also cited above, distinguished it on that ground. Phelps held that asset value was an important factor, but rarely, if ever, the exclusive determining factor. Woodward was in the same vein. In the *Libby* case, net asset value was assigned a weighting of 20 per cent.

The Canadian jurisprudence reviewed above, although it places primary emphasis on the earnings method, reserves as well a role for net asset values. The basic concept currently accepted by valuation theorists is that a business is worth only what it can earn, except where it is worth less on earnings basis than the amount that would be realized if it were liquidated.

However, Professor Bonbright rang a note of caution when he wrote at p. 264 vol. I of his celebrated textbook:

> But a careful appraisal of the physical assets is indispensable as a guide to the forecast of earning power; and the tendency of modern financial writers to ignore the inventories and the balance sheets in favor of earnings statements is an excessive reaction from the opposite error of earlier days.

He stated also at p. 240 of vol. I:

> In fact . . . the costliness of the assets possessed by the business and necessary for its continuance may have an important, though an indirect, bearing on future earnings. Hence, even though recognizing prospective earning power as the sole consideration, the appraiser cannot intelligently make his forecast of earnings without reference to the costliness and the physical and functional condition of the separate assets.

[Mr. Wise] rejected the assets method as a direct method of valuation in the present case, because Domglas was a going concern. Therefore, he felt that a prudent investor would be primarily interested in acquiring the right to future earnings and dividends. Also, he pointed out the specialized nature and the consequent illiquidity of much of the assets. He therefore did not attempt to fix any value for the assets.

However, he recognized in his report the fact that a higher tangible asset backing diminishes the risk in making an investment, and is therefore a positive consideration in the determination of a multiple in the earnings approach.

At pp. 4 and 5 of his report, Ex. P-5, Mr. Turnbull calculated the estimated depreciated replacement cost of the common shareholders' equity in Domglas, based upon the December 31, 1977, balance sheet, Sched. II to that exhibit as adjusted. He arrived at the figure of $40.12 per common share.

In his report, Ex. I-15, at pp. 16 to 21, Mr. Gajewski, using the same Domglas balance sheet, but with seven areas of adjustment, fixed an asset value of $55.18 per common share. He indicated that he calculated the asset values "in order to corroborate the investment value".

Hence, all three expert witnesses did not assign a direct valuation role to asset values. Mr. Wise's report limited its role to a factor in fixing the multiple; while Mr. Gajewski limited its role to corroboration of the investment value. Mr. Turnbull did not assign it any role whatsoever.

As to the book value of the shares, it was $22.96 each on December 31, 1977; $23.11 on March 31, 1978; and $23.74 on April 30, 1978. None of the experts took book value as such into account, and rightly so.

"Book value" is the term commonly used to describe the value at which property is recorded in the financial accounts of its owner. Usually, property is recorded at historical cost less, in the case of depreciable property, the amount of accumulated depreciation. Book value and current value are thus very different concepts. Because of rising prices, book values of real estate and certain other assets are often much less than realizable values in current markets. For example, in its financial accounts, Domglas carried its land at original cost; although much of that land had been acquired many years ago and was obviously worth much more as at valuation date. The same would apply to other fixed assets, where the depreciated replacement cost as a valuation date would be far more than the depreciated book value.

It must therefore be concluded that the book value as such will play no part in the carrying out by this Court of its task of fixing a fair value of the shares of the dissenting shareholders as at valuation date.

C. The Earnings (or Investment Value) Approach

As already alluded to above, this approach is the generally accepted method to value a business as a going concern. It reflects the principle that commercial and industrial property is worth what it can earn.

In terms of economics, this concept is known as the "capital value theory". That theory holds that anticipated future earning power is the sole matter of consequence, since past earnings are — to use Professor Bonbright's expression — "already water under the mill".

The relevance of reported earnings lies in their justifying an inference as to what may reasonably be expected in the future, i.e., "prospective earnings", which in turn are capitalized at an appropriate rate of return. Thus, present value is based wholly upon anticipated income. Capitalized earning power is necessarily forward looking. Hence, valuation unavoidably involves prophecy or forecasting. As Mr. Justice O.W. Holmes of the United States Supreme Court wrote in *Ithica Trust Co. v. United States*:

> The value of property [as] of a certain date, like all values, as the word is used in law . . . depends largely on more or less certain prophecies of the future . . .

Once the appraiser fixes the most probable prospective net earnings, it is reasonable to assume that the chances of a more favorable record would roughly balance the chances of the opposite.

When employing the earnings approach, the appraisal process comprises the capitalization of the income derivable from the property in question. Thus, the earnings approach is a two-stage exercise:

  (a) to arrive at the most probable and reasonable prospective net earnings; i.e., a stream of maintainable earnings projected into the near future;

  (b) to capitalize those projected net earnings at an appropriate rate; i.e., to fix an appropriate multiple — or price: earnings ratio.

The capitalization rate, or multiplier, applied to earnings will vary with the quality of the enterprise, and hence of its earnings. In addition to that quality, other factors affecting the multiplier include, but are not limited to, the net tangible asset backing of the enterprise, its short, medium and longer term probabilities for growth and profitability (both as to itself in particular and as to its industry and the economy in general), and the quality of its management and its workforce, including the general state of its labor relations. These matters were discussed above in the sections of this judgment entitled "Business History and Position of Domglas" and "Financial Analysis".

D. The Combined Approach

An obvious illustration of the use of this approach is the *Libby* case, discussed above. There, the appraiser and the Court fixed three different per share values by applying separately each of the three approaches described above. The three values thus derived were then weighted, based upon the particular facts and circumstances of the case.

The combined approach to share valuation gives recognition to the principle that such valuation is not based as much on a priori concepts as it is on empirical criteria . . .

As Professor Bonbright recalled at p. 1071 of vol. II of his book, where he cited the judgment in the *Ford Motor* case:

earnings are the test of success of the past and the indication of the future. The other statistics — of production, sales, etc. — and the description of the management and its methods and plans, serve to give depth and perspective to the earnings. Such other facts help to indicate the safety with which the earnings may be relied upon as indicating a normal or healthy condition. They are significant, not of their own weight or force but only in their relation to earnings. . . . This is likewise true of the tangible assets.

In the light of the jurisprudence and doctrine cited and referred to in the present judgment, as well as the expert evidence and all the relevant facts and circumstances pertaining to Domglas, this Court has no hesitation in adopting the investment value (earnings) approach, in order to fix a fair value as of the close of business on the valuation date, of the common shares of Domglas held by the dissenting shareholders on that date.

That is the benchmark approach in valuing a business as a going concern, where no liquidation is postulated.

The net tangible asset backing of the Domglas shares will be one factor, among others, which the Court will draw upon to establish an appropriate price: earnings multiple.

"Fair market value" is defined by Campbell, at pp. 3-12 in "Canada Valuation Service" as:

> The highest price available in an open and unrestricted market between informed, prudent parties, acting at arm's length and under no compulsion to act, expressed in terms of money or money's worth.

At p. 6 of "Business and Securities Valuation", the authors defined fair market value as:

> the highest price obtainable in an open and unrestricted market between knowledgeable and willing parties dealing at arm's length who are fully informed and not under any compulsion to act.

Those definitions come very close to Professor Bonbright's definition of "intrinsic value", cited above at p. *[92]*, which he in turn seems to equate with "fair market value".

Contrary to the premise of Mr. Wise that "fair value" means "intrinsic value", this Court is of the opinion, seeing all the principles and considerations discussed heretofore in this judgment, that "intrinsic value" or "real value" is synonymous with "fair market value".

Had Parliament intended CBCA s. 184 to invoke the concept of "intrinsic value", it would have used the term "fair market value", as it had done theretofore in numerous other enactments.

In legislating the term "a fair value", Parliament conveyed upon the Court the equitable jurisdiction and the obligation to fix a value which is fair, just and equitable, having regard to all of the circumstances; including, in particular, a situation which is tantamount to an expropriation of the shares held by the minority shareholders.

Campbell would appear to agree that "fair value" is something other than "intrinsic value", when he wrote at p. 7-108 of his "Canada Valuation Service":

> Because these Business Corporations Acts do not define the term "fair value" or adopt other value terms that would assist in its meaning, it may be that the term "fair value" in these Acts mean something other than "intrinsic value" as defined and discussed in this article.

In cases of the "squeeze-out" of the dissenting shareholders, which is equivalent to an expropriation, "fair value" goes beyond the concept of "intrinsic value", in that the former must include a premium for forcible taking, and is not subject to a minority discount.

In this Court's opinion, in a "squeeze-out" situation, as exists in the case at Bar, the absence of a discount in valuing a minority holding and the increment or premium for forcible taking are the essence of the distinction between "fair market value" and "fair value".

The Court will, therefore, first calculate and establish the "fair market value" of the dissenting shareholders' shares; and from there go on to fix "a fair value" for those shares.

Mr. Wise testified, and counsel for the petitioner argued that, theoretically at least, the "fair value" of a given share can be less than its "fair market value". This Court disagrees. Within the context of CBCA s. 184, if the fair market value of share "X" is $Y, how can any sum less than $Y be its fair value? Conceptually, the "fair value" of a given share can be equal to or greater than, but never less than, its "fair market value".

The payment by the petitioner of "a fair value", even if more than the "intrinsic value" of the shares, is the price that must be paid by it for the privilege of effecting the amalgamation over the protest of the dissenting shareholders, who in effect are being ousted from the corporation.

In proceeding through the necessary stages; i.e., the fixing of an appropriate level of net maintainable earnings, the selection of a multiple and the awarding of a premium for forcible taking, at each step the Court must make its determination in such a manner that it will be fair, just and equitable to the dissenting shareholders provided, however, that no injustice is done to the petitioner . . .

Notes

1 *Smeenk v. Dexleigh Corp.*(1990), 74 O.R. (2d) 385, 1990 CarswellOnt 130 (H.C.), additional reasons at (1990), 72 D.L.R. (4th) 609, affirmed (1993), 105 D.L.R. (4th) 193 (C.A.), is another appraisal remedy case that discusses valuation principles. Foodex Inc was primarily involved in the business of operating restaurants and Hatleigh Corporation was an investment company that owned, among other things, all of the common and junior preference shares of Foodex. Both corporations were struggling under heavy debt loads, and were advised to amalgamate. On June 8, 1984 the amalgamation of Foodex and Hatleigh was approved by special meetings of the shareholders of the two corporations, and the new corporation Dexleigh was formed. The applicants were holders of Foodex preference shares and Hatleigh class A shares. They dissented in the amalgamation and were offered by Dexleigh $1.30 per share for Foodex preference shares and $1.00 per share for Hatleigh class A shares. The Foodex shares had traded at $1.05 before the amalgamation plans were announced, and had last traded before the valuation date at $1.30. The Hatleigh shares were admittedly valueless, as the corporation was insolvent, but had last traded at $0.90. The

dissenters applied to the court to have the fair value of the shares determined.

In the course of his judgement, Henry J. set out several principles which flow from the statute and judicial decisions by which he was-guided in making the valuation:

1. There is no onus on the applicants to demonstrate that the value represented by the company's offer is too low. The court must itself value the shares of the dissenting shareholders; however, any party who asserts a proposition must prove it by a preponderance of the evidence on the balance of probabilities. This case, however, does not necessarily depend upon onus unless the balance or scale needs to be tipped in favour of one party over the other (the usual rule).

2. The court must proceed on the basis of evidence offered by the parties. Where expert evidence is offered the court should be cautious in exercising its discretion to reject it. Where the court has offered the evidence of one expert only whose opinion is uncontroverted in any material respect the court cannot ignore it.

3. Valuation of shares under s. 190 of the Act is a matter of assessment in accordance with the facts of the particular case. It is not proper for the court to adopt a rigid formula and to view the matter as one of seeking mathematical precision. Whatever the decision, there is an important element of judgment involved and particular attention must be given to seeking a value that is fair having regard to all the circumstances; this invokes the equitable jurisdiction of the court.

4. The advantages of hindsight are not available either to the applicants or to the court. It is the policy of the Act to divorce the value of the shares on the valuation date from the effects of the amalgamation whether anticipated or *ex post facto*. Events that were not known on the valuation date or which occurred thereafter are therefore, in ordinary circumstances, not relevant to the issue which is to determine fair value on the valuation date; where they may nevertheless have some relevance or probative value they should on the basis of the same principle be given little weight.

5. The applicants are not entitled to obtain the benefits of the amalgamation, having dissented from the transaction. By dissenting the applicants elected to participate in neither the benefits nor the perceived detriments and risks of the amalgamation; they chose not to invest in the proposed arrangements and the resulting enterprise. The applicants in this case were not "squeezed out" or expropriated but were offered, with the other shareholders, a continuing interest in the amalgamated corporation. This interest and any benefits or risks flowing from it, the applicants declined in favour of referring the matter of their compensation to the court.

Henry J. found on the evidence that the Foodex shares had no value on the earnings or income approach, no value on the assets approach, and, after eliminating the value added by the announcement of the amalgamation, $1.05 by the market value approach. Their value was set at $1.05. The Hatleigh shares were found to have no value.

2   The court has discretion to select a valuation method to use. What method is selected depends upon the facts of the case. Factors include: whether the corporation is publicly traded and at what volume, the ease of asset valuation, and the likelihood of liquidation. For cases utilizing market value, see *Montgomery v. Shell Canada Ltd.* (1980), 111 D.L.R. (3d) 116, 3 Sask. R. 19, 1980 CarswellSask 113 (Q.B.) and *Lough v. Canadian Natural Resources Ltd.* (1983), 45 B.C.L.R. 335, 1983 CarswellBC 161 (S.C.), where market value was favoured because the corporations involved were highly traded. See also *Silber v. BGR Precious Metals Inc.* (1998), 41 O.R. (3d) 147, 1998 CarswellOnt 2994 (Gen. Div.), affirmed (2001), 46 O.R. (3d) 255 (C.A.), where market value was favoured because the corporation was a closed-end investment fund, where shares could not be redeemed but had to be traded on the open market.

3   If the events behind the need for a valuation amount to a forcible taking of the shares (for example, a transaction that "squeezes out" some shareholders), should this be taken into account in the valuation of those shares? While *Domglas Inc. v. Jarislowsky, Fraser & Co.*, 13 B.L.R. 135, [1980] C.S. 925, 1980 CarswellQue 51 (S.C.), affirmed (1982), 138 D.L.R. (3d) 521, 1982 CarswellQue 32 (C.A.), held that a forcible taking premium applied, this decision appears to have been reversed. See *Locicero v. B.A.C.M. Industries Ltd.* (1984), 28 B.L.R. 172, 31 Man. R. (2d) 208, 1984 CarswellMan 18 (Q.B.), which was reversed on appeal but ultimately restored by the Supreme Court, [1988] 1 S.C.R. 399, 1988 CarswellMan 138, 1988 CarswellMan 256, and *Brant Investments Ltd. v. KeepRite Inc.* (1991), 3 O.R. (3d) 289, 1991 CarswellOnt 133 (C.A.).

4   On the appraisal right generally, see Krishna, "Determining the 'Fair Value' of Corporate Shares" (1988), 13 C.B.L.J. 132, and MacIntosh, "The Shareholders' Appraisal Right in Canada: A Critical Reappraisal" (1986), 24 Osgoode Hall L.J. 201.

9. WINDING-UP

The corporation statutes provide for liquidation and winding-up to take place voluntarily by shareholders' resolution or involuntarily by court order (*e.g.*, see, generally, ss. 207–228 of the CBCA, ss. 312–353 of the BCBCA and ss. 191–244 of the O.B.C.A.).

In the context of shareholder remedies, the dissolution order is the most drastic form of shareholder relief. Most statutes provide for a shareholder application to the court for such an order on the grounds that it is "just and equitable" to do so. See subparagraph 214(1)(b)(ii) of the CBCA, s. 324(1)(b) of the BCBCA and s. 207(1)(b)(iv) of the O.B.C.A.

HUBERMAN: "Winding-up of Business Corporations"
Ziegel, *Studies in Canadian Company Law* Vol. II (1973)
at p. 281 (footnotes omitted)

2. THE GENERAL NATURE OF THE RELIEF

The courts have, in the exercise of their powers under the "just and equitable" rule, made it abundantly clear that there are no fixed outside limits to the rule but rather that each case must be decided on its own facts. Indeed, where appropriate, the courts have, over the years, expanded the rule into new areas as fresh circumstances and situations have arisen and as the courts' reformulation of standards of intra-corporate conduct have developed. Thus, parallel to, and underlying, the expansion of the "just and equitable" rule there has been a corresponding imposition of stricter standards of behavior on the directors and majority shareholders in their treatment of minority shareholders. Similarly, there has been a growing recognition by the courts of the special nature and needs of the close corporation or, as some courts prefer to call it, the partnership in the guise of a company.

The power of the court to make a winding-up order is within the realm of its equitable jurisdiction and, as is traditional in courts of equity, the jurisdiction is construed liberally. Thus it has been said:

> The words "just and equitable" are words of the widest significance, and do not limit the jurisdiction of the Court to any case. It is a question of fact, and each case must depend upon its own circumstances.

And further:

> Nor . . . can any general rule be laid down as to the nature of the circumstances which have to be borne in mind in considering whether the case comes within the phrase.

In addition, it is clear from the legislation that the courts have been granted a broad discretion under the "just and equitable" rule. This is not to say that such discretion is unbounded, for, as was pointed out by Lord Clyde in *Baird v. Lees*:

> This discretion must, however, be judicially exercised. It is not enough for the Court in exercising it to have, in the familiar phrase of a decree-arbitral, "God and a good conscience" before its eyes; grounds must be given which can be examined and justified.

As to the general approach that the court should take in any given case, Lord Shaw stated in *Loch v. John Blackwood Ltd.* that, in considering whether it was "just and equitable" to make a winding-up order, the court's consideration:

> . . . ought to proceed upon a sound induction of all the facts of the case, and should not exclude, but should include circumstances which bear upon the problem of continuing or stopping courses of conduct which substantially impair those rights and protections to which shareholders, both under statute and contract, are entitled.

It should be pointed out, however, that running through the cases under the "just and equitable" rule, and under each of the categories herein discussed, are several fundamental propositions. The most basic of these is that there is a well-recognized reluctance on the part of the courts to interfere in the internal affairs of a corporation. As one judge put it:

> While the words "just and equitable" are clearly intended to be elastic in their application in order that as the case arises injustice and inequity may be prevented, it is a common ground that a very strong case must be made to justify the interference of the Court in the internal management of a company's affairs.

To the same effect, a leading Canadian judge has stated that: "The remedy is drastic, and hence must be addressed to a serious condition affecting the proper conduct or management of the company's affairs."

This reluctance to interfere is based on several-known "rules", variously called the "internal management" rule, the "business judgment" rule, and the principal of "majority rule". Simply put, these rules come down to nothing more than this — the courts believe strongly that the majority of a corporation is entitled to govern the corporation as it, and not the court, sees fit and the majority will be allowed to do so free from court interference, unless its conduct is so gross as to shock the conscience of the court.

Not all courts are as reluctant as others to grant winding-up orders. Those that are reluctant tend invariably to fall back on the standard principles of majority rule and the like. The less reluctant courts manage skillfully to avoid reference to these time-worn clichés. Hopefully, in the discussion which follows, the foregoing matters will become apparent.

3. CATEGORIES UNDER THE "JUST AND EQUITABLE" RULE

The natural tendency of text-writers and judges alike is to categorize the relevant cases within a given area of law so that they may be more easily handled, discussed and applied. This writer proposes to do likewise, in order to make the task at hand more manageable, though it is felt appropriate at this point to add the following caveat:

Facts rendering it just and equitable that a company should be wound up cannot be resolved into categories. Cases upon the subject are to be read with this always in mind. They merely illustrate the diversity of the circumstances calling for an exercise of the Court's discretion in winding up a company because it is just and equitable to do so.

With this admonition in mind, it is now proposed to consider the circumstances which will amount to a "just and equitable" cause.

There are no fixed definitions of what circumstances will constitute sufficient grounds under the broad "just and equitable" rule although a few jurisdictions have sought to supplement the "just and equitable" rule by legislating specific related grounds which might conceivably also fall under the rule.

There emerge from the cases four principal relevant categories which will be analyzed and discussed presently under the headings (1) "loss of substratum", (2) "justifiable lack of confidence", (3) "deadlock", and (4) "the partnership analogy" . . .

In Re German Date Coffee Company
(1882), 20 Ch. D. 169 (C.A.)

A company was formed for the purpose of acquiring a German patent in order to manufacture coffee from dates. The company was unable to acquire the patent but acquired instead a Swedish patent which was equally suitable. The company established a plant in Hamburg which operated at a profit. A petition was filed by two shareholders to have the company wound-up on the grounds that there was a complete failure of the corporate objects. Kay J. found that the whole substratum of the company had disappeared and granted the petition to wind up the company. The company appealed.

BAGGALLAY L.J.: . . . It appears to me that the principle involved in the decision of *In re Suburban Hotel Company* (1867), 2 Ch. App. 737 at 742, by Lord Cairns amounts to this, that if you have proof of the impossibility of carrying on the business contemplated by the company at the time of its formation, that is a sufficient ground for winding up the company. Therefore the question arises in the present case, is there an impossibility of carrying out the objects of the company? I cannot entertain any doubt, having regard to the memorandum of association, and the view I take of the memorandum is verified by the surrounding circumstances, that the real contemplated object of the company at the time when it was formed was to carry out the manufacture of German date coffee, to be manufactured from dates, to be manufactured in Germany under a patent that was actually granted or about to be granted, and that in the contemplation of all parties the granting of the letters patent in Germany for the working of this invention was the basis of the company. No doubt in this case, as in many other cases, you have a variety of general words added which, if they are to be construed by themselves, would give powers to carry on almost any possible business which could be suggested. These must be taken within certain limits, and those limits are, that they must be regarded as ancillary to the purport of the scheme for which the company was formed. It appears to me, from the memorandum of association so construed, that the business of the company was the manufacturing of coffee by virtue of a patent already obtained, or to be obtained, with the benefit of any improvement that might be made by the patentee or the company in connection with that patent.

Now, is there an utter impossibility in carrying on the business of the company? It appears to me from the evidence that there is. Not only is there very strong evidence that the obtaining of these letters patent was contemplated by all parties who took shares, but the holders of 27,000 shares, being more than one quarter of all the shares in the company, had their names removed from the register of shareholders, on the ground that they had been deceived by a statement in the prospectus that the patent had been already obtained.

It appears to me beyond all question that there is an impossibility of carrying on the business of the company, and I think that the order Mr. Justice Kay made is quite correct. I feel bound to say I entirely go with him in the enunciation of the law applicable to the case, and his criticisms on the cases. [The concurring judgments of Lindley L.J. and Jessel M.R. are omitted.]

Appeal dismissed.

See also the decision in *Re Tivoli Freeholds Ltd.*, [1972] V.R. 445.

Loch v. John Blackwood, Ltd.
[1924] A.C. 783 (P.C.)

LORD SHAW of DUNFERMLINE: A good many years ago Mr. John Blackwood established an engineering business in Barbados and carried it on until his death in January, 1904. Under the provisions of his will his estate fell to be divided one-half to Mrs. Rebecca Thomson McLaren, the wife of Mr. William McLaren, and one-quarter each to his niece Mrs. Loch and to his nephew (Mrs. Loch's brother) James Blackwood Rodger lately deceased; the shares to be paid to Mrs. Loch and Mr. Rodger when they reached the age of 30.

Authority was given to his trustees to convert his business into a company, with powers to his trustees to act as directors and to Mr. McLaren to have the supreme control and management of matters connected with the business. The trustees were James Murphy (who died in 1911 and never acted in the trusts); Mr. William McLaren (the testator's sister's husband); and Mr. McLaren's clerk Henry Allan Yearwood.

A company was accordingly formed on January 2, 1905. In the year 1916 Mrs. Loch and James Blackwood Rodger had both attained the age of

30. The latter died in December, 1919. The board of directors now consists of Mr. McLaren, his wife Mrs. McLaren, who was appointed in 1913, and Mr. Yearwood. Under this directorate, the business of the company appears to have been energetically managed and to have amassed considerable profits.

The arrangement of the capital was this: the total amount was 40,000 in F-I shares; 20,000 of these were allotted to Mrs. McLaren; of the remaining 20,000, 10,000 should have gone to Mrs. Loch and 10,000 to Mr. Rodger. Mrs. Loch, however, was allotted 9,999; Mr. Rodgers, 9,998; and the three shares left over were allotted one to Mr. McLaren and one each to Mr. Yearwood and Mr. King (Mrs. McLaren's nominees; the first being Mr. McLaren's clerk and the second his solicitor). This was quite a natural and proper arrangement; but, of course, in the event of a division of opinion in the family between what may be called the McLaren interest on the one hand, and the interest of the nephew and niece on the other, the preponderance of voting power lay with the former. It is thus seen that although taking the form of a public company the concern was practically a domestic and family concern. This consideration is important, as also is the preponderance of voting power just alluded to.

In the petition for winding up eight different reasons are assigned therefor. The first is: that the statutory conditions as to general meetings have not been observed, the second, that balance sheets, profit and loss accounts and reports have not been submitted in terms of the articles of the company; and the third is that the conditions under the statute and articles as to audit have not been complied with. All these allegations are true, and it seems naturally to follow from the preponderance already alluded to, that there is at least considerable force in the fifth reason that it is impossible for the petitioners to obtain any relief by calling a general meeting of the company. There are further submissions — namely, that the company and the managing director, Mr. McLaren, have refused to submit the value of the shares to arbitration, and that without winding up it is impossible for the petitioners to realize the true value of their shares. But the principal ground of the petition is that in the circumstances to be laid before the court it is just and equitable that the company should be ordered to be wound up. This last ground was affirmed by the Court of Common Pleas. [The winding-up order of the Court of Common Pleas was set aside by the West Indian Court of Appeal.]

With regard to the first three submissions made in the petition, it was strenuously argued on behalf of the company, which practically means the directorate or the McLaren interest, that however true it might be that owing to the informal way in which the books of the company had been kept it appeared as if both the statute and the articles of association had been violated in various particulars and that no general meetings of the company had been held, and no auditors properly appointed, and it was certain that no balance sheets, profit and loss accounts and reports had been submitted for the critical years 1919 and 1920, still these were no grounds for winding up. Other applications, it was said, might competently be made to the court to compel the statute and articles to be properly complied with. It may be doubtful whether such a course of conduct lasting in several particulars since its inception until now, would be insufficient as a ground for winding the company up. But their Lordships think it unnecessary to give any separate decision upon such a point.

In their opinion, elements of that character in the history of the company, together with the fact that a calling of a meeting of shareholders would lead admittedly to failure and be unavailable as a remedy, cannot be excluded from the point of view of the court in a consideration of the justice and equity of pronouncing an order for winding up. Such a consideration, in their Lordship's view, ought to proceed upon a sound induction of all the facts of the case, and should not exclude, but should include circumstances which bear upon the problem of continuing or stopping courses of conduct which substantially impair those rights and protections to which shareholders, both under statute and contract, are entitled. It is undoubtedly true that at the foundation of applications for winding up, on the "just and equitable" rule, there must lie a justifiable lack of confidence in the conduct and management of the company's affairs. But this lack of confidence must be grounded on conduct of the directors, not in regard to their private life or affairs, but in regard to the company's business. Furthermore the lack of confidence must spring not from dissatisfaction at being outvoted on the business affairs or on what is called the domestic policy of the company. On the other hand, wherever the lack of confidence is rested on a lack of probity in the conduct of the company's affairs, then the former is justified by the latter, and it is under statute just and equitable that the company be wound up.

The judgment of the court below appears to have proceeded upon the view that this statutory prescription for winding up under the sixth subsection — namely, when the Court is of opinion that it is just and equitable that this should be done — is restricted to cases *ejusdem generis* with those enumerated in the other sub-ss. 1-5 of s. 127 of the Barbados *Companies Act*.

The Board, having fully considered these authorities, the judgments and the arguments, are of opinion that this is not the law. . . .

The cases set forth in sub-ss. 1-5 separately are: (1) if the company has by special resolution resolved that the company be wound up by the Court; (2) if default is made in filing the statutory report or in holding the statutory meeting; (3) if the company does not commence its business within a year from its incorporation, or suspends its business for a whole year; (4) if the number of members is reduced below five; and (5) if the company is unable to pay its debts. It seems plain enough that beyond these cases there is the whole category of fraudulent administration under which a company's property might be imperilled or transferred into the pockets of its directors, when the case for winding up would be of supreme urgency. Yet if the arguments as to *ejusdem generis* were sound, it would logically exclude such a case from the grounds for winding up, which is absurd. It has been long stated that the element of fraud could not be so dealt with.

The cases need not be further referred to in detail; but in the opinion of the Board it is in accordance with the laws of England, of Scotland and of Ireland that the *ejusdem generis* doctrine (as supposed to have been laid by Lord Cottenham) does not operate so as to confine the cases of winding up to those strictly analogous to the instances of the first five sub-sections of s. 129 of the British Act. It so happens, however, that, in several instances, there have occurred circumstances analogous to those of the present in regard to the two other points noted above — namely, the domestic nature of the company and the permanent preponderance of voting power. And accordingly one or two of such cases may be cited. . . .

The present Lord President of the Court of Session (Lord Clyde) in *Baird v. Lees*, [1924] S.C. 83, at 92, discusses the section and the *ejusdem generis* doctrine in exactly the same spirit. His words are as follows:

> I have no intention of attempting a definition of the circumstances which amount to a "just and equitable" cause. But I think I may say this. A shareholder puts his money into a company on certain conditions. The first of them is that the business in which he invests shall be limited to certain definite objects. The second is that it shall be carried on by certain persons elected in a specified way. And the third is that the business shall be conducted in accordance with certain principles of commercial administration defined in the statute, which provide some guarantee of commercial probity and efficiency. If shareholders find that these conditions or some of them are deliberately and consistently violated and set aside by the action of a member and official of the company who wields an overwhelming voting power, and if the result of that is that, for the extrication of their rights as shareholders, they are deprived of the ordinary facilities which compliance with the Companies Acts would provide them with, then there does arise, in my opinion, a situation in which it may be just and equitable for the Court to wind up the company.

It only remains to apply the doctrines thus expressed to the circumstances of the present case. Their Lordships forgo unnecessary details. They are of opinion that the learned Greaves C.J. is correct when he says that:

> The directors in control since the death of Blackwood Rodger have, I think, laid themselves open to the suspicion that by omitting to hold general meetings, submit accounts and recommend a dividend, their object was to keep the petitioners in ignorance of the truth and acquire their shares at an under value.

The Board agrees with these views. In the opinion which they have formed, Mr. McLaren, for reason not unnatural, had come to be of opinion that the business owed much of its value and prosperity to himself. But he appears to have proceeded to the further stage of feeling that in these circumstances he could manage the business as if it were his own. Had Mrs. Loch and Mr. Rodger, or after his death Mr. Rodger's executor, obtained a dividend which year by year represented in any reasonable measure a just declaration of the undoubted profits of the concern, they might no doubt have been content to allow this state of matters to go on; but although on one or two occasions Mr. McLaren paid trifling and fragmentary sums to Mrs. Loch, neither she nor the Rodger family have ever obtained any dividend at all. And it is not to be wondered at that in the transaction now about to be mentioned they completely lost confidence in Mr. McLaren, and had only too great justification for doing so.

It appears that Mr. McLaren viewed with the highest disrelish the testamentary arrangements made by Mr. J.B. Rodger, who died in December, 1919, and he expresses his opinion upon that subject in a somewhat extraordinary letter of February 24, 1920, going so far as to suggest that another and prior will of Mr. Rodger ought to be substituted for his last will. It is difficult to understand what he conceived this has to do with the management of the business, or the distribution of profits therein. But it is certain that Mr. McLaren then proceeded with much urgency and vigor to attempt to acquire the shares of Mrs. Loch and of Mr. Rodger's executor for himself, thereby consolidating the entire concern in himself and his wife.

The substantial fact which their Lordships think to be proved is that in 1920 the assets of that business, apart from any allowance for goodwill, very substantially exceed the £40,000 of the company's nominal capital. A skilled accountant called in after the proceedings commenced placed the amount somewhere about £80,000: but it is sufficient to take the facts simply as their Lordships have just put them.

This most satisfactory state of the company's finances was fully realized by Mr. and Mrs. McLaren.

Upon May 1, 1920, Mr. McLaren, Mr. Yearwood and Mrs. McLaren, at a director's meeting, agreed:

> That the financial position of the firm was such that the directors unanimously agreed that they could with every confidence partly discharge the chairman's deferred salary; to meet that it was agreed that the £12,500 5 percent War Loan be transferred to his name and become his properly absolutely including the six months' interest now due. . . .
> It was further agreed that the chairman's salary be increased from £1,000 to £2,000 per annum from January 1, 1920.

It may be noted that the company's own minutes form the most important evidence in the case, and that, owing probably to the view of the statute taken as already mentioned, they are not referred to in the judgment in the Court of Appeal.

No notice was given to the respondents, as shareholders, of this piece of business being contemplated, and no notice was given of what had been done. Four days after this extraordinary transaction, Mr. McLaren wrote to Mrs. Loch's husband a letter dated May 5, 1920, proposing to her that £10,000 should be given by him as the cumulative value of Mrs. Loch's shares and Mr. J.B. Rodger's executor's shares. These shares in all amounted to one-half of the capital of the company — namely £20,000 — and, as already mentioned, it is evident that the true value of assets much exceeded this amount. The proposal was to buy Mrs. Loch and the Rodger family out for £10,000. But a further suggestion, which in some way seems to have been mixed up with the umbrage felt by Mr. McLaren in regard to the contents of Mr. Rodger's will, was made, and that was that Mrs. Loch should be a participant in a scheme whereby the £10,000 to be paid should be distributed — £8,000 to herself and only £2,000 to the Rodger family.

Their Lordships do not desire to characterize these suggestions in the language which perhaps they fully deserve. The Rodger family, entitled to one-fourth of the holding in the company, nominally £10,000, but in reality of a much higher value, were to be bought off for £2,000 and Mrs. Loch was to be the agent in this scheme. No confidence in the directorate could survive such a proposal. To crown all this, as was afterwards discovered, the £10,000 could be comfortably paid by Mr. McLaren out of the £12,500 which, four days before, he and his wife and clerk had voted to himself out of the funds of the company. Their Lordships express no surprise at the instant repudiation of Mr. McLaren's proposals by Mrs. Loch — a repudiation which is creditable to her — and at the application for a winding up of the company being made. Upon the principles already set forth in this judgment that application must succeed. The broad ground is that confidence in its management was, and is, and that most justifiably, at an end. A further narrative of the facts is unnecessary, although some of them are grave.

It must, however, be said in justice to Mr. McLaren that after the parties were at arm's length the £12,500 was refunded and the minute rescinded. Further, being advised that the increase of salary from £1,100 to £2,000 was wrong he abandoned the same from February, 1922, and at their Lordships' Bar, he being present, an assurance was given that the two years' increase already drawn — namely £1,800 — would forthwith be paid to the company.

Their Lordships will humbly advise His Majesty that the appeal should be allowed with costs and the order of Court of Common Pleas of Barbados restored with costs in both courts below.

Appeal allowed.

In Re Yenidje Tobacco Co. Ltd.
[1916] 2 Ch. 426 (C.A.)

LORD COZENS-HARDY M.R.: This is an appeal from a decision of Astbury J., who ordered this private company to be compulsorily wound up. I think it right to consider what is the precise position of a private company such as this and in what respects it can be fairly called a partnership in the guise of a private company.

In the present case there were two tobacco manufacturers, one Rothman and the other Weinberg. They were minded to amalgamate their businesses. They formed a private limited company, one certainly of a most peculiar kind. Under the constitution of that company they are the sole shareholders in the company; the only voting power is given to the "A" shareholders, and although the holdings of the two members including the "B" shares and preference shares are unequal, one having a larger holding than the other, yet with regard to the only shares which give the power of voting, that is the "A" shares, they each hold an equal number and consequently have equal voting rights. The articles of association provide that there shall be no casting vote, that one director shall form a quorum, and that in the event of any particular disagreement between the directors the matter in dispute shall be referred to arbitration; but there is no provision whatever in the articles, and I cannot imagine such a provision, that in the general management of the company all disputes between the directors shall go to arbitration, and certainly, having regard to the result of the one arbitration which has been held, it would be absurd to suggest that the working out of that provision is inexpensive. There was one dispute about a Mr. Litiger which was referred to two arbitrators who could not agree, and then an umpire was appointed, and the result was that the parties were some 18 days before the arbitrators and umpire, the costs alone of the arbitrators and umpire amount to upwards of £1,000, to say nothing of the costs of the two parties, each of whom had to pay his own costs.

In those circumstances, supposing it had been a private partnership, an ordinary partnership between two people having equal shares, and there being no other provision to terminate it, what would have been the position? I think it is quite clear under the law of partnership, as has been asserted in this Court for many years and is now laid down by the *Partnership Act*, that the state of things might be a ground for dissolution of the partnership for the reasons which are stated by Lord Lindley in his book on Partnership at p. 657 in the passage which I will read, and which, I think, is quite justified by the authorities to which he refers: "Refusal to meet on matters of business, continued quarrelling, and such a state of animosity as precludes all reasonable hope of reconciliation and friendly co-operation have been held sufficient to justify a dissolution. It is not necessary, in order to induce the court to interfere, to show personal rudeness on the part of one partner to the other, or even any gross misconduct as a partner. All that is necessary is to satisfy the court that it is impossible for the partners to place that confidence in each other which each has a right to expect, and that such impossibility has not been caused by the person seeking to take advantage of it."

Now here we have this fact. Mr. Rothman has commenced an action charging Mr. Weinberg with fraud in obtaining the agreement under which he, Rothman, sold his business to the company. I ask myself the question: When one of the two partners has commenced, and has not discontinued, an action charging his co-partner with fraud in the inception of the partnership, is it likely, is it reasonable, is it common sense, to suppose those two partners can work together in the manner in which they ought to work in the conduct of the partnership business? Can they do so when things have reached such [an impasse], as they have here, that after an arbitration lasting 18 days, an arbitration on the only point which was referred, which terminated in favor of Mr. Weinberg, and to which Mr. Rothman declines to give effect, in this sense, that although the award decide that Litiger had not been dismissed and ought to be continued as a servant of the firm until removed, Mr. Rothman will not allow him to come and do his business, so that he, Litiger, is in the happy position of now receiving his wages of £5 a week without being allowed to do any work for the company in respect of which he is a servant?

The matter does not stop there. It is proved that these two directors are not on speaking terms, that the so-called meetings of the board of directors have been almost a farce or comedy, the directors will not speak to each other on the board, and some third person has to convey communications between them which ought to go directly from one to the other.

It is impossible to say that it is not just and equitable that that state of things should not be allowed to continue, and that the court should not intervene and say this is not what the parties contemplated by the arrangement into which they entered? They assumed, and it is the foundation of the whole of the agreement that was made, that the two would act as reasonable men with reasonable courtesy and reasonable conduct in every way towards each other, and arbitration was only to be resorted to with regard to some particular dispute between the directors which could not be determined in any other way. Certainly, having regard to the fact that the only two directors will not speak to each other, and no business which deserves the name of business in the affairs of the company can be carried on, I think the company should not be allowed to continue. I have treated it as a partnership, and under the *Partnership Act* of course the application for a dissolution would take the form of an action, but this is not a partnership strictly, it is not a case in which it can be dissolved by action. But ought not precisely the same principles to apply to a case like this where in substance it is a partnership in the form or the guise of a private company? It is a private company, and there is no way to put an end to the state of things which now exists except by means of a compulsory order. It has been urged upon us that, although it is admitted that the "just and equitable" clause is not to be limited to cases *ejusdem generis*, it has nevertheless been held, according to the authorities, not to apply except where the substratum of the company has gone or where there is a complete deadlock. Those are the two instances which are given, but I should be very sorry, so far as my individual opinion goes, to hold that they are strictly the limits of the "just and equitable" clause as found in the *Companies Act*. I think that in a case like this we are bound to say that circumstances which would justify the winding up of a partnership between these two by action are circumstances which should induce the Court to exercise its jurisdiction under the just and equitable clause and to wind up the company.

Astbury J. dealt with this case, as it seems to me, in a most satisfactory way, and at the end of his judgment he says that he tried to suggest a solution: he suggested that the two should continue or try to continue for six months to see if they could get on better or that they should appoint one or more additional directors to assist them in the business; but this neither would do. If ever there was a case of deadlock I think it exists here; but, whether it exists or not, I think the circumstances are such that we ought to apply, if necessary, the analogy of the partnership law and to say that this company is now in a state which could not have been contemplated by the parties when the company was formed and which ought to be terminated as soon as possible. We are told we ought not to do it because the company is prosperous, making large profits, rather larger profits than before the disputes became so acute. I think one's knowledge of what one sees in the streets is sufficient to account for that, having regard to the number of cigarettes that are sold, and we can take judicial notice of that in judging whether the business is much larger than it was before. Whether such profits would be made in circumstances like this or not, it does not seem to me to remove the difficulty which exists. It is contrary to the good faith and essence of the agreement between the parties that the state of things which we find here should be allowed to continue.

In my opinion the appeal fails and ought to be dismissed with costs.

WARRINGTON L.J.: . . . In substance, therefore, it seems to me these two people are really partners. It is true they are carrying on the business by means of the machinery of a limited company, but in substance they are partners; the litigation in substance is an action for dissolution of the partnership, and I think we should be unduly bound by matters of form if we treated either the relations between them as one than that of partners or the litigation as other than an action brought by one for the dissolution of the partnership against the other; but one result which of course follows from the fact that there is this entity called a company is that, in order to obtain what is equivalent to a dissolution of the partnership, the machinery for winding up has to be resorted to. Now, if this had been an ordinary partnership and an action had been brought for dissolution, it seems to me quite clear that the plaintiff, who is the petitioner in this case, would have had sufficient ground for a dissolution of partnership according to the ordinary principle by which the Court is guided in such matters. Then s. 129 of the *Companies (Consolidation) Act, 1908*, which defines the grounds upon which the Court in the case of a company can make an order for winding up, includes the provision that such an order may be made if the Court is of opinion that it is just and equitable that the company should be wound up. At one time it was thought, and there was judicial opinion in support of it, that an order to bring the case within that provision of the *Companies Act* it must be shown to be *ejusdem generis* with a certain number of other cases which are specified in a previous part of the section; but that opinion has long been abandoned, and the Court has in more cases than one expressed the view that a company may be wound up if, for example, the state of things is such that what may be called a deadlock has been arrived at in the management of the business of the company. I am prepared to say that in a case like the present, where there are only two persons interested, where there are no shareholders other than those two, where there are no means of overruling by the action of a general meeting of shareholders the trouble which is occasioned by the quarrels of the two directors and shareholders, the company ought to be wound up if there exists such a ground as would be sufficient for the dissolution of a private partnership at the suit of one of the partners against the other. Such ground exists in the present case. I think, therefore, that it is just and equitable that the company should be wound up.

There is only one other point to which I ought to refer. It is said that according to the constitution of the company there is provided a means by which the quarrels of these directors can be overridden for the benefit and advantage of the company and the deadlock can be got rid of, and the means suggested is the provision in article 106 for reference to arbitration; but in my judgment, that article does not contemplate a case such as the present, where, in the daily intercourse between the two directors, they are unwilling to speak to each other and discuss the affairs of the company. It relates, I think, to specific cases where a particular resolution important to the company cannot be passed because of a dispute or difference between the two directors, and it is therefore necessary to obtain the authority of some third person who will say what is to be done. It seems to me it has no reference to the ordinary everyday business of the company and its conduct, and that it really does not provide the means of getting rid of the difficulties which are encountered in the present case.

[Pickford L.J. concurred in the result.]

Appeal dismissed.

Notes

1 *Ebrahimi v. Westbourne Galleries Ltd.*, [1972] 2 All E.R. 492, [1973] A.C. 360 (H.L.), which deals with the just and equitable winding up on the so-called "partnership analogy", may be found in Chapter 7 and is also discussed in the section of this chapter dealing with the oppression remedy.

2 Section 214 of the CBCA is not limited to the "just and equitable" ground for a court ordered dissolution. Paragraph 214(1)(a) mentions grounds for a dissolution which are similar to those for granting an oppression order under s. 241. The draftsmen of the CBCA explained the section as follows:

Paragraph (a) of that subsection [ss.(1)] takes account of the strict limits which the courts have imposed on the "just and equitable" rule in paragraph (b)(ii). It is unlikely that the courts will be able to free themselves from the weight of the established precedents without statutory assistance. Paragraph (a) therefore contains a set of more relaxed criteria which, we hope, the courts may find useful in those cases where dissolution appears to be the most equitable solution, but which would be excluded under the "just and equitable" rule. As long as the "just and equitable" rule is not the only basis upon which dissolution may be sought — and the other criteria in s. 17.07(1) [214] prevent this — then the established precedents are worth keeping. Paragraph (b)(ii) of s. 17.07(1) is therefore a residual provision, retained so that a useful fund of case law is not discarded. (Proposals for a New Business Corporations Law for Canada.)

Also, it should be noted that the wide powers available to the court in granting relief from oppression under s. 241 include an order liquidating and dissolving the corporation. (See also ss. 207 and 248 of the O.B.C.A., which are comparable to the CBCA provisions in this respect.)

3 In a company that is analogous to a partnership, a lack of trust and cooperation between "partners" may act to incapacitate the company in the same sense that actual voting deadlock could. Winding-up may be ordered in such a situation. In *Bondi Better Bananas Ltd., Re*, [1951] O.R. 845, 1951 CarswellOnt 115 (C.A.), Aylesworth J.A. said (at p.855 [O.R.]):

We think the principles governing the dissolution of partnerships apply to the circumstances in which these two gentlemen find themselves as equal owners of the capital stock and in equal control of this private company, and if this be so authority is not required for the proposition that "continued quarrelling, and such a state of animosity as precludes all reasonable hope of reconciliation and friendly co-operation" is sufficient to justify the order . . .

See also *Rogers v. Agincourt Holdings Ltd.* (1976), 1 B.L.R. 102, 1976 CarswellOnt 35 (C.A.); *Kapeluck v. Professional Industries Ltd.* (1983), 25 Sask. R. 58, 1983 CarswellSask 279 (Q.B.); and *King City Holdings Ltd. v. Preston Springs Gardens Inc.* (2001), 14 B.L.R. (3d) 277, 2001 CarswellOnt 1364 (S.C.J.).

4 On a winding-up application, the court is not limited to a decision between winding-up and doing nothing. The court may make an order for relief as under the applicable oppression remedy section. See, *e.g.*, CBCA s.214(2). The courts have also stated that winding-up is an extreme remedy and should sometimes not be granted if other remedies would suffice. See *Witlin v. Bergman* (1995), 25 O.R. (3d) 761, 1995 CarswellOnt 1204 (C.A.); and *Gold v. Rose* (2001), 2001 CarswellOnt 5 (S.C.J. [Commercial List]). The result is that while it may be "just and equitable" to order winding-up, another remedy may be ordered.